MOVIES MADE FOR TELEVISION

MOVIES MADE FOR TELEVISION

THE TELEFEATURE AND THE MINI-SERIES
1964–1979

ALVIN H. MARILL

ARLINGTON HOUSE PUBLISHERS
WESTPORT, CONNECTICUT

Library of Congress Cataloging in Publication Data

Marill, Alvin H
Movies made for television.

Includes index.
1. Television broadcasting of films.
I. Title
PNI992.8.F5M34   791.45'75   80-22924
ISBN 0-87000-451-4

Manufactured in the United States of America

9 8 7 6 5 4 3 2 1

CONTENTS

A VIEW BY QUINN MARTIN

Having spent twenty years in prime time, I have been asked to do this foreword. I humbly accept the assignment in the hope that it may trigger the imagination of potential filmmakers.

I've been asked to differentiate between the TV movie and the theatrical movie and to make some sort of statement about some of the series I've done.

First, the TV movie. It has evolved in many ways, but most important it is presently filling a void in a genre not made today in theatrical films. That void is the small, intense personal drama. This started about ten years ago with *Brian's Song,* with James Caan and Billy Dee Williams, and a recent example is *Friendly Fire* with Carol Burnett and Ned Beatty. *Brian's Song* is a beautifully made film about the death from cancer of a professional football player and his relationship with his best friend and his family. *Friendly Fire* is the powerful story of a midwestern housewife who takes on the Pentagon, trying to find the truth about her son's death in Vietnam. The mother's story probably put more illumination on the Vietnam War than any film to date. *Brian's Song* examines the death of a young man in his prime and the interaction of all those around him. I think it is the most profound film ever made on the subject of death.

I bring up TV films like these as benchmarks against the theatrical films that were successful in the same time span. They run from *Butch Cassidy and the Sundance Kid* to *Jaws* to *Star Wars* to *Alien.* The difference is easily detected. The TV film is small, intense and personal, while the theatrical film is big external entertainment.

A few of the TV movies I've made prove the general thought. *A Home of Our Own* is the true story of a Catholic priest who went to Mexico to die. He was cured by a doctor in a small village and is still alive today. The priest caught an orphan stealing from the church and adopted him. Dissolve to today: Father Wasson takes care of 2,000 orphans, raising the money personally. This TV film stars Jason Miller. *Incident in San Francisco,* which stars Richard Kiley, is about a man doing a Good Samaritan deed which almost costs him his life. *Murder or Mercy* is a story about euthanasia which made a strong point about the need for dignity in death. Melvyn Douglas and Mildred Dunnock star.

There are two reasons for television making the more intense personal drama. One is economic; the other is the technical restriction of the TV screen.

There is a saying that the art form changes as the technology changes. When we can get a six-foot screen with the workings inside for the price of a regular color television set, you will see big external movies made for the home. That's when pay TV will come in and there will be a major change in the industry.

As to series television, the first major success I had was "The Untouchables" starring Robert Stack. Out of the rest, I particularly liked "The Fugitive" with David Janssen, "The Streets of San Francisco" with Karl Malden and Michael Douglas, "The FBI" with Efrem Zimbalist, Jr., and "Barnaby Jones" with Buddy Ebsen. The common denominator in all these series is the idealization of the human spirit —that man can overcome his problems by accepting responsibility for his own destiny.

When I first moved into the Samuel Goldwyn Studios, my next door neighbor was the proprietor of the studio, Goldwyn himself. I got to know him quite well, and one of the things he liked to state was that a good producer was, above all, a good story editor and a good film editor. Goldwyn was correct. If your script is right and the film is edited correctly, you are going to make a successful film, with one caveat. That, in my opinion, is the cast. In the final assembly someone has to be up there on the screen acting out that good script.

In closing, I would like to encourage all those who would like to make their mark in the entertainment business. There is always room for the talented person who is willing to work for what he believes. It's an exciting business waiting to attract exciting people.

INTRODUCTION

Movies made for television. *A Case of Rape* to *The Feminist and the Fuzz. Duel* to *QB VII. The Autobiography of Miss Jane Pittman* to *Charlie's Angels. Cindy* to *Helter Skelter. The Execution of Private Slovik* to *Zuma Beach. Evil Roy Slade* to *Eleanor and Franklin*. The range is as wide as any theatrical offerings over the past seventy years, and esthetically as well as technically—within its restricted time limits and on a quarter of the budget—the equal of what is done for the big screen. On the high end, quality that represents television at its best; on the low, bread and butter fare generally several notches above standard series episodes as contemporary counterparts of the fondly recalled theatrical "B" movie.

The made-for-television movie as generally accepted today is just over fifteen years old but has taken rapid strides to catch up with its bigger (theatrical) brother in its approach to virtually any subject tackled theatrically. It is limited merely by "viewer sensibility" consideration and other guidelines that eliminate nudity, profanity and assorted explicit mayhem, and by the physical dimension of time allotments and the home receiver itself that confines its use of scope for outdoor dramas and cast-of-thousands spectacles. These considered, the telefeature today more than matches its theatrical counterpart (which ultimately shows up on television anyway) in plots, production values and comparable star power.

Those escapist pieces of the early days, generally with lots of closeups of familiar TV faces and themes that stayed generally in the mystery/crime/law-and-order rut or situation comedy fluff motif or fast-and-furious adventure plotting (war movies as well as Westerns), have given way to more mature themes that explore such topics as teenage suicide and alcoholism, homosexuality, single parenthood, battered children, problems of the aging and the aged, cancer, wife beating, rape, urban terrorism, Vietnam, and the like. And, ironically, time considerations have allowed television ever increasingly to offer "full-length" filmings of literary works by James Michener, Harold Robbins, Irwin Shaw, Thomas Wolfe, Conrad Richter, Irving Wallace, James T. Farrell, et al., best-selling authors' best-selling books before and after the fact, that could not be done except in condensed form in theatrical movies. Would Alex Haley's *Roots* have been effective trimmed to, say, three hours in a theatrical version? Could Michener's *Centennial,* sprawled over twenty-six hours on television, have been telescoped coherently for the wide screen? Or the John Jakes Revolutionary War sagas?

Television has offered "complete" film versions of *From Here to Eternity, Studs Lonigan,* and even *Black Beauty*—what the movies (in the first two cases at least) couldn't show, as the network promotions for them stressed. And it has offered an altered (re-edited and resequenced) production of *The Godfather,* reassembled by its director, Francis Ford Coppola, into a *new,* ten-hour television film spread over several nights. Only the most dedicated moviegoer would even consider sitting through a marathon showing of this length.

There really is no subject too big for television to pursue. Nor is there a lack of "stars"—the majority home-grown and cultivated into instant identification the way movie personalities were groomed under the studio system of Hollywood's halcyon days. Stardom in TV movies and stardom in movies, however, are not necessarily equal. Elizabeth Montgomery is a star on TV; Elizabeth Taylor is not. Elizabeth Montgomery virtually guarantees high ratings when one of her television movies airs. So do Barbara Eden, Suzanne Somers, Darren McGavin, Hal Holbrook, Cloris Leachman, and Michael Landon. These are television *stars:* familiar names and faces that perhaps mean next-to-nothing on movie theatre marquees, but superstars they are—on TV. Fanny Brice's legendary observation about Esther Williams' screen importance in direct relationship to her wetness is easily paraphrased here: Ruth Buzzi (or James Arness or Kristy McNichol or Jack Lord or any of "Charlie's Angels") on television is a star; in the movies, she ain't.

TV moviemaking has become vital for the apprenticeship it also has offered to a whole generation of directors who, during the 1970s, began attracting the attention of critics and film enthusiasts alike for their important theatrical work. Most notable, of course, has been Steven Spielberg, one-time TV wunderkind. After doing series episodes (*Marcus Welby, M.D., The Psychiatrist, The Name of the Game* and *Columbo,* among others) as a brash young Universal contract director just out of his teens, Spielberg leaped to prominence originally by directing Joan Crawford in one segment of the multi-part pilot telefeature *Night Gallery* (1969) and then went on to the Gothic horror tale with Sandy Dennis, *Something Evil* (1970), the cult man-vs.-machine thriller *Duel* (1971), and the electronic journalism in the wake of Watergate chiller, *Savage* (1973). Then the big screen called—and the big time as well.

John Badham and Randal Kleiser also did their early film directing in television before bursting onto the theatrical movie scene with two of the biggest grossing films of the 1970s: *Saturday Night Fever* and *Grease,* respectively. Michael Crichton, surgeon-turned-novelist, made his directing debut with the made-for-TV *Pursuit* in 1972, and Peter Hyams, former jazz musician and Chicago television news anchorman, made his with *Rolling Man* and *Goodnight My Love* (both also 1972).

Michael Ritchie, Joseph Sargent and Stuart Rosenberg also directed TV movies as their first feature work after turning out various series and anthology dramas, while other prominent directorial names associated nearly exclusively with TV films throughout the 1970s after toiling in the theatrical movie vineyards include those of John Korty, Boris Sagal, Richard A. Colla, Paul Wendkos and Leonard Horn. Some of their colleagues similarly are regarded as basically television movie directors (with lots of series work to their credit) whose names turn up on an occasional theatrical features. Representative is Lamont Johnson, a former "B" actor who moved behind the camera in TV during the 1950s to assemble an extensive list of directing credits and whose most highly regarded big or little screen works happen to be telefeatures: *My Sweet Charlie* (1970), *That Certain Summer* (1972), *The Execution of Private Slovik* (1974), and *Fear on Trial* (1975). These deal with such mature TV themes as race relations, homosexuality, military desertion and blacklisting. (Another, a little thriller called *You'll Like My Mother,* was a telefeature that escaped to movie houses for its premiere in 1972.) The most prolific TV-movie directors working today are David Lowell Rich and William A. Graham; with more than sixty telefeatures between them, they seem to thrive on moviemaking and appear to be at home behind virtually any camera.

The made-for-TV movie genre, while not attracting all of the alumnae who did the bulk of their early work in television (Robert Altman, Sam Peckinpah, Arthur Penn, Franklin Schaffner, John Frankenheimer, Martin Ritt, Sydney Pollack, Sidney Lumet, et al.), has brought back to the medium such directors as Burt Kennedy, Ralph Nelson and Andrew McLaglen. It also has enticed old guard Hollywood veteran George Cukor (contemporaries Alfred Hitchcock, William Wyler, George Marshall, George Sidney, John Ford and others also have directed on TV but not in the field of telefeatures) as well as international figures such as Franco Zeffirelli, Michael Cacoyannis, Tony Richardson and Jan Kadar, each making his American TV directing debut with telefeatures.

The encyclopedia of made-for-television movies that follows, along with a complete filmography of their principal actors and their directors, requires some ground rules. Covered are approximately a thousand mini-series and films made expressly for television. Each premiered on the networks in prime time between the start of the 1964–65 TV season and the end of the 1978–79 one. Each was made to fill a two-hour time slot (approximately 100 minutes in length to accommodate commercials), although a number were produced to fit into a ninety-minute period (seventy-nine minutes in running time), and some in recent years were three hours or longer. Many subsequently have been released theatrically abroad, and selected ones, such as *Brian's Song* and *My Sweet Charlie,* have been given test movie theatre engagements since their network premieres.*

Telefeatures, for purposes of this book, are films produced as separate entities, not as episodes of continuing series—thus eliminating segments, for instance, of "Columbo," "McCloud," "McMillan and Wife," "The Name of the Game" and "How the West Was Won" which were aired as ninety-minute or two-hour films and often later found their way into syndication as "TV movies." Also not included are those two-hour specials such as "Police Story" and "Emergency," which are irregularly shown continuations of the original hit series, and special film productions made during the late 1960s for the United Nations (television showings here and theatrical releases abroad of *The Poppy Is Also a Flower, Who Has Seen the Wind?* and *Carol for Another Christmas,* among others).

The original Disney movies made specifically for "The Wonderful World of Disney" (and its predecessors going back to 1954) are not included herein since they are shown exclusively on that anthology-style family-oriented show and never go into normal syndication— although many receive regular theatrical release overseas. A case often has been made for *Davy Crockett, King of the Wild Frontier* (from Disney's 1954–55 debut season) as being the first "TV movie," although actually it was a later theatrical release of three separate Davy Crockett adventures with Fess Parker and Buddy Ebsen, each airing at least one month apart.

Another category that will remain undocumented for purposes of this book is the movie strung together from several individual series episodes and later passed off as a telefeature in syndication packages. Examples: *The Forty-Eight Hour Mile,* taken from two entirely different episodes of the Darren McGavin series, "The Outsider" (1968–69); *Slay Ride,* stitched together from the final two "Cade's County" series (1971–72) episodes with Glenn Ford; *The Last of the Powerseekers,* which turns out to be the initial three "chapters" of "Harold Robbins' The Survivors," the abortive series (1969–70) that brought Lana

Turner to television; *Magnificent Thief,* the initial 90-minute episode of Robert Wagner's "It Takes a Thief" series (1968–69).

Also not included are various filmed dramas originally produced as part of television anthologies in the 1960s, such as "Kraft Suspense Theatre" and the "Bob Hope Chrysler Theatre"—two-part episodes that later were edited into a single film and shown subsequently as TV movies. Robert Altman's offbeat thriller, *Nightmare in Chicago,* initially was shown on two nights a week apart on the former series as *Once Upon a Savage Night.* And from the latter anthology came such subsequent "movies" as *Asylum for a Spy* with Robert Stack (as the original two-parter it was called *Memorandum for a Spy*); the behind-the-Hollywood-scenes drama, *The Movie Maker,* the Rod Steiger telefeature that initially was shown in two parts as *A Slow Fade to Black;* and the Cold War spy thriller, *Code Name: Heraclitus,* with Stanley Baker.

Still another group of films not indexed herein: those diverted into theatrical release instead of having intended television premieres— although they all subsequently took their natural route to TV. Leading the list is, ironically, *The Killers,* filmed as the initial entry in the "Project 120" series, an ambitious undertaking by NBC and Universal Pictures, in the fall of 1964 that would evolve into the format generally accepted as the television movie as we know it. Directed by Don Siegel and starring, among others, Ronald Reagan in his last job as an actor, the movie at the time was deemed too violent for home viewing and was shunted off to movie houses by Universal, television's prime film supplier, along with a number of other features originally intended for TV.** Also released first to theatres were such made-for-TV movies as *Hot Rod to Hell* with Dana Andrews and Jeanne Crain battling teenage punks; Rod Serling's adaptation of Irving Wallace's *The Man* featuring James Earl Jones as a black U.S. Senator who accidentally falls heir to the presidency; *Warning Shot,* a detective movie in which David Janssen becomes involved with a star-laden cast of suspects; *Scott Joplin,* the film biography of the famed ragtime composer with Billy Dee Williams in the starring role; and the aforementioned *You'll Like My Mother* and *Buck Rogers in the 25th Century.*

All of these titles will be conspicuously absent from the following chronologically arranged A to Z *(The Abduction of Saint Anne* to *Zuma Beach)* listing through the years in order of premiere date. Lengthy productions spanning no more than two nights are being considered here as television movies. Those running longer are mini-series. All are accompanied by cast and credits, a very brief story line, notes of interest where called for, and awards and nominations to those cited by the National Academy of Television Arts and Sciences. The films then are listed alphabetically and cross-indexed by code number, and the subsequent section offers a filmography of the principal actors and each of the directors. Space limitations prohibit inclusion of *every* player, but an attempt was made to list not only the "stars" but also those supporting actors and actresses most widely recognized by television viewers.

Although every film is not represented by a scene still, more than 300 of them are, and for these photos and other invaluable assistance, I am indebted to ABC-TV, CBS-TV, NBC-TV, Universal City Studios, Inc., Time-Life Television, Viacom, Screen Gems, Aaron Spelling Productions, Quinn Martin Productions, and the Doug McClelland Collection. Sincere thanks also to Jim Meyer, John Cocchi, Stephen Klain, Dennis Belafonte, James Marill, David McGillivray, Leonard Maltin, Vincent Terrace, Guy Giampapa, the staff of the Theatre Collection of the Lincoln Center Library for the Performing Arts in New York, and the New York chapter of the National Academy of Television Arts and Sciences for their complete cooperation in my research.

Alvin H. Marill

---

*The 1979 theatrical features *Battlestar Galactica* and *Buck Rogers in the 25th Century* actually are pared-down versions of the initial episode of each of the two TV space series.

**Among others which Universal diverted to theatrical release first were remakes in the 1960s of *The Plainsman, Beau Geste, The Paleface*

(newly titled *The Shakiest Gun in the West*), *Against All Flags* (renamed *The King's Pirate*) and *Man Without a Star* (as *A Man Called Gannon*); assorted hoss-operas *Ride to Hangman's Tree, Journey to Shiloh* and *Gunfight in Abilene;* action dramas *Jigsaw, Company of Killers, The Young Warriors, Lost Flight* and *Valley of Mystery;* and comedies *Nobody's Perfect, Rosie, Munster, Go Home* and *The Reluctant Astronaut.*

MADE-FOR-TV MOVIES: 1964-1979

The date is that of the film's
premiere on the network.

1964–65 SEASON

0001
SEE HOW THEY RUN
10/7/64 Universal (2 hours)

Producer: Jack Laird
Director: David Lowell Rich
Teleplay: Michael Blankfort
Based on his novel *The Widow Makers*
Photography: Lionel Lindon
Music: Lalo Schifrin
Editor: George Jay Nicholson

Martin Young	JOHN FORSYTHE
Orlando Miller	SENTA BERGER
Augusta Flanders	JANE WYATT
Tirza Green	PAMELA FRANKLIN
Baron Frood	FRANCHOT TONE
Elliott Green	LESLIE NIELSEN
Rudy	GEORGE KENNEDY
Maggie Green	JAMI FIELDS
Jamsey Green	JACKIE JONES

and: John van Dreelan, Harlan Warde, Robert Carricart

A chase drama involving three youngsters who are stalked by syndicate killers after unwittingly taking damaging evidence exposing a crooked international cartel for which their father had been murdered.

0002
THE HANGED MAN
11/18/64 Universal (2 hours)

Producer: Ray Wagner
Director: Don Siegel
Teleplay: Jack Laird and Stanford Whitmore
From the novel by Dorothy B. Hughes
Photography: Bud Thackery
Music: Stanley Wilson
Art Director: John J. Lloyd
Editor: Richard Belding

Harry Pace	ROBERT CULP
Arnie Seeger	EDMOND O'BRIEN
Lois Seeger	VERA MILES
Gaylord Greb	NORMAN FELL
Whitey Devlin	GENE RAYMOND
Celine	BRENDA SCOTT
Uncle Picaud	J. CARROLL NAISH
Otis Honeywell	PAT BUTTRAM
Hotel Clerk	EDGAR BERGEN
Xavier	ARCHIE MOORE
The Boy	RANDY BOONE
Al	AL LETTIERI
Bellboy	SEYMOUR CASSEL
TV Newsman	SCOTT HALE
Themselves	STAN GETZ and ASTRUD GILBERTO

Siegel's second made-for-tv movie (his first, *The Killers,* had been diverted to theatrical distribution, having originally been deemed too violent for television) is a remake of the chase melodrama *Ride the Pink*

Robert Culp in THE HANGED MAN (1964)

Vera Miles in THE HANGED MAN (1964)

Horse (1947), set this time in New Orleans during Mardi Gras. A gunman sets out to avenge the supposed murder of a friend and finds himself neck-deep in trouble with a powerful union official. One of the top songs of the day, "The Girl from Ipanema," was worked in by Stan Getz and Astrud Gilberto when the action lagged.

1965–66 SEASON

0003
SCALPLOCK
4/10/66 Columbia (2 hours)

Producer: Herbert Hirschman
Director: James Goldstone
Teleplay: Steven Kandel
From a story by James Goldstone and Steven Kandel
Photography: Fred Gately
Music: Richard Markowitz
Editor: Richard C. Meyer

Ben Calhoun	DALE ROBERTSON
Barnabus Rogers	ROBERT RANDOM
Martha Grenier	DIANA HYLAND
Joanna Royce	SANDRA SMITH
John Pendennis	LLOYD BOCHNER
Frontiersman	DAVID SHEINER
Nehemiah	JAMES WESTERFIELD
Standish	JOHN ANDERSON
Dave Tarrant	TODD ARMSTRONG
Brooks	ROBERT CINDER
Nils Tovald	ROGER TORREY
Judge Biddle	CLIFF HALL

and: Woodrow Parfrey, James Doohan, Herbert Voland, Eddie Firestone, Stephanie Hill, Harry Swogger, Ed Griffith, Harry Basch, Paul Sorensen, Howard Morton, Sydna Scott, Jerry Summers

This Western, a pilot for Dale Robertson's series *The Iron Horse* (1966–68), set up the subsequent premise in which a dapper frontier gambler wins a railroad line in a poker game and has his hands full holding it from the clutches of various conniving bad guys. Robert Random, Robert Cinder and Roger Torrey continued as regulars in the series along with Robertson.

Anthony Franciosa and Jill St. John in FAME IS THE NAME OF THE GAME (1966)

1966–67 SEASON

0004
FAME IS THE NAME OF THE GAME
11/26/66 Universal (2 hours)

Producer: Ranald MacDougall
Director: Stuart Rosenberg
Teleplay: Ranald MacDougall
Based on the novel *One Woman* by Tiffany Thayer
Photography: John F. Warren
Music: Benny Carter
Art Director: John J. Lloyd
Editor: Edward W. Williams

Jeff Dillon	ANTHONY FRANCIOSA
Leona	JILL ST. JOHN
Ben Welcome	JACK KLUGMAN
Glenn Howard	GEORGE MACREADY
Griffin	JACK WESTON
Peggy Maxwell	SUSAN SAINT JAMES
Cruikshank	LEE BOWMAN
Belle	MELODIE JOHNSON
Eddie	ROBERT DUVALL
Pat	NANETTE FABRAY
Dizzy	JAY C. FLIPPEN

and: George Furth, Nick Colasanto, Ena Hartman, John Hoyt, John Francis

In this TV remake of the 1949 Alan Ladd movie *Chicago Deadline,* a brash big-time investigative reporter, looking into the death of a call girl, uncovers her diary and tries to find her killer among the names contained in it. Franciosa subsequently shared star billing (on a rotating basis) with Gene Barry and Robert Stack in the weekly series based on this film, "The Name of the Game" (1968–71), in which Susan Saint James, "introduced" here, also was a regular. Former musical comedy star Nanette Fabray did a rare acting part in this movie which was written and produced by her husband.

0005
THE DOOMSDAY FLIGHT
12/13/66 Universal (2 hours)

Producer: Frank Price
Director: William A. Graham
Teleplay: Rod Serling
Photography: William Margulies
Music: Lalo Schifrin
Assistant Director: Joseph Cavalier
Art Director: Frank Arrigo
Editor: Robert F. Shugrue

Special Agent Frank Thompson	JACK LORD
The Man	EDMOND O'BRIEN
Captain Anderson	VAN JOHNSON
Jean	KATHERINE CRAWFORD
George Ducette	JOHN SAXON
Chief Pilot Shea	RICHARD CARLSON
Engineer Chipps	TOM SIMCOX
Army Corporal	MICHAEL SARRAZIN
Feldman	EDWARD ASNER
Bartender	MALACHI THRONE
Willoughby	ROBERT PICKERING
Mrs. Thompson	JAN SHEPARD
FBI Agent Balaban	GREG MORRIS
Mr. Rierdon	DAVID LEWIS

Robert Horton in THE DANGEROUS DAYS OF KIOWA JONES (1966)

L.A. Dispatcher	HOWARD CAINE
Seaton	JOHN KELLOGG
Virginia	BERNADETTE HALE
Elderly Woman	CELIA LOVSKY
Speedjet Messenger	DEE POLLOCK
Co-Pilot Reilly	EDWARD FAULKNER
Bomb Disposal Man	DON WILLBANKS
Charlie	DON STEWART

A controversial thriller about a madman who puts the lives of a group of travelers in jeopardy by planting an altitude-activated bomb aboard a plane in an extortion plot against the airline. Serling's screenplay was so detailed—creating a device that would explode below 5,000 feet—that a subsequent real-life incident using an almost identical premise caused this film to be withdrawn from distribution for a number of years.

0006
THE DANGEROUS DAYS OF KIOWA JONES
12/25/66 MGM (2 hours)

Producers: Max E. Youngstein and David Karr
Associate Producer: Hank Moonjean
Director: Alex March
Teleplay: Frank Fenton and Robert W. Thompson
From the novel by Clifton Adams
Photography: Ellsworth Fredricks
Music: Samuel Matlovsky

Title Song: Steve Karliski and Larry Kolber
Sung by Hank Williams, Jr.
Assistant Director: Al Jennings
Art Director: George W. Davis
Editor: John McSweeney

Kiowa Jones	ROBERT HORTON
Amilia Rathmore	DIANE BAKER
Bobby Jack Wilkes	SAL MINEO
Skoda	NEHEMIAH PERSOFF
Marshal Duncan	GARY MERRILL
Dobie	ROBERT H. HARRIS
Roy	LONNY CHAPMAN
Otto	ROYAL DANO
Jesse	ZALMAN KING
Jelly	DEAN STANTON
Morgan	VAL AVERY

A Western about a drifter who is deputized by a dying marshal to deliver two killers to prison and his efforts to elude a pair of bounty hunters who want his charges. This was a pilot for a prospective series that failed to materialize.

0007
HOW I SPENT MY SUMMER VACATION
1/7/67 Universal (2 hours)

Producer: Jack Laird
Director: William Hale
Teleplay: Gene Kearney

Photography: Bud Thackery
Music: Lalo Schifrin
Assistant Director: Frank Losee
Art Director: Henry Larrecq
Editor: Douglas Stewart

Jack Washington	ROBERT WAGNER
Ned Pine	PETER LAWFORD
Mrs. Pine	LOLA ALBRIGHT
Lewis Gannet	WALTER PIDGEON
Nikki Pine	JILL ST. JOHN
Pucci	MICHAEL ANSARA
The Greek	LEN LESSER
Jewelry Dealer	ALBERTO MORIN
Mr. Amin	RALPH SMILEY
Yoshiro	TIGER JOE MARSH
Miss Karali	JONI WEBSTER
The Interviewer	LYN PETERS
Spanish Sailor	ASHER DANN
Croupier	PETER CAMLIN
Croupier's Assistant	FRANK DELFINO
1st Spaniard	FRANCISCO ORTEGA
2nd Spaniard	VICTOR DUNLOP
1st Guard	HORST EBERSBERG
Helicopter Pilot	PETER PASCAL
Waiter	ROLF SEDAN

An offbeat thriller (well received in Great Britain where it was shown theatrically under the title *Deadly Roulette*) tells of a ne'er-do-well with an obsession that he is the victim of a conspiracy after compiling a dossier on the activities of a mysterious billionaire.

13

Robert Taylor in RETURN OF THE GUNFIGHTER (1967)

0008
THE LONGEST HUNDRED MILES
1/21/67 Universal (2 hours)

Producer: Jack Leewood
Director: Don Weis
Teleplay: Winston Miller
From a story by Hennie Leon
Adapted by Paul Mason
Photography: Ray Flin
Music: Franz Waxman
Assistant Director: Luis Calasanz
Editor: Richard G. Wray

Cpl. Steve Bennett	DOUG McCLURE
Laura Huntington	KATHARINE ROSS
Father Sanchez	RICARDO MONTALBAN
Miguel	RONALD REMY
Lupe	HELEN THOMPSON
Pedro	BERTING LABRA

A war story set in the Philippines, with American GI, an army nurse, a local priest and a busload of native children fleeing the enemy. Distinguishing this movie: Franz Waxman's only television film score.

0009
RETURN OF THE GUNFIGHTER
1/29/67 King Bros./MGM (2 hours)

Producers: Frank King and Maurice King
Associate Producer: Herman King
Director: James Neilson
Teleplay: Robert Buckner
From a story by Burt Kennedy and Robert Buckner
Photography: Ellsworth Fredericks
Music: Hans J. Salter
Assistant Director: Carl Beringer

Art Directors: George W. Davis and James W. Sullivan
Editor: Richard Heermance

Ben Wyatt	ROBERT TAYLOR
Anisa	ANA MARTIN
Lee Sutton	CHAD EVERETT
Will Parker	MORT MILLS
Clay Sutton	LYLE BETTGER
Sundance	JOHN DAVIS CHANDLER
Frank Boone	MICHAEL PATE
Lomax	BARRY ATWATER
Butch Cassidy	JOHN CRAWFORD
Judge Ellis	WILLIS BOUCHEY
Luis Domingo	RODOLFO HOYOS
Wid Boone	READ MORGAN
Sam Boone	HENRY WILLIS
Cowboy	ROBERT SHELTON
Dance Hall Girls	LORETTA MILLER and JANELL ALDEN

An aging gunman and a wounded saddle tramp team up to help a Mexican girl avenge the death of her parents, murdered for their land.

0010
WINGS OF FIRE
2/14/67 Universal (2 hours)

Producer/Director: David Lowell Rich
Teleplay: Stirling Silliphant
Photography: Bud Thackery
Music: Samuel Matlovsky
Assistant Director: Edward K. Dodds
Aerial Photography: Ray Fernstrom
Art Director: Frank Arrigo
Editor: Tony Martinelli

Kitty Sanborn	SUZANNE PLESHETTE
Taff Malloy	JAMES FARENTINO
Max Clarity	LLOYD NOLAN
Lisa	JULIET MILLS
Hal Random	JEREMY SLATE
Doug Sanborn	RALPH BELLAMY
Scott	GARY CROSBY
Luis Passos	JAIME SANCHEZ

A melodramatic tale of a headstrong aviatrix who enters an international air race to save her father's floundering business and to soothe the hurt of an old flame who returned home with a new wife in tow.

0011
THE SCORPIO LETTERS
2/19/67 MGM (2 hours)

Producer/Director: Richard Thorpe
Teleplay: Adrian Spies and Jo Eisinger
From the novel by Victor Canning
Photography: Ellsworth Fredericks
Music: Dave Grusin
Assistant Director: Dale Hutchinson
Art Directors: George W. Davis and Addison Hehr
Editor: Richard Farrell

Joe Christopher	ALEX CORD
Phoebe Stewart	SHIRLEY EATON
Burr	LAURENCE NAISMITH
Philippe Sorieh (Scorpio)	OSCAR BEREGI
Mr. Harris	LESTER MATTHEWS
Terry	ANTOINETTE BOWER
Hinton	ARTHUR MALET
Bratter	BARRY FORD
Garin	EMILE GENEST
Paul Fretoni	VINCENT BECK
Miss Gunther	ILKA WINDISH
Tyson	LAURIE MAIN

Gian	ANDRE PHILIPPE
Lodel	HARRY RAYBOULD
Maria	DANIELLE DeMETZ

A spy thriller involving an American who is enlisted by British Intelligence to replace one of its recently murdered agents and smash a ring of blackmailers—James Bond style—headed by a nefarious figure known as Scorpio. One of the early telefeatures filmed on location rather than on the old back lot.

0012

THE BORGIA STICK
2/25/67 Universal (2 hours)

Producer: Richard Lewis
Director: David Lowell Rich
Teleplay: A. J. Russell
Photography: Morris Hartzband
Music: Kenyon Hopkins
Songs: George Benson
Assistant Director: Joel Glickman
Art Director: Robert Gundlach
Editor: Sidney Katz

Tom Harrison	DON MURRAY
Eve Harrison	INGER STEVENS
Hal Carter	BARRY NELSON
Anderson	FRITZ WEAVER
Alton	SORRELL BOOKE
Davenport	MARC CONNELLY
Ruth	KATHLEEN MAGUIRE
Craigmeyer	DANA ELCAR
Dr. Helm	BARNARD HUGHES
Wilma	SUDI BOND
Rigley	FREDERICK ROLF
Willoughby	HUGH FRANKLIN
Man from Toledo	RALPH WAITE
Louise	VALERIE ALLEN
Smith	JOHN RANDOLPH

and: Doreen Lang, House Jameson

A suspense thriller about a surburban couple who discover they are pawns for a powerful crime syndicate and the problems they face trying to break with it and go straight—especially after learning that their contract with the gang carries no escape clause.

0013

WINCHESTER '73
3/14/67 Universal (2 hours)

Producer: Richard E. Lyons
Director: Herschel Daugherty
Teleplay: Stephen Kandel and Richard L. Adams
Based on the screenplay by Borden Chase and Robert L. Richards
Photography: Bud Thackery
Music: Sol Kaplan
Assistant Director: Joseph Cavalier
Art Director: Frank Arrigo
Editor: Richard G. Wray

Lin McAdam	TOM TRYON
Dakin McAdam	JOHN SAXON
Bart McAdam	DAN DURYEA
The Preacher	JOHN DREW BARRYMORE
Larouge	JOAN BLONDELL
High-Spade Johnny Dean	JOHN DEHNER
Meriden	BARBARA LUNA
Ben McAdam	PAUL FIX
Dan McAdam	DAVID PRITCHARD

and: John Doucette, Jack Lambert, John Hoyt, Jan Arvan, Robert Bice, Ned Romero, George Keymas

In this remake of the 1950 James Stewart Western of the same title, brother opposes brother—ex-con against law officer—for possession of the famed repeating rifle, and a long chase begins. Interestingly, Dan Duryea appeared in both versions: a bad guy doing nasty things to James Stewart in the original, the good guy cousin to the protagonists in the telefeature. Veteran actress Joan Blondell made her TV-movie debut here as a boistrous saloon keeper.

0014

IRONSIDE
3/28/67 Universal (2 hours)

Producer: Collier Young
Director: James Goldstone
Teleplay: Don M. Mankiewicz
Based on a story by Collier Young
Photography: John F. Warren
Music: Quincy Jones
Assistant Director: Joseph Cavalier
Art Director: Loyd S. Papez
Editor: Edward W. Williams

Chief Robert Ironside	RAYMOND BURR
Honor Thompson	GERALDINE BROOKS
Scoutmaster	WALLY COX
Ellen Wells	KIM DARBY
Doctor	DAVID SHEINER
Det. Sgt. Ed Brown	DON GALLOWAY
Eve Whitfield	BARBARA ANDERSON
Mark Sanger	DONALD MITCHELL
Sister Agatha	LILIA SKALA
Commissioner Randall	GENE LYONS
Dr. Schley	JOEL FABIANI
Baby Peggy Marvel	AYLLENE GIBBONS
Announcer	TERRENCE O'FLAHERTY
Wheels Montana	EDDIE FIRESTONE

Raymond Burr found another powerful character as a wheelchair-bound San Francisco chief of detectives, crippled by a sniper's bullet, in this pilot movie for the long-run follow-up series (1967–75) to his equally long-run "Perry Mason." Joining Burr in the series as regulars were Don Galloway, Donald Mitchell and Barbara Anderson (later replaced by Elizabeth Bauer). For the movie, Burr and writer Mankiewicz were each Emmy-nominated.

Alex Cord in THE SCORPIO LETTERS (1967)

Henry Fonda and Anne Baxter in STRANGER ON THE RUN (1967)

16

1967–68
SEASON

0015
STRANGER ON THE RUN
10/31/67 Universal (2 hours)

Producer: Richard E. Lyons
Director: Donald Siegel
Teleplay: Dean Riesner
From a story by Reginald Rose
Photography: Bud Thackery
Music: Leonard Rosenman
Title Song: Kay Scott
Sung by Bill Anderson
Assistant Director: Earl J. Bellamy
Art Director: William D. DeCinces
Editor: Richard G. Wray

Ben Chamberlain	HENRY FONDA
Valverda Johnson	ANNE BAXTER
Vince McKay	MICHAEL PARKS
O. E. Hotchkiss	DAN DURYEA
George Blaylock	SAL MINEO
Mr. Gorman	LLOYD BOCHNER
Matt Johnson	MICHAEL BURNS
Leo Weed	TOM REESE
Dickory	BERNIE HAMILTON
Alma Britten	MADLYN RHUE

and: Zalman King, Walter Burke, Rodolfo Acosta, George Dunn, Pepe Hern

In his TV-movie debut, Fonda is a drifter who finds himself wrongly accused of murder by a hostile sheriff and chased into the desert with a horse, some supplies, a one-hour start, and a deadly posse on his heels. Anne Baxter also entered television moviemaking with this one—and director Don Siegel left it.

0016
THE OUTSIDER
11/21/67 Universal (2 hours)

Producer: Roy Huggins
Director: Michael Ritchie
Teleplay: Roy Huggins
Photography: Bud Thackery
Music: Pete Rugolo
Assistant Director: Henry Kline
Art Director: Frank Arrigo
Editors: Carl Pingitore and David Rawlins

David Ross	DARREN McGAVIN
Collin Kenniston III	SEAN GARRISON
Peggy Leyden	SHIRLEY KNIGHT
Honora Dundas	NANCY MALONE
Marvin Bishop	EDMOND O'BRIEN
Mrs. Kozzek	ANN SOTHERN
Ernest Grimes	JOSEPH WISEMAN
Lt. Wagner	OSSIE DAVIS
Mrs. Bishop	AUDREY TOTTER
Sgt. Delgado	MARIO ALCALDE

and: Anna Hagan, Mme. Spivy, Kent McCord

In the pilot movie for the moderately successful single-season series (1968–69), a hard-nosed private eye, an ex-con, finds that he is the chief suspect when the girl he is trailing in an embezzling case is slain with his gun in his office.

0017
PRESCRIPTION: MURDER
2/20/68 Universal (2 hours)

Producer/Director: Richard Irving
Teleplay: Richard Levinson and William Link
Based on their play

Photography: Ray Rennahan
Music: Dave Grusin
Assistant Director: George Bisk
Art Director: Russell Kimball
Editor: Richard G. Wray

Lieut. Columbo	PETER FALK
Dr. Roy Flemming	GENE BARRY
Joan Hudson	KATHERINE JUSTICE
Burt Gordon	WILLIAM WINDOM
Carol Fleming	NINA FOCH

and: Anthony James, Virginia Gregg, Andrea King, Susanne Benton, Ena Hartman, Sherry Boucher, Tom Williams, Jim Creech, Don Stewart

In the first of two telefeature pilots for the "Columbo" series (1971–78), the wily, rumpled Los Angeles police lieutenant—one of TV's great fictional personalities—plays an engaging cat-and-mouse game with a prominent psychiatrist who thinks he has created the perfect crime in the murder of his wife. Originally staged several years earlier in a coast-to-coast tour (but never reaching Broadway), the play co-starred Joseph Cotten and his wife, Patricia Medina, with Columbo being portrayed by Thomas Mitchell in his last stage appearance. When creators Levinson and Link subsequently planned to bring their detective to television, their original choice for the part was Bing Crosby. Only when he turned them down did they select Peter Falk.

0018
SHADOW OVER ELVERON
3/5/68 Universal (2 hours)

Producer: Jack Laird
Director: James Goldstone
Teleplay: Chester Krumholz
Based on the novel by Michael Kingsley
Photography: William Margulies
Music: Leonard Rosenman
Assistant Director: Donald Baer
Art Director: Alexander A. Mayer
Editor: Edward Biery

Dr. Matthew Tregaskis	JAMES FRANCISCUS
Sheriff Verne Drover	LESLIE NIELSEN
Joanne Tregaskis	SHIRLEY KNIGHT
Barney Conners	FRANCHOT TONE
Luke Travers	JAMES DUNN
Justin Pettit	DON AMECHE
Tino	VIC DANA
Arturo Silvera	THOMAS GOMEZ
Emily Masian	JOSEPHINE HUTCHINSON
Merle	STUART ERWIN
Jessie Drover	JILL BANNER

and: Clinton Sundberg, Robert Osterloh, Kent McWirter (McCord), Wright King

A young physician trying to clear a local youth of a murder charge runs afoul of local corruption and a sadistic sheriff who has the town in his hip pocket. This film marked the last role for veteran actor Franchot Tone.

1968–69
SEASON

0019
HAWAII FIVE-O
9/20/68 Leonard Freeman Productions/CBS Television (2 hours)

Producer: Leonard Freeman
Director: Paul Wendkos
Teleplay: Leonard Freeman
Photography: Richard Rawlings

Music: Morton Stevens
Art Director: Gibson Holley
Editor: Ira Haymann

Steve McGarrett	JACK LORD
Rosemary Quong	NANCY KWAN
Brent	LESLIE NIELSEN
Miller	ANDREW DUGGAN
Governor	LEW AYRES
Jonathan Kaye	JAMES GREGORY
Wo Fat	KHIGH DHEIGH
Danny Williams	TIM O'KELLY
Chin Ho Kelly	KAM FONG
Detective Kono	ZULU

and: Philip Ahn, Mitzi Hoag, Noah Keen, Wright Esser, Bill Saito, Baird Miller, Gertrude Flynn, Dale Isimoto, Russell Thorsen, Newell Tarrant, Yankee Chang, Iris Rainer, Mark LeBuse, Soon Taik-Oh, Maxine Saltonstall, Kaai Hayes, Ati Soo, Richard Kusa, Stirling Mossman and the Gang

Special law officer Steve McGarrett tracks down Red Chinese operatives and their spy ring in Honolulu in this realistic pilot for the long-running series that premiered one week after the telefeature and was one of the top-rated weekly shows for more than a decade. Lord became a major TV personality and Khigh Dheigh turned up frequently to recreate his role as McGarrett's long-time nemesis, Wo Fat. Tim O'Kelly and veteran actor Lew Ayres relinquished their original parts to James MacArthur and Richard Denning, respectively, while Kam Fong and Zulu remained with the original cast for a number of years.

0020
SPLIT SECOND TO AN EPITAPH
9/26/68 Universal (2 hours)

Executive Producer: Frank Price
Producer: Paul Mason
Director: Leonard J. Horn
Teleplay: Sig Salkowitz and Don M. Mankiewicz
Created by Collier Young
Photography: Bud Thackery
Music: Quincy Jones
Editor: Edward W. Williams

Chief Robert Ironside	RAYMOND BURR
Det. Sgt. Ed Brown	DON GALLOWAY
Eve Whitfield	BARBARA ANDERSON
Mark Sanger	DON MITCHELL
Dr. Ben Stern	JOSEPH COTTEN
Father Dugan	TROY DONAHUE
Sister Agatha	LILIA SKALA
Ernie Clark	ANDREW PRINE
Louise Prescott	MARGARET O'BRIEN
Albee	DON STROUD
Ralph Fellows	MEL SCOTT

In the second "Ironside" movie, the Chief has his spine jolted during a hospital encounter with a narcotics pusher, not only raising the possibility for an operation that might cure his paralysis but putting him in jeopardy because he can identify the man who had just shot a guard.

0021
ISTANBUL EXPRESS
10/22/68 Universal (2 hours)

Producer/Director: Richard Irving
Associate Producer: Jerrold Freedman
Teleplay: Richard Levinson and William Link
Photography: Benjamin H. Kline
Music: Oliver Nelson
Assistant Director: Burt Astor
Second Unit Director: Hal Polaire
Art Director: John J. Lloyd
Editor: Richard G. Wray

Jayne Meadows and Steve Allen in NOW YOU SEE IT, NOW YOU DON'T (1968)

Haggarty	RICHARD X. SLATTERY
Capt. Boyle	JAMES WESTERFIELD
Dr. Von Ganza	THAN WYENN
Inspector Delon	MICHAEL FOX
Miss Ross	LUCILLE MEREDITH
Taxi Driver	JOSEPH COREY
Nori	RICHARD KIEL
Mr. Stockman	ROY ROBERTS
Achmed	JOHN ANISTON
Hamid	MICHAEL FOREST
George	GEORGE NEISE
Belly Dancer	TAMIA LOMANI

A bumbling art expert, hired by an insurance company to protect a Rembrandt on loan from the Louvre, schemes to steal it in this gag-ridden comedy that originally was to have been called, more aptly, *The Midnight Oil*.

0023
HEIDI
11/17/68 Omnibus Productions (2 hours)

Producers: Frederick Brogger and James Franciscus
Director: Delbert Mann
Teleplay: Earl Hamner, Jr.
Based on the novel by Johanna Spyri
Photography: Klaus von Tautenfeld
Music: John Williams
Performed by the Hamburg Symphony Orchestra
Song "A Place of My Own" by John Williams and Rod McKuen
Sung by Rod McKuen
Editor: D. J. Cohen

Herr Sesseman	MAXIMILLIAN SCHELL
Fraulein Rottenmeier	JEAN SIMMONS
Grandfather	SIR MICHAEL REDGRAVE
Heidi	JENNIFER EDWARDS
Father Richter	WALTER SLEZAK
Dr. Raboux	PETER VAN EYCK
Klara	ZULEIKA ROBSON
Viertel	ELIZABETH NEUMAN

and: John Moulder-Brown, Miriam Spoerri, John Crawley

A superb fourth film version of the all-time favorite children's novel and the first in a series of movies based on literary classics put together by Frederick Brogger and James Franciscus (through their Omnibus Productions) and director Delbert Mann. *David Copperfield, Jane Eyre* and the theatrical *Kidnapped* followed. Making her acting debut in the title role: the daughter of Blake Edwards and Julie Andrews. This film always will occupy a place in television history as the program which preempted the final crucial minutes of an important (to sports fans, at least) football game causing not only switchboard havoc at the network but also several newspaper editorials about viewer priorities.

0024
COMPANIONS IN NIGHTMARE
11/23/68 Universal (2 hours)

Producer/Director: Norman Lloyd
Teleplay: Robert L. Joseph
Associate Producer: John Wallace Hyde
Photography: William Margulies
Music: Bernard Herrmann
Assistant Director: Earl J. Bellamy, Jr.
Art Director: Alexander A. Mayer
Editor: Douglas Stewart

Michael London	GENE BARRY
Cheval	JOHN SAXON
Mila Darvos	SENTA BERGER
Leland McCord	TOM SIMCOX
Peggy Coopersmith	MARY ANN MOBLEY
Doctor Lenz	WERNER PETERS
Shepherd	DONALD WOODS
Captain Granicek	JACK KRUSCHEN
Kapel	JOHN MARLEY
Claude	PHILIP BOURNEUF
Englishwoman	NORMA VARDEN
Henri, the Conductor	EMILE GENEST
Gustav	MOUSTACHE

An espionage adventure against a European backdrop that has a secret agent posing as an art dealer and dodging bombs, seductive women and a trainload of assassins while trying to retrieve a dead scientist's top secret research notes.

0022
NOW YOU SEE IT, NOW YOU DON'T
11/11/68 Universal (2 hours)

Producer: Roland Kibbee
Director: Don Weis
Teleplay: Roland Kibbee
Photography: John L. Russell
Music: Lyn Murray
Assistant Director: Henry Kline
Art Director: Loyd S. Papez
Editor: Edward W. Williams

Jeremiah Klay	JONATHAN WINTERS
Gabrielle Monet	LUCIANA PALUZZI
Herschel Lucas	STEVEN ALLEN
Ida	JAYNE MEADOWS
Prince Haroun	JACK WESTON
Herman	LEWIS CHARLES
Moville	MARCEL HILLAIRE

Eric Nicholson	GIG YOUNG
Carlotta Mauridge	ANNE BAXTER
Jeremy Siddack	PATRICK O'NEAL
Julia Klanton	DANA WYNTER
Dr. Neesden	LESLIE NIELSEN
Dr. Lawrence Strelson	MELVYN DOUGLAS
Richard Lyle	WILLIAM REDFIELD
Sara Nicholson	BETTYE ACKERMAN
Lt. Adam McKay	LOU GOSSETT
Phillip Rootes	STACY HARRIS

and: Thomas Bellin, Gregory Mullavey, David Fresco, Connie Hunter, Syl Lamont

A psychological thriller involving a number of hand-picked professionals going through group therapy together—and one of them turns out to be a murderer. Veteran actor Melvyn Douglas made his TV movie debut here as the renowned psychiatrist who brings them all to his elegant estate.

0025
SOMETHING FOR A LONELY MAN
11/26/68 Universal (2 hours)

Producer: Richard E. Lyons
Director: Don Taylor
Teleplay: John Fante and Frank Fenton
Photography: Benjamin H. Kline
Music: Jack Marshall
Assistant Director: Frank Losee
Art Director: Henry Larrecq
Editor: Robert F. Shugrue

(Below) **William Redfield, Dana Wynter, Melvyn Douglas, Gig Young, Anne Baxter and Patrick O'Neal in COMPANIONS IN NIGHTMARE (1968)**

Susan Clark and Dan Blocker in SOMETHING FOR A LONELY MAN (1968)

John Killibrew	DAN BLOCKER
Mary Duren	SUSAN CLARK
Sam Batt	JOHN DEHNER
Angus Duren	WARREN OATES
Pete Duren	PAUL PETERSON
Eben Duren	DON STROUD
R. J. Hoferkamp	HENRY JONES
Bleeck	SANDY KENYON
Old Man Wolenski	EDGAR BUCHANAN
Rafe Runkel	TOM NOLAN

and: Conlan Carter, Dub Taylor, Grady Sutton, Joan Shawlee, Ralph Neff, Iron Eyes Cody

A gentle Western with Blocker in his own starring TV-movie role as a blacksmith outcast who tries to atone to the townsfolk who followed him West and built a town later bypassed by the railroad and who finally finds the way—with the love of a good woman, a book of Emerson's essays, and a steam engine that derails nearby.

0026
SHADOW ON THE LAND
12/4/68 Screen Gems/Columbia (2 hours)

Producer: Matthew Rapf
Director: Richard C. Sarafian
Teleplay: Nedrick Young
Photography: Fred Koenekamp
Music: Sol Kaplan
Art Director: Ross Bellah
Editor: Henry Batista

Lt. Col. Andy Davis	JACKIE COOPER
General Bruce	JOHN FORSYTHE
Rev. Thomas Davis	GENE HACKMAN
Abby Tyler	CAROL LYNLEY
Maj. Shepherd McCloud	MARC STRANGE
Captain Everett	JANICE RULE
Timothy Willing	MIKE MARGOTTA
Arnold	BILL WALKER
Felting	SCOTT THOMAS
General Hemstead	MYRON HEALEY
Drucker	FREDERIC DOWNS
Lt. Allen	JONATHAN LIPPE

and: Mickey Sholda, Ronnie Eckstein, Sandy Kevin, Ken Swofford, Kay Stewart, Paul Sorenson, Paulene Myers

A provocative attempt to show America under the grip of a totalitarian government and a secret underground force battling an iron-fisted dictator. Former child star Jackie Cooper returned to acting in this one after many years as a television executive, producer and director. Gene Hackman, on the other hand, made one of his last TV acting appearances before hitting the big time in films.

0027
ESCAPE TO MINDANAO
12/7/68 Universal (2 hours)

Producer: Jack Leewood
Director: Don McDougall
Teleplay: Harold Livingston
From a story by Orville H. Hampton
Photography: Ray Flin
Music: Lyn Murray
Assistant Director: Nick Miranda
Art Director: Napoleon Enriquez
Editor: Richard G. Wray

Joe Walden	GEORGE MAHARIS
Captain Kramer	NEHEMIAH PERSOFF
Lt. Takahashi	JAMES SHIGETA
Lt. Parang	RONALD REMY

James Farentino and Dorothy Provine in THE SOUND OF ANGER (1968)

Anne Kramer	WILLI KOOPMAN
Sokuri	VIC DIAZ
Captain Aquino	EDDIE ARENAS
Zairin	GIL DeLEON
Viray	ANDRES CENTENERA
Sgt. Major	VIC UEMATSU

Two American POWs break out of a Japanese jungle prison camp with their captors' secret decoding device and try to reach freedom despite being slowed by an opportunistic sea captain, his pretty daughter and a black marketeer.

0028
THE SOUND OF ANGER
12/10/68 Universal (2 hours)

Producer: Roy Huggins
Director: Michael Ritchie
Teleplay: Dick Nelson
From a story by Roy Huggins
Photography: Eugene Polito
Music: Pete Rugolo
Assistant Director: Phil Bowles
Art Director: Alexander A. Mayer
Editor: Carl Pingitore

Walter Nichols	BURL IVES
Brad Darrell	GUY STOCKWELL
Neil Darrell	JAMES FARENTINO
Marge Carruthers	DOROTHY PROVINE
Gerald Thompson	CHARLES AIDMAN
Judge Prentiss	JAY C. FLIPPEN
Barbara Keeley	LYNDA DAY
Barry Kochek	DAVID MACKLIN
Andrew Pearce	DANA ELCAR
Ann Kochek	COLLIN WILCOX

and: John Milford, Shannon Farnon, Nina Roman, George Murdock, Gene Dynarski, Arch Whiting

A courtroom drama involving two attorneys, brothers as well as partners in a law firm that is called on to represent a young man accused of murdering his girlfriend's wealthy father, and the gruff senior partner who guides them through the intricacies of the case. This was the initial pilot for "The Lawyers" segment of "The Bold Ones," the series (1969–72) that presented on a rotating basis dramas involving medicine, the law and the police. The formidable Burl Ives continued in the subsequent series along with James Farentino, while Guy Stockwell was replaced by Joseph Campanella.

0029
THE SUNSHINE PATRIOT
12/16/68 Universal (2 hours)

Producer: Joel Rogosin
Director: Joseph Sargent
Teleplay: Gustave Field, Joel Rogosin and John Kneubuhl
From a story by Gustave Field
Photography: Gerald Perry Finnerman
Music: Stanley Wilson
Assistant Director: George Bisk
Art Director: Howard E. Johnson
Editor: Budd Small

Michael Ross	
Arthur Selby	CLIFF ROBERTSON
Brancie Hagen	DINA MERRILL
Imre Hyneck	LUTHER ADLER
Morris Vanders	WILFRID HYDE-WHITE
Dr. Novack	LILIA SKALA
Iris	ANTOINETTE BOWER
Benedeck	DONALD SUTHERLAND
Janosi	SANDOR SZABO
Scopes	CLARKE GORDON
Beamis	WOODROW PARFREY

Shirley Booth in THE SMUGGLERS (1968)

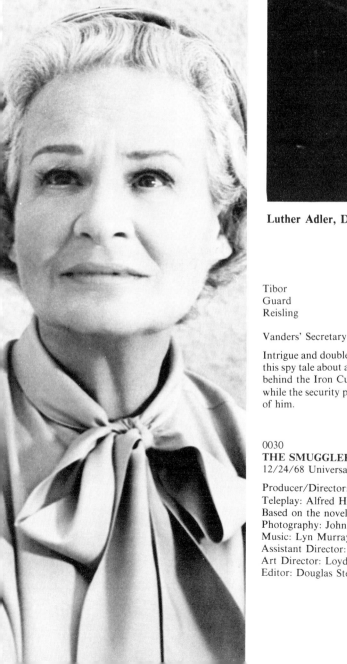

Luther Adler, Dina Merrill and Cliff Robertson in THE SUNSHINE PATRIOT (1968)

Tibor	VICTOR BRANDT
Guard	DANNY KLEGA
Reisling	CHARLES H. RADILAC
Vanders' Secretary	JILL CYRZON

Intrigue and double-identity are the prime elements in this spy tale about a secret agent trying to get out from behind the Iron Curtain with some crucial microfilm while the security police are only a step or two in back of him.

0030
THE SMUGGLERS
12/24/68 Universal (2 hours)

Producer/Director: Norman Lloyd
Teleplay: Alfred Hayes
Based on the novel by Elizabeth Hely
Photography: John F. Warren
Music: Lyn Murray
Assistant Director: Edward K. Dodds
Art Director: Loyd S. Papez
Editor: Douglas Stewart

Mrs. Hudson	SHIRLEY BOOTH
Jo Hudson	CAROL LYNLEY
Willi Rabon	KURT KASZNAR
Alfredo Faggio	DAVID OPATOSHU
Antoine Cirret	DONNELLY RHODES
Anna	ILKA WINDISH
Inspector Brunelli	EMILIO FERNANDEZ
Harry Miller	CHARLES DRAKE
Piero	MICHAEL J. POLLARD
Adrianna	GAYLE HUNNICUTT

and: Albert Szabo, Ralph Manza, Rico Cattani

In her only TV movie, Shirley Booth is an elderly American tourist on the Continent who, with her pretty stepdaughter, unwittingly becomes involved in a smuggling plot and a slight case of murder. This movie had the dubious distinction of being interrupted halfway through by the arrival of Apollo 8 in the vicinity of the Moon on Christmas Eve—and it was never seen in its entirety on the network.

21

Jack Webb and Harry Morgan in DRAGNET (1969)

Diane Baker and James Franciscus in TRIAL RUN (1969)

0031
DRAGNET
1/27/69 Universal/Mark VII Ltd. (2 hours)

Producer/Director: Jack Webb
Associate Producer: Burt Nodella
Teleplay: Richard L. Breen
Photography: Walter Strenge
Music: Lyn Murray
Dragnet Theme: Walter Schumann
Assistant Director: Edward K. Dodds
Art Director: Richard Kimball
Editor: Richard Belding

Sgt. Joe Friday	JACK WEBB
Officer Bill Gannon	HARRY MORGAN
Don Negler	VIC PERRIN
Mrs. Eve Kruger	VIRGINIA GREGG
Capt. Hugh Brown	GENE EVANS
Sgt. Dave Bradford	JOHN ROSEBORO
George Freeman	BOBBY TROUP
Melvin Gannon	TOM WILLIAMS
Carl Rockwell	JACK RAGOTZY
William Smith	ROGER TIL
Claude LeBorg	GERALD MICHENAUD
Freddie	BRUCE WATSON
Ricky Markell	HERB ELLIS
Max Shelton	EDDIE FIRESTONE
Eve Sorenson	ELIZABETH ROGERS
Hotel Desk Clerk	KENT McCORD

In this pilot for the successful revival version of the classic TV series, Sergeant Joe Friday and partner Bill Gannon doggedly track down the killer of two models. Curiously, this pilot was premiered two years *after* the second "Dragnet" series returned to the air for its three-year run (1967–70), mirroring the success Jack Webb had with the original between 1951 and 1959. This TV-movie version, filmed in 1966, is often confused in television listings with Webb's 1954 theatrical version of the same title. Unexplained is why, in this version and the new series, Joe Friday was "demoted" to sergeant after attaining the rank of lieutenant by the time the original faded from view in the late 1950s.

0032
TRIAL RUN
1/18/69 Universal (2 hours)

Producer: Jack Laird
Associate Producer: Jerrold Freedman
Director: William A. Graham
Teleplay: Chester Krumholz
From a story by Richard Levinson and William Link
Photography: Alric Edens
Music: Stanley Wilson
Art Director: Robert MacKichan
Editor: Douglas Stewart

Louis Coleman	JAMES FRANCISCUS
Lucille Harkness	JANICE RULE
Jason Harkness	LESLIE NIELSEN
Carole Trenet	DIANE BAKER
Leo D'Agosta	JOHN VERNON
Noel Ferguson	DAVID SHEINER
Charles Andrews	FRED BEIR
Tyler Peters	PAUL CARR
Mrs. Menderes	LILI VALENTY
Henry Wycoff	JACK COLLINS
Karlson	WILLIAM BRAMLEY
Larkin	BARTLETT ROBINSON
Jeanne	VICKI MEDLIN
Herself	HAZEL SCOTT
Themselves	THE HOLT-YOUNG TRIO

A drama involving an ambitious young attorney, the adoring secretary who tries to help him advance his career, and his employer, a famed lawyer burdened with an unfaithful wife.

0033
ANY SECOND NOW
2/11/69 Universal (2 hours)

Producer/Director: Gene Levitt
Associate Producer: Paul Freeman
Teleplay: Gene Levitt
From a story by Gene Levitt, Robert Mitchell and Harold Jack Bloom
Photography: Jack Marta
Music: Leonard Rosenman
Assistant Director: Kenny Williams
Art Director: Howard E. Johnson
Editor: David Eric Rawlins

Paul Dennison	STEWART GRANGER
Nancy Dennison	LOIS NETTLETON
Dr. Raul Valdez	JOSEPH CAMPANELLA
Jane Peterson	DANA WYNTER
Senora Vorhis	KATY JURADO
Howard Lenihan	TOM TULLY
Mrs. Hoyt	MARION ROSS
American Girl	EILEEN WESSON

and: Bob Hastings, Francine York, Victor Millan, Luis de Cordova, Bill McCright, John Aladdin, Dallas Mitchell

A photographer tries to knock off his rich young wife after she has caught him playing around, but his plan to kill her for her money before she can divorce him goes awry when the automobile accident he has rigged merely causes her to temporarily lose her memory—which could return any second now. This was Stewart Granger's initial made-for-TV movie.

0034
DEADLOCK
2/22/69 Universal (2 hours)

Producer: William Sackheim
Director: Lamont Johnson
Teleplay: Chester Krumholz, Robert E. Thompson and William Sackheim
From a story by Roland Wolpert and William Sackheim
Photography: Vilis Lapenieks
Music: Stanley Wilson
Song "Even When You Cry" sung by The Blossoms
Assistant to the Producer: John Badham
Assistant Director: Ralph Ferrin
Art Director: John T. McCormack
Editor: Edward M. Abroms

Lt. Sam Danforth	LESLIE NIELSEN
Leslie Washburn	HARI RHODES
Edward Logan	ALDO RAY
Lucinda	RUBY DEE
Melissa	BEVERLY TODD
Coley Walker	MAX JULIEN
George Stack	DANA ELCAR
Gamel	MELVIN STEWART
Ski	ROGER BOWEN

and: James McEachin, Fred Williamson, Walter Reed, Charles Lampkin

In this pilot for "The Protectors," the single season (1969–70) cop element of "The Bold Ones" series, the conflict between a white police officer and a black D.A. is established after violence flares in the ghetto when a black youth is killed by a cop and a white newspaperman covering the story is then murdered. Nielsen, one of the busiest actors in television, and Rhodes, who

Stewart Granger and Lois Nettleton in ANY SECOND NOW (1969)

Leslie Nielsen and Hari Rhodes in DEADLOCK (1969)

Carrie Snodgress *(center)* in THE WHOLE WORLD IS WATCHING (1969)

later changed his first name from Hari to Harry, continued opposing each other, despite a grudging respect, in the series.

0035
FEAR NO EVIL
3/3/69 Universal (2 hours)

Producer: Richard Alan Simmons
Associate Producer: David Levinson
Director: Paul Wendkos
Teleplay: Richard Alan Simmons
From a story by Guy Endore
Photography: Andrew J. McIntyre
Music: Billy Goldenberg
Assistant Director: Kenny Williams
Art Director: Howard E. Johnson
Editor: Byron Chudnow

David Sorell	LOUIS JOURDAN
Myles Donovan	CARROLL O'CONNOR
Paul Varney	BRADFORD DILLMAN
Harry Snowden	WILFRID HYDE-WHITE
Barbara	LYNDA DAY
Mrs. Varney	MARSHA HUNT
Ingrid Dorne	KATHARINE WOODVILLE
Wyant	HARRY DAVIS

and: Ivor Barry, Jeanne Buckley, Robert Sampson, Lyn Peters, Susan Brown

A supernatural thriller involving a worldly psychiatrist specializing in the occult who becomes involved with a man possessed by an antique mirror and his fiancée who discovers that it can return her boyfriend, killed in an auto accident, back from the dead. Louis Jourdan reprised his role of David Sorell later, along with Wilfrid Hyde-White as Harry Snowden, in *Ritual of Evil* (1970).

0036
THE WHOLE WORLD IS WATCHING
3/11/69 Universal (2 hours)

Executive Producer: Roy Huggins
Producer: Jo Swerling, Jr.
Associate Producers: Steve Heilpern and Carl Pingitore
Director: Richard A. Colla
Teleplay: Richard Levinson and William Link
Photography: E. Charles Straumer
Music: Pete Rugolo
Assistant Director: Marty Hornstein
Art Director: Robert Luthardt
Editor: Robert L. Kimble

Walter Nichols	BURL IVES
Brian Darrell	JOSEPH CAMPANELLA
Neil Darrell	JAMES FARENTINO
Chancellor Graham	HAL HOLBROOK
Officer Platt	STEVE IHNAT
The Governor	STEPHEN McNALLY
Gil Bennett	RICK ELY
Ed Shepp	DENNIS OLIVIERI
Jim Church	ROY POOLE
Huston	DANA ELCAR
Megan Baker	CARRIE SNODGRESS
Debbie	EILEEN WESSON
2nd Judge	KERMIT MURDOCK
Mrs. Harbeson	JUANITA MOORE
Student Witness	CHARLES BREWER
Arresting Officer	JOHN RAGIN
Dr. Sloan	BENNES MARDENN
Jail Guard	STUART NISBET

A student radical, accused of murdering a cop during a campus revolt, welcomes a court confrontation and then refuses to take the stand, despite the urging of the three high-priced lawyers he has hired to represent him in this second pilot to "The Lawyers" segment of "The Bold Ones" series. Hal Holbrook won an Emmy nomination for his performance in this one.

0037
THEN CAME BRONSON
3/24/69 MGM (2 hours)

Producer: Robert H. Justman
Director: William A. Graham
Teleplay: Denne Bart Petticlerc
Photography: Ray Flin
Music: George Duning
Assistant Director: Fred Gammon
Art Directors: George W. Davis and Gabriel Scognamillo
Editor: Hugh S. Fowler

Jim Bronson	MICHAEL PARKS
Temple Brooks	BONNIE BEDELIA
Papa Bear	AKIM TAMIROFF

Inspector Otis	GARY MERRILL
Gloria Oresco	SHEREE NORTH
Nick Oresco	MARTIN SHEEN
Editor Carson	BERT FREED
Boots	GENE DYNARSKI
Eddie	LAWRENCE HAUBEN
Railroad Clerk	PETER BROCCO
Barker	ART METRANO
Troy	BRUCE MARS

A young newspaperman drops out following his friend's suicide, sets out cross-country on his motorcycle in his quest for the meaning of life and befriends a runaway bride, another searching soul, in this variation of the "Route 66" series—becoming involved weekly in the lives of diverse people subsequently during the 1969–70 TV season. Veteran actor Akim Tamiroff made his farewell TV appearance in this one.

0038
MARCUS WELBY, M.D.
3/26/69 Universal (2 hours)
(subsequently titled *A Matter of Humanities*)

Robert Young and James Brolin in MARCUS WELBY, M.D. (1969)

Executive Producer: David Victor
Producer: David J. O'Connell
Director: David Lowell Rich
Teleplay: Don M. Mankiewicz
From a story by David Victor
Photography: Russell L. Metty
Music: Leonard Rosenman
Assistant Director: Phil Bowles
Art Director: George Patrick
Editor: Gene Palmer

Marcus Welby	ROBERT YOUNG
Steven Kiley	JAMES BROLIN
Myra Sherwood	ANNE BAXTER
Tina Sawyer	SUSAN STRASBERG
Dr. Andrew Swanson	LEW AYRES
Tiny Baker	TOM BOSLEY
Lew Sawyer	PETER DEUEL
Sandy Welby	SHEILA LARKEN
Ray Wells	MERCER HARRIS
Consuelo Guadalupe-Lopez	PENNY STANTON
Kenji Yamashita	RICHARD LOO

and: Lawrence Linville, Ben Wright, Ron Stokes, Allison McKay, Craig Littler, Sheila Rogers, Fran Ryan

The pilot film for the long-run (1969–76) series introduced the kindly small-town general practitioner who, following a mild coronary, grudgingly brings in an independent, motorcycling young associate to help share his work load. Welby's lady friend and his family, part of the plot of this movie, were written out of the subsequent series, with only his medical sidekick, Steven Kiley, and their secretary/nurse, Consuelo (later played by Elena Verdugo), remaining as regulars.

Edward G. Robinson in U.M.C. (1969)

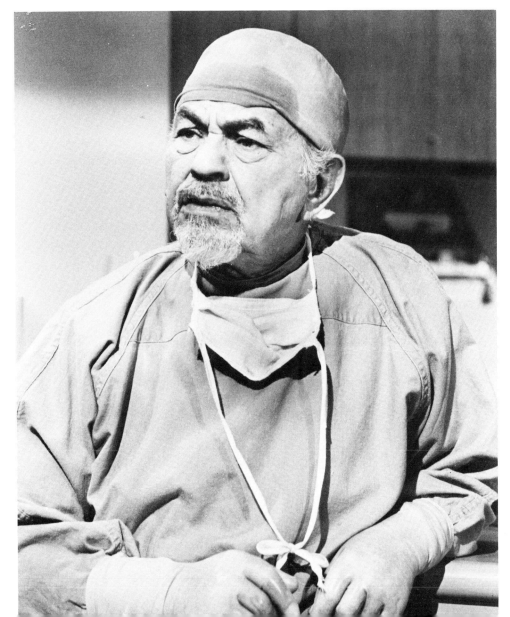

0039
U.M.C.
4/17/69 MGM (2 hours)
(subsequently titled *Operation Heartbeat*)

Producer: Frank Glicksman
Director: Boris Sagal
Teleplay: A. C. Ward
Photography: Joseph Lashelle
Music: George Romanis
Art Directors: George W. Davis and Marvin Summerfield
Editor: Henry Batista

Dr. Joseph Gannon	RICHARD BRADFORD
Dr. Lee Forestman	EDWARD G. ROBINSON
Dr. Paul Lochner	JAMES DALY
Joanna Hanson	KIM STANLEY
Dr. George Barger	MAURICE EVANS
Clifford Coswell	KEVIN McCARTHY
Thomas Jarris	J. D. CANNON
Raymond Hanson	WILLIAM WINDOM
Tim Martin	DON QUINE
Mike Carter	SHELLEY FABARES
Chief Resident	JAMES SHIGETA
Dr. Harold Tawn	WILLIAM MARSHALL
Eve Wilcox	AUDREY TOTTER
Dr. Corlane	ALFRED RYDER
Judge	ROBERT EMHARDT
Angela	ANGELA CARTWRIGHT
Dr. Dave Falconer	MICHAEL EVANS
Technician	JASON WINGREEN
Johnson	TIM O'KELLY
Intern	MEL CARTER

Edward G. Robinson's dignified performance as the aging surgeon whose heart transplant gets his protégé slapped with a lawsuit after the donor's wife charges that her husband was allowed to die so that the young doctor could save his mentor highlights this pilot movie for the popular "Medical Center" series (1969–76). Chad Everett assumed the part originated by Richard Bradford (who virtually disappeared as Everett's star ascended), while James Daly and Audrey Totter continued as regulars.

1969–70 SEASON

0040
SEVEN IN DARKNESS
9/23/69 Paramount (90 min)

Producer: Richard Newton
Director: Michael Caffey
Teleplay: John W. Bloch
Based on the novel *Against Heaven's Hand* by Leonard Bishop
Photography: Howard R. Schwartz
Music: Mark Bucci
Art Director: William Campbell
Editor: Robert Swanson

Sam Fuller	MILTON BERLE
Mark Larsen	SEAN GARRISON
Emily Garth	DINA MERRILL
Alex Swain	BARRY NELSON
Larry Wise	ARTHUR O'CONNELL
Ramon Rahas	ALEJANDRO REY
Christine	ELIZABETH WALKER
Deborah	LESLEY ANN WARREN

Blind passengers of a plane crash struggle to reach safety after their flight goes down in a mountainous area. Milton Berle's TV-movie debut further solidified his talents as a dramatic actor.

0041
THE IMMORTAL
9/30/69 Paramount (90 min)

Producer: Lou Morheim
Director: Joseph Sargent
Teleplay: Lou Morheim and Robert Specht
From the story *The Immortals* by James E. Gunn
Photography: Howard R. Schwartz
Music: Dominic Frontiere
Art Director: William Campbell
Editor: David Wages

Ben Richards	CHRISTOPHER GEORGE
Jordan Braddock	BARRY SULLIVAN
Dr. Matthew Pearce	RALPH BELLAMY
Janet Braddock	JESSICA WALTER
Sylvia Cartwright	CAROL LYNLEY
Locke	VINCENT BECK
Doctor	MARVIN SILBERSCHER
Pilot	WILLIAM SARGENT
Mechanic	JOSEPH BERNARD

A test driver, discovered to possess a rare blood type that temporarily halts disease and aging, finds that he's suddenly being stalked by the greedy seeking a second or third lifetime who want a transfusion, voluntarily or otherwise. In the brief series that began a year later (1970–71), Christopher George resumed his role as the continually pursued hero, with Carol Lynley occasionally turning up as his old girlfriend.

0042
THE OVER-THE-HILL GANG
10/7/69 Thomas/Spelling Productions (90 min)

Producers: Aaron Spelling and Shelly Hull
Director: Jean Yarbrough
Teleplay: Jameson Brewer
Photography: Henry Cronjager
Music: Hugo Friedhofer
Art Director: Paul Sylos, Jr.
Editor: Joe Gluck

Capt. Oren Hayes	PAT O'BRIEN
Nash Crawford	WALTER BRENNAN
Gentleman George	CHILL WILLS
Jason Finch	EDGAR BUCHANAN
Cassie	GYPSY ROSE LEE
Judge Amos Polk	ANDY DEVINE
Sheriff Clyde Barnes	JACK ELAM
Mayor Nard Lundy	EDWARD ANDREWS
Jeff Rose	RICK NELSON
Hannah Rose	KRIS NELSON
Amos	WILLIAM SMITH

In this comedy Western, a retired Texas Ranger and three aged pals help to clean up a town run by a crooked mayor, a drunken judge and a trigger-happy sheriff. This marked the TV-movie debuts of both Rick Nelson and Gypsy Rose Lee, and it was the latter's farewell acting appearance.

0043
WAKE ME WHEN THE WAR IS OVER
10/14/69 Thomas/Spelling Productions (90 min)

Executive Producers: Danny Thomas and Aaron Spelling
Producers: Gene Nelson and Sid Morse
Director: Gene Nelson
Teleplay: Frank Peppiatt and John Aylesworth
Photography: Arch R. Dalzell
Music: Fred Steiner
Art Director: Tracy Bousman
Editor: Leon Carrere

Lt. Roger Carrington	KEN BERRY
Baroness Marlene	EVA GABOR
Eva	DANIELLE DeMETZ
Major Erich Mueller	WERNER KLEMPERER
Colonel	JIM BACKUS
Erhardt	HANS CONRIED

and: Martin Kosleck, Alan Hewitt, Parley Baer, Woodrow Parfrey

A comedy about a World War II pilot who falls out of his plane and is hidden by a baroness to protect him from the enemy—long after the war has ended.

0044
THE LONELY PROFESSION
10/21/69 Universal (2 hours)

Executive Producer: Roy Huggins
Producer: Jo Swerling, Jr.
Associate Producers: Steve Heilpern and Carl Pingitore
Director: Douglas Heyes
Teleplay: Douglas Heyes
From his novel *The Twelfth of Never*
Photography: Ralph Woolsey
Music: Pete Rugolo
Songs sung by Barbara McNair
Assistant Director: Marty Hornstein
Art Director: Robert Luthardt
Editor: Robert Watts

Lee Gordon	HARRY GUARDINO
Charles Van Cleve	DEAN JAGGER
Donna Travers	BARBARA McNAIR

Harry Guardino, Dina Merrill and Troy Donahue in THE LONELY PROFESSION (1969)

George Maharis and Janet Leigh in THE MONK (1969)

Martin Bannister	JOSEPH COTTEN
Karen Menardos	INA BALIN
Beatrice Savarona	DINA MERRILL
Freddie Farber	JACK CARTER
Julian Thatcher	TROY DONAHUE
Lt. Joseph Webber	STEPHEN McNALLY
Dominic Savarona	FERNANDO LAMAS

and: Kermit Murdock, Hal Hopper, Vince Williams, Duane Grey, John Ragin

A detective tale about a no-nonsense private eye who looks into the murder of the mistress of one of the world's wealthiest men. Originally this was to have been called *The Savarona Syndrome,* and it was a pilot for a series that failed to materialize.

0045
THE MONK
10/21/69 Thomas/Spelling Productions (90 min)

Executive Producer: Ron Jacobs
Producers: Aaron Spelling and Tony Barrett
Director: George McCowan
Teleplay: Blake Edwards
From a story by Tony Barrett and characters created by Blake Edwards

Lorne Greene and Anthony Quayle in DESTINY OF A SPY (1969)

Photography: Fleet Southcott
Music: Earle Hagen
Art Director: Tracy Bousman
Editor: Bob Lewis

Gus Monk	GEORGE MAHARIS
Janice Barnes	JANET LEIGH
Wideman	RICK JASON
Danny Gouzenko	CARL BETZ
Tinker	JACK ALBERTSON
Lt. Ed Heritage	RAYMOND ST. JACQUES
Leo Barnes	WILLIAM SMITHERS
Hip Guy	JACK SOO
Lisa Daniels	LINDA MARSH

and: Edward G. Robinson, Jr., Mary Wickes, Joe Besser, George Burrafato, Walter Reed, George Saurel, John Hancock, Bob Nash

This unsuccessful private eye series pilot was developed by Blake Edwards, trying to recapture the glory of his earlier *Peter Gunn* and *Mr. Lucky.* A gumshoe named Monk is somewhat embarrassed after finding himself the prime suspect in the murder of an underworld attorney who had hired him to guard a valuable envelope containing incriminating evidence on a syndicate bigwig.

0046
DESTINY OF A SPY
10/27/69 Universal   (2 hours)

Producer: Jack Laird
Director: Boris Sagal
Teleplay: Stanford Whitmore
From the novel *The Gaunt Woman* by John Blackburn
Photography: Arthur Grant
Music: Ron Grainger
Art Director: Bernard Robinson
Editor: Archie Ludski

Peter Vanin	LORNE GREENE
Megan Thomas	RACHEL ROBERTS
Colonel Malendin	ANTHONY QUAYLE
Sir Martin Rolfe	JAMES DONALD
General Kirk	HARRY ANDREWS
John Flack	PATRICK MAGEE
Julius Bates	PATRICK NEWELL
Superintendent Pode	RAYMOND HUNTLEY
Igor Trubenoff	OLAF POOLEY
Karl Kronig	VICTOR BEAUMONT
Elena Vanin	JANINA FAYE
Elizaveta	JOSEPHINE STUART

and: Angela Pleasence, Mary Kerridge

A rambling espionage tale, filmed in London, about a veteran Russian spy who is brought out of retirement for a sabotage task in the West and finds himself falling in love with an attractive British double agent.

0047
THE YOUNG LAWYERS
10/28/69 Paramount (90 min)

Producer: William P. DeAngelo
Director: Harvey Hart
Teleplay: Michael Zager
Photography: Howard R. Schwartz
Music: Lalo Schifrin
Art Director: William Campbell
Editor: Donald R. Rode

Michael Cannon	JASON EVERS
Ann Fielding	JUDY PACE
Aaron Silverman	ZALMAN KING
David Harrison	TOM FIELDING
Ron Baron	MICHAEL PARKS
Frank Baron	KEENAN WYNN
Bonnie Baron	ANJANETTE COMER
Jay Spofford	GEORGE MACREADY

and: Richard Pryor, James Shigeta, Barry Atwater, Dick Bass, Louise Latham, Georg Stanford Brown

Life in a student-manned legal aid office in Boston. In their first case, the young lawyers find themselves defending a couple of black musicians accused of beating a racist cabdriver. The subsequent series (1970–71) starred Lee J. Cobb as the boss, along with Pace and King.

0048
THE PIGEON
11/4/69 Thomas/Spelling Productions (90 min)

Executive Producers: Danny Thomas and Aaron Spelling
Producer: Alex Gottlieb
Director: Earl Bellamy
Teleplay: Edward Lasko
From a story by Stanley Andrews
Photography: Henry Cronjager
Music: Billy May
Art Director: Paul Sylos, Jr.
Editor: Ben Ray

Larry Miller	SAMMY DAVIS, JR.
Elaine Hagen	DOROTHY MALONE
Barbara Hagen	VICTORIA VETRI
John Stambler/Kane	RICARDO MONTALBAN
Dave Williams	PAT BOONE
Lt. Frank Miller	ROY GLENN, SR.
Mrs. Macready (Landlady)	PATSY KELLY
1st Thug (Carl)	NORMAN ALDEN
2nd Thug	BERNIE DOBBINS

and: Bill Quinn, Judy Jordan, Francis DeSales, Allen Pierson, Monica Peterson

A light-hearted detective show about an eager investigator who insists on protecting a girl who doesn't want his help.

0049
NIGHT GALLERY
11/8/69 Universal (2 hours)

Producer: William Sackheim
Associate Producer: John Badham
Directors: Boris Sagal, Steven Spielberg and Barry Shear
Teleplays: Rod Serling
Photography: Richard Batcheller and William Margulies
Music: Billy Goldenberg
Assistant Directors: Ralph Ferrin and Marty Hornstein
Art Director: Howard E. Johnson
Editor: Edward M. Abroms

Claudia Menlo	JOAN CRAWFORD
Osmond Portifoy	OSSIE DAVIS
Joseph Strobe	RICHARD KILEY
Jeremy	RODDY McDOWALL
Dr. Frank Heatherton	BARRY SULLIVAN
Resnick	TOM BOSLEY
Hendricks	GEORGE MACREADY
Bleum	SAM JAFFE
Gretchen	NORMA CRANE
Carson	BARRY ATWATER
1st Agent	GEORGE MURDOCK
Packer	BYRON MORROW
Louis	GARRY GOODROW
1st Nurse	SHANNON FARNON
Doctor	RICHARD HALE

This three-part drama anthology spawned the popular TV series (1971–73). In the first, directed by Sagal, a young man who murders his uncle for his promised inheritance becomes possessed by a painting of the family cemetery (Ossie Davis, Roddy McDowall and George Macready star). In the second, instrumental in making an important director out of a young Spielberg, a blind millionairess buys the eyes of an indebted gambler to see for twelve hours (Joan Crawford, Barry Sullivan and Tom Bosley). In the third, under Shear, a fugitive Nazi is recognized by a concentration camp victim during a visit to a Buenos Aires art museum (Richard Kiley and Sam Jaffe).

0050
THE SPY KILLER
11/11/69 Halsan Productions/ABC, Inc. (90 min)

Executive Producer: Harold Cohen
Producer: Jimmy Sangster
Director: Roy Baker
Teleplay: Jimmy Sangster
From his novel *Private I*
Photography: Arthur Grant
Music: Philip Martel
Assistant Director: Roy Batt
Art Director: Scott Macgregor
Editor: Spencer Reeve

John Smith	ROBERT HORTON
Max	SEBASTIAN CABOT
Mary Harper	JILL ST. JOHN
Miss Roberts	ELEANOR SUMMERFIELD
Igor	LEE MONTAGUE
Alworthy	DOUGLAS SHELDON
Police Sergeant	ROBERT RUSSELL
Danielle	BARBARA SHELLEY
Dunning	DONALD MORLEY
Diaman	KENNETH WARREN
Gar	PHILIP MARDOC

and: Michael Segal, Timothy Bateson, Douglas Blackwell, Sonny Caldinez, John Slavid, Anthony Stamboulieh

Filmed in the autumn of 1968 back to back with *Foreign Exchange* (shown in the U.S. initially in January 1970), this spy tale focuses on a private eye who finds himself framed for murder by his old employer, the British Secret Service, and pressed into locating a mysterious notebook filled with names of agents working for Red China.

0051
RUN A CROOKED MILE
11/18/69 Universal (2 hours)

Executive Producer: Charles F. Engel
Producer: Ian Lewis
Director: Gene Levitt
Teleplay: Trevor Wallace
Photography: Arthur Grant
Music: Mike Leander
Assistant Director: Bert Batt
Art Director: Bernard Robinson
Editor: Bert Rule

Richard Stuart	LOUIS JOURDAN
Elizabeth Sutton	MARY TYLER MOORE
Dr. Ralph Sawyer	WILFRID HYDE-WHITE
Caretaker	STANLEY HOLLOWAY
Sir Howard Nettleton	ALEXANDER KNOX
Peter Martin	TERENCE ALEXANDER
Inspector Huntington	RONALD HOWARD
Lord Dunnsfield	LAURENCE NAISMITH
Sergeant Hooper	NORMAN BIRD
Chairman	ERNEST CLARK
Business Spokesman	BERNARD ARCHER

A thriller about a math teacher, vacationing in Europe, who stumbles onto a plot to manipulate the international gold standard and becomes the prime target of high-level conspirators.

0052
THE BALLAD OF ANDY CROCKER
11/18/69 Thomas/Spelling Productions (90 min)

Producers: Danny Thomas and Aaron Spelling
Associate Producer: Stuart Margolin
Director: George McCowan
Teleplay: Stuart Margolin
Photography: Henry Cronjager
Music: Billy May
Title song by Murray McLeod and Stuart Margolin
Art Director: Paul Sylos, Jr.
Editor: Bob Lewis

Andy Crocker	LEE MAJORS
Lisa	JOEY HETHERTON
Mack	JIMMY DEAN
Joe Bob	BOBBY HATFIELD
David	MARVIN GAYE
Lisa's Mother	AGNES MOOREHEAD
Earl	PAT HINGLE
Karen	JILL HAWORTH

and: Claudia Bryar, Lee DeBroux, Charlie Briggs, Lisa Todd, Jackie Russell, Barbara Leigh, Joe Higgins, Harry Harvey, Warren Peterson

The first TV movie to deal with the Vietnam War, written by actor Stuart Margolin (he's Angel on "The Rockford Files"), finds a returning veteran discovering that his girlfriend has been forced into marriage, his small business is in ruins and buddies are in short supply. In the part of the girl's shrewish mother, veteran actress Agnes Moorehead made her TV-movie debut.

0053
IN NAME ONLY
11/25/69 Screen Gems/Columbia (90 min)

Executive Producer: Harry Ackerman
Producer/Director: E. W. Swackhamer
Teleplay: Bernard Slade
Photography: Fred H. Jackman
Music: Sunset Editorial
Art Directors: Ross Bellah and Robert Peterson
Editor: Norman Wallerstein

Steve Braden	MICHAEL CALLEN
Jill Willis	ANN PRENTISS
Aunt Theda	EVE ARDEN
Ruth Clayton	RUTH BUZZI
Tony Caruso	CHRISTOPHER CONNELLY
Peter Garrity	BILL DAILY
Esther Garrity	ELINOR DONAHUE
Bert Clayton	HERB EDELMAN
Elwy Pertwhistle	PAUL FORD
Mrs. Caruso	ELSA LANCHESTER
Sgt. Mulligan	HERBERT VOLAND
Haskell	ALAN REED
Debbie Caruso	HEATHER YOUNG

In this romantic comedy, a carbon copy of *We're Not Married* (1952), several couples discover they were joined in illegal wedlock by a pair of marriage consultants who set about to rectify the situation.

0054
THREE'S A CROWD
12/2/69 Screen Gems/Columbia (90 min)

Producer: Jon Epstein
Director: Harry Falk
Teleplay: Nate Monaster and Harry Winkler
From a story by Nate Monaster

Robert Conrad, Diane Baker and Howard Duff in THE D.A.: MURDER ONE (1969)

Photography: Lathrop Worth
Music: Boyce and Hart
Conducted by Don Costa
Art Directors: Ross Bellah and Howard Campbell
Editor: William Martin

Jim Carson	LARRY HAGMAN
Jessica Carson	JESSICA WALTER
Ann Carson	E. J. PEAKER
Dr. Pike	HARVEY KORMAN
Norman (Elevator Operator)	NORMAN FELL
Ralph Wilcox	STU GILLIAM
Drunk	MICKEY DEEMS
Mona	SHELLEY MORRISON

An Enoch Arden-themed comedy about a pilot who ends up with two wives in separate cities, mixing elements of Guinness' *The Captain's Paradise* and the Cary Grant-Irene Dunne classic, *My Favorite Wife.*

0055
THE D.A.: MURDER ONE
12/8/69 Universal/Mark VII Ltd. (2 hours)

A Jack Webb Production
Executive Producer: Robert H. Forward
Producer: Harold Jack Bloom
Associate Producer: Edward K. Dodds
Director: Boris Sagal
Teleplay: Harold Jack Bloom

Photography: Alric Edens
Music: Frank Comstock
Assistant Director: Ralph Ferrin
Art Director: George C. Webb
Editor: Tony Martinelli

Paul Ryan	ROBERT CONRAD
District Attorney	LYNN D. COMPTON
Mary Brokaw	HOWARD DUFF
Nicholas Devaney	DIANE BAKER
Andrushian	J. D. CANNON
	GERALD S. O'LOUGHLIN
Dr. Stuart	ALFRED RYDER
Cherniss	SCOTT BRADY
Ramirez	CARLOS ROMERO
Dr. Enright	DANA ELCAR
Dr. Grainger	DAVID OPATOSHU
Charles Lloyd	PATRIC KNOWLES
Judge Tanner	ALAN HEWITT
Vee Ryan	FREDRICKA MYERS
Larry Triplett	CHUCK DANIEL
Dr. Ellis Anders	FORD RAINEY
Judge Skinner	DEAN HARENS

A deputy district attorney shows up his superiors by proving that an attractive nurse has murdered her rich husbands and relatives through insulin overdoses. This was the pilot for the subsequent series (1971–72) that

starred Conrad, who was joined in it by Harry Morgan, Julie Cobb (Lee J.'s little girl) and Ned Romero as regulars.

0056
DAUGHTER OF THE MIND
12/9/69 20th Century-Fox (90 min)

Producer/Director: Walter Grauman
Associate Producer: William Kayden
Teleplay: Luther Davis
Based on the novel *The Hand of Mary Constable*
by Paul Gallico
Photography: Jack Woolf
Music: Robert Drasnin
Assistant Director: Larry Powell
Art Directors: Jack Martin Smith and Philip Barber
Editor: Michael Economou

Dr. Alex Lauder	DON MURRAY
Prof. Samuel Constable	RAY MILLAND
Lenore Constable	GENE TIERNEY
Tina Cryder	BARBARA DANA
Saul Wiener	EDWARD ASNER
Mary Constable	PAMELYN FERDIN
Arnold Bessmer	WILLIAM BECKLEY
Dr. Paul Cryder	IVOR BARRY
Dr. Frank Ferguson	GEORGE MACREADY
Mr. Bosch	JOHN CARRADINE
Helga	VIRGINIA CHRISTINE
Devi Bessmer	CECILE OZORIO
General Augstadt	FRANK MAXWELL
Enemy Agent	BILL HICKMAN
Technician	HAL FREDERICK

In this chiller mixing espionage with the supernatural, a cybernetics professor believes that his dead daughter is communicating with him from beyond the grave. The film was Gene Tierney's debut telefeature.

0057
SILENT NIGHT, LONELY NIGHT
12/16/69 Universal (2 hours)

Producer: Jack Farren
Director: Daniel Petrie
Teleplay: John Vlahos
From the play by Robert Anderson
Photography: Jack Marta
Music: Billy Goldenberg
Assistant Director: Harker Wade
Art Director: William D. DeCines
Editor: Budd Small

John Sparrow	LLOYD BRIDGES
Katherine Johnson	SHIRLEY JONES
Jennifer Sparrow	LYNN CARLIN
Janet	CARRIE SNODGRESS
Philip	ROBERT LIPTON
Ginny	CLORIS LEACHMAN
Paul Johnson	RICHARD EASTHAM
Jerry Johnson	STEFAN ARNGRIM
Mae	NYDIA WESTMAN
Dr. Hyatt	WOODROW PARFREY
Mac (Local Cabbie)	EDWARD R. LEADBETTER
Walter (Desk Clerk)	WALTER BOUGHTON
Saleswoman	AMZIE STRICKLAND
Young Ginny	MARJORIE ANNE SHORT
Young John	JEFFREY BRIDGES

Don Murray and Ray Milland in DAUGHTER OF THE MIND (1969)

Lloyd Bridges and Shirley Jones in SILENT NIGHT, LONELY NIGHT (1969)

During the Christmas holidays, a brief interlude is shared by two lonely people in a New England college town—he's there to visit his wife, a mental patient there; she's there visiting her son after discovering her husband's infidelity. On Broadway in 1959, the Lloyd Bridges-Shirley Jones roles were played by Henry Fonda and Barbara Bel Geddes.

0058
THE SILENT GUN
12/16/69 Paramount (90 min)

Producer: Bruce Lansbury
Director: Michael Caffey
Teleplay: Clyde Ware
From a format developed by Bob Kane
Photographer: Howard R. Schwartz
Music: Leith Stevens
Art Director: William Campbell
Editor: Donald R. Rode

Brad Clinton	LLOYD BRIDGES
Billy Reed	JOHN BECK
John Cole	ED BEGLEY
Joe Henning	EDD BYRNES
Sam Benner	PERNELL ROBERTS
Louise Cole	SUSAN HOWARD

and: Michael Forest, Trace Evans, Bob Diamond, Barbara Rhoades, Walker Edminston, Elizabeth Perry, Arte Lewis

An offbeat Western about a gunfighter who carries an unloaded pistol after nearly shooting an innocent child, is made sheriff of a wide-open town, and rides into frays on the strength of his reputation.

0059
HONEYMOON WITH A STRANGER
12/23/69 20th Century-Fox (90 min)

Producer: Robert Jacks
Associate Producer: Clarence Eurist

Eric Braeden and Barbara Steele in HONEYMOON WITH A STRANGER (1969)

Janet Leigh and Rossano Brazzi in HONEYMOON WITH A STRANGER (1969)

Director: John Peyser
Teleplay: David P. Harmon and Henry Slesar
Based on novel *Piege pour un homme Suel* by Robert Thomas
Photography: Rafael Pacheco de Usa
Music: Mark Bucci
Art Director: Santiago Otanon Fernandez
Editor: Joe Gluck

Sandra Latham	JANET LEIGH
Captain Sevilla	ROSSANO BRAZZI
Ernesto (1)	JOSEPH LENZI
Ernesto (2)	CESARE DANOVA
Juanito	JUAN ELIZE
Frederico Caprio	ERIC BRAEDEN
Carla	BARBARA STEELE
Sergeant	SANCHO GRACIA
Policeman	RAOUL ANTHONY

Honeymooning in Italy, a young bride wakes up to discover that her husband is gone and an imposter is in his place, but she cannot convince the police of the switch.

0060
GIDGET GROWS UP
12/30/69 Screen Gems/Columbia (90 min)

Producer: Jerome Courtland
Director: James Sheldon
Teleplay: John McGreevey
Based on the novel *Gidget Goes to New York* by Frederick Kohner

Photography: John Morley Stephens
Music: Shorty Rogers
Art Directors: Ross Bellah and Howard Campbell
Editor: Aaron Nibley

Gidget Lawrence	KAREN VALENTINE
Alex	EDWARD MULHARE
Jeff "Moondoggie" Griffin	PAUL PETERSON
Louis B. Latimer	PAUL LYNDE
Russell Lawrence	BOB CUMMINGS
Bibi Crosby	NINA FOCH
Ambassador Post	WARNER ANDERSON
Diana	SUSAN BATSON
Lee	HAL FREDERICK

and: Michael Lembeck, Gunilla Knudson, Doreen Lang, Margot Jane, Donald Symington, Harlen Carrather, Helen Funai

In the fourth Gidget movie (the first made for television), our heroine has given up surfing off California to become a UN guide in Manhattan and carry on a long-distance romance with her childhood sweetheart, now an Air Force officer in Greenland.

Ricardo Montalban and Keir Dullea in BLACK WATER GOLD (1970)

William Shatner and Richard Basehart in SOLE SURVIVOR (1970)

0061
BLACK WATER GOLD
1/6/70 Metromedia (MPC) (90 min)

Executive Producer: M. J. Rivkin
Producer/Director: Alan Landsburg
Teleplay: Erwan Kahane
From a story by Alan Landsburg
Photography: Andrew Laszlo
Music: Mike Curb and Jerry Steiner
Editor: John Soh

Dr. Chris Perdeger	KEIR DULLEA
Lyle Fawcett	BRADFORD DILLMAN
Thais	FRANCE NUYEN
Ray Sandage	ARON KINCAID
Ali Zayas	RICARDO MONTALBAN
Eagan Ryan	LANA WOOD
Kefalos	JACQUES AUBUCHON
Roger	PAUL HAMPTON
Jason	STUART TYRONE

A scuba bum joins a marine archeologist and a Mexican historian in the race to reach a treasure from a sunken Spanish galleon ahead of a well-armed dilettante and his associates.

0062
SOLE SURVIVOR
1/9/70 Cinema Center 100 (2 hours)

Executive Producer: Steve Shagen
Producer: Walter Burr
Director: Paul Stanley
Teleplay: Guerdon Trueblood
Photography: James Crabe
Music: Paul Glass
Art Director: Bill Smith
Editor: Renn Reynolds

Major Michael Devlin	VINCE EDWARDS
General Russell Hamner	RICHARD BASEHART
Lt. Col. Joe Gronke	WILLIAM SHATNER
Tony	LOU ANTONIO
Gant	LARRY CASEY
Brandy	DENNIS COONEY
Elmo	BRAD DAVID
Mac	PATRICK WAYNE
Corey	ALAN CAILLOU

Julie Harris, Eve Plumb and Christopher George in THE HOUSE ON GREENAPPLE ROAD (1970)

Beddo	TIMUR BASHTU
British Pilot	JOHN WINSTON
Captain Patrick	DAVID CANNON
General Shurm	NOAH KEEN
British Co-Pilot	IAN ABERCROMBIE
Older Senator	BART BURNS
Amanda	JULIE BENNETT

The ghosts of the crew of a bomber that crashed in the Libyan desert during World War II return to haunt the navigator, now a general, whom they accuse of desertion when he joins an investigation team sifting through the newly found wreckage twenty-five years later. This was the maiden production of a new film company formed by CBS.

0063
THE HOUSE ON GREENAPPLE ROAD
1/11/70 Quinn Martin Productions (2¼ hours)*

Executive Producer: Quinn Martin
Producer: Adrian Samish
Director: Robert Day
Teleplay: George Eckstein
Based on the novel by Harold R. Daniels
Photography: Robert Hoffman
Music: Duane Tatro

Art Director: James D. Vance
Editor: Thomas Ness

Lt. Dan August	CHRISTOPHER GEORGE
Marian Ord	JANET LEIGH
Leona Miller	JULIE HARRIS
George Ord	TIM O'CONNOR
Mayor Jack Parker	WALTER PIDGEON
Chief Frank Untermyer	BARRY SULLIVAN
Sgt. Charles Wilentz	KEENAN WYNN
Sal Gilman	MARK RICHMAN
Paul Durstine	WILLIAM WINDOM
Bill Foley	BURR DeBENNING
Lillian Crane	LYNDA DAY
Connie Durstine	JOANNE LINVILLE
Sheriff Muntz	EDWARD ASNER
Margaret Ord	EVE PLUMB

A crime drama involving a dogged plainclothes cop, a meek salesman accused of murdering his promiscuous wife, and a corpse than cannot be found. The subsequent "Dan August" series (1970–71) starred Burt Reynolds, Norman Fell and Richard Anderson in the roles originally played by Christopher George, Keenan Wynn and Barry Sullivan.

*Subsequently cut to two hours.

0064
FOREIGN EXCHANGE
1/13/70 Halsan Productions (90 min)

Executive Producer: Harold Cohen
Producer: Jimmy Sangster
Director: Roy Baker
Teleplay: Jimmy Sangster
Based on his novel
Photography: Arthur Grant
Music: Philip Martell
Assistant Director: Roy Batt
Art Director: Scott MacGregor
Editor: Spencer Reeve

John Smith	ROBERT HORTON
Max	SEBASTIAN CABOT
Mary Harper	JILL ST. JOHN
Leo	DUDLEY FOSTER
Johns	CLIVE GRAHAM
Karkov	GEORGE ROUBICEK
Borensko	ERIC POHLMANN
Boreman	ERIC LONGWORTH

and: Eleanor Summerfield, Michael Segal, Timothy Bateson, Blake Butler, Constantin de Goguel, Warren Stanhope, Anthony Stamboulieh, Carol Dilworth Carol Cleveland, Anna Gilchrist, Martin Wyldeck, Terence Brady

In this sequel to *The Spy Killer* (1969), an ex-British Secret Service agent is pursuaded to negotiate a spy exchange with Russia, only to find himself ensconced in devious political shenanigans.

0065
MY SWEET CHARLIE
1/20/70 Universal (2 hours)

Executive Producer: Bob Banner
Producers: Richard Levinson and William Link
Director: Lamont Johnson
Teleplay: Richard Levinson and William Link
Based on the novel and play by David Westheimer
Photography: Gene Polito
Music: Gil Melle
Assistant Director: Ralph Ferrin
Art Director: Robert Luthardt
Editor: Edward M. Abroms

Marlene Chambers	PATTY DUKE
Charles Roberts	AL FREEMAN, JR.
Treadwell	FORD RAINEY
Mr. Larrabee	WILLIAM HARDY
Mrs. Larrabee	CHRIS WILSON

and: Archie Moore, Noble Willingham

A pregnant white southern girl and a black New York lawyer, both on the run, meet in a boarded-up house in rural Texas and develop a close friendship for their mutual survival. Patty Duke won an Emmy for her acting—the first given to a TV-movie performance—and Levinson and Link were given Emmys for their original teleplay. In the spring of 1970, *My Sweet Charlie* received a limited theatrical release, including a Manhattan showing—none too successfully.

0066
CARTER'S ARMY
1/27/70 Thomas/Spelling Productions (90 min)

Producers: Danny Thomas and Aaron Spelling
Associate Producer: Shelley Hull
Director: George McCowan
Teleplay: Aaron Spelling and David Kidd
Photography: Arch R. Dalzell
Music: Fred Steiner
Art Director: Paul Sylos, Jr.
Editor: George Brooks

Patty Duke and Al Freeman, Jr., in MY SWEET CHARLIE (1970)

Roosevelt Grier, Stephen Boyd, Richard Pryor and Glynn Turman in CARTER'S ARMY (1970)

Capt. Beau Carter	STEPHEN BOYD
Lt. Edward Wallace	ROBERT HOOKS
Anna	SUSAN OLIVER
Big Jim	ROOSEVELT GRIER
Doc	MOSES GUNN
Jonathan Crunk	RICHARD PRYOR
George Brightman	GLYNN TURMAN
Lewis	BILLY DEE WILLIAMS
General Clark	PAUL STEWART
Robinson	BOBBY JOHNSON
Fuzzy	NAPOLEON WHITING

A redneck army captain becomes the commanding officer of an all-black rear-eschelon service company and is ordered to hold an important dam against the enemy.

0067
THE MOVIE MURDERER
2/2/70 Universal (2 hours)

Producer: Jack Laird
Director: Boris Sagal
Teleplay: Stanford Whitmore
From a story by Bernard Taper and Stanford Whitmore
Photography: Lionel Lindon
Music: Stanley Wilson
Assistant Director: Carl Beringer
Art Director: Henry Bumstead
Editor: Frank E. Morriss

Angus MacGregor	ARTHUR KENNEDY
Alfred Fisher	WARREN OATES
Mike Beaudine	TOM SELLECK
Collier Landis	JEFF COREY
Ellen Farrington	NORMA CRANE
Karel Kessler	ROBERT WEBBER
Cliff Thomas	RUSSELL JOHNSON
Lois Warwick	NITA TALBOT
Jimmy Apache	SEVERN DARDEN
Willie Peanuts	ELISHA COOK
J. M. Cole	DAVID ASTOR
Martin Moss	HENRY JONES
King Kong	STEVE SANDOR
Hotel Clerk	NED GLASS
Linderman	WOODROW PARFREY
Beaver	SALLY ANN RICHARDS

Suzanne Pleshette and Ed Nelson in ALONG CAME A SPIDER (1970)

Arthur Kennedy and Tom Selleck in THE MOVIE MURDERER (1970)

Arson Lieutenant	FRANK CAMPANELLA
Pete Holland	MARK ALLEN
Jacob Silas	MILTON FROME

An aging fire insurance investigator pits his long experience against modern computer methods to track down a professional arsonist who is torching movie film.

0068
ALONG CAME A SPIDER
2/3/70 20th Century-Fox (90 min)

Executive Producer: Alan A. Armer
Producer: Bill Faralla
Director: Lee H. Katzin
Teleplay: Barry Oringer
Based on the novel *Sweet Poison* by Leonard Lee
Photography: Robert Moreno
Music: David Rose
Art Director: Ed Graves
Editor: Desmond Marquette

Anne Banning/Janet Furie	SUZANNE PLESHETTE
Martin Becker	ED NELSON
Sam Howard	ANDREW PRINE
Adrienne Klein	BROOKE BUNDY
Dist. Atty. Freiberg	RICHARD ANDERSON
Frank Dietzler	WRIGHT KING
Judge Romagna	BARRY ATWATER
Dr. Schuster	MILTON SELZER
Dr. Blake	FRANK FERGUSON
Dr. Newman	VIRGINIA GREGG
Herbie	JOHNNIE COLLINS III
Dr. Hernandez	JOE E. TATA

A research scientist's widow, seeking to avenge her husband's murder at the hand of his colleague, conceals her true identity and embarks on an affair with the man she suspects.

0069
CUTTER'S TRAIL
2/10/70 CBS Studio Center (2 hours)

Producer: John Mantley
Director: Vincent McEveety
Teleplay: Paul Savage
Photography: Richard Batcheller
Music: John Parker
Assistant Director: Paul Nichols
Editor: Howard A. Smith

Ben Cutter	JOHN GAVIN
Paco Avila	MANUEL PADILLA, JR.
Amelita Avila	MARISA PAVAN
Maggie	BEVERLY GARLAND
General Spalding	JOSEPH COTTEN
Santillo	NEHEMIAH PERSOFF
Froteras	J. CARROLL NAISH
Tuttle	SHUG FISHER
Clay Wooten	KEN SWOFFORD
Alex Bowen	VICTOR FRENCH
Kyle Bowen	BOB RANDOM
Thatcher	ROBERT TOTTEN
Orville Mason	TOM BROWN

A formula Western about a U.S. marshal who finds his town nearly destroyed by Mexican bandits during his absence and vows to track down the desperadoes in their home territory—with the help of a young Mexican mother and her son. Reversing the usual process, this film premiered as a ninety-minute movie and subsequently was shown as a two-hour hoss opera.

Marisa Pavan, Manuel Padilla and John Gavin in CUTTER'S TRAIL (1970)

John Gavin and Beverly Garland in CUTTER'S TRAIL (1970)

0070

THE CHALLENGE
2/10/70 20th Century-Fox (90 min)

Producers: Jay Cipes and Ed Palmer
Director: Allen Smithee
Teleplay: Marc Norman
Photography: John M. Nicholaus
Music: Harry Geller
Art Directors: Jack Martin Smith and Ed Graves
Editors: Stanford Tischler and Joe Gluck

Jacob Gallery	DARREN McGAVIN
Gen. Lewis Meyers	BRODERICK CRAWFORD
Yuro	MAKO
Overman	JAMES WHITMORE
Lyman George	SKIP HOMEIER
Dr. Nagy	PAUL LUKAS
Bryant	SAM ELLIOTT
Clarence Opano	ADOLPH CAESAR
Swiss Official	ANDRE PHILIPPE
Sarah	ARIANHE ULMER
Scientist	DAVIS ROBERTS
Defense Secretary	BYRON MORROW
Army Colonel	BILL ZUCKERT
Doctor	GENE LeBELL
Sergeant	LEW BROWN
Soldier	EDDIE GUARDINO
Submarine Captain	GARRY WALBERG
Marine Colonel	BILL QUINN
Army Captain	MICHAEL HINN

This offbeat war movie has an armed conflict between
the United States and an Asian country reduced to the
lowest common denominator, with one surrogate soldier from each country in a fight to the death on a
deserted island.

0071

McCLOUD: WHO KILLED MISS U.S.A.?
2/17/70 Universal (2 hours)
(subsequently titled *Portrait of a Dead Girl*)

Producer: Leslie Stevens
Associate Producer: John Strong
Director: Richard A. Colla
Teleplay: Stanford Whitmore, Richard Levinson
and William Link
From a story by Stanford Whitmore
Photography: Ben Colman
Music: David Shire
Song: "Another Way" lyrics by Richard Maltby, Jr.
Assistant Directors: Edward K. Dodds and Steve
Marshall

Mako and Darren McGavin in THE CHALLENGE (1970)

John McMartin and Anne Baxter in RITUAL OF EVIL (1970)

Darren McGavin in THE CHALLENGE (1970)

Art Director: Henry Bumstead
Editors: Robert L. Kimble and Bob Kagey

Marshal Sam McCloud	DENNIS WEAVER
Whitman	CRAIG STEVENS
Peter B. Clifford	MARK RICHMAN
Chris Coughlin	DIANA MULDAUR
Sgt. Joe Broadhurst	TERRY CARTER
Peralta	MARIO ALCALDE
Father Nieves	RAUL JULIA
James Waldron	SHELLY NOVACK
Adrienne Redman	JULIE NEWMAR
Billy	MICHAEL BOW
Ramos	NEFTI MILLET
Merri Ann Coleman	KATHY STRITCH
Guard	ALBERT POPWELL
2nd Reporter	IRA COOK
1st Deputy	GREGORY SIERRA
2nd Deputy	TONY DANTE
Black Reporter	VICTOR BOZEMAN
1st Reporter	BILL BALDWIN
Vejar	RON HENRIQUEZ
Receptionist	LEE PULFORD
Chico	ROBERTO VARGAS

Recycled from Don Siegel's Clint Eastwood film, *Coogan's Bluff* (1969), this pilot movie for the long-run "McCloud" series (1971–76) brings a modern-day western marshal to New York with a subpoenaed witness, only to have him kidnapped and then finding himself dragged into a murder case involving Puerto Rican militants, a lady novelist, a Wall Street lawyer and a dead beauty queen. Weaver was joined in the series by Terry Carter and (occasionally) Diana Muldaur, while Mark Richman's role of police commissioner was taken over by J. D. Cannon.

0072
THE CHALLENGERS
2/20/70 Universal (2 hours)

Producer: Roy Huggins
Associate Producer: Frederick Shorr
Director: Leslie H. Martinson
Teleplay: Dick Nelson
From a story by Robert Hamner and John Thomas James
Photography: Jack Marta
Music: Pete Rugolo
Assistant Director: Les Berke
Art Director: John T. McCormack
Editors: Edward A. Biery and Nick Archer

Jim McCabe	DARREN McGAVIN
Cody Scanlon	SEAN GARRISON
Paco	NICO MINARDOS
Stephanie York	ANNE BAXTER
Ritchie	RICHARD CONTE
Nealy	FARLEY GRANGER
Mary McCabe	JULIET MILLS
Angel de Angelo	SAL MINEO
Catherine Burroughs	SUSAN CLARK
Jules	MICHAEL EVANS
Brad York	WILLIAM SYLVESTER
Ambrose	JOHN HOLLAND
Bryan Toomey	ALAN CAILLOU

Racing drivers compete here for the Grand Prix. Filmed in March 1968, it originally was scheduled for airing on March 28, 1969 but was preempted because of the death of Dwight D. Eisenhower.

0073
RITUAL OF EVIL
2/23/70 Universal (2 hours)

Producer: David Levinson
Director: Robert Day
Teleplay: Robert Presnell, Jr.
Based on characters created by Richard Alan Simmons

UNIVERSAL *presenta*
DARREN McGAVIN
SEAN GARRISON
NICO MINARDOS

sfida sulla PISTA DI FUOCO

ANNE BAXTER · RICHARD CONTE · FARLEY GRANGER · JULIET MILLS · SAL MINEO · SUSAN CLARK
DICK NELSON · ROBERT HAMNER · JOHN THOMAS JAMES · LESLIE H. MARTINSON · ROY HUGGINS · TECHNICOLOR · UNIVERSAL · PUBLIC ARTS

Advertisement for Italian theatrical release of THE CHALLENGERS (1970)

Susan Clark and Sean Garrison in THE CHALLENGERS (1970)

Vince Edwards and Kim Hunter in DIAL HOT LINE (1970)

Photography: Lionel Lindon
Music: Billy Goldenberg
Assistant Director: Carl Beringer
Art Director: William D. DeCinces
Editor: Douglas Stewart

David Sorell	LOUIS JOURDAN
Jolene Wiley	ANNE BAXTER
Leila Barton	DIANA HYLAND
Edward Bolander	JOHN McMARTIN
Harry Snowden	WILFRID HYDE-WHITE
Loey Wiley	BELINDA MONTGOMERY
Aline Wiley	CARLA BORELLI
Larry Richmond	GEORG STANFORD BROWN
Sheriff	REGE CORDIC
Mora	DEHL BERTI
Hippie	RICHARD ALAN KNOX
Newscaster	JOHNNY WILLIAMS
1st Reporter	JIMMY JOYCE
2nd Reporter	JAMES LaSANE

Further excursions into black magic and the occult occur in this sequel to *Fear No Evil* (1969) with Louis Jourdan and Wilfrid Hyde-White recreating their roles. This movie was called *Next Time, My Love* during production and has a noted psychiatrist delving into the death of a patient, a young heiress.

0074
QUARANTINED
2/24/70 Paramount (90 min)

Producer: Lou Morheim
Director: Leo Penn
Teleplay: Norman Katkov
Photography: Howard R. Schwartz
Music: George Duning
Art Director: William Campbell
Editor: Donald R. Rode

Dr. Larry Freeman	GARY COLLINS
Dr. John Bedford	JOHN DEHNER
Peggy Bedford	SUSAN HOWARD
Dr. Bud Bedford	GORDON PINANT
Dr. Tom Bedford	DAN FERRONE
Ginny Pepper	SHARON FARRELL
Wilbur Mott	WALLY COX
Mr. Berryman	SAM JAFFE
Martha Atkinson	TERRY MOORE
Nurse Nelson	VIRGINIA GREGG

and: Greg Mullavey, Marilyn Hassett, Vince Howard, Joe Bernard, Jan Peters, Madison Arnold

This unsuccessful pilot is set in a clinic run by a renowned medical family. The plot has them trying to stem a cholera epidemic and save the life of a film star who is fighting treatment.

0075
MISTER JERICO
3/3/70 I.T.C. (90 min)

Producer: Julian Wintle
Director: Sidney Hayers
Teleplay: Philip Levine
From a story by David T. Chantler
Photography: Alan Hume
Music: Laurie Johnson
Song by George Martin and Don Black
Sung by Lulu
Art Director: Harry Pottle
Editor: Lionel Selwyn

Dudley Jerico	PATRICK MACNEE
Susan	CONNIE STEVENS
Victor Russo	HERBERT LOM
Wally	MARTY ALLEN
Angelo	LEONARDO PIERONI
Nolan	BRUCE BUA
Merle	JOANNE DAINTON
Hotel Clerk	PAUL DARROW
Maid	JASMINA HILTON
Felipe	PETER YAPP

A charming conman teams up with a pretty blonde in his attempt to separate a crooked millionaire from a fabulous diamond. Macnee, better known at the time as John Steed of "The Avengers," made his initial TV-movie debut—to American audiences at least—in this comedy adventure.

0076
DIAL HOT LINE
3/8/70 Universal (2 hours)

Producer: William Sackheim
Associate Producer: John Badham
Director: Jerry Thorpe
Teleplay: Carol Sobieski
From a story by Carol Sobieski and Don Ingalls
Photography: Jack Marta
Music: Oliver Nelson
Song "Hey, Does Somebody Care?" written and sung by Linda Perhaps
Art Director: George C. Webb
Editor: Edward M. Abroms

David Leopold	VINCE EDWARDS
Tag (Tasmania Australia Gibson)	CHELESA BROWN
Kevin	MICHAEL LARRAIN
Ann	JUNE HARDING
Jimmy	FELTON PERRY
Mrs. Edith Carruthers	KIM HUNTER
Pam Carruthers	LANE BRADBURY
Joe	ELLIOTT STREET
Dr. Stone	G. D. SPRADLIN
Earl	ROBERT PRATT
Peter	MICHAEL McGREEVEY
Sam	JAMES GRIFFITH
4th Board Member	KERMIT MURDOCK
Stevie	VINNIE VAN PATTEN

The concept that eventually became Vince Edwards' "Matt Lincoln" series (1970–71) revolves around a psychiatric telephone service with Edwards as head man and several younger players taking to the street —in the best tradition of "The Mod Squad"—and getting involved with people with myriads of problems. The later series, although short-lived, did not affect Edwards' career adversely, but the other four regulars never went on to become household names. John Badham, the pilot's associate producer, subsequently moved into directing and did such moneymakers as *Saturday Night Fever* and *Dracula* for the big screen, as well as several television movies.

0077
THE MASK OF SHEBA
3/9/70 MGM (2 hours)

Producer: Sam Rolfe
Director: David Lowell Rich
Teleplay: Sam Rolfe
Photography: Gabriel Torres and Harold Wellman
Music: Lalo Schifrin
Art Directors: George W. Davis and Marvin
Summerfield
Editor: John Dunning

Dr. Roan Morgan	ERIC BRAEDEN
Travis	STEPHEN YOUNG
Dr. Joanna Glenville	CORINNE COMACHO
Dr. Max van Condon	WALTER PIDGEON
Sarah Kramer	INGER STEVENS
Bondalok	JOSEPH WISEMAN
Condor	WILLIAM MARSHALL
Peter	CHRISTOPHER CAREY
Jason	LINCOLN KILPATRICK

Intrigue, romance and the customary angry natives are
the major elements in this tale of a hunt for a priceless
gold mask in the jungles of Ethiopia.

0078
THE LOVE WAR
3/10/70 Thomas/Spelling Productions (90 min)

Producer: Aaron Spelling
Director: George McCowan
Teleplay: Guerdon Trueblood and David Kidd
Photography: Paul Uhl
Music: Dominic Frontiere
Assistant Director: Wes Barry
Art Director: Tracy Bousman
Editor: Bob Lewis

Kyle	LLOYD BRIDGES
Sandy	ANGIE DICKINSON
Bal	HARRY BASCH
Ted	DAN TRAVANTY

and: Allen Jaffe, Bill McLean, Byron Foulger, Pepper
Martin

A science-fiction thriller involving aliens from two
warring planets who take human form and continue
their battle in a small California town.

0079
HUNTERS ARE FOR KILLING
3/12/70 Cinema Center 100 (2 hours)

Producer: Hugh Benson
Director: Bernard Girard
Teleplay: Charles Kuenstle
Photography: Gerald Perry Finnerman
Music: Jerry Fielding
Art Directors: James D. Vance and Michael S.
Glick
Editor: Edward Mann

L. G. Floran	BURT REYNOLDS
Keller Floran	MELVYN DOUGLAS
Barbara Soline	SUZANNE PLESHETTE
Rudy LeRoy	LARRY STORCH
Wade Jamilton	MARTIN BALSAM
Raymond Pera	PETER BROWN
Holly Farnell	JILL BANNER
Hank Phillips	DONALD BARRY
Richard Soline	ANGUS DUNCAN
Carl Farnell	IVOR FRANCIS
Jimmy Ramirez	A. MARTINEZ

Eric Braeden, Walter Pidgeon, Corinne Comacho and Stephen Young in
THE MASK OF SHEBA (1970)

Martin Balsam, Peter Brown and Melvyn Douglas in **HUNTERS ARE FOR KILLING** (1970)

A drifter comes home after serving time for manslaughter to claim his share of his mother's estate and settle things with his abrasive stepfather, unforgiving since he holds the ex-con responsible for his own son's death. Burt Reynolds made his TV-movie debut in this one, and during the succeeding decade he acted in just one other telefeature.

0080
DAVID COPPERFIELD
3/15/70 Omnibus Productions/Sagittarius Productions (2 hours)

Producer: Frederick H. Brogger
Associate Producer: Hugh Attwooll
Director: Delbert Mann
Teleplay: Jack Pulman
Based on the novel by Charles Dickens
Photography: Ken Hodges
Music: Malcolm Arnold
Art Director: Alex Vetchinsky
Editor: Peter Boita

David Copperfield   ROBIN PHILLIPS
Agnes Wickfield   SUSAN HAMPSHIRE
Betsy Trotwood   EDITH EVANS
Mr. Peggotty   MICHAEL
                           REDGRAVE

Richard Attenborough and Laurence Olivier in DAVID COPPERFIELD (1970)

Roger Davis and Joan Hackett in THE YOUNG COUNTRY (1970)

Mr. Micawber	RALPH RICHARDSON
Mrs. Micawber	WENDY HILLER
Steerforth	CORIN REDGRAVE
Dora	PAMELA FRANKLIN
Uriah Heep	RON MOODY
Mr. Murdstone	JAMES DONALD
Mr. Dick	EMLYN WILLIAMS
Mr. Creakle	LAURENCE OLIVIER
Mr. Tungay	RICHARD ATTENBOROUGH
Clara Peggotty	MEGS JENKINS
Jane Murdstone	ANNA MASSEY
Barkis	CYRIL CUSACK
Traddles	NICHOLAS PENNELL
Emily	SINEAD CUSACK

and: Andrew McCulloch, Isobel Black, Donald Layne-Smith, James Hayter, Helen Cotterill, Kim Craik, Alistair Mackenzie, Christopher Moran, Jeffrey Chandler, Brian Tipping, Alison Blair, Liam Redmond, Gordon Rollings, George Woodbridge, William Lyon-Brown, Christine Ozanne, Phoebe Shaw, Robert Lankesheer

A moody, sentimental fifth film version of the Dickens classic (the first in nearly thirty-five years) with a stellar cast composed of the giants of the British acting community providing much needed support to the virtual unknown in the title role. Laurence Olivier's cameo as Creakle won him an Emmy nomination.

0081
THE YOUNG COUNTRY
3/17/70 Universal (90 min)

Producer/Director: Roy Huggins
Associate Producers: Carl Pingitore and Steve Heilpern
Teleplay: Roy Huggins
Photography: Vilis Lapenieks
Music: Pete Rugolo
Assistant Director: Richard Bennett
Art Director: Joseph Alves, Jr.
Editor: Robert Watts

Sheriff Matt Fenley	WALTER BRENNAN
Clementine Hale	JOAN HACKETT
Aaron Grimes/Ira Greebe	WALLY COX
Honest John Smith	PETER DEUEL
Stephen Foster Moody	ROGER DAVIS
Hotel Manager	SKIP YOUNG
Parker	STEVE SANDOR
Harvey "Fat" Chance	ROBERT DRISCOLL MILLER
Randy Willis	RICHARD VAN FLEET

and: Elliott Street, Barbara Gates, Luis Delgado, Thomas Ballin

This lighthearted Western finds a footloose young gambler searching for the owner of a mysterious fortune.

0082
A CLEAR AND PRESENT DANGER
3/21/70 Universal (2 hours)

Producer: William Sackheim
Associate Producer: John Badham
Director: James Goldstone
Teleplay: A. J. Russell and Henri Simoun
From a story by S. S. Schweitzer and A. J. Russell
Photography: Bill Butler
Music: Billy Goldenberg
Assistant Director: Donald Roberts
Art Director: John J. Lloyd
Editors: Edward A. Biery and Richard M. Sprague

Hays Stowe	HAL HOLBROOK
Senator Stowe	E. G. MARSHALL
Jordan Boyle	JOSEPH CAMPANELLA
Dr. Chanute	JACK ALBERTSON
Salem Chase	PAT HINGLE
Erin Stowe	SHARON ACKER
Howard Eagar	JAMES DOUGLAS
Professor Duke	MIKE KELLIN
Beiseker	JEFF COREY
House	BERNIE HAMILTON
Elliot Morse	MICHAEL BELL
Norma Stowe	CINDY EILBACHER
Amanda Shamokin	ADRIENNE MARDEN
Health Commissioner	HARRY BASCH
Preston Gardiner	ROBERT HEINZ
Nurse	MARIAN COLLIER

A U.S. Senator's concerned son takes up the cause against air pollution when an old friend of the family dies of emphysema and finds himself becoming involved in a senatorial race joining his father. The first TV movie involving environmental problems, this served as the pilot to "The Senator" element of the rotating series under the umbrella title of "The Bold Ones." It proved to be too good and a shade too controversial for television (Holbrook, Acker and Eilbacher continued their roles in the series and were joined by Michael Tolan in the role originated by Campanella) and lasted only one season (1970–71), being virtually pressured off the airwaves. Hal Holbrook won an Emmy nomination for his performance in the TV movie and the following year again for his work in the series.

1970–71 SEASON

0083
THE BROTHERHOOD OF THE BELL
9/17/70 Cinema Center 100 (2 hours)

Executive Producer: Hugh Benson
Producer: David Karp
Director: Paul Wendkos

Hal Holbrook and Sharon Acker in A CLEAR AND PRESENT DANGER (1970)

Teleplay: David Karp
Photography: Robert B. Hauser
Music: Jerry Goldsmith
Art Director: William Smith
Editor: Carroll Sax

Prof. Andrew Paterson	GLENN FORD
Vivian Paterson	ROSEMARY FORSYTH
Chad Harmon	DEAN JAGGER
Harry Masters	MAURICE EVANS
Mike Paterson	WILL GEER
Dr. Konstantin Horvathy	EDUARD FRANZ
Bart Harris	WILLIAM CONRAD
Philip Dunning	ROBERT PINE

Dean Jagger and Glenn Ford in THE BROTHERHOOD OF THE BELL (1970)

Julie Harris and Anthony Perkins in HOW AWFUL ABOUT ALLAN (1970)

Joan Hackett and Anthony Perkins in HOW AWFUL ABOUT ALLAN (1970)

Jerry Fielder	WILLIAM SMITHERS
Thaddeus Burns	LOGAN FIELD
Betty Fielder	LIZABETH HUSH

and: Leon Lontoc, Dabney Coleman, Virginia Gilmore, Joe Brooks, Robert Clarke, Marc Hannibal, Scott Grahame

Glenn Ford and Rosemary Forsyth both made their TV acting debuts in this tale of a successful professor who is presented with a due bill from a club he had joined years earlier—a secret society whose power to achieve monetary and professional security for its members is equalled only by its determination to punish those standing in its way. His job now is to prevent a long-time colleague and friend from a Communist bloc country from accepting a professorship.

0084
HOW AWFUL ABOUT ALLAN
9/22/70 Aaron Spelling Productions (90 min)

Executive Producer: Aaron Spelling
Producer: George Edwards
Director: Curtis Harrington
Teleplay: Henry Farrell
Based on his novel
Photography: Fleet Southcott
Music: Laurence Rosenthal
Art Director: Tracy Bousman
Editor: Richard Darrell

Allan Colleigh	ANTHONY PERKINS
Elizabeth Colleigh	JULIE HARRIS
Olive	JOAN HACKETT
Raymond Colleigh	KENT SMITH
Dr. Ellins	ROBERT H. HARRIS
Harold Dennis	BILL BOWLES
Eric	TRENT DOLAN
Allan as a Child	GENE LAWRENCE
Elizabeth as a Child	JEANETTE HOWE

and: Molly Dodd, William Erwin

A chiller about a man who is tormented by guilt over his father's death and tormented by strange voices and an unseen menace.

0085
SAN FRANCISCO INTERNATIONAL
9/29/70 Universal (2 hours)

Executive Producer: Frank Price
Producers: William Read Woodfield and Allan Balter
Associate Producer: John Orland
Director: John Llewellyn Moxey
Teleplay: William Read Woodfield and Allan Balter
Photography: Andrew Jackson
Music: Pat Williams
Assistant Director: Ricci R. Rondell
Art Director: Henry Larrecq
Editors: Budd Small and John Elias

Jim Conrad	PERNELL ROBERTS
Bob Hatten	CLU GULAGER
Katie Barrett	BETH BRICKELL
Lester Scott	VAN JOHNSON
Ross Edwards	DAVID HARTMAN
Tina Scott	NANCY MALONE
Davey Scott	TEDDY ECCLES
Clifford Foster Evans	WALTER BROOKE
William Sturtevant	CLIFF POTTS
Joan Edwards	JILL DONOHUE
Frank Davis	CHUCK DANIEL
George Woodruff	DANA ELCAR
Stayczek	TAB HUNTER
Dan	ROBERT SORRELLS
Amato	JIM B. SMITH

Senator	JASON WINGREEN
Sgt. Dobkin	MARC HANNIBAL
Congressman	FRANK GERSTLE

Daily doings at a huge airport, not the least of which is a possible $3 million hijacking while the manager and his staff are already wrestling with everything from a kidnapping to a shaky marriage. The subsequent series (1970–71) starred Lloyd Bridges, taking over for Pernell Roberts, and Clu Gulager.

0086
NIGHT SLAVES
9/29/70 Bing Crosby Productions (90 min)

Producer: Everett Chambers
Director: Ted Post
Teleplay: Everett Chambers and Robert Specht
Based on the novel by Jerry Sohl
Photography: Robert B. Hauser
Music: Bernardo Segall
Art Director: Howard Hollander
Editor: Michael Kahn

Clay Howard	JAMES FRANCISCUS
Marjorie Howard	LEE GRANT
Matt Russell	SCOTT MARLOWE
Fess Beany (Noel)	ANDREW PRINE
Annie Fletcher (Naillil)	TISHA STERLING
Sheriff Henshaw	LESLIE NIELSEN
Mrs. Crawford	VIRGINIA WRIGHT
Mr. Hale	MORRIS BUCHANAN
Spencer	CLIFF CARNELL
Jeff Pardee	VICTOR ISAY
Joe Landers	RAYMOND MAYO
Mr. Fletcher	JOHN KELLOGG
Dr. Smithers	RUSSELL THORSON
May	NANCY VALENTINE

A science-fiction thriller about a man who finds himself stranded in a sleepy western town with his wife and then becomes romantically involved with a beautiful woman who holds the key to the mystery of the strange force that has turned the townspeople into zombies.

0087
BUT I DON'T WANT TO GET MARRIED!
10/6/70 Aaron Spelling Productions (90 min)

Producer: Aaron Spelling
Director: Jerry Paris
Teleplay: Roland Wolpert
Photography: Fleet Southcott
Music: George Duning
Art Director: William Creeber
Editor: Aaron Stell

Walter Benjamin	HERSCHEL BERNARDI
Evelyn Harris	SHIRLEY JONES
Bernard	BRANDON CRUZ
Mrs. Vale	NANETTE FABRAY
Hope	JUNE LOCKHART
Miss Spencer	TINA LOUISE
Laura	SUE LYON
Hallie	KAY MEDFORD
Mr. Good	HARRY MORGAN
Olga	JOYCE VAN PATTEN
Carl	TEDDY ECCLES
Mrs. Borg	KATHLEEN FREEMAN
Harry	JERRY PARIS

An accountant finds himself a widower after eighteen years of marriage and the quarry of a herd of husband-hunters.

Van Johnson and Nancy Malone in SAN FRANCISCO INTERNATIONAL (1970)

Tisha Sterling and James Franciscus in NIGHT SLAVES (1970)

Edward G. Robinson and Ruth Roman in THE OLD MAN WHO CRIED WOLF (1970)

0088
THE OLD MAN WHO CRIED WOLF
10/13/70 Aaron Spelling Productions (90 min)

Executive Producer: Aaron Spelling
Producer/Director: Walter Grauman
Teleplay: Luther Davis
From a story by Arnold Horwitt
Photography: Arch R. Dalzell
Music: Robert Drasnin
Assistant Director: Max Stein
Art Director: Paul Sylos
Editor: Art Seid

Emile Pulska	EDWARD G. ROBINSON
Stanley Pulska	MARTIN BALSAM
Peggy Pulska	DIANE BAKER
Frank Jones	PERCY RODRIGUES
Lois	RUTH ROMAN
Dr. Morheim	EDWARD ASNER
Hudson Ewing	MARTIN E. BROOKS
Detective Green	PAUL PICERNI
Abe Stillman	SAM JAFFE
Detective Seroly	ROBERT YURO
Carl	BILL ELLIOTT
Leon	JAMES E. WATSON
Mrs. Raspili	NAOMI STEVENS
Miss Cummings	VIRGINIA CHRISTINE
Pawnbroker	JAY C. FLIPPEN
Louie	PEPE BROWN

An old man, unable to convince anyone—even his own family—that he has been a witness to the brutal murder of a long-time friend, sets out to find the killer himself.

0089
THE OTHER MAN
10/19/70 Universal (2 hours)

Producer: William Frye
Director: Richard A. Colla
Teleplay: Michael Blankfort and Eric Bercovici
Based on the novel by Margaret Lynn
Photography: E. Charles Straumer
Music: Michel Colombier
Assistant Director: Marty Hornstein
Art Director: John J. Lloyd
Editor: Robert L. Kimble

Johnny Bryant	ROY THINNES
Paul Maitland	ARTHUR HILL
Kathy Maitland	JOAN HACKETT
Denise Gray	TAMMY GRIMES
Lt. Lorca	RODOLFO HOYOS
Mrs. Baird	VIRGINIA GREGG
Mrs. Turley	ANNE COLLINGS
George Dunning	JAMES GAVIN
Maria Soledad	ZOLYA TALMA

The neglected wife of an ambitious D.A. drifts into an affair with the ex-con he had helped send away, and when her lover is found murdered, she cannot shake the idea that her husband is the killer.

0090
WILD WOMEN
10/20/70 Aaron Spelling Productions (90 min)

Executive Producer: Aaron Spelling
Producer: Lou Morheim
Associate Producer: Shelley Hull
Director: Don Taylor

Teleplay: Lou Morheim and Richard Carr
Based on the novel *The Trailmakers* by Vincent Forte
Photography: Fleet Southcott
Music: Fred Steiner
Supervised by George Duning
Art Director: Tracy Bousman
Editor: Aaron Stell

Killian	HUGH O'BRIAN
Jean Marshek	ANNE FRANCIS
Maude Webber	MARILYN MAXWELL
Lottie Clampett	MARIE WINDSOR
Nancy Delacourt	SHERRY JACKSON
Colonel Donahue	ROBERT F. SIMON
Captain Charring	RICHARD KELTON
Mit-O-Ne	CYNTHIA HULL
Lt. Santos	PEPE CALLAHAN

and: Ed Call, John Neris, Loie Bridge, Troy Melton, Jay Kaufmann, Chuck Hicks, Jim Boles, Thomas Montgomery, Kaye Elhardt, Michael Keep, Pedro Regas

Five female convicts are recruited to help secretly transport arms into Mexican-held Texas in 1840.

0091
THE AQUARIANS
10/24/70 Universal/Ivan Tors Productions (2 hours)

Producer: Ivan Tors
Director: Don McDougall
Teleplay: Leslie Stevens and Winston Miller
From a story by Ivan Tors and Allan Caillou

Photography: Clifford Poland
Music: Lalo Schifrin
Underwater sequences directed by Ricou Browning
Underwater sequences photographed by Jordan Klein
Art Director: Gene Harris
Editor: Erwin Dumbrille

Dr. Luis Del Gado	RICARDO MONTALBAN
Alfred Vreeland	JOSE FERRER
Official (and spoken introduction)	LESLIE NIELSEN
Ledring	CHRIS ROBINSON
Barbara Brand	KATE WOODVILLE
Bob Exeter	LAWRENCE CASEY
Jerry Hollis	TOM SIMCOX
Ehrlich	CURT LOWENS
Jean Hollis	ELSA INGRAM
Norma	JOAN MURPHY

and: Austin Stoker, Napoleon Reed, Henry Mortimer, Phil Philbin, Dan Chandler, Ted Swanson, William Evenson, Ken Harris, Roger Phillips, Myron Natwick, Harlan Warde

A noted scientist and his team of underwater explorers go deep-sea diving to hunt the villain who has stolen the world's supply of nerve gas and is polluting the ocean. Adventure below sea level, Ivan Tors-style, in his initial plunge into the field of TV movies after his success with "Flipper" and others.

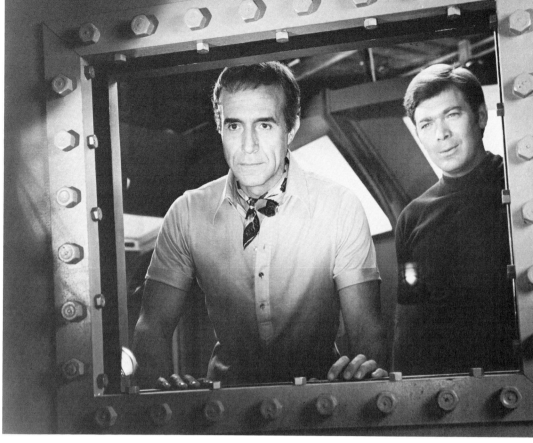

Ricardo Montalban and Tom Simcox in THE AQUARIANS (1970)

Joan Hackett and Arthur Hill in THE OTHER MAN (1970)

0092
THE HOUSE THAT WOULD NOT DIE
10/27/70 Aaron Spelling Productions (90 min)

Producer: Aaron Spelling
Director: John Llewellyn Moxey
Teleplay: Henry Farrell
Based on the novel *Ammie, Come Home* by Barbara Michaels
Photography: Fleet Southcott
Music composed by Laurence Rosenthal
Conducted by George Duning
Art Director: Tracy Bousman
Editor: Art Seid

Ruth Bennett	BARBARA STANWYCK
Pat McDougal	RICHARD EGAN
Stan Whitman	MICHAEL ANDERSON, JR.
Sara Dunning	KATHERINE WINN
Sylvia Wall	DOREEN LANG
Delia McDougal	MABEL ALBERTSON

Barbara Stanwyck made her TV-movie debut in this tale of witchcraft, black magic and unsettled ghosts in an inherited house in Amish country.

0093
BERLIN AFFAIR
11/2/70 Universal (2 hours)

Producers: E. Jack Neuman and Paul Donnelly
Director: David Lowell Rich
Teleplay: Peter Penduik and E. Jack Neuman
From a story by Elliot West
Photography: Michael Marszalek
Music: Francis Lai
Art Director: Hans Jurgen Kiebach
Editor: Edward M. Abroms

Killian	DARREN McGAVIN
Mallicent	FRITZ WEAVER
Paul Strand	BRIAN KELLY
Languin	CLAUDE DAUPHIN
Wendi	PASCALE PETIT
Galt	DERREN NESBITT

47

Albert	CHRISTIAN ROBERTS
Andrea	KATHIE BROWNE
Juliet	MARIAN COLLIER
Klaus	REINHARD KOLLDEHOFF
Mildred	HEIDRUN HANKAMMER
Copy Girl	GITTA SCHUBERT
Vendor	MANFRED MEURER
Blonde	ISABELLE ERVENS

This foreign intrigue thriller has a one-time spy forced by a murder-for-hire syndicate to hunt down and kill his best friend and former colleague.

0094
TRIBES
11/10/70 20th Century-Fox (90 min)

Producer: Marvin Schwartz
Director: Joseph Sargent
Teleplay: Tracy Keenan Wynn and Marvin Schwartz
Photography: Russell Metty
Music: Al Capps and Marty Cooper
Supervised by Lionel Newman
Assistant Director: Bruce Fowler
Art Directors: Jack Martin Smith and Richard Day
Editor: Patrick Kennedy

Sergeant Drake	DARREN McGAVIN
DePayster	EARL HOLLIMAN
Adrian	JAN-MICHAEL VINCENT
Quentin	JOHN GRUBER
Sidney	DANNY GOLDMAN
Sanchez	RICHARD YNIGUEZ
Marchelus	ANTONE CURTIS
Scrunch	PETER HOOTEN
Armstrong	DAVID BUCHANAN
Morton	RICK WEAVER

This social comedy/drama pits a veteran Marine Corps drill instructor against a long-haired hippie who refuses to adapt to the military way of life. Perceptive writing won Emmy Awards for Wynn (son of Keenan, grandson of Ed) and Schwartz. It was shown theatrically in Great Britain and elsewhere under the title *The Soldier Who Declared Peace*.

0095
THE INTRUDERS
11/10/70 Universal (2 hours)

Producer: James Duff McAdams
Director: William A. Graham
Teleplay: Dean Riesner
From a story by William Lansford
Photography: Ray Flin
Music: Dave Grusin
Assistant Director: Roger Slager
Art Director: Loyd S. Papez
Editor: J. Howard Terrill

Sam Garrison	DON MURRAY
Leora Garrison	ANNE FRANCIS
Col. William Bodeen	EDMOND O'BRIEN
Billy Pye	JOHN SAXON
Cole Younger	GENE EVANS
Elton Dykstra	EDWARD ANDREWS
Theron Pardo	SHELLY NOVACK
Whit Dykstra	DEAN STANTON
Jesse James	STUART MARGOLIN
Bob Younger	ZALMAN KING

and: Phillip Alford, John Hoyt, Harrison Ford, Marlene Tracy, Ken Swofford, Robert Donner, Edward Faulkner, James Gammon, Gavin MacLeod, Len

Wayland, Mickey Sholdar, Kay E. Kuter, Ted Gehring, Robert P. Lieb, William Phipps

This Western drama finds a town in crisis as the James/Younger gang rides in, and the local marshal, having lost both his nerve and his skill with a pistol, is put to the test. Originally this was to have been titled *Death Dance at Madelia*.

0096
THE OVER-THE-HILL GANG RIDES AGAIN
11/17/70 Thomas/Spelling Productions (90 min)

Executive Producers: Danny Thomas and Aaron Spelling
Producer: Shelly Hull
Director: George McCowan
Teleplay: Richard Carr
Photography: Fleet Southcott III
Music: David Raksin
Art Director: Tracy Bousman
Editor: Richard Farrell

Nash Crawford	WALTER BRENNAN
The Baltimore Kid	FRED ASTAIRE
Jason Fitch	EDGAR BUCHANAN
Amos Polk	ANDY DEVINE
George Agnew	CHILL WILLS
Sam Braham	PAUL RICHARDS
Katie	LANA WOOD
The Mayor	PARLEY BAER
Stableman	WALTER BURKE
Mrs. Murphy	LILLIAN BRONSON
Parson	JONATHAN HOLE
Best Man	BURT MUSTIN
Cowboy	DON WILBANKS
Drifter	PEPPER MARTIN

In this sequel to *The Over-the-Hill Gang* (1969), the old-time comrades-in-arms join forces to sober up an old buddy, a down-and-out drunk, and restore his reputation. Fred Astaire made his TV-movie debut in this one and appeared in his only Western role.

Anne Francis and Don Murray in THE INTRUDERS (1970)

Lilli Palmer and David McCallum in HAUSER'S MEMORY (1970)

0097
NIGHT CHASE
11/20/70 Cinema Center 100 (90 min)

Executive Producer: Nathaniel Lande
Producer: Collier Young
Director: Jack Starrett
Teleplay: Marvin A. Gluck
From a story by Collier Young
Photography: Fred J. Koenekamp
Music: Laurence Rosenthal
Art Director: Bill Smith
Editor: Carroll Sax

Adrian Vico	DAVID JANSSEN
Ernie Green	YAPHET KOTTO
Beverly Dorn	VICTORIA VETRI
Proprietor	ELISHA COOK, JR.
Old Fisherman	JOSEPH DeSANTIS
Young Fisherman	RICHARD ROMANUS
Jumbo	MEL BERGER
Vico's Wife	KAREN CARLSON

and: John Carter, Laurie Main, Edward Faulkner, Dan Kemp, Sonora McKeller, Robert Rothwell, Stafford Morgan, Bill Katt, Lorna Thayer, Robert Kino, Robert Wheeler, John Hall, Armando Diaz, John Steadman, Sam Nudell, Clay Tanner

A suspense tale of a wealthy businessman's frantic flight from the scene of his wife's shooting and his unexpected relationship with the hardened cab driver he hires to drive him to the Mexican border. The original title: *The Man in the Back Seat.*

0098
HAUSER'S MEMORY
11/24/70 Universal (2 hours)

Producer: Jack Laird
Director: Boris Sagal
Teleplay: Adrian Spies
Based on the novel by Curt Siodmack
Photography: Petrus Schloemp
Music: Billy Byers
Assistant Director: Weiland Liebske
Art Director: Ellen Schmidt
Editor: Frank E. Morriss

Hillel Mondoro	DAVID McCALLUM
Karen Mondoro	SUSAN STRASBERG
Anna	LILLI PALMER
Kramer	HELMUT KANTNER
Slaughter	LESLIE NIELSEN
Dorsey	ROBERT WEBBER
Renner	HERBERT FLEISCHMANN
Von Kungen	HANS ELWENSPOCK
Shepilov	PETER CAPELL
Angelika	BARBARA LASS
Kucera	PETER EHRLICH
Koroviev	GUNTHER MEISNER
Gessler	OTTO STERN
Sorsen	MANFRED REDDEMANN
Bak	ART BRAUSS
Dieter	JOCHEN BUSSE
Young Anna	BARBARA CAPELL

A Cold War thriller about a scientist who is recruited by the CIA to inject himself with the brain fluid of a dying colleague in order to preserve missile-defense secrets, but who soon discovers that he is leading a double life—torn between his own wife and his fellow scientist's widow, a Nazi sympathizer.

49

Carol Lynley, Jane Wyatt and Lois Nettleton in WEEKEND OF TERROR (1970)

Simon Zuniga	BURT REYNOLDS
Carroll Reunard	INGER STEVENS
Sheriff Tackaberry	ROYAL DANO
Henry Burroughs	JAMES BEST
Manuel	RODOLFO ACOSTA
Freddy Toms	DON DUBBINS
Clarice	JOYCE JAMESON
Detective	BARNEY PHILLIPS
Asa	HERMAN RUDIN
Santana	EDDIE LITTLE SKY
Helen Polino	MARSHA MOORE

and: Ken Lynch, Martin G. Soto, Rosemary Eliot

A Papago Indian returns to his people after serving time in prison and vows to find his brother's killer. Originally titled *The Tradition of Simon Zuniga,* this movie gave Inger Stevens her final role.

0101
WEEKEND OF TERROR
12/8/70 Paramount (90 min)

Producer: Joel Freeman
Director: Jud Taylor
Teleplay: Lionel E. Siegel
Photography: Les Shorr
Music: Richard Markowitz
Art Director: Walter M. Jeffries
Editor: Donald R. Rode

Eddie	ROBERT CONRAD
Larry	LEE MAJORS
Sister Meredith	CAROL LYNLEY
Sister Ellen	LOIS NETTLETON
Sister Frances	JANE WYATT
Papich	KEVIN HAGEN
Wedemeyer	TODD ANDREWS

and: Ann Doran, Gregory Sierra, Ford Lile, Barbara Bennett, Byron Clark, William Lally, Buck Young

Three kidnapped nuns realize that their abductors need only one of them alive—as a substitute for a hostage they accidentally killed.

0102
BREAKOUT
12/8/70 Universal (2 hours)

Producer/Director: Richard Irving
Teleplay: Sy Gomberg
Photography: Ray Flin
Music: Shorty Rogers
Assistant Director: Joseph Cavalier
Art Director: Henry Larrecq
Editor: Milton Shifman

Joe Baker	JAMES DRURY
Pipes	RED BUTTONS
Ann Baker	KATHRYN HAYS
Skip Manion	WOODY STRODE
Frank McCready	SEAN GARRISON
Marian	VICTORIA MEYERLINK

and: Bert Freed, Mort Mills, William Mims, Harold J. Stone, Don Wilbanks, Kenneth Tobey, Ric Roman

A prison escape movie involving a tough convict who concocts a foolproof plan for breaking out to be near his wife and the $50,000 in stolen loot that landed him there in the first place.

0103
THE PSYCHIATRIST: GOD BLESS THE CHILDREN
12/14/70 Universal (2 hours)
(subsequently titled *Children of the Lotus Eater*)

Executive Producer: Norman Felton
Producer: Edgar Small
Director: Daryl Duke
Teleplay: Jerrold Freedman

0099
CROWHAVEN FARM
11/24/70 Aaron Spelling Productions (90 min)

Executive Producer: Aaron Spelling
Producer/Director: Walter Grauman
Teleplay: John McGreevey
Photography: Fleet Southcott
Music: Robert Drasnin
Art Director: Tracy Bousman
Editor: Aaron Stell

Maggie Porter	HOPE LANGE
Ben Porter	PAUL BURKE
Kevin Pierce	LLOYD BOCHNER
Nate Cheever	JOHN CARRADINE
Dr. Terminer	MILTON SELZER
Harold Dane	CYRIL DELAVANTI
Felicia	PATRICIA BARRY
Jennifer	CINDY EILBACHER
Mercy Lewis	VIRGINIA GREGG
Madeleine Wardwell	JUNE DAYTON
Sam Wardwell	WOODROW PARFREY
Claire Allen	LOUISE TROY
Fritz Allen	ROSS ELLIOTT
Patrolman Hayes	WILLIAM SMITH
Henry Pearson	PITT HERBERT
Police Chief	DENNIS CROSS

An occult tale of a middle-class couple who inherit a farm and move in to try to patch up their strained marriage, only to be confronted by the supernatural.

0100
RUN, SIMON, RUN
12/1/70 Aaron Spelling Productions (90 min)

Producer: Aaron Spelling
Director: George McGowan
Teleplay: Lionel E. Siegel
Photography: Arch R. Dalzell
Music: The Orphanage
Art Director: Paul Sylos
Editor: Art Seid

James Drury and Kathryn Hays in BREAK-OUT (1970)

From a story by Richard Levinson and William Link
Production Consultant: Jerrold Freedman
Story Consultant: Jack Laird
Photography: Richard C. Glouner
Music: Roger Kellaway
Art Director: William D. DeCines
Editor: Robert F. Shugrue

Dr. James Whitman	ROY THINNES
Casey T. Pope	PETER DEUEL
Dr. Bernard Altman	LUTHER ADLER
Teddy	JOHN RUBINSTEIN
Kendell	JOY BANG
Sheriff Glenn	NORMAN ALDEN
Fritz	BARRY BROWN
Persephone	KATHERINE JUSTICE
Mrs. Pilgrim	MARION ROSS
Dr. Lewis	GILBERT GREEN
Ellen	SHANNON FARNON
Weasel	DAVID ALAN BAILEY
Pusher	MICHAEL C. GWYNNE
Maxwell	JOHN LASELL
Danny	DANNY SMALLER
Michael	MICHAEL LAIRD
Beatrice	LYNN HAMILTON
Jane	JACKIE BURROUGHS
Cathy	GLORIA MANON
Don	PHILIP E. PINE
Mary	VIRGINIA VINCENT
Art	GEORGE SPERDAKOS
Steve	JERE BRIAN
Themselves	THE STAPLE SINGERS

(Beatrice, Jane, Cathy, Don, Mary, Art, Steve — Therapy Group)

A hip psychiatrist teams up with an ex-addict to combat drug addiction in a small town in this pilot for *The Psychiatrist* (Thinnes and Adler continuing their roles) in the spring of 1971—a six-week feature that was the third of the elements in the "Four-In-One" series. Others: *San Francisco International* (which, like *The Psychiatrist,* did not attract enough viewers to warrant renewal), *McCloud* and *Night Gallery.*

0104
THE MAN WHO WANTED TO LIVE FOREVER
12/15/70 Palomar Pictures International (90 min)

Executive Producers: Edgar Scherick and Henry Denker
Producer: Terry Dene
Director: John Trent
Teleplay: Henry Denker
Photography: Marc Champion
Music: Dorothy Clamen
Art Director: Jack McAdam
Editors: M. C. Manne and Ron Wisman

Dr. McCarter Purvis	STUART WHITMAN
Dr. Enid Bingham	SANDY DENNIS
T. M. Trask	BURL IVES
McBride	TOM HARVEY
Dr. Wilfrid Morton	ROBERT GOODIER
Dr. John Emmett	RON HARTMANN
Dr. George Simmons	JACK CRELEY
Dr. Carl Bryant	ALLAN DOREMUS
Clinton	KENNETH JAMES
Dr. Franz Heinemann	JOSEPH SHAW
Pianist	CLEM HARBOURG

and: Harvey Fisher, Robert Warner, James Forrest, Robert Mann, John Davies

Joy Bang and Peter Deuel in THE PSYCHIATRIST: GOD BLESS THE CHILDREN (1970)

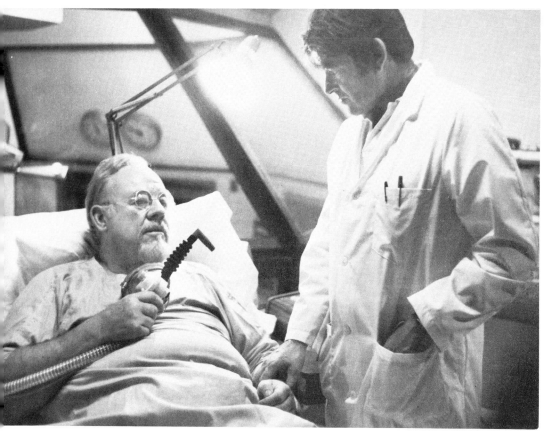

Burl Ives and Stuart Whitman in THE MAN WHO WANTED TO LIVE FOREVER (1970)

A brilliant heart surgeon discovers that a private medical research foundation is being used as a cover for sinister purposes. The working title for this film was *Heartfarm* while in production in the Bugaboo Mountains of British Columbia. In its later theatrical release overseas, its title became *The Only Way Out Is Dead.*

same name with Deuel and Murphy followed, beginning several weeks after the initial showing of this film and continuing through early January 1973. When actor Deuel committed suicide in mid-1972, Roger Davis was brought in to replace him.

0105
ALIAS SMITH AND JONES
1/5/71 Universal (2 hours)

Executive Producer: Frank Price
Producer: Glen A. Larson
Director: Gene Levitt
Teleplay: Matthew Howard and Glen A. Larson
From the story by Glen A. Larson
Photography: John Morley Stephens
Music: Billy Goldenberg
Art Director: George C. Webb
Editor: Bob Cagey

Hannibal Hayes (Joshua Smith)	PETER DEUEL
Jed Kid Curry (Thaddeus Jones)	BEN MURPHY
Deputy Harker	FORREST TUCKER
Miss Porter	SUSAN SAINT JAMES
Sheriff Lom Trevors	JAMES DRURY
Miss Birdie	JEANETTE NOLAN
Wheat	EARL HOLLIMAN
Marshal	JOHN RUSSELL
Kyle	DENNIS FIMPLE
Kane	BILL FLETCHER
Logo	BILL McKINNEY
Shields	CHARLES DIERKOP
Pincus	PETER BROCCO
Outlaws	SID HAIG
	JOHN HARPER
	JON SHANK

A lighthearted Western about a pair of notorious outlaws who take the governor's offer of amnesty, offered through a lawman friend, if they'll bring in a vicious desperado and his gang—and then discover that their amnesty has other strings attached. A series of the

0106
THE D.A.: CONSPIRACY TO KILL
1/11/71 Universal/Mark VII Ltd. (2 hours)

A Jack Webb Production
Producer: Robert H. Forward
Director: Paul Krasny
Teleplay: Stanford Whitmore
Photography: Alric Edens
Music: Frank Comstock
Art Director: Arch Bacon
Editors: Robert F. Shugrue and Richard M. Sprague

Deputy D.A. Paul Ryan	ROBERT CONRAD
Chief Vincent Kovac	WILLIAM CONRAD
Luanne Gibson	BELINDA MONTGOMERY
Thomas Bertrand	DON STROUD
James Fletcher	STEVE INHAT
Robert Ramirez	ARMANDO SILVESTRE
Rochelle DeHaven	LINDA MARSH
Attorney Stevens	ROGER PERRY
Ramona Bertrand	LESLIE PARRISH
Arthur DeHaven	MICHAEL STRONG
Mrs. Grimes	ANN MORGAN GUILBERT
Ray Shadlock	TOM GEAS
Judge Virginia Adamson	VIRGINIA GREGG
Walter Gibson	THOMAS HUFF

and: Olan Soule, Stacy Harris, James McEachin, Morgan Sterne, Lew Brown, William Wintersole, Ray Ballard, Joe E. Tate, Sonja Dunson, Arthur Balinger, Arleen Starr, Thomas J. Huff, Ron Cavallo, Dick Congey, Dallas Mitchell, David Tyrone, Andrew MacHeath, Larry Levine, Don Edwards, Ralph Gambina, Cisco Andrade

This was the sequel to *The D.A.: Murder One* (1969) and the second pilot for the short-lived series "The D.A." (1971–72) that starred Robert Conrad, Harry Morgan, Julie Cobb and Ned Romero.

0107
ASSAULT ON THE WAYNE
1/12/71 Paramount (90 min)

Producer: Bruce Lansbury
Director: Marvin Chomsky
Teleplay: Jackson Gillis
Photography: Howard R. Schwartz
Music: Leith Stevens
Art Director: William Campbell
Editor: Donald R. Rode

The Admiral	JOSEPH COTTEN
Cmdr. Phil Kettenring	LEONARD NIMOY
Lt. Dave Burston	LLOYD HAYNES
Skip Langley	DEWEY MARTIN
Capt. Frank Reardon	WILLIAM WINDOM
Orville Kelly	KEENAN WYNN
Dr. Dykers	MALACHI THRONE

and: Sam Elliott, Ivor Barry, Ron Masak, Lee Stanley, David Thorpe, Dale Tarter, Gordon Hoban, John Winston

Intrigue aboard a nuclear sub with foreign agents infiltrating the crew to get their hands on a top secret device.

0108
DO YOU TAKE THIS STRANGER?
1/18/71 Universal (2 hours)

Executive Producer: Roy Huggins
Producer: Jo Swerling, Jr.
Director: Richard T. Heffron
Teleplay: Matthew Howard
Photography: Lionel Lindon
Music: Pete Rugolo
Art Director: John J. Lloyd
Editor: John Dumas

Murray Jarvis	GENE BARRY
Steven Breck	LLOYD BRIDGES
Rachel Jarvis	DIANE BAKER
Dr. Robert Carson	JOSEPH COTTEN
G. R. Jarvis	SIDNEY BLACKMER
Mildred Crandall	SUSAN OLIVER
Night Man	ARTHUR MALET
Dr. Bamber	IVOR BARRY
Florence	CARA BURGESS

and: Byron Webster, Bart Burns, Marc Seaton, Linda Marie

A social climber schemes to inherit one million dollars by trading identities with a dying man. Working and pre-release titles for this one were *A Knock at the Wrong Door* and *Strangers and Lovers.*

0109
DR. COOK'S GARDEN
1/19/71 Paramount (90 min)

Producer: Bob Markell
Associate Producer: George Goodman
Director: Ted Post
Teleplay: Art Wallace
Based on the play by Ira Levin
Photography: Urs Ferrer
Music: Robert Drasnin
Art Director: Bill Molyneaux
Editor: John McSweeney

Dr. Leonard Cook	BING CROSBY
Jim Tennyson	FRANK CONVERSE
Jane Rausch	BLYTHE DANNER
Dora Ludlow	ABBY LEWIS

Elias Hart	BARNARD HUGHES
Essie Bullitt	BETHEL LESLIE
Ted Rausch	STAATS COTSWORTH
Billy	JORDAN REED
Ruth Hart	HELEN STENBORG
Mary Booth	CAROL MORLEY
Harry Bullitt	FRED BURREL
The Reverend	TOM BARBOUR

Crosby's only TV movie has him cast against type as a small-town doctor who sees to it that the bad people in his community die before their time and the good live longer—like the flowers in his garden. In the 1967 play which had a brief Broadway run, Burl Ives was the kindly general practitioner with a warped sense of community service.

0110
THE FEMINIST AND THE FUZZ
1/26/71 Screen Gems/Columbia (90 min)

Producer: Claudio Guzman
Director: Jerry Paris
Teleplay: James Henerson
Photography: Emil Oster
Music: Jack Elliott and Allyn Ferguson
Art Director: Ross Bellah and Phillip Bennett
Editor: Bud Molin

Dr. Jane Bowers	BARBARA EDEN
Officer Jerry Frazer	DAVID HARTMAN
Dr. Debby Inglefinger	JO ANNE WORLEY
Wyatt Foley	HERB EDELMAN
Lilah McGuinness	JULIE NEWMAR
Warren Sorenson	JOHN McGIVER
Kitty Murdock	FARRAH FAWCETT
Dr. Horace Bowers	HARRY MORGAN
Dr. Howard Lassiter	ROGER PERRY
Joe	ARTHUR BATANIDES

and: Sheila James, Jill Choder, Merri Robinson, Penny Marshall, Patti Chandler, Amanda Pepper, Judy March, John Garwood

A familiar TV sitcom plot that makes roommates of a dedicated women's libber and a male chauvinist cop.

0111
CITY BENEATH THE SEA
1/27/71 20th Century-Fox/Motion Pictures International (2 hours)

Producer/Director: Irwin Allen
Associate Producers: George E. Swink and Sidney Marshall
Teleplay: John Meredyth Lucas
From a story by Irwin Allen
Photography: Kenneth Peach
Music: Richard LaSalle
Assistant Director: Les Warner
Art Directors: Rodger E. Maus and Stan Jolley
Special Effects: L. B. Abbott and John C. Caldwell
Editor: James Baiotto

Adm. Michael Matthews	STUART WHITMAN
Brett Matthews	ROBERT WAGNER
Lia Holmes	ROSEMARY FORSYTH
Cmdr. Woody Paterson	ROBERT COLBERT
Elena	SUSANNA MIRANDA
Dr. Aguila	BURR DeBENNING
The President	RICHARD BASEHART
Dr. Zeigler	JOSEPH COTTEN
Dr. Talty	JAMES DARREN
Mr. Barton	PAUL STEWART
Capt. Hunter	SUGAR RAY ROBINSON
Professor Holmes	WHIT BISSELL

Diane Baker and Gene Barry in DO YOU TAKE THIS STRANGER? (1971)

Sugar Ray Robinson, Robert Wagner and Stuart Whitman in CITY BENEATH THE SEA (1971)

Bill Holmes	LARRY PENNELL
General Putnam	TOM DRAKE
Blonde Woman	SHEILA MATHEWS
Quinn	CHARLES DIERKOP

and: Bill Bryant, Bob Dowdell, Edward G. Robinson, Jr., John Lee, Glenna Sergent, Ray Didsbury, Erik Nelson

Presumably intended as a follow-up to his successful *Voyage to the Bottom of the Sea* TV series, this elaborate Irwin Allen pilot has a group of 21st-century colonists inhabiting earth's first underwater city, called Pacifica, and pitting the predictable good guys against various alien forces. In its theatrical release overseas, this TV movie was known as *One Hour to Doomsday*.

0112
SAM HILL: WHO KILLED THE MYSTERIOUS MR. FOSTER?
2/1/71 Universal (2 hours)

Executive Producer: Roy Huggins
Producer: Jo Swerling, Jr.
Director: Fielder Cook
Teleplay: Richard Levinson and William Link
Photography: Gene Polito
Music: Pete Rugolo
Assistant Director: Richard Bennett
Art Director: Robert E. Smith
Editors: John Dumas and Gloryette Clark

Deputy Sam Hill	ERNEST BORGNINE
Jethro	STEPHEN HUDIS
Jody Kenyon	JUDY GEESON
Simon Anderson	WILL GEER
Mal Yeager	J. D. CANNON
Doyle Pickett	BRUCE DERN
Toby	SAM JAFFE
Abigail Booth	CARMEN MATHEWS
Judge Hathaway	JOHN McGIVER
Kilpatrick	SLIM PICKENS
Reverend Foster	G. D. SPRADLIN

and: Jay C. Flippen, Woodrow Parfrey, George Furth, Milton Selzer, Dub Taylor, Ted Gehrig, Robert Gooden, Dennis Fimple

In this Western series pilot (unrealized), an alcoholic drifter finds himself unchallenged in his run for sheriff in a small town, but campaigning means that he must find the killer of a visiting preacher.

0113
THE NEON CEILING
2/8/71 Universal (2 hours)

Producer: William Sackheim
Director: Frank A. Pierson
Teleplay: Carol Sobieski and Henri Simoun
From a story by Carol Sobieski
Photography: Edward Rosson
Music: Billy Goldenberg
Art Director: Alexander A. Mayer
Editor: Robert F. Shugrue

Jones	GIG YOUNG
Carrie Miller	LEE GRANT
Paula Miller	DENISE NICKERSON
Harry	HERB EDELMAN
Dr. Miller	WILLIAM SMITHERS
Ferriswheel Man	ROBERT PRATT
Highway Patrolman	JAMES McEACHIN

A runaway wife, fleeing middle-class boredom with her teenage daughter, lands in a truck-stop diner in the California desert run by a gruff, beer-drinking recluse living in a fantasy world that is a creative work of art. Lee Grant won an Emmy for her performance; Gig Young was nominated for his.

Gig Young and Lee Grant in THE NEON CEILING (1971)

0114
LOVE, HATE, LOVE
2/9/71 Aaron Spelling Productions (90 min)

Executive Producer: Aaron Spelling
Producer: Joan Harrison
Director: George McGowan
Teleplay: Eric Ambler
Photography: Arch R. Dalzell
Music: Lyn Murray
Art Director: Paul Sylos
Editor: George Brooks

Russ Emery	RYAN O'NEAL
Sheila Blunden	LESLEY WARREN
Leo Price	PETER HASKELL
Tom Blunden	HENRY JONES
Mary Blunden	JEFF DONNELL
Eddie	JACK MULLANEY
Wally	STANLEY ADAMS
Karen	SHANNON FARNON
Lt. Hank Robins	RYAN McDONALD
Patrolman	FRED HOLLIDAY
Secretary	CHARLENE POLITE

O'Neal's TV movie debut casts him as a glib engineer who steals the heart of a fashion model. She in turn jilts her jet setter fiancé who turns out to be a psychotic.

0115
MAYBE I'LL COME HOME IN THE SPRING
2/16/71 Metromedia Productions (90 min)

Executive Producer: Charles Fries
Producer/Director: Joseph Sargent
Teleplay: Bruce Feldman
Photography: Russell Metty
Music: Earl Robinson

Songs "Maybe I'll Come Home in the Spring" by
Roger Atkins and Helen Miller and "A Different
Day" by Earl Robinson and Bruce Feldman
Sung by Linda Ronstadt
Editor: Pembroke J. Herring

Denise Miller	SALLY FIELD
Claire Miller	ELEANOR PARKER
Ed Miller	JACKIE COOPER
Susie Miller	LANE BRADBURY
Flack	DAVID CARRADINE

A young runaway, going from middle-class suburbia
to the heart of the hippie drug culture, returns home
only to find deepening family conflicts and parental
bickering—and realizes what it threatens to do to her
younger sister.

0116
SARGE: THE BADGE OR THE CROSS
2/22/71 Universal (2 hours)

Executive Producer: Richard A. Colla
Producer: David Levinson
Director: Richard A. Colla
Teleplay: Don M. Mankiewicz
Photography: Jacques R. Marquette
Music: Dave Grusin
Art Directors: Joseph Alves, Jr. and Sidney Z.
Litwack
Editor: Robert L. Kimble

Sarge Swanson	GEORGE KENNEDY
Al Matteo	RICARDO MONTALBAN
Nico	NICO MINARDOS
Carol Swanson	DIANE BAKER
Father Terrence	STEWART MOSS
Valerie	SALLIE SHOCKLEY
Arnie Bigelow	LARRY GATES
Kenji Takichi	HAROLD SAKATA
Mama Bain	NAOMI STEVENS
Bishop Andrade	HENRY WILCOXON
Charlie	STANLEY LIVINGSTON
Father Frank Dinsmore	DANA ELCAR
Chief Dewey	RAMON BIERI
Rector	WALTER BROOKE
Hawley	CHARLES TYNER
Tyler	DAVID HUDDLESTON

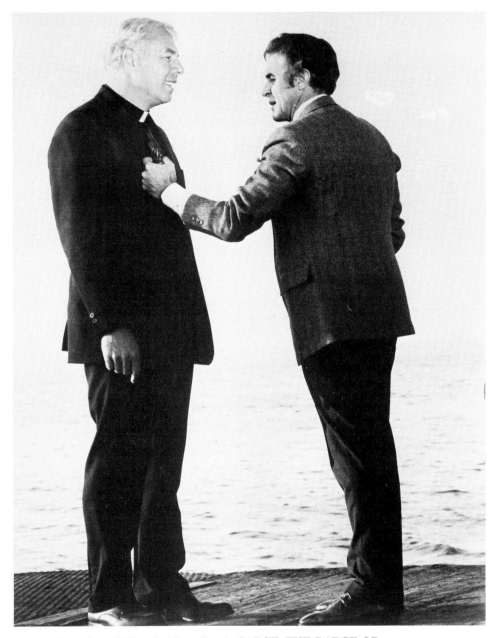

George Kennedy and Ricardo Montalban in SARGE: THE BADGE OR
THE CROSS (1971)

**Eleanor Parker, Jackie Cooper and Sally Field in MAYBE I'LL COME HOME IN THE
SPRING (1971)**

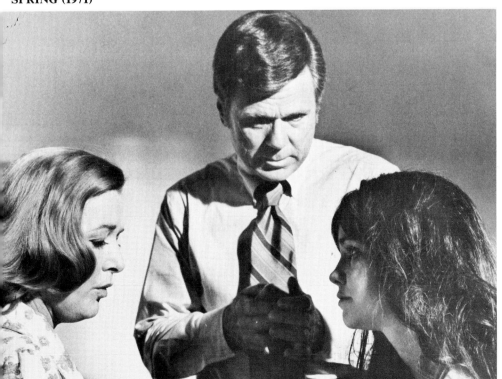

A suspense drama about a veteran cop who turns to
the priesthood after his wife is shot to death, and three
years later is assigned to a parish where he encounters
the assassin who originally had been gunning for him.
This was the first of two feature-length pilots for
Kennedy's first TV series "Sarge" that had a half-
season run beginning the following September.

0117
LONGSTREET
2/23/71 Paramount (90 min)

Executive Producer: Stirling Silliphant
Producer/Director: Joseph Sargent
Teleplay: Stirling Silliphant
Based on characters created by Baynard Kendrick
Photography: Howard R. Schwartz
Music: Robert Drasnin
Art Director: William Campbell
Editor: George J. Nicholson

Michael Longstreet	JAMES FRANCISCUS
Duke Paige	BRADFORD DILLMAN
Dr. Dan Stockton	JOHN McINTIRE

James Franciscus in LONGSTREET (1971)

Peter Falk, Peter Lawford and Vic Morrow in A STEP OUT OF LINE (1971)

Alice Longstreet	JEANETTE NOLAN
Nikki Bell	MARTINE BESWICK
Lt. Kirk Gantry	BARRY RUSSO
Ingrid Longstreet	JUDY JONES
Dr. Richards	BARNEY PHILIPS
Von Marks	MARTIN KOSLECK
Nurse	LISABETH FIELD
Inspector	LINCOLN DEMYAN
Police Sergeant	JAMES DeCLOSS

A New Orleans-based insurance investigator, blinded in an explosion, tracks down the man who killed his wife and took his sight. This was the pilot to the short-lived series (1971–72) that starred Franciscus, with Peter Mark Richman replacing Bradford Dillman as his boss and Marlyn Mason taking over the role of his braille teacher/romantic interest from Martine Beswick. Of interest: Bruce Lee had a continuing part instructing Longstreet in the art of kung fu.

0118
A STEP OUT OF LINE
2/26/71 Cinema Center 100 (2 hours)

Producer: Steve Shagan
Director: Bernard McEveety
Teleplay: S. S. Schweitzer and Steve Shagan
From a story by Albert Ruben
Photography: James Crabe
Music: Jerry Goldsmith
Art Director: Albert Heschong
Editor: Robert Y. Takagi

Harry Connors	PETER FALK
Joe Rawlins	VIC MORROW
Art Stoyer	PETER LAWFORD
Gillian Frances	JO ANN PFLUG
Linda Connors	LYNN CARLIN
Jack Berger	TOM BOSLEY
Det. John Riddle	JOHN RANDOLPH
Sorenson	WALLARD SAGE
Angie Rawlins	SUSAN ADAMS
Frank Presnell	STUART KLITSNER
Dr. Finnerman	LEONARD STONE
Doreen	DONICA D'HONDT
Announcer	RUSS HODGES

Three businessmen, Korean War buddies, attempt to solve their financial problems by pulling off an elaborate bank heist. Falk is a disgruntled insurance agent, Morrow a structural engineer and Lawford a playboy TV director in this caper tale.

0119
INCIDENT IN SAN FRANCISCO
2/28/71 Quinn Martin Productions (2 hours)

Executive Producer: Quinn Martin
Producers: Arthur Fellows and Adrian Samish
Associate Producer: Howard Alston
Director: Don Medford
Teleplay: Robert Dozier
Based on the story *Incident at 125th St.* by J. E. Brown
Photography: William Spencer
Music: Pat Williams
Art Director: George B. Chan
Editor: Richard Brockway

Robert Harmon	RICHARD KILEY
Lt. Brubaker	LESLIE NIELSEN
Sam Baldwin	DEAN JAGGER
Mario Cianelli	JOHN MARLEY
Arthur Andrews	TIM O'CONNOR
Lois Harmon	PHYLLIS THAXTER
Sophia Cianelli	RUTH ROMAN
Herschel Rosen	DAVID OPATASHU
Odessa Carter	CLAUDIA McNEIL
Penny Carter	TRACY REED
Henry Carter	JULIUS HARRIS
Alfred Cianelli	TOM NARDINI
Jeff Marshall	CHRISTOPHER CONNELLY

and: Richard O'Brien, Ken Lynch, Victoria Vetri, John Considine, William Traylor, Dennis Olivieri, Robert Pine, Fred Sadoff, Radames Pera, Bill Quinn

A young reporter crusades to clear a good samaritan who is charged with murdering a mugger after the victim and witnesses fail to corroborate his story. This pilot was for a proposed series to have starred Connelly as the newshound, O'Connor as the cynical city editor, and Jagger as the tough editor-in-chief.

0120
RANSOM FOR A DEAD MAN
3/1/71 Universal (2 hours)

Executive Producer: Richard Irving
Producer: Dean Hargrove
Director: Richard Irving
Teleplay: Dean Hargrove
From a story by Richard Levinson and William Link
Photography: Lionel Lindon
Music: Billy Goldenberg
Art Director: John J. Lloyd
Editor: Edward M. Abroms

Lieutenant Columbo	PETER FALK
Leslie Williams	LEE GRANT
Michael Clarke	JOHN FINK
Carlson	HAROLD GOULD
Margaret Williams	PATRICIA MATTICK
Hammond	PAUL CARR
Phil	JED ALLEN
Richard	CHARLES MacAULEY
Attorney	HENRY BRANDT
Pat	JEAN BYRON
Perkins	RICHARD ROAT
Celia	NORMA CONNOLLY
Paul Williams	HARLAN WADE
Crowell	BILL WALKER
Bert	TIMOTHY CAREY
Judge	JUDSON MORGAN
Priest	RICHARD O'BRIEN
Gloria	CELESTE YARNELL
Nancy	LISA MOORE
Waitress	LOIS BATTLE
Mechanic	REGINALD FENDERSON

A clever lady lawyer hatches an intricate plan to do away with her wealthy husband for his fortune and then finds herself parrying with a rumpled but wily homicide detective who would go on to have a long-running TV series (1971–78). Lee Grant received an Emmy nomination for her performance.

0121
YUMA
3/2/71 Aaron Spelling Productions (90 min)

Producer: Aaron Spelling
Director: Ted Post
Teleplay: Charles Wallace
Photography: John Morley Stephens
Music: George Duning
Art Director: Paul Sylos
Editor: Art Seid

Marshal Dave Harmon	CLINT WALKER
Nels Decker	BARRY SULLIVAN
Julie Williams	KATHRYN HAYS
Mules McNeil	EDGAR BUCHANAN
Arch King	MORGAN WOODWARD
Major Lucas	PETER MARK RICHMAN
Captain White	JOHN KERR
Sanders	ROBERT PHILLIPS
Andres	MIGUEL ALEJANDRO
Rol King	NEIL RUSSELL
Sam King	BRUCE GLOVER

A Western adventure about a tough marshal's efforts to clean up a frontier town filled with brawling cattlemen, crooked officials and various bad guys out to discredit him.

0122
VANISHED
3/8–9/71 Universal (4 hours)

Executive Producer: David Victor
Producer: David J. O'Connell
Director: Buzz Kulik
Teleplay: Dean Riesner
Based on the novel by Fletcher Knebel
Photography: Lionel Lindon
Music: Leonard Rosenman
Assistant Director: Jim Fargo
Art Director: John J. Lloyd
Editor: Robert Watts

Pres. Paul Roudebush	RICHARD WIDMARK
Jill Nichols	SKYE AUBREY
Johnny Cavanaugh	TOM BOSLEY
Gene Culligan	JAMES FARENTINO
Jerry Frytag	LARRY HAGMAN
Nick McCann	MURRAY HAMILTON
Arnold Greer	ARTHUR HILL
Larry Storm	ROBERT HOOKS
Arthur Ingram	E. G. MARSHALL
Sue Greer	ELEANOR PARKER
Dave Paulick	WILLIAM SHATNER

Dean Jagger and Tim O'Connor in INCIDENT IN SAN FRANCISCO (1971)

E. G. Marshall and Richard Widmark in VANISHED (1971)

Sen. Earl Gannon	ROBERT YOUNG
General Palfrey	STEPHEN McNALLY
Beverly	SHEREE NORTH
Loomis	ROBERT LIPTON
Captain Cooledge	JIM DAVIS
Descowicz	MICHAEL STRONG
Grace	CATHERINE McLEOD
Gretchen Greer	CHRISTINE BELFORD
Cincom Commander	DENNY MILLER
Themselves	CHET HUNTLEY BETTY WHITE MARTIN AGRONSKY HERBERT KAPLOW

and: Russell Johnson, Herb Vigran, Neil Hamilton, Stacy Keach, Sr., Ilka Windish, Carleton Young, Stacy Harris, Helen Kleeb, Susan Kussman, Don Pedro Colley, Judy Jordan, Richard Dix, Nancy Lee Dix, Earl Ebi, Athena Lorde, Kevin Hagen, Randolph Mantooth, Russ Conway, Clark Howart, Gil Stewart, Art Balinger, Barry Atwater, James Hong, Lawrence Linville, Leo G. Morrell, Perry Ribiero, Vince Howard, Stephen Colt, Francis DeSales, Fred Holliday, William Boyett, Dick Kleiner, Vernon Scott, Joseph Finnigan

A thriller about the mysterious disappearance of a senior presidential advisor. This first long-form TV movie, shown in two parts (actual running time minus commercials totaled three hours and ten minutes), paved the way for subsequent filmed mini-series. Both Richard Widmark, in his TV acting debut, and Robert Young, playing against character as a rascally Southern senator, received Emmy nominations.

0123
RIVER OF GOLD
3/9/71 Aaron Spelling Productions (90 min)

Executive Producer: Aaron Spelling
Producers: Mort Fine and David Friedkin
Director: David Friedkin
Teleplay: Salvatore C. Puedes
Photography: Alex Phillips, Jr.
Music: Fred Steiner
Art Director: Paul Sylos
Editor: George Brooks

Evelyn Rose	RAY MILLAND
Anna	SUZANNE PLESHETTE
Riley Briggs	DACK RAMBO
Marcus McAllister	ROGER DAVIS
Julie	MELISSA NEWMAN
Tomas	JORGE LUKE
Angel	PEDRO ARMENDARIZ, JR.
Rodrigo	JOSE CHAVEZ
Cepeda	EDUARDO LOPEZ ROJAS
Jay Marstron	TEDDY STAUFFER
Tine Marstron	BARBARA ANGELI
Priest	FRANCISCO CORDOVA

A pair of beach bums drift to Acapulco in search of a beautiful young woman and a sunken treasure.

0124
TRAVIS LOGAN, D.A.
3/11/71 Quinn Martin Productions (2 hours)

Executive Producer: Quinn Martin
Producers: Adrian Samish and Arthur Fellows
Director: Paul Wendkos
Teleplay: Adrian Samish and Arthur Fellows
Photography: Robert L. Morrison

Music: Pat Williams
Art Director: William Craig Smith
Editor: Marston Fay

Travis Logan	VIC MORROW
Mark	CHRIS ROBINSON
Jerry	JAMES CALLAHAN
Matthew Sand	HAL HOLBROOK
Eve	BROOKE BUNDY
Lucille Sand	BRENDA VACCARO
Chuck Bentley	GEORGE GRIZZARD
George Carnera	SCOTT MARLOWE
Judge Rose	EDWARD ANDREWS
Dr. Reichart	MICHAEL STRONG
Mrs. Tice	JOSEPHINE HUTCHINSON
First Reporter	JAMES CHANDLER
Tony Carnera	RICHARD ANGAROLA

This prospective series pilot has a hard-nosed prosecutor doggedly trying to crack a homicide case in which the defense's plea of temporary insanity is the plan to cover the perfect murder, the result of a love triangle.

0125
HARPY
3/12/71 Cinema Center 100 (2 hours)

Executive Producer: Hugh Benson
Producer/Director: Gerald Seth Sindell
Teleplay: William Wood
From a story by T. K. Brown III
Photography: Robert B. Hauser
Music: David Shire
Art Director: Bill Smith
Editor: Norman Colbert

Peter Clune	HUGH O'BRIAN
Marian	ELIZABETH ASHLEY
John	TOM NARDINI
Alison Reed	MARLYN MASON
Don Haskins	MARK MILLER
Mrs. Reed	LINDA WATKINS

An offbeat melodrama about a brooding architect who trains eagles, his grasping ex-wife who is trying to break up his impending marriage to his secretary, and his young Indian companion who helps to thwart her plans with the aid of a harpy eagle.

0126
BANYON
3/15/71 Warner Bros. (2 hours)

Executive Producer: Richard Alan Simmons
Producer: Ed Adamson
Director: Robert Day
Teleplay: Ed Adamson
Photography: Lamar Boren
Music: Leonard Rosenman
Art Director: Ed Graves
Editor: Jamie Caylor

Myles C. Banyon	ROBERT FORSTER
Lt. Pete Cordova	DARREN McGAVIN
Lee Jennings	JOSÉ FERRER
Diane Jennings	ANJANETTE COMER
Harry Sprague	HERB EDELMAN
Peggy Revere	HERMIONE GINGOLD
Ruth Sprague	LESLIE PARRISH
Victor Pappas	RAY DANTON
Irene Fortolla	DIERDRE DANIELS
Eddie Dolan	STANLEY ADAMS
Linda	CARLA BORELLI
Sonny Arnheim	TED HARTLEY

David	PAUL HAMPTON
Clayton	ALVIN CHILDRESS
Carl Horner	JOE RUSKIN

and: Jeff Morris, Ann Randall, John Lawrence, Ned Glass, Jason Wingreen, John Craig, Florence Lake, Cathleen Cordell, Robert Shields

An atmospheric pilot for the series (1972-73) about a private eye working the Los Angeles beat circa 1937. In this outing, he's embarrassed when a girl—his client—is found murdered in his office with his gun. The subsequent series starring Forster found Joan Blondell (in Hermione Gingold's pilot role) as the head of the secretarial school who kept Banyon supplied with temporary help, and Richard Jaeckel playing Banyon's reluctant police contact in the department.

0127
IN SEARCH OF AMERICA
3/23/71 Four-Star Productions (90 min)

Executive Producer: Richard M. Rosenbloom
Producer: William Froug
Directord: Paul Bogart
Teleplay: Lewis John Carlino
Photography: Fred J. Koenekamp
Music: Fred Myrow
Art: Mort Rabinowitz
Editor: Richard R. Reilly

Ben Olson	CARL BETZ
Jenny Olson	VERA MILES
Mike Olson	JEFF BRIDGES
Grandma Rose	RUTH McDEVITT
Kathy	RENEE JARRETT
Ray Chandler	HOWARD DUFF
Cora Chandler	KIM HUNTER
J.J.	MICHAEL ANDERSON, JR.
Nick	SAL MINEO
Anne	TYNE DALY
Bodhi	GLYNN TURMAN

A college dropout convinces his family to re-examine its goals and gets them to chuck it all for a cross-country odyssey in a 1928 Greyhound bus—or, the family that stays together. . .

0128
JANE EYRE
3/24/71 Omnibus Productions/Sagittarius Productions (2 hours)

Producer: Frederick H. Brogger
Associate Producer: Hugh Attwooll
Director: Delbert Mann
Teleplay: Jack Pulman
Based on the novel by Charlotte Bronte
Photography: Paul Beeson
Music: John Williams
Art Director: Vetchinsky
Editor: Peter Boita

Edward Rochester	GEORGE C. SCOTT
Jane Eyre	SUSANNAH YORK
St. John Rivers	IAN BANNEN
Mr. Brocklehurst	JACK HAWKINS
Blanche Ingram	NYREE DAWN PORTER
Mrs. Fairfax	RACHEL KEMPSON
Mason	KENNETH GRIFFITH
John	PETER COPLEY
Mr. Eshton	CLIVE MORTON
Mrs. Eshton	FANNY ROWE
Amy	SUSAN LAWE
Louise	ANGHARAD REES
Lord Ingram	CARL BERNARD
Lady Ingram	NAN MUNRO
Colonel Dent	HUGH LATIMER

Beau Bridges and Carl Betz in IN SEARCH OF AMERICA (1971)

Mrs. Dent	SHEILA BROWNRIGG
Child Jane Eyre	SARAH GIBSON
Mrs. Rochester	JEAN MARSH

and: Jeremy Child, Peter Blythe, Helen Goss, Louise Pajo, Kara Wilson, Michele Dotrice, Lockwood West, Barbara Young, Rosalyn Landor, Helen Lindsay, Sharon Rose, Anne Korwin, Stella Tanner, Arthur Howard

A lavish, first color filming of Charlotte Bronte's classic Gothic romance with Emmy-nominated performances by George C. Scott and Susannah York highlighting this ninth screen version of the tale. It also had been staged several times on live television—a "Studio One" adaptation in 1949, for one, starred Charlton Heston at the very beginning of his career. John Williams' score for this TV film earned him an Emmy nomination in addition to those given to its two stars for acting.

0129
CANNON
3/26/71 Quinn Martin Productions (2 hours)

Executive Producer: Quinn Martin
Producers: Adrian Samish and Arthur Fellows
Director: George McGowan
Teleplay: Ed Hume
Photography: John A. Alonzo
Music: Robert Drasnin
Art Director: Phil Barber
Editor: Jerry Young

Frank Cannon	WILLIAM CONRAD
Diana Langston	VERA MILES
Lt. Kelly Redfield	J. D. CANNON
Christie	LYNDA DAY
Calhoun	BARRY SULLIVAN
Eddie	KEENAN WYNN
Virgil Holley	MURRAY HAMILTON
Magruder	EARL HOLLIMAN
Jake	JOHN FIEDLER
Herb Mayer	LAWRENCE PRESSMAN
Red Dunleavy	ROSS HAGEN

In this pilot for the long-running series (1971–77), a portly, well-heeled investigator looks into the murder of an old flame's husband and becomes enmeshed in a web of small-town corruption. Long-time character actor Conrad finally attained stardom with this role. Previously he had been one of the great radio voices, a frequent screen and TV villain, a motion picture producer and director, and often narrator of Quinn Martin's various productions on television.

0130
THE SHERIFF
3/30/71 Screen Gems/Columbia (90 min)

Executive Producer: Marvin Worth
Producer: Jon Epstein
Director: David Lowell Rich
Teleplay: Arnold Perl

Photography: Emil Oster
Music: Dominic Frontiere
Art Directors: Ross Bellah and Cary Odell
Editor: Howard Kunin

James Lucas	OSSIE DAVIS
Harve Gregory	KAZ GARAS
Sue-Anne Lucas	RUBY DEE
Vance Lucas	KYLE JOHNSON
Kinsella	JOHN MARLEY
Larry Walters	ROSS MARTIN
Almy Gregory	LYNDA DAY
Paulsen	EDWARD BINNS
Cliff Wilder	MOSES GUNN
Janet Wilder	BRENDA SYKES

and: Joel Fluellen, Austin Willis, Parley Baer

A rape case tears apart a small California town as a black sheriff and his white deputy go after an insurance salesman suspected of attacking a black coed.

0131
O'HARA, UNITED STATES TREASURY: OPERATION COBRA
4/2/71 Universal/Mark VII Ltd. (2 hours)

Executive Producers: Jack Webb and James B. Moser
Producer: Leonard B. Kaufman
Director: Jack Webb
Teleplay: James B. Moser
Photography: Alric Edens
Aerial Photography: James Gavin
Music: Ray Heindorf and William Lava
"U.S. Treasury March" by Ray Heindorf
Art Director: William D. DeCines
Editor: Warren H. Adams

James O'Hara	DAVID JANSSEN
Fran Harper	LANA WOOD
Marty Baron	JEROME THOR
Harry Fish	GARY CROSBY
Agent Joe Flagg	CHARLES McGRAW
Agent Garrick	JACK GING
Agent Ben Hazzard	STACY HARRIS
Keegan	WILLIAM CONRAD
Foreword spoken by	JACK WEBB

Narcotics agents break up a dope smuggling ring in the standard, efficient, Jack Webb-produced manner. Janssen went on to play O'Hara in the 1971–72 series, upholding law and order valiantly.

0132
ESCAPE
4/6/71 Paramount (90 min)

Producer: Bruce Lansbury
Director: John Llewellyn Moxey
Teleplay: Paul Playdon
Photography: Al Francis
Music: Lalo Schifrin
Art Director: Walter M. Jeffries
Editor: John Loeffler

Cameron Steele	CHRISTOPHER GEORGE
Dr. Henry Walding	WILLIAM WINDOM
Susan Walding	MARLYN MASON
Nicholas Slye	AVERY SCHREIBER
Charles Walding	JOHN VERNON
Evelyn Harrison	GLORIA GRAHAME
Lewis Harrison	WILLIAM SCHALLERT
Gilbert	HUNTZ HALL
Dan	MARK TAPSCOTT
Roger	GEORGE CLIFTON
Trudy	LUCILLE BENSON

and: Lisa Moore, Chuck Hicks, Ed Call, Lester Fletcher, Merriana Henrig, Caroline Ross

An escape artist and his sidekick/assistant attempt to rescue a kidnapped scientist and thwart a dastardly plan to rule the world in this unsuccessful pilot to a proposed series.

0133
POWDERKEG
4/16/71 Filmways/Rodphi Productions (2 hours)

Executive Producer: Phil Feldman
Producer/Director: Douglas Heyes
Teleplay: Douglas Heyes
Photography: John Morley Stephens
Music: John Andrew Tartaglia
Art Director: Jack Martin Smith
Editor: Russ Schoengarth

Hank Bracket	ROD TAYLOR
Johnny Reach	DENNIS COLE
Chucho Morales	FERNANDO LAMAS
Cyrus Davenport	JOHN McINTIRE
Juanita Sierra-Perez	LUCIANA PALUZZI
Paco Morales	MICHAEL ANSARA
Beth Parkinson	TISHA STERLING
Ricardo Sandoval	RENI SANTONI
Miss Baker	MELODIE JOHNSON
Major Bull Buckner	WILLIAM BRYANT

and: Joe DeSantis, Jay Novello, Jim L. Brown, Roy Jenson

A lighthearted adventure in the pre-World War I West with Taylor and Cole playing a pair of troubleshooters hired to retrieve a hijacked train. They continued their roles and battled early twentieth-century crime in the short-lived late 1971 series "Bearcats!"

0134
THE CITY
5/17/71 Universal (2 hours)

Producer: Frank Price
Director: Daniel Petrie
Teleplay: Howard Rodman
Photography: Jack Marta
Music: Billy Goldenberg
Song "Satisfied With You" by Billy Goldenberg and Bobby Russell
Sung by Bobby Russell
Art Director: Howard E. Johnson
Editors: Robert Watts and Larry Lester

Mayor Thomas Jefferson

Alcala	ANTHONY QUINN
Sheridan Hugotor	E. G. MARSHALL
Sealy Graham	ROBERT REED
Ira Groom	PAT HINGLE
Holland Yermo	JOHN LARCH
Unknown Man	KAZ GARAS
Sabina Menard	SKYE AUBREY
Mrs. Lockney	PEGGY McCAY
Victoria Ulysses	LORRAINE GARY
Detective Loop	EMANUEL SMITH
Detective Kosse	PAUL LEES
Plainclothesman	JOHN F. MILHOLLAND
Mrs. Cintra	PABLITA VELARDE HARDIN
Ambulance Attendant	JIM SMITH
La La Lajilla	SUE ANN CARPENTER
Bangi Fox	JAMES L. McCONKEY
Virginia Fox	MARJORIE M. SANFORD
Bishop Martin Bremend	W. ROBERT STEVENS
Commune Hippie	SCOTT BRITT

and: Doyle Randall, Ed Pennybacker, Phil Mead, Robert McCoy, Judson Ford, Manuel J. Gallegos, Howard R. Kirk, Thomas Dycus, Felicita Jojola, Jose

Rod Taylor in POWDERKEG (1971)

Anthony Quinn in THE CITY (1971)

ristopher George in ESCAPE (1971)

Rey Toledo, Eulojia Rubio, Winona Margery Haury, Ken Dunnagan, James R. Eaton, Bud Conlan, Ross Elder, Ben L. Abruzzo, Belle Abeytia

Quinn's powerhouse TV-movie debut as a shirt-sleeved mayor in Albuquerque who solves urban as well as personal problems later led him to reprise the role in the brief (1971) series that was retitled "The Man and the City."

1971–72 SEASON

0135
OWEN MARSHALL, COUNSELOR AT LAW
9/12/71 Universal (2 hours)
(subsequently titled *A Pattern of Morality*)

Executive Producer: David Victor
Producer: Douglas Benton
Director: Buzz Kulik
Teleplay: Jerry McNeely
From a story by David Victor and Jerry McNeely
Photography: Walter Strenge
Music: Elmer Bernstein
Art Director: George Patrick
Editor: Robert F. Shugrue

Owen Marshall	ARTHUR HILL
Joan Baldwin	VERA MILES
Dr. Eric Gibson	JOSEPH CAMPANELLA
D.A. Dave Blankenship	WILLIAM SHATNER
Raymond "Cowboy" Leatherberry	BRUCE DAVISON
Jim McGuire	TIM MATHESON
Judge Lynn Oliver	DANA WYNTER
Dr. Thomas Hershey	RAMON BIERI
Murray Gale	SORRELL BOOKE
Melissa Marshall	CHRISTINE MATCHETT
Baird Marshall	RICK LENZ
Frieda Krause	JOAN DARLING
Dr. Ray Baldwin	WALTER BROOKE
Gloria Leatherberry	KATHY LLOYD
Innkeeper	DONALD BARRY

A successful, recently divorced lawyer defends a hippie accused of murdering a wealthy housewife in this pilot to the hit TV series (1971–74). Arthur Hill continued in the title role, as did Joan Darling (later to become a respected producer and director) in the part of his secretary. Lee Majors signed on as his associate and David Soul became one of his legmen.

0136
THE PRIEST KILLER
9/14/71 Universal (2 hours)

Executive Producer: Richard A. Colla
Producer: David Levinson
Director: Richard A. Colla
Teleplay: Robert Van Scoyk and Joel Oliansky
Photography: Jacques R. Marquette
Music: David Shire
Art Director: Joseph Alves, Jr.
Editor: Robert L. Kimble

Chief Robert T. Ironside	RAYMOND BURR
Sarge Swanson	GEORGE KENNEDY
Sgt. Ed Brown	DON GALLOWAY
Mark Sanger	DON MITCHELL
Martha Gordon	LOUISE LATHAM
Vincent Wiertel	ANTHONY ZERBE
Father Miles	PETER BROCCO
Father McMurtry	ROBERT SAMPSON
Father Wendell	ROBERT SHAYNE
Publisher	KERMIT MURDOCK
Author	FRED SLYTER
Patrolman	MAX GAIL

and: Ned Romero, David Huddleston, Ann Doran, Regis J. Cordic, Kit Woodhouse, Allison McKay, Thomas Bellin

Wheelchair-bound Ironside and cop-turned-priest Sarge Swanson team up to solve a series of murders among the clergy in this second pilot to Kennedy's "Sarge" show which ran for several months in late 1971.

0137
THE FORGOTTEN MAN
9/14/71 Grauman Productions (90 min)

Executive Producer: Walter Grauman
Producer: Philip Barry
Director: Walter Grauman
Teleplay: Mark Rogers
Photography: Michel Hugo
Music: Dave Grusin
Editor: Frank Keller

Lt. Joe Hardy	DENNIS WEAVER
Anne Wilson	LOIS NETTLETON
Marie Hardy Forrest	ANNE FRANCIS
William Forrest	ANDREW DUGGAN
Captain Jackson	PERCY RODRIGUES
Sharon Hardy	PAMELYN FERDIN
Major Everett	ROBERT DOYLE
Major Thon	JAMES HONG
Colonel Thompson	FRANK MAXWELL
Lt. Diamonte	CARL REINDEL
Major Parkman	JOHN S. RAGIN
Surgeon	VERNON WEDDLE

An American POW reportedly killed in action returns from Vietnam to find his wife remarried, his daughter adopted, his business sold and his life completely changed.

0138
TERROR IN THE SKY
9/17/71 Paramount (90 min)

Producer: Matthew Rapf
Director: Bernard Kowalski
Teleplay: Richard Nelson and Stephen and Elinor Karpf
Based on the novel *Runway Zero 8* by Arthur Hailey
Photography: Howard R. Schwartz
Music: Pat Williams
Art Director: Jack DeShields
Editor: Argyle Nelson

George Spencer	DOUG McCLURE
Janet Turner	LOIS NETTLETON
Dr. Ralph Baird	RODDY McDOWALL
Marty Treleavek	LEIF ERICKSON
Milton	KEENAN WYNN
Capt. Wilson	KENNETH TOBEY
Stewart	SAM MELVILLE
Ellen	PATRICIA MATTICK
McCann	CHRISTOPHER DARK
Mrs. McCann	LORETTA LEVERSEE
Controller	JACK GING
Harry Burdick	LEONARD STONE

This TV carbon of Hailey's *Airport* has crew and passengers stricken by food poisoning, forcing a washed-up helicopter pilot on board to land the plane with the help of a stewardess. Previously it had been the basis for a drama *Flight into Danger* on TV's "Alcoa Hour" (1956) and then was made as *Zero Hour*, a 1957 theatrical film with Dana Andrews and Linda Darnell.

0139
ONCE UPON A DEAD MAN
9/17/71 Universal (2 hours)

Executive Producer: Leonard Stern
Producer: Paul Mason
Director: Leonard Stern
Teleplay: Chester Krumholz and Leonard Stern
Photography: Stanley M. Lazan
Music: Jerry Fielding
Art Director: John J. Lloyd
Editor: Michael Economou

Commissioner Stewart McMillan	ROCK HUDSON
Sally McMillan	SUSAN SAINT JAMES
Chief Andy Yeakel	JACK ALBERTSON
Andre Stryker	RENE AUBERJONOIS
Edmond Corday	KURT KASZNAR
Wortzel	JONATHAN HARRIS
Gregory Constantine	HERB EDELMAN
Sergeant Enright	JOHN SCHUCK
John Patterson	JAMES WAINRIGHT
Mme. Jamac	LILYAN CHAUVIN
Dewhawk	FRANK ORSATTI
Dr. Hinton	STACY KEACH, SR.
Emily Hull	LINDA WATKINS
Etienne Jacoby	GERALD HIKEN

A San Francisco police commissioner is dragged into a charity auction theft and a mysterious murder by his kooky wife. Rock Hudson made his TV acting debut in this pilot to his hit "McMillan and Wife" series (1971–77). Susan Saint James and John Schuck were the other holdovers from the pilot.

0140
THE BIRDMEN
9/18/71 Universal (90 min)
(subsequently titled *Escape of the Birdmen*)

Producer: Harve Bennett
Co-Producer: Harris Tatleman
Director: Philip Leacock
Teleplay: David Kidd
Photography: Jack Marta
Music: David Rose
Art Director: Henry Bumstead
Editor: Robert F. Shugrue

Major Harry Cook	DOUG McCLURE
Halden Brevik	RENE AUBERJONOIS
Schiller	RICHARD BASEHART
Colonel Morgan Crawford	CHUCK CONNORS
Tanker	MAX BAER, JR.
Focus Flaherty	DON KNIGHT
Fits	TOM SKERRITT
Sparrow	GREG MULLAVEY
Donnelly	BARRY BROWN
Davies	PAUL KOSLO
Bridski	GENADII BIEGOULOFF
Helmut Weber	ROLF NIEHUS
Konrad	PETER HELLMANN
Gunter	KARL SWENSON
Chef	KARL BRUCK

A group of allied POWs held by the Germans plot an unusual breakout from an impregnable medieval castle. They plan to escape by glider and soar into Switzerland.

0141
CONGRATULATIONS, IT'S A BOY!
9/21/71 Aaron Spelling Productions (90 min)

Producer: Aaron Spelling
Director: William A. Graham
Teleplay: Stanley Z. Cherry

Photography: Arch R. Dalzell
Music: Basil Poledouris and Richard Baskin
Art Director: Paul Sylos
Editor: Art Seid

Johnny Gaines	BILL BIXBY
Eydie	DIANE BAKER
Al Gaines	JACK ALBERTSON
Ethel Gaines	ANN SOTHERN
Rhonda	KAREN JENSEN
B.J.	DARRELL LARSON
Herb	TOM BOSLEY
Rose	JEFF DONNELL
Riva	JUDY STRANGIS
Tom	ROBERT H. HARRIS

A happy bachelor's swinging life is disrupted by the arrival of a teenager who claims to be his son. *So's Your Old Man!* was this movie's original pre-airing title.

0142
LOCK, STOCK AND BARREL
9/24/71 Universal (90 min)

Producer: Richard Alan Simmons
Director: Jerry Thorpe
Teleplay: Richard Alan Simmons
Photography: Russell Metty and Harry J. May
Music: Pat Williams
Art Director: William D. DeCinces
Editor: Edward M. Abroms

Clarence Bridgeman	TIM MATHESON
Roselle Bridgeman	BELINDA MONTGOMERY
Punck Logan	CLAUDE AKINS
Brucker	JACK ALBERTSON
Sergeant Markey	NEVILLE BRAND
Reverend Willie Pursle	BURGESS MEREDITH
Sam Hartwig	ROBERT EMHARDT
Micah Brucker	JOHN BECK
Corporal Fowler	CHARLES DIERKOP
Kane	JOE DiREDA
Deville	TIMOTHY SCOTT
Plye	MILIS WATSON
Butcher	DAN JENKINS
Jean	MARLENE TRACY

An amiable Western about a young frontier couple who elope, are pursued by the girl's displeased father and brothers, are joined by an escaped convict, and become involved with a phony preacher.

0143
A TATTERED WEB
9/24/71 Metromedia Productions (90 min)

Executive Producer: Charles W. Fries
Producer: Bob Markell
Director: Paul Wendkos
Teleplay: Art Wallace
Photography: Michel Hugo

Music: Robert Drasnin
Art Director: Lawrence G. Paull
Editor: Jack McSweeney

Sgt. Ed Stagg	LLOYD BRIDGES
Steve Butler	FRANK CONVERSE
Tina Butler	SALLIE SHOCKLEY
Sgt. Joe Marcus	MURRAY HAMILTON
Willard Edson	BRODERICK CRAWFORD
Louise Campbell	ANNE HELM
Sam Jeffers	JOHN FIEDLER
Sgt. Harry Barnes	VAL AVERY
Lt. Preston	WALTER BROOKE
Mr. Harland	WHIT BISSELL
Mrs. Simmons	ELLEN CORBY
Bert Korawicz	ROY JENSON
Bartender	JOE BERNARD
Police Surgeon	JAMES HONG
Selma Marcus	ALISON McKAY

A detective discovers his son-in-law cheating on his daughter, confronts the other woman and accidentally kills her, and then attempts to pin the crime on a wino.

0144
THE DEADLY DREAM
9/25/71 Universal (90 min)

Producer: Stan Shpetner
Director: Alf Kjellin
Teleplay: Barry Oringer

Diane Baker, Darrell Larson and Bill Bixby in CONGRATULATIONS, IT'S A BOY! (1971)

Photography: Jack Marta
Music: Dave Grusin
Art Director: Loyd S. Papez
Editor: Robert L. Kimble

Dr. Jim Hanley	LOYD BRIDGES
Laurel Hanley	JANET LEIGH
Dr. Howard Geary	CARL BETZ
Dr. Harold Malcolm	LEIF ERICKSON
Kagan	DON STROUD
Delgreve	RICHARD JAECKEL
Dr. Farrow	PHILLIP PINE
Dr. Goodman	HERBERT NELSON

A research scientist is driven to the brink by a recurring dream that he is marked for death by a mysterious tribunal, and soon he is unable to separate his dreams from reality—and vice versa.

0145
FIVE DESPERATE WOMEN
9/28/71 Aaron Spelling Productions (90 min)

Producer: Aaron Spelling
Director: Ted Post
Teleplay: Marc Norman and Walter Black
From a story by Larry Gordon
Photography: Arch R. Dalzell
Music: Paul Glass
Art Director: Paul Sylos
Editor: Art Seid

Lucy	ANJANETTE COMER
Jim Meeker	BRADFORD DILLMAN
Dorian	JOAN HACKETT
Joy	DENISE NICHOLAS
Gloria	STEFANIE POWERS
Mary Grace	JULIE SOMMARS
Wylie	ROBERT CONRAD
Mrs. Brown	CONNIE SAWYER
Mrs. Miller	BEATRICE MANLEY
Man on Beach	PATRICK WALTZ

Five college pals, meeting on a private island for a reunion, find themselves stalked by a mental institution escapee.

0146
RIVER OF MYSTERY
10/1/71 Universal (2 hours)

Producer: Steve Shagan
Director: Paul Stanley

Teleplay: Albert Ruben
Photography: Gabriel Torres Garces
Music: Luis Bonfa
Art Director: Robert Machado
Editor: Richard G. Wray

Phil Munger	VIC MORROW
Ernie Dorata	CLAUDE AKINS
Garwood Drum	NIALL MacGINNIS
Elena	LOUISE SOREL
El Alacron	NICO MINDARDOS
R. J. Twitchell	EDMOND O'BRIEN
Torres	CICERO SHADLER
Cleo	DILMA LOES
Pablo	WALDIR MAIA
Gold	EARL PARKER

A pair of free-lance explosives experts find jungle adventure while being stalked by a revolutionary leader and a diamond hunter in this tale filmed in South America early in 1969.

0147
THE DEADLY HUNT
10/1/71 Four Star International (90 min)

Executive Producer: David Levy
Producer/Director: John Newland
Teleplay: Jerry Ludwig and Eric Bercovici
Based on the novel by Pat Stadley
Photography: Fred Koenekamp
Music: Vic Mizzy
Art Director: Walter Neumiester
Editor: Henry Berman

Ryab	TONY FRANCIOSA
Mason	PETER LAWFORD

Janet Leigh and Lloyd Bridges in
THE DEADLY DREAM (1971)

Julie Sommars, Denise Nicholas, Stefanie Powers, Anjanette Comer and Joan Hackett in FIVE DESPERATE WOMEN (1971)

Louise Sorel, Claude Akins and Vic Morrow in RIVER OF MYSTERY (1971)

Tony Franciosa and Peter Lawford in THE DEADLY HUNT (1971)

Martha Cope	ANJANETTE COMER
Cliff Cope	JIM HUTTON
Peter Burton	TIM McINTIRE
Danny	TOM HAUFF
Ferraches	BOB GEORGE
Uncle Claude	IVOR HARRIES
Jeb	WALLY McSWEEN
McKeever	BILL BARRINGER
Perkins	DAVID GLYN-JONES
Joe	DEREK GLYN-JONES

A young businessman and his wife on a hunting trip find themselves the quarry of two paid assassins and caught in a forest fire.

0148
SWEET, SWEET RACHEL
10/2/71 ABC Inc. (90 min)

Producer: Stan Shpetner
Director: Sutton Roley
Teleplay: Anthony Lawrence
Photography: James Crabe
Music: Laurence Rosenthal
Art Director: Paul Sylos
Editors: James Potter and Harry Coswick

Dr. Lucas Darrow	ALEX DREIER
Rachel Stanton	STEFANIE POWERS
Arthur Piper	PAT HINGLE
Lillian Piper	LOUISE LATHAM
Dr. Tyler	STEVE IHNAT
Nora Piper	BRENDA SCOTT

Steve Ihnat, Stefanie Powers, Chris Robinson and Alex Dreier in SWEET, SWEET RACHEL (1971)

Van Heflin, Michael Cole and Janet Margolin in THE LAST CHILD (1971)

Carey	CHRIS ROBINSON
Houseman	MARK TAPSCOTT
Doctor	WILLIAM BRYANT
Minister	LEN WAYLAND
Paul Stanton	ROD McCAREY
Surgeon	JOHN ALVIN
Medical Examiner	JOHN HILLERMAN

An ESP expert (played by former news commentator Alex Dreier) uses his powers to search for a psychic employing telepathy to commit murder. The series "The Sixth Sense" (Jan.–Dec. 1972) spun off from this movie—without Dreier. Gary Collins starred.

0149
THE LAST CHILD
10/5/71 Aaron Spelling Productions (90 min)

Executive Producer: Aaron Spelling
Producer: William Allyn
Director: John Llewellyn Moxey
Teleplay: Peter S. Fisher
Photography: Arch R. Dalzell
Music: Laurence Rosenthal
Art Director: Paul Sylos
Editor: Art Seid

Alan Miller	MICHAEL COLE
Howard Drum	HARRY GUARDINO
Karen Miller	JANET MARGOLIN
Sen. Quincy George	VAN HEFLIN
Barstow	EDWARD ASNER
Iverson	KENT SMITH
Sandy	MICHAEL LARRAIN
Dr. Tyler	PHILIP BOURNOUF
Shelley	BARBARA BABCOCK
Silverman	VICTOR IZAY

This futuristic drama, containing Van Heflin's last performance, focuses on a young couple trying to circumvent the government's edict that limits each family to only one child. Heflin is a retired U.S. Senator who tries to help them in this film originally to have been called *The Day They Took the Babies Away*.

0150
THE IMPATIENT HEART
10/8/71 Universal (2 hours)

Producer: William Sackheim
Director: John Badham
Teleplay: Alvin Sargent
Photography: Jacques R. Marquette
Music: David Shire
Art Director: Joseph Alves, Jr.
Editor: Edward M. Abroms

Grace McCormack	CARRIE SNODGRESS
Frank Pescadero	MICHAEL BRANDON
Murray Kane	MICHAEL CONSTANTINE
Nellie Santchi	MARIAN HAILEY
Mr. Hernandez	HECTOR ELIZONDO
Brewster Crowley	BRAD DAVID

and: Harry Davis, Victor Millan, Penny Stanton, Anna Navarro, John Bakos, Lyvonne Walder, Linda Dangeil, Yuki Shimoda, Ralph Moody

A social worker throws herself into others' problems but finds that she cannot motivate the man she loves. During production, this film was titled *McCormack*.

0151
THE FACE OF FEAR
10/8/71 Quinn Martin Productions (90 min)

Executive Producer: Quinn Martin
Producers: Arthur Fellows and Adrian Samish
Director: George McGowan

Angie Dickinson and Richard Crenna in THIEF (1971)

Teleplay: Edward Hume
Based on the novel *Sally* by E. V. Cunningham
Photography: Ben Colman
Music: Morton Stevens
Art Director: Bill Smith
Editor: Marston Fay

Sgt. Frank Ortega	RICARDO MONTALBAN
Lt. George Coye	JACK WARDEN
Sally Dillman	ELIZABETH ASHLEY
Tamworth	DANE CLARK
Glenn Kennedy	ROY POOLE
Patsy Fain	CHARLES DIERKOP
Peter Sargent Fennington	BURR DeBENNING
Dr. Landsteiner	REGIS J. CORDIC

A young Iowa schoolteacher thinks she is dying of leukemia, goes to San Francisco where she hires a syndicate killer to take her life, then changes her mind and tries to cancel the contract with the help of the local police.

0152
THIEF
10/9/71 Metromedia Productions/Stonehenge (90 min)

Executive Producer: Dick Berg
Producer: Ron Roth
Director: William A. Graham
Teleplay: John D. F. Black
Photography: Michel Hugo
Music: Ron Grainger
Art Director: Art Stolnitz
Editor: Jim Benson

Neal Wilkinson	RICHARD CRENNA
Jean Melville	ANGIE DICKINSON
Charles Herrod	CAMERON MITCHELL
Herman Gray	HURD HATFIELD
James Calendar	ROBERT WEBBER
Beffy	BRUCE KIRBY
Jack Cutter	MICHAEL LERNER
Junkie	MICHAEL C. GWYNNE
Party Hostess	MARY GREGORY
Swinger	ED PECK
Mrs. Risman	BARBARA PERRY
Bob Rifleman	RICHARD STAHL
Matron	JO DeWINTER

A suave professional burglar wants to break with his criminal past but is forced to pull one last job to make good on a gambling debt. Winner of the 1971 Edgar Award from the Mystery Writers of America as the Best TV Suspense Film, and nominated for an Emmy as Best Written Original Drama of 1971. Original title: *A Day in the Life of a Burglar*.

0153
A TASTE OF EVIL
10/12/71 Aaron Spelling Productions (90 min)

Producer: Aaron Spelling
Director: John Llewellyn Moxey
Teleplay: Jimmy Sangster
Photography: Arch R. Dalzell
Music: Robert Drasnin
Art Director: Paul Sylos
Editor: Art Seid

Miriam Jannings	BARBARA STANWYCK
Susan Wilcox	BARBARA PARKINS
Dr. Michael Lomas	RODDY McDOWALL
Harold Jannings	WILLIAM WINDOM
John	ARTHUR O'CONNELL
Sheriff	BING RUSSELL
Young Susan	DAWN FRAME

Returning from a mental institution following a traumatic rape experience, a young woman finds herself the target of someone trying to drive her insane.

0154
MARRIAGE: YEAR ONE
10/15/71 Universal (2 hours)

Executive Producer: Norman Felton
Producer: Stephen Karpf
Director: William A. Graham
Teleplay: Stephen and Elinor Karpf
Photography: William Margulies
Music: David Shire
Art Director: William D. DeCinces
Editor: Douglas Stewart

Jane Duden	SALLY FIELD
L. T. Mellons	ROBERT PRATT
Warren Duden	WILLIAM WINDOM
Grandma Duden	AGNES MOOREHEAD
Golonkas	NEVILLE BRAND
Bernie	BOB BALABAN
Phil	LONNY CHAPMAN
Lemberg	MICHAEL LERNER
Shirley Lemberg	SUSAN SILO
Emma Teasley	CICELY TYSON
Dan	RANDOLPH MANTOOTH
Luke	ROBERT LIPTON
Mechanic	MANTAN MORELAND

Robert Pratt and Sally Field in MARRIAGE: YEAR ONE (1971)

Suzanne Pleshette, Paul Smith and Richard Boone in IN BROAD DAYLIGHT (1971)

Cloris Leachman, Fred Beir and Hal Holbrook in SUDDENLY SINGLE (1971)

and: Essex Smith, Alison Rose, Lorri Davis, Stanley Clay, Annazette Chase, Carol Swenson, Paulene Myers, Charles Steel, Stuart Nisbet

Cutesy love story about a fourth-year medical student who marries a free-thinking heiress and then insists that they live on his meager earnings.

0155
IN BROAD DAYLIGHT
10/16/71 Aaron Spelling Productions (90 min)

Executive Producer: Aaron Spelling
Producer: Robert Mirisch
Director: Robert Day
Teleplay: Larry Cohen
Photography: Arch R. Dalzell
Music: Leonard Rosenman
Art Director: Paul Sylos
Editor: Edward Mann

Tony Chappel	RICHARD BOONE
Kate Todd	SUZANNE PLESHETTE
Elizabeth Chappel	STELLA STEVENS
Lt. Bergman	JOHN MARLEY
Alex Crawford	FRED BEIR
Captain Moss	WHIT BISSELL
Charles (Doorman)	PAUL SMITH
Teenager	DANIEL SPELLING
Mother	BARBARA DODD
Dr. Grant	KEN SANSOM
Cunningham	SAM EDWARDS
Driver	BUDDY LEWIS
Sgt. Wilkes	FRANK BELLU
Manager	AL C. WARD

A blind actor discovers that his wife is cheating on him with his best friend and plots an elaborate double murder.

0156
SUDDENLY SINGLE
10/19/71 Chris-Rose Productions (90 min)

Producers: Robert W. Christianson and Rick Rosenberg
Director: Jud Taylor
Teleplay: Stephen and Elinor Karpf and Arnold and Lois Peyser
Photography: David Walsh
Music: Billy Goldenberg
Art Director: Perry F. Ferguson II
Editor: Folmar Blangsted

Larry Hackett	HAL HOLBROOK
Evelyn Baxter	BARBARA RUSH
Jackie	MARGOT KIDDER
Marlene	AGNES MOOREHEAD
Frankie Ventura	MICHAEL CONSTANTINE
Conrad	HARVEY KORMAN
Joanne Hackett	CLORIS LEACHMAN
Beverly	PAMELA RODGERS
Bennie	DAVID HUDDLESTON
Ted	FRED BEIR
Frank	STEVE DUNNE
Singer	KATE PORTER

A bittersweet tale of a newly divorced man trying to find a place for himself in the world of swinging singles.

0157
GOODBYE RAGGEDY ANN
10/22/71 Metromedia Productions (90 min)

Executive Producer: Fielder Cook
Producer: Jack Sher
Director: Fielder Cook

Teleplay: Jack Sher
Photography: Earl Rath
Music: Wladimir Selinsky
Art Director: Robert E. Smith
Editor: Philip Anderson

Brooke Collier	MIA FARROW
Harlan Webb	HAL HOLBROOK
Paul Jamison	JOHN COLICOS
Louise Walters	MARLENE WARFIELD
David Bevin	ED FLANDERS
Jules Worthman	MARTIN SHEEN
Jerry	WALTER KOENIG
Kim	MARGUERITA CHAN
Clerk	MAXINE STUART
Woman in Line	BARBARA DAITCH
Man in Line	TONY DiMILO
Tony	BUCK KARTALIAN
Autograph Seeker	NORA MARLOWE
Woman Officer	TONI GILMAN
Receptionist	PAM DIXON

A sensitive Hollywood writer tries to talk a young down-on-her-luck actress out of suicide in this movie marking Mia Farrow's telefeature debut.

0158
DEATH TAKES A HOLIDAY
10/23/71 Universal (90 min)

Producer: George Eckstein
Director: Robert Butler
Teleplay: Rita Larkin
From Walter Ferris' adaptation of the play by Alberto Casella
Photography: Michael Margulies
Music: Laurindo Almeida
Art Director: Eugene Lourie
Editor: Michael Economou

Peggy Chapman	YVETTE MIMIEUX
David Smith	MONTE MARKHAM
Selena Chapman	MYRNA LOY
John Cummings	BERT CONVY
Judge Earl Chapman	MELVYN DOUGLAS
Sen. Earl Chapman, Jr.	KERWIN MATHEWS
Marion Chapman	PRISCILLA POINTER
Martin Herndon	AUSTIN WILLIS
Tony Chapman	COLBY CHESTER
Ellen Chapman	MAUREEN REAGAN
TV Announcers	REGIS J. CORDIC MARIO MACHADO

In this updated remake of the 1934 movie that starred Fredric March, Death in human form comes to earth to learn why people hang onto life so tenaciously and unexpectedly falls in love with a beautiful young woman. The film reunited veteran actors Melvyn Douglas and Myrna Loy for the first time since the 1940s when they worked together in *Third Finger— Left Hand* (1940) and *Mr. Blandings Builds His Dream House* (1948).

(Left) **Yvette Mimieux and Monte Markham in DEATH TAKES A HOLIDAY (1971)**
(Below) **Doug McClure and Meg Foster in THE DEATH OF ME YET (1971)**

0159
THE DEATH OF ME YET
10/27/71 Aaron Spelling Productions (90 min)

Producer: Aaron Spelling
Director: John Llewellyn Moxey
Teleplay: A. J. Russell
Based on a novel by Whit Masterson
Photography: Tim Southcott
Music: Pete Rugolo
Art Director: Tracy Bousman
Editor: Art Seid

Edward Young/Paul Towers	DOUG McCLURE
Joe Chalk	DARREN McGAVIN
Sybil Towers	ROSEMARY FORSYTH
Robert Barnes	RICHARD BASEHART
Alice	MEG FOSTER
Hank Keller	DANA ELCAR
Marilyn Keller	JEAN ALLISON
George Dickman	STEVE DUNN
Nora Queen	SCOTTIE MacGREGOR
Nylec	ALLEN JAFFE
Jerry	SAM EDWARDS
Redstone	JOHN KROGA

A small-town newspaper editor, a pillar of his community, discovers that his hidden past has caught up with him and an Iron Curtain agent who knew him in his other life has been sent to kill him.

0160
MURDER ONCE REMOVED
10/29/71 Metromedia Productions (90 min)

Executive Producer: Charles W. Fries
Producer: Robert Markell
Director: Charles S. Dubin
Teleplay: Irving Gaynor Neiman
Photography: Robert C. Moreno
Music: Robert Drasnin
Art Director: Lawrence G. Paull
Editor: Jack McSweeney

Dr. Ron Wellesley	JOHN FORSYTHE
Frank Manning	RICHARD KILEY
Lisa Manning	BARBARA BAIN
Lt. Phil Procter	JOSEPH CAMPANELLA
Nurse Regis	RETA SHAW
Fred Kramer	WENDELL BURTON
Officer Bates	LARRY HADDON

A deadly love triangle involves a scheming doctor who tries to inveigle his patient's wealthy wife to dump her husband for him, and together they hatch the perfect crime.

0161
A LITTLE GAME
10/30/71 Universal (90 min)

Executive Producer: Richard Irving
Producer: George Eckstein
Director: Paul Wendkos
Teleplay: Carol Sobieski
Based on the novel by Fielden Farrington
Photography: Harry Wolf
Music: Robert Prince
Art Director: Frank Arrigo
Editor: Michael Economou

Elaine Hamilton	DIANE BAKER
Paul Hamilton	ED NELSON
Dunlap	HOWARD DUFF
Laura	KATY JURADO

(Above) Richard Kiley and John Forsythe in MURDER ONCE REMOVED (1971)
(Left) Christopher Shea and Ed Nelson in A LITTLE GAME (1971)
(Below) Ted Bessell and Patty Duke in TWO ON A BENCH (1971)

Robert Mueller	MARK GRUNER
Stu Parker	CHRISTOPHER SHEA
Secretary	HELEN KLEEB

A hostile youngster who will stop at nothing to break up his mother's marriage is suspected of homicide, and his stepfather fears that he may be the boy's next victim.

0162
TWO ON A BENCH
11/2/71 Universal (90 min)

Producer: Richard Levinson
Director: Jerry Paris
Teleplay: Richard Levinson and William Link
Photography: Harry Wolf
Music: Mike Post and Pete Carpenter

Art Director: Walter L. Simonds
Editor: Stefan Arnsten

Macy Kramer	PATTY DUKE
Preston Albright	TED BESSELL
Brubaker	ANDREW DUGGAN
Dr. Stanley Remington	JOHN ASTIN
Mrs. Kramer	ALICE GHOSTLEY
Kingston	TERRY CARTER
Luckins	DICK BALDUZZI
Mr. Hayes	ROBERT CORNTHWAITE
Harriet	JEANNIE BERLIN
Ralph	GARY WAYNESMITH
Agent	KEN SANSOM

Wacky comedy about a hip young lady and a square stockbroker who meet on a park bench in Boston and are picked up as international spies.

0163
A HOWLING IN THE WOODS
11/5/71 Universal (2 hours)

Producer: Douglas Benton
Director: Daniel Petrie
Teleplay: Richard DeRoy
Based on the novel by Velda Johnson
Photography: Jack Marta
Music: Dave Grusin
Art Director: Howard E. Johnson
Editor: Robert F. Shugrue

Liza Crocker	BARBARA EDEN
Eddie Crocker	LARRY HAGMAN
Justin Conway	JOHN RUBINSTEIN
Rose Saines	VERA MILES
Sally Bixton	TYNE DALY
Sharon	RUTA LEE

Mel Warren	GEORGE MURDOCK
Bud Henshaw	FORD RAINEY
Betsy Warren	LISA GERRITSEN
Lonnie Henshaw	BILL VINT
Apperson	KARL SWENSON

The "other side" of the co-stars of TV's long-running "I Dream of Jeannie" shows up in this chiller about a disillusioned housewife vacationing in the wilds, her incompatible husband who is trying to get her to come home, and a starving dog with a baleful howl.

0164
BLACK NOON
11/5/71 Fenady Associates/Screen Gems (90 min)

Producer: Andrew J. Fenady
Director: Bernard Kowalski
Teleplay: Andrew J. Fenady
Photography: Keith Smith
Music: George Duning
Art Director: John Beckman
Editor: Dann Kahn

Rev. John Keyes	ROY THINNES
Lorna Keyes	LYN LORING
Deliverance	YVETTE MIMIEUX
Caleb Hobbs	RAY MILLAND
Moon	HENRY SILVA
Bethia	GLORIA GRAHAME
Jacob	WILLIAM BRYANT
Ethan	BUDDY FOSTER
Joseph	HANK WORDEN

An occult Western about a circuit-riding minister and his wife who are caught up in a web of witchcraft involving a mute beauty and a satanical gunfighter.

Larry Hagman and Barbara Eden in A HOWLING IN THE WOODS (1971)

Roy Thinnes and Lyn Loring in BLACK NOON (1971)

0165
REVENGE
11/6/71 Mark Carliner Productions (90 min)

Producer: Mark Carliner
Director: Jud Taylor
Teleplay: Joseph Stefano
Based on the novel by Elizabeth Davis
Photography: John A. Alonzo
Music: Dominic Frontiere
Art Director: Joseph Jennings
Editor: John F. Link II

Amanda Hilton	SHELLEY WINTERS
Frank Klaner	BRADFORD DILLMAN
Mark Hembric	STUART WHITMAN
Diane Klaner	CAROL ROSSEN
Peter Marsh	ROGER PERRY
Ed Lucas	GARY CLARKE
Jimmy Klaner	JOHNNY SCOTT LEE
Nancy Grover	LESLIE CHARLETON

A deranged mother takes revenge on the man she thinks seduced her daughter by caging him in her basement while his wife uses ESP in a frantic search to find him.

0166
DO NOT FOLD, SPINDLE OR MUTILATE
11/9/71 Lee Rich Productions (90 min)

Executive Producer: Lee Rich
Producer: Robert L. Jacks
Director: Ted Post
Teleplay: John D. F. Black
Based on a novel by Doris Miles Disney
Photography: Stanley Cortez
Music: Jerry Goldsmith
Editor: Folmar Blangsted

**Stuart Whitman and Shelley Winters
in REVENGE (1971)**

Sophie Tate Curtis	HELEN HAYES
Sussy Tryon	MYRNA LOY
Shelby Saunders	MILDRED NATWICK
Elizabeth Gibson	SYLVIA SIDNEY
Mal Weston	VINCE EDWARDS
Lt. Hallum	JOHN BERADINO
Sgt. Lutz	LARRY D. MANN
Cutter	PAUL SMITH
Brenda	BARBARA DAVIS
Jonas	GARY VINSON
Trudy	DODO DENNEY
Hostess	PATRICIA WYNAND
Ralph	JOHN MITCHUM

Four elderly ladies with time on their hands create a fictional girl for a computer dating service and get involved with a psychopath. Helen Hayes, in her first TV movie, was Emmy-nominated for her performance.

0167
THE HARNESS
11/12/71 Universal (2 hours)

Producer: William Sackheim
Director: Boris Sagal
Teleplay: Leon Tokatyan and Edward Hume
Based on the story by John Steinbeck
Photography: Russell Metty
Music: Billy Goldenberg
Art Director: Alexander A. Mayer
Editor: Frank Morriss

Julie Sommars and Lorne Greene in THE HARNESS (1971)

James Olson and Elliott Street in PAPER MAN (1971)

Peter Randall	LORNE GREENE
Jennifer Shagaras	JULIE SOMMARS
Roy Kern	MURRAY HAMILTON
Tor Shagaras	LEE HARCOURT MONTGOMERY
Emma Randall	LOUISE LATHAM
Doc Marn	HENRY BECKMAN
Millie Chappel	JOAN TOMPKINS
Edgar Chappel	ROBERT KARNES
Minister	JOHN LASSELL
Charlie (Banker)	WILLIAM LANTEAU

A gentle Steinbeck tale about a farmer who is dominated by his ailing wife until a free-minded young woman turns up at his ranch with her eight-year-old son.

0168
PAPER MAN
11/12/71 20th Century-Fox (90 min)

Executive Producer: Walter Grauman
Producer: Anthony Wilson
Director: Walter Grauman
Teleplay: James D. Buchanan and Ronald Austin
From a story by Anthony Wilson
Photography: Jack Woolf
Music: Duane Tatro
Art Director: Rodger Maus
Editor: Jack McSweeney

Avery Jensen	DEAN STOCKWELL
Karen McMillan	STEFANIE POWERS
Jerry	JAMES STACY
Joel Fisher	ELLIOTT STREET
Lisa	TINA CHEN
Art Fletcher	JAMES OLSON
Sheriff	ROSS ELLIOTT
Secretary	MARCY LAFERTY
Father	ROBERT PATTEN
Mother	SUE TAYLOR
Avery as a Boy	JOHNNY SCOTT LEE
Doctor	JASON WINGREEN

and: Dan Barton, Bob Golden, Len Wayland, Dean Harens

A suspense drama that begins with a group of college students who create an identity for a fictitious credit card-holder after feeding data into a computer and snowballs into a scheme that leaves three of them dead.

0169
DUEL
11/13/71 Universal (90 min)

Producer: George Eckstein
Director: Steven Spielberg
Teleplay: Richard Matheson
From his short story in *Playboy*
Photography: Jack A. Marta
Music: Billy Goldenberg
Art Director: Robert S. Smith
Editor: Frank Morriss

David Mann	DENNIS WEAVER
Gas Station Attendant	TIM HERBERT
Old Man	CHARLES STEEL
Cafe Owner	EDDIE FIRESTONE
Waitress	SHIRLEY O'HARA
Lady at Snakarama	LUCILLE BENSON
Man in Car	ALEXANDER LOCKWOOD
Woman in Car	AMY DOUGLASS
Man in Cafe	GENE DYNARSKI
Truck Driver	CARY LOFTIN

Peter Lawford and Harry Morgan in ELLERY QUEEN: DON'T LOOK BEHIND YOU (1971)

A suspense classic and subsequent cult movie that "made" director Steven Spielberg, pitting a traveling salesman against a ten-ton tanker truck on a lonely stretch of highway. Emmy award-nominated for his work was cinematographer Jack A. Marta. The theatrical version shown outside of the United States, and lately in festivals in this country, runs somewhat longer with additional footage devoted to the salesman's home life.

0170
MR. AND MRS. BO JO JONES
11/16/71 20th Century-Fox (90 min)

Producer: Lester Linsk
Director: Robert Day
Teleplay: William Wood
Based on a novel by Ann Head
Photography: Edward Rossen
Music: Fred Karlin
Art Director: Merrill Pye
Editor: Harry Coswick

Bo Jo Jones	DESI ARNAZ, JR.
Julie Greher	CHRISTOPHER NORRIS
Mr. Greher	DAN DAILEY
Mrs. Greher	DINA MERRILL
Mr. Jones	TOM BOSLEY
Mrs. Jones	LYNN CARLIN

Grandmother	JESSIE ROYCE LANDIS
Lee	SUSAN STRASBERG
Joan Hartlane	JEANNE ARNOLD
Evan Clark	NICK HAMMOND
Nurse	PHYLLIS LOVE
Charlie Saunders	LARRY WILCOX

and: Michael Freeman, Julie Benjamin, Maidee Severn

Two high school seniors try to adjust to adult responsibilities when her unexpected pregnancy forces them into marriage.

0171
ELLERY QUEEN: DON'T LOOK BEHIND YOU
11/19/71 Universal (2 hours)

Executive Producer: Edward J. Montagne
Producer: Leonard J. Ackerman
Director: Barry Shear
Teleplay: Ted Leighton
Based on the novel *Cat of Many Tales* by Ellery Queen
Photography: William Margulies
Music: Jerry Fielding
Art Director: Alexander A. Mayer
Editor: Samuel E. Waxman

Ellery Queen	PETER LAWFORD
Inspector Richard Queen	HARRY MORGAN
Dr. Cazalis	E. G. MARSHALL

Christy	SKYE AUBREY
Celeste	STEFANIE POWERS
Mrs. Cazalis	COLEEN GRAY
Commissioner	MORGAN STERNE
Sergeant Velie	BILL ZUCKERT

and: Bob Hastings, Than Wyenn, Tim Herbert, Robin Raymond, Buddy Lester, Bill Lucking, Pat Delany, Victoria Hale, Billy Sands

Pilot for a prospective new Ellery Queen series, marred by the miscasting of too-suave Lawford in the leading role. This film, taken from the 1949 mystery by Queen (pseudonym as well as principal character for Frederick Dannay and Manfred Lee), has the sleuth involved in a series of murders, with victims having numerically descending ages and males being strangled with blue cords, females with pink ones.

0172
THE CABLE CAR MURDER
11/19/71 Warner Bros. (90 min)*

Producer: E. Jack Neuman
Director: Jerry Thorpe
Teleplay: Herman Miller

Photography: Fred Koenekamp
Music: Jerry Goldsmith
Art Director: Bill Malley
Editors: Alex Beaton and John W. Holmes

Inspector Lou Van Alsdale	ROBERT HOOKS
Sgt. Pat Cassidy	JEREMY SLATE
Howard McBride	ROBERT WAGNER
Kathy Cooper	CAROL LYNLEY
Capt. E. J. Goodlad	SIMON OAKLAND
Dr. Charles Bedford	JOSE FERRER
Frederick D. Cooper	JOHN RANDOLPH
Fred Trench	DON PEDRO COLLEY
Lulu	JOYCE JAMESON
Inspector Poole	WESLEY LAU
Don Cope	JAMES McEACHIN
Harold Britten	LAWRENCE COOK
J. P. Moose	H. B. HAGGERTY
Rainie Lewis	TA-TANISHA
Ernie Deeds	MILTON STEWART
Rafael	MARIO PEEBLES
Victor Shoddy	FRED CARSON

A syndicate contract killing in broad daylight of a shipping tycoon's son on a San Francisco cable car leads two police detectives into a complex search for the killer, involving a drugs kingpin, the victim's sister, a family business associate, the dead man's physician friend, and the impatient captain of police. This pilot film for a series that was to have starred Hooks, Slate and Oakland never went beyond the telefeature stage.

*Subsequently shown as *Cross Current* as a two hour movie.

0173
THE RELUCTANT HEROES
11/23/71 Aaron Spelling Productions (90 min)

Executive Producer: Aaron Spelling
Producer: Robert Mirisch
Director: Robert Day
Teleplay: Herman Hoffman and Ernie Frankel
Photography: Arch R. Dalzell
Music: Frank DeVol
Art Director: Paul Sylos
Editor: Art Seid

Lt. Parnell Murphy	KEN BERRY
Sgt. Marion Bryce	CAMERON MITCHELL
Cpl. Leroy Sprague	WARREN OATES

Shelley Winters and Arthur Kennedy in A DEATH OF INNOCENCE (1971)

Pvt. Carver LeMoyne	DON MARSHALL
Cpl. Bill Lukens	JIM HUTTON
Pvt. Sam Rivera	TRINI LOPEZ
Capt. Luke Danvers	RALPH MEEKER
Pvt. Golden	RICHARD YOUNG
Cpl. Bates	MICHAEL ST. GEORGE
Korean Officer	SOON-TAIK OH

An army tale about an egghead ninety-day-wonder who relies on ancient tactics he remembers from the history books to save his beleaguered squad on an important mission in Korea. Original title: *The Egghead on Hill 656.*

0174
A DEATH OF INNOCENCE
11/26/71 Mark Carliner Productions (90 min)

Producer: Mark Carliner
Director: Paul Wendkos
Teleplay: Joseph Stefano
Based on the novel by Zelda Popkin
Photography: Ben Colman

Music: Morton Stevens	
Art Director: Joseph R. Jennings	
Editor: Gene Fowler	
Elizabeth Cameron	SHELLEY WINTERS
Marvin Hirsh	ARTHUR KENNEDY
Buffie Cameron	TISHA STERLING
Annie LaCossitt	ANN SOTHERN
Charles Cameron	JOHN RANDOLPH
Alexander Weisberg	HAROLD GOULD
Cara Fellman	ANTOINETTE BOWER
Helen McCloud	PEGGY McCAY
Jimmy Rekko	RICHARD BRIGHT
Joe LaCossitt	TONY YOUNG
Miss Santiago	PILAR SEVRAT
Mary Fingerhut	DOREEN LONG
Klein	BARNEY PHILLIPS
Judge Morahan	REGIS J. CORDIC

Courtroom drama of the ordeal of a small-town mother who comes to Manhattan from Idaho to attend her daughter's murder trial, bewildered by the pace of big city life but steadfastly standing beside the girl despite the evidence against her. Kim Stanley originally was to have played the mother of the co-defendant, but a foot injury caused her to be replaced by Ann Sothern, the real-life mother of Tisha Sterling, the accused girl.

0175
THE FAILING OF RAYMOND
11/27/71 Universal (90 min)

Producer: George Eckstein
Director: Boris Sagal
Teleplay: Adrian Spies
Photography: Ben Colman
Music: Pat Williams
Art Director: William D. DeCinces
Editor: John Kaufman, Jr.

Mary Bloomquist	JANE WYMAN
Allan McDonald	DANA ANDREWS
Raymond	DEAN STOCKWELL
Sgt. Manzak	MURRAY HAMILTON
Cliff Roeder	TIM O'CONNOR
Dr. Abel	PAUL HENREID
History Teacher	PRISCILLA POINTER
Latin Teacher	MARY JACKSON
Librarian	ADRIENNE MARDEN
Girl Patient	CATHERINE LOUISE SAGAL
City Editor	ROBERT KARNES
Store Owner	RAY BALLARD

A spinster school teacher, on the eve of her retirement, finds that she is marked for death by a mentally deranged former student she had flunked ten years earlier.

0176
EARTH II
11/28/71 MGM (2 hours)

Producers: William Read Woodfield and Allan Balter
Director: Tom Gries
Teleplay: William Read Woodfield and Allan Balter
Photography: Michel Hugo
Music: Lalo Schifrin
Art Directors: George W. Davis and Ed Carfango
Special Effects: J. McMillan Johnson
Editor: Henry Berman

David Seville	GARY LOCKWOOD
Frank Karger	ANTHONY FRANCIOSA
Jim Capa	SCOTT HYLANDS
Dr. Loren Huxley	HARI RHODES
Pres. Charles Carter	
Durant	LEW AYRES
Lisa Karger	MARIETTE HARTLEY
Walter Dietrich	GARY MERRILL
Ilyana Kovalefskii	INGA SWENSON
Matt Karger	BRIAN DEWEY
Anton Kovalefskii	EDWARD BELL
Hannah Young	DIANA WEBSTER
Steiner	BART BURNS
Hazlitt	JOHN CARTER
Chairman	HERBERT NELSON
Russian	SERGE TSCHERNISCH
Technician	VINCE CANNON
Surgeon	DAVID SACHS
West	BOB HOY

An elaborate space movie focusing on the day-to-day operation of a futuristic space station nation, Earth II, inhabited by 2,000 persons and functioning as a laboratory and an eye in space for Earth I. A soap opera sub-plot is attached to this imaginative production.

Dean Stockwell and Jane Wyman in THE FAILING OF RAYMOND (1971)

James Caan and Billy Dee Williams in BRIAN'S SONG (1971)

0177
BRIAN'S SONG
11/30/71 Screen Gems/Columbia (2 hours)

Producer: Paul Junger Witt
Director: Buzz Kulik
Teleplay: William Blinn
Based on the book *I Am Third* by Gale Sayers
Photography: Joseph Biroc
Music: Michel Legrand
Art Director: Ross Bellah
Editor: Bud S. Isaacs

Brian Piccolo	JAMES CAAN
Gale Sayers	BILLY DEE WILLIAMS
Coach George Halas	JACK WARDEN
Joy Piccolo	SHELLEY FABARES
Linda Sayers	JUDY PACE
J. C. Caroline	BERNIE CASEY
Ed McCaskey	DAVID HUDDLESTON
Doug Atkins	RON FEINBERG

and: Jack Concannon, Abe Gibron, Ed O'Bradovich, Dick Butkus, Mario Machado, Bud Furillo, Stu Nahan, Happy Hairston

One of the most critically acclaimed of all made-for-TV movies, and one of the most watched, this was a finely told and acted story of Brian Piccolo, running back for the Chicago Bears, his lasting rivalry and friendship with fellow player Gale Sayers, and his losing battle with cancer. The film was an Emmy-winner as Best Dramatic Program (1971–72), and Emmy awards also were given to William Blinn for his tele-play and to Jack Warden for his performance as Coach Halas. Caan and Williams also were nominated. The title theme by Michel Legrand has become a standard. Columbia Pictures later released the film theatrically, with a major premiere in Chicago, but withdrew it because of lack of business (virtually everybody had already seen it for free on television).

0178
DESPERATE MISSION
12/3/71 20th Century-Fox (2 hours)

Executive Producer: Aaron Rosenberg
Producer: David Silver
Associate Producer: Joseph Silver
Director: Earl Bellamy
Teleplay: Jack Guss and Richard Collins
Photography: John Stahl, Jr.
Music: Jerry Goldsmith
Art Director: Alfred Ybarra
Editor: Russell Schoengarth

Joaquin Murieta	RICARDO MONTALBAN
Three-Finger Jack	SLIM PICKENS
Morgan	ROSEY GRIER
Otilia	INA BALIN
Shad Clay	EARL HOLLIMAN
Arkansaw	JIM McMULLAN
Claudina	MIRIAM COLON
Diego Campos	ARMANDO SILVESTRE
Gant	ROBERT J. WILKE
Don Miguel Ruiz	ANTHONY CARUSO
Yuma	CHARLES HORVATH
Croncracker	ALAN PINSON
Frankie	BEN ARCHIBEK

and: Lina Marin, Victor Eberg, Barbara Turner, Ivan Scott, Tamara Girina, Miguel Fernandez, Juan Garcia, Jose Galvez, Francisco Cordova, Eldon Bourke, Eddra Gale, Juan Edwards

Western hokum about Mexican bandit-folk hero Joaquin Murieta, here shown to be a frontier Robin Hood, fighting a bunch of ruthless hombres and, with three cohorts, righting wrongs done to harassed pioneers. Filmed in 1969, it was initially shown theatrically outside the United States in 1970 under the title *Joaquin Murieta*.

0179
THE DEVIL AND MISS SARAH
12/4/71 Universal (90 min)

Producer: Stan Shpetner
Director: Michael Caffey
Teleplay: Calvin Clements
Photography: Harry Wolf
Music: David Rose
Art Director: Arch Bacon
Editor: Budd Small

Rankin	GENE BARRY
Gil Turner	JAMES DRURY
Sarah Turner	JANICE RULE
Marshal Duncan	CHARLES McGRAW
Stoney	SLIM PICKENS

Holmes	LOGAN RAMSEY
Appleton	DONALD MOFFAT

A legendary western outlaw with satanic powers, being escorted to justice by a homesteading couple, uses hypnosis to possess the wife's soul and to help him make his getaway.

0180
IF TOMORROW COMES
12/7/71 Aaron Spelling Productions (2 hours)

Executive Producer: Aaron Spelling
Producer: Richard Newton
Director: George McGowan
Teleplay: Lew Hunter
Photography: Arch R. Dalzell
Music: Gil Melle
Art Director: Paul Sylos
Editor: Art Seid

Eileen Phillips	PATTY DUKE
David Tayaneka	FRANK LIU
Miss Cramer	ANNE BAXTER
Frank Phillips	JAMES WHITMORE
Sheriff	PAT HINGLE
Tadashi	MAKO
Father Miller	JOHN McLIAM
Midori	BEULAH QUO
Harlan	MICHAEL McGREEVEY
Helen Phillips	KAY STEWART
Itachiro	BENNETT OHTA
Coslow	BERT REMSEN

A young couple, a California girl and a Japanese-American boy, ignore local prejudices and marry secretly—on December 7, 1941, minutes before the announcement that Pearl Harbor has been bombed. *The Glass Hammer* was the title of this film while it was in production.

Anne Francis in MONGO'S BACK IN TOWN (1971)

0181
HOW TO STEAL AN AIRPLANE
12/10/71 Universal (2 hours)

(subsequently titled *Only One Day Left Before Tomorrow*)

Executive Producer: Roy Huggins
Producer: Jo Swerling, Jr.
Associate Producers: Robert Foster, Philip de Guere, Jr. and Carl Pingitore
Director: Leslie Martinson
Teleplay: Robert Foster and Philip de Guere, Jr.
Photography: Jack Marta
Music: Pete Rugolo
Song "Sadness of a Happy Time" lyrics by Norman Gimbel
Sung by Claudine Longet
Art Director: Frank Arrigo
Editors: Budd Small and John Dumas

Sam Rollins	PETER DEUEL
Evan Brice	CLINTON GREYN
Luis Ortega	SAL MINEO
Michelle Chivot	CLAUDINE LONGET
Jan	KATHERINE CRAWFORD
Dorothy	JULIE SOMMARS

Two adventurous gringos take on the job of reclaiming a stolen jet from the son of a banana republic dictator. Filmed in late 1968 under the title *Only One Day Left Before Tomorrow,* this one sat in a vault for over two years before reluctantly being shown. In later syndication, it reverted to its original title.

0182
MONGO'S BACK IN TOWN
12/10/71 Bob Banner Associates (90 min)

Executive Producer: Bob Banner
Producer: Tom Egan
Director: Marvin Chomsky
Teleplay: Herman Miller
Based on the novel by E. Richard Johnson
Photography: Arch R. Dalzell
Music: Mike Melvoin
Art Director: Albert Heschong
Editor: Howard Smith

Lt. Pete Tolstad	TELLY SAVALAS
Vicki	SALLY FIELD
Angel	ANNE FRANCIS
Mike Nash	CHARLES CIOFFI
Gordon	MARTIN SHEEN
Mongo Nash	JOE DON BAKER
Rocco	JOHNNY HAYMER
Kanole	HARRY BASCH
Owl Eyes	HOWARD DAYTON
Freddie	NED GLASS
Trembles	ANGELO ROSSITO

This sadistic tale of a professional gunman who is hired by his brother, a syndicate kingpin, to rub out a gangland rival comes from a novel written by a convicted murderer serving time in the Minnesota State Prison.

0183
SEE THE MAN RUN
12/11/71 Universal (90 min)

Producer: Stan Shpetner
Director: Corey Allen
Teleplay: Mann Rubin
Photography: Gerald Perry Finnerman
Music: David Shire
Art Director: Joseph Alves, Jr.
Editor: Lovel Ellis

Ben Taylor	ROBERT CULP
Joanne Taylor	ANGIE DICKINSON
Dr. Thomas Spencer	EDDIE ALBERT
Helene Spencer	JUNE ALLYSON

Sammy Davis, Jr., and Ernest Borgnine in THE TRACKERS (1971)

Capt. Dan Dorsey   CHARLES CIOFFI
Peggi Larson   ANTOINETTE
    BOWER
Ralph Larson   ROSS ELLIOTT
Mike   MICHAEL BELL
Dex   ROBERT LIPTON
Serviceman   JOHN GODDARD

A bizarre tale of a struggling actor who casts himself as the middleman in a kidnap plot after being mistakenly called with a ransom demand, and decides to cut himself in for half of the payoff money. The film marked June Allyson's return to moviemaking after a twelve-year absence. Initially this was to be titled *The Second Face*.

0184
THE TRACKERS
12/14/71 Aaron Spelling Productions (90 min)

Producers: Aaron Spelling and Sammy Davis, Jr.
Director: Earl Bellamy
Teleplay: Gerald Gaiser
From a story by Aaron Spelling and Sammy Davis, Jr.
Photography: Tim Southcott
Music: Johnny Mandell
Art Director: Paul Sylos
Editor: Saul Caplan

Zeke Smith   SAMMY DAVIS, JR.
Sam Paxton   ERNEST BORGNINE
Dora Paxton   JULIE ADAMS
Becky Paxton   CONNIE KRESKI
Sheriff Naylor   JIM DAVIS
Ben Vogel   ARTHUR
    HUNNICUTT
El Grande   CALEB BROOKS
Dilworth   NORMAN ALDEN
Higgins   LEO GORDON
Captain   ROSS ELLIOTT
Father Gomez   DAVID REYNARD

A Western pilot that teams up a strong-willed black frontier scout and a stubborn rancher in a reluctant alliance to find out who killed the latter's son and made off with his daughter. *No Trumpets, No Drums* was the title during production.

0185
THEY CALL IT MURDER
12/17/71 20th Century-Fox (2 hours)

Executive Producer: Cornwell Jackson
Producer/Director: Walter Grauman
Teleplay: Sam Rolfe
Based on the novel *The D.A. Draws a Circle* by Erle Stanley Gardner
Photography: Jack Woolf
Music: Robert Drasnin
Art Director: Merrill Pye
Editors: Michael Economou and Neil Travis

Doug Selby   JIM HUTTON
A. B. Carr   LLOYD BOCHNER
Jane Antrim   JESSICA WALTER
Frank Antrim   LESLIE NIELSEN
Sylvia Martin   JO ANN PFLUG
Rona Corbin   NITA TALBOT
Doris Kane   CARMEN
    MATHEWS
Sheriff Brandon   ROBERT J. WILKE
Chief Larkin   EDWARD ASNER

Gardner's small-town district attorney, Doug Selby, came to TV in this pilot that has him investigating a swimming pool murder of a gambler, a questionable car crash and a huge insurance claim. Hutton was more successful subsequently in bringing another fictional detective, Ellery Queen, to television. The "Doug Selby" pilot was filmed in 1969.

0186
DEAD MEN TELL NO TALES
12/17/71 20th Century-Fox (90 min)

Executive Producer: Walter Grauman
Producer: William Kayden
Director: Walter Grauman
Teleplay: Robert Dozier
Based on the novel by Kelley Roos
Photography: Jack Woolf
Music: Robert Drasnin
Art Director: Merrill Pye
Editor: Charles Freeman

Larry Towers   CHRISTOPHER
    GEORGE
Midge Taylor   JUDY CARNE
Lisa Martin   PATRICIA BARRY
Tom Austin   RICHARD
    ANDERSON
Sam Mirakian   LARRY D. MANN
Karl   KEVIN HAGEN
Polly Grant   JOAN SHAWLEE
Mike Carter   LINCOLN
    KILPATRICK, JR.
Sgt. Corso   FRED SADOFF
Alan   ERIC SINCLAIR
Bud Riley   MIKE
    LOOKINLAND

**Brenda Vaccaro, Roddy McDowall and Vincent Price in
WHAT'S A NICE GIRL LIKE YOU . . . ? (1971)**

80

Mrs. Riley	JUDITH HART
Mrs. Carter	ELLA EDWARDS
Darrow	LEN WAYLAND
Bartender	BILL QUINN
Mr. Riley	RICHARD O'BRIEN
Mack	JOHN DENNIS
Suntan Lady	LORNA THAYER

A chase thriller that has a travel photographer finding himself the quarry of paid assassins who have mistaken him for somebody else.

0187
WHAT'S A NICE GIRL LIKE YOU . . . ?
12/18/71 Universal (90 min)

Producer: Norman Lloyd
Director: Jerry Paris
Teleplay: Howard Fast
Based on the novel *Shirley* by E. V. Cunningham
Photography: Harry Wolf
Music: Robert Prince
Art Director: Alexander A. Mayer
Editor: Richard M. Sprague

Shirley Campbell	BRENDA VACCARO
Lt. Joe Burton	JACK WARDEN
Albert Soames	RODDY McDOWALL
Cynthia	JO ANNE WORLEY
Morton Stillman	EDMOND O'BRIEN
William Spevin	VINCENT PRICE
Adam Newman	MORGAN STERNE
Fats Detroit	MICHAEL LERNER
Selzer	GINO CONFORTI
Flint	ARTHUR BATANIDES
Mr. Foley	CURT CONWAY
Francis Malone	ROBERT DOYLE
Louis (Waiter)	JOHNNY SILVER
Elderly Woman	MAUDIE PRICKETT

A Bronx working girl is drawn into an elaborate extortion plot after being kidnapped by a gang of sophisticated con men who force her, because of her remarkable resemblance, to impersonate a wealthy socialite.

0188
THE HOMECOMING
12/19/71 Lorimar Productions (2 hours)

Executive Producer: Lee Rich
Producer: Robert L. Jacks
Director: Fielder Cook
Teleplay: Earl Hamner, Jr.
Based on his novel
Photography: Earl Rath
Music: Jerry Goldsmith
Art Director: Bob Smith
Editors: Marjorie and Gene Fowler, Jr.

Olivia Walton	PATRICIA NEAL
John-Boy Walton	RICHARD THOMAS
Grandpa Walton	EDGAR BERGEN
Grandma Walton	ELLEN CORBY
Hawthorne Dooley	CLEAVON LITTLE
Emily Baldwin	DOROTHY STICKNEY
Charlie Snead	WILLIAM WINDOM
John Walton	ANDREW DUGGAN
Ike Godsey	WOODROW PARFREY
Mary Ellen	JUDY NORTON
Erin	MARY ELIZABETH McDONOUGH
Elizabeth	KAMI COTLER
Ben	ERIC SCOTT
Jim-Bob	DAVID S. HARPER
Jason	JON WARMSLEY
Sheriff Bridges	DAVID HUDDLESTON

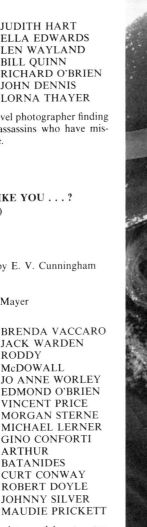

Patricia Neal and Cleavon Little in THE HOMECOMING (1971)

City Lady	SALLY CHAMBERLAIN
Claudie Dooley	DONALD LIVINGSTON

This was the pilot movie for "The Waltons" (which began its long run in September 1972), recounting the events of one day—Christmas Eve, 1933—in the lives of a rural American mountain family. Later called *The Homecoming—A Christmas Story*, it won a Christopher Award as well as Emmy nominations for actress Patricia Neal, director Fielder Cook and author Earl Hamner, Jr. (who based the story apparently on his own youthful recollections and was the model for "John-Boy"). Hamner previously had written the story in another form which turned up on the screen as *Spencer's Mountain* (1963) with Henry Fonda and Maureen O'Hara as the parents. When "The Waltons" turned up as a series, Michael Learned, Ralph Waite and Will Geer took over the roles created by Patricia Neal, Andrew Duggan and Edgar Bergen, while most of the others in the cast continued in the parts they originated.

0189
GIDGET GETS MARRIED
1/4/72 Screen Gems/Columbia (90 min)

Executive Producer: Harry Ackerman
Producer/Director: E. W. Swackhamer
Teleplay: John McGreevey

Based on characters created by Frederick Kohner
Photography: Joseph Biroc
Music: Mike Post and Pete Carpenter
Song "Good Morning Love" by Jack Keller and John Carter
Art Directors: Ross Bellah and Carl Anderson
Editor: Hugh Chaloupka

Gidget Lawrence	MONIE ELLIS
Jeff Stevens	MICHAEL BURNS
Otis Ramsey	DON AMECHE
Claire Ramsey	JOAN BENNETT
Russ Lawrence	MACDONALD CAREY
Louis B. Lattimer	PAUL LYNDE
Medley Blaine	ELINOR DONAHUE
Nancy Lewis	CORINNE CAMACHO
Tom Blaine	ROGER PERRY
Anatole	LARRY GELMAN
Minister	BURKE BYRNES
Richie	TIGER WILLIAMS
Vince Blaine	GENE ANDRUSCO
Bob Ramsey	RADEMAS PERA

and: Judy McConnell, Susan Spell, Joe Bernard, Dennis Fimple, Victoria Meyerink, Jimmy Bracken, Nicholas Beauvy

The last screen adventure of Gidget has her married off, finally, and rebelling against the social caste system in her husband's company. Monie Ellis, daughter of veteran actress Mona Freeman, followed a long line of

up-and-coming actresses in the starring role: Sandra Dee (1959), Deborah Walley (1961), Cindy Carol (1963), Sally Field (1965 TV series), and Karen Valentine (1969 TV movie). Like one or two of her predecessors, Monie Ellis seems to have vanished from the show business scene.

0190
KILLER BY NIGHT
1/7/72 Cinema Center 100 (2 hours)

Producer: Fred Engel
Director: Bernard McEveety
Teleplay: David P. Harmon
Photography: Robert B. Hauser
Music: Quincy Jones
Art Director: Jack T. Collis
Editor: Raymond Daniels

Dr. Larry Ross	ROBERT WAGNER
Dr. Tracey Morrow	DIANE BAKER
Capt. George Benson	GREG MORRIS
Sgt. Phil "Sharkey" Gold	THEODORE BIKEL
Warren Claman	ROBERT LANSING
Sister Sarah	MERCEDES McCAMBRIDGE
Dr. Carlos Madeira	PEDRO ARMENDARIZ, JR.
Marley	MICHAEL EVANS
Dr. Bradville	ROBERT CORNTHWAITE
Sam Kenyon	KELLY THORDSEN
Professor Langley	IVOR FRANCIS
Counterman	JOHN CRAWFORD
Hotel Clerk	BRYAN O'BYRNE
Frank Roland	BILL BRYANT
Dr. Jacobs	JASON WINGREEN
Nurse Maggie	NORA MARLOWE
Manager	IRWIN CHARONE

A doctor's battle to stem a diphtheria outbreak puts him in conflict with a police captain who is using all his manpower to track down a cop-killer. Many elements of this one revive memories of Elia Kazan's stunning *Panic in the Streets* (1950). The original title until the eve of airing: *The City by Night*.

Monie Ellis and Macdonald Carey in GIDGET GETS MARRIED (1972)

Robert Wagner, Greg Morris and Theodore Bikel in KILLER BY NIGHT (1972)

(*Above*) **Robert Lansing and Mercedes McCam-bridge in KILLER BY NIGHT (1972)**
(*Right*) **Susan Clark and Monte Markham in THE ASTRONAUT (1972)**

0191
THE ASTRONAUT
1/8/72 Universal (2 hours)

Producer: Harve Bennett
Director: Robert Michael Lewis
Teleplay: Gerald DiPego, Charles R. Kuenstle,
Robert S. Biheller, Harve Bennett
From a story by Charles R. Kuenstle and Robert S.
Biheller
Photography: Alric Edens
Music: Gil Melle
Art Director: George C. Webb
Editors: Les Green and John Kaufman, Jr.

Kurt Anderson	JACKIE COOPER
Eddie Reese/Col. Brice	
Randolph	MONTE MARKHAM
Dr. Wylie	RICHARD ANDERSON
John Phillips	ROBERT LANSING
Gail Randolph	SUSAN CLARK
Don Masters	JOHN LUPTON
Tom Everett	WALTER BROOKE
Astronaut Higgins	JAMES SIKKING
Carl Samuels	PAUL KENT
Toni Scott	LORETTA LEVERSEE

Top space officials, fearing for the future of the program, substitute a look-alike for an astronaut who died
during a Mars mission.

George Peppard in THE BRAVOS (1972)

Ben Lawler	L. Q. JONES
Captain MacDowall	GEORGE MURDOCK
Garrett Chase	BARRY BROWN
Captain Detroville	DANA ELCAR
Sergeant Marcy	JOHN KELLOGG
Raeder	BO SVENSON
Peter Harkness	VINCENT VAN PATTEN
Santana	JOAQUIN MARTINEZ
Kate	KATE McKEOWN
Corporal Love	CLINT RITCHIE
Lieut. Lewis	RANDOLPH MANTOOTH
Sergeant Boyd	MICHAEL BOW

A rugged Western about the commander of a beleaguered cavalry post whose precarious friendship with the area's Indians is destroyed, resulting in his son's abduction.

0193
THE NIGHT STALKER
1/11/72 ABC, Inc. (2 hours)

Producer: Dan Curtis
Director: John Llewellyn Moxey
Teleplay: Richard Matheson
From an unpublished story by Jeff Rice
Photography: Michel Hugo
Music: Robert Colbert
Art Director: Trevor Wallace
Editor: Desmond Marquette

Carl Kolchak	DARREN McGAVIN
Gail Foster	CAROL LYNLEY
Joe Vincenzo	SIMON OAKLAND
Bernie Jenks	RALPH MEEKER
Sheriff Warren Butcher	CLAUDE AKINS
Chief Ed Masterson	CHARLES McGRAW
D. A. Tom Payne	KENT SMITH
Mazurji	LARRY LINVILLE
Dr. O'Brien	JORDAN RHODES
Janos Skorzeny	BARRY ATWATER
Fred Hurley	STANLEY ADAMS
Mickey Crawford	ELISHA COOK, JR.

A flip, down-on-his-luck newspaper reporter stumbles across a modern-day vampire who is murdering Las Vegas showgirls, but he cannot convince his own editor, let alone the police, of the identity of the crazed maniac. The now-cult comedy thriller that eventually spawned the regrettably brief series of the same name (1974–75) with McGavin and Oakland continuing their roles was the highest rated made-for-TV movie up to that time.

0194
EMERGENCY!
1/15/72 Universal/Mark VII Ltd. (2 hours)

Executive Producer: Jack Webb
Producer: Robert A. Cinader
Associate Producer: William Stark
Director: Jack Webb
Teleplay: Harold Jack Bloom and Robert A. Cinader
Photography: Jack Marta
Music: Nelson Riddle
Art Director: John J. Lloyd
Editor: Warren H. Adams

Dr. Kelly Brackett	ROBERT FULLER
Nurse Dixie McCall	JULIE LONDON
Dr. Joe Early	BOBBY TROUP
John Gage	RANDOLPH MANTOOTH
Roy DeSoto	KEVIN TIGHE
Officer Pete Malloy	MARTIN MILNER
Officer Jim Reed	KENT McCORD
Sen. Mike Wolski	JACK KRUSCHEN

0192
THE BRAVOS
1/9/72 Universal (2 hours)

Executive Producer: David Victor
Producer: Norman Lloyd
Director: Ted Post
Teleplay: Christopher Knopf and Ted Post
From a story by David Victor, Douglas Benton and Christopher Knopf

Photography: Enzo Martinelli
Music: Leonard Rosenman
Art Director: Russell C. Forrest
Editors: Robert L. Kimble and Michael R. McAdam

Maj. John Harkness	GEORGE PEPPARD
Jackson Buckley	PERNELL ROBERTS
Heller Chase	BELINDA MONTGOMERY

and: Ann Morgan Guilbert, Lew Brown, Arthur Balinger, Virginia Gregg, Herb Vigran, Colby Chester, Ron Pinnard, Kathryn Kelly Wiget, Bert Holland, Don Ross

The pilot movie to the hit series about Los Angeles' paramedics and their interaction with the fire department and hospital system—told briskly in the proven, clipped-dialogue Jack Webb style that had served so well in "Dragnet" and "Adam-12" (its two stars turn up here to give this film a Webb continuity). The five leads continued in the series (1972–77), and then first Fuller and then London and Troup (married in real life) were phased out during the occasional "Emergency!" specials during the 1977–78 season. Tighe and Mantooth also provided the voices to their characters in the Saturday morning animated series.

0195
MADAME SIN
1/15/72 ITC Productions (2 hours)

Executive Producer: Robert Wagner
Producer: Julius Wintle and Lou Morheim
Director: David Greene
Teleplay: David Greene and Barry Oringer
Photography: Tony Richmond
Music: Michael Gibbs
Art Director: Brian Eatwell
Editor: Peter Tanner

Darren McGavin and Barry Atwater in THE NIGHT STALKER (1972)

Bette Davis and Robert Wagner in MADAME SIN (1972)

Sandy Dennis, Darren McGavin and Ralph Bellamy in SOMETHING EVIL (1972)

Rose Malone	ROSALIE WILLIAMS
Sarah	CHARLOTTE KNIGHT
Eben	JASON WINGREEN
Madeline Erickson	MARJORIE BENNETT
Cab Driver	JOE E. ROSS
Doorman	ALLEN JENKINS

and: Dick Wilson, Bonnie Kammerman, Carol Speed

A comedy about two urban couples who decide to chuck big-city life and return to nature, only to find that rural living has its own set of infuriating problems.

0197
SOMETHING EVIL
1/21/72 Belford Productions/CBS International (2 hours)

Producer: Alan Jay Factor
Director: Steven Spielberg
Teleplay: Robert Clouse
Photography: Bill Butler
Music: Wladimir Selinsky
Art Director: Albert Heschong
Editor: Allan Jacobs

Marjorie Worden	SANDY DENNIS
Paul Worden	DARREN McGAVIN
Gehrmann	JEFF COREY
Harry Lincoln	RALPH BELLAMY
Ernest Lincoln	JOHN RUBINSTEIN
Stevie Worden	JOHNNY WHITTAKER
Beth	LAURIE HAGAN
John	DAVID KNAPP
Laurie Worden	SANDY and DEBBIE LEMPERT
Schiller	HERB ARMSTRONG
Irene	MARGARET AVERY
Hackett	NORMAN BARTHOLD
Mrs. Hackett	SHEILA BARTHOLD
Mrs. Faraday	LOIS BATTLE
Mrs. Gehrmann	BELLA BRUCK
Secretary	LYNN CARTWRIGHT

and: John J. Fox, Alan Frost, Carl Gottlieb, John Hudkins, Crane Jackson, Michael Macready, Paul Micale, Margaret Muse, John Nolan, Bruno VeSota, Connie Hunter Ragaway, Elizabeth Rogers, Steven Spielberg

A horror tale about a young couple moving into a Bucks County, Pennsylvania, farmhouse, unaware that it is occupied by an unseen presence that is trying to possess the wife.

0198
THE PEOPLE
1/22/72 Metromedia/American Zoetrope (90 min)

Executive Producer: Francis Ford Coppola
Producer: Gerald I. Isenberg
Director: John Korty
Teleplay: James M. Miller
Based on the novel *Pilgrimage* by Zenna Henderson
Photography: Edward Rosson
Music: Carmine Coppola
Art Director: Jack DeGovia
Editor: Patrick Kennedy

Melodye Amerson	KIM DARBY
Dr. Curtis	WILLIAM SHATNER
Valency	DIANE VARSI
Sol Diemus	DAN O'HERLIHY
Karen Dingus	LAURIE WALTERS
Francker	CHRIS VALENTINE

Madame Sin	BETTE DAVIS
Tony Lawrence	ROBERT WAGNER
Malcolm DeVere	DENHOLM ELLIOTT
Cmdr. Teddy Cavandish	GORDON JACKSON
Monk	DUDLEY SUTTON
Barbara	CATHERINE SCHELL
Connors	PAUL MAXWELL
Nikko	PIK-SEN LIM
Braden	DAVID HEALEY
White	ALAN DOBIE
Holidaymaker	ROY KINNEAR
Fisherman	AL MANCINI
Willoughby	CHARLES LLOYD PACK
Lengett	ARNOLD DIAMOND
Dr. Henriques	FRANK MIDDLEMASS

In her initial movie for television, Bette Davis is a ruthless, all-powerful mystery woman who abducts an ex-CIA agent and forces him to help her steal an ultra modern Polaris submarine. This pilot to a prospective series was a personal project of co-star Robert Wagner, here acting as the film's executive producer.

0196
GETTING AWAY FROM IT ALL
1/18/72 Palomar Pictures International (90 min)

Executive Producer: Leon I. Mirell
Producers: Ira Skutch and Howard Felsher
Director: Lee Philips
Teleplay: Roy Kammerman
Photography: William K. Jurgensen
Music: Vic Mizzy
Art Director: Joseph R. Jennings
Editors: George Jay Nicholson and Stanley Frazen

Fred Clark	LARRY HAGMAN
Helen Clark	BARBARA FELDON
Mark Selby	GARY COLLINS
Alice Selby	E. J. PEAKER
May Brodey	VIVIAN VANCE
Mike Lorimar	JIM BACKUS
Capt. Frank Coffin	BURGESS MEREDITH
Hank (Postmaster)	PAUL HARTMAN
Jeremiah	J. PAT O'MALLEY
April Brodey	MELISSA NEWMAN
Herbie	RANDY QUAID
Charlie Erickson	JOHN QUALEN
Jeb	HAL SMITH

Bethie	JOHANNA BAER
Talitha	STEPHANIE VALENTINE
Kiah	JACK DALLGREN
Thann	ANDREW CRICHTON
Matt	DAVID PETCH
Dita	DOROTHY DRADY
Maras	MARY ROSE McMASTER
Obla	ANNE WALTERS
Bram	TONY DARIO

A supernatural thriller involving a young teacher in an isolated California community who discovers that her pupils and their parents possess special powers and a secret bond.

Chris Valentine and Kim Darby in THE PEOPLE (1972)

Dorothy McGuire and Lew Ayres in SHE WAITS (1972)

0199
WOMEN IN CHAINS
1/25/72 Paramount (90 min)

Producer: Edward K. Milkis
Director: Bernard Kowalski
Teleplay: Rita Larkin
Photography: Howard R. Schwartz
Music: Charles Fox
Music Director: Kenyon Hopkins
Art Director: Bill Ross
Editor: Argyle Nelson

Tyson	IDA LUPINO
Sandra Parker/Sally Porter	LOIS NETTLETON
Dee Dee	JESSICA WALTER
Melinda	BELINDA MONTGOMERY
Helen Anderson	PENNY FULLER
Barney	JOHN LARCH
Leila	NEILE ADAMS
Althea	HAZEL MEDINA
Alice	KATHY CANNON
Billie	LUCILLE BENSON
Simpson	JOYCE JAMESON
Maggie	JUDY STRANGIS

A lady parole officer has herself imprisoned in order to examine charges of brutality but is trapped when the only other person who knows why she is there is killed. Playing a sadistic prison superintendent, Ida Lupino (in her TV-movie debut) virtually reprised a similar role fifteen years earlier in *Women's Prison*.

0200
SHE WAITS
1/28/72 Metromedia (90 min)

Executive Producer: Charles W. Fries
Producer/Director: Delbert Mann
Associate Producer: Mort Zarcoff
Teleplay: Art Wallace
Photography: Charles F. Wheeler
Music: Morton Stevens
Art Director: Lawrence G. Paull
Editor: John Schreyer

Laura Wilson	PATTY DUKE
Mark Wilson	DAVID McCALLUM
Dr. Sam Carpenter	LEW AYRES
Sarah Wilson	DOROTHY McGUIRE
Angela Medina (Mrs. M)	BEULAH BONDI
David Brody	JAMES CALLAHAN
Kurawicz	NELSON OLMSTEAD

A murdered woman seeks vengeance and possesses her husband's new bride in this well-acted ghost story. This marked Dorothy McGuire's first TV movie as well as her television comeback after a fifteen-year absence.

0201
THE SCREAMING WOMAN
1/29/72 Universal (90 min)

Producer: William Frye
Director: Jack Smight
Teleplay: Merwin Gerard
Based on the short story by Ray Bradbury
Photography: Sam Levitt
Music: John Williams
Art Director: John E. Chilberg II
Costumes: Edith Head
Editor: Robert F. Shugrue

Laura Wynant	OLIVIA de HAVILLAND
Carl Nesbitt	ED NELSON
Caroline Wynant	LARAINE STEPHENS
George Tresvant	JOSEPH COTTEN
Dr. Amos Larkin	WALTER PIDGEON
Howard Wynant	CHARLES KNOX ROBINSON
Evie Carson	ALEXANDRA HAY
Police Sergeant	LONNY CHAPMAN
Ken Bronson	CHARLES DRAKE
Harry Sands	RUSSELL C. WIGGINS
David (Deputy)	GENE ANDRUSCO
Bernice Wilson	JOYCE CUNNINGHAM
Martin (Servant)	JAN ARVAN
Ted Wilson	RAY MONTGOMERY
Slater	JOHN ALDERMAN

Martin Landau in WELCOME HOME, JOHNNY BRISTOL (1972)

Alan Alda in TRUMAN CAPOTE'S THE GLASS HOUSE (1972)

A contemporary Gothic horror story that has a dowager, an ex-mental patient, discovering a woman buried alive and screaming for help on the grounds of her sprawling estate, but her family feels that her mind has snapped and refuses to believe the bizarre story in its greed to get hold of her money if she is declared incompetent. Olivia de Havilland made her TV movie debut in this one, with Joseph Cotten replacing Ray Milland in the role of her lawyer.

0202
WELCOME HOME, JOHNNY BRISTOL
1/30/72 Cinema Center 100 (2 hours)

Producer: Arthur Joel Katz
Director: George McGowan
Teleplay: Stanley R. Greenberg
Photography: Robert L. Morrison
Music: Lalo Schifrin
Art Director: Bill Molyneaux
Editor: Carroll Sax

Capt. Johnny Bristol	MARTIN LANDAU
Anne Palmer	JANE ALEXANDER
Dr. Berdahl	BROCK PETERS
Graytak	MARTIN SHEEN
Sergeant McGill	PAT O'BRIEN
Harry McMartin	FORREST TUCKER
Margaret Bristol	MONA FREEMAN
Virginia (Sister Theresa)	JANE ELLIOTT
Mrs. Tyson	CLAUDIA BRYAR
Minister	JOHN HOYT
Colonel Anderson	SIMON SCOTT
Mr. Bristol	MARK ROBERTS
Loughton	JAMES McEACHIN
Shuster	ALAN BERGMAN
Franks	RICHARD EVANS
Young Johnny Bristol	GERALD MICHENAUD

A Vietnam POW tries to return to the hometown he dreamed of in captivity, but can find no trace of it.

0203
TRUMAN CAPOTE'S THE GLASS HOUSE
2/4/72 Tomorrow Entertainment (2 hours)

Executive Producer: Roger Gimbel
Producers: Robert W. Christiansen and Rick Rosenberg
Director: Tom Gries
Teleplay: Tracy Keenan Wynn
From a story by Truman Capote and Wyatt Cooper
Photography: Jules Brenner
Music: Billy Goldenberg
Editor: Gene Fowler, Jr.

Hugo Slocum	VIC MORROW
Brian Courtland	CLU GULAGER
Lennox Beach	BILLY DEE WILLIAMS
Allan Campbell	KRISTOFFER TABORI
Warden Auerbach	DEAN JAGGER
Jonathan Paige	ALAN ALDA
Bibleback	LUKE ASKEW
Ajax	SCOTT HYLANDS
Sinclair	EDWARD BELL
Steve Berino	TONY MANCINI
Pagonis	G. WOOD
Officer Brown	ROY JENSON
Bree	ALLAN VINT

A grim, award-winning portrait of prison life as seen through the eyes of two newcomers—an idealistic rookie guard (Gulager) and a college professor up for manslaughter (Alda). Tom Gries received an Emmy Award for his direction; Gene Fowler, Jr. was nominated for his editing.

0204
HARDCASE
2/1/72 Hanna-Barbera Productions (90 min)

Executive Producers: Joseph Barbera and William
Hanna
Producer: Matthew Rapf
Director: John Llewellyn Moxey
Teleplay: Harold Jack Bloom and Sam Rolfe
Photography: Rosalio Solano
Music: Pat Williams
Art Director: Jose Rodriguez Granada
Editor: Mike Pozen

Jack Rutherford	CLINT WALKER
Rozaline	STEFANIE POWERS
Simon Fuegus	PEDRO ARMENDARIZ, JR.
Booker Llewellyn	ALEX KARRAS
Felipe	E. LOPEZ ROJAS
Major Tovar	LUIS MIRANDO
Luis Comacho	MARTIN LASALLE

The first live-action film from the famed producers of
animated cartoons, beginning with Tom and Jerry, is
a period Western about a soldier of fortune who discovers that his wife has sold his ranch and run off with
a Mexican revolutionary.

0205
WHEN MICHAEL CALLS
2/5/72 Palomar International (90 min)

Executive Producer: Edgar Scherick
Producer: Gil Shiva
Director: Philip Leacock
Teleplay: James Bridges
Based on the novel by John Farris
Photography: Reg Morris and Don Wilder
Music: Lionel Newman
Editor: P. A. James

Doremus Connelly	BEN GAZZARA
Helen Connelly	ELIZABETH ASHLEY
Craig	MICHAEL DOUGLAS
Peggy Connelly	KAREN PEARSON
Dr. Britton	LARRY REYNOLDS
Sheriff Hap Washbrook	ALBERT S. WAXMAN
Harry Randall	ALAN McRAE
Elsa Britton	MARIAN WALDMAN
Peter	CHRIS PELLETT
Enoch Mills	STEVE WESTON
Sam	ROBERT WARNER
Quinlan	JOHN BETHUNE
Professor Swen	WILLIAM OSLER
Amy	MICHELE CHICOINE

A mystery thriller about a woman tormented by phone
calls from a nephew who supposedly died fifteen years
earlier.

0206
SECOND CHANCE
2/8/72 Metromedia Productions (90 min)

Executive Producer: Danny Thomas
Producer: Harold D. Cohen
Director: Peter Tewksbury
Teleplay: Michael Morris
Photography: Ed Rossen
Art Director: Paul Sylos
Editor: Jack Wolz

Geoff Smith	BRIAN KEITH
Ellie Smith	ELIZABETH ASHLEY
Dr. Julius Roth	KENNETH MARS
Stan Petryk	WILLIAM WINDOM

Clint Walker and Stefanie Powers in HARDCASE (1972)

Elizabeth Ashley in WHEN MICHAEL CALLS (1972)

89

Brian Keith and Juliet Prowse in SECOND CHANCE (1972)

Gloria Petryk	PAT CARROLL
Roberto Gazzari	AVERY SCHREIBER
Maxie Hill	ROSEY GRIER
Martha Foster	JULIET PROWSE
Charlene	ANN MORGAN GUILBERT
Jimmy Smith	MARK SAVAGE
Charley Whitehead	NED WERTIMER
Stella Hill	EMILY YANCY
Lester Fern	VERN WEDDLE
Hardin	BRET PARKER
Dr. Strick	BOB NICHOLS
Dr. Willard	OLIVE DUNBAR

A serio-comedy about a rich stockbroker who buys a ghost town in Nevada to create a community for "losers" seeking another chance in life.

0207
CRAWLSPACE
2/11/72 Titus Productions (90 min)

Executive Producer: Herbert Brodkin
Producer: Robert "Buzz" Berger
Director: John Newland*
Teleplay: Ernest Kinoy
Based on the novel by Herbert Lieberman
Photography: Urs Furrer
Music: Jerry Goldsmith

Art Director: Robert Gundlach
Editor: Carl Lerner

Albert Graves	ARTHUR KENNEDY
Alice Graves	TERESA WRIGHT
Richard Atlec	TOM HAPPER
Emil Birge	EUGENE ROCHE
Harlow	DAN MORGAN
Dave Freeman	MATHEW COWLES

A middle-aged, childless couple discover that a young handyman, hired to fix their furnace, has moved into the crawlspace in their cellar, and they make him part of their family. Director Newland replaced Buzz Kulik in mid-production during the filming in Norwalk, Connecticut.

*Replaced Buzz Kulik.

0208
THE HOUND OF THE BASKERVILLES
2/12/72 Universal (90 min)

Executive Producer: Richard Irving
Producer: Stanley Kallis
Director: Barry Crane
Teleplay: Robert E. Thompson
Based on the novel by Arthur Conan Doyle
Photography: Harry Wolf
Art Director: Howard E. Johnson
Editor: Bill Mosher

Sherlock Holmes	STEWART GRANGER
Dr. Watson	BERNARD FOX
George Stapleton	WILLIAM SHATNER
Dr. John Mortimer	ANTHONY ZERBE
Laura Frankland	SALLY ANN HOWES
Arthur Frankland	JOHN WILLIAMS
Sir Henry Baskerville	IAN IRELAND
Beryl Stapleton	JANE MERROW
Inspector Lestrade	ALAN CALLIOU
John Barrymore	BRENDAN DILLON
Eliza Barrymore	ARLINE ANDERSON
Billy Cartwright	BILLY BOWLES
Seldon	CHUCK HICKS
Mrs. Mortimer	KAREN KONDAN

The oft-filmed Conan Doyle classic (it had been made at least eight times previously) and the first American color version about how Holmes and Watson solve the baffling murder of an heir to the Baskerville fortune on the misty English moors. This was the pilot to a prospective Sherlock Holmes series that was to have rotated with the adventures of Hildegarde Withers and Nick Carter (with Eve Arden and Robert Conrad, respectively) in a regular program bringing to TV three popular fictional detectives. None of the three went beyond the pilot stage.

Bernard Fox and Stewart Granger in THE HOUND OF THE BASKERVILLES (1972)

Arthur Kennedy and Teresa Wright in CRAWLSPACE (1972)

0209
PROBE
2/12/72 Warner Bros. (2 hours)
(subsequently cut to 90 min and retitled *Search*)

Producer: Leslie Stevens
Associate Producer: John Christopher Strong
Director: Russ Mayberry
Created by Leslie Stevens
Teleplay: Leslie Stevens
Photography: John Morley Stephens
Music: Dominic Frontiere
Editor: Bill Brame

Hugh Lockwood	HUGH O'BRIAN
Heideline "Uli" Ullman	ELKE SOMMER
Harold L. Streeter	JOHN GIELGUD
B. C. Cameron	BURGESS MEREDITH
Gloria Harding	ANGEL TOMPKINS
Frieda Ullman	LILIA SKALA
Dr. Laurent	KENT SMITH
Cheyne	ALFRED RYDER
Kurt von Niestst	BEN WRIGHT
Brugge	JULES MAITLAND

and: Albert Popwell, Robert Boon, A Martinez, Ginny Golden, Byron Chung, Jan Daley, Gun Sundberg, Joanne Frank, Jaclyn Smith

In this chase thriller, the pilot for the TV series "Search" (1972–73), a space-age detective, Lockwood, monitored and directed by mission control center, investigates the disappearance of a fabulous gem collection. O'Brian, Meredith and Angel Tompkins continued in the short-lived series, and were joined by Tony Franciosa and Doug McClure.

John Gielgud, Elke Sommer and Hugh O'Brian in PROBE (1972)

Connie Stevens in CALL HER MOM (1972)

(Left) John Astin in EVIL ROY SLADE (1972)
(Above) Pam Austin and Dick Shawn in EVIL ROY SLADE (1972)

0210
CALL HER MOM
2/15/72 Screen Gems/Columbia (90 min)

Executive Producer: Douglas S. Cramer
Producer: Herb Wallerstein
Director: Jerry Paris
Teleplay: Kenny Solms and Gail Parent
Photography: Emil Oster
Song "Come On-a My House" by Ross Bagdasarian and William Saroyan
Sung by Connie Stevens
Art Directors: Ross Bellah and John Beckman
Editors: Jim Faris and Bob Moor

Angie Bianco	CONNIE STEVENS
President Hardgrove	VAN JOHNSON
Dean Walden	CHARLES NELSON REILLY
Jonathan Calder	JIM HUTTON
Helen Hardgrove	GLORIA DeHAVEN
Ida	THELMA CARPENTER
Roscoe	BILL TEPPER
Jeremy	ALFIE WISE
Woody	JOHN DAVID CARSON
Bruno	CORBETT MONICA
Wilson	MIKE JONAS EVANS
Feigelbaum	STEVE VINOVICH
Chip	MIKE MALMBOURG
Woman	KATHLEEN FREEMAN
Mr. Guinness	HERB RUDLEY
Waiter	FRITZ FELD
Jeremy's Father	RAYMOND BAKEWELL

and: William Malloy, Ray Ballard, Peter Hobbs, Jonathan Hole

A sexy waitress becomes a housemother in a fraternity house and involves the college in a nationwide women's lib controversy. Gloria DeHaven, playing the ex-chorus girl wife of college president Van Johnson, replaced Ann Miller who in turn had replaced Cyd Charisse.

0211
EVIL ROY SLADE
2/18/72 Universal (2 hours)

Executive Producer: Howie Horwitz
Producers: Garry Marshall and Jerry Belson
Director: Jerry Paris
Teleplay: Garry Marshall and Jerry Belson
Photography: Sam Leavitt
Music: Stuart Margolin, Murray McLeod and Jerry Riopelle
Art Director: Alexander A. Mayer
Editor: Richard M. Sprague

Nelson Stool	MICKEY ROONEY
Marshal Bing Bell	DICK SHAWN
Clifford Stool	HENRY GIBSON
Logan Delp	DOM DeLUISE
Flossie	EDIE ADAMS
Betsy Potter	PAM AUSTIN
Harry Fern	MILTON BERLE
Evil Roy Slade	JOHN ASTIN
Lee	ARTHUR BATANIDES
Snake	LARRY HANKIN
Foss (Telegrapher)	MILTON FROME
Alice Fern	LUANA ANDERS

Preacher	ROBERT LIBERMAN
Smith	EDMUND CAMBRIDGE
Aggie Potter	CONNIE SAWYER
Claire Beckendorf	ALICE NUNN
Turhan	PAT MORITA
Billy	BILLY SANDS
Randolph	LEONARD BARR
Toy Cowboy	JIM WAGERMAN

A comedy Western involving a rotten outlaw whose villainy knows no bounds, a pretty but bubbleheaded schoolmarm who tries to reform him, and an egotistical singing marshal out to capture him. This feature-length film was the second pilot to an unrealized series called "Sheriff Who?" in which the bad guys were the regulars and the good guys and "guest" lawmen were killed off every week.

0212
MAN ON A STRING
2/18/72 Screen Gems/Columbia (90 min)

Producer: Douglas S. Cramer
Associate Producer: Joseph Goodson
Director: Joseph Sargent
Teleplay: Ben Maddow
Photography: Ed Rossen
Art Director: Ross Bellah
Editor: Asa Clark

Lt. Pete King	CHRISTOPHER GEORGE
William Connaught	WILLIAM SHALLERT
Mickey Brown	MICHAEL BASELEONE

Joel Grey and Christopher George in MAN ON A STRING (1972)

Robert Conrad and Shelley Winters in THE ADVENTURES OF NICK CARTER (1972)

Danny Brown	KEITH CARRADINE
Big Joe Brown	JOEL GREY
Angela Canyon	KITTY WINN
Cowboy	PAUL HAMPTON
Jake Moniker	JACK WARDEN
Carlo Buglione	J. DUKE RUSSO
Counterman	JACK BERNARDI
Billy Prescott	LINCOLN DEMYAN
Motor Officer	BOB GOLDEN
Scarred Man	JEROME GUARDINO
Judge	BYRON MORROW
Anita	CAROLYN NELSON
Pipe Smoker	JAMES SIKKING
Officer Jack	RICHARD YNIGUEZ
Sergeant	GARRY WALBERG

A government undercover agent, out to smash a crime ring, finds himself in the middle of a mob war in this pilot for a proposed new version of the old TV series "Tightrope" (1959–60) that had made a star of Mike Connors.

0213
THE ADVENTURES OF NICK CARTER
2/20/72 Universal (90 min)

Executive Producer: Richard Irving
Producer: Stan Kallis
Director: Paul Krasny

Teleplay: Ken Pettus
Photography: Alric Edens
Music: John Andrew Tartaglia
Art Director: Henry Bumstead
Editor: Robert F. Shugrue

Nick Carter	ROBERT CONRAD
Bess Tucker	SHELLEY WINTERS
Otis Duncan	BRODERICK CRAWFORD
Capt. Dan Keller	NEVILLE BRAND
Neal Duncan	PERNELL ROBERTS
Hallelujah Harry	PAT O'BRIEN
Lloyd Deams	SEAN GARRISON
Joyce Jordan	LARAINE STEPHENS
Freddy Duncan	DEAN STOCKWELL
Roxy O'Rourke	BROOKE BUNDY
Plush Horse Singer	JAYE P. MORGAN
Dr. Zimmerman	SORRELL BOOKE
Max	NED GLASS
Arch	JOSEPH MOROSS
Flo	ARLENE MARTEL
Sam Bates	BYRON MORROW

and: Arthur Peterson, Booth Colman, Warren Parker, Larry Watson, Leon Lontoc, James McCallion, Charles Davis, William Benedict, Elizabeth Harrower, Deidre Hudson

Nick Carter learns that a fellow private eye's death is tied into the disappearance of a wealthy playboy's wife, and he hunts for the killer among the social register as well as the dregs of 1912 New York.

0214
KUNG FU
2/22/72 Warner Bros. (90 min)

Producer/Director: Jerry Thorpe
Teleplay: Ed Spielman and Howard Friedlander
From a story by Ed Spielman

Photography: Richard Rawlings
Music: Jim Helms
Art Director: Eugene Lourie
Technical Advisor: David Chow
Editor: John C. Horger

Caine	DAVID CARRADINE
Dillon	BARRY SULLIVAN
Raif	ALBERT SALMI
McKay	WAYNE MAUNDER
Han Fei	BENSON FONG
Master Kan	PHILIP AHN
Master Sun	RICHARD LOO
Master Po	KEYE LUKE
Chuen	VICTOR SEN YUNG
Middle Caine	KEITH CARRADINE
Boy Caine	RADAMES PERA
Jenson	ROY FULLER
Fong	ROBERT ITO
Teh	JOHN LEONING
Little Monk	DAVID CHOW

A young Chinese-American, fleeing a murder charge in China, becomes the champion of oppressed laborers building the transcontinental railroad in the American West of the 1870s. This was the pilot for the popular series (1972–75).

0215
TO ALL MY FRIENDS ON SHORE
2/25/72 Jemmin & Jamel Productions (90 min)

Executive Producer: William H. Cosby, Jr.
Producer/Director: Gilbert Cates
Teleplay: Allan Sloane
From a story by Bill Cosby
Photography: Urs Furrer
Music: William H. Cosby, Jr.
Editor: Angelo Ross

Blue	BILL COSBY
Serena	GLORIA FOSTER

Vandy	DENNIS HINES
Tempo	TEDDY THOMPSON
First Doctor	RAY MASON
Dr. Fogson	DENNIS TATE

An airport redcap, whose single-minded dream to move his family out of the ghetto has cut him off from them, until faced with the shattering news that his only son has contacted sickle-cell anemia. Allan Sloane was awarded an Emmy for his original teleplay.

0216
TWO FOR THE MONEY
2/26/72 Aaron Spelling Productions (90 min)

Producer: Aaron Spelling
Director: Bernard Kowalski
Teleplay: Howard Rodman
Photography: Arch R. Dalzell
Art Director: Paul Sylos
Editor: Art Seid

Larry Dean	ROBERT HOOKS
Chip Bronx	STEPHEN BROOKS
Cody Guilford	WALTER BRENNAN
Judith Gap	CATHERINE BURNS
Sheriff Harley	NEVILLE BRAND
Bethany Hagen	SHELLEY FABARES
Mrs. Gap	ANNE REVERE
Mrs. Castle	MERCEDES McCAMBRIDGE
Morris Gap	RICHARD DREYFUSS
Doctor	SKIP HOMEIER
Hospital Administrator	MICHAEL FOX
Waitress	MADY MAGUIRE

Two cops quit the force to become private detectives and are quickly thrust into the search for a killer who has eluded the authorities for twelve years.

Stephen Brooks and Robert Hooks in TWO FOR THE MONEY (1972)

Sharon Farrell and Peter Haskell in THE EYES OF CHARLES SAND (1972)

James Stacy and Susan Hayward in HEAT OF ANGER (1972)

0217

THE EYES OF CHARLES SAND
2/29/72 Warner Bros. (90 min)

Producer: Hugh Benson
Director: Reza Badiyi
Teleplay: Henry Farrell and Stanford Whitmore
From a story by Henry Farrell
Photography: Ben Colman
Art Director: Eugene Lourie
Editor: Carroll Sax

Charles Sand	PETER HASKELL
Aunt Alexandra	JOAN BENNETT
Katharine Winslow	BARBARA RUSH
Emily Parkhurst	SHARON FARRELL
Jeffrey Winslow	BRADFORD DILLMAN
Dr. Paul Scott	ADAM WEST
Raymond	GARY CLARKE
Dr. Ballard	IVOR FRANCIS
Gardner	OWEN BUSH
Trainer	DONALD BARRY
Groom	LARRY LEVINE

A young man inherits the ability to see visions from beyond the grave after his uncle's sudden death and is pursuaded to investigate a girl's story about her brother's alleged murder. Although no music score is credited because of a composer's strike against TV film packagers at the time, Henry Mancini happened to recognize much of his *Wait Until Dark* score which Warner Bros. had in its vault and subsequently sued the film's producer.

0218

HEAT OF ANGER
3/3/72 Metromedia Productions (90 min)

Executive Producer: Dick Berg
Producer: Ron Roth
Director: Don Taylor
Teleplay: Fay Kanin
Photography: Robert C. Moreno
Art Director: Lawrence G. Paull
Editor: John F. Link II

Jessie Fitzgerald	SUSAN HAYWARD
Gus Pride	JAMES STACY
Frank Galvin	LEE J. COBB
Vincent Kagel	FRITZ WEAVER
Stella Galvin	BETTYE ACKERMAN
Chris Galvin	JENNIFER PENNY
Obie	MILLS WATSON
Ray Carson	RAY SIMMS
Mr. Stoller	JACK SOMMAK
Fran	LYNETTE METTY
Jean Carson	TYNE DALY

and: Arnold Mesches, Lucille Benson, Noah Keen, Inez Pedroza

A woman attorney and her young associate defend a wealthy contractor, accused of murdering an iron worker who was having an affair with his teenage daughter. Susan Hayward replaced ailing Barbara Stanwyck in this pilot for a prospective Stanwyck series that was to have been called "Fitzgerald and Pride."

0219

A VERY MISSING PERSON
3/4/72 Universal (90 min)

Executive Producer: Richard Irving
Producer: Edward J. Montagne
Director: Russ Mayberry
Teleplay: Phil Reisman, Jr.
Based on the novel *Hildegarde Withers Makes the Scene* by Stuart Palmer and Fletcher Flora
Photography: William Margulies

Eve Arden and Dennis Rucker in A VERY MISSING PERSON (1972)

Celeste Holm and Laurence Luckinbill in THE DELPHI BUREAU (1972)

Music: Vic Mizzy
Art Director: William Tuntke
Editor: Richard M. Sprague

Hildegarde Withers	EVE ARDEN
Oscar Piper	JAMES GREGORY
Aletha Westering	JULIE NEWMAR
Captain Westering	RAY DANTON
Sister Isobel/Leonore Gregory	SKYE AUBREY
Al Fister	DENNIS RUCKER
Onofre	ROBERT EASTON
Eberhardt	WOODROW PARFREY
James Malloy	BOB HASTINGS
Delmar Faulkenstein	PAT MORITA
Judge	EZRA STONE
Bernadine Toller	LINDA GILLIN
Ora	DWAN SMITH
Dr. Singer	PETER MORRISON JACOBS
Mrs. Singer	SAVANNAH BENTLEY
Mariette	UDANA POWER

An ex-schoolmarm turns detective when police ask for her aid in finding a missing heiress in this pilot project to bring to TV the Hildegarde Withers character popularized in films in the 1930s by Edna May Oliver.

0220
FIREBALL FORWARD
3/5/72 20th Century-Fox (2 hours)

Producer: Frank McCarthy
Director: Marvin Chomsky
Teleplay: Edmund H. North
Photography: Robert L. Morrison
Music: Lionel Newman
Theme "The Longest Day" by Paul Anka
Art Directors: Jack Martin Smith and Bill Malley
Editors: Pembroke J. Herring, Charles L. Freeman and Harry Coswick

Maj. Gen. Joe Barrett	BEN GAZZARA
Jean Duval	RICARDO MONTALBAN
Helen Sawyer	ANNE FRANCIS
Colonel Talbot	DANA ELCAR
Corps Commander	EDWARD BINNS
Sgt. Andrew Collins	MORGAN PAULL
Captain Bauer	CURT LOWENS
Major Larkin	L. Q. JONES
Col. Douglas Graham	EDDIE ALBERT
Colonel Avery	ROBERT PATTEN
Capt. Tony Sanchez	RICHARD YNIGUEZ
General Dawson	KENNETH TOBEY

A standard war movie that not only has stalwart Ben Gazzara taking over a hard-luck division at the front

but also utilizes lots of extra footage from *Patton* which Frank McCarthy, producer of that movie and this, had in abundance.

0221
THE DELPHI BUREAU
3/6/72 Warner Bros. (2 hours)

Producer: Sam Rolfe
Director: Paul Wendkos
Teleplay: Sam Rolfe
Photography: Ben Colman
Music: Harper McKay
Art Director: Eugene Lourie
Editor: Dann Cahn

Glenn Garth Gregory	LAURENCE LUCKINBILL
Sybil Van Loween	CELESTE HOLM
Matthew Keller	DEAN JAGGER
Stokely	CAMERON MITCHELL
Randy Jamison	BRADFORD DILLMAN
Charlie Taggart	BOB CRANE
April Thompson	JOANNA PETTET
Joe Dobkin	DAVID SHEINER
Mrs. Loveless	LUCILLE BENSON
Luke	KEVIN HAGEN

Charlotte	JUNE VINCENT
Old Timer	DUB TAYLOR
Sheriff Morgan	FRANK MARTH
Alice (Boarder)	PAMELA FERDIN
Drunk	ROBERT OSTERLOH

and: Judy Baldwin, William Stevens, Joseph Mell, K. L. Smith

A suspense drama that has a government agent with a photographic memory assigned to solve the disappearance of an entire fleet of old Air Force planes. Luckinbill again played the talented operative in the subsequent series (1972–73) with Celeste Holm repeating her role, later to be replaced by Anne Jeffreys.

0222
THE ROOKIES
3/7/72 Aaron Spelling Productions (90 min)

Producer: Aaron Spelling
Director: Jud Taylor

Teleplay: William Blinn
From a story by Rita Larkin
Photography: Arch R. Dalzell
Music: Elmer Bernstein
Art Director: Paul Sylos
Editor: Art Seid

Sgt. Eddie Ryker	DARREN McGAVIN
Neil Montgomery	PAUL BURKE
Sniper	CAMERON MITCHELL
Jared Whitman	ROBERT F. LYONS
Terry Webster	GEORG STANFORD BROWN
Mike Danko	SAM MELVILLE
Willie Gillis	MICHAEL ONTKEAN
Kevin Lassiter	JEFFREY POMERANTZ
Jill Danko	JENNIFER BILLINGSLEY
Birgitta Whitman	MONIKA SVENSON
Toby Loomis	LOGAN RAMSEY

Molly Lassiter	DAVY DAVISON
Ranch Instructor	ARCH JOHNSON
Officer Shaw	ROBERT L. WILKIE

Police recruits and their wives try to adjust to the ways of being part of a metropolitan police force. This was the pilot for the hit series (1972–75) starring Brown, Melville and Ontkean, along with Kate Jackson (in the part played by Jennifer Billingsley in this film).

0223
BANACEK: DETOUR TO NOWHERE
3/20/72 Universal (2 hours)

Producer: George Eckstein
Director: Jack Smight
Teleplay: Anthony Wilson
Photography: Sam Levitt
Music: Billy Goldenberg
Art Director: George C. Webb
Editor: Robert Watts

Thomas Banacek	GEORGE PEPPARD
Charlie Kirkland	CHRISTINE BELFORD
Sheriff Jessup	DON DUBBINS
Felix Mulholland	MURRAY MATHESON
Earl Lewis	RUSSELL WIGGINS
Arthur Patrick McKinney	CHARLES KNOX ROBINSON
Jay Drury	RALPH MANZA
Cavanaugh	GEORGE MURDOCK
Geoff Holden	ED NELSON
Deputy Bill Makey	BILL VINT
Joe Hawk	VIC MOHICA

also: Lou Frizzell, Gene Dynarski, Mario Machado, J. Pat O'Malley, Dee Gardner, Hank Sharon, Larry Burrel

An urbane, Boston-based insurance investigator attempts to locate an armored car filled with gold bullion that vanished in the middle of a deserted Texas highway. This film spawned the TV series with Peppard (1972–74).

0224
JIGSAW
3/26/72 Universal (2 hours)

Producer: Stanley Kallis
Director: William A. Graham
Teleplay: Robert E. Thompson
Photography: Michael Margulies
Music: Robert Drasnin
Art Director: Bill Kenny
Editor: Jim Benson

Lt. Frank Dain	JAMES WAINWRIGHT
Lilah Beth Cummings	VERA MILES
Harrison Delando	ANDREW DUGGAN
Det. Ed Burtelson	EDMOND O'BRIEN
Dr. Gehlen	MARSHA HUNT
Mrs. Cummings	IRENE DAILEY
D. A. Dan Bellington	RICHARD KILEY
Timmy Cummings	GENE ANDRUSCO
Psychologist	MILTON SELZER
Motel Clerk	ELLIOTT STREET
Mr. Cummings	KEN LYNCH
Adele Collier	PAMELA ROGERS
Waitress	JENNIFER SHAW
Motel Manager	CLAUDIA BRYAR
Cab Driver	FELTON PERRY

and: Ted Gehring, Charles Lampkin, J. H. Lawrence, Ed Peck, Casey MacDonald, Adrian Ricard, Lou Krugman, Helen Baron, Vert Holland

Darren McGavin and Sam Melville in THE ROOKIES (1972)

Roy Scheider and Richard Basehart in ASSIGNMENT: MUNICH (1972)

In this pilot for the 1972–73 series, a detective specializing in missing-persons cases finds himself accused of murder after being found unconscious in the apartment of a slain state official. Wainwright proved to be a rather unlikely though likeable TV series hero.

0225
ASSIGNMENT: MUNICH
4/30/72 MGM (2 hours)

Executive Producer: Robert H. Justman
Producers: Eric Bercovici and Jerry Ludwig
Director: David Lowell Rich
Teleplay: Eric Bercovici and Jerry Ludwig
Photography: Mike Marszelek
Music: George Romanis
Art Director: Otto Pischinger
Editor: William B. Gulick

Maj. Barney Caldwell	RICHARD BASEHART
Jake Webster	ROY SCHEIDER
Inspector Hoffman	WERNER KLEMPERER
Doug Mitchell	ROBERT REED
George	KEENAN WYNN
Gus	MIKE KELLIN
Cathy Lange	LESLEY WARREN
Fritz	KARL-OTTO ALBERTY
Hilda	MARIA LUCCA
Harry Lange	GERRY CRAMPTON

Undercover agent Webster, using his bar as a front, vies with three assassins to locate a stolen fortune in Germany for which a man was murdered after leaving prison. Ultimately, in series form, the locale was changed, along with the title (to "Assignment: Vienna") and the three regulars, following a legal action against Roy Scheider. The actor, expecting big things for himself in movies after winning an Oscar nomination for *The French Connection,* balked at continuing in the part of Jake Webster and was sued by the producers. In the 1972–73 series, Robert Conrad took over the role, Charles Cioffi was signed to play Caldwell, and Anton Diffring was Hoffman.

0226
THE CATCHER
6/2/72 HBL Productions/Screen Gems (2 hours)

Executive Producer: Herbert B. Leonard
Producer: Stanley Neufeld
Director: Allen H. Miner

Teleplay: David Freeman
Photography: Irving Lippman
Music: Bill Walker
Title song by Jackie DeShannon and Kiel Martin
Sung by Jackie DeShannon
Song "Not for Long" written and sung by Kiel Martin
Art Director: Ross Bellah
Editor: Sig Neufeld, Jr.

Noah Hendricks	MICHAEL WITNEY
Sam Callender	JAN-MICHAEL VINCENT
Joe Cade	TONY FRANCIOSA
Sara Faber	CATHERINE BURNS
Kate	ANNE BAXTER
Mike Keller	MIKE KELLIN
Armand Faber	DAVID WAYNE
Wes Watkins	KIEL MARTIN
Amy Lee Cade	JACKIE DeSHANNON
Andy	ANDY ROBINSON
Shooting Gallery Attendant	MARSHALL EFRON
Himself	PIANO RED

and: Naomi Borden, Jacqueline Bergaud, David Williams

A Seattle ex-cop and a Harvard graduate team up to locate fugitives, errant husbands and other missing persons, and are hired to undertake a cross-country search for a runaway coed in this pilot that never caught on. This modern bounty hunter-themed film was made in 1970.

1972–73 SEASON

0227
THE LONGEST NIGHT
9/12/72 Universal (90 min)

Producer: William Frye
Director: Jack Smight
Teleplay: Merwin Gerard
Photography: Sam Leavitt
Music: Hal Mooney
Art Director: John J. Lloyd
Editor: Robert F. Shugrue

Alan Chambers	DAVID JANSSEN
John Danbury	JAMES FARENTINO
Norma Chambers	PHYLLIS THAXTER
Ellen Gunther	SKYE AUBREY
Wills	MIKE FARRELL
Karen Chambers	SALLIE SHOCKLEY
Barris	JOEL FABIANI
Father Chase	CHARLES McGRAW
Harvey Eaton	RICHARD ANDERSON
Officer Jones	JOHN KERR
Frank Cavanaugh	ROBERT CORNTHWAITE
Dr. Steven Clay	ROSS ELLIOTT

A fact-based drama about a wealthy co-ed who is kidnapped and imprisoned underground in a coffin with a limited life-support system while her parents and police engage in an agonizing four-day search for her before she suffocates.

0228
THE FAMILY RICO
9/12/72 CBS Inc. (90 min)

Producer: George LeMaire
Director: Paul Wendkos
Teleplay: David Karp
Based on the novel *The Brothers Rico* by George Simenon

Karen Valentine, Lesley Warren, Buddy Ebsen and Sandra Dee in THE DAUGHTERS OF JOSHUA CABE (1972)

Buddy Ebsen and Jack Elam in THE DAUGHTERS OF JOSHUA CABE (1972)

Photography: Robert B. Hauser
Music: Dave Grusin
Art Director: Albert Heschong
Editor: Carroll Sax

Eddie Rico	BEN GAZZARA
McGee	JACK CARTER
Boston Phil	DANE CLARK
Mike Lamont	LEIF ERICKSON
Gino Rico	JAMES FARENTINO
Sid Kubik	JOHN MARLEY
Nick Rico	SAL MINEO
Malakas (Mario Felici)	JOHN RANDOLPH
Mama Rico	JO VAN FLEET
Nora Malakas	SIAN BARBARA ALLEN
George Lamont	MICHAEL ANDERSON, JR.
John Ryan	ALAN VINT
Angelo	TOM PEDI
Accountant	RICHARD GITTINGS
Chauffeur	ALBERTO MORIN

A drama about underworld pressures on a crime syndicate chief, played by Gazzara, who is torn between his love for a younger brother who defects and his own loyalty to the organization. The 1957 theatrical version of the story, *The Brothers Rico,* starred Richard Conte and Kathryn Grant, who had just become Mrs. Bing Crosby.

0229
THE DAUGHTERS OF JOSHUA CABE
9/13/72 Spelling/Goldberg Productions (90 min)

Executive Producers: Aaron Spelling and Leonard Goldberg
Producer: Richard E. Lyons
Associate Producer: Robert Monroe
Director: Philip Leacock
Teleplay: Paul Savage
Photography: Arch R. Dalzell
Music: Jeff Alexander
Art Director: Bud Brooks
Editor: Art Seid

Joshua Cabe	BUDDY EBSEN
Charity	KAREN VALENTINE
Mae	LESLEY WARREN
Ada	SANDRA DEE
Blue Wetherall	DON STROUD
Codge Collier	HENRY JONES
Bitterroot	JACK ELAM
Amos Wetherall	LEIF ERICKSON
Cole Wetherall	MICHAEL ANDERSON, JR.
Deke Wetherall	PAUL KOSLO
Sister Mary Robert	JULIE MANNIX
Arnie	RON SOBLE
Billy Jack	BILL KATT

An amiable Western about a fur trapper who, in a scheme to keep his land holdings in the wake of a homesteading law, recruits a prostitute, a thief and a pickpocket to portray his daughters.

0230
THE STREETS OF SAN FRANCISCO
9/16/72 Quinn Martin Productions (2 hours)

Executive Producer: Quinn Martin
Producers: Arthur Fellows and Adrian Samish
Director: Walter Grauman
Teleplay: Ed Hume
Based on the novel *Poor, Poor Ophelia* by Carolyn Weston
Photography: William Spencer
Music: Pat Williams

Karl Malden in THE STREETS OF SAN FRANCISCO (1972)

Art Director: Hoyle Barrett
Editor: Richard Brockway

Lt. Mike Stone	KARL MALDEN
David J. Farr	ROBERT WAGNER
Inspector Steve Keller	MICHAEL DOUGLAS
Capt. A. R. Malone	ANDREW DUGGAN
Saretti	TOM BOSLEY
Lindy	JOHN RUBINSTEIN
Sally Caswell	CARMEN MATHEWS
Joe Caswell	EDWARD ANDREWS
Gregory Praxas	LAWRENCE DOBKIN
Holly Jean Berry	KIM DARBY
Kenji	MAKO

Scott Jacoby and Herschel Bernardi in NO PLACE TO RUN (1972)

| Del Berry | BRAD DAVID |
| Mrs. Saretti | NAOMI STEVENS |

and: Lou Frizzell, June Vincent

A street-smart veteran cop and his young college-educated partner go after the killer of a girl by systematically piecing together her last moves and come upon her junkie brother, a closed-mouth corporation lawyer and someone claiming to be her uncle. This pilot to the hit series (1972–77) marked Karl Malden's TV movie debut and his first work in the medium in more than twenty years.

0231
THE WOMAN HUNTER
9/19/72 Bing Crosby Productions (90 min)

Executive Producer: Andrew J. Fenady
Producer: Jerome L. Epstein
Director: Bernard Kowalski
Teleplay: Brian Clemens and Tony Williamson
From a story by Brian Clemens
Photography: Gabriel Torres
Music: George Duning
Art Director: Stan Jolley
Editor: Melvin Shapiro

Dina Hunter	BARBARA EDEN
Jerry Hunter	ROBERT VAUGHN
Paul Carter	STUART WHITMAN
George	SYDNEY CHAPLIN
Vardy	ENRIQUE LUCERO
Raconteur	LARRY STORCH
Victor	VICTOR HUGO JAUREQUI

| Mrs. Trice | NORMA STORCH |
| Señora Amalia | AURORA MUÑOZ |

A wealthy woman, vacationing in Acapulco with her stuffy husband, stumbles upon evidence that she is being stalked by an international jewel thief and murderer.

0232
NO PLACE TO RUN
9/19/72 ABC Circle Films (90 min)

Executive Producers: Aaron Spelling and Leonard Goldberg
Producer: Paul Junger Witt
Director: Delbert Mann
Teleplay: James G. Hirsch
Photography: Ralph Woolsey
Music: George Aliceson Tipton
Title song written and sung by Paul Williams
Art Director: Bud Brooks
Editor: Gene Milford

Hyam L. Malsh	HERSCHEL BERNARDI
Bonnie Howard	STEFANIE POWERS
Remus	NEVILLE BRAND
Dr. Sam Golinski	TOM BOSLEY
Doug	SCOTT JACOBY
Landlady	KAY MEDFORD*
Jay Fox	LARRY HAGMAN
Used Car Salesman	ROBERT DONNER
Bill Ryan	WESLEY LAU
Motel Manager	WOODROW PARFREY

Highway Patrolman	WILL J. WHITE
Girl on Bus	SUSAN SULLIVAN
Cabbie	LARRY WATSON

When an adopted boy's parents are killed and the authorities threaten to keep the boy's ailing but loving grandfather from gaining custody, the pair run away together. John Badham, the film's original director, left when the project was suspended because of Herschel Bernardi's illness, and was replaced by Delbert Mann.

*Replaced Nancy Walker.

0233
HAUNTS OF THE VERY RICH
9/20/72 ABC Circle Film (90 min)

Producer: Lillian Gallo
Director: Paul Wendkos
Teleplay: William Wood
From a story by T. K. Brown
Photography: Ben Colman
Music: Dominic Frontiere
Art Director: Eugene Lourie
Editor: Fredric Steinkamp

Dave Woodbrough	LLOYD BRIDGES
Ellen Blunt	CLORIS LEACHMAN
Albert Hunsicker	EDWARD ASNER
Annette Larrier	ANNE FRANCIS
Lyle	TONY BILL

Laurie	DONNA MILLS
Rev. John Fellows	ROBERT REED
Seacrist	MOSES GUNN
Rita	PHYLLIS HILL
Delmonico	MICHAEL LEMBECK
Miss Upton	SUSAN FOSTER
Miss Vick	BEVERLY GILL
Harris	TODD MARTIN
Ham Radio Operator	SAMMY JACKSON

Seven people who arrive at an idyllic tropical resort after receiving a mysterious invitation find their dream of paradise turning into a hellish nightmare with little chance of escape.

0234
DEADLY HARVEST
9/26/72 CBS, Inc. (90 min)

Producer: Anthony Wilson
Director: Michael O'Herlihy
Teleplay: Dan Ullman
Based on the novel *Watcher in the Shadows* by Geoffrey Household
Photography: Earl Rath
Music: Morton Stevens
Editor: Bud S. Isaacs

Anton Solca	RICHARD BOONE
Jenny	PATTY DUKE
Stefan Groza	MICHAEL CONSTANTINE
Vartamian	JACK KRUSCHEN
Sheriff Bill Jessup	MURRAY HAMILTON
McAndrews/George Anson	FRED CARSON
Franklin	JACK DeMAVE
Charley (Deputy)	BILL McKEEVER
Peterson	RICHARD ROAT
Roger	RICHARD TURNER
Caretaker	FREDDY MAO
Attendant	JOSEF RODRIGUEZ

and: T. J. Howard, Stephen Lodge

An Iron Curtain defector who has lived peacefully for years as a Napa Valley wine grower discovers that he's being stalked by an enemy from his past.

0235
MOON OF THE WOLF
9/26/72 Filmways (90 min)

Executive Producer: Edward S. Feldman
Producers: Everett Chambers and Peter Thomas
Director: Daniel Petrie
Teleplay: Alvin Sapinsley
Based on the novel by Leslie H. Whitten
Photography: Richard C. Glouner
Music: Bernardo Segall
Art Director: James G. Hulsey
Editor: Richard Halsey

Sheriff Aaron Whitaker	DAVID JANSSEN
Louise Rodanthe	BARBARA RUSH
Andrew Rodanthe	BRADFORD DILLMAN
Dr. Druten	JOHN BERADINO
Lawrence Burrifors	GEOFFREY LEWIS
Gurmandy Sr.	ROYAL DANO
Gurmandy Jr.	JOHN CHANDLER
Sara	CLAUDIA McNEIL
Hugh Burrifors	PAUL R. DeVILLE
Sam Cairns	DAN PRIEST
Deputy	ROBERT PHILLIPS
Nurse	SERENA SANDE

Lloyd Bridges and Cloris Leachman in HAUNTS OF THE VERY RICH (1972)

Bradford Dillman in MOON OF THE WOLF (1972)

After several townspeople are savagely murdered, a Louisiana bayou sheriff searches for a crazed killer and becomes convinced that he's chasing a modern-day werewolf.

0236
SAY GOODBYE, MAGGIE COLE
9/27/72 Spelling/Goldberg Productions (90 min)

Producers: Aaron Spelling and Leonard Goldberg
Director: Jud Taylor
Teleplay: Sandor Stern
Photography: Tim Southcott
Music: Hugo Montenegro
Title song sung by Dusty Springfield
Art Director: Tracy Bousman
Editor: Bill Mosher

Dr. Maggie Cole	SUSAN HAYWARD
Dr. Lou Grazzo	DARREN McGAVIN
Dr. Sweeney	MICHAEL CONSTANTINE
Lisa Downey	MICHELE NICHOLS
Hank Cooper	DANE CLARK
Myrna Anderson	BEVERLY GARLAND
Mrs. Downey	JEANETTE NOLAN
Fergy	MAIDIE NORMAN
Dr. Ben Cole	RICHARD ANDERSON
Mr. Alessandro	FRANK PUGLIA

Susan Hayward and Darren McGavin in SAY GOODBYE, MAGGIE COLE (1972)

Doug McClure, Barbara Feldon (top), Connie Stevens and Alan Alda in PLAYMATES (1972)

Anderson	RICHARD CARLYLE
Pathologist	PETER HOBBS
Isadore Glass	HARRY BASCH
Night Nurse	LEIGH ADAMS
Ivan Dvorsky	JAN PETERS
Brig	ROBERT CLEAVERS

A pretty research doctor, suddenly widowed, is inveigled by a gruff street doctor to put away the mourning band and join him in his clinic in a Chicago slum area. The title role marked the end of Susan Hayward's long film career.

0237
PLAYMATES
10/3/72 ABC Circle Films (90 min)

Producer: Lillian Gallo
Director: Theodore J. Flicker
Teleplay: Richard Baer
Photography: Joseph Biroc
Music: Jack Elliott and Allyn Ferguson
Art Director: Peter M. Wooley
Editor: Lovel Ellis

Marshall Barnett	ALAN ALDA
Patti Holvey	CONNIE STEVENS
Lois Barnett	BARBARA FELDON
Kermit Holvey	DOUG McCLURE
Roger (Man in Gallery)	SEVERN DARDEN
Man in Kiddieland	ROGER BOWEN
Amy	EILEEN BRENNAN
Eric Barnett	BRYAN SCOTT
Johnny Holvey	TIGER WILLIAMS
Estelle Chase	ELOISE HARDT
Nick	JIM ANTONIO
Bikini Girl No. 1	VALERIE FITZGERALD
Bikini Girl No. 2	DEBBIE DOZIER

A romantic comedy involving two divorced men who become friends and then secretly begin dating the other's ex-wife, causing even more complications than their original marriages did.

(Left) **Richard Crenna in FOOTSTEPS (1972)**
(Above) **Bill Overton and Richard Crenna in FOOTSTEPS (1972)**

0238
FOOTSTEPS
10/3/72 Metromedia Productions (90 min)
(subsequently titled *Footsteps: Nice Guys Finish Last*)

Executive Producer: Dick Berg
Producer: Lynn Stalmaster

Director: Paul Wendkos
Teleplay: Alvin Sargent and Richard E. Thompson
Based on the novel *Paddy* by Hamilton Maule
Photography: Alan Stensvold
Music: Dennis Gold
Art Director: Peter M. Wooley
Editor: John Martinelli

Paddy O'Connor	RICHARD CRENNA
Sarah Allison	JOANNA PETTET
Bradford Emmons	FORREST TUCKER
Jonas Kane	CLU GULAGER
Frank Powell	NED BEATTY
Martha Hagger	MARY MURPHY
Jessie Blake	BEAH RICHARDS
J. J. Blake	BILL OVERTON
Brewster	ALLEN GARFIELD
Zimmerman	AL LETTIERI
Gas Station Attendant	ROBERT CARRADINE
Meat Inspector	LOU FRIZZELL
Reporter	JAMES WOODS
Crowther	JACK COLVIN
Doreen	JENNIFER LEE
Minister	WOODROW CHAMBLISS
Drill Major	MICHAEL SHAW

A win-or-else coach, hired to whip a small college football team into shape, finds himself in trouble with heavy gamblers on the squad's success, who plan to set the odds.

0239
ROLLING MAN
10/4/72 ABC Circle Films (90 min)

Executive Producer: Aaron Spelling
Producers: Stephen and Elinor Karpf
Director: Peter Hyams
Teleplay: Stephen and Elinor Karpf
Photography: Earl Rath
Music: Murray McLeod and Stuart Margolin
Art Director: Albert Brenner
Editors: Don Ernst and W. R. Wormell

Lonnie McAfee	DENNIS WEAVER
Harold Duncan	DON STROUD
Bebe Lotter	DONNA MILLS
Lyman	JIMMY DEAN
Ruby	SHEREE NORTH
Chuck	SLIM PICKENS
Grandmother	AGNES MOOREHEAD
Crystal	LINDA SCOTT
Mildred Slye	DEVRA KORWIN
Lester	DONALD LARKIN
Clifford	JACK HALEY
Announcer	JOE NIXON

Shaken by the death of his wife and the disappearance of his young sons while he spent four years in prison, a simple man tries to rebuild his life while searching for the missing boys.

Sheree North and Dennis Weaver in ROLLING MAN (1972)

Dennis Weaver and Jimmy Dean in ROLLING MAN (1972)

0240
HEC RAMSEY
10/8/72 Universal/Mark VII Ltd. (2 hours)
(subsequently titled *The Century Turns*)

Executive Producer: Jack Webb
Producer: William Finnegan
Director: Daniel Petrie
Teleplay: Harold Jack Bloom
Photography: Robert B. Hauser
Music: Fred Steiner
Art Director: Robert Luthardt
Editor: Edward A. Biery

Hec Ramsey	RICHARD BOONE
Chief Oliver Stamp	RICK LENZ
Nora Muldoon	SHARON ACKER
Doc Amos C. Coogan	HARRY MORGAN
Ben Ritt	R. G. ARMSTRONG
Steve Ritt	ROBERT PRATT
Judge Leroy Tate	RAY MIDDLETON
Earl Enright	DICK VAN PATTEN
Sgt. Juan Mendoza	PERRY LOPEZ
Andy Muldoon	DENNIS RUCKER

and: Bill Vint, Brian Dewey, Ron Turbeville

An aging lawman in the turn-of-the-century West finds himself out of step with the times and reluctantly accepts a job as deputy to an inexperienced, college-educated cop in this light-hearted pilot for the series (1972–74) that was one of the rotating elements of the "NBC Sunday Mystery Movie." Boone and Lenz continued in their roles along with (occasionally) Sharon Acker and Harry Morgan.

0241
NIGHT OF TERROR
10/10/72 Paramount (90 min)

Producers: Thomas L. Miller and Edward K. Milkis
Director: Jeannot Szwarc
Teleplay: Cliff Gould
Photography: Howard R. Schwartz
Music: Robert Drasnin
Art Director: William Campbell
Editor: Mike Vejar

Capt. Caleb Sark	MARTIN BALSAM
Celeste Davillo	CATHY BURNS
Brian DiPaulo	CHUCK CONNORS
Linda Daniel	DONNA MILLS
Bronsky	AGNES MOOREHEAD
Washington	VIC VALLARO
Pete Manning	JOHN KARLEN
Chris Arden	PETER HOOTEN
Dr. Whitacomb	DAVID SPIELBERG
Dr. Cannard	WILLIAM GRAY ESPY
Chairlady	MARY GRACE CANFIELD
Phone Man	BART LaRUE
Steve Martin	JOHNNY MARTINO

A Syndicate killer relentlessly pursues a pretty young teacher who doesn't know what he's after, although he has already killed twice to get it.

0242
VISIONS . . .
10/10/72 CBS, Inc. (90 min)
(subsequently titled *Visions of Death*)

Producer: Leonard Freeman
Director: Lee H. Katzin

Donna Mills and Martin Balsam in NIGHT OF TERROR (1972)

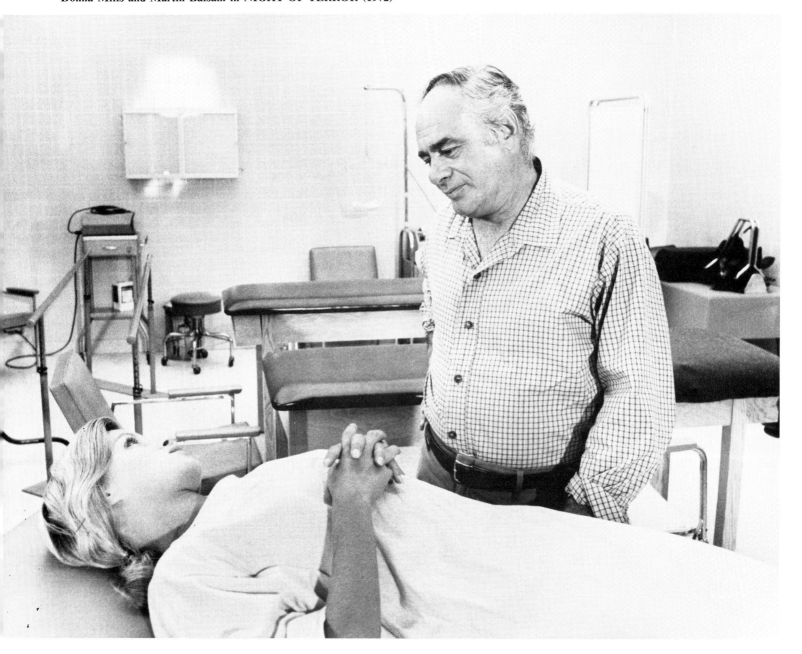

Paul Burke and Lee Grant in LIEUTENANT SCHUSTER'S WIFE (1972)

James Farentino and Barbara Bouchet in COOL MILLION (1972)

Teleplay: Paul Playdon
Photography: John A. Alonzo
Music: Morton Stevens
Art Director: Albert Heschong
Editor: Ira Heymann

Prof. Mark Lowell	MONTE MARKHAM
Susan Schaeffer	BARBARA ANDERSON
Lt. Phil Keegan	TELLY SAVALAS
Bert Hayes	TIM O'CONNOR
George Simpson	JOE SIROLA
Martin Binzech	LONNY CHAPMAN
Sgt. Ted Korel	JIM ANTONIO
Ellis	RICHARD ERDMAN
Steve Curtis	VAL DeVARGAS
Mrs. Metcalf	ELIZABETH MOORE
Andrews	ROBERT DoQUI

A clairvoyant professor who alerts police that someone is about to plant a bomb discovers that he is their prime suspect.

0243
LIEUTENANT SCHUSTER'S WIFE
10/11/72 Universal (90 min)

Producer: Steven Boscho
Director: David Lowell Rich
Teleplay: Steven Boscho and Bernie Kuboff
Photography: Bud Thackery
Music: Gil Melle
Art Director: Loyd S. Papez
Editor: John M. Woodcock

Ellie Schuster	LEE GRANT
Capt. Patrick Lonergan	JACK WARDEN

Lt. Danny Reilly	DON GALLOWAY
Champagne Joe Carroll	NEHEMIAH PERSOFF
Lady	EARTHA KITT
Lt. Lou Schuster	PAUL BURKE
Abbott	MURRAY MATHESON
Tony Butrick	GEORGE BRENLIN
Detective McCann	ROBERT DoQUI
Guido	LEW PALTER
Junkie	JOHN HERZFELD

A policeman's widow becomes determined to clear his name after learning that he was accused of being on the take, and following his shooting in an ambush she tracks down the real killer.

0244
COOL MILLION
10/16/72 Universal (2 hours)
(subsequently titled *Mask of Marcella*)

Executive Producer: George Eckstein
Producer: David J. O'Connell
Director: Gene Levitt
Teleplay: Larry Cohen
Photography: Gabor Pogany
Music: Robert Prince
Art Director: Aurelio Crugnola
Editor: Michael Economou

Jefferson Keyes	JAMES FARENTINO
Inspector Duprez	JOHN VERNON
Carla Miles	BARBARA BOUCHET

Adrienne/Marcella Pascal	CHRISTINE BELFORD
Cossack	JACKIE COOGAN
Mme. Martine	LILA KEDROVA
Dr. Emile Snow	PATRICK O'NEAL
Tomlin	GUIDO ALBERTI

and: John Karlen, Michael Hargitay, Jacques Herlin, Frederich Ober, Massimo Serato, Anthony Dawson, Bennes Mendenn, Debile Vargas

An international private investigator whose fee is one million dollars hunts for an heiress who has not been seen for thirteen years when her tycoon father dies under mysterious circumstances. Filmed on location in Greece and Italy, this pilot emerged in series form with Farentino during the 1972–73 season.

0245
SANDCASTLES
10/17/72 Metromedia Productions (90 min)

Executive Producer: Charles W. Fries
Producer: Gerald I. Isenberg
Director: Ted Post
Teleplay: Stephen and Elinor Karpf and James M. Miller
Photography: Alan Stensvold
Music: Paul Glass
Editor: Thomas McCarthy

Alexis	HERSCHEL BERNARDI
Jenna Hampshire	BONNIE BEDELIA
Michael	JAN-MICHAEL VINCENT

Barbara Bain, Richard Boone and Michael Dunn in GOODNIGHT MY LOVE (1972)

George Kennedy and Vera Miles in A GREAT AMERICAN TRAGEDY (1972)

Sarah	MARIETTE HARTLEY
Frank Watson	GARY CROSBY
Ruth Watson	LORETTA LEVERSEE
Paul Fiedler	LLOYD GOUGH
George Peterson	WILLIAM LONG, JR.
Sascha	WILLIAM HANSEN
Sister	MIMI DAVIS
Driver	DICK VALENTINE
Sherry	JODY HAUBER

A ghostly romance between a lonely young girl and the handsome victim of an auto accident who had died in her arms but later is discovered wandering on the beach. This was the first TV movie using a single camera videotape system, later being transferred to film.

0246
GOODNIGHT MY LOVE
10/17/72 ABC Circle Films (90 min)

Producer: Ward Sylvester
Director: Peter Hyams
Teleplay: Peter Hyams
Photography: Earl Rath
Music: Harry Betts
Assistant Director: Kurt Neumann
Art Director: Peter M. Wooley
Editor: James Mitchell

Frank Hogan	RICHARD BOONE
Arthur Boyle	MICHAEL DUNN
Susan Lakely	BARBARA BAIN
Julius Limeway	VICTOR BUONO
Michael Tarlow	GIANNI RUSSO
Edgar	JOHN QUADE
Wheezer	WALTER BURKE
Sally	LOU WAGNER
Sidney	LOU CUTELL
Reardon	JOHN LAWRENCE
Nightclub Singer	JAN DALEY

and: Luke Andreas, Don Calfa, Vic Vallardo

This private-eye spoof has a seedy, down-and-out detective and his partner, an erudite dwarf, being drawn by a voluptuous blonde into a missing persons case leading to murder in the seamy underworld of 1946 Los Angeles.

0247
A GREAT AMERICAN TRAGEDY
10/18/72 Metromedia Productions (90 min)

Executive Producers: Charles W. Fries and Gerald I. Isenberg
Producer: Ronald Shedlo
Director: J. Lee Thompson
Teleplay: Caryl Ledner
Photography: J. J. Jones
Music: George Duning
Editor: Henry Berman

Brad Wilkes	GEORGE KENNEDY
Gloria Wilkes	VERA MILES
Rob Stewart	WILLIAM WINDOM
Carol	SALLIE SHOCKLEY
Mark Reynolds	KEVIN McCARTHY
Julie Wilkes	HILARIE THOMPSON
Rick	JAMES WOODS
Paula Braun	NATALIE TRUNDY
Trudy Stewart	NANCY HADLEY
Leslie Baker	ROBERT MANDAN
Johnny	TONY DOW
Claire	MARCIA MAE JONES

An aerospace engineer is laid off and faces the economic realities of middle-class living, going through the agony of fruitless job interviews and mounting debts while seeing his wife go back to work and his marriage dissolve. Initially the film was called *A New American Tragedy*.

0248
SHORT WALK TO DAYLIGHT

10/24/72 Universal (90 min)

Producer: Edward J. Montagne
Director: Barry Shear
Teleplay: Philip Reisman, Jr. and Gerald DiPego
From a story by Edward J. Montagne
Photography: Terry K. Meade and Ed Brown
Music: Pat Williams
Art Director: John J. Lloyd
Special Effects: Albert Whitlock
Editor: Sam E. Waxman

Tom Phelan	JAMES BROLIN
Alvin	DON MITCHELL
Ed Mullins	JAMES McEACHIN
Dorella	ABBEY LINCOLN
Joanne	BROOKE BUNDY
Jax	LARAZO PEREZ
Sylvia	SUZANNE CHARNY
Sandy	LAURETTE SPANG
Conductor	FRANKLIN COVER

Eight terrified people, trapped in a New York subway tunnel when a devastating earthquake levels the city, desperately try to find a way out.

0249
FAMILY FLIGHT

10/25/72 Universal (90 min)

Producer: Harve Bennett
Director: Marvin Chomsky
Teleplay: Guerdon Trueblood
Photography: Emil Oster
Music: Fred Steiner
Art Director: John J. Lloyd
Editor: Chuck K. McClelland

Jason Carlyle	ROD TAYLOR
Florence Carlyle	DINA MERRILL
David Carlyle	KRISTOFFER TABORI
Carol Rutledge	JANET MARGOLIN
Aircraft Carrier Captain	GENE NELSON
Officer of the Deck	RICHARD ROOT
1st Controller	PAUL KENT
2nd Controller	JAMES SIKKING
Frank Gross	BILL ZUCKERT
Driver	ED BEGLEY, JR.
3rd Controller	ARTHUR TURNER

A flying vacation to Mexico for a troubled family turns into a near-hopeless battle for survival following a crash landing in an isolated section of Baja, California.

0250
THE BOUNTY MAN

10/31/72 ABC Circle Films (90 min)

Producers: Aaron Spelling and Leonard Goldberg
Director: John Llewellyn Moxey
Teleplay: Jim Byrnes
Photography: Ralph Woolsey
Music: The Orphanage
Art Director: Rolland M. Brooks
Editor: Art Seid

Kincaid	CLINT WALKER
Angus Keough	RICHARD BASEHART
Billy Riddle	JOHN ERICSON
Mae	MARGOT KIDDER
Tom Brady	GENE EVANS
Sheriff	ARTHUR HUNNICUTT

Don Mitchell, Abbey Lincoln, Suzanne Charny, Brooke Bundy, Laurette Spang, James McEachin and James Brolin in SHORT WALK TO DAYLIGHT (1972)

Dina Merrill and Rod Taylor in FAMILY FLIGHT (1972)

Clint Walker, Margot Kidder and John Ericson in THE BOUNTY MAN (1972)

Driskill	REX HOLMAN	Janet Salter	HOPE LANGE	George Benson	JIM BACKUS
Tully	WAYNE SUTHERLIN	Mr. Early (Conductor)	JAMES McEACHIN	Edna Benson	HENNY BACKUS
		Jody Bonner	JAN SHEPPARD	Lucy Kane	ABBY DALTON
Hargus	PAUL HARPER	Artist	CLARKE GORDON	Harold Kane	WALLY COX
Rufus	DENNIS CROSS	Mrs. Michele	CAROLYN BUONO	Virginia Wolfe	NANETTE FABRAY
Santana	VINCENT ST. CYR			Mrs. Vogel	SELMA DIAMOND
Gault	GLENN WILDER			Mr. Tracy	JOHN LARCH
Baker	ROB TOWNSEND			John Doolittle	CLINT KIMBROUGH

and: Patti Steele, Myron Natwick

An acclaimed drama illuminating the conflict between a divorced homosexual and his teenage son. Holbrook, Sheen, Jacoby and Lange all were nominated for Emmy Awards, and Lamont Johnson won the Directors Guild of America Award.

A bounty hunter in the Old West and his long-time rival are both after the reward for a young killer—dead or alive—but find themselves menaced by the outlaw's gang of cut-throats.

Toland	FRANK LATIMORE
Jamie Burke	JAMIE MacDOUGALL

and: Michael Lerner, Barbara Pilaven, Bud Walls, Casey MacDonald, Nona Medici, Bruno Boschetti, Linda De Felice

A language student living in Rome hires on as a tour guide and falls for a mysterious stowaway who is sought by the police in this filmed-on-location stellar (by TV standards) romp.

0251
THAT CERTAIN SUMMER
11/1/72 Universal (90 min)

Producers: Richard Levinson and William Link
Director: Lamont Johnson
Teleplay: Richard Levinson and William Link
Photography: Vilis Lapenieks
Music: Gil Melle
Art Director: William D. DeCinces
Editor: Edward M. Abroms

Doug Salter	HAL HOLBROOK
Gary McClain	MARTIN SHEEN
Phil Bonner	JOE DON BAKER
Laureen Hyatt	MARLYN MASON
Nick Salter	SCOTT JACOBY

0252
MAGIC CARPET
11/6/72 Universal (2 hours)

Producer: Ranald MacDougall
Director: William A. Graham
Teleplay: Ranald MacDougall
Photography: Pietro Portalupi
Music: Lyn Murray
Art Director: Franco Fumagelli
Editor: Richard G. Wray

Timothea Lamb	SUSAN SAINT JAMES
Josh Tracy	ROBERT PRATT
Roger Warden	CLIFF POTTS
Renato Caruso	ENZO CERUSICO

0253
THE CROOKED HEARTS
11/8/72 Lorimar Productions (90 min)

Executive Producer: Lee Rich
Producer: Allen S. Epstein
Director: Jay Sandrich
Teleplay: A. J. Russell
Based on the novel *Miss Lonelyhearts 4122* by Colin Watson

Photography: Joseph Biroc
Music: Billy Goldenberg
Art Director: Jan Scott
Editor: Gene Fowler, Jr.

Laurita Dorsey	ROSALIND RUSSELL
Rex Willoughby	DOUGLAS FAIRBANKS, JR.
Sgt. Daniel Shane	ROSS MARTIN
Frank Adamic	MICHAEL MURPHY
Lillian Stanton	MAUREEN O'SULLIVAN
James Simpson	KENT SMITH
Edward (Desk Clerk)	DICK VAN PATTEN
Taxi Driver	PATRICK CAMPBELL
Writer	LIAM DUNN
Waitress	PENNY MARSHALL
Fisherman	KENNETH TOBEY
Security Guard	BILL ZUCKERT

A charming but somewhat larcenous widow attempts to snare a rich bachelor through a lonelyhearts club, but her scheme boomerangs into a deadly cat-and-mouse game. This marked the TV-movie debut of both Rosalind Russell and Douglas Fairbanks, Jr., and was the last film role for the veteran actress.

0254
THE VICTIM
11/14/72 Universal (90 min)

Producer: William Frye
Director: Herschel Daugherty
Teleplay: Merwin Gerard

Hal Holbrook, Scott Jacoby and Martin Sheen in THAT CERTAIN SUMMER (1972)

Elizabeth Montgomery and George Maharis in THE VICTIM (1972)

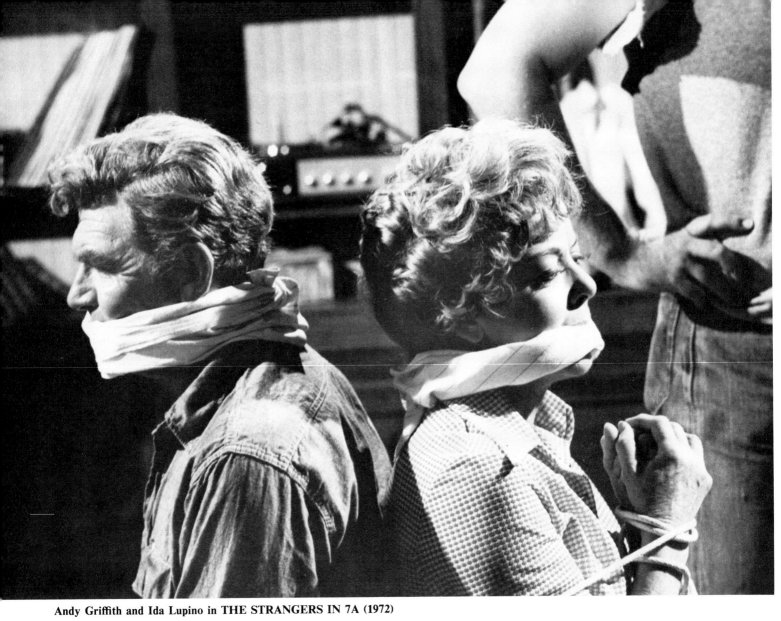

Andy Griffith and Ida Lupino in THE STRANGERS IN 7A (1972)

Michael Brandon and Ida Lupino in THE STRANGERS IN 7A (1972)

Jennifer Salt and Cornel Wilde in GARGOYLES (1972)

From a story by MacIntoch Malmar
Photography: Michael Joyce
Music: Gil Melle
Art Director: Henry Bumstead
Editor: Douglas Stewart and John Kaufman, Jr.

Katherine Wainwright	ELIZABETH MONTGOMERY
Mrs. Hawks	EILEEN HECKART
Edith Jordan	SUE ANE LANGDON
Ben Chappel	GEORGE MAHARIS
Susan Chappel	JESS WALTON
Highway Patrolman	RICHARD DERR
1st Patrolman	ROSS ELLIOTT
George (Butler)	GEORGE JUE
2nd Patrolman	JOE FURLONG

A wealthy woman is trapped by a fierce storm in the house with no electricity or phone, her murdered sister's body hidden in the basement, and a killer waiting for an opportunity to make her his next victim.

0255
THE STRANGERS IN 7A
11/14/72 Palomar International (90 min)

Producer: Mark Carliner
Director: Paul Wendkos
Teleplay: Eric Roth
Based on the novel by Fielden Farrington
Photography: Robert B. Hauser
Music: Morton Stevens

Art Director: James G. Hulsey
Editor: Bud S. Isaacs

Artie Sawyer	ANDY GRIFFITH
Iris Sawyer	IDA LUPINO
Billy	MICHAEL BRANDON
Riff	JAMES A. WATSON, JR.
Virgil	TIM McINTIRE
Claudine	SUSANNE HILDUR
Mrs. Layton	CONNIE SAWYER
Danny (Bartender)	JOE MELL
Miss Simpson	VICTORIA CARROLL
Pete	SQUIRE FRIDELL
Woman	VIRGINIA VINCENT
Policeman	MARC HANNIBAL
Old Woman	CHARLOTTE KNIGHT

A building superintendent and his wife are held hostage in their apartment by a sadistic would-be bank robber and his spaced-out accomplices.

0256
GARGOYLES
11/21/72 Tomorrow Entertainment (90 min)

Executive Producer: Roger Gimbel
Producers: Robert W. Christiansen and Rick Rosenberg
Director: B. W. L. Norton

Teleplay: Stephen and Elinor Karpf
Photography: Earl Rath
Music: Robert Prince
Assistant Director: Claude Binyon, Jr.
Editor: Frank P. Keller

Mercer Boley	CORNEL WILDE
Diana Boley	JENNIFER SALT
Mrs. Parks	GRAYSON HALL
Head Gargoyle	BERNIE CASEY
James Reeger	SCOTT GLENN
Police Chief	WILLIAM STEVENS
Uncle Willie	WOODROW CHAMBLISS
Jesse	JOHN GRUBER
Ray	TIM BURNS
Buddy	JIM CONNELL

and: Mickey Alzola, Greg Walker, Rock Walker

A horror tale involving an anthropologist researching his book on demonology with his photographer daughter in a bizarre adventure that has a group of gargoyles, descendants of a monster whose skeleton the two have stumbled on, menacing the pair in order to retrieve the bones of their ancestor.

0257
ALL MY DARLING DAUGHTERS
11/22/72 Universal (90 min)

Executive Producer: David Victor
Producer: David J. O'Connell
Director: David Lowell Rich

Julie Harris, Eleanor Parker, Jill Haworth and Sally Field in HOME FOR THE HOLIDAYS (1972)

Teleplay: John Gay
From a story by Robert Presnell, Jr. and Stan Dreben
Photography: Walter Strenge
Music: Billy Goldenberg
Art Director: Russell G. Forrest
Editor: Richard G. Wray

Judge Charles Raleigh	ROBERT YOUNG
Miss Freeling	EVE ARDEN
Matthew Cunningham	RAYMOND MASSEY
Susan	DARLEEN CARR
Robin	JUDY STRANGIS
Jennifer	SHARON GLESS
Charlotte	FAWNE HARRIMAN
Andy O'Brien	DARRELL LARSON
Jerry Greene	JERRY FOGEL
Bradley Coombs	COLBY CHESTER
Biff Brynner	MICHAEL RICHARDSON
Anthony Stephanelli	BRUCE KIRBY, JR.
District Attorney	JOHN LUPTON
Defense Attorney	RICHARD ROAT
Witness	VIRGINIA GREGG

This plotline involves a judge with four daughters, four prospective sons-in-law, and four weddings scheduled for the same day.

0258
HOME FOR THE HOLIDAYS
11/28/72 ABC Circle Films (90 min)

Executive Producers: Aaron Spelling and Leonard Goldenberg
Producer: Paul Junger Witt
Associate Producer: Tony Thomas
Director: John Llewellyn Moxey
Teleplay: Joseph Stefano
Photography: Leonard J. South
Music: George Aliceson Tipton
Art Director: Rolland M. Brooks
Editor: Allan Jacobs

Christine Morgan	SALLY FIELD
Joanna	JILL HAWORTH
Elizabeth Hall Morgan	JULIE HARRIS
Alex Morgan	ELEANOR PARKER
Benjamin Morgan	WALTER BRENNAN
Dr. Ted Lindsay	JOHN FINK
Sheriff Nolan	MED FLORY

A suspense tale in which ailing Walter Brennan summons his three daughters home for Christmas and asks them to kill his much younger wife (Julie Harris) who he suspects is trying to poison him. It marked Brennan's last screen role.

0259
THE HEIST
11/29/72 Paramount (90 min)

Producers: Thomas L. Miller and Edward K. Milkis
Director: Don McDougall
Teleplay: Lionel E. Siegel
Photography: Al Francis
Music: Robert Drasnin
Art Director: William Campbell
Editor: Mike Vejar

Joe Craddock	CHRISTOPHER GEORGE
Diane Craddock	ELIZABETH ASHLEY
Lt. Nicholson	HOWARD DUFF
Pat Dillon	NORMAN FELL
John Cadiski	MICHAEL BELL
Tom Logan	CLIFF OSMOND
Owens	ROBERT MANDAN
Wendy Craddock	KAMI COTLER
Slausen	DEL MONROE
Ridley	COLIN HIGGINS
D'Amico	ARTHUR BATANIDES
Maxwell	STACY KEACH, SR.

Christopher George and Howard Duff in THE HEIST (197

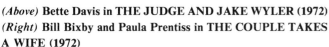

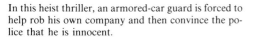

(Above) **Bette Davis in THE JUDGE AND JAKE WYLER (1972)**
(Right) **Bill Bixby and Paula Prentiss in THE COUPLE TAKES A WIFE (1972)**

In this heist thriller, an armored-car guard is forced to help rob his own company and then convince the police that he is innocent.

0260
THE JUDGE AND JAKE WYLER
12/2/72 Universal (2 hours)

Producers: Richard Levinson and William Link
Associate Producer: Jay Benson
Director: David Lowell Rich
Teleplay: David Shaw, Richard Levinson and William Link
Photography: William Margulies
Music: Gil Melle
Art Director: Alexander A. Mayer
Editor: Budd Small

Judge Meredith	BETTE DAVIS
Jake Wyler	DOUG McCLURE
Anton Granicek	ERIC BRAEDEN
Alicia Dodd	JOAN VAN ARK
Frank Morrison	GARY CONWAY
Lt. Wolfson	LOU JACOBI
Quint	JAMES McEACHIN
Caroline Dodd	LISABETH HUSH
Robert Dodd	KENT SMITH
Chloe Jones	BARBARA RHOADES
James Rockmore	JOHN RANDOLPH
Mr. Gilbert	MILT KAMEN
Sen. Joseph Pritchard	JOHN LUPTON

and: Michael Fox, Rosanna Huffman, Eddie Quillan, Celeste Yarnell, Ray Ballard, Virginia Capers, Myron Natwick, Harriett E. MacGibbon, Stuart Nisbet, Steven Peck, Don Diamond, Margarita Cordova, Khalil Ben Bezaleel

A light-hearted whodunit involving a retired lady judge, who is a hypochondriac now running a private detective agency, with a charming ex-con as her leg man and various parolees helping in the day-to-day operation. This prospective pilot failed to catch on and later was tried once more with Lee Grant and Lou Antonio in the Davis/McClure roles.

0261
THE COUPLE TAKES A WIFE
12/5/72 Universal (90 min)

Producer: George Eckstein
Director: Jerry Paris
Teleplay: Susan Silver
Photography: Bud F. Mautino
Music: Dick DeBenedictis
Art Director: Joseph Alves, Jr.
Editors: Aaron Stell and Bill Brame

Jeff Hamilton	BILL BIXBY
Barbara Hamilton	PAULA PRENTISS
Mrs. Flanagan	MYRNA LOY
Randy Perkins	ROBERT GOULET
Marion Randolph	NANETTE FABRAY
David	LARRY STORCH
Jennifer Allen	VALERIE PERRINE
Christy Hamilton	MIA BENDIXSON
Mindy Hamilton	DANA LAURITA
Paula	PENNY MARSHALL
Ginger	DWAN SMITH
Maria	CARMEN ZAPATA

and: Helen Kleeb, Bert Holland

An independent-minded couple, each insisting on a business career, decide to hire a second "wife"—someone who looks like a model and works like a scrubwoman—to take care of the house and kids, but the three-way arrangement threatens to break up the marriage.

0262
A WAR OF CHILDREN
12/5/72 Tomorrow Entertainment (90 min)

Executive Producer: Roger Gimbel
Producer/Director: George Schaefer
Teleplay: James Costigan
Photography: Chris Challis
Music: Jerry Fielding
Editor: Anne V. Coates

Nora Tomelty	VIVIEN MERCHANT
Maureen Tomelty	JENNY AGUTTER
Frank Tomelty	JOHN RONANE
Donal Tomelty	DANNY FIGGIS
Reg Hogg	ANTHONY ANDREWS
Meg McCullum	AIDEEN O'KELLY
Ian McCullum	OLIVER MAGUIRE
Robbie McCullum	DAVID MEREDITH
Seamus Lynch	PATRICK DAWSON
British Lieutenant	DESMAN NEALON
British Soldier	STUART KNEE

and: Kathleen Delaney, Brenda Doyle, Maura Keeley, Arthur O'Sullivan, Pat Laffan, Conor Evans, Paul Wilson

This Emmy Award-winning drama, chosen the Outstanding Program of the 1972–73 TV season, depicted two middle-class Belfast families—one Protestant, one Catholic—that discovered themselves engulfed in the surrounding violence that turned their years of friendship to bitter hatred which ultimately filtered to their children's lives.

0263
PURSUIT
12/12/72 ABC Circle Films (90 min)

Executive Producer: Lee Rich
Producer: Robert L. Jacks
Director: Michael Crichton
Teleplay: Robert Dozier
Based on the novel *Binary* by John Lange (Michael Crichton)
Photography: Robert L. Morrison
Music: Jerry Goldsmith
Art Director: Robert Smith
Editor: Gene Fowler, Jr.

Steven Graves	BEN GAZZARA
James Wright	E. G. MARSHALL
Robert Phillips	WILLIAM WINDOM
Dr. Peter Nordmann	JOSEPH WISEMAN
Lewis	JIM McMULLAN
Timothy Drew	MARTIN SHEEN
Dr. Wolff	WILL KULUVA
Agent	HANK BRANDT
Capt. Morrison	QUINN REDECKER

and: Joe Brooks, Robert Cleaves, Conrad Beckman

A government agent tries to keep an extremist from decimating with stolen nerve gas a city where a political convention is underway in this suspense thriller that marked the directorial debut of surgeon-turned-novelist Michael Crichton.

0264
EVERY MAN NEEDS ONE
12/13/72 ABC Circle Films (90 min)

Executive Producers: Aaron Spelling and Leonard Goldberg
Producer/Director: Jerry Paris
Teleplay: Carl Kleinschmitt
Photography: William T. Cline
Music: Jack Elliott and Allyn Ferguson
Art Director: Rolland M. Brooks
Editor: Bob Wyman

Beth Walden	CONNIE STEVENS
David Chase	KEN BERRY
Pauline Kramer	GAIL FISHER
Bob Rasmussen	STEVE FRANKEN
Walt	HENRY GIBSON
Marty Ranier	JERRY PARIS
Louise Lathrop	LOUISE SOREL
David's Mother	NANCY WALKER
Nancy	CAROL WAYNE
Bus Driver	STANLEY ADAMS
Hotel Clerk	OGDEN TALBOT
McMillan	BUCK GEE

A swinging bachelor architect is pressured into hiring a dedicated women's libber as his assistant and finds himself falling for her.

0265
THE SNOOP SISTERS
12/18/72 Universal (2 hours)
(subsequently titled *Female Instinct*)

Executive Producer: Leonard Stern
Producer: Douglas Benton
Director: Leonard Stern

(Right) **Ken Berry and Connie Stevens in EVERY MAN NEEDS ONE (1972)**

(Below) **Ben Gazzara, William Windom and Jim McMullan in PURSUIT (1972)**

Mildred Natwick, Art Carney and Helen Hayes in THE SNOOP SISTERS (1972)

Teleplay: Leonard Stern and Hugh Wheeler
From a story by Allan Sharpe
Photography: Harry L. Wolf
Music: Jerry Fielding
Art Director: Kenneth Reid
Editor: Edward W. Williams

Ernesta Snoop	HELEN HAYES
Gwendolyn Snoop Nicholson	MILDRED NATWICK
Barney	ART CARNEY
Norma Treat	PAULETTE GODDARD
Charlie	CHARLIE CALLAS
Mary Nero	JILL CLAYBURGH
Melvin Kaplan	BILL DANA
Milo Perkins	ED FLANDERS
Alexander Scalamandre	KURT KASZNAR
Julius Nero	ED PLATT
Warren Packer	KENT SMITH
Charles Corman	CRAIG STEVENS
Anton de Tourolet	FRITZ WEAVER
Lt. Steven Ostrowski	LAWRENCE PRESSMAN
Pinky Allen	GLORIA STROOK
Frank	IGGIE WOOLFINGTON
Detective	BART BURNS

An engaging comedy-mystery about a couple of eccentric mystery writers, a spinster and her widowed sister, who turn detective to hunt down the killer of a faded movie star (Paulette Goddard, who came out of retirement to play the role) with the help of their ex-con bodyguard/chauffeur, hired by their police lieutenant nephew to keep them out of trouble. This was the pilot for the brief series (1973–74): four episodes as rotating elements of the "NBC Tuesday Mystery Movie." Actresses Hayes and Natwick distinguished the series and were joined by actor/director Lou Antonio and game show host Bert Convy in the two roles originated by Art Carney and Lawrence Pressman.

0266
YOUR MONEY OR YOUR WIFE
12/19/72 Brentwood Productions (90 min)

Executive Producer: Alexander H. Cohen
Producer: Everett Rosenthal
Director: Allen Reisner
Teleplay: J. P. Miller
Based on the novel *If You Want To See Your Wife Again* by John Craig
Photography: Dick Kratina
Music: Elliott Lawrence
Art Director: Peter Dohanos
Editors: Dorton Fallick and Barbara Franks

Dan Cramer	TED BESSELL
Laurel Plunkett	ELIZABETH ASHLEY
Josh Darwin	JACK CASSIDY
Jill Bennett	BETSY VON FURSTENBERG
Bo Tinsley	RICHARD PEABODY
Richard Bannister	GRAHAM JARVIS
Himself	ALFRED DRAKE
Jeannie	PAT CAREY
TV Director	ALEX CORT
Fair	LOUIS EDMONDS
Vinnie	PETER LIGHTSTONE

A wacky comedy caper about a TV script writer taking revenge on an actress who walks out on his program to become the wife of the wealthy sponsor, putting a damper on many careers, by writing her into a kidnapping scheme and then turning fiction into fact.

0267
THE WEEKEND NUN
12/20/72 Paramount (90 min)

Producers: Thomas L. Miller and Edward K. Milkis
Director: Jeannot Szwarc
Teleplay: Ken Trevey
Photography: Ronald W. Browne
Music: Charles Fox
Art Director: William Campbell
Editor: Rita Roland

Sister Mary Damian/Marjorie Walker	JOANNA PETTET
Chuck Jardine	VIC MORROW
Mother Bonaventure	ANN SOTHERN
Sid Richardson	JAMES GREGORY
Bobby Sue Prewitt	BEVERLY GARLAND
Andree Prewitt	KAY LENZ
Rick Seiden	MICHAEL CLARK
Bernetta	TINA ANDREWS
Priest	JUDSON PRATT

and: Barbara Werle, Lynn Borden, Marian Ross, Stephen Rogers, Ann Summers

Drama based on the life of Joyce Duco, with Joanna Pettet as a young nun torn between the reality of her secular job as a daytime juvenile probation officer and the vows she has taken with the Church. Original title: *Matter of the Heart.*

0268
CLIMB AN ANGRY MOUNTAIN
12/23/72 Warner Bros. (2 hours)

Executive Producer: Herbert E. Solow
Director: Leonard Horn
Teleplay: Joseph Calvelli and Sam Rolfe
Photography: Michel Hugo
Music: George Duning
Editors: Neil Travis and Nicholas M. Archer

Sheriff Elisha Cooper	FESS PARKER
May Franklin	MARJ DUSAY
Sunny	ARTHUR HUNNICUTT
Lt. Frank Bryant	BARRY NELSON
Joey Chilko	JOE KAPP
Sheila Chilko	STELLA STEVENS
Michael Cooper	CLAY O'BRIEN
Christina Cooper	JEWEL BRANCH
Javis Dwiggins	RICHARD BRIAN HARRIS
Buck Moto	CASEY TIBBS
Huggins	KENNETH WASHINGTON
Minister	J. C. McELROY

A widowed rancher sheriff clashes with a hard-nosed New York cop over the techniques for pursing a fugitive Indian up the side of California's Mount Shasta.

Elizabeth Ashley and Ted Bessell in YOUR MONEY OR YOUR WIFE (1972)

0269
FIREHOUSE
1/2/73 Metromedia Productions/Stonehenge (90 min)

Executive Producer: Dick Berg
Producer: Joe Manduke
Director: Alex March
Teleplay: Frank Cucci
Photography: Alan Stensvold
Music: Tom Scott
Art Director: Rodger Maus
Editor: John A. Martinelli

Shelly Forsythe	RICHARD ROUNDTREE
Spike Ryerson	VINCE EDWARDS
Captain Parr	ANDREW DUGGAN
Hank Myers	RICHARD JAECKEL
Michelle Forsythe	SHEILA FRAZIER
Sonny Caputo	VAL AVERY
Dalzell	PAUL LeMAT
Ernie Bush	MICHAEL LERNER
Mamu	MEL SCOTT
Doyle	HOWARD CURTIS
Landlord	JOSHUA SHELLEY

Conflict erupts within a close-knit engine company of a big city fire department when a black recruit and a bigoted white veteran clash during a wave of suspected arson in the ghetto. Pilot to the short-lived series that began a run in January 1974, with James Drury (replacing Vince Edwards) and Richard Jaeckel.

Vic Morrow and Joanna Pettet in THE WEEKEND NUN (1972)

Vince Edwards and Richard Roundtree in FIREHOUSE (1973)

0270
THE 500-POUND JERK
1/2/73 Wolper Productions (90 min)

Executive Producer: David L. Wolper
Producer: Stan Margulies
Director: William Kronick
Teleplay: James P. Henderson
Photography: Herbert Raditschnig
Music: Neal Hefti
Editor: James T. Heckert

Gil Davenport	JAMES FRANCISCUS
Karen Walsh	HOPE LANGE
Hughie Rae Feather	ALEX KARRAS
Natalya	CLAUDIA BUTENUTH
Mickey	RICK PARSE
Lermontov	HEINZ VIERTALER
Martin Bloore	VICTOR SPINETTI
Glabov	RALPH WOLTER
Himself	HOWARD COSELL

Hope Lange and James Franciscus in THE 500-POUND JERK (1973)

Chuck Connors (and Paul Fix in photo) in SET THIS TOWN ON FIRE (1973)

An ad-man's dreams of grooming a gentle hillbilly giant into an overnight weight-lifting champion, have him win a gold medal, and then endorse a breakfast cereal are shattered when his protégé falls in love with a petite Russian gymnast and almost ignites an international incident.

0271
SET THIS TOWN ON FIRE
1/8/73 Universal (2 hours)
(subsequently titled *The Profane Comedy*)

Executive Producer: Roy Huggins
Producer/Director: David Lowell Rich
Associate Producer: Carl Pingitore
Teleplay: John Thomas James
Photography: Gene Polito
Music: Pete Rugolo
Art Director: Robert Luthardt
Editor: John Dumas

Buddy Bates	CHUCK CONNORS
Andy Wells	CARL BETZ
Molly Thornburgh	LYNDA DAY
Brad Wells	CHARLES ROBINSON
Henry Kealey	JOHN ANDERSON
Walter Stafford	JEFF COREY
Carl Rickter	JAMES WESTERFIELD
Senator Porter	PAUL FIX
Shirley Hammond	NANCY MALONE
Stabler	VAUGHN TAYLOR
Alice Whittier	JOAN TOMPKINS
Chief Murdoch	TOL AVERY
Motel Manager	SAM EDWARDS
Chuck	BING RUSSELL
Ralph	BOB RODES
Chairman	BILL QUINN

and William Blakewell, Maurice Wells, Ray Montgomery, Drew R. Handley, James Gavin, Michael Masters, Jim Neumarker, Vince Deadrick, Mary L. DeCinces

After serving seven years for manslaughter, a man returns home to run for mayor following the disclosure that the local newspaper editor whose eyewitness testimony had put him behind bars now has second thoughts and the town drunk now has confessed to the crime. Filmed in 1969 as *The Profane Comedy* (its once and future title), it gathered dust in a Universal vault for nearly four years.

0272
THE DEVIL'S DAUGHTER
1/9/73 Paramount (90 min)

Producers: Thomas L. Miller and Edward K. Milkis
Director: Jeannot Szwarc
Teleplay: Colin Higgins
Photography: J. J. Jones
Music: Laurence Rosenthal
Art Director: William Campbell
Editor: Rita Roland

Lilith Malone	SHELLEY WINTERS
Diane Shaw	BELINDA J. MONTGOMERY
Steve Stone	ROBERT FOXWORTH
Mr. Howard	JONATHAN FRID
Mrs. Stone	MARTHA SCOTT
Judge Wetherby	JOSEPH COTTEN
Susan Sanford	BARBARA SAMMETH
Alice Shaw	DIANE LADD
Janet Poole	LUCILLE BENSON
Margaret Poole	THELMA CARPENTER
Alikhine	ABE VIGODA

Joseph Cotten and Belinda J. Montgomery in THE DEVIL'S DAUGHTER (1973)

Shelley Winters and Belinda J. Montgomery in THE DEVIL'S DAUGHTER (1973)

Father MacHugh	IAN WOLFE
Pastor Dixon	ROBERT CORNTHWAITE
Fedora	ROZELLE GAYLE
Turk	NICK BOLIN
Landlady	LILLIAN BRONSON

A young girl whose mother had sold her soul to the devil in infancy is now called to the fold by Satan (in the guise of Shelley Winters) who tries to marry her off to a fellow demon. This devil-worshipping horror tale was assembled by the producers and the writer of such later collaborations as *Silver Streak* and *Foul Play*.

0273
HUNTER
1/9/73 CBS, Inc. (90 min)

Producer: Bruce Geller
Director: Leonard Horn
Teleplay: Cliff Gould
Created by Bruce Geller
Photography: Jerry Sims
Music: Lalo Schifrin
Art Director: Allen Smith
Editors: Mel Shapiro and Patrick Kennedy

David Hunter/Praetorius	JOHN VERNON
Alain Praetorius	STEVE IHNAT
Anne Novak	SABINA SCHARF
Owen Larkdale	EDWARD BINNS
Cirrak	FRITZ WEAVER
Mishani	RAMON BIERI
McDaniel	JOHN SCHUCK
Girl	BARBARA RHOADES

Alfred Blunt	ROGER BOWEN	Cecil Tabor	PAT HINGLE	Deaver Wallace	WILLIAM SHATNER
Tyson	WOODROW PARFREY	Horace Speare	HARI RHODES	Edmund Schilling	MURRAY HAMILTON
Albert Treadway	LONNY CHAPMAN	Naomi Speare	JANET MacLACHLAN	Dominic Leopold	GILBERT ROLAND
Dr. Miles	ED FLANDERS	Mrs. Murdock	SHEREE NORTH	Attorney Gallagher	JOHN KERR
Dr. Abrams	SHELDON ALLMAN	Stacy Garrett	THOMAS EVANS	Louise Trenier	KATHY LLOYD
Lubbock	DAVY JONES	Billy Keith	JOSEPH BOTTOMS	John Pine	WESLEY LAU
Griggs	TONY VAN BRIDGE	Darren Fox	DAMON DOUGLAS	Miles Henderson	DONALD BARRY
Donnelly	LAWRENCE COOK	Buchanan	JAMES WHEATON	Luke Burgess	DAVID DOYLE
Gunner	WALTER STOCKER	Bubba Speare	WILBUR GOODY	Mayor	GORDON PINSENT
				Arthur Trenier	JAMES DAVIDSON

In this pilot for a projected spy series by the man who gave "Mission: Impossible" to TV, a fatal racetrack crash in which a government agent is critically injured uncovers an enemy brainwashing scheme, and another agent assumes his colleague's identity to expose the plot. Made in 1971 and originally scheduled for a spring 1972 airing, *Hunter* finally emerged after nearly two years on the shelf.

and: Bill Zuckert, Thom Charney, Morris Buchanan

A racial drama involving a liberal southern sheriff who brings into his home a northern black delinquent, the son of the man who had saved his life in Korea.

and: Jerry Thor, Mark Jenkins, Jenny Kulik, Marlene Clark, Susan Stafford, Tony Giorgio, Valentine de Vargas, Marian Collier, Roland LaStarza, Earl Ebi, Nicholas Konakas, Michele Nichols, Michael W. Siokey, Owen Orr, Jed Allen, Robyn Millian

A small-time hood is murdered as he is about to blow the whistle on the syndicate in this pilot for a prospective series about the day-to-day operations of the U.S. Attorney's office in the Justice Department.

0274
TROUBLE COMES TO TOWN
1/10/73 ABC Circle Films (90 min)

Producer: Everett Chambers
Director: Daniel Petrie
Teleplay: David Westheimer
Photography Richard C. Glouner
Music: Tom Scott
Song "Good Morning World" by Cheryl Dilcher
Editor: James Mitchell

Sheriff Porter Murdock LLOYD BRIDGES

0275
INCIDENT ON A DARK STREET
1/13/73 20th Century-Fox (2 hours)

Executive Producer: David Gerber
Producer: E. Jack Neumann
Director: Buzz Kulik
Teleplay: E. Jack Neumann
Photography: Charles F. Wheeler
Music: Elmer Bernstein
Editor: Rita Roland

Joseph Dubbs	JAMES OLSON
Pete Gallagher	DAVID CANARY
Paul Hamilton	ROBERT PINE
Frank Romeo	RICHARD CASTELLANO

0276
FRANKENSTEIN
1/16-17/73 Dan Curtis Productions (3 hours)

Producer: Dan Curtis
Director: Glenn Jordan
Teleplay: Sam Hall (Part 1) and Richard Landau (Part 2)
Based on the novel by Mary Shelley
Photography: Ben Colman

Hari Rhodes and Lloyd Bridges in TROUBLE COMES TO TOWN (1973)

Music: Robert Cobert
Art Director: Trevor Williams
Editor: Dennis Virkler

Dr. Victor Frankenstein	ROBERT FOXWORTH
Elizabeth Lavenza	SUSAN STRASBERG
Monster	BO SVENSON
Agatha DeLacey	HEIDI VAUGHN
Alphonse Frankenstein	PHILIP BOURNEUF
Henri Clerval	ROBERT GENTRY
Charles DeLacey	JON LORMER
Professor Waldman	WILLIAM HANSEN
Otto Roget	JOHN KARLEN
Hugo	GEORGE MORGAN
Felix	BRIAN AVERY
Safie	MALILA SAINT DUVAL
William Frankenstein	WILLIE AMES
Bride of the Monster	ROSELLA OLSON

Dan Curtis' retelling of the all-time Gothic horror classic, one of the favorite subjects among moviemakers. This was a two-parter shown in ninety-minute segments on successive nights as part of ABC's late night "Wide World of Mystery" series.

0277
THE NIGHT STRANGLER
1/16/73 ABC Circle Films (90 min)

Producer/Director: Dan Curtis
Teleplay: Richard Matheson
Based on characters created by Jeff Rice
Photography: Robert B. Hauser
Music: Robert Cobert
Art Director: Trevor Williams
Monster Makeup: William J. Tuttle
Editor: Folmar Blangsted

Carl Kolchak	DARREN McGAVIN
Louise Harper	JO ANN PFLUG
Joe Vincenzo	SIMON OAKLAND
Capt. Roscoe Schubert	SCOTT BRADY
Titus Berry	WALLY COX
Professor Crabwell	MARGARET HAMILTON
Llewellyn Crossbinder	JOHN CARRADINE
Charisma Beauty (Gladys Weems)	NINA WAYNE
Dr. Christopher Webb	IVOR FRANCIS
Dr. Richard Malcolm	RICHARD ANDERSON
Wilma Krankhamer	VIRGINIA PETERS
Janie	KATE MURTAGH
Ethel Murray	REGINA PARTON

A monster-chasing reporter finds himself searching Seattle for a killer whose grisly record seems to stretch back more than a century, making an appearance every twenty-one years. This sequel to *The Night Stalker* (1971) led to the near-cult "Kolchak" series (1974–75) that had Darren McGavin trying week after week to convince Simon Oakland, his skeptical editor, of the most bizarre monster stories. Original title: *The Time Killer.*

0278
THE VOYAGE OF THE YES
1/16/73 Bing Crosby Productions (90 min)

Producer: Andrew J. Fenady
Director: Lee H. Katzin
Teleplay: William Stratton
Photography: John A. Alonzo
Music: Richard Markowitz
Song "El Condor Pasa" sung by Desi Arnaz, Jr. and Mike Evans
Technical Advisor: Hilyard Brown
Editor: Mel Shapiro

Darren McGavin in THE NIGHT STRANGLER (1973)

Cal Markwell	DESI ARNAZ, JR.
Orlando B. Parker	MIKE EVANS
Agatha Markwell	BEVERLY GARLAND
Arnold Markwell	SKIP HOMEIER
Pretty	SCOEY MITCHLLL
Opal Parker	DELLA REESE
Dick Stanwood	DICK POWELL, JR.
Lieutenant Matthews	STEVE MARLO
Peter Reed	ED McCREADY
Doctor	STEVE FRANKEN
Philip Blemsley	BEN WRIGHT

Two teenagers embark on a 2,600-mile journey from California to Hawaii in a sailboat, battling the elements as well as their own prejudices.

0279
FEMALE ARTILLERY
1/17/73 Universal (90 min)

Producer: Winston Miller
Director: Marvin Chomsky
Teleplay: Bud Freeman
From a story by Jack Sher and Bud Freeman
Photography: Enzo A. Martinelli
Music: Frank DeVol
Art Director: Sydney Z. Litwack
Editors: John Elias, John Kaufman, Jr. and Albert J. Zuniga

Deke Chambers	DENNIS WEAVER
Martha Lindstrom	IDA LUPINO
Sybil Townsend	SALLY ANN HOWES
Charlotte Paxton	LINDA EVANS
Brian Townsend	LEE HARCOURT MONTGOMERY
Frank Taggert	ALBERT SALMI
Amelia Craig	NINA FOCH
Sarah Gallado	ANNA NAVARRO
Sam	CHARLES DIERKOP
Johnny	NATE ESFORMES
Squat	LEE DeBROUX
Scotto	ROBERT SORRELLS

and: Bobby Eilbacher, Robby Weaver

A comedy western that has a tough outlaw joining forces with a contingent of pioneer women against a vicious gang that wants the money he secretly hid in the ladies' wagon train.

Desi Arnaz, Jr., and Mike Evans in THE VOYAGE OF THE YES (1973)

Desi Arnaz, Jr., and Beverly Garland in THE VOYAGE OF THE YES (1973)

0280
GO ASK ALICE
1/24/73 Metromedia Productions (90 min)

Executive Producer: Charles Fries
Producer: Gerald I. Isenberg
Director: John Korty
Teleplay: Ellen M. Violett
Photography: Earl Rath
Music: Joel Sill, Michael O'Martin and Bill Schnee
Art Director: Rodger Maus
Editor: Henry Berman

Alice	JAMIE SMITH-JACKSON
Sam	WILLIAM SHATNER
Psychiatrist	RUTH ROMAN
Joel Clements	WENDELL BURTON
Dorothy	JULIE ADAMS
Priest	ANDY GRIFFITH
Jan	ANN RUYMAN
Beth Bonds	MIMI SAFFIAN
Chris	JENNIFER EDWARDS
Richie	DANIEL MICHAEL MANN
Tim	MICHAEL MORGAN
Jean	JEANNE AVERY
Ted	FREDERICK HERRICK
Bill	ROBERT CARRADINE
Tom	GARY MARSH

A drama based on the actual diary of a teenage girl caught in a web of drug addiction who, with the help of her family and true friends, desperately tries to fight her way back to the real world after a bad LSD trip.

0281
BIRDS OF PREY
1/30/73 Tomorrow Entertainment (90 min)

Executive Producer: Roger Gimbel
Producer: Alan A. Armer
Director: William A. Graham
Teleplay: Robert Boris
From a story by Rupert Hitzig and Robert Boris
Photography: Jordan Cronenweth
Music: Jack Elliott and Allyn Ferguson
Assistant Director: Phil Rawlins
Aerial Supervisor: Jim Gavin
Editor: Jim Benson

Harry Walker	DAVID JANSSEN
Jim McAndrew	RALPH MEEKER
T.J.	ELAYNE HEILVEIL
Captain Slater	HARRY KLEKAS
Inspector Sinclair	SAM DAWSON
Trucker	DON WILBANKS
Police Pilot	GAVIN JAMES
Robbers	WAYNE WILKINSON
	LARRY PEACEY
	LARRY DOLL

A suspense thriller about a World War II ace turned traffic reporter for a Salt Lake City radio station who witnesses a bank robbery from his helicopter and is drawn into an aerial duel with the gang.

0282
A COLD NIGHT'S DEATH
1/30/73 ABC Circle Films (90 min)

Executive Producers: Aaron Spelling and Leonard Goldberg
Producer: Paul Junger Witt
Director: Jerrold Freedman
Teleplay: Christopher Knopf
Photography: Leonard J. South
Music: Gil Melle
Art Director: Rolland M. Brooks
Editor: David Berlatsky

Dr. Robert Jones	ROBERT CULP
Dr. Frank Enari	ELI WALLACH
Val Adams	MICHAEL C. GWYNNE

An offbeat psychological horror tale in which two scientists, snowbound in an Arctic research station while looking into the death of a colleague, find themselves stalked by an unknown force. *The Chill Factor* was its original title during production.

0283
BAFFLED!
1/30/73 Arena Productions/I.T.C. (2 hours)

Executive Producer: Norman Felton
Producer/Director: Philip Leacock
Associate Producer: John Oldknow
Teleplay: Theodore Apstein
Photography: Ken Hodges
Music: Richard Hill
Art Director: Harry Pottle
Editor: Bill Blunden

Tom Kovack	LEONARD NIMOY
Michele Brent	SUSAN HAMPSHIRE
Mrs. Farraday	RACHEL ROBERTS
Andrea Glenn	VERA MILES
Jennifer Glenn	JEWEL BLANCH
Louise Sanford	VALERIE TAYLOR
George Tracewell	RAY BROOKS
Peggy Tracewell	ANGHARAD REES

Jamie Smith-Jackson and Andy Griffith in GO ASK ALICE (1973)

Robert Culp and Eli Wallach in A COLD NIGHT'S DEATH (1973)

Verelli	CHRISTOPHER BENJAMIN
Duncan Sanford/John Parrish	MIKE MURRAY
Hopkins	EWAN ROBERTS
Dr. Reed	MILTON JOHNS
TV Interviewer	AL MANCINI

and: John Rae, Patsy Smart, Shane Rimmer, Roland Brand, Bill Hutchinson, Frank Mann, Michael Sloan, Dan Meaden

An American race driver has visions that are premonitions of danger and joins with a lady psychiatrist, specializing in ESP, to prevent future tragedies and sort out his unaccountable images.

0284
SNATCHED
1/31/73 ABC Circle Films (90 min)

Executive Producers: Aaron Spelling and Leonard Goldberg
Producer: Tony Thomas
Director: Sutton Roley
Teleplay: Rick Husky
Photography: Leonard J. South
Music: Randy Edelman
Art Director: Rolland M. Brooks
Editor: Howard Kunin

Duncan Ward	HOWARD DUFF
Bill Sutter	LESLIE NIELSEN
Kim Sutter	SHEREE NORTH
Barbara Maxville	BARBARA PARKINS
Frank McCloy	ROBERT REED

Leonard Nimoy and Susan Hampshire in BAFFLED! (1973)

Tisha Sterling, Sheree North and Barbara Parkins in SNATCHED (1973)

Richard Burton and Elizabeth Taylor in DIVORCE HIS/DIVORCE HERS (1973)

Paul Maxville	JOHN SAXON
Robin Wood	TISHA STERLING
Boone	ANTHONY ZERBE
Whit	RICHARD DAVALOS
Cheech	FRANK McRAE
Russell	BART LaRUE
1st Detective	HOWARD PLATT
2nd Detective	JOHN GILGREEN

The wives of three wealthy men are kidnapped and held for $3,000,000 in ransom, but one husband refuses to pay his share.

0285
DIVORCE HIS/DIVORCE HERS
2/6–7/73 World Film Services (90 min each)

Executive Producer: John Heyman
Producers: Terence Baker and Gareth Wigen
Director: Waris Hussein
Teleplay: John Hopkins
Photography: Ernst Wild and Gabor Pogany
Music: Stanley Myers
Art Director: Roy Stannard
Costumes: Edith Head
Editor: John Bloom

Jane Reynolds	ELIZABETH TAYLOR
Martin Reynolds	RICHARD BURTON
Diana Proctor	CARRIE NYE
Donald Trenton	BARRY FOSTER
Turi Livicci	GABRIELE FERZETTI
Franca	DANIELLA SURINA
Kaduna	RUDOLPH WALKER
Tommy Reynolds	MARK COLLEANO
Judith Reynolds	EVA GRIFFITH
Peggy	ROSALYN VANDOR
Minister	THOMAS BAPTISTE
Angus McIntyre	RONALD RUDD
Gina	MARIETTA SCHUPP

In their TV movie debuts, Elizabeth Taylor and Richard Burton co-starred in this unusual two-part film—actually two films or two stories running concurrently—delving into the dissolution of an eighteen-year marriage through the eyes of both parties.

0286
TENAFLY
2/12/73 Universal (90 min)

Executive Producers: Richard Levinson and William Link
Producer: Jon Epstein
Director: Richard A. Colla
Teleplay: Richard Levinson and William Link
Photography: Emil Oster
Music: Gil Melle
Art Director: George C. Webb
Editor: Robert L. Kimble

Harry Tenafly	JAMES McEACHIN
Ted Harris	ED NELSON
Lt. Sam Church	DAVID HUDDLESTON
Ken Shepherd	JOHN ERICSON
Charlie Rush	MEL FERRER
Lorrie	ROSANNA HUFFMAN
Ruth Tenafly	LILLIAN LEHMAN
Aunt Gertrude	LILLIAN RANDOLPH
Uncle Walter	BILL WALKER
Herbert Tenafly	PAUL M. JACKSON, JR.
Mrs. Castle	ANNE SEYMOUR

and: Bert Holland, Leonard Stone, Devan Smith, Jack Denton, Don Bexley, Jackie Russell

In this pilot for the short-lived "Tenafly" series with McEachin (1973–74), a potpourri of slice-of-life comedy and straight-ahead detective mystery, a black private eye investigates the murder of a radio talk-show host's wife.

Eleanor Parker, Louis Jourdan, Farrah Fawcett (Miss Texas) and Barbi Benton (Miss Iowa) in
THE GREAT AMERICAN BEAUTY CONTEST (1973)

0287
THE GREAT AMERICAN BEAUTY CONTEST
2/13/73 ABC Circle Films (90 min)

Executive Producers: Aaron Spelling and Leonard
Goldberg
Producer: Everett Chambers
Director: Robert Day
Teleplay: Stanford Whitmore
Photography: James Crabe
Music: Ken Wannberg
Art Director: Rolland M. Brooks
Editor: James Mitchell

Peggy Lowery	ELEANOR PARKER
Dan Carson	BOB CUMMINGS
Ralph Dupree	LOUIS JOURDAN
Gloria Rockwell	JOANNA CAMERON
Angelique Denby	SUSAN DAMANTE
T. L. Dawson	FARRAH FAWCETT
Melinda Wilson	KATHY BAUMANN
Pamela Parker	TRACY REED
Joe Bunch	LARRY WILCOX
Kay Earnshaw	PATRICIA BARRY
Elliott	RYAN MacDONALD
Miss Utah	CHRISTOPHER NORRIS
Miss Iowa	BARBI BENTON
Texas Chaperone	BRETT SOMERS
Newsmen	WILL TUSHER
	VERNON SCOTT
Judges	MORTON MOSS
	JOAN CROSBY
	JOE PILCHER
	NORMA LEE BROWNING

The pursuit by America's loveliest girls for a coveted beauty crown is threatened by a scandal which implicates a judge, a former winner and one of the five finalists.

0288
THE HORROR AT 37,000 FEET
2/13/73 CBS, Inc. (90 min)

Producer: Anthony Wilson
Director: David Lowell Rich
Teleplay: Ron Austin and Jim Buchanan
From a story by V. X. Appleton
Photography: Earl Rath
Music: Morton Stevens
Art Director: James G. Hulsey
Editor: Bud Isaacs

Ernie Slade	CHUCK CONNORS
Len Farlee	BUDDY EBSEN
Mrs. Pinder	TAMMY GRIMES
Manya	LYN LORING
Sheila O'Neill	JANE MERROW
Annalik	FRANCE NUYEN
Paul Kovalik	WILLIAM SHATNER
Aaron O'Neill	ROY THINNES
Dr. Enhalla	PAUL WINFIELD
Holcombe	WILL HUTCHINS
Margot	DARLEEN CARR
Sally	BRENDA BENET

and: H. M. Wynant, Mia Bendixsen, Russell Johnson

A people-in-jeopardy fantasy which finds the baggage hold of a jetliner swarming with a gaggle of ghosts preparing to exact revenge on the passengers in first class.

0289
THE GREAT MAN'S WHISKERS
2/13/73 Universal (2 hours)

Producer: Adrian Scott
Director: Philip Leacock
Teleplay: John Paxton
Based on a play by Adrian Scott
Photography: John F. Warren
Music: Earl Robinson
Songs "The Wilderness Man" (sung by Dean Jones) and "Things That Go Bump in the Night" (sung by Isabel Sanford) by E. Y. Harburg and Earl Robinson
Art Director: George C. Webb
Editor: John Elias

James E. Cooper	DEAN JONES
Aunt Margaret Bancroft	ANN SOTHERN
Abraham Lincoln	DENNIS WEAVER
Andrew Hogan	JOHN McGIVER
Ballad Singer	HARVE PRESNELL
Katherine Witherby	BETH BRICKELL
Elizabeth Cooper	CINDY EILBACHER
Joseph Somerby	RICHARD ERDMAN
Ella	ISABEL SANFORD
Pearl	NICOLE MEGGERSON
Major Underwood	JOHN HILLERMAN
Miss Albright	MAUDIE PRICKETT
Paddleford	WOODROW CHAMBLISS
Whately	ALVIN HAMMER
Philbrick	CHARLES LANE

Dennis Weaver, Cindy Eilbacher, Isabel Sanford and Nicole Meggerson in
THE GREAT MAN'S WHISKERS (1973)

Jack Klugman and Sammy Davis, Jr., in POOR DEVIL (1973)

Marilyn Fox, Sissy Spacek and Shirley Jones in THE GIRLS OF HUNTINGTON HOUSE (1973)

A comedy-drama, filmed in 1969, about how a letter from a ten-year-old girl urged President Lincoln to grow a beard and altered America's most famous face.

0290
POOR DEVIL
2/14/73 Paramount (90 min)

Executive Producers: Arne Sultan and Earl Barret
Producer: Robert Stambler
Director: Robert Scheerer
Teleplay: Arne Sultan, Earl Barret and Richard Baer
Photography: Howard R. Schwartz
Music: Morton Stevens
Art Director: Monty Elliott
Editors: Robert Kern and Mike Vejar

Sammy	SAMMY DAVIS, JR.
Lucifer	CHRISTOPHER LEE
Burnett Emerson	JACK KLUGMAN
Chelsea	EMILY YANCY
Crawford	ADAM WEST
Bligh	GINO CONFORTI
Frances Emerson	MADLYN RHUE

and: Alan Manson, Stephen Coit, Jo DeWinter, Owen Bush

A comedy about Satan's bumbling disciple who, after 1,400 years of failure to secure a single soul for his boss, gets one last chance when he sets his sights on a gambler. This unsuccessful pilot was for a prospective series for Sammy Davis, Jr.

0291
THE GIRLS OF HUNTINGTON HOUSE
2/14/73 Lorimar Productions (90 min)

Executive Producer: Lee Rich
Producer: Robert L. Jacks
Director: Alf Kjellin
Teleplay: Paul Savage
Based on the novel by Blossom Elfman
Photography: Andrew Jackson
Music: Tom Scott
Title song written and sung by Paul Williams
Art Director: Ed Graves
Editors: Marjorie and Gene Fowler, Jr.

Anne Baldwin	SHIRLEY JONES
Doris McKenzie	MERCEDES McCAMBRIDGE
Gail Dorn	PAMELA SUE MARTIN
Sam Dutton	WILLIAM WINDOM
Sara	SISSY SPACEK
Sara's Mother	NANCY MALONE
Mary Lou	DEBBIE DOZIER
Cookie	MARILYN FOX
Marilyn Dutton	BARBARA MALLORY
Nurse Caulfield	HELEN PAGE CAMP
Miss Rodriguez	CARMEN ZAPATA
Sandy	DARRELL LARSON
Baby	BONNIE VAN DYKE
Tina	TINA ANDREWS
Wanda	MARY MALONADO
Harold	DAMON DOUGLAS
Rose Beckwith	SCOTTIE MacGREGOR
Mrs. Conover	RUTH WARSHAWSKY
Gail's Mother	DOLORES DORN
Sara's Father	NOBLE WILLINGHAM
Agnes Swenton	QUEENIE SMITH

An unmarried teacher in a school for unwed mothers finds herself increasingly drawn to her students' problems, leading to a deep emotional crisis.

0292
A BRAND NEW LIFE
2/20/73 Tomorrow Entertainment (90 min)

Producers: Robert W. Christiansen and Rick Rosenberg
Director: Sam O'Steen
Teleplay: Jerome Kass and Peggy Chantler Dick
From a story by Peggy Chantler Dick
Photography: David M. Walsh
Music: Billy Goldenberg
Assistant Director: Claude Binyon, Jr.
Art Director: Ed Graves
Editor: William Ziegler

Victoria Douglas	CLORIS LEACHMAN
Jim Douglas	MARTIN BALSAM
Eleanor	MARGE REDMOND
Harry	GENE NELSON
Mother	MILDRED DUNNOCK
Berger	WILFRID HYDE-WHITE
Sarah White	KAREN PHILIPP
Dr. Arliss	LLOYD BATISTA
Jessica Hiller	BARBARA COLBY
Burt	HUNTER VAN LEER
Nancy	AMY ROBINSON
Dr. Kalman	ELIZABETH HARROWER

and: Lois Walden, Ann Urcan, Marcy Casey, Jennifer Kulik, Tony Mancini, Dee Gregory, Dick Kay Hong, Marilyn Powell

Cloris Leachman won one of her assortment of Emmy Awards for her performance in this melodrama centering on a middle-aged couple's reaction to the prospect of their first child after eighteen years of marriage.

0293
AND NO ONE COULD SAVE HER
2/21/73 Associated London Films (90 min)

Executive Producer: Beryl Virtue
Producer: William Allyn
Director: Kevin Billington
Teleplay: Anthony Skene
Photography: Austin Dempster
Music: Ron Grainger
Editor: Keith Palmer

Fern O'Neil	LEE REMICK
Patrick Dooley	MILO O'SHEA
Sam O'Neil	FRANK GRIMES
Fitzgerald	LIAM REDMOND
Maid	JENNIE LINDEN
Mrs. Benet	SHELAGH FRASER
Boland	EDWARD GOLDEN
Miss O'Connor	MAY CLUSKEY
O'Toole	RONAN SMITH

and: Harold Goldblatt, Mary Ollis, Robert Lang, Paul Maxwell

A middle-aged American heiress (Lee Remick in her TV-movie debut) frantically searches for her banker husband who boarded a plane for Ireland and then disappeared. This was the maiden film made for American TV by the Robert Stigwood Group, which evolved into RSO, producers of films like *Saturday Night Fever* and *Grease*.

0294
THE NORLISS TAPES
2/21/73 Metromedia Productions (90 min)

Executive Producer: Charles Fries
Producer/Director: Dan Curtis
Teleplay: William F. Nolan

Roy Thinnes and Angie Dickinson in THE NORLISS TAPES (1973)

Photography: Ben Colman
Music: Robert Cobert
Art Director: Trevor Williams
Special Effects: Roger George
Editor: Dick Van Enger

David Norliss	ROY THINNES
Ellen Sterns Cort	ANGIE DICKINSON
Sheriff Hartley	CLAUDE AKINS
Marsha Sterns	MICHELE CAREY
Mme. Jeckiel	VONETTA McGEE
Charles Langdon	HURT HATFIELD
Sanford Evans	DON PORTER
James Cort	NICK DIMITRI
The Demon	BOB SCHOTT

and: Bryan O'Byrne, Edmund Gilbert, Robert Mandan, Stanley Adams, George DiCenzo

In Dan Curtis' warmed-over, more straightforward version of his *Night Stalker,* a pilot for a prospective new series, a humorless investigative reporter chasing down the supernatural stumbles onto the walking dead and finds himself in the clutches of a demon-spirit.

0295
THE STRANGER
2/26/73 Bing Crosby Productions (2 hours)

Executive Producer: Andrew J. Fenady
Producer: Alan A. Armer
Co-Producer: Gerald Sanford
Director: Lee H. Katzin
Teleplay: Gerald Sanford
Photography: Keith C. Smith
Music: Richard Markowitz
Art Director: Stan Jolley
Editor: Nick Archer

Neil Stryker	GLENN CORBETT
Benedict	CAMERON MITCHELL
Bettina Cooke	SHARON ACKER
Professor MacAuley	LEW AYRES
Max Greene	GEORGE COULOURIS
Henry Maitland	STEVE FRANKEN
Carl Webster	DEAN JAGGER
Dr. Revere	TIM O'CONNOR
Steve Perry	JERRY DOUGLAS
Mike Frome	ARCH WHITING
Eric Sconer	H. M. WYNANT
Secretary	VIRGINIA GREGG

and: Buck Young, Steven Marlo, William Bryant, Margaret Field, Philip Manson, Alan Foster, Ben Wright, Gregg Shannon, Jon Blake, William Harlow, Peggy Stewart, James Chandler, Heather McCoy, Jeanne Bates, Joie Magidow, Kathleen M. Schultz

A science-fiction thriller about an astronaut's frantic efforts to come home after crashing on Terra, the twin planet of Earth, and finding himself marked for extermination.

Steven Marlo, Jerry Douglas and Glenn Corbett in THE STRANGER (1973)

0296

I LOVE A MYSTERY
2/27/73 Universal (2 hours)

Producer: Frank Price
Director: Leslie Stevens
Teleplay: Leslie Stevens
Based on the radio series by Carlton E. Morse
Photography: Ray Rennahan
Music: Oliver Nelson
Assistant Director: Frank Losee
Art Director: John J. Lloyd
Editor: Robert F. Shugrue

Randolph Cheyne	IDA LUPINO
Jack Packard	LES CRANE
Doc Long	DAVID HARTMAN
Reggie York	HAGAN BEGGS
Job Cheyne	JACK WESTON
Alexander Archer	DON KNOTTS
Gordon Elliott	TERRY-THOMAS
Charity	MELODIE JOHNSON
Faith	KAREN JENSEN
Hope	DEANNA LUND

and: Peter Mamakos, Andre Philippe, Lewis Charles, Francine York

Surfacing six years after being made and eagerly awaited by old-time radio buffs, this send-up of the fondly remembered mystery show had insurance detectives Jack Packard, Doc Long and Reggie York searching for a mysterious billionaire. Not to be confused with the 1945 film of the same name, also based on the radio show.

0297

CALL TO DANGER
2/27/73 Paramount (90 min)

Producer: Laurence Heath
Director: Tom Gries
Teleplay: Laurence Heath
Photography: Ronald W. Brown
Music: Laurence Rosenthal
Art Director: William Campbell
Editor: John Loeffler and Chuck Freeman

Doug Warfield	PETER GRAVES
Carrie Donovan	DIANA MULDAUR
Edward McClure	JOHN ANDERSON
Emmet Jergens	CLU GULAGER
April Tierney	TINA LOUISE
Joe Barker	STEPHEN McNALLY
Marla Hayes	INA BALIN
Frank Mulvey	MICHAEL ANSARA
Dave Falk	ROY JENSEN
Tony Boyd	WILLIAM JORDAN
Reed	EDWARD BELL
Adams	PAUL MANTEE
Police Sergeant	WESLEY LAU
Danny	VICTOR CAMPOS
Rosalind	LESLEY WOODS
Chairman	BART BARNES
Reynolds	DAN FRAZER

A federal undercover agent recruits a computer-selected jack-of-all-trades in a scheme to rescue a syndicate witness who has been kidnapped and stashed away in a heavily fortified West Coast enclave.

0298

CONNECTION
2/27/73 D'Antoni Productions (90 min)

Executive Producer: Philip D'Antoni
Producer: Jacqueline Babbin
Director: Tom Gries
Teleplay: Albert Ruben
Photography: Dick Kratina
Music: John Murtaugh

Melodie Johnson, Deanna Lund and Karen Jensen in I LOVE A MYSTERY (1973)

Art Director: Ed Wittstein
Editor: Norman Gay

Frank Devlin	CHARLES DURNING
Everett Hutchneker	RONNY COX
Hannah	ZOHRA LAMPERT
Sy McGruder	DENNIS COLE
June McGruder	HEATHER MacRAE
Himself	HOWARD COSELL
Pillo	MIKE KELLIN
Eleanor Warren	DANA WYNTER
Det. Phaelen	TOM ROSQUI
Beejay	RICHARD BRIGHT
Dewey	JOE KEYES, JR.

An out-of-work newspaperman, trying to keep a step ahead of his alimony payments, becomes the go-between for a jewel thief and the insurance company that wants to settle.

0299
YOU'LL NEVER SEE ME AGAIN
2/28/73 Universal (90 min)

Executive Producer: Harve Bennett
Producer: David J. O'Connell
Director: Jeannot Szwarc
Teleplay: William Wood and Gerald DiPego
Based on the short story by Cornell Woolrich
Photography: Walter Strenge
Music: Richard Clements
Art Director: Sydney Z. Litwack
Editor: Richard G. Wray

Ned Bliss	DAVID HARTMAN
Mary Alden	JANE WYATT
Will Alden	RALPH MEEKER
Vicki Bliss	JESS WALTON
Lt. John Stillman	JOSEPH CAMPANELLA
Bob Sellini	COLBY CHESTER
Sam	BO SVENSON
Ben	BILL VINT
Murdock	GEORGE MURDOCK

This mystery thriller finds a husband searching for his young wife who has disappeared following a domestic tiff and uncovering evidence implicating himself as her murderer.

0300
HONOR THY FATHER
3/1/73 Metromedia Productions (2 hours)

Executive Producer: Charles W. Fries
Producer: Harold D. Cohen
Director: Paul Wendkos
Teleplay: Lewis John Carlino
Based on the novel by Gay Talese
Photography: Arthur Ornitz
Music: George Duning
Art Director: Rodger Maus
Editor: Richard Halsey

Salvatore "Bill" Bonanno	JOSEPH BOLOGNA
Rosalie Bonanno	BRENDA VACCARO
Joe "Bananas" Bonanno	RAF VALLONE
Frank Labruzzo	RICHARD CASTELLANO
Joseph Magliocco	JOE DeSANTIS
Gaspare di Gregorio	GILBERT GREEN
Stefano Magaddino	MARC LAWRENCE
Joe Notario	LOUIS ZORICH
Perrone	FELICE ORLANDI
Pete Notario	JAMES J. SLOYAN

Narrated by JOSEPH CAMPANELLA

and: Robert Burr, Antonia Rey, Carmine Caridi, Henry Farentino, Frank Albanese

Barbara Rush and Lloyd Bridges in CRIME CLUB (1973)

The success of *The Godfather* encouraged this adaptation of Gay Talese's 1971 best-selling novel about life inside the Mafia, a fact-based drama revolving around the collapse of the Joseph Bonanno family. The real-life Bonanno was kidnapped in 1964 and was not heard from for over eighteen months.

0301
BROCK'S LAST CASE
3/5/73 Talent Associates-Norton Simon Inc./Universal (2 hours)

Executive Producer: Leonard B. Stern
Producer: Roland Kibbee
Director: David Lowell Rich
Teleplay: Martin Donaldson and Alex Gordon
Photography: Russell T. Metty
Music: Charles Gross
Editor: Frank Morriss

Lt. Max Brock	RICHARD WIDMARK
Arthur Goldencorn	HENRY DARROW
Ellen Ashley	BETH BRICKELL
Jack Dawson	DAVID HUDDLESTON
Jake Hinkley	HENRY BECKMAN
J. Smiley Krenshaw	WILL GEER
Joe Cuspis	JOHN ANDERSON
Stretch Willis	MICHAEL BURNS
Sam Wong	PAT MORITA
Red-Eye	VIC MOHICA
Alma Gam	JEAN ALLISON
Doctor	VAUGHN TAYLOR
Judge	DUB TAYLOR

A comedy drama about a New York cop who retires to his small ranch in the West and is reluctantly drawn into a local case of an Indian accused of killing a sheriff with a bow and arrow. This pilot for a series that never materialized looked suspiciously like a reworking of "McCloud" in reverse.

0302
CRIME CLUB
3/6/73 CBS, Inc. (90 min)

Executive Producer: Frank Glicksman
Producer: Charles Larson
Director: David Lowell Rich
Teleplay: Charles Larson
Photography: Robert L. Morrison
Music: George Romanis
Art Director: Albert Heschong
Editor: Fred Chulack

Paul Cord	LLOYD BRIDGES
Judge Roger Knight	VICTOR BUONO

Dina Merrill, Barbara Stanwyck and Leslie Nielsen in THE LETTERS (1973)

Lee Majors in THE SIX-MILLION DOLLAR MAN (1973)

Robert London	PAUL BURKE
Jack Kilburn	WILLIAM DEVANE
Nick Kelton	DAVID HEDISON
Hilary Kelton	CLORIS LEACHMAN
Anne Dryden	BELINDA MONTGOMERY
Denise London	BARBARA RUSH
Deputy Wade Wilson	MARTIN SHEEN
Joey Parrish	MILLS WATSON
Sheriff Art Baird	FRANK MARTH
Roy Evans	EUGENE PETERSON
Hugh London	RICHARD LAWRENCE HATCH
Phone Supervisor	JOAN TOMPKINS
Frederick (Valet)	STEPHEN COIT
John (Butler)	ALAN NAPIER
Information Clerk	CLAIBORNE CARY
Cab Driver	JAMES McCALLION

A fraternity of public and private investigators looks into the suspicious death in an auto accident of the son of one of its members' long-time, wealthy lady friend. This was yet another pilot for a prospective series for Lloyd Bridges.

0303
THE LETTERS
3/6/73 ABC Circle Films (90 min)

Executive Producers: Aaron Spelling and Leonard Goldberg
Producer: Paul Junger Witt
Associate Producer: Tony Thomas
Directors: Gene Nelson and Paul Krasny
Teleplays: James Hirsch, Ellis Marcus and Hal Sitowitz
Photography: Tim Southcott
Music: Pete Rugolo
Art Director: Tracy Bousman
Editor: Carroll Sax

Episodes:
"The Andersons: Dear Elaine"

Paul Anderson	JOHN FORSYTHE
Elaine Anderson	JANE POWELL
Laura Reynolds	LESLEY WARREN
Stewardess	TRISH MAHONEY
Paul Anderson, Jr.	GARY DUBIN
Lisa	MIA BENDIXON

"The Parkingtons: Dear Penelope"

Penelope Parkington	DINA MERRILL
Derek Childs	LESLIE NIELSEN
Geraldine Parkington	BARBARA STANWYCK
Michael	GIL STUART
Minister	ORVILLE SHERMAN

"The Forresters: Dear Karen"

Karen Forrester	PAMELA FRANKLIN
Mrs. Forrester	IDA LUPINO
Joe Randolph	BEN MURPHY
Sonny	SHELLY NOVACK
Billy	FREDERICK HERRICK
Sally	ANN NOLAND
Officer	BRICK HUSTON
1st Man	CHARLES PICERNI

and HENRY JONES as The Postman

Three interconnected stories about nine people whose lives are drastically changed by letters delayed a year in delivery.

0304
THE SIX-MILLION DOLLAR MAN
3/7/73 Universal (90 min)

Producer/Director: Richard Irving
Teleplay: Henri Simon
Based on the novel *Cyborg* by Martin Caidin
Photography: Emil Oster
Music: Gil Melle
Art Director: Raymond Beal
Editors: Budd Small and Richard M. Sprague

Steve Austin	LEE MAJORS
Jean Manners	BARBARA ANDERSON
Dr. Rudy Wells	MARTIN BALSAM
Oliver Spencer	DARREN McGAVIN
Mrs. McKay	DOROTHY GREEN
Prisoner	CHARLES KNOX ROBINSON
Geraldton	IVOR BARRY
Young Woman	ANNE WHITFIELD
General	GEORGE WALLACE
Dr. Ashburn	ROBERT CORNTHWAITE
Saltillo	OLAN SOULE
Woman	NORMA STORCH
Nudaylah	MAURICE SHERBANEE

A test pilot, all but killed in a crash, is "remade" through the science of bionics into a superman superior to the flesh-and-blood man he had been. The popular series that followed (1973–78) had Majors repeating his role, with Richard Anderson and Alan Oppenheimer taking over the parts created by McGavin and Balsam.

0305
THE MARCUS-NELSON MURDERS
3/8/73 Universal (3 hours)

Executive Producer: Abby Mann
Producer: Matthew Rapf
Director: Joseph Sargent
Teleplay: Abby Mann
Suggested by *Justice in the Back Room* by Selwyn Rabb
Photography: Mario Tosi
Music: Billy Goldenberg
Art Director: John J. Lloyd
Editors: Carl Pingitore and Richard M. Sprague

Theo Kojak	TELLY SAVALAS
Teddy Hopper	MARJOE GORTNER
Jake Weinhaus	JOSE FERRER
Det. Dan Corrigan	NED BEATTY
Mario Portello	ALLEN GARFIELD
Lewis Humes	GENE WOODBURY
Det. Matt Black	WILLIAM WATSON
Det. Lou Jacarrino	VAL BASIGLIO
Ruthie	LORRAINE GARY
Bobby Martin	ROGER ROBINSON
Ginny	HARRIET KARR

and: Chita Rivera, Lloyd Gough, Antonia Rey, Bruce Kirby, Robert Walden, Lynn Hamilton, Lawrence Pressman, John Sylvester White, Carolyn Nelson, Paul Jennings, Helen Page Camp, Ellen Moss, George Savalas, Alan Manson, Fred Holliday, Henry Brown, Jr., Joshua Shelley, Patricia O'Connel, Alex Colon, Ben Hammer, Tol Avery, Bill Zuckert, Elizabeth Berger, Lora Kaye, Steven Gravers

Gene Woodbury, Telly Savalas and Allen Garfield in THE MARCUS-NELSON MURDERS (1973)

Robert Webber and James Stewart in HAWKINS ON MURDER (1973)

The acclaimed TV adaptation of Selwyn Rabb's book based on the Wylie-Hoffert murders in Manhattan in 1963, resulting in the case that ultimately led to the Supreme Court's Miranda decision three years later. Both director Sargent and writer Mann won Emmy Awards, and Telly Savalas received a nomination for his role which skyrocketed him to stardom in the subsequent hit series (1973–78), playing in this film a hard-boiled detective who fights to keep a black teenager from being wrongly convicted of the killings of two women. After its initial showing, it was re-edited to 2½ hours and retitled *Kojak and the Marcus-Nelson Murders.*

0306
HAWKINS ON MURDER
3/13/73 Arena-Leda Productions/MGM (90 min) (subsequently titled *Death and the Maiden*)

Executive Producer: Norman Felton

Producer: David Karp
Director: Jud Taylor
Teleplay: David Karp
Photography: Earl Rath
Music: Jerry Goldsmith
Art Director: Joseph R. Jennings
Editor: Henry Berman

Billy Jim Hawkins	JAMES STEWART
R. J. Hawkins	STROTHER MARTIN
Edith Dayton-Thomas	BONNIE BEDELIA
Julia Dayton	KATE REID
Joseph Harrelson	DAVID HUDDLESTON
Dr. Aaronson	DANA ELCAR
Vivian Vincent	ANTOINETTE BOWER
Captain Bates	CHARLES McGRAW
Carl Vincent	ROBERT WEBBER
Theresa Ruth Colman	MARGARET MARKOV
Judge	IVAN BONAR

and: Don Diamond, Tim Hallick, Inez Pedroza, Dennis Robertson, Bill Robles, Virginia Hawkins

In his TV movie debut, a pilot to his subsequent short-lived series (1973–74), James Stewart is a homespun West Virginia lawyer who defends an heiress charged with three murders. Strother Martin, as his cracker-barrel sheriff cousin and legman, also appeared in the series.

0307
THE BAIT
3/13/73 ABC Circle Films (90 min)

Executive Producers: Aaron Spelling and Leonard Goldberg

140

Producer: Peter Nelson
Director: Leonard Horn
Teleplay: Don Mankiewicz and Gordon Cotler
Based on the novel by Dorothy Uhnak
Photography: Gert Anderson
Music: Jack Elliott and Allyn Ferguson
Art Director: Rolland M. Brooks
Editors: Leon Carrere and Neil Travis

Tracy Fleming	DONNA MILLS
Capt. Gus Maryk	MICHAEL CONSTANTINE
Earl Stokey	WILLIAM DEVANE
Nora	JUNE LOCKHART
Liz Fowler	ARLENE GOLONKA
Solomon	NOAM PITLIK
Eddie Nugent	THALMUS RASULALA
Gianni Ruggeri	GIANNI RUSSO

Denise	XENIA GRATSOS
Mickey	BRAD SAVAGE
Big Mike	TIMOTHY CAREY
Newsdealer	DON KEEFER
Nancy	MITZI HOAG

and: Wendy Wagner, James Melinda, John Dennis, Paul Pepper, James O. Rear, Irenee Byatt, Vince Cannon

An undercover policewoman risks her life as she lures a homicidal rapist into a trap.

0308
CLASS OF '63
3/14/73 Metromedia Productions/Stonehenge
(90 min)

Executive Producer: Dick Berg
Producer: Lynn Stalmaster
Director: John Korty
Teleplay: Lee Kalcheim
Photography: Alan Stensvold
Music: Tom Scott
Art Director: Rodger Maus
Editor: John A. Martinelli

Joe Hart	JAMES BROLIN
Louise Swerner	JOAN HACKETT
Mickey Swerner	CLIFF GORMAN
Dr. Pillard	WOODROW CHAMBLISS
Dave McKay	ED LAUTER
Brandon George	COLBY CHESTER
Dan (Bartender)	GRAHAM BECKET
Lenny Hill	TOM PETERS
Girl	ANN NOLAND
Young Wife	JESSICA RAINS
Alumnus Husband	LOU PICETTI

Strother Martin and James Stewart in HAWKINS ON MURDER (1973)

James Brolin, Joan Hackett and Cliff Gorman in CLASS OF '63 (1973)

A campus reunion is the setting for a jealous husband to take revenge on his wife's former lover, his college rival, still convinced that the two are seeing each other after all these years.

0309
MR. INSIDE/MR. OUTSIDE
3/14/73 D'Antoni Productions (90 min)

Executive Producer: Philip D'Antoni
Producer: George Goodman
Associate Producer: Kenneth Utt
Director: William A. Graham
Teleplay: Jerome Coopersmith
Based on an account by Sonny Grosso
Photography: Dick Kratina
Music: Charles Gross
Editor: Murray Solomon

Det. Rick Massi	TONY LoBIANCO
Det. Lou Isaacs	HAL LINDEN
Lt. Valentine	PAUL VALENTINE
Renee Isaacs	MARCIA JEAN KURTZ

Luber	STEFAN SCHNABEL
Brack	PHIL BRUNS
Arnie	ARNOLD SOBOLOFF
Hooker	MELODY SANTANGELO
Frederick Wakeman	ED VAN NUYS
Emergency Sergeant	ROBERT RIESEL

and: Brigit Winslow, Randy Jergenson, Tony Palmer

Two New York cops, one losing an arm in a shootout, buck the system to track a foreign embassy official in their efforts to bust a drug ring in this pilot for a prospective series.

0310
JARRETT
3/17/73 Screen Gems/Columbia (90 min)

Executive Producer: David Gerber
Producer: Richard Maibaum
Director: Barry Shear

Teleplay: Richard Maibaum
Photography: Irving Lippman
Music: Jack Elliott and Allyn Ferguson
Art Director: Ross Bellah
Editor: Jack Holmes

Sam Jarrett	GLENN FORD
Bassett Cosgrove	ANTHONY QUAYLE
Rev. Vocal Simpson	FORREST TUCKER
Sigrid Larsen	LARAINE STEPHENS
Luluwa	YVONNE CRAIG
Spencer Loomis	RICHARD ANDERSON
Karoufi	HERB JEFFRIES
Dr. Carey	ELLIOTT MONTGOMERY

and: Lee Kolina, Joe Herrera, Bob Schott

An unrealized series project for Glenn Ford as an erudite investigator specializing in fine arts cases, here tangling with an urbane villain, a bogus preacher, and his nubile, snake dancer niece while tracking down some missing rare biblical scrolls.

142

0311
THE MAGICIAN
3/17/73 Paramount (90 min)

Producer: Barry Crane
Director: Marvin Chomsky
Teleplay: Laurence Heath
From a story by Joseph Stefano
Photography: Robert Hoffman
Music: Pat Williams
Art Director: William Campbell
Editors: Donald R. Rode, Larry Strong and Mike Vejar

Anthony Dorian	BILL BIXBY
Max Pomeroy	KEENE CURTIS
Lulu	JOAN CAULFIELD
Nora Coogan	KIM HUNTER
Sallie Baker	ELIZABETH ASHLEY
Joseph Baker	BARRY SULLIVAN
Ridgeway	ALLEN CASE
Mme. Parga	SIGNE HASSO
Jerry	JIM WATKINS
Mary Rose Coogan	ANNE LOCKHART

and: Richard Van Fleet, Toni Crespi, Lorelei and Cami Sebring

In this pilot for the 1973–74 series, a dapper magician uses the wizardry of his craft to help people in distress and exposes a staged plane crash when asked by the mother of one of the victims to check into a possible conspiracy. In the later series, Bixby, Curtis and Watkins were joined by Joseph Sirola as the fictional manager of Hollywood's real-life House of Magic, the club frequented by magicians where the shows were filmed. The title of this TV movie and the subsequent series had nothing to do, of course, with Ingmar Bergman's famed, similarly titled 1959 classic.

0312
THE RED PONY
3/18/73 Universal/Omnibus Productions (2 hours)

Producer: Frederick Brogger
Director: Robert Totten
Associate Producer: Ray Kellogg
Teleplay: Robert Totten and Ron Bishop
Based on the book by John Steinbeck
Photography: Andrew Jackson, Frank Phillips and Lloyd Ahern
Music: Jerry Goldsmith
Editor: Marsh Hendry

Carl Tiflin	HENRY FONDA
Ruth Tiflin	MAUREEN O'HARA
Jess Taylor	BEN JOHNSON
Grandfather	JACK ELAM
Jody Tifflin	CLINT HOWARD
Gitano	JULIAN RIVERO
Dearie	LIEUX DRESSLER
Toby	ROY JENSON
James Creighton	RICHARD JAECKEL
Orville Frye	WOODROW CHAMBLISS
Sonny Frye	LINK WYLER
Sheriff Bill Smith	RANCE HOWARD
Barton	WARREN DOUGLAS
Sarah Taylor	YVONNE WOOD
Miss Willis	SALLY CARTER-IHNAT
Mr. Sing/Mr. Green	VICTOR SEN YUNG

and: Kurt Sled, Jerry Fuentes, David Markham, Clay Radovitch, Clifford Hodge, Heather Totten, Debbie Steele, Verne Ellenwood, Joe Sardello, Bob Roe

A handsome color remake of the 1949 movie from the Steinbeck novella—here without the Billy Buck character—telling of a turn-of-the-century California farm family and the attachment of their sensitive young son to his horse after being unable to establish an understanding with his gruff father.

0313
THE POLICE STORY
3/20/73 Screen Gems/Columbia (2 hours)

Producer: David Gerber
Associate Producer: Christopher Morgan
Director: William A. Graham
Teleplay: E. Jack Neuman
Created by Joseph Wambaugh
Photography: Robert L. Morrison
Music: Jerry Goldsmith
Art Directors: Ross Bellah and Robert Peterson
Editor: Rita Roland

Sgt. Joe LaFrita	VIC MORROW
Lt. Dave Blodgett	EDWARD ASNER
Jenny Dale	DIANE BAKER
Martha LaFrita	INA BALIN
Ray Gonzales	SANDY BARON
Slow Boy	CHUCK CONNORS
Sgt. Solly Piccolini	HARRY GUARDINO
Chief Harry Stahlgaher	RALPH MEEKER
K.T.	MEL SCOTT
Kurt Mueller	DAVID DOYLE
Sgt. Chick Torpi	JOHN BENNETT PERRY
Harriet Parsons	KIM HAMILTON
Marnie	BARBARA RHOADES
Patti	DIANNE HULL
Arnie Dillon	BYRON MABE

and: Hal Williams, Joe Bernard, James Luisi, Michael Baseleon, John Karlen, Taylor Larcher

A solid cop movie that served as the pilot to the acclaimed anthology series (1973–77) which focused on various aspects of police work with different leading players every week (aside from one or two recurring roles). The TV-movie pitted a hard-nosed cop, in charge of a special felony squad, against a trigger-happy gunman who knows his way around the law.

0314
MURDOCK'S GANG
3/20/73 Don Fedderson Productions (90 min)

Executive Producer: Don Fedderson
Producer: Edward H. Feldman
Director: Charles S. Dubin
Teleplay: Edmond H. North
Photography: Michael Joyce
Music: Frank DeVol
Art Director: Perry Ferguson II
Editor: Charles Van Enger

Bartley James Murdock	ALEX DREIER
Laura Talbot	JANET LEIGH
Harold Talbot	MURRAY HAMILTON
Roger Bates	WILLIAM DANIELS
Dave Ryker	HAROLD GOULD
Glenn Dixon	DON KNIGHT
Bert Collins	WALTER BURKE
Larry DeVans	COLBY CHESTER
Terry	DONNA BETZ
Red Harris	NORMAN ALDEN
Ed Lyman	ED BERNARD
Denver Briggs	CHARLES DIERKOP
Mickey Carr	DAVE MORICK
Frank Winston	MILTON SELZER
Barney Pirelli	FRANK CAMPANELLA
Dr. Barkis	FRED SADOFF
Hellstrom	EDDIE FIRESTONE
George	WILLIAM FLETCHER
Ryler's Secretary	KAREN ARTHUR
Deputy	LARRY McCORMICK

A flamboyant, disbarred attorney and his staff of ex-cons are hired by a multimillionaire to find an embezzling bookkeeper, uncovering a trail of murder, suicide, blackmail and double-dealing in this unsuccessful series pilot.

0315
BEG, BORROW . . . OR STEAL
3/20/73 Universal (90 min)

Producer: Stanley Kallis
Director: David Lowell Rich

Alex Dreier (seated left) with Donna Benz, Ed Bernard, Colby Chester, Norman Alden and Walter Burke in MURDOCK'S GANG (1973)

Teleplay: Paul Playdon
From a story by Grant Sims and Paul Playdon
Photography: Harkness Smith
Music: Richard Markowitz
Editor: Carl T. Pingitore

Victor Cummings	MIKE CONNORS
Lester Yates	KENT McCORD
Cliff Norris	MICHAEL COLE
Kevin Turner	JOEL FABIANI
Hal Cooper	HENRY BECKMAN
Alex Langley	RUSSELL JOHNSON
Walter Beal	LOGAN RAMSEY
Ray Buren	RON GLASS
Lt. Collier	ROGER PERRY
Steve Ramsey	BARNEY PHILLIPS
Marty	PAUL FIERO
Brubaker	LEONARD STONE
Larry LaCava	FRANK MARTH
Dwight Stone	FRANCIS DeSALES
Jerry	WILL J. WHITE
Guard	JOHN DAVEY

Three ex-TV cops hop to the other side of the law in this caper movie with a twist—a complex museum robbery is pulled off by a resourceful team: one with no legs (Connors), one with no eyes (McCord) and one with no hands (Cole).

0316
TOMA
3/21/73 Universal (90 min)

Producer: Jo Swerling, Jr.
Director: Richard T. Heffron
Teleplay: Edward Hume and Gerald DiPego
Photography: Vilis Lapenieks
Music: Pete Rugolo
Editors: John Dumas and Gloryette Clark

David Toma	TONY MUSANTE
Inspector Spooner	SIMON OAKLAND
Patty Toma	SUSAN STRASBERG
Tully	MICHAEL BASELEON
Frank Barber	ROBERT YURO
Marlowe	DAVID SPIELBERG
Harrison	RON SOULE
Prolaci	NICHOLAS COLASANTO
Donzer	ABE VIGODA
Sam Hooper	PHILIP THOMAS
Bags Rolland	DAVID MAURO
Vinnie Cecca	DAVID TOMA

Based on the exploits of David Toma, real-life Newark, New Jersey plainclothes detective with a talent for disguises, this pilot to the subsequent series (1973–74) has the independent-minded cop bucking his superiors to stalk the leader of a syndicate's numbers racket. Musante, Oakland and Strasberg had the same roles in the series which lasted only one season because Musante tired of it. Later, it was reworked and disguised slightly to become "Baretta," Robert Blake's series.

0317
TOM SAWYER
3/23/73 Universal/Hal Roach Productions (90 min)

Executive Producer: Earl A. Glick
Producer: Trevor Wallace
Director: James Neilson
Teleplay: Jean Holloway
Based on the novel by Mark Twain
Photography: Fred Mandl
Music: Hal Mooney

Michael Cole and Mike Connors in BEG, BORROW . . . OR STEAL (1973)

Production Designer: Trevor Wallace
Editor: John McSweeney

Tom Sawyer	JOSH ALBEE
Huckleberry Finn	JEFF TYLER
Muff Potter	BUDDY EBSEN
Aunt Polly	JANE WYATT
Injun Joe	VIC MORROW
Judge Thatcher	JOHN McGIVER
Becky Thatcher	KAREN PEARSON
Mary Sawyer	SUE PETRIE

and: Scott Fisher, Chris Wiggins, Murray Westgate, Dawn Greenlogh, Leonard Bernardo, Gwen Thomas, Bob Goodier, David Yorstan, Kay Hawtrey, Al Bernardo, Colin Fox, Scott Carlson, Ricky O'Neill, Chris Pellett, Susan Stacey, Alysia Pascaris, Leo Leyden, Peter Mews

This Mark Twain classic, a film perennial, retells the familiar tale of several young friends on an adventurous summer in the sleepy Mississippi River town of Hannibal, Missouri. A theatrical *Tom Sawyer*, musicalized, also was released in 1973, some weeks after the TV version which, technically, was a remake of the 1938 movie (before that, it had been filmed in 1917 and 1930).

0318
GENESIS II
3/23/73 Warner Bros. (90 min)

Producer: Gene Roddenberry
Director: John Llewellyn Moxey
Teleplay: Gene Roddenberry
Photography: Gerald Perry Finnerman
Music: Harry Sukman
Art Director: Hilyard Brown
Editor: George Watters

Dylan Hunt	ALEX CORD
Lyra-a	MARIETTE HARTLEY
Isiah	TED CASSIDY
Isaac Kimbridge	PERCY RODRIGUES
Singh	HARVEY JASON
Yuloff	TITOS VANDIS
Astrid	LINDA GRANT
Primus	MARJEL BARRETT
Brian	TOM PACE
Overseer	LEON ASKIN
Janus	LIAM DUNN
Harper-Smythe	LYNNE MARTA
Slan-u	HARRY RAYBOULD
Lu-Chan	BEULAH QUO
Tyranian Teacher	RAY YOUNG

and: Ed Ashley, Dennis Young, Robert Hathaway, Bill Striglos, David Westburg, Tammi Bula, Teryl Wills, Didi Conn

A science-fiction fantasy from the creator of "Star Trek." Hoping to duplicate its success, this movie focuses on a twentieth-century NASA scientist who finds himself in a futuristic society after being preserved in suspended animation. It was reworked in 1974 as the TV movie *Planet Earth*.

Susan Strasberg and Tony Musante in TOMA (1973)

0319
CHASE
3/24/73 Universal/Mark VII Ltd. (90 min)

Producer/Director: Jack Webb
Teleplay: Stephen J. Cannell
Photography: Jack Marta
Music: Oliver Nelson
Art Director: John J. Lloyd
Editor: Warren H. Adams

Capt. Chase Reddick	MITCHELL RYAN
Norm Hamilton	REID SMITH
Steve Baker	MICHAEL RICHARDSON
Fred Sing	BRIAN FONG
Nora Devlin	BRENDA SCOTT
Chief Dawson	ALBERT REED
Thomas L. Traynor	JOHN CHANDLER
Joe Salizar	VALENTIN DeVARGAS
Mae Monroe	ANN MORGAN GUILBERT

and: Virginia Gregg, Pedro Gonzalez-Gonzalez, Herb Vigran, Gavin James, Bert Holland, Sam Edwards, Ron Henriquez

A special police unit goes out after a cop killer in this pilot to another Jack Webb series that ran briefly during the 1973–74 season. Ryan continued as the head of the unit, and Wayne Maunder and Gary Crosby signed on, along with Reid Smith, Michael Richardson, Brian Fong and Albert Reed.

0320
PARTNERS IN CRIME
3/24/73 Universal (90 min)

Executive Producers: Richard Levinson and William Link
Producer: Jon Epstein
Director: Jack Smight
Teleplay: David Shaw
Photography: Jack Marta
Music: Gil Melle
Art Director: Raymond Beal
Editor: Robert F. Shugrue

Judge Meredith Leland	LEE GRANT
Sam Hatch	LOU ANTONIO
Ralph Elsworth	BOB CUMMINGS
Walt Connors	HARRY GUARDINO
Frank Jordan	RICHARD JAECKEL
Lt. Fred Harnett	CHARLES DRAKE
Judge Charles Leland	JOHN RANDOLPH
Roger Goldsmith	RICHARD ANDERSON
Oscar	WILLIAM SCHALLERT
Margery Jordan	LORRAINE GARY
Bartender	DONALD BARRY
Trooper	GARY CROSBY

and: Alex Henteloff, Vic Tayback, Maxine Stewart

In this reworking of *The Judge and Jake Wyler* (1972), a lady judge-turned-detective and her ex-con associate go in search of $750,000 in bank robbery loot. Lee Grant and Lou Antonio stepped into the roles done earlier by Bette Davis and Doug McClure.

0321
HITCHED
3/31/73 Universal (90 min)

Producer: Richard Alan Simmons
Director: Boris Sagal
Teleplay: Richard Alan Simmons
Photography: Gerald Perry Finnerman
Music: Pat Williams
Editor: Frank Morriss

Roselle Bridgeman	SALLY FIELD
Clare Bridgeman	TIM MATHESON
Banjo Reilly	NEVILLE BRAND
Sam/Bart Dawson	SLIM PICKENS
Henry	JOHN FIEDLER
Ben Barnstable	DENVER PYLE
Pete Hutter	JOHN McLIAM
Rainbow McLeod	KATHLEEN FREEMAN
Reese	DON KNIGHT
Jay Appleby	BO SVENSON

and: Bill Zuckert, Charles Lane

The further adventures of those teenaged newlyweds of the Old West who were introduced in the TV-movie *Lock, Stock and Barrel* (1971), with Sally Field taking over the role originated by Belinda Montgomery.

0322
SAVAGE
3/31/73 Universal (90 min)

Executive Producers: Richard Levinson and William Link
Producer: Paul Mason

Director: Steven Spielberg
Teleplay: Mark Rodgers, Richard Levinson and William Link
Photography: Bill Butler
Music: Gil Melle
Editor: Edward M. Abroms

Paul Savage	MARTIN LANDAU
Gail Abbott	BARBARA BAIN
Joel Ryker	WILL GEER
Peter Brooks	PAUL RICHARDS
Allison Baker	MICHELLE CAREY
Judge Daniel Stern	BARRY SULLIVAN
Lee Raynolds	SUSAN HOWARD
Ted	DABNEY COLEMAN
Russell	PAT HARRINGTON
Jerry	JACK BENDER

A TV journalist investigates the compromising photo of a Supreme Court nominee in this pilot for a prospective series for ex-"Mission: Impossible" stars Martin Landau and Barbara Bain. It marked director Steven Spielberg's farewell to the TV vineyards where he had started only four years earlier. Originally this movie was titled *Watch Dog.*

0323
THE MAN WHO DIED TWICE
4/13/73 Cinema Center 100 (2 hours)

Producer: Steve Shagan
Director: Joseph Sargent
Teleplay: Jackson Gillis
Photography: James Crabe
Music: John Parker
Editor: Howard A. Smith

Erik Seward	STUART WHITMAN
Denise	BRIGITTE FOSSEY
Joe	JEREMY SLATE
Cumberland	BERNARD LEE
Harry	SEVERN DARDEN
Poldo	BRUNO BARNABE
Kincaid	PETER DAMON
Jenkins	RALPH NEVILLE

Originally called *A Spanish Portrait* when filmed in 1970 and then put on the shelf, this movie follows an aimless drifter and painter in Spain who surfaces after seven years, only to find himself plagued by art forgeries and a crooked dealer.

0324
THE ADVENTURES OF DON QUIXOTE
4/23/73 Universal/BBC-TV (2 hours)

Producer: Gerald Savory
Director: Alvin Rakoff
Teleplay: Hugh Whitmore
Based on J. M. Cohen's translation of the novel by Miguel Cervantes
Photography: Peter Bartlett
Music: Michel Legrand
Editor: Dave King

Don Quixote	REX HARRISON
Sancho Panza	FRANK FINLAY
Dulcinea	ROSEMARY LEACH
Duke	ROBERT EDDISON
Village Priest	BERNARD HEPTON
Innkeeper	PAUL WHITSUN-JONES
Barber	MURRAY MELVIN
Monk	ROGER DELGADO

and: Ronald Lacey, Gwen Nelson, Francoise Pascal, Brian Spink, John Hollis, Walter Sparrow, Jon Mattoche, Michael Golden, Brian Coburn, Athol Coats

An atmospheric dramatization of Cervantes' seventeenth-century tale of the self-proclaimed Spanish knight who travels the countryside with his squire, tilting at windmills as if they were dragons and trying

to reform a bawdy peasant girl. This was the first of a series of co-productions and trade-offs between Universal-TV and the British Broadcasting Corporation. This was the tenth filming of the classic novel, following closely on the heels of the movie version of the musical *Man of La Mancha.* Some months later came a filmed ballet adaptation with Nureyev, and still to be seen (if ever) is Orson Welles' long-planned, possibly aborted production of the tale.

0325
THE MAN WITHOUT A COUNTRY
4/24/73 Norman Rosemont Entertainment, Inc. (90 min)

Producer: Norman Rosemont
Director: Delbert Mann
Teleplay: Sidney Carroll
Based on the novel by Edward Everett Hale
Photography: Andrew Lazlo
Music: Jack Elliott and Allyn Ferguson
Production Designer: Jan Scott
Editor: Gene Milford

Philip Nolan	CLIFF ROBERTSON
Frederick Ingham	BEAU BRIDGES
Arthur Danforth	PETER STRAUSS
Captain Vaughan	ROBERT RYAN
Col. A. B. Morgan	WALTER ABEL
Slave on Ship	GEOFFREY HOLDER
Secretary of the Navy	SHEPPARD STRUDWICK
Aaron Burr	JOHN CULLUM
Mrs. Graff	PATRICIA ELLIOTT
Counsel	LAURENCE GUITTARD

and: Alexander Clark, Guy Spaull, Peter Coffield, Addison Powell, Geddeth Smith, Dick Sabol, Peter Weller, Jimmy Williams, Wince Carroll, William Myers

This classic about the man who renounced his country and lived to regret it received a sparkling production here with a tour-de-force performance by Cliff Robertson, aging sixty years as Philip Nolan. Previously it had been filmed three times as a silent movie and once (in 1938) as a short for Vitaphone. This version was the first full-scale sound adaptation of Hale's 1863 novel.

0326
THE PICTURE OF DORIAN GRAY
4/23–24/73 Dan Curtis Productions (90 min each)

Producer: Dan Curtis
Director: Glenn Jordan
Teleplay: John Tomerlin
Based on the novel by Oscar Wilde
Photography: Ben Colman
Music: Robert Cobert
Art Director: Trevor Williams
Editor: Dennis Virkler

Dorian Gray	SHANE BRIANT
Sir Harry Wotton	NIGEL DAVENPORT
Basil Hallward	CHARLES AIDMAN
Felicia	FIONNUALA FLANAGAN
Beatrice	LINDA KELSEY
Sibyl Vane	VANESSA HOWARD
Alan Campbell	JOHN KARLEN
Madame De Ferrol	DIXIE MARQUIS
Victor	BRENDAN DILLON

Oscar Wilde's eerie tale about a handsome Englishman who retains his youth while his portrait ages was given a two-part tape-to-film adaptation. Earlier there had been five silent film versions plus the classic production with Hurd Hatfield in 1945 and its 1970 remake.

0327

HAPPINESS IS A WARM CLUE
(filmed 1970–71) Universal (2 hours)
(subsequently retitled *The Return of Charlie Chan*)

Executive Producer: John J. Cole
Producer: Jack Laird
Director: Daryl Duke
Teleplay: Gene Kearney
From a story by Simon Last and Gene Kearney
Photography: Richard C. Glouner
Music: Robert Prince
Art Director: Frank Arrigo
Editor: Frank Morriss

Charlie Chan	ROSS MARTIN
Andrew Kidder	RICHARD HAYDN
Ariane Hadrachi	LOUISE SOREL
Paul Hadrachi	JOSEPH HINDY
Irene Hadrachi	KATHLEEN WIDDOES
Lambert	DON GORDON
Noel Adamson	PETER DONAT
Alexander Hadrachi	LESLIE NIELSEN
Peter Chan	ROCKY GUNN
Doreen Chan	VIRGINIA LEE
Stephen Chan	SOON TAIK-OH
Oliver Chan	ERNEST HARADA
Fielding	WILLIAM NUNN
Sylvia Grombach	PAT GAGE
Dr. Howard Jamison	TED GREENHALGH
Inspector McKenzie	GRAHAM CAMPBELL
Richard Lovell	NEIL DAINARD
Giancarlo Tui	JOHN GUILIANI
Anton Grombach	OTTO LOWY
Jan Chan	PEARL HONG
Mai-Ling Chan	ADELE YOSHIODA

Plans to bring Charlie Chan back to TV in this mystery involving the legendary sleuth and a wealthy Greek ship tycoon aboard the latter's yacht off the coast of Vancouver resulted in this curiously disappointing TV movie with a stranger history. Filmed on location in late 1970, it premiered on British television in July 1973 and subsequently disappeared, only to resurface six years later (7/17/79) under a new title for its first American showing—tucked away on late night TV.

1973–74 SEASON

0328

DRIVE HARD, DRIVE FAST
9/11/73 Universal (2 hours)

Executive Producer: Roy Huggins
Producer: Jo Swerling, Jr.
Associate Producers: Steve Heilpern and Carl Pingitore
Director: Douglas Heyes
Teleplay: Matthew Howard
From a story by John Thomas James
Photography: Gene Polito
Music: Pete Rugolo
Art Director: Robert Luthardt
Editor: John Dumas

Mark Driscoll	BRIAN KELLY
Carole Bradley	JOAN COLLINS
Deek La Costa	HENRY SILVA
Eric Bradley	JOSEPH CAMPANELLA
Ellen Bradley	KAREN HUSTON
Fielder	TODD MARTIN
Blond Man	CHARLES H. GRAY
Cartier	PATRICK WHYTE
Gerald Ives	JOHN TRAYNE
Comandante Morales	FRANK RAMIREZ

Ross Martin as Charlie Chan in HAPPINESS IS A WARM CLUE (1973)

and: Budd Albright, Michael Carr, Jacques Denbeaux, Hal Hopper, Socorro Serrano, Abel Franco, Luis Delgado, Ref Sanchez

A murder drama, filmed in 1969, about a race car driver who finds himself part of a deadly romantic triangle and his life threatend by a machete-wielding mystery man.

0329

COFFEE, TEA OR ME?
9/11/73 CBS, Inc. (90 min)

Producer: Mark Carliner
Director: Norman Panama
Teleplay: Ralph Ross, Albert E. Lewin and Norman Panama

John Davidson, Michael Anderson, Jr., and Karen Valentine in COFFEE, TEA OR ME? (1973)

Based on the book by Trudy Baker and Rachel Jones
Photography: William Cline
Music: Morton Stevens
Art Director: Perry Ferguson II
Editor: Bud S. Isaacs

Carol Burnham/Byrnes	KAREN VALENTINE
Dennis Burnham	JOHN DAVIDSON
Tommy Byrnes	MICHAEL ANDERSON, JR.
Susan Edmonds	LOUISE LASSER
Waiter	LOU JACOBI
Lisa Benton	ERICA HAGEN
Doctor	GEORGE COULOURIS
Mrs. Fitzgerald	NORA MARLOWE
Captain	KENNETH TOBEY
Businessman	JAMES SIKKING
Salesgirl	VIRGINIA SCOTT KING
Salesgirl	PHILIPPA HARRIS

Stewardess	MARCY LAFFERTY
Dee Dee	CYNTHIA HARRIS

A romantic comedy which takes Alec Guinness' *The Captain's Paradise* and changes the gender, with an airline stewardess juggling a crammed romantic life that includes one husband in Los Angeles and another in London.

0330
DELIVER US FROM EVIL
9/11/73 Playboy Films (90 min)

Producer: Ron Roth
Director: Boris Sagal
Teleplay: Jack B. Sowards
Photography: Bill Butler
Music: Andrew Belling
Editor: Jim Benson

Walter "Cowboy" McAdams	GEORGE KENNEDY
Nick Fleming	JAN-MICHAEL VINCENT

Steven Dennis	BRADFORD DILLMAN
Arnold Fleming	CHARLES AIDMAN
Dixie	JIM DAVIS
Al Zabrocki	JACK WESTON
Skyjacker	ALLEN PINSON

Stumbling onto an injured skyjacker who parachuted into the mountains with $600,000 in ransom, five greenhorn hikers kill the fugitive and fight the elements and each other for the money.

0331
SHE LIVES
9/12/73 ABC Circle Films (90 min)

Executive Producer: Lawrence Turman
Producer: Stan Margulies
Director: Stuart Hagmann
Teleplay: Elizabeth Gill
Based on the novel by Paul Neimark
Photography: Ronald W. Browne
Songs "Time in a Bottle" written and sung by Jim Croce, "Circles" written and sung by Harry

(Left) Susan Dey and Estelle Parsons in TERROR ON THE BEACH (1973)

(Below) Jack Weston, George Kennedy, Charles Aidman *(right rear)*, Bradford Dillman and Jim Davis in DELIVER US FROM EVIL (1973)

Chapin, "Ashes, the Rain and I" by James Gang, and "Rock & Roll Mood" by Dennis Lambert
Art Director: Tracy Bousman
Editor: Rita Roland

Andy Reed	DESI ARNAZ, JR.
Pam Rainey	SEASON HUBLEY
Dr. Wellman	ANTHONY ZERBE
Al Reed	MICHAEL MARGOTTA
Dr. Osikawa	JACK SOO
Dr. Mayhill	JAY ROBINSON
Lab Instructor	BILL STRIGLOS
Sue Stern	JENI KULIK
Cashier	ELEANOR ZEE
Dean's Secretary	KAREN ANDERS
Newspaper Ad Girl	DIANE CIVITA
Janitor	EDDIE QUILLAN
Policeman	CLAY TANNER
Dr. Wellman's Nurse	SHARON MADIGAN
Little Girl	JENNY GOMAN

Two lonely college students meet through a newspaper ad and share an idyllic love until the girl discovers she has a terminal illness, and the couple begin a frantic search to find a doctor, researcher or anyone who can help them.

0332
TERROR ON THE BEACH
9/18/73 20th Century-Fox (90 min)

Producer: Alan Jay Factor
Co-producer: Walter Beakel
Director: Paul Wendkos
Teleplay: Bill Svanoe
Photography: William K. Jurgensen
Music: Billy Goldenberg
Art Director: Rodger Maus
Editor: Richard Halsey

Neil Glynn	DENNIS WEAVER
Arlene Glynn	ESTELLE PARSONS
Steve Glynn	KRISTOFFER TABORI
Jerry	SCOTT HYLANDS
Dee Dee Glynn	SUSAN DEY
David	MICHAEL CHRISTIAN
Frank	HENRY OLEK

Gail	ROBERTA COLLINS
Helen	CAROLE ITA WHITE
Jenny	BETSY SLADE
Mickey	JACKIE GIROUX
Fisherman	WALTER BEAKEL
Ranger	DAVID KNAPP

A family outing turns into a nightmare when a gang of young thugs begins a campaign of harassment.

0333
DYING ROOM ONLY
9/18/73 Lorimar Productions (90 min)

Executive Producer: Lee Rich
Producer: Allen S. Epstein
Director: Philip Leacock
Teleplay: Richard Matheson
From his short story
Photography: John Morley Stephens
Music: Charles Fox
Assistant Director: Kurt Neumann
Art Director: Ed Graves
Editor: Bill Mosher

Jean Mitchell	CLORIS LEACHMAN
Jim Cutler	ROSS MARTIN
Tom King	NED BEATTY
Vi	LOUISE LATHAM
Sheriff	DANA ELCAR
Bob Mitchell	DABNEY COLEMAN
Lou McDermott	RON FEINBERG

A rest stop at a dingy roadside diner in the desert becomes a terrifying ordeal for a woman when her

Ross Martin and Cloris Leachman in DYING ROOM ONLY (1973)

Roy Thinnes in SATAN'S SCHOOL FOR GIRLS (1973)

husband mysteriously disappears in the washroom and her search for him is thwarted by the surly proprietor and his sinister friend.

0334
SATAN'S SCHOOL FOR GIRLS
9/19/73 Spelling/Goldberg Productions (90 min)

Producers: Aaron Spelling and Leonard Goldberg
Director: David Lowell Rich
Teleplay: Arthur A. Ross
Photography: Tim Southcott
Music: Laurence Rosenthal
Art Director: Tracy Bousman
Editor: Leon Carrere

Elizabeth Sayres	PAMELA FRANKLIN
Dr. Clampett	ROY THINNES
Roberta Lockhart	KATE JACKSON
Dr. Delacroix	LLOYD BOCHNER
Debbie Jones	JAMIE SMITH-JACKSON
Mrs. Williams	JO VAN FLEET
Martha Sayres	TERRY LUMLEY
Lucy Dembrow	GWYNNE GILFORD
Jody Keller	CHERYL JEAN STOPPELMOOR (CHERYL LADD)
Detective	FRANK MARTH
Gardener	BILL QUINN
Sheriff	BING RUSSELL

A young woman's investigation into the seemingly un-motivated suicide of her sister leads her to an exclusive girls' school where she soon finds herself in the same satanic grip that drove her sister and others to their deaths.

0335
SHE CRIED "MURDER!"
9/25/73 Universal (90 min)

Producer: William Frye
Director: Herschel Daugherty
Teleplay: Merwin Gerard
From a story by Roy Moore
Photography: Harry Makin
Music: John Cacavas
Art Director: Loyd S. Papez
Editor: John Kaufman

Inspector Joe Brody	TELLY SAVALAS
Sara Cornell	LYNDA DAY GEORGE
Detective Stepanek	MIKE FARRELL
Maggie Knowlton	KATE REID
Chris Cornell	JEFF TONER
David Sinclair	STU GILLARD
John McKenzie	ROBERT GOODIER
Sister Maria Teresa	AILEEN SEATON

and: Hope Garber, Len Birman, Murray Westgate

A young widow, in New York to resume a modeling career, sees a woman pushed violently into the path of an oncoming subway train and reports the accident to the police. In answer to her call, two detectives are sent to get her statement and she recognizes one of them as the killer.

0336
HIJACK!
9/26/73 Spelling/Goldberg Productions (90 min)

Producers: Aaron Spelling and Leonard Goldberg
Associate Producer: Peter Dunne
Director: Leonard Horn
Teleplay: Michael Kelly, James Buchanan and Ronald Austin
From a story by Michael Kelly
Photography: Arch R. Dalzell

Alan Alda, Louise Lasser and Ruth Gordon in ISN'T IT SHOCKING? (1973)

Music: Jack Elliott and Allyn Ferguson
Art Director: Paul Sylos
Editor: Leon Carrere

Jake Wilkinson	DAVID JANSSEN
Donny McDonald	KEENAN WYNN
Eileen Noonan	LEE PURCELL
Mrs. Briscoe	JEANETTE NOLAN
Frank Kleiner	WILLIAM SCHALLERT
Mr. Noonan	TOM TULLY
Bearded Man	RONALD FEINBERG
Man with Glasses	JOHN ZEE
Highway Patrolman	WILLIAM MIMMS
Helicopter Pilot	JAMES W. GAVIN

Two veteran truckers are hired to haul a top-secret cargo from Los Angeles to Houston and are challenged by a series of hijacking attempts by a group who will stop at nothing to prevent delivery.

0337
RUNAWAY!
9/29/73 Universal (90 min)

Executive Producer: Harve Bennett
Producer/Director: David Lowell Rich
Teleplay: Gerald DiPego
Photography: Bud Thackery
Music: Hal Mooney
Art Director: Loyd S. Papez
Editor: Douglas Stewart

Holly Gibson	BEN JOHNSON
Les Reaver	BEN MURPHY
Nick Staffo	ED NELSON
Carol Lerner	DARLEEN CARR
Mark Shedd	LEE H. MONTGOMERY
John Shedd	MARTIN MILNER
Ellen Staffo	VERA MILES
Prof. Jack Dunn	RAY DANTON
Dispatcher	FRANK MARTH
Fireman	BING RUSSELL
Conductor	JOHN McLIAM
Herb Elkhart (Brakeman)	LOU FRIZZELL
Chief Dispatcher	FRANK MAXWELL
College Man	KIP NIVEN
Coed	LAURETTE SPANG
Dr. Phillips	ROSS ELLIOTT
Screaming Girl	KELLEY MILES
Bill Travers	JUDSON PRATT
Man in Shock	THAN WYENN

A suspense thriller about a bunch of weekend skiers (familiar TV faces all) who sweat out a harrowing journey down a mountainside in a runaway train. Theatrically, in Great Britain, this film was known, cleverly, as *The Runaway Train*.

0338
ISN'T IT SHOCKING?
10/2/73 ABC Circle Films (90 min)

Producers: Ron Bernstein and Howard Rosenman
Director: John Badham
Teleplay: Lane Slate
Photography: Jack Woolf
Music: David Shire
Art Director: Roland M. Brooks
Editor: Henry Berman

Sheriff Dan Barnes	ALAN ALDA
Blanche	LOUISE LASSER
Justin Oates	EDMOND O'BRIEN
Marge Savage	RUTH GORDON
Dr. Lemuel Lovell	WILL GEER
Doc Lovell	DOROTHY TRISTAN
Jesse Chapin	LLOYD NOLAN

Robert Sterling and June Allyson in LETTERS FROM THREE LOVERS (1973)

Leonard Frey, Doug McClure and Rene Auberjonois in SHIRTS/SKINS (1973)

Ma Tate	PAT QUINN
Myron Flagg	LIAM DUNN
Michael	MICHAEL POWELL
Hattie	JACQUELINE ALLAN McCLURE

An inexperienced small-town sheriff is confronted with the mysterious deaths of the local senior citizens, an ingenious killer, and some very odd goings-on.

0339
LETTERS FROM THREE LOVERS
10/3/73 Spelling/Goldberg Productions (90 min)

Producers: Aaron Spelling and Leonard Goldberg
Director: John Erman
Teleplays: Ann Marcus and Jerome Kass
Photography: Tim Southcott
Music: Pete Rugolo
Art Director: Tracy Bousman
Editor: Leon Carrere

Monica	JUNE ALLYSON
Jack	KEN BERRY
Maggie	JULIET MILLS
Angie	BELINDA MONTGOMERY
Vincent	MARTIN SHEEN
Bob	ROBERT STERLING
Joshua	BARRY SULLIVAN
Sam	LYLE WAGGONER
Messenger	LAWRENCE ROSENBERG

152

Thompson	DAN TOBIN
Wilson	LOGAN RAMSEY
Eddie	LOU FRIZZELL
Al	JAMES McCALLION
Donna	ELLEN WESTON
Girl at Pool	KATHY BAUMANN
Joanne	JUNE DAYTON
Maitre d'	ROGER TIL

and HENRY JONES as The Postman

This successor to *The Letters* (1973)—and the second pilot for a proposed series—once more offers three interconnected stories in which three letters, delayed a year, change the lives of a young couple separated by a jail sentence, a suburban housewife involved in a love affair, and two vacationers pretending to be wealthy.

0340
THE ALPHA CAPER
10/6/73 Universal (90 min)

Executive Producer: Harve Bennett
Associate Producer: Arnold Turner
Producer: Aubrey Schenck
Director: Robert Michael Lewis
Teleplay: Elroy Schwartz
Photography: Enzo A. Martinelli
Music: Oliver Nelson
Art Director: John J. Lloyd
Editor: Richard Belding

Mark Forbes	HENRY FONDA
Mitch	LEONARD NIMOY
Scat	JAMES McEACHIN
Hilda	ELENA VERDUGO
Lee Saunders	JOHN MARLEY
Tudor	LARRY HAGMAN
Harry Balsam	NOAH BEERY
Harlan Moss	TOM TROUPE
Minister	WOODROW PARFREY
Policeman	VIC TAYBACK
Police Captain	KENNETH TOBEY
John Woodbury	PAUL KENT
Henry Kellner	JAMES B. SIKKING
Tow Truck Driver	PAUL SORENSEN
Sergeant	WALLY TAYLOR

A heist movie in which a parole officer forced into retirement teams up with three ex-cons to pull off a hijacking of a thirty-million-dollar gold shipment. The main interest is in seeing Fonda as a criminal mastermind in this film that was shown theatrically overseas as *Inside Job*.

0341
SHIRTS/SKINS
10/9/73 MGM (90 min)

Executive Producer: Burt Nodella
Producers: Bruce W. Paltrow, Hugh Benson
Director: William A. Graham
Teleplay: Bruce W. Paltrow
Photography: Michel Hugo
Music: Jerry Fielding
Editor: Henry Berman

Sidney Krebs	RENE AUBERJONOIS
Teddy Bush	BILL BIXBY
Jerry Axelrod	LEONARD FREY
Dr. Francis Murphy	DOUG McCLURE
Dr. Benny Summer	McLEAN STEVENSON
Dick Dubin	ROBERT WALDEN
Rose Axelrod	AUDREY CHRISTIE
Lynn Bush	LORETTA SWIT
Herbie Bush	JOHN KARLEN
Brown	RON GLASS
Father Braddock	MARTIN BRADDOCK
Arlene	JESSICA RAINS

Perlman	WILLIAM HANSEN
Cop	BARNEY PHILLIPS
Cop	JOSEPH PERRY
Patient	SANDY WARD

A sardonic comedy about six businessmen who find their zest for life rekindled when a simple bet after their weekly basketball game turns into a zany anything-goes hide-and-seek contest.

0342
DON'T BE AFRAID OF THE DARK
10/10/73 Lorimar Productions (90 min)

Executive Producer: Lee Rich
Producer: Allen S. Epstein
Director: John Newland
Teleplay: Nigel McKeand
Photography: Andrew Jackson
Music: Billy Goldenberg
Art Director: Ed Graves
Editor: Michael McCroskey

Sally Farnham	KIM DARBY
Alex Farnham	JIM HUTTON*
Joan	BARBARA ANDERSON
Harris	WILLIAM DEMAREST
Francisco Perez	PEDRO ARMENDARIZ, JR.
Ethel	LESLEY WOODS
Doctor	ROBERT CLEAVES
Policeman	STERLING SWANSON

Kim Darby in DON'T BE AFRAID OF THE DARK (1973)

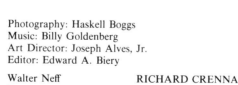

Tony Curtis and Kim Novak in THE THIRD GIRL FROM THE LEFT (1973)

Kim Novak in THE THIRD GIRL FROM THE LEFT (1973)

George	J. H. LAWRENCE
Tom	WILLIAM SYLVESTER
Bob	DON MALLON

and: Felix Silla, Tamarra DeTreaux, Patty Mahoney

A trim chiller that has a young couple inheriting an old mansion inhabited by demon-like creatures who are determined to make the wife one of their own.

*Replaced George Hamilton.

0343
DOUBLE INDEMNITY
10/13/73 Universal (2 hours)

Executive Producer: David Victor
Producer: Robert F. O'Neill
Director: Jack Smight
Teleplay: Steve Boscho
Based on the screenplay by Raymond Chandler and Billy Wilder of the novel *Three of a Kind* by James M. Cain

Photography: Haskell Boggs
Music: Billy Goldenberg
Art Director: Joseph Alves, Jr.
Editor: Edward A. Biery

Walter Neff	RICHARD CRENNA
Barton Keyes	LEE J. COBB
Phyllis Dietrickson	SAMANTHA EGGAR
Edward Norton	ROBERT WEBBER
Dietrickson	ARCH JOHNSON
Lola Dietrickson	KATHLEEN CODY
Jackson	JOHN FIEDLER
Donald Franklin	JOHN ELERICK
Sam Bonventura	GENE DYNARSKI
Neff's Secretary	JOAN PRINGLE
Porter	KEN RENARD
Redcap	ARNOLD TURNER
Conductor	RAND BROOKS
Norton's Secretary	JOYCE CUNNING
Charlie	TOM CURTIS
George	JOHN FURLONG

A TV remake of Billy Wilder's film classic (1944) about a scheming wife who inveigles an insurance agent into helping her bump off her husband and of the dogged investigator, the agent's boss, who stalks them after deciding that the man's death was not accidental.

0344
THE THIRD GIRL FROM THE LEFT
10/16/73 Playboy Films (90 min)

Executive Producer: Hugh Hefner
Producer: Ron Roth
Director: Peter Medak
Teleplay: Dory Previn
Photography: Gayne Rescher
Music: Dory Previn
Choreography: Miriam Nelson
Art Director: Frank Arrigo
Editor: Jim Benson

Gloria Joyce	KIM NOVAK
Joey Jordan	TONY CURTIS
David	MICHAEL BRANDON
Zimmy	GEORGE FURTH
Melanie	BARBI BENTON

antha Eggar and Richard Crenna in

JBLE INDEMNITY (1973)

Peter Boyle and Scott Jacoby in THE MAN WHO COULD TALK TO KIDS (1973)

Murray	LOUIS GUSS	Susie Detweiler	TYNE DALY	Freeman Sharkey	RAYMOND MASSEY
Hugh	MICHAEL CONRAD	Tom Lassiter	ROBERT REED	Hester Madigan	MERCEDES
Bradford	LARRY BISHOP	Dina Pingitore	DENISE		McCAMBRIDGE
Madelaine	ANNE RAMSEY		NICKERSON	George Oldenberg	RIP TORN
Gaye	JENNIFER SHAW	Cunningham	JACK WADE	Joanna Spencer	LOUISE SOREL
Stage Manager	BERN HOFFMAN	Carling	DUDLEY KNIGHT	General Dunbar	JAMES
		Mrs. Broadwhite	HANNA		WAINWRIGHT
			HERTELENDY	Sen. Burt Haines	DABNEY COLEMAN
				Col. Doug Henderson	JOSEPH

Kim Novak and Tony Curtis made their TV-movie debuts in this drama of an aging chorus girl who falls for an attentive young delivery boy after deciding that her long-time love affair with a nightclub comic is not headed anywhere.

Isolated from his heartbroken parents in his own solitary world, a troubled boy allows one special man to penetrate his lonely fortress and bring the family back together.

	CAMPANELLA
President Jeremy Haines	TOD ANDREWS
General Colton	RICHARD
	EASTHAM

and the voice of Howard K. Smith

A political thriller based on the 1967 novel by Robert J. Serling (Rod's brother) about an incompetent vice president who is left in control of the government when Air Force One mysteriously disappears with the President aboard.

0345

THE MAN WHO COULD TALK TO KIDS
10/17/73 Tomorrow Entertainment (90 min)

Producers: Robert W. Christiansen and Rick Rosenberg
Director: Donald Wrye
Teleplay: Douglas Day Stuart
Photography: Gene Polito
Music: Fred Karlin
Art Director: Charles Fultz
Editor: Walter Thompson

Charlie Detweiler	PETER BOYLE
Kenny Lassiter	SCOTT JACOBY
Honor Lassiter	COLLIN
	WILCOX-HORNE

0346

THE PRESIDENT'S PLANE IS MISSING
10/23/73 ABC Circle Films (2 hours)

Producer: Mark Carliner
Director: Daryl Dyke
Teleplay: Ernest Kinoy and Mark Carliner
Based on the novel by Robert J. Serling
Photography: Richard C. Glouner
Music: Gil Melle
Art Director: James G. Hulsey
Editor: John F. Link II

Vice Pres. Kermit	
Madigan	BUDDY EBSEN
Mark Jones	PETER GRAVES
Gunther Damon	ARTHUR KENNEDY

0347

MONEY TO BURN
10/27/73 Universal (90 min)

Producer: Harve Bennett
Director: Robert Michael Lewis
Teleplay: Elroy Schwartz
Photography: Enzo A. Martinelli

Suzanne Benton, Dean Jones and Barbara Eden in GUESS WHO'S SLEEPING IN MY BED? (1973)

Music: Oliver Nelson
Art Director: Joseph Alves, Jr.
Editor: Les Green

Jed Finnegan	E. G. MARSHALL
Emily Finnegan	MILDRED NATWICK
Caesar Rodriguez	ALEJANDRO REY
Calvin Baker	CLEAVON LITTLE
Warden Caulfield	DAVID DOYLE
Neil Davis	CHARLES McGRAW
Big Maury Kowalski	RONALD FEINBERG
Guard Sergeant	LOU FRIZZELL
Team Leader	ROBERT KARNES
Guard	LEW BROWN
Parking Lot Attendant	PAUL SORENSON

A light-hearted caper tale about an ingenious convict who manages to counterfeit one million dollars in the prison print shop and, with the aid of his wife, executes a complex scheme to swap the phony bills for real ones in the U.S. Treasury.

0348
ORDEAL
10/30/73 20th Century-Fox (90 min)

Producer: William Bloom
Director: Lee H. Katzin

Teleplay: Frances Cockerell and Leon Tokatyan
From a story by Frances Cockerell
Photography: William K. Jurgensen
Music: Pat Williams
Art Director: Jack Senter
Editor: Joseph Silver

Richard Damian	ARTHUR HILL
Kay Damian	DIANA MULDAUR
Andy Folsom	JAMES STACY
Eliot Frost	MACDONALD CAREY
Sheriff Geeson	MICHAEL ANSARA
Dep. Sheriff Fred	ARCH WHITING
Dep. Sheriff Joe	BILL CATCHING

Left to die in the desert by his wife and her lover, an arrogant businessman fights desperately for survival in order to exact his revenge and discovers an inner strength that changes his life.

0349
GUESS WHO'S SLEEPING IN MY BED?
10/31/73 ABC Circle Films (90 min)

Producer: Mark Carliner
Director: Theodore J. Flicker
Teleplay: Pamela Herbert Chais
Based on her play *Six Weeks in August*
Photography: John A. Alonzo

Music: Morton Stevens
Art Director: Walter M. Simonds
Editor: John A. Martinelli

Francine Gregory	BARBARA EDEN
George Gregory	DEAN JONES
Mitchell Bernard	KENNETH MARS
Chloe Gregory	SUZANNE BENTON
Mrs. Guzmando	RETA SHAW
Adam	TODD LOOKINLAND
Dolores	DIANA HERBERT
Waiter	WALTER BEAKEL

A romantic comedy about a divorcée who wakes up one morning to find her penniless ex-husband, his new wife, their eight-week-old baby and their lion-chasing dog camped on her doorstep looking for a place to call home for a while.

0350
LINDA
11/3/73 Universal (90 min)

Producer: William Frye
Director: Jack Smight
Teleplay: Merwin Gerard
Photography: Leonard J. South
Music: John Cacavas

John McIntire and Ed Nelson in LINDA (1973)

Art Director: George C. Webb
Editor: Edward A. Biery

Linda Reston	STELLA STEVENS
Paul Reston	ED NELSON
Marshall Journeyman	JOHN McINTIRE
Jeff Braeden	JOHN SAXON
Chief Vernon	FORD RAINEY
Anne Braeden	MARY ROBIN-REDD
Brownell	JOHN FINK
Officer Carr	ALAN FUDGE
Louella	JOYCE CUNNING
Officer Ramsey	ROSS ELLIOTT
Young Man	GARY MORGAN

A calculating woman kills her lover's wife, then sets about framing her own husband for the murder.

0351
THE GIRL MOST LIKELY TO . . .
11/6/73 ABC Circle Films (90 min)

Producer: Everett Chambers
Director: Lee Philips
Teleplay: Joan Rivers and Agnes Gallin
From a story by Joan Rivers
Photography: Richard C. Glouner
Music: Bernardo Segall
Art Director: Joseph R. Jennings
Editors: George Jay Nicholson and Diane Adler

Miriam Knight	STOCKARD CHANNING
Det. Ralph Varone	EDWARD ASNER
Prof. David Tilson	JIM BACKUS
Dr. Green	JOE FLYNN
Coach	CHUCK McCANN

Minister	CYRIL DELAVANTI
Dr. Hankim	CARL BALLANTINE
House Mistress	RUTH McDEVITT
Heidi Murphy	SUZANNE ZENOR
Dr. Ted Gates	FRED GRANDY
Moose Meyers	LARRY WILCOX
Herman Anderson	WARREN BERLINGER
Fred Ames	DANIEL SPELLING

and: Florence Lake, Victor Izay, Bill Zuckert, Reb Brown, Warren Burton, Angela Clarke, Dennis Dugan, Annette O'Toole, Bobby Griffin, Charles Pinte, Bob Hanley, Lonny Stevens, Mary Linn, Florence London, John Kirby, Jack Kutchel

A black comedy about the trials of an ugly girl who undergoes plastic surgery and then takes revenge on those who have been mean to her through a series of bizarre killings.

0352
MY DARLING DAUGHTERS' ANNIVERSARY
11/7/73 Universal (90 min)

Executive Producer: David Victor
Producer: David J. O'Connell
Director: Joseph Pevney
Teleplay: John Gay
Photography: Walter Strenge
Music: Hal Mooney
Art Director: Howard E. Johnson
Editor: Sam E. Waxman

Judge Charles Raleigh	ROBERT YOUNG
Maggie Cartwright	RUTH HUSSEY
Matthew Cunningham	RAYMOND MASSEY
Susan	DARLEEN CARR
Andy	DARRELL LARSON
Robin	JUDY STRANGIS
Jerry	JERRY FOGEL
Jennifer	SHARON GLESS
Brad	COLBY CHESTER
Charlotte	LARA PARKER
Biff	ALAN VINT
Carter	BEN WRIGHT

and: Anna Lee, Anne Loos, Gail Bonney, Carmen Zapata, Lois January, Bert Holland, John Day

In this sequel to *All My Darling Daughters* (1972) all the darling daughters get as anniversary presents the news that their widowed dad is about to get married. This film reunited Robert Young and Ruth Hussey after those golden years at MGM in *Honolulu, Maisie, Northwest Passage,* and *H. M. Pulham, Esq.* It was also Raymond Massey's film swan song after a long screen career.

0353
SUNSHINE
11/9/73 Universal (2½ hours)

Producer: George Eckstein
Director: Joseph Sargent
Teleplay: Carol Sobieski
Suggested by the journals of Jacquelyn Helton
Photography: Bill Butler
Music: John Denver
Assistant Director: Jim Fargo
Art Director: George C. Webb
Editors: Budd Small and Richard M. Sprague

Dr. Carol Gillman	BRENDA VACCARO
Kate Hayden	CRISTINA RAINES
Sam Hayden	CLIFF DeYOUNG
Nora	MEG FOSTER
Weaver	BILL MUMY
Jill Hayden	LINDSAY GREENBUSH
David	ALAN FUDGE
Givits	COREY FISCHER
Jill at 2½ years	ROBIN BUSH

Jill at 6 months	SARAH VALENTINI
Dr. Wilde	JAMES HONG
Bartender	NOBLE WILLINGHAM
Nurse	ADRIAN RICARD
Interviewer	BILL STOUT

A sentimental film based on an actual case history of a cancer victim, taken from a tape-recorded diary, involving a young dropout living in the wilderness with her boyfriend, who is a struggling musician, and her baby daughter.

0354
DEATH RACE
11/10/73 Universal (90 min)

Executive Producer: Harve Bennett
Producer: Terry K. Meade
Director: David Lowell Rich
Teleplay: Charles Kuenstle
Photography: Terry K. Meade
Music: Milton Rosen*
Editors: Les Green and Carl Pingitore

Gen. Ernst Beimler	LLOYD BRIDGES
Arnold McMillan	ROY THINNES
Stoeffer	ERIC BRAEDEN
Lt. Del Culpepper	DOUG McCLURE
Voelke	DENNIS RUCKER

and: Ivor Barry, Dennis Dugan, William Beckley, Eric Micklewood

A war movie pitting a crippled American fighter plane against a Nazi tank in a desert duel.

*Rosen's score was written originally for a 1967 World War II yarn called *The Young Warriors.*

0355
TRAPPED
11/14/73 Universal (90 min)

Executive Producer: Richard Irving
Producer: Gary L. Messenger
Director: Frank DeFelitta
Teleplay: Frank DeFelitta
Photography: Fred Mandl
Music: Gil Melle
Assistant Director: Howard K. Kazanjian
Animal Actions Director: Karl Miller
Art Director: George C. Webb
Editor: Richard Belding

Chuck Brenner	JAMES BROLIN
Elaine Moore	SUSAN CLARK
David Moore	EARL HOLLIMAN
Sgt. Connaught	ROBERT HOOKS
Connie Havenmeyer	IVY JONES
Bartender	BOB HASTINGS
Carrie	TAMMY HARRINGTON
Steward	MARCO LOPEZ
Stewardess	ERICA HAGEN
Waitress	MARY ROBINSON
Mr. Higgins	ELLIOTT LINDSEY

A thriller about a man who is accidentally locked in a department store overnight and finds himself held at bay by six vicious Doberman guard dogs. Cinematographer Fred Mandl's contribution was cited for an Emmy Award nomination.

0356
THE AFFAIR
11/20/73 Spelling/Goldberg Productions (90 min)

Producers: Aaron Spelling and Leonard Goldberg
Associate Producer: Parke Perine
Director: Gilbert Cates
Teleplay: Barbara Turner
Photography: Jerry Hirschfeld

Robert Young and Ruth Hussey in MY DARLING DAUGHTERS'
ANNIVERSARY (1973)

Lloyd Bridges in DEATH RACE (1973)

Natalie Wood and Robert Wagner in THE AFFAIR (1973)

Bette Davis in SCREAM, PRETTY PEGGY (1973)

Bette Davis and Ted Bessell in SCREAM, PRETTY PEGGY (1973)

Music: George Aliceson Tipton
Song "I Can't See You Anymore" by Renee
Armand and Jim Gordon
Sung by Natalie Wood
Art Director: Tracy Bousman
Editor: Folmar Blangsted

Courtney Patterson	NATALIE WOOD
Marcus Simon	ROBERT WAGNER
Jamie Patterson	BRUCE DAVISON
Jennifer	JAMIE SMITH-JACKSON
Frank	PAT HARRINGTON
Mr. Patterson	KENT SMITH
Bobbie	PAUL RYAN
Mrs. Patterson	FRANCES REID
Howard	MARK ROBERTS
Annie Simon	ANNA ARIES
Peter	STEVE RISKES
Evan	BRETT ERICSON

Natalie Wood returned to TV after an eighteen-year absence to co-star with her husband, Robert Wagner, in this bittersweet tale of a crippled lady songwriter and the sensitive lawyer who becomes her first love. The original title until the eve of airing: *Love Song*. The actress not only made her TV movie debut in this one but also sang the film's theme song.

0357
SCREAM, PRETTY PEGGY
11/24/73 Universal (90 min)

Producer: Lou Morheim
Director: Gordon Hessler
Teleplay: Jimmy Sangster and Arthur Hoffe
Photography: Leonard G. South
Music: Robert Prince
Art Director: Joseph Alves, Jr.
Editor: Larry Strong

Jeffrey Elliot	TED BESSELL
Peggy Johns	SIAN-BARBARA ALLEN
Mrs. Elliot	BETTE DAVIS
George Thornton	CHARLES DRAKE
Dr. Saks	ALLAN ARBUS
Agnes Thornton	TOVAH FELDSHUH
Student	JOHNIE COLLINS III
Office Girl	JESSICA RAINS
Jennifer Elliot	CHRISTIANE SCHMIDTNER

An average horror tale, spiced with a dash or two of *Psycho*, about a sculptor who hires college coeds as housekeepers for the mansion he shares with his recluse mother and his supposedly insane sister.

0358
CRY RAPE!
11/27/73 Leonard Freeman Productions (90 min)

Executive Producer: Leonard Freeman
Producer: Will Lorin
Director: Corey Allen
Teleplay: Will Lorin
Photography: Jack Woolf
Art Director: Albert Heschong
Editor: Jack Gleason

Betty Jenner	ANDREA MARCOVICCI
Andy Coleman	PETER COFFIELD
Liam Price	GREG MULLAVEY
Detective Sloane	JOSEPH SIROLA
Mrs. Coleman	LESLEY WOODS
Jenny Coleman	PATRICIA MATTICK
Detective Kroger	JAMES LUISI
Jim Bryan	ROBERT HOGAN

Janie Warren	JANA BELLAN
Ben Warren	HOWARD PLATT
Dist. Atty. Ritchie	PAUL COMI
Dr. Lang	RICHARD EVANS
John Curzon	GEORGE MURDOCK
Officer Hill	LAWRENCE BAME
Sam Lesinski	LEW HORN
Judge Newcombe	WHIT BISSELL
Thomas Kirby	FRANK MAXWELL
Louise Jennings	HAZEL MEDINA
Hilda Brownlee	ANNE ANDERSON
Jerry Cohen	JOBY BAKER
Jim Hadley	PAUL MANTEE

and: Carol Larson, Frank Farmer, Ken Washington, Barbara George, Paul Lichtman, Dick Gittings, Willard Gage, Sandra Belson, Don Eitner, Tony DiMilo

A candid drama that examines the effects of rape on both the victim and the accused as well as their families and acquaintances.

0359
OUTRAGE!
11/28/73 ABC Circle Films (90 min)

Producer: Michael C. Green
Director: Richard T. Heffron
Teleplay: William Wood
Photography: John Morley Stephens
Music: Jimmie Haskell
Art Director: Walter M. Simonds
Editor: Ronald J. Fagan

Dr. John Kiler	ROBERT CULP
Muriel Kiler	MARLYN MASON
Thelma	BEAH RICHARDS
Mrs. Chandler	JACQUELINE SCOTT
Deputy Tottif	RAMON BIERI
Vance Chandler	THOMAS LEOPOLD
Mr. Chandler	MARK LENNARD
Ron	NICHOLAS HAMMOND

Phil	DON DUBBINS
Judge Cox	IVOR FRANCIS

In this film one man decides to wage war against a gang of teenage punks besieging an affluent community. Based on a true incident, this story originally was titled *One Angry Man.*

0360
LISA, BRIGHT AND DARK
11/28/73 Bob Banner Associates (90 min)

Executive Producer: Bob Banner
Producer: Tom Egan
Director: Jeannot Szwarc
Teleplay: Lionel E. Siegel
Based on the novel by John Neufeld
Photography: Richard C. Glouner
Music: Rod McKuen
Editor: Keith Olson

Margaret Schilling	ANNE BAXTER
William Schilling	JOHN FORSYTHE
Lisa Schilling	KAY LENZ
Elizabeth	ANN LOCKHART
Mary Nell	DEBRALEE SCOTT
Betsy	JAMIE SMITH-JACKSON
Brian	ANSON WILLIAMS

and: Erin Moran, Stu Klitsner, Richard Stahl, Jessica Myerson, Larry Casey

A teenager, in the throes of a nervous breakdown, is helped by three girlfriends who try to draw her out with attempts at their own style of group therapy.

0361
CATHOLICS
11/29/73 A Sidney Glazier Production (90 min)

Executive Producer: Sidney Glazier
Producer: Barry Levinson
Director: Jack Gold
Teleplay: Brian Moore

Based on his novel
Photography: Gerry Fisher
Music: Carl Davis
Art Director: John Clark
Editor: Anne V. Coates

The Abbot	TREVOR HOWARD
Father Kinsella	MARTIN SHEEN
Father General	RAF VALLONE
Father Manus	CYRIL CUSACK
Father Matthew	ANDREW KEIR
Brother Kevin	MICHAEL GAMBON
Brother Donald	LEON VITALE
Father Terrence	TOM JORDAN
Father Walter	GODFREY QUIGLEY
Brother Paul	JOHN KELLY
Brother Alphonsus	RICHARD OLIVER
Brother Sean	PATRICK LONG
Brother John	GILBERT McINTYRE
Brother Michael	CONNOR EVANS
Brother Pius	SEAMUS HEALY
Brother Martin	JOHN FRANKLIN
Brother Malachy	CECIL SHERIDAN
Brother Daniel	LIAM BURK
Father Colum	FRANK HOWARD
Brother Benedict	JOHN PINE
Dirty Monk	DERRY POWER
Boatman	JOE PILKINGTON
Publican	GEOFFREY GOLDEN

This acclaimed religious drama, set in the future, brings theological adversaries head to head—the Vatican's emissary of change and a strong-willed abbot clinging to the old ways.

0362
FRANKENSTEIN: THE TRUE STORY
11/30–12/1/73 Universal (4 hours)

Producer: Hunt Stromberg, Jr.
Director: Jack Smight
Teleplay: Christopher Isherwood and Don Bachardy

Michael Sarrazin (on table) and Leonard Whiting in FRANKENSTEIN: THE TRUE STORY (1973)

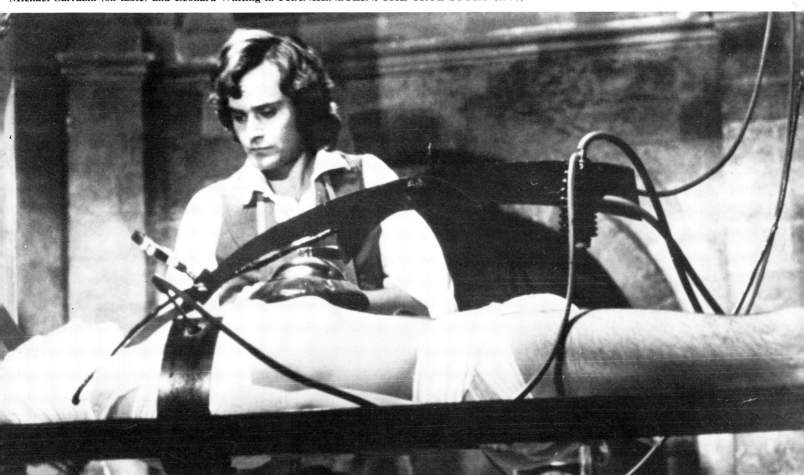

Based on the novel by Mary Shelley
Photography: Arthur Ibbetson
Music: Gil Melle
Art Director: Wilfrid Shingleton
Editor: Richard Marden

Dr. Polidori	JAMES MASON
Dr. Victor Frankenstein	LEONARD WHITING
Henri Clerval	DAVID McCALLUM
Agatha/Prima	JANE SEYMOUR
Elizabeth Fanschawe	NICOLA PAGET
The Creature	MICHAEL SARRAZIN
Sir Richard Fanschawe	MICHAEL WILDING
Lady Fanschawe	CLARISSA KAYE
Mrs. Blair	AGNES MOOREHEAD
Francoise DuVal	MARGARET LEIGHTON
Mr. Lacey	RALPH RICHARDSON
Chief Constable	JOHN GIELGUD
Sea Captain	TOM BAKER
Felix	DALLAS ADAMS
Young Man	JULIAN BARNES
Passenger in Coach	ARNOLD DIAMOND

A literate retelling of Mary Shelley's Gothic horror classic with the accent here on character instead of terror, establishing an offbeat relationship between the doctor and his creature. Subsequently this film was edited down to two hours or so for theatrical showings overseas and for TV syndication in the United States.

0363
A SUMMER WITHOUT BOYS
12/4/73 Playboy Productions (90 min)

Executive Producer: Hugh Hefner
Producer: Ron Roth
Director: Jeannot Szwarc
Teleplay: Rita Larkin
Photography: Mario Tosi
Music: Andrew Belling
Songs sung by Helen O'Connell
Editor: Jim Benson

Ellen Hailey	BARBARA BAIN
Abe Battle	MICHAEL MORIARTY
Ruth Hailey	KAY LENZ
Lenore Atkins	DEBRALEE SCOTT
Mrs. LaCava	MILDRED DUNNOCK
Joe	RIC CARROTT
Burt	MICHAEL LEMBECK
Gladys Potter	SUE TAYLOR
Quincy	B. KIRBY, JR.
Mr. Collins	NED WERTIMER
Mrs. Margolis	JAN BURRELL
Mrs. Denning	DIANE HILL
Mrs. Battle	CLAUDIA BRYAR
Rikki	JESSICA RAINS

A middle-aged woman, suffering through the final moments of a dissolving marriage in the early 1940s, tries to get away from it all at a summer lodge where she finds that she is her daughter's rival for the attentions of the handsome handyman.

0364
BLOOD SPORT
12/5/73 Danny Thomas Productions (90 min)

Executive Producer: Paul Junger Witt
Producer: Tony Thomas
Director: Jerrold Freedman
Teleplay: Jerrold Freedman
Photography: Richard C. Glouner
Music: Randy Edelman
Editor: Jerry Shepard

Dwayne Birdsong	BEN JOHNSON
David Lee Birdsong	GARY BUSEY
Coach Marshall	LARRY HAGMAN
Dennis Birdsong	BILL LUCKING
Mr. Schmidt	DAVID DOYLE
Mary Louise Schmidt	MIMI SAFFIAN
Mrs. Birdsong	PEGGY REA
Michael Braun	CRAIG RICHARD NELSON
Bubba Montgomery	MICHAEL TALBOTT
Frank Dorsdale	VAL AVERY
Blanche Birdsong	JEAN CLAYTON

Holly	MISTY ROWE
Mr. Millsaps	WILLIAM HANSEN
Reuben	MICHAEL LEMBECK

A high school athlete is torn between the ambitions of his father, who wants him to get a football scholarship, and his coach, looking for a winning season. *Poetry in Motion* was the original title.

0365
MANEATER
12/8/73 Universal (90 min)

Producer: Robert F. O'Neill
Director: Vince Edwards
Teleplay: Vince Edwards, Marcus Demian and Jimmy Sangster
From a story by Vince Edwards
Photography: Haskell Boggs
Music: George Romanis
Art Director: William Newberry
Editor: John F. Schreyer

Nick Baron	BEN GAZZARA
Gloria Baron	SHEREE NORTH
Carl Brenner	RICHARD BASEHART
Shep Saunders	KIP NIVEN
Polly	LAURETTE SPANG
Paula Brenner	CLAIRE BRENNAN
Louis	STEWART RAFFILL
1st Ranger	LOU FERRAGHER
2nd Ranger	JERRY FITZPATRICK

Two city couples on a camping trip become the prey for a pair of hungry tigers set on them by a mad animal trainer, in this film not only written by Vince Edwards but marking his TV-movie directorial debut.

0366
KEY WEST
12/10/73 Warner Bros. (2 hours)

Producer: Anthony S. Martin
Director: Philip Leacock
Teleplay: Anthony S. Martin
Photography: Ted Voigtlander and Ben Colman

Barbara Bain and Michael Moriarty in A SUMMER WITHOUT BOYS (1973)

Ben Johnson in BLOOD SPORT (1973)

Sheree North and Ben Gazzara in MANEATER (1973)

Music: Frank DeVol
Editor: Bill Brame

Steve Cutler	STEPHEN BOYD
Candy Rhodes	WOODY STRODE
Ruth Frazier	TIFFANY BOLLING
General Luker	SIMON OAKLAND
Senator Scott	WILLIAM PRINCE
Prescott Webb	FORD RAINEY
Chief Miller	DON COLLIER
Sam Olsen	GEORGE "SHUG" FISHER
Brandi	SHEREE NORTH
Rick	EARL HINDMAN
George	STEPHEN MENDILLO
Carol Luker	VIRGINIA KISER

An ex-CIA operative, running a boat service in Florida with an old buddy, finds himself the target of an eccentric tycoon with a score to settle and becomes involved in a chase for evidence incriminating a U.S. Senator in this pilot for a prospective series.

0367
THE CAT CREATURE
12/11/73 Screen Gems/Columbia (90 min)

Producer: Douglas S. Cramer
Associate Producer: Wilford Lloyd Baumes
Director: Curtis Harrington
Teleplay: Robert Bloch
From a story by Douglas S. Cramer, Wilford Lloyd Baumes and Robert Bloch
Photography: Charles Rosher
Music: Leonard Rosenman

Art Directors: Ross Bellah and Carey Odell
Editor: Stan Ford

Rina Carter	MEREDITH BAXTER
Roger Edmonds	DAVID HEDISON
Hester Black	GALE SONDERGAARD
Hotel Clerk	JOHN CARRADINE
Lieut. Marco	STUART WHITMAN
Sherry Hastings	RENEE JARRETT
Thief	KEYE LUKE
Frank Lucas	KENT SMITH
Deputy Coroner	MILTON PARSONS
Prof. Reinhart	JOHN ABBOTT
Pawnshop Clerk	PETER LORRE, JR.
Donovan	VIRGIL FRYE
Bert	WILLIAM SIMS

In this chiller, a valentine to the fondly remembered horror B-movie, the theft of an amulet from the mummy of an Egyptian priestess sets off a reign of terror that involves an archeology professor, a mysterious shopkeeper, a pretty salesgirl and an Oriental thief.

0368
MESSAGE TO MY DAUGHTER
12/12/73 Metromedia Productions (90 min)

Executive Producer: Charles Fries
Producer: Gerald I. Isenberg
Director: Robert Michael Lewis
Teleplay: Rita Larkin
Photography: Richard C. Glouner
Music: Fred Myrow
Art Director: Rodger Maus
Editor: John F. Link II

Kent Smith in THE CAT CREATURE (1973)

Janet Thatcher	BONNIE BEDELIA
John Thatcher	MARTIN SHEEN
Miranda Thatcher	KITTY WINN
Mrs. Oliver	NEVA PATTERSON
Dave	MARK SLADE
Steve	JERRY AYRES
Frank	KING MOODY
Phil	BOB GOLDSTEIN
Woman on Train	LUCILLE BENSON
Abortionist	JOHN CRAWFORD
Doctor	JOHN LASELL

and: Richard McMurray, Jan Shutan, Peg Shirley, Della Thomas, Dick Balducci, Laurie Brooks Jefferson, Jeni Kulik

A confused teenager finds emotional strength in the tapes recorded years earlier by her dying mother.

163

0369

THE BORROWERS

12/14/73 Walt DeFaria Productions/20th Century-Fox (90 min)

Executive Producer: Duane C. Bogie
Producers: Walt DeFaria and Warren L. Lockhart
Director: Walter C. Miller
Teleplay: Jay Presson Allen
Based on the book by Mary Norton
Music: Rod McKeun
Songs sung by Rod McKuen and Shelby Flint
Additional Music: Billy Byers
Special Effects: Douglas Trumbull
Art Director: Bill Zamprik

Pod Clock	EDDIE ALBERT
Homily Clock	TAMMY GRIMES
Aunt Sophy	DAME JUDITH ANDERSON
Arrietty Clock	KAREN PEARSON
Nephew	DENNIS LARSON
Mrs. Crampfurl	BEATRICE STRAIGHT
Mr. Crampfurl	BARNARD HUGHES
Ernie	MURRAY WESTGATE
Tom	DANNY McILVARY

An engaging fantasy about a family of inches-tall little people who live beneath the floorboards of a Victorian country house in peace and quiet until discovered by an eight-year-old boy. The film was Emmy-nominated as Outstanding Children's Special, with nominations also going to Dame Judith Anderson and director Walter C. Miller.

0370

MIRACLE ON 34th STREET

12/14/73 20th Century-Fox (2 hours)

Producer: Norman Rosemont
Director: Fielder Cook
Teleplay: Jeb Rosebrook
Based on the screenplay by George Seaton from the story by Valentine Davies
Photography: Earl Rath
Music: Sid Ramin
Art Director: Jan Scott
Editor: Gene Milford

Karen Walker	JANE ALEXANDER
Bill Schaffner	DAVID HARTMAN
Dr. Henry Sawyer	RODDY McDOWALL
Kris Kringle	SEBASTIAN CABOT
Susan Walker	SUZANNE DAVIDSON
Horace Shellhammer	JIM BACKUS
R. H. Macy	DAVID DOYLE
Judge Harper	TOM BOSLEY
District Attorney	JAMES GREGORY
Mr. Gimbel	ROLAND WINTERS
Reindeer Keeper	LIAM DUNN
Richardson	CONRAD JANIS
Celeste	ELLEN WESTON

A heartwarming color update of the 1947 movie classic telling whimsically of the department store Santa Claus, the little girl who believes in him, and his trial to prove he really is Kris Kringle.

0371

THE GLASS MENAGERIE

12/16/73 Talent Associates/Norton-Simon (2 hours)

Producer: David Susskind
Director: Anthony Harvey
Teleplay: Tennessee Williams
Photography: Billy Williams
Music: John Barry
Art Director: Trevor Williams
Editor: John Bloom

Amanda Wingfield	KATHARINE HEPBURN
Tom	SAM WATERSTON
Laura	JOANNA MILES
The Gentleman Caller (Jim O'Connor)	MICHAEL MORIARTY

Katharine Hepburn made her television acting debut in this poetic adaptation of Tennessee Williams' wistful play about the memories and hopes of the Wingfield family during the 1930s. Filmed once before in 1950 with Gertrude Lawrence, this version offered Emmy Award-winning performances by Joanna Miles and Michael Moriarty (both in the supporting category).

0372

I HEARD THE OWL CALL MY NAME

12/18/73 Tomorrow Entertainment (90 min)

Executive Producer: Roger Gimbel
Producer/Director: Daryl Duke
Teleplay: Gerald DiPego
Based on the book by Margaret Craven
Photography: Bill Butler
Music: Peter Matz
Art Director: Barry Lavender
Editor: Richard Halsey

Father Tark Brian	TOM COURTENAY
Bishop	DEAN JAGGER
Jim Wallace	PAUL STANLEY
Keetah	MARIANNE JONES
George P. Hudson	GEORGE CLUTESI
Alan Spencer	KEITH PEPPER
Marta Stevens	MARGARET ATLEO

A young American priest, in his search for greater knowledge, finds that his schooling has hardly prepared him for his mission to a remote Canadian Indian village in British Columbia.

0373

WHAT ARE BEST FRIENDS FOR?

12/18/73 ABC Circle Films (90 min)

Producer: Lillian Gallo
Director: Jay Sandrich
Teleplay: Rubin Carson and J. A. Vargas
Photography: Ben Colman
Music: Jack Elliott and Allyn Ferguson
Art Director: Eugene Lourie
Editor: John A. Martinelli

Paul Nesbitt	TED BESSELL
Adele Ross	LEE GRANT
Frank Ross	LARRY HAGMAN
Valerie Norton	BARBARA FELDON
Evelyn Huston	NINA TALBOT
Barry Chambers	GEORGE FURTH
Dr. Otto Ludwig	ALAN OPPENHEIMER
Roberta	PATRICIA HARTY
Deborah Nesbitt	CORINNE COMACHO
Keith	ROGER PERRY
Marge	BARBARA RHOADES

and: Linda Morrow, Shirley O'Hara, Jo Marie Ward, Guy Remsen, Salvatore Corsitto

An amiable comedy about the determined efforts of a married couple to find a girl for their recently divorced best friend.

0374

PIONEER WOMAN

12/19/73 Filmways (90 min)

Producers: Edward S. Feldman and Robert M. Rosenbloom
Director: Buzz Kulik
Teleplay: Suzanne Clauser
Photography: Charles F. Wheeler
Music: Al DeLory
Editor: Rita Roland

Maggie Sergeant	JOANNA PETTET
John Sergeant	WILLIAM SHATNER
Robert Douglas	DAVID JANSSEN
Joe Wormser	LANCE LeGAULT
Sarah Sergeant	HELEN HUNT
Jeremy Sergeant	RUSSELL BAER
Philippa Wormser	LINDA KUPECEK
Slim Hall	LLOYD BERRY
William Seymour	ROBERT KOONS
Trudy Seymour	AGATHA MERCER
Jake	JOHN SCOTT
Jordan Seymour	LES KIMBER
Henry Seymour	JOHN MURRELL
Frank	FRANK EDGE
Mrs. Hill	UNA PULSON

The hardships of homesteading in the Wyoming Territory in 1867 are brought into focus through the eyes of a wife and mother when her husband is killed and the decision whether or not to remain on the frontier is hers to make.

0375

A DREAM FOR CHRISTMAS

12/24/73 Lorimar Productions (2 hours)

Executive Producer: Lee Rich
Producer: Walter Coblenz
Director: Ralph Senesky
Teleplay: John McGreevey and Mark Hodge
From a story by Earl Hamner, Jr.
Photography: Frank V. Phillips
Music: David Rose
Art Director: Ed Graves
Editors: Bill Mosher, Anthony Wollner and Gene Fowler, Jr.

Rev. Will Douglas	HARI RHODES
Grandma Reese	BEAH RICHARDS
Sarah Douglas	LYNN HAMILTON
Joey Douglas	GEORGE SPELL
Bradley Douglas	MARLIN ADAMS
George Briggs	ROBERT DoQUI
Emmarine Douglas	TA RONCE ALLEN
Arthur Rogers	JOEL FLUELLEN
Fannie Mitchell	JUANITA MOORE
Becky Douglas	BEBE REDCROSS
Donald Freeland	CLARENCE MUSE
Cousin Clara	DOROTHY MEYER

and: Saria Grant, Maidie Norman, Dennis Hines, Zara Cully, Frances E. Williams

An all-black cast shines in this pilot for a proposed series involving a southern minister who is assigned to a poor parish in California with the congregation drifting away and the church scheduled for demolition. The hope here was for writer Earl Hamner to repeat his success with "The Waltons."

0376

INDICT AND CONVICT

1/6/74 Universal (2 hours)

Executive Producer: David Victor
Producer: Winston Miller
Director: Boris Sagal
Teleplay: Winston Miller
Based on the book by Bill Davidson
Photography: Bill Butler

Helen Hunt, Joanna Pettet, Russell Baer and William Shatner in PIONEER WOMAN (1973)

Hari Rhodes, Joel Fluellen and Clarence Muse in A DREAM OF CHRISTMAS (1973)

Michelle Phillips and Melvyn Douglas in DEATH SQUAD (1974)

Music: Jerry Goldsmith
Art Director: John T. McCormack
Editor: Robert F. Shugrue

Bob Mathews	GEORGE GRIZZARD
Mike Belano	RENI SANTONI
Joanna Garrett	SUSAN HOWARD
Timothy Fitzgerald	ED FLANDERS
DeWitt Foster	ELI WALLACH
Sam Belden	WILLIAM SHATNER
Judge Christine Taylor	MYRNA LOY
Mel Thomas	HARRY GUARDINO
Norman Hastings	KIP NIVEN
Phyllis Dorfman	RUTA LEE
Frank Rogers	DEL RUSSEL
Barbara Mathews	MARIE CHEATHAM
Pathologist	ALFRED RYDER

and: Eunice Christopher, Arlene Martel, Henry Beckman, Michael Petaki

This courtroom drama finds prosecutor Grizzard against his deputy D.A. pal Shatner who is accused of murdering his wife and her lover although he was 150 miles away at the time of the killing.

0377
F. SCOTT FITZGERALD AND "THE LAST OF THE BELLES"
1/7/74 Titus Productions, Inc. (2 hours)

Executive Producer: Herbert Brodkin
Producer: Robert Berger

Director: George Schaefer
Teleplay: James Costigan
Photography: Ed Brown
Music: Don Sebesky
Art Director: Jack DeGovia
Choreography: George Bunt
Costume Designer: Joseph Aulisi
Consultant: Frances Scott Fitzgerald Smith
Editor: Sidney Katz

F. Scott Fitzgerald	RICHARD CHAMBERLAIN
Zelda Fitzgerald	BLYTHE DANNER
Ailie Calhoun	SUSAN SARANDON
Andy McKenna	DAVID HUFFMAN
Earl Shoen	ERNEST THOMPSON
Bill Knowles	RICHARD HATCH
Capt. John Haines	JAMES NAUGHTON
Scottie	LESLIE WILLIAMS
John Biggs	ALBERT STRATTON
Philippe	ALEX SHEAFE

and: Sasha Van Scherler, Thomas A. Stewart, Norman Barrs, Early Sydnor, Brooke Adams, Cynthia Woll, Tom Fitzsimmons, Kate Wilkinson, Jane Hoffman, Dan Browning, Jr. Don Ferguson, Ralph E. Flanders, Brandon Galloway

A dramatization intertwining a part of the lives of the famed American writer and his flamboyant wife with one of the author's short stories, a semi-fictional account of their first meeting in Montgomery, Alabama while he was a soldier in 1919.

0378
NIGHTMARE
1/8/74 CBS, Inc. (90 min)

Producer: Mark Carliner
Director: William Hale
Teleplay: David Wiltse
Photography: Robert B. Hauser
Music: Peter Link
Art Director: James G. Hulsey
Editor: Bud S. Isaacs

Howard Falson	RICHARD CRENNA
Jan Richards	PATTY DUKE ASTIN
Det. Rausch	VIC MORROW
Tayor	PETER BROMILOW
Superintendent	ARCH JOHNSON
Linda	ARLENE GOLONKA
George	RICHARD SCHAAL
Louise	DOREEN LANG
Mrs. Ramsey	MARYESTHER DENVER
Albert	NORBERT SCHILLER

and: Mary Boylan, Wright King, Christopher Joy, James Gavin

A thriller involving a murder witness who, unable to convince police that the killer is in the apartment across the courtyard from his, realizes that he is the next target of the sniper.

0379
THE DEATH SQUAD
1/8/74 Spelling/Goldberg Productions (90 min)

Producers: Aaron Spelling and Leonard Goldberg
Director: Harry Falk
Teleplay: James Buchanan and Ronald Austin
Photography: Tim Southcott
Music: Dave Grusin
Art Director: Tracy Bousman
Editor: Stefan Arnstein

Eric Benoit	ROBERT FORSTER
Joyce Kreski	MICHELLE PHILLIPS
Connie Brennan	CLAUDE AKINS
Allen Duke	MARK GODDARD
Captain Earl Kreski	MELVYN DOUGLAS
Hartman	KENNETH TOBEY
Vern Acker	GEORGE MURDOCK
Harmon	JESSE VINT
Andrece	STEPHEN YOUNG
Sharon	JULIE COBB
The Chief	BERT REMSEN

A television carbon of Clint Eastwood's *Magnum Force* (1973), this movie likewise has a hard-nosed cop going after a self-styled assassination squad of bad cops who are methodically eliminating criminals they feel were wrongly exonerated in court. Forster is the one rooting out the bad apples.

0380
SHOOTOUT IN A ONE-DOG TOWN
1/9/74 Hanna-Barbera Productions (90 min)

Producer: Richard E. Lyons
Director: Burt Kennedy
Teleplay: Larry Cohen and Dick Nelson
From a story by Larry Cohen
Photography: Robert B. Hauser
Music: Hoyt Curtin
Editor: Warner E. Leighton

Zack Wells	RICHARD CRENNA
Letty Crandell	STEFANIE POWERS
Handy	JACK ELAM
Henry Gillis	ARTHUR O'CONNELL
Reynolds	MICHAEL ANSARA
Hall	DUB TAYLOR
Gabe	GENE EVANS
Billy Boy	MICHAEL ANDERSON, JR.
Petry	RICHARD EGAN
Preston	JOHN PICKARD
Little Edgar	JAY RIPLEY

and: Jerry Catlin, Henry Nelson Wills, Eric Valdez

This lean Western with overtones of *High Noon* finds a small-town banker pitted against a vicious gang who will stop at nothing to steal the $200,000 in his vault. Originally this was to have been called simply *The Bank*.

0381
MRS. SUNDANCE
1/15/74 20th Century-Fox (90 min)

Producer: Stan Hough
Director: Marvin Chomsky
Teleplay: Christopher Knopf
Photography: Michel Hugo
Music: Pat Williams
Art Director: Carl Anderson
Editor: Jack McSweeney

Etta Place	ELIZABETH MONTGOMERY
Jack Maddox	ROBERT FOXWORTH
Charles Siringo	L. Q. JONES
Walt Putney	ARTHUR HUNNICUTT
Fanny Porter	LORNA THAYER
Mrs. Lee	LURENE TUTTLE
Mary Lant	CLAUDETTE NEVINS
Merkle	BYRON MABE
Ben Lant	ROBERT DONNER
Avery	DEAN SMITH
Davis	JACK WILLIAMS
David	TODD SHELHORSE

With fond memories of her life with the Sundance Kid, Etta Place leads a fugitive's existence, with a price on her head and bounty hunters on her trail, until rumors reach her that the supposedly dead Sundance still lives.

0382
SCREAM OF THE WOLF
1/16/74 Metromedia Productions (90 min)

Executive Producer: Charles Fries
Producer/Director: Dan Curtis
Associate Producer: Robert Singer
Teleplay: Richard Matheson
Based on the story *The Hunter* by David Chase
Photography: Paul Lohmann
Music: Robert Cobert
Art Director: Walter M. Simonds
Editor: Richard Harris

John Wetherby	PETER GRAVES
Byron Douglas	CLINT WALKER
Sandy Miller	JO ANN PFLUG
Sheriff Vernon Bell	PHILIP CAREY
Grant	DON MEGOWAN
Deputy Crane	BRIAN RICHARDS
Student	LEE PAUL

Richard Crenna in SHOOTOUT IN A ONE DOG TOWN (1974)

Boy	JAMES STORM
Girl	BONNIE VAN DYKE
Lake	DEAN SMITH
Deputy Bill	GRANT OWENS
Coroner	ORVILLE SHERMAN

and: Vernon Weddle, William Baldwin, Douglas Bungert, Kenneth Stimson

A once-famous hunter comes out of retirement to help track down what seems to be a mad killer wolf and discovers that it is no mere animal he is stalking but an animal that may take human form.

0383
SKYWAY TO DEATH
1/19/74 Universal (90 min)

Producer: Lou Morheim
Director: Gordon Hessler
Teleplay: David Spector
Photography: J. J. Jones
Music: Lee Holdridge
Art Director: William Campbell
Editor: Bud Hoffman

Martin Leonard	ROSS MARTIN
Nancy Sorenson	STEFANIE POWERS
Barney Taylor	BOBBY SHERMAN
Sam Nichols	TIGE ANDREWS
Ann Leonard	NANCY MALONE
Bill Carter	DAVID SHEINER

Andrew Tustin	JOHN ASTIN
Bob Parsons	JOSEPH CAMPANELLA
Aunt Louise	RUTH McDEVITT
Steve Kramer	SEVERN DARDEN
Walter Benson	BILLY GREEN BUSH
Kathy Reed	LISSA MORROW

A standard "lives in peril" movie with a dozen or so passengers trapped on an aerial tramway 8,500 feet in the air.

0384
GET CHRISTIE LOVE!
1/22/74 Wolper Productions (90 min)

Executive Producer: Lawrence Turman
Producer: Peter Nelson
Director: William A. Graham
Teleplay: George Kirgo
Based on the novel *The Ledger* by Dorothy Uhnak
Photography: Meredith Nicholson
Music: Jack Elliott and Allyn Ferguson
Editor: Jim Benson

Christie Love	TERESA GRAVES
Casey Reardon	HARRY GUARDINO
Helena Varga	LOUISE SOREL
Enzo Cortino	PAUL STEVENS
Greenberg	ANDY ROMANO

Amy	DEBBIE DOZIER
Gwen Fenley	TRACY ROBERTS
Loomis	LEE PAUL

and: Lynne Holmes, Bill Henderson, Titos Vandis, Davis Roberts, Richard Hurst, Byron Chung

A foxy female cop goes undercover to bust a drug empire in this pilot for the first of the policewoman series (1974–75), in which shapely Miss Graves was joined by Charles Cioffi (in the role originated by Guardino) and Jack Kelly as their boss. Graves, the eye-popping bikini girl of the old "Laugh-In" series, subsequently disappeared from television to take up religious causes.

0385
THE QUESTOR TAPES
1/23/74 Universal (2 hours)

Executive Producer: Gene Roddenberry
Producer: Howie Hurwitz
Director: Richard A. Colla
Teleplay: Gene Roddenberry and Gene L. Coon
From a story by Gene Roddenberry
Photography: Michael Margulies
Music: Gil Melle
Art Director: Phil Barber
Special Effects: Albert Whitlock

Editorial Supervisor: Richard Belding
Editors: Robert L. Kimble and Jerry Williams

Cicely Tyson and Michael Murphy in THE AUTOBIOGRAPHY OF MISS JANE PITTMAN (1974)

Questor	ROBERT FOXWORTH
Jerry Robinson	MIKE FARRELL
Darrow	JOHN VERNON
Vaslovik	LEW AYRES
Dr. Chen	JAMES SHIGETA
Dr. Michaels	ROBERT DOUGLAS
Lady Helen Trimbal	DANA WYNTER
Allison Sample	ELLEN WESTON
Dr. Bradley	MARJEL BARRETT
Dr. Gorlov	REUBEN SINGER
Administrative Assistant	WALTER KOENIG
Dr. Audret	FRED SADOFF
Randolph	GERALD SANDERSON PETERS
Stewardess	EYDSE GIRARD
Immigration Officer	ALAN CAILLOU
Colonel Henderson	LAL BAUM
Secretary	PATTI CIBBISON

An unsuccessful pilot by Gene ("Star Trek") Roddenberry about a sophisticated android looking for his true identity, hoping to locate his missing creator through the use of his computerized brain.

0386
PRAY FOR THE WILDCATS
1/23/74 ABC Circle Films (2 hours)

Producer: Anthony Wilson
Director: Robert Michael Lewis
Teleplay: Jack Turley
Photography: John Morley Stephens
Music: Fred Myrow
Art Director: Bill Malley
Editor: Les Green

Sam Farragut	ANDY GRIFFITH
Warren Summerfield	WILLIAM SHATNER
Lila Summerfield	LORRAINE GARY
Krissie Kincaid	JANET MARGOLIN
Paul McIlvian	ROBERT REED
Terry Maxon	MARJOE GORTNER
Nancy McIlvian	ANGIE DICKINSON
Howard Norkan	JOHN BARBOUR
Michael	SKIP BURTON
Loris	MARILYN MEARN
Captain Guiterrez	JOHN BRASCIA
Mr. Perkins	WILLIAM WINTERSOLE
Doctor Harris	PAUL KENT

A hard-driving executive induces three advertising men, seeking his business, to accompany him on a wild motorcycle trip into Mexico, jeopardizing their careers, their families and their lives.

0387
HEATWAVE!
1/26/74 Universal (90 min)

Producer: Herbert F. Solow
Director: Jerry Jameson
Teleplay: Peter Allen Fields and Mark Weingart
From a story by Herbert F. Solow
Photography: Enzo A. Martinelli
Music: Fred Steiner
Art Director: Robert Jillson
Editors: Doug Young and J. Jerry Williams

Frank Taylor	BEN MURPHY
Laura Taylor	BONNIE BEDELIA
Dr. Grayson	LEW AYRES
Arnold Brady	DAVID HUDDLESTON
Toler	JOHN ANDERSON
Prescott	DANA ELCAR
Harry	ROBERT HOGAN
Jerry	LIONEL JOHNSTON
Susan	JANIT BALDWIN

Cicely Tyson in THE AUTOBIOGRAPHY OF MISS JANE PITTMAN (1974)

and: Clete Roberts, Joe Perry, Naomi Stevens, Donald Mantooth, Robert DoQui, Richard Bull, Stuart Nisbet, Christine Bennett

During a severe heat wave, the courageous determination of a young husband and his pregnant wife ultimately inspires the survivors in a mountain town to unite in an effort to save a life.

0388
THE GIRL WHO CAME GIFT-WRAPPED
1/29/74 Spelling/Goldberg Productions (90 min)

Producer: Aaron Spelling and Leonard Goldberg
Director: Bruce Bilson
Teleplay: Susan Silver
Photography: Tim Southcott
Music: Jack Elliott and Allyn Ferguson
Art Director: Tracy Bousman
Editor: John Woodcock

Sandy	KAREN VALENTINE
Michael Green	RICHARD LONG
Harold	TOM BOSLEY
Patti	FARRAH FAWCETT
Stanley	DAVE MADDEN
Miss Markin	RETA SHAW
Sylvia	LOUISE SOREL
Cindy	PATTI CUBBISON
Larry	MICHAEL HAYNES
Louise	SHELLEY MORRISON

A small-town beauty with wide eyes, great ambitions and empty pockets is presented to a wealthy and jaded magazine publisher as a bikinied birthday present by his business associates.

0389
THE AUTOBIOGRAPHY OF MISS JANE PITTMAN
1/31/74 Tomorrow Entertainment (2 hours)

Producers: Robert W. Christiansen and Rick Rosenberg
Director: John Korty
Teleplay: Tracy Keenan Wynn

Based on the novel by Ernest J. Gaines
Photography: James Crabe
Music: Fred Karlin
Production Designer: Michael Haller
Makeup: Stan Winston and Rick Barker
Editor: Sid Levin

Jane Pittman	CICELY TYSON
Big Laura	ODETTA
Mme. Gautier	JOSEPHINE PREMICE
Sheriff Guidry	TED AIRHART
Tee-Bob	SIDNEY ARROYO
Jimmy (age 7)	ERIC BROWN
Freedom Investigator	WOODROW CHAMBLISS
Amma Dean	BARBARA CHANEY
Long-Haired Boy	NOEL CRAVENZE
Master Bryant	RICHARD DYSART
"Unc" Isom	JOEL FLUELLEN
Etienne	JERRY GREEN
Mr. Clyde	JAMES GOODMAN
Elbert Cluveau	WILL HARE
Colonel Dye	DAVID HOOKS
Mary	ELNORA B. JOHNSON
Trooper Brown	DUDLEY KNIGHT
Little Ned (age 5)	DERRICK MILLS
Quentin Lerner	MICHAEL MURPHY
Ticey (Young Jane)	VALERIE O'DELL
Joe Pittman	ROD PERRY
Master Robert	ROY POOLE
Ned	THALMUS RASULALA
Ned (age 15)	DAN SMITH
Vivian	CAROL SUTTON
Timmy	TONY THOMAS
Mary Agnes	ALANA VILLAVASO
Elder Banks	BILL WALKER
Mistress Bryant	COLLIN WILCOX-HORNE
Jimmy	ARNOLD WILKERSON
Lena	BEATRICE WINDE

Winner of nine Emmy Awards, including Outstanding Drama of the 1973–74 season, this was one of the most acclaimed TV movies ever, highlighted by Cicely Tyson's Emmy-winning performance as the (fictional)

169

woman who was born into slavery in the 1850s and lived to see the Civil Rights movement a century later. Director John Korty and writer Tracy Keenan Wynn also received Emmy Awards. Additionally, they won the Directors Guild of America and Writers Guild of America awards, respectively, and the film was given the prestigious Christopher Award.

0390
KILLDOZER
2/2/74 Universal (90 min)

Producer: Herbert F. Solow
Director: Jerry London
Teleplay: Theodore Sturgeon and Ed MacKillop
Based on the novella by Theodore Sturgeon
Photography: Terry K. Meade
Music: Gil Melle
Art Director: James Martin Buchanan
Special Effects: Albert Whitlock
Editor: Fabien Tordjmann

Lloyd Kelly	CLINT WALKER
Dennis Holvig	CARL BETZ
Chub Foster	NEVILLE BRAND
Jules "Dutch" Krasner	JAMES WAINWRIGHT
Al Beltran	JAMES A. WATSON, JR.
Mack McCarthy	ROBERT URICH

A man-vs.-machine thriller pitting a group of construction workers against a murderous bulldozer controlled by an alien being.

0391
SMILE, JENNY, YOU'RE DEAD
2/3/74 Warner Bros. (2 hours)

Producer/Director: Jerry Thorpe
Teleplay: Howard Rodman
Photography: Jack Woolf
Music: Billy Goldenberg
Art Director: Walter Herndon
Editors: Mel Shapiro and Michael A. Hoey

Harry Orwell	DAVID JANSSEN
Col. John Lockport	JOHN ANDERSON
Lt. Humphrey Kenner	HOWARD da SILVA
Meade DeRuyter	MARTIN GABEL
Milt Bosworth	CLU GULAGER
Roy St. John	ZALMAN KING
Charley English	TIM McINTIRE
Jennifer English	ANDREA MARCOVICCI
Liberty Cole	JODIE FOSTER
Fashion Photographer	HARVEY JASON
Mildred	BARBARA LEIGH
Lt. Richard Marum	VICTOR ARGO
Julia	ELLEN WESTON
Assistant Photographer	CHET WINFIELD

This pilot for Janssen's "Harry-O" series (1974–76) had the ex-cop moonlighting as a private investigator looking into the murder of a cop friend's son-in-law and becoming emotionally involved with his daughter who happens to be the chief suspect in the killing.

0392
THE MIGRANTS
2/3/74 CBS Television, Inc. (90 min)

Producer/Director: Tom Gries
Associate Producer: Paul A. Helmick
Teleplay: Lanford Wilson
From a story by Tennessee Williams
Photography: Dick Kratina
Music: Billy Goldenberg
Editor: Bud S. Isaacs

Viola Barlow	CLORIS LEACHMAN

Carl Betz and Clint Walker in KILLDOZER (1974)

Carl Betz, James Watson, Jr. (seated) and James Wainwright in KILLDOZER (1974)

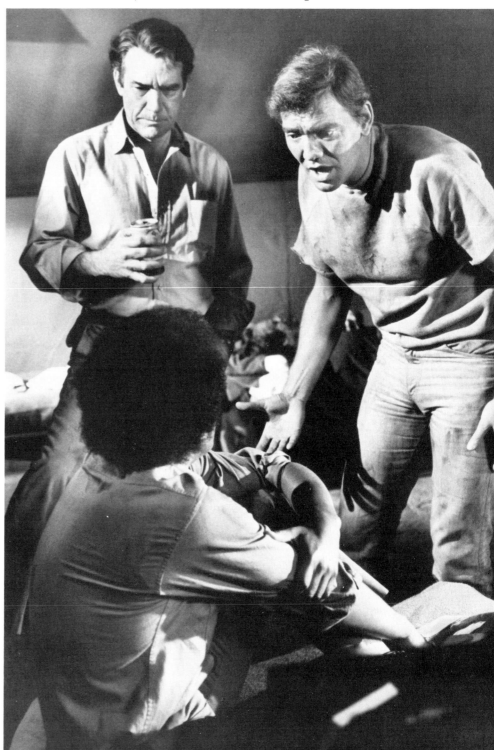

David Janssen and Andrea Marcovicci in SMILE, JENNY, YOU'RE DEAD (1974)

Kathy Cannon and John Saxon in CAN ELLEN BE SAVED? (1974)

Lyle Barlow	RON HOWARD
Wanda Trimpin	SISSY SPACEK
Betty	CINDY WILLIAMS
Mr. Barlow	ED LAUTER
Molly Barlow	LISA LUCAS
Hec Campbell	MILLS WATSON
Tom Trimpin	DAVID CLENNON
Billie Jean Barlow	DINAH ENGLUND
Johnson	BRAD SULLIVAN
Doctor	LEON RUSSOM
Rose Daw	CLAUDIA McNEIL
Father	TOM ROSQUI
Sheriff	DOLPH SWEET
Miss Travers	MARI GORMAN

and: Wally Parnell, George Castellini, Henry Newman, Richard DeFeo, Rudolph Tillman, Joseph Brady, Billy Pope, Sol Weiner

A stark look at the lives of migratory farm workers, focusing on one family. The film was Emmy-nominated as the Outstanding Drama of the 1973–74 season, and nominations also went to director Tom Gries, actress Cloris Leachman, cinematographer Dick Kratina, and composer Billy Goldenberg.

0393
CAN ELLEN BE SAVED?
2/5/74 ABC Circle Films (90 min)

Producer: Everett Chambers
Director: Harvey Hart
Teleplay: Emmett Roberts
Photography: Earl Rath
Music: The Orphanage
Art Director: Jan Scott
Editors: George Jay Nicholson and Ronald J. Fagan

Arnold Lindsey	LESLIE NIELSEN
Joseph	MICHAEL PARKS
Bea Lindsey	LOUISE FLETCHER

171

John Ireland and Broderick Crawford in THE PHANTOM OF HOLLYWOOD (1974)

Earl Holliman and Hope Lange in I LOVE YOU, GOODBYE (1974)

Ellen Lindsey	KATHY CANNON
James Hallbeck	JOHN SAXON
Rachael	RUTANYA ALDA
Mary	CRISTINA HART
Bob	BILL KATT
Daniel	DENNIS REDFIELD
Joanne	KATHLEEN QUINLAN
Randy	SCOTT COLOMBY

An exorcism movie involving a girl whose search for herself becomes the object of an intense struggle between her parents and members of a religious commune. Initially this was entitled *Children of God*.

0394
CRY PANIC
2/6/74 Spelling/Goldberg Productions (90 min)

Producers: Aaron Spelling and Leonard Goldberg
Director: James Goldstone
Teleplay: Jack B. Sowards
Photography: Tim Southcott
Music: Jack Elliott and Allyn Ferguson
Art Director: Tracy Bousman
Editor: Folmar Blangsted

Dennis Ryder	JOHN FORSYTHE
Sheriff Ross Cabot	EARL HOLLIMAN
Chuck Braswell	RALPH MEEKER
Doc Potter	NORMAN ALDEN
Ethel Hanson	CLAUDIA McNEIL
Julie	ANNE FRANCIS
Dozier	EDDIE FIRESTONE
Taylor	JASON WINGREEN
Lipscombe	GENE TYBURN
Jackson	HARRY BASCH

A drama about a man who accidentally runs over and kills a pedestrian on the outskirts of a small town whose citizens, including the sheriff, are hiding a deadly secret about the victim.

0395
DRACULA
2/8/74 Universal/Dan Curtis Productions (2 hours)

Producer/Director: Dan Curtis
Associate Producer: Robert Singer
Teleplay: Richard Matheson
Based on the novel by Bram Stoker
Photography: Oswald Morris
Music: Robert Cobert
Assistant Director: Derek Kavanagh
Art Director: Trevor Williams
Special Effects: Kit West
Editor: Richard A. Harris

Count Dracula	JACK PALANCE
Arthur Holmwood	SIMON WARD
Dr. Van Helsing	NIGEL DAVENPORT
Mrs. Westerna	PAMELA BROWN
Lucy Westerna	FIONA LEWIS
Mina Murray	PENELOPE HORNER
Jonathan Harker	MURRAY BROWN
Dracula's Wives	VIRGINIA WETHERALL BARBARA LINDLEY SARAH DOUGLAS
Innkeeper	GEORGE PRAVDA
Innkeeper's Wife	HANNA-MARIA PRAVDA
Zookeeper	REG LYE
Priest	FRED STONE
Whitby Inn Maid	SANDRA CARON
Whitby Inn Clerk	ROY SPENCER
Stockton-on-Tees Clerk	JOHN CHALLIS

172

Midvale Shipping Clerk	NIGEL GREGORY
Richmond Shipping Clerk	JOHN PENNINGTON
Coast Guard	MARTIN READ
Madam Kirstoff	GITTA DENISE

A lavish, atmospheric new version of Bram Stoker's classic tale of horror with Jack Palance heading a stellar British cast as the bloodthirsty count.

0396
THE ELEVATOR
2/9/74 Universal (90 min)

Producer: William Frye
Director: Jerry Jameson
Teleplay: David Ketchum, Bruce Shelley and Rhoda Blecker
Photography: Matthew F. Leonetti
Music: John Cacavas
Art Director: Leroy G. Deane
Editors: Philip Haberman and J. Jerry Williams

Eddie Holcomb	JAMES FARENTINO
Marvin Ellis	RODDY McDOWALL
Dr. Stuart Reynolds	CRAIG STEVENS
Pete Howarath	DON STROUD
Edith Reynolds	TERESA WRIGHT
Amanda Kenyon	MYRNA LOY
Irene Turner	CAROL LYNLEY
Wendy Thompson	ARLENE GOLONKA
Robert Peters	BARRY LIVINGSTON
Mrs. Peters	JEAN ALLISON
Alan Rambeau	BOB FISHER

and: Paul Sorenson, Ed Deemer, Will J. White, Jack Griffin, Jason Wingreen

A claustrophobic armed robber, fleeing from his latest job, finds himself trapped with a group of people between floors in a high-rise building.

Dick Van Dyke in THE MORNING AFTER (1974)

0397
THE PHANTOM OF HOLLYWOOD
2/12/74 MGM (90 min)

Executive Producer: Burt Nodell
Producer/Director: Gene Levitt
Teleplay: Robert Thom and George Shenk
From a story by George Shenk
Photography: Gene Polito
Music: Leonard Rosenman
Art Director: Edward Carfagno
Phantom Makeup: William Tuttle
Editor: Henry Batista

Randy Cross	SKYE AUBREY
Otto Vonner/Karl Vonner	JACK CASSIDY
Jonathan	JACKIE COOGAN
Captain O'Neal	BRODERICK CRAWFORD
Ray Burns	PETER HASKELL
Lieut. Gifford	JOHN IRELAND
Roger Cross	PETER LAWFORD
Wickes	KENT TAYLOR
Fogel	BILL WILLIAMS
Mrs. Wickes	CORINNE CALVET
Joe (Watchman)	REGIS TOOMEY
Studio Engineer	BILLY HALOP
Duke	GARY BURTON
Al	JOHN LUPTON
Clyde	FREDD WAYNE

and: Carl Byrd, Edward Cross, Bill Stout, Damon Douglas, George Nolan

A masked monster goes on a deadly rampage aimed at those selling his home, the legendary MGM back lot.

0398
I LOVE YOU, GOODBYE
2/12/74 Tomorrow Entertainment (90 min)

Producers: Robert W. Christiansen and Rick Rosenberg
Director: Sam O'Steen
Teleplay: Diana Gould
Photography: Andrew Jackson
Music: Billy Goldenberg
Art Director: Walter Scott Herndon
Editor: Howard S. Deane

Karen Chandler	HOPE LANGE
Tom Chandler	EARL HOLLIMAN
Alex Shield	MICHAEL MURPHY
Gwen	PATRICIA SMITH
Pam Parks	MARY MURPHY
Julie Chandler	KERRI SHUTTLETON
Steve Chandler	BRIAN ANDREWS
David Chandler	STEPHEN HUDIS
Alton Stockard	MILT KOGAN
Nancy	ELAINE SCURRY
Ann	DEIRDRE FLYNN
Joy	LOIS WALDEN
Katie	JESSICA STUART
Ria	BRENDA SMITH
Salesgirl	MADGE SINCLAIR

and: Alan Paige, Elizabeth Harrower, Hannah Hertelendy, Tony Mancini, Booth Colman, Betty Pairad, Bernie Valentine, Maureen Dawson

Frustrated by the role society has forced on her as a wife and mother, a suburbanite abandons her family in an effort to find a more challenging and fulfilling life.

0399
THE MORNING AFTER
2/13/74 Wolper Productions (90 min)

Executive Producer: Lawrence Turman
Producer: Stan Margulis
Director: Richard T. Heffron
Teleplay: Richard Matheson
Based on the novel by Jack B. Weiner
Photography: Michel Hugo
Music: Mike Post and Pete Carpenter
Art Director: Ben Kasazkaw
Editor: David Newhouse

Charlie Lester	DICK VAN DYKE
Fran Lester	LYNN CARLIN
Rudy King	DON PORTER
Frank Lester	ROBERT HOVER
Karen Lester	JEWEL BLANCH
Carol Lester	CAROLYN AMES
Dr. Tillman	RICHARD DERR
Dr. Emmett	JOSHUA BRYANT
Toni	LINDA LAVIN
Danny Lester	DERMOTT DOWNS
Rita	JOYCE EASTON
Telly	SANDY WARD
Jim Doherty	JIM B. RAYMOND
Kathy Doherty	PENNY CUNARD
Stewart	DOUG JOHNSON

Peter Bromilow, Donna Mills and Stewart Moss in LIVE AGAIN, DIE AGAIN (1974)

Dick Van Dyke made his TV dramatic debut in this drama about a successful public relations writer whose refusal to admit that he is an alcoholic causes him to lose his self-respect, his career, his family and almost his life. Van Dyke's performance earned him an Emmy nomination.

0400
LIVE AGAIN, DIE AGAIN
2/16/74 Universal (90 min)

Executive Producer: David Victor
Producer: Robert F. O'Neill
Director: Richard A. Colla
Teleplay: Joseph Stefano
Based on the novel *Come to Mother* by David Sale
Photography: Michael Margulies
Music: George Romanis
Art Director: George C. Webb
Editor: David Newhouse and Jamie Caylor

Joe Dolan	CLIFF POTTS
Caroline Carmichael	DONNA MILLS
Thomas Carmichael	WALTER PIDGEON
James Carmichael	MIKE FARRELL
Sissie O'Neil	GERALDINE PAGE
Marcia Carmichael	VERA MILES
Betty Simpson	LURENE TUTTLE
Wilson	STEWART MOSS
Miss Moritz	IRENE TEDROW
Dr. Felman	PETER BROMILOW
Larry Brice	WALKER EDMISTON
Old Friends	FLORENCE LAKE TOM CURTIS

A cryogenics tale about a woman's re-emergence after being frozen for more than thirty years following her death from rheumatic fever—and facing her now aged husband (Walter Pidgeon), her neurotic grown daughter (Vera Miles) and her confused son (Mike Farrell).

0401
A CASE OF RAPE
2/20/74 Universal (2 hours)

Executive Producer: David Levinson
Producer: Louis Randolph
Director: Boris Sagal
Teleplay: Robert E. Thompson
From a story by Louis Randolph
Photography: Terry K. Meade
Music: Hal Mooney
Art Director: George C. Webb
Editor: Richard Bracken

Ellen Harrod	ELIZABETH MONTGOMERY
Leonard Alexander	WILLIAM DANIELS
Larry Retzliff	CLIFF POTTS
Muriel Dyer	ROSEMARY MURPHY
David Harrod	RONNY COX
Marge Bracken	PATRICIA SMITH
Det. Riley	KEN SWOFFORD
Det. Parker	JONATHAN LIPPE
Judge	ROBERT KARNES

and: Sandy Kenyon, Gerald Hiken, Debbie Lytton

A tough drama about a middle-class housewife whose rape experience made her feel not only humiliation but the feeling that she was the guilty party following her husband's waning trust and the harsh courtroom interrogation leading to sympathy for the accused. The sensitive performance by Elizabeth Montgomery earned her an Emmy nomination (editor Richard Bracken also received one, as did director Boris Sagal) for this acclaimed movie which, at the time, became the second highest rated made-for-television film ever.

0402
IT'S GOOD TO BE ALIVE
2/22/74 Metromedia Productions (2 hours)

Executive Producers: Charles Fries and Larry Harmon
Producer: Gerald I. Isenberg
Director: Michael Landon
Teleplay: Steven Gethers

Based on the book by Roy Campanella
Photography: Ted Voigtlander
Music: Michel Legrand
Editor: John A. Martinelli

Roy Campanella	PAUL WINFIELD
Sam Brockington	LOU GOSSETT
Ruthe Campanella	RUBY DEE
Walter O'Malley	RAMON BIERI
Campanella's Father	JOE DeSANTIS
David Campanella	TY HENDERSON
Surgeon	LLOYD GOUGH
Roy Campanella (as a boy)	ERIC WOODS
Man at Accident	LEN LESSER
Preacher	STYMIE BEARD
Attendant	PAUL SAVIOR
Boy	STANLEY CLAY
Pee Wee Reese	JOE E. TATA

and: Nina Roman, Stuart Nisbet, Buck Young, Richard Hurst, Gene Tyburn, Willie McIntyre, Jr., Benny Nickleberry, Byron Nickleberry, Azalie Nickleberry, Roy Campanella, Roxie Campanella, Joni Campanella, Tony Campanella, Routh Campanella

This movie details the struggles of former Brooklyn Dodger catcher Roy Campanella to adapt to life in a wheelchair following his crippling automobile accident in 1959. Cinematographer Ted Voigtlander was Emmy-nominated.

0403
HITCHHIKE!
2/23/74 Universal (90 min)

Producer: Jay Benson
Director: Gordon Hessler
Teleplay: Yale M. Udoff
From a story by Yale M. Yudoff
Photography: Leonard J. South
Music: Gil Melle
Art Director: Art Bacon
Editor: John F. Schreyer

Claire Stevens	CLORIS LEACHMAN
Keith Miles	MICHAEL BRANDON
Gardner	HENRY DARROW
Hadley	CAMERON MITCHELL
Stefanie	SHERRY JACKSON
Mary Reardon	CLAIBORNE CARY
Ken Reardon	LINDEN CHILES
Sgt. Hanrathy	JOHN ELERICK
Ken Reardon, Jr.	JEFF WILLIAMS
Tim Moore	LES LANNON
Agatha Carlyle	ELIZABETH KERR
Matt Benton	JACK MANNING
Dr. Schlesinger	NADYNE TURNEY
Counterman	EDDIE QUILLAN
Sheriff Bentley	JAMES GRIFFITH
Gas Station Owner	TERRY WILSON

A woman heading for a vacation unwittingly picks up a murderer and begins a relationship with him that jeopardizes her life during his desperate attempt to elude the police. Originally this was to have been titled *Crisscross*.

0404
MANHUNTER
2/26/74 Quinn Martin Productions (90 min)

Executive Producer: Quinn Martin
Producer: Adrian Samish
Director: Walter Grauman
Teleplay: Sam H. Rolfe
Photography: Jacques R. Marquette
Music: Duane Tatro
Art Director: George B. Chan
Editor: Richard Brockway

Dave Barrett	KEN HOWARD
Frank Clinger	GARY LOCKWOOD
Ben Marks	TIM O'CONNOR
Walt Hovis	JAMES OLSON
Ann Louise Hovis	STEFANIE POWERS
Aaron Denver	JOHN ANDERSON
Charles "Crutch" Shanks	L. Q. JONES
James Barrett	FORD RAINEY
Paul Tate	ROBERT HOGAN
Henry Stratemeyer	R. G. ARMSTRONG
Max Chabriol	LUKE ASKEW
May	MARIE WINDSOR
Alvin Davidson	BEN FRANK
Wilcox Barnes	ROBERT PATTEN
Susan Tate	MARY CROSS
Mrs. Barrett	CLAUDIA BRYAR
Elizabeth Barrett	SHIRLEY O'HARA

and: Lou Frizzell, Hilary Thompson, Russell Thorsen

A World War I ex-marine turns 1930s bounty hunter and goes after Bonnie-and-Clyde style bank robbers who murdered his former girlfriend. Ken Howard later starred in the TV series (1974–75) as the Depression Era crimefighter tracking down wanted criminals for the reward money.

0405
KILLER BEES
2/26/74 RSO Films Inc. (90 min)

Producers: Howard Rosenman and Ron Bernstein
Director: Curtis Harrington
Teleplay: John William Corrington and Joyce Corrington
Photography: Jack Woolf
Music: David Shire
Production Designer: Joel Schumacher
Editors: John W. Holmes and Robert P. Daniels

Edward van Bohlen	EDWARD ALBERT
Victoria Wells	KATE JACKSON
Madame van Bohlen	GLORIA SWANSON
Dr. Helmut van Bohlen	ROGER DAVIS
Mathias	DON McGOVERN
Rudolf van Bohlen	CRAIG STEVENS
Jeffreys	JOHN S. RAGIN
Zeb Tucker	LIAM DUNN
Roseanna	HEATHER ANN BOSTAIN

and: Donald Gentry, Jack Perkins, Robert L. Balzar, Daniel Woodworth, John Getz

Gloria Swanson made her TV-film debut as an iron-willed matriarch (with a German accent) who not only dominates a family of California winegrowers but also maintains a strange power over a colony of bees thriving in her vineyard.

0406
UNWED FATHER
2/27/74 Wolper Productions (90 min)

Executive Producer: Lawrence Turman
Producer: Stan Margulies
Director: Jeremy Kagan
Teleplay: W. Hermanos and Carol Evan McKeand
From a story by W. Hermanos
Photography: Jules Brenner
Music: Jerry Fielding
Art Director: Howard E. Johnson
Editors: Pat Kennedy and John Levin

Peter	JOSEPH BOTTOMS
Vicky Simmons	KAY LENZ
Estelle	BEVERLY GARLAND
Judy Simmons	KIM HUNTER
Scott Simmons	JOSEPH CAMPANELLA
Gum	WILLIE AAMES
Principal	WILLIAM H. BASSETT
Judge	WILLIAM HANSEN
Mrs. Howell	GINA ALVARADO
Butler	ED BERNARD
Donna	MICHELLE ART

Joseph Bottoms in UNWED FATHER (1974)

| Jeff | RICHARD GILLILAND |
| Gloria | JAN HILL |

and: Joan Crosby, Michael Talbott, Marni Alexander

A teenage father battles with his girlfriend, her wealthy parents, his own family and the courts in his attempt to gain legal custody of his illegitimate child.

0407
HOUSTON, WE'VE GOT A PROBLEM
3/2/74 Universal (90 min)

Executive Producer: Harve Bennett
Producer: Herman Saunders
Director: Lawrence Doheny
Teleplay: Rick Nelson

Photography: J. J. Jones
Music: Richard Clements
Art Director: Lester L. Green
Editor: Robert F. Shugrue

Steve Bell	ROBERT CULP
Lou Matthews	CLU GULAGER
Tim Cordell	GARY COLLINS
Angie Cordell	SANDRA DEE
Gene Kranz	ED NELSON
Lisa Bell	SHEILA SULLIVAN
Shimon Levin	STEVE FRANKEN
Abraham Levin	ROBERT CORFF
Kerwin	JACK HOGAN
Lousma	QUINN REDEKER
Donna	BARBARA BALDWIN
Mrs. Levin	ZOLYA TOLMA
Mel Anderson	GEOFFREY SCOTT
Mike Matthews	ERIC SHEA

| Newsman | JAMES N. HARRELL |
| Astronaut in Simulator | BRIG. GEN. THOMAS P. STAFFORD |

A thriller about the struggle to return the Apollo 13 astronauts safely to earth after their moon-bound spacecraft was damaged by an explosion, in this film based on actual events of the abortive mission.

0408
THE STRANGER WHO LOOKS LIKE ME
3/6/74 Filmways (90 min)

Executive Producer: Edward S. Feldman
Producer: Lillian Gallo
Director: Larry Peerce
Teleplay: Gerald DiPego
Photography: Mario Tosi
Music: George Aliceson Tipton
Title song written and sung by Paul Williams
Art Director: Lawrence G. Paull
Editor: Eve Newman

Chris Schroeder	BEAU BRIDGES
Joanne Denver	MEREDITH BAXTER
Mr. Denver	WALTER BROOKE
Mrs. Denver	NEVA PATTERSON
Emma Verko	WHITNEY BLAKE
Paul	WOODROW CHAMBLISS
Mr. Gilbert	FORD RAINEY
Mrs. Weiner	MAXINE STUART
Carol Sutton	PATRICIA HARTY
Mrs. Quayle	MARY MURPHY
Bob	BILL VINT

and: Anne Barton, Warren Miller, Linda Morrow, Warren Seabury, Victor Bevine, Cecil Elliot, Jan Arvan, Biff Elliot, Tom Moses, Sylvia Walden, Millie Slavin, Hampton Fancher, Jocelyn Jones, Susan Adams, Patrick Duffy

The drama of an adopted girl searching for her real mother with the help of a young man who also is looking for the parents who gave him up. Meredith Baxter's real-life mother, Whitney Blake, plays the real mother of the girl in the story.

0409
MOUSEY
3/9/74 Universal/Associated British Films (90 min)

Executive Producer: Beryl Vertue
Producer: Aida Young
Director: Daniel Petrie
Teleplay: John Peacock
Photography: Jack Hildyard
Music: Ron Grainger
Assistant Director: David Tringham
Art Director: Roy Stannard
Editor: John Trumper

George Anderson	KIRK DOUGLAS
Laura Anderson	JEAN SEBERG
David Richardson	JOHN VERNON
Mrs. Richardson	BESSIE LOVE
Sandra	BETH PORTER
Inspector	SAM WANAMAKER
Private Detective	JAMES BRADFORD
Nancy	SUZANNE LLOYD
Simon	STUART CHANDLER
Miss Wainwright	VALERIE COLGAN
Martha	MAVIS VILLIERS
Harry	ELLIOTT SULLIVAN
Barman	BOB SHERMAN
Headmaster	JAMES BERWICK
Miss Carter	MARGO ALEXIS

Cathy Lee Crosby in WONDER WOMAN (1974)

and: Robert Henderson, Louis Negin, Jennifer Watts, Toby Sibbald, Don Fellows, Francis Napier, Roy Stephens, Elsa Pickthorne

Cast somewhat against type in his first made-for-TV movie, Kirk Douglas is a milquetoast biology teacher in Nova Scotia who learns during divorce proceedings that he is not the father of his wife's son and stops at nothing to take vengeance on her in a cat and mouse game. *Cat and Mouse* was the theatrical title of this film as shown in Great Britain.

0410
WONDER WOMAN
3/12/74 Warner Bros. (90 min)

Executive Producer: John D. F. Black
Producer: John G. Stephens
Director: Vincent McEveety
Teleplay: John D. F. Black
Photography: Joseph Biroc
Music: Artie Butler
Art Director: Philip Bennett
Editor: Gene Ruggiero

Diana Prince	CATHY LEE CROSBY
Steve Trevor	KAZ GARAS
Abner Smith	RICARDO MONTALBAN
George Calvin	ANDREW PRINE
Ahnjayla	ANITRA FORD
Hippolyte	CHARLENE HOLT
Joe	ROBERT PORTER
Bob	JORDAN RHODES
Colonel Henkins	RICHARD X. SLATTERY
Dia	BEVERLY GILL
Tina	SANDY GABRIOLA
Zoe	ROBERTA BREHM
Cass	DONNA GARRETT

The initial project to bring the 1940s comic book heroine to television had her entering the 1970s after leaving her native island home to fight for justice in the world beyond and using her wisdom and strength to recover vital documents from a charming but ruthless international spy and his ego-driven associate. Tennis star Cathy Lee Crosby (no relation to Bing) made a valiant effort to bring this live-action cartoon to life.

0411
TELL ME WHERE IT HURTS
3/12/74 Tomorrow Entertainment (90 min)

Executive Producer: Roger Gimbel
Producer: Herbert Hirschman
Director: Paul Bogart
Teleplay: Fay Kanin
Photography: David Walsh
Music: David Shire
Editor: Mike McLean

Connie	MAUREEN STAPLETON
Joe	PAUL SORVINO
Reva	DORIS DOWLING
Agnes	ROSE GREGORIO
Lynn	AYN RUYMAN
Lou	JOHN RANDOLPH
Louise	LOUISE LATHAM
Marge	SCOTTIE MacGREGOR
Edna	PEARL SHEAR
Naomi	PATRICIA SMITH
Jane	FAY KANIN

and: Maxine Stuart, James Foote, Mark Roberts, Tracy Bogart, Marcy Lafferty, David Ankrum, James Dale, Eugene Troobnick, Gerald L. Ray, Ted Swanson

Ned Beatty (left) and Martin Sheen in THE EXECUTION OF PRIVATE SLOVIK (1974)

A housewife, increasingly disenchanted with her homemaker role, searches for new meaning in her life and organizes a discussion group, changing the lives of her six closest friends. Fay Kanin was awarded an Emmy for her original teleplay.

0412
THE EXECUTION OF PRIVATE SLOVIK
3/13/74 Universal (2½ hours)

Executive Producers: Richard Levinson and William Link
Producer: Richard Dubleman
Director: Lamont Johnson
Teleplay: Richard Levinson and William Link
Based on the novel by William Bradford Huie
Photography: Bill Butler
Music: Hal Mooney
Assistant Director: Jim Fargo
Art Director: Walter Tyler
Editor: Frank Morriss

Eddie Slovik	MARTIN SHEEN
Antoinette Slovik	MARICLARE COSTELLO
Father Stafford	NED BEATTY
Jimmy Feedek	GARY BUSEY
Dunn	MATT CLARK
Lt. Col. Leacock	BEN HAMER
Major Fellman	WARREN KEMMERLING
Brockmeyer	CHARLES HAID
Margaret	KATHRYN GRADY
Joe Sirelli	PAUL LAMBERT

and: Jon Cedar, Joseph George, Laurence Haddon, James Burr-Johnson, Tom Ligon, Bill McKinney, Paul Shenar, George Sperdakos, William Traylor, Sandy Ward

Martin Sheen received an Emmy nomination for his portrayal of the only American soldier to be executed for desertion since the Civil War, going to the firing squad in 1945. The film, Emmy-nominated as Outstanding Drama of the 1973–74 season, is a dramatiza-

Dean Jagger, Steve Forrest and Cameron Mitchell in THE HANGED MAN (1974)

tion of William Bradford Huie's controversial 1954 book which, several years after publication, Frank Sinatra had acquired and planned to film, using a screen adaptation by Albert Maltz, one of Hollywood's "unfriendly ten." Sinatra was later pressured by various groups to drop Maltz; instead he completely abandoned his project. For the TV production, Emmy Award nominations also were given to director Lamont Johnson, writers Levinson and Link, art director Walter Tyler and editor Frank Morriss (who won).

0413
THE HANGED MAN
3/13/74 Fenady Associates/Bing Crosby Productions (90 min)

Producer: Andrew J. Fenady
Director: Michael Caffey
Teleplay: Ken Trevey
Photography: Keith C. Smith
Music: Richard Markowitz
Editor: Nick Archer

James Devlin	STEVE FORREST
Lew Halleck	CAMERON MITCHELL
Carrie Gault	SHARON ACKER
Josiah Lowe	DEAN JAGGER
Nameless	WILL GEER
Soledad Villegas	BARBARA LUNA
Father Alvaro	RAFAEL CAMPOS
Billy Irons	BRENDON BOONE
Benjamin Gault	BOBBY EILBACHER
Judge Bayne	RAY TEAL
Joe Janney	STEVEN MARLO
Eubie Turpin	JOHN MITCHUM
Dr. Nye	WILLIAM BRYANT
Ab Wilkes	HANK WORDEN

and: John Pickard, Michael Masters, Bill Catching, Peter J. Ellington, Danny Zapien, Jud McCabe, Ralph Anderson

An ex-gunslinger who survives his own hanging turns into a mystical avenger fighting for justice in the Old West, coming first to the help of a young widow who is trying to keep her silver mine from the clutches of an unscrupulous land baron.

0414
NIGHT GAMES
3/16/74 Paramount (90 min)

Executive Producer: E. Jack Neumann
Producers: Thomas L. Milkis and Edward K. Miller
Director: Don Taylor
Teleplay: E. Jack Neumann
Photography: Howard R. Schwartz
Music: Lalo Schifrin
Art Director: William Campbell
Editor: Donald R. Rode

Tony Petrocelli	BARRY NEWMAN
Patsy Petrocelli	SUSAN HOWARD
Pete Toley	ALBERT SALMI
D. D. Franklin	LUKE ASKEW
Pauline Hannigan	STEFANIE POWERS
Thelma Lattimer	JOANNA CAMERON
Jenny Kenedisis	ANJANETTE COMER
Dale Hannigan	JON CYPHER
D. A. Julio Martinez	HENRY DARROW
Dutch Armbreck	RALPH MEEKER
Clayton Nichols	WILLIAM PRINCE

Judge Medford   DENNIS PATRICK
Judge Ambrose   ROBERT EMHARDT

and: William Hanson, Richard O. Hurst, Sherry Love, Larry Thor, Katey Sweatman, Ernest Neumann

An unorthodox Harvard-educated lawyer, trying to carve out a practice in a small Arizona town with his young bride, defends a pretty socialite accused of murdering her husband in this pilot for the "Petrocelli" series (1974–76). Barry Newman originated the character in the theatrical feature *The Lawyer* (1970), and he continued the role, along with Susan Howard and Albert Salmi, in the later series.

0415
TWICE IN A LIFETIME
3/16/74 Martin Rackin Productions (90 min)

Producer: Martin Rackin
Director: Herschel Daugherty
Teleplay: Martin Rackin and Robert Pirosh
Photography: Arch R. Dalzell
Music: Al Capps
Art Director: Bill Malley
Editor: Carroll Sax

Vince Boselli	ERNEST BORGNINE
Flo	DELLA REESE
Lewis	ERIC LANEUVILLE
Carlos	VITO SCOTTI
Pete Lazich	SLIM PICKENS
Hank Davis	HERB JEFFRIES
Kipp	WARREN VANDERS
Ron Talley	ARTE JOHNSON

and: Sheila Wells, Allison McKay

A lovable old salt, who operates a salvage tug, and his pal, the gal who runs a waterfront cafe, clash with the unscrupulous dock foreman who is trying to throw his weight around in this pilot for a prospective series for Borgnine.

0416
MEN OF THE DRAGON
3/20/74 Wolper Productions (90 min)

Executive Producer: Stan Margulies
Producer: Barney Rosenzweig
Director: Harry Falk
Teleplay: Denne Bart Petitclerc
Photography: Frank Phillips
Music: Elmer Bernstein
Martial Arts Supervisor: David Chow
Editor: Neil Travis

Jan Kimbro	JARED MARTIN
Lisa Kimbro	KATI SAYLOR
Li-Teh	ROBERT ITO
Balashev	JOSEPH WISEMAN
Sato	LEE TIT WAR
Tao	DAVID CHOW
Madame Wu	HSAI HO LAN
O-Lan	NANG SHEEN CHIOU
Inspector Endicott	BILL JERVIS

and: Bobby To, Victor Kan, Herman Chan

Three karate/kung fu experts run up against a gang of modern slavers in this unsuccessful pilot for a series designed to cash in on the current martial arts movie craze.

0417
SIDEKICKS
3/21/74 Warner Bros. (90 min)

Producer/Director: Burt Kennedy
Teleplay: William Bowers
Based on characters created by Richard Alan Simmons

Photography: Robert B. Hauser
Music: David Shire
Art Director: Bill Malley
Editor: Michael Pozen

Quince	LARRY HAGMAN
Jason	LOU GOSSETT
Prudy Jenkins	BLYTHE DANNER
Boss	JACK ELAM
Sheriff Jenkins	HARRY MORGAN
Sam	GENE EVANS
Tom	NOAH BEERY
Max	HAL WILLIAMS
Ed	DICK PEABODY
Drunk	DENVER PYLE
Luke	JOHN BECK

and: Dick Haynes, Tyler McVey, Billy Shannon

Based on the 1971 comedy Western *Skin Game*, this lark, a pilot for a prospective series that never materialized, had a couple of hapless post-Civil War con artists, one black, one white, on the sagebrush trail trying to collect a $15,000 bounty on an outlaw's head. Lou Gossett recreated the role he played in the original film, while Larry Hagman stepped in to replace James Garner.

0418
SENIOR YEAR
3/22/74 Universal (90 min)

Producer: David Levinson
Director: Richard Donner
Teleplay: M. Charles Cohen
Photography: Jack Woolf
Music: James DiPasquale
Art Director: Walter M. Simonds
Editor: Richard Bracken

Jeff Reed	GARY FRANK
Anita Cramer	GLYNNIS O'CONNOR
Moose Kerner	BARRY LIVINGSTON
Evie Mortenson	DEBRALEE SCOTT
Stash	SCOTT COLOMBY
Charlie	LIONEL JOHNSTON
Lucille Reed	JAY W. McINTOSH
Danny Reed	MICHAEL MORGAN
Ruth Cramer	JAN SHULTAN
Walter Cramer	JOHN S. RAGIN
Paul Reed	DANA ELCAR

and: Chris Nelson, Christopher Norris, Randi Kallan, Teresa Medaris, Cheryl Linde, Bonnie Van Dyke, Wallace Rooney, Ted Gehring, Maida Severn, Al Dunlap

High school in the 1950s as seen through the eyes of five carefree seniors is depicted in this pilot for the short-lived series "Sons and Daughters" (September-November 1974), with much of the same cast.

0419
REMEMBER WHEN
3/23/74 Danny Thomas Productions/The Raisin Co. (2 hours)

Executive Producer: Danny Thomas
Producer: Paul Junger Witt
Associate Producer: Tony Thomas
Director: Buzz Kulik
Teleplay: Herman Raucher
Photography: Richard C. Glouner
Music: George Aliceson Tipton
Art Director: Bill Smith
Choreography: Miriam Nelson
Editor: Rita Roland

Joe Hodges	JACK WARDEN
Dick Hodges	WILLIAM SCHALLERT

Joanna	JAMIE SMITH-JACKSON
Frankie Hodges	ROBBY BENSON
Beverly	MARGARET WILLOCK
Annie Hodges	NAN MARTIN
Warren Thompson	TIM MATHESON
Kraus the Butcher	ROBERT MIDDLETON
Shirley	MURIEL LANDERS
Zack	BURTON GILLIAM
Wesso	FRANK DELFINO
Jimmy	CHARLES HAID

A sentimental World War II tale of a small-town Connecticut family with four boys in combat, oozing with warmth and innocence, and shining with the performance of Jack Warden as the live-in bachelor uncle. The original title for this: *Four Stars in the Window*.

0420
A CRY IN THE WILDERNESS
3/26/74 Universal (90 min)

Producer: Lou Morheim
Director: Gordon Hessler
Teleplay: Stephen and Elinor Knarpf
From a story by Gilbert Wright
Photography: J. J. Jones
Music: Robert Prince
Editor: Bud Hoffman

Sam Hadley	GEORGE KENNEDY
Delda Hadley	JOANNA PETTET
Gus Hadley	LEE H. MONTGOMERY
Bess Millard	COLLIN WILCOX-HORNE
Rex Millard	ROY POOLE
Hainie	LIAM DUNN
Griffey	BING RUSSELL
Old Woman	IRENE TEDROW
Doctor	ROBERT BRUBAKER

and: Paul Sorenson, Troy Melton, Anne Seymour, Bob Hoy

A farmer, bitten by a rabid skunk, has himself chained inside his barn to protect his family from his oncoming madness—and then learns that a flood is on the way.

0421
BIG ROSE
3/26/74 20th Century-Fox (90 min)

Producer: Joel Rogosin
Director: Paul Krasny
Teleplay: Andy Lewis
Photography: Andrew Jackson
Music: Robert Prince
Music Supervisor: Lionel Newman
Art Director: Jack Senter
Editors: Clay Bartels and Jack McSweeney

Rose Winters	SHELLEY WINTERS
Ed Mills	BARRY PRIMUS
Lt. John Moore	LONNY CHAPMAN
Gunther	MICHAEL CONSTANTINE
Nina	JOAN VAN ARK
Marian	PEGGY WALTON
Troy	PAUL MANTEE
Blass	PAUL PICERNI
James Mayhew	YALE SUMMERS
Waitress	LENORE KASDORF

and: Burt Mustin, Jennifer Rhodes, Mary Wilcox, Jennifer Shaw

In this pilot for a prospective series for Shelley Winters, she plays a brash private detective who with her young partner investigates why a wealthy contractor is the victim of an extortion plot.

0422

THE ROCKFORD FILES
3/27/74 Universal (90 min)

Executive Producer: Jo Swerling, Jr.
Producer: Stephen J. Cannell
Director: Richard T. Heffron
Teleplay: Stephen J. Cannell
From a story by John Thomas James
Photography: Lamar Boren
Music: Pete Carpenter and Mike Post
Art Director: Robert Luthardt
Editor: John Dumas

Jim Rockford	JAMES GARNER
Sara Butler	LINDSAY WAGNER
Jerry Grimes	WILLIAM SMITH
Mildred Elias	NITA TALBOT
Dennis Becker	JOE SANTOS
Angel	STUART MARGOLIN
Joseph Rockford	ROBERT DONLEY
Morrie Talbot	PAT RENELIA
Nick Butler	BILL MUMY
Danford Baker	MIKE STEELE

The pilot for Garner's hit TV series that debuted in the fall of 1974 has the ex-con-turned-private-eye investigating the death of a skid row bum after being convinced by the man's daughter that he was murdered. Santos and Margolin continued in the series in recurring roles, and Noah Beery was brought in to replace Robert Donley as Rockford's dad.

0423

A TREE GROWS IN BROOKLYN
3/27/74 20th Century-Fox (90 min)

Producer: Norman Rosemont
Director: Joseph Hardy
Teleplay: Blanche Hanalis, Tess Slesinger and Frank Davis
Based on the novel by Betty Smith
Photography: Charles F. Wheeler
Music: Jerry Goldsmith
Art Director: Jan Scott
Editor: Gene Milford

Johnny Nolan	CLIFF ROBERTSON
Katie Nolan	DIANE BAKER
McShane	JAMES OLSON
Francie Nolan	PAMELYN FERDIN
Aunt Sissy	NANCY MALONE
Neely Nolan	MICHAEL-JAMES WIXTED
Barker	LIAM DUNN
Miss Tilford	ANNE SEYMOUR
Miss Martin	ALLYN ANN McLERIE

A sentimental tale, remade from the 1945 classic with an eye toward a possible series, of an impoverished family in a 1912 New York tenement with an alcoholic father and a strong-willed mother.

0424

LITTLE HOUSE ON THE PRAIRIE
3/30/74 NBC Productions (2 hours)

Executive Producer: Ed Friendly
Producer/Director: Michael Landon
Teleplay: Blanche Hanalis
Based on the novel by Laura Ingalls Wilder
Photography: Ted Voigtlander
Music: David Rose
Art Director: Trevor Williams
Editor: John Loeffler

Charles Ingalls	MICHAEL LANDON
Caroline Ingalls	KAREN GRASSLE
Laura Ingalls	MELISSA GILBERT
Mary Ingalls	MELISSA SUE ANDERSON
Carrie Ingalls	LINDSAY SIDNEY GREEN BUSH
Edwards	VICTOR FRENCH
Soldat Du Chene	VIC MOHICA
Brave	CAL BELLINI
1st Indian	SAM VLAHOS
2nd Indian	RICHARD ALARIAN
Grandmother	MARIAN BREEDLER

This faithful adaptation of the charming book about a family's attempts to adjust to life on the Kansas frontier became the forerunner to the long-run TV series which Michael Landon not only starred in but also produced and frequently wrote and directed.

James Garner in THE ROCKFORD FILES (1974)

0425
HONKY TONK
4/1/74 MGM (90 min)

Executive Producer: Douglas Heyes
Producer: Hugh Benson
Director: Don Taylor
Teleplay: Douglas Heyes
Photography: Joseph Biroc
Music: Jerry Fielding
Art Director: Henry Bumstead
Editor: Harry Batista

Candy Johnson	RICHARD CRENNA
Gold Dust	STELLA STEVENS
Judge Cotton	WILL GEER
Lucy Cotton	MARGOT KIDDER
Brazos	JOHN DEHNER
Roper	GEOFFREY LEWIS
Slade	GREGORY SIERRA
Dr. Goodwin	ROBERT CASPER

and: James Luisi, Richard Stahl, Stephen Coit, Dub Taylor, John Quade, Dennis Fimple, Richard Evans

Loosely based on the Clark Gable-Lana Turner-Claire Trevor 1941 movie (at least the character names of the principals match), this light-hearted Western follows the exploits of two hapless con men operating in the boom towns of the Old West.

0426
THE GIRL ON THE LATE, LATE SHOW
4/1/74 Screen Gems/Columbia (90 min)

Executive Producer: David Gerber
Producer: Christopher Morgan
Director: Gary Nelson
Teleplay: Mark Rodgers
Photography: Robert L. Morrison
Music: Richard Markowitz
Art Directors: Ross Bellah and Robert Peterson
Editor: Richard C. Meyer

William Martin	DON MURRAY
F. J. Allen	BERT CONVY
Lorraine	YVONNE DeCARLO
Carolyn Parker	GLORIA GRAHAME
Johnny Leverett	VAN JOHNSON
Inspector DeBiesse	RALPH MEEKER
Norman Wilder	CAMERON MITCHELL
Librarian	MARY ANN MOBLEY
Sergeant Scott	JOE SANTOS
Paula	LARAINE STEPHENS
Bruno Walters	JOHN IRELAND
John Pahlman	WALTER PIDGEON
Pat Clauson	SHERRY JACKSON
Detective	FELICE ORLANDI
Studio Guard	FRANKIE DARRO

A mystery drama with a Hollywood background and lots of familiar screen faces as TV producer Don Murray inquires around town about faded film queen Gloria Grahame and unwittingly triggers a series of murders.

0427
THE GUN AND THE PULPIT
4/3/74 Danny Thomas Productions (90 min)

Executive Producer: Paul Junger Witt
Producer: Paul Maslansky
Associate Producer: Tony Thomas
Director: Daniel Petrie
Teleplay: William Bowers
Based on the novel by Jack Erlich
Photography: Richard C. Glouner
Music: George Aliceson Tipton
Editor: Terrence Anderson

Ernie Parsons	MARJOE GORTNER
Billy One-Eye	SLIM PICKENS
Mr. Ross	DAVID HUDDLESTON
Jason McCoy	GEOFFREY LEWIS
Sadie Underwood	ESTELLE PARSONS
Sally Underwood	PAMELA SUE MARTIN
Head of Posse	JEFF COREY
Adams	KARL SWENSON
Luther	JON LORMER
Tom Underwood	ROBERT PHILLIPS
Max	LARRY WARD
Dixie	JOAN GOODFELLOW

and: Walter Barnes, Melanie Fullerton, Steve Tackett, Jason Clark, Kimo Owens, Charles Young, Ron Nix, Roy Gunsburg

A fugitive gunfighter, disguised as a preacher, is faced with defending townspeople at the mercy of a crooked land baron.

0428
DR. MAX
4/4/74 CBS, Inc. (90 min)

Producer/Director: James Goldstone
Teleplay: Robert L. Joseph
Photography: Terry K. Meade
Music: Billy Goldenberg
Art Director: Joseph R. Jennings
Editor: Folmar Blangsted

Dr. Max Gordon	LEE J. COBB
Gloria Gordon	JANET WARD
Alex Gordon	ROBERT LIPTON
Lester Opel	DAVID SHEINER
Libby Opel	KATHERINE HELMOND
Dr. Scott Herndon	SORRELL BOOKE
Mrs. Camacho	MIRIAM COLON
Rafael Camacho	PANCHITO GOMEZ
Dr. Jules Grogin	JOHN LEHNE
Jean	DELLA THOMAS
Luis Camacho	CAESAR CORDOVA
Dr. John Poole	GRANVILLE VAN DUSEN

and: Marie Earle, Henry Strosier, Alice Rodriguez, Erin Connor, Jon DuBois, Anthony J. Cadorette

A curmudgeony big-city doctor's concern for his patients in a rundown Baltimore neighborhood puts him at odds with his own family. This is a similar contemporary version of the Paul Muni film *The Last Angry Man* (1959), which itself was remade as a TV movie and shown first several weeks after this one.

0429
THE FAMILY KOVACK
4/5/74 Playboy Films (90 min)

Executive Producer: Ed Rissien
Producer: Ron Roth
Director: Ralph Senensky
Teleplay: Adrian Spies
Photography: William Margulies
Music: Harry Sukman
Art Director: Robert Clatworthy
Editor: Jim Benson

Vinnie Kovack	JAMES SLOYAN
Ma Kovack	SARAH CUNNINGHAM
Butch Kovack	ANDY ROBINSON
Karen Kovack	TAMMI BULA
Lennie Kovack	RICHARD GILLILAND
Jill	RENNE JARRETT
Mrs. Linsen	MARY LaROCHE
Jo-Jo Linsen	PHIL BRUNS

Charlie	PAUL BRYAR
Mr. Manzak	PETER BROCCO
Mr. Czablinski	BARUCH LUMET
Thelma	NORMA THAYER
Albert	JIMMY JETER
Nurse	DOROTHY MAYER

A tightly-knit family headed by a beleaguered Chicago widow rallies behind the eldest son when he is charged with bribing a city health department inspector in this pilot for a possible series.

0430
THE STORY OF JACOB AND JOSEPH
4/7/74 Screen Gems/Columbia (2 hours)

Producer: Mildred Freed Alberg
Director: Michael Cacoyannis
Teleplay: Ernest Kinoy
Photography: Ted Moore and Austin Dempster
Music: Mikis Theodorakis
Art Director: Kuli Sander
Editor: Kevin Connor

Jacob	KEITH MICHELL
Joseph	TONY LoBIANCO
Rebekah	COLLEEN DEWHURST
Laban	HERSCHEL BERNARDI
Isaac	HARRY ANDREWS
Esau	JULIAN GLOVER
Rachel	YONA ELIAN
Pharaoh	YOSEPH SHILOAH
Potiphar's Wife	RACHEL SHORE
Potiphar	BENNES MAARDEN
Reuben	YEHUDA EFRONI
Butler	YOSSI GRABBER
Judah	SHMUEL ATZMON
Baker	AMNON MESKIN

Narrated by ALAN BATES

A biblical drama, in two parts—the tale of Jacob and Esau and the legend of Joseph and his brothers—told by director Michael Cacoyannis in his first TV movie.

0431
MELVIN PURVIS: G-MAN
4/9/74 American-International Pictures (90 min)

Executive Producer: Paul R. Picard
Producer/Director: Dan Curtis
Teleplay: John Milius and William F. Nolan
From a story by John Milius
Photography: Jacques R. Marquette
Music: Robert Cobert
Art Director: Trevor Williams
Editors: Richard Harris and Corky Ehlers

Melvin Purvis	DALE ROBERTSON
George "Machine Gun" Kelly	HARRIS YULIN
Katherine Ryan Kelly	MARGARET BLYE
Charles Parlmetter	MATT CLARK
Thomas "Buckwheat" Longmaker	ELLIOTT STREET
Tony Redecci	JOHN KARLEN
Eugene Farber	DAVID CANARY
Sam Cowley	STEVE KANALY
Nash Covington	WOODROW PARFREY
Thatcher Covington	DICK SARGENT

and: Jim Hill, Don McGowan, Max Kleven, Eddie Quillan, Hank Rolike, Ben Pinson, Bill Madden, Darrell Fetty

A breezy, fictional account of the dogged pursuit by cigar-chomping lawman Purvis of notorious public enemy Machine Gun Kelly throughout the Midwest in

Gene Wilder and Bob Newhart in THURSDAY'S GAME (1974)

1933. Writers Milius and Nolan portray Purvis as pure bravado swathed in a flamboyant fur-collared overcoat, and Kelly's gang as a collection of inept buffoons.

0432
THURSDAY'S GAME
4/14/74 ABC Circle Films (2 hours)

Producer: James L. Brooks
Associate Producer: Lew Gallo
Director: Robert Moore
Teleplay: James L. Brooks
Photography: Joseph Biroc
Music: Billy Goldenberg
Song "This Is What You Call Happy" by Dory Previn and Mike Settle
Art Director: Trevor Williams
Editors: Fred Steinkamp and Diane Adler

Harry Evers	GENE WILDER
Marvin Ellison	BOB NEWHART
Lynne Evers	ELLEN BURSTYN
Lois Ellison	CLORIS LEACHMAN
Mrs. Reynolds	MARTHA SCOTT
Miss Bender	NANCY WALKER
Ann Menzenne	VALERIE HARPER
Joel Forrest	ROB REINER
Mel Leonard	NORMAN FELL
Mike	GINO CONFORTI
Bob	RICHARD SCHALL
Dave	ROBERT SAMPSON
Dick	DICK GAUTIER
David Evers	GERALD MICHENAUD
Mr. Wood	JOHN ARCHER

and: Jonathan Kidd, Barbara Barnett, Jed Allen, Bill Callaway, Sidney Clute, Chris Sarandon, Charles Skull, Carol Worthington, Ric Mancini

A delightful adult comedy with a stellar cast dealing with the marital and business problems of a couple of middle-aged men who continue their night out with the boys even after the breakup of their Thursday evening poker game. Made in 1971 as a theatrical release, it was shelved for several years before eventually being given a television premiere.

0433
TURN OF THE SCREW
4/15–16/74 Dan Curtis Productions (90 min each)

Producer/Director: Dan Curtis
Associate Producer: Tim Steele
Assistant Director: Art Seidel
Teleplay: William F. Nolan
Based on the novel by Henry James
Photography: Ben Colman
Music: Robert Cobert
Art Director: Trevor Williams
Editor: Dennis Virkler

Jane Cubberly	LYNN REDGRAVE
Miles	JASPER JACOB
Flora	EVA GRIFFITH
Mrs. Grose	MEGS JENKINS
Mr. Frericks	JOHN BARTON
Luke	ANTHONY LANGDON
Timothy	BENEDICT TAYLOR
Peter Quint	JAMES LAURENSON
Miss Jessel	KATHRYN SCOTT

A thriller about a troubled English governess hired to take charge of a pair of precocious but strangely disturbing orphans beset by demons. This tape-to-film adaptation of Henry James' 1898 novelette, shown in two parts originally, is occult director Dan Curtis' version of the horror perennial, frequently staged during TV's golden age of drama (Ingrid Bergman had made her American TV acting debut in the 1959 production) and filmed as *The Innocents* in 1961 with Deborah Kerr.

0434
WINTER KILL
4/15/74 Andy Griffith Enterprises/MGM (2 hours)

Executive Producer: Richard O. Linke
Producer: Burt Nodella
Director: Jud Taylor
Teleplay: Joseph Michael Hayes
From a story by David Karp
Photography: Frank Stanley
Music: Jerry Goldsmith
Art Director: Albert Brenner
Editor: Henry Berman

Sheriff Sam McNeill	ANDY GRIFFITH
Dr. Hammond	JOHN LARCH
Bill Carter	TIM O'CONNOR
Peter Lockhard	LAWRENCE PRESSMAN
Mayor Bickford	EUGENE ROCHE
Charley Eastman	CHARLES TYNER
Grace Lockhard	JOYCE VAN PATTEN
Betty	SHEREE NORTH
Deputy Jerry Troy	JOHN CALVIN
Doris	LOUISE LATHAM
Harvey	ROBERT F. SIMON
Cynthia Howe	ELAYNE HEILVEIL
Dave Michaels	NICK NOLTE
Mildred Young	RUTH McDEVITT
Ben	WALTER BROOKE

and: Devra Korwin, David Frankham, Wes Stern, Vaughn Taylor

The sheriff of a ski resort town is challenged by a murderer who leaves spray-painted messages next to his victims for the perplexed lawman. This was a pilot film for a proposed Andy Griffith series that failed to materialize, although several hour-long attempts later turned up with the star doggedly trying to make the concept (slightly altered) a viable prospect.

0435
THE LAST ANGRY MAN
4/16/74 Screen Gems/Columbia (90 min)

Executive Producer: Gerald I. Eisenberg
Producer: Ernest A. Laslo
Director: Jerrold Freedman
Teleplay: Gerald Green
Based on his novel
Photography: Jacques R. Marquette
Music: Gil Melle
Art Directors: Ross Bellah and Robert Peterson
Editor: John F. Link II

Dr. Sam Abelman	PAT HINGLE
Sarah Abelman	LYNN CARLIN
Myron Malcolm	PAUL JABARA
Eunice Abelman	TRACY BOGART
Dr. Max Vogel	SORRELL BOOKE
Penny	PENNY STANTON
Mr. Parelli	TITOS VANDIS
Mrs. Parelli	PEPE SERITA
Frankie Parelli	MICHAEL MARGOTTA
Dr. McCabe	ANDREW DUGGAN
Nurse	ANN DORAN
Petey Parelli	DAVID ROY
Paul Parelli	PAUL HENRY ITKIN

An irascible depression era doctor who practices in a Brooklyn tenement neighborhood takes an interest in a local teenager whose hostile behavior he eventually attributes to a brain tumor. This film, a remake of the 1959 movie with Paul Muni in his last screen role, was the pilot for a series that never got on the air.

0436
NAKIA
4/17/74 Screen Gems/Columbia (90 min)

Executive Producer: David Gerber
Producer: Peter Katz
Director: Leonard Horn
Teleplay: Christopher Trumbo, Michael Butler and Sy Salkowitz
From a story by Christopher Trumbo and Michael Butler
Photography: Ric Waite
Music: Leonard Rosenman
Art Director: Ross Bellah
Editors: Arthur D. Hilton and David Wages

Nakia Parker	ROBERT FORSTER
Sheriff Sam Jericho	ARTHUR KENNEDY
Samantha Lowell	LINDA EVANS
Naiche	CHIEF GEORGE CLUTESI
Diane Little Eagle	MARIA-ELENA CORDERO
Deputy Hubbell	JOE KAPP
Elliott	TAYLOR LARCHER
Alva Chambers	STEPHEN McNALLY
McMasters	GEORGE NADER
Sally	BARBARA SIGEL
Half Cub	JED HORNER, JR.
Sheila	HELENE NELSON
Fincher	ROBERT DONNER
Indiana Johnny	JAY VARELLA
Peter	JOE RENTERIA

An American Indian deputy sheriff is caught in the middle of a community dispute when the tribe tries to save an historic mission from a housing developer.

Forster and Kennedy continued their roles in the short-lived series that followed (1974–75). Strong overtones of *Billy Jack* (1972) were spotted in both the telefeature and the later series.

0437
THE CHADWICK FAMILY
4/17/74 Universal (90 min)

Executive Producer: David Victor
Producer: David O'Connell
Director: David Lowell Rich
Teleplay: David Victor
From a story by David Victor and John Gay
Photography: Walter Strenge
Music: Hal Mooney
Art Director: Howard E. Johnson
Editor: Richard G. Wray

Ned Chadwick	FRED MacMURRAY
Valerie Chadwick	KATHLEEN MAGUIRE
Joan Chadwick McTaggert	DARLEEN CARR
Lisa Chadwick	JANE ACTMAN
Tim Chadwick	STEPHEN NATHAN
Eileen Chadwick Hawthorne	LARA PARKER
Fargo	JOHN LARCH
Alex Hawthorne	ALAN FUDGE
Lee Wu-Tsaung	FRANK MICHAEL LIU
Duffy McTaggert	BARRY BOSTWICK
Cindy Hawthorne	CARLENE GOWER
Sari Hawthorne	KIM DURSO
Jimmy Hawthorne	EBEN GEORGE
Elly	MARGARET LINDSAY
Dr. Simon	WALTER BROOKE
Madame Wu-Tsaung	PAT LI
Danny	BRUCE BOXLEITNER

and: Judson Morgan, Elliott Montgomery, Ray Ballard, Sharon Cintron, Jan Gerstel, Carle Bensen, Morton Lewis

After many years with "My Three Sons," Fred Mac-Murray made his TV movie debut in this pilot about a concerned father whose brood consists of one son, three daughters, two sons-in-law, and the Chinese-American boyfriend of the youngest girl. The concept worked better later as "Eight Is Enough."

Arthur Kennedy in NAKIA (1974)

0438
MURDER OR MERCY
4/19/74 Quinn Martin Productions (90 min)

Executive Producer: Quinn Martin
Producer: Adrian Samish
Director: Harvey Hart
Teleplay: Douglas Davis Stewart
Photography: William Standish
Music: Pat Williams
Art Director: George B. Chan
Editor: Richard Brockway

Sam Champion	BRADFORD DILLMAN
Dr. Paul Harelson	MELVYN DOUGLAS
Lois Harelson	MILDRED DUNNOCK
Amos Champion	DENVER PYLE
Henry Balin	DON PORTER
Dr. Peter Peterson	DAVID BIRNEY
Dr. Eric Stoneman	ROBERT WEBBER
Nurse Cantelli	BETTYE ACKERMAN
Judge	KENT SMITH
Elena Champion	BONNIE BARTLETT
Dr. Raymond Ecksworth	ARTHUR FRANZ
Arraignment Judge	REGIS J. CORDIC
Bailiff	LINDSAY WORKMAN
Dr. Chadway	WARREN PARKER
Coroner	STEPHEN COIT

An eminent physician, accused of his wife's mercy-killing, is defended by a retired attorney and his ambitious lawyer son. This film's plot more than vaguely resembles *An Act of Murder* (1948) that starred Fredric March and his wife, Florence Eldridge.

0439
NICKY'S WORLD
4/19/74 Tomorrow Entertainment, Inc. (90 min)

Executive Producer: Bob Markell
Producer: Joe Manduke
Director: Paul Stanley
Teleplay: William Katz and Edward Adler
Photography: Harvey Genkins
Music: Charles Gross
Art Director: Ben Kasazkaw
Editor: David Newhouse

George Kaminios	CHARLES CIOFFI
Paul Kaminios	GEORGE VOSKOVEC
Irene Kaminios	OLYMPIA DUKAKIS
Electra	DESPO
Nicky Kaminios	MARK SHERA
Torres	RENE ENRIQUEZ
Helen	EMILY BINDIGER
Elizabeth	PHYLLIS GLICK
Block	JOEL FABIANI
Gus	ERIC O'HANLAN
Shelton	GLENN WALKEN
Larry	MICHAEL MULLINS
Mrs. Mylonas	RITA KARLIN
Russell	JAMES BRODERICK

and: Chris Campell, Mark Vahanian, Leonard Parker, Richard MacKenzie, Ted Beniades

A close-knit Greek-American family, jeopardized when its Manhattan bakery goes up in flames, looks desperately for ways to solve the financial dilemma of repossession and property without destroying its heritage.

0440
LARRY
4/23/74 Tomorrow Entertainment, Inc. (90 min)

Executive Producer: Herbert Hirschman
Producers: Mitchell Brower and Robert Lovenheim
Director: William A. Graham
Teleplay: David Seltzer
From a true case history by Dr. Robert McQueen
Photography: Terry K. Meade
Music: Peter Matz
Editor: Ronald J. Fagan

Larry Herman	FREDERICK FORREST
Nancy Hockworth	TYNE DALY
Dr. McCabe	MICHAEL McGUIRE
Tom Corman	ROBERT WALDEN
Maureen Whitten	KATHERINE HELMOND
Workman	TIM RYAN
Waitress	BARBARA SLOANE
Customer	DAVID GARFIELD
Clothing Salesman	TED SWANSON
Cop	JON CEDAR
Cashier	KATY SEGAL
Prostitute	DANA BRADY

and: Ray Fry, Elizabeth Gill, Chris Hubbard, Don Rizzan, Ted Lange, Linda Redfearn

An acclaimed drama about a man, mistakenly confined to a mental institution for his first twenty-six years, who is discovered to have normal intelligence and is faced with the task of becoming physically self-sufficient to live in the outside world.

0441
PLANET EARTH
4/23/74 Warner Bros. (90 min)

Executive Producer: Gene Roddenberry
Producer: Robert H. Justman
Director: Marc Daniels
Teleplay: Gene Roddenberry and Juanita Bartlett
From a story by Gene Roddenberry
Photography: Arch R. Dalzell
Music: Harry Sukman
Art Director: Robert Kinoshita
Editor: George Watters

Dylan Hunt	JOHN SAXON
Harper-Smythe	JANET MARGOLIN
Isiah	TED CASSIDY
Baylok	CHRISTOPHER CARY
Marg	DIANA MULDAUR

John Saxon, Janet Margolin, Ted Cassidy and Christopher Carey in PLANET EARTH (1974)

Villar	JOHANA DeWINTER
Yuloff	MARJEL BARRETT
Dr. Jonathan Connor	JAMES D. ANTONIO, JR.
Treece	SALLY KEMP
Delba	CLAIRE BRENNAN
Bronta	CORINNE CAMACHO
Thetis	SARAH CHATLIN
Kreeg Commandant	JOHN QUADE
Kreeg Captain	RAYMOND SUTTON
Dr. Kimbridge	RAI TASCO
Gorda	ARON KINCAID
Skylar	PATRICIA SMITH
Partha	JAMES BACON
Kyla	JOAN CROSBY

An American astronaut, cast into the year 2133 through suspended animation, is captured and enslaved by a female-dominated society in the science fiction reworking by Gene Roddenberry of his *Genesis II* (1973).

0442
QB VII
4/29–30/74 Screen Gems/Columbia (6½ hours)

Producer: Douglas S. Cramer
Director: Tom Gries
Teleplay: Edward Anhalt
Based on the novel by Leon Uris
Photography: Robert L. Morrison and Paul Beeson
Music: Jerry Goldsmith
Production Concept: Wilford Lloyd Baumes
Art Directors: Ross Bellah and Maurice Fowler
Editors: Byron "Buzz" Brandt and Irving C. Rosenblum

Abe Cady	BEN GAZZARA
Dr. Adam Kelno	ANTHONY HOPKINS
Angela Kelno	LESLIE CARON
Lady Margaret Alexander Weidman	LEE REMICK
Samantha Cady	JULIET MILLS
David Shawcross	DAN O'HERLIHY
Robert Highsmith	ROBERT STEPHENS
Tom Bannister	ANTHONY QUAYLE
Dr. Stanislaus Lotaki	MILO O'SHEA
Clinton-Meek	SIR JOHN GIELGUD
Dr. Parmentier	DAME EDITH EVANS
Justice Gilroy	JACK HAWKINS
Natalie	JUDY CARNE
Ben Cady	KRISTOFFER TABORI
Morris Cady	JOSEPH WISEMAN
Stephen Kelno	ANTHONY ANDREWS
Lena Kronska	SIGNE HASSO
Dr. Mark Tessler	SAM JAFFE
Semple	ALAN NAPIER
Sheik Hassan	GREGOIRE ASLAN
Sue Scanlon	LANA WOOD
Igor Zaminski	JULIAN GLOVER
American Ambassador	ROBERT HUTTON
Dr. Melcher	MICHAEL GOUGH

and: Vladek Sheybel, Milos Kirek, Geoffrey Keen, Michael-James Wixted, Suzanne Fleuret, Louis Selwyn

An absorbing adaptation of Uris' best-selling novel telling the story of two successful men, an American writer and a Polish doctor, whose careers lead to a confrontation in a London courtroom when the former accuses the latter of having performed illegal operations in a Nazi prison camp years earlier and is sued for libel. The longest made-for-TV movie to date received thirteen Emmy Award nominations including Outstanding Special, as well as for directing, writing, music, cinematography, art, editing and graphic design. Lee Remick, Jack Hawkins (in his last screen

Ben Gazzara and Lee Remick in QB VII (1974)

Juliet Mills and Ben Gazzara in QB VII (1974)

Kim Darby and Martin Sheen in THE STORY OF PRETTY BOY FLOYD (1974)

Martin Sheen in THE STORY OF PRETTY BOY FLOYD (1974)

Eleanor Strome	VERA MILES
Jean Broadhurst	JO ANN PFLUG
Mrs. Snow	DAME JUDITH ANDERSON
Sheriff Tremaine	JACK KLUGMAN
Joe Kelsey	ARCH JOHNSON
Willy Coggins	BILL McKINNEY
Fritz Snow	LEE PAUL
Ronny Broadhurst	JAN JOHN TANZA
Jerry Kilpatrick	JUDSON MORGAN
Newscaster	BILL STOUT

Peter Graves, completely miscast as private eye Lew Archer, goes after the kidnappers of an old flame's young son and gets mixed up in a series of murders going back fifteen years. This was the pilot for the subsequent very short-lived (six episodes) series "Archer" that began in January 1975 and starred Brian Keith, a better but not ideal choice.

THE STORY OF PRETTY BOY FLOYD
5/7/74 Universal (90 min)

Executive Producer: Roy Huggins
Producer: Jo Swerling, Jr.
Director: Clyde Ware
Teleplay: Clyde Ware
Photography: J. J. Jones
Music: Pete Rugolo
Art Director: Alfeo Bocchicchio
Editors: Chuck McClelland and Gloryette Clark

Charles Arthur Floyd	MARTIN SHEEN
Ruby Hardgrave	KIM DARBY
Bradley Floyd	MICHAEL PARKS
Ma Floyd	ELLEN CORBY
E. W. Floyd	JOSEPH ESTEVEZ
Mary Floyd	KITTY CARL
Melvin Purvis	GEOFFREY BINNEY
Bill Miller	BILL VINT
Shine Rush	MILLS WATSON
Dominic Mirell	ABE VIGODA
Eddie Ferchetti	STEVEN KEATS
George Burtwell	ROD McCAREY
Suggs	FORD RAINEY
Secretary	ANN DORAN
Juanita	ARLENE FABER
Phil Donnati	FRANK CRISTI
Decker	TED GEHRING
Deputy	RON APPLEGATE

and: Amzie Strickland, Misty Rowe, Sandra Escamilla

An affecting version of the Floyd saga telling of the Oklahoma farm boy who, to escape poverty, becomes enmeshed in a life of crime and ends up as one of the most notorious bank robbers of the 1930s. Sheen and his real-life brother, Joseph Estevez, played Pretty Boy and one of his two brothers.

0445
LUCAS TANNER
5/8/74 Universal (90 min)

Executive Producer: David Victor
Producer: Jerry McNeely
Director: Richard Donner
Teleplay: Jerry McNeely
Photography: Harry L. Wolf
Music: David Shire
Art Director: Sydney Z. Litwack
Editor: Richard Bracken

Lucas Tanner	DAVID HARTMAN
Margaret Blumenthal	ROSEMARY MURPHY
Joyce Howell	KATHLEEN QUINLAN
Craig Willeman	RAMON BIERI
Himself	JOE GARAGIOLA

role), Anthony Quayle and Juliet Mills all were nominated for supporting performances. Quayle and Mills won, as did Jerry Goldsmith (music), Phill Norman (graphic design), and Brandt and Rosenblum (editing).

0443
THE UNDERGROUND MAN
5/6/74 Paramount (2 hours)

Executive Producer: Howard W. Koch
Producer: Philip L. Parslow
Director: Paul Wendkos
Teleplay: Douglas Heyes
Based on the novel by Ross MacDonald
Photography: Earl Rath
Music: Richard Hazzard
Theme: Marvin Hamlisch
Art Director: Jack DeShields
Editor: Richard Rabjohn

Lew Archer	PETER GRAVES
Marty Nickerson	SHARON FARRELL
Beatrice Broadhurst	CELESTE HOLM
Stanley Broadhurst	JIM HUTTON
Sue Crandall	KAY LENZ
Cassidy	BIFF McGUIRE

Nancy Howell	NANCY MALONE
Mr. Howell	MICHAEL BASELEON
Glendon	ROBBIE RIST
Jaytee	ALAN ABELEW

A high school teacher's career is threatened because of a student's death when the rumor is spread that his negligence killed the boy. The 1974–75 series also starred Hartman as the problem-solving teacher and Rosemary Murphy as the principal.

0446
IN TANDEM
5/8/74 D'Antoni Productions (90 min) (subsequently titled *Movin' On*)

Executive Producer: Philip D'Antoni
Producer: Barry J. Weitz
Director: Bernard Kowalski
Teleplay: Robert Collins and Herb Meadow
Photography: Dennis Dalzell
Music: Don Ellis
Special Effects: Ira Anderson, Jr.
Editor: Howard Deane

Sonny Pruitt	CLAUDE AKINS
Will Chandler	FRANK CONVERSE
Diangelo	RICHARD ANGAROLA
Connie	SONDRA BLAKE
Betty	ANN COLMAN
Myrna	JANIS HANSEN
Guido	TITOS VANDIS
Emilio	ERNEST SARRACINO

Gypsy truckers—a tough veteran driver and his young college-educated partner—come to the aid of embattled citrus growers in this pilot for the 1974–75 series about these free-spirited, civic-minded teamsters. Akins and Converse also starred in the series, making pit stops in various locations around the country, much the same way that Martin Milner and George Maharis had done years earlier in the "Route 66" series.

0447
THE HEALERS
5/22/74 Warner Bros. (2 hours)

Executive Producer: Jerry Thorpe
Producer: John Furia, Jr.
Director: Tom Gries
Teleplay: John Furia, Jr., and Howard Dimsdale
Photography: Jack Woolf
Music: David Shire
Art Director: Walter Herndon
Editor: Michael A. Hoey

Dr. Robert Kier	JOHN FORSYTHE
Joe Tate	PAT HARRINGTON
Claire	KATE WOODVILLE
Ann Kilmer	SEASON HUBLEY
Dr. Albert Scanlon	ANTHONY ZERBE
Laura Kier	BEVERLY GARLAND
Dr. Ernest Wilson	JOHN McINTIRE
Barbara	LOUISE SOREL
Kennedy Brown	LANCE KERWIN
Dr. Tony Balinowski	MICHAEL C. GWYNNE
Nikki Kier	SHELLY JUTTNER

and: Christian Juttner, Ellen Weston, Julio Medina, Jay W. MacIntosh, Priscilla Garcia, Anne Newman, Stach Pierce, James Storm, Paul Mantee, Angela Gibbs, Casey McDonald, Jim Boles, Dick Valentine, Jacqueline Weiss, Gavin O'Herlihy, Liam Dunn, Bill McKinney

In this pilot for an unrealized series called "Crisis!" the director of a big-city medical center faces the predictable multitude of doctor show problems, from a threatened rebellion among the research staff to a surgeon's unauthorized use of drugs to the obligatory lack of funds to run the hospital to nagging personal difficulties.

1974–75 SEASON

0448
BORN INNOCENT
9/10/74 Tomorrow Entertainment, Inc. (2 hours)

Executive Producers: Robert W. Christiansen and Rick Rosenberg
Producer: Bruce Cohn Curtis
Director: Donald Wrye
Teleplay: Gerald DiPego
Photography: David M. Walsh
Music: Fred Karlin
Editor: Mark Winetrobe

Chris Parker	LINDA BLAIR
Barbara Clark	JOANNA MILES
Mrs. Parker	KIM HUNTER
Mr. Parker	RICHARD JAECKEL
Emma Lasko	ALLYN ANN McLERIE
Miss Murphy	MARY MURPHY
Denny	JANIT BALDWIN
Moco	NORA HEFLIN
Josie	TINA ANDREWS
Tom Parker	MITCH VOGEL
Janet	SANDRA EGO

A sensationally promoted juvenile delinquency film about a fourteen-year-old girl's struggles to adjust after being sent to a tough detention home. A graphic sequence depicting a broom-handle rape of Linda Blair (in her TV-movie debut) subsequently was deleted but made the film the focal point of a highly publicized lawsuit against the network in 1978.

0449
HURRICANE
9/10/74 Metromedia Productions (90 min)

Executive Producer: Charles Fries
Producer: Edward J. Montagne
Director: Jerry Jameson
Teleplay: Jack Turley
Based on the novel *Hurricane Hunters* by William C. Anderson
Photography: Matthew F. Leonetti
Music: Vic Mizzy
Art Director: Bill Malley
Editor: Art Seid

Paul Damon	LARRY HAGMAN
Major Stoddard	MARTIN MILNER
Louise Damon	JESSICA WALTER
Hank Stoddard	BARRY SULLIVAN
Lee Jackson	MICHAEL LEARNED
Bert Pearson	FRANK SUTTON
Dr. McCutcheon	WILL GEER
Pappy	LONNY CHAPMAN
Suzanne	AYN RUYMEN
Richie Damon	BARRY LIVINGSTON
Captain Mackey	JIM ANTONIO
Barker	RIC CARROTT
Newscaster	JACK COLVIN

Linda Blair and Janit Baldwin in BORN INNOCENT (1974)

and: Alan Landers, Charles Lampkin, Maggie Malooly, Read Morgan, Jessica Rains, Paul Tulley

In this film hurricane hunters Hagman and Milner are in a desperate race to avoid disaster as a violent storm threatens to devastate a Gulf Coast town.

0450
SAVAGES
9/11/74 Spelling/Goldberg Productions (90 min)

Producers: Aaron Spelling and Leonard Goldberg
Associate Producer: Shelley Hull
Director: Lee H. Katzin
Teleplay: William Wood
Based on the novel *Death Watch* by Robb White
Photography: Tim Southcott
Music: Murray McCloud
Art Director: Tracy Bousman
Editor: John Woodcock

Horton Maddock	ANDY GRIFFITH
Ben Whiting	SAM BOTTOMS
George Whiting	NOAH BEERY
Sheriff Hamilton	JAMES BEST
Deputy Haycroft	RANDY BOONE
Les Hanford	JIM ANTONIO
The Doctor	JIM CHANDLER

A wealthy New York attorney, on a western hunting trip, turns into a deranged hunger after accidentally killing an old prospector and then deliberately stalking his young guide to protect his own reputation.

0451
THE SEX SYMBOL
9/17/74* Screen Gems/Columbia (90 min)

Producer: Douglas S. Cramer
Director: David Lowell Rich
Teleplay: Alvah Bessie
Based on his 1966 novel *The Symbol*
Photography: J. J. Jones
Music: Jeff Williams
Title theme by Francis Lai and conducted by Henry Mancini
Art Director: Ross Bellah
Editor: Byron "Buzz" Brandt

Kelly Williams (Emmaline Kelly)	CONNIE STEVENS
Agatha Murphy	SHELLEY WINTERS
Manny Fox	JACK CARTER
Jack P. Harper	WILLIAM CASTLE
Senator Grant O'Neal	DON MURRAY
Calvin Bernard	JAMES OLSON
Nikos Fortis	NEHEMIAH PERSOFF
Joy Hudson	MADLYN RHUE
Phil Bamberger	MILTON SELZER
Rick Roman	TONY YOUNG
Buck Wischnewski	WILLIAM SMITH
Edward Kelly	RAND BROOKS
Voice of Dr. Otto Litsky	MALACHI THRONE**
Investigator	FRANK LOVERDE
Public Relations Man	BING RUSSELL
Tom Brown	DENNIS RUCKER

Shelley Winters in THE SEX SYMBOL (1974)

Jackie Cooper, Stella Stevens and Cleavon Little in THE DAY THE EARTH MOVED (1974)

and: Joseph Turkel, Jack Collins, Rita Guerrero, Bill McGovern, Albert Able, Herb Graham, Burr Smidt

A thinly disguised drama based on Marilyn Monroe's life and death, with Connie Stevens flaunting her undeniable charms, Shelley Winters as a Hollywood gossip columnist, Don Murray as an attractive married U.S. Senator, Nehemiah Persoff as a European-accented studio czar, James Olson as a cerebral artist who becomes the star's husband, *et al.* Apparently anticipating a libel suit, ABC Television yanked this film prior to its original premiere and tried to keep it under wraps.

*Originally scheduled 3/5/74.

**Eduard Franz redubbed the voice for theatrical showings overseas.

0452
TERROR ON THE 40th FLOOR
9/17/74 Metromedia Productions (2 hours)

Executive Producer: Charles Fries
Producer: Ed Montagne
Director: Jerry Jameson
Teleplay: Jack Turley
From a story by Ed Montagne and Jack Turley
Photography: Matthew F. Leonetti
Music: Vic Mizzy
Art Director: Sidney Z. Litwack
Editor: Art Seid

Daniel Overland	JOHN FORSYTHE
Howard Foster	JOSEPH CAMPANELLA
Lee Parker	LYNN CARLIN
Darlene Foster	ANJANETTE COMER
Ginger Macklin	LAURIE HEINEMAN
Kelly Freeman	DON MEREDITH
Betty Carson	KELLY JEAN PETERS
Mrs. Overland	PIPPA SCOTT
Captain Harris	MARK TAPSCOTT

and: Norman Alden, Danny Goldman, Hank Brandt

In television's carbon of *The Towering Inferno,* seven people are trapped in a skyscraper penthouse during an office party, and nobody knows they are there.

0453
THE DAY THE EARTH MOVED
9/18/74 ABC Circle Films (90 min)

Producers: Bobby Sherman and Ward Sylvester
Director: Robert Michael Lewis
Teleplay: Jack Turley and Max Jack
From a story by Jack Turley
Photography: Charles F. Wheeler
Music: Bobby Sherman
Art Director: Bill Malley
Editor: John F. Link II

Steve Barker	JACKIE COOPER
Kate Barker	STELLA STEVENS
Harley Copeland	CLEAVON LITTLE
Judge Backsler	WILLIAM WINDOM
Helen Backsler	BEVERLY GARLAND
Miss Porter	LUCILLE BENSON
Angela	TAMMY HARRINGTON
Officer Ferguson	KELLY THORDSEN
Evelyn Ferguson	ELLEN BLACK
Henry Butler	E. J. ANDRE
Chief	SID MELTON

An aerial photography team tries to alert a small town about an impending earthquake, but no one believes the duo until the tremors start and the walls begin to collapse.

Michael Sacks and Burt Young in THE GREAT NIAGARA (1974)

Richard Boone in THE GREAT NIAGARA (1974)

0454
THE GREAT NIAGARA
9/24/74 Playboy Films (90 min)

Producer: Ron Roth
Director: William Hale
Teleplay: Robert E. Thompson
Photography: Gayne Rescher
Music: Peter Link
Art Director: Walter Scott Herndon
River Sequences: Jim Sarten and Breck O'Neill
Editor: Jim Benson

Aaron Grant	RICHARD BOONE
Lonnie Grant	MICHAEL SACKS
Carl Grant	RANDY QUAID
Lois	JENNIFER SALT
Ace Tully	BURT YOUNG
Smitty	LES RUBIE
Young Mountie	DAVID SCHURMANN
Doctor	JACK VON EVERA
Driver	JONATHAN WHITE

An offbeat Depression-era drama about an embittered old cripple whose obsession with conquering the river and the falls endangers his sons' lives by forcing them to challenge the waters in a barrel.

0455
THE STRANGE AND DEADLY OCCURRENCE
9/24/74 Metromedia Productions (90 min)

Executive Producer: Charles Fries
Producer: Sandor Stern
Director: John Llewellyn Moxey
Teleplay: Lane Sloan and Sandor Stern
Photography: Frank Holgate
Music: Robert Prince
Editor: John A. Martinelli

Bradford Dillman and Glenn Ford in THE DISAPPEARANCE OF FLIGHT 412 (1974)

Michael Rhodes	ROBERT STACK
Christine Rhodes	VERA MILES
Sheriff Berlinger	L. Q. JONES
Felix	HERB EDELMAN
Audrey	DENA DIETRICH
Dr. Gilgreen	TED GEHRING
Melissa Rhodes	MARGARET WILLOCK
Ardie Detweiler	JAMES McCALLION

A family's move to a new home in a remote area coincides with a series of mysterious accidents, and they soon realize that someone is deadly serious about getting them out of the house.

0456
THE CALIFORNIA KID
9/25/74 Universal (90 min)

Executive Producer: Paul Mason
Producer: Howie Horwitz
Director: Richard T. Heffron
Teleplay: Richard Compton
Photography: Terry K. Meade
Music: Lucio DeJesus
Art Director: Raymond Beal
Editor: Robert F. Shugrue

Michael McCord	MARTIN SHEEN
Sheriff Roy Childress	VIC MORROW
Maggie	MICHELLE PHILLIPS
Deputy	STUART MARGOLIN
Buzz Stafford	NICK NOLTE
Sissy	JANIT BALDWIN
Lyle Stafford	GARY MORGAN
Don McCord	JOE ESTEVEZ
Jack	DONALD MANTOOTH
Judge Hooker	FREDERIC DOWNS
Charley	MICHAEL RICHARDSON

and: Norman Bartlold, Britt Leach, Barbara Collentine, Gavin O'Herlihy, Jack McCulloch, Ken Johnson, Sandy Brown, Trent Dolan, Monika Henreid

After a number of speeders have deliberately been sent to their deaths by a psychotic sheriff in a small-town speed trap, the brother of a recent victim rolls into town in his hot rod and forces the lawman into a high speed duel. Real-life brothers Sheen and Estevez played fictional brothers in this one, billed by ABC Television as its 200th "Movie of the Week" at its premiere showing.

0457
THE STRANGER WITHIN
10/1/74 Lorimar Productions (90 min)

Executive Producers: Philip Capice and Lee Rich
Producer: Neil T. Maffeo
Director: Lee Philips
Teleplay: Richard Matheson
From his short story
Photography: Michael Margulies
Music: Charles Fox
Art Director: Hilyard Brown
Editor: Samuel E. Beetley

Ann Collins	BARBARA EDEN
David Collins	GEORGE GRIZZARD
Phyllis	JOYCE VAN PATTEN
Bob	DAVID DOYLE
Dr. Edward Klein	NEHEMIAH PERSOFF

A chiller about an expectant mother whose bizarre actions are controlled by her unborn baby. Originally this was to have been titled *Trespass*.

0458
THE DISAPPEARANCE OF FLIGHT 412
10/1/74 Cinemobile Productions (90 min)

Executive Producer: Gerald L. Adler
Director: Jud Taylor
Teleplay: George Simpson and Neal Burger
Photography: Robert B. Hauser
Music: Morton Stevens
Art Director: Albert Heschong
Editor: Carroll L. Sax

Col. Pete Moore	GLENN FORD
Major Mike Dunning	BRADFORD DILLMAN
Capt. Roy Bishop	DAVID SOUL
Capt. Cliff Riggs	ROBERT F. LYONS
Colonel Trottman	GUY STOCKWELL
Lt. Tony Podryski	GREG MULLAVEY
Lt. Ferguson	STANLEY CLAY
General Enright	KENT SMITH
Smith	JONATHAN LIPPE
White	JACK GING

190

Nina Moore	CYNTHIA HAYWARD
Col. Freeman Barnes	SIMON SCOTT
McCheer	EDWARD WINTER

Narrated by HERB ELLIS

and: Jesse Vint, Morris Buchanan, Brent Davis, Kevin Kerchival, Donald Scott

After two jets mysteriously disappear while pursuing UFOs and the Air Force officially refuses to recognize the incident, flight commander Glenn Ford disobeys orders from the military complex to learn what happened to his men.

0459
DEATH SENTENCE
10/2/74 Spelling/Goldberg Productions (90 min)

Producers: Aaron Spelling and Leonard Goldberg
Associate Producer: Shelley Hull
Director: E. W. Swackhamer
Teleplay: John Neufeld
Based on the novel *After the Trial* by Eric Roman
Photography: Tim Southcott
Music: Laurence Rosenthal
Art Director: Tracy Bousman
Editor: Leon Carrere

Susan Davies	CLORIS LEACHMAN
Don Davies	LAURENCE LUCKINBILL
John Healy	NICK NOLTE
Lubell	ALAN OPPENHEIMER
Tanner	WILLIAM SCHALLERT
Elaine Croft	YVONNE WILDER
Lowell Bracken	HERB VOLAND
Emily Boylan	HOPE SUMMERS
Judge	PETER HOBBS
Mrs. Cottard	DOREEN LANG
Martin Gorman	MURRAY MacLEOD
Trooper	BING RUSSELL
Mae Sinclair	MEG WYLIE
Mr. Bowman	LEW BROWN
Marilyn Healy	C. J. HINCKS

and: Vernon Weddle, Robert Cleaves, Jack Collins, Dick Winslow, Pat Patterson, Morgan Englund, Dinah Englund

A juror in a murder case comes to the conclusion that the wrong man is on trial, and then finds her own life threatened by the real killer—her husband.

0460
WHERE HAVE ALL THE PEOPLE GONE?
10/8/74 Metromedia Productions (90 min)

Executive Producer: Charles Fries
Producer: Gerald Isenberg
Director: John Llewellyn Moxey
Teleplay: Lewis John Carlino and Sandor Stern
From a story by Lewis John Carlino
Photography: Michael Margulies
Music: Robert Prince
Editor: John A. Martinelli

Steven Anders	PETER GRAVES
Jenny	VERNA BLOOM
David Anders	GEORGE O'HANLON, JR.
Deborah Anders	KATHLEEN QUINLAN
Michael	MICHAEL-JAMES WIXTED
Guide	NOBLE WILLINGHAM
Tom Clancy	DOUG CHAPIN

Mother	JAY W. MacINTOSH
Man with Gun	DAN BARROWS
Man at Store	KEN SANSOM

A father and his two children struggle to survive after a lethal virus, the aftermath of a mysterious radiation explosion, kills most of the earth's population.

0461
HIT LADY
10/8/74 Spelling/Goldberg Productions (90 min)

Producers: Aaron Spelling and Leonard Goldberg
Associate Producer: Shelley Hull
Director: Tracy Keenan Wynn
Teleplay: Yvette Mimieux
Photography: Tim Southcott
Music: George Aliceson Tipton
Art Director: Tracy Bousman
Editor: Sid Levin

Angela de Vries	YVETTE MIMIEUX
Jeffrey Baine	JOSEPH CAMPANELLA
Roarke	CLU GULAGER
Doug Reynolds	DACK RAMBO
Buddy McCormack	KEENAN WYNN
Eddie	ROY JENSEN
Webb	PAUL GENGE
Hansen	DEL MONROE
Woman at Airport	MITZI HOAG

Yvette Mimieux wrote this story and stars as a professional artist who moonlights (primarily in bikini) as a syndicate killer. Writer Tracy Keenan Wynn made his directorial debut with this movie, working for the first time with his father, Keenan Wynn.

0462
LOCUSTS
10/9/74 Paramount (90 min)

Executive Producer: Michael Donohew
Producer: Herbert Wright
Associate Producer: Judith Coppage
Director: Richard T. Heffron
Teleplay: Robert Malcolm Young
Photography: Jack Woolf
Music: Mike Post and Pete Carpenter
Special Effects: John Burke
Editor: Neil MacDonald

Amos Fletcher	BEN JOHNSON
Donny Fletcher	RON HOWARD
Claire Fletcher	KATHERINE HELMOND
Sissy Fletcher	LISA GERRITSEN
Janet Willimer	BELINDA BALASKI
Aaron	RANCE HOWARD
Cully Cullitan	ROBERT CRUSE
Ace Teverley	WILLIAM SPEERSTRA
Blauser	BOB KOONS
Tom	ROBERT HOFFMAN
Jim	LES KIMBER
Mrs. Heusen	JACQUELINE DUNCKEL
Hank	JACK GOTH
Lilah	NANCY DUNCKEL
Dr. Brant	MICHAEL ZAWADSKI

Strikingly similar to the short story chiller *Laningen and the Ants* (filmed by Paramount in 1953 as *The Naked Jungle*), this tale has a menacing swarm of locusts advancing on the Midwest, forcing a young World War II pilot, discharged as unfit to fly, to attempt to conquer his personal terror and dispel his father's shame.

0463
ALOHA MEANS GOODBYE
10/11/74 Universal (2 hours)

Executive Producer: David Lowell Rich
Producer: Sam Strangis
Director: David Lowell Rich
Teleplay: Dean Riesner and Joseph Stefano
Based on a novel by Naomi A. Hintze
Photography: J. J. Jones
Music: Charles Fox
Art Director: William Campbell
Editor: Richard Sprague

Sara Moore	SALLY STRUTHERS
Pamela Crane	JOANNA MILES
Dr. David Kalani	HENRY DARROW
Dr. Lawrence Maddox	JAMES FRANCISCUS
Dr. Da Costa	FRANK MARTH
Torger Nilsson	LARRY GATES
Dr. Frank Franklin	RUSSELL JOHNSON
Christian Nilsson	COLIN LOSBY
Mrs. Kalani	PAT LI
Connie	TRACY REED
Blind Girl	DAWN LYN
Stewardess	ANNE SCHEDEEN

A young schoolteacher in Hawaii fights for her life against both a rare blood disease and an unscrupulous surgeon in need of a heart-transplant donor.

0464
FER-DE-LANCE
10/18/74 Leslie Stevens Productions (2 hours)

Executive Producer: Leslie Stevens
Producer: Dominic Frontiere
Associate Producer: Clifford Wenger
Director: Russ Mayberry
Teleplay: Leslie Stevens
Photography: John Morley Stephens
Music: Dominic Frontiere
Special Effects: Thomas L. Fisher
Editor: Bill Butler

Russ Bogan	DAVID JANSSEN
Elaine Wedell	HOPE LANGE

Yvette Mimieux in HIT LADY (1974)

Joe Voit	IVAN DIXON	
Commander Kirk	JASON EVERS	
Lt. Nicholson	CHARLES KNOX ROBINSON	
Lt. Whitehead	BEN PIAZZA	
Torquale	GEORGE PAN	
Liz McCord	SHERRY BOUCHER	
Masai Ikeda	ROBERT ITO	
Mayne Bradley	BILL MIMS	
Suan Kuroda	SHIZUKO HOSHI	
Chief Hughes	RICHARD LePORE	
Terezita	SANDRA EGO	
Shaman	FELIPE TURICH	
Compton	FRANK BONNER	
Commander Scott	ROBERT BURR	

and: Alain Patrick, Richard Guthrie, Bill Catching, Elvenn Harvard

A disaster movie that has terror stalking a striken sub, wedged deep below the sea and crawling with deadly vipers. In Great Britain, this film was released theatrically as *Death Dive,* a somewhat more descriptive title.

0465
THE LAW
10/22/74 Universal (2½ hrs.)

Producer: William Sackheim
Director: John Badham
Teleplay: William Sackheim and Joel Oliansky
Photography: Michael Margulies
Music adapted from Gilbert and Sullivan's *The Mikado*
Art Director: Raymond Beal
Editor: Frank Morriss

Murray Stone	JUDD HIRSCH
Gene Carey	JOHN BECK
Bobbie Stone	BONNIE FRANKLIN
Judge Rebeccah Fornier	BARBARA BAXLEY
Jules Benson	SAM WANAMAKER
Leonard Caporni	ALLAN ARBUS
Thomas Q. Rachel	JOHN HILLERMAN
William Bright	GARY BUSEY
Judge Arnold Lerner	GERALD HIKEN
Cliff Wilson	MICHAEL BELL
Maxwell Fall	HERB JEFFERSON, JR.
Arthur Winchell	FRANK MARTH
Judge Philip Shields	JOHN SYLVESTER WHITE
Speaker at Bar Dinner	ROBERT Q. LEWIS

and: Logan Ramsey, Sandy Ward, George Wyner, Ernie Anderson, Reb Brown, Dennis Burkley, Don Calfa, Helen Page Camp, Alex Colon, Regis J. Cordic, Ted Gehring, Corey Fisher, Pamela Hensley, Milt Kogan, Luis Moreno, Joel Oliansky, Eugene Peterson, Anne Ramsey, Brad Sullivan, Keith Walker, Chris White, Alex Wilson

A sensational homicide trial is the focal point of this incisive examination of the inner working of a large city's legal system and was the Emmy Award-winner as the Outstanding Dramatic Special of the 1974–75 TV season. Director John Badham also was nominated.

0466
TRAPPED BENEATH THE SEA
10/22/74 ABC Circle Films (2 hours)

Producer: Frank Capra, Jr.
Director: William A. Graham
Teleplay: Stanford Whitmore
Photography: Terry K. Meade
Music: Al Kasha and Joel Hirschhorn
Art Director: Philip M. Jeffries
Underwater Photography: John Lamb
Special Effects: Cliff Wenger
Editors: Ronald J. Fagan and Marshall Neilan

Victor Bateman	LEE J. COBB
T. C. Hollister	MARTIN BALSAM
Sam Wallants	JOSHUA BRYANT
Jack Beech	PAUL MICHAEL GLASER
Grace Wallants	BARRA GRANT
Cmdr. Prestwick	WARREN KEMMERLING
Gordon Gaines	CLIFF POTTS
Chris Moffet	LAURIE PRANGE
Cmdr. Hanratty	PHILLIP R. ALLEN
POI Stanton	REDMOND GLEESON
Jeff Turley	ROGER KERN
Captain Osborn	S. JOHN LAUNER
Jimmy	ROD PERRY
Cmdr. Robbins	WILLIAM WINTERSOLE
Seaman Schrier	HUNTER VON LEER

Narrated by HOWARD K. SMITH

and: Simon Deckard, Fredric Franklyn, Norman Honath, Andy Knight

A drama based on the true story of four men entombed in a mini-sub off the coast of Florida in 1973.

0467
BAD RONALD
10/23/74 Lorimar Productions (90 min)

Executive Producer: Lee Rich
Producer: Philip Capice
Director: Buzz Kulik
Teleplay: Andrew Peter Marin
Based on a novel by John Holbrook Vance
Photography: Charles F. Wheeler
Music: Fred Karlin
Art Director: Ed Graves
Editor: Samuel E. Beetley

Ronald Wilby	SCOTT JACOBY
Mrs. Wood	PIPPA SCOTT
Sergeant Lynch	JOHN LARCH
Mr. Wood	DABNEY COLEMAN
Elaine Wilby	KIM HUNTER
Mr. Roscoe	JOHN FIEDLER
Mrs. Schumacher	LINDA WATKINS
Babs Wood	CINDY FISHER
Althea Wood	CINDY EILBACHER
Ellen Wood	LISA EILBACHER
Duane Mathews	TED ECCLES
Aunt Margaret	LESLEY WOODS
Mrs. Mathews	ANETA CORSAUT
Laurie Mathews	LINDA PURL
Carol Mathews	ANGELA HOFFMAN

A family with three daughters moves into an old house, unaware that it has a secret room occupied by a teenage murderer.

0468
STRANGE HOMECOMING
10/29/74 Alpine Productions/Worldvision (90 min)

Executive Producer: Charles Fries
Producers: Eric Bercovici and Jerry Ludwig
Director: Lee H. Katzin
Teleplay: Eric Bercovici and Jerry Ludwig
Photography: Howard R. Schwartz
Music: John Parker
Art Director: Joe Jennings
Editor: Nick Archer

Jack Halsey	ROBERT CULP
Elaine Halsey	BARBARA ANDERSON
Bill Halsey	GLEN CAMPBELL
Bobby Halsey	LEIF GARRETT
Winston	JOHN CRAWFORD
Floyd	VICTOR BRANDT

Earl Gates	GERRIT GRAHAM
Peggy Harwood	WHITNEY BLAKE
Sandy Halsey	TARA TALBOY
Otis	ARCH WHITING
Mel	BILL BURTON

A small-town sheriff (Glen Campbell in his TV movie debut) is visited for the first time in nearly twenty years by his brother, a thief-turned-killer.

0469
THE MARK OF ZORRO
10/29/74 20th Century-Fox (90 min)

Producers: Robert C. Thompson and Rodrick Paul
Director: Don McDougall
Teleplay: Brian Taggert
Based on the novel *The Curse of Capistrano* by Johnston McCulley
Photography: Jack Woolf
Music: Dominic Frontiere
Musical Supervisor: Lionel Newman
Theme Material: Alfred Newman
Editor: Bill Martin

Don Diego/Zorro	FRANK LANGELLA
Captain Esteban	RICARDO MONTALBAN
Don Alejandro Vega	GILBERT ROLAND
Isabella Vega	YVONNE DeCARLO
Inez Quintero	LOUISE SOREL
Don Luis Quintero	ROBERT MIDDLETON
Teresa	ANNE ARCHER
Frey Felipe	TOM LACY
Sergeant Gonzales	GEORGE CERVERA
Duenna Maria	INEZ PEREZ
Rodrigo	JOHN ROSE
Antonio	JAY HAMMER
Miguel	ALFONSO TAFOYA
Dock Worker	ROBERT CARRICART

"TV's first movie swashbuckler," as this remake of the old Tyrone Power classic was billed, had Frank Langella portraying the dashing avenger of the oppressed people of early California, a dandified weakling by day, a masked-and-caped crusader by night.

0470
DEATH CRUISE
10/30/74 Spelling/Goldberg Productions (90 min)

Producers: Aaron Spelling and Leonard Goldberg
Director: Ralph Senensky
Teleplay: Jack B. Sowards
Photography: Tim Southcott
Music: Pete Rugolo
Art Director: Tracy Bousman
Editor: John Woodcock

Jerry Carter	RICHARD LONG
Sylvia Carter	POLLY BERGEN
James Radney	EDWARD ALBERT
Mary Frances Radney	KATE JACKSON
Elizabeth Mason	CELESTE HOLM
David Mason	TOM BOSLEY
Dr. Burke	MICHAEL CONSTANTINE
Captain Vettori	CESARE DANOVA
Lynn	AMZIE STRICKLAND
Barrere	ALAIN PATRICK
Room Steward	MAURICE SHERBANEE

Three couples, all mysterious winners of a pleasure cruise, find that their tickets have guaranteed them a one-way passage to death.

0471
THE GREATEST GIFT
11/4/74 Universal (2 hours)

Producer: Dean Hargrove
Director: Boris Sagal
Teleplay: Abby Mann
From the novel *Ramey* by Jack Farris
Photography: Steven Larner
Music: Dick DeBenedictis
Song "Look How Far We've Come" sung by Denis Brooks
Assistant Director: Alan Crosland
Art Director: Dick T. Smith
Editors: Douglas Stewart and Howard Epstein

The Reverend Holvak	GLENN FORD
Elizabeth Holvak	JULIE HARRIS
Ramey Holvak	LANCE KERWIN
Hog Yancy	HARRIS YULIN
Amos Goodloe	CHARLES TYNER
Deacon Hurd	DABBS GREER
Julie Mae Holvak	CARI ANNE WARDER
Eli Wiggins	ALBERT SMITH
Willis Graham	FURMAN WALTERS
Tincey Bell	LESLIE THORSEN
Mrs. Goodloe	ELSIE TRAVIS
Abraham Morrison	KEN RENARD
Jim Friedland	J. DON FURGUSON
Narrator	BURT DOUGLAS

An impoverished small-town preacher struggles to provide for his family while leading a dwindling congregation, battling restless church deacons and standing up to a bullying sheriff in a small southern town in 1940. The subsequent short-lived series, "The Family Holvak" (9/7/75–10/27/75), reteamed Ford, Harris and Kerwin but was moved back in time to the Depression days.

0472
ONLY WITH MARRIED MEN
11/4/74 Spelling/Goldberg Productions (90 min)

Executive Producers: Aaron Spelling and Leonard Goldberg
Producer: Jerome L. Davis
Associate Producer: Shelley Hull
Director: Jerry Paris
Teleplay: Jerome L. Davis
Photography: Tim Southcott
Music: Jack Elliott and Allyn Ferguson
Art Director: Tracy Bousman
Editor: John Woodcock

Dave Andrews	DAVID BIRNEY
Jill Garrett	MICHELE LEE
Dr. Harvey Osterman	JOHN ASTIN
Marge West	JUDY CARNE
Murray West	DOM DeLUISE
Jordan Robbins	GAVIN MacLEOD
Alan Tolan	DAN TOBIN
Tina	SIMONE GRIFFETH
Sheila Osterman	YOLANDA GALARDO
Chef	FRITZ FELD
Alfreda	JAN NARRAMORE
Charlotte	ROYCE WALLACE
Maitre d'	MIKE PERROTTA
Doris	LORA KAYE
Minister	JOHN HART
Ann West	MICHELE STACY
Peter West	PATRICK LABORTEAUX

A comedy about a sexy girl who only wants to date married men and a sly bachelor who pretends to be married to avoid a long-term involvement with anyone.

0473
THE GREAT ICE RIP-OFF
11/6/74 ABC Circle Films (90 min)

A Dan Curtis Production
Producer/Director: Dan Curtis
Associate Producer: Robert Singer
Teleplay: Andrew Paul Marin
Photography: Paul Lohmann
Music: Robert Cobert
Art Director: Bill Malley
Editor: Richard A. Harris

Willy Calso	LEE J. COBB
Harkey Rollins	GIG YOUNG
Helen Calso	GRAYSON HALL
Checker	ROBERT WALDEN
Georgie	MATT CLARK
Archie	GEOFFREY LEWIS
Sam	HANK GARRETT
Cab Driver	BILL SMILLIE
Boat Proprietor	ORIN CANNON
Bus Driver	NORMAN A. HONATH
Thompson	JERRY AUGUST
Bus Official	EDGAR DANIELS

and: Jason Dunn, Al Hansen, John Hart, Marcia Lewis, Robert Nadder

A heist comedy pitting a dogged retired cop against a dapper gangster and his cohorts who, with four million dollars in diamonds in their possession, use a cross-country bus to make their getaway.

0474
THE FBI STORY: THE FBI VERSUS ALVIN KARPIS, PUBLIC ENEMY NUMBER ONE
11/8/74 Quinn Martin Productions/Warner Bros. (2 hours)

Executive Producer: Quinn Martin
Producer: Philip Saltzman
Director: Marvin Chomsky
Teleplay: Calvin Clements
Photography: Jacques R. Marquette
Music: Duane Tatro
Art Director: James D. Vance
Editor: Jerry Young

Alvin Karpis	ROBERT FOXWORTH
Maynard Richards	DAVID WAYNE
Shirley	KAY LENZ
Fred Barker	GARY LOCKWOOD
Colette	ANNE FRANCIS
Earl Anderson	CHRIS ROBINSON
J. Edgar Hoover	HARRIS YULIN
Ma Baker	EILEEN HECKART
Alex Denton	JAMES GAMMON
Dr. Williams	ROBERT EMHARDT
Vicky Clinton	ALEXANDRA HAY
Bernice Griffiths	JANICE LYNDE
Arthur (Doc) Barker	CHARLES CYPHERS
Smith	GERALD McRANEY
Frank	FRED SADOFF
Chief of Detectives	KELLY THORDSEN
Senator McKellar	WHIT BISSELL

and: Lenore Kasdorf, Charles Bateman, Mark Roberts, Byron Mabe, Betty Anne Rees, Robert Patten, Arch Whiting, Eric Scott, Claudia Bryar, Jeff Davis, John Cilgreen, Queen Smith, Bill Zuckert, Dallas Mitchell, James Sikking, Donovan Jones, Richard Roat.

The title tells it all in this meticulously restaged first film in a series by producer Quinn Martin based on landmark FBI cases. Through the 1978–79 season, only two others followed, indicating perhaps that Martin lost interest or Bureau cooperation.

0475
BRIEF ENCOUNTER
11/12/74 Carlo Ponti-Cecil Clarke Productions (90 min)

Executive Producer: Duane C. Bogie
Producer: Cecil Clarke
Director: Alan Bridges
Teleplay: John Bowen
Based on the play *Still Life* by Noel Coward
Photography: Arthur Ibbetson
Music: Cyril Ornadel
Editor: Peter Weatherly

Alec Harvey	RICHARD BURTON
Anna Jesson	SOPHIA LOREN
Graham Jesson	JACK HEDLEY
Mrs. Gaines	ROSEMARY LEACH
Melanie Harvey	ANN FIRBANK
Dolly	GWEN CHERRELL

and: Benjamin Edney, John LeMesurier, Jumoke Debayo, Madeline Hinde, Marco Orlandini, Patricia Franklin, Ernest C. Jennings, Jacki Harding, Maggie Walker, Christopher Hammond, Norman Mitchell

An updated version of the 1946 film classic (based on Noel Coward's 1936 drama) retelling the bittersweet tale of two married strangers who meet by chance in an English train station and drift into a short but poignant romance. Sophia Loren made her TV acting debut not as the proper British lady of the original but as an Italian-born housewife married into the English middle-class for seventeen years.

0476
ALL THE KIND STRANGERS
11/12/74 Cinemation Industries (90 min)

Executive Producer: Jerry Gross
Producer: Roger Lewis
Director: Burt Kennedy
Teleplay: Clyde Ware
Photography: Gene Polito and Robert B. Hauser
Music: Ron Frangipane
Song "What Are You Living For?" written and sung by Regis Hall
Editor: Folmar Blangsted

Jimmy	STACY KEACH
Carol Ann	SAMANTHA EGGAR
Peter	JOHN SAVAGE
John	ROBBY BENSON
Martha	ARLENE FABER
Gilbert	TIM PARKISON
Rita	PATTI PARKISON
James	BRENT CAMPBELL
Baby	JOHN CONNELL

A drama about seven strange orphans with vicious dogs who turn a remote farmhouse into a prison for unsuspecting travelers who will either become their parents or disappear permanently.

0477
THE GUN
11/13/74 Universal (90 min)

Producers: Richard Levinson and William Link
Director: John Badham
Teleplay: Richard Levinson and William Link
From a story by Jay Benson, Richard Levinson and William Link
Photography: Stevan Larner
Art Director: Walter M. Simonds
Editor: Frank Morriss

Art Hilliard	STEPHEN ELLIOTT
Fran	JEAN LeBOUVIER
Howie	WALLACE ROONEY
Wayne	DAVID HUFFMAN

Natcho	PEPE SERNA
Gloria	EDITH DIAZ
Senor Peralta	FELIPE TURICH
Frank	VAL DeVARGAS
Walt Kelsy	RAMON BIERI
Wilke	MICHAEL McGUIRE
Tom	RON THOMPSON
Braverman	JOHN SYLVESTER WHITE
Gil Strauss	RICHARD BRIGHT
Beryl Strauss	MARICLARE COSTELLO
Kenny	RANDY GRAY

The odyssey of an American handgun and the dramatic way it reshapes the lives of its various owners, in a plot similar to the famed overcoat in *Flesh and Fantasy* (1943).

0478

IT COULDN'T HAPPEN TO A NICER GUY
11/19/74 The Jozak Company (90 min)

Executive Producer: Gerald I. Isenberg
Producer: Arne Sultan
Associate Producer: Gerald W. Abrams

Director: Cy Howard
Teleplay: Arne Sultan and Earl Barret
Photography: Matthew F. Leonetti
Music: Fred Karlin
Editors: Christopher Holmes and Carroll Sax

Harry Walters	PAUL SORVINO
Janet Walters	MICHAEL LEARNED
Ed Huxley	BOB DISHY
Ken Walters	ADAM ARKIN
Sergeant Riggs	ED BARTH
Stu Dotney	ROGER BOWEN
Wanda Olivia Wellman	JOANNA CAMERON
Judge A. J. White	BARBARA CASON
Sgt. Rose Templeton	ELAINE SHORE
Warren Morgan	G. WOOD
Alan Ronston	GRAHAM JARVIS
Mrs. Carter	SANDRA DEEL

and: Dick Yarmy, Edward Marshall, Lorna Thayer, Ruth Warshawsky, Carl Franklin, Jack Frey, Arlen Stewart, Patricia Heider

A comedy about a mild-mannered man who cries "Rape!" and can't convince anybody he was seduced and abandoned on a lonely highway by a gorgeous woman with a Cadillac and a gun.

0479

THE VIRGINIA HILL STORY
11/19/74 RSO Films, Inc. (90 min)

Executive Producers: Deane Barclay and Howard Rosenman
Producer: Aaron Rosenberg
Director: Joel Schumacher
Teleplay: Joel Schumacher and Juleen Compton
From a story by Juleen Compton
Photography: Jack Woolf
Music: David Shire
Assistant Director: Claude Binyon, Jr.
Art Director: Walter McKegen
Editor: David Rawlins

Virginia Hill	DYAN CANNON
Bugsy Siegel	HARVEY KEITEL
Leo Ritchie	ALLEN GARFIELD
Nick Rubanos	JOHN VERNON
Senator Estes Kefauver	HERBERT ANDERSON
Leroy Small	ROBBY BENSON
Mousie	JOHN QUADE
Auctioneer	LIAM DUNN
Halley	CONRAD JANIS

The fact-based story of Virginia Hill, girlfriend of one-time Los Angeles gangster Bugsy Siegel, who was slain in gangland fashion in 1947.

Bernie Casey and Laurence Luckinbill in PANIC ON THE 5:22 (1974)

0480
PANIC ON THE 5:22
11/20/74 Quinn Martin Productions (90 min)

Executive Producer: Quinn Martin
Producer: Anthony Spinner
Director: Harvey Hart
Teleplay: Eugene Price
Photography: William W. Spencer
Music: Richard Markowitz
Art Director: Richard Y. Haman
Editor: Pembroke J. Herring

Countess Hedy Maria	
Tovarese	INA BALIN
Wendell Weaver	BERNIE CASEY
Tony Ebsen	LINDEN CHILES
Harlan Jack Gardner	ANDREW DUGGAN
Hal Rodgers	DANA ELCAR
Jerome Hartford	EDUARD FRANZ
Mary Ellen Lewis	LYNDA DAY GEORGE
Lawrence Lewis	LAURENCE LUCKINBILL
Emil Linz	RENI SANTONI
Frankie Scamantino	JAMES SLOYAN
Eddie Chiario	ROBERT WALDEN
Dudley Stevenson	DENNIS PATRICK
Dr. Cruikshank	ROBERT MANDAN
George Lincoln	CHARLES LAMPKIN
Charlie	JOSEPH PERRY
A. C. Thompson	BYRON MORROW
Shoeshine Boy	DERICK STROUD
Harry Kinney	GEORGE KRAMER
Rick Apollo	SAN DeFAZIO

Terror rides a private railroad car where passengers
have only their wits as weapons against three armed
men determined to rob and kill them.

0481
GREAT EXPECTATIONS
11/24/74 Transcontinental Film Productions
(2 hours)

Producer: Robert Fryer
Associate Producer: Johnny Goodman
Director: Joseph Hardy
Teleplay: Sherman Yellen
Based on the novel by Charles Dickens
Photography: Freddie Young
Music: Maurice Jarre
Performed by the New Philharmonia Orchestra of
London
Production Designer: Terence Marsh
Art Director: Alan Tomkins
Costumes: Elizabeth Haffenden and Joan Bridge
Editor: Bill Butler

Pip	MICHAEL YORK
Estella	SARAH MILES
Magwich	JAMES MASON
Miss Havisham	MARGARET LEIGHTON
Pumplec	ROBERT MORLEY
Jaggers	ANTHONY QUAYLE
Joe Gargery	JOSS ACKLAND
Mrs. Gargery	RACHEL ROBERTS
Biddy	HEATHER SEARS
Herbert Pocket	ANDREW RAY
Young Pip	SIMON GIPPS-KENT
Bentley Drummle	JAMES FAULKNER
Wemmick	PETER BULL
Scarred Convict	SAM KYDD
Mr. Wopsle	JOHN CLIVE
Mrs. Wopsle	PATSY SMART

and: Dudley Sutton, Celia Hewitt, Maria Charles,
Elaine Garreau, Eric Chitty, Edward Brayshaw, Tow
Owen, Noel Trevarthen, Richard Beaumont, Paul El-
lison, Michael Howart, Ben Cross, Geoffrey Greenhill,
John Wireford

Joan Hackett and Tuesday Weld in REFLECTIONS OF MURDER (1974)

A sumptuous remake of the Dickens classic that previously had been filmed in black and white in 1917, 1934,
and 1947 (the definitive version). The latest version
was produced as a musical with an original score by
Norman Sachs and Mel Mandel, but none of the songs
appeared in the final print for reasons never explained.

0482
REFLECTIONS OF MURDER
11/24/74 ABC Circle Films (2 hours)

An Aaron Rosenberg/Charles Lederer Production
Producer: Aaron Rosenberg
Director: John Badham

Teleplay: Carol Sobieski
Based on the novel *Celle Qui N'Etait Plus* by Pierre
Boileau and Thomas Narcejac
Photography: Mario Tosi
Music: Billy Goldenberg
Adapted from "The Well-Tempered Clavichord" by
J. S. Bach
Production Design: Boris Leven
Editor: David Rawlins

Vicky	TUESDAY WELD
Claire Elliott	JOAN HACKETT
Michael Elliott	SAM WATERSTON
Mrs. Turner	LUCILLE BENSON
Jerry Steele	MICHAEL LERNER

Jack Palance and Keith Carradine in THE GODCHILD (1974)

Coroner	ED BERNARD	Rourke	JACK PALANCE	Music: Fred Karlin	
Mr. Turner	R. G. ARMSTRONG	Sgt. Dobbs	JACK WARDEN	Art Director: Stan Jolley	
Chip	LANCE KERWIN	Lieut. Lewis	KEITH CARRADINE	Editor: Carroll L. Sax	
Keithe	JOHN LEVIN	Crees	ED LAUTER		
Cop on Freeway	JESSE VINT	Sanchez	JOSE PEREZ	Peter "Punch" Travers	GLENN FORD
Mr. Griffiths	WILLIAM TURNER	Cpl. Crawley	BILL McKINNEY	Jody Travers	PAM GRIFFIN
Peter	JAMES A.	Loftus	JESSE VINT	Lil Charny	RUTH ROMAN
	NEWCOMBE	Virginia	FIONNUALA	Margaret Howell Grant	KATHLEEN
David	SAM HENRIOT		FLANAGAN		WIDDOES
Photographer	DON SPARKS	Denton	JOHN QUADE	Dan Baxter	PARLEY BAER
Woman	SANDRA COBURN	William	SIMON DECKARD	Jen Kingsley	SUSAN BROWN
Maid	RITA CONDE	Shaw	ED BAKEY	Franz Butz	DONALD BARRY
		Nathaniel Mony	KERMIT MURDOCH	Mrs. Stilts (Midget)	BILLY BARTY
				Woody	MEL STEWART
				Aurora	CYNTHIA
					HAYWARD

The wife and former mistress of a tyrannical schoolmaster team up to murder him but he diabolically haunts them with his macabre influence following the baffling disappearance of his body. An exciting remake of Henri-Georges Clouzot's French classic, *Les Diaboliques* (1955).

0483
THE GODCHILD
11/26/74 MGM (90 min)

An Alan Neuman Production
Executive Producer: Charles Robert McLain
Producer: Richard Collins
Director: John Badham
Teleplay: Ron Bishop
Based on a short story in the *Saturday Evening Post* by Peter B. Kyne
Photography: Stevan Larner
Music: David Shire
Art Director: Robert E. Smith
Editor: Frank Morriss

An update of the oft-filmed *The Three Godfathers*, previously made in 1916 with Harry Carey, repeating his role in John Ford's 1919 version *(Marked Men)*, in William Wyler's 1929 adaptation *(Hell's Heroes)* with Charles Bickford, in Richard Boleslavski's 1936 production with Chester Morris and Walter Brennan, and in John Ford's Technicolor version with John Wayne in 1948, dedicated to Harry Carey. Three Civil War prisoners, fleeing from both Confederates and Apaches, risk their freedom and lives to aid a dying woman and become guardians of her newborn child.

0484
PUNCH AND JODY
11/26/74 Metromedia Productions (90 min)

Executive Producer: Charles Fries
Producer: Dick Berg and Douglas Benton
Director: Barry Shear
Teleplay: John McGreevey
Photography: Robert B. Hauser

and: Patti Mahoney, Pat Morita, Peter Ford

A circus grifter finds his life suddenly complicated by the arrival of the teenage daughter he never knew about. This pilot for a prospective series for Ford also included in its cast Ford's new wife, Cynthia Hayward, as well as his son Peter from his marriage to Eleanor Powell.

0485
ROBINSON CRUSOE
11/27/74 A BBC-TV Production (2 hours)

Producer: Cedric Messina
Director: James MacTaggart
Teleplay: James MacTaggart
Based on the book by Daniel Defoe
Photography: Brian Tufano
Music: Wilfred Josephs

Conducted by Marcus Dods
Editor: Ken Pearce

Robinson Crusoe	STANLEY BAKER
Man Friday	RAM JOHN HOLDER
The Sea Captain	JEROME WILLIS

The classic eighteenth-century saga of a man's struggle to survive after being shipwrecked on an uninhabited island. This was the initial production in an exchange program between NBC-TV and Great Britain's BBC and the fifteenth (at least) film version of the Defoe tale.

0486
THINGS IN THEIR SEASON
11/27/74 Tomorrow Entertainment, Inc. (90 min)

Executive Producer: Philip Barry, Jr.
Producer: Herbert Hirschman
Director: James Goldstone
Teleplay: John Gay
Photography: Terry K. Meade
Music: Ken Lauber
Art Director: Ed Graves
Editor: Edward A. Biery

Peg Gerlach	PATRICIA NEAL
Carl Gerlach	ED FLANDERS
Andy Gerlach	MARC SINGER
Judy Pines	MEG FOSTER
Willie McCreevy	CHARLES HAID
Millie Havemeyer	DOREEN LANG
John Tillman	MED FLORY
M.C.	JIM KASTEN
Clifford Canby	OLIVER JACQUES
Harold Redman	A. R. BOWLES
Auctioneer	JAMES ESCH
Harvey	RON TIMM
Mrs. Weldy	SHARON RYBACKI
Vera Steelwright	MARCIE REICHE

A sentimental family drama about the growing apart—and together—of a household of Wisconsin dairy farmers when the son decides to get married and move away and the mother discovers she has incurable leukemia and only a short time to live.

0487
THE RED BADGE OF COURAGE
12/3/74 20th Century-Fox (90 min)

Executive Producer: Norman Rosemont
Producer: Charles B. Fitzsimmons
Director: Lee Philips
Teleplay: John Gay
Based on the novel by Stephen Crane
Photography: Charles F. Wheeler
Music: Jack Elliott
Music Supervisor: Lionel Newman
Art Director: Bill Malley
Editor: George Jay Nicholson

Henry Fleming	RICHARD THOMAS
Jim Conklin	MICHAEL BRANDON
Wilson	WENDELL BURTON
The Tattered Man	CHARLES AIDMAN
The Cheery Soldier	WARREN BERLINGER
Sergeant	LEE DeBROUX
Mother	FRANCESCA JARVIS
Colonel	GEORGE SAWAYA
General	HANK HENDRICK
Lieutenant	JOHN COX
Fat Soldier	TINY WELLS
Corporal	NORMAN STONE

Narrated by JACK DeLEON

The Civil War classic, filmed previously in 1951 by John Huston, revolving around a young Union soldier's flight in terror from his first battle and the ultimate inner resolve that leads him back to battle.

0488
BETRAYAL
12/3/74 Metromedia Productions (90 min)

Executive Producer: Charles Fries
Producer: Gerald I. Isenberg
Associate Producer: Gerald W. Abrams
Director: Gordon Hessler
Teleplay: James Miller
Based on the novel *Only Couples Need Apply* by Doris Miles Disney
Photography: Jacques R. Marquette
Music: Ernest Gold
Editor: John A. Martinelli

Helen Mercer	AMANDA BLAKE
Gretchen	TISHA STERLING
Harold Porter	DICK HAYMES
Jay	SAM GROOM
Fred Hawkes	BRITT LEACH
Roy	EDWARD MARSHALL
Police Sergeant	TED GEHRING
Highway Patrolman	DENNIS CROSS
Mr. Hall	ERIC BROTHERSON
Eunice Russell	LUCILLE BENSON
Savings Officer	VERNON WEDDLE
Betty (Waitress)	RENEE BOND

Amanda Blake, in her TV movie debut and her first role after eighteen years on *Gunsmoke*, is a lonely widow who hires a young woman companion, unaware that the girl and her boyfriend are killer-extortionists planning to make her their next victim. Dick Haymes also made his initial TV movie appearance in this one.

0489
THE TRIBE
12/11/74 Universal (90 min)

Producer: George Eckstein
Director: Richard A. Colla
Teleplay: Lane Slate
Photography: Rexford Metz
Music: Hal Mooney
Art Director: William Newberry
Editor: Robert F. Shugrue

Mathis	VICTOR FRENCH
Gorin	WARREN VANDERS
Cana	HENRY WILCOXON
Jen	ADRIANA SHAW
Gato	STEWART MOSS
Rouse	SAM GILMAN
Sarish	TANI PHELPS GUTHRIE
Perron	MARK GRUNER
Hertha	MEG WYLIE
Ardis	NANCY ELLIOT
Orda	JEANNINE BROWN
Kiska	DOMINIQUE PINASSI
The Neanderthal	JACK SCALICI

This was a most distinctive TV movie set in caveman days, as a tribe of Cro-Magnons fight starvation and the viciously primitive Neanderthals at the dawn of history 100,000 years ago.

0490
ROLL, FREDDY, ROLL!
12/17/74 ABC Circle Films (90 min)

Producer: Bill Persky and Sam Denoff
Director: Bill Persky
Teleplay: Bill Persky and Sam Denoff
Photography: John Morley Stephens
Music: Jack Elliott and Allyn Ferguson
Art Director: Bill Malley
Editor: Jerry Shepard

Freddy Danton	TIM CONWAY
Big Sid Kane	JAN MURRAY
Tommy Danton	MOOSIE DRIER
Sidni Kane	BARRA GRANT
Admiral Norton	SCOTT BRADY
Don Talbert	ROBERT HOGAN
Evelyn Danton Kane	RUTA LEE
Theodore Menlo	HENRY JONES
Skating Rink Attendant	DANNY WELLS
Rita	EDWINA GOUGH
Gas Station Attendant	SAM DENOFF

A mild-mannered computer programmer lives on roller skates for seven days to compete for attention with his son's stepfather and to win a place in the Guinness Book of Records.

0491
THIS WAS THE WEST THAT WAS
12/17/74 Universal (90 min)

Executive Producer: Roy Huggins
Producer: Jo Swerling, Jr.
Director: Fielder Cook
Teleplay: Sam H. Rolfe
Photography: Earl Rath
Music: Dick DeBenedictis
Assistant Director: Bob Birnbaum
Art Director: Walter M. Simonds
Editors: Gloryette Clark and Fred Knudtson

Wild Bill Hickok	BEN MURPHY
Calamity Jane	KIM DARBY
Sarah Shaw	JANE ALEXANDER
J. W. McCanles	ANTHONY FRANCIOSA
Blind Pete	STUART MARGOLIN
Carmedly	STEFAN GIERASCH
Buffalo Bill Cody	MATT CLARK
Oscar Wellman	BILL McKINNEY
Hearts	W. L. LeGAULT

and: Roger Robinson, Luke Askew, Woodrow Parfrey, Milton Selzer, Bruce Glover, Dimitra Arliss, Wayne Sutherlin, Ronnie Clair Edwards

Narrated by ROGER DAVIS

A lighthearted look at the saga of Wild Bill Hickok and his relationship with Calamity Jane as he is targeted for revenge by some tough gunfighters.

0492
THE RANGERS
12/24/74 Universal/Mark VII Ltd. (90 min)

Executive Producer: Jack Webb
Producer: Edwin Self
Director: Chris Nyby III
Teleplay: Robert A. Cinader, Michael Donavan and Preston Wood
Photography: Robert H. Wyckoff
Music: Lee Holdridge
Art Director: James Martin Buchanan
Editor: Bill Parker and John Kaufman, Jr.

Ranger Tim Cassidy	JAMES G. RICHARDSON
Ranger Matt Harper	COLBY CHESTER
Chief Ranger Jack Moore	JIM B. SMITH
Edie	LARAINE STEPHENS
Bob	LAURENCE DELANEY
Frank	MICHAEL CONRAD
Sam	ROGER BOWEN

and: Carl Roger Breedlove, Dave Birkoff

This was the pilot for the short-lived "Sierra" series (Sept.–Dec. 1974)—it was shown two weeks *after* the series was cancelled—revolving around the rescue operations of the U.S. park rangers. The series starred Richardson along with Ernest Thompson and Jack Hogan in the roles here played by Colby Chester and Jim B. Smith, plus Susan Foster as a lady ranger.

0493
JUDGE DEE AND THE MONASTERY MURDERS
12/29/74 ABC Circle Films (2 hours)

Producer: Gerald I. Isenberg
Director: Jeremy Kagan
Teleplay: Nicholas Meyer
Based on the novel *Judge Dee at the Haunted Monastery* by Robert Van Gulick
Photography: Gene Polito
Music: Leonard Rosenman
Production Designer: Jan Scott
Editors: Patrick Kennedy and John Farrell

Judge Dee	KHIGH ALX DHIEGH
Tao Gan	MAKO
Kang I-Te	SOOK-TAIK OH
Jade Mirror	MIIKO TAKA
Celestial Wife	IRENE TSU
Miss Ting	SUESIE ELENE
Prior	JAMES HONG
Bright Flower	BEVERLY KUSHIDA
White Rose	CHING HOCSON
Pure Faith	YUKI SHIMODA
Tsung Lee	ROBERT SADANG
Lord Sun Ming	KEYE LUKE
Mrs. Pao	FRANCES FONG
True Wisdom	TOMMY LEE
Driver No. 1	RICHARD LEE-SUNG
Motai	TADASHI YAMASHITA

A handsomely produced detective movie set in seventh-century China, with a totally distinctive sleuth faced with an unusual case involving his three wives, a killer bear, three murders, a one-armed lady, a dead monk, a chamber of horrors, a vengeful swordsman, a lovesick juggler, a kidnapped nun—and a nagging head cold. Every role—major, supporting or extra—is portrayed by an Oriental, making this another TV movie first.

0494
THE LOG OF THE BLACK PEARL
1/4/75 Universal/Mark VII Ltd. (2 hours)

Executive Producer: Jack Webb
Producer: William Stark
Director: Andrew McLaglen
Teleplay: Harold Jack Bloom
From a story by Harold Jack Bloom, Eric Bercovici and Jerry Ludwig
Photography: Gabriel Torres
Music: Laurence Rosenthal
Art Director: James Martin Buchanan
Editor: John Kaufman, Jr.

Captain Fitzsimmons	RALPH BELLAMY
Christopher Sand	KIEL MARTIN
Jock Roper	JACK KRUSCHEN
Michael Devlin	GLENN CORBETT
Lila Bristol	ANNE ARCHER
Alexander Sand	HENRY WILCOXON
Eric Kort	JOHN ALDERSON
Fenner	EDWARD FAULKNER
Archie Hector	PEDRO ARMENDARIZ, JR.

Benjamin Velasquez	JOSE ANGEL ESPINOSA
Stockbroker	DALE JOHNSON

A young businessman receives a cryptic message from his seafaring grandfather, triggering the search for a sunken treasure and an expedition threatened by sabotage.

0495
THE SPECIALISTS
1/6/75 Mark VII Ltd./Universal (90 min)

Executive Producer: Robert A. Cinader
Director: Richard Quine
Teleplay: Robert A. Cinader and Preston Wood
Photography: F. Bud Maurtino
Music: Billy May
Editor: Chuck McClelland

Dr. William Nugent	ROBERT YORK (URICH)
Dr. Christine Scofield	MAUREEN REAGAN
Dr. Edward Grey	JACK HOGAN
Dick Rawdon	JED ALLEN
Dr. Al Marsdan	ALFRED RYDER
Dr. Burkhart	HARRY TOWNES
Resident Doctor	LILLIAN LEHMAN
Ruth Conoyer	CORINNE CAMACHO
Eileen	ANNE WHITFIELD

and: Jackie Coogan, David Lewis, Tom Scott, Chris Anders

The pilot film for a never-produced series called "Vector," in which a team of U.S. Public Health epidemiologists must trace the cause of health hazards that may start epidemics. Several plot threads: an entire grammar school is afflicted with an unidentified itching rash; a female victim of a rare strain of venereal disease is resistant to standard treatment; a group of European travelers are felled by typhoid; a series of unexplained accidents plague soap factory workers.

0496
TARGET RISK
1/6/75 Universal (90 min)

Executive Producer: Jo Swerling, Jr.
Producer: Robert F. O'Neill
Director: Robert Scheerer
Teleplay: Don Carlos Dunaway
Photography: Bill Butler
Music: Eumir Deodato
Editor: John A. Martinelli

Lee Driscoll	BO SVENSON
Linda Flayly	MEREDITH BAXTER
Simon Cusack	KEENAN WYNN
Ralph Sloan	JOHN P. RYAN
Julian Ulrich	ROBERT COOTE
Marty	PHIL BRUNS
Bill Terek	CHARLES SHULL

and: Lee Paul, Jack Bender, William Hansen

A bonded courier, whose girlfriend is abducted while they are on a date, is blackmailed into faking a diamond robbery in this pilot for a series that never got off the ground.

0497
THE DREAM MAKERS
1/7/75 MGM (90 min)

Executive Producer: Charles Robert McLain
Producer/Director: Boris Sagal
Teleplay: Bil Svanoe
Photography: Howard R. Schwartz

Music: Fred Karlin
Songs co-written and sung by Kenny Rogers
Art Director: Robert Gundlach
Editor: Jim Benson

Sammy Stone	JAMES FRANCISCUS
Mary Stone	DIANE BAKER
Manny Wheeler	JOHN ASTIN
Earl	KENNY ROGERS
Jesse	MICKEY JONES
Sally	JAMIE DONNELLY
Carol	DEVON ERICSON
Barry	STEVEN KEATS
Mike	MICHAEL LERNER
Dave	RON THOMPSON
Dean Holden	JOHN LUPTON

and: Lois Walden, David Mann, Erica Yohn, Ron Rifkin, Regis J. Cordic

A college professor becomes a top recording company executive, only to be swept out of a job in the wake of a payola scandal.

0498
MILES TO GO BEFORE I SLEEP
1/8/75 Tomorrow Entertainment, Inc. (90 min)

A Roger Gimbel Production
Executive Producer: Philip Barry
Producer: Herbert Hirschman
Director: Fielder Cook
Teleplay: Judith Parker and Bill Svanoe
From a story by Judith Parker
Photography: Terry K. Meade
Music: Vladimir Selinsky
Art Director: Ed Graves
Editor: Mike McLean

Ben Montgomery	MARTIN BALSAM
Robin Williams	MACKENZIE PHILLIPS
Maggie Stanton	KITTY WINN
Lisa	PAMELYN FERDIN
Hattie	DOROTHY MEYER
Kate Stanton	ELIZABETH WILSON
Ruth	FLORIDA FREEBUS
Jenny	SUSAN LYNN MATHEWS
Kathy	WENDY WRIGHT-HAY
Susan	ALMA COLLINS

and: John Goff, Lillian Randolph, Vicki Kriegler, Sheldon Allman, Tom Atkins, Rose Gregorio

An idealistic drama about a lonely old man trying to fulfill his life by aiding a teenage delinquent living at a rehabilitation center in Boston.

0499
LET'S SWITCH
1/7/75 Universal (90 min)

Producer: Bruce Johnson
Director: Alan Rafkin
Teleplay: Peter Lefcourt, Ruth Brooks Flippen, Andy Chubby Williams and Sid Arthur
From a story by Peter Lefcourt
Photography: Stevan Larner
Music: Harry Geller
Editor: Albert J. Zuniga

Lacy Colbert	BARBARA EDEN
Kate Fleming	BARBARA FELDON
Sidney King	GEORGE FURTH
Ross Daniels	RICHARD SCHAAL
Randy Colbert	PAT HARRINGTON
Morgan Ames	BARRA GRANT
Alice Wright	PENNY MARSHALL

Linette Robbin	JOYCE VAN PATTEN
Flo Moore	KAYE STEVENS
Greta Bennett	BARBARA CASON
LaRue Williams	RON GLASS
Inez Dulin	BELA BRUCK

and: Bill Balance, Tanya Matarazzo, Jerry Bishop, Roger Til, Paul Hansen, Donald Mantooth, Reb Brown, Mary Ann Kosica

Comedy adventures result when a hip woman's magazine editor and a pretty suburban housewife swap lives.

0500
THE MISSING ARE DEADLY
1/8/75 Lawrence Gordon Productions (90 min)

Executive Producer: Lawrence Gordon
Producer: Allen S. Epstein
Director: Don McDougall
Teleplay: Kathryn and Michael Michaelian
Photography: Tim Southcott
Music: Gil Melle
Art Director: Rodger Maus
Editor: Frank Capacchione

Dr. Margolin	ED NELSON
Dr. Durov	LEONARD NIMOY
David Margolin	GEORGE O'HANLON, JR.
Jeff Margolin	GARY MORGAN
Mr. Warren	JOSE FERRER
Michelle	KATHLEEN QUINLAN
Mrs. Robertson	MARJORIE LORD
Dr. Martinez	ARMAND ALZAMORA
Captain Franklin	JOHN MILFORD
Mrs. Bates	IRENE TEDROW
Grocer	STUART NISBET

A suspense tale about the search for an emotionally disturbed teenager who has taken from his father's research laboratory a rat infected with an incurable virus that can kill one hundred million people in three weeks.

0501
THE COUNT OF MONTE CRISTO
1/10/75 Norman Rosemont Productions/ITC (2 hours)

Producer: Norman Rosemont
Production Supervisor: Richard McWhorter
Director: David Greene
Teleplay: Sidney Carroll
Based on the novel by Alexandre Dumas
Photography: Aldo Tonti
Music: Allyn Ferguson
Art Director: Walter Patriarca
Editor: Gene Milford

Edmond Dantes	RICHARD CHAMBERLAIN
Mondego	TONY CURTIS
Abbe Faria	TREVOR HOWARD
DeVillefort	LOUIS JOURDAN
Danglars	DONALD PLEASENCE
Valentine De Villefort	TARYN POWER
Mercedes	KATE NELLIGAN
Jacopo	ANGELO INFANTI
M. Morrell	HAROLD BROMLEY
Andrea Benedetto	CARLO PURI
Caderousse	ALESSIO ORLANDO
Albert Mondego	DOMINIC GUARD
Haydee	ISABELLE de VALVERT
M. Dantes	RALPH MICHAEL
Noirtier De Villefort	ANTHONY DAWSON

and: Dominic Barto, Harry Baird, George Willing, David Mills, John Karlsen, Bill Vanders, Eddy Fay, Marco Tulli, Brian Vreeland, Troy Patterson, Gino Marturano, Lou Waldon, Franco Mazzieri, Ciro Ellias, Loris Perera, Albert Rueprechet, Renzo Marignano, Jean Mas, Andrea Fantasia, Lars Bloch, Richard Watson, George Higgins, Piero Gerlini, Michael Colton, Bondi Esterhazy

A sumptuous new version of the adventure classic which already had been filmed more than a dozen times. Louis Jourdan, who plays DeVillefort this time, was Edmond Dantes in the 1961 adaptation. Both Richard Chamberlain and Trevor Howard won Emmy Award nominations for their performances.

0502
STOWAWAY TO THE MOON
1/10/75 20th Century-Fox (2 hours)

Producer: John Cutts
Director: Andrew V. McLaglen
Teleplay: Jon Boothe and William R. Shelton
Based on the novel by William R. Shelton
Photography: J. J. Jones
Music: Pat Williams
Art Director: Allen E. Smith
Special Effects: Joe Zomar
Editor: John Schreyer

Charlie Engelhardt	LLOYD BRIDGES
Astronaut Rick Lawrence	JEREMY SLATE
Astronaut Ben Pelham	JAMES McMULLAN
Astronaut Dave Anderson	MORGAN PAULL
Eli "E.J." Mackernutt	MICHAEL LINK
Jacob Avril	JOHN CARRADINE
Dr. Jack Smathers	JAMES CALLAHAN
Tom Estes	KEENE CURTIS
Eli Mackernutt, Sr.	EDWARD FAULKNER
Whitehead	WALTER BROOKE
Mary Mackernutt	BARBARA FAULKNER
Hans Hartman	JON CEDAR
Joey Williams	STEPHEN ROGERS
News Commentator	CHARLES "PETE" CONRAD

A lighthearted drama of a spirited young boy's adventures aboard a manned space flight. This eleven-year-old with a consuming interest in space travel hides aboard a rocket ship before it blasts off for the moon.

0503
THE DEAD DON'T DIE
1/14/75 The Douglas S. Cramer Co. (90 min)

Executive Producers: Douglas S. Cramer and Wilford Lloyd Baumes
Producer: Henry Colman
Director: Curtis Harrington
Teleplay: Robert Block
Photography: James Crabe
Music: Robert Prince
Art Director: Robert Kinoshita
Editor: Ronald Fagan

Don Drake	GEORGE HAMILTON
Jim Moss	RAY MILLAND
Vera LaValle	LINDA CRISTAL
Lieutenant Reardon	RALPH MEEKER
Frankie Specht	JAMES McEACHIN
Levenia	JOAN BLONDELL
Perdido	REGGIE NADLER
Ralph Drake	JERRY DOUGLAS
Undertaker	MILTON PARSONS

and: William O'Connell, Yvette Vickers, Brendon Dillon, Russ Grieves, Bill Smiley

This supernatural period piece set in the mid-1930s has a sailor becoming drawn into the netherworld while trying to prove that his brother was wrongly executed for murder.

0504
SATAN'S TRIANGLE
1/14/75 Danny Thomas Productions (90 min)

Executive Producers: Paul Junger Witt and Tony Thomas
Producer: James Roykos

Kim Novak and Doug McClure in SATAN'S TRIANGLE (1975)

Director: Sutton Roley
Teleplay: William Read Woodfield
Photography: Leonard J. South
Music: Johnny Pate
Editors: Bud Molin and Dennis Virkler

Eva	KIM NOVAK
Haig	DOUG McCLURE
P. Martin	ALEJANDRO REY
Hal	JIM DAVIS
Strickland	ED LAUTER
Pagnolini	MICHAEL CONRAD
Salao	TITOS VANDIS
Juano	ZITTO KAZANN
Swedish Captain	PETER BOURNE
Coast Guard Captain	HANK STOHL
Miami Rescue Radio Officer	TOM DEVER
Miami Rescue Lieutenant	TRENT DOLAN

Strange ocean phenomena force a woman, the lone survivor of a shipwreck, and two Coast Guard helicopter pilots, her would-be rescuers, to pay the price for trespassing in the Devil's Place.

0505
THE HATFIELDS AND THE McCOYS
1/15/75 Charles Fries Productions (90 min)

Executive Producer: Charles Fries
Producer: George Edwards
Director: Clyde Ware
Teleplay: Clyde Ware
Photography: Fred H. Jackman
Music: Ken Lauber
Editor: Nick Archer

Devil Anse Hatfield	JACK PALANCE
Pandall McCoy	STEVE FORREST
Johnse Hatfield	RICHARD HATCH
Rose Ann McCoy	KAREN LAMM
Jim McCoy	JAMES KEACH
Cotton Top	JOHN CALVIN
Bob Hatfield	ROBERT CARRADINE
Calvin McCoy	GERRIT GRAHAM
Ellison Hatfield	MORGAN WOODWARD
Levicy Hatfield	VIRGINIA BAKER
Sarah McCoy	JOAN CAULFIELD
Troy Hatfield	JOE ESTEVEZ
Mary Hatfield	BROOKE PALANCE
Cap Hatfield	JIM BOHAN
Allifair McCoy	CHARLEY YOUNG
Tolbert McCoy	DARRELL FETTY
T. C. Crawford (and narrator)	DICK DINMAN

A retelling of the most famous feud in American history, the legendary mountain war between the Hatfields and the McCoys, covered previously in Samuel Goldwyn's *Roseanna McCoy* (1949). Palance is remarkably subdued as the pipe-smoking Hatfield patriarch, with his ex-wife Virginia Baker and his daughter Brooke as members of the clan.

0506
DEATH STALK
1/21/75 Wolper Pictures (90 min)

Executive Producers: Herman Rush and Ted Bergman
Producer: Dick Caffey
Director: Robert Day
Teleplay: Steven Kandel and John W. Bloch
Based on the novel by Thomas Chastain
Photography: Leonard J. South and Michel Hugo
Music: Pete Rugolo
Editors: James T. Heckert and Chuck Montgomery

Jack Trahey	VINCE EDWARDS
Pat Trahey	ANJANETTE COMER
Hugh Webster	ROBERT WEBBER
Cathy Webster	CAROL LYNLEY
Brunner	VIC MORROW
Cal Shepherd	NEVILLE BRAND
Frank Cody	NORMAN FELL
Roy Joad	LARRY WILCOX

A kidnap thriller that finds two men desperately trying to save their wives who have been abducted by four escaped convicts fleeing down a treacherous river in rubber rafts.

0507
THE ABDUCTION OF SAINT ANNE
1/21/75 Quinn Martin Productions (90 min)
(subsequently titled *They've Kidnapped Anne Benedict*)

Executive Producer: Quinn Martin
Producer: John Wilder
Director: Harry Falk
Teleplay: Edward Hume
Based on the novel *The Issue of the Bishop's Blood* by Thomas Patrick McMahon
Photography: Jack Swain
Music: George Duning
Art Director: James Martin Buchanan
Editor: Walter Hannemann

Dave Hatcher	ROBERT WAGNER
Bishop Francis Paul Logan	E. G. MARSHALL
Carl Gentry	LLOYD NOLAN
Anne Benedict	KATHLEEN QUINLAN
Ted Morrisey	WILLIAM WINDOM
Pete Haggerty	JAMES GREGORY
Angel Montoya	A MARTINEZ
Sister Patrick	RUTH McDEVITT
Frank Benedict	ALFRED RYDER
Wayne Putnam	GEORGE McCALLISTER
Vanjack	TONY YOUNG
Mother Michael	MARTHA SCOTT
Father Rubacava	VIC MOHICA
Sheriff Townsend	PATRICK CONWAY
Woody	ROY JENSON

A cynical detective and a Roman Catholic bishop from the Vatican team up to investigate the reported miraculous powers of a beautiful seventeen-year-old girl being held captive in the home of her father, an ailing syndicate kingpin, whose associates will stop at nothing to keep her imprisoned.

0508
A SHADOW IN THE STREETS
1/28/75 Playboy Productions (90 min)

Executive Producer: Hugh Hefner
Producers: John D. F. Black and Richard D. Donner
Director: Richard D. Donner
Teleplay: John D. F. Black
Photography: Gayne Rescher
Music: Charles Bernstein
Editor: David Rawlins

Pete Mackey	TONY LoBIANCO
Gina Pulaski	SHEREE NORTH
Len Raeburn	DANA ANDREWS
Siggy Taylor	ED LAUTER
Debby	JESSE WELLES
Leroy	BILL HENDERSON
Bense	DICK BALDUZZI
Cavelli	JOHN SYLVESTER WHITE
Lee	LEE DeBROUX
Lila	LIEUX DRESSLER

Steemson   RICHARD KIETH
Gardner   SHERWOOD PRICE
Hazlett   JACK O'LEARY

This pilot for a prospective TV series dealt with a tough ex-convict who tries to build a new life on the outside as a parole agent in an experimental paraprofessional program.

0509
THE DAUGHTERS OF JOSHUA CABE RETURN
1/28/75 Spelling/Goldberg Productions (90 min)

Executive Producers: Aaron Spelling and Leonard Goldberg
Producer: Richard E. Lyons
Director: David Lowell Rich
Teleplay: Kathleen Hite
Photography: Tim Southcott
Music: Jeff Alexander
Art Director: Tracy Bousman
Editor: Frank P. Keller

Joshua Cabe	DAN DAILEY
Bitteroot	DUB TAYLOR
Ada	RONNE TROUP
Charity	CHRISTINA HART
Mae	BROOKE ADAMS
Essie	KATHLEEN FREEMAN
Will	CARL BETZ
Miner	ARTHUR HUNNICUTT
Sergeant Maxwell	TERRY WILSON
Jim Finch	RANDELL CARVER
Jenny Finch	JANE ALICE BRANDON
Claver	ROBERT BURTON
Vickers	GREG LEYDIG

In the second of the "Joshua Cabe" movies—this one with an entirely different cast—the three shady ladies, hired by a rascally old rancher to pose as his daughters, are outwitted by the real father of one, who kidnaps his own daughter and holds her for a ransom Cabe can't pay.

0510
DEATH BE NOT PROUD
2/4/75 Good Housekeeping Presentation/Westfall Productions Inc. (2 hours)

Executive Producer: Charles G. Mortimer, Jr.
Producer/Director: Donald Wrye
Teleplay: Donald Wrye
Based on *Death Be Not Proud,* a memoir by John Gunther
Photography: Michael Chapman
Music: Fred Karlin
Editor: Maury Winetrobe

John Gunther	ARTHUR HILL
Frances Gunther	JANE ALEXANDER
Johnny Gunther	ROBBY BENSON
Dr. Tracy Putnam	LINDEN CHILES
Frank Boyden	RALPH CLANTON
Mary Wilson	WENDY PHILLIPS

The moving true story adapted from John Gunther's book about the life and early death from a brain tumor of his teenage son in 1947. An Emmy Award nomination went to cinematographer Michael Chapman.

0511
ALL CREATURES GREAT AND SMALL
2/4/75 Talent Associates, LTD/EMI (2 hours)

Producers: David Susskind and Duane C. Bogie
Associate Producer: Cecil F. Ford
Director: Claude Whatham

Teleplay: Hugh Whitemore
Based on the books *If Only They Could Talk* and
And It Shouldn't Happen to a Vet by James Herriot
Photography: Peter Suschitzky
Music: Wilfred Josephs
Music Director: Marcus Dods
Production Designer: Geoffrey Drake
Editor: Ralph Sheldon

James Herriot	SIMON WARD
Siegfried Farnon	ANTHONY HOPKINS
Helen Alderson	LISA HARROW
Tristan Farnon	BRIAN STIRNER
Cranford	FREDDIE JONES
Soames	T. P. McKENNA
Miss Harbottle	BRENDA BRUCE
Mr. Alderson	JOHN COLLIN
Mrs. Hall	CHRISTINE BUCKLEY
Connie	JANE COLLINS
Farmer in Cinema	FRED FEAST
Joyce	GLYNNE GELDART
Dinsdale's Uncle	HAROLD GOODWIN
Mrs. Seaton	DOREEN MANTLE
Headwaiter	JOHN NETTLETON
Mrs. Pumphrey	DAPHNE OXENFORD
Mr. Dean	BERT PALMER
Geoff Mallock	JOHN REES
Pamela	JENNY RUNACRE
Brenda	JANE SOLO

A gentle, episodic account of author Herriot's apprenticeship in the mid-1930s to an eccentric rural English veterinarian and his awkward courtship of a farmer's daughter. The film was tested briefly after its TV premiere in theatrical release in the U.S. following a semi-successful New York engagement.

0512
ALL TOGETHER NOW
2/5/75 RSO Films (90 min)

Executive Producers: Deane Barkley and Howard Rosenman
Producer: Ron Bernstein
Director: Randal Kleiser
Teleplay: Jeff Andrus and Rubin Carson
From a story by Rubin Carson
Photography: Gene Polito
Music: John Rubinstein
Songs by John Rubinstein and Tim McIntyre
Editors: Bob Wyman and Larry Robinson

Bill Lindsay	JOHN RUBINSTEIN
Carol Lindsay	GLYNNIS O'CONNOR
Andy Lindsay	BRAD SAVAGE
Susan Lindsay	HELEN HUNT
Nicki	DORI BRENNER
Charles Drummond	BILL MACY
Helen Drummond	JANE WITHERS
Mike	LARRY BISHOP
Jerry	ADAM ARKIN
Rafe	MOOSIE DRIER
Joe	TIGER WILLIAMS
Attorney	BRAD TRUMBULL
Chauffeur	FRANK VENTGEN
Carla	DEBORAH SHERMAN
Girlfriend	LYLE ANNE MORSE
Store Manager	EDWIN MILLS

A film inspired by the actual story of four orphaned children who have thirty days to prove they can remain together as a family without adult supervision. John Rubinstein (son of legendary pianist Artur Rubinstein) stars as the oldest, and he also wrote the film's music. Two other second generation actors also appear: Adam Arkin (son of Alan) and Larry Bishop (son of Joey).

0513
THE LEGEND OF LIZZIE BORDEN
2/10/75 Paramount (2 hours)

Producer: George LeMaire
Associate Producer: William Bast
Director: Paul Wendkos
Teleplay: William Bast
Photography: Robert B. Hauser
Music: Billy Goldenberg
Art Director: Jack DeShields
Editor: John A. Martinelli

Robby Benson in DEATH BE NOT PROUD (1975)

Elizabeth Montgomery in THE LEGEND OF LIZZIE BORDEN (1975)

Lizzie Borden	ELIZABETH MONTGOMERY
Bridget Sullivan	FIONNUALA FLANAGAN
Hosea Knowlton	ED FLANDERS
Emma Borden	KATHERINE HELMOND
George Robinson	DON PORTER
Andrew Borden	FRITZ WEAVER
Sylvia Knowlton	BONNIE BARTLETT
Dr. Bowen	JOHN BEAL
Abby Borden	HELEN CRAIG
Mayor Coughlin	ALAN HEWITT
Alice Russell	GAIL KOBE

An ethereal retelling, stylishly produced, of the story of the New England spinster accused of the axe murders of her father and stepmother in nineteenth-century Fall River, Massachusetts. Emmy Award nominations went to Elizabeth Montgomery, art director Jack DeShields, set decorator Henry Gordon, editor John A. Martinelli, and costume designer Guy Verhille. DeShields and Gordon won.

0514
SARAH T.—PORTRAIT OF A TEENAGE ALCOHOLIC
2/11/75 Universal (2 hours)

Producer: David Levinson
Director: Richard Donner
Teleplay: Richard and Esther Shapiro
Photography: Gayne Rescher
Music: Jim DiPasquale
Art Director: Jack Chilberg II
Editor: Richard Bracken

Sarah Travis	LINDA BLAIR
Jean Hodges	VERNA BLOOM
Matt Hodges	WILLIAM DANIELS
Jerry Travis	LARRY HAGMAN
Dr. Marvin Kittredge	MICHAEL LERNER
Ken Newkirk	MARK HAMILL
Margaret	HILDA HAYNES
Nancy	LAURETTE SPANG
Mr. Peterson	M. EMMET WALSH
Marsha Cooper	KAREN PURCIL

A drama about a fifteen-year-old girl (Linda Blair again in another of her inevitable put-upon-teenager roles) who is unable to cope with her problems and the lack of love at home and becomes an alcoholic.

0515
THE TRIAL OF CHAPLAIN JENSEN
2/11/75 20th Century-Fox (90 min)

A Monash/Preissman Production
Executive Producer: Paul Monash
Producer: Ron Preissman
Director: Robert Day
Teleplay: Loring Mandel
Based on the book by Chaplain Andrew Jensen and Martin Abrahamson
Photography: Earl Rath
Music: Dave Grusin
Art Director: Carl Anderson
Editors: Aaron Stell and J. Frank O'Neill

Chaplain Andrew Jensen	JAMES FRANCISCUS
Kathleen Jensen	JOANNA MILES
Louise Kennelly	LYNDA DAY GEORGE
Adrienne Hess	DOROTHY TRISTAN
Budd Rogers	CHARLES DURNING
Lieutenant Kastner	HARRIS YULIN
Lieutenant Levin	HOWARD PLATT
Captain Atherton	ALAN MANSON
Clark Jensen	DENNIS LARSON
Donald Jensen	STEVEN KUNZ
Jane A. Johnston	BETTY URICH
Irene Daniels	SALLY CARTER IHNAT

The true account of the ordeal of a chaplain, the only U.S. naval officer ever to be court-martialed solely on charges of adultery.

0516
A CRY FOR HELP
2/12/75 Universal (90 min)

Executive Producers: Richard Levinson and William Link
Producer: Howie Hurwitz
Director: Daryl Duke
Teleplay: Peter S. Fischer
Photography: Richard C. Glouner
Music: Gil Melle
Art Director: Jack T. Collis
Editors: Douglas Stewart and Frank Morriss

Harry Freeman	ROBERT CULP
Ingrid Brunner	ELAYNE HEILVEIL
Paul Church	KEN SWOFFORD
George Rigney	JULIUS HARRIS
Buddy Marino	CHUCK McCANN
Philip Conover	MICHAEL LERNER
Richie Danko	BRUCE BOXLEITNER
Sgt. Lou Shirley	LEE DeBROUX
Brother Stephen Tyler	GRANVILLE VAN DUSEN
Hank Buchek	KEN SYLK
Eddie Frisch	JOSEPH GEORGE
Irene Schullman	JEAN ALLISON
Arthur Schullman	DONALD MANTOOTH
Quinn Shaw	RUDOLPH WILLRICH
Mae Dowd	LIEUX DRESSLER
Tony Garafolas	RALPH MANZA

Charles Durning and James Franciscus in THE TRIAL OF CHAPLAIN JENSEN (1975)

Robert Culp and Elayne Heilweil in A CRY FOR HELP (1975)

Maureen Stapleton and Charles Durning in QUEEN OF THE STARDUST BALLROOM (1975)

A cynical radio talk show host, who daily insults his audience, receives a suicide threat from a nameless young girl and frantically tries to get his listeners to locate her before she can carry out her threat. During production, this film was called *End of the Line*.

0517
QUEEN OF THE STARDUST BALLROOM
2/13/75 Tomorrow Entertainment, Inc. (2 hours)

Producers: Robert W. Christiansen and Rick Rosenberg
Director: Sam O'Steen
Teleplay: Jerome Kass
Photography: David M. Walsh
Music: Billy Goldenberg
Original score by Billy Goldenberg and Alan and Marilyn Bergman
Songs: "Who Gave You Permission?," "Pennies and Dreams," "A Big Mistake," "Call Me a Fool," "Suddenly There's You" and "I Love To Dance"

Choreography: Marge Champion
Editor: William H. Ziegler

Bea Asher	MAUREEN STAPLETON
Al Green	CHARLES DURNING
Davis Asher	MICHAEL BRANDON
Jennifer	ELIZABETH BERGER
Johnny	LEWIS CHARLES
Pauline Krimm	NATALIE CORE
Louis	ALAN FUDGE
Sylvia	FLORENCE HALOP
Martha	DANNA HANSEN
Angie	JACQUELYN HYDE
Marie	HOLLY IRVING
Harry	GIL LAMB
Emily	NORA MARLOWE
Helen	CHARLOTTE RAE
Petie	GUY RAYMOND
Diane	BEVERLY SANDERS
Jack	MICHAEL STRONG
Moe	CLAUDE STROUD
Shirley	RUTH WARSHAWSKY
Band Vocalist	MARTHA TILTON

and Orrin Tucker and His Orchestra

A striking, Emmy Award-winning drama with music about a suddenly widowed housewife who finds that her acute problems are loneliness and the well-meaning attempts at comfort by her family and friends. She discovers a new life and companionship at a local ballroom where she meets a married mailman who becomes her regular dance partner and tender friend. Both Stapleton and Durning received Emmy nominations, while David Walsh, Marge Champion, Billy Goldenberg and Alan and Marilyn Bergman all won. Sam O'Steen received the Directors Guild of America Award and Jerome Kass won the Writers Guild of America Award for his teleplay. *Queen of the Stardust Ballroom* subsequently was expanded into the Broadway musical *Ballroom* and opened in December 1978.

0518
ADVENTURES OF THE QUEEN
2/14/75 20th Century-Fox (2 hours)

Producer: Irwin Allen
Director: David Lowell Rich
Teleplay: John Gay
Photography: Jack Woolf
Music: Richard LaSalle
Production Designer: Stan Jolley
Editor: Bill Brame

Capt. James Morgan	ROBERT STACK
Dr. Peter Brooks	DAVID HEDISON
J. L. Dundeen	RALPH BELLAMY
Martin Reed	BRADFORD DILLMAN
Robert Dwight	SORRELL BOOKE
Ted Trevor	BURR DeBENNING
John Howe	JOHN RANDOLPH
Ann Trevor	ELLEN WESTON
Matthew Evans	LINDEN CHILES
Claudine Lennart	SHEILA MATTHEWS
Jim Greer	MILLS WATSON
Phillips	FRANK MARTH
Riley	RICHARD X. SLATTERY
Betsy Schuster	FRANCINE YORK
Bill Schuster	VITO SCOTTI
Forbes	RUSSELL JOHNSON
Irene McKay	ELIZABETH ROGERS
Barbara	LARA PARKER
Walter Fletcher	PAUL CARR
Fedderson	THAN WYENN

A luxury cruise ship is threatened with destruction—with all aboard—as part of a deadly vendetta against a multi-millionaire passenger in true Irwin Allen seagoing disaster style. The liner Queen Mary provided the backdrop for this suspense movie.

0519
THE LAST DAY
2/15/75 Paramount (2 hours)

Producer: A. C. Lyles
Director: Vincent McEveety
Teleplay: Jim Byrnes and Steve Fisher
From a story by Steve Fisher and A. C. Lyles
Photography: Robert B. Hauser
Music: Carmine Coppola
Art Director: Jack DeShields
Editor: Mike Vejar

Will Spence	RICHARD WIDMARK
Dick Broadwell	CHRISTOPHER CONNELLY
Bob Dalton	ROBERT CONRAD
Charlie Connelly	GENE EVANS
Gratt Dalton	RICHARD JAECKEL
Emmet Dalton	TIM MATHESON
Betty Spence	BARBARA RUSH
Bill Powers	TOM SKERRITT
Daisy	LORETTA SWIT
Ransom Payne	MORGAN WOODWARD
Julie Johnson	KATHLEEN CODY
Player	JON LOCKE
Clerk	BRYAN O'BYRNE

Narrated by HARRY MORGAN

A trim A. C. Lyles Western (like the type he made in the 1960s with a stellar cast of veteran actors) that has the Dalton gang riding again, forcing a retired gunman to use his weapons once more in the climactic battle at Coffeyville, Kansas.

0520
THE SECRET NIGHT CALLER
2/18/75 Charles Fries Productions/Penthouse Productions (90 min)

Executive Producer: Florence Small
Producer: Art Stolnitz
Director: Jerry Jameson
Teleplay: Robert Presnell, Jr.
Photography: Matthew F. Leonetti
Music: John Parker
Art Director: Perry Ferguson II
Editor: George W. Brooks

Freddy Durant	ROBERT REED
Pat Durant	HOPE LANGE
Jan Durant	ROBIN MATTSON
Dr. Mayhill	MICHAEL CONSTANTINE
Kitty	SYLVIA SIDNEY
Chloe	ELAINE GIFTOS
Charlotte	ARLENE GOLONKA
Mr. Henry	THAYER DAVID
Ruth	MARLA ADAMS
District Attorney	ROBERT DOYLE

A respectable family man suffers from a compulsion to make obscene telephone calls.

0521
THE FAMILY NOBODY WANTED
2/19/75 Universal (90 min)

Executive Producer: David Victor
Producer: William Kayden
Director: Ralph Senensky
Teleplay: Suzanne Clauser

Shirley Jones in THE FAMILY NOBODY WANTED (1975)

Based on the 1954 best-seller by Helen Doss
Photography: Jack Woolf
Music: George Romanis
Art Director: Ira Diamond
Editor: Chuck McClelland

Helen Doss	SHIRLEY JONES
Carl Doss	JAMES OLSON
Mrs. Bittner	KATHERINE HELMOND
Elmer Franklin	WOODROW PARFREY
James Collins	BEESON CARROLL
Eunice Franklin	CLAUDIA BRYAR
Mrs. Kimberly	ANN DORAN
Judge Goldman	LINDSAY WORKMAN

The Children:

Donny	WILLIE AAMES
Rick	ERNEST ESPARZA III
Tina	DAWN BIGLAY
Tony	GUILLERMO SAN JUAN
Lynette	JINA TAN
Pam	TINA TOYOTA
Aram	HAIG MOVSESIAN
Ton	TIM KIM
Debby	SHERRY LYNN KUPAHU
Andy	MICHAEL and ROBERT STADNIK
Angela	KNAR KESHISHIAN

A heartwarming drama recounting the true story of a minister and his wife who put together a family of twelve racially mixed children.

0522
ATTACK ON TERROR: THE FBI VERSUS THE KU KLUX KLAN
2/20–21/75 Quinn Martin Productions (4 hours)

Executive Producer: Quinn Martin
Producer: Philip Saltzman
Director: Marvin Chomsky
Teleplay: Calvin Clements
Photography: Jacques R. Marquette
Music: Mundell Lowe
Art Director: Bill Kenney
Editor: Jerry Young

Ollie Thompson	NED BEATTY
George Greg	JOHN BECK
Dave Keene	BILLY GREEN BUSH
Paul Mathison	DABNEY COLEMAN
Inspector Ryder	ANDREW DUGGAN
Ralph Paine	ED FLANDERS
Attorney Clay	GEORGE GRIZZARD
Roy Ralston	L. Q. JONES
Ed Duncan	GEOFFREY LEWIS
Jean Foster	MARLYN MASON
Don Foster	WAYNE ROGERS
Ben Jacobs	PETER STRAUSS
Glen Tuttle	RIP TORN
Dee Malcom	MILLS WATSON
Harry Dudley	JAMES HAMPTON
Linn Jacobs	SHEILA LARKIN
Steve Bronson	ANDREW PARKS
Charles Gilmore	HILLY HICKS
Aaron Cord	LUKE ASKEW
Jailer Sutton	JOHN McLIAM
Bea Sutton	MARTINE BARTLETT
Thurston Carson	LOGAN RAMSEY

Narrated by WILLIAM CONRAD

and: Arthur Adams, Curtis Lee Harris, Hal Lynch, Taylor Larcher, Rosalind Miles, Paulene Myers, Arch Whiting, Johnny Haymer, Hal Riddle, Mark Edward Hall, Roy Applegate, Albert Morgenstern, Jerry Ayres, Jim Bohan, Jeanie Capps, Jessie Lee Fulton, Jim Gough

A fact-based drama, from the FBI files, detailing the story of three civil rights workers who were murdered in Mississippi in 1964 and the subsequent investigation leading to the conviction of seven Ku Klux Klansmen. This was the second in Quinn Martin's series of landmark FBI cases.

Beverly Hope Atkinson, Lee Remick and Jill Clayburgh in HUSTLING (1975)

0523
HUSTLING
2/22/75 Filmways (2 hours)

Producer: Lillian Gallo
Director: Joseph Sargent
Teleplay: Fay Kanin
Based on the book by Gail Sheehy
Photography: Bill Butler
Music: Jerry Fielding
Editor: George Jay Nicholson

Fran Morrison	LEE REMICK
Orin Dietrich	MONTE MARKHAM
Wanda	JILL CLAYBURGH
Swifty	ALEX ROCCO
Dee Dee	MELANIE MAYRON
Gizelle	BEVERLY HOPE ATKINSON
Keough	DICK O'NEILL
Gustavino	BURT YOUNG

Barbara Anderson and Don Galloway in YOU LIE SO DEEP, MY LOVE (1975)

Lester Traube	PAUL BENEDICT	David Hartman	MARC SINGER	Photography: Leonard J. South
Geist	JOHN SYLVESTER WHITE	Sherry Williams	KAY LENZ	Music: Elliot Kaplan
		Mike	WENDELL BURTON	Art Director: Ira Diamond
Harold Levine	ALLAN MILLER	Dr. Cavaliere	WILLIAM WINDOM	Editor: Asa Clark
		Dr. Schroeder	JOSEPH CAMPANELLA	

A drama about an investigative reporter (obviously based on Gail Sheehy) for a New York-based news magazine who digs into the multi-million dollar prostitution business in Manhattan in search of the real profiteers. Emmy Award nominations went to Jill Clayburgh for her acting and Fay Kanin for her writing.

Fred Hartman	JACK WARDEN
Ida Mae Hartman	DOROTHY TRISTAN
Bill	DIRK BENEDICT
Bobbi Hartman	NANCY WOLFE
Nancy	MARCIA STRASSMAN
Danny	WYNN IRWIN
David (age 8)	CHRISTIAN JUTTNER
Bobbi (age 10)	ALISON LEEMAN

Neal Collins	DON GALLOWAY
Susan Collins	BARBARA ANDERSON
Jennifer Pierce	ANGEL TOMPKINS
Uncle Joe Padway	WALTER PIDGEON
Ellen	ANNE SCHEDEEN
The Foreman	RUSSELL JOHNSON
The Maid	VIRGINIA GREGG
Tom File	ROBERT ROTHWELL
Phyllis	BOBBI JORDAN
Jordan	PITT HERBERT

0524
JOURNEY FROM DARKNESS
2/25/75 Bob Banner Associates (2 hours)

Executive Producer: Bob Banner
Producers: Tom Egan and Stephen Pouliot
Director: James Goldstone
Teleplay: Peggy Chandler Dick
From a story by Peggy Chandler Dick and Stephen Pouliot
Photography: Michel Hugo
Music: Ken Lauber
Art Director: Jan Scott
Editor: Edward A. Biery

A brilliant blind student fights a seemingly hopeless battle to gain acceptance into medical school.

0525
YOU LIE SO DEEP, MY LOVE
2/25/75 Universal (90 min)

Producer/Director: David Lowell Rich
Teleplay: John Neufeld and Robert Hamner
From a story by William L. Stuart and Robert Hamner

A desperate man wants love and money—his girlfriend has one, his wife has the other—and he will stop at nothing to get both, including murder.

0526
SOMEONE I TOUCHED
2/26/75 Charles Fries Productions (90 min)

Executive Producer: Dick Berg
Producer: Wayne Weisbart
Associate Producer: John A. Ireland

James Olson and Cloris Leachman in SOMEONE I TOUCHED (1975)

Director: Lou Antonio
Teleplay: James Henerson
From a story by Patricia Winter and James Henerson
Photography: Stevan Larner
Music: Al Kasha and Joel Hirschhorn
Title song sung by Cloris Leachman
Editor: John F. Link II

Laura Hyatt	CLORIS LEACHMAN
Sam Hyatt	JAMES OLSON
Terry	GLYNNIS O'CONNOR
Frank Berlin	ANDY ROBINSON
Jean	ALLYN ANN McLERIE
Paul Wrightwood	KENNETH MARS
Enid	LENKA PETERSON
Dr. Klemperer	PEGGY FEURY
Phil	FRED SADOFF
Frank	LES LANNOM
Bess	CYNTHIA TOWNE
Eddie	RICHARD GUTHERIE
John	GRANVILLE VAN DUSEN

When venereal disease infects a young woman and an expectant mother and her husband, the question of who contacted it from whom arises. Glynnis O'Connor and Lenka Peterson—daughter and mother in real life—are daughter and mother in this odd-themed movie.

0527
IN THIS HOUSE OF BREDE
2/27/75 Tomorrow Entertainment, Inc. (2 hours)

Executive Producer: Philip Barry
Producer/Director: George Schaefer
Teleplay: James Costigan
Based on the novel by Rumer Godden
Photography: Chris Challis
Music: Peter Matz
Art Director: Carmen Dillon
Editor: Ronald J. Fagan

Philippa	DIANA RIGG
Joanne	JUDI BOWKER
Catherine	GWEN WATFORD
Agnes	PAMELA BROWN
Richard	DENNIS QUILLEY
David	NICHOLAS CLAY
Emily	GLADYS SPENCER
Penny	JULIA BLALOCK
Miss Bowen	FRANCES ROWE
Diana	CHARLOTTE MITCHELL
Jeremy	PETER SPROULE
Cynthia	MARGARET HEERY
Margaret	ELIZABETH BRADLEY
Beatrice	DERVLA MOLLOY
Jane	ANN RYE
Ellen/Renata	CATHERINE WILLMER
Maura	VALERIE LUSH

and: Janette Legge, Stacey Tendetter, Peter Geddis, Janet Davies, Yasuko Nagazumi, Michi Takeda, Frances Kearney, Sanae Fukua, Michiko Sukomoro, Jun Majima, Brian Hawkesley, Hugh Morton, Gerald Case, N. K. Sonoda

A sophisticated London widow renounces a successful business career—and the man who loves her—to become a cloistered Benedictine nun. Diana Rigg won an Emmy Award nomination for her performance in the lead role.

0528
WHO IS THE BLACK DAHLIA?
3/1/75 The Douglas S. Cramer Co. (2 hours)

Executive Producers: Douglas S. Cramer and Wilford L. Baumes
Producer: Henry Colman
Director: Joseph Pevney
Teleplay: Robert W. Lenski
Photography: Al Francis
Music: Dominic Frontiere
Art Director: James B. Hulsey
Editor: Carroll Sax

Sgt. Harry Hansen	EFREM ZIMBALIST, JR.
Sgt. Finis Brown	RONNY COX
Capt. Jack Donahoe	MACDONALD CAREY
Elizabeth Short	LUCIE ARNAZ
Bevo Means	TOM BOSLEY
Dr. Waltere Coppin	LINDEN CHILES
Police Matron	GLORIA DeHAVEN
P.X. Manager	JOHN FIEDLER
Miles Harmon	RICK JASON
Lee Jones	HENRY JONES
Mrs. Fowler	JUNE LOCKHART
Grandmother	MERCEDES McCAMBRIDGE
Susan Winters	DONNA MILLS
Soldier on Highway	MURRAY McLEOD
Mr. Short	FRANK MAXWELL
Diane Fowler	BROOKE ADAMS
Reporter	JOHN FINK
Casting Man	LEE DeBROUX
A. Redfield	TED GEHRING
Boarder	LANA WOOD
Jim Richardson	DON KEEFER
Salesman	HENRY BECKMAN

A fact-based mystery drama about a Los Angeles detective's obsession with finding the slayer of a starstruck young woman, dubbed the Black Dahlia because of her black hair and penchant for black clothing, whose body was found in a vacant lot in 1947. (The case remains unsolved.)

0529
WINNER TAKE ALL
3/3/75 The Jozak Company (2 hours)

Executive Producer: Gerald I. Isenberg
Producer: Nancy Malone
Associate Producer: Gerald W. Abrams
Director: Paul Bogart
Teleplay: Caryl Ledner
Photography: Terry K. Meade
Music: David Shire
Editor: Folmar Blangsted

Eleanor Anderson	SHIRLEY JONES
Bill Anderson	LAURENCE LUCKINBILL
Rick Santos	SAM GROOM
Edie Gould	JOYCE VAN PATTEN
Beverly Craig	JOAN BLONDELL
Anne Barclay	SYLVIA SIDNEY
Leonard Fields	JOHN CARTER
Stacy Anderson	LORI BUSK

Arnie	WYNN IRWIN	Helen Dixon	ANNE FRANCIS
Man at Track	AL LANTIERI	Rudi Franco	PERCY RODRIGUES
Sara	CARMEN ZAPATA	Susie Mansham	ANNE SEYMOUR

and: Jason Wingreen, Joe Hacker, Alex Nicol, Alice Backes, Michael Toma, Chris West, Sue Taylor

A woman's compulsion to gamble threatens to ruin her marriage—especially after losing $30,000 of her husband's savings. Originally, this film was entitled *Time Lock*.

0530
THE LAST SURVIVORS
3/4/75 Bob Banner Associates (90 min)

Executive Producer: Bob Banner
Producer: Tom Egan
Director: Lee H. Katzin
Teleplay: Douglas Day Stewart
Photography: Michel Hugo
Music: Michael Melvoin
Art Director: Frederic P. Hope
Editors: Melvin Shapiro and George Watters

Alexander Holmes	MARTIN SHEEN
Marilyn West	DIANE BAKER
Marcus Damian	TOM BOSLEY
Duane Jeffreys	CHRISTOPHER GEORGE
Michael Larrieu	BRUCE DAVISON

Inez Haynes	BETHEL LESLIE
Sid Douglas	MEL STEWART
Nancy Victor	MARGARET WILLOCK
David Broadhead	LONNY CHAPMAN
Mrs. Peters	BEULAH QUO
Prosecutor	EUGENE ROCHE
Captain Harris	WILLIAM BRYANT
Linda Collison	LINDA DANO
Don West	STEVE FRANKEN
Billy Wright	LEIF GARRETT
Francis Askin	ALEX HENTELOFF
Checkerman	ANDREW STEVENS

This uncredited remake of the Tyrone Power movie *Abandon Ship* (1957) recounts the agony of a ship's officer who must decide which passengers in an over-crowded lifeboat are to be sacrificed so that the majority can survive an approaching typhoon.

0531
TRILOGY OF TERROR
3/4/75 ABC Circle Films (90 min)

Producer/Director: Dan Curtis
Associate Producer: Robert Singer

Teleplays: "Julie" and "Millicent and Therese" by William F. Nolan, from short stories by Richard Matheson; and "Amelia" by Richard Matheson, based on his short story "Prey"
Photography: Paul Lohmann
Music: Robert Cobert
Art Director: Jan Scott
Editor: Les Green

Millicent Larimore ⎫	
Therese Larimore ⎪	
Julie Eldridge ⎬	
Amelia ⎭	KAREN BLACK
Chad Foster	ROBERT BURTON
Thomas Anman	JOHN KARLEN
Dr. Chester Ramsey	GEORGE GAYNES
Eddie Nells	JAMES STORM
Arthur Moore	GREGORY HARRISON
Anne Richards	KATHRYN REYNOLDS
Tracy	TRACY CURTIS
Motel Clerk	ORIN CANNON

Three bizarre stories with Karen Black playing four tormented women. In "Millicent and Therese" she is both a plain-looking woman, almost a recluse, and her amoral sister whom she taunts by revealing to her current boyfriend her past escapades. In "Julia" she is a sexually repressed teacher who is blackmailed by one of her students for past indiscretions in which she

Karen Black in TRILOGY OF TERROR (1975)

played an unwilling part. And in "Amelia" she is a mother-dominated young woman who buys a fetish doll for a new male companion and discovers that the creature is alive and ready to create a reign of terror for her.

0532
THE DESPERATE MILES
3/5/75 Universal (90 min)

Executive Producer: Joel Rogosin
Producers: Robert Greenwald and Frank von Zerneck
Director: Daniel Haller
Teleplay: Arthur Ross and Joel Rogosin
From a story by Arthur Ross
Photography: Jack Woolf
Music: Robert Prince
Song "Many Miles to Morning" by Robert Prince, Bill Dyer and Joel Rogosin
Sung by Denny Brooks
Editors: J. Howard Terrill and Chuck McClelland

Joe Larkin	TONY MUSANTE
Ruth Merrick	JOANNA PETTET
Mrs. Larkin	JEANETTE NOLAN
Jill	LYNN LORING
Dr. Bryson	JOHN LARCH
Ruiz	PEPE ZERNA
Ted	MICHAEL RICHARDSON
Lou	SHELLY NOVACK
Al	RICHARD REICHEG
Mr. Rhodes	STACY KEACH, SR.
Truck Driver	JOHN CHANDLER

and: John Elerick, Kathy Cronkite, Previs Atkins

A disabled Vietnam veteran, out to prove that a person does not have to be helpless, embarks on a grueling 130-mile trip in a wheelchair, an odyssey in which his life is endangered by a paranoid truck driver.

0533
LOVE AMONG THE RUINS
3/6/75 ABC Circle Films (2 hours)

Producer: Allan Davis
Director: George Cukor
Teleplay: James Costigan
Photography: Douglas Slocombe
Music: John Barry
Art Director: Carmen Dillon
Costumes: Margaret Furse
Editor: John F. Burnett

Jessica Medlicott	KATHARINE HEPBURN
Sir Arthur Granville-Jones	LAURENCE OLIVIER
J. F. Devine	COLIN BLAKELY
Druce	RICHARD PEARSON
Fanny Pratt	JOAN SIMS
Alfred Pratt	LEIGH LAWSON
Hermione Davis	GWEN NELSON
The Judge	ROBERT HARRIS

An outstanding, multi-award-winning romantic comedy, written especially for Hepburn and Olivier, acting together for the first time and each winning an Emmy Award. Hepburn plays an aging actress being sued for breach of promise and Olivier is a blunt barrister, her one-time lover, who must destroy her reputation to protect her fortune. George Cukor made his TV directorial debut here and also won an Emmy, as did James Costigan for his witty, elegant teleplay. The film also won Emmy Awards for art and set decoration and for costumes, and was given the Peabody Award in addition.

0534
SEARCH FOR THE GODS
3/9/75 Warner Bros. (2 hours)

Executive Producer: Douglas S. Cramer
Producer: Wilford Lloyd Baumes
Director: Jud Taylor

Tony Musante (in wheelchair) in THE DESPERATE MILES (1975)

Teleplay: Ken Pettus
From a story by Herman Miller
Photography: Matthew F. Leonetti
Music: Billy Goldenberg
Art Director: James B. Hulsey
Editor: Art Seid

Shan Mullins	KURT RUSSELL
Willie Longfellow	STEPHEN McHATTIE
Dr. Henderson	RALPH BELLAMY
Genara Juantez	VICTORIA RACIMO
Raymond Stryker	RAYMOND ST. JACQUES
Tarkanian	ALBERT PAULSEN
Lucio	JOHN WAR EAGLE
Wheeler	CARMEN ARGENZIANO
Elder	JOE DAVID MARCUS
Council Indian	JOE MARCUS, JR.
Jailer	LARRY BLAKE
Glenn	JACKSON D. KANE

Three young people search for a priceless medallion in their quest for evidence of ancient visitors to earth.

0535
SWITCH
3/10/75 Universal (90 min)

Producer: Glen Larson
Director: Robert Day
Teleplay: Glen Larson
Photography: John Morley Stephens and Ben Coleman
Music: Stu Phillips
Art Director: George Renne
Editors: Budd Small and Frank Morriss

Pete Ryan	ROBERT WAGNER
Frank MacBride	EDDIE ALBERT
Phil Beckman	CHARLES DURNING
Maggie	SHARON GLESS
Captain Griffin	KEN SWOFFORD
Malcolm	CHARLIE CALLAS
Murray Franklin	ALAN MANSON
Alice	JACLYN SMITH
Chuck Powell	GREG MULLAVEY

An ex-con and a retired cop, partners in an investigation agency, try to prove that a safecracker with a previous record is innocent of a diamond heist and pin the crime on the police by laying an intricate trap. Wagner and Albert went on to recreate their roles in the later series (1975–77).

0536
THE BIG RIPOFF
3/11/75 Universal (90 min)

Producers: Roland Kibbee and Dean Hargrove
Director: Dean Hargrove
Created and written by Dean Hargrove and Roland Kibbee
Photography: Bill Butler
Music: Dick DeBenedictis
Art Director: Loyd S. Papez
Editor: Robert L. Kimble

McCoy	TONY CURTIS
Brenda Brooks	BRENDA VACCARO
Silky Gideon Gibbs	ROSCOE LEE BROWNE
Frank Darnell	LARRY HAGMAN
C. J. Bishop	JOHN DEHNER
Jimmie Kelson	MORGAN WOODWARD
Grace Bishop	LYNN BORDEN
Captain of Ship	VITO SCOTTI
Peabody	WOODROW PARFREY

Katharine Hepburn and Laurence Olivier in LOVE AMONG THE RUINS (1975)

Lucy Meredith	PRISCILLA POINTER
Art	NATE ESFORMES
Phil	LEN LESSER
Notch	FUDDLE BAGLEY
Security Chief	ED PECK
Hersh	ALAN FUDGE

and: Robert Symonds, Charles Macauley, Carl Mathis Craig, Trina Parks, Billy Varga, Ted Christy, Jack Krupnick, Linda Gray, Jeffrey Kibbee, Barry Cahill, Robert Ball, John Lawrence Shaw, Owen Hithe Pace, Phil Diskin, Howard Storm, Manuel DePina, Jerry Mann, Linda Evans, Mario Gallo, William Benedict, Don Fenwick, Nancy Belle Fuller, Larry Burrell, James V. Christy, Wayne Bartlett, Tyree Glenn, Jr., Tobar Mayo, Tom McFadden, Brian O'Mullin, Carol Ann Susi, Ben Gage

This was the pilot for Curtis' "McCoy" series (1975–76) with an elaborate "sting" which he concocts to recover $250,000 in ransom from the kidnappers of a millionaire's wife.

0537
CAGE WITHOUT A KEY
3/14/75 Columbia Pictures (2 hours)

Executive Producer: Douglas S. Cramer
Producer/Director: Buzz Kulik
Teleplay: Joanna Lee
Photography: Charles F. Wheeler
Music: Jerry Fielding
Art Director: Ross Bellah
Editor: Roland Gross

Valerie Smith	SUSAN DEY
Tommy	JONELLE ALLEN
Buddy Goleta	SAM BOTTOMS
Ben Holian	MICHAEL BRANDON
Joleen	ANNE BLOOM
Betty Holian	KAREN CARLSON
Angel Perez	EDITH DIAZ
Suzy Kurosawa	SUESIE ELENE
Sarah	DAWN FRAME
Mrs. Little	KATHERINE HELMOND
Jamie	VICKY HUXSTABLE
Mrs. Turner	KAREN MORROW
Noreen	LANI O'GRADY
Wanda Polsky	MARGARET WILLOCK

and: Marc Alaimo, Lewis Charles, Jerry Crews, Edward Cross, Ann D'Andrea, Jo Ella Deffenbaugh, Al Dunlap, Annette Ensley

A high school girl gets trapped in a web of circumstances after accepting a ride with a strange boy who then forces her at gunpoint to assist him in a robbery during which he kills a clerk, and both are caught and charged with first-degree murder. Convicted and sent to a women's detention center, the girl discovers that her horrifying experience has just begun. Several similarities, intentional or not, to the Patty Hearst case can easily be glimpsed in this movie.

0538
THE IMPOSTER
3/18/75 Warner Bros. (90 min)

Executive Producer: Richard Bluel
Producer: Robert Stambler
Director: Edward M. Abroms
Teleplay: Jon Sevorg and Ken August
Characters created by E. Jack Neuman
Photography: Howard R. Schwartz
Music: Gil Melle
Art Director: Leroy Deane
Editor: Carl Pingitore

Joe Tyler	PAUL HECHT
Victoria Kent	NANCY KELLY
Julie Watson	MEREDITH BAXTER
Carl Rennick	JACK GING
Margaret Elliott	BARBARA BAXLEY
Sheriff Turner	JOHN VERNON
Barney West	EDWARD ASNER
Teddy Durham	PAUL JENKINS
Dwight Elliott	JOSEPH GALLISON
Del Gazzo	VICTOR CAMPOS
Jennings	BRUCE GLOVER
Reager	SHERWOOD PRICE
April	SUZANNE DENOR
Dance Director	RONNIE SCHELL
Glover	GEORGE MURDOCK

An ex-Army intelligence officer accepts $5,000 to impersonate a wealthy contractor targeted for assassination and uncovers a conspiracy to loot a land development company. This was a pilot film (made in early 1974) for a project that failed to materialize.

0539
ELLERY QUEEN
3/23/75 Universal (90 min)
(Subsequently retitled *Too Many Suspects*)

Producers: Richard Levinson and William Link
Director: David Greene
Teleplay: Richard Levinson and William Link
Based on the novel *The Fourth Side of the Triangle* by Ellery Queen
Photography: Howard R. Schwartz
Music: Elmer Bernstein
Art Director: George C. Webb
Editor: Douglas Stewart

Jim Hutton in ELLERY QUEEN (1975)

Ellery Queen	JIM HUTTON
Inspector Richard Queen	DAVID WAYNE
Carson McKell	RAY MILLAND
Marion McKell	KIM HUNTER
Tom McKell	MONTE MARKHAM
Simon Brimmer	JOHN HILLERMAN
District Attorney	JOHN LARCH
Ben Waterson	TIM O'CONNOR
Monica Gray	NANCY MEHTA
Eddie Carter	WARREN BERLINGER
Announcer	HARRY VON ZELL
Gail Stevens	GAIL STRICKLAND
Sergeant Velie	TOM REESE
Ramon	VIC MOHICA
Maid	DWAN SMITH

and: James Lydon, Basil Hoffman, Ross Elliott, John Finnegan, Rosanna Huffman

An atmospheric whodunit set in the 1940s that involves an author-criminologist in one of the cases stumping his New York City police inspector father—the murder of a famed fashion designer. Hutton and Wayne continued their roles in the subsequent series (1975–76) that also had John Hillerman in a recurring role of pompous radio detective Simon Brimmer (a character not in the Ellery Queen mysteries).

0540
CROSSFIRE
3/24/75 Quinn Martin Productions (90 min)

Executive Producer: Quinn Martin
Producer: Philip Saltzman
Director: William Hale
Teleplay: Philip Saltzman
Photography: Michael Joyce

Music: Pat Williams
Art Director: Richard Y. Haman
Editor: Harry Kaye

Vince Rossi	JAMES FARENTINO
Captain McCardle	RAMON BIERI
Dave Ambrose	JOHN SAXON
Lane Fielding	PATRICK O'NEAL
Sheila Fielding	PAMELA FRANKLIN
Bert Ganz	HERB EDELMAN
Arthur Peabody	LOU FRIZZELL
Jimmy	JOSEPH HINDY
Bartender	NED GLASS

and: Garry Walberg, Richard Lawson, George Spell, Buck Young, Dennis Robertson, Byron Chung, Read Morgan, Renie Radich, Matt Pelto, Frank DeKova

A cop-show pilot that failed with an undercover officer volunteering to get kicked off the force in order to infiltrate the underworld and learn who has been laundering money being used to corrupt city officials.

0541
THE RUNAWAY BARGE
3/24/75 Lorimar Productions (90 min)

Executive Producer: Lee Rich
Producer/Director: Boris Sagal
Teleplay: Stanford Whitmore
Based on an idea by Sara Macon

Photography: Fredric J. Koenekamp
Music: Nelson Riddle
Songs by Al Kasha and Joel Hirschhorn
Art Director: Ed Graves
Editor: Tony Wollner

Ezel Owens	BO HOPKINS
Danny Worth	TIM MATHESON
Capt. Buckshot Bates	JIM DAVID
Ray Blount	NICK NOLTE
June Bug	DEVON ERICSON
Reba	CHRISTINA HART
Bingo	JAMES BEST
Madge	LUCILLE BENSON
Sooey	CLIFTON JAMES
Whispering Walley	DOM PLUMLEY
Rouge LeBlanc	BEAU GIBSON

and: G. W. Bailey, John O. White, Bill Rowley, James Paul, David Carlton, Joneal Joplin, Chuck Gunel

An adventure drama involving three modern-day Mississippi boatmen who find themselves neck-deep in a kidnapping and hijacking plot.

0542
HUCKLEBERRY FINN
3/25/75 ABC Circle Films (90 min)

Producer: Steven North
Director: Robert Totten
Teleplay: Jean Holloway

Based on the book by Mark Twain
Photography: Andrew Jackson
Music: Earl Robinson
Song "Mississippi (Said the River, I'm Your Friend)" by Earl Robinson and Steven North
Sung by Roy Clark
Art Director: Peter M. Wooley
Editors: Diane Adler and Marsh Hendry

Huckleberry Finn	RON HOWARD
Tom Sawyer	DONNY MOST
Mark Twain	ROYAL DANO
Jim Watson	ANTONIO FARGAS
The King	JACK ELAM
The Duke	MERLE HAGGARD
Pap Finn	RANCE HOWARD
Widow Douglas	JEAN HOWARD
Arch	CLINT HOWARD
Old Doc	SHUG FISHER
Aunt Polly	SARAH SELBY
Harvey Wilkes	WILLIAM L. ERWIN
Ben Rucker	FREDERIC DOWNS
Silas Phelps	JAMES ALMANZAR
Mary Jane	PATTY WEAVER
Auctioneer	WOODROW CHAMBLISS

The Mark Twain perennial with freckle-faced Ron Howard and most of his family—father Rance, mother Jean, brother Clint—in this TV update of the classic. Previous Huck Finns on film were Lewis Sargent in 1919, Junior Durkin (1931) in the Jackie

Ron Howard and Royal Dano in HUCKLEBERRY FINN (1975)

Cooper movie about Tom Sawyer, Mickey Rooney (1939), Eddie Hodges (1960) and Jeff East (to Johnny Whittaker's Tom Sawyer) in both 1973 and 1974.

0543
THE RUNAWAYS
4/1/75 Lorimar Productions (90 min)

Executive Producer: Lee Rich
Producer: Philip Capice
Director: Harry Harris
Teleplay: John McGreevey
Based on a novel by Victor Canning
Photography: Russell Metty
Music: Earle Hagen
Art Director: Ed Graves
Editor: Marjorie Fowler

Angela Lakey	DOROTHY McGUIRE
Joe Ringer	VAN WILLIAMS
George Collingwood	JOHN RANDOLPH
Alice Collingwood	NEVA PATTERSON
Johnny Miles	JOSH ALBEE
Mrs. Wilson	LENKA PETERSON
Lew Brown	STEVE FERGUSON
Haines	DON MATHESON
Bob Davis	TIERRE TURNER
Mrs. Pickerel	JANICE CARROLL
Al Pritchard	JOHN PICKARD
Rita Armijo	GINA ALVARADO
Captain Baker	LEONARD STONE
Kelly	GEORGE REYNOLDS
Mr. Morgan	NORMAN ANDREWS

An adventure drama about a teenage boy who runs away from his foster home after wrongly being accused of theft and soon crosses paths with a young leopard which has escaped from a wild-animal compound during a lightning storm. Both are befriended by a brusque lady kennel owner with a heart of gold.

0544
DEAD MAN ON THE RUN
4/2/75 A Sweeney/Finnegan Production (90 min)

Executive Producer: Bob Sweeney
Producer: William Finnegan
Director: Bruce Bilson
Teleplay: Ken Pettus
Photography: Robert Collins
Music: Harry Geller
Editor: Ira Heymann

Jim Gideon	PETER GRAVES
Libby Stockton	KATHERINE JUSTICE
Brock Dillon	PERNELL ROBERTS
Jason Monroe	JOHN ANDERSON
Meg	DIANA DOUGLAS
Father Sebastian	MILLS WATSON
Fletcher	TOM ROSQUI
"Rocky" Flanagan	JACK KNIGHT
DiMosco	JOE E. TATA
Alan Stockton	HANK BRANDT
Hollander	STOCKER FONTELIEU
Sam Daggett	DONALD HOOD
Antoine LeClerc	EUGENE AUTRY

A special government agent, investigating the murder of a colleague, stumbles onto a plot to cover up a political assassination in this pilot for a prospective TV series using New Orleans as a backdrop.

0545
CRIME CLUB
4/3/75 Universal (90 min)

Executive Producer: Matthew Rapf
Producer: Jim McAdams
Director: Jeannot Szwarc
Teleplay: Gene R. Kearney
Photography: Gayne Rescher
Music: Gil Melle
Art Director: Peter M. Wooley
Editors: Jim Benson and Sigmund Neufeld, Jr.

John "Jake" Keesey	SCOTT THOMAS
Daniel Lawrence	EUGENE ROCHE
Alex Norton	ROBERT LANSING
Byron Craine	BIFF McGUIRE
Angela Swoboda	BARBARA RHOADES
Frank Swoboda	MICHAEL CRISTOFER
Peter Karpf	DAVID CLENNON
D. R. Schroeder	MARTINE BESWICK
Lieutenant Doyle	M. E. WALSH
Pam Agostino	KATHY BELLER
Mary Jo	JENNIFER SHAW
Gamos	CARL GOTTLIEB
Jack Dowd	REGIS J. CORDIC

and: Rosanna Huffman, Dolores Quinlan, Erica Yohn, John Durren, Diane Harper, Robert Burton

Aided by a defense attorney and an investigative reporter, the head of an exclusive club dedicated to crime prevention sets out to learn who is behind a series of icepick murders for which a loser craving public attention has confessed. This was another movie pilot for an programming idea that never made it to series form.

0546
KATE McSHANE
4/11/75 Paramount (90 min)

Producer: E. Jack Neuman
Associate Producer: Richard Rosetti
Director: Marvin Chomsky
Created and written by E. Jack Neuman
Photography: Richard Kline
Music: John Cacavas
Art Director: Monty Elliott
Editor: Donald R. Rode

Kate McShane	ANNE MEARA
Pat McShane	SEAN McCLORY
Ed McShane	CHARLES HAID
Angelo Romero	CAL BELLINI
Charlotte Randall Chase	CHRISTINE BELFORD
Harold Cutler	CHARLES CIOFFI
Judge Graham Platte	LARRY GATES
Dr. Nate Tishman	STEFAN GIERASCH
Dr. Frank McCabe	ALAN FUDGE
Secretary	MARIAN SELDES

A flamboyant Denver lady lawyer, with the help of her father, a retired cop who does the leg work for her investigations, and her brother, a Jesuit priest and university law professor, unravels a murder case of a society woman who allegedly stabbed her husband. This was the pilot for Anne Meara's short-lived series (1975–76).

0547
THE TURNING POINT OF JIM MALLOY
4/12/75 Columbia Pictures (90 min)

Executive Producer: David Gerber
Producers: Peter Katz and James H. Brown
Director: Frank D. Gilroy
Teleplay: Frank D. Gilroy

The collection of short stories entitled *The Doctor's Son* by John O'Hara
Photography: Gerald Perry Finnerman
Music: Johnny Mandel
Art Directors: Ross Bellah and John Beckman
Editor: Ken Zemke

Jim Malloy	JOHN SAVAGE
Dr. Mike Malloy	BIFF McGUIRE
Mrs. Malloy	PEGGY McKAY
Ray Whitehead	GIG YOUNG
Edith Evans	KATHLEEN QUINLAN
Lonnie	JANIS PAIGE
Dr. Enright	ALLAN MILLER
Lintzie	FRANK CAMPANELLA
Bo-Peep	ROSALIND MILES
Mr. Kelly	JOHN McLIAM
Terry	JANIS HANSEN
Mrs. Ingram	SARAH CUNNINGHAM
Mr. Evans	NOAH KEEN
Mrs. Evans	DOLORES DORN
Harry Longden	JOHN HOYT
Arthur Pond	ROBERT GINTY
Mr. Winfield	WALLACE ROONEY
Mr. Pell	IVOR FRANCIS
A. J. Conrad	BYRON MORROW
Officer Dorelli	JOHN DURREN

Life in John O'Hara's small Pennsylvania town of Gibbsville with the son of the town doctor returning home after being kicked out of Yale and finding a new career on the town's newspaper. Originally it was called *John O'Hara's Gibbsville,* which became the title for the short-lived (late 1976) series that starred John Savage and Gig Young.

0548
STRIKE FORCE
4/12/75 D'Antoni-Weitz Television Production (90 min)

Producers: Philip D'Antoni and Barry Weitz
Associate Producer/Creator: Sonny Grosso
Director: Barry Shear
Teleplay: Roger O. Hirson
Photography: Jack Priestley
Music: John Murtaugh
Art Director: Robert Gundlach
Editor: Murray Solomon

Det. Joey Gentry	CLIFF GORMAN
Agent Jerome Ripley	DONALD BLAKELY
Trooper Walter Spenser	RICHARD GERE
Captain Peterson	EDWARD GROVER
Sol Terranova	JOE SPINELL

and: Marilyn Chris, Mimi Cecchini, Billy Longo, Arnold Soboloff, Carl Don, Allan Rich, Randy Jurgenson

A streetwise New York detective teams up with a federal agent and a state trooper (in this pilot for a proposed series) to bust a narcotics case.

0549
I WILL FIGHT NO MORE FOREVER
4/14/75 David Wolper Productions (2 hours)

Executive Producer: David L. Wolper
Producer: Stan Margulies
Director: Richard T. Heffron
Teleplay: Jeb Rosebrook and Theodore Strauss
Photography: Jorge Stahl
Music: Gerald Fried
Editor: Robert K. Lambert

Gen. Oliver O. Howard	JAMES WHITMORE
Chief Joseph	NED ROMERO

Captain Wood	SAM ELLIOTT
Wahlitits	JOHN KAUFFMAN
Olloket	EMILIO DELGADO
Rainbow	NICK RAMUS
Toma	LINDA REDFEARN
White Bird	FRANK SALSEDO
Looking Glass	VINCENT ST. CYR
Colonel Gibbon	DELROY WHITE

A dramatization of a tragic part of U.S. history in which the leader of the Nez Perce Indians refused to take his tribe to a reservation in 1877, trying instead to lead them to safety in Canada, with the cavalry in pursuit trying to stop the escape. Emmy Award nominations went to writers Jeb Rosebrook and Theodore Strauss and to editor Robert K. Lambert.

0550
THE SWISS FAMILY ROBINSON
4/15/75 Irwin Allen Productions/20th Century-Fox (2 hours)

Producer: Irwin Allen
Director: Harry Harris
Teleplay: Ken Trevey
Based on the book by Johann Wyss
Photography: Fred Jackman
Music: Richard LaSalle
Production Designer: Stan Jolley
Editors: Bill Brame and William DeNicholas

Karl Robinson	MARTIN MILNER
Lottie Robinson	PAT DELANY
Jeremiah Worth	CAMERON MITCHELL
Fred Robinson	MICHAEL-JAMES WIXTED
Ernie Robinson	ERIC OLSON
Helga Wagner	CINDY FISHER
Charles Forsythe	JOHN VERNON
Suramin	GEORGE DiCENZO
Nate Bidwell	JOHN CRAWFORD

A new version, and a pilot for the 1975–76 series, of the adventure classic about a family striving together to survive on a remote island following a shipwreck and facing an invasion by pirates in search of a golden idol.

DELANCEY STREET: THE CRISIS WITHIN
4/19/75 Paramount (90 min)

Executive Producer: Emmet G. Lavery, Jr.
Producer: Anthony Wilson
Associate Producer: Robert Foster
Director: James Frawley
Teleplay: Robert Foster
Photography: Robert B. Hauser
Music: Lalo Schifrin
Art Director: William Campbell
Editor: Mike Vejar

John McCann	WALTER McGINN
Joe	CARMINE CARIDI
Robert John Holtzman	MICHAEL CONRAD
Otis James	LOU GOSSETT
Philip Donaldson	MARK HAMILL
Mrs. Donaldson	BARBARA BOSTOCK
Ms. Sommerville	BARBARA CASON
Tony	ANTHONY CHARNOTA
Rudolfo	HECTOR ELIAS
Richard Copell	JOHN KARLEN
Jeff Donaldson	JOHN RAGAN
Suzie Franklin	JERRI WOODS
George Miles	JOSEPH X. FLAHERTY

Ruby James	SYLVIA SOARES
Mary	LEIGH FRENCH

and: Bart Cardinelli, David Moody, Bill Toliver, James Jeter, M. P. Murphy

A drama based on the work of John Maher, founder of the Delancey Street Foundation, a self-help rehabilitation center dedicated to recycling ex-junkies, ex-convicts and others. This was an unsuccessful pilot for a proposed weekly series with Walter McGinn.

0552
LAST HOURS BEFORE MORNING
4/19/75 Charles Fries Productions/MGM (90 min)

Executive Producer: Charles Fries
Producer: Malcolm Stuart
Director: Joseph Hardy
Teleplay: Robert Garland and George Yanok
Photography: Gene Polito
Music: Pete Rugolo
Production Designer: Richard Sylbert
Editor: John A. Martinelli

Bud Delaney	ED LAUTER
Justice Sullivan	THALMUS RASULALA
Sergeant Hagen	GEORGE MURDOCK
Shirley	SHEILA SULLIVAN
Vivian Pace	RHONDA FLEMING
Theo "Lucky" English	ROBERT ALDA
Ty Randolph	KAZ GARAS
Mr. Pace	DON PORTER
Yolanda Marquez	VICTORIA PRINCIPAL
Peter Helms	PETER DONAT
Bruno Gant	MICHAEL BASELEON
Elmo	WILLIAM FINLEY
Buck Smith	ART LUND

and: George DiCenzo, John Harkins, John Quade, Philip Bruns, Michael Stearns, Elaine Pepparde, Redmond Gleeson

Atmospheric private eye film set in the 1940s about a hotshot house detective and ex-cop who moonlights by chasing deadbeats and finds himself investigating the connection between an arrogant gambler's murder and a beautiful film star's jewel robbery.

0553
FORCE FIVE
4/28/75 Universal (90 min)

Producers: Michael Gleason and David Levinson
Director: Walter Grauman
Teleplay: Michael Gleason and David Levinson
Photography: Jack Swain
Music: James DiPasquale
Art Director: Jack E. Chilberg II
Editor: Richard Bracken

Lt. Roy Kessler	GERALD GORDON
James T. O'Neil	NICK PRYOR
Lester White	JAMES HAMPTON
Arnie Kogan	ROY JENSON
Vic Bauer	BILL LUCKING
Michael Dominick	BRADFORD DILLMAN
Norman Ellsworth	DAVID SPIELBERG
Arthur Haberman	NORMAN BURTON
Frankie Hatcher	VICTOR ARGO
Steve Ritchie	LEE PAUL
Ginger	BELINDA BALASKI
Reggie Brinkle	ROD HAASE
Patty	NANCY FULLER
Shirley Cole	CLAIRE BRENNAN
Detective Felcher	GEORGE LOROS

A special police undercover unit composed of ex-cons chosen for their particular skills investigates the vicious syndicate beating of a star basketball player whose father vows to take vengeance if he catches the attackers first. This prospective series pilot cleverly adapted the plot hook of *The Dirty Dozen* and its coutless carbon copies, switching the characters to contemporary police work under a hard-nosed, no-nonsense leader.

0554
THEY ONLY COME OUT AT NIGHT
4/29/75 MGM (90 min)

Executive Producer: Everett Chambers
Producer: Robert Monroe
Associate Producer: Richard M. Rosenbloom
Director: Daryl Duke
Created and written by Al Martinez
Photography: Richard C. Glouner
Music: The Orphanage
Editor: Henry Batista

John St. John	JACK WARDEN
Tallchief	CHARLES YNFANTE
Helen St. John	MADELINE THORNTON-SHERWOOD
Lieutenant Baylor	JOE MANTELL
Det. Lee Masters	TIM O'CONNOR
David Kanlan	DICK DINMAN
Mrs. Eichman	LILI VALENTY
Receptionist	BARBARA LUNA
Petulia	KING SOLOMON III (SOLOMON KARRIEM)
Mrs. Owens	MELENDY BRITT
Eichman Daughter	CONSTANCE PFEIFER
Woman Pharmacist	DOROTHY DELLS
Elderly Woman	NEDRA VOLZ
Pharmacy Clerk	ADELE YOSHIOKA

This pilot for Warden's "Jigsaw John" series (1975–76) has him playing a dyspeptic middle-aged homicide investigator looking into a string of robbery-slayings of elderly women in Los Angeles.

0555
RETURNING HOME
4/29/75 Lorimar Productions/Samuel Goldwyn Productions (90 min)

Executive Producer: Lee Rich
Producer: Herbert Hirschman
Director: Daniel Petrie
Teleplay: John McGreevey and Bill Svanoe
Photography: Richard L. Rawlings
Music: Ken Lauber
Art Director: Phil Barber
Editors: Marjorie Fowler and Mike McCroskey

Al Stephensen	DABNEY COLEMAN
Fred Derry	TOM SELLECK
Homer Parish	JAMES R. MILLER
Millie Stephensen	WHITNEY BLAKE
Peggy Stephensen	JOAN GOODFELLOW
Marie Derry	SHERRY JACKSON
Wilma Parish	LAURIE WALTERS
Capt. Will Tobey	JAMES A. WATSON, JR.
Mrs. Parish	LENKA PETERSON
Mrs. Cameron	PAT SMITH
Mr. Cameron	RICHARD O'BRIEN
Vern Miller	BOOTH COLMAN
Butch	LOU FRIZZELL

Laurie Walters and James R. Miller in RETURNING HOME (1975)

A nostalgic war drama based on the 1946 Goldwyn classic *The Best Years of Our Lives*, following three returning World War II veterans as they face the challenge of adjusting to civilian life. Coleman takes the Fredric March role and Selleck the part played by Dana Andrews, while non-professional actor James Miller (a Vietnam bilateral amputee who is deputy sheriff in Sidney, Montana) enacts the character created by Harold Russell (in his only film).

0556
STARSKY AND HUTCH
4/30/75 Spelling/Goldberg Productions (90 min)

Executive Producers: Aaron Spelling and Leonard Goldberg
Producer: Joseph P. Naar
Director: Barry Shear
Teleplay: William Blinn
Photography: Arch R. Dalzell
Music: Lalo Schifrin
Art Director: Archie Bacon
Editor: John Woodcock

Ken Hutchinson	DAVID SOUL
Dave Starsky	PAUL MICHAEL GLASER
Fat Rolly	MICHAEL LERNER
Huggy Bear	ANTONIO FARGAS
Captain Doby	RICHARD WARD

Frank Tallman	GILBERT GREEN
Henderson	ALBERT MORGANSTERN
Zane	RICHARD LYNCH
Cannell	MICHAEL CONRAD
Coley	BUDDY LESTER
Gretchen	CAROL ITA WHITE

In this pilot for the hit series that began in September 1975, an unorthodox pair of undercover cops investigate a double homicide and discover that they were the intended victims.

0557
NEVADA SMITH
5/3/75 A Rackin-Hayes Production/MGM (90 min)

Producers: Martin Rackin and John Michael Hayes
Director: Gordon Douglas
Created and written by Martin Rackin and John Michael Hayes
Based on characters created by Harold Robbins
Photography: Gabriel Torres
Music: Lamont Dozier
Editor: John C. Horger

Nevada Smith	CLIFF POTTS
Jonas Cord	LORNE GREENE
Frank Hartlee	ADAM WEST
Red Fickett	WARREN VANDERS

Two Moon	JORGE LUKE
Brill	JERRY GATLIN
Davey	ERIC CORD
McLane	JOHN McKEE
Perkins	ROGER CUDNEY
MacBaren	ALAN GEORGE
Belva	LORRAINE CHANEL

In this pilot for an unrealized Western series, the half-breed gunslinger and his former mentor introduced in the theatrical feature of the same title in 1966 and before that in 1964's *The Carpetbaggers* join forces to escort a shipment of explosives across the Utah territory. Potts and Greene had the roles played earlier by Steve McQueen and Brian Keith (in the namesake movie) and by Alan Ladd and Leif Erickson in *The Carpetbaggers*.

0558
THE BARBARY COAST
5/4/75 Paramount (2 hours)

Producer: Douglas Heyes
Director: Bill Bixby
Created and written by Douglas Heyes
Photography: Robert B. Hauser
Music: John Andrew Tartaglia
Art Director: Jack DeShields
Costume Designer: Guy Verhille
Editors: Neil MacDonald and Steven C. Brown

Jeff Cable	WILLIAM SHATNER
Cash Conover	DENNIS COLE
Lieutenant Tully	CHARLES AIDMAN
Diamond Jack Bassiter	MICHAEL ANSARA
Florrie Roscoe	NEVILLE BRAND
Flame	BOBBI JORDAN
Moose Moran	RICHARD KIEL
Robin Templar	JOHN VERNON
Clio Du Bois	LYNDA DAY GEORGE
Chief Macdonald Keogh	LEO GORDON
Sergeant Hatch	BOB HOY
Bret Hollister	TERRY LESTER
Brant Hollister	SIMON SCOTT
Gibbon	TODD MARTIN
Mr. Speece	BYRON WEBSTER
Jacques Fouchet	LOUIS de FARRA
Philippe Despard	BILL BIXBY

and: Erik Silju, Michael Carr, Lucien Lanvin Martin, Roberta McElroy, Lidia Kristen, Charles Picerni

A government undercover agent and the dashing owner of a boomtown San Francisco casino team up to expose an elaborate extortion plot devised by a Confederate Army officer in this pilot for the short-lived (late 1975) series that bore a striking resemblance to the fondly-remembered "Wild, Wild West." William Shatner repeated his role of Cable (along with his makeup trunk of exotic disguises), Doug McClure took over the part of Conover from Dennis Cole, and Richard Kiel continued as the casino's giant bouncer. For the TV movie, art director Jack DeShields and set decorator Reg Allen received Emmy Award nominations.

0559
ONE OF OUR OWN
5/5/75 Universal (2 hours)

Executive Producer: Matthew Rapf
Producer: Jack Laird
Director: Richard Sarafian
Teleplay: Jack Laird
Photography: Howard R. Schwartz
Music: Hal Mooney
Art Director: Jack T. Collis
Editor: Douglas Stewart

Dr. Jake Goodwin	GEORGE PEPPARD
Dr. Moresby	WILLIAM DANIELS
Carole Simon	LOUISE SOREL
LeRoy Atkins	STROTHER MARTIN
Dr. Norah Purcell	ZOHRA LAMPERT
Dr. Helmut Von Schulthers	OSCAR HOMOLKA
Dr. Felipe Ortega	VICTOR CAMPOS
Dr. Madison	PETER HOOTEN
Dr. Janos Varga	ALBERT PAULSEN
Sanantonio	GIORGIO TOZZI
Frances Hollander	JACQUELINE BROOKES
Felix Needham	BEN MASTERS
Grance Chang	MARY VON TOY
Scotty	MAXINE STUART
Rose Sanantonio	ROSE GREGORIO
Bill Hinshaw	WILLIAM TRAYLOR
Mavis Porter	ELEANOR ZEE
Sabina	TRISH NOBLE
Adrian Hollander	SCOTT McKAY
Debbie Hinshaw	WENDY PHILLIPS
Muriel Emhardt	FRANCES OSBORNE
Dr. Korngold	MILT KOGAN
Myrna	KAREN KNOTTS
Glick	LARRY GELMAN

A hospital drama involving a neurosurgeon/chief of services who faces numerous crises—including saving a fellow doctor's life after an incompetent physician makes an erroneous diagnosis. This was the pilot for Peppard's short-lived "Doctors Hospital" series (1975–76), that had Lampert, Campos and Paulsen continuing their roles as surgeons at Lowell Memorial Hospital.

0560
THE INVISIBLE MAN
5/6/75 Universal (90 min)

Executive Producer: Harve Bennett
Producer: Steven Bochco
Director: Robert Michael Lewis
Teleplay: Steven Bochco
From a story by Harve Bennett and Steven Bochco
Adapted from the novel by H. G. Wells
Photography: Enzo A. Martinelli
Music: Richard Clements
Art Director: Frank T. Smith
Editor: Robert F. Shugrue

Dr. Daniel Weston	DAVID McCALLUM
Kate Weston	MELINDA FEE
Walter Carlson	JACKIE COOPER
Dr. Nick Maggio	HENRY DARROW
Rick Steiner	ALEX HENTELOFF
General Turner	ARCH JOHNSON
Blind Man	JOHN McLIAM
Gate Guard	TED GEHRING

A scientist working on laser beam projection in a Think Tank discovers a way of making himself invisible, then flees with his secret rather than permit it to be used by the military. This updated version of the Wells science-fiction classic, filmed initially in 1933 and copied countless times since, was the pilot to the brief series, with McCallum, Fee, and Craig Stevens in the role originated by Cooper, that ran for several weeks in the fall of 1975.

0561
THE RETURN OF JOE FORRESTER
5/6/75 Columbia Pictures (90 min)

Executive Producers: David Gerber and Stanley Kallis
Producer: Christopher Morgan
Director: Virgil W. Vogel
Teleplay: Mark Rogers
Production Consultant: Joseph Wambaugh
Photography: Emmett Bergholz
Music: Richard Markowitz
Art Directors: Ross Bellah and Robert Peterson
Editor: Arthur D. Hilton

Joe Forrester	LLOYD BRIDGES
Georgia Cameron	PAT CROWLEY
Jake Mandel	JIM BACKUS
Lieutenant Eaker	DANE CLARK
Sergeant Callan	DEAN STOCKWELL
Claudine	DELLA REESE
Irene	JANIS PAIGE
The Golfer	TOM DRAKE
Massage Parlor Owner	EDIE ADAMS
Dr. Belding	HARI RHODES
Commander	CHARLES DRAKE
Sergeant Malone	EDDIE EGAN
Plums	DON STROUD

and: Rudy Solari, Shelley Novack, Ted Gehring

An aging street cop goes after a gang of toughs involved in several robbery-rapes on his beat in this pilot (a spin-off from "Police Story") for the 1975–76 series. The veteran cop concept also was the basis for "The Blue Knight" series at the same time—and that too was based on a Joseph Wambaugh creation.

0562
MATT HELM
5/7/75 Columbia Pictures (90 min)

Executive Producer: Irving Allen
Producer/Director: Buzz Kulik
Teleplay: Sam H. Rolfe
Photography: Charles F. Wheeler
Music: Jerry Fielding
Art Directors: Ross Bellah and John Beckman
Editor: Les Green

Matt Helm	ANTHONY FRANCIOSA
Maggie Gantry	ANN TURKEL
Claire Kronski	LARAINE STEPHENS
Shawcross	PATRICK MACNEE
Harry Paine	JOHN VERNON
Sergeant James	VAL BISOGLIO
Sergeant Hanrahan	GENE EVANS
Charlie Danberry	MICHAEL C. GWYNNE
Seki	HARI RHODES
Thomas McCauley III	JAMES SHIGETA
Alice	CATHERINE BACH
Drone	RICHARD BUTLER
Taylor	FRANK CAMPANELLA
Champion	PAUL PICERNI
Saleslady	JOAN SHAWLEE

Intrepid secret agent-turned-private eye Matt Helm finds himself involved with an international black market operation in heavy munitions when he tries to protect a beautiful movie star whose life is endangered. The pilot, with Franciosa taking up where Dean Martin left off after four Helm movies, spawned the brief series (Sept. 1975–Jan. 1976) starring Franciosa, Laraine Stephens, Gene Evans and Jeff Donnell.

0563
SHELL GAME
5/9/75 Thoroughbred Productions (90 min)

Producer: Harold Jack Bloom
Director: Glenn Jordan
Teleplay: Harold Jack Bloom
Photography: Jerry Hirschfeld
Music: Lenny Stack
Art Director: Walter L. Simonds
Editor: Aaron Stell

Max Castle	JOHN DAVIDSON
Stoker Frye	TOMMY ATKINS
Stephen Castle	ROBERT SAMPSON
Lola Ramirez	MARIE O'BRIEN
Lyle Rettig	JACK KEHOE
Shirley	JOAN VAN ARK
Mrs. Margolin	LOUISE LATHAM
Susan	KAREN MACHON
Carruthers	ROBERT SYMONDS
Bellhop	GARY SANDY
Carmichael	CLIFF EMMICH
Sammy	LANCE TAYLOR, SR.
Tim Carson	GARY PAGETT
Louis	PETE GONNEAU
Countess	SIGNE HASSO

and: Deborah Sherman, Jason Wingreen, Frank Corsentino, Mike Tillman, Don Diamond

A heist romp that has a convicted con man risking another prison term by setting out in Robin Hood style to fleece the crooked head of a big charity fund who has been diverting the money to cover gambling losses. This *Sting* carbon, spurred by the enormous success of the Newman-Redford movie, turned out to be an unsuccessful pilot for a series with singer John Davidson.

0564

THE BLUE KNIGHT
5/9/75 Lorimar Productions (90 min)

Executive Producer: Lee Rich
Producer: John Furia, Jr.
Director: J. Lee Thompson
Teleplay: Albert Ruben
Based on the book by Joseph Wambaugh
Photography: Richard L. Rawlings
Music: Henry Mancini
Art Director: Phil Barber
Editor: Samuel E. Beetley

William A. "Bumper" Morgan	GEORGE KENNEDY
Det. Charley Bronski	ALEX ROCCO
Edwin Beall	GLYNN TURMAN
Moody Larkin	VERNA BLOOM
Frank Zugarelli	MICHAEL MARGOTTA
Piskor	SETH ALLEN
Wimpey	JOHN STEADMAN
Detective Harriman	RICHARD HURST
Randy	BART BURNS
Leroy "Tank" Whittier	JI-TU CUMBUKA
Personnel Officer	WALTER BARNES
The Dutchman	MARC ALAIMO
Joel Stebbins	ERIC CHRISTMANS
Desk Sergeant	JOSEPH WAMBAUGH

and: Britt Leach, Hoke Howell, Reid Cruickshanks, Don Hamner, Howard Hesseman, Harry Caesar, John Dennis, Valentine Villarreal, Lieux Dressler, Curtis Henderson, Richard Kalk

Veteran street cop Bumper Morgan searches for the killer of an aging colleague in the Los Angeles barrio in this pilot for the 1975–76 series. Kennedy took over the role originated in the 1973 telefeature by William Holden.

0565

THE FIRST 36 HOURS OF DR. DURANT
5/13/75 Columbia Pictures (90 min)

Executive Producer: Stirling Silliphant
Producer: James H. Brown
Director: Alexander Singer
Teleplay: Stirling Silliphant
Photography: Gerald Perry Finnerman
Music: Leonard Rosenman
Art Directors: Ross Bellah and Robert Purcell
Editor: Jack Kampschroer

Dr. Chris Durant	SCOTT HYLANDS
Dr. Konrad Zane	LAWRENCE PRESSMAN
Nurse Katherine Gunther	KATHERINE HELMOND
Nurse Clive Olin	KAREN CARLSON
Dr. Lynn Peterson	RENNE JARRETT
Dr. Alex Keefer	ALEX HENTELOFF
Dr. Hutchins	DANA ANDREWS
Graham	MICHAEL CONRAD
Dr. Bryce	PETER DONAT
Dr. Atkinson	DAVID DOYLE
Dr. Baxter	JAMES NAUGHTON
Mr. Wesco	DENNIS PATRICK
Mrs. Graham	JOYCE JAMESON
Surgical Secretary	JANET BRANDT
Dr. Dorsett	DAVIS ROBERTS

An idealistic young surgical resident confronts the realities of medical ethics with a life and a career at stake during his first hectic hours on call at a big city hospital.

0566

PROMISE HIM ANYTHING . . .
5/14/75 ABC Circle Films (90 min)

Producers: Mitchell Brower and Robert Lovenheim
Director: Edward Parone
Teleplay: David Freeman
Photography: Howard R. Schwartz
Music: Nelson Riddle*
Art Director: Peter M. Wooley
Editor: John F. Burnett

Pop	EDDIE ALBERT
Paul Hunter	FREDERIC FORREST
Marjorie Sherman	MEG FOSTER
Silver	WILLIAM SCHALLERT
Judge Jason Melbourne	TOM EWELL
Chuck	STEVEN KEATS
Tom	EDWARD BELL
Lucille	JOYCE JAMESON
Cop	ALDO RAY
Housewife	ELLEN BLAKE
Karen	JUDY CASSMORE
Mother	PEGGY REA
Lyle	HUNTER VON LEER

and: Tom Hatten, Pearl Shear, Mary Grace Canfield, Patty Regan

A bachelor has high hopes when he takes out a girl whose computer dating card read suggestively "Anything goes," but when he learns that nothing goes, he hauls her into court for breach of promise.

*Variations on Cole Porter's "Anything Goes" as sung by Diana Trask.

0567

FRIENDLY PERSUASION
5/18/75 International Television Productions/Allied Artists (2 hours)

Executive Producers: Emanuel L. Wolf and Herbert B. Leonard
Producer/Director: Joseph Sargent
Teleplay: William P. Wood
Based on the books *Friendly Persuasion* and *Except for Me and Thee* by Jessamyn West
Photography: Mario Tosi
Music: John Cacavas
Title Theme: Dmitri Tiomkin
Art Director: Jim Spencer
Editors: George Jay Nicholson and Edward J. Forsyth

Jess Birdwell	RICHARD KILEY
Eliza Birdwell	SHIRLEY KNIGHT
Sam Jordan	CLIFTON JAMES
Josh	MICHAEL O'KEEFE
Labe	KEVIN O'KEEFE
Mattie	TRACIE SAVAGE
Little Jess	SPARKY MARCUS
Swan Stebeney	PAUL BENJAMIN
Enoch	ERIK HOLLAND
Lily Truscott	MARIA GRIMM
Burk	BOB MINOR

A loving remake of William Wyler's 1956 film classic, with Kiley and Knight in the Gary Cooper and Doro-

Lee Remick and William Holden in THE BLUE KNIGHT (1973)

Lark Geib, Michael-James Wixted, Robert Preston and Brad Savage in MY FATHER'S HOUSE (1975)

Cliff Robertson in MY FATHER'S HOUSE (1975)

thy McGuire roles as a Quaker couple who, when forced to a painful decision by their convictions, risk their lives to help a pair of runaway slaves.

0568
DEATH AMONG FRIENDS
5/20/75 Douglas S. Cramer Company/Warner Bros. (90 min)
(subsequently titled *Mrs. R—Death Among Friends*)

Executive Producers: Douglas S. Cramer and Wilford Lloyd Baumes
Producer: Alex Beaton
Director: Paul Wendkos
Teleplay: Stanley Ralph Ross
Photography: Terry K. Meade
Music: Jim Helms
Special Effects: Joe Unsinn
Editor: George Watters

Lt. Shirley Ridgeway	KATE REID
Captain Lewis	JOHN ANDERSON
Manny Reyes	A MARTINEZ
Buckner	MARTIN BALSAM
Chico Donovan	JACK CASSIDY
Otto Schiller	PAUL HENREID
Connie	PAMELA HENSLEY
Sheldon Casey	WILLIAM SMITH
Lisa Manning	LYNDA DAY GEORGE
Morgan	DENVER PYLE

Nancy	ROBYN HILTON
Carol	KATHERINE BAUMANN

A lady homicide detective tries to solve the murder of an international financier in this pilot for a prospective but unrealized series.

0569
SKY HEIST
5/26/75 Warner Bros. (2 hours)

Executive Producer: Andrew J. Fenady
Producer: Rick Rosner
Director: Lee H. Katzin
Teleplay: William F. Nolan, Rick Rosner and Stanley Ralph Ross
Photography: Michel Hugo
Music: Leonard Rosenman
Editors: Dann Kahn, Bill Neel and Rick Wormell

Sgt. Doug Trumbell	DON MEREDITH
Capt. Monty Ballard	JOSEPH CAMPANELLA
Deputy Jim Schiller	LARRY WILCOX
Deputy Pat Connelly	KEN SWOFFORD
Terry Hardings	STEFANIE POWERS
Ben Hardings	FRANK GORSHIN
Lisa	SHELLEY FABARES
Deputy Rick Busby	RAY VITTE
Nan Paige	NANCY BELLE FULLER
Lt. Bill Hammon	JAMES DARIS

and: John Davey, R. B. Sorko-Ram, James Chandler, Steven Marlo, Robert Jordan, Philip Mansour, Peter Colt, William Harlow, Joe Ohar, Ed McReady, Leslie Thompson, Stan Barrett, Richard Reed, Steve Franken, Bill Catching, Al Wyatt, George R. Wilbur, Buck Young, Stanley Ralph Ross, Hunter Von Leer, Renny Rocker, Arch Whiting, Jim Conners, Trent Dolan, Maralyn Thomas, Hank Worden, Suzanne Marie Somers, Gloria Fioramonti

A husband and wife team devise an ingenious plan to steal ten million dollars in gold bullion, hijacking a police helicopter as a diversionary tactic.

0570
MY FATHER'S HOUSE
6/1/75 Filmways (2 hours)

An Edward S. Feldman/David Sontag Production
Executive Producer: Edward S. Feldman
Producer: David Sontag
Director: Alex Segal
Teleplay: David Seltzer and David Sontag
Based on the novel by Philip Kunhardt, Jr.
Photography: David M. Walsh
Music: Charles Fox
Art Director: George Reune
Editor: Marion Rothman

Tom Lindholm, Jr.	CLIFF ROBERTSON
Tom Lindholm, Sr.	ROBERT PRESTON
Mrs. Lindholm, Sr.	EILEEN BRENNAN

Judith Lindholm	ROSEMARY FORSYTH
Anna	RUTH McDEVITT
Tom, Jr. (as a boy)	MICHAEL-JAMES WIXTED
Steven	MICHAEL CORNELISON
Brad	BRAD SAVAGE
Susan	LARK GEIB
Paula	GAIL STRICKLAND
Ellen	CARLENE OLSON

and: Lil Greenwood, Kerri Osborn, Kelli Osborn, Victoria Clark, Hilary Clark, Laurie Main, Clark Gordon, Arthur Bernard, Dilart Heyson, Madgel Dean, Cris Capen

A drama about a heart attack patient, a busy, highly paid executive, who reflects upon his happy childhood and the way he was brought up in a simpler age. Although playing father and son, Preston and Robertson, sharing star billing, never appear together in this film.

0571
A GIRL NAMED SOONER
6/18/75 Frederick Brogger Associates/20th Century-Fox (2 hours)

Executive Producer: Frederick Brogger
Producer: Fred Hamilton
Director: Delbert Mann
Teleplay: Suzanne Clauser
Based on her novel
Photography: Ralph Woolsey
Music: Jerry Goldsmith
Supervised by Lionel Newman
Production Design: Jan Scott
Editor: Jack Holmes

Elizabeth McHenry	LEE REMICK
R. J. "Mac" McHenry	RICHARD CRENNA
Sheriff Phil Rotteman	DON MURRAY
Selma Goss	ANNE FRANCIS
Old Mam Hawes	CLORIS LEACHMAN
Sooner	SUSAN DEER
Jim Seevey	MICHAEL GROSS
Teacher	NANCY BELL
Harvey Drummond	KEN HARDIN
Judith Ann Drumond	TONIA SCOTTI

A drama about an abandoned young girl, raised in the hill country of Indiana by an eccentric bootlegging old crone, who becomes the ward of a childless couple.

0572
MAN ON THE OUTSIDE
6/29/75 Universal (2 hours)

Executive Producer: David Victor
Producer: George Eckstein
Director: Boris Sagal
Teleplay: Larry Cohen
Photography: Mario Tosi
Music: Elliot Kaplan
Art Director: Walter M. Simonds
Editors: Douglas Stewart and Bud Hoffman

Wade Griffin	LORNE GREENE
Gerald Griffin	JAMES OLSON
Mark Griffin	LEE H. MONTGOMERY
Nora Griffin	LORRAINE GARY
Sandra Ames	BROOKE BUNDY
Lieutenant Matthews	KEN SWOFFORD
Ames	WILLIAM C. WATSON
Scully	BRUCE KIRBY
Mr. Arnold	CHARLES KNOX ROBINSON
Benny	GARRY WALBERG

Ellen	JEAN ALLISON
Stella Daniels	RUTH McDEVITT
Ruben Hammer	SCATMAN CROTHERS

A retired police captain storms angrily out of retirement when his son is shot down before his eyes and his grandson is kidnapped by a syndicate killer in this pilot for Lorne Greene's brief "Griff" series, which went off the air eighteen months *before* this film was aired. (Series dates: 9/23/73–1/4/74)

0573
STRANGE NEW WORLD
7/13/75 Warner Bros. (2 hours)

Executive Producers: Walon Green and Ronald F. Graham
Producer: Robert E. Larson
Director: Robert Butler
Teleplay: Walon Green, Ronald F. Graham and Al Ramus
Photography: Michael Margulies
Music: Richard Clements and Elliot Kaplan
Art Director: Jack Martin Smith
Editor: David Newhouse

Capt. Anthony Vico	JOHN SAXON
Dr. Allison Crowley	KATHLEEN MILLER
Dr. William Scott	KEENE CURTIS
The Surgeon	JAMES OLSON
Tana	MARTINE BESWICK
Sprang	REB BROWN
Sirus	FORD RAINEY
Badger	BILL McKINNEY
Daniel	GERRIT GRAHAM
Araba	CYNTHINA WOOD
Lara	CATHERINE BACH

and: Norland Benson, Dick Farnsworth

A science-fiction adventure with three astronauts returning to earth after 180 years in suspended animation and finding scientists who have developed eternal life and primitives who live with jungle beasts. This pilot film for a prospective series subsequently was edited to ninety minutes from its original two-hour running time for syndicated showings.

1975–76 SEASON

0574
MOBILE TWO
9/2/75 Universal/Mark VII Ltd. (90 min)

Executive Producer: Jack Webb
Producer: William Bowers
Director: David Moessinger
Teleplay: David Moessinger and James M. Miller
Photography: Enzo A. Martinelli
Music: Nelson Riddle
Editor: Robert Leeds

Peter Campbell	JACKIE COOPER
Maggie Spencer	JULIE GREGG
Doug McKnight	MARK WHEELER
Roger Brice	EDD BYRNES
Bill Hopkins	JACK HOGAN
Father John Lucas	JOE E. TATA
Phillip Ganzer	HARRY BARTELL
Lt. Don Carter	BILL BOYETT

A seasoned broadcast journalist, an ex-boozer, gets the chance to again prove himself as a television news reporter in this pilot for the short-lived "Mobile One" series that premiered ten days after this movie's initial airing and ran through the end of the year.

0575
MEDICAL STORY
9/4/75 David Gerber Productions/Columbia (2 hours)

Executive Producer: Abby Mann
Producer: Christopher Morgan
Director: Gary Nelson
Teleplay: Abby Mann
Photography: Jules Brenner
Music: Arthur Morton
Theme: Jerry Goldsmith
Art Directors: Ross Bellah and Zoltan Muller
Editor: Richard Sprague

Dr. Steve Drucker	BEAU BRIDGES
Dr. Matthews	CLAUDE AKINS
Joe Bick	WENDELL BURTON
Dr. Maxwell	SIDNEY CHAPLIN
Dr. William Knowland	JOSE FERRER
Dr. Federicci	HAROLD GOULD
Fritzi Donnelly	HARRIET KARR
Phyllis Lenahan	SHIRLEY KNIGHT
Dr. Reiber	CARL REINER
Dr. Patterson	FORD RAINEY
Mrs. Drayden	MADYLYN RHUE
Miss McDonald	MARTHA SCOTT

and: Theodore Wilson, Shelley Novack, Lillian Bronson, Marilyn Nix

Paralleling the successful format of its sister show "Police Story," this pilot for the short-lived anthology series pits an idealistic intern against three established doctors over the question of whether a young actress should have a hysterectomy. Executive producer-writer Abby Mann was said to have based this story on the near-fatal experience of his wife, Harriet Karr, who plays the ailing actress.

0576
THE KANSAS CITY MASSACRE
9/19/75 ABC Circle Films (2 hours)

Producer/Director: Dan Curtis
Associate Producer: Robert Singer
Teleplay: Bronson Howitzer and William F. Nolan
From a story by Bronson Howitzer
Photography: Paul Lohmann
Music: Robert Cobert
Art Director: Trevor Williams
Editors: Richard A. Harris and Dennis Virkler

Melvin Pervis	DALE ROBERTSON
Charles Arthur "Pretty Boy" Floyd	BO HOPKINS
Adam Richetti	ROBERT WALDEN
Frank Nash	MILLS WATSON
Hubert Tucker McElway	SCOTT BRADY
Verne Miller	MATT CLARK
Sam Cowley	JOHN KARLEN
Vi Morland	LYN LORING
Lester Gillis "Baby Face" Nelson	ELLIOTT STREET
Johnny Lazia	HARRIS YULIN
Captain Jackson	PHILIP BRUNS
Wilma Floyd	SALLY KIRKLAND
John Dillinger	WILLIAM JORDAN
Alvin Karpis	MORGAN PAULL
Larry DeVol	JIM STORM
Gov. Garfield Burns	LESTER MADDOX

Robertson here reprises his role of the flamboyant Melvin Purvis that he originated in Dan Curtis' *Melvin Purvis, G-Man* (1974) and takes on the crime cartel formed by Pretty Boy Floyd, John Dillinger, Baby Face Nelson, Alvin Karpis and others. Their crime wave ended in the notorious Kansas City massacre of June 17, 1933. Of interest: Harris Yulin, who portrayed J. Edgar Hoover in the 1974 TV movie, *The FBI Versus Alvin Karpis*, here is on the other side of the law as a vicious crime czar; and former Georgia governor, Lester Maddox made his movie debut in a small role as the governor of Oklahoma.

0577
DEATH SCREAM
9/26/75 RSO Films (2 hours)
(subsequently titled *The Woman Who Cried Murder*)

Executive Producer: Ron Bernstein
Producer: Deanne Barkley
Director: Richard T. Heffron
Teleplay: Stirling Silliphant
Photography: Gene Polito
Music: Gil Melle
Editor: David Newhouse

Det. Nick Rodriguez	RAUL JULIA
Det. Dave Lambert	JOHN P. RYAN
Det. Johnny Bellon	PHILLIP CLARK
Judy	LUCIE ARNAZ
Peter Singleton	EDWARD ASNER
Mr. Jacobs	ART CARNEY
Betty May	DIAHANN CARROLL
Carol	KATE JACKSON
Mrs. Singleton	CLORIS LEACHMAN
Hilda Murray	TINA LOUISE
Mrs. Jacobs	NANCY WALKER
Kosinsky	ERIC BRAEDEN
Alice Whitmore	ALLYN ANN McLERIE
Jimmy	TODD SUSMAN
Jenny Storm	BELINDA BALASKI

(Below) **Dale Robertson in THE KANSAS CITY MASSACRE (1975)**
(Right) **Raul Julia in DEATH SCREAM (1975)**

Sissy Spacek, Art Carney, Jane Wyatt and Henry Winkler in KATHERINE (1975)

Sissy Spacek in KATHERINE (1975)

Mrs. Kosinsky	DIMITRA ARLISS
Mr. Whitmore	WILLIAM BRYANT
Mrs. Daniels	JOAN GOODFELLOW
Lady Wing Ding	THELMA HOUSTON
Det. Ross	BERT FREED
Det. Hughes	DON PEDRO COLLEY
Joey	TONY DOW
Teila	HELEN HUNT
Mary	SALLY KIRKLAND

An all-star suspense drama about a young woman whose murder was witnessed by fifteen of her neighbors who did nothing to help and refused to cooperate with the police. Based on an actual event, this was filmed under the title *Homicide* and in its repeat showing was called *The Woman Who Cried Murder.*

0578
FEAR ON TRIAL
10/2/75 Alan Landsburg Productions (2 hours)

Executive Producers: Alan Landsburg and Laurence D. Savadove
Producer: Stanley Chase
Director: Lamont Johnson
Teleplay: David W. Rintels
Based on the autobiography by John Henry Faulk
Music Supervisors: William Loose and Jack Tillar
Art Director: John Lloyd
Editor: Tom Rolfe

Louis Nizer	GEORGE C. SCOTT
John Henry Faulk	WILLIAM DEVANE
Laura Faulk	DOROTHY TRISTAN

Stan Hopp	WILLIAM REDFIELD
Herb Steinmann	MILT KOGAN
Gerry Dickler	ALLAN MILLER
Thomas Bolan	JOHN LEHNE
Harry	BEN PIAZZA
Hartnett	JOHN HARKINS
Tom Murray	JOHN McMARTIN
Paul	PAUL HECHT
Nan Claybourne	LOIS NETTLETON
Mike Collins	JOHN HOUSEMAN
Saul	JUDD HIRSCH
Himself	DAVID SUSSKIND
Himself	MARK GOODSON
Judge Abraham N. Geller	BRUCE GELLER*
Anne Steinmann	DOROTHY RICE
Paul Martinson	PAUL JENKINS
Hall	CLIFFORD DAVID
Art Beresford	NICHOLAS PRYOR

and: William Traylor, Mona Bruns, John Lasell, Irene Robinson, Susan Kirschner, Kim Webster, Alice Backes, Maxine Cooper, Madeline Lee, Mary Alan Hokanson, Manuel Depina, Thomas Duncan, William Hellinger, Sean Peters, Alan Rachins, John M. Reed

This Emmy-nominated film follows the troubles stalking John Henry Faulk, a folksy, homespun radio-television personality of the early 1950s whose broadcasting career was abruptly cut off during the blacklisting of the era. Retaining attorney Louis Nizer, he went to court and successfully sued for libel, obtaining a $3,500,000 judgment, although he never again came back to network radio or television. The character portrayed by Lois Nettleton actually was Kim Hunter, the actress and fellow blacklistee, who refused to allow her name to be used in this teleplay, for which

222

David Rintels won an Emmy. William Devane, Lois Nettleton and director Lamont Johnson were also nominated.

*Geller, the creator and developer of such TV series as "Mission: Impossible" and "Mannix," played the role of his own father, the presiding judge at the trial of Faulk vs. Aware, Inc.

0579
KATHERINE
10/5/75 The Jozak Company (2 hours)

Producer: Gerald I. Isenberg
Associate Producer: Gerald W. Abrams
Director: Jeremy Paul Kagan
Teleplay: Jeremy Paul Kagan
Photography: Frank Stanley
Art Director: Perry Ferguson II
Editor: Patrick Kennedy

Thornton Alman	ART CARNEY
Katherine Alman	SISSY SPACEK

Bob Kline	HENRY WINKLER
Margot Weiss Goldman	JULIE KAVNER
Emily Alman	JANE WYATT
Juan	HECTOR ELIAS
Liz Alman Parks	JENNY SULLIVAN
Miss Collins	MARY MURPHY
Vega	RENE ENRIQUEZ
Julio	JORGE CERVERA, JR.
Jessica	NIRA BARAB
Father Echeverra	JOE DeSANTIS
Lillian Colman	BARBARA ILEY
Frizzy	ANN NOLAND
Jennie	TA-RONCE ALLEN

and: John Hawker, Brad Rearden, Buck Young

The socialite-to-revolutionary evolution of a pampered young heiress whose concern leads her first to the Peace Corps and ultimately to a group of political terrorists bent on changing the system. Art Carney, as her father in this film paralleling the Patty Hearst case, received an Emmy nomination as Best Supporting Actor. Originally shown as a two hour movie, it subsequently has been cut down to ninety minutes.

0580
SWEET HOSTAGE
10/10/75 Brut Productions (2 hours)

Executive Producer: George Barrie
Producers: Richard E. Lyons and Sidney D. Balkin
Director: Lee Philips
Teleplay: Ed Hume
Based on the novel *Welcome to Xanadu* by Nathaniel Benchley
Photography: Richard C. Glouner
Music: Luchi De Jesus
Song "Strangers on a Carousel" by George Barrie and Bob Larimer
Sung by Steven Michael Schwartz
Art Director: Phil Barber
Editor: George Jay Nicholson

Doris Mae Withers	LINDA BLAIR
Leonard Hatch	MARTIN SHEEN
Mrs. Withers	JEANNE COOPER
Mr. Withers	BERT REMSEN
Sheriff Emmet	LEE DeBROUX
Harry Fox	DEHL BERTI
Mr. Smathers	AL HOPSON
Hank Smathers	BILL STERCHI

Martin Sheen and Linda Blair in SWEET HOSTAGE (1975)

Martin Sheen in SWEET HOSTAGE (1975)

and: Roberto Valentino DeLeon, Michael C. Eiland, Mary Michael Carnes, Don Hann, Ross Elder, Chris Williams

A bizarre drama of a young woman who is kidnapped by an escaped mental patient and whisked away to his remote mountain cabin, where her abductor becomes her teacher, friend and lover.

0581
THE DEADLY TOWER
10/18/75 MGM (2 hours)

Executive Producer: Richard Caffey
Producer: Antonio Calderon
Director: Jerry Jameson
Teleplay: William Douglas Lansford

Photography: Matthew F. Leonetti
Music: Don Ellis
Special Effects: Cliff Wenger
Editor: Tom Stevens

Charles Whitman	KURT RUSSELL
Off. Ramiro Martinez	RICHARD YNIGUEZ
Lt. Elwood Forbes	JOHN FORSYTHE
Allan Crum	NED BEATTY
Lieutenant Lee	PERNELL ROBERTS
Capt. Fred Ambrose	CLIFTON JAMES
C. Y. Foss	PAUL CARR
Bill Davis	ALAN VINT
Mano	PEPE SERNA
Vinnie Martinez	MARIA ELENA CORDERO

Narrated by GILBERT ROLAND

A vivid re-creation of the Texas Tower massacre of August 4, 1966, during which disturbed student Charles Whitman holed up with a gun in the tower of the University of Texas and began firing on people below, killing thirteen and wounding thirty-four.

0582
A HOME OF OUR OWN
10/19/75 Quinn Martin Productions (2 hours)

Executive Producer: Quinn Martin
Producer: Fred Baum
Director: Robert Day
Teleplay: Blanche Hanalis
Photography: Jacques R. Marquette
Music: Laurence Rosenthal
Art Director: Richard Y. Haman
Editor: Jerry Young

Father William Wasson	JASON MILLER
Hilario	PANCHO CORDOVA
Julio (as a child)	GUILLERMO DAN JUAN
Julio (as an adult)	ENRIQUE NOBI
Police Captain	PEDRO ARMENDARIZ, JR.
The Bishop	RICHARD ANGAROLA
Elena de la Paz	CARMEN ZAPATA
Chicken Farmer	FARNESIO de BERNAL
Magdalena (as a child)	ROSARIO ALVAREZ
Sister Philomena	NANCY RODMAN

A drama based on the work of Father William Wasson, the founder and director of a home for orphaned children in Mexico.

0583
THE UFO INCIDENT
10/20/75 Universal (2 hours)

Producer/Director: Richard A. Colla
Co-Producer: Joe L. Cramer
Teleplay: S. Lee Pogostin and Hesper Anderson
From the book *The Interrupted Journey* by John G. Fuller
Photography: Rexford Metz
Music: Billy Goldenberg
Art Director: Peter M. Wooley
Editor: Richard Bracken

Barney Hill	JAMES EARL JONES
Betty Hill	ESTELLE PARSONS
Dr. Benjamin Simon	BARNARD HUGHES
Gen. James Davison	DICK O'NEILL
Jack MacRainey	BEESON CARROLL
Lisa MacRainey	TERRENCE O'CONNOR
The Leader	LOU WAGNER

Narrated by VIC PERRIN

and: Eric Murphy, Eric Server

A talkative drama, reportedly fact-based, about the interracial New Hampshire couple who claim to have been taken aboard a UFO in September 1961 and examined medically by strange extraterrestrial creatures. The original title before initial airing: *Interrupted Journey*.

0584
BABE
10/23/75 MGM (2 hours)

Producers: Stanley Rubin and Norman Felton
Associate Producer: Joanna Lee
Director: Buzz Kulik
Teleplay: Joanna Lee
Based on the autobiography *This Life I've Led* by Babe Didrickson Zaharias
Photography: Charles F. Wheeler
Music: Jerry Goldsmith
Art Directors: Preston Ames and Dave Marshall
Editor: Henry Berman

Babe Didrickson	SUSAN CLARK
George Zaharias	ALEX KARRAS
Col. William J. McComb	SLIM PICKENS
Hanna Marie Didrickson	JEANETTE NOLAN
Lily Didrickson	ELLEN GEER
Dr. Tatum	FORD RAINEY
Johnson	ARCH JOHNSON
Father	PHILIP BOURNEAUF
Grantland Rice	BYRON MORROW
Heckler	HERB VIGRAN
Hospital Spokesman	JAMES GRIFFITH
Sportscaster	STUART NATHAN
Jimmy	GREG NARRY
Joe	MICKEY SHOLDAR
Sister Tarsisis	MEG WYLIE
Sue Ellen	KATHLEEN CODY
Nurse	JENI GERBER
Randy	DICK DINMAN

Susan Clark here gave an Emmy Award-winning performance as America's foremost woman athlete who won two Olympic track-and-field gold medals in 1932 and went on to become a world champion golfer. The film traces her development as an athlete, her battles to be accepted in sports, her marriage to wrestler-turned-promoter George Zaharias (played by ex-football pro Alex Karras), and her losing struggle with cancer. In addition to an Emmy for its star, the movie also received a nomination as the Outstanding Special of 1975–76, and director Buzz Kulik and writer Joanna Lee were nominated for their work, as were composer Jerry Goldsmith, cinematographer Charles Wheeler, editor Henry Berman and makeup artist William Tuttle.

0585
THE LIVES OF JENNY DOLAN
10/27/75 Ross Hunter Productions/Paramount (2 hours)

Executive Producer: Ross Hunter
Producer: Jacque Mapes
Director: Jerry Jameson
Teleplay: James Lee
From a format developed by Richard Alan Simmons
Photography: Matthew F. Leonetti
Music: Pat Williams
Art Director: Preston Ames
Editor: George Brooks

Jenny Dolan	SHIRLEY JONES
Joe Rossiter	STEPHEN BOYD
Nancy Royce	LYNN CARLIN
Orlando	JAMES DARREN
David Ames	FARLEY GRANGER
Ralph Stantlow	GEORGE GRIZZARD
Dr. Wes Dolan	DAVID HEDISON
Lieutenant Nesbitt	STEPHEN McNALLY
Sanders	IAN McSHANE
Camera Shop Proprietor	PERNELL ROBERTS
Dr. Laurence Mallen	PERCY RODRIGUEZ
Mrs. Owens	COLLIN WILCOX-JONES
Andrea Hardesty	DANA WYNTER
Alan Hardesty	CHARLES DRAKE
Springfield	JESS OPPENHEIMER
Eddie Owens	PAUL CARR
Landlady	VIRGINIA GREY
Interne	TONY YOUNG

Veteran producer Ross Hunter came to television with this drama (a pilot for a prospective series) about a glamorous newspaper reporter who is assigned to investigate the assination of a political figure.

0586
THE NIGHT THAT PANICKED AMERICA
10/31/75 Paramount (2 hours)

Executive Producer: Anthony Wilson
Producer/Director: Joseph Sargent
Teleplay: Nicholas Meyer and Anthony Wilson
Radio Play written by Howard Koch
Photography: Jules Brenner
Music: Frank Comstock
Art Director: Monty Elliott
Creative Consultant: Paul Stewart
Editors: Bud S. Isaacs, Tony Radecki and George Jay Nicholson

Orson Welles	PAUL SHENAR
Hank Muldoon	VIC MORROW
Stefan Grubowski	CLIFF DeYOUNG
Jess Wingate	MICHAEL CONSTANTINE
Paul Stewart	WALTER McGINN
Ann Muldoon	EILEEN BRENNAN
Linda Davis	MEREDITH BAXTER
Norman Smith	TOM BOSLEY
Reverend Davis	WILL GEER
Walter Wingate	JOHN RITTER
Carl Philips	GRANVILLE VAN DUSEN
Tex	BRUTON GILLIAM
Howard Koch	JOSHUA BRYANT
Radio Actor 1	RON RIFKIN
Radio Actor 2	WALKER EDMISTON
Radio Actor 3	CASEY KASEM
Radio Actor 4	MARCUS J. GRAPES
Charlie	LIAM DUNN
Toni (Sound Effects Girl)	SHELLEY MORRISON
Announcer	ART HANNES

A drama recalling the widespread fright caused by the famous Halloween night 1938 radio broadcast, Orson Welles' Mercury Theater adaptation of H. G. Wells' *The War of the Worlds* (meticulously recreated), which sent millions into the streets convinced that America was being invaded by Martians. Nicholas Meyer and Anthony Wilson won Emmy Award nominations for their original teleplay. Also cited were editors Bud S. Isaacs, Tony Radecki and George Jay Nicholson. This was another two-hour movie that subsequently was edited down to ninety minutes for its network rerun (in 1977) and syndicated showings.

0587
BEYOND THE BERMUDA TRIANGLE
11/6/75 Playboy Productions, Inc. (90 min)

Executive Producer: Paul Donnelly
Producer: Ron Roth
Associate Producer: Brenda Beckett
Director: William A. Graham
Teleplay: Charles A. McDaniel
Photography: Gayne Rescher
Music: Harry Sukman
Editor: Michael McLean

Harry Ballinger	FRED MacMURRAY
Jed Horn	SAM GROOM
Claudia	DONNA MILLS
Jill	SUZANNE REED
Wendy	DANA PLATO
Caldas	DAN WHITE
Doyle	RIC O'FELDMAN
Linder	JOHN DiSANTI
Borden	WOODY WOODBURY
Myra	JOAN MURPHY

A retired businessman probes into mysterious ship and plane disappearances off the Florida coast after his friends and his fiancée are involved. Originally this one was titled *Beyond This Place There Be Dragons*.

0588
THE SILENCE
11/6/75 Palomar Pictures International (90 min)

Executive Producer: Edgar J. Scherick
Producer: Bridget Poteer
Director: Joseph Hardy
Teleplay: Stanley R. Greenberg
Photography: Jack Priestley
Music: Maurice Jarre
Art Director: Mel Bourne
Editor: Alan Heim

Cadet James Pelosi	RICHARD THOMAS
Stanley Greenberg	CLIFF GORMAN
Captain Nichols	GEORGE HEARN
Captain Harris	PERCY GRANGER
Colonel Mack	JAMES MITCHELL
Court President	JOHN KELLOGG
Cadet Captain	CHARLES FRANK
Mr. Pelosi	ANDREW DUNCAN
Andy	MALCOLM GROOM
Red Sash	PETER WELLER
Tom Thorne	MICHAEL COOKE
Mr. Keene	JOHN CARPENTER
Elaine	CYNTHIA GROVER

This fact-based drama has a West Point cadet reliving for a TV playwright his experiences of being subjected to total exile after being accused of violating the school's honor code.

0589
HEY, I'M ALIVE!
11/7/75 Charles Fries Productions/Worldvision (90 min)

Executive Producer: Charles Fries
Producer/Director: Lawrence Schiller
Teleplay: Rita Larkin
Based on the book by Helen Klaban with Beth Day
Photography: Richard Moore
Music: Frank DeVol
Art Director: Cam Porteous
Editor: Millie Moore

Ralph Flores	EDWARD ASNER
Helen Klaban	SALLY STRUTHERS
Glen Sanders	MILTON SELZER
Jeff Lawson	HAGAN BEGGS
Sheryl Flores	MARIA HERNANDEZ
Mrs. Flores	CLAUDINE MELGRAVE

A dramatization of the 1963 plane crash in which an adventurous young woman and an older man survived in the frozen Yukon wilderness for forty-nine days, subsisting on melted snow.

0590

THE NEW, ORIGINAL WONDER WOMAN
11/7/75 The Douglas S. Cramer Co./Warner Bros.
(90 min)

Producer: Douglas S. Cramer
Director: Leonard J. Horn
Teleplay: Stanley Ralph Ross
Based on characters created by Charles Moulton
Photography: Dennis Dalzell
Music: Charles Fox
Title Song: Charles Fox and Norman Gimbel
Titles and Animation: Phil Norman
Art Director: James G. Hulsey
Costumes: Donfeld
Editor: Carroll Sax

Lyle Waggoner and Lynda Carter in THE NEW, ORIGINAL WONDER WOMAN (1975)

Diana Prince	LYNDA CARTER
Major Steve Trevor	LYLE WAGGONER
General Blankenship	JOHN RANDOLPH
Ashley Norman	RED BUTTONS
Queen Hippolyte	CLORIS LEACHMAN
Marcia	STELLA STEVENS
Kapitan Drangel	ERIC BRAEDEN
Bad Guy	SEVERN DARDEN
The Doctor	FANNIE FLAGG
Nicholas	HENRY GIBSON
Colonel Von Balasko	KENNETH MARS

and: Helen Verbit, Fritzi Burr, Ian Wolfe, Tom Rosqui

The popular comic books superwoman from the 1940s, the legendary Amazonian princess with the magic golden lasso, the invisible airplane and the bullet-deflecting bracelets, among other devices, performs incredible feats of skill and daring to save the life of handsome army air force pilot Steve Trevor and then pits her superior powers against Nazi spies who will stop at nothing to eliminate her. This pilot for the 1975–78 series was the first of several subsequent films developed from popular comic book heroes (Spider-Man, The Incredible Hulk, Captain America and others), and the series that followed was aired on an irregular basis on ABC during the first season (set in the 1940s) before moving over to CBS as a weekly show with a contemporary setting, in which Wonder Woman was allied with the son of the original Steve Trevor. Carter and Waggoner continued their characterizations.

0591

ERIC
11/10/75 Lorimar Productions   (2 hours)

Executive Producers: Lee Rich and Philip Capice
Producer: Herbert Hirschman
Director: James Goldstone
Teleplay: Nigel McKeand and Carol Evan McKeand
From the book by Doris Lund
Photography: Terry K. Meade
Music: Dave Grusin
Song "Loving Somebody" written and sung by John Savage
Art Director: Phil Barber
Editor: Edward A. Biery

Lois Swenson	PATRICIA NEAL
Stanley Swenson	CLAUDE AKINS
Marilyn Porter	SIAN-BARBARA ALLEN
Paul Swenson	MARK HAMILL
Dr. Duchesnes	NEHEMIAH PERSOFF
Eric Swenson	JOHN SAVAGE
Murphy	TOM CLANCY
Tom	JAMES G. RICHARDSON
Linda Swenson	EILEEN McDONOUGH
Mrs. Harris	KATHERINE SQUIRE

A young man learns that he has terminal cancer but vows not to give up without an all-out fight in this drama based on Doris Lund's memoir of her son's last year.

0592

FOSTER AND LAURIE
11/13/75 Charles Fries Productions Inc.   (2 hours)

Executive Producer: Charles Fries
Producer: Arthur Stolnitz
Director: John Llewellyn Moxey
Teleplay: Albert Ruben

Based on the book by Al Silverman
Photography: John Nicholaus
Music: Lalo Schifrin
Art Director: Perry Ferguson II
Editor: Bud S. Isaacs

Rocco Laurie	PERRY KING
Gregory Foster	DORIAN HAREWOOD
Adelaide Laurie	TALIA SHIRE
Jacqueline Foster	JONELLE ALLEN
Sims	ROGER AARON BROWN
Dealer	VICTOR CAMPOS
Mr. Rosario	RENE ENRIQUEZ
Sergeant Bray	CHARLES HAID
Max	ERIC LANEUVILLE
Johnson	OWEN HITHE PACE
Ianucci	DAVID PROVAL
Commissioner	WALLACE ROONEY
Sergeant Petrie	EDWARD WALSH
Addict	JAMES WOODS

This was a film chronicle of the true-life story of two New York City patrolmen who in 1972 were killed in a brutal ambush, victims of militant extremists attempting to create a wave of terror in the Police Department.

0593

GUILTY OR INNOCENT: THE SAM SHEPPARD MURDER CASE
11/17/75 Universal (3 hours)

Executive Producer: Harve Bennett
Producer: Harold Gast
Director: Robert Michael Lewis
Teleplay: Harold Gast
From a story by Lou Randolph
Photography: Stevan Larner
Music: Lalo Schifrin
Art Director: William Campbell
Editor: Robert F. Shugrue

Dr. Sam Sheppard	GEORGE PEPPARD
Atty. Philip J. Madden	BARNARD HUGHES
F. Lee Bailey	WALTER McGINN
Walt Adamson	WILLIAM WINDOM
Ilse Brandt	NINA VAN PALLANDT
Prosecutor Simons	GEORGE MURDOCK
Fred Stoner	JOHN CRAWFORD
Jack	JOHN CARTER
Medical Examiner	JOHN HARKINS
Marilyn Sheppard	CLAUDETTE NEVINS
Dr. Richard Sheppard, Sr.	WILLIAM DOZIER
Detective Moore	JACK KNIGHT
Supreme Court Justice	PAUL FIX
Judge Edwards	RUSSELL THORSEN
Jerry Wyman	JAMES WHITMORE III

and: Paul Kent, Kathleen Crawford, William Sylvester, Stewart Moss, Charlotte Moore, Smith Evans

A drama about the headline-making murder case involving Dr. Sam Sheppard, the Cleveland osteopathic surgeon, convicted of the July 4, 1954 slaying of his wife Marilyn, the ten years he spent in prison, and his subsequent life until his death in 1970.

0594

MURDER ON FLIGHT 502
11/21/75 Spelling/Goldberg Productions   (2 hours)

Executive Producers: Aaron Spelling and Leonard Goldberg
Producer: David Chasman
Director: George McCowan
Teleplay: David P. Harmon

Lesley Warren and Franco Nero in THE LEGEND OF VALENTINO (1975)

Photography: Arch R. Dalzell
Music: Laurence Rosenthal
Art Director: Alfeo Bocchicchio
Editor: Allan Jacobs

Dr. Kenyon Walker	RALPH BELLAMY
Mona Briarly	POLLY BERGEN
Otto Gruenwaldt	THEODORE BIKEL
Jack Marshall	SONNY BONO
Ray Garwood	DANE CLARK
Claire Garwood	LARAINE DAY
Paul Barons	FERNANDO LAMAS
Robert Davenport	GEORGE MAHARIS
Karen White	FARRAH FAWCETT-MAJORS
Det. Daniel Myerson	HUGH O'BRIAN
Ida Goldman	MOLLY PICON
Charlie Perkins	WALTER PIDGEON
Captain Larkin	ROBERT STACK
Vera Franklin	BROOKE ADAMS
Millard Kensington	DANNY BONADUCE
Dorothy Saunders	ROSEMARIE STACK
Marilyn Stonehurst	ELIZABETH STACK
Arnold Goldman	STEVE FRANKEN
Bomb Man	PEPPER MARTIN

A road-company *Airport* with a stellar cast being menaced by a maniac on a transatlantic jet who has murdered once and threatens to kill again. Rock-jawed Robert Stack is the stalwart, unflappable pilot; his wife Rosemarie and daughter Elizabeth have key roles.

0595
THE LEGEND OF VALENTINO
11/23/75 Spelling/Goldberg Productions (2 hours)

Producers: Aaron Spelling and Leonard Goldberg
Writer/Director: Melville Shavelson
Photography: Arch R. Dalzell
Music: Charles Fox
Choreography: Anita Mann
Art Director: Tracy Bousman
Editor: John Woodcock

Rudolph Valentino	FRANCO NERO
June Mathis	SUZANNE PLESHETTE
Jack Auerbach	JUDD HIRSCH
Laura Lorraine	LESLEY WARREN
Jesse Lasky	MILTON BERLE
Natacha Rambova	YVETTE MIMIEUX
Sam Baldwin	HAROLD J. STONE
Nazimova	ALICIA BOND
Rex Ingram	MICHAEL THOMA
Silent Star	CONNIE FORSLUND
Constance Carr	BRENDA VENUS
Mexican Mayor	RUBEN MORENO
Madame Tullio	PENNY STANTON
Teenage Girl	JANE ALICE BRANDON

Romantic fiction—a term used by the network to describe it and blunt any possible lawsuits—based on the life and myth of the screen's first and most famous male sex symbol.

0596
THE ART OF CRIME
12/3/75 Universal (90 min)

Executive Producer: Richard Irving
Producer: Jules Irving
Director: Richard Irving
Teleplay: Martin Smith and Bill Davidson
Based on the novel *Gypsy in Amber* by Martin Smith
Photography: Jack Priestley and Bernie Abrahmson
Music: Gil Melle
Art Directors: William Campbell and May Callas
Editor: Frederic Baratta

Roman Grey	RON LEIBMAN
Parker Sharon	DAVID HEDISON
Dany	JILL CLAYBURGH
Det. Sgt. Harry Isadore	EUGENE ROCHE
Beckwith Sloan	JOSE FERRER
Hillary	DIANE KAGAN
Nanoosh	CLIFF OSMOND
Madame Vera	DIMITRA ARLISS
Kore	MIKE KELLIN
Dodo	LOUIS GUSS
Gypsy Queen	TALLY BROWN

A pilot for a prospective series dealing with a gypsy private eye who is dragged into a homicide case from his other job—as an antique dealer—when one of his colleagues is accused of the crime.

227

(Above) Douglas V. Fowley and Rod Taylor in THE OREGON TRAIL (1976)

(Below) Jane Alexander *(Left)* and Edward Herrmann *(Right)* in ELEANOR AND FRANKLIN (1976)

James Arness and Bruce Boxleitner in THE MACAHANS (1976)

0597
THE OREGON TRAIL
1/10/76 Universal (2 hours)

Producer: Michael Gleason
Director: Boris Sagal
Teleplay: Michael Gleason
Photography: Jack Woolf
Music: David Shire
Art Director: A. C. Montenaro
Editor: Jamie Caylor

Evan Thorpe	ROD TAYLOR
Jessica Thorpe	BLAIR BROWN
Painted Face Kelly	DAVID HUDDLESTON
Eli Thorpe	DOUGLAS V. FOWLEY
Andrew Thorpe	ANDREW STEVENS
William Thorpe	TONY BECKER
Rachel Thorpe	GINA MARIA SMIKA
Thomas Hern	G. D. SPRADLIN
Deborah Randal	LINDA PURL

and: George Kermas, Eddie Little Sky

A pioneer family pulls up stakes, packs its belongings and heads west for the rewards of free land and a freer life. The series that followed this pilot film ran briefly from September to December 1977.

0598
ELEANOR AND FRANKLIN
1/11–12/76 A Talent Associates Ltd. Production (4 hours)

Executive Producer: David Susskind
Producers: Harry R. Sherman and Audrey Maas
Director: Daniel Petrie
Teleplay: James Costigan
Based on the book by Joseph P. Lash
Story Consultants: Franklin D. Roosevelt, Jr. and Joseph P. Lash
Photography: Paul Lohmann and Edward R. Brown
Music: John Barry
Production Design: Jan Scott
Editor: Michael Kahn

Eleanor Roosevelt (age 18–60)	JANE ALEXANDER
Franklin Roosevelt (age 20–50)	EDWARD HERRMANN
Sara Delano Roosevelt	ROSEMARY MURPHY
Anna Hall	PAMELA FRANKLIN
Elliott Roosevelt, Sr.	DAVID HUFFMAN
Eleanor Roosevelt (age 14)	MACKENZIE PHILLIPS
Mlle. Souvestre	LILIA SKALA
Louis Howe	ED FLANDERS
Daisy	HELEN KLEEB
Grace Tully	PEGGY McCAY
Laura Delano	ANNA LEE
Mary Hall	IRENE TEDROW
Corinne Robinson	DEVON ERICSON
Alice Roosevelt (age 14–20)	LINDA PURL
Theodore Roosevelt	WILLIAM PHIPPS
Franklin Roosevelt (age 16)	TED ECCLES
Lucy Mercer	LINDA KELSEY
Joe McCall	EDWARD WINTER

and: Sari Price, Timothy Jecko, Harry Holcombe, Len Wayland, Brett Salomon, Hilary Stolla, Tiffani Boli, Elie Liardet, Irene Robinson, Shannon Terhune, Lindsay Crouse, Evan Morgan, Lidia Kristen, Cynthia Latham, John Earle Burnett, Ellen Drake, Derrick Lynn-Thomas, Ned Wilson, Carl Blackwell Lester, Steve Tanner, Nora Heflin, Cherry Davis, Alvin Childress, Teresa Steenhoek, Vaughn Taylor, Arthur Adams, Jack Stauffer

An acclaimed, multi-award-winning production based on Lash's Pulitzer Prize-winning best-seller, with the story of the Roosevelts, from early youth to FDR's death in 1945, told through the recollections of the widowed Eleanor. Chosen Outstanding Special (1975–76 season) in the Emmy Awards ceremony, the production also won Emmys for Daniel Petrie (director), Rosemary Murphy (supporting actress), James Costigan (original teleplay), Paul Lohmann and Edward R. Brown (photography), Joe I. Tompkins (costume design), Del Armstrong and Mike Westmore (makeup), Jan Scott and Anthony Mondello (art director and set decorator), and Michael Kahn (editor). Neither Jane Alexander nor Edward Herrmann, each nominated, won however, nor did Irene Tedrow or Lilia Skala, both nominated for Best Supporting Actress.

0599
THE MACAHANS
1/19/76 An Albert S. Ruddy Production/MGM (2½ hours)

Executive Producer: John Mantley
Producer: Jim Byrnes
Director: Bernard McEveety
Teleplay: Jim Byrnes
Photography: Edward R. Plante
Music: Jerrold Immel
Art Director: Carl Anderson
Editor: Robbe Roberts

Zeb Macahan	JAMES ARNESS
Kate Macahan	EVA MARIE SAINT
Timothy Macahan	RICHARD KILEY
Seth Macahan	BRUCE BOXLEITNER
Laura Macahan	KATHRYN HOLCOMB
Jeb Macahan	WILLIAM KIRBY CULLEN
Jessie Macahan	VICKI SCHRECK
Dutton	GENE EVANS
Vic	VIC MOHICA
Grandpa Macahan	FRANK FERGUSON
Grandma Macahan	ANN DORAN
Jethro	BEN WILSON
Doc Dodd	MEL STEVENS
Chief Bear Dance	RUDY DIAZ
Hale Crowley	JOHN CRAWFORD

Narrated by WILLIAM CONRAD

A buckskin-clad mountain scout helps to move his parents, his brother and sister-in-law and their four children westward in 1860 ahead of the impending war in this sweeping drama based on the film *How the West Was Won*. James Arness returned to acting in this one after twenty years as Matt Dillon in "Gunsmoke," and he later continued in the once-in-a-while series (1977–79), also called *How the West Was Won*.

0600
LOUIS ARMSTRONG—CHICAGO STYLE
1/25/76 Charles Fries Productions (90 min)

Executive Producer: Dick Berg
Producers: Stan Myles, Jr. and Betty L. Myles
Director: Lee Philips
Teleplay: James Lee
Photography: Richard C. Glouner
Music: Benny Carter
Art Director: Perry Ferguson III
Editors: Bud S. Isaacs and Richard Halsey

Louis Armstrong	BEN VEREEN
Red Cleveland	RED BUTTONS
Alma Rae	MARGARET AVERY
Lil Armstrong (Lil Hardin)	JANET MacLACHLAN
Jack Cherney	LEE DeBROUX
Florence Cleveland	KAREN JENSEN
The Man	ALBERT PAULSEN
Charles Rudolph	BILL HENDERSON
Mrs. Thomas	KETTY LESTER
Cummins	STACK PIERCE
Detective	FRANCIS X. SLATTERY
Desk Sergeant	WALLACE ROONEY

and: Jason Wingreen, Victor Arnold, Vincent Merotrano

An incident in the life of jazz great Louis Armstrong when, in 1931, he was booked into a small Chicago night spot, turning down a lucrative offer to move over to a club run by gangsters. His manager is bribed to secretly frame him on a marijuana charge, and he is forced to leave town—ironically (after the film ends) going to Europe where he was to skyrocket to international fame. Ben Vereen made his dramatic acting debut playing the young Satchmo.

0601
WIDOW
1/22/76 Lorimar Productions (2 hours)

Executive Producers: Lee Rich and Philip Capice
Producer: John Furia, Jr.
Director: J. Lee Thompson
Teleplay: Barbara Turner
Based on the novel by Lynn Caine
Photography: Richard Rawlings
Music: Billy Goldenberg
Art Director: Ed Graves
Editor: Bill Mosher

Lynn Caine	MICHAEL LEARNED
Richard	BRADFORD DILLMAN
Martin Caine	FARLEY GRANGER
Violet Brown	CAROL ROSSEN
Vivian	LOUISE SOREL
Harold	ROBERT LANSING
Jon Caine	ERIC OLSON
Buffy Caine	MICHELLE STACY
Carmen	CARMEN MATHEWS
Paula	KATE WOODVILLE
Matty	AMZIE STRICKLAND

A drama about a woman with two children who tries to adjust emotionally after the sudden death of her husband.

0602
DARK VICTORY
2/5/76 Universal (3 hours)*

Executive Producer: Richard Irving
Producer: Jules Irving
Director: Robert Butler
Teleplay: M. Charles Cohen
Based on the 1934 play by George Emerson Brewer, Jr. and Bertram Bloch
Photography: Michael Margulies
Music: Billy Goldenberg
Art Director: William H. Tuntke
Editor: John Dumas

Katherine Merrill	ELIZABETH MONTGOMERY
Dr. Michael Grant	ANTHONY HOPKINS
Dolores Marsh	MICHELE LEE
Eileen	JANET MacLACHLEN
Manny	MICHAEL LERNER
Jeremy	JOHN ELERICK
Dr. Kassiter	HERBERT BERGHOF
Archie	VIC TAYBACK
Sandy	MARIO ROCCUZZO
Veronica	JULIE ROGERS

and: Michael Toma, James Ingersoll, Deborah White, Eric Server, Edgar Daniels, Jack Manning

An updated version of the 1939 Bette Davis movie and the 1967 one with Susan Hayward in this poignant love story of a terminally ill TV producer whose love for her doctor gives her the determination to go on. Billy Goldenberg was Emmy Award-nominated for his musical score.

*Subsequently cut to two hours for its repeat network showing and syndicated runs.

0603
MALLORY: CIRCUMSTANTIAL EVIDENCE
2/8/76 Universal (2 hours)

Producer: William Sackheim
Director: Boris Sagal
Teleplay: Joel Oliansky and Joseph Polizzi
Photography: Russell Metty
Music: James DiPasquale
Art Director: John Corso
Editor: Robert F. Shugrue

Daniel Mallory	RAYMOND BURR
Angelo Rondello	ROBERT LOGGIA
Cliff Wilson	ROGER ROBINSON
Joe Celli	MARK HAMILL
John Shields	PETER MARK RICHMAN
Roberto Ruiz	A MARTINEZ
Tony Garcia	VIC MOHICA
Bob Lattimer	EUGENE ROCHE
Judge Paul Pieter	ALLAN RICH

Farley Granger and Michael Learned in WIDOW (1976)

Stephen McHattie and Michael Brandon in JAMES DEAN (1976)

Richmond	PETER STIRLING
Sandra Wiley	JOYCE EASTON
Ron Wymer	CLIFF EMMICH
George	BILL LUCKING
Cole	STANLEY KAMEL

After many years, first as Perry Mason and then as Robert T. Ironside, Burr starred in this pilot about a prominent lawyer with a tarnished reputation who defends a young man charged with committing homicide in prison.

0604
JAMES DEAN
2/19/76 The Jozak Company (2 hours)

Executive Producers: Gerald I. Isenberg and Gerald Abrams
Producers: William Bast and John Forbes
Director: Robert Butler
Teleplay: William Bast
Photography: Frank Stanley
Music: Billy Goldenberg

Art Director: Perry Ferguson III
Editor: John A. Martinelli

James Dean	STEPHEN McHATTIE
Bill Bast	MICHAEL BRANDON
Chris White	CANDY CLARK
Dizzy Sheridan	MEG FOSTER
Reva Randall	JAYNE MEADOWS
James Whitmore	DANE CLARK

Claire Folger	KATHERINE HELMOND
JoAnne	HEATHER MENZIES
Arlene	LELAND PALMER
Norma	AMY IRVING
Psychiatrist	ROBERT FOXWORTH
Secretary	CHRIS WHITE

An offbeat look at the screen legend by writer William Bast who had roomed with James Dean when both were aspiring actors in the early 1950s.

0605
THE LINDBERGH KIDNAPPING CASE
2/26/76 Columbia Pictures (3 hours)

Executive Producer: David Gerber
Producer/Director: Buzz Kulik
Teleplay: J. P. Miller
Photography: Charles F. Wheeler
Music: Billy Goldenberg
Art Directors: Ross Bellah and Carl Anderson
Editor: Rita Roland

Charles Lindbergh	CLIFF DeYOUNG
Bruno Richard Hauptmann	ANTHONY HOPKINS
Dr. John Francis Condon	JOSEPH COTTEN
Violet Sharpe	DENISE ALEXANDER
Anne Morrow Lindbergh	SIAN-BARBARA ALLEN
Edward J. Reilly	MARTIN BALSAM
Col. H. Norman Schwarzkopf	PETER DONAT
Mr. Anderson	JOHN FINK
Koehler	DEAN JAGGER
Gov. Hal Hoffman	LAURENCE LUCKINBILL
Chief Harry Wolfe	FRANK MARTH
Lt. Jim Finn	TONY ROBERTS
John Curtis	ROBERT SAMSON
David Wilentz	DAVID SPIELBERG
Dr. Schonfeld	JOSEPH STERN
Betty Gow	KATE WOODVILLE
Fred Huisache	KEENAN WYNN
Judge Trenchard	WALTER PIDGEON
Andrew Phelps	BILL QUINN

A dramatization of the 1932 kidnapping of the Lindbergh infant, the search for the abductor, and his capture, trial and execution three years later. Anthony Hopkins won an Emmy for his acting in this movie which itself was nominated as Outstanding Special, as were J.P. Miller (original teleplay), Rita Roland (editor) and Bob Christenson and Denita Cavett (costume design).

0606
GRIFFIN AND PHOENIX
2/27/76 An ABC Circle Film (2 hours)

Executive Producer: Paul Junger Witt
Producer: Tony Thomas
Director: Daryl Duke
Teleplay: John Hill
Photography: Richard C. Glouner
Music: George Aliceson Tipton
Title song written and sung by Paul Williams
Art Director: Bill Malley
Editor: O. Nicholas Brown

Geoffrey Griffin	PETER FALK
Sarah Phoenix	JILL CLAYBURGH
Jean Griffin	DOROTHY TRISTAN
George Griffin	JOHN LEHNE
Old Man	GEORGE CHANDLER
Dr. Glenn	JOHN HARKINS

Peter Falk in GRIFFIN AND PHOENIX (1976)

Professor	MILTON PARSONS
Dr. Thompson	IRWIN CHARONE
Dr. Feinberg	BEN HAMMER
Jody	SALLY KIRKLAND
Randy Griffin	RANDY FAUSTINO
Bob Griffin	STEPHEN ROGERS
Usher	ROD HASSE
Dr. Harding	KEN SANSOM

and: Russell Shannon, Caroline Yablans

Two lonely people, both terminally ill, have a short-lived love affair, sharing a series of adventures in which they live out their childhood dreams. This film was called *Today Is Forever* for its theatrical showings overseas. Richard C. Glouner won an Emmy Award nomination for his cinematography.

0607
YOUNG PIONEERS
3/1/76 An ABC Circle Film (2 hours)

Producer: Ed Friendly
Director: Michael O'Herlihy
Teleplay: Blanche Hanalis
Based on the novels *Young Pioneers* and *Let the Hurricane Roar* by Rose Wilder Lane
Photography: Robert L. Morrison
Music: Laurence Rosenthal
Production Designer: Jan Scott
Editor: Allan LaMastra

David Beaton	ROGER KERN
Molly Beaton	LINDA PURL
Dan Grey	ROBERT HAYS

Nettie Peters	SHELLY JUTTNER
Mr. Peters	ROBERT DONNER
Mr. Swenson	FRANK MARTH
Doyle	BRENDAN DILLON
Mr. Beaton	CHARLES TYNER
Dr. Thorne	JONATHAN KIDD
Clerk	ARNOLD SOBOLOFF
Mrs. Swenson	BERNICE SMITH
Eliza	JANIS FAMISON
Man in Land Office	DENNIS FIMPLE

Teenaged newlyweds use their unbeatable courage and love for each other to tame the Dakota wilderness in the 1870s.

0608
McNAUGHTON'S DAUGHTER
3/4/76 Universal (2 hours)

Executive Producer: David Victor
Producer: David J. O'Connell
Director: Jerry London
Teleplay: Ken Trevey
From a story by David Victor and Ken Trevey
Photography: Sy Hoffberg
Music: David Shire
Art Director: Howard E. Johnson
Editors: John Elias and Richard Watts

Laurel McNaughton	SUSAN CLARK
D. A. Charles Quintero	RICARDO MONTALBAN
Lew Farragut	JAMES CALLAHAN
Ed Hughes	JOHN ELERICK
Cassy Garnett	LOUISE LATHAM
Grace Coventry	VERA MILES
Moses Bellman	RALPH BELLAMY
Colin Pierce	MIKE FARRELL
Randall Jardine	RAMON BIERI
Aprili	TINA ANDREWS
Zareb Parker	ROGER AARON BROWN
Judge	IVOR FRANCIS
Juror	JEFF DONNELL

Carlos Ruiz	RAUL ARROYO
Roy Strickling	CLIFF EMRICH
Jerry Loftus	JOEY ARESCO

and: Kelly Lange, Martin Speer, Phil Diskin, Louise Fitch, Ted Chapman, Dale Ishimoto, Rod Gist, Joe La Due, Charles Wagenheim, Ed Arnold, Ben Frommer, Jack Bender.

A series pilot about a lady deputy district attorney, here assigned the task of trying to pin a murder rap on a "saint," a beloved religious crusader accused of killing her young lover. The series, in fact, never materialized.

0609
ONE OF MY WIVES IS MISSING
3/5/76 Spelling/Goldberg Productions (90 min)

Executive Producers: Aaron Spelling and Leonard Goldberg
Producer: Barney Rosenzweig
Director: Glenn Jordan
Teleplay: Pierre Marton
Based on the play *Trap for a Single Man* by Robert Thomas
Photography: Arch R. Dalzell
Music: Billy Goldenberg
Art Director: Paul Sylos
Editor: Aaron Stell

Murray Levine	JACK KLUGMAN
Elizabeth Corban	ELIZABETH ASHLEY
Daniel Corban	JAMES FRANCISCUS
Father Kelleher	JOEL FABIANI
Mrs. Foster	RUTH McDEVITT
Sidney	MILTON SEIZER
Bert	TONY COSTELLO

A small-town detective faces a baffling case when the missing wife of a wealthy man suddenly reappears but the distraught husband claims that she is not his wife but an imposter.

0610
THE ENTERTAINER
3/10/76 RSO Productions (2 hours)

Producers: Beryl Vertue and Marvin Hamlisch
Associate Producer: Robert T. Skodis
Director: Donald Wrye
Teleplay: Elliott Baker
Based on the play by John Osborne
Photography: James Crabe
Music: Marvin Hamlisch
Songs by Marvin Hamlisch and Robert Joseph
Song "The Only Way to Go" by Marvin Hamlisch and Tim Rice
Musical sequences choreographed by Ron Field
Art Director: Bob MacKichan
Editors: William H. Reynolds and Ralph Winters

Archie Rice	JACK LEMMON
Billy Rice	RAY BOLGER
Phoebe Rice	SADA THOMPSON
Jean	TYNE DALY
Frank	MICHAEL CRISTOFER
Bambi	ANNETTE O'TOOLE
Mr. Pasko	MITCH RYAN
Mrs. Pasko	ALLYN ANN McLERIE
Charlie	DICK O'NEIL
Charleen	LEANNA JOHNSON HEATH
Lilly	RITA O'CONNOR
Bakery Clerk	ALAN DeWITT

A semi-musical adaptation of the stage and screen drama (both of which starred Laurence Olivier) about a second-rate vaudevillian, still struggling at middle age for success and stardom. The setting is changed from the original British to an American seaside resort and has Emmy Award-nominated performances by Lemmon, Bolger and Sada Thompson, with Elliott Baker's adaptation and James Crabe's cinematography also cited. For Lemmon, who began acting on television in its infancy, this marked his first dramatic TV work in nearly seventeen years. It also marked Ray

Jill Clayburgh and Peter Falk in GRIFFIN AND PHOENIX (1976)

Bolger's television movie debut and reunited him with Allyn Ann McLerie, his co-star both on stage and screen in *Where's Charley?*

0611
FAREWELL TO MANZANAR
3/11/76 Korty Films, Inc./Universal (2 hrs, 10 min)

Executive Producer: George J. Santoro
Producer/Director: John Korty
Teleplay: Jeanne Wakatsuki Houston, James D. Houston and John Korty
Based on the book by Jeanne Wakatsuki Houston and James D. Houston
Photography: Hiro Narita
Music: Paul Chihara
Production Designer: Robert Kinoshita
Editor: Eric Albertson

Ko Wakatsuki	YUKI SHIMODA
Misa/Jeanne Wakatsuki	NOBU McCARTHY
Young Jeanne	DORI TAKESHITA
Koro	AKEMI KIKUMURA
Teddy Wakatsuki	CLYDE KASATU
Fukimoto	MAKO
Zenahiro	PAT MORITA
Richard Wakatsuki	JAMES SAITO
Alice	MOMO YASHIMA
Lois	GRETCHEN CORBETT
Captain Curtis	KIP NIVEN
Lou Frizzell	LOU FRIZZELL
Narrator	GRETA CHI

This true story examines the bitterness and sorrow of the internment of Japanese Americans during World War II. Emmy Award nominations went to Jeanne Wakatsuki Houston, James D. Houston and John Korty for the teleplay and to Hiro Narita for his cinematography.

0612
JAMES A. MICHENER'S DYNASTY
3/13/76 David Paradine Television, Inc. (2 hours)

Executive Producer: David Frost
Producer: Buck Houghton
Director: Lee Philips
Teleplay: Sidney Carroll
From a story by James Michener
Creative Consultant: James Michener
Photography: Henry Cronjager
Music: Gil Melle
Art Director: Perry Ferguson II
Editor: George Jay Nicholson

Jennifer Blackwood	SARAH MILES
Matt Blackwood	STACY KEACH
John Blackwood	HARRIS YULIN
Mark Blackwood	HARRISON FORD
Amanda Blackwood	AMY IRVING
Creed Vauclose	GRANVILLE VAN DUSEN
Sam Adams	CHARLES WELDON
Carver Blackwood	GERRIT GRAHAM
Young Sam	STANLEY CLAY
Harry Blackwood	TONY SWARTZ
Benjamin McCullum	JOHN CARTER
Lucinda	STEPHANIE FAULKNER
Majors	RAYFORD BARNES
Margaret McCullum	SARI PRICE
Ernst Schmidt	NORBERT SCHILLER
Dr. Klauber	IAN WOLFE
McHenry	GUY RAYMOND
Ross	DON EITNER
Alfred Brinkerhoff	JAMES HOUGHTON

and: J. Jay Saunders, Brent Jones, William Challee, Francis DeSales, Mark Saegers, Wonderful Smith, Gary Lee Cooper, Michelle Stacy, Dennis Larson, Peter Haas, Brian Busta, Debbie Fresh

The saga of a pioneer family—husband, wife and brother-in-law—torn by jealousy, deception and rivalry in love and business as they seek their fortune on the Ohio frontier. The story, originally entitled *The Americans* and covering a thirty-five-year period starting in the 1820s, looks to be a trial run for Michener's subsequent American epic, *Centennial.*

0613
TIME TRAVELERS
3/19/76 An Irwin Allen Production/20th Century-Fox (90 min)

Producer: Irwin Allen
Director: Alex Singer
Teleplay: Jackson Gillis
From a story by Irwin Allen and Rod Serling
Photography: Fred Jackman
Music: Morton Stevens
Art Director: Eugene Lourie
Editor: Bill Brame

Dr. Clint Earnshaw	SAM GROOM
Jeff Adams	TOM HALLICK
Dr. Joshua P. Henderson	RICHARD BASEHART
Jane Henderson	TRISH STEWART
Dr. Helen Sanders	FRANCINE YORK
Dr. Cummings	BOOTH COLMAN
Dr. Stafford	WALTER BURKE
Sharkey	DORT CLARK
Irish Girl	KATHLEEN BRACKEN
Betty	VICTORIA MEYERINK
Chief Williams	BAYNES BARRON
News Vendor	ALBERT COLE
Police Sergeant	RICHARD WEBB

A pilot movie in which Irwin Allen, recycling his earlier hit series *The Time Tunnel*, has a young doctor and a research scientist, in search of a cure for a deadly epidemic, being whisked back through time to Chicago in 1871 on the eve of the great Chicago fire hoping to find the physician who then had stumbled on a cure but whose records were destroyed in the conflagration. Footage from 20th Century-Fox's spectacular *In Old Chicago* (1938) was incorporated into this movie, tinted in sepia to recreate the fire sequences.

0614
CHARLIE'S ANGELS
3/21/76 Spelling/Goldberg Productions (90 min)

Executive Producers: Aaron Spelling and Leonard Goldberg
Producers: Ivan Goff and Ben Roberts
Associate Producer: Shelley Hull
Director: John Llewellyn Moxey
Teleplay: Ivan Goff and Ben Roberts
Photography: Arch R. Dalzell
Music: Jack Elliott and Allyn Ferguson
Art Director: Paul Sylos
Editor: Allan Jacobs

Sabrina	KATE JACKSON
Jill Monroe	FARRAH FAWCETT-MAJORS
Kelly	JACLYN SMITH
John Bosley	DAVID DOYLE
Scott Woodville	DAVID OGDEN STIERS
Rachel LeMaire	DIANA MULDAUR
Beau Creel	BO HOPKINS
Henry Bancroft	JOHN LEHNE
Aram Kolegian	TOMMY LEE JONES
Wilder	GRANT OWENS
Hotel Clerk	KEN SANSOM
Miguel	DANIEL NUNEZ
Hicks	RON STEIN
Bathing Beauty	COLETTE BERTRAND
Sheriff Hopkins	RUSS GRIEVE

and the voice of John Forsythe as Charlie

This was the pilot for the hit TV series that began in September 1976, with three attractive females who work for a very private investigator, a man they have never seen or met, and must use their wiles to con the manager of a vineyard into revealing the whereabouts of the body of his wealthy boss whom he killed years earlier.

0615
MOST WANTED
3/21/76 Quinn Martin Productions (90 min)

Executive Producer: Quinn Martin
Producer: John Wilder
Director: Walter Grauman
Teleplay: Laurence Heath
Photography: Jack Swain
Music: Pat Williams
Art Director: Richard Y. Haman
Editor: Jerry Young

Lincoln Evers	ROBERT STACK
Charlie Benson	SHELLY NOVACK
Lee Herrick	LESLIE CHARLESON
Tom Roybo	TOM SELLECK
Melissa	SHEREE NORTH
Sister Beth	KITTY WINN
Mayor Stoddard	PERCY RODRIGUES
Phil Benedict	JACK KEHOE
Reverend Benson	STEPHEN McNALLY
Jean Evers	MARJ DUSAY
Harkness	ROGER PERRY
Goldberg	FRED SADOFF

In this pilot for the short-lived Robert Stack series, a specialized police unit, made up of a dedicated homicide detective, a lady psychologist, an undercover cop and an electronic gadgetry expert, tracks down the merciless killer whose victims have included Catholic nuns.

0616
BRINK'S: THE GREAT ROBBERY
3/26/76 Quinn Martin Productions/Warner Bros. (2 hours)

Executive Producer: Quinn Martin
Producer: Philip Saltzman
Director: Marvin Chomsky
Teleplay: Robert W. Lenski
Photography: Jacques R. Marquette
Music: Richard Markowitz
Art Director: Paul Haman
Editor: Jerry Young

Paul Jackson	CARL BETZ
Agent Donald Nash	STEPHEN COLLINS
Ernie Heideman	BURR DeBENNING
Mario Russo	MICHAEL GAZZO
Danny Conforti	CLIFF GORMAN
James McNally	DARREN McGAVIN
Julius Mareno	ART METRANO
Agent Norman Houston	LESLIE NIELSEN
Maggie Hefner	JENNY O'HARA
Ted Flynn	BERT REMSEN
Dennis Fisher	JERRY DOUGLAS
Det. Russ Shannon	LAURENCE HADDON
Les Hayes	PHILIP KENNEALLY
Jerry Carter	BYRON MABE
Thomas Preston	BARNEY PHILLIPS
Neighbor Lady	AMZIE STRICKLAND

Narrated by MARVIN MILLER

and: Frank Borone, David Bradon, Hank Brandt, Dort Clark, Nick Ferris, Mary LaRoche, Terry Lumley, Stuart Nisbet, John Perak, Artie Spain

The third film in Quinn Martin's productions from the annals of the FBI recreates the infamous January 17, 1950 Brink's Incorporated robbery in Boston involving the theft of $2,750,000 and the Bureau's dogged pursuit of the perpetrators, whose names were changed for this movie in the traditional protection of their privacy.

0617
HELTER SKELTER
4/1–2/76 Lorimar Productions (4 hours)

Executive Producers: Lee Rich and Philip Capice
Producer/Director: Tom Gries
Based on the book by Vincent Bugliosi with Curt Gentry
Photography: Jules Brenner
Teleplay: J P Miller
Music: Billy Goldenberg
Art Director: Phil Barber
Editors: Byron "Buzz" Brandt and Bud S. Isaacs

Vincent Bugliosi	GEORGE DiCENZO
Charles Manson	STEVE RAILSBACK
Susan Atkins	NANCY WOLFE
Linda Kasabian	MARILYN BURNS
Patricia Krenwinkel	CHRISTINA HART
Leslie Van Houten	CATHEY PAINE
Aaron Stovitz	ALAN OPPENHEIMER
Danny DeCarlo	RUDY RAMOS
Ronnie Howard	SONDRA BLAKE
Rosner	GEORGE GARRO
Lt. Sam Brenner	VIC WERBER
Everett Scoville	HOWARD CAINE
Paul Watkins	JASON RONARD
Judge Charles Older	SKIP HOMEIER
Sgt. Phil Cohen	MARC ALAIMO
Charles "Tex" Watson	BILL DURKIN
Sgt. Manuel Gris	PHILLIP R. ALLEN
Leno LaBianca	AL CHECCO

and: David Clennon, James E. Broadhead, Anne Newman Mantee, Joyce Easton, Jon Gries, Edward Bell, Roy Jenson, Paul Mantee, Ray Middleton, Anthony Herrera, Robert Hoy, Stanley Ralph Ross, Bart Burns, Jerry Dunphy, George Putnam, Linden Chiles, Carol Ita White, Richard Venture, Bert Conway, Larry Pennel, Josh Albee, Steve Gries, Bill Sorrells, Robert Ito, Barbara Mallory

An explosive dramatization of the best-seller about the Charles Manson "family" and the trial of the Tate-LaBianca murderers. One of the biggest made-for-TV movie productions to its time, with 115 speaking parts, and the highest-rated television film of all during the two nights it took to unfold. Emmy Award nominations went to director Tom Gries, to composer Billy Goldenberg and to editors Byron "Buzz" Brandt and Bud S. Isaacs.

0618
THE MANHUNTER
4/3/76 Universal (2 hours)

Producer: Ron Roth
Director: Don Taylor
Teleplay: Meyer Dolinsky
Based on a novel by Wade Miller
Photography: Benjamin H. Kline
Music: Benny Carter
Art Director: Henry Larrecq
Editor: Howard G. Epstein

Mara Bocock	SANDRA DEE
David Farrow	ROY THINNES
Rafe Augustine	ALBERT SALMI
Carl Auscher	SORRELL BOOKE
Walter Sinclair	DAVID BRIAN
Pa Bocock	ROYAL DANO
Ma Bocock	MADELEINE SHERWOOD
Clel Bocock	WILLIAM SMITH
Teresa Taylor	MADLYN RHUE
Himself	AL HIRT
Prof. Mike Mellick	PITT HERBERT
Police Sergeant	LEW BROWN
Stephen Sinclair	RICHARD VAN FLEET
Fronie	ERIC LANEUVILLE

and: Joe Pepi, Jeff Burton, Mel Berger, William Fawcett, Foster Brooks, Sharon Johnson

A big-game hunter is hired to track down a bank robbery suspect in the Louisiana swamp country and becomes involved with the wife of his quarry. Filmed in 1968, this film first saw the light of day on British television in 1972 and finally was given a belated American premiere more than four years later.

0619
THE KILLER WHO WOULDN'T DIE
4/4/76 Paramount (2 hours)

Producers: Ivan Goff and Ben Roberts
Director: William Hale
Teleplay: Cliff Gould
From a story by Cliff Gould, Ivan Goff and Ben Roberts
Photography: Gert Anderson
Music: Georges Garvarentz
Art Director: Joseph R. Jennings
Editor: Neil MacDonald

Kirk Ohanian	MIKE CONNORS
Anne Roland	SAMANTHA EGGAR
Ara	GREGOIRE ASLAN
Heather	MARIETTE HARTLEY
Commissioner Moore	PATRICK O'NEAL
Keller	CLU GULAGER
David Lao	JAMES SHIGETA
McDougall	ROBERT COLBERT
Commissioner Wharton	ROBERT HOOKS
Flo	LUCILLE BENSON
Soong	PHILIP AHN
Doug	CHRISTOPHER GARDNER
Steve	TONY BECKER
Chew	KWAN HI LIM
Jun	LESLIE HOWARD FONG, JR.

A former cop who now operates a charter boat service following the unsolved bombing murder of his wife is called on to look into the killing of a close friend, an undercover agent, and ends up in Hawaii entangled in a network of intrigue and espionage. This pilot to an unsold series called "Ohanian" (which happens to be Mike Connors' real last name) returned Connors to the TV screen following the demise of his long-running "Mannix."

0620
A MATTER OF WIFE . . . AND DEATH
4/10/76 Columbia Pictures (90 min)

Producer: Robert M. Weitman
Director: Marvin J. Chomsky
Teleplay: Don Ingalls
Photography: Emmett Bergholz
Music: Richard Shores
Art Director: Robert Peterson
Editor: David Wages

Shamus	ROD TAYLOR
Lt. Vince Promuto	JOE SANTOS
Blinky	EDDIE FIRESTONE
Snell	LUKE ASKEW
Joe Ruby	JOHN COLICOS
Paulie Baker	TOM DRAKE
Helen Baker	ANITA GILLETTE
Bruno	CHARLES PICERNI
Carol	ANNE ARCHER
Springy	LARRY BLOCK
Heavy	DICK BUTKUS
Angie	MARC ALAIMO
Dottore	CESARE DANOVA
Zelda	LYNDA CARTER

and: Gene LeBell, Dick Butler, Gary Cashdollar, Leonard D'John, Walter Wonderman, Lloyd McLinn, A. G. Vitanza, Stephanie Faulkner, Bobby Bavin, Tony Ballen, Abe Alvarez, Don Ray Hall

A free-wheeling private eye attempts to track down the killers of a small-time hood and finds himself neck-deep in a big-time gambling operation. This pilot to a prospective series called "Shamus" was an attempt to duplicate the success of the theatrical feature that was a big hit for Burt Reynolds.

0621
CONSPIRACY OF TERROR
4/10/76 Lorimar Productions (90 min)

Executive Producer: Lee Rich
Producer: Charles FitzSimmons
Director: John Llewellyn Moxey
Teleplay: Howard Rodman
Based on the book by David Delman
Photography: Fred Koenekamp
Music: Neal Hefti
Art Director: Ed Graves
Editor: Dick Wormell

Jacob Horowitz	MICHAEL CONSTANTINE
Helen Horowitz	BARBARA RHOADES
Barbara Warnall	MARICLARE COSTELLO
Fred Warnall	ROGER PERRY
Mr. Dale	LOGAN RAMSEY
Mr. Slate	JON LORMER
Arthur Horowitz	DAVID OPATOSHU
David Horowitz	JED ALLEN
Leslie Horowitz	ARLENE MARTEL
Lieutenant Rossos	NORMAN BURTON
Roger Gordon	ERIC OLSON
Rabbi	STEWART MOSS

and: Ken Sansom, Paul Bryar, Beverly Bremers, Paul Smith, Murray McLeod, Bruce Kirby, Judi Stein, Charles Cooper, John Finnegan, Bob Golden, Anthony Aiello, Shelly Morrison

A husband and wife detective team investigates satanism in suburbia when not squabbling over visits to his parents who never forgave him for marrying out of the faith. This pilot movie never proceeded to series form.

0622
JUDGE HORTON AND THE SCOTTSBORO BOYS
4/22/76 Tomorrow Entertainment Productions (2 hours)

Executive Producer: Thomas W. Moore
Producer: Paul Leaf
Director: Fielder Cook
Teleplay: John McGreevey
Based on the book *Scottsboro—A Tragedy of the American South* by Dan T. Carter
Photography: Mario Tosi
Assistant Director: Dwight Williams

Art Director: Frank Smith
Editor: Eric Albertson

Judge James Edwin Horton	ARTHUR HILL
Mrs. Horton	VERA MILES
Sam Liebowitz	LEWIS J. STADLEN
D. A. Tom Knight	KEN KERCHEVAL
Victoria Price	ELLEN BARBER
Ruby Bates	SUSAN LEDERER
Lester Carter	TOM LIGON
Haywood Patterson	DAVID HARRIS
Andy Wright	RONY CLANTON
Willie Roberson	WALLACE THOMPSON
Olen Montgomery	GREGORY WYATT
Leroy Wright	LARRY BUTTS
Ramsey	PAUL BENJAMIN
Captain Burleson	BARRY SNIDER
Joe Brodsky	ROBERT FIELDS
Orville Gilley	BRUCE WATSON

A dramatization of the headline-making case in the 1930s of the controversial rape trial involving nine young black men and two white women, and of the embattled southern judge whose initial decision to free them made him a pariah in the community and ruined his career. The nine ultimately were convicted but the case subsequently was overturned by the U.S. Supreme Court. Horton died in 1967, the last of the Scottsboro boys in 1978. Fielder Cook (director) and John McGreevey (writer) each won an Emmy Award nomination for the film.

0623
SERPICO: THE DEADLY GAME
4/24/76 Dino DeLaurentiis Productions/Paramount (2 hours)

Producer: Emmet G. Lavery, Jr.
Associate Producer: Arthur E. McLaird
Director: Robert Collins
Teleplay: Robert Collins
Based on the book by Peter Maas
Photography: Donald M. Morgan
Music: Elmer Bernstein
Art Director: Frank Smith
Editor: Patrick Kennedy

Frank Serpico	DAVID BIRNEY
The Professor	ALLEN GARFIELD
Alec Rosen	BURT YOUNG
Sullivan	TOM ATKINS
Carol	LANE BRADBURY
Kim	CHRISTINE JONES
Mr. Serpico	WILL KULUVA
David Doyle	WALTER McGINN
Pasquale	MARIO ROCCUZZO
Goldman	SYDNEY LASSICK
Joe Simone	ANTHONY CHARNOTA
Carothers	CARL LEE
Atkins	RICHARD C. ADAMS
Polo	MADISON ARNOLD

This was the pilot for the 1976–77 "Serpico" series with David Birney, in the role originated on the screen by Al Pacino, as the New York undercover cop battling corruption in and out of the department.

0624
LAW OF THE LAND
4/29/76 Quinn Martin Productions (2 hours)

Executive Producer: Quinn Martin
Producer: John Wilder
Director: Virgil W. Vogel
Teleplay: John Wilder and Sam Rolfe
Photography: William Spencer
Music: John Parker
Art Director: Albert Heschong
Editor: Marston Fay

Sheriff Pat Lambrose	JIM DAVIS
Quirt	DON JOHNSON
Tom Condor	CAL BELLINI
Brad Jensen	NICHOLAS HAMMOND
Selina Jensen	DARLEEN CARR
Jane Adams	BARBARA PARKINS
Jacob	MOSES GUNN
Travis Carrington	ANDREW PRINE
Andy Hill	GLENN CORBETT
Dudley	CHARLES MARTIN SMITH
Rev. Mr. Endicott	DANA ELCAR
E. J. Barnes	WARD COSTELLO
Dwight Canaway	PAUL STEVENS

and: Barney Phillips, Patti Jerome, Regis J. Cordic

Originally called *The Deputies,* this pilot movie for a prospective series (referred to as "The Rookies" on horseback) follows a frontier lawman and his young deputies in their frantic search for a psychopath with a vendetta against prostitutes.

0625
TWIN DETECTIVES
5/1/76 Charles Fries Productions (90 min)

Executive Producer: Charles Fries
Producer: Everett Chambers
Director: Robert Day
Teleplay: Robert Specht
From a story by Robert Carrington, Robert Specht and Everett Chambers
Photography: Earl Rath
Music: Tom Scott
Songs "Spinning the Wheel" and "Hard on Me" sung by The Hudson Brothers
Art Director: Michael Bauch
Editor: James Potter

Tony Thomas	JIM HAGER
Shep Thomas	JON HAGER
Billy Jo Haskins	LILLIAN GISH
Leonard Rainier	PATRICK O'NEAL
Ben Sampson	MICHAEL CONSTANTINE
Cartwright	OTIS YOUNG
Sheila Rainier	BARBARA RHOADES
Marvin Telford	DAVID WHITE
Dr. Hudson	FRED BIER
Nancy Pendleton	LYNDA DAY GEORGE
Jennie	RANDY OAKES
Lt. Martinez	JAMES VICTOR
Hutchins	FRANK LONDON
Bartender	BILLY BARTY

Identical twin detectives use their look-alike images to appear to be in two places at the same time in an attempt to expose a psychic con group, but become involved in a deadly game when a beautiful medium turns up murdered. This unsuccessful pilot for a series with The Hager Twins, country singers who were regulars on TV's "Hee Haw," marked the TV movie debut for veteran actress Lillian Gish, whose lengthy career spanned the entire history of motion pictures to that time.

0626
FUTURE COP
5/1/76 Paramount (90 min)

Executive Producer: Gary Damsker
Producer: Anthony Wilson
Director: Jud Taylor
Teleplay: Anthony Wilson
Photography: Terry K. Meade
Music: Billy Goldenberg
Art Director: Jack DeShields
Editors: Ronald J. Fagan and Steven C. Brown

Cleaver	ERNEST BORGNINE
Haven	MICHAEL SHANNON
Bundy	JOHN AMOS
Forman	JOHN LARCH
Klausmeier	HERBERT NELSON
Avery	RONNIE CLAIR EDWARDS
Paterno	JAMES LUISI
Dorfman	STEPHEN PEARLMAN
Young Rookie	JAMES DAUGHTON
Grandmother	SHIRLEY O'HARA

An old-line street cop is assigned a rookie partner who happens to be an android programmed in a lab. The subsequent short-lived 1977 series also starred Borgnine, Shannon and Amos, as did another TV movie, *Cops and Robin* (1978), which recycled what the producers felt continued to be a viable concept.

0627
THE KEEGANS
5/3/76 Universal (90 min)

Producer: George Eckstein
Director: John Badham
Teleplay: Dean Riesner
Photography: Stevan Larner
Music: Paul Chihara
Art Director: Ira Diamond
Editor: Jamie Caylor

Larry Keegan	ADAM ROARKE
Pat Keegan	SPENCER MILLIGAN
Brandy Keegan	HEATHER MENZIES
Tim Keegan	TOM CLANCY
Mary Keegan	JOAN LESLIE
Rudi Portinari	PAUL SHENAR
Helen Hunter McVey	PRISCILLA POINTER
Tracy McVey	JANIT BALDWIN
Penny Voorhees Keegan	PENELOPE WINDUST
Lt. Marco Ciardi	JUDD HIRSCH
Vinnie Cavell	ROBERT YURO
Angie Carechal	SMITH EVANS
Martha Carechal	ANNA NAVARRO
Don Guido Carechal	GEORGE SKAFF
Bill Richardson	MICHAEL McGUIRE
Slim Montana	JAMES LOUIS WATKINS

An investigative magazine reporter sets out to prove the innocence of his brother, a professional football player who is accused of murdering his sister's brutal attacker, found to be tied in with the syndicate.

0628
BANJO HACKETT: ROAMIN' FREE
5/3/76 Bruce Lansbury Productions/Columbia Pictures (2 hours)

Producer: Bruce Lansbury
Associate Producer: Mel Swope
Director: Andrew V. McLaglen
Teleplay: Ken Trevey
Photography: Al Francis
Music: Morton Stevens
Art Directors: Ross Bellah and Carl Braunger
Editors: Dann Cahn and David Wages

Banjo Hackett	DON MEREDITH
Jubal Winner	IKE EISENMANN
Mollie	JENNIFER WARREN
Sam Ivory	CHUCK CONNORS
Tip Conaker	DANIEL O'HERLIHY
Judge Janeway	JEFF COREY
Lady Jane Gray	GLORIA DeHAVEN
Sheriff Tadlock	L. Q. JONES

Jethro Swain	JAN MURRAY
Flora Dobbs	ANNE FRANCIS
Lijah Tuttle	SLIM PICKENS
Elmore Mintore	DAVID YOUNG
Luke Mintore	RICHARD YOUNG
Blacksmith	STAN HAZE

An amiable Western about an itinerant horse trader who travels the frontier in 1880 with his orphaned nine-year-old nephew in quest of the boy's prize Arabian mare, stolen by a ruthless bounty hunter. This pilot project never made it to series form.

0629
LAW AND ORDER
5/6/76 Paramount (3 hours)*

Producer: E. Jack Neuman
Director: Marvin J. Chomsky
Teleplay: E. Jack Neuman
Based on the novel by Dorothy Uhnak
Photography: Jacques R. Marquette
Music: Richard Hazard
Art Director: Robert Smith
Editors: Donald R. Rode and Gerald J. Wilson

Dep. Chief Brian O'Malley	DARREN McGAVIN
Johnny Morrison	KEIR DULLEA
Aaron Levine	ROBERT REED
Inspector Ed Shea	JAMES OLSON
Karen Day	SUZANNE PLESHETTE
Rita Wusinski	TERI GARR
Lieutenant Lenihan	BIFF McGUIRE
Mary	JEANETTE NOLAN
Sgt. Brian O'Malley, Sr.	SCOTT BRADY
Pat Crowley	WILL GEER
Patrick O'Malley	ART HINDLE
Arthur Pollack	ALLAN ARBUS
Mary-Ellen Crowley	WHITNEY BLAKE
Pete Caputo	JAMES WHITMORE, JR.
Mrs. Brian O'Malley, Sr.	LUREEN TUTTLE
Captain Toomey	JAMES FLAVIN

and Paul Jenkins, Robert Hegyes, Beverly Hope Atkinson, Brad Dexter, Redmond Gleeson, Jack Knight, Patrick O'Moore, Frank Ramirez, Marion Collier, Fredd Wayne, Paul Lichtman, Don Priest, Harry Basch

Three generations of New York City cops are the focal point of this saga revolving primarily around the deputy chief of public affairs caught up in the politics and intrigue of the department, the discovery that his father had been on the take, and the news that his youngest son is having second thoughts about carrying on the family tradition.

*Subsequently edited to two hours for syndicated showings.

0630
BRENDA STARR
5/8/76 David L. Wolper Productions (90 min)

Executive Producer: Paul Mason
Producer: Bob Larson
Director: Mel Stuart
Teleplay: George Kirgo
From a story by Ira Barmak and George Kirgo
Based on the syndicated comic strip by Dale Messick
Photography: Ted Voigtlander
Music: Lalo Schifrin
Art Director: Art Tunkle
Editor: Jack Kampschroer

Brenda Starr	JILL ST. JOHN
Roger Randall	JED ALLAN
A. J. Livwright	SORRELL BOOKE
Hank O'Hare	TABI COOPER

Lance O'Toole	VICTOR BUONO
Carlos Vegas	JOEL FABIANI
Luisa Santamaria	BARBARA LUNA
Kentucky Smith	MARCIA STRASSMAN
Lassiter	TORIN THATCHER
Dax Leander	ART ROBERTS
Tommy	ROY APPLEGATE

The intrepid comic strip newspaperwoman follows a hot tip on a billionaire recluse and finds herself involved in voodoo, millions in extortion money, and strange doings in the jungles of Brazil.

0631
KISS ME, KILL ME
5/8/76 Columbia Pictures (90 min)

Executive Producer: Stanley Kallis
Associate Producer: Jay Daniel
Director: Michael O'Herlihy
Teleplay: Robert E. Thompson
Photography: Meredith Nicholson
Music: Richard Markowitz
Art Directors: Ross Bellah and Robert Peterson
Editor: Arthur D. Hilton

Stella Stafford	STELLA STEVENS
Dan Hodges	MICHAEL ANDERSON, JR.
Captain Logan	DABNEY COLEMAN
Harry Gant	CLAUDE AKINS
Douglas Lane	BRUCE BOXLEITNER
Lieutenant Dagget	ALAN FUDGE
Sergeant Hovak	BRUCE GLOVER
James Deukmajian	MORGAN PAULL
Maureen Coyle	TISHA STERLING
Leonard Hicks	CHARLES WELDON
Jimmy (Morgue Attendant)	PAT O'BRIEN
Edward Fuller	ROBERT VAUGHN

A pilot movie about a lady investigator for the district attorney's office and her relentless search for the killer of a young teacher who appeared to have been a pillar of the community.

0632
GEMINI MAN
5/10/76 Universal (2 hours)
(subsequently cut to 90 minutes and retitled *Code Name: Minus One*)

Executive Producer: Harve Bennett
Producer: Robert F. O'Neill
Director: Alan Levi
Teleplay: Leslie Stevens
Adapted from the novel *The Invisible Man* by H. G. Wells
Photography: Enzo A. Martinelli
Music: Billy Goldenberg
Art Director: David Marshall
Editor: Robert F. Shugrue

Sam Casey	BEN MURPHY
Dr. Abby Lawrence	KATHERINE CRAWFORD
Leonard Driscoll	RICHARD DYSART
Dr. Harold Schuyler	DANA ELCAR
Charles Edward Royce	PAUL SHENAR
Vince Rogers	QUINN REDEKER
Captain Ballard	H. M. WYNANT
Captain Whelan	LEN WAYLAND
Receptionist	CHERYL MILLER

and: Michael Lane, Gregory Walcott, Austin Stoker, Jim Raymond, Richard Kennedy, Robert Forward

In this recycling of the unsuccessful TV series "The Invisible Man," a brash special agent finds himself capable of invisibility from the after-effects of an underwater explosion during a government salvage oper-

ation and uses his new-found "talent" to prove the incident was sabotage. Unfortunately, his invisibility is a transient affliction, and he must do his out-of-sight undercover work in a specified time. This pilot too spawned a brief series during the 1976–77 season.

0633
THE QUEST
5/13/76 David Gerber Productions/Columbia Pictures (2 hours)

Executive Producer: David Gerber
Associate Producer: Marvin Miller
Producer: Christopher Morgan
Director: Lee H. Katzin
Teleplay: Tracy Keenan Wynn
Photography: Robert L. Morrison
Music: Richard Shores
Art Director: Carl Anderson
Editor: Ken Zemke

Quentin Baudine	TIM MATHESON
Morgan Baudine/Two Persons	KURT RUSSELL
Tank Logan	BRIAN KEITH
H. H. Small	KEENAN WYNN
Earl	WILL HUTCHINS
Shea	NEVILLE BRAND
Shadrack Peltzer	CAMERON MITCHELL
Sheriff Moses	MORGAN WOODWARD
China	IRENE YAH-LING SUN
Blanchard	ART LUND
Young Gunslinger	MARK LAMBERT
Blacksmith	GREGORY WALCOTT
Old Indian	IRON EYES CODY
Luke	LUKE ASKEW

Two brothers search the western frontier for their sister who was taken away as a child and is living with Indians in this pilot for the short-lived series (1976–77) that is more than faintly reminiscent of the story line of John Ford's *The Searchers* (1956). Adding some distinction to this movie are an offbeat horse/camel race and the performance of Brian Keith as a dissolute old timer, a crippled ex-gunman on the run from just about every lawman in the West.

0634
RETURN TO EARTH
5/14/76 A King-Hitzig Production (90 min)

Executive Producers: Alan King and Rupert Hitzig
Producer/Director: Jud Taylor
Teleplay: George Malko
Based on the book by Edwin E. "Buzz" Aldrin, Jr. and Wayne Warga
Photography: Frank Stanley
Music: Billy Goldenberg
Editor: Ronald J. Fagan

Col. Edwin E. "Buzz" Aldrin, Jr.	CLIFF ROBERTSON
Joan Aldrin	SHIRLEY KNIGHT
Dr. Sam Mayhill	CHARLES CIOFFI
Col. Edwin E. Aldrin	RALPH BELLAMY
Marianne	STEFANIE POWERS
Andy Aldrin	KRAIG METZINGER
Jan Aldrin	ALEXANDRA TAYLOR
Mike Aldrin	TONY MARKS
Dr. Hotfield	STEVE PEARLMAN
Al Davis	STEFAN GIERASCH

The true story of Apollo 11 astronaut Buzz Aldrin who, two years after his historic moon landing in 1969, had a breakdown, was hospitalized for psychiatric treatment, and subsequently lost his wife and children.

0635
HIGH RISK
5/15/76 Danny Thomas Productions/MGM
(90 min)

Executive Producer: Paul Junger Witt
Producer: Robert E. Relyea
Associate Producer: Tony Thomas
Director: Sam O'Steen
Teleplay: Robert Carrington
Photography: Matthew F. Leonetti
Music: Billy Goldenberg
Art Director: Jan van Tamelen
Editor: Robbe Roberts

Sebastian	VICTOR BUONO
Guthrie	JOSEPH SIROLA
Walker-T	DON STROUD
Sandra	JOANNA KARA CAMERON
Daisy	RONNE TROUP
Erik	WOLF ROTH
Ambassador Henriques	RENE ENRIQUEZ
Quincey	JOHN FINK
Aide	GEORGE SKAFF
Butler	WILLIAM BECKLEY

A light-hearted tale of derring-do as six former circus performers engage in a caper to carry off a priceless artifact from a Washington, D.C. embassy in broad daylight. This was an unsuccessful series pilot.

0636
PANACHE
5/15/76 Warner Bros. (90 min)

Executive Producer: E. Duke Vincent
Producer: Robert E. Relyea
Director: Gary Nelson
Teleplay: E. Duke Vincent
Photography: Donald M. Morgan
Music: Frank DeVol
Art Director: Fernando Carrere
Editor: Les Green

Panache	RENE AUBERJONOIS
Donat	DAVID HEALY
Alain	CHARLES FRANK
Rochefort	CHARLES SEIBERT
Treville	JOHN DOUCETTE
Anne	AMY IRVING
Louis	HARVEY SOLIN
Cardinal Richelieu	JOSEPH RUSKIN
M. Durant and Pere Joseph	LIAM DUNN
Laval	PEGGY WALTON
Horseman	MICHAEL O'KEEFE
Chevreuse	MARJORIE BATTLES
Montvallier	PAUL JENKINS
Lisa	LISA EILBACHER
Duchess Montvallier	JUDITH BROWN
First Guard	ROBERT KARVELAS

A stylish comedy swashbuckler mixing romance, masterful swordplay, political treachery, and twentieth-century pratfalls in seventeenth-century France—obviously inspired by the success of Richard Lester's versions of *The Three Musketeers* and *The Four Musketeers*. This film, which lives up to its title, was the pilot for an unrealized series.

0637
F. SCOTT FITZGERALD IN HOLLYWOOD
5/16/76 A Titus Production (2 hours)

Executive Producer: Herbert Brodkin
Producer: Robert Berger
Director: Anthony Page
Teleplay: James Costigan
Consultant: Sheilah Graham
Photography: James Crabe
Music: Morton Gould
Art Director: Jack DeGovia
Editor: Sidney Katz

F. Scott Fitzgerald	JASON MILLER
Zelda Fitzgerald	TUESDAY WELD
Sheilah Graham	JULIA FOSTER
Dorothy Parker	DOLORES SUTTON
The Starlet	SUSANNE BENTON
Marvin Margulies	MICHAEL LERNER
Alan Campbell	TOM LIGON
Rupert Wahler	JOHN RANDOLPH
Edwin Knopf	TOM ROSQUI
Helen (The Hostess)	AUDREY CHRISTIE
The Maid	HILDA HAYNES
Lucius Krieger	PAUL LAMBERT
Detmar	JOSEPH STERN
"Schwab's" Waitress	JACQUE LYNN COLTON
Zelda's Nurse	NORMA CONNOLLY
Mrs. Taft	SARAH CUNNINGHAM
Lenny Schoenfeld	JAMES WOODS

A drama dealing with the famed novelist's two markedly contrasting stays in the film capital: first in 1927, at the height of his popularity with the widespread acclaim for *The Great Gatsby*, when he and Zelda dazzled Hollywood; then in 1937, with Zelda in a sanitarium and expenses mounting, when a romance developed with ambitious columnist Sheilah Graham that bolstered him in his bouts with illness and alcoholism. Much of the same creative talent also was involved with the earlier *F. Scott Fitzgerald and "The Last of the Belles"* (1974).

0638
SHARK KILL
5/20/76 D'Antoni/Weitz Productions (90 min)

Executive Producer: Philip D'Antoni
Producer: Barry Weitz
Associate Producer: Robert Dijoux
Director: William A. Graham
Teleplay: Sandor Stern
Photography: Terry K. Meade
Music: George Romanis
Editor: Art Seid

Cabo Mendoza	RICHARD YNIGUEZ
Rick Dayner	PHILLIP CLARK
Carolyn	JENNIFER WARREN
Bonnie	ELIZABETH GILL
Luis	VICTOR CAMPOS
Bearde	DAVID HUDDLESTON
Helena Mendoza	CARMEN ZAPATA
Franey	JIMMIE B. SMITH
Maria	ROXANNA BONILLA-GIANNINI
Banducci	RICHARD FORONJY

Two ocean-oriented adventurers set sail in search of a man-killing great white shark.

0639
THE DARK SIDE OF INNOCENCE
5/20/76 Warner Bros. (90 min)

Executive Producer: Jerry Thorpe
Producer: Phil Mandelker
Director: Jerry Thorpe
Teleplay: Barbara Turner
Photography: Charles G. Arnold
Music: Peter Matz
Art Director: Philip Jeffries
Editors: Neil Travis and Jack Harnish

Jesse Breton	JOANNA PETTET
Nora Hancock	
Mulligan	ANNE ARCHER
Stephen Hancock	JOHN ANDERSON
Kathleen Hancock	KIM HUNTER
Skip Breton	LAWRENCE CASEY
Heather	GAIL STRICKLAND
Maggie Hancock	CLAUDETTE NEVINS
Jason Hancock	ROBERT SAMPSON
Dennis Hancock	JAMES HOUGHTON
Rebecca Hancock	ETHELLIN BLOCK
Gabriela Hancock	DENISE NICKERSON
Michael Hancock	DENNIS BOWEN
Rodney Breton	KRISTOPHER MARQUIS
Kim Breton	TIGER WILLIAMS
Topher Mulligan	SHANE BUTTERWORTH
Tony	GEOFFREY SCOTT

A drama involving three generations of a family in middle-class suburbia: an affluent housewife who feels that life is passing her by, the daughter she embitters by walking out on the family, and the mother whose traditional values are shaken by the woman's divorce. This was a pilot for a prospective series that never got on the air.

0640
THE CALL OF THE WILD
5/22/76 Charles Fries Productions (2 hours)

Executive Producer: Charles Fries
Producer: Malcolm Stuart
Director: Jerry Jameson
Teleplay: James Dickey
Based on the 1903 book by Jack London
Photography: Matthew F. Leonetti
Music: Peter Matz
Art Director: Joel Schiller
Editor: Tom Stevens

John Thornton	JOHN BECK
Francois	BERNARD FRESSON
Prospector	JOHN McLIAM
Simpson	DONALD MOFFAT
Stranger	MICHAEL PATAKI
Rosemary	PENELOPE WINDUST
Redsweater	BILLY GREEN BUSH
Guitar Player	JOHNNY TILLOTSON
Will	RAY GUTH
Stoney	DENNIS BURKLEY

Jack London's classic tale of two men, a trapper and a prospector, who, with the aid of a magnificent dog, battle the frozen Klondike in an effort to reach gold country. Clark Gable had starred in William Wellman's 1935 version, and Charlton Heston headed a multi-national cast in the 1974 remake.

0641
THE NEW DAUGHTERS OF JOSHUA CABE
5/29/76 Spelling/Goldberg Productions (90 min)

Executive Producers: Aaron Spelling and Leonard Goldberg
Producer: Paul Savage
Director: Bruce Bilson
Teleplay: Paul Savage
From a story by Margaret Armen
Photography: Dennis Dalzell
Music: Jeff Alexander
Art Director: Al Smith
Editor: John Woodcock

Sheriff Joshua Cabe	JOHN McINTIRE
Bitterroot	JACK ELAM
Essie Cargo	JEANETTE NOLAN

Charity	LIBERTY WILLIAMS
Ada	RENNE JARRETT
Mae	LEZLIE DALTON
Warden Mannering	JOHN DEHNER
Dutton	GEOFFREY LEWIS
Codge Collier	SEAN McCLORY
Matt Cobley	JOEL FABIANI
The Judge	FORD RAINEY
Clel Tonkins	LARRY HOVIS
Jim Pickett	JAMES LYDON
Billy Linaker	RANDALL CARVER

Rascally Joshua Cabe is back for his third go-around (John McIntire takes over for Dan Dailey who previously took over for Buddy Ebsen) and is wrongly convicted of murder, so his "daughters" devise a daring plot to smuggle him out of prison and cheat the hangman.

0642
THE RETURN OF THE WORLD'S GREATEST DETECTIVE
6/16/76 Universal (90 min)

Producer: Roland Kibbee and Dean Hargrove
Director: Dean Hargrove
Teleplay: Roland Kibbee and Dean Hargrove
Photography: William Mendenhall
Music: Dick DeBenedictis
Art Director: William Campbell
Editor: John Kaufman, Jr.

Sherman Holmes	LARRY HAGMAN
Dr. Joan Watson	JENNY O'HARA
Lt. Nick Tinker	NICHOLAS COLASANTO
Himmel	WOODROW PARFREY
Landlady	HELEN VERBIT
Spiner	IVOR FRANCIS
Judge Clement Harley	CHARLES MACAULEY
Dr. Collins	RON SILVER
Vince Cooley	SID HAIG
Psychiatrist	BOOTH COLMAN
Mrs. Slater	LIEUX DRESSLER
Detective	FUDDLE BAGLEY
Klinger	BENNY RUBIN

and: Robert Snively, Jude Farese, George Brenlin, Al Dunlap, Jefferson Kibbee

A bumbling Los Angeles cop falls off his motorcycle, and as the result of a concussion he comes to the conclusion that he is really Sherlock Holmes. With the aid of a woman psychiatric social worker named Watson, he then sets out to solve the puzzling murder of an embezzler.

0643
LANIGAN'S RABBI
6/17/76 Universal (2 hours)

Executive Producer: Leonard B. Stern
Producers: Robert C. Thompson and Rod Paul
Director: Lou Antonio
Teleplay: Don M. Mankiewicz and Gordon Cotler
Based on the novel *Friday the Rabbi Slept Late* by Harry Kemelman
Photography: Andrew Jackson
Music: Leonard Rosenman
Art Director: Norman R. Newberry
Editor: Volney Howard III

Police Chief Paul Lanigan	ART CARNEY
Rabbi David Small	STUART MARGOLIN
Kate Lanigan	JANIS PAIGE
Miriam Small	JANET MARGOLIN
Myra Galen	LORRAINE GARY

Morton Galen	ROBERT REED
Willie Norman	ANDREW ROBINSON
Jim Blake	JIM ANTONIO
Al Becker	DAVID SHEINER
Bobbi Whittaker	BARBARA CARNEY
Osgood	ROBERT DOYLE
Stanley	WILLIAM WHEATLEY
Basserman	STEFFAN ZACHARIAS
Mrs. Blake	BARBARA FLICKER

A mystery-comedy about a rabbi and an Irish police chief who form an unlikely alliance to solve the homicide of a housekeeper whose body was found on the doorstep of the synagogue. This was the pilot film to the series that played during the 1976–77 season with Art Carney and Bruce Solomon (taking over for Stuart Margolin, who was otherwise occupied with "The Rockford Files" series).

0644
WOMAN OF THE YEAR
7/28/76 MGM (2 hours)

Executive Producer: Jud Taylor
Producer: Hugh Benson
Director: Jud Taylor
Teleplay: Joseph Bologna, Renee Taylor and Bernard M. Kahn
Based on the original screenplay by Ring Lardner, Jr. and Michael Kanin
Photography: David M. Walsh
Music: Fred Karlin
Art Director: Preston Ames
Costumes by Moss Mabry
Editor: Bob Wyman

Sam Rodino	JOSEPH BOLOGNA
Tess Harding	RENEE TAYLOR
Phil Whitaker	DICK O'NEILL
Gerald Howe	ANTHONY HOLLAND
Pinkey Barbiki	DICK BAKALYAN
Pizzo	CHUCK BERGANSKY
Himself	HUGH DOWNS
Harding	GEORGE GAYNES
Dimitri Subakov	LEON BELASCO
Justice of the Peace	JOHN FIEDLER
Alma	VIRGINIA CHRISTINE
Editor Clayton	REGIS J. CORDIC
Ralph Rodino	BURT YOUNG

This sophisticated comedy, a remake of the 1942 classic that teamed Tracy and Hepburn for the first time, is about the offbeat romance and stormy marriage of a nonchalant sportswriter and a sophisticated international reporter who work on the same newspaper.

0645
PERILOUS VOYAGE
7/29/76 Universal (2 hours)

Producer: Jack Laird
Associate Producer: Jerrold Freedman
Director: William A. Graham
Teleplay: Robert Weverka, Sidney Stebel and Oscar Millard
Photography: Bud Thackery
Music: Gil Melle
Art Director: George Patrick
Editor: Carl Pingitore

Antonio DeLeon	MICHAEL PARKS
Virginia Monroe	LEE GRANT
Steve Monroe	WILLIAM SHATNER
General Salazar	FRANK SILVERA
Dr. Henry Merrill	VICTOR JORY
Captain Humphreys	CHARLES McGRAW

Alicia Salazar	LOUISE SOREL
Maggie Merrill	BARBARA WERLE
Reynaldo Solis	MICHAEL TOLAN
Rico	STUART MARGOLIN
Colonel	VALENTIN DeVARGAS

An alcoholic banana republic revolutionary hijacks a ship carrying armaments and holds a group of passengers hostage. This one sat on the shelf for eight years following its production in 1968. At that time its title was *The Revolution of Antonio DeLeon*.

0646
THE INVASION OF JOHNSON COUNTY
7/31/76 Roy Huggins Productions/Universal (2 hours)

Executive Producer: Jo Swerling, Jr.
Producer: Roy Huggins
Director: Jerry Jameson
Teleplay: Nicholas E. Baehr
Photography: Rexford Metz
Music: Mike Post and Pete Carpenter
Art Director: Alexander A. Mayer
Editors: Gloryette Clark, Chuck McClelland and Jim Benson

Sam Lowell	BILL BIXBY
George Dunning	BO HOPKINS
Major Walcott	JOHN HILLERMAN
Frank Canton	BILLY GREEN BUSH
Colonel Van Horn	STEPHEN ELLIOTT
Richard Allen	LEE DeBROUX
Irvine	M. EMMET WALSH
Sheriff Angus	MILLS WATSON
Teschmacher	ALAN FUDGE
Deputy Sheriff Brooks	LUKE ASKEW
Maj. Edward Fershay	EDWARD WINTER

and: David Donner, Ted Gehring

A footloose Bostonian and a Wyoming cowboy team up in the Old West to block a private army's land-grab scheme against a bunch of small-time ranchers.

1976–77 SEASON

0647
DEATH AT LOVE HOUSE
9/3/76 Spelling/Goldberg Productions (90 min)

Executive Producers: Aaron Spelling and Leonard Goldberg
Producer: Hal Sitowitz
Associate Producer: Shelley Hull
Director: E. W. Swackhamer
Teleplay: Jim Barnett
Photography: Dennis Dalzell
Music: Laurence Rosenthal
Art Director: Paul Sylos
Editor: John Woodcock

Joel Gregory (Jr. & Sr.)	ROBERT WAGNER
Donna Gregory	KATE JACKSON
Clara Josephs	SYLVIA SIDNEY
Lorna Love (in flashback)	MARIANNA HILL
Marcella Geffenhart	JOAN BLONDELL
Conan Carroll	JOHN CARRADINE
Denise Christian	DOROTHY LAMOUR
Oscar	BILL MACY
Bus Driver	JOSEPH BERNARD
Eric Herman	JOHN A. ZEE
Director	ROBERT GIBBONS

Policeman AL HANSEN
Actor in Film CROFTEN
HARDESTER

Curious over the relationship that his artist-father had with a famous film queen in the 1930s, a young writer and his wife accept the challenge of writing a movie script about the legendary star, gain access to her old mansion, occupied by a lone caretaker, and find themselves menaced by her spirit which reaches out from her glass tomb. Filmed on the fabulous Harold Lloyd estate under the title *The Shrine of Lorna Love*.

0648
BRIDGER
9/10/76 Universal (2 hours)

Producer/Director: David Lowell Rich
Teleplay: Merwin Gerard
Photography: Bud Thackery
Music: Elliot Kaplan
Art Director: Loyd S. Papez
Editor: Boyd Clark

Jim Bridger	JAMES WAINWRIGHT
Kit Carson	BEN MURPHY
Joe Meek	DIRK BLOCKER
Jennifer Melford	SALLY FIELD
President Andrew Jackson	JOHN ANDERSON
Daniel Webster	WILLIAM WINDOM
Shoshone Woman	MARGARITA CORDOVA
Doctor	TOM MIDDLETON
Modoc Leader	ROBERT MIANO
Paiute Chief	SKEETER VAUGHAN
Crow Chief	X. BRANDS
Army Lieutenant	W. T. ZACHA
Presidential Aide	KEITH EVANS
David Bridger	CLAUDIO MARTINEZ

A true-life adventure of legendary mountain man Jim Bridger who, with the fate of the Pacific Northwest at stake, is given forty days to blaze a trail through the Rockies to the California coast and told that failure means loss of the territory to England. This two hour movie was cut to ninety minutes for its rerun and subsequent syndication.

0649
STREET KILLING
9/12/76 ABC Circle Films (90 min)

Executive Producer: Everett Chambers
Producer: Richard Rosenbloom
Director: Harvey Hart
Teleplay: Bill Driskill
Photography: David M. Walsh
Music: J. J. Johnson
Art Director: Peter M. Wooley
Editors: David McCann and Argyle Nelson, Jr.

Gus Brenner	ANDY GRIFFITH
Howard Bronstein	BRADFORD DILLMAN
Al Lanier	HARRY GUARDINO
Louis Spillane	ROBERT LOGGIA
Bud Schiffman	DON GORDON
J. D. Johnson	ADAM WADE
Louise	ANNA BERGER
Darlene Lawrence	DEBBIE WHITE
Susan Brenner	SANDY FAISON
Kitty Brenner	GIGI SEMONE
Wally Barnes	JOHN O'CONNELL
Leonard	FRED SADOFF
Carelli	PAUL HECHT
Dr. Vinton	GERRIT GRAHAM
Mitchell Small	STAN SHAW
Daniel Bronstein	BEN HAMMER

0650
JUST AN OLD SWEET SONG
9/14/76 MTM Enterprises, Inc. (90 min)

Producer: Philip Barry
Director: Robert Ellis Miller
Teleplay: Melvin Van Peebles
Photography: Terry K. Meade
Music: Peter Matz
Title song by Melvin Van Peebles
Art Director: Ray Beal
Editor: Argyle Nelson

Priscilla Simmons	CICELY TYSON
Nate Simmons	ROBERT HOOKS
Grandma	BEAH RICHARDS
Joe Mayfield	LINCOLN KILPATRICK
Aunt Velvet	MINNIE GENTRY
Mr. Claypool	EDWARD BINNS
Trunk	SONNY JIM GAINES
Helen Mayfield	MARY ALICE
Darlene	TIA RANCE
Junior	KEVIN HOOKS
Highpockets	ERIC HOOKS

A sentimental tale of a contemporary black family from Detroit whose two-week vacation in the South leads to a variety of changes in their lives. Robert Hooks' real-life sons played his fictional sons in the story. Pilot to a prospective series called "Down Home." A second one-hour movie in 1978 had basically the same cast, except for Madge Sinclair replacing Cicely Tyson.

0651
KINGSTON: THE POWER PLAY
9/15/76 Universal (2 hours)

Executive Producer: David Victor
Producer: David J. O'Connell
Director: Robert Day
Teleplay: Dick Nelson
From a story by David Victor and Dick Nelson
Photography: Sy Hoffberg
Music: Leonard Rosenman
Art Director: Howard E. Johnson
Editor: Richard G. Wray

R. B. Kingston	RAYMOND BURR
Tony Kolsky	JAMES CANNING
Beth Kelly	PAMELA HENSLEY
Laura Frazier	LENKA PETERSON
Avery Stanton	BRADFORD DILLMAN
Helen Martinson	DINA MERRILL
Pat Martinson	BIFF McGUIRE
Sam Trowbridge	ROBERT SAMPSON
Lieutenant Vokeman	MILT KOGAN
Father Reardon	R. G. ARMSTRONG
Senator Hobath	ROBERT MANDAN
Dealey	MARTIN KOVE
Ethelmae Turner	CLAIRE BRENNAN
Dr. Eberly	STACY KEACH, SR.

This was the pilot film for Burr's brief (Spring 1977) series about an investigative reporter given a free hand by the head of a chain of newspapers and TV stations, here uncovering a plot to use nuclear power plants to take over the world.

0652
THE LOVE BOAT
9/18/76 A Douglas S. Cramer Production (2 hours)

Producer: Douglas S. Cramer
Associate Producer: Henry Colman
Directors: Richard Kinon and Alan Myerson
Teleplays: "Mona Lisa Speaks" by Carl Kleinschmitt, "Mr. and Mrs. Havlicek Aboard" by Robert Iles and James R. Stein, "Are There Any Real Love Stories?" by Dawn Aldredge and Marion C. Freeman, and "Till Death Do Its Part" by Carl Kleinschmitt
Suggested by *The Love Boat* by Jeraldine Saunders
Photography: Tim Southcott
Music: Charles Fox
Art Director: Tracy Bousman
Editors: Jerry Dronsky and Bob Moore

Donald Richardson	DON ADAMS
George Havlicek	TOM BOSLEY
Monica Richardson	FLORENCE HENDERSON
Stan Nichols	GABRIEL KAPLAN
Willard	HARVEY KORMAN
Iris Havlicek	CLORIS LEACHMAN
Andrew Canaan	HAL LINDEN
Ellen Carmichael	KAREN VALENTINE

Your "Love Boat" Crew:	
The Captain	TED HAMILTON
The Doctor (O'Neil)	DICK VAN PATTEN
The Bartender (Isaac)	THEODORE WILSON
The Yeoman Purser (Gopher)	SANDY HELBERG
The Steward	JOSEPH SICARI
The Cruise Director (Gerry)	TERRI O'MARA
Appearing in the Lounge	RICHARD STAHL and KATHRYN ISH

and:	
Arnold Merrit	JIMMY BAIO
Louella McKenzie	JOYCE JAMESON
Rita Merrit	BEVERLY SAUNDERS
The First Officer	WILLIAM BASSETT
The Photographer	DAVID MAN
Juanita Havlicek	LAURETTE SPANG
Binaca	JETTE SEEAR
Richard Garrett III	RIC CARROTT
Momma	MONTANA SMOVER

This was the pilot for the hit series, packed with familiar TV names and faces, interweaving several comedy stories of the misadventures of passengers and crew aboard a California to Mexico cruise ship.

0653
THE MILLION DOLLAR RIP-OFF
9/22/76 Charles Fries Productions (90 min)

Executive Producer: Charles Fries
Producer: Edward J. Montagne
Director: Alexander Singer
Teleplay: Andrew Peter Marin
Based on a screenplay by William J. Devane and John Pleshette
Photography: Jules Brenner
Music: Vic Mizzy
Art Director: Robert MacKichan
Editor: Sam Waxman

Muff Kovak	FREDDIE PRINZE
Lt. Ralph Fogherty	ALLEN GARFIELD
Lil	CHRISTINE BELFORD
Helene	LINDA SCRUGGS BOGART
Jessie	JOANNA DeVARONA
Kitty	BROOKE MILLS
Lubeck	JAMES SLOYAN
Sgt. Frank Jarrett	BOB HASTINGS
Hennessy	GARY VINSON
Brown	ROBERT P. LIEB
Funeral Director	COLIN HAMILTON

Prinze, in his only dramatic film role, is an ex-con electronics whiz who, with the aide of four female accomplices, steals a bundle from the Chicago Transit Authority, much to the annoyance of a dyspeptic detective who has been keeping an eye on him since he left prison. The original story, interestingly, was written by two of the more prolific TV actors of the era, presumably as a vehicle for one or both of them.

0654
DAWN: PORTRAIT OF A TEENAGE RUNAWAY
9/27/76 The Douglas S. Cramer Co. (2 hours)

Producer: Douglas S. Cramer
Director: Randal Kleiser
Teleplay: Darlene Young
Photography: Jacques R. Marquette
Music: Fred Karlin
Song: "Comin' Home Again" by Fred and Meg Karlin
Sung by Shaun Cassidy
Art Director: James G. Hulsey
Editor: Carroll Sax

Dawn Wetherby	EVE PLUMB
Alexander	LEIGH J. McCLOSKEY
Dawn's Mother	LYNN CARLIN
Harry	WILLIAM SCHALLERT
Counterwoman	ANNE SEYMOUR
Susie	JOAN PRATHER
Frankie Lee	MARGUERITE DeLAIN
Swan	BO HOPKINS
Donald Umber	GEORG STANFORD BROWN
Dr. Roberts	DAVID KAPP
Randy	STEPHANIE BURCHFIELD
Melba	KAAREN RAGLAND

The fifteen-year-old daughter of a cocktail waitress goes to the big city to become a prostitute when she can't find legitimate work.

0655
FRANCIS GARY POWERS: THE TRUE STORY OF THE U-2 SPY INCIDENT
9/29/76 Charles Fries Productions (2 hours)

Executive Producer: Charles Fries
Producers: Edward J. Montagne and John B. Bennett
Director: Delbert Mann
Teleplay: Robert E. Thompson
Based on the book *Operation Overflight* by Francis Gary Powers with Curt Gentry
Photography: Vilis Lapenieks
Music: Gerald Fried
Art Director: Walter Scott Herndon
Editor: Sam Waxman

Francis Gary Powers	LEE MAJORS
Oliver Powers	NOAH BEERY, JR.
Rudenko	NEHEMIAH PERSOFF
Mrs. Powers	BROOKE BUNDY
Bissell	WILLIAM DANIELS
James Donovan	JAMES GREGORY
DeGaulle	MARCEL HILLAIRE
Ivan Vasilev	ALF KJELLIN
John McCone	BIFF McGUIRE
Robert Kennedy	JIM McMULLEN
Grinev	DAVID OPATOSHU
Wheatley	CHARLES KNOX ROBINSON
Allen Dulles	LEW AYRES
Ida Powers	KATHERINE BARD

Eisenhower	JAMES FLAVIN
Khrushchev	THAYER DAVID

A dramatization of the historic U-2 incident in which a CIA spy pilot was shot down over the Soviet Union in the early 1960s and brought to trial. Powers ultimately was returned to the United States in a prisoner swap, and during the later years he became a helicopter traffic reporter for a Los Angeles radio station. He was killed in a copter crash while on duty in late 1977.

0656
WANTED: THE SUNDANCE WOMAN
10/1/76 20th Century-Fox (2 hours)
(subsequently titled *Mrs. Sundance Rides Again*)

Executive Producer: Stan Hough
Producer: Ron Preissman
Director: Lee Philips
Teleplay: Richard Fielder
Photography: Terry K. Meade
Music: Fred Karlin
Art Director: Arch Bacon
Editor: Samuel E. Beetley

Etta Pace	KATHARINE ROSS
Charlie Siringo	STEVE FORREST
Lola Watkins	STELLA STEVENS
Dave Riley	MICHAEL CONSTANTINE
Mattie Riley	KATHERINE HELMOND
Pancho Villa	HECTOR ELIZONDO
Fierro	HECTOR ELIAS
The Sheriff	WARREN BERLINGER
Major Vasquez	JORGE CERVERA
Elsie	LUCILLE BENSON

Katharine Ross repeats her portrayal of Etta Pace (from *Butch Cassidy and the Sundance Kid*) in this adventure of the fugitive who, alone and desperate following the deaths of Butch and Sundance, seeks help from Pancho Villa in exchange for guns and ammunition.

0657
HOW TO BREAK UP A HAPPY DIVORCE
10/6/76 Charles Fries Productions (90 min)

Executive Producer: Charles Fries
Producers: Gerald Gardner and Dee Caruso
Director: Jerry Paris
Teleplay: Gerald Gardner and Dee Caruso
Photography: Richard A. Kelley
Music: Nelson Riddle
Editors: Bob Moore and Bud Molin

Ellen Dowling	BARBARA EDEN
Tony Bartlett	HAL LINDEN
Carter Dowling	PETER BONERZ
Eve	MARCIA RODD
Mr. Henshaw	HAROLD GOULD
Mrs. Henshaw	BETTY BRESSLER
Jennifer Hartman	LIBERTY WILLIAMS
Man with Hangover	CHUCK McCANN
Harassed Waiter	ARCHIE HAHN
Man at Concert	EDWARD ANDREWS
Professor Schofield	DAVID KETCHUM
Conductor	CARL BALLANTINE
Soprano	MARY JO CATLETT
Marilyn	LEIGH FRENCH
Gallery Guide	BARBARA MINKUS
Lance Colson	FRED WILLARD

and: Ivy Jones, Shirley Prestia, Janis Jamison, Sandra Maley, Roy Stuart, Alberto Sarno, Robert Karvelas, Eileen Dietz, Harriet Gibson, Dale Johnson, Andrew J. Paris, Linda Ann Stewart

A sight-gag-happy farce, loaded with cameos by familiar TV faces, about a divorcée's campaign to make her ex-husband jealous in order to win him back.

0658
THE GREAT HOUDINIS
10/8/76 An ABC Circle Film (2 hours)

Writer/Director: Melville Shavelson
Photography: Arch R. Dalzell
Music: Peter Matz

Adrienne Barbeau, Geoffrey Lewis, Ruth Gordon and Paul Michael Glaser in THE GREAT HOUDINIS (1976)

Sally Struthers and Vivian Vance in THE GREAT HOUDINIS (1976)

Art Director: Tracy Bousman
Editor: John Woodcock

Harry Houdini (Erich Weiss)	PAUL MICHAEL GLASER
Bess Houdini	SALLY STRUTHERS
Cecilia Weiss	RUTH GORDON
Minnie	VIVIAN VANCE
Daisy White	ADRIENNE BARBEAU
Rev. Arthur Ford	BILL BIXBY
Theo Weiss	JACK CARTER
Conan Doyle	PETER CUSHING
Rev. LeVeyne	NINA FOCH
Superintendent Melville	WILFRID HYDE-WHITE
Dr. Crandon	GEOFFREY LEWIS
Lady Doyle	MAUREEN O'SULLIVAN
Slater	CLIVE REVILL
Margery Crandon	BARBARA RHOADES
Conductor	JEROME THOR

A biographical dramatization of the life and times of the world-renowned illusionist and escape artist whose glittering career masked a deep obsession with the occult, culminated by a vow that he would one day speak from the beyond, a promise he made to his wife on his deathbed in 1926. Ruth Gordon won an Emmy Award nomination for her performance as Houdini's mother.

0659
HAVING BABIES
10/17/76 The Jozak Company (2 hours)

Executive Producers: Gerald I. Isenberg and Gerald W. Abrams
Producer: Lew Gallo
Director: Robert Day
Teleplay: Peggy Elliott
Photography: Jacques R. Marquette
Music: Earl Hagen
Song "Paper Bridges" with lyrics by Al Kasha and Joel Hirschhorn
Sung by Maureen McGovern
Art Director: Peter M. Wooley
Editor: John F. McSweeney

Frank Gorman	DESI ARNAZ, JR.
Allie Duggin	ADRIENNE BARBEAU
George McNamara	RONNY COX
Ralph Bancini	HARRY GUARDINO
Hal Bergstrom	TOM KENNEDY
Grace Fontreil	VICKI LAWRENCE
Max Duggin	RICHARD MASUR
Mickey Paterno	GREG MULLAVEY
Laura Gorman	LINDA PURL
Mrs. Fontreil	JAN STERLING
Beth Paterno	KAREN VALENTINE
Al Schneider	ABE VIGODA
Sally McNamara	JESSICA WALTER

Four couples experience childbirth by the "natural" Lamaze method in this TV pilot to the subsequent series. Original title: *Giving Birth*.

0660
SCOTT FREE
10/13/76 Cherokee Productions/Universal (90 min)

Executive Producers: Meta Rosenberg and Stephen J. Cannell
Producer: Alex Beaton
Director: William Wiard
Teleplay: Stephen J. Cannell
Photography: Jacques R. Marquette
Music: Mike Post and Pete Carpenter
Art Director: Seymour Klate
Editor: Howard S. Deane

Tony Scott	MICHAEL BRANDON
Kevin Southerland	STEPHEN NATHAN
Holly	SUSAN SAINT JAMES
James Donaldson	ROBERT LOGGIA
Ed McGraw	KEN SWOFFORD
Max	ALLAN RICH
Al	PAUL KOSLO
Lillle Lion	CAL BELLINI
Santini	MICHAEL LERNER
George Running Bear	DEHL BERTI

and: Robert Casper, Harvey Downing, Bart Burns

James Garner's production company made this pilot film about a free-wheeling professional gambler, here sought by the syndicate, a band of Indians and the Feds, all interested in a piece of land he won in a poker game.

0661
SHERLOCK HOLMES IN NEW YORK
10/18/76 20th Century-Fox (2 hours)

Executive Producer: Nancy Malone
Producer: John Cutts
Director: Boris Sagal
Teleplay: Alvin Sapinsley
Based on the character created by Arthur Conan Doyle
Photography: Michael Margulies
Music: Richard Rodney Bennett
Conducted by Leonard Rosenman
Art Director: Lawrence G. Paull
Costumes: Hal Hoff and Shannon Litten
Editor: Samuel E. Beetley

Sherlock Holmes	ROGER MOORE
Professor James Moriarty	JOHN HUSTON
Dr. John Watson	PATRICK MACNEE
Mortimer McGraw	GIG YOUNG
Irene Adler	CHARLOTTE RAMPLING
Inspector Lafferty	DAVID HUDDLESTON
Frau Reichenbach	SIGNE HASSO
Daniel Furman	LEON AMES
Heller	JOHN ABBOTT
Hotel Haymarket Proprietor	JACKIE COOGAN
Nicole Romaine	MARIA GRIMM
Mrs. Hudson	MARJORIE BENNETT
Scott Adler	GEOFFREY MOORE

There is an affectionate bow to the master sleuth in this lavishly produced original that has Holmes rushing to New York City after discovering that his old nemesis, Moriarty, not only has kidnapped the son of his (Holmes') long-time love, actress Irene Adler, but also has hatched a scheme to steal the world's gold supply, squirreled away under Union Square in lower Manhattan.

0662
AMELIA EARHART
10/25/76 Universal (3 hours)

Producer: George Eckstein
Director: George Schaefer
Teleplay: Carol Sobieski
Photography: Ted Voigtlander
Music: David Shire
Art Director: William H. Tuntke
Aerial Sequences: Frank Tallman
Editor: Jim Benson

Amelia Earhart	SUSAN CLARK
G. P. Putnam	JOHN FORSYTHE
Paul Mantz	STEPHEN MACHT
Neta Snook ("Snookie")	SUSAN OLIVER
Pidge Earhart	CATHERINE BURNS
Amy Earhart	JANE WYATT
Mr. Earhart	CHARLES AIDMAN
Sid Isaacs	ED BARTH
Radio Operator	DAVID HUFFMAN
Fred Norman	BILL VINT
Bill Stultz	JACK COLVIN
Alan Bradford	KIP NIVEN
Dr. Paterson	JOHN ARCHER
Miss Perkins	FLORIDA FROEBUS
Billy Putnam	LANCE KERWIN
Young Amelia	KIM DIAMOND
Broadcaster	LOWELL THOMAS

and: Colleen Camp, Ann Morgan Guilbert, Garry Walberg, Robert Ridgley, Priscilla Morrill, Steve Kanaly, Sari Price, Nora Morgan, Jack Bannon, Doris Singleton, Michael LeClair, Kathleen O'Malley

An ambitious movie biography of the famed aviatrix and her marriage to a noted publisher. Emmy nominations went to Susan Clark as Best Actress, Susan Oliver as Best Supporting Actress, and William Tuntke and Richard Freedman for their art direction and set decoration.

0663
RICHIE BROCKELMAN: MISSING 24 HOURS
10/27/76 Universal (90 min)

Executive Producers: Stephen J. Cannell and Steven Bochco
Producer: William F. Phillips
Director: Hy Averback
Teleplay: Stephen J. Cannell and Steven Bochco
Photography: William Mendenhall

Music: Mike Post and Pete Carpenter
Art Director: Lester L. Green
Editor: John Elias

Richie Brockelman	DENNIS DUGAN
Elizabeth Morton	SUZANNE PLESHETTE
Mr. Brockelman	NORMAN FELL
Mrs. Brockelman	HELEN PAGE CAMP
Sharon Peterson	BARBARA BOSSON
Davenport	LLOYD BOCHNER
Darcy Davenport	SHARON GLESS
Arnold Springfield	WILLIAM WINDOM
Rider	HAROLD SYLVESTER
McNeil	NED WILSON
Marine	HUNTER VON LEER
Hooker	GLORIA LeROY

and: Ted Gehring, Lew Palter, W. T. Zacha, Tom Falk, George Fisher

A neophyte gumshoe with more nerve than know-how joins the big leagues when hired by an amnesia victim who not only cannot explain why she's being sought by a gunman but who also believes that she is involved in a murder. Brockelman originally was introduced on James Garner's "The Rockford Files" with the idea of making him Rockford's sidekick. Instead the character was written into this pilot film and then spun-off into a very brief "Richie Brockelman" series in 1977 that never caught on, even after Brockelman made another appearance on "The Rockford Files" and again was tried in series.

0664
LOOK WHAT'S HAPPENED TO ROSEMARY'S BABY
10/29/76 Paramount (2 hours)
(subsequently titled *Rosemary's Baby II*)

Producer: Anthony Wilson
Director: Sam O'Steen
Teleplay: Anthony Wilson
Based on characters created by Ira Levin
Photography: John A. Alonzo
Music: Charles Bernstein
Art Director: Lester D. Gobruegge
Editor: Bob Wyman

Adrian/Andrew	STEPHEN McHATTIE
Rosemary Woodhouse	PATTY DUKE ASTIN
Holtzman	BRODERICK CRAWFORD
Minnie Castavet	RUTH GORDON
Laykin	LLOYD HAYNES
Peter Simon	DAVID HUFFMAN
Marjean Dorn	TINA LOUISE
Guy Woodhouse	GEORGE MAHARIS
Roman Castavet	RAY MILLAND
Ellen	DONNA MILLS
Adrian/Andrew (age 8)	PHILIP BOYER
Dr. Lister	BRIAN RICHARDS

This sequel to Roman Polanski's 1968 chiller traces the growth to adulthood of the half-human/half-demon child whose life is a macabre battleground between human and satanic forces. Ruth Gordon recreates her original film role, and Patty Duke Astin and George Maharis take over where Mia Farrow and John Cassavetes left off. Originally this one was to have been titled simply *Rosemary's Baby II*—and that's what it was called in syndication.

0665
STALK THE WILD CHILD
11/3/76 Charles Fries Productions (90 min)

Executive Producer: Charles Fries
Producers: Stanley Bass and Paul Wendkos

Director: William Hale
Teleplay: Peter Packer
Photography: Harry May
Music: John Rubinstein
Art Director: Robert MacKichan
Editor: David Newhouse

Dr. James Hazard	DAVID JANSSEN
Maggie	TRISH VAN DEVERE
Cal (as a youth)	BENJAMIN BOTTOMS
Cal (as a young man)	JOSEPH BOTTOMS
Andrea	JAMIE SMITH JACKSON
Gault	ALLAN ARBUS
Secretary	MARCIA WARNER
Ellen Mott	FRAN RYAN
Menzies	JEROME THOR

A young boy raised by wild dogs is found and taken to a university where an attempt is made to civilize him.

0666
NIGHTMARE IN BADHAM COUNTY
11/5/76 An ABC Circle Film (2 hours)

Executive Producer: Douglas S. Cramer
Producer: Wilford Lloyd Baumes
Director: John Llewellyn Moxey
Teleplay: Jo Heims
Photography: Frank Stanley
Music: Charles Bernstein
Art Director: Jan Scott
Editor: Carroll Sax

Cathy Phillips	DEBORAH RAFFIN
Diane Emery	LYNNE MOODY
Sheriff Dannen	CHUCK CONNORS
Dulcie	FIONNUALA FLANAGAN
Greer	TINA LOUISE
Superintendent Deaner	ROBERT REED
Sarah	DELLA REESE
Smitty	LANA WOOD
The Judge	RALPH BELLAMY

Two college coeds find their vacation drive across the country turning into a nightmare when one is attacked by a small-town sheriff and both are then beaten, degraded and locked into a corrupt prison farm with no way to tell their parents or friends where they are.

0667
21 HOURS AT MUNICH
11/7/76 A Filmways Production (2 hours)

Executive Producer: Edward S. Feldman
Producers: Frank von Zerneck and Robert Greenwald
Director: William A. Graham
Teleplay: Edward Hume and Howard Fast
Based on the book *The Blood of Israel* by Serge Groussard
Photography: Jost Vacano
Music: Laurence Rosenthal
Art Director: Herta Pischinger
Editor: Ronald J. Fagan

Chief of Police Manfred Schreiber	WILLIAM HOLDEN
Annaliese Graes	SHIRLEY KNIGHT
Issa	FRANCO NERO
Chancellor Willy Brandt	RICHARD BASEHART
General Zvi Zamir	ANTHONY QUAYLE
Interior Minister Bruno Merk	NOEL WILLIAM
Hans Dietrich Genscher	GEORG MARISCHKA

Broderick Crawford and Marjoe Gortner in MAYDAY AT 40,000 FEET (1976)

and: Kathleen Bracken, Bill Catching, Norland Benson, Philip Baker Hall, Bert Williams, Buck Young, Bill Harlow, Alan Foster, Garry McLarty

An airliner has been disabled and the lives of its terrified passengers depend on the untried skills of its co-pilot after the pilot is seriously wounded by a killer who had boarded during a stopover.

0669
THE BOY IN THE PLASTIC BUBBLE
11/12/76 Spelling/Goldberg Productions
(2 hours)

Executive Producers: Aaron Spelling and Leonard Goldberg Goldberg
Producers: Joel Thurm and Cindy Dunne
Associate Producer: Shelley Hull
Director: Randal Kleiser
Teleplay: Douglas Day Stewart
From a story by Joseph Morgenstern and Douglas Day Stewart
Photography: Arch R. Dalzell
Music: Mark Snow
Song "What Would They Say?" written and sung by Paul Williams
Art Director: Paul Sylos
Editor: John F. McSweeney

Tod Lubitch	JOHN TRAVOLTA
Gina Biggs	GLYNNIS O'CONNOR
Johnny Lubitch	ROBERT REED
Mickey Lubitch	DIANA HYLAND
Dr. Ernest Gunther	RALPH BELLAMY
Martha Biggs	KAREN MORROW
Pete Biggs	HOWARD PLATT
Roy Slater	JOHN FRIEDRICH
Gwen	VERNEE WATSON
Himself	BUZZ ALDRIN

A teenager, born with no immunities and forced to live in an incubator-like environment isolating him from any direct human contact, is faced with a life-or-death decision when he falls in love with the girl next door. Diana Hyland, playing the boy's mother, won an Emmy Award for her performance. Writers Douglas Day Stewart and Joseph Morgenstern were cited with Emmy nominations.

0670
SYBIL
11/14–15/76 Lorimar Productions (4 hours)

Executive Producers: Peter Dunne and Philip Capice
Producer: Jacqueline Babbin
Director: Daniel Petrie
Teleplay: Stewart Stern
Based on the book by Flora Rheta Schreiber
Photography: Mario Tosi
Music: Leonard Rosenman
Lyrics by Alan and Marilyn Bergman
Production Design: Tom H. John
Editors: Michael McLean and Rita Roland

Dr. Cornelia Wilbur	JOANNE WOODWARD
Sybil Dorsett	SALLY FIELD
Richard J. Loomis	BRAD DAVIS
Hattie	MARTINE BARTLETT
Frieda Dorsett	JANE HOFFMAN
Dr. Quinoness	CHARLES LANE
Grandma Dorsett	JESSAMINE MILNER
William Dorsett	WILLIAM PRINCE
Young Sybil	NATASHA RYAN
Matthew Loomis	MICHAEL CREBBS

and: Penelope Allen, Camila Ashland, Gina Petrushka, Paul Tulley, Elizabeth Ann Beesley, Virginia Campbell, Cathy Lynn Lesko

Israeli Gutfreund	PAUL SMITH
Moshe Weinberger	MARTIN GILAT
Golda Meir	ELSE QUECKE
Mohamed Kadiff	MICHAEL DEGEN
Avery Brundage	JAMES HURLEY

and: Djamchid Soheli, Walter Kohut, Jan Niklan, Ernst Lenart, Osman Ragheb, Franz Rudnick, Heinz Feldhaus, David Hess, Erik Falk, Bernhard Melcer, Herbert Fox, Eppaminondas Sodukos, Wilfried von Aacken, Abraham Gabison, Ulrich Haupt, Carmelo Celso, Sammy Kazian, Franz Gunther Heider, Julio Pinheiro, Reto Feurer, Joachim Eisler, Dan Van Husen

A dramatization of the events surrounding the 1972 Olympics massacre when eight Arab terrorists killed eleven Israeli athletes. A well-made, thoughful film that had the dubious distinction of premiering opposite the initial TV showing of *Gone with the Wind,* gathering virtually no audience, but receiving an Emmy Award nomination as the Outstanding Drama Special of the 1976–77 season and another for editor Ronald J. Fagan.

0668
MAYDAY AT 40,000 FEET
11/12/76 A. J. Fenady Associates/Warner Bros.
(2 hours)

Producer: Andrew J. Fenady
Director: Robert Butler
Teleplay: Austin Ferguson, Dick Nelson and Andrew J. Fenady
Based on the novel *Jet Stream* by Austin Ferguson
Photography: William K. Jurgensen
Music: Richard Markowitz
Art Director: Robert Kinoshita
Editor: Nick Archer

Captain Pete Douglas	DAVID JANSSEN
Mike Fuller	DON MEREDITH
Stan Burkhart	CHRISTOPHER GEORGE
Dr. Joseph Mannheim	RAY MILLAND
Cathy Armello	LYNDA DAY GEORGE
Susan MacKenzie	MAGGIE BLYE
Greco	MARJOE GORTNER
Marshal Riese	BRODERICK CRAWFORD
Harry Jensen	TOM DRAKE
Cindy Jensen	CHRISTOPHER NORRIS
Belson	HARI RHODES
Glen Meyer	WARREN VANDERS
Terry Dunlap	SHANI WALLACE
Kitty Douglas	JANE POWELL
Kent	WILLIAM BRYANT
Wynberg	JOHN PICKARD
Controller	STEVE MARLO
Doctor	JIM CHANDLER
Surgeon	PHILIP MANSOUR
Forenzo	AL MOLINARO

An acclaimed production (Emmy Award winner as Outstanding Special) in which Sally Field won an Emmy as Best Actress for playing a young woman so disturbed by childhood experiences that she develops sixteen distinct personalities. A third Emmy Award went to Stewart Stern for his teleplay, and a fourth was given for the score by Leonard Rosenman and Alan and Marilyn Bergman. Of interest is that Joanne Woodward, here playing the psychiatrist, gave her own Oscar-winning performance as a similar multi-personality woman in *Three Faces of Eve* (1957), and was Emmy-nominated for her role here, losing to her co-star. Cinematographer Mario Tosi also received an Emmy nomination.

0671
THE DISAPPEARANCE OF AIMEE
11/17/76 Tomorrow Entertainment (2 hours)

Executive Producer: Thomas W. Moore
Producer: Paul Leaf
Director: Anthony Harvey
Teleplay: John McGreevey
Photography: James Crabe
Music: Steve Byrne
Art Director: Chuck Rosen
Costumes: Edith Head
Editor: Gerry Greenberg

Sister Aimee McPhearson	FAYE DUNAWAY
Minnie Kennedy	BETTE DAVIS
Dist. Att. Asa Keyes	JAMES SLOYAN
Asst. D.A. Joseph Ryan	JAMES WOODS
Captain Cline	JOHN LEHNE
Emma Shaffer	LELIA GOLDONI
S. I. Gilbert	SEVERN DARDEN
Kenneth Ormiston	WILLIAM JORDAN
Judge Blake	SANDY WARD
Wallace Moore	BARRY BROWN
Benedict	IRBY SMITH
Clerk	HARTLEY SILVER

A dramatization of the unexplained six-week disappearance in 1926 of evangelist Aimee Semple McPhearson after which a court hearing had to decide whether she had been kidnapped to Mexico as she claimed or had been trysting with a married man as the police and her mother (played by Bette Davis) suspected. This was Faye Dunaway's TV movie debut in a role that was scheduled to be played by Ann-Margret.

0672
REVENGE FOR A RAPE
11/19/76 Albert S. Ruddy Productions (2 hours)

Executive Producer: Richard R. St. Johns
Producer: Alan P. Horowitz
Director: Timothy Galfas
Teleplay: Yabo Yablonsky
From a story by Albert S. Ruddy
Photography: Robert E. Collins
Music: Jerrold Immel
Editor: Allan Jacobs

Travis Green	MIKE CONNORS
Sheriff Paley	ROBERT REED
Amy Green	TRACY BROOKS SWOPE
Raleigh	DEANNA LUND
Cooper	LARRY WATSON
Curly	JOCK LIVINGSTON
Chuck	GLENN WILDER
Dr. Bird	ROGER DRESSLER
Nurse	SHIRLEY BARCLAY
Farley	JOE AUSTIN

A compelling drama of a man who becomes a lone vigilante tracking down the three men who attacked his wife while on a camping trip.

0673
I WANT TO KEEP MY BABY
11/19/76 CBS, Inc. (2 hours)

Executive Producer: Jerry Thorpe
Producer: Joanna Lee
Director: Jerry Thorpe
Teleplay: Joanna Lee
Photography: Frank Stanley
Music: George Aliceson Tipton
Song "Child with a Child" by Craig Lee and Hermine Hilton
Sung by Salli Terri
Art Director: Ray Beal
Editor: Alex Beaton

Sue Ann Cunningham	MARIEL HEMINGWAY
Donna Jo Martelli	SUSAN ANSPACH
Ralph Martelli	JACK RADER
Don DeReda	VINCE BEGATTA
Renee DeReda	DORI BRENNER
Rae Finer	RHEA PEARLMAN
Chuck Ryan	JONATHAN JONES
Gregg	HERB WILLIAMS
Miranda	LISA PELICAN
Andy	JOHN MEGNA

A drama about a fifteen-year-old girl who becomes pregnant and decides to raise the baby herself. The film marked the TV acting debut of Mariel Hemingway, the granddaughter of Ernest Hemingway.

0674
THE SAVAGE BEES
11/22/76 Alan Landsburg/Don Kirshner Production (2 hours)

Executive Producers: Alan Landsburg, Merrill Grant and Don Kirshner
Producer/Director: Bruce Geller
Teleplay: Guerdon Trueblood
Photography: Richard C. Glouner
Music: Walter Murphy
Editors: George Hively and Bud Friedgen

Sheriff Donald McKew	BEN JOHNSON
Jeff DuRand	MICHAEL PARKS
Rufus	PAUL HECHT
Jeannie Devereaux	GRETCHEN CORBETT
Dr. Mueller	HORST BUCHOLZ
Police Lieutenant	BRUCE FRENCH
Deputy Mayor Peligrino	JAMES BEST

A swarm of killer bees from South America threatens New Orleans at the height of the Mardi Gras weekend. A neat little thriller that won an Emmy in the category of Film Sound Mixing.

0675
FLOOD
11/24/76 Irwin Allen Productions/20th Century-Fox (2 hours)
(formally titled "Irwin Allen's Production of 'Flood' ")

Martin Milner, Robert Culp and Cameron Mitchell in FLOOD! (1976)

Laurence Olivier and Maureen Stapleton in CAT ON A HOT TIN ROOF (1976)

Executive Producer: Irwin Allen
Director: Earl Bellamy
Teleplay: Don Ingalls
Photography: Lamar Boren
Music: Richard LaSalle
Production Design: Stan Jolley
Special Effects Photography: L. B. Abbott
Editor: Bill Brame

Steve Banning	ROBERT CULP
Paul Blake	MARTIN MILNER
Mary Cutler	BARBARA HERSHEY
John Cutler	RICHARD BASEHART
Abbie Adams	CAROL LYNLEY
Franklin (Fisherman)	RODDY McDOWALL
Sam Adams	CAMERON MITCHELL
Andy Cutler	ERIC OLSON
Alice Cutler	TERESA WRIGHT
Daisy Kempel	FRANCINE YORK
Dr. Ted Horne	WHIT BISSELL
Charlie Davis	JAMES GRIFFITH
Emma Fisher	ANN DORAN
Johnny Lowman	LEIF GARRETT
Al Spangler	JACK COLLINS
Nancy Lowman	ELIZABETH ROGERS
Mrs. Wilson	EDNA HELTON
Mrs. Parker	GLORIA STUART

Irwin Allen's first made-for-TV disaster movie follows the course charted by its wide-screen big brothers, only this time it's a small town about to be devastated by a flood when a faulty dam bursts. At a reported cost of $2.5 million, this was, according to network publicity, the most expensive film made to that time for television. A companion Irwin Allen movie called *Fire* was aired several weeks later, and then each was trimmed to ninety minutes and rerun as a TV double bill subsequently.

0676
BEAUTY AND THE BEAST
12/3/76 Palm Films Ltd. (90 min)

Executive Producer: Thomas M. C. Johnston
Producer: Hank Moonjean
Director: Fielder Cook
Teleplay: Sherman Yellen
Photography: Jack Hildyard
Music: Ron Goodwin
Assistant Director: David Tringham
Art Director: Elliott Scott
Editor: Freddie Wilson

The Beast	GEORGE C. SCOTT
Belle Beaumont	TRISH VAN DEVERE
Lucy	VIRGINIA McKENNA
Edward Beaumont	BERNARD LEE
Susan	PATRICIA QUINN
Anthony	MICHAEL HARBOUR
Nicholas	WILLIAM RELTON

A striking adaptation of the children's classic about the beautiful maiden who agrees to marry a beast and live in his magical castle in order to save her father's life. George C. Scott, who played the role in a boar's head mask, received an Emmy Award nomination as Best Actor, and nominations also went to Albert Wolsky for his costume designs and to Del Acevedo, John Chambers and Dan Striepke for their unusual make-up creations.

0677
SMASH-UP ON INTERSTATE 5
12/3/76 A Filmways Production (2 hours)

Executive Producer: Edward S. Feldman
Producer: Roger Lewis
Director: John Llewellyn Moxey
Teleplay: Eugene Price and Robert Presnell, Jr.
Based on the novel *Expressway* by Elleston Trevor
Photography: John M. Nicholaus
Music: Bill Conti
Production Designer: W. Stewart Campbell
Special Effects: Howard Jensen
Editor: John A. Martinelli

Sgt. Sam Marcum	ROBERT CONRAD
Barbara Hutton	SIAN BARBARA ALLEN
Al Pearson	BUDDY EBSEN
Danny	HERB EDELMAN
Dale	DAVID GROH
Lee Bassett	SCOTT JACOBY
Officer Estevez	JOE KAPP
Burnsey	SUE LYON
Erica	VERA MILES
Laureen	DONNA MILLS
June Pearson	HARRIET NELSON
Pete	GEORGE O'HANLON, JR.
Trudy	TERRY MOORE
Officer Berman	DAVID NELSON
Officer Hutton	TOMMY LEE JONES
Andy	JOEL PARKS
Randy	BARRY HAMILTON

This drama depicts the lives of an all-star cast prior to their involvement in a massive thirty-nine-car crash on a Southern California freeway over a holiday weekend.

0678
CAT ON A HOT TIN ROOF
12/6/76 Granada Television Ltd. (2 hours)

Producers: Derek Granger and Laurence Olivier
Director: Robert Moore
Teleplay: Tennessee Williams
From his Pulitzer Prize-winning play
Theme music arranged by Michael Lankester from
the music of Henry Purcell
Incidental Music: Derek Hilton
Costumes: Jane Robinson
Set Design: Peter Phillips

Big Daddy	LAURENCE OLIVIER
Margaret	NATALIE WOOD
Brick	ROBERT WAGNER
Big Mama	MAUREEN STAPLETON
Gooper	JACK HEDLEY
Mae	MARY PEACH
Dixie	HEIDI RUNDT
Sonny	SEAN SAXON
Buster	MARK TAYLOR
Trixie	ELIZABETH CAPARROS
Polly	JENNIFER HUGHES
Lacey	SAM MANSERAY
Daisy	GLADYS TAYLOR
Brightie	NADIA CATOUSE
Sookey	GEORGE HARRIS
Small	MEL TAYLOR
Doc Baugh	DAVID HEALY

This was the premiere of Laurence Olivier's "Tribute
to American Theatre," offering an adaptation of
Tennessee Williams' 1955 Pulitzer Prize-winning play
about the conflicts, weaknesses and strengths of a Mississippi family, portrayed, with three exceptions, by an
all-British cast.

0679
VICTORY AT ENTEBBE
12/13/76 David L. Wolper Productions (3 hours)

Executive Producer: David L. Wolper
Producer: Robert Guenette
Associate Producer: Albert J. Simon
Director: Marvin J. Chomsky
Teleplay: Ernest Kinoy
Photography: James Kilgore
Music: Charles Fox
Production Design: Edward Stephenson
Editors: Jim McElroy and Mike Gavaldon

German Terrorist	HELMUT BERGER
Yakov Shlomo	THEODORE BIKEL
Chana Vilnofsky	LINDA BLAIR
Hershel Vilnofsky	KIRK DOUGLAS
Col. Yonatan "Yonni" Netanyahu	RICHARD DREYFUSS
Mordecai Gur	STEFAN GIERASCH
Benjamin Wise	DAVID GROH
President Idi Amin	JULIUS HARRIS*
Mrs. Wise	HELEN HAYES
Yitzhak Rabin	ANTHONY HOPKINS
Shimon Peres	BURT LANCASTER
Captain Dukas	CHRISTIAN MARQUAND
Edra Vilnofsky	ELIZABETH TAYLOR
Nomi Haroun	JESSICA WALTER
Gen. Dan Shomron	HARRIS YULIN
Natan Haroun	ALLAN MILLER
German Woman	BIBI BESCH
Aaron Olav	DAVID SHEINER
Moshe Meyer	SEVERN DARDEN
Yaakobi	BEN HAMMER
Gamal Fahmy	ANTHONY JAMES

Kirk Douglas in VICTORY AT ENTEBBE (1976)

Richard Dreyfuss, Harris Yulin, Burt Lancaster and Stefan Gierasch in
VICTORY AT ENTEBBE (1976)

Jaif	VICTOR MOHICA
Nan Peyser	SAMANTHA HARPER

and: Phil Sterling, Erica Yohn, Lilyan Chauvin, Miriam Bird Nethery, Zitto Kazan, Jessica St. John, Kristine Wayborn, Austin Stoker, Dimitri Logothetis, Jenny Maybrook, Than Wyenn, Eunice Christopher, Pitt Herbert, Barbara Carney, Michael Mullins, Vera Mandell

The first of two dramatic re-creations of the July 4, 1976 Israeli lightning raid on the airport at Entebbe, Uganda, to rescue a planeload of hostages who had been taken by Palestinian hijackers. Rushed into release, this was shown initially on videotape and later converted to film for theatrical showings outside of the United States. Ernest Kinoy received an Emmy Award nomination for his teleplay.

*Replaced Godfrey Cambridge, who died during production.

Susan Anspach and Ralph Waite in THE SECRET LIFE OF JOHN CHAPMAN (1976)

0680
YOUNG PIONEERS' CHRISTMAS
12/17/76 An ABC Circle Film (2 hours)

Producer: Ed Friendly
Director: Michael O'Herlihy
Teleplay: Blanche Hanalis
Photography: Robert L. Morrison
Music: Laurence Rosenthal
Art Director: Jan M. Van Tamelen
Editor: Allan La Mastra

Molly Beaton	LINDA PURL
David Beaton	ROGER KERN
Dan Gray	ROBERT HAYS
Nettie Peters	KAY KIMLER
Mr. Peters	ROBERT DONNER
Loftus	BRITT LEACH
Yancy	ARNOLD SOBOLOFF
Doyle	BRENDAN DILLON
Pike	RAND BRIDGES
Charlie Peters	BRIAN MELROSE
Flora Peters	SHERRI WAGNER

A young frontier couple put aside the grief of losing their infant son to extend a gift of friendship and help bring a joyous holiday to the Dakota wilderness in this sequel to the earlier *The Young Pioneers* (1976). A brief "Young Pioneers" series followed in January 1977.

0681
THE LONELIEST RUNNER
12/20/76 NBC Television (90 min)

Producer/Director: Michael Landon
Teleplay: Michael Landon
Photography: Ted Voigtlander
Music: David Rose
Art Director: Walter M. Jeffries
Editor: John Loeffler

John Curtis (as a youth)	LANCE KERWIN
Arnold Curtis	BRIAN KEITH
Alice Curtis	DeANN MEARS
Nancy Rizzi	MELISSA SUE ANDERSON
Himself	RAFER JOHNSON
John Curtis (as an adult)	MICHAEL LANDON
Tony	RANDY FAUSTINO
Donnie	DERMOTT DOWNS
Doctor	WALKER EDMINSON
Security Guard	HERB VIGRAN

A teenage loner who happens to be a gifted athlete must cope with personal shame and the angry accusations of his parents, especially his demanding mother, over his chronic bed-wetting, although his shame ironically results in his eventually becoming an Olympic gold-medalist runner. Michael Landon based this story on his own teenage experiences. Photographer Ted Voigtlander and editor John Loeffler each received an Emmy nomination.

0682
THE SECRET LIFE OF JOHN CHAPMAN
12/27/76 The Jozak Company (90 min)

Executive Producer: Gerald I. Isenberg
Producer: Gerald W. Abrams
Director: David Lowell Rich
Teleplay: Albert Ruben
Based on the book *Blue Collar Journal* by John R. Coleman
Photography: Jacques R. Marquette
Music: Fred Myrow
Art Director: Trevor Williams
Editor: John A. Martinelli

John Chapman	RALPH WAITE
Wilma	SUSAN ANSPACH
Gus Reed	PAT HINGLE
Meredith Chapman	ELAYNE HEILVEIL
Andy Chapman	BRAD DAVIS
College Chairman	MAURY COOPER
Charlie	REUBEN SIERRA
Victor	GARDNER HAYES
Dammit Stanley	BILL TREADWELL
Al	TEOTHA DENNARD
Grady	JOHN AYLWARD
Wally	CURTIS JACKSON
Factory Clerk	PETER FISHER
Manager	JOHN ROEDER

and: Zoaunne Leroy, Richard Arnold, Thomas Moss, Earnest M. Simon, Norman Bernard, Richard Hawkins, Joe Brazil

A true-life drama about a college president who takes a sabbatical from his position with a small Eastern college to work as a laborer and experience a life style different from his regulated existence.

0683
GREEN EYES
1/3/77 Lorimar Productions (2 hours)

Executive Producers: Lee Rich and Philip Capice
Producers: David Seltzer and John Erman
Director: John Erman
Teleplay: David Seltzer
From a story by David Seltzer and Eugene Logan
Photography: Terry K. Meade
Music: Fred Karlin
Art Director: Phil Barber
Editor: John W. Wheeler

Lloyd Dubeck	PAUL WINFIELD
Margaret Sheen	RITA TUSHINGHAM
Noel Cousins	JONATHAN LIPPE
Em Thuy	VICTORIA RACIMO
Trung	LEMI
Mrs. Dubeck	ROYCE WALLACE
Hal	ROBERT DoQUI
V.A. Officer	FRED SADOFF
Mr. Cousins	DABBS GREER
Mrs. Cousins	CLAUDIA BRYAR
Minh	JOSEPH HIEU

Disillusioned and uncertain about his future, a Vietnam veteran journeys back to Southeast Asia to search among thousands of war orphans for the son he left behind.

0684
BENNY AND BARNEY: LAS VEGAS UNDERCOVER
1/9/77 Universal (90 min)

Producer: Glen A. Larson
Director: Ron Satlof
Teleplay: Glen A. Larson
Photography: Ronald W. Brown
Music: Stu Phillips
Art Director: Alexander A. Meyer
Editor: Ronald J. Fagan

Benny Kowalski	TERRY KISER
Barney Tuscom	TIMOTHY THOMERSON
Lieut. Callan	JACK COLVIN
Margie Parks	JANE SEYMOUR
Jules Rosen	JACK CASSIDY
Jack Davis	HUGH O'BRIAN
Joey Gallion	PAT HARRINGTON
Manager	RODNEY DANGERFIELD
Higgie	MARTY ALLEN
Drunk	GEORGE GOBEL
Paul Mizener	BOBBY TROUP
Sergeant Ross	MICHAEL PATAKI
Will Dawson	DICK GAUTIER
Jake Tuttle	TED CASSIDY

and: Don Marsh, J. P. Finegan, Rosalind Miles

Two undercover cops find their avocation—a musical act—helpful in tapping informants on the Las Vegas Strip regarding the alleged kidnapping of a top entertainer. This pilot was for a series that never materialized. Original title (until eve of premiere): *Benny and Barney, The Aristocrats.*

0685
RAID ON ENTEBBE
1/9/77 Edgar J. Scherick Associates/20th Century-Fox (3 hours)

Executive Producers: Edgar J. Scherick and Daniel H. Blatt
Associate Producer: Robin S. Clark
Director: Irvin Kershner
Teleplay: Barry Beckerman
Photography: Bill Butler

David Opatoshu and Peter Finch in RAID ON ENTEBBE (1977)

2nd Unit Photography: Terry K. Meade
Music: David Shire
Production Design: W. Stewart Campbell
Art Director: Kirk Axtell
Editors: Bud S. Isaacs, Nick Archer and Art Seid

Yitzhak Rabin	PETER FINCH
Daniel Cooper	MARTIN BALSAM
Wilfrid Bose	HORST BUCHHOLZ
Maj. Gen. Benny Pelod	JOHN SAXON
Dora Bloch	SYLVIA SIDNEY
Mordechai Gur	JACK WARDEN
President Idi Amin	YAPHET KOTTO
Gen. Dan Shamron	CHARLES BRONSON
Shimon Peres	TIGE ANDREWS
Capt. Michel Bacos	EDDIE CONSTANTINE
Yaakobi	WARREN KEMMERLING
Yigal Allon	ROBERT LOGGIA
Menachem Begin	DAVID OPATOSHU
Pasco Cohen	ALLAN ARBUS
Gabriele Krieger	MARICLARE COSTELLO
Col. Yonatan "Yonni" Netanyahu	STEPHEN MACHT
Sammy Berg	JAMES WOODS
Bar Lev	LOU GILBERT
Terrorist	ALEX COLON
Mr. Sager	ROBIN GAMMELL
Lieut. Grut	AHARON IPALE
Mr. Harvey	HARVEY LEMBECK
Goldbaum	BILLY SANDS
Mrs. Sager	MILLIE SLAVIN

and: Pearl Shear, Rene Assa, Barbara Allyne Bennet, Anna Berger, Stanley Brock, Peter Brocco, Fred Cardoza, Lauren Frost, Larry Gelman, Bill Gerber, Dov Gottesfeld, Hanna Hertelendy, Dinah Manoff, Caryn Matchinga, Harlee McBride, George Petrie, Louis Quinn, Kim Richards, Tom Rosqui, Steve Shaw, Martin Speer

This was the second star-laden dramatization of the Israeli rescue of plane-bound hostages taken during a Palestinian hijacking on July 4, 1977. Cinematographer Bill Butler won an Emmy Award for his work. Others nominated were Peter Finch (his last screen role), Martin Balsam and Yaphet Kotto, director Irvin Kershner, writer Barry Beckerman, composer David Shire, and editors Bud S. Isaacs, Nick Archer and Art Seid. Charles Bronson returned to television acting in this one (without top billing and even listed *below* the title) after a decade away in his successful search for movie stardom.

0686
THE DEATH OF RICHIE
1/10/77 Henry Jaffe Enterprises, Inc. (2 hours)

Executive Producer: Charles B. FitzSimmons
Producer: Michael Jaffe
Director: Paul Wendkos
Teleplay: John McGreevey
Based on the book *Richie* by Thomas Thompson
Photography: Robert B. Hauser
Music: Fred Karlin
Art Director: James G. Hulsey
Editor: Michael Economou

George Werner	BEN GAZZARA
Richie Werner	ROBBY BENSON
Carol Werner	EILEEN BRENNAN
Russell Werner	LANCE KERWIN
Brick	CHARLES FLEISCHER
Peanuts	CLINT HOWARD
Mark	HARRY GOLD
Sheila	CINDY EILBACHER
Betty Firmani	ROSE GREGORIO
Judge Feinberg	ANNE NEWMAN-MANTEE
Pat	SEAN ROCHE
Mrs. Norton	SHIRLEY O'HARA
Elaine	JENNIFER RHODES

Hugh O'Brian in FANTASY ISLAND (1977)

A confused teenager turns to drugs, leading to erratic outbursts in school and violent quarrels with his straight-arrow father.

0687
THE CITY
1/12/77 Quinn Martin Productions (90 min)

Executive Producer: Quinn Martin
Producer: John Wilder
Director: Harvey Hart
Teleplay: John Wilder
Photography: Jacques R. Marquette
Music: John Elizalde
Art Director: Herman Zimmerman
Editors: Ray Daniels and James Gross

Lt. Matt Lewis	ROBERT FORSTER
Sgt. Brian Scott	DON JOHNSON

Capt. Lloyd Bryant	WARD COSTELLO
Wes Collins	JIMMY DEAN
Eugene Banks	MARK HAMILL
Carol Carter	SUSAN SULLIVAN
Dr. Hank Cullen	FELTON PERRY
Girl at Hospital	LESLIE ACKERMAN
Burt Frescura	PAUL CAVONIS
Jed Haynes	PAUL FIX
Mel Greenwall	JOBY BAKER

Narrated by WILLIAM CONRAD

A police-drama pilot featuring two Los Angeles cops scouring the city in search of a psychotic with a deadly grudge against a country-western singer.

0688
FANTASY ISLAND
1/14/77 Spelling/Goldberg Productions (2 hours)

Producers: Aaron Spelling and Leonard Goldberg
Director: Richard Lang
Teleplay: Gene Levitt
Photography: Arch R. Dalzell
Music: Laurence Rosenthal
Art Director: Paul Sylos
Editor: John Woodcock

Roarke	RICARDO MONTALBAN
Arnold Greenwood	BILL BIXBY
Francesca	SANDRA DEE
Grant Baines	PETER LAWFORD
Liz Hollander	CAROL LYNLEY
Paul Henley	HUGH O'BRIAN
Eunice Hollander Baines	ELEANOR PARKER
Michelle	VICTORIA PRINCIPAL
Charles Hollander	DICK SARGENT
Connie Raymond	CHRISTINA SINATRA
Tattoo	HERVE VILLECHAIZE
Hunter #1	JOHN McKINNEY
Hunter #2	CEDRIC SCOTT
Hunter #3	PETER MacLEAN
Bartender	IAN ABERCROMBIE
Barmaid	ELIZABETH DARTMOOR

In this pilot to the hit series which began in the fall of 1977, a planeload of wealthy vacationers land on a glamorous island paradise for the weekend, where for $50,000 each they can live out their most compelling fantasies. Suave Montalban and his short man Friday, Villechaize, continued welcoming familiar TV faces in the weekly series.

0689
LITTLE LADIES OF THE NIGHT
1/16/77 Spelling-Goldberg Productions (2 hours)

Executive Producers: Aaron Spelling and Leonard Goldberg
Producer: Hal Sitowitz
Director: Marvin J. Chomsky
Teleplay: Hal Sitowitz
Photography: Dennis Dalzell
Music: Jerry Fielding
Art Director: Paul Sylos
Editor: George Brooks

Lyle York	DAVID SOUL
Russ Garfield	LOU GOSSETT
Hailey Atkins	LINDA PURL
Comfort	CLIFTON DAVIS
Marilyn Atkins	CAROLYN JONES
Frank Atkins	PAUL BURKE
Maureen	LANA WOOD
Karen Brodwick	KATHLEEN QUINLAN
Finch	VIC TAYBACK

Miss Colby	KATHERINE HELMOND
Maggie	DOROTHY MALONE
Matron	BIBI OSTERWALD
Mrs. Brodwick	SANDRA DEEL
Wally	CLAUDE EARL JONES
Brady	DAVID HAYWARD

and: James Ray, Tom McDonald, Byron Morrow, Matt Bennett, Connie Sawyer

A one-time pimp turned big-city cop takes an interest in a teenage runaway who has been drawn into the hard world of prostitution after being shunned by her parents. Originally this was to have premiered in September 1976.

0690
STONESTREET: WHO KILLED THE CENTERFOLD MODEL?
1/16/77 Universal (90 min)

Executive Producer: David J. Connell
Producer: Leslie Stevens
Director: Russ Mayberry
Teleplay: Leslie Stevens
Photography: Terry K. Meade
Music: Pat Williams
Art Director: John E. Chilberg II
Editor: Robert F. Shugrue

Liz Stonestreet	BARBARA EDEN
Max Pierce	JOSEPH MASCOLO
Jessica Hilliard	JOAN HACKETT
Elliot Osborn	RICHARD BASEHART
Mrs. Schroeder	LOUISE LATHAM
Arlene	ELAINE GIFTOS
Eddie Schroeder	JAMES INGERSOLL
Della Bianco	SALLY KIRKLAND
Chuck Voit	VAL AVERY
Dale Anderson	ROBERT BURTON
Davis	GINO CONFORTI
Erna	LaWANDA PAGE
Watch Commander	RYAN MacDONALD
Amory Osborn	ANN DUSENBERRY

A pilot movie about a female private eye who goes undercover as a porno actress to unravel the case of a prominent industrialist's missing daughter.

0691
THE MAN IN THE IRON MASK
1/17/77 Norman Rosemont Productions/ITC Entertainment Ltd. (2 hours)

Producer: Norman Rosemont
Director: Mike Newell
Teleplay: William Bast
Based on the novel by Alexandre Dumas
Photography: Freddie Young
Music: Allyn Ferguson
Art Director: David Tringham
Costume Designer: Olga Lehmann
Editor: Bill Blunden

King Louis XIV/Philippe	RICHARD CHAMBERLAIN
Fouquet	PATRICK McGOOHAN
D'Artagnan	LOUIS JOURDAN
Louise de la Valliere	JENNY AGUTTER
Duval	IAN HOLM
Colbert	SIR RALPH RICHARDSON
Queen Maria Theresa	VIVIEN MERCHANT
Anne of Austria	BRENDA BRUCE
Armand	ESMOND KNIGHT
Baisemeaux	GODFREY QUIGLEY
Percerin	EMRYS JAMES

Claude	DENIS LAWSON
Henriette	ANNE ZELDA
Blacksmith	STACY DAVIS

and: Gene Renex, Pierre Marteville, John Cording

A stylish new version of the Dumas swashbuckler, mixing fact and fictitious derring-do and telling of Louis XIV's identical twin. It already had been filmed a half-dozen times in several variations. This production earned Emmy Award nominations for writer William Bast and costumer Olga Lehmann.

0692
THE LOVE BOAT II
1/21/77 Aaron Spelling Productions (2 hours)

Executive Producers: Aaron Spelling and Douglas S. Cramer
Producer: Henry Colman
Director: Hy Averback
Teleplays: "Unfaithfully Yours" by Carl Kleinschmitt; "Here's Looking at You, Love" by Dawn Aldredge and Marion C. Freeman; "For the Love of Sandy" by Aldredge, Freeman and Leonora Thuna; and "The Heckler" by Steve Pritzker
Photography: Arch R. Dalzell
Music: Charles Fox
Art Director: Tracy Bousman
Editor: Jerry Dronsky

Jim Berkley	KEN BERRY
Ralph Manning	BERT CONVY
Eva McFarland	CELESTE HOLM
Elaine Palmer	HOPE LANGE
Linda Morley	KRISTY McNICHOL
Stephen Palmer	ROBERT REED
Robert Grant	CRAIG STEVENS
Pat McFarland	MARCIA STRASSMAN
Roger	LYLE WAGGONER
Donna Morley	DIANA CANOVA
Angela	TRACY BROOKS SWOPE
Dr. Livingston	WESLEY ADDY
Amy Mitchell	CANDICE AZZARA

and Your "Love Boat" Crew:

Gopher (Purser)	FRED GRANDY
Dr. O'Neill	BERNIE KOPELL
Isaac (Bartender)	TED LANGE
Captain Madison	QUINN REDECKER
Sandy Summers (Cruise Director)	DIANE STILWELL

The sequel to *The Love Boat* (1976), this second pilot to the subsequent hit series once again offered an all-star TV cast setting sail for romance under the watchful eyes of a totally new crew, several of whom (Grandy, Kopell and Lange) were signed on for the later weekly voyage which began setting sail in September 1977.

0693
JOHNNY, WE HARDLY KNEW YE
1/27/77 Talent Associates Ltd./Jamel Productions, Inc. (2 hours)

Executive Producer: David Susskind
Producer: Lionel Chetwynd
Associate Producer: Peter Dohanos
Director: Gilbert Cates
Teleplay: Lionel Chetwynd
Based on the 1972 book by Kenneth P. O'Donnell and David F. Powers with Joe McCarthy
Photography: Edward R. Brown
Music: Garry Sherman
Production Design: Peter Dohanos
Editor: Stephen A. Rotter

John F. Kennedy	PAUL RUDD
Ambassador Joseph P. Kennedy	WILLIAM PRINCE
John F. "Honey Fitz" Fitzgerald	BURGESS MEREDITH
David F. Powers	KEVIN CONWAY
Joe Kane	RICHARD VENTURE
Mrs. Rose Kennedy	SHIRLEY RICH
Billy Sutton	TOM BERENGER
Legion Commander	DAVID F. POWERS
Father Robinson	JOSEPH BOVA
Powers' Sister	PADDY CROFT
Mrs. Murphy	MARY DIVENY
Softy McNamara	KENNETH McMILLAN
Sullivan	SEAN GRIFFIN
Tip Tobin	JOHN RAMSEY
Bubba	RON McLARTY

and: Bob O'Connell, Brian Dennehy, Bernie McInerney, E. Brian Dean, Chip Olcott, Elizabeth Moore, Rebecca Sand, Joanne Dusseau, Bernie Passeltiner

The dramatization of a chapter in the best-selling book, focusing on young John Kennedy's first run for office as he sought a congressional seat in the 1946 election.

0694
YESTERDAY'S CHILD
2/3/77 Paramount (90 min)

Producer: William Kayden
Directors: Corey Allen and Bob Rosenbaum
Teleplay: Michael Gleason
Based on the novel *Night of Clear Choice* by Doris Miles Disney
Photography: Robert B. Hauser
Music: Dominic Frontiere
Art Director: Joseph J. Jennings
Editor: Michael Economou

Laura Talbot	SHIRLEY JONES
John Talbot	ROSS MARTIN
Cliff Henley	CLAUDE AKINS
Emma Talbot	GERALDINE FITZGERALD
Ann Talbot	STEPHANIE ZIMBALIST
Sanford Grant	PATRICK WAYNE
Seth Talbot	DANIEL ZIPPI
Lieutenant Spano	GEORGE MURDOCK
Doctor	BOOTH COLMAN
Noel Talbot	TERENCE SCAMMELL

A seventeen-year-old girl turns up on the doorstep of a wealthy family claiming to be the daughter who was kidnapped fourteen years earlier.

0695
TAIL GUNNER JOE
2/6/77 Universal (3 hours)

Producer: George Eckstein
Director: Jud Taylor
Teleplay: Lane Slate
Photography: Ric Waite
Music: Billy May
Art Director: Lawrence G. Paull
Editor: Bernard J. Small

Joseph McCarthy	PETER BOYLE
Paul Cunningham	JOHN FORSYTHE
Logan	HEATHER MENZIES
Joseph Welch	BURGESS MEREDITH
Sen. Margaret Chase Smith	PATRICIA NEAL
Mrs. DeCamp	JEAN STAPLETON
Librarian	TIM O'CONNOR
Senator Lucas	PHILIP ABBOTT
Middleton	WESLEY ADDY
Sylvester	NED BEATTY
Jean Kerr	KAREN CARLSON
Wisconsin Farmer	JOHN CARRADINE
Logan's Boss	CHARLES CIOFFI
Sarah	DIANA DOUGLAS
Eisenhower	ANDREW DUGGAN
Armitage	HENRY JONES
Publisher	MURRAY MATHESON
Farmer	ANDREW PRINE
General Larkin	JOHN RANDOLPH
General Zwicker	WILLIAM SCHALLERT
Drew Pearson	ROBERT F. SIMON
Harry Truman	ROBERT SYMONDS
Senator Symington	LIN McCARTHY
General George Marshall	JOHN ANDERSON
Dean Acheson	ALAN HEWITT
Robert F. Kennedy	SAM CHEW, JR.
Senator Bolland	HERB VOLAND
Richard M. Nixon	RICHARD M. DIXON

and: Allan Miller, Addison Powell, Allan Oppenheimer, Allan Rich, Simon Scott, Bill Quinn, Kelly Jean Peters

An ambitious production of questionable accuracy spanning the rise and fall of Senator Joseph R. McCarthy as uncovered by a fictional veteran newsman and the ambitious young lady investigative reporter assigned to assist him. Emmy Awards went to Burgess Meredith for his portrayal of Joseph Welch and to Lane Slate for his original teleplay. Also nominated were Peter Boyle, Patricia Neal, director Jud Taylor and cinematographer Ric Waite.

0696
NIGHT TERROR
2/7/77 Charles Fries Productions (90 min)

Executive Producer: Charles Fries
Producers: Joel Glickman and Daniel Selznick
Director: E. W. Swackhamer
Teleplay: Carl Babler and Richard DeNeut
Photography: Vilis Lapenieks
Music: Fred Steiner
Editor: Aaron Stell

Carol Turner	VALERIE HARPER
The Killer	RICHARD ROMANUS
Man in Sports Car	NICHOLAS PRYOR
Old Derelict	JOHN QUADE
Walter Turner	MICHAEL TOLAN
Aunt Vera Willis	BEATRICE MANLEY
Carolyn Turner	QUINN CUMMINGS
Buddy	DAMON RASKIN
Indian Woman	MADELEINE TAYLOR HOLMES
Indian Man	JOHN WAR EAGLE

and: Jan Burrell, Gary Springer, Gary Barton, Dinah Manhoff, Linda Lukens, Frank Lugo, Charles Parks, Edward Cross

A housewife becomes the quarry of a psychopathic killer after she sees him shoot down a highway patrolman.

0697
THE LAST DINOSAUR
2/11/77 A Rankin/Bass Production (2 hours)

Producers: Arthur Rankin, Jr. and Jules Bass
Associate Producer: Benni Korzen
Directors: Alex Grasshoff and Tom Kotani
Teleplay: William Overgard
Photography: Shoji Ukda

Music: Maury Laws
Song "He Is the Last Dinosaur" by Maury Laws
and Jules Bass
Sung by Nancy Wilson
Art Director: Katzov Satsoya
Editor: Barry Walter

Masten Thrust	RICHARD BOONE
Frankie Banks	JOAN VAN ARK
Bunta	LUTHER RACKLEY
Chuck Wade	STEVEN KEATS
Barney	CARL HANSEN
Prehistoric Girl	MAMIYA SEKIA
Dr. Kawamoto	TATSU NAKAMURA
Expedition Captain	WILLIAM ROSS

The world's richest man, trapped in a pocket of time without weapons, is pursued by a primitive tribe while hunting the last living dinosaur, his obsession in life. The Japanese special effects provide an added touch to this Saturday matinee-type adventure tale.

0698
THE SPELL
2/20/77 Charles Fries Productions (90 min)

Executive Producers: Charles Fries and Dick Berg
Producer: David Manson
Director: Lee Philips
Teleplay: Brian Taggert
Photography: Matthew F. Leonetti
Music: Gerald Fried
Art Director: Robert MacKichan
Special Effects: Larry Roberts
Editor: David Newhouse

Marion Matchett	LEE GRANT
Rita Matchett	SUSAN MYERS
Jo Standish	LELIA GOLDONI
Kristina Matchett	HELEN HUNT
Dale Boyce	JACK COLVIN
Glenn Matchett	JAMES OLSON
Stan Restin	JAMES GREENE
Rian Bellamy	WRIGHT KING
Jill	BARBARA BOSTOCK
Jackie Segal	DONEY OATMAN

A study in the occult with more than a passing similarity to Brian de Palma's *Carrie* (1977). An overweight teenager, taunted by schoolmates and unloved at home, turns her supernatural powers on her tormentors.

0699
SECRETS
2/20/77 The Jozak Company (2 hours)

Executive Producer: Gerald I. Isenberg
Producer: Gerald W. Abrams
Director: Paul Wendkos
Teleplay: James Henerson
Photography: Richard C. Glouner
Music: George Aliceson Tipton
Song "Dream Away" written and sung by Susan Blakely
Art Director: Trevor Williams
Editor: John A. Martinelli

Andrea Fleming	SUSAN BLAKELY
Herb Fleming	ROY THINNES
Helen Warner	JOANNE LINVILLE
Ed Warner	JOHN RANDOLPH
Laura Fleming	MELODY THOMAS
Dr. Lee	FRANCES LEE McCAIN
Phyllis Turner	CHARLOTTE STEWART
Larry Bleier	ANTHONY EISLEY
Chrissie	MICHELLE STACY
Joanne Weese	ROSEANNE COVY
Joel Corcoran	ANDREW STEVENS

Phyllis Turner	CHARLOTTE STEWART
Andrea (age 7)	ELIZABETH CHESHIRE
Cab Driver	BRYAN CUTLER
Piano Tuner	PAUL ITKIN

An unhappily married young woman succumbs to her sexual fantasies and becomes compulsively promiscuous in a desperate attempt to find the "secret" of happiness that her mother had convinced her was hers.

0700
SST—DEATH FLIGHT
2/25/77 ABC Circle Films (2 hours)
(subsequently titled *SST: Disaster in the Sky*)

Producer: Ron Roth
Director: David Lowell Rich
Teleplay: Robert L. Joseph, Meyer Dolinsky and William Roberts
From a story by Guerdon Trueblood
Photography: Joseph Biroc
Music: John Cacavas
Art Director: Peter M. Wooley
Editor: Pembroke J. Herring

Carla Stanley	BARBARA ANDERSON
Tim Vernon	BERT CONVY
Paul Whitley	PETER GRAVES
Marshall Cole	LORNE GREENE
Anne Redding	SEASON HUBLEY
Mae	TINA LOUISE
Les Phillips	GEORGE MAHARIS
Willy Basset	BURGESS MEREDITH
Hank Fairbanks	DOUG McCLURE
Lyle Kingman	MARTIN MILNER
Dr. Ralph Therman	BROCK PETERS
Capt. Jim Walsh	ROBERT REED
Nancy Kingman	SUSAN STRASBERG
Angela Garland	MISTY ROWE
David	BILLY CRYSTAL
Bob Connors	JOHN DeLANCIE
Kathy	CHRYSTIE JENNER
Carter	REGIS PHILBIN
Flight Engineer	ROBERT ITO

The inaugural flight of America's first supersonic transport is launched with a celebrity-studded passenger list (familiar TV faces all), but the plane may never land. During filming, this was called *Flight of the Maiden,* and for its overseas showings it is titled simply *Death Flight.*

0701
THE STRANGE POSSESSION OF MRS. OLIVER
2/28/77 The Schpetner Company (90 min)

Producer: Stan Schpetner
Associate Producer: Richard Matheson
Director: Gordon Hessler
Teleplay: Richard Matheson
Photography: Frank Stanley
Music: Morton Stevens
Editors: Frank E. Morriss and Jerry L. Garcia

Miriam Oliver	KAREN BLACK
Greg Oliver	GEORGE HAMILTON
Mark	ROBERT F. LYONS
Housekeeper	LUCILLE BENSON
Mrs. Dempsey	JEAN ALLISON
Saleslady	GLORIA LeROY
Bartender at Beach	BURKE BYRNES
Dance Partner in Bar	ASHER BRAUNER

and: Charles Cooper, William Irwin, Danna Hansen, Delos V. Smith, Nancy Hahn Leonard, Macon McCalman, Bob Palmer, Sunny Woods

A housewife, seeking to change her ordinary routine, alters her hairstyle, makeup and wardrobe, and gradually takes on the personality of another woman—who had died five years earlier.

0702
IN THE GLITTER PALACE
2/27/77 The Writers' Company/Columbia Pictures (2 hours)

Executive Producer: Stanley Kallis
Producers: Jerry Ludwig and Jay Daniel
Director: Robert Butler
Teleplay: Jerry Ludwig
Photography: Gerald Perry Finnerman
Music: John Parker
Art Directors: Ross Bellah and Zoltan Muller
Editor: Richard Bracken

Vincent Halloran	CHAD EVERETT
Ellen Lange	BARBARA HERSHEY
Roy Danko	ANTHONY ZERBE
Raymond Travers	HOWARD DUFF
Casey Walker	DIANA SCARWID
Nate Redstone	DAVID WAYNE
Grace Mayo	TISHA STERLING
Judge Kendis Winslow	SALOME JENS
Roger	RON RIFKIN
Fred Ruggiero	RON MASAK
Merrill	PAUL STEVENS
Daisy Dolon	CAROLE COOK
Harry Brittenham	ROBERT SAMPSON
Ricki	LYNNE MARTA

and: Booth Colman, Gloria Le Roy, Carole Mallory, Stanley Kamel, Lee Delano, Paul Bryar, Lucetta Jenison, Paula Shaw, Romo Vincent

A murder melodrama in which a defense lawyer-detective is urged by his ex-girl friend to defend her lesbian lover, charged with a killing of which she claims she is innocent.

0703
MINSTREL MAN
3/2/77 Roger Gimbel Productions/First Artists (2 hours)

Executive Producer: Roger Gimbel
Producers: Mitchell Brower and Robert Lovenheim
Director: William A. Graham
Teleplay: Richard Shapiro and Esther Mayesh Shapiro
Photography: Michael Margulies
Music: Fred Karlin
Choreography: Donald McKayle
Art Director: Hilyard Brown
Editor: Ronald J. Fagan

Harry Brown, Jr.	GLYNN TURMAN
Charlie Bates	TED ROSS
Rennie Brown	STANLEY CLAY
Jessamine	SAUNDRA SHARP
Tambo	ART EVANS
Harry Brown, Sr./Fat Man	GENE BELL
George	EARL BILLINGS
Young Harry, Jr.	ANTHONY AMOS
Young Rennie	AMECHI UZODINMA
Robert	ARTHUR ROOKS
Tess	CAROL SUTTON
Tobias Finch	WILBER SWARTZ
Oliver Turpin	ROBERT EARLE
Carmichael	DON LUTENBACHER
Pitchman	BILLY HOLLIDAY
Fair Manager	ROBERT L. HARPER

The era of black minstrelsy as captured in the lives of two brothers, one an extroverted song-and-dance man determined to break tradition and own his own minstrel troupe in a field dominated by black-faced whites, the other an introverted and innovative composer struggling to break away from the stereotypes haunting black minstrel artists. Fred Karlin received an Emmy Award nomination for his musical score.

0704
MAN FROM ATLANTIS
3/4/77 Solow Production Company (2 hours)

Executive Producer: Herbert F. Solow
Producer: Robert H. Justman
Director: Lee H. Katzin
Teleplay: Mayo Simon
Photography: William Cronjager
Music: Fred Karlin
Art Director: J. Smith Poplin
Special Effects: Tom Fisher
Editor: Gary Griffin

Mark Harris	PATRICK DUFFY
Dr. Elizabeth Merrill	BELINDA MONTGOMERY
Ernie Smith	DEAN SANTORO
Adm. Dewey Pierce	ART LUND
Mr. Schuburt	VICTOR BUONO
Cmdr. Phil Roth	LAWRENCE PRESSMAN
Lt. Ainsley	MARK JENKINS
Lt. Cmdr. Johnson	ALLEN CASE
Dr. Doug Berkley	JOSHUA BRYANT

and: Steve Franken, Virginia Gregg

A science-fiction drama about a water-breathing humanoid, the last survivor of an underwater habitat called Atlantis, and his encounter with earthlings. The subsequent series was short-lived (September-December 1977).

0705
A CIRCLE OF CHILDREN
3/10/77 Edgar J. Sherick Productions, Inc./20th Century-Fox (2 hours)

Executive Producers: Edgar J. Scherick and Daniel H. Blatt
Producer: Steven Gethers
Associate Producer: Robin S. Clark
Director: Don Taylor
Teleplay: Steven Gethers
From the novel by Mary MacCracken
Photography: Gayne Rescher
Music: Nelson Riddle
Title song by Steve Hines and Steven Gethers
Sung by Carmen McRae
Art Director: Lawrence G. Paull
Editor: Sheldon Kahn

Mary MacCracken	JANE ALEXANDER
Helga	RACHEL ROBERTS
Dan Franklin	DAVID OGDEN STIERS
Doris Fleming	NAN MARTIN
Brian O'Connell	MATTHEW LABORTEAUX
Larry MacCracken	PETER BRANDON
Chris	JASON TYLER
Sarah Johnson	KYLE RICHARDS
Elizabeth MacCracken	SUSAN PRATT
Mrs. O'Connell	JUDY LEWIS
Dr. Marino	RAY BUKTENICA
Mrs. Grady	PEARL SHEAR

and: Christopher West, Niki Dantine, William Tragoe

An affluent suburbanite's life is changed by a demanding challenge as a volunteer at a school for emotionally disturbed children when her own structured existence, stale marriage and now independent college-age daughter no longer provide fulfillment. Steven Gethers' teleplay earned him an Emmy Award nomination.

0706
ELEANOR AND FRANKLIN: THE WHITE HOUSE YEARS
3/13/77 A Talent Associates Ltd. Production (3 hours)

Executive Producer: David Susskind
Producer: Harry R. Sherman
Director: Daniel Petrie
Teleplay: James Costigan
Based on the book *Eleanor and Franklin* by Joseph P. Lash
Story Consultants: Franklin D. Roosevelt, Jr. and Joseph P. Lash
Photography: James Crabe
Music: John Barry
Production Design: Jan Scott
Editors: Rita Roland and Michael S. McLean

Eleanor Roosevelt	JANE ALEXANDER
Franklin D. Roosevelt	EDWARD HERRMANN
Missy Lehand	PRISCILLA POINTER
Louis Howe	WALTER McGINN
Sara Delano Roosevelt	ROSEMARY MURPHY
Anna Roosevelt	BLAIR BROWN
Theodore Roosevelt	DAVID HEALY
Grace Tully	PEGGY McKAY
Harry Hopkins	DONALD MOFFAT
Malvina Thompson	TONI DARNAY
Dr. Carr	JOHN BEAL
Marian Anderson	BARBARA CONRAD
Plog	MORGAN FARLEY
Robert Dunlap	MARK HARMON
Laura Delano	ANNA LEE
Lucy Mercer	LINDA KELSEY
Ike Hoover	COLIN HAMILTON
James Roosevelt	RAY BAKER
John Roosevelt	BRIAN PATRICK CLARKE
Elliott Roosevelt	DON HOWARD
Franklin D. Roosevelt, Jr.	JOSEPH HACKER
Irvin McDuffie	CHARLES LAMPKIN

A further look into the lives of FDR and Eleanor Roosevelt during their twelve-year residence at 1600 Pennsylvania Avenue, reuniting most of the cast and technical crew responsible for the multiple-award-winning first film (1976). Equally as honored (with seventeen Emmy nominations), this film was chosen Outstanding Special of the Year, and Emmy Awards went to director Daniel Petrie, editors Rita Roland and Michael S. McLean, production designer Jan Scott, set decorator Anne D. McCulley, and costume designer Joe I. Tompkins. Nominations also went to Jane Alexander, Edward Herrmann, Rosemary Murphy, Walter McGinn, Mark Harmon, writer James Costigan, composer John Barry, cinematographer James Crabe, and others in several technical categories.

0707
THE DEADLIEST SEASON
3/16/77 Titus Productions, Inc. (2 hours)

Executive Producer: Herbert Brodkin
Producer: Robert Berger
Associate Producer: Tom DeWolfe
Director: Robert Markowitz
Teleplay: Ernest Kinoy
From a story by Ernest Kinoy and Tom King
Photography: Alan Metzger
Music: Dick Hyman
Art Director: Richard Bianchi
Editor: Stephen A. Rotter

Gerry Miller	MICHAEL MORIARTY
George Graff	KEVIN CONWAY
Tom Feeney	SULLY BOYAR
Carole Eskanazi	JILL EIKENBERRY
D.A. Horace Meade	WALTER McGINN
Sharon Miller	MERYL STREEP
Al Miller	ANDREW DUGGAN
Bertram Fowler	PATRICK O'NEAL
Dave Eskanazi	PAUL D'AMATO
Bill Cairns	MASON ADAMS
Coach Bryant	MEL BOUDROT
Trainer Doyle	TOM QUINN
Judge Reinhardt	RONALD WEYAND

Kevin Conway and Michael Moriarty in THE DEADLIEST SEASON (1977)

Michael Moriarty in THE DEADLIEST SEASON (1977)

Referee Merritt	DINO NARRIZANO
President MacCloud	GEORGE PETRIE
Eddie Miller	EDDIE MORAN
Rene Beavois	FRANK BONGIORNO
Waiter	RUDY HORNISH
Dectective Forscher	ALAN NORTH
Jury Foreman	IAN STUART

A professional hockey player, compelled by his drive to succeed and by financial pressures to adopt a more aggresive playing style, gets involved with violence on the ice, resulting in the death of a player and a man-slaughter charge against him.

0708
MURDER AT THE WORLD SERIES
3/20/77 An ABC Circle Film (2 hours)

Producer: Cy Cermak
Director: Andrew V. McLaglen
Teleplay: Cy Cermak
Photography: Richard C. Glouner
Music: John Cacavas
Art Director: Elayne Ceder
Editors: Richard A. Harris and John F. Link II

Margot Mannering	LYNDA DAY GEORGE
Harvey Murkison	MURRAY HAMILTON

Lois Marshall	KAREN VALENTINE
Moe Gold	GERALD S. O'LOUGHLIN
Larry Marshall	MICHAEL PARKS
Karen Weese	JANET LEIGH
The Governor	HUGH O'BRIAN
Alice Dakso	NANCY KELLY
Severino	JOHNNY SEVEN
Lisa	TAMARA DOBSON
Sam Druckman	JOSEPH WISEMAN
Cisco	BRUCE BOXLEITNER
Gary Vawn	LARRY MAHAN
Frank Gresham	COOPER HUCKABEE
Kathy	MAGGIE WELLMAN
Jane Torres	CYNTHIA AVILA
Barbara Gresham	MONICA GAYLE

A troubled young man, bent on avenging the Houston Astro baseball team's rejection of him, plots a bizarre kidnapping during the final two games of the World Series in Houston and places the lives of five innocent women in jeopardy. The original title for this movie: *The Woman in Box 359.*

0709
THE LIFE AND ASSASSINATION OF THE KINGFISH
3/21/77 Tomorrow Entertainment Inc. (2 hours)

Executive Producer: Thomas W. Moore
Producer: Paul Leaf
Writer/Director: Robert Collins
Photography: Ric Waite
Music: Fred Karlin
Song "Kingfish" written and sung by Randy Newman
Editor: Pat Kennedy

Huey Long	EDWARD ASNER
Manners	NICHOLAS PRYOR
Rose Long	DIANE KAGAN
Earl Long	FRED COOK
Alice Grosjean	DORRIE KAVANAUGH
J.R.	GARY ALLEN
Harley Bozeman	DONEGAN SMITH
Seymour Weiss	STANLEY REYES
Murphy Roden	ROD MASTERSON
Russell Long	STEVEN RAMAY

and: Eliot Keener, J. Frank Lucas, Jake Staples, Wilbur Swartz, Robert Adams, Don Lutenbacher, Patrick McNamara, Tom Alden, Edward Hoerner, Jean Mayre

A lavishly detailed dramatization of the events leading up to the 1935 assassination of Huey Long, Louisiana's Depression-era governor and U.S. Senator. An Emmy Award nomination went to Ric Waite for his cinematography. Original title: *Every Man a King.*

0710
FLIGHT TO HOLOCAUST
3/27/77 Aycee Productions/First Artists (2 hours)

Producer/Creator: A. C. Lyles
Director: Bernard L. Kowalski
Teleplay: Robert Heverly and Anthony Lawrence
Photography: Matthew F. Leonetti
Music: Paul Williams
Title song written and sung by Paul Williams
Art Director: Lyle Wheeler
Special Effects: Joe Unsinn
Editor: Mike Vejar

Les Taggart	PATRICK WAYNE
Mark Gates	CHRISTOPHER MITCHUM

Scotty March	FAWNE HARRIMAN	Katharine Hepburn	TOVAH FELDSHUH
Rick Bender	DESI ARNAZ, JR.	Billie Dove	LEE PURCELL
George Beam	SID CAESAR	George	JIM ANTONIO
Ed Davis (Engineer)	RORY CALHOUN	Fiorello LaGuardia	SORRELL BOOKE
Dr. Jeff Evans	GREG MORRIS	Lewis Milestone	MARTY BRILL
Wilton Bender	LLOYD NOLAN	Jane Russell	MARLA CARLIS
Colorado Davis	PAUL WILLIAMS	Jimmy	LEE JONES
Gordon Stokes	ROBERT PATTEN		DeBROUX
Linda Michaels	ANNE SCHEDEEN	Production Manager	ROY ENGEL
TV Commentator	BILL BALDWIN	Barnes	ARTHUR FRANZ
Sheila	KATHRYN BAUMANN	Shirley Whitehead	DENISE GALIK
Mrs. Bender	SHIRLEY O'HARA	Jenks	HOWARD HESSEMAN
Woman in Elevator	ARGENTINA BRUNETTI	Mrs. Hughes	TANNIS G. MONTGOMERY

and: John Dewey Carter, Bob Hoy, Don Reid, Bill Deiz, Louis Elias, Marilyn Fox, Robert Gooden, Barry Hamilton, Victor Izay, Ed McCready

Professional troubleshooters are called to a skyscraper where a private plane has crashed and is lodged in the side of the building at the twentieth floor level.

0711
SOMETHING FOR JOEY
4/6/77 MTM Productions (2 hours)

Producer: Jerry McNeely
Associate Producer: Roger Young
Director: Lou Antonio
Teleplay: Jerry McNeely
Photography: Gayne Rescher
Music: David Shire
Art Director: Sydney Z. Litwack
Editor: Gary Griffin

Anne Cappelletti	GERALDINE PAGE
John Cappelletti, Sr.	GERALD S. O'LOUGHLIN
John Cappelletti	MARC SINGER
Joey Cappelletti	JEFF LYNAS
Joyce Cappelletti (narrator)	LINDA KELSEY
Marty Cappelletti	BRIAN FARRELL
Jean Cappelletti	KATHLEEN BELLER
Mike Cappelletti	STEVEN GUTTENBERG
Joe Paterno	PAUL PICERNI
Eddie O'Neil	STEPHEN PARR
Archbishop	DAVID HOOKS
Mrs. Frome	JUNE DAYTON
Dr. Wingreen	JAMES KAREN
Dr. Klunick	DAVID GARFIELD
Mark	KEVIN McKENZIE

A dramatization of the true-life relationship between 1973 Heisman Trophy-winning football star John Cappelletti and his brother, Joey, stricken with leukemia. Director Lou Antonio and writer Jerry McNeely both received Emmy Award nominations.

0712
THE AMAZING HOWARD HUGHES
4/13–14/77 Roger Gimbel Productions/EMI Television (4 hours)

Executive Producer: Roger Gimbel
Producer: Herbert Hirschman
Director: William A. Graham
Teleplay: John Gay
Based on the book *Howard: The Amazing Mr. Hughes* by Noah Dietrich and Bob Thomas
Photography: Jules Brenner and Michael Margulies
Music: Laurence Rosenthal
Production Design: Stan Jolley
Editor: Aaron Stell

Howard Hughes	TOMMY LEE JONES
Noah Dietrich	ED FLANDERS
Wilbur Peterson	JAMES HAMPTON

General Hap Arnold	WALTER O. MILES
Henry J. Kaiser	GARRY WALBERG
Jean Peters	CAROL BAGDASARIAN
Robert Maheu	BART BURNS
Floyd Odlum	THAYER DAVID

Senator Brewster	BARRY ATWATER
Senator Ferguson	WILLIAM DOZIER
Saunders	BARNEY PHILLIPS
Himself	JIM BACON

and: John S. Ragin, John Lupton, Art Gilmore, Ray Ballard, Robert Baron, James Beach, Morgan Brittany, Susan Buckner, Ray Buktenica, Sid Conrad, Jack Denbo, John Dennis, Steve Doubet, Shay Duffin, S. J. Launer, Joel Lawrence, Jim McKrell, Glenn Miller, Myron Natwick, Kim O'Brien, Andy Romano, Jetta Seear, John Bellah, Thom Carney, Peter Dane, Hal England, Gene Handsaker, Ed Harris, Ted Hartley, Wayne Heffley, Russ McGinn, Marvin Miles, Ken Sansom, Ken Scott, Dave Shelley, Wayne Thomas, Jerome Thor, Bert Williams

An intriguing if lethargic look at the life of Howard Hughes from his takeover of the Hughes Tool Co. at eighteen, through his rapidly expanding business ventures. The film covers his interests ranging from golf

Patrick Wayne, Fawne Harriman and Christopher Mitchum in FLIGHT TO HOLOCAUST (1977)

and aviation to filmmaking and Hollywood starlets, his involvement in the Senate probe pertaining to war profits, his growing isolation and phobias, and his death in April 1976.

0713
SNOWBEAST
4/28/77 Douglas Cramer Productions (2 hours)

Executive Producer: Douglas S. Cramer
Producer: Wilford Lloyd Baumes
Director: Herb Wallerstein
Teleplay: Joseph Stefano
Photography: Frank Stanley
Music: Robert Prince
Art Director: Steven Sardanis
Editors: Carroll Sax and Neil Travis

Gar Seberg	BO SVENSON
Ellen Seberg	YVETTE MIMIEUX
Tony Rill	ROBERT LOGAN
Sheriff Paraday	CLINT WALKER
Carrie Rill	SYLVIA SIDNEY
The Beast	MICHAEL J. LONDON
Buster	THOMAS BABSON
Jennifer	KATHY CHRISTOPHER
Heidi	ANNE McENCROE

and: Jacquie Betts, Richard Jamison, Liz Jury, Ric Jury, Ros McClung, Prentiss Rowe, Victor Raider-Wexler

A killer beast on the rampage terrorizes a ski resort during a winter carnival. Yvette Mimieux and Sylvia Sidney replaced Donna Mills and Gloria Swanson respectively.

0714
THE POSSESSED
5/1/77 Warner Bros. (90 min)

Executive Producer: Jerry Thorpe
Producer: Philip Mandelker
Director: Jerry Thorpe
Teleplay: John Sacret Young
Executive Story Consultant: William Blinn
Photography: Charles G. Arnold
Music: Leonard Rosenman
Assistant Director: Erich von Stroheim II
Art Director: Frederic Hope
Special Effects: Joe Unsinn
Editor: Michael A. Hoey

Kevin Leahy	JAMES FARENTINO
Louise Gelson	JOAN HACKETT
Ellen Sumner	CLAUDETTE NEVINS
Sgt. Taplinger	EUGENE ROCHE
Paul Winjam	HARRISON FORD
Weezie Sumner	ANN DUSENBERRY
Lane	DIANA SCARWID
Celia	DINAH MANOFF
Alex	CAROL JONES
Marty	P. L. SOLES
Barry	ETHELINN BLOCK

and: Susan Walden, Lawrence Bame, James R. Parkes, Catherine Cunneff

A defrocked minister—and free-lance exorcist—battles the forces of evil apparently responsible for a rash of mysterious fires threatening an isolated girls' school.

0715
ROGER & HARRY: THE MITERA TARGET
5/2/77 Bruce Lansbury Productions/Columbia Pictures (90 min)
(subsequently titled *Love for Ransom*)

Executive Producer: Bruce Lansbury
Producer: Anthony Spindler

Director: Jack Starrett
Teleplay: Alvin Sapinsley
Photography: Fred Jackman
Music: Jack Elliott and Allyn Ferguson
Art Director: Ross Bellah
Editor: David Wages

Roger Quentin	JOHN DAVIDSON
Harry Jaworsky	BARRY PRIMUS
Kate Wilson	CAROLE WAGNER MALLORY
Joanna March	ANNE RANDALL STEWART
Curt Blair	RICHARD LYNCH
Arthur Pennington	HARRIS YULIN
Cindy St. Claire	SUSAN SULLIVAN
Claude DuCloche	TITOS VANDIS
Sylvester March	BIFF McGUIRE
David Peterson	ALAN McRAE
Heller	VAUGHN ARMSTRONG
Cutts	HENRY SUTTON
Mankowitz	JAMES O'CONNELL
Lt. Shelley	ROBERT DoQUI
TV Reporter	FRED HOLLIDAY

The pilot movie for a series that never materialized, dealing with a pair of free-wheeling investigators who specialize in recovering lost and stolen objects as well as missing or kidnapped persons, and who here are hired by a millionaire businessman whose daughter apparently was spirited out of the country.

0716
CODE NAME: DIAMOND HEAD
5/3/77 Quinn Martin Productions (90 min)

Executive Producer: Quinn Martin
Producer: Paul King
Director: Jeannot Szwarc
Teleplay: Paul King
Photography: Jack Whitman
Music: Morton Stevens
Art Director: George B. Chan
Editor: James Gross

Johnny Paul	ROY THINNES
Tso-Tsing	FRANCE NUYEN
Zulu	ZULU
Captain MacIntosh	WARD COSTELLO
H. K. Muldoon	DON KNIGHT
Sean Donavan Father Horton Colonel Butler	IAN McSHANE
Ernest Graeber	ERIC BRAEDEN
Cmdr. Yarnell	DENNIS PATRICK
Edward Sherman	ALEX HENTELOFF
Sakai	FRANK MICHAEL LIU
Hero Yamamoto	ERNEST HARADA
Tanner	LEE STETSON
Dr. En-Ping	HARRY ENDO
Father Murphy	ERIC CHRISTMAS

and: Terrence Brady, Dan Cicogni, Cynthia Cookinham

An American undercover agent in Hawaii duels a master of disguises hired by a foreign power to steal a top secret formula in this unsuccessful pilot for a TV series.

0717
FIRE!
5/8/77 Irwin Allen Productions/Warner Bros. (2 hours)
(formally titled "Irwin Allen's Production of 'Fire!' ")

Executive Producer: Irwin Allen
Director: Earl Bellamy
Teleplay: Norman Katkov and Arthur Weiss

From a story by Norman Katkov
Photography: Dennis Dalzell
Music: Richard La Salle
Art Director: Ward Preston
Special Effects: Cliff Wenger
Special Photographic Effects: L. B. Abbott
Editor: Bill Brame

Sam Brisbane	ERNEST BORGNINE*
Martha Wagner	VERA MILES
Dr. Peggy Wilson	PATTY DUKE ASTIN
Dr. Alex Wilson	ALEX CORD
Harriet Malone	DONNA MILLS
Doc Bennett	LLOYD NOLAN
Larry Durant	NEVILLE BRAND
Walt Fleming	TY HARDIN
Dan Harter	GENE EVANS
Bill Clay	JAMES W. GAVIN
Ted	PATRICK CULLITAN
Frank	ERIK ESTRADA
Judy	MICHELLE STACY

A forest fire started by a convict to cover his escape from a road gang threatens to destroy a mountain community. Later this two-hour movie was cut to ninety minutes and put on TV's first disaster double bill teamed with Irwin Allen's *Flood* (6/11/78).

*Replaced Fred MacMurray.

0718
DANGER IN PARADISE
5/12/77 Filmways (2 hours)

Executive Producer: Perry Lafferty
Producers: Bill and Pat Finnegan
Director: Marvin J. Chomsky
Teleplay: William Wood
Photography: Robert Collins
Music: Jack Elliott and Allyn Ferguson
Art Director: Albert Heschong
Editor: O. Nicholas Brown

Mitch Fears	CLIFF POTTS
Barrett Fears	JOHN DEHNER
Marla Fears	INA BALIN
Oscar	BILL LUCKING
Reva	JEAN MARIE HON
Bobby Fears	MICHAEL MULLINS
Karen	LUCIA STRAIGER
Carson Fears	RICHARD McKENZIE
Stephen	HARRY MOSES
Candy	SANDY WILL

and: Moe Keale, Elizabeth Smith, Richard Ventura, Anthony Charnota, Noel Conlon, Wayne Heffley, Denny Miller, Dave Clannon, Peter Brandon, Lynette Chun

This was the pilot for the brief 1977–78 series "Big Hawaii," with an angry young man fighting his scheming stepmother for control of his ill father's huge island ranch-estate.

0719
THE SAN PEDRO BUMS
5/13/77 Aaron Spelling Productions (90 min)

Executive Producers: Aaron Spelling and Douglas S. Cramer
Producer: E. Duke Vincent
Director: Barry Shear
Teleplay: E. Duke Vincent
Photography: Arch R. Dalzell
Music: Pete Rugolo
Art Director: Paul Sylos
Editors: Carroll Sax and Michael S. McLean

Buddy	CHRISTOPHER MURNEY
Boychick	JEFFRY DRUCE
Dancer	JOHN MARK ROBINSON
Stuf	STUART PANKIN
Moose	DARRYL McCULLOGH
Turk	BILL LUCKING
Pop	TITOS VANDIS
Sgt. Yost	RAMON BIERI
Mrs. McClory	JEANNE COOPER
Ramirez	JORGE CERVERA, JR.
Mr. McClory	KEVIN HAGEN
Mr. Donelli	DICK BALDUZZI
Louise	LOUISE HOVEN
Suzy	SUSAN MULLEN
Margo	LISA REEVES
Pam	SUSAN WALDEN

In this pilot for the brief series beginning in September 1977, five rough-and-tumble pals, living on a leaky boat, try to collar a gang of waterfront toughs after a robbery in which their buddy was the victim.

0720
ALEXANDER: THE OTHER SIDE OF DAWN
5/16/77 Douglas Cramer Productions (2 hours)

Executive Producer: Douglas S. Cramer
Producer: Wilford Lloyd Baumes
Director: John Erman
Teleplay: Walter Dallenbach
From a story by Walter Dallenbach and Dalene Young
Photography: Gayne Rescher
Music: Fred Karlin
Art Director: Carl Anderson
Editor: Neil Travis

Alexander Duncan	LEIGH J. McCLOSKEY
Dawn Wetherby	EVE PLUMB
Myra	JULIET MILLS
Landlady	JEAN HAGEN
Eddie Duncan	LONNIE CHAPMAN
Ray Church	EARL HOLLIMAN
Charles Selby	ALAN FEINSTEIN
Buddy	ASHER BRAUNER
Clara Duncan	DIANA DOUGLAS
Singer	MISS FRANCES FAYE

and: Fred Sadoff, Alice Hirson, John Devlin, Mark Baker, Jack Rader, Claudia Bryar, Gary Campbell, Noel Conlon, Daria Cook, Pat Corely, Robert Drye, Yolanda Galardo, Colin Hamilton, Wayne Haffley, Lincoln Kilpatrick, Jr., Damu King, Jonathan R. Banks, Larry Rosenberg, Richard Saunders, Talia Balsam, Matt Bennett, P. J. Soles, Ben Marley, John Gries, George Whiteman

A male hustler has no end of trouble trying to find legitimate work in this sequel to *Dawn: Portrait of a Teenage Runaway* (1976), and he soon finds himself involved with a gay football pro.

0721
COVER GIRLS
5/18/77 Columbia Pictures (90 min)

Executive Producer: David Gerber
Producers: Charles FitzSimons and Mark Rodgers
Director: Jerry London
Teleplay: Mark Rodgers
Photography: William K. Jurgensen
Music: Richard Shores
Art Directors: Ross Bellah and Robert Peterson
Editors: Arthur D. Hilton and Stanley Wohlberg

Monique	JAYNE KENNEDY
Linda	CORNELIA SHARPE
James Andrews	DON GALLOWAY
Bradner	VINCE EDWARDS
Paul Richards	MICHAEL BASELEON
Karl	DeVEREN BOOKWALTER
Fritz Porter	JERRY DOUGLAS
Sven	SEAN GARRISON
Johnny Wilson	DON JOHNSON
Michael	GEORGE LAZENBY
Football Player	BILL OVERTON
Photographer	ELLEN TRAVOLTA

and: Eric Holland, Paul Dumont, Maurice Marsac, James Almanzar, Todd Martin, Lenore Stevens, Fritzi Burr, June Whitley Taylor, Peter Gunnean, Brian Baker, Kien Chinh, Ben Frommer, Carolyn Brand, Bob Hastings

A road company "Charlie's Angels" that never made it to a series format, featuring here a pair of high fashion models who combine photo assignments around the world with work as espionage agents.

0722
PINE CANYON IS BURNING
5/18/77 Universal (90 min)

Executive Producer: Robert A. Cinader
Producers: Gino Grimaldi and Hannah Shearer
Director: Chris Nyby III
Teleplay: Robert A. Cinader
Photography: Frank Thackery
Music: Lee Holdridge
Art Director: George Renne
Editor: Albert Zuniga

Capt. William Stone	KENT McCORD
Margaret Stone	MEGAN McCORD
Michael Stone	SHANE SINUTKO
Sandra	DIANA MULDAUR
Capt. Ed Wilson	ANDREW DUGGAN
Charlie Edison	DICK BAKALYAN
Anne Walker	BRIT LIND
Whitey Olson	CURTIS CREDEL

and: Sandy McPeak, Larry Deraney, Joan Roberts

A pilot film out of the Jack Webb municipal-services-salute school that has a widowed fireman with two kids transferring to a one-man fire-rescue station in the Los Angeles foothills, permitting him to stay in the field and still be at home nights.

0723
RED ALERT
5/18/77 Jozak Productions/Paramount Pictures (2 hours)

Executive Producers: Gerald Isenberg and Gerald W. Abrams
Producer: Barry Goldberg
Associate Producer: Richard Briggs
Director: William Hale
Teleplay: Sandor Stern
Based on the novel *Paradigm Red* by Harold King
Photography: Ric Waite
Music: George Aliceson Tipton
Art Director: Jim Spencer
Editor: John A. Martinelli

Frank Brolen	WILLIAM DEVANE
Carl Wyche	MICHAEL BRANDON
Judy Wyche	ADRIENNE BARBEAU
Henry Stone	RALPH WAITE
Larry Cadwell	DAVID HAYWARD
Sheriff Sweeney	M. EMMET WALSH

Lou Banducci	MALCOLM WITTMAN
Bill Yancy	DON WISEMAN
Harry Holland	HOWARD FINCH
Stover	CHARLES KROHN
Mrs. Kerwin	DIXIE TAYLOR
Howard Ives	JIM SIEDOW
Marie	LOIS FLECK

A suspense thriller about an accident at a nuclear power plant in which a mysterious breakdown causes a giant computer to erroneously detect escaped radiation and seal off the building, trapping fourteen technicians inside.

0724
THE DEADLY TRIANGLE
5/19/77 Columbia Pictures (90 min)

Executive Producer: Barry Weitz
Producer: Robert Stambler
Director: Charles S. Dubin
Teleplay: Carl Gottlieb
Photography: Al Francis
Music: Dick DeBenedictis
Art Director: Ross Bellah
Editors: Mike Vejar and Greg Prange

Bill Stedman	DALE ROBINETTE
Archie Sykes	TAYLOR LACHER
Red Bayliss	GEOFFREY LEWIS
Charles Cole	ROBERT LANSING
Edith Cole	DIANA MULDAUR
Joanne Price	LINDA SCRUGGS BOGART
Merrie Leonard	MAGGIE WELLMAN
Dwight Thatcher	JAMES COLEMAN
Wayne	TOM McFADDEN
Ernst Haag	ROBERT WEISSER

and: Victor Brandt, Gary Wood, Carl Gottlieb, Paul Ramlow, Ned Bell, Ruth Lieder, Terry E. Cole, Mark Abel, Stanley L. Springer, Paula Wakefield, Lorraine Curtis, Kandi Demaray, Alexander Higgins

An ex-Olympic ski champion becomes the sheriff in his hometown, Sun Valley, just in time to investigate the slaying of a member of a ski team that has come to the resort for training. This was the first of two pilot movies for a never-aired "Stedman" series.

0725
ROSETTI AND RYAN: MEN WHO LOVE WOMEN
5/19/77 Universal (2 hours)

Executive Producer: Leonard B. Stern
Producer: Jerry Davis
Director: John Astin
Teleplay: Don M. Mankiewicz, Gordon Dotler and Sam Rolfe
Photography: William Mendenhall
Music: Peter Matz
Art Director: George Reune
Editor: James T. Hackert

Joseph Rosetti	TONY ROBERTS
Frank Ryan	SQUIRE FRIDELL
Jessica Hornesby	JANE ELLIOT
Beverly Dresden	SUSAN ANSPACH
Judge Proctor Hardcastle	DICK O'NEILL
Druscilla Gerard	ROBERTA LEIGHTON
Benny	AL MOLINARO
Sister Constanza	ANDREA HOWARD
Judge Marcus Black	WILLIAM MARSHALL
Medical Examiner	RICHARD STAHL
Sgt. Pete Agopian	BILL DANA
Sylvia Crawford	PATTY DUKE ASTIN

Greta Gerber   BARBARA ALSTON
Ma Rosetti   PENNY STANTON

and: Rene Enriquez, Bobby Herbeck, Kip King, Art Koustik, Larry Block, Bill Boyett, Frank Bongiorno, John Bentley, Gloria Strook, Loren Berman, Hope Alexander, Ruth Manning, Choo-Li Chi, Bob Golden, James F. O'Connell, Ralph Hoopes, Ed McCready, Alan Austin, Michael Ericson, Luana Anders, Roger Price, Delos V. Smith, Jr., Rita O'Connor, Diane Lander, Carol O'Leary, Heather Lowe, John Wyler, Sterling Swanson, Will Gill, Jr., Jodi Carlsen, Paul Micale

A couple of resourceful, free-wheeling criminal attorneys with an eye for the ladies confront a no-nonsense judge while trying to clear an heiress in the slaying of her husband, although her explanation that a mysterious intruder did it provides them with a rather weak case. The subsequent series with Roberts and Fridell lasted for several months in late 1977.

0726
DELTA COUNTY, U.S.A.
5/20/77 Leonard Goldberg Productions/Paramount (2 hours)

Executive Producer: Leonard Goldberg
Producers: Robert Greenwald and Frank von Zerneck
Director: Glenn Jordan
Teleplay: Thomas Rickman
Photography: William Cronjager, Jr.
Music: Jack Elliott and Allyn Ferguson
Art Director: Jack Collins
Editors: Gordon Scott and Richard Wormell

Jack the Bear   JIM ANTONIO
Terry Nicholas   JEFF CONAWAY
Bo   ROBERT HAYS
Val Nicholas   ED POWER
Kate McCain Nicholas   JOANNA MILES
John McCain, Jr.   PETER DONAT
Dossie Wilson   LOLA ALBRIGHT
Jonsie Wilson   MICHELE CAREY
Vonda   LEIGH CHRISTIAN
Cap McCain   JOHN McLIAM
Bevo   JAMES CRITTENDEN
McCain   DONEY OATMAN
Joe Ed   JOE PENNY
Robbie Jean   TISCH RAYE
Billy Wingate   PETER MASTERSON
Doris Ann   MORGAN BRITTANY
Biggie   DENNIS BURKLEY

Delta County is "Peyton Place" relocated in a staid southern community, with the communications barrier between the generations as solid as ever.

0727
SPECTRE
5/21/77 20th Century-Fox (2 hours)

Executive Producer: Gene Roddenberry
Producer: Gordon L. T. Scott
Director: Clive Donner
Teleplay: Gene Roddenberry and Samuel B. Peebles
From a story by Gene Roddenberry
Photography: Arthur Ibbetson
Music: John Cameron
Art Director: Arthur Witherick
Editor: Peter Tanner

William Sebastian   ROBERT CULP
Dr. Hamilton   GIG YOUNG
Mitri Cyon   JOHN HURT
Inspector Cabell   GORDON JACKSON
Anitra Cyon   ANN BELL
Sir Geoffrey Cyon   JAMES VILLIERS

Lilith   MAJEL BARRETT
Sydna   JENNY RUNACRE

and: Angela Grant, Linda Benson, Michael Latimer

This demonology tale, sumptuously produced, has a world-famed American criminologist and his usually tipsy doctor friend summoned to England to investigate a suspicious wealthy financier and learn that supernatural forces are at work in his Playboy-style estate.

0728
LUCAN
5/22/77 MGM (90 min)

Executive Producer: Barry Lowen
Producer/Director: David Greene
Teleplay: Michael Zagor
Photography: Harry May
Music: Fred Karlin
Art Director: Brian Eatwell
Editor: Scott Conrad

Lucan   KEVIN BROPHY
Mickey   STOCKARD CHANNING
Larry McElwaine   NED BEATTY
Gene Boone   WILLIAM JORDAN
Dr. Hoagland   JOHN RANDOLPH
Casey   LOU FRIZZELL
Coach Dalton   BEN DAVIDSON
Rantzen   GEORGE WYNER
President Davies   HEDLEY MATTINGLY
Jess   JOHN FINNEGAN
Coffin   RICHARD C. ADAMS
Lucan (age 10)   TODD OLSEN
Policeman   GEORGE REYNOLDS
Woman   VIRGINIA HAWKINS

A twenty-year-old who spent the first ten years of his life running wild in the forest after being raised by predatory animals now strikes out on his own in search of his identity. Subsequently, this became a once-in-a-while series during the 1977–78 season.

0729
GOOD AGAINST EVIL
5/22/77 Frankel-Bolen Productions/20th Century-Fox (90 min)

Executive Producers: Lin Bolen and Ernie Frankel
Director: Paul Wendkos
Teleplay: Jimmy Sangster
Photography: Jack Woolf
Music: Lalo Schifrin
Music Supervisor: Lionel Newman
Art Director: Richard Y. Haman
Editors: Art Seid and George Hively

Andy Stuart   DACK RAMBO
Jessica Gordon   ELYSSA DAVALOS
Mr. Rimmin   RICHARD LYNCH
Father Kemschler   DAN O'HERLIHY
Father Wheatley   JOHN HARKINS
The Woman   JENNY O'HARA
Sister Monica   LEILA GOLDONI
Irene   PEGGY McCAY
Dr. Price   PETER BRANDON
Linday Isley   KIM CATTRALL
Cindy Isley   NATASHA RYAN
The Doctor   RICHARD SANDERS
Beatrice   LILLIAN ADAMS
Agnes   ERICA YOHN
Brown   RICHARD STAHL

Lieutenant Taggert   SANDY WARD
Merlin   ISAAC GOZ

An exorcism movie in which a young couple is beset by evil forces—she's been spoken for by the devil.

0730
THE MAN WITH THE POWER
5/24/77 Universal (2 hours)

Producer: Allan Balter
Director: Nicholas Sgarro
Teleplay: Allan Balter
Photography: J. J. Jones
Music: Pat Williams
Art Director: George Reune
Editors: Jerrold Ludwig and Chuck McClelland

Eric Smith   BOB NEILL
Agent Walter Bloom   TIM O'CONNOR
Paul   VIC MORROW
Princess Siri   PERSIS KHAMBATTA
Farnsworth   ROGER PERRY
Major Sajid   RENE ASSA
Shanda   NOEL deSOUZA
Driver   JAMES INGERSOLL
Dilling   BILL FLETCHER

A pseudo science-fiction pilot about a man who has inherited unique powers from his father, a native of another planet, enabling him to move objects, bend iron and perform other amazing feats through eye concentration, and who here is given the task of guarding a beautiful Bengal heiress on her visit to America.

0731
GOLDENROD
6/1/77 Talent Associates Ltd./Film Funding Ltd. of Canada (2 hours)

Executive Producer: David Susskind
Producers: Lionel Chetwynd and Gerry Arbeid
Associate Producer: Duane Howard
Director: Harvey Hart
Teleplay: Lionel Chetwynd
Based on the novel by Herbert Harker
Photography: Harry Makin
Music: Franklin Boyd
Art Director: Gerry Holmes
Editor: Peter Shatalow

Jess Gifford   TONY LoBIANCO
Shirley Gifford   GLORIA CARLIN
John Tyler Jones   DONALD PLEASENCE
Ethan Gifford   WILL DARROW McMILLAN
Keno McLaughlin   DONNELLY RHODES
George Gifford   IAN McMILLAN
Mrs. Gunderson   PATRICIA HAMILTON
Johnson   ED McNAMARA

A once-successful champion of the Western Canadian rodeo circuit in the 1950s is crippled in the ring, ending his winning streak and breaking up his marriage. Left with responsibility of raising two young sons after his wife deserts him, he finds his life changing when he discovers strength and direction in his eldest boy, coming into his own young manhood.

0732
RANSOM FOR ALICE!
6/2/77 Universal (90 min)

Producer: Franklin Barton
Director: David Lowell Rich
Teleplay: Jim Byrnes
Photography: Jacques R. Marquette

Music: David Rose
Art Director: David Marshall
Editor: Sam Waxman

Clint Kirby	GIL GERARD
Jenny Cullen	YVETTE MIMIEUX
Pete Phelan	CHARLES NAPIER
Harry Darew	GENE BARRY
Johnson	JOHN DENNAN
Alice Halliday	LAURIE PRANGE
Jess Halliday	BARNARD HUGHES
Whitaker Halliday	ROBERT HOGAN
Isaac Pratt	HARRIS YULIN
Nick Vithanian	MARC VAHANIAN
Toby	MILLS WATSON
Yankee Sullivan	GAVIN MacLEOD
James	ANTHONY JAMES

This cop movie, an unsuccessful pilot for a prospective series and set in Seattle during the 1890s, finds a deputy marshal and his female partner working as undercover agents trying to locate a teenage girl and bust a gang of white slavers.

0733
NOWHERE TO HIDE
6/5/77 Mark Carliner Productions/Viacom Enterprises (90 min)

Executive Producer: Mark Carliner
Producers: Rift Fournier and Edward Anhalt
Director: Jack Starrett
Teleplay: Edward Anhalt
Photography: Jacques R. Marquette
Music: Ray Ellis
Editor: Jack Horgor

Ike Scanlon	LEE VAN CLEEF
Joey Faber	TONY MUSANTE
Deputy Ted Willoughby	CHARLES KNOX ROBINSON
Linda Faber	LELIA GOLDONI
Frankie Faber	NOEL FOURNIER
Charles Montague	RUSSELL JOHNSON
Alberto Amarici	EDWARD ANHALT

Narrated by JOHN RANDOLPH

and: David Proval, Clay Tanner, John McLaughlin, Robert Hevelone, Richard Narita, Stafford Morgan, Blackie Dammett, Bud Davis, Vince Di Paolo, John Alderman, John Stefano, Bill Yeager

Lee Van Cleef's TV-movie debut was in this pilot for a prospective series called "Scanlon," the name of a street-wise U.S. marshal assigned here to protect a former syndicate hit man who is testifying against his ex-boss.

0734
A SENSITIVE, PASSIONATE MAN
6/6/77 Factor-Newland Productions (2 hours)

Producer: Alan Jay Factor
Director: John Newland
Teleplay: Rita Larkin
Based on a novel by Barbara Mahoney
Photography: Michael Margulies
Music: Bill Conti
Title song written by David Janssen, Carol Connors and Bill Conti
Sung by Melba Moore
Art Director: Elayne Barbara Ceder
Editor: Michael Economou

Marjorie Delaney	ANGIE DICKINSON
Michael Delaney	DAVID JANSSEN
Pat Morris	MARICLARE COSTELLO
Jack Morris	RICHARD VENTURE
Dan Delaney	TODD LOOKINLAND

Kerry Delaney	JUSTIN RANDI
John Chapin	RHODES REASON
Dr. Lazerow	RICHARD BULL

An affluent couple's seemingly happy marriage is threatened by the husband's alcoholism.

0735
CHARLIE COBB: NICE NIGHT FOR A HANGING
6/9/77 Universal (2 hours)

Executive Producers: Richard Levinson and William Link
Producer: Peter S. Fischer
Director: Richard Michaels
Teleplay: Peter S. Fischer
Photography: Andrew Jackson
Music: Mike Post and Pete Carpenter
Art Director: John E. Chilberg II
Editor: Howard S. Deane

Charlie Cobb	CLU GULAGER
McVea	RALPH BELLAMY
Charity	BLAIR BROWN
Waco	CHRISTOPHER CONNELLY
Conroy	GEORGE FURTH
Miss Cumberland	CARMEN MATHEWS
Angelica	TRICIA O'NEIL
Sheriff Yates	PERNELL ROBERTS
Martha McVea	STELLA STEVENS

In this pilot for a prospective Western detective series, a private eye of the 1870s is hired to deliver a California rancher's long-missing daughter to him, despite numerous efforts to thwart the plan involving the rancher's new wife, his top hand, and a crooked sheriff.

0736
COREY: FOR THE PEOPLE
6/12/77 Columbia Pictures (90 min)

Executive Producer: Buzz Kulik
Producer: Jay Daniel
Director: Buzz Kulik
Teleplay: Alvin Boretz
Photography: Gerald Perry Finnerman
Music: Ed Kelakoff
Art Director: Ross Bellah
Editor: Rita Roland

Dan Corey	JOHN RUBINSTEIN
D.A. Patrick Shannon	EUGENE ROCHE
Det. Phil Gilman	WYNN IRWIN
Judge Taylor	FRANK CAMPANELLA
Johnson	YALE McCLOSKEY
Peters	KIP NIVEN
Nick Wolfe	STEVE PEARLMAN
Katie Ryan	JOAN PRINGLE
Justin Milford	BILL QUINN
Arnie Finnager	ARNOLD SOBOLOFF
Laura Casey	ANN SWEENY
Janet Hanley	LANA WOOD
Dr. Paul Hanley	RONNY COX
Roger	RICHARD VENTURE
Harriet Morgan	CAROL ROSSEN
Sam Myers	STEPHEN BURLEIGH
Judy Corey	DEBORAH RYAN
Judge Stone	PITT HERBERT

A lowly assistant D.A. bucks the system and files capital charges against a socialite in the murder of her doctor-husband, suspecting that she is more than the battered wife killing her spouse in self-defense. This

was a proposed pilot for a series for Artur Rubinstein's actor/musician son John.

0737
THE WAR BETWEEN THE TATES
6/13/77 Talent Associates Ltd. (2 hours)

Executive Producer: David Susskind
Producer: Frederick Brogger
Director: Lee Philips
Teleplay: Barbara Turner
Based on the novel by Alison Lurie
Photography: Zale Magder
Music: John Barry
Art Director: Earl Preston
Editor: George Jay Nicholson

Erica Tate	ELIZABETH ASHLEY
Brian Tate	RICHARD CRENNA
Danielle	ANN WEDGEWORTH
Wendy Dehagen	ANNETTE O'TOOLE
Sanford Finkelstein	GRANVILLE VAN DUSEN
Mathilda Tate	LAURA PATRICK
Jeffrey Tate	SHAWN CAMBELL
Leonard	COLIN FOX
Roo	JULIE PHILIPS
Celia	MINA BADIYI
Chuck	MICHAEL J. REYNOLDS
Girl in Bookstore	REBECCA APPLEBAUM

A small-town college professor's wife discovers that he is having an affair with one of his students, and he is forced to resolve a crisis in his once orderly life. Barbara Turner's adaptation of Alison Lurie's book won her an Emmy Award nomination.

0738
THE 3,000 MILE CHASE
6/16/77 Universal (2 hours)

Executive Producer: Roy Huggins
Producer: Jo Swerling, Jr.
Director: Russ Mayberry
Teleplay: Philip DeGuere, Jr.
From a story by Roy Huggins
Photography: Charles G. Arnold
Music: Elmer Bernstein
Art Director: Mark Hassbinder
Editors: Larry Lester and Lawrence J. Vallario

Matthew Considine/ Marty Scanlon	CLIFF DeYOUNG
Paul Dvorak/ Leonard Staveck	GLENN FORD
Rachel Kane	BLAIR BROWN
Frank Oberon	DAVID SPIELBERG
Emma Dvorak	PRISCILLA POINTER
Ambrose Finn	BRENDAN DILLON
Livingston	LANE ALLAN
Inspector	JOHN ZENDA
Santeen	CARMEN ARGENZIANO
Richette	TOM BOWER
Prosecutor	ROGAR AARON BROWN
Vince Leone	TITOS VANDIS
Richards	MARC ALAIMO

and: Michael J. London, Stephen Coit, Abraham Alvarez, Tanya Swerling, Hugh Gillin, June Whitely Taylor, George Fisher

A professional courier's efforts to deliver a key witness cross-country to a New York court appearance comes under attack by professional gunmen in this pilot film for a prospective series.

0739
THE PRINCE OF CENTRAL PARK
6/17/77 Lorimar Productions (90 min)

Executive Producer: Philip Capice
Producer/Director: Harvey Hart
Teleplay: Jeb Rosebrook
Based on the novel by Evan H. Rhodes
Photography: Victor Kemper
Music: Arthur B. Rubinstein
Art Director: Hank Aldrich
Editor: Marjorie Fowler

Mrs. Miller	RUTH GORDON
Jay Jay	T. J. HARGRAVE
Laurie	LISA RICHARD
Elmo	MARC VAHANIAN
Alice	EDA REISS MERIN
Ardis	CAROL GUSTAFSON
Kristin	BROOKE SHIELDS
Mme. Dupres	BRENDA CURRIN
Rodney	BRUCE HOWARD WEBSTER
Rodney's Father	WILLIAM KNIGHT
Boy in Cafeteria	MIKE BROWN
Busboy	TONY TRAVIS

and: Kim Webster, Jo Flores Chase, Carol Nadell, Estelle Omens, J. Herbert Kerr, Ellin Ruskin, Dan Hedaya

A lonely widow who frequents Central Park becomes emotionally involved with two orphaned youngsters who have built an oasis for themselves there after fleeing from a foster home.

0740
EXO-MAN
6/18/77 Universal (2 hours)

Executive Producer: Richard Irving
Producer: Lionel E. Siegel
Director: Richard Irving
Teleplay: Martin Caidin and Howard Rodman
From a story by Martin Caidin and Henri Simoneon
Photography: Enzo A. Martinelli
Music: Dana Kaproff
Art Director: John R. Corso
Editor: Howard Leeds

Nicholas Conrad	DAVID ACKROYD
Emily Frost	ANNE SCHEDEEN
Raphael Torres	A MARTINEZ
Kermit Haas	JOSE FERRER
Martin	JACK COLVIN
Travis	HARRY MORGAN
Rogers	DONALD MOFFAT
D.A. Kamenski	KEVIN McCARTHY
Eddie Rubinstein	JONATHAN SEGAL
Dominic Leandro	JOHN MOIO
Jim Yamaguchi	RICHARD NARITA

This pilot movie for a proposed series is about a professor, paralyzed in an attack by syndicate hit-men, who creates an exo-suit to make him mobile again—and superhuman.

0741
THE MAGNIFICENT MAGNET OF SANTA MESA
6/19/77 Columbia Pictures (90 min)

Executive Producer: David Gerber
Producers: Hy Averback and Jim Brown
Director: Hy Averback
Teleplay: Gerald Gardner and Dee Caruso
Photography: William K. Jurgensen
Music: Jack Elliott and Allyn Ferguson
Art Directors: Ross Bellah and James G. Hulsey
Editor: Asa Boyd

Freddie Griffith	MICHAEL BURNS
Cal Bixby	DICK BLASUCCI
Ida Griffith	JANE CONNELL
Mr. Undershaft	KEENE CURTIS
Marcie Hamilton	SUSAN BLANCHARD
Mr. Kreel	CONRAD JANIS
Willard Bensinger	TOM POSTON
C. B. Macauley	SUSAN SULLIVAN
J. J. Strange	HARRY MORGAN

and: Loni Anderson, Alex Sharp, Zachary A. Charles, Jack Frey, Martin Asarow, Hal Floyd, Gary Giem, Linda McClure, William Hubbard Knight, Lindy Davis

A Disney-like comedy about a naive young scientist whose employers try to steal his invention—an energy disk that can solve the world's energy crisis. Originally this film had been scheduled to premiere nearly three months earlier under the title *Adventures of Freddie.*

0742
MULLIGAN'S STEW
6/20/77 Paramount (90 min)

Producer: Joanna Lee
Director: Noel Black
Teleplay: Joanna Lee
Photography: Terry K. Meade
Music: George Aliceson Tipton
Art Director: Ken Reid
Editor: Kenneth Koch

Michael Mulligan	LAWRENCE PRESSMAN
Jane Milligan	ELINOR DONAHUE
Mark	JOHNNY WHITAKER
Adam "Moose" Freeman	CHRISTOPHER CIAMPA
Jimmy	K. C. MARTEL
Melinda	JULIE HADDOCK
Steve	SUZANNE CROUGH
Polly	LORY KOCHHEIM
Kimmy	SUNSHINE LEE
Mr. Hollenbeck	ALEX KARRAS
Matt Hollenbeck	JOHNNY TIMKO
Zandor	ZANDOR TAYLOR
Polo	JAIME POLA

and: Katy Kurtzman, David Jolliffe, Jamie Silvani, Adam Gunn, Steve Butts, Paul Lambert, Pamela Serpe, Lynn Holly, Sally Marr

A struggling high school football coach, his wife and three growing children take in four more who were being raised by his sister and her husband before dying in a plane crash. This was the pilot for the short-lived 1977–78 series with Pressman and Donahue.

0743
PANIC IN ECHO PARK
6/23/77 Edgar J. Scherick Associates, Inc. (90 min)

Producers: Edgar J. Scherick and Daniel Blatt
Associate Producer: Robert Greenhut
Director: John Llewellyn Moxey
Teleplay: Dalene Young
Photography: Robert B. Hauser
Music: Johnnie Spence
Song sung by Dorian Harewood
Art Director: Gene Callahan
Editor: Bud S. Isaacs

Dr. Michael Stoner	DORIAN HAREWOOD
Dr. Tishman	ROBIN GAMMELL
Cynthia	CATLIN ADAMS
Harold Dickerson	NORMAN BARTHOLD
Fallen Reilly	RAMON BIERI

Dr. Gavin O'Connor	REGIS J. CORDIC
Mason	VERNON WEDDLE
Tony Lamberti	GEORGE BRENLIN
Angie	TAMU
Ebony	JANE ELLIOTT

and: James Hong, David Clennon, Movita

An undisciplined but dedicated black doctor spends his off-duty hours tracing the cause of an apparent epidemic afflicting tenants of a slum building of East Los Angeles, with the help of local teenagers, and is accused by city officials of precipitating a panic. This pilot film never materialized into a series.

0744
TERRACES
6/27/77 Charles Fries Productions/Worldvision (90 min)

Executive Producer: Charles Fries
Producer/Director: Lila Garrett
Teleplay: Lila Garrett and George Kirgo
Photography: Leonard J. South
Music: Peter Matz
Art Director: Robert MacKichan
Editor: David Newhouse

Dr. Roger Cabe	LLOYD BOCHNER
Roberta Robbins	JANE DULO
Martin Robbins	ARNY FREEMAN
Beth Loomis	ELIZA GARRETT
Gregg Loomis	BILL GERBER
Julie Bordon	KIT McDONOUGH
Chalane Turner	JULIE NEWMAR
Alex Bengston	JAMES PHIPPS
Dorothea Cabe	LOLA ALBRIGHT
Steve	TIMOTHY THOMERSON
Vogel	ALLEN RICH
Louis Parizzi (Doorman)	RALPH MANZA

A drama about various people who share adjoining terraces in a high-rise apartment building.

0745
THE QUINNS
7/1/77 Daniel Wilson Productions (90 min)

Producer: Daniel Wilson
Director: Daniel Petrie
Teleplay: Sidney Carroll
Photography: Arthur J. Ornitz
Music: John Scott
Art Director: Mel Bourne
Editors: Sidney and Virginia Scott

Bill	BARRY BOSTWICK
Elizabeth	SUSAN BROWNING
Liam	LIAM DUNN
Rita	PAT ELLIOTT
Peggy	GERALDINE FITZGERALD
Michael	PETER MASTERSON
Laurie	PENNY PEYSER
Tom	WILLIAM SWETLAND
Eugene Carmody	PAT CORELY
Millicent Priestley	BLAIR BROWN
Renee Carmody	VIRGINIA VESTOFF

A drama about three generations of Irish-American firefighters in the New York City Fire Department—and their careers, romances and growing pains.

0746
DOG AND CAT
7/22/77 Largo Productions (90 min)

Executive Producer: Lawrence Gordon
Producer: Robert Singer
Director: Bob Kelljan

Teleplay: Walter Hill, Owen Morgan, Henry Rosenbaum and Haywood Gould
From a story by Owen Morgan
Created by Walter Hill
Photography: Robert L. Morrison
Music: Barry De Vorzon
Art Director: Steve Sarandis
Editor: Dennis Virkler

Jack Ramsey	LOU ANTONIO
J. Z. Kane	KIM BASINGER
Captain Kipling	MATT CLARK
Ralph Travan	CHARLES CIOFFI
Shirley	RICHARD LYNCH
Nicholas Evans	DALE ROBINETTE
Roeanne	JANIT BALDWIN
David Storey	GEOFFREY SCOTT
Velman	LESLIE WOOD
Gonzo	MATT BENNETT
Trog	WALT DAVIS
Zink Kauffen	DICK WESSON

This pilot for the brief series (spring 1977) shown *after* the series went off the air has a veteran police detective losing his long-time partner in a shooting during a routine stakeout to collar a hood in the porno rackets and then has his spirits sinking further when he is assigned to work "dog and cat" with a green lady cop.

1977–78 SEASON

0747
OPERATION PETTICOAT
9/4/77 Universal (2 hours)

Executive Producer: Leonard Stern
Producer: David J. O'Connell
Director: John Astin
Teleplay: Leonard Stern
From a story by Paul King and Joe Stone
Photography: Frank Thackery
Music: Artie Butler
Art Director: John J. Jeffries
Editor: Clay Bartels

Lt. Cmdr. Matthew Sherman	JOHN ASTIN
Lt. Nick Holden	RICHARD GILLILAND
Major Edna Hayward	YVONNE WILDER
The Admiral	JACKIE COOPER
Yeoman Hunkle	RICHARD BRESTHOFF
Ensign Stovall	CHRISTOPHER J. BROWN
Seaman Dooley	KRAIG CASSITY
Chief Herbert Molumphrey	WAYNE LONG
Williams	RICHARD MARION
Seaman Gossett	MICHAEL MAZES
Chief Tostin	JACK MURDOCK
Seaman Horwich	PETER SCHUCK
Lt. Watson	RAYMOND SINGER
Seaman Broom	JIM VARNEY
Lt. Dolores Crandell	MELINDA NAUD
Lt. Barbara Duran	JAMIE LEE CURTIS
Lt. Ruth Colfax	DORRIE THOMSON
Lt. Claire Reid	BOND GIDEON
Admiral Hatfield	GEORGE O. PETRIE

This pilot movie (complete with laugh track) for the subsequent one season-plus series—with much of the same cast during the first season and a complete overhaul during the initial weeks of the second—is the TV remake of the 1959 Cary Grant-Tony Curtis comedy about a World War II submarine painted shocking pink and numbering among its crew five nurses rescued from battle. Interestingly, one of them is played by Jaimie Lee Curtis, daughter of Tony (and Janet Leigh), who co-starred in the original.

0748
JAMES AT 15
9/15/77 20th Century-Fox (2 hours)

Executive Producers: Martin Manulis and Joseph Hardy
Producer: Martin Manulis
Director: Joseph Hardy
Teleplay: Dan Wakefield
Based on his book
Photography: Charles F. Wheeler
Music: Richard Baskin
Supervised by Lionel Newman
Art Director: Kim Swardos
Editor: J. Frank O'Neill

James Hunter	LANCE KERWIN
Alan Hunter	LINDEN CHILES
Meg Hunter	LYNN CARLIN
Sandy Hunter	KIM RICHARDS
Lacey Stevens	MELISSA SUE ANDERSON
Rip Lindeman	VINCENT VAN PATTEN
Robin	KATE JACKSON
Kathy Hunter	DIERDRE BERTHONG
Richie Gammons	MARC McCLURE
Tiger	DENNIS RUCKER
Mrs. Larsen	JENIFER SHAW
Mrs. Stevens	K CALLAN

This was the pilot movie for the brief series that began in November 1977, later was retitled "James at 16," and subsequently disappeared. James is introduced here as a smitten teenager who is separated from his girl when his family moves to Boston from Oregon and, heartsick in his new urban surroundings, runs away, meets an attractive hitchhiking art student on the road, and learns several valuable lessons about life. Kate Jackson won an Emmy Award nomination for her performance.

0749
THE HOSTAGE HEART
9/9/77 Andrew J. Fenady Associates Production/MGM (2 hours)

Executive Producer: Andrew J. Fenady
Director: Bernard McEveety
Teleplay: Andrew J. Fenady, Charles Sailor and Eric Kaldor
Based on the novel by Gerald Green
Photography: Matthew F. Leonetti
Music: Fred Karlin
Art Director: Marvin Summerfield
Editor: Melvin Shapiro

Dr. Eric Lake	BRADFORD DILLMAN
Chris LeBlanc	LORETTA SWIT
Steve Rockewicz	VIC MORROW
Martha Lake	SHARON ACKER
John Trask	STEPHEN DAVIES
Chief Reinhold	GEORGE DiCENZO
Arnold Stade	CAMERON MITCHELL
Fiona	BELINDA J. MONTGOMERY
James Cardone	PAUL SHENAR
Dr. Motzkin	ALLAN RICH
Dr. Licata	PETER PALMER
Brian O'Donnel	ROBERT WALDEN
Bateman Hooks	CARL WEATHERS
Don Harris	HARI RHODES

Terrorists plot a bizarre kidnapping, breaking into an operating room where a billionaire is undergoing heart surgery and holding him for a ten million dollar ransom.

0750
BILLY: PORTRAIT OF A STREET KID
9/12/77 Mark Carliner Productions, Inc. (2 hours)

Producer: Mark Carliner
Director: Steven Gethers
Teleplay: Steven Gethers
Based on the book *Peoples* by Robert C. S. Downs
Photography: William K. Jurgensen
Music: Fred Karlin
Editor: Carroll Sax

Billy Peoples	LeVAR BURTON
Dr. Fredericks	OSSIE DAVIS
George	DOLPH SWEET
Luis	CHICK VENNERA
Roseanne	TINA ANDREWS
Mrs. Peoples	ROXIE ROKER
Justin	T. K. CARTER
Dr. Silver	MICHAEL CONSTANTINE
Miss Beverly	SHARON ULLRICH
Mrs. Bedford	DIANA DOUGLAS
Hospital Roommate	LEONARD BARR

A drama about a ghetto youth's efforts to escape from his dismal existence and his chance at a future as a veterinarian's assistant.

0751
SEX AND THE MARRIED WOMAN
9/13/77 Universal (2 hours)

Executive Producer: George J. Santoro
Producer/Director: Jack Arnold
Teleplay: Michael Norell
Photography: Ben Coleman
Music: Gerald Fried
Art Director: Jack DeGovia
Costumes: Edith Head
Editors: Jamie Caylor and Robert Watts

Alan Fitch	BARRY NEWMAN
Leslie Fitch	JOANNA PETTET
Uncle June	KEENAN WYNN
Louie Grosscup	DICK GAUTIER
Arnie Fish	LARRY HOVIS
Irma Caddish	JAYNE MEADOWS
Heidi Lomax	NITA TALBOT
Virginia Ladysmith	FANNIE FLAGG
Jim Cutler	CHUCK McCANN
Duke Skaggs	F. MURRAY ABRAHAM
Peter Nebben	ANGUS DUNCAN
Carolyn Fish	JEANNE LANGE
Stan Oberfeld	JOHN LAWRENCE

and: Marco Battaglia, Robin Cohen, Liz Ingleson, Jessica Rains, Bryan O'Byrne, Gregg Forest, Andy Stone, Rori King, Lance Gordon, Roy Stuart, Jordan Rhodes, Jack Stryker, Lin Shaye, Jackie Joseph, Tamar Cooper, Dennis McCarthy, Maureen Reagan, Hugh Benson, Bill Dyer, Pamela Davenport, Laura Gile, Judith Woodbury, June Fenley, Kathy Longinaker, Sharri Zak, Dave Armstrong

A whimsical tale of how success can ruin a good marriage which is thrown into turmoil when the wife achieves sudden fame after publication of her book on her neighbors' sex lives.

0752
RELENTLESS
9/14/77 CBS Television, Inc. (90 min)

Producer: Fred Baum
Associate Producer: Sy Kasoff
Director: Lee H. Katzin
Teleplay: Sam H. Rolfe
Based on a novel by Brian Garfield
Photography: Jack Whitman
Music: John Cacavas

Nicholas Hammond in SPIDER-MAN (1977)

Art Director: Albert Heschong
Editor: Richard Bracken

Sam Watchman	WILL SAMPSON
Paul Vickers	MONTE MARKHAM
Major Leo Hargit	JOHN HILLERMAN
Annie Lansford	MARIANNA HILL
Buck	LARRY WILCOX
Jack Hanratty	ANTONY PONZINI
Walker	JOHN LAWLOR
Lt. Dan Barraclough	TED MARKLAND
Dwayne Terry	DAVID PENDLETON
Sgt. Ed Kleber	RON FOSTER
Cal	DON STARR
Jasper Simalee	DANNY ZAPIAN

and: Steve Schemmel, Richard Kennedy, Pat Bolt, Earl Smith, Mel Todd, Dick Armstrong, Carroll Reynolds

A taciturn Arizona state trooper pits his Indian skills against modern military combat tactics as he pursues a band of bank robbers who have pulled off a combat-style heist, killed his doting uncle and taken a ranch woman hostage while withdrawing into the snowy mountains.

0753
SPIDER-MAN
9/14/77 Charles Fries Productions (90 min)

Executive Producers: Charles Fries and Daniel R. Goodman

Producer: Edward J. Montagne
Director: E. W. Swackhamer
Teleplay: Alvin Boretz
Script Consultant: Stan Lee
Photography: Fred Jackman
Music: Johnnie Spence
Art Director: James B. Hulsey
Editor: Aaron Stell

Peter Parker	NICHOLAS HAMMOND
J. Jonah Jameson	DAVID WHITE
Captain Barbera	MICHAEL PATAKI
Robbie Robinson	HILLY HICKS
Judy Tyler	LISA EILBACHER
Delivery Man	DICK BALDUZZI
Aunt May	JEFF DONNELL
Monahan	BOB HASTINGS
Purse Snatcher	BARRY CUTLER
Professor Noah Tyler	IVOR FRANCIS
Edward Byron	THAYER DAVID

and: Norman Rice, Len Lesser, Ivan Bonnar, Carmelita Pope, George Cooper, Robert Snively, Kathryn Reynolds, Harry Caesar, Roy West, Jim Storm, Ron Gilbert, Larry Anderson, James E. Brodhead

A comic-book superhero who gained mysterious powers after being bitten by a radioactive spider pursues an evil extortionist whose mind-control plot threatens the lives of ten innocent people. This pilot movie previewed a series of once-in-a-while programs during the 1977 season and thereafter.

0754
CURSE OF THE BLACK WIDOW
9/16/77 Dan Curtis Productions/ABC Circle Films (2 hours)
(subsequently titled *Love Trap*)

Executive Producer: Dan Curtis
Producer: Steven North
Associate Producer: Steven P. Reicher
Director: Dan Curtis
Teleplay: Robert Blees and Earl Wallace
From a story by Robert Blees
Photography: Paul Lohmann and Stevan Larner
Music: Robert Cobert
Art Director: Phil Barber
Special Effects: Roy Downey
Editor: Leon Carrere

Mark Higbie	TONY FRANCIOSA
Leigh Lockridge	DONNA MILLS
Laura Lockridge	PATTY DUKE ASTIN
Mrs. Lockridge	JUNE LOCKHART
Olga	JUNE ALLYSON
Ragsdale	MAX GAIL
Aspa Soldado	JEFF COREY
Flaps	ROZ KELLY
Lazlo Cozart	SID CAESAR
Lt. Gully Conti	VIC MORROW
Carlo Lenzi	MICHAEL DeLANO
Jeff Wallace	ROBERT BURTON
Oakes (Zoo Watchman)	BRYAN O'BYRNE
Jennifer	ROSANNA LOCKE
Hank (Morgue Attendant)	ROBERT NADER
Gymnast	TRACY CURTIS
Popeye	H. B. HAGERTY
Summers (Town Clerk)	BRUCE FRENCH

A chiller about the search for an elusive killer whose victims are found wrapped in a strange, spider-like web.

0755

YOUNG JOE, THE FORGOTTEN KENNEDY
9/18/77 An ABC Circle Film (2 hours)

Producer: William McCutchen
Director: Richard T. Heffron
Teleplay: M. Charles Cohen
Based on the biography *The Lost Prince: Young Joe, The Forgotten Kennedy* by Hank Searls
Photography: Stevan Larner
Music: John Barry
Art Director: William Malley
Editor: Ronald J. Fagan

Joseph Kennedy, Jr.	PETER STRAUSS
Vanessa Hunt	BARBARA PARKINS
Joseph Kennedy, Sr.	STEPHEN ELLIOTT
Kathleen Kennedy	DARLEEN CARR
Delaney	SIMON OAKLAND
Mike Krasna	ASHER BRAUNER
Joe, Jr. (age 14)	LANCE KERWIN
Simpson	PETER FOX
Ray Pierce	STEVE KANALY
Willy	ROBERT ENGLUND
Rose Kennedy	GLORIA STROOCK
Elinor	TARA TALLBOY
Hank Riggs	BEN FUHRMAN
Commander Devril	JAMES SIKKING
Greenway	KEN SWOFFORD
Jack Kennedy	SAM CHEW
Ted Kennedy	PATRICK LABORTEAUX
Bob Kennedy	SHANE KERWIN
Jean Kennedy	MARGIE ZECH
Rosemary Kennedy	KRISTIN LARKIN
Eunice Kennedy	ROSANNE COVY
Pat Kennedy	DIERDRE BERTHONG

and: Lawrason Driscoll, Kim O'Brien, Michael Irving, Gardner Hayes

A drama about the eldest Kennedy brother who undertook a perilous World War II mission that would bring him home a hero and achieve the family dream of a Kennedy in the White House. The film was Emmy Award-nominated as the Outstanding Special of the 1977–78 TV season. Editor Ronald J. Fagan also received an Emmy nomination for his work.

0756

THE GIRL IN THE EMPTY GRAVE
9/20/77 MGM-TV (2 hours)

Executive Producer: Richard O. Linke
Producers: Lane Slate and Gordon A. Webb
Director: Lou Antonio
Teleplay: Lane Slate
Photography: Gayne Rescher
Music: Mundell Lowe
Art Director: Leon R. Harris
Editor: Gary Griffin

Abel Marsh	ANDY GRIFFITH
Courtland Gates	JONATHAN BANKS
Deputy Malcolm	JAMES CROMWELL
Gloria	MITZI HOAG
Deputy Fred	CLAUDE EARL JONES
David Alden	GEORGE GAYNES
MacAlwee	BYRON MORROW
Gilda	MARY ROBIN REDD
Jedediah Partridge	ROBERT F. SIMON
Doc	SHARON SPELMAN
Harry	LEONARD STONE
Deputy John	HUNTER VON LEER
Dr. Peter Cabe	EDWARD WINTER

In this pilot film for a series about a small-town police chief, an investigation is launched after a girl, believed to have died months earlier, turns up at the funeral of her murdered parents. Andy Griffith, in search of a successful follow-up series to "The Andy Griffith Show," played his familiar homespun law enforcer, this time without laughs, and without a series.

0757

A KILLING AFFAIR
9/21/77 Columbia Pictures (2 hours)
(subsequently titled *Behind the Badge*)

Executive Producer: David Gerber
Producer: James H. Brown
Director: Richard C. Sarafian
Teleplay: E. Arthur Kean
Photography: Al Francis
Music: Richard Shores
Art Directors: Ross Bellah and Robert Peterson
Editor: Ken Zemke

Vikki Eaton	ELIZABETH MONTGOMERY
Woodrow York	O. J. SIMPSON
Beverly York	ROSALIND CASH
Detective Shoup	JOHN MAHON
Judge Cudahy	PRISCILLA POINTER
Captain Bullis	ALLAN RICH
Buck Fryman	CHARLIE ROBINSON
Flagler	JOHN P. RYAN
Kenneth Switzer	DEAN STOCKWELL
Lt. Scotty Neilson	DOLPH SWEET
Todd York	TODD BRIDGES
Lukens Switzer	FRED STUTHMAN
Cooks	JOHN STEADMAN
Cabrillo	MICHAEL SURRELL
Sergeant Boyle	STEPHEN PARR
Kagel	ED KNIGHT
Sergeant Gould	MICHAEL J. LONDON
Macy	MORGAN FARLEY
Mrs. Macy	GEORGIA SCHMIDT

and: Natalie Core, Eleanor Zee, Karmin Murcelo, Tony Perez, Jay Ingram, Joanna Lehmann, Sari Price, Robert Phalen, Gil Stuart, Valentina Quinn, Cheryl Carter, Mary Maldonado, Danil Torppe, Tim Wead, Yolanda Marquez, Jim Veres, Fil Formicola, Bill Jackson, Frank Doubleday, Bill J. Stevens

A white woman detective and her black partner are caught up in a love affair while working on a series of vicious crimes.

0758

KILL ME IF YOU CAN
9/25/77 Columbia Pictures (2 hours)

Producer: Peter Katz
Director: Buzz Kulik
Teleplay: John Gay
Photography: Gerald Perry Finnerman
Music: Bill Conti
Art Directors: Ross Bellah and Carl Braunger
Technical Consultant: Rosalie S. Asher
Editor: Les Green

Caryl W. Chessman	ALAN ALDA
Rosalie Asher	TALIA SHIRE
George Davis	JOHN HILLERMAN
Judge Fricke	BARNARD HUGHES
Virginia Gibbons	VIRGINIA KISER
Warden Teets	EDWARD MALLORY
J. Miller Leavy	WALTER McGINN
Bill Edmunds	BEN PIAZZA
Judge Lewis Goodman	JOHN RANDOLPH
Hart (Jury Foreman)	HERB VIGRAN
Mrs. Asher	MAXINE STEWART
Sara Loper	ROSE MORTILLO

A fact-based drama about Caryl Chessman, California's notorious "red light bandit" who was captured in 1948 and spent twelve years on death row in San Quentin before his execution in May 1960. Alda's performance got him an Emmy Award nomination.

0759

IN THE MATTER OF KAREN ANN QUINLAN
9/26/77 Warren V. Bush Productions (2 hours)

Executive Producer: Warren V. Bush
Producer: Hal Sitowitz

Peter Strauss and Barbara Parkins in YOUNG JOE, THE FORGOTTEN KENNEDY (1977)

Director: Hal Jordan
Teleplay: Hal Sitowitz
Photography: Arch R. Dalzell
Music: Bill Conti
Art Director: Les Gobruegge
Editor: Sidney M. Katz

Joe Quinlan	BRIAN KEITH
Julie Quinlan	PIPER LAURIE
Paul Armstrong	DAVID HUFFMAN
Mary Ellen Quinlan	STEPHANIE ZIMBALIST
Father Tom	BIFF McGUIRE
Dr. Mason	DAVID SPIELBERG
Dr. Julius Korein	BERT FREED
Sister Mary Luke	LOUISE LATHAM
Karen	MARY ANNE GRAYSON

A fact-based drama about the ordeal of a New Jersey couple over whether to keep their comatose teenage daughter alive on life-supporting machines or let her die with dignity. (The girl lapsed into a coma in the spring of 1975, and at the end of 1979 she was still alive.)

0760

THE TRIAL OF LEE HARVEY OSWALD
9/30–10/1/77 Charles Fries Productions (4 hours)

Executive Producer: Charles Fries
Producer: Richard Freed
Director: David Greene
Teleplay: Robert E. Thompson
Photography: Vilis Lapenieks
Music: Fred Karlin
Art Director: John Schiller
Supervising Editor: Michael Economou
Editor: Allan Jacobs

Anson "Kip" Roberts	BEN GAZZARA
Matthew Arnold Watson	LORNE GREENE
Jan Holder	FRANCES LEE McCAIN
Paul Ewbank	LAWRENCE PRESSMAN
Melvin Johnson	CHARLIE ROBINSON
Ed Blandings	GEORGE WYNER
Marina Oswald	MO MALONE
Lee Harvey Oswald	JOHN PLESHETTE
Oswald's Mother	ANNABELLA WEENICK
James Kleist	WILLIAM JORDAN
Michael Brandon	CHARLES CYPHERS
Evita Alesio	MARISA PAVAN
Judge Claymoor	JACK COLLINS

The bizarre story behind the man accused of assassinating John F. Kennedy and what might have happened had he been brought to trial. The title is all that is left of the 1967 off-Broadway play by Amram Ducovny and Leon Friedman. John Pleshette, whose resemblance to the real Oswald is remarkable, is the brother of actress Suzanne Pleshette.

0761

JUST A LITTLE INCONVENIENCE
10/2/77 Universal (2 hours)

Executive Producer: Lee Majors
Producer: Allan Balter
Director: Theodore J. Flicker
Teleplay: Theodore J. Flicker and Allan Balter
Photography: Duke Callaghan
Music: Jimmie Haskell
Art Director: David Marshall
Editor: Bernard J. Small

Frank Logan	LEE MAJORS
Kenny Briggs	JAMES STACY

Nikki Klausing	BARBARA HERSHEY
B-Girl	LANE BRADBURY
Dave Erickson	JIM DAVIS
Major Bloom	CHARLES CIOFFI
Bartender	JOHN FUREY
Harry	BOB HASTINGS

A Vietnam veteran attempts to rehabilitate his buddy who has become bitter and withdrawn after losing an arm and a leg in war action—a loss that he feels his friend could have prevented. This film marked actor James Stacy's return to TV (he previously had acted in the theatrical movie *Posse* with Kirk Douglas) following a crippling motorcycle accident, and earned him an Emmy Award nomination.

0762

MURDER IN PEYTON PLACE
10/3/77 20th Century-Fox (2 hours)

Producer: Peter Katz
Director: Bruce Kessler
Teleplay: Richard DeRoy
Based on characters created by Grace Metalious
Photography: Gert Anderson
Music: Laurence Rosenthal
Main Theme: Franz Waxman
Supervised by Lionel Newman
Art Director: Rodger Maus
Editor: Bud S. Isaacs

Constance MacKenzie	DOROTHY MALONE*
Dr. Michael Rossi	ED NELSON*
Elliot Carson	TIM O'CONNOR*
Jill Harrington	JOYCE JILLSON*
Norman Harrington	CHRISTOPHER CONNELLY*
Betty Anderson Roerick	JANET MARGOLIN
Ellen Considine	MARJ DUSAY
Tommy Crimpton	JAMES BOOTH
Steven Cord	DAVID HEDISON
Stella Chernak	STELLA STEVENS
Stan Haley	JONATHAN GOLDSMITH
Denise Haley	CHARLOTTE STEWART
Springer	KAZ GARAS
Carla Cord	LINDA GRAY

and, as she appeared in the original, MIA FARROW (in film clips)

also:

Bonnie Buehler	KIMBERLY BECK
Bo Buehler	ROYAL DANO
Mae Buehler	PRISCILLA MORRILL
Billie Kaiserman	DAVID KYLE
Jay Kamens	NORMANN BURTON
Kaiserman	CHARLES SIEBERT

and: Chris Nelson, Robert Deman, Gale Sladstone, Fred Lerner, Jerome Thor, Catherine Bach

A suspense drama focusing on the mysterious killings of Rodney Harrington and Allison MacKenzie (Ryan O'Neal and Mia Farrow in the original series) as part of a diabolical plot to tear the community apart by a former resident, now powerful and wealthy, who has secretly returned seeking revenge.

*Recreating their original roles from the 1964–69 series.

0763

MARY JANE HARPER CRIED LAST NIGHT
10/5/77 Paramount (2 hours)

Producer: Joanna Lee
Associate Producer: Ralph Riskin

Director: Allen Reisner
Teleplay: Joanna Lee
Photography: Gayne Rescher
Music: Billy Goldenberg
Art Director: Ken Reid
Editor: Kenneth R. Koch

Rowena Harper	SUSAN DEY
Dr. Orrin Helgerson	JOHN VERNON
Tom Atherton	KEVIN McCARTHY
Dr. Angela Buccieri	TRICIA O'NEIL
Dave Williams	BERNIE CASEY
Laura Atherton	PRISCILLA POINTER
Mr. Bernards	PHILLIP R. ALLEN
Mary Jane Harper	NATASHA RYAN
Dr. Mark Handelman	RAY BUKTENICA
Judy	RHEA PERLMAN
Judge F. F. Carlson	IVAR BONARD
Dr. Sutterman	JAMES KAREN
Bill Harper	CHIP LUCIA
Mrs. Ramish	SANDRA DEEL
Jeanne Williams	ELIZABETH ROBINSON
Joy	LINDA GILLIAN
Nancy West	FRITZI BURR

and: Pierrino Mascarino, Brandi Tucker, Pat Ast, Susan Hickey, Chris Ciampa, Connie Izay, Read Morgan

Child abuse is the subject of this film dealing with a deeply troubled young mother whose serious psychiatric problems lead her to take them out on her daughter. Editor Kenneth R. Koch received an Emmy Award nomination.

0764

ESCAPE FROM BROGEN COUNTY
10/7/77 Paramount (2 hours)

Executive Producer: Howard W. Koch
Producers: Frank von Zerneck and Robert Greenwald
Director: Steven Hilliard Stern
Teleplay: Christopher Knopf and Judith Parker
From a story by Christopher Knopf
Photography: Fred Jackman
Music: Charles Bernstein
Art Director: Mark Mansbridge
Editor: Mike Brown

Maggie Bowman	JACLYN SMITH
Ambler Bowman	MITCH RYAN
Abe Rand	HENRY GIBSON
Judge Henry Martin	PAT HINGLE
Harry Webb	PHILIP ABBOTT
Jack Kern	MICHAEL PARKS
Emily Martin	JULIE MANNIX
Sheriff Mason	JOHN QUADE
Pearson	FRED WILLARD
Hunnicutt	GEORGE MEMMOLI
Bo Walker	DOUGLAS DIRKSON
Reese Dreux	ALAN FUDGE

and: Debi Storm, Dave Adams, Murray Kramer, Marian Gibson, Jac Zacha, Drummond Barclay, Curtis Pratt, Sarah D. Alvarado

A tyrannical political kingpin in the Southwest attempts to keep his young wife a virtual prisoner of his power and insane desire to dominate her, stripping her of her human and legal rights.

0765

BLACK MARKET BABY
10/7/77 Brut Productions (2 hours)

Executive Producer: James Green
Producer: Milton Sperling
Director: Robert F. Day

Teleplay: Andrew Peter Marin
Based on the novel *A Nice Italian Girl* by Elizabeth Christman
Photography: Richard C. Glouner
Music: Richard Bellis and George Wilkins
Art Director: Carl Anderson
Editor: George Jay Nicholson

Anne Macarino	LINDA PURL
Steve Aletti	DESI ARNAZ, JR.
Mrs. Carmino	JESSICA WALTER
Mr. Carmino	DAVID DOYLE
Dr. Andrew Brantford	TOM BOSLEY
Herbert Freemont	BILL BIXBY
Mrs. Krieg	LUCILLE BENSON
Linda Cleary	ANNIE POTTS
Babs	TRACY BROOKE SWOPE
Albert Macarino	ALLEN JOSEPH
Mario Macarino	MARK THOMPSON
Aunt Imelda	ARGENTINA BRUNETTI
Uncle Sanchi	TOM PEDI
Mrs. Yamato	BEULAH QUO

and: Robert Resnick, Stuart Nisbet, James Oliver, James Fraracci, Shelly Hoffman, Ivana Moore, Andrew Marin

A young college girl becomes pregnant, and she and the father-to-be are caught in the middle of a desperate struggle with a black market adoption ring out to take their baby. The original pre-airing title to this was *A Dangerous Love,* and theatrically overseas it was called *Don't Steal My Baby.*

0766
KILLER ON BOARD
10/10/77 Lorimar Productions (2 hours)

Executive Producers: Lee Rich and Peter Dunne
Producer: Sandor Stern
Director: Philip Leacock
Teleplay: Sandor Stern
Photography: William H. Cronjager
Music: Earle Hagen
Song "Take My Hand" by Carl Friberg and Sandor Stern
Sung by Trudy Desmond
Art Director: Ed Graves
Editor: Bill Mosher

Oscar Billingham	CLAUDE AKINS
Norma Walsh	PATTY DUKE ASTIN
Marvin Luck	LEN BIRMAN
Dr. Paul Jeffries	FRANK CONVERSE
Marshall Snowden	WILLIAM DANIELS
Glenn Lyle	GEORGE HAMILTON
Dr. Ned Folger	MURRAY HAMILTON
Julie	SUSAN HOWARD
Mitch	JEFF LYNAS
Jan	JANE SEYMOUR
Beatrice Richmond	BEATRICE STRAIGHT
Dr. Berglund	MICHAEL LERNER
Dr. Alvarez	THALMUS RASULALA
Buddy Sterpa	JOHN ROPER
Meade	FRED LERNER
Debra Snowden	BONNIE BARTLETT
Miguel	RAFAEL CAMPOS

and: Joshua Bryant, Fritzi Burr, John Durran, Edward Gallardo, Trudy Desmond, Jay Valera, John Dewey-Carter, Patrick McNamara, Norman J. Andrews, Rudy Challenger, Jim Storm, Robert S. Busch, Kandy Berley, Lee F. Stetson, Gene Massey, Howard Curtis, Johnny Walker, Jr., Wallace W. Landford,

Dane A. Taylor, Donald R. Smith, Joseph W. Vida, Matt Christian, David Hinton, Rene Paulo

A cruise ship, with a traditional roster of TV faces, is swept with fear and panic when hit by a mysterious, deadly virus, disrupting the fun and games.

0767
THE GIRL CALLED HATTER FOX
10/12/77 Roger Gimbel Productions/EMI Television (2 hours)

Executive Producer: Roger Gimbel
Producer/Director: George Schaefer
Teleplay: Darryl Ponicsan
Based on the book by Marilyn Harris
Photography: Howard R. Schwartz
Music: Fred Karlin
Art Director: Herman Zimmerman
Editor: Sidney M. Katz

Dr. Teague Summer	RONNY COX
Nurse Rhinehart	CONCHATA FERRELL
Claude	JOHN DURREN
Hatter Fox	JOANELLE ROMERO
Dr. Levering	DONALD HOTTEN
Mr. Winton	S. JOHN LAUNER
Mango	MIRA SANTERA
Policeman	DANNY VILLANEUEVA
Bartender	WILLIAM FARRINGTON
Belle	JEANNIE STEIN
Reverend	JACK McGUIRE
Indian Nurse	MONA LAWRENCE

and: Robert Jones, Arthur Wagner, Hardy Phelps, David Leyba, Denise Montoya, Sabra Wilson, Virginia Bird, Caroline Rackley, Biff Yeager, Billy Beck, Adam Williams, Renn Durren, Deborah Brown

A battle of wills between a concerned young doctor and ancient Indian witchcraft, with the future of a teenage Indian girl, sent to a state reformatory as an incorrigible, at stake.

0768
THE NIGHT THEY TOOK MISS BEAUTIFUL
10/24/77 Don Kirshner Productions (2 hours)

Executive Producers: Don Kirshner and Merrill Grant
Producer: George Lefferts
Director: Robert Michael Lewis
Teleplay: George Lefferts
From a story by Lou LaRose
Photography: Jules Brenner
Music: Walter Murphy
Music Supervisor: Don Kirshner
Choreography: James Starbuck
Art Director: Steven P. Sardanis
Editors: Robert Swanson and Les Green

Paul Fabiani	GARY COLLINS
Mike O'Toole	CHUCK CONNORS
Rolly Royce	HENRY GIBSON
Damon Faulkner	PETER HASKELL
Cindy Lou Barrett	KAREN LAMM
Layla Burden	SHEREE NORTH
Reba Bar Lev	VICTORIA PRINCIPAL
Omar Welk	GREGORY SIERRA
Marv Barker	PHIL SILVERS
Kate Malloy	STELLA STEVENS
April Garland	ROSANNE KATON
Buck	JONATHAN BANKS
Smitty	WILLIAM BASSETT
Mrs. Barrett	MARCIA LEWIS
Hector	SANTOS MORALAS
Barney Jessup	BURKE BYRNES
Toni McDuff	SUZETTE CARROLL

and: Lillian Muller, Phoebe Dorin, Al Rossi, James Jeter, Bill Overton, Pat Corley, Paul Kent

A hijacking caper involving an airliner carrying not only five beauty contest finalists but also a dangerous laboratory mutation to be used for bacterial warfare.

0769
THE GREATEST THING THAT ALMOST HAPPENED
10/26/77 Charles Fries Productions (2 hours)

Executive Producer: Charles Fries and Malcolm Stuart
Producer: Herbert Hirschman
Associate Producer: Tony Ganz
Director: Gilbert Moses
Teleplay: Peter S. Beagle
Based on the novel by Don Robertson
Photography: Joseph M. Wilcots
Music: David Shire
Art Director: Bill Ross
Editor: David Newhouse

Morris Bird III	JIMMIE WALKER
Morris Bird, Jr.	JAMES EARL JONES
Julie Sutton	DEBORAH ALLEN
Sandra Bird	TAMU
Miss Goldfarb	VALERIE CURTIN
Hoover Sissle	KEVIN HOOKS
Samuelson	SORRELL BOOKE
Coach	WILLIAM TRAYLOR
Dr. Brimson	DARRYL ZWERLING
Horton	SAM LAWS
Bonner	HARRY CAESAR
Aunt Edythe	SAUNDRA SHARP

In the 1950s a teenage athlete learns that he has leukemia, and his winning spirit is threatened as he faces a major basketball tournament just before Christmas, while his dad's struggle to maintain his own self-respect often blinds him to his son's emotional needs.

0770
HAVING BABIES II
10/28/77 The Jozak Company (2 hours)

Executive Producer: Gerald W. Abrams
Producer: Richard Briggs
Director: Richard Michaels
Teleplay: Elizabeth Clark
From a story by Ann Marcus
Photography: Michael P. Joyce
Music: Fred Karlin
Art Director: William M. Hiney
Editor: John A. Martinelli

Aaron Canfield	TONY BILL
Arthur Magee	CLIFF GORMAN
Sally Magee	CAROL LYNLEY
Martha Cooper	LEE MERIWETHER
Trish Canfield	PAULA PRENTISS
Jeff Kramer	NICHOLAS PRYOR
Lou Plotkin	WAYNE ROGERS
Dr. Julie Farr	SUSAN SULLIVAN
Paula Plotkin	CASSIE YATES
Danny Magee	ROBBIE RIST
Jenny Cooper	TRACY MARSHAK
Chris Williams	MICHAEL ST. CLAIR

and: Tracy Bogart, Belinda Balaski, Patrick Collins, Rhea Perlman, Cal Haynes, Valerie Robinson, Stacy Swor, Rosanna Arquette, Alice Borden, Marcia Martin, Vinton Freedley III, Sandy McPeak, Linda Lyons, John Medici, Nicholas Beavvy

Like its predecessor *Having Babies* (1976), this film focuses on several couples, the emotional crises involving birth and adoption, and hospital personnel's participation in their lives. Susan Sullivan's character of

Carol Lynley and Paula Prentiss in HAVING BABIES II (1977)

Dr. Julie Farr became the pivotal role in this one which served as a pilot to a "Having Babies" series that ran briefly in early 1978 and almost immediately had its title changed to "Julie Farr, M.D."

0771
SHARON: PORTRAIT OF A MISTRESS
10/31/77 Moonlight Productions, Inc./Paramount (2 hours)

Producer: Frank von Zerneck
Director: Robert Greenwald
Teleplay: Nancy Greenwald
Photography: Fred Jackman
Music: Roger Kellaway
Song "The Days Have No Names" by Roger Kellaway and Gene Lees
Sung by Sarah Vaughn
Art Director: Dan Lomino
Editor: Jerry Young

Sharon Blake	TRISH VAN DEVERE
Ed Dowling	PATRICK O'NEAL
Carol	JANET MARGOLIN
Timothy	SAM GROOM
David	MEL FERRER
Mrs. Blake	GLORIA DeHAVEN
Anne Dowling	ROSE GREGORIO
Dr. Greenspan	ARTHUR STORCH
Terri	SALOME JENS
Exercise Instructor	GOWER CHAMPION
Jill	JULIE MANNIX
Bill Winston	STEPHEN BRADLEY

This film details a professional woman's romantic life through a series of affairs with married men because she is unable to make a lasting commitment.

0772
THE INCREDIBLE HULK
11/4/77 Universal (2 hours)

Producer/Director: Kenneth Johnson
Teleplay: Kenneth Johnson
Based on characters created for Marvel Comic Books
Photography: Howard R. Schwartz
Music: Joseph Harnell
Art Director: Charles R. Davis
Editors: Jack Schoengarth and Alan Marks

Dr. David Bruce Banner	BILL BIXBY
Dr. Elaina Marks	SUSAN SULLIVAN
Jack McGee	JACK COLVIN
The Hulk	LOU FERRIGNO
Mrs. Jessie Maier	SUSAN BATSON
Ben	CHARLES SIEBERT
Martin Bram	MARIO GALLO
Policeman	ERIC SERVER
B. J. Maier	ERIC DEVON
Jerry	JAKE MITCHELL
Laura Banner	LARA PARKER
Minister	WILLIAM LARSEN
Girl at Lake	OLIVIA BARASH
Man at Lake	GEORGE BRENLIN
Mrs. Epstein	JUNE WHITLEY TAYLOR
Young Man	TERENCE LOCKE

The comic-book tale of the mild-mannered scientist who accidentally gains the secret to superhuman strength that manifests itself when he becomes enraged. This was the pilot for the popular TV series that began in the fall of 1977.

0773
PETER LUNDY AND THE MEDICINE HAT STALLION
11/6/77 Ed Friendly Productions (2 hours)

Producer: Ed Friendly
Director: Michael O'Herlihy
Teleplay: Jack Turley
Based on the novel *San Domingo, The Medicine Hat Stallion* by Marguerite Henry
Photography: Robert L. Morrison
Music: Morton Stevens
Editor: Paul Frederick LaMastra

Peter Lundy	LEIF GARRETT
Brisly	MILO O'SHEA
Emily Lundy	BIBI BESCH
Adam	JOHN QUADE
Grandma Lundy	ANN DORAN
Jim Baxter	BRAD REARDEN
Jethro Lundy	MITCH RYAN
Alexander Majors	JOHN ANDERSON
Lefty Slade	CHARLES TYNER
Red Cloud	NED ROMERO
Muggeridge	JAMES LYDON

and: Ned Romero, James Lydon

An engaging saga of a teenage frontier lad who becomes a rider for the Pony Express in the Nebraska Territory shortly before the Civil War. An Emmy Award nomination went to this film as Outstanding Children's Special of 1977–78.

0774
TELETHON
11/6/77 ABC Circle Films (2 hours)

Producer: Robert Lovenheim
Director: David Lowell Rich
Teleplay: Roger Wilton
Photography: Jacques R. Marquette
Music: Peter Matz
Art Director: Bill Kenny
Editor: Howard Epstein

Dorothy Goodwin	POLLY BERGEN
Matt Tallman	LLOYD BRIDGES
Mart Rand	RED BUTTONS
Charlie Barton	EDD BYRNES
Irv Berman	DICK CLARK
Elaine Cotten	JANET LEIGH
Arnold Shagan	JOHN MARLEY
Tom Galvin	KENT McCORD
Kim	EVE PLUMB
Roy Hansen	DAVID SELBY
Fran	JILL ST. JOHN
June	RANDI OAKES
Lorna	SHEILA SULLIVAN
Himself	DAVE BURTON
Himself	JIMMIE WALKER
Himself	SUGAR RAY ROBINSON

Romance, intrigue, danger and possibly murder are among the behind-the-scenes elements surrounding a multimillion-dollar fund-raising telethon with an all-star TV cast assembled against a Las Vegas backdrop.

0775
INTIMATE STRANGERS
11/11/77 Charles Fries Productions (2 hours)

Executive Producer: Charles Fries
Producer: Richard and Esther Shapiro
Director: John Llewellyn Moxey
Teleplay: Richard and Esther Shapiro
Photography: Robert B. Hauser
Music: Fred Karlin
Art Director: Bill Ross
Editor: Walter Hannemann

Donald Halston	DENNIS WEAVER
Janis Halston	SALLY STRUTHERS
Karen Renshaw	TYNE DALY
Mort Burns	LARRY HAGMAN
Donald's Father	MELVYN DOUGLAS
Chris Halston	BRIAN ANDREWS
Peggy Halston	QUINN CUMMINGS
Dr. James Morgan	JULIAN BURTON
Marilyn Burns	ELLEN TRAVOLTA
Bridget	ELLEN BLAKE
Simpson (Rest Home Director)	REGIS J. CORDIC

and: James Keane, Ed Walsh, Barbara Iley, Jack Stauffer, Carol Vogel, Dolores Dorn, Judy Farrell

A contemporary drama of a couple who find that their deep love for each other can not overcome the emotions threatening to destroy their marriage, and she becomes a battered wife. The original title for this: *Battered!* Tyne Daly garnered an Emmy Award nomination as Best Supporting Actress.

0776
THE LAST HURRAH
11/16/77 O'Connor/Becker Productions/Columbia (2 hours)

Executive Producer: Terry Becker
Producers: Mike Wise and Franklin R. Levy
Director: Vincent Sherman
Teleplay: Carroll O'Connor
Based on the novel by Edwin O'Connor
Photography: Gerald Perry Finnerman
Music: Peter Matz
Art Directors: Ross Bellah and Robert Purcell
Editors: Les Green and Bernard Balmuth

Frank Skeffington	CARROLL O'CONNOR
Prudy Cass	LESLIE ACKERMAN
Amos Force	JOHN ANDERSON
Roger Shanley	DANA ANDREWS

Lou Ferrigno in THE INCREDIBLE HULK (1977)

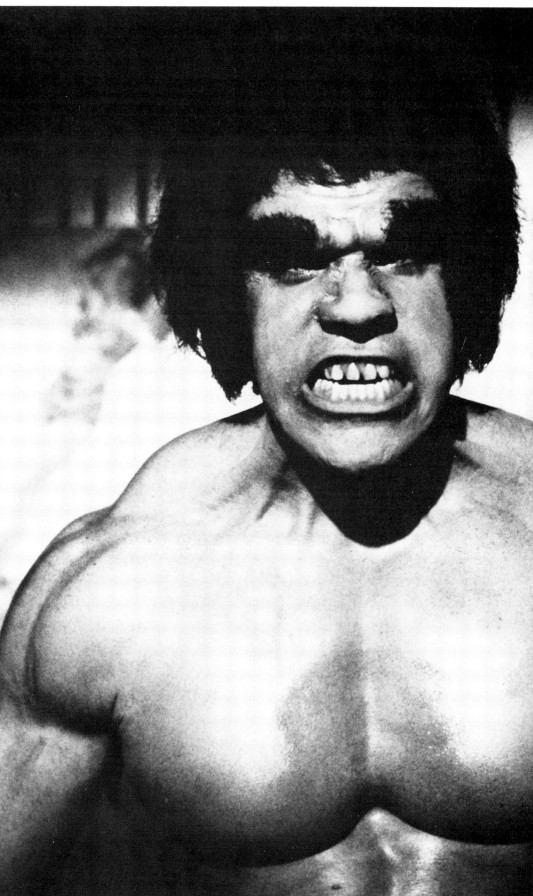

Nat Gardiner	ROBERT BROWN
Sam Weinberg	JACK CARTER
Ditto Boland	TOM CLANCY
John Gorman	BRENDAN DILLON
Hack Wiles	ARTHUR FRANZ
George Sherrard	ALAN HAMEL
Clare Gardiner	MARIETTE HARTLEY
Cardinal Burke	BURGESS MEREDITH
Winslow	STEWART MOSS
Norman Cass	PATRICK O'NEAL
Dr. Mike Santangelo	PAUL PICERNI
Robert Skeffington	PATRICK WAYNE
Maeve Skeffington	KITTY WINN
Herb Ripley	MEL STEWART
Grace Minihan	KATHARINE BARD
Jimmy Minihan	BILL QUINN

and: Sandy Kenyon, James Sikking, Art Batanides, William Benedict, Ricki Williams, Harry Basch, Lane Allan, George Barrows, Jack Griffith, Sal Vecchio, Paul Napier, Mike Walden, Dennis McMullen, Lane McCormick, Barbara Schillaci, Paul Lawrence, Elise O'Connor

Carroll O'Connor wrote and starred in this second screen adaptation of the 1956 best-seller (previously filmed by John Ford in 1958 with Spencer Tracy) about the aging and ailing head of a big-time political machine who schemes to stay in power and win a fourth term. Emmy nominations went to Burgess Meredith and Mariette Hartley for supporting actor and actress.

0777
CONTRACT ON CHERRY STREET
11/19/77 Columbia (3 hours)

Executive Producer: Renee Valente
Producer: Hugh Benson
Director: William A. Graham
Teleplay: Edward Anhalt
Based on the book by Philip Rosenberg
Photography: Jack Priestley
Music: Jerry Goldsmith
Art Director: Robert Gundlach
Editor: Eric Albertson

Deputy Inspector Frank Hovannes	FRANK SINATRA
Tommy Sinardos	JAY BLACK
Emily Hovannes	VERNA BLOOM
Capt. Ernie Weinberg	MARTIN BALSAM
Vincenzo Seruto	JOE DeSANTIS
Baruch Waldman	MARTIN GABEL
Ron Polito	HARRY GUARDINO
Al Palmini	JAMES LUISI
Lou Savage	MICHAEL NOURI
Eddie Manzaro	MARCO ST. JOHN
Roberto Obregon	HENRY SILVA
Jack Kittens	RICHARD WARD
Bob Halloran	ADDISON POWELL
Fran Marks	STEVE INWOOD
Otis Washington	JOHNNY BARNES
Phil Lombardi	LENNY MONTANA
Richie Saint	MURRAY MOSTON
Mickey Sinardos	ROBERT DAVI
Jeff Diamond	NICKY BLAIR
Flo Weinberg	ESTELLE OMONS
Cecelia	RUTH RIVERA
Paul Gold	SOL WEINER

Sinatra's TV-movie debut had him playing a hard-driven New York cop who explodes after his close friend and team partner is gunned down and decides to operate outside of established procedures to break an organized crime ring.

0778
MARY WHITE
11/19/77 Radnitz/Mattel Productions, Inc. (2 hours)

Producer: Robert B. Radnitz
Director: Jud Taylor
Teleplay: Caryl Ledner
Based on the writings of William Allen White
Photography: Bill Butler
Music: Leonard Rosenman
Production Designer: Ward Preston
Editor: Fred Chulack

William Allen White	ED FLANDERS
Sallie White	FIONNULA FLANAGAN
William L. White	TIM MATHESON
Sir James M. Barrie	DONALD MOFFAT
Jane Addams	DIANA DOUGLAS
Mary White	KATHLEEN BELLER
Richard Sloan III	HOWARD McGILLIN
Selina	KAKI HUNTER
John Rice	WILLIAM KUHIKE
Mr. Andrews	HENRY STROZIER
Ellie Rogers	VALERIE COTTON
Tom	PAUL FREDERICKSON
Tod	JACK MEYER

A sensitive story of a young girl and her moving relationship with her famed father, Pulitzer Prize-winning journalist William Allen White, and the profound change in his life following her tragic death at sixteen in a horseback riding accident in 1921. Caryl Ledner received an Emmy Award for the adaptation of White's book.

0779
LAST OF THE MOHICANS
11/23/77 Schick Sunn Classics (2 hours)

Executive Producer: Charles E. Sellier, Jr.
Producer: Robert Stabler
Director: James L. Conway
Teleplay: Stephen Lord
Based on the novel by James Fenimore Cooper
Photography: Henning Schellerup
Music: Bob Summers
Art Director: Charles Bennett
Editors: Steve Michael and Jim Webb

Hawkeye	STEVE FORREST
Chingachgook	NED ROMERO
Major Heyward	ANDREW PRINE
Uncas	DON SHANKS
Magua	ROBERT TESSIER
Alice Morgan	JANE ACTMAN
Cora Morgan	MICHELE MARSH
David Gamut	ROBERT EASTON
General Webb	WHIT BISSELL

and: Dehl Berti, John G. Bishop, Beverly Rowland, Coleman Lord

A "Classics Illustrated" version of the adventure tale about the intrepid white hunter who, with two Indian blood brothers, aids a British officer trying to escort two women through hostile territory. The two-hour production subsequently was cut to 90 minutes.

0780
THE HUNTED LADY
11/28/77 Quinn Martin Productions (2 hours)

Executive Producer: Quinn Martin
Producer: William Robert Yates
Director: Richard Lang
Teleplay: William Robert Yates
Photography: Paul Lohmann
Music: Laurence Rosenthal
Art Director: George B. Chan
Editor: James Gross

Susan Reilly	DONNA MILLS
Robert Armstrong	LAWRENCE CASEY
Capt. John Shannon	ANDREW DUGGAN
Sgt. Stanley Arizzio	ALAN FEINSTEIN
Mr. Eckert	GEOFFREY LEWIS
Lt. Henry Jacks	MICHAEL McGUIRE
Carol Arizzio	JENNY O'HARA
Max Devine	QUINN REDECKER
Dr. Arthur Sills	ROBERT REED
Uncle George	WILL SAMPSON
Angie	MARIO ROCCUZZO
David Todd	RICHARD YNIGUEZ
James Radford	DAVID DARLOW
Johnny Ute	PANCHITO GOMEZ
Senator Roger Clements	MARK MILLER
Cathy Clements	PATTI KOHOON
Lewis Clements	ROBERT NATHAN

and: Jess Walton, Hank Brandt, Taylor Larcher, Richard Herd, Vince Howard, Eric Server, Danny Wells, Charles Alvin Bell, James Chandler, Carl Mathis Craig, Tim Haldeman, Byron Mabe, Kathleen O'Malley, Sean Michael Rice

An undercover policewoman becomes a target for elimination by a crime syndicate and must flee for her life after being framed for murder in this prospective series pilot which bore a close resemblance to "The Fugitive" with a change of sex.

0781
IT HAPPENED AT LAKE WOOD MANOR
12/2/77 Alan Landsburg Productions, Inc. (2 hours)
(subsequently titled *Panic at Lakewood Manor*)

Executive Producer: Alan Landsburg
Producer: Peter Nelson
Director: Robert Scheerer
Teleplay: Guerdon Trueblood and Peter Nelson
Photography: Bernie Abramson
Music: Kim Richmond
Art Director: Ray Beal
Special Effects: Roy Downey
Editor: George Fowley, Jr.

Gloria Henderson	SUZANNE SOMERS
Mike Carr	ROBERT FOXWORTH
Ethel Adams	MYRNA LOY
Valerie Adams	LYNDA DAY GEORGE
Tony Fleming	GERALD GORDON
Vince	BERNIE CASEY
Richard Cyril	BARRY VAN DYKE
Linda Howard	KAREN LAMM
Peggy Kenter	ANITA GILLETTE
Tommy West	MOOSIE DRIER
White	STEVE FRANKEN
Fire Chief	BRIAN DENNEHY
Marjorie West	BARBARA BROWNELL

and: Bruce French, Stacy Keach, Sr., Rene Enriquez, Vincent Cobb

Terror from the depths of the earth traps a group of fun-seekers at a lavish summer resort in this thriller that initially was to have been called simply *Ants!*

0782
DEADLY GAME
12/3/77 MGM (2 hours)

Executive Producer: Richard O. Linke
Producer: Gordon A. Webb
Director: Lane Slate

Teleplay: Lane Slate
Photography: Gayne Rescher
Music: Mundell Lowe
Art Director: Leon R. Harris
Editor: Gary Griffin

Abel Marsh	ANDY GRIFFITH
Gloria	MITZI HOAG
Malcolm Rossiter, Jr.	JAMES CROMWELL
Deputy Fred	CLAUDE EARL JONES
"Doc" Susan Glascow	SHARON SPELLMAN
Deputy John	HUNTER VON LEER
Col. Edward Stryker	DAN O'HERLIHY
Amy Franklin	REBECCA BALDING
Whit	EDDIE FOY, JR.
Frieda Beasley	FRAN RYAN
Sergeant Redman	MED FLORY
Jake	JOHN PEREK
Vernon Brea	STEFFAN ZACHARIAS

and: Ysabel McCloskey, Miriam Byrd Nethery, Chuck Gradi, Ted Noose, O. W. Tuthill, Christopher Tenney, Ellen Blake

The second Abel Marsh pilot film, a sequel to *The Girl in the Empty Grave* (1977), deals with a military conspiracy surrounding the destruction and scandal caused by chemical spillage from an army tanker truck.

0783
CAPTAINS COURAGEOUS
12/4/77 Norman Rosemont Productions (2 hours)

Producer: Norman Rosemont
Director: Harvey Hart
Teleplay: John Gay
Based on the novel by Rudyard Kipling
Photography: Philip Lathrop
Music: Allyn Ferguson
Production Designer: Hilyard M. Brown
Editor: John McSweeney

Disko Troop	KARL MALDEN
Harvey Cheyne	JONATHAN KAHN
Dan	JOHNNY DORAN
Little Penn	NEVILLE BRAND
Long Jack	FRED GWYNNE
Tom Platt	CHARLES DIERKOP
Salters	JEFF COREY
Harvey Cheyne, Sr.	FRITZ WEAVER
Manuel	RICARDO MONTALBAN
Cook	STAN HAZE
Phillips	REDMOND GLEESON
Chief Steward	SHAY DUFFIN
Mr. Atkins	MILTON FROME
Mrs. Cheyne	STANJA LOWE

A remake of the all-time adventure classic that starred Spencer Tracy, Freddie Bartholomew and Melvyn Douglas in 1937 and told of a spoiled rich kid who grows up fast under the care of a crusty sea captain after falling overboard from his father's ship.

0784
THE GATHERING
12/4/77 Hanna-Barbera Productions, Inc.
(2 hours)

Executive Producer: Joseph Barbera
Producer: Harry R. Sherman
Associate Producer: Terry Morse, Jr.
Director: Randal Kleiser
Teleplay: James Poe
Photography: Dennis Dalzell
Music: John Barry
Production Designer: Jan Scott
Editor: Allan Jacobs

Edward Asner and Maureen Stapleton in THE GATHERING (1977)

Adam Thornton	EDWARD ASNER
Kate Thornton	MAUREEN STAPLETON
Julie Pelham	REBECCA BALDING
Clara	SARAH CUNNINGHAM
George Pelham	BRUCE DAVISON
Helen Thornton	VERONICA HAMEL
Bud Thornton	GREGORY HARRISON
Bob Block	JAMES KAREN
Tom Thornton	LAWRENCE PRESSMAN
Dr. John Hodges	JOHN RANDOLPH
Peggy Thornton	GAIL STRICKLAND
Roger	EDWARD WINTER
Toni Thornton	STEPHANIE ZIMBALIST
Reverend Powell	JOHN HUBBARD
Mary (Maid)	MARY BRADLEY MARABLE
Tiffany	MAUREEN READINGER
Joey	RONALD READINGER

A crusty businessman, facing his last Christmas, makes an eleventh hour attempt to pull together the family which he shattered by allowing them to become second to his work and which he left years earlier. The Emmy-winner as Outstanding Special of 1977–78, with nominations also going to Maureen Stapleton, director Randal Kleiser, writer James Poe, production designer Jan Scott and set decorator Anne D. McCulley.

0785
THE STORYTELLER
12/5/77 Universal (2 hours)

Executive Producers: Richard Levinson and William Link
Director: Robert Markowitz
Teleplay: Richard Levinson and William Link
Photography: Terry K. Meade
Music: David Shire and Hal Mooney
Art Director: Lawrence G. Paull
Editor: Bud S. Isaacs

Ira Davidoff	MARTIN BALSAM
Sue Davidoff	PATTY DUKE ASTIN
Marion Davidoff	DORIS ROBERTS
Mrs. Eberhardt	ROSE GREGORIO
Arthur Huston	JAMES DALY
Randolph	JON KORKES
Anthony	DICK ANTHONY WILLIAMS
Frank Eberhardt	TOM ALDREDGE
Louis Kellogg	DAVID SPIELBERG
Paul Temperson	JAMES STALEY
Lee Gardner	PETER MASTERSON
Phil Curry	MILT KOGAN
Russ Whitman	IVAN BONAR

and: Susan Adams, Shelby Balik, Richard LeFlore, Lieux Dressler

A veteran television writer is troubled by charges that his teleplay motivated a boy to actions that caused his death. Richard Levinson and William Link received Emmy Award nominations for their original story.

0786
IT HAPPENED ONE CHRISTMAS
12/11/77 Universal (2½ hours)

Producers: Marlo Thomas and Carole Hart
Director: Donald Wrye
Teleplay: Lionel Chetwynd

From the story *The Greatest Gift* by Philip Van Doren Stern
Photography: Conrad Hall
Music: Stephen Lawrence
Art Director: John J. Lloyd
Editors: Robbe Roberts and Bill Martin

Mary Hatch	MARLO THOMAS
Henry F. Potter	ORSON WELLES
George Hatch	WAYNE ROGERS
Clara	CLORIS LEACHMAN
Uncle Willie	BARNEY MARTIN
Violet	KAREN CARLSON
Mr. Gower	DICK O'NEIL
Mrs. Bailey	DORIS ROBERTS
Martini	CLIFF NORTON
Peter Bailey	RICHARD DYSART
Harry Bailey	CHRIS GUEST
Bert Andrews	MORGAN UPTON
Mary (age 12)	LYNN WOODLOCK
Ernie Baker	ARCHIE HAHN
Cousin Tillie	CEIL CABOT
Sam Wainwright	JIM LOVELETT
Judge	ROBERT EMHARDT
Sassini	GINO CONFORTI
Doctor	BRYAN O'BYRNE
Nick (Bartender)	MED FLORY

A new version of Frank Capra's 1947 classic *It's a Wonderful Life* with a gender switch—Marlo Thomas for James Stewart, Wayne Rogers for Donna Reed, and Cloris Leachman for Henry Travers. Emmy Award nominations went to Cloris Leachman as well as to art director John J. Lloyd and set decorator Hal Gausman.

0787
SUNSHINE CHRISTMAS
12/12/77 Universal (2 hours)

Producer: George Eckstein
Director: Glenn Jordan
Teleplay: Carol Sobieski
Photography: Edward Rosson
Music Coordinator: Tony Berg
Art Director: William Tuntke
Costumes: Edith Head
Editor: Gordon Scott

Sam Hayden	CLIFF DeYOUNG
Jill	ELIZABETH CHESHIRE
Weaver	BILL MUMY
Corey Grivits	COREY FISCHER
Nora	MEG FOSTER
Bertha Hayden	EILEEN HECKART
Joe Hayden	PAT HINGLE
Cody	BARBARA HERSHEY
Hugh Bob	JAMES KEANE
Stanley	DOUGLAS V. FOWLEY
Ray Griff	MICHAEL ALLDREDGE

In the sequel to *Sunshine* (1973) and the brief series that followed it, musician Sam Hayden, moody over the marriage of his sometime lover, decides to take his adopted young daughter home to Texas to celebrate Christmas with his family, and he rekindles a romance with a childhood sweetheart.

0788
THE INCREDIBLE ROCKY MOUNTAIN RACE
12/17/77 Schick Sunn Classics (2 hours)

Executive Producer: Charles E. Sellier, Jr.
Producer: Robert Stabler

Director: James L. Conway
Teleplay: Tom Chapman and David O'Malley
Photography: Henning Schellerup
Music: Robert Summers
Art Director: Charles Bennett
Editor: John F. Link II

Mark Twain	CHRISTOPHER CONNELLY
Mike Fink	FORREST TUCKER
Eagle Feather	LARRY STORCH
Jim Bridger	JACK KRUSCHEN
Crazy Horse	MIKE MAZURKI
Farley Osmond	PARLEY BAER
Simon Hollaway	WHIT BISSELL
Mayor Calvin Mercer	BILL ZUCKERT
Sheriff Benedict	DON HAGGERTY
Milford Petrie	SAM EDWARDS
Virginia City Sheriff	SANDY GIBBON
Burton	WILLIAM KAZELE
Bill Cody	JOHN HANSEN

and: Robert Easton, Greg Brickman, Thomas Chapman, Hugh Burritt, Prentiss Rowe, Warren Ewing, David O'Malley, Allen Wood, Michael Roud, Earl Smith, Dennis R. Williams

A lighthearted Western involving a madcap grudge race from Missouri to California between a young Mark Twain and his long-time rival, Mike Fink, with the aid of a slightly daft Indian.

0789
DON'T PUSH, I'LL CHARGE WHEN I'M READY
12/18/77 Universal (2 hours)

Producer/Director: Nathaniel Lande
Associate Producer: Lloyd Richards
Teleplay: Al Ramus and John Shaner
Photography: Lionel Lindon
Music: Lyn Murray
Title song sung by Rita Gardner
Art Director: Henry Bumstead
Editor: Robert L. Kimble

Wendy Sutherland	SUE LYON
Angelo Rossini	ENZO CERUSICO
Sgt. Ed Hutchins	DWAYNE HICKMAN
Teodoro Bruzizi	CESAR ROMERO
Major Ralph Watson	EDWARD ANDREWS
Santola	SOUPY SALES
Himself	JERRY COLONNA
Tony Esposito	GINO CONFORTI
Fabrizio	MIKEL ANGEL
Phil Parsons	PARLEY BAER
Lauren	VICTORIA MEYERINK
Oliver	KENNETH TOBEY
Announcer	AVERY SCHREIBER

and: Byron Morrow, Dick Simmons, Robert Ball, Lee Delano

An old-fashioned service comedy—the kind Bob Hope used to make in the 1940s—telling of the misadventures of an Italian POW who is drafted into the American army during World War II. Made in 1969, it was produced and directed by Bob Hope's son-in-law, with Italian actor Enzo Cerusico, remembered by TV trivia buffs as the one-time star of the series "My Friend Tony" (1969), in the lead. This film premiered not in TV's prime time but on NBC's late night network movie on a quiet Sunday.

0790
WILMA
12/19/77 Cappy Productions, Inc. (2 hours)

Executive Producer: Cappy Petrash Greenspan
Producer/Director: Bud Greenspan
Teleplay: Bud Greenspan
Photography: Arthur Ornitz
Music: Irwin Bazelon
Art Director: Ned Parsons
Editor: William Cahn

Wilma Rudolph	SHIRLEY JO FINNEY
Blanche Rudolph	CICELY TYSON
Coach Temple	JASON BERNARD
Ed Rudolph	JOE SENECA
Robert Eldridge (age 18)	DENZEL WASHINGTON, JR.
Coach Gray	CHARLES BLACKWELL
Doctor Gordon	NORMAN MATLOCK
Robert Eldridge (age 12)	LARRY SCOTT
Wilma (age 12)	REJANE MAGLOIRE
Wilma (age 4)	PIPER CARTER
Mae Faggs	PAULETTE PEARSON
Martha Hudson	ANDREA FRIERSON
Tootie	STACEY GREEN
Pappy Marshall	DURY COX
Doctor Williams	ROGER ASKEW
Principal	J. FRANKLIN TAYLOR

A fact-based drama of the childhood years of a Tennessee girl who overcame physical handicaps with her parents' encouragement and became a champion track sprinter, winning three gold medals in the 1960 Rome Olympics.

0791
TELL ME MY NAME
12/20/77 Talent Associates, Ltd. (2 hours)

Executive Producers: David Suskind and Frederick Brogger
Producer: Donald W. Reid
Teleplay: Joanna Lee
Based on the book by Mary Carter
Director: Delbert Mann
Photography: Zale Magder
Music: Hagood Hardy and Mickey Erbe
Art Director: Karen Bromley
Supervising Editor: Gene Milford
Editor: Kent Anthony

Porter McPhail	ARTHUR HILL
Emily McPhail	BARBARA BARRIE
Uncle Tyler	BARNARD HUGHES
Alexandra/Sarah	VALERIE MAHAFFEY
P. J.	GLENN ZACHAR
Timmy	DOUGLAS McKEON
Lucy	DEBORAH TURNBULL
Thurmond	MURRAY WESTGATE
Catherine	DAWN GREENHALGH

The story of a middle-aged wife and mother with two young sons who is forced to face the truth about her life after being confronted by her teenage daughter, born out of wedlock and given up for adoption, who has returned seeking the truth about her origins.

0792
MAD BULL
12/21/77 Steckler Productions/Filmways (2 hours)

Executive Producer: Len Steckler
Producer: Richard M. Rosenbloom
Directors: Walter Doniger and Len Steckler
Teleplay: Vernon Zimmerman
Photography: Jacques R. Marquette
Music: Al DeLory
Art Director: William Hiney
Editor: Scott Conrad

Iago "Mad Bull" Karkus	ALEX KARRAS
Christina Sebastiani	SUSAN ANSPACH
Duke Sallow	NICHOLAS COLASANTO
Sweeper	ELISHA COOK, JR.
Eddie Creech	DANNY DAYTON
Anthoney "The Executioner" Yarkus	CHRIS DeROSE
Yapopotsky, "The Cave Man"	RICHARD KARRON
Jack, "The White Knight" Braden	STEVE SANDOR
Theo Karkus	TITOS VANDIS
Coley Turner	TRACY WALTER
TV Announcer	BILL BALDWIN
Earl Lewis	DENNIS BURKLEY
TV Interviewer	WALKER EDMISTON
Queenie	EDDRA GALE
Mr. Clean	H. B. HAGGERTY
Delia	LAURIE HEINEMAN
Black Bart	ERNIE HUDSON
Dr. Bradford	HARRY LANDERS
Alex Karkus	K. C. MARTEL
Tidy	MIKE MAZURKI
Rafferty	EDDIE QUILLAN

and: Billy Varga, Jimmy Lennon, Rozelle Gayle, Regis Philbin, Harry Landers, Charlie Waggenheim, Russell Shannon, Ila Britton, Bonnie Wiseman, Virginia Peters, Douglas Deane, Al Dunlap, Bradley Lieberman, Merie Earle, Dolores Sandoz, Kathleen Hiethala, Simmy Bow, Patrick Campbell, Dale Ishimoto, Hal Smith

A love story between a hulking wrestler, whose life in the ring has little meaning, and an attractive woman who sees through his muscleman veneer to discover a sensitive human being.

0793
CHRISTMAS MIRACLE IN CAUFIELD, U.S.A.
12/26/77 20th Century-Fox (2 hours)

Producer: Lin Bolen
Director: Jud Taylor
Teleplay: Dalene Young
Photography: Terry K. Meade
Music: Fred Karlin
Art Director: James B. Hulsey
Editor: Peter Perasheles

Mathew Sullivan	MITCHELL RYAN
Johnny	KURT RUSSELL
Arthur	ANDREW PRINE
Grampa	JOHN CARRADINE
Rachel Sullivan	BARBARA BABCOCK
Caufield	DON PORTER
Matilda Sullivan	KAREN LAMM
Kelly Sullivan	MELISSA GILBERT
Willie	BILL McKINNEY
Carrie	SHELBY LEVERINGTON

Tim Sullivan	ROSS HARRIS
Storekeeper	ROBERT M. JEFFRIES
Bob	STEPHEN EARLEY

and: Jim McKrell, Phill Adams, Sean Fallon Walsh, Skip Lundby

A dramatic re-creation of the Christmas Eve 1951 coal mine disaster in which union workers, threatened with replacement by scabs, were forced to enter an unsafe mine and then were trapped underground by an explosion.

0794
TARANTULAS: THE DEADLY CARGO
12/28/77 Alan Landsburg Productions (2 hours)

Executive Producer: Alan Landsburg
Producer: Paul Freeman
Director: Stuart Hagmann
Teleplay: Guerdon Trueblood and John Groves
Photography: Robert L. Morrison
Music: Mundell Lowe
Art Director: Raymond Beal
Editor: Corky Ehlers

Bert Springer	CLAUDE AKINS
Joe Harmon	CHARLES FRANK
Cindy Beck	DEBORAH WINTERS
Chief Beasley	SANDY McPEAK
Mayor Douglas	BERT REMSEN
Doc Hodgins	PAT HINGLE
Buddy	TOM ATKINS
Fred	HOWARD HESSEMAN
Rich Finley	CHARLES SIEBERT
Sylvan	JOHN HARKINS
Honey Lamb	NOELLE NORTH
Gloria Beasley	PENELOPE WINDUST
Frank	EDWIN OWENS
Harry Weed	LANNY HORN
H. L. Williams	JEROME GUARDINO
Chuck Beck	MATTHEW LABORTEAUX

The crash of a cargo plane unleashes a horde of deadly tarantulas and allows them to move unchecked through a southwestern town.

0795
COME BACK, LITTLE SHEBA
12/31/77 Granada Television Ltd. (2 hours)

Executive Producer: Derek Granger
Artistic and Creative Producer: Laurence Olivier
Director: Silvio Narizzano
Teleplay: William Inge
From his prize-winning play
Incidental Music: John McCabe
Theme music by Henry Purcell, adapted by Michael Lankester
Production Designer: Eugene Ferguson

Doc Delaney	LAURENCE OLIVIER
Lola	JOANNE WOODWARD
Marie	CARRIE FISHER
Mrs. Coffman	PATIENCE COLLIER
Turk	NICHOLAS CAMPBELL
Postman	BILL HOOTKINS
Milkman	BOB SHERMAN
Telegraph Boy	SHERIDAN E. RUSSELL

Brice	JAY BENEDICT
Ed	BRUCE BOA
Elmo	ED DEVEREAUX

The second Olivier "Tribute to American Theatre" brought to television Inge's play about a sensitive man trying to fight alcoholism and understand his loving but inadequate wife who mourns the disappearance of her youth and her little dog. Originally Robert Mitchum was to have played Doc Delaney in this presentation, staged around the same time as Olivier's previous *Cat on a Hot Tin Roof.* Carrie Fisher, the daughter of Debbie Reynolds and Eddie Fisher, made her TV acting debut here.

0796
THE FOUR FEATHERS
1/1/78 Norman Rosemont Productions/Trident Films, Ltd. (2 hours)

Producer: Norman Rosemont
Associate Producer: Bruce Sharman
Director: Don Sharp
Teleplay: Gerald DiPego
Based on the 1902 novel by A. E. W. Mason
Photography: John Coquillon
Music: Allyn Ferguson
Art Director: Herbert Westbrook
Costume Designer: Olga Lehmann
Editor: Eric Boyd-Perkins

Harry Feversham	BEAU BRIDGES
Jack Durrance	ROBERT POWELL
William Trench	SIMON WARD
Ethne Eustace	JANE SEYMOUR
Gen. David Feversham	HARRY ANDREWS
Thomas Willoughby	DAVID ROBB
Wembol (Valet)	RICHARD BEALE
Colonel Eustace	ROBIN BAILEY
The Sgt. Major	JOHN HALLAM
Lieut. Bradley	JULIAN BARNES
Mrs. Feversham	MARY MAUDE
The Old Major	FRANK GATLIFF
The Old Colonel	ROBERT FLEMYNG
John (Butler)	ROBERT JAMES
Harry Feversham (age 7)	ALEXANDER BIRD
Harry Feversham (age 14)	JONATHAN SCOTT-TAYLOR
Army Nurse	PAULINE YATES
Colonel of North Surreys	NEIL HALLET
Abou Fatma	RICHARD JOHNSON

The fifth filming of the adventure classic about a British soldier in the 1880s who fights to regain his honor after being given four white feathers, symbols of cowardice. Previously made in 1921, 1929, 1939 and 1956. Olga Lehmann received an Emmy Award-nomination for her period costumes.

0797
BREAKING UP
1/2/78 A Time-Life Television Production (2 hours)

Executive Producer: David Susskind
Producer: Frederick Brogger
Director: Delbert Mann
Teleplay: Loring Mandel
Photography: Gil Taylor
Music: Walt Levinsky
Art Director: Ben Edwards
Editor: Gene Milford

JoAnn Hammil	LEE REMICK
Tom Hammil	GRANVILLE VAN DEUSEN
Amy Hammil	VICKI DAWSON
T. C. Hammil	DAVID STAMBAUGH
Tony	FRED J. SCOLLAY
Gabe	STEPHEN JOYCE
Edie	CYNTHIA HARRIS

Ira	MICHAEL LOMBARD
Louise Crawford	MEG MUNDY
George	ED CROWLEY
Mickey	LINDA SORENSEN
Vancrier	KEN McMILLAN
Haberle	JAMES NOBLE
Vic	BRUCE GRAY
Toby	LOIS MARKEL
Alice	JILL ANDRE
Robert Crawford	FRANK LATIMORE

A drama about a woman who faces a harrowing fight to rediscover her personal identity when her husband of fifteen years announces that he is leaving her and their children to search for the indefinable joy he feels is missing from his life. Subsequently a one-hour pilot called *Tom and JoAnn* was aired (with Elizabeth Ashley and Joel Fibiani) to test the waters for a prospective series. Emmy Award nominations went to director Delbert Mann and to Loring Mandel for his teleplay.

0798
FOREVER
1/6/78 Roger Gimbel Productions/EMI Television (2 hours)

Executive Producer: Roger Gimbel
Producers: Marc Trabulus and Merrit Malloy
Director: John Korty
Teleplay: A. J. Carothers and Joanna Crawford
Based on the novel by Judy Blume
Photography: David Myers
Music: Fred Karlin
Art Director: Herman Zimmerman
Editor: Robert Dalva

Kath Danziger	STEPHANIE ZIMBALIST
Michael	DEAN BUTLER
Artie	JOHN FRIEDRICH
Erica	BETH RAINES
Sybil	DIANA SCARWID
Theo Maxton	JORDAN CLARKE
Mr. Danziger	TOM DAHLGREN
Mrs. Danziger	JUDY BROCK
Grandpa	WOODROW CHAMBLISS
Grandma	ERICA CHAMBLISS

and: Judith Wilson, Sid Hollister, Dan Caldwell, Lois Marie Hunter, Robert F. Vandervort

A romantic drama about a teenage girl's first love and the perennial adolescent dilemma of whether to give herself to him in order to hang on to him.

0799
SUPERDOME
1/9/78 ABC Circle Films (2 hours)

Producer: William Frye
Director: Jerry Jameson
Teleplay: Barry Oringer
From a story by Barry Oringer and Bill Svanoe
Photography: Matthew F. Leonetti
Music: John Cacavas
Art Director: Bill Kenney
Editor: J. Terry Williams

Mike Shelley	DAVID JANSSEN
Joyce	EDIE ADAMS
P. K. Jackson	CLIFTON DAVIS
Doug Collins	PETER HASKELL
Dave Walecki	KEN HOWARD
Nancy Walecki	SUSAN HOWARD
Chip Green	VAN JOHNSON
Sonny	VONETTA McGEE
Lainie	DONNA MILLS
George Beldridge	ED NELSON
Fay Bonelli	JANE WYATT
Brooks	SHELLY NOVACK
Gail	ROBIN MATTSON

McCauley	TOM SELLECK
Mooney	MARVIN FLEMING
Caretta	LES JOSEPHSON
Moses	BUBBA SMITH
Tony	MICHAEL PATAKI
Whitley	M. EMMET WALSH
Hennerson	DICK BUTKUS
Announcer	CHARLIE JONES

A silent killer stalks New Orleans and threatens the Super Bowl football game, putting a roster full of familiar TV faces in jeopardy in this mini-version of *Two Minute Warning*.

0800
A LOVE AFFAIR: THE ELEANOR AND LOU GEHRIG STORY
1/15/78 Charles Fries Productions/Stonehenge Productions (2 hours)

Executive Producers: Charles Fries and Dick Berg
Producer: David Manson
Director: Fielder Cook
Teleplay: Blanche Hanalis
Based on the book *My Luke and I* by Eleanor Gehrig and Joseph Durso
Photography: Michel Hugo
Music: Eddy Lawrence Manson
Art Director: Herman Zimmerman
Editor: David Newhouse

Eleanor Gehrig	BLYTHE DANNER
Lou Gehrig	EDWARD HERRMANN
Mrs. Gehrig	PATRICIA NEAL
Joe McCarthy	GERALD S. O'LOUGHLIN
Babe Ruth	RAMON BIERI
Eleanor's Mother	JANE WYATT
Claire Ruth	GEORGIA ENGEL
Dr. Canlan	MICHAEL LERNER
Dr. Charles Mayo	DAVID OGDEN STIERS
Dorothy	GAIL STRICKLAND
Kitty	VALERIE CURTIN
Jennifer	JENNIFER PENNY
Sophie Tucker	LAINIE KAZAN
Joe Durso	ROBERT BURR
Tony Lazzeri	JAMES LUISI
Yankee Executive	WYNN ERWIN
Bill Dickey	WILLIAM WELLMAN, JR.

A sentimental retelling of the love story of baseball immortal Lou Gehrig and his wife, told from her point of view. Originally this was to have premiered in October 1977, but ironically it was pre-empted by the World Series. Instead it had its initial airing opposite the Super Bowl Game! An Emmy Award nomination went to Blanche Hanalis for her adaptation of Eleanor Gehrig's book.

0801
NOWHERE TO RUN
1/16/78 MTM Productions (2 hours)

Producer: Jim Byrnes
Director: Richard Lang
Teleplay: Jim Byrnes
Based on the novel by Charles Einstein
Photography: Charles G. Arnold
Music: Jerrold Immel
Art Director: Albert Heschong
Editor: Gary Griffin

Harry Adams	DAVID JANSSEN
Marian Adams	STEFANIE POWERS
Herbie Stoltz	ALLEN GARFIELD
Amy Kessler	LINDA EVANS
Marian's Mother	NEVA PATTERSON
Marian's Father	JOHN RANDOLPH

David Janssen and Linda Evans in NOWHERE TO RUN (1978)

Joe Anasto	ANTHONY EISLEY
McEnerney	JAMES KEACH
Charleen	AHNA CAPRI
Kaufman	LANCE LeGAULT
Christos	LIONEL DECKER
Spence	CHARLES SIEBERT
Dr. Steinberg	RICHARD McKENZIE

A disgruntled husband devises a winning blackjack system as part of an elaborate scheme to leave his overbearing, unfaithful wife and start a new life, despite the fact that she has hired an inept, down-at-the-heels private detective to keep an eye on him.

0802
THE OTHER SIDE OF HELL
1/17/78 Aubrey-Lyon Productions (3 hours)

Executive Producer: James T. Aubrey
Producers: Ronald Lyon and Jim Milio
Director: Jan Kadar
Teleplay: Leon Tokatyan
Photography: Adam Hollander
Music: Leonard Rosenman
Art Director: James Murakami
Editor: Ralph Winters

Frank Dole	ALAN ARKIN
Jim Baker	ROGER E. MOSLEY

Johnson	MORGAN WOODWARD
Donahue	SEAMON GLASS
Miller	SHAY DUFFIN
The Rev. Wyler	RICHARD HAWKINS
Pudgy Man	AL CHECCO
Morelli	LEONARD STONE
Carlo	TONY KARLOFF
Guard	NICKY BLAIR
Louise Dole	BARBARA DANA

A man who enters a hospital for the criminally insane in an irrational state but regains his sanity after several years desperately tries to win his release after witnessing attacks on patients by guards. Production began on this as *The Next Howling Wind* and then it was to have been called *Escape from Hell.*

0803
RETURN TO FANTASY ISLAND
1/20/78 A Spelling-Goldberg Production (2 hours)

Executive Producers: Aaron Spelling and Leonard Goldberg
Producer: Michael Fisher
Associate Producer: Shelly Hull
Director: George McGowan
Teleplay: Marc Brandell
Photography: Arch R. Dalzell
Music: Laurence Rosenthal
Art Director: Alfeo Bocchicchio
Editor: John Woodcock

Roarke	RICARDO MONTALBAN
Margo Dean	ADRIENNE BARBEAU
Charles Fleming	HORST BUCHHOLZ
Brian Faber	JOSEPH CAMPANELLA
Pierre	GEORGE CHAKIRIS
Mr. Grant	JOSEPH COTTEN
Lucy Faber	PAT CROWLEY
Mrs. Grant	LARAINE DAY
Benson	GEORGE MAHARIS
Raoul	CAMERON MITCHELL
Kito	FRANCE NUYEN
Janet Fleming	KAREN VALENTINE
Tattoo	HERVE VILLECHAIZE

and: John Zaremba, Kevi Kendall, Kristine Ritzke, Nancy McKeon

This second feature-length pilot for the hit series that began in January 1978 offered more dreams fulfilled for six lucky people on a plush island resort. Originally it was to have been titled simply *Fantasy Island II* and had been scheduled to premiere two months earlier.

0804
STANDING TALL
1/21/78 Quinn Martin Productions (2 hours)

Executive Producer: Quinn Martin
Producer: Marty Katz
Director: Harvey Hart
Teleplay: Franklin Thompson
Photography: Stevan Larner
Music: Richard Markowitz
Art Director: George B. Chan
Editor: James Gross

Luke Shasta	ROBERT FORSTER
Lonny Moon	WILL SAMPSON
Nate Rackley	L. Q. JONES
Sheriff Brumfield	ROBERT DONNER
Elroy Bones	RON HAYES
George Fewster	BUCK TAYLOR

Jill Shasta	LINDA EVANS
Major Hartline	CHUCK CONNORS
Anne Klinger	FAITH QUABIUS
Ginny Tarver	DANI JANSSEN
Bob Workett	LEE JONES-DeBROUX
Tom Sparkman	ROBERT GENTRY
Strickland	EDDIE FIRESTONE
Captain Hinton	BRYAN MONTGOMERY
Hodges	REGIS J. CORDIC
Judge Lang	DAVID LEWIS

A small-time half-breed cattle rancher, struggling to eke out a Depression-era existence, is subjected to a terror campaign after refusing to sell out to a ruthless land baron.

0805
THE DARK SECRET OF HARVEST HOME
1/23–24/78 Universal (5 hours)

Producer: Jack Laird
Director: Leo Penn
Teleplay: Jack Guss (Part 1) and Charles E. Israel (Part 2)
Adapted by James and Jennifer Miller
Based on the novel *Harvest Home* by Thomas Tryon
Photography: Charles Correll, Frank V. Phillips and Ken Dickson
Music: Paul Chihara
Art Director: Philip Barber
Editors: Robert Watts and Robert F. Shugrue

Widow Fortune	BETTE DAVIS
Nick Constantine	DAVID ACKROYD
Kate Constantine	ROSANNA ARQUETTE
Jack Stump	RENE AUBERJONOIS
Justin Hooke	JOHN CALVIN
Amys Penrose	NORMAN LLOYD
Maggie Dodd	LINDA MARSH
Beth Constantine	JOANNA MILES
Worthy Pettinger	MICHAEL O'KEEFE
Richard	RICHARD VENTURE
Sophie Hooke	LAURIE PRANG
Tamar Penrose	LENA RAYMOND
Missy Penrose	TRACY GOLD
Ty Harth	MICHAEL DURRELL
Roy Soakes	DICK DUROCK
Robert Dodd	STEPHEN JOYCE
Jimmy Minerva	STEPHEN GUSTAFSON

and: Phoebe Alexander, Bill Balhatchet, Kathleen Howland, John Daheim, Lori Street, Martin Shakar, Grayce Grant

and the voice of Donald Pleasence

A suspense drama chronicling the events that beset a New York commercial artist when he and his wife and daughter move to a rustic New England village they visited during their travels, only to find a ritualistic life style full of foreboding secrets. Costumer Bill Jobe was Emmy Award-nominated for his creations.

0806
THE DEFECTION OF SIMAS KUDIRKA
1/23/78 The Jozak Company/Paramount (2 hours)

Executive Producers: Gerald I. Eisenberg and Gerald W. Abrams
Producer: Richard Briggs
Director: David Lowell Rich
Teleplay: Bruce Feldman
Photography: Jacques R. Marquette

Music: David Shire
Art Director: William Hiney
Editor: John A. Martinelli

Simas Kudirka	ALAN ARKIN
Cmdr. Edward Devon	RICHARD JORDAN
Capt. Vladimir Popov	DONALD PLEASENCE
Gruzauskas	GEORGE DZUNDZA
Phillip Chadway	JOHN McMARTIN
Genna Kudirka	SHIRLEY KNIGHT
Cmdr. Burkalis	MARVIN SILBERSHER
Mott	PETER EVANS
Blain	TED SHACKELFORD
Dr. Paegle	BARTON HEYMAN
Kabek	JACK BLESSING
Baltrunar	NICHOLAS GUEST
Petras	MATTHEW ARKIN
Asst. Supervisor	SALEM LUDWIG

and: Bok Richardson, Don Warlock, Jr., Nick Saunders

A fact-based drama about the Luthuanian seaman who made an abortive attempt for freedom in 1970 by leaping from a Russian ship to the deck of an American Coast Guard cutter in Portsmouth, New Hampshire. Director David Lowell Rich and editor John A. Martinelli each received an Emmy Award for this film, which also gained nominations for Donald Pleasence (Supporting Actor), Bruce Feldman (Teleplay) and David Shire (Music).

0807
THE BERMUDA DEPTHS
1/27/78 Rankin/Bass Productions (2 hours)

Producers: Arthur Rankin, Jr. and Jules Bass
Associate Producer: Benni Korzen
Director: Tom Kotani
Teleplay: William Overgard
From a story by Arthur Rankin, Jr.
Photography: Jeri Sopanen
Music: Maury Laws
Song "Jennie" by Maury Laws and Jules Bass
Art Director: Katzov Satsoya
Editor: Barry Walter

Paulis	BURL IVES
Magnus	LEIGH McCLOSKEY
Eric	CARL WEATHERS
Jennie	CONNIE SELLECCA
Doshan	JULIE WOODSON
Delia	RUTH ATTAWAY

Scientists pursuing the mysteries of the deep are threatened by a beautiful girl who seems to have returned from the dead and by a prehistoric sea creature that dwells in the deadly Bermuda Triangle.

0808
NIGHT CRIES
1/29/78 Charles Fries Productions (2 hours)

Executive Producers: Charles Fries and Dick Berg
Producer: David Manson
Director: Richard Lang
Teleplay: Brian Taggert
Photography: Charles G. Arnold
Music: Paul Chihara
Art Director: Bill Ross
Editor: David Newhouse

Jeannie Haskins	SUSAN SAINT JAMES
Mitch Haskins	MICHAEL PARKS
Peggy Barton	JAMIE SMITH JACKSON
Nurse Green	DELORES DORN
Mrs. Delesande	CATHLEEN NESBITT
Dr. Whelan	WILLIAM CONRAD
Dr. Medlow	BRITT LEACH
Bea Pryor	SAUNDRA SHARP
Mrs. Thueson	DIANA DOUGLAS
Mrs. Whitney	ELLEN GEER
Cynthia	LEE KESSLER

and: Carl Byrd, James Keane, Jennifer Penny

A suspense tale about a young woman tormented by terrifying dreams that indicate her dead child is alive and in danger.

0809
SEE HOW SHE RUNS
2/1/78 CLN Productions, Inc. (2 hours)

Producer: George Englund
Director: Richard T. Heffron
Teleplay: Marvin A. Gluck
Photography: Ron Lautore
Music: Jimmie Haskell
Art Director: Charles Bailey
Editor: Gary Griffin

Betty Quinn	JOANNE WOODWARD
Larry Quinn	JOHN CONSIDINE
Janey Quinn	LISSY NEWMAN
Kathy Quinn	MARY BETH MANNING
John Matusak	BARNARD HUGHES
Evelyn	BARBARA MEEK
Handsome Man	JAMES HOUGHTON
Holly	LINDA PETERSON
Grillo	CHRIS ANASTASIO

and: Harvey Reed, Tom Kemp, Nancy James, Annette Miller

Joanne Woodward won an Emmy Award for her performance as a middle-aged housewife and mother (one of her fictional daughters was played by real-life daughter Lissy Newman) who, after spending a lifetime giving to others, decides to claim a piece for herself and enters the grueling twenty-six-mile Boston marathon as an obsessive means of self-expression. Composer Jimmie Haskell also received an Emmy for his score. A stage musical, *A Long Way to Boston*, based on this TV-movie, opened at the Goodspeed Opera House in Connecticut in 1969, but never got to Broadway. Nancy Dussault and Shelley Bruce had the roles played in the film by Joane Woodward and daughter Lissy.

0810
THE GREAT WALLENDAS
2/2/78 A Daniel Wilson Production (2 hours)

Executive Producer: Daniel Wilson
Producer: Linda Marmelstein
Director: Larry Elikann
Teleplay: Jan Hartman
Photography: Robert Bailin
Music: Joe Weber and Bill Soden
Art Director: Richard Bianchi
Editors: Eric Albertson and Pat McMahon

Karl Wallenda	LLOYD BRIDGES
Jenny Wallenda	BRITT EKLAND
Helen Wallenda	TAINA ELG
Jana Schmidt	CATHY RIGBY
Herman Wallenda	JOHN VAN DREELIN
Arnold Fielding	MICHAEL McGUIRE
Gunther Wallenda	BEN FUHRMAN
Lotte Schmidt	TRAVIS HUDSON
Mario Wallenda	BRUCE ORNSTEIN
Dick Faughnan	STEPHEN PARR
Dieter Schmidt	WILLIAM SADLER

Edith Wallenda	ISA THOMAS
Gene Hallow	CASEY BIGGS
Nurse	LUCINDA BRIDGES

A drama based on the legendary circus family, its spectacular but tragic career, and its unique aerial act that includes the seven-member pyramid that led to the 1962 accident in which two of the troupe were killed and another permanently paralyzed.

0811
CRUISE INTO TERROR
2/3/78 Aaron Spelling Productions (2 hours)

Executive Producers: Aaron Spelling and Douglas S. Cramer
Producer: Barry Oringer
Director: Bruce Kessler
Teleplay: Michael Braverman
Photography: Arch R. Dalzell
Music: Gerald Fried
Art Director: Alfeo Bocchicchio
Editors: Dennis Virkler and John Wright

Simon	DIRK BENEDICT
Matt Lazarus	FRANK CONVERSE
Rev. Charles Mather	JOHN FORSYTHE
Neal Barry	CHRISTOPHER GEORGE
Sandra Barry	LYNDA DAY GEORGE

Judy Haines	JOANN HARRIS
Lil Mather	LEE MERIWETHER
Dr. Isiah Bakkun	RAY MILLAND
Andy (Captain)	HUGH O'BRIAN
Marilyn Magnesun	STELLA STEVENS
Debbie Porter	HILARY THOMPSON
Bennett	MARSHALL THOMPSON
Emanuel	RUBEN MORENO
Nathan	ROGER E. MOSLEY

Evil emanates from an ancient sarcophagus brought aboard a pleasure cruise ship peopled by a predictably stellar TV cast. Originally this was to have been called *Voyage into Evil.*

0812
DEADMAN'S CURVE
2/3/78 Roger Gimbel Productions/EMI Television (2 hours)

Executive Producers: Roger Gimbel and Tony Converse
Producer: Pat Rooney
Associate Producer: Jacob Zilberg
Director: Richard Compton
Teleplay: Dalene Young
From a story by Paul Morantz
Photography: William Cronjager

Music: Fred Karlin
Art Director: Herman Zimmerman
Editor: Aaron Stell

Jan Barry	RICHARD HATCH
Dean Torrence	BRUCE DAVISON
Annie	PAMELA BELLWOOD
Dr. Vivian Sheehan	FLOY DEAN
Susan	DENISE DUBARRY
Linda	PRISCILLA CORY
Billy	KELLY WARD
Nancy	EDDIE BENTON
Mr. Barry	GEORGE WALLACE
Mrs. Barry	JUNE DAYTON
Himself	DICK CLARK
The Jackal	WOLFMAN JACK
Mr. Torrence	HANK BRANDT
Rainbow	SUSAN SULLIVAN
Himself	MIKE LOVE
Himself	BRUCE JOHNSTON

and: David Byrd, Art Bradford, Leonard Stone, James Oliver, Noah Keen

A movie biography based on the meteoric careers of Jan and Dean, the popular singing duo of the late 1950s and 1960s who immortalized the day's California surfing sound, and the tragic auto accident in 1966 that ended their rise when Jan was nearly killed and was hospitalized, either comatose or severely crippled, for more than three years.

John Considine, Lissy Newman and Joanne Woodward in SEE HOW SHE RUNS (1978)

0813
RING OF PASSION
2/4/78 20th Century-Fox (2 hours)

Executive Producer: Sheldon A. Saltman
Producer: Lou Morheim
Director: Robert Michael Lewis
Teleplay: Larry Forrester
Photography: Jules Brenner
Music: Bill Conti
Art Director: Richard Y. Haman
Editor: Sidney M. Katz

Joe Louis	BERNIE CASEY
Max Schmeling	STEPHEN MACHT
Damon Runyon	ALLEN GARFIELD
John Roxborough	PERCY RODRIGUES
Paul Gallico	JOSEPH CAMPANELLA
Anny Ondra Schmeling	BRITT EKLAND
Max Machon	NORMAN ALDEN
Chappie Jackson	JULIUS HARRIS
Joe Jacobs	MORDECAI LAWNER
Mike Jacobs	AL LEWIS
Nazi Official	JOHNNY HAYMER
Julian Black	MEL STEWART
Marva Trotter Louis	DENISE NICHOLAS
Lilly Brooks	BEAH RICHARDS
Adolph Hitler	BARRY DENNAN
Roosevelt	STEPHEN ROBERTS

and: David Moody, Patrick O'Hara, Dan Ayer, Joshua Shelley, Shaka Cumbaka, Tom Kelly, Rod McCarey, Jack Bernardi, Wonderful Smith, Clay Hodges, Sarina C. Grant, Joni Palmer, Warren Munson

A fact-based drama about the two Louis-Schmeling heavyweight fights and the way both boxers became unwilling symbols of political ideologies just prior to World War II. Originally titled *Countdown to the Big One.*

0814
THE INITIATION OF SARAH
2/6/78 Charles Fries Productions (2 hours)

Executive Producers: Charles Fries and Dick Berg
Producer: Jay Benson
Director: Robert Day
Teleplay: Don Ingalls, Carol Saraceno and Kenette Gfeller
From a story by Tom Holland and Carol Saraceno
Photography: Ric Waite
Music: Johnny Harris
Art Director: Herman Zimmerman
Special Effects: Cliff Wenger
Editor: Tony DiMarco

Sarah	KAY LENZ
Miss Erica	SHELLEY WINTERS
Mrs. Goodwin	KATHRYN CROSBY
Patti	MORGAN BRITTANY
Jennifer	MORGAN FAIRCHILD
Paul Yates	TONY BILL
Laura	ELIZABETH STACK
Mouse	TISA FARROW
Bobbi	DEBORAH RYAN
Barbara	NORA HEFLIN
Scott	ROBERT HAYS
Allison	TALIA BALSAM
Tommy	DOUG DAVIDSON

and: Jennifer Gay, Susan Duvall, Karen Purcil, Madeline Kelly, Michael Talbot, Debi Fries, Albert Owens

Strange goings-on involve a naive college coed in the bizarre rites of an old sorority. Kathryn Crosby, playing a house mother, returned to filmmaking here in her first appearance following Bing's death. Mia Farrow's

sister, Van Heflin's niece and Martin Balsam's daughter were among the other campus girls of questionable powers.

0815
RUBY AND OSWALD
2/8/78 Alan Landsburg Productions, Inc. (3 hours)
(Subsequently retitled *Four Days in Dallas,* edited to 2 ½ hours)

Executive Producer: Alan Landsburg
Producer: Paul Freeman
Director: Mel Stuart
Teleplay: John McGreevey and Michael McGreevey
Photography: Matthew F. Leonetti
Art Director: Ray Beal
Editors: Corky Ehlers and George Hively

Jack Ruby	MICHAEL LERNER
Lee Harvey Oswald	FREDERIC FORREST
Eva	DORIS ROBERTS
Capt. J. Will Fritz	LOU FRIZZELL
Robert Oswald	BRUCE FRENCH
District Attorney Wade	SANDY McPEAK
Marina Oswald	LANNA SAUNDERS
Chief Curry	SANDY WARD
Judge Johnston	JAMES E. BRODHEAD
George Paulsen	BRIAN DENNEHY
Little Lynn	GWYNNE GILFORD
Clyde Gaydosh	GORDON JUMP
Andy Armstrong	ERIC KILPATRICK
George	WALTER MATHEWS
Ike Pappas	MICHAEL PATAKI
Nat Ryan	AL RUSCIO
Phyllis Noonan	JODEAN RUSSO
Agent Kelley	RICHARD SANDERS
Wanda Killiem	VICKERY TURNER

and: Max Anderson, Lewis Arquette, Robert Bryan Berger, Dean Brooks, Ed Call, Raymond Colbert, Molly Dodd, David Leroy Dorr, Jessie Lee Fulton, John William Galt, Phyllis Glick, Margie Gordon, James Hall, Bill Joyce, Delbert Henry Knight, Sr., Jim Lough, Chip Lucia, Lilah McCarthy, Dick McGarvin, John R. Maclean, Jim Mendenhall, Anthony Palmer, George Paul, Richard Roat, Michael Schwartz, Adriana Shaw, Amanda Sherman, Bill Sorrells, Jon Terry, Lesley Woods, Rabbi Hillel Silverman

A dramatic re-creation of the four-day span preceding and following the assassination of John F. Kennedy in November 1963, drawn from authenticated events and eye-witness accounts.

0816
THE PRESIDENT'S MISTRESS
2/10/78 A Stephen Friedman/Kings Road Production (2 hours)

Executive Producer: Stephen Friedman
Producer: Herbert Hirschman
Director: John Llewellyn Moxey
Teleplay: Tom Lazarus
Based on the novel by Patrick Anderson
Photography: Robert L. Morrison
Music: Lalo Schifrin
Production Designer: W. Stewart Campbell
Editor: John A. Martinelli

Ben Morton	BEAU BRIDGES
Margaret "Mugsy" Evans	SUSAN BLANCHARD
Jim Gilkrest	JOEL FABIANI
Ed Murphy	LARRY HAGMAN
Craig	DON PORTER
Lt. Gordon	THALMUS RASULALA
Gwen Bowers	GAIL STRICKLAND
Anatoly	TITOS VANDIS
Donna Morton	KAREN GRASSLE

Tuesday Weld in A QUESTION OF GUILT (1978)

Bradley	MICHAEL BELL
Jan	JANICE CARROLL
Claire Whitmore	PATRICIA WILSON
Bill Kincaid	RICHARD BALIN
Josef	GREGORY GAY
Phil (Doorman)	JOHN S. FOX
Analyst	ELLEN TRAVOLTA

and: Virginia Wing, Steve Shaw, Jason Wingreen, Wes Dawn, Biff Yeager, Laurie Jefferson, Morton Lewis, Connie Sawyer, Anita Dangler, Juli Bridges, Tom Moses, Dale Ware, Abagail Shelton

A young government courier is caught in a deadly cover-up after discovering that his murdered sister was not only the mistress of a U.S. President but also a Soviet spy.

0817
THREE ON A DATE
2/17/78 ABC Circle Films (2 hours)

Executive Producers: Danny Thomas and Ronald Jacobs
Producer: David Shapiro
Director: Bill Bixby
Teleplay: Dale McRaven
Based on a book by Stephanie Buffington
Photography: Charles W. Short
Music: George Aliceson Tipton
Art Director: Michael Bauch
Editors: Tom Stevens and Jack McSweeney

Marge Emery	JUNE ALLYSON
Angela Ross	LONI ANDERSON
Andrew	RAY BOLGER
Donald Lumis	JOHN BYNER
Eve Harris	DIDI CONN
Leonard	GARY CROSBY
Emcee	GEOFF EDWARDS
Joan	CAROL LAWRENCE
Valerie Owens	MEREDITH MacRAE
Bob Oakes	RICK NELSON
Roger Powell	PATRICK WAYNE
Stephanie Barrington	FORBESY RUSSELL

Philip Halzerson, Tuesday Weld and Stephen Pearlman in A QUESTION OF GUILT (1978)

Ernest	JAMES HAMPTON
Frank	HOWARD T. PLATT
Gabe	RICHARD LIBERTINI
Allen Lunalilo	BRANSCOMBE RICHMOND
Man in Airport	DANNY THOMAS

The adventures of four couples, winners on a television game show, and their young chaperone on a Hawaiian holiday. A *Love Boat* carbon, set ashore.

0818
THE GHOST OF FLIGHT 401
2/19/78 Paramount (2 hours)

Producer: Emmet G. Lavery, Jr.
Director: Steven Hilliard Stern
Teleplay: Robert Malcolm Young
Based on the book by John G. Fuller
Photography: Howard R. Schwartz
Music: David Raksin
Art Director: Dan Lomino
Editor: Harry Keller

Dom Cimoli	ERNEST BORGNINE
Jordan Evanhower	GARY LOCKWOOD
Val	TINA CHEN
Prissy Frazier	KIM BASINGER
Dutch	TOM CLANCY
Bert Stockwell	HOWARD HESSEMAN
Loft	RUSSELL JOHNSON
Bill Bowdish	ROBERT F. LYONS
Les Garrick	ALLAN MILLER
Barton	ALAN OPPENHEIMER
Maria Cimoli	CAROL ROSSEN
Matt Andrews	EUGENE ROCHE
Dana	BEVERLY TODD
Mrs. Collura	ANGELA CLARKE
Marshall	JOHN QUADE
Ron Smith	MARK L. TAYLOR
Bailey	BYRON MORROW

and: Lynn Wood, Anna Mathias, Tony Mattlanga, Luis Avalos, Deborah Harmon, Meeno Peluce.

A supernatural mystery involving an actual plane crash in December 1972 in the Florida Everglades and the subsequent legend growing from it about the recurring presence on other flights of the ghostly figure of its captain. For his photography, Howard R. Schwartz won an Emmy Award nomination.

0819
WILD AND WOOLY
2/20/78 Aaron Spelling Productions (2 hours)

Executive Producers: Aaron Spelling and Douglas S. Cramer
Producer: Earl W. Wallace
Director: Philip Leacock
Teleplay: Earl W. Wallace
Photography: Jack Swain
Music: Charles Bernstein
Art Directors: Allen Smith and Paul Sylos
Editors: Howard Kunin and Dennis Duckwell

Lacey Sommers	CHRIS DeLISLE
Liz Hannah	SUSAN BIGELOW
Shiloh	ELYSSA DAVALOS
Delaney Burke	DOUG McCLURE
Teddy Roosevelt	DAVID DOYLE
Otis Bergen	ROSS MARTIN
Warden Willis	VIC MORROW
Tobias Singleton	PAUL BURKE
Megan	JESSICA WALTER
Jessica	SHERRY BAIN
Sean	CHARLES SIEBERT
Burgie	MED FLOREY
Demas Scott	ROBERT J. WILKIE
Mark Hannah	KENNETH TOBEY

and: Eugene Butler, Joan Crosby, Wayne Grace, Jim Lough, Bill Smillie

A Western adventure—a "Charlie's Angels" on horseback—involving three comely females who meet in a territorial prison, engineer a daring escape, and find themselves in a race against time to prevent the assassination of Teddy Roosevelt.

0820
A QUESTION OF GUILT
2/21/78 Lorimar Productions (2 hours)

Executive Producers: Lee Rich and Philip Capice
Producer: Peter Katz
Director: Robert Butler
Teleplay: Jack and Mary Willis
Photography: Ric Waite
Music: Artie Kane
Art Director: Jan Van Tamelen
Editor: Mike McCroskey

Doris Winters	TUESDAY WELD
Det. Louis Kazinsky	RON LEIBMAN
Lt. Tom Wharton	PETER MASTERSON
Mel Duvall	ALEX ROCCO
Dr. Rosen	VIVECA LINDFORS
Elizabeth Carson	LANA WOOD
Herman Golub	STEPHEN PEARLMAN
Asst. D.A. Verrell	RON RIFKIN
Det. Dick Tracher	DAVID WILSON
Larry Winters	JIM ANTONIO
McCartney	M. EMMETT WALSH
Mrs. Wharton	KELLY JEAN PETERS
Miriam Hamlish	MARI GORMAN
Mrs. Winters	KATHERINE BARD

and: Lisa Richards, Robert Costanza, James Ingersoll, Nicky Blair, Brian Farrell, Sid McCoy, Michael Fairman, John Fitzpatrick, Philip Halverson, Bernard Behrens

Inspired by the Alice Crimmins case in New York, this drama focuses on an attractive woman whose personal life style is viewed by many as distasteful and who later is accused of murdering her young daughter.

277

0821

SPECIAL OLYMPICS

2/22/78 Roger Gimbel Productions/EMI Television
(2 hours)
(subsequently titled *A Special Kind of Love*)

Executive Producer: Roger Gimbel
Producers: Merrit Malloy and Marc Tabulous
Director: Lee Philips
Teleplay: John Sacret Young
Photography: Matthew F. Leonetti
Music: Peter Matz
Art Director: James Murakami
Editor: George Jay Nicholson

Carl Gallitzin	CHARLES DURNING
Elmira Gallitzin	IRENE TEDROW
Janice Gallitzin	MARE WINNINGHAM
Michael Gallitzin	PHILIP BROWN
Matthew Gallitzin	GEORGE PARRY
Doug Ransom	HERB EDELMAN
Sherrie Hensley	DEBRA WINGER
Trina Cunningham	CONSTANCE McCASHIN
Dr. Brennaman	JAMES CALVIN NELSON

A widowed father struggles to hold together his family of three teenagers, one of whom is mentally retarded and enrolled in a state school for "special" children where he finds self-fulfillment in his love of sports, emulating his older, athletic brother.

0822

DR. SCORPION

2/24/78 Universal (2 hours)

Executive Producer: Stephen J. Cannell
Producer: Alex Beaton
Director: Richard Lang
Teleplay: Stephen J. Cannell
Photography: Charles Correll
Music: Mike Post and Pete Carpenter
Art Director: John J. Lloyd
Editors: Diane Adler and George R. Rohrs

John Shackelford	NICK MANCUSO
Tania Reston	CHRISTINE LAHTI
Bill Worthington	RICHARD T. HERD
Sharon Shackelford	SANDRA KERNS
Dr. Cresus	ROSCOE LEE BROWNE
The Dane	DENNY MILLER
Terry Batliner	GRANVILLE VAN DEUSEN
Admiral Gunwilder	PHILIP STERLING
Eddie	LINCOLN KILPATRICK
Lieut. Reed	JOSEPH RUSKIN
Whitey Ullman	BILL LUCKING

A live-action comic book adventure in which a power-mad genius threatens world peace with a scheme involving the theft of the country's atomic missiles, and only one man stands in his way.

0823

THADDEUS ROSE AND EDDIE

2/24/78 CBS Television, Inc. (2 hours)

Producers: Dan Paulson and Rod Sheldon
Director: Jack Starrett
Teleplay: William D. Wittliff
Photography: Robert Jessup
Music: Charles Bernstein
Art Director: Albert Heschong
Editor: Carroll Sax

Thaddeus Rose	JOHNNY CASH
Carlotta	DIANE LADD
Eddie Lee Haskell	BO HOPKINS
Crystal	JUNE CARTER CASH
Alvin Karl	JAMES HAMPTON
Judge	NOBLE WILLINGHAM
Singer	CLAY TANNER
Vioreen	ANNABELLE WEENICK
Pablo	JESUS ROSALES MORALES

and: Sarah Novell, John Starrett Berry, Greg Gault, John O'Conner White, Steve Schneider

The adventures of two good old boys from Texas, no-account buddies who are finally forced to face reality for themselves and for their girlfriends. Johnny and June Carter Cash made their TV acting debuts in this film.

0824

A DEATH IN CANAAN

3/1/78 Chris-Rose Productions/Warner Bros.
(2½ hours)

Producers: Robert W. Christiansen and Rick Rosenberg
Director: Tony Richardson
Teleplay: Thomas Thompson and Spencer Eastman
Based on the book by Joan Barthel
Photography: James Crabe
Music: John Addison
Art Director: Robert Jillson
Editor: Bud Smith

Joan Barthel	STEFANIE POWERS
Peter Reilly	PAUL CLEMENS
Lt. Bragdon	TOM ATKINS
Mildred Carston	JACQUELINE BROOKES
Barney Parsons	BRIAN DENNEHY
Rita Parsons	CONCHATA FERRELL
Sergeant Case	CHARLES HAID
Thomas Lanza	FLOYD LEVINE
Sgt. Tim Scully	KENNETH McMILLAN
Father Mark	GAVAN O'HERLIHY
Dr. Samura	YUKI SHIMODA
Jim Barthel	JAMES SUTORIUS
Teresa Noble	BONNIE BARTLETT
Judge Revere	WILLIAM BRONDER
Judge Vincet	PAT CORLEY
Sweeney	TRENT DOLAN
Corporal Sebastian	CHARLES HALLAHAN
Sarah Gibbons	SALLY KEMP

and: Doreen Lang, Lane Smith, Michael Talbott, Marc Vahanian, Paige Mellon, Dan Miller, Brad Willis, Brian McGibbon, Olan Shepard

A dramatization of the non-fictional account of Connecticut townspeople, rising to the defense of a local teenager charged with the mutilation murder of his mother in September 1973, and outraged at the police handling of the case. Clemens, son of actress Eleanor Parker, made his film acting debut here. This movie also marked the American TV directing debut of Tony Richardson and was Emmy Award-nominated as Outstanding Special of the 1977–78 season.

0825

SKI LIFT TO DEATH

3/3/78 The Jozak Company/Paramount (2 hours)

Executive Producer: Gerald W. Abrams
Producers: Richard Briggs and Bruce J. Sallan
Director: William Wiard
Teleplay: Laurence Heath
Photography: Roland S. Smith
Music: Barry DeVorzon
Art Director: Trevor Williams
Editor: Jerry Wilson

Lee Larson	DEBORAH RAFFIN
Dick Elston	CHARLES FRANK
Ben Forbes	HOWARD DUFF
Ron Corley	DON GALLOWAY
Vicki Gordon	GAIL STRICKLAND
Mike Sloan	DON JOHNSON
Andrea Mason	VERONICA HAMEL
Marv Gillman	CLU GULAGER
Wendy Bryant	LISA REEVES
Clevenger	PIERRE JALBERT
Ski Patroller	SUZY CHAFFEE

A suspense thriller centering on several people trapped in two derailed ski lift gondolas and facing possible death—a couple of ski champions whom a sports promoter is trying to link together romantically, an ex-mobster and a professional assassin who is stalking him.

0826

HAVING BABIES III

3/3/78 The Jozak Company/Paramount (2 hours)

Executive Producers: Gerald I. Isenberg and Gerald W. Abrams
Producer: B. W. Sandefur
Director: Jackie Cooper
Teleplay: Pamela Chais
Photography: William K. Jurgenson
Music: Lee Holdridge
Song: "There Will Always Be Love" by Lee Holdridge and Alan and Marilyn Bergman
Art Director: Frank T. Smith
Editor: Jerry Young

Dr. Julie Farr	SUSAN SULLIVAN
Dr. Ron Daniels	DENNIS HOWARD
Kelly Williams	BEVERLY TODD
Dr. Blake Simmons	MITCHELL RYAN
Leslee Wexler	PATTY DUKE ASTIN
Dawn	KATHLEEN BELLER
Chuck	PHIL FOSTER
Marnie Bridges	JAMIE SMITH JACKSON
Russ Bridges	MICHAEL LEMBECK
Gloria Miles	RUE McCLANAHAN
Jim Wexler	RICHARD MULLIGAN

The third pilot movie for the subsequent "Having Babies" series which quickly was retitled "Julie Farr, M.D.," and soon afterward disappeared, all during the last few weeks of the 1977–78 season. Patty Duke Astin won another of her various Emmy Award nominations for her performance.

0827

LAST OF THE GOOD GUYS

3/7/78 Columbia Pictures (2 hours)

Producer: Jay Daniel
Director: Theodore J. Flicker
Teleplay: John D. Hess, Theodore J. Flicker and Clark Howard
Photography: Emmett Bergholz
Music: Dana Kaproff
Art Directors: Ross Bellah and Robert Peterson
Editor: Robert L. Swanson

Sergeant Nichols	ROBERT CULP
Officer Johnny Lucas	DENNIS DUGAN
Officer Tash Namaguchi	RICHARD NARITA

Officer Marv Pulaski	JI-TU CUMBUKA	Daniel Cooper	CHRIS PETERSON	
Officer George Talltree	HAMPTON FANCHER	Sarah Cooper	KATY KURTZMAN	
		Joseph T. Antonelli	HARRIS YULIN	

Officer Marv Pulaski — JI-TU CUMBUKA
Officer George Talltree — HAMPTON FANCHER
Lill O'Malley — MARLYN MASON
Sgt. Frank O'Malley — LARRY HAGMAN
Marnie — ELTA BLAKE
Dr. Cropotkin — JONATHAN HARRIS
Mr. Stit — ROGER BOWEN
El Caliph — ERNIE HUDSON
Benita Juarez Zapata — CHU CHU MALAVE

and: Merie Erle, Howard Honig, James Hong, Mart Tobin, Ed Leonard, Ina Gold, Joi Staton

A comedy-drama about a bunch of police rookies who conspire to convince their hard-nosed sergeant that a seriously ill fellow officer, two weeks away from retirement, is on the job, and who, when he suddenly dies, try to hide the fact so that his family can collect his full benefits.

0828
WHEN EVERY DAY WAS THE FOURTH OF JULY
3/12/78 A Dan Curtis Production (2 hours)

Producer/Director: Dan Curtis
Teleplay: Lee Hutson
From a story by Dan Curtis and Lee Hutson
Photography: Frank Stanley
Music: Walter Scharf
Art Director: Jack DeGovia
Editor: Ted Virkler

Ed Cooper — DEAN JONES
Millie Cooper — LOUISE SOREL

Daniel Cooper — CHRIS PETERSON
Sarah Cooper — KATY KURTZMAN
Joseph T. Antonelli — HARRIS YULIN
Albert Cavanaugh (The Snow Man) — GEOFFREY LEWIS
Off. Mike Doyle — SCOTT BRADY
Mrs. Najarian — RONNIE CLAIRE EDWARDS

Herman Gasser — BEN PIAZZA
Judge Henry J. Wheeler — HENRY WILCOXON
Red Doyle — ERIC SHEA
Robert Najarian — MICHAEL PATAKI
Dr. Alexander Moss — WOODROW PARFREY

Narrated by DAN CURTIS

and: H. B. Haggerty, Moosie Drier, Scott Kimball, Tiger Williams

Fictionalized from events during producer/director/writer Dan Curtis' boyhood in Bridgeport, Connecticut, in the 1930s, this sentimental drama tells of a local attorney who succumbs to the pleas of his nine-year-old daughter and agrees to defend on homicide charges a mute handyman the girl has befriended, thought to be the town "weirdo" after being shell-shocked during World War I.

0829
PERFECT GENTLEMEN
3/14/78 Paramount (2 hours)

Executive Producer: Bud Austin
Producer/Director: Jackie Cooper
Teleplay: Nora Ephron

Photography: William K. Jurgensen
Music: Dominic Frontiere
Art Director: James Claytor
Editor: Jerry Dronsky

Lizzie Martin — LAUREN BACALL
Mama Cavagnaro — RUTH GORDON
Sophie Rosenman — SANDY DENNIS
Annie Cavagnaro — LISA PELIKAN
Ed Martin — ROBERT ALDA
Murray Rosenman — STEPHEN PEARLMAN
Vinnie Cavagnaro — STEVE ALLIE COLLURA
Mr. Appleton — DICK O'NEILL
Nick Auletta — RICK GARIA
Johnson — ROBERT KYA-HILL
Desk Clerk — KEN OLFSON
Frankie Fox — RALPH MANZA

Lauren Bacall made her TV-movie debut in this amusing caper film about three women with totally different backgrounds but sharing a common bond in that each needs a large sum of money and each has a husband in prison, and with the help of a safecracking old lady they pull off a million dollar heist.

0830
KEEFER
3/16/78 David Gerber Productions/Columbia Pictures (2 hours)

Executive Producers: David Gerber and Bill Driskill
Producer: James H. Brown
Director: Barry Shear

Ruth Gordon in PERFECT GENTLEMEN (1978)

Teleplay: Bill Driskill and Simon Muntner
Photography: Gerald Perry Finnerman
Music: Duane Tatro
Art Directors: Ross Bellah and James G. Hulsey
Editor: Ken Zemke

Keefer	WILLIAM CONRAD
Benny	MICHAEL O'HARE
Angel	CATHY LEE CROSBY
Amy	KATE WOODVILLE
Beaujolais	BRIONI FARRELL
Kleist	JEREMY KEMP
Maureau	MARCEL HILLAIRE
Hegel	BILL FLETCHER
Rudy	IAN ABERCROMBIE
Benson	JACK L. GING
Bemmel	RICHARD SANDERS
Vorst	NORBERT WEISSER
Sergeant	WILLIAM H. BASSETT
Duval	STEFFAN ZACHARIAS
Madame Cerral	NATALIE CORE
Jacques	ALAIN PATRICK
Folger	ANDRE LANDZAAT

The pilot movie for a prospective series, with Conrad playing the leader of a crack group of secret agents operating behind enemy lines during World War II.

0831
DOCTORS' PRIVATE LIVES
3/20/78 David Gerber Productions/Columbia Pictures (2 hours)

Executive Producer: David Gerber
Producer: Robert Stambler
Director: Steven Hilliard Stern
Teleplay: James Henerson
From a story by Peggy Elliott and James Henerson
Photography: Howard R. Schwartz
Music: Richard Markowitz
Art Directors: Ross Bellah and John Beckman
Editors: David Wages and Ronald LaVine

Dr. Jeffrey Latimer	JOHN GAVIN
Dr. Beth Demery	DONNA MILLS
Dr. Mike Wise	ED NELSON
Frances Latimer	BARBARA ANDERSON
Sylvia	BETTYE ACKERMAN
Irv	JOHN RANDOLPH
Dr. Rick Calder	RANDY POWELL
Phyllis	FAWNE HARRIMAN
Kenny	LEIGH McCLOSKEY
Kitty	KIM HAMILTON
Mona Wise	ELINOR DONAHUE
Howard Weese	JOHN LUPTON
Harriet Wise	VIOLA HARRIS
Lou Wise	ROSS ELLIOTT
Sheila	ROBIN MATTSON
Tania	PAMM KENNEALLY

Two famed heart surgeons find their lives in turmoil when personal passions clash with medical ethics in this pilot for a prospective hospital-based series that finally emerged (briefly) in the spring of 1979.

0832
CINDY
3/24/78 John Charles Walters Production
(2 hours)

Producers: James L. Brooks, Stan Daniels, David Davis, Ed. Weinberger
Director: William A. Graham
Teleplay: James L. Brooks, Stan Daniels, David Davis, Ed. Weinberger
Photography: Larry Boelens
Music and Lyrics: Stan Daniels
Additional Music/Musical Director: Howard Roberts
Choreography: Donald McKayle
Art Director: Jim Vance
Editors: Kenneth Kotch and Vince Humphrey

Cindy	CHARLAINE WOODARD
Father	SCOEY MITCHLLL
Sara Hayes (Stepmother)	MAE MERCER
Olive	NELL-RUTH CARTER
Venus	ALAINA REED
Michael Simpson	CLEAVANT DERRICKS
Captain Joe Prince	CLIFTON DAVIS
Miles Archer	W. BENSON TERRY
Wilcox	JOHN HANCOCK
Recruiter	RICHARD STAHL
Sergeant	NOBLE WILLINGHAM

A sparkling musical updating to World War II Harlem of the Cinderella story, featuring an all-black cast, with an original score and several twists at the end. Charlaine Woodard and Nell-Ruth Carter later were reunited in the Broadway smash *Ain't Misbehavin'* for which the latter won the Tony Award.

0833
COPS AND ROBIN
3/28/78 Paramount (2 hours)

Executive Producers: Tony Wilson and Gary Damsker
Producer: William Kayden
Director: Allen Reisner
Teleplay: John T. Dugan, Brad Radnitz and Dawning Forsyth
Photography: Howard R. Schwartz
Music: Charles Bernstein
Art Director: Dan Lomino
Editor: Jerry Young

Joe Cleaver	ERNEST BORGNINE
John Haven	MICHAEL SHANNON
Sergeant Bundy	JOHN AMOS
Robin Loren	NATASHA RYAN
Dr. Alice Alcott	CAROL LYNLEY
Wayne Dutton	TERRY KISER
Dist. Atty. Garfield	PHILIP ABBOTT
Richards	RICHARD BRIGHT
Jim Loren	JEFF DAVIDY
Richard	JAMES YORK
Carl Tyler	GENE RUTHERFORD
Detective Furie	J. KENNETH CAMPBELL
Dutton's Lawyer	WALTER COSTELLO
Judge Wheeler	IVAN BONNAR

An aging street cop and his partner, a robot programmed to be the perfect policeman, are assigned to protect the five-year-old daughter of the widow who witnessed the killing of her police officer husband and now is stalked by the gangster who murdered him. This film, which premiered on NBC, tried to breath new life into the previous season's ABC show "Future Cop," in turn recycled from the 1977 TV movie of that name, also with Borgnine, Shannon and Amos.

0834
CRISIS IN SUN VALLEY
3/29/78 Columbia Pictures (2 hours)

Executive Producer: Barry Weitz
Producer: Robert Stambler
Director: Paul Stanley
Teleplays: "Outward Bound" by Carl Gottlieb and "The Vanishing Kind" by Alvin Boretz
Photography: Al Francis
Music: Dick DeBenedictis
Art Director: Ross Bellah
Editor: Mike Vejar and Greg Prange

Sheriff Bill Stedman	DALE ROBINETTE
Deputy Archie Sykes	TAYLOR LARCHER
Buchanan	BO HOPKINS
Sheila	TRACY BROOKS SWOPE
Poole	PAUL BRINEGAR
Derry	JASON JOHNSON
Hubbard	JOHN McINTIRE
Thorndike	KEN SWOFFORD
Eva	SUSAN ADAMS
Shuyler	CHARLES FLEISHER
Lester	LARRY FLASH JENKINS
Jenny	JULIE PARSONS
Adler	MAX KLEVEN
Scott	TONY JEFFERSON
Sandy	DEBORAH WINTERS
Baker	WAYNE KEFFLEY
Reynolds	GRANT OWENS

and: Mark Simeon, Mike Hoover, Lorraine Curtis, Gary Williams, Mickey Livingston, Bill Quinn, Beverly Johnson, Paul Ramlow, Mike Susak, Tom Drougas, Niall McGinnis, Lori Hughes, Marcia Stringer

In another unrealized go at a series called "Stedman," dealing with a sheriff and his deputy in a sleepy ski town, this follow-up to *The Deadly Triangle* (1977) tied together two pilot films in which Stedman and Sykes contend with a group of urbanites planning a dangerous mountain climb and then investigate sabotage in a condominium development.

0835
LOVE'S DARK RIDE
4/2/78 Mark VII Ltd./Worldvision (2 hours)

Producer: Joseph M. Teritero
Director: Delbert Mann
Teleplay: Ann Beckett, Kane O'Connor and Dennis Nemec
From a story by Ann Beckett and Kane O'Connor
Photography: Robert Wycoff
Music: Tom Sullivan, John D'Andrea and Michael Lloyd
Art Director: William F. O'Brien
Editor: Richard Greer

Stephen P. Ehlers	CLIFF POTTS
Nancy Warren	CARRIE SNODGRESS
Diana	JANE SEYMOUR
Tom Scott	GRANVILLE VAN DUSEN
Dr. Brad Smith	TOM SULLIVAN
Karl Sears	SHELLY NOVACK
Dr. Kanlan	BASIL HOFFMAN
Dave Ramsey	FRED BEIR
Dr. Rush	BILL DEIZ
John Ehlers	JOHN WALDRON
David Ehlers	JIMMY MAIR
Debbie	JUDY JORDAN WEST

A young advertising executive, blinded in a gun accident, falls in love with a nightclub entertainer he has befriended, and through her he attempts to rebuild his life and career. Blind actor-musician Tom Sullivan lends a degree of authenticity to this reportedly true story as a blind psychiatrist who helps the film's hero

0836
A FAMILY UPSIDE DOWN
4/9/78 A Ross Hunter-Jacque Mapes
Film/Paramount (2 hours)

Producers: Ross Hunter and Jacque Mapes
Director: David Lowell Rich
Teleplay: Gerald DiPego
Photography: Joseph Biroc
Music: Henry Mancini
Art Director: Preston Ames
Editor: Richard Bracken

Emma Long	HELEN HAYES
Ted Long	FRED ASTAIRE
Mike Long	EFREM ZIMBALIST, JR.
Carol Long	PAT CROWLEY
Wendy	PATTY DUKE ASTIN
Scott Long	BRAD REARDON
Instructor	GARY SWANSON
Painter	DAVID HASKELL
Charlie Case	FORD RAINEY
Waiter	JIM MONTOYA
Paula	KIM HAMILTON
Wes Allen	NORWOOD SMITH
Mrs. Taka	MIIKO TAKA
Rhonda	BELINDA PALMER
Al	KARL HELD
Dr. Russo	PHILLIP ALLEN

and: Charles Walker II, Gail Landry, Bob Marsic, Lanna Saunders, Ernestine Barrier, Nolan Leary, Peter Rich, Matthew Tobin, Owen Cunningham

Fred Astaire won an Emmy Award as Best Actor and Helen Hayes received a nomination as Best Actress for their performances as a retired house painter and his loving wife of forty years who face an emotional crisis when he has a heart attack that makes both of them dependent on their grown children and leads to a separation. Efrem Zimbalist, Jr. and Patty Duke Astin also were cited for their acting with Emmy Award nominations, as was cinematographer Joseph Biroc.

0837
TO KILL A COP
4/10–11/78 David Gerber Productions/Columbia Pictures (4 hours)

Executive Producer: David Gerber
Producer: James H. Brown
Director: Gary Nelson
Teleplay: Ernest Tidyman
Based on the book by Robert Daley
Photography: Gayne Rescher
Music: Lee Holdridge
Assistant Directors: Stanley Neufeld and Ron Walsh
Art Directors: Ross Bellah and Ward Preston
Technical Advisor: Sonny Grosso
Editors: Donald R. Rode and Harry Kaye

Chief Earl Eischied	JOE DON BAKER
Everett Walker	LOUIS GOSSETT, JR.
Police Commissioner	PATRICK O'NEAL
Martin Delahanty	DESI ARNAZ, JR.
Agnes Cusack	CHRISTINE BELFORD
Paula	EARTHA KITT
Capt. Cornworth	GEORGE DiCENZO
Det. Baker	JULIUS HARRIS
Betty Eischied	JOYCE VAN PATTEN
Lt. Fitzgerald	KEN SWOFFORD
Ralph O'Connor	ALAN FUDGE
Albert Hoyt	ROSEY GRIER
Florence Kowski	DIANA MULDAUR
Capt. Finnerty	ALAN OPPENHEIMER
Chief Ed Palmer	EDDIE EGAN
Mark D	GENE WOODBURY

Butch	KIM DELGADO
Capt. Pete Rolfe	ROBERT HOOKS
Inspector James Gleason	SCOTT BRADY
Charles	NATHAN GEORGE
Myron Klopfman	MILTON SELZER

and: Ric Mancini, Rosalind Miles, Sonny Grosso, Joe Maross, David Toma, Allen Price

A police action drama dealing with a maverick chief of detectives with two cop killings and a rash of bank robberies on his hands who is forced to wage war against a back-stabbing police commissioner with political ambitions and a black revolutionary leader plotting a police massacre. Emmy Award nominations went to editors Donald R. Rode and Harry Kaye. Joe Don Baker reprised his role in the series "Eischied" that began in the fall of 1979.

0838
THE TWO-FIVE
4/14/78 Universal (90 min)

Executive Producer: R. A. Cinader
Producers: Gian R. Grimaldi and Hannah L. Shearer
Director: Bruce Kessler
Teleplay: R. A. Cinader and Joseph Polizzi
Photography: Frank P. Beascoechea
Music: Peter Matz
Art Director: George Renne
Editor: James J. Heckart

Charlie Morgan	DON JOHNSON
Frank Sarno	JOE BENNETT
Vinnie Lombardo	MICHAEL DURRELL
Commander Malloy	GEORGE MURDOCK
Captain Carter	JOHN CRAWFORD
Dale Von Krieg	CARLENE WATKINS
Angel	TARA BUCKMAN
Waldo	MARTY ZAGON
Pierre Menoir	JACQUES AUBUCHON
Chief	RICHARD O'BRIEN
Ralston	SANDY McPEAK
Bandit	HENRY OLEK
Cliff Roberts	CURTIS CREDEL

A police show pilot movie dealing with two eager beaver cops who try to set up a major narcotics bust anonymously because their eccentric commander wants to keep his precinct out of the limelight.

0839
STICKING TOGETHER
4/14/78 Blinn/Thorpe Productions for Viacom Enterprises (90 min)

Producers: William Blinn and Jerry Thorpe
Director: Jerry Thorpe
Teleplay: William Blinn
Photography: Charles G. Arnold
Music: John Rubinstein
Art Director: Gibson Holley
Editor: Byron Chudnow

Cuda Weber	CLU GULAGER
Kevin MacKenzie	SEAN ROCHE
Bridget MacKenzie	LORI WALSH
Michael MacKenzie	SEAN MARSHALL
Celia MacKenzie	RANDI KIGER
Timothy MacKenzie	KEITH MITCHELL
Lead Actor	RICHARD VENTURE
Miss Farrell	DEBORAH WHITE
Miss Steigler	GWEN ARNER
Grace Geary	TALIA BALSAM
Officer Stanbery	SANTOS MORALES
Big Ben Kalikini	MOE KEALE

Little Ben Kalikini	SEAN TYLER HALL
Mrs. Kalikini	LEINAALA HEINA

A Hawaii beach bum finds himself surrogate uncle to five orphaned children, helping them stay together, in this pilot movie for a planned TV series which turned up briefly in the spring of 1979 as "The MacKenzies of Paradise Cove."

0840
VEGA$
4/25/78 Aaron Spelling Productions (2 hours)

Executive Producers: Aaron Spelling and Douglas S. Cramer
Producer: E. Duke Vincent
Director: Richard Lang
Teleplay: Michael Mann
Photography: Arch R. Dalzell
Music: Dominic Frontiere
Art Director: Paul Sylos
Editor: Howard Kunin

Dan Tanna	ROBERT URICH
Harlon Twoleaf	WILL SAMPSON
Costigan	CHICK VENNERA
Nate Destefano	MICHAEL LERNER
Marilyn	ELISSA LEEDS
Tom Cirko	RED BUTTONS
Loretta Ochs	JUNE ALLYSON
Johnny Crystal	EDD BYRNES
Rosie	SCATMAN CROTHERS
Merle Ochs	JACK KELLY
George Nelson	GREG MORRIS
Bernie Roth	TONY CURTIS
Larry Johnson	COLBY CHESTER
Beatrice	PHYLLIS DAVIS
Angie	JUDY LANDERS
Charlene	DIANE PARKINSON
Hugh	JOHN QUADE
Julie	KATHERINE HICKLAND
Hank Adamek	JASON WINGREEN
Bella Archer	NAOMI STEVENS
Charlie	NED GLASS

A flashy private eye in Las Vegas searches for a runaway teenage girl and runs into a murder investigation in this pilot for the hit series that began in the fall of 1978.

0841
SIEGE
4/26/78 Titus Productions, Inc. (2 hours)

Executive Producer: Herbert Brodkin
Producer: Robert Berger
Associate Producer: Thomas DeWolfe
Director: Richard Pearce
Teleplay: Conrad Bromberg
Photography: Alan Metzger
Music: Charles Gross
Art Director: Robert Gundlach
Editor: Stephen A. Rotter

Henry Fancher	MARTIN BALSAM
Lillian Gordon	SYLVIA SIDNEY
Simon	DORIAN HAREWOOD
Lt. Don Riegel	JAMES SUTORIUS
Mrs. Shapiro	RASCHEL NOVIKOFF
Mrs. Terranova	ANTONIA REY
Mr. Lubin	ALBERT M. OTTHEIMER
Mrs. Doyle	LESSLIE NICOL
Mr. Johnson	TED BUTLER
Mr. Hegen	JOE SULLIVAN
Mrs. Mikowski	JETY HERLICK
Mrs. Comacho	MILA CONWAY

Martin Balsam and Sylvia Sidney in SIEGE (1978)

Sergeant Doan	LLOYD HOLLAR
Sergeant Dermudez	ALEX COLON
Ronald	LARRY SCOTT
Mikey	PETER ACEVEDO
Carlos	DADI PINERO
Renee	WANDA VELEZ

A drama about a community of senior citizens who are terrorized by a ruthless neighborhood gang. After learning that the police are stymied because the victims are too scared to testify against the bullying leader, the semi-retired toolmaker decides to take a stand.

0842
GO WEST, YOUNG GIRL
4/27/78 Bennett-Katleman Productions/Columbia Pictures (90 min)

Executive Producers: Harve Bennett and Harris Katleman
Producer: George Yanok
Director: Alan J. Levi
Teleplay: George Yanok
Photography: Gerald Perry Finnerman

Music: Jerrold Immel
Title song by John Stewart and Jerrold Immel
Art Director: Ross Bellah
Editors: Sam Vitale and Ronald Lavine

Netty Booth	KAREN VALENTINE
Gilda Corin	SANDRA WILL
Deputy Shreeve	STUART WHITMAN
Billy	RICHARD JAECKEL
Nestor	MICHAEL BELL
Chato	CAL BELLINI
Reverend Crane	DAVID DUKES
Captain Anson	CHARLES FRANK
Griff	RICHARD KELTON
Fanchon	WILLIAM LARSEN
Ingalls	JOHN QUADE
Payne	GREGG PALMER
Librado	PEPE CALLAHAN

A lighthearted Western about a peppery New England lady who goes west to seek her fortune by writing of her experiences, and the attractive widow of a cavalry officer, both of whom go in search of Billy the Kid, teaming up to outwit gamblers, bounty hunters, and rough-and-tumble lawmen.

0843
KILLING STONE
5/2/78 Universal (2 hours)

Producer/Director: Michael Landon
Teleplay: Michael Landon
Photography: Ted Voigtlander
Music: David Rose
Art Director: Walter M. Jeffries
Editor: Jerry Taylor

Gil Stone	GIL GERARD
Sheriff Harky	J. D. CANNON
Sen. Barry Tyler	JIM DAVIS
Christopher Stone	MATTHEW LABORTEAUX
Ellen Rizzi	CORINNE MICHAELS
Harold Rizzi	JOSHUA BRYANT
Earl Stone	NEHEMIAH PERSOFF
Daniel Tyler	DICK DeCOIT
Cindy	VALENTINA QUINN
Barney Dawes	KEN JOHNSON
Bobby Joe	DAN McBRIDE

and: Barbara Collentine, Robert L. Gibson, Richard Grayling, Clint Young, Dick Alexander, Roy Gunzburg, Charlcie Garrett, Dave Adams

Returning from prison after serving ten years on trumped-up charges, a free-lance writer tries to uncover the truth behind a homicide involving the son of a U.S. Senator in this pilot for a prospective series.

0844
HOME TO STAY
5/2/78 Time-Life Television (2 hours)

Executive Producers: David Susskind and Frederick Brogger
Producer: Donald W. Redd
Director: Delbert Mann
Teleplay: Suzanne Clauser
Based on the novel *Grandpa and Frank* by Janet Majerus
Photography: Reg Morris
Music: Hagood Hardy
Art Director: Ben Edwards
Editor: Gene Milford

Grandpa George	HENRY FONDA
Frank McDermott	MICHAEL McGUIRE
Aunt Martha	FRANCES HYLAND
Joey Brewster	DAVID STAMBAUGH
Clara Hirshman	PIXIE BIGELOW
Richard	LOUIS DEL GRANDE
Hildy	TRUDY YOUNG
Mrs. Strickmeyer	DORIS PETRIE
Frances	ELEANOR BEACROFT
Sarah	KRISTEN VIGARD
Petrie	DAVE THOMAS
Bill Brewster	DAVID HUGHES
Edith Brewster	JUDY SINCLAIR
Farmer	LEN DONCHEFF
Policeman	JAMES D. MORRIS
Neighbor	SANDRA SCOTT

A teenage girl sets off on an odyssey with her spirited but frail grandfather to thwart her uncle's plan to place the old man in a home for the aged. Filmed in Canada, this story is set in Illinois farm country.

0845
MANEATERS ARE LOOSE!
5/3/78 A Mona Production with Finnegan Associates (2 hours)

Executive Producer: Robert D. Wood
Producer: William Finnegan
Director: Timothy Galfas
Teleplay: Robert W. Lenski
Based on the book *Maneater* by Ted Willis
Photography: Hugh Gagnier
Music: Gerald Fried
Editor: Howard A. Smith

John Gosford	TOM SKERRITT
David Birk	STEVE FORREST
Gordon Hale	G. D. SPRADLIN
Toby Waites	HARRY MORGAN
Jim Taggert	FRANK MARTH
Tom Purcell	JOSH BRYANT
Edith Waites	PRISCILLA MORRILL
Penny Halpern	JENNIFER SHAW
May Purcell	DIANA MULDAUR
McCallum	DABNEY COLEMAN
Sheriff Rondel	ARTHUR ROBERTS

and: Tony Swartz, Susan Adams, Carol Jones, Anita Dangler, Phil Brown, Harry Northup, John Welsh, Kit McDonough, Tom Mahoney, Richard Caine, Kurt Andon, Pat Van Patten

Terror stalks a small California community when a broke and depressed animal owner and trainer is forced to abandon his tigers and let them fend for themselves in the nearby wilderness.

0846
WITH THIS RING
5/5/78 The Jozak Company/Paramount (2 hours)

Executive Producer: Gerald W. Abrams
Producer: Bruce J. Sallan
Director: James Sheldon
Teleplay: Terence Mulcahy
Photography: Roland S. Smith
Music: George Aliceson Tipton
Art Director: Charles Hughes
Editor: Jerry Dronsky

Peter	TONY BILL
Edward	TOM BOSLEY
Dolores Andrews	DIANA CANOVA
Viola Andrews	BARBARA CASON
Jilly Weston	JOYCE DeWITT
Gen. Albert Harris	JOHN FORSYTHE
Tom Burkhardt	SCOTT HYLANDS
James	DONNY MOST
Alvin Andrews	DICK VAN PATTEN
Evelyn Harris	BETTY WHITE
Kate	DEBORAH WHITE
Dirk	PETER JASON
Neil Dankworth	HARRY MOSES
Claude	MARTY ZAGON
Bill	CHARLES THOMAS MURPHY
Lenny	HOWARD GEORGE
Mr. Pheeb	DARRELL ZWERLING
Lisa Harris	MARY FRANCIS CROSBY

A romantic comedy about various engaged couples and their families who, as wedding dates rapidly approach, are caught up in a whirlwind of emotional crises, from past loves and parental pressure to social and financial obligations. Diana Canova is the actress daughter of former hillbilly movie star Judy Canova; Mary Frances Crosby is Bing's daughter, in her TV movie debut.

0847
MURDER AT THE MARDI GRAS
5/10/78 The Jozak Company/Paramount (2 hours)

Executive Producer: Gerald W. Abrams
Producers: Richard Nader and Matthew N. Herman
Director: Ken Annakin
Teleplay: Stanley Ralph Ross
Photography: Roland Smith
Music: Peter Matz
Art Director: William M. Hiney
Editor: Howard Epstein

Herself	BARBI BENTON
Julie Evans	DIDI CONN
Jack Murphy	BILL DAILY
Harry Benson	DAVID GROH
Randy Brian	GREGG HENRY
Jim Bob Jackson	HARRY MORGAN
Larry Cook	RON SILVER
Janet Murphy	JOYCE VAN PATTEN
Mickey Mills	DAVID WAYNE
Himself	WOLFMAN JACK

and: Laverne Hooker, Duncan McCord, Andrea Piwetz, Don Hood, Louis Dezseran, Don Lutenbacher, Joe Millane

A bubble-brained Philadelphia waitress witnesses a murder during the Mardi Gras festivities in New Orleans and finds herself stalked by the killer.

0848
LEAVE YESTERDAY BEHIND
5/14/78 ABC Circle Films (2 hours)

Producer: Paul Harrison
Director: Richard Michaels
Teleplay: Paul Harrison
Photography: Ric Waite
Music: Fred Karlin
Title song by Fred Karlin and sung by Shandi Sinnamon
Production Designer: Michael Baugh
Editor: John A. Martinelli

Paul Stallings	JOHN RITTER
Marny Clarkson	CARRIE FISHER
Doc	BUDDY EBSEN
Mr. Clarkson	ED NELSON
Connie	CARMEN ZAPATA
David Lyle	ROBERT URICH
Betty Stallings	BARBARA STUART
Howard Stallings	WALTER MASLOW
Kim	LUCIA STRALSER
Laura	CAROL ANN WILLIAMS
Biff	JOSH HALL
Dan	DAN HARRISON

A happy-go-lucky veterinary student, paralyzed for life in a college polo meet, finds love with a young woman who leaves her fiancé to help him overcome his handicap.

0849
GETTING MARRIED
5/17/78 Paramount (2 hours)

Producers: Frank von Zerneck and Robert Greenwald
Director: Steven Hilliard Stern
Associate Producer: Linda Solomon
Teleplay: John Hudock
Photography: Howard R. Schwartz
Music: Craig Safan
Song "Now That I've Found You" by John Hudock
Art Director: Dan Lomino
Editor: Kurt Kirschler

Michael Carboni	RICHARD THOMAS
Kristy Lawrence	BESS ARMSTRONG
Sylvia Carboni	DENA DIETRICH
Wayne Spanka	FABIAN
Howie Lesser	MARK HARMON
Vera Lesser	KATHERINE HELMOND
Phil Lawrence	VAN JOHNSON
Jenny	MIMI KENNEDY
Catherine Lawrence	AUDRA LINDLEY
Paula	JULIE MANNIX
Burt Carboni	VIC TAYBACK
Wedding Director	RICHARD DEACON

and: Bryan O'Byrne, Claude Stroud, Mark Lenard, Iris Adrian, Jerome Guardino, Barney Morris, Ken Medlock, Ann Ryerson, Jeanne Bates, Tony Matranga, Guy Remsen

Romantic fluff about an aspiring young songwriter, who works in a TV newsroom as an assistant director, and the girl, the station's attractive newscaster, he decides he is going to marry, despite her own plans to wed somebody else in less than a week.

0850
LACY AND THE MISSISSIPPI QUEEN
5/17/78 A Lawrence Gordon
Production/Paramount (90 min)

Executive Producer: Lawrence Gordon
Supervising Producer: Robert Singer
Producer: Lew Gallo
Director: Robert Butler
Teleplay: Kathy Donnell and Madeline
DiMaggio-Wagner
Photography: Ted Voigtlander
Music: Barry DeVorzon
Art Director: Eugene Lourie
Editor: Richard Freeman

Kate Lacy	KATHLEEN LLOYD
Queenie	DEBRA FEUER
Isaac Harrison	EDWARD ANDREWS
Willie Red Fire	JACK ELAM
Reynolds	MATT CLARK
Webber	LES LANNOM
Jennings	CHRISTOPHER LLOYD
Parker	JAMES KEACH
Sam Lacy	ANTHONY PALMER
Bixby	DAVID BYRD
Reverend	ALVY MOORE
Mitchell Beacon	SANDY WARD
Madam Josephine	ELIZABETH ROGERS
Lord Percival Winchester	DAVID COMFORT

and: Cliff Pellow, Robert Casper, Jacquelyn Gaschen, John D. Gowans, Mickey Jones, Dan Magiera, Scott Mulhern, Bill Martel, Gordon Metcalfe, Linda Morrow, Garrett Pearson, Ava Readdy, Kathi Sawyer, Steve Tannen, Candice Courtney, Alan Koss

This lighthearted Western was an unsuccessful series pilot in which two sisters—a gun-toting tomboy and a beauty with an engaging smile—team up to track down a pair of train robbers, suspects in the shooting of their father.

0851
THE BEASTS ARE ON THE STREETS
5/18/78 Hanna-Barbera Productions (2 hours)

Executive Producer: Joseph Barbera
Producer: Harry R. Sherman
Director: Peter Hunt
Teleplay: Laurence Heath
From a story by Frederic Louis Fox
Photography: Charles G. Arnold
Music: Gerald Fried
Art Director: Kirk Axtell
Editor: Argyle Nelson

Dr. Claire McCauley	CAROL LYNLEY
Kevin Johnson	DALE ROBINETTE
Jim Scudder	BILLY GREEN BUSH
Eddie Morgan	PHILIP MICHAEL THOMAS
Rick	CASEY BIGGS
Al	BURTON GILLIAM
Lucetta	SHARON ULLRICK
Mrs. Jackson	ANNA LEE
Claire's Daughter	MICHELLE WALLING
Trucker	BILL THURMAN

and: Laura Whyte, Vernelle Jesse, Carter Mullaly

Panic grips a small community after a tanker truck crashes through a fence at a wild animal park, freeing dozens of dangerous beasts.

0852
TRUE GRIT
5/19/78 Paramount (2 hours)

Producer: Sandor Stern
Director: Richard T. Heffron
Teleplay: Sandor Stern
Based on characters created by Charles Portis
Photography: Stevan Larner
Music: Earle Hagen
Art Director: Arch Bacon
Editor: Jerry Young

Rooster Cogburn	WARREN OATES
Mattie	LISA PELIKAN
Annie	LEE MERIWETHER
Joshua	JAMES STEPHENS
Christopher	JEFF OSTERHAGE
Daniel	LEE HARCOURT MONTGOMERY
Sheriff	RAMON BIERI
Clerk	JACK FLETCHER
Rollins	PARLEY BAER
Skorby	LEE DeBROUX
Chaka	FRED COOK
Harrison	REDMOND GLEESON

The further adventures of Rooster Cogburn, the rascally Western hero played in *True Grit* (1969) and *Rooster Cogburn* (1975) by John Wayne, has him battling injustice in his own unorthodox way while contending with a teenage girl bent on reforming him.

0853
HUNTERS OF THE REEF
5/20/78 A Writers Company
Production/Paramount (2 hours)

Executive Producer: Stanley Kallis
Producer: Ben Chapman
Director: Alex Singer
Teleplay: Eric Bercovici
Characters created by Peter Benchley
Photography: Andrew Laszlo
Music: Richard Markowitz
Production Designer: Jack DeShields
Editors: Gerard J. Wilson and Arthur Hilton

Jim Spanner	MICHAEL PARKS
Tracey Russell	MARY LOUISE WELLER
Panama Cassidy	WILLIAM WINDOM
Winston L. T. St. Andrew	FELTON PERRY
Mike Spanner	MOOSIE DRIER
La Salle	STEVEN MACHT
Kris La Salle	KATY KURTZMAN

An action adventure in this pilot for a proposed series entitled "Peter Benchley's Mysteries of the Deep" (this film's original title), pitting a salvage boat captain against a better equipped competitor in a race to locate a sunken wreck in shark-infested waters off the Florida coast.

0854
ZIEGFELD: THE MAN AND HIS WOMEN
5/21/78 A Frankovich Production/Columbia
Pictures (3 hours)

Executive Producer: Mike Frankovich
Producer/Director: Buzz Kulik
Teleplay: Joanna Lee
Photography: Gerald Perry Finnerman
Music: Dick DeBenedictis
Production Designer: John DeCuir
Choreography: Miriam Nelson
Technical Advisor: Patricia Ziegfeld Stephenson
Editor: Les Green

Flo Ziegfeld	PAUL SHENAR
Billie Burke	SAMANTHA EGGAR
Anna Held	BARBARA PARKINS
Marilyn Miller	PAMELA PEADON
Lillian Lorraine	VALERIE PERRINE
Will Rogers	GENE McLAUGHLIN
Eddie Cantor	RICHARD SHEA
Fanny Brice	CATHERINE JACOBY
Bert Williams	DAVID DOWNING
Nora Bayes	INGA SWENSON
Jack Norworth	RON HUSSMAN
Martha	FRANCES LEE McCAIN
Abe Erlanger	CLIFF NORTON
Flo's Father	DAVID OPATOSHU
Charles Frohman	NEHEMIAH PERSOFF
Joseph Ervin	RICHARD B. SHULL
Frank Carter	WALTER WILSON
Pat Ziegfeld	TARA TALBOY
Goldie	JESSICA RAINES

and: Howard Dayton, Michael Francis Blake, Ken Kuehn, Bob Fraser, Hy Pyke

The life and times of the flamboyant showman who built his legendary Follies around beautiful women, as told by the women in his life. This film received seven Emmy Award nominations, and Gerald Perry Finnerman won for his photography, John DeCuir for his production design, and Richard C. Goddard for his set decoration. Other nominations included Dick DeBenedictis (music), Les Green (editing) and Grady Hunt (costumes).

0855
JUST ME AND YOU
5/22/78 Roger Gimbel Productions for EMI
Television (2 hours)

Executive Producer: Roger Gimbel
Producer: William S. Gilmore, Jr.
Director: John Erman
Teleplay: Louise Lasser
Photography: Gayne Rescher
Music: Fred Karlin
Art Director: W. Stewart Campbell
Editor: Tina Hirsch

Jane Alofsin	LOUISE LASSER
Michael Linsey	CHARLES GRODIN
Waitress	JULIE BOVASSO
Old Man	PAUL FIX
Max	MICHAEL ALDREDGE
Connie	MIRIAM BYRD-NETHERY
Gas Station Owner	NOBLE WILLINGHAM

and: Mark Syers, Tony DiBenedetto, Marcella Lowery, David Thomas, Rosemary Angelis, Jeff Engle, Kate Murtagh, Belle Ellig, Sam Edwards, Dennis Erdman, Michael Morgan

Louise ("Mary Hartman, Mary Hartman") Lasser wrote this comedy-drama about a slightly daffy New Yorker with a compulsion to talk who shares a cross-country drive with a down-to-earth salesman—and wrote herself into the lead role.

0856
KATE BLISS AND THE TICKER TAPE KID
5/26/78 Aaron Spelling Productions (2 hours)

Executive Producers: Aaron Spelling and Douglas S. Cramer
Associate Producer: Shelley Hull

Producer: Richard E. Lyons
Director: Burt Kennedy
Teleplay: William Bowers and John Zodorow
From a story by John Zodorow
Photography: Lamar Boren
Music: Jeff Alexander
Art Directors: Al Bocchicchio and Paul Sylos
Editor: Jack Harnish

Kate Bliss	SUZANNE PLESHETTE
Clint Allison	DON MEREDITH
Hugo Peavey	HARRY MORGAN
The Sheriff	DAVID HUDDLESTON
Lord Seymour Devery	TONY RANDALL
William Blackstone	BURGESS MEREDITH
Joe	BUCK TAYLOR
Bud Dozier	JERRY HARDIN
Fred Williker	GENE EVANS
Tim	DON COLLIER
Betty Dozier	ALICE HIRSON
Deputy Luke	HARRY CAREY, JR.
Devery's Foreman	DONALD BARRY

A comedy Western about a turn-of-the-century lady investigator who goes to the wide-open spaces to capture a gang of outlaws led by a charming Robin Hood of the plains, leading a band of dispossessed ranchers against a stuffy English land baron who has cheated them out of their property.

0857
THE COURAGE AND THE PASSION
5/27/78 David Gerber Productions/Columbia Pictures (2 hours)

Executive Producers: David Gerber and Vince Edwards
Producer: Jay Daniel
Director: John Llewellyn Moxey
Teleplay: Richard Fielder
Photography: John M. Nicholaus
Music: Richard Shores
Art Directors: Ross Bellah and Robert Peterson
Editors: Donald R. Rode and David Wages

Col. Joe Agajanian	VINCE EDWARDS
Sgt. Tom Wade	DESI ARNAZ, JR.
Lt. Lisa Rydell	TRISHA NOBLE
Capt. Kathy Wood	LINDA FOSTER
Airman Donald Berkle	ROBERT GINTY
Maj. Stanley Norton	ROBERT HOOKS
Nick Silcox	PAUL SHENAR
Brett Gardener	LARAINE STEPHENS
Col. Jim Gardener	DON MEREDITH
Gen. Sam Brewster	MONTY HALL
Janet Sayers	MELODY ROGERS
Tuyet Berkle	IRENE YAHLING SUN
Tracy	DONNA WILKES
Emily	ELLEN TRAVOLTA
Lt. Hogan	WES PARKER

and: Robert Englund, Owen Humble, Richard Salamanca, Jody Landers, Brett Hadley, David L. Anderson, Ron Kelly, Adina Ross, Gary Cashdollar, Jerry Fitzpatrick, Allan Koss, Michael Twain, Mark Robin

The private lives and personal problems of air force test pilots on a sprawling base called Joshua Tree, which was to have been the title for this movie and the prospective series that programmers hoped it would spawn, created by and starring Vince Edwards.

0858
DEATH MOON
5/31/78 Roger Gimbel Productions/EMI Television (2 hours)

Executive Producer: Roger Gimbel
Producer: Jay Benson
Director: Bruce Kessler
Teleplay: George Schenck
Photography: Jack Whitman
Music: Paul Chihara
Art Directors: Herman Zimmerman and Gibson Holley
Editor: Tony DiMarco

Tapalua	FRANCE NUYEN
Jason Palmer	ROBERT FOXWORTH
Rick Bladen	JOE PENNY

Robert Foxworth and France Nuyen in DEATH MOON (1978)

Diane May	BARBARA TRENTHAM
Lt. Russ Cort	DOLPH SWEET
Sherry Weston	DEBRALEE SCOTT
Earl Wheelie	CHARLES HAID
Mrs. Jennings	JOAN FREEMAN
Vince Tatupu	BRANSCOMBE RICHMOND
Tami Waimea	CAROLE KAI
Mr. Jennings	MITCH MITCHELL
Dr. Restin	ALBERT HARRIS
Julie Chin	LYDIA LEI KAYAHARA
Dr. Erlich	DON POMES
Wolf Man Dancer	JOSE BULATAO

and: Terry Takada, Donna White, Bob Witthans, Robert I. Preston, Carole Avery, Alan Vicencio, Chris Bailey

An overworked executive vacationing in Hawaii finds that his romance with an attractive businesswoman he meets there is threatened by the supernatural powers of a strange native curse.

0859
TOP SECRET
6/4/78 Jemmin, Inc./Sheldon Leonard Productions (2 hours)

Executive Producer: Sheldon Leonard
Producer: David Levinson
Director: Paul Leaf
Teleplay: David Levinson
Photography: Gabor Pogany
Music: Teo Macero and Stu Gardner
Art Director: Pier-Luigi Basile
Editor: Michael Economou

Aaron Strickland	BILL COSBY
McGee	TRACY REED
Carl Vitale	SHELDON LEONARD
Judith	GLORIA FOSTER
Murphy	GEORGE BRESLIN
Gino	PAOLO TURCO
Pietro	LUCIANO BARTOLI
Rosa	MARISA MERLINI

and: Francesca DeSapio, Leonard Treviglio, Byran Rostram, Craig Hill, Walter Williams, Nat Bush

A hip American agent and his foxy associate try to recover a hundred pounds of stolen plutonium in Italy before it can be used by terrorists.

0860
LOVE IS NOT ENOUGH
6/12/78 Universal (2 hours)

Producer: Stanley L. Robinson
Director: Ivan Dixon
Teleplay: Arthur Ross
Photography: Lamar Boren
Music: Coleridge-Taylor Perkinson
Art Director: Sherman Loudermilk
Editor: Larry Strong

Mike Harris	BERNIE CASEY
David Harris	STUART K. ROBINSON
Liz Morris	RENNE BROWN
Richard Allen	DAIN TURNER
Angie Adams	CAROL TILLERY BANKS
J.P.	LIA JACKSON
Tommy	EDDIE SINGLETON
Cousin Charley Adams	STU GILLIAM
Harry Foreman	JAMES LUISI
Guitarist	JAMES CANNING

and: Mel Carter, Chesley Uxbridge, Douglas Grant, Art Kimbro, Ben Hartigan, Deborah Pratt, David Westberg, Phyllis Applegate, Lois Warden, Bill Duke, Warren Miller, Jesse Dizon, Jack Wells, Daniel Free, John Zenda, Pamela Jones, Mike Swan, Carol Baxter, Clarence Floyd III, Vince Howard, Raphael Baker, Lisa D. Ray, Kendall McCarthy

An amiable comedy-drama about a black family which moves from Los Angeles to Detroit in search of a better life. "Harris and Company," the series that spun off from this film, ran briefly in the spring of 1979.

0861
BIG BOB JOHNSON AND HIS FANTASTIC SPEED CIRCUS
6/27/78 Playboy Productions/Paramount (2 hours)

Executive Producers: R. W. Goodwin and Edward L. Rissen
Producer: Bob Gantman
Director: Jack Starrett
Teleplay: Bob Comfort and Rick Kellard
Photography: Robert Jessup
Music: Mark Snow
Art Director: Jack DeShields
Editor: Leon Carrere

Big Bob Johnson	CHARLES NAPIER
Vikki Lee Sanchez	MAUD ADAMS
Julie Hunsacker	CONSTANCE FORSLUND
W. G. Blazer	ROBERT STONEMAN
Lawrence Stepwell III	WILLIAM DANIELS
Half-Moon Muldoon	BURTON GILLIAN
Timothy Stepwell	RICK HURST
Alfie	TOM McFADDEN
Earl	CLAY TURNER
Jesse	JAMES BOND III

and: Buck Flower, Stafford Morgan, Jean Mayre, Sylvia "Kuumba" Williams, Brother Dave Garner

A rambunctious comedy about a ragtag auto racing team that helps an heir to gain the inheritance his uncle is trying to snatch from him, and finds itself in a race from one end of Louisiana to the other that pits one Rolls-Royce against another.

0862
DADDY, I DON'T LIKE IT LIKE THIS
7/12/78 CBS Entertainment (2 hours)

Executive Producer: Merrit Malloy
Producer: Jay Daniel
Director: Adell Aldrich
Teleplay: Burt Young
Photography: Donald M. Morgan
Music: David Shire
Art Directors: Albert Heschong and David Jenkins
Editor: John M. Holmes

Carol Agnelli	TALIA SHIRE
Rocco Agnelli	BURT YOUNG
Peter	DOUG McKEON
Margaret	ERICA YOHN
Sister Theresa	TRESA HUGHES
Michael	BOBBY CASSIDY
Girl in Hotel Room	MELANIE GRIFFITH
Tommy	JAMIE AFF
Marge	CONSTANCE McCASHIN
Bob	LEE WEAVER
Mother Superior	BEVERLY MAY
Store Owner	FRANK ROBLES
Morty	MORTON LEWIN

and: Jessica James, John Wylie, Raymond Barry, Vicky Perry, Diane Stilwell, Clinton Allmon, Jennifer Cooke, Bob Mora, Wayne Harding, Adam Monti, Susie Cebulski, Mathew Anton, Chris Langer, Shawn Firtell, G. Adam Gifford, Eric Ohanien, Larry Silvestri, Brendan Ward

The unfulfilled dreams of his parents and the tensions created at home cause life to become a nightmare for a youngster who seeks release in a withdrawal to his own world. Actor Burt Young (an Oscar nominee for *Rocky*) wrote the story with a starring role for himself, and Adell Aldrich, the daughter of director Robert Aldrich, made her TV directing debut here.

0863
THE HUNCHBACK OF NOTRE DAME
7/18/78 A BBC-TV Production (2 hours)

Producer: Cedric Messina
Director: Alan Cooke
Teleplay: Robert Muller
Based on the novel by Victor Hugo
Music: Wilfred Josephs
Conducted by Marcus Dods
Performed by The Ambrosian Singers with John McCarthy
Art Director: Don Taylor
Choreographer: Geraldine Stephenson

Archdeacon Claude Frolio	KENNETH HAIGH
Quasimodo	WARREN CLARKE
Esmeralda	MICHELLE NEWELL
Pierre	CHRISTOPHER GABLE
Jehan	DAVID RINTOUL
Phoebus	RICHARD MORANT
Fleur-de-Lys	HENRIETTA BAYNES
Madame Gondelaurier	RUTH GORING
Clopin	TONY CAUNTER
La Falourdel	LIZ SMITH
Robin	JOHN RATCLIFF
Cardinal	TERENCE BAYLER

A new tape-to-film production of Victor Hugo's classic focusing on the hunchback bellringer of the Cathedral of Notre Dame in fifteenth-century Paris, filmed six times previously between 1906 and 1957.

0864
THE COMEDY COMPANY
7/21/78 A Merrit Malloy-Jerry Adler Production/MGM (2 hours)

Executive Producer: Jerry Adler
Producer: Merrit Malloy
Director: Lee Philips
Teleplay: Lee Kalcheim
Photography: Matthew F. Leonetti
Music: Tom Scott
Art Director: Robert MacKichan
Editors: Axel Hubert and Gene Mathews

Barney Bailey	JACK ALBERTSON
Russell Dodd	LAWRENCE-HILTON JACOBS
Lester Dietz	HERBERT EDELMAN
Ellen Dietz	JOYCE VAN PATTEN
Linda Greg	SUSAN SULLIVAN
Paul Lester	MICHAEL BRANDON
Jake	ABE VIGODA
Himself	GEORGE BURNS
Jerry	ERNST EMLING
Red	JEFF DOUCETTE
Roger Dustleman	HOWARD HESSEMAN

Harry Fenner	DON CALFA
Sid Weller	BEN FUHRMAN
Hickey McDay	CHRISTOPHER ROBERTS

and: Ann Weldon, Lindsey V. Jones, Carole Goldman, Trish Soodik, Peggy Sandvig, Lee Stein, Gertrude Garner, Ginger Farrell, Reginald Farmer, Laurel Barnett, Jeffrey Richman, Patti Jerome, Robert Kino, Johnny Haymer, Patrick Laborteaux, Jeffrey Winner, Donald Hooten, Judy Thomas, John Davey, Lee Kalcheim, Victor Cesario

An ex-comedian fights to keep a failing nightclub alive as a showcase for aspiring young comics.

0865
THE LAST TENANT
7/25/78 Titus Productions, Inc. (2 hours)

Executive Producer: Herbert Brodkin
Producer: Robert Berger
Associate Producer: Thomas DeWolfe
Director: Jud Taylor
Teleplay: George Rubino
Photography: Sol Negrin
Music: Dick Hyman
Art Director: Patrizia von Brandenstein
Editor: Robert Reitano

Joey	TONY LoBIANCO
Frank	LEE STRASBERG
Carol	CHRISTINE LEHTI
Marie	JULIE BOVASSO
Carl	DANNY AIELLO
Vinnie	JEFFREY DeMUNN
Connie	ANNE DeSALVO
Carmine	VICTOR ARNOLD
Mrs. Farelli	JOANNA MERLIN
Mrs. Korowski	RUTH JARASLOW
Lucy	ANTONIA REY
Frankie	EVAN MICHAEL TURZ

A drama of family members facing decisions about the care of their elderly father who can no longer safely live alone, and the effects on the oldest son whose pending marriage has been placed in jeopardy. George Rubino won an Emmy for his original teleplay, and Sol Negrin received a nomination for his photography.

1978–79 SEASON

0866
SERGEANT MATLOVICH VS. THE U.S. AIR FORCE
8/21/78 Tomorrow Entertainment, Inc. (2 hours)

Executive Producer: Thomas W. Moore
Producer/Director: Paul Leaf
Teleplay: John McGreevey
Photography: Mario Tosi
Music: Teo Mascero
Art Director: Bill Sully
Editor: Thomas Stanford

Leonard Matlovich	BRAD DOURIF
Capt. Larsen Jaenicke	FRANK CONVERSE
Father Veller	WILLIAM DANIELS
Mat's Father	STEPHEN ELLIOTT
Mat's Mother	RUE McCLANAHAN
David Addlestone	DAVID SPIELBERG
Lt. Col. Applegate	MITCH RYAN
Susan Hewman	BARRA GRANT
Colonel Grand	ALFRED RYDER
G-2 Captain	DAVID OGDEN STIERS
Jason	MARC SINGER

Colonel Benton	DONALD MOFFAT
Amy	ELLEN HOLLY
Josh	HARRISON PAIGE
Major Holloway	WILLIAM BOGERT

A strong drama based on the true story of an Air Force sergeant's fight to stay in the service after admitting his homosexuality.

0867
FLYING HIGH
8/28/78 Mark Carliner Productions, Inc. (2 hours)

Producer: Mark Carliner
Associate Producer: Robin S. Clark
Director: Peter Hunt
Teleplay: Marty Cohan and Dawn Aldredge
Photography: William K. Jurgensen
Music: Jonathan Tunick
Theme: David Shire
Editor: Carroll Sax

Pam Bellagio	KATHRYN WITT
Marcy Bower	PAT KLOUS
Lisa Benton	CONNIE SELLECCA
Captain March	HOWARD PLATT
Connie Martin	MARCIA WALLACE
Paul Mitchell	JIM HUTTON
Burt Stahl	DAVID HAYWARD
Bagranditello, Jr.	MARTIN SPEER
Papa Bagranditello	VAL BISOLLIO
Sally	LYNN MARIE JOHNSTON
Desk Clerk	RICHARD HICK
Dale	CASEY BIGGS
Mrs. Bellagio	CARMEN ZAPATA
Miss Simmons	LILYAN CHAUVIN
Mr. Bellagio	LOUIS ZITO

and: Catherine Campbell, Cyndi James-Reese, Victoria Shaw, Story White, Karen Rushmore, Rita Wilson, Marianne Bunch, Derrick Lynn-Thomas, Brion James, Steve Shaw, Janear Hines, Ann Higgins

The pilot movie for the subsequent series dealing with the adventures of three airline stewardesses, fast friends after surviving their "stew" training.

0868
THE NEW MAVERICK
9/3/78 Cherokee Productions/Warner Bros. (2 hours)

Executive Producer: Meta Rosenberg
Producer: Bob Foster
Director: Hy Averback
Teleplay: Juanita Bartlett
Photography: Andrew Jackson
Music: John Rubinstein
Original Theme: David Buttolph
Art Director: John J. Jeffries
Editors: Diane Adler and George Rohrs

Bret Maverick	JAMES GARNER
Ben Maverick	CHARLES FRANK
Bart Maverick	JACK KELLY
Nell McGarahan	SUSAN BLANCHARD
Judge Crupper	EUGENE ROCHE
Poker Alice	SUSAN SULLIVAN
Vinnie	GEORGE LOROS
Leveque	WOODROW PARFREY
Dobie	GARY ALLEN
Flora Crupper	HELEN PAIGE CAMP
Homer	JACK GARNER
Lambert (undertaker)	GRAHAM JARVIS

Recycling the legendary comedy Western series (1957–62), this pilot for a prospective new run for

"Maverick" has brothers Bret and Bart (Garner and Kelly recreating their original roles) joining forces with the eager but inexperienced son of their British cousin Beau (played in the earlier series by Roger Moore) in a free-wheeling adventure involving with a female card-sharp, a corrupt judge, an ill-tempered gunrunner, a gang of train robbers and a crafty farm girl. Charles Frank and Susan Blanchard returned when the new series premiered in the fall of 1979 as *Young Maverick*.

0869
LITTLE MO
9/5/78 Mark VII Ltd./Worldvision (3 hours)

Executive Producer: Jack Webb
Producer: George Sherman
Director: Daniel Haller
Teleplay: John McGreevey
Photography: Harry Wolf
Music: Billy May and Carl Brandt
Art Director: Carl Anderson
Technical Advisor: Nancy Chaffee Kiner
Editors: Michael Berman, Bill E. Garst, Doug Hines and Bob Swanson

Maureen Connolly	GLYNNIS O'CONNOR
Eleanor "Teach" Tennant	MICHAEL LEARNED
Jess Connolly	ANNE BAXTER*
Gus Berste	CLAUDE AKINS
Wilbur Folsom	MARTIN MILNER
Sophie Fisher	ANNE FRANCIS
Norman Brinker	MARK HARMON
Nelson Fisher	LESLIE NIELSEN
Aunt Gert	ANN DORAN
Himself	TONY TRABERT

and: Fred Holiday, Len Wayland, Stacy Keach, Sr.

A fact-based drama about the tennis great who, as a teenager, was the first woman to win the Grand Slam of Tennis, became world-renowned as "Little Mo," and died of cancer in 1969 at the age of thirty-four.

*Replaced Lana Turner

0870
HAPPILY EVER AFTER
9/5/78 Tri-Media II, Inc./Hamel-Somers Entertainment (2 hours)

Executive Producer: Philip Barry
Producer: Robert Lovenheim
Director: Robert Scheerer
Teleplay: Garry Michael White
Photography: Edward R. Brown
Music: Peter Matz
Song "You Made a Believer Out of Me" by Bobby Gosh
Sung by Suzanne Somers
Special Musical Material: Peter Matz and Mitzie Welch
Production Designer: Stan Jolley
Editor: Larry Heath

Mattie	SUZANNE SOMERS
Jack	BRUCE BOXLEITNER
Ross Ford	ERIC BRAEDEN
Richy	JOHN RUBINSTEIN
Lewis Gordon	BILL LUCKING
Construction Boss	RON HAYES
Del Gregory	ARCH JOHNSON
Reverend Hale	AL CHECCO
Mrs. Hale	PATSY GARRETT
Tennis Court Manager	WILLIAM LANTEAU
Jenny Wilson	GLORIA MANNERS
Dealer	RENO NICHOLS
Al	BILLY SNYDER

and: Ed King Cross, Steve Eastin, Charles Bracy, Bill Cross, Scott Sachs

Suzanne Somers appears in her first TV starring role in this romantic comedy about an aspiring singer torn between making the most of her one chance at fame in Las Vegas or giving her heart to a love-struck mountain man.

0871
DR. STRANGE
9/6/78 Universal (2 hours)

Executive Producer: Philip DeGuere
Producer: Alex Beaton
Director: Philip DeGuere
Teleplay: Philip DeGuere
Based on Marvel Comics Group characters created by Stan Lee
Photography: Enzo A. Martinelli
Music: Paul Chihara
Art Director: William H. Tuntke
Editor: Christopher Nelson

Dr. Stephen Strange	PETER HOOTEN
Wong	CLYDE KUSATSU
Morgan Le Fay	JESSICA WALTER
Clea	EDDIE BENTON
Lindmer	JOHN MILLS
Dr. Frank Taylor	PHILIP STERLING
Sarah	JUNE BARRETT
Nurse	SARAH RUSH
The Nameless One	DAVID HOOKS
Head Nurse	DIANA WEBSTER
Department Chief	BLAKE MARION
Intern	BOB DELEGALL
Orderly	FRANK CATALANO
Magician	LARRY ANDERSON
Agnes Carson	INEZ PEDROZA
Mrs. Sullivan	LADY ROWLANDS

An occult drama in which a young psychiatrist joins an urbane, world-weary sorcerer when the latter's ancient adversary, an unearthly beauty with the power to possess men's souls, once again appears to spread her evil magic. This tongue-in-cheek tale, laced with all manner of wizardry, was the pilot for a prospective series, joining other comic book heroes on the airwaves.

0872
THE CRITICAL LIST
9/11–12/78 MTM Productions (4 hours)

Producer: Jerry McNeely
Director: Lou Antonio
Teleplay: Jerry McNeely
Based on the novels *Skeletons* and *Critical List* by Dr. Marshall Goldberg
Photography: Charles Correll
Music: James DiPasquale
Art Director: Richard G. Berger
Editor: Jerrold L. Ludwig

Dr. Dan J. Lassiter	LLOYD BRIDGES
Dr. Kris Lassiter	MELINDA DILLON
Charles Sprague	BUDDY EBSEN
Angela Adams	BARBARA PARKINS
Dr. Nick Sloan	ROBERT WAGNER
Nels Freiberg	KEN HOWARD
Ned Josephson	LINWOOD McCARTHY
Dr. Jack Hermanson	JAMES WHITMORE, JR.
Jordon Donnelly	ROBERT HOGAN
Dr. Albert Dubron	SCOTT MARLOWE
Dr. Hill	FELTON PERRY
Jimmy Regosi	PAT HARRINGTON
Lem Harper	LOU GOSSETT, JR.
Matt Kinsella	RICHARD BASEHART

Lloyd Bridges in THE CRITICAL LIST (1978)

Dr. Henry de Jong	BEN PIAZZA
Nan Forrester	JOANNE LINVILLE
Sidney Hammond	EUGENE PETERSON
Detweiler	JIM ANTONIO
Sprony	JOHN LARCH
Andrew Vivienne	BRAD DAVID
Dr. Kenderly	WRIGHT KING

Two two-hour pilot films are strung together here in which a hospital director in line for a federal cabinet post first finds that his private life may jeopardize the opportunity and then discovers himself in the middle of a scandal involving stolen federal health funds.

0873
THE CLONE MASTER
9/13/78 Mel Ferber Productions/Paramount (2 hours)

Executive Producer: Mel Ferber
Producer: John D. F. Black
Director: Don Medford
Teleplay: John D. F. Black
Photography: Joseph Biroc
Music: Glen Paxton
Art Director: Daniel Lomino
Editor: Jerry Young

Dr. Simon Shane	ART HINDLE
Gussie	ROBYN DOUGLASS
Walt	JOHN VAN DREELAN
Bender	ED LAUTER
Fiezer	MARIO ROCCUZZO
Ezra Louthin	RALPH BELLAMY
Admiral Millus	STACY KEACH, SR.

and: Lew Brown, Bill Sorrells, Ken Sansom

A science-fiction series pilot involving a biochemist, working on a top-secret government project, who clones thirteen perfect replicas of himself and sends them forth to fight evil wherever it might exist in the world.

0874
THE ISLANDER
9/16/78 Universal (2 hours)

Producer: Glen A. Larson
Director: Paul Krasny
Teleplay: Glen A. Larson
Photography: Ron Browne
Music: Stu Phillips
Art Director: Ira Diamond
Editor: Bud Small

Gable McQueen	DENNIS WEAVER
Shauna Cooke	SHARON GLESS
Lieut. Larkin	PETER MARK RICHMAN
Trudy Engles	BERNADETTE PETERS
Sen. Gerald Stratton	ROBERT VAUGHN
Bishop Hatch	JOHN S. RAGIN
Al Kahala	DICK JENSEN
Kimo	ED KAAHEA
Paul Lazarro	SHELDON LEONARD
Simms	GEORGE WYNER
Paco	ZITTO KAZAAN
Mac's Wife	LEANN HUNLEY
Wallace	GLENN CANNON

and: Jimmy Borges, Daniel Kamekona, Burt Marshall, Moe Keale, John Fitzgibbon, Galen W. Y. Kam, Kwan Hi Lin, Bob Sevey

A mystery-adventure set in Hawaii. This series pilot never got anywhere. It's about a retired mainland lawyer who buys a small Honolulu hotel and finds himself in a murderous situation involving a runaway grand jury witness, a ruthless mobster, and a racket-busting U.S. Senator framed for beating up an airline stewardess.

0875
ARE YOU IN THE HOUSE ALONE?
9/20/78 Charles Fries Productions (2 hours)

Executive Producers: Charles Fries and Dick Berg
Producer: Jay Benson
Director: Walter Grauman
Teleplay: Judith Parker
Based on the novel by Richard Peck
Photography: Jack Swain
Music: Charles Bernstein
Art Director: Bill Ross
Editor: Tony DiMarco

Gail Osborne	KATHLEEN BELLER
Anne Osborne	BLYTHE DANNER
Neil Osborne	TONY BILL
Allison	ROBIN MATTSON
Jessica Hirsh	TRICIA O'NEIL
Phil Lawver	DENNIS QUAID
Chris Elden	ALAN FUDGE
Steve Pastorini	SCOTT COLOMBY
Rouillard	ELLEN TRAVOLTA
E. K. Miller	RANDY STUMPF

Malevich	MAGDA HAROUT
Pamela	SAUNDRA SHARP
Doctor	MICHAEL BOND
Policewoman	LOIS ARENO
Hostess	SANDRA GILES
Billy	TED GEHRING

and: Richard Molinare, David Leon, Art Kimbro, Jayne Lyn Martin

A thriller about a beautiful high school student who becomes the target of a terror campaign that eventually leads to rape in this adaptation of the Edgar Mystery Award-winning novel.

0876
OVERBOARD
9/25/78 Factor-Newland Productions (2 hours)

Producer: Alan Jay Factor
Director: John Newland
Teleplay: Hank Searles
Based on his novel
Photography: Robert C. Moreno
Music: Carol Connors Shaw
Editor: Michael Economou

Lindy Garrison	ANGIE DICKINSON
Mitch Garrison	CLIFF ROBERTSON
Dugan	ANDREW DUGGAN
Shawn	STEPHEN ELLIOTT
Dr. Medlow	SKIP HOMEIER
Bernie Bertelli	MICHAEL STRONG
Jean-Paul	LEWIS VAN BERGEN

and: Christina Shigedomi, Acajou, Gary Edwards, Joan Cox

A flashback story, filmed in French Polynesia, in which Angie Dickinson spends two hours bobbing around in the ocean after having fallen overboard from lawyer-husband Cliff Robertson's forty-foot sailboat, recalling her life with him and the fling she had ashore with a French playboy.

0877
BATTERED
9/26/78 Henry Jaffe Enterprises, Inc. (2 hours)

Executive Producer: Henry Jaffe
Producer: Michael Jaffe
Director: Peter Werner
Teleplay: Karen Grassle and Cynthia Lovelace Sears
Photography: John Bailey
Music: Don Peake
Art Director: Daniel Lomino
Editor: Carol Littleton

Susannah Hawks	KAREN GRASSLE
Andrew Sinclair	LeVAR BURTON
Michael Hawks	MIKE FARRELL
Ginny Sinclair	CHIP FIELDS
Edna Thompson	JOAN BLONDELL
Bill Thompson	HOWARD DUFF
Doris Thompson	DIANA SCARWID
Stevie	KEITH MITCHELL
Helen	KETTY LESTER
Professor Hayden	LEONARD BARR

and: Kris Mersky, Alex Colon, Barbara Bishop

A drama interweaving the stories of three women of varied backgrounds and ages whose marriages are complicated by the tragedy of wife-beating.

0878
ONE IN A MILLION: THE RON LeFLORE STORY
9/26/78 Roger Gimbel Productions/EMI Television (2 hours)

Executive Producers: Roger Gimbel and Tony Converse
Producer: William S. Gilmore, Jr.
Associate Producers: Michael and Carole Raschella
Director: William A. Graham
Teleplay: Stanford Whitmore
Based on the book *Breakout* by Ron LeFlore with Jim Hawkins
Photography: Jorden Croneweth
Music: Peter Matz
Art Director: William B. Fosser
Editor: Aaron Stell

Ron LeFlore	LeVAR BURTON
Georgia LeFlore	MADGE SINCLAIR
John LeFlore	PAUL BENJAMIN
Jimmy Karalla	JAMES LUISI
Himself	BILLY MARTIN
Pee Wee Spencer	ZAKES MOKAE
Gerald LeFlore	LARRY B. SCOTT
Leroy	YAUMILTON BROWN
Antoine	WALTER KING
Umpire	JIMMY SPINKS
Himself	JAMES BUTSICARIS
Ralph Houk	JOHN R. McKEE
Mickey Stanley	MATT STEPHENS
Prison Board Chairman	TONY MOKUS
Themselves	AL KALINE
	NORM CASH
	JIM NORTHRUP
	BILL FREEHAN

The true story of baseball star Ron LeFlore from his days as a street-corner punk with no future to his days behind bars on a petty robbery conviction and his ultimate once-in-a-lifetime chance with the Detroit Tigers, where he became an outstanding baseball player.

0879
ZUMA BEACH
9/27/78 Edgar Scherick & Associates Production/Warner Bros. (2 hours)

Executive Producers: Edgar J. Scherick and Daniel H. Blatt
Producers: Bruce Cohn Curtis and Brian Grazer
Director: Lee H. Katzin
Teleplay: William Schwartz and John Carpenter
Photography: Hector Figueroa
Music: Dick Halligan
Song "Don't Run Away" by Carol Connors and Dick Halligan
Sung by Suzanne Somers
Art Director: Al Manser
Editors: Robert L. Swanson and Bobbie Shapiro

Bonnie Katt	SUZANNE SOMERS
Jerry McCabe	STEVEN KEATS
David Hunter	MARK WHEELER
Cathy	KIMBERLY BECK
Billy	PERRY LANG
J.D.	MICHAEL BIEHN
Norman	BIFF WARREN
Stan	LES LANNOM
Beverly	ROSANNE ARQUETTE
Frank	GARY IMHOFF
Johnson	LEONARD STONE
Rick	STEVE FRANKEN
Nancy	P. J. SOLES

and: Ben Marley, Richard Molinare, Tanya Roberts, Shelley Johnson, Tim Hutton, Joshua Daniel, Gary Pendergast, Bobby Doran, Victor Brandt

A fading rock star goes to the beach on the last day of summer to unwind and forget about her faltering career, only to become involved with the problems of a group of teenagers out for surf and sun.

0880
THE USERS
10/1/78 An Aaron Spelling Production (2½ hours)

Executive Producers: Aaron Spelling and Douglas S. Cramer
Producer: Dominick Dunne
Director: Joseph Hardy
Teleplay: Robert J. Shaw
Based on the novel by Joyce Haber
Photography: Richard L. Rawlings
Music: Maurice Jarre
Art Directors: Frank Swig and Paul Sylos
Editor: Byron "Buzz" Brandt

Elena Schneider	JACLYN SMITH
Randy Brent	TONY CURTIS
Warren Ambrose	RED BUTTONS
Marty Lesky	ALAN FEINSTEIN
Grace St. George	JOAN FONTAINE
Reade Jamieson	JOHN FORSYTHE
Adam Baker	GEORGE HAMILTON
Henry Waller	DARREN McGAVIN
Nancy Baker	CARRIE NYE
Marina Brent	MICHELLE PHILLIPS
Harvey Parkes	MICHAEL BASELEON
Kip Nathan	JOHN PLESHETTE
Elena's Mother	JOANNE LINVILLE
Andrew Lyons	DOUGLAS WARNER
Himself	ARMY ARCHERD

and: Pat Ast, Walter George Alton, Judy Landers

A small-town girl with a drab past falls in love with a fading screen star and masterminds his spectacular professional and personal comeback. Screen veteran Joan Fontaine made her TV-movie debut here as a Hollywood socialite.

0881
LITTLE WOMEN
10/2–3/78 Universal (4 hours)

Producer: David Victor
Director: David Lowell Rich
Teleplay: Suzanne Clauser
Based on the novel by Louisa May Alcott
Photography: Joseph Biroc
Music: Elmer Bernstein
Art Director: Howard E. Johnson
Costumes: Edith Head
Editors: James Benson and Donald Douglas

Meg March	MEREDITH BAXTER BIRNEY
Jo March	SUSAN DEY
Amy March	ANN DUSENBERRY
Beth March	EVE PLUMB
Marmee	DOROTHY McGUIRE
Grandpa Lawrence	ROBERT YOUNG
Aunt March	GREER GARSON
Laurie	RICHARD GILLILAND
John Brooke	CLIFF POTTS
Professor Bhaer	WILLIAM SHATNER
Reverend March	WILLIAM SCHALLERT
Hannah	VIRGINIA GREGG
Mrs. Kirke	JOYCE BULIFANT
Frank Vaughn	JOHN DeLANCIE
Sally Gardiner	CARLENE WATKINS
J. T. Dashwood	LOGAN RAMSEY
Mrs. Hummel	CAROL BAXTER

A lavish fourth filming of the classic novel of family life during the Civil War (previously made in 1919, 1933 and 1949), and the sixth (at least) TV presentation, sparking a weekly series that began in January 1979. Dorothy McGuire, playing Marmee here and in the series, had been scheduled to portray Meg in David O. Selznick's abortive 1947 movie version, while Greer Garson made her TV-movie debut in this sugarplum production (Mildred Natwick took over her role in the later series).

0882
BJ AND THE BEAR
10/4/78 Universal (2 hours)

Executive Producer: Glen A. Larson
Producers: John Peyser and Christopher Crowe
Director: Bruce Bilson
Teleplay: Glen A. Larson and Christopher Crowe
Photography: Sy Hoffman
Aerial Photography: Frank Holgate
Music: Glen A. Larson
Art Director: Vince Cresciman
Editor: Michael S. Murphy

Billie Joe "BJ" McKay	GREG EVIGAN
Sheriff Lobo	CLAUDE AKINS
Perkins	MILLS WATSON
Stilts	PENNY PEYSER
Col. Whitmore	JULIUS HARRIS
Store Proprietor	WOODROW PARFREY
Marcia	KRISTINE DeBELL
Willie	ANTOINETTE STELLA
Julie	ELENA EILEEN FRANK

and: Harry Townes, Dennis Fimple, Ted Gehring, Mario Roccuzzo, Kimberly Cameron, Jane Steele, Pamela Jean Bryant, Angela Capre, Barbara Stephenson, Leslie Winston, Kory Lynn, Walt Davis, William

Greer Garson, Susan Dey, Dorothy McGuire, Eve Plumb, Virginia Gregg and Meredith Baxter Birney (front row); Robert Young, Richard Gilliland, Ann Dusenberry, William Shatner, William Schallert and Cliff Potts (back row) in LITTLE WOMEN (1978)

Stephens, Ross Borden, Tom Newman, Irene Kelly, J. Andrew Kenny, Chip Johnson

An action adventure featuring a guitar-plucking independent trucker who travels with a fun-loving chimp, hauls anything, and finds himself caught up with a bunch of girls trying to flee a white slaver who happens to be the local sheriff. The series based on this film began in January 1979, with Evigan the only holdover (along, of course, with the chimp known as "The Bear"). Subsequently, in the fall of 1979, "The Misadventures of Sheriff Lobo" spun off from this with Claude Akins and Mills Watson returning to play Lobo and his thick-headed deputy.

0883
SECRETS OF THREE HUNGRY WIVES
10/9/78 Penthouse Productions (2 hours)

Executive Producers: Florence Small and Alan Surgal
Producer: Robert A. Papazian
Director: Gordon Hessler
Teleplay: Jo Heims
Photography: William Cronjager
Music: Johnny Parker
Art Director: Sidney Z. Litwack
Editor: Gary Griffin

Christina Wood	JESSICA WALTER
Karen McClure	GRETCHEN CORBETT
Vicki Wood	EVE PLUMB
Lynn Briskin	HEATHER MacRAE
Mark Powers	JAMES FRANCISCUS
Bill McClure	CRAIG STEVENS
Insp. George Dunbar	RAYMOND ST. JACQUES
Harry Briskin	JOHN REILLY
Myrtle Hollander	ERICA YOHN
Carl Wood	RICHARD ROAT
Det. Bennett	DUANE TUCKER

Three prominent women are suspected in the slaying of an amoral zillionaire who has been having affairs with each.

0884
A GUIDE FOR THE MARRIED WOMAN
10/13/78 20th Century-Fox (2 hours)

Producer: Lee Miller
Director: Hy Averback
Teleplay: Frank Tarloff
From a story by Frank Tarloff, Jewel Jaffe and Jerry Rainbow
Photography: Ric Waite
Music: Jack Elliott and Allyn Ferguson
Song "Nothing Stays the Same" sung by Maureen McGovern
Art Director: David Habel
Editor: Samuel E. Beetley

Julie	CYBILL SHEPHERD
Jerry	CHARLES FRANK
Marvin	JOHN HILLERMAN
Helen	ELAINE JOYCE
Fantasy Man	RICHARD KELTON
Fred Hurley	PETER MARSHALL
Employment Lady	EVE ARDEN
Doctor	JOHN BERADINO
Man No. 3	JOHN BYNER
Eloise	MARY FRANCES CROSBY
Ed	BILL DANA
Shirley	BONNIE FRANKLIN
Man No. 4	GEORGE GOBEL
Bill	BERNIE KOPELL
Marty	TOM POSTON
Marsha	SARAH PURCELL

Chuck	BOB SEGRAM
Tennis Pro	CHUCK WOOLERY
Maggie	BARBARA FELDON

and: Carmen Zapata, Dick Yarmy, Steven Mond, Allison Balson

A romantic comedy about a housewife who rebels against being taken for granted by her husband and dreams about finding new romantic adventures in her life. Cybill Shepherd made her television film debut as the star of this semi-sequel to writer Frank Tarloff's 1967 movie *A Guide for the Married Man.*

0885
HUMAN FEELINGS
10/16/78 Crestview Productions/Worldvision (90 min)*

Producer: Herbert Hirschman
Director: Ernest Pintoff
Teleplay: Henry Bloomstein
Photography: William K. Jurgenson
Music: John Cacavas
Art Director: Bill Ross
Editor: Angelo Ross

God (Mrs. G)	NANCY WALKER
Miles Gordon	BILLY CRYSTAL
Verna Gold	PAMELA SUE MARTIN
Phil Sawyer	SQUIRE FRIDELL
Gloria Prentice	DONNA PESCOW
Johnny Turner	ARMAND ASSANTE
Garcia	RICHARD DIMITRI
Robin Dennis	JACK CARTER
Waiter	PAT MORITA
Lester	JOHN FIEDLER
Eddie	ANTHONY CHARNOTA
Frank	TOM PEDI
Detective	JAMES WHITMORE, JR.
Guard #1	SCOTT WALKER

A pilot movie (complete with laugh-track) dealing with the day-to-day workings of God herself, here threatening to destroy Las Vegas if six righteous people cannot be found there in seven days, and it's up to an eager-to-please young angel, a frustrated clerk-typist in the heavenly music department, to try to hold off the total devastation while disguised as a mortal.

*(Expanded to 2 hours for its initial network repeat and the laugh track was eliminated.)

0886
MORE THAN FRIENDS
10/20/78 Reiner-Mishkin Production/Columbia Pictures (2 hours)

Executive Producers: Rob Reiner and Phil Mishkin
Producer: Norman S. Powell
Director: Jim Burrows
Teleplay: Rob Reiner and Phil Mishkin
Photography: Jack Swain and Sol Negrin (New York sequences)
Music: Fred Karlin
Art Directors: Ross Bellah and Don Roberts
Editor: Lee Burch

Maddy Pearlman	PENNY MARSHALL
Alan Corkus	ROB REINER
Gertie	KAY MEDFORD
William Kane	PHILLIP R. ALLEN
Josh Harrington	DABNEY COLEMAN
Beverly	FAWNE HARRIMAN
Avery Salminella	HOWARD HESSEMAN
Terry Christopher	MICHAEL McKEAN
Frances Harrington	CLAUDETTE NEVINS

Ralphie	JOE PANTOLIANO
Himself	ARMY ARCHERD

A romantic comedy, loosely based on the early courtship of Rob Reiner and his wife Penny Marshall. It's about a young couple who can't make up their minds whether they just want to be bosom buddies or uncommitted lovers and their embattled relationship between 1958 and 1971 when her show business aspirations take her to Hollywood and his struggles to be a novelist keep him in the Bronx.

0887
LIKE MOM, LIKE ME
10/22/78 CBS Entertainment, Inc. (2 hours)

Producer: Nancy Malone
Director: Michael Pressman
Teleplay: Nancy Lynn Schwartz
Based on the novel by Sheila Schwartz
Photography: Brianne Murphy
Music: Lee Holdridge
Art Director: Albert Heschong
Editor: Millie Moore

Althea Gruen	LINDA LAVIN
Jennifer Gruen	KRISTY McNICHOL
Philip Sanford	PATRICK O'NEAL
Henry Millen	MAX GAIL
Tao Wolf	STACEY NELKIN
Peter	MICHAEL LeCLAIR
Michael Gruen	LAWRENCE PRESSMAN
Kevin	CLARK BRANDON
Woodhill	MICHAEL THOMA
Sam Light	CARROLL REYNOLDS
Doorman	RICHARD BLAKE
Desk Clerk	CARVER BARNERS
Waitress	BABBETT BRAM
Jackie	NANCY MALONE

The problems of a college professor and her teenage daughter facing a new life after being deserted by the husband/father are explored in this drama. Nancy Malone, an actress in the 1940s who found a new career as a TV executive, produced this film and plays a small role.

0888
KATIE: PORTRAIT OF A CENTERFOLD
10/23/78 Moonlight Productions/Warner Bros. (2 hours)

Producers: Frank von Zerneck and Robert Greenwald
Director: Robert Greenwald
Teleplay: Nancy Audley
Photography: Donald Morgan
Music: Charles Bernstein
Art Director: David Marshall
Editor: Gary Griffin

Katie McEvera	KIM BASINGER
Marietta Cutler	VIVIAN BLAINE
M.C.	FABIAN
Elliot Bender	TAB HUNTER
Gunther	DON JOHNSON
Deborah Pintoff	VIRGINIA KAISER
Myrtle Cutler	DOROTHY MALONE
Aunt Isabel	NAN MARTIN
Madelaine	MELANIE MAYRON
Cindy Holland	TERRI NUNN
Sullie Toulours	DON STROUD
Preston de Cordiva	GLYNN TURMAN
Joshua Holland	BEAU GORDON
Taylor	JAMES CRITTENDEN
Blaze Adams	JANET WOOD

and: Dick Dinman, Victor Eschbach, Ron Prince, Peter von Zerneck, Michael Mislove, Ken Medlock, Rusty Cole, Catherane Skillien

A naive Texas beauty queen seeking Hollywood stardom quickly learns the realities of the business after encountering an unethical modeling school.

0889
DONNER PASS: THE ROAD TO SURVIVAL
10/24/78 Schick Sunn Classics (2 hours)

Executive Producer: Charles E. Sellier, Jr.
Producer: James Simmons
Director: James L. Conway
Teleplay: S. S. Schweitzer
Photography: Henning Schellerup
Music: Bob Summers
Art Director: Paul Staheli
Editor: Trevor Jolley

James Reed (and narrator)	ROBERT FULLER
Keyser	ANDREW PRINE
William Eddy	MICHAEL CALLAN
Margaret Reed	DIANE McBAIN
Patrick Breen	JOHN ANDERSON
George Donner	JOHN DOUCETTE
Mary Graves	CYNTHIA EILBACHER
Sutter	ROYAL DANO
Will McKutchwon	GREGORY WALCOTT
Charles Stanton	LANCE LeGAULT
Uncle Billy Graves	WHIT BISSELL
Mrs. Breen	PEG STEWART

and: Reid Cruickshanks, Robert Carricart, Rudy Diaz, Brian Erickson, John Hansen, Paul Grace, Barta Lee Heiner, Augustin Vallejo, George Barrows, Rick Jury, Elaine Daniels, Michael Ruud, Jorge Moreno

A "Classics Illustrated" version of American history and the fight waged by a pioneer to save the lives of his family and others in a wagon train who find themselves trapped in deep mountain snows and facing starvation that leads them to (unspecified) cannibalism.

0890
DESPERATE WOMEN
10/25/78 Lorimar Productions (2 hours)

Executive Producer: Lee Rich
Producer: Robert Stambler
Director: Earl Bellamy
Teleplay: Jack B. Sowards
Photography: Jorges Stahl
Music: Dick DeBenedictis
Song "Ballad of Desperate Women" by Dick DeBenedictis and Sally Stevens
Sung by Beau Charles
Art Director: Ed Graves
Editor: Sam Vitale

Esther Winters	SUSAN SAINT JAMES
Benjamin Ward	DAN HAGGERTY
Selena Watson	RONEE BLAKLEY
Joanna Dance	ANN DUSENBERRY
Amy	SUSAN MYERS
Terry	RANDY POWELL
Lt. Spangler	MAX GAIL
Black Jack Ketcham	MICHAEL DELANO
Tulsa Red	TAYLOR LARCHER
Charlie	TIGER WILLIAMS
Sgt. Mulrooney	BOB HOY
Jonas Scurlock	JAMES GRIFFITH
Two Feathers	RUDY DIAZ

and: John Crawford, Clint Ritchie, William Vaughan, Ed Fury

A laconic ex-hired gun in the Old West teams up with three scrappy female prisoners abandoned in the desert, two orphaned children, an Army deserter, and a group of cantankerous animals, all of whom try to outsmart and outshoot a ratty gang of desperadoes trying to retrieve their boss' girlfriend and the saddletramp's secret cargo.

0891
THE GRASS IS ALWAYS GREENER OVER THE SEPTIC TANK
10/25/78 A Joe Hamilton Production (2 hours)

Producer: Joe Hamilton
Associate Producer: Robert Wright
Director: Robert Day
Teleplay: Dick Clair and Jenna McMahon
Based on the book by Erma Bombeck
Photography: Steve Poster
Music: Peter Matz
Art Director: Paul Barnes
Costumes: Bob Mackie
Editor: Peter Kirby

Dorothy Benson	CAROL BURNETT
Jim Benson	CHARLES GRODIN
Ralph Corliss	ALEX ROCCO
Leslie Corliss	LINDA GRAY
Lester Wentworth	ROBERT SAMPSON
Helen Wentworth	VICKI BELMONTE
Hal Watson	CRAIG RICHARD NELSON
Kelly Benson	ANNRAE WALTERHOUSE
Steve Benson	ERIC STOLTZ
Davie Benson	DAVID HOLLANDER
Dollie Sullivan	PAT WILSON
Marci	EDWINA GOUGH
Brother Bud	FRANK REILLY
Mr. Loring	MORGAN UPTON

A comedy-drama about a New York couple who decided to dump the hassle of the big city, pack up the kids and move to what they think is the easy life of suburbia. Carol Burnett made her TV-movie debut in this film which followed her departure from the grind of weekly television after ten years of "The Carol Burnett Show."

0892
COTTON CANDY
10/26/78 A Major H Production (2 hours)

Producer: John Thomas Lenox
Associate Producer: Rance Howard
Director: Ron Howard
Teleplay: Ron and Clint Howard
Photography: Robert Jessup
Music: Joe Renzetti
Songs by Joe Renzetti and Charles Martin Smith
Art Director: Cyndy Severson
Editor: Robert J. Kern, Jr.

George Smally	CHARLES MARTIN SMITH
Corky MacFearson	CLINT HOWARD
Brenda Mathews	LESLIE KING
Barry Bates	KEVIN LEE MILLER
Julio Guererro	MANUEL PADILLA, JR.
Bart Bates	DINO SCOFIELD
Torbin Bequette	MARK WHEELER
George's Father	ALVY MOORE
George's Mother	JOAN CROSBY
Coach Grimes	RAY LePERE
Bremmercamp	RANCE HOWARD

and: William H. Burkett, Lonnie Hearn, Jessie Lee Fulton, Eugene S. Lee, David May, Kimo Schutze,

Darlene Gratz, Marty Bingfeldt, David Ellzy, Jay Fountain, Nick Alexander

An engaging comedy about a group of high school misfits who form a rock band. Ron Howard (of "Happy Days") directed from an original script he wrote with his brother Clint, one of the film's stars. Their father Rance also acted in it and was associate producer.

0893
KISS MEETS THE PHANTOM OF THE PARK
10/28/78 Hanna-Barbera/Kiss Productions (2 hours)

Executive Producer: Joseph Barbera
Producer: Terry Morse, Jr.
Director: Gordon Hessler
Teleplay: Jan-Michael Sherman and Don Buday
Photography: Robert Caramico
Music: Hoyt Curtin
Fight Scene Music: Fred Karlin
Art Director: James G. Hulsey
Editor: Peter E. Berger

KISS	PETER CRISS
	ACE FREHLEY
	GENE SIMMONS
	PAUL STANLEY
Abner Devereaux	ANTHONY ZERBE
Calvin Richards	CARMINE CARIDI
Melissa	DEBORAH RYAN
Sam	TERRY WEBSTER
Chopper	JOHN DENNIS JOHNSTON
Slime	JOHN LISBON WOOD
Dirty Dee	LISA JANE PERSKY

The bizarrely costumed rock group KISS made its acting debut, with the four thwarting a mad scientist attempting to destroy their careers by making robot KISS replicas and turning them loose to create havoc in an amusement park.

0894
CRASH
10/29/78 Charles Fries Productions, Inc. (2 hours)

Executive Producer: Charles Fries and Malcolm Stuart
Producer: Edward J. Montagne
Director: Barry Shear
Teleplay: Donald S. Sanford and Steve Brown
Based on the book by Rob and Sarah Elder
Photography: Jacques R. Marquette and James Pergola (Florida sequence)
Music: Eddy Lawrence Manson
Art Director: Alexander A. Mayer
Editor: Samuel E. Waxman

Carl Tobias (and narrator)	WILLIAM SHATNER
Veronica Daniels	ADRIENNE BARBEAU
Camille Lawrence	BROOKE BUNDY
Mike Tagliarino	CHRISTOPHER CONNELLY
Emily Mulwray	LORRAINE GARY
Jerry Grant	RON GLASS
Lesley Fuller	SHARON GLESS
Standish	BRETT HALSEY
Sophie Cross	JOYCE JAMESON
Evan Walsh	GEORGE MAHARIS
Philip Mulwray	ED NELSON
Larry Cross	GERALD S. O'LOUGHLIN
Elderly Passenger	ARTIE SHAW
Alvin Jessop	JOE SILVER
Ginny Duffy	LARAINE STEPHENS
Ray Ordway	W. K. STRATTON

Osario	RICHARD YNIGUEZ
Cecilia Tagliarino	MARIA MELENDEZ
Claypool	GEORGE MURDOCK

and: Donald Barry, Maria Elena Cordero, Lureen Tuttle, Shirley O'Hara

A dramatization of the jetliner crash into the Florida Everglades in December, 1972, and the rescue of seventy-three passengers (103 died), made up primarily of recognizable TV personalities plus famed bandleader Artie Shaw in his TV-movie debut. This crash also was the basis for the earlier TV movie *The Ghost of Flight 401*, which had Ernest Borgnine as its captain.

0895
SUMMER OF MY GERMAN SOLDIER
10/30/78 Highgate Productions (2 hours)

Producer: Linda Gottlieb
Director: Michael Tuchner
Teleplay: Jane-Howard Hammerstein
Based on the novel by Bette Greene
Photography: Peter Sova
Music: Stanley Meyers
Production Supervisor: Patricia von Zippridot
Art Director: Carl Copeland
Editor: Michael Taylor

Patty Bergen	KRISTY McNICHOL
Anton Reiker	BRUCE DAVISON
Ruth	ESTHER ROLLE
Harry Bergen	MICHAEL CONSTANTINE
Mrs. Bergen	BARBARA BARRIE
Pierce	JAMES NOBLE
Sharon Bergen	ROBYN ELAIN LIVELY
Sister Parker	MARGARET HALL
Mrs. Benn	ANNE HANEY
Mr. Jackson	J. DON FERGUSON

A bittersweet story of a teenage Jewish girl who falls in love with an escaped Nazi prisoner of war in a small Georgia town during World War II. Esther Rolle won the Emmy as Outstanding Supporting Actress in a Limited Series or Special for her performance in this film which also was nominated as the Outstanding Drama of the 1978–79 season. In addition, Jane-Howard Hammerstein received an Emmy Award nomination for her teleplay.

0896
DEVIL DOG: THE HOUND OF HELL
10/31/78 Zeitman-Landers-Roberts Productions (2 hours)

Executive Producer: Jerry Zeitman
Producer: Lou Morheim
Director: Curtis Harrington
Teleplay: Stephen and Elinor Karpf
Photography: Gerald Perry Finnerman
Music: Artie Kane
Art Director: William Cruse
Editor: Ronald J. Fagan

Mike Barry	RICHARD CRENNA
Betty Barry	YVETTE MIMIEUX
Bonnie Barry	KIM RICHARDS
Charlie Barry	IKE EISENMANN
Shaman	VICTOR JORY
George	LOU FRIZZELL
Miles Amory	KEN KERCHEVAL
Dunworth	R. G. ARMSTRONG
Red-Haired Lady	MARTINE BESWICK
Newscaster	BOB NAVARRO
Mrs. Hadley	LOIS URSONI

Doctor	JERRY FOGEL
Superintendent	WARREN MUNSON

and: Shelley Curtis, Deborah Karpf, Jan Burrell, Kevin McKenzie, Jack Carol, Dana Laurita, James Reynolds, E. A. Sirianni

A chiller involving a suburban family which falls under the spell of a dog imbued with the spirit of the devil, premiering on television, quite naturally, on Halloween.

0897
STRANGER IN OUR HOUSE
10/31/78 Inter Planetary Pictures Inc./Finnegan Associates (2 hours)

Executive Producers: Max A. and Michelle H. Keller
Producers: Pat and Bill Finnegan
Director: Wes Craven
Teleplay: Max A. Keller and Glenn M. Benest
Based on the novel *Summer of Fear* by Lois Duncan
Photography: William K. Jurgensen
Music: Michael Lloyd and John D'Andrea
Art: Joe Aubel
Editor: Howard E. Smith

Rachel Bryant	LINDA BLAIR
Julia	LEE PURCELL
Tom Bryant	JEREMY SLATE
Mike Gallagher	JEFF McCRACKEN
Peter Bryant	JEFF EAST
Leslie Bryant	CAROL LAWRENCE
Professor Jarvis	MACDONALD CAREY
Bobby Bryant	JAMES JARNAGIN
Dr. Morgan	GWIL RICHARDS
Anne	KERRY ARQUETTE
Marge Trent	BEATRICE MANLEY
Mrs. Gallagher	PATRICIA WILSON
Mr. Wilson	ED WRIGHT
Carolyn	FRAN DRESCHER
Sheriff	BILLY BECK
Elizabeth	NICOLE KELLER

A thriller about a young girl's encounter with witchcraft when a cousin turns up at her house and begins using supernatural powers to dominate the family. Linda Blair once again was the put-upon one in this film originally to have been called *Summer of Fear*, the title of the source novel.

0898
THOU SHALT NOT COMMIT ADULTERY
11/1/78 Edgar J. Scherick Productions, Inc. (2 hours)

Executive Producers: Edgar J. Scherick and Daniel H. Blatt
Producers: Bryan Hickox and Brian Grazer
Director: Delbert Mann
Teleplay: Calder Willingham and Del Reisman
Photography: Robert B. Hauser
Music: Paul Chihara
Art Director: John Braden
Editor: Bud S. Isaacs

Sally Kimball	LOUISE FLETCHER
Vic Tannehill	WAYNE ROGERS
Bill Dent	BERT CONVY
Jack Kimball	ROBERT REED
Boneyard	HAL WILLIAMS
Stewardess	SHANNON WILCOX
JoJo	JESSE DIZON

and: Lucy Dee Flippin, Donald Petrie

In this initial entry in a projected series on contemporary interpretations of the Ten Commandments, the wife of a paralytic becomes involved in an extramarital affair—with his permission.

0899
HOW TO PICK UP GIRLS!
11/3/78 A King-Hitzig Production (2 hours)

Executive Producer: Alan King
Producer: Rupert Hitzig
Director: Bill Persky
Teleplay: Jordan Crittenden, Peter Gethers, David Handler and Bill Persky
Inspired by the book by Eric Weber
Photography: Alan Metzger
Music: Don Sebesky
Songs by John Loeffler
Art Director: Ronald Baldwin
Editor: Craig McKaig

Robbie Harrington	DESI ARNAZ, JR.
Sally Clabrook	BESS ARMSTRONG
Donald Becker	FRED McCARREN
Dana Greenberg	POLLY BERGEN
Chandler Corey	RICHARD DAWSON
Manny Shiller	ALAN KING
Nathan Perlmutter	ABE VIGODA
Cynthia Miller	DEBORAH RAFFIN
Frank Cavanaugh	RUDOLPH WILLRICH
Pam	FORBSEY RUSSELL
Denise	HOLLIS WINICH

The amusing adventures of an unsophisticated small-town lad who arrives in New York, moves in with his swinging buddy, and surprisingly becomes an authority on the ways and wiles of women as he enters the world of big-time girl-chasing. The star here is not Desi Arnaz, Jr. but Fred McCarren, despite the billing.

0900
THE TIME MACHINE
11/5/78 Schick Sunn Classics (2 hours)

Executive Producers: Charles E. Sellier, Jr. and James L. Conway
Producer: James Simmons
Director: Henning Schellerup
Teleplay: Wallace Bennett
Based on the novel by H. G. Wells
Photography: Stephen W. Gray
Music: John Cacavas
Art Director: Paul Staheli
Editor: Trevor Jolley

Neil Perry	JOHN BECK
Weena	PRISCILLA BARNES
Bean Worthington	ANDREW DUGGAN
Agnes	ROSEMARY DeCAMP
John Bedford	JACK KRUSCHEN
Ralph Branly	WHIT BISSELL
Ariel	JOHN HANSEN
General Harris	R. G. ARMSTRONG
Sheriff Finley	JOHN DOUCETTE
Henry Haverson	PARLEY BAER

and: John Zaremba, Peg Stewart, Bill Zuckert, Hyde Clayton, Craig Clyde, Scott D. Curran, Debbie Dutson, Buck Flower, Paul Grace, Tom Kelly, Maurice Grandmaison, Julie Parrish, Walt Price, H. E. O. Redford, Michael Rudd, Scott Wilkinson, James Lyle Strong, Kerry Summers

A "Classics Illustrated" adaptation (updated to the 1970s) of the Wells classic about a scientific wizard who invents a device to transport himself back and forth in time and gets a bleak look at the future when visiting an alien civilization.

0901
RAINBOW
11/6/78 Ten-Four Productions (2 hours)

Executive Producers: Gregory Strangis and William Hogan

Director: Jackie Cooper
Teleplay: John McGreevey
Based on the book by Christopher Finch
Photography: Howard R. Schwartz
Music: Charles Fox
Art Director: Bill Ross
Editor: Jerry Dronsky

Judy Garland	ANDREA McARDLE
Frank Gumm	DON MURRAY
Roger Edens	MICHAEL PARKS
Ida Koverman	RUE McCLANAHAN
Will Gilmore	NICHOLAS PRYOR
George Jessel	JACK CARTER
Jinnie Gumm	DONNA PESCOW
Janey Gumm	ERIN DONOVAN
Louis B. Mayer	MARTIN BALSAM
Ethel Gunn	PIPER LAURIE
Mickey Rooney	MOOSIE DRIER
Jackie Cooper	JOHNNY DORAN
Arthur Freed	PHILIP STERLING

and: Ben Frank, Don Sherman, Albert Morgenstern, Vincent Duke Milana, Mary Gregory, David Eibel, Frank Bonner, Judith Searle, Selma Archerd, Stanley Kamel, John Murat, Carol Lombard

A musical drama tracing the life of a young Judy Garland (ages 10 to 17) during her rise from struggling vaudeville performer to the star of *The Wizard of Oz*. Cinematographer Howard R. Schwartz received an Emmy Award for his contribution.

0902
FIRST YOU CRY
11/8/78 MTM Productions, Inc. (2 hours)

Producer: Philip Barry
Director: George Schaefer
Teleplay: Carmen Culver
Based on the book by Betty Rollin
Photography: Edward R. Brown
Music: Peter Matz
Art Director: Albert Heschong
Editor: James Galloway

Betty Rollin	MARY TYLER MOORE
Arthur Herzog	ANTHONY PERKINS
David Towers	RICHARD CRENNA
Erica Wells	JENNIFER WARREN
Dr. Brennerman	RICHARD DYSART
Daniel Easton	DON JOHNSON
Mrs. Rollin	FLORENCE ELDRIDGE
Anne	PATRICIA BARRY
Marsha	ANTOINETTE BOWER
Cal Connors	JAMES A. WATSON, JR.
Dr. Sanford Elby	DONALD BISHOP
Robin	ROBIN ROSE
Notions Clerk	WILLIAM LANTEAU

and: Vivi Janis, Carole Hemingway, Sari Price, Eda Reiss Merin, Leigh Hamilton

A dramatization of the true story of NBC news correspondent Betty Rollin and her experience with a mastectomy that shook her emotions, her marriage and her outlook on life. Fredric March's widow, Florence Eldridge, made a rare acting appearance as Rollin's mother in one of the only jobs she has ever taken without her husband. The film received four Emmy Award nominations: Outstanding Drama, Best Actress in a Special, Music Score and Editing.

0903
BETRAYAL
11/13/78 Roger Gimbel Productions/EMI Television (2 hours)

Executive Producers: Roger Gimbel and Tony Converse
Producer: Marc Trabulus
Director: Paul Wendkos
Teleplay: Jerrold Freedman and Joanna Crawford
Based on the book by Lucy Freeman and Julie Roy
Photography: Gayne Rescher
Music: Paul Chihara
Art Director: William Stewart Campbell
Editor: Dann Cahn

Julie Roy	LESLEY ANN WARREN
Dr. Hartogs	RIP TORN
Loren Plotkin	RICHARD MASUR
Bob Cohen	RON SILVER
Pat	BIBI BESCH
Victor Slavin	JOHN HILLERMAN
Jane	JANE MARLA ROBBINS
Carol Stockwood	PEGGY ANN GARNER
Dr. Todson	FRED SADOFF
Judge Allan Myers	STEPHEN ELLIOTT
Adam	RICHARD KARLAN
Man in Bar	BOB DELEGALL
Dr. Van Hoving	RICHARD SEFF

A dramatization of the 1971 case involving a young woman who sued her psychiatrist for luring her into a sexual relationship with him under the guise of therapy.

0904
LADY OF THE HOUSE
11/14/78 Metromedia Productions (2 hours)

Executive Producer: William Kayden
Directors: Ralph Nelson and Vincent Sherman
Teleplay: Ron Koslow
Photography: Robert L. Morrison
Music: Fred Karlin
Art Director: Sidney Z. Litwack
Editor: John A. Martinelli

Sally Stanford	DYAN CANNON
Ernest de Paulo	ARMAND ASSANTE
Julia de Paulo	ZOHRA LAMPERT
Helen Proctor	SUSAN TYRELL
Acapico	JESSE DIZON
Kate de Paulo	MAGGIE COOPER
Ray Navarette	ANTHONY CHARNOTA
Rosette	COLLEEN CAMP
Mary	MIM HAMILTON
John David	SAM FREED
Mayor Jim	MELVIN BELLI
Mayor Collins	CHARLIE MURPHY
Young Marcy	CHRISTOPHER NORRIS
Sgt. John Guffy	TOM ROSQUI

A dramatization of the life of the flamboyant San Francisco madam of the 1930s and 1940s who retired in 1950 to open a restaurant in Sausalito, California, despite local opposition, and who became the town's mayor from 1976 to 1978.

BUD AND LOU
11/15/78 Bob Banner Associates (2 hours)

Executive Producer: Bob Banner
Producers: Robert C. Thompson and Clyde B. Phillips
Director: Robert C. Thompson

Teleplay: George Lefferts
Based on the book by Bob Thomas
Photography: Richard C. Glouner
Music: Fred Karlin
Art Director: Serge Krizmann
Editor: Dann Cahn

Bud Abbott	HARVEY KORMAN
Lou Costello	BUDDY HACKETT
Anne Costello	MICHELE LEE
Eddie Sherman	ARTE JOHNSON
Alan Randall	ROBERT REED
Ted Collins	WILLIAM TREGOE
Gene Duffy	DANNY DAYTON

A fact-riddled behind-the-scenes drama about the stormy partnership of the famed comedy team that came out of burlesque to conquer radio, movies and television (the last never once mentioned in this film).

0906
HAROLD ROBBINS' THE PIRATE
11/21–22/78 A Howard W. Koch Production/Warner Bros. (4 hours)

Executive Producer: Paul R. Picard
Producer: Howard W. Koch
Associate Producer: Skip Ward
Director: Ken Annakin
Teleplay: Julius J. Epstein
Based on the novel by Harold Robbins
Photography: Roland (Ozzie) Smith
Music: Bill Conti
Art Director: Phil Jeffries
Editor: Howard Epstein

Baydr Al Fay	FRANCO NERO
Jordana Mason	ANNE ARCHER
Leila	OLIVIA HUSSEY
Rashid	IAN McSHANE
Samir	CHRISTOPHER LEE
Yasfir	MICHAEL CONSTANTINE
Dick Carriage	JAMES FRANCISCUS
Hamid	ARMAND ASSANTE
Terry Sullivan	STUART WHITMAN
Ben Ezra	ELI WALLACH
Maryam	CAROL BAGDASARIAN
Prince Feiyad	JEFF COREY
Mrs. Mason	MARJORIE LORD
Jabir	FERDY MAYNE
General Eshnev	MICHAEL PATAKI
Ramadan	MURRAY SALEM

and: Edward Ansara, Dimitra Arliss, Peter Brandon, Leon Charles, Renato Cibelli, Edith Diaz, Patricia Donahue, Antonia Ellis, Ina Gould, Magda Harout, Tina Johnson, Ben Kahlon, Zitto Kazann, Stacy Keach, Sr., Martine Kelly, Ali Kiani, Manuel Kichian, Gloria Manos, Macon McCallman, Mark McIntire, Mustapha Bourth Ouchama, Alain Patrick, Meeno Peluce, Desiree Richards, Jane Marla Robbins, Leo Rossi, Natasha Ryan, Clement St. George, Naomi Stevens, Roger Til, Dick Wilson

Elaborate Harold Robbins fiction dealing with a handsome Israeli, raised by an influential Arab, who comes into conflict with his heritage when he is entrusted with managing his country's oil fortunes and must deal with a fanatical terrorist group led by his daughter.

0907
THE THIEF OF BAGHDAD
11/23/78 Palm Films Ltd. (2 hours)

Executive Producer: Thomas M. C. Johnston
Producer: Aida Young
Director: Clive Donner

Teleplay: A. J. Carothers
Adapted by Andrew Birkin
Photography: Denis Lewiston
Music: John Cameron
Art Director: Edward Marshall
"Magic Carpet" by John Stears and Dick Hewitt
Editor: Peter Tanner

Hasan	RODDY McDOWALL
Prince Taj	KABIR BEDI
Abu Bakar	FRANK FINLAY
Perizadah	MARINA VLADY
The Caliph	PETER USTINOV
Wazir Jandur	TERENCE STAMP
Princess Yasmine	PAVLA USTINOV
Gatekeeper	IAN HOLM
Genie	DANIEL EMILFORK

And: Ahmed el-Shenawi, Kenji Tanaki, Neil Mc-Carthy, Vincent Wong, Leone Greene, Bruce Monague, Arnold Diamondi, Raymond Llewellyn, Geoffrey Cheshire, Gabor Vernon, Kevork Malikyan, Michael Chesdon, Ahmed Khail, Yasher Adem, George Little

The fourth filming of the Arabian Nights fantasy about a friendly thief who helps a handsome prince overcome an evil wizard to win a beautiful princess and a kingdom. Not to be overlooked, of course, are the inevitable flying carpet and the giant genie-in-a-magic-lamp.

0908
A QUESTION OF LOVE
11/26/78 Viacom Productions (2 hours)

Producers: William Blinn and Jerry Thorpe
Associate Producer: Michael A. Hoey
Director: Jerry Thorpe
Teleplay: William Blinn
Photography: Charles G. Arnold
Music: Billy Goldenberg
Art Director: Stephen M. Berger
Editor: Byron Chudnow

Linda Ray Guettner	GENA ROWLANDS
Barbara Moreland	JANE ALEXANDER
Dwayne Stabler	NED BEATTY
Mike Guettner	CLU GULAGER
Joan Saltzman	BONNIE BEDELIA
Richard Freeman	JAMES SUTORIOUS
Billy Guettner	KEITH MITCHELL
David Guettner	JOSH ALBEE
Mrs. Hunnicutt	JOCELYN BRANDO
Dr. Tippit	GWEN ARNER
Dr. Berwick	JOHN HARKINS
Susan Moreland	NANCY McKEON
The Judge	S. JOHN LAUNER

A sensitive drama about a mother who battles to keep her son when her ex-husband sues for custody because she is a lesbian and has moved in with her lover. Original title: *A Purely Legal Matter.*

0909
A FIRE IN THE SKY
11/26/78 Bill Driskill Productions (3 hours)

Executive Producer: Bill Driskill
Producer: Hugh Benson
Director: Jerry Jameson
Teleplay: Dennis Nemec and Michael Blankfort
Based on a story by Paul Gallico
Photography: Matthew F. Leonetti
Music: Paul Chihara
Art Directors: Ross Bellah and Dale Hennessy
Special Effects: Joseph A. Unsinn
Editor: J. Terry Williams

Jason Voight	RICHARD CRENNA
Sharon Allan	ELIZABETH ASHLEY
David Allan	DAVID DUKES
Jennifer Dreiser	JOANNA MILES
Paul Gilliam	LLOYD BOCHNER
Stan Webster	MERLIN OLSEN
President	ANDREW DUGGAN
Carol	MAGGIE WELLMAN
Governor	NICHOLAS COSTER
Lustus	WILLIAM BOGERT
Ann Webster	JENNY O'HARA
Tom Reardon	MICHAEL BIEHN
Mrs. Reardon	DIANA DOUGLAS
Paula Gilliam	CYNTHIA EILBACHER

A fiery comet is hurtling toward Phoenix, Arizona, and an astronomer's desperate warnings fall on deaf ears among city officials in this lengthy disaster tale

Franco Nero in THE PIRATE (1978)

highlighted by some striking special effects and miniature work. Publicity releases for this movie insisted that a record (for a TV film) 5,700 extras were used in the exodus sequences and that the miniature work was the most extensive ever created for television. Emmy Award nominations went to this film for Special Effects and Sound Editing.

0910
AND I ALONE SURVIVED
11/27/78 Jerry Leider/OJL Productions (2 hours)

Executive Producer: Jerry Leider
Producer: Burt Nodella
Director: William A. Graham
Teleplay: Lane Slate
Based on the book by Lauren Elder and Shirley Streshinsky

Photography: Jordan Cronenweth
Music: Laurence Rosenthal
Art Director: C. E. Guzman
Editor: Ronald J. Fagan

Lauren Elder	BLAIR BROWN
Jay Fuller	DAVID ACKROYD
Irene Elder	VERA MILES
Bob Elder	G. D. SPRADLIN
Jean	MAGGIE COOPER
Carol	MICHELLE STACY
Craig Elder	CHRISTOPHER ALLPORT
Carla	ELIZABETH CHESHIRE
Harry	CHARLES H. GRAY
Kaminsky	PAT CORLEY

A dramatization of the story of a woman's ordeal following a plane crash in the Sierra Nevadas that killed her two companions in April 1976.

0911
SOMEONE IS WATCHING ME!
11/29/78 Warner Bros. (2 hours)

Executive Producer: Richard Kobritz
Producer: Anna Cottle
Director: John Carpenter
Teleplay: John Carpenter
Photography: Robert B. Hauser
Music: Harry Sukman
Art Director: Phil Barber
Editor: Jerry Taylor

Leigh Michaels	LAUREN HUTTON
Paul Winkless	DAVID BIRNEY
Sophie	ADRIENNE BARBEAU
Gary Hunt	CHARLES CYPHERS
Leone	JAMES MURTAUGH
Steve	GRAINGER HINES
Burley Man	LEN LESSER
Frimsin	JOHN MAHON
Police Inspector	J. JAY SAUNDERS
TV Announcer	MICHAEL LAURENCE
Herbert Stiles	GEORGE SKAFF

A suspense tale about a career gal who becomes the target of a terror campaign by an unknown man in a neighboring high rise and who takes matters into her own hands when she can not get protection from the police. *High Rise* was the original title for this one.

0912
OUTSIDE CHANCE
12/2/78 New World Productions/Miller-Begun Television (2 hours)

Executive Producer: Roger Corman
Producer: Jeff Begun
Director: Michael Miller
Teleplay: Ralph Gaby Wilson and Michael Miller
Photography: Willy Kurant
Music: Michael Dunne and Lou Levy
Art Director: John Carter
Editor: Bruce Logan

Dinah Hunter	YVETTE MIMIEUX
Larry O'Brien	ROYCE D. APPLEGATE
Clair	BEVERLY HOPE ATKINSON
Mavis	SUSAN BATSON
Miss Hopkins	BABS BRAM
Deputy Hobie	FREDRIC COOK
Sheriff Dempsey	SEVERN DARDEN
Tony Hunter	HOWARD HESSEMAN
Doctor	LEE FERGUS
Bill Hill	JOHN LAWLER

Katherine	BETTY THOMAS
Alfred	BRITT LEACH
Luther	CHARLES YOUNG
Mirror Glasses	KIMO OWENS
Dale	IRA MILLER
Lola	NANCY NOBLE
Tootie	ROBIN SHERWOOD
Arnold Bradfield	DICK ARMSTRONG
Matron	JANINA T. WHITE
Jimmy (Diesel Driver)	JERRY HAMLIN

A lady advertising executive finds herself in a small-town jail after being terrorized on a drive from Los Angeles to New York by two hitchhikers who steal her car and leave her unconscious by the roadside. She becomes a fugitive after killing her jailer during a rape attempt and breaking out with one of the hitchhikers who could prove her innocence. This is the same story, with a twist, as the unexpectedly successful *Jackson County Jail* (1976), also with Yvette Mimieux and the same technical crew headed by director Michael Miller, with much of the footage from that film telescoped to set up the premise for the new one.

0913
SUDDENLY, LOVE
12/4/78 Ross Hunter Productions (2 hours)

Producers: Ross Hunter and Jacque Mapes
Associate Producer: Marvin Miller
Director: Stuart Margolin
Teleplay: Katherine Coker
Photography: Robert B. Hauser
Music: David Rose
Art Director: Kim Swados
Editors: Richard Bracken and Sidney Wolinsky

Regina Malloy	CINDY WILLIAMS
Jack Graham	PAUL SHENAR
Mrs. Malloy	EILEEN HECKART
Mrs. Graham	JOAN BENNETT
Mr. Graham	LEW AYRES
Dr. Luria	KURT KASZNAR
Helen Malloy	KRISTINE DeBELL
Mr. Webster	HAYDEN ROARKE
Regina (age 8)	LULU BAXTER
Jane	NANCY FOX
Male Student	MAX KELLER

and: John Creamer, Richard Rorke, Linwood Boomer, Brian Fuld, Douglas Anderson, Jim Galante, Christopher Norris, Diane Chesney, Claudia Bryar, Robert Street, Monica Mancini, Chris Mancini

Young lovers—she's a child of the ghetto, determined to escape her alcoholic, bickering parents; he's a socially prominent attorney with a long-standing health problem—attempt to defy every obstacle to their romance and ultimate marriage.

0914
MY HUSBAND IS MISSING
12/5/78 Bob Banner Associates (2 hours)

Executive Producer: Bob Banner
Producer: John Herman Shaner and Al Ramus
Director: Richard Michaels
Teleplay: John Herman Shaner and Al Ramus
Photography: Michael Margulies
Music: Joseph Wells
Art Director: Carl Anderson
Editors: Richard C. Myers and Ann Mills

Kathy Eaton	SALLY STRUTHERS
Derek Mackenzie	TONY MUSANTE
Quan Dong	JAMES HONG
Francesca Bellini	MARTINE BESWICK
Paul Eaton	SAM FREED
Boisson	JEFF DAVID
Receptionist	NAM LOC
Vice Consul	SHIZUKO HOSHI
Peasant Woman	LIEN DAO

Woman	LAN TRAN
Old Man	TRAN TE
Tuc Dow	TUNG-GIANG

A young wife journeys to North Vietnam in an effo[rt] to find her husband, an American flier reported miss[ing] in action, and is joined by a cynical Canadia[n] correspondent on the trail of a human interest stor[y].

0915
STEEL COWBOY
12/6/78 Roger Gimbel Productions/EMI Televisi[on] (2 hours)

Executive Producers: Roger Gimbel and Tony Converse
Producer: R. J. Lewis
Director: Harvey Laidman
Teleplay: Douglas Wheeler and Bill Kerby
From a story by Douglas Wheeler
Photography: Frank Holgate
Music: Charles Bernstein
Art Director: Alan Manson
Editor: Aaron Stell

Clayton Davis	JAMES BROLIN
K. W. Hicks	RIP TORN
Jesse Davis	JENNIFER WARRE[N]
Johnnie	MELANIE GRIFFITH
Gloria	JULIE COBB
Arky	LOU FRIZZELL
Pink Pincus	STROTHER MARTIN
Miller	ALBERT POPWELL
Bobby "Bob" Hicks	JOHN DENNIS JOHNSTON
Tiny Pollard	BOB SCHOTT

and: Don Calfa, Rudy Diaz, Bob Hoy, Scott Thomp[son], Jack O'Leary, Stanley Brock, Anthony Charnot[a], Miriam Byrd Netherly, Bo Gibson, Larry Spalding, Stuart Gillard

An independent trucker, trying to keep his marriag[e] alive and his rig out of the hands of bill collectors, agrees to haul a cargo of stolen cattle with his good old-boy buddy.

0916
THE GIFT OF LOVE
12/8/78 An Osmond Production (2 hours)

Executive Producers: The Osmond Brothers and Toby Martin
Producer: Mitchell Brower
Director: Don Chaffey
Teleplay: Caryl Ledner
Inspired by *The Gift of the Magi* by O. Henry
Photography: Charles F. Wheeler
Music: Fred Karlin
Art Director: Hilyard Brown
Editors: John R. Hoger and Herbert Carr

Beth Atherton	MARIE OSMOND
Rudi Miller	TIMOTHY BOTTOMS
Agnes	BETHEL LESLIE
Constance Schuyler	JUNE LOCKHART
William Schuyler	DONALD MOFFAT
O. Henry (and narrator)	DAVID WAYNE
Alfred Browning	JAMES WOODS
Mary O'Halloran	SONDRA WEST
Franz Hollner	ROBERT PIERCE
Griggs	FRED STUTHMAN
Mrs. Mooney	PEGGY REA
Maeve O'Halloran	ANNE RAMSEY

Marie Osmond made her dramatic acting debut play[ing] a poor little rich girl who loses her heart to a[n] penniless immigrant in New York of the Gay Ninetie[s] in this variation of the O. Henry tale that has the girl cutting and selling her long hair to buy a watch for her husband who has sold his priceless watch to buy a set of jeweled combs for his wife—all of which, naturally, happens in the final minutes of this film.

0917
A REAL AMERICAN HERO
12/9/78 Bing Crosby Productions, Inc. (2 hours)

Executive Producer: Charles A. Pratt
Producer: Samuel A. Peeples
Director: Lou Antonio
Teleplay: Samuel A. Peeples
Based on characters created by Mort Briskin
Photography: Charles Correll
Music: Walter Scharf
Song "Walking Tall" by Walter Scharf and Don Black
Sung by Don Williams
Art Director: Jack Poplin
Editor: Houseley Stevenson

Buford Pusser	BRIAN DENNEHY
Carl Pusser	FORREST TUCKER
Til Johnson	BRIAN KERWIN
Danny Boy Mitchell	KEN HOWARD
Carrie Todd	SHEREE NORTH
Debbie Pride	LANE BRADBURY
Mick Rogers	BRAD DAVID
Grady Coker	EDWARD CALL
Obra Eaker	W. O. SMITH
Dwana Pusser	JULIE THRASHER
Mike Pusser	JASON HOOD
Grandma Pusser	ANN STREET
Lloyd Tatum	GEORGE BOYD
Amelia Biggins	MAUREEN BURNS
Miles Conway	CHARLIE BRIGGS
Sabrina Marlowe	ELIZABETH LANE

Law-and-order Selma, Tennessee sheriff Buford Pusser, the resourceful, club-wielding real-life folk hero whose career inspired three ultra-violent movies, returns to wage a relentless battle against a dapper local moonshiner in this TV feature. Brian Dennehy assumed the role played originally by Joe Don Baker in the hugely successful *Walking Tall* and by Bo Svenson in the two sequels. Forrest Tucker, who was Buford's dad in the last, recreates his role in this TV version.

0918
A WOMAN CALLED MOSES
12/11–12/78 Henry Jaffe Enterprises Inc. (4 hours)

Executive Producer: Henry Jaffe
Producers: Ike Jones and Michael Jaffe
Director: Paul Wendkos
Teleplay: Lonne Elder III
Based on the book by Marcy Heidish
Photography: Robert B. Hauser
Music: Coleridge-Taylor Perkinson
Title song by Van McCoy and sung by Tommie Young
Art Director: Ray Beal
Editors: Stan Frazer and Frank Mazzola

Harriet Ross Tubman	CICELY TYSON
Thomas Garrett	WILL GEER
William Still	ROBERT HOOKS
Andrew Coleman	JAMES WAINWRIGHT
Daddy Ben Ross	JASON BERNARD
Doc Thompson	CLIFFORD DAVID
Bernette Wilson	JUDYANN ELDER
Stewart	JOHN GETZ
Aunt Juba	MAE MERCER
Tazwell Robinson	HARRY RHODES
McCracken	JAMES SIKKING
Shadrack Davis	CHARLES WELDON

John Tubman	DICK ANTHONY WILLIAMS
Molly	MARILYN COLEMAN
Susan	CECILIA HART
Mama Ritt Ross	ANN WALDON

Narrated by ORSON WELLES

A dramatization of the life of the legendary slave who escaped to freedom and returned to the South many times to rescue others via her underground railroad.

0919
THE JORDAN CHANCE
12/12/78 Roy Huggins Productions/R.B. Productions/Universal (2 hours)

Executive Producer: Roy Huggins
Producer: Jo Sweling, Jr.
Director: Jules Irving
Teleplay: Stephen J. Cannell
From a story by John Thomas James and Stephen J. Cannell
Photography: Enzo A. Martinelli
Music: Pete Rugolo
Art Director: John J. Jeffries
Editor: Larry Lester

Frank Jordan	RAYMOND BURR
Brian Klosky	TED SHACKELFORD
Jimmy Foster	JAMES CANNING
Karen Wagner	JEANNIE FITZSIMMONS
Virna Stewart	STELLA STEVENS
Sheriff DeVega	GEORGE DiCENZO
Jasper Colton	JOHN McINTIRE
Lee Southerland	PETER HASKELL
Elena Delgado	MARIA-ELENA CORDERO
Sid Burton	GERALD McRANEY
Lew Mayfield	JOHN DENNIS
Mike Anderson	GRANT OWEN
Judge Miller	MICHAEL DON WAGNER

and: Walt Davis, Rod Hasse, Sylvia Hayes, Nancy Jeris, Julia Benjamin, Ellen Blake, Tom Stewart

Burr again portrays a no-nonsense lawyer in this pilot for a prospective series, this time a prominent attorney who in early life spent seven years behind bars for a crime he did not commit and now has established a foundation dedicated to helping those wrongly accused and unjustly convicted, giving them "The Jordan Chance."

0920
LOVEY: A CIRCLE OF CHILDREN, PART II
12/13/78 Time-Life Television (2 hours)

Executive Producer: David Susskind
Producers: Frederick Brogger and Diana Kerew
Director: Jud Taylor
Teleplay: Josh Greenfield
Based on the book *Lovey, A Very Special Child* by Mary MacCracken
Photography: Ron Lautore
Music: Jerry Fielding
Art Director: Karen Bromley
Editor: Gene Milford

Mary MacCracken	JANE ALEXANDER
Cal MacCracken	RONNY COX
Hannah ("Lovey")	KRIS McKEON
Brian	JEFF LYNAS
Rufus	GUY COSTLEY
Jamie	DREW BUETTOW
Doris Stevens	AVRIL GENTLES
Patty	HELEN SHAVER

Elizabeth	KAREN ALLEN
Mrs. Rosnic	DIANE KAGAN
Bernie Serino	DANNY AIELLO
Ellen	CAROLINE YEAGER
Ed	JAMES NOBLE

In this sequel to *A Circle of Children* (1977), Jane Alexander recreates her original role as a teacher of disturbed children who must make decisions regarding her own life and the progress of her students.

0921
THE NEW ADVENTURES OF HEIDI
12/13/78 Pierre Cossette Enterprises Inc. (2 hours)

Executive Producer: Pierre Cossette
Producer: Charles B. FitzSimmons
Director: Ralph Senesky
Teleplay: John McGreevey
Based on characters created by Johanna Spyri
Photography: John M. Nicholas
Music and Lyrics: Buz Kohan
Production Designer: Michael Baugh
Editor: Gene Fowler

Heidi	KATY KURTZMAN
Grandfather	BURL IVES
Dan Wyler	JOHN GAVIN
Mady	MARLYN MASON
Peter	SEAN MARSHALL
Elizabeth Wyler	SHERRIE WILLS
Chef Andre	ALEX HENTELOFF
The Wild Man	CHARLES AIDMAN
Cousin Tobias	WALTER BROOKE
Cousin Martha	AMZIE STRICKLAND
Mother Gertrude	MOLLY DODD
Sister Agnes	ADRIENNE MARDEN

and: Arlen Stuart, Barry Cahill, Bartlett Robinson, Fred Lerner, Lola Mason, Buck Young, Karl Ellis

The long-familiar Heidi tale is given a contemporary setting—as the young heroine leaves her familiar Swiss mountain for the bright lights of Manhattan—and a musical background.

0922
LONG JOURNEY BACK
12/15/78 Lorimar Productions (2 hours)

Executive Producers: Lee Rich and Philip Capice
Producer: Robert Lovenheim
Director: Mel Damski
Teleplay: Audrey Davis Levin
Based on an article by Judith Ramsey
Photography: Stevan Larner
Music: Fred Karlin
Art Director: John E. Chilburg III
Editors: Herbert H. Dow and John P. Farrell

Vic Casella	MIKE CONNORS
Laura Casella	CLORIS LEACHMAN
Celia Casella	STEPHANIE ZIMBALIST
Amy Casella	KATY KURTZMAN
Steve	HOWARD McGILLIN
Dr. Rojas	LUIS AVALOS
Dr. Roberts	NICOLAS COSTER
Dr. Chisholm	LEE CHAMBERLIN
Cal	JOHN LAMONT

This film depicts a teenage girl's courageous fight following a crushing school bus accident that leaves her physically and emotionally handicapped.

0923

WHO'LL SAVE OUR CHILDREN?
12/16/78 Time-Life Television (2 hours)

Executive Producer: David Susskind
Producer/Director: George Schaefer
Teleplay: William Hanley
Based on the book by Rachel Maddux
Photography: Don Wilder
Music: Fred Karlin
Production Designer: Trevor Williams
Editor: Sidney M. Katz

Sarah Laver	SHIRLEY JONES
Matt Laver	LEN CARIOU
Lurene Garver	CASSIE YATES
Bob Garver	DAVID HAYWARD
Dodie Hart	CONCHATA FERRELL
Nellie Henderson	FRANCES STERNHAGEN
Marjory Garver	LEE ANN MITCHELL
Tommy Garver	DAVID SCHOTT
John Drake	JORDON CHARNEY
Oscar Taylor	FRANZ RUSSELL

A childless couple become foster parents to two young children who have been deserted by their irresponsible parents, but when they attempt to adopt them legally after falling in love with them and raising them, are rebuffed when the natural parents sue to reclaim their offspring.

0924

THE NATIVITY
12/17/78 D'Angelo-Bullock-Allen Productions/20th Century-Fox (2 hours)

Executive Producers: Ray Allen and Harvey Bullock
Producer: William P. D'Angelo
Director: Bernard L. Kowalski
Teleplay: Millard Kaufman and Mort Fine
Photography: Gabor Pogany
Music: Lalo Schifrin
Art Director: Luciano Spadoni
Editors: Robert Phillips and Jerry Dronsky

Mary	MADELINE STOWE
Joseph	JOHN SHEA
Anna	JANE WYATT
Zacharias	PAUL STEWART
Elizabeth	AUDREY TOTTER
Joachim	GEORGE VOSKOVEC
Zipporah	JULIE GARFIELD
Menachem	JAMIL ZAKKAI
Diomedes	FREDDIE JONES
Nestor	JOHN RHYS-DAVIES
Flavius	MORGAN SHEPPARD
Salome	KATE O'MARA
Herod	LEO McKERN
Eleazar	GEOFFREY BEEVERS
Preacher	BARRIE HOUGHTON
Census Taker	JACOB WITKIN
Innkeeper	JACK LYNN

This film offers a reverent retelling of the courtship of Mary and Joseph and the first Christmas.

0925

THE WINDS OF KITTY HAWK
12/17/78 Charles Fries Productions (2 hours)

Executive Producer: Charles Fries
Associate Producer: Tony Ganz
Producer: Lawrence Schiller
Director: E. W. Swackhamer
Teleplay: Jeb Rosebrook and William Kelley
Photography: Dennis Dalzell
Music: Charles Bernstein
Art Director: Sidney Z. Litwack
Editor: John A. Martinelli

Wilbur Wright	MICHAEL MORIARTY
Orville Wright	DAVID HUFFMAN
William Tate	TOM BOWER
H. A. Toumlin	ROBIN GAMMELL
Glenn Curtiss	SCOTT HYLANDS
Alexander Graham Bell	JOHN RANDOLPH
Kate Wright	KATHRYN WALKER
Bishop Milton Wright	EUGENE ROCHE
Prof. Samuel Langley	JOHN HOYT
Tom Tate	ARI ZELTZER
Harlan Mumford	LEW BROWN
Agnes Osborne	CAROLE TRU FOSTER
Elizabeth Mayfield	MO MALONE
Ace Hutchin	DABBS GREER
William Howard Taft	ROSS DURFEE

and: Robert Casper, Frank Farmer, Lawrence Haddon, Tom Lawrence, Charles Macaulay, Stephen Zacharias, Vaughn Armstrong

The Wright Brothers' story and their efforts to fly, stunningly filmed and first shown on the seventy-fifth anniversary of their historic flight. Dennis Dalzell (cinematographer) and John A. Martinelli (editor) received Emmy Award nominations for their work, but the film won in only one category: Film Sound Mixing.

0926

THE DEERSLAYER
12/18/78 Schick Sunn Classics Productions (90 min)

Executive Producers: Charles E. Sellier, Jr. and James L. Conway
Producer: Bill Conford
Director: Dick Friedenberg
Teleplay: S. S. Schweitzer
Based on the novel by James Fenimore Cooper
Photography: Paul Hipp
Music: Bob Summers and Andrew Belling
Art Director: Scott Lindquist
Editor: Carl Kress

Hawkeye	STEVE FORREST
Chingachgook	NED ROMERO
Hutter	JOHN ANDERSON
Rivenoak	VICTOR MOHICA
Judith Hutter	JOAN PRATHER
Hurry Harry March	CHARLES DIERKOP
Lt. Plowden	BRIAN DAVIES
Sieur de Beaujeur	TED HAMILTON
Hetty Hutter	MADELINE STOWE
Tamenund	RUBEN MORENO

and: Alma Bettran, Rosa Maria Hudson, Andrew William Lewis, Stephen Craig Taylor

A "Classics Illustrated" film treatment of Cooper's Leatherstocking Tale of 1841 that has Hawkeye and his blood brother Chingachgook teaming up to rescue a chief's daughter from the hands of her enemies.

0927

THE MILLIONAIRE
12/19/78 A Don Fedderson Production (2 hours)

Producer/Creator: Don Fedderson
Director: Don Weis
Teleplay: John McGreevey
Photography: Michael Joyce
Music: Frank DeVol
Art Director: David Scott
Editor: Harry Keller

Arthur Haines	MARTIN BALSAM
Paul Mathews	EDWARD ALBERT
Eddie Reardon	BILL HUDSON
Mike Reardon	MARK HUDSON
Harold Reardon	BRETT HUDSON
Maggie Haines	PAT CROWLEY
Kate Mathews	PAMELA TOLL
George Jelks	ALLAN RICH
Marshall Wayburn	JOHN IRELAND
George Mathews	RALPH BELLAMY
Mrs. Mathews	JANE WYATT
Oscar Pugh	WILLIAM DEMAREST
Michael Anthony	ROBERT QUARRY

and: Talia Balsam, Michael Minor, Milt Kogan, Sally Kemp, Patricia Hindy, P. R. Paul, Domingo Abriz, Paul Jackson, Edith Diaz, Penelope Jackson, Ann Greer, Patrick Driscoll, Buck Young

Three people's lives are drastically changed when they are suddenly given one million dollars each by an eccentric billionaire in this pilot to a prospective new series which the producers hoped would equal the success of the original one that ran from 1955 to 1960—with Robert Quarry now in the role of Michael Anthony (then played by Marvin Miller), executive secretary to the mysterious John Beresford Tipton, and deliverer of those weekly tax-free million-dollar cashier's checks.

0928

ISHI: THE LAST OF HIS TRIBE
12/20/78 An Edward and Mildred Lewis Production (2 hours)

Executive Producers: Edward and Mildred Lewis
Producer: James F. Sommers
Director: Robert Ellis Miller
Teleplay: Dalton and Christopher Trumbo
Based on the book *Ishi in Two Worlds* by Theodora Kroeber Quinn
Photography: Woody Omens
Music: Maurice Jarre
Art Director: Mort Rabinowitz
Editors: Argyle Nelson, Jr. and Harold Wilner

Prof. Benjamin Fuller	DENNIS WEAVER
Ishi as Man	ELOY PHIL CASADOS
Lushi as Teenager	DEVON ERICSON
Elder Uncle	GENO SILVA
Ishi as Teenager	JOSEPH RUNNING ROX
Grandmother	LOIS RED ELK
Timawi as Teenager	GREGORY NORMAN CRUZ
Mother	ARLIENE NOFCHISSEY WILLIAMS
Ishi as Boy	MICHAEL MEDINA
Lushi as Girl	PATRICIA GANERA
Timawi as Boy	EDDY MARQUEZ
Tad Fuller	DENNIS DIMSTER
Sheriff Lockhart	WAYNE HEFLEY

and: Peter Brandon, Missy Gold, Jay W. MacIntosh, Ernest D. Paul

A touching dramatization of a short chapter of American history, tracing the life of the last Yahi Indian from his childhood to his death in 1917 and the story of his friendship with an anthropologist after his discovery in northern California in 1911. The late Dalton Trumbo died before finishing the teleplay which his son completed.

0929

A CHRISTMAS TO REMEMBER
12/20/78 George Englund Enterprises (2 hours)

Producer/Director: George Englund
Teleplay: Stewart Stern

Based on the novel *The Melodeon* by Glendon Swarthout
Photography: Gayne Rescher
Music: Jimmie Haskell
Art Director: Alexander A. Mayer
Editor: Gary Griffin

Daniel Larson	JASON ROBARDS
Emma Larson	EVA MARIE SAINT
Russell McCloud	GEORGE PARRY
Mildred McCloud	JOANNE WOODWARD
Danny Larson	BRYAN ENGLUND
Louise Hockmeyer	MARY BETH MANNING
Lolly Hockmeyer	NORA MARTIN
Ralph Youngquist	ARVID CARLSON
Beulah Youngquist	MILDRED CARLSON
Russell McCloud (as Adult)	ALEX MAYER
Lolly Hockmeyer (as Adult)	PAMELA DANSER
Tal Fellow	GUY PAUL
Oskar Hockmeyer	ALLEN HAMILTON
Lil Hockmeyer	SALLY CHAMBERLIN
Preacher	LOWELL ANDERSON

An elderly farm couple take in their city-bred adolescent grandson for the holidays during the darkest days of the Depression, and the old man, embittered by the death of his only son in World War I, gradually opens his heart to the boy as both learn the importance of a giving relationship. Joanne Woodward plays a cameo as the boy's mother.

0930
TERROR OUT OF THE SKY
12/26/78 Alan Landsburg Productions (2 hours)

Executive Producer: Alan Landsburg
Producer: Peter Nelson
Director: Lee H. Katzin
Teleplay: Guerdon Trueblood, Peter Nelson and Doris Silverton
Photography: Michel Hugo
Music: William Goldstein
Art Director: Alan Manser
Editor: George Hively

David Martin	EFREM ZIMBALIST, JR.
Nick Willis	DAN HAGGERTY
Jeannie	TOVAH FELDSHUH
Earl Logan	LONNY CHAPMAN
Eric	IKE EISENMANN
Gladstone	STEVE FRANKEN
Eli Nathanson	BRUCE FRENCH
Colonel Mangus	RICHARD HERD
Groves	JOE E. TATA
Agent	ELLEN BLAKE
Starrett	PHILIP BAKER POINDEXTER
Mike	CHARLES HALLAN
Tibbles	STEVE TANNEN
Sergeant	MELINDA PETERSON
Computer Operator	TONY LA TORRE
Boy Tibbles	BILL QUINN
Old Dermott	

Two bee specialists and a free-lance pilot go all-out to prevent another invasion force of killer bees in this sequel to *The Savage Bees* (1976) which originally was to have been titled *The Revenge of the Savage Bees.*

0931
LES MISERABLES
12/27/78 Norman Rosemont Productions/ITV Entertainment (3 hours)

Producer: Norman Rosemont
Associate Producer: Ron Carr
Director: Glenn Jordan
Teleplay: John Gay
Based on the novel by Victor Hugo
Photography: Jean Tournier
Music: Allyn Ferguson
Productions Designer: Wilfred Shingleton
Editor: Bill Blunden

Jean Valjean	RICHARD JORDAN
Inspector Javert	ANTHONY PERKINS
Fauchelevent	CYRIL CUSACK
Bishop Myriel	CLAUDE DAUPHIN
Gillenormand	JOHN GIELGUD
Thenardier	IAN HOLM
Sister Simplice	CELIA JOHNSON
Magliorie	JOYCE REDMAN
The Prioress	FLORA ROBSON
Marius	CHRISTOPHER GUARD
Cosette	CAROLINE LANGRISHE
Fantine	ANGELA PLEASENCE

and: David Swift, Timothy Morand, William Squire, Geoffrey Russell, Caroline Blakiston, Robin Scobey, Michael Sheard, Dexter Fletcher, Joanna Price, Dave Hill, John Moreno

A lavish remake of the classic about the escaped convict, a woodcutter who had been imprisoned for stealing a loaf of bread to feed his starving family, and the dogged police inspector who dedicates himself to hounding the man until he can again be put behind bars. An Emmy Award nomination went to director Glenn Jordan.

0932
THE INCREDIBLE JOURNEY OF DOCTOR MEG LAUREL
1/2/79 Columbia Pictures (3 hours)

Executive Producer: Ron Samuels
Producer: Paul Radin
Director: Guy Green
Teleplay: Michael Berk, Douglas Schwartz and Joseph Fineman
Photography: Al Francis
Music: Gerald Fried
Art Director: Jack DeShields
Editor: Gloryette Clark

Dr. Meg Laurel	LINDSAY WAGNER
Granny Arrowroot	MISS JANE WYMAN
Effie Webb	DOROTHY McGUIRE
Judge Adamson	ANDREW DUGGAN
Harley Moon	GARY LOCKWOOD
Joe	BROCK PETERS
Thom Laurel	JOHN REILLY
Doug Slocomb	CHARLES TYNER
Sin Eater	JAMES WOODS
Messerschmidt	WOODROW PARFREY
Mrs. Slocomb	PEGGY WALTON
Becca	KATHI SOUCIE
Laurie Mae Moon	TRACEY GOLD
Sophie Pride	CHERILYN PARSONS
Jacob Barth	GARY GRAHAM
Joel	RAY YOUNG
Rose Hooper	GLORIA STUART
Granny Bacon	MARY ELLEN O'NEILL

and: Tom Spratley, Meegan King, David Gregory, Henry Gayle Sanders, Dee Croxton, Hazel Johnson, Pauline McFadgen, Stephanie Smith, Carolyn Jane Reed, Ronald Peterson, John Driscoll, Sam Jones, Philip G. Schultz, Dan Kemp, Diane Fetterly, Sharon McGrath, Marta Nichols, Genevieve Beauvais

A big-city lady doctor returns to her roots in the backwoods of the Blue Ridge Mountains to bring modern medicine to the local folks in the Appalachia of the 1930s and finds herself at odds with the homespun ways of the local medicine woman. Originally this was titled *The Outlander.* Veteran actress Jane Wyman returned to filmmaking here and was accorded the seldom used billing "Miss Jane Wyman."

0933
SOME KIND OF MIRACLE
1/3/79 Lorimar Productions (2 hours)

Executive Producers: Lee Rich and Philip Capice
Producer: George LeMaire
Director: Jerrold Freedman
Teleplay: Mary and Jack Wills
From their book *But There Are Always Miracles*
Photography: Tak Fujimoto
Music: Jimmie Haskell and Robie Porter
Art Director: James H. Spencer
Editor: David Berlatsky

Joe Dine	DAVID DUKES
Maggie Nicoff	ANDREA MARCOVICCI
Dr. Mark Spencer	MICHAEL C. GWYNNE
Sam	ART HINDLE
Dr. Hopstone	DICK ANTHONY WILLIAMS
Hal	JOHN HERZFELD
Frank	BRUNO KIRBY
Ruth Nicoff	NANCY MARCHAND
Arthur Nicoff	STEPHEN ELLIOTT
Harriet	MARILYN CHRIS
Marge	KATHERINE PASS
Elvis	ART EVANS
Aide	MICHAEL LaGUARDIA
Janet	LEE KESSLER
Al	AL RUSCIO

and: James Veres, Susan Bredhoff, Anton Greene, Marion Scherer, Jerry DeWilde, Jean Holloway, Lou Carello, Brad Parks, Walker Edminston, Maureen Lee, Jill Lent

A drama about the emotional and physical shock faced by a TV newscaster and his fiancée, a newspaper reporter, following a surfing accident which paralyzes him and puts him in a wheelchair for life.

0934
PLEASURE COVE
1/3/79 Lou Shaw Production for the David Gerber Co./Columbia Pictures (2 hours)

Producer: Mel Swope
Director: Bruce Bilson
Teleplay: Lou Shaw
Photography: Jack A. Whitman, Jr.
Music: Perry Botkin, Jr.
Art Director: Ray Beal
Editors: J. Terry Williams and John Farrell

Raymond Gordon	TOM JONES
Kim Parker	CONSTANCE FORSLUND
Julie	MELODY ANDERSON
Chip Garvey	JERRY LACY
Henry Sinclair	JAMES MURTAUGH
Osaki	ERNEST HARADA
Martha Harrison	JOAN HACKETT
Bert Harrison	HARRY GUARDINO
Helen Perlmutter	SHELLEY FABARES

Scott	DAVID HASSELHOFF	Barbara Harlich	SHIRLEY KNIGHT
Joe	RON MASAK	Damschroeder	TONY LoBIANCO
Gayle Tyler	BARBARA LUNA	Peter Scoggin III	JAMES VINCENT McNICHOL
Sally	TANYA ROBERTS	Carrie Harlich	JOY LeDUC
Zelda Golden	RHODA BATES	Camille Scoggin	JENNIFER WARREN
Fat Man at Bar	ROBERT EMHARDT	Peter Scoggin, Jr.	RICHARD JAECKEL
Jack	DAVID ANKRUM	Kachatorian	ANNE SCHEDEEN
Willard	SANDY CHAMPION	Lisa	ELIZABETH CHESHIRE
Donald	WES PARKER	Laura	TIFFANY ANN FRANCIS
		Sally	MISSY FRANCIS

and Les Brown and His Band of Renown

A landlocked carbon of "Love Boat" was this pilot for a prospective series, interweaving several lighthearted plots about vacationers at a posh resort—one of whom is Tom Jones, making his acting debut as a charming rogue with criminal intentions.

The story of two adolescents whose personal relationship blossoms and whose professional relationship matures as they attempt to reach their goal—the national figure skating championships.

0935
AMATEUR NIGHT AT THE DIXIE BAR AND GRILL
1/8/79 Motown/Universal (2 hours)

Executive Producer: Rob Cohen
Producer: Lauren Shuler
Director: Joel Schumacher
Teleplay: Joel Schumacher
Photography: Ric Waite
Music: Bradford Craig
Art Directors: Ray Brandt and Henry Berman
Editor: Anthony Redmond

Mac	VICTOR FRENCH
Sharee	CANDY CLARK
Fanny	LOUISE LATHAM
Cowboy	DON JOHNSON
Snuffy McCann	JAMIE FARR
Lettie Norman	SHEREE NORTH
Sharon Singleton	TANYA TUCKER
Marvin Laurie	JEFF ALTMAN
Vera Elvira	PAT AST
Moss Tillis	ED BEGLEY, JR.
Roy	GARY BISIG
Marcy	JOAN GOODFELLOW
Milt Cavanaugh	HENRY GIBSON
Harry	RICK HURST
Duke	HOWARD ITZKOWITZ
Doreen Reese	ROZ KELLY
Joanne Nutter	MELINDA NAUD
Anita	MARY McCUSKER
Big Arnold	DENNIS BURKLEY
Laurie Jean	KYLE RICHARDS
Frank Smith	TIMOTHY SCOTT

and: Dennis Quaid, Allan Warnick, Gloria Torres, Tanya Lee Russell, Bob Louden, Bill Dietz, Bob Schott, Richard Collier, Corey David Rand, Brenda White, Michele Michaels, Barbara Wiggins, Bernice Criswell

A drama, similar to Robert Altman's *Nashville,* surrounding the preparations by employees, patrons and hopefuls for a roadhouse country and western talent show.

0936
CHAMPIONS: A LOVE STORY
1/13/79 Warner Bros. (2 hours)

Executive Producer: Philip Mandelker
Associate Producer: Anna Cottle
Producer: John Sacret Young
Director: John A. Alonzo
Teleplay: John Sacret Young
Photography: John A. Alonzo
Music: John Rubinstein
Art Director: Tracy Bousman
Editor: Bernard J. Small

0937
DALLAS COWBOYS CHEERLEADERS
1/14/79 Aubrey/Hamner Productions (2 hours)

Executive Producers: James T. Aubrey and Robert Hamner
Producer/Director: Bruce Bilson
Teleplay: Robert Hamner
Photography: Don Birnkrant
Music: Jimmie Haskell
Choreographer: Texie Waterman
Art Director: Ray Beal
Coordinator and Technical Advisor of the Dallas Cowboys Cheerleaders: Suzanne Mitchell
Editor: Ira Haymann

Laura Cole	JANE SEYMOUR
Suzanne Mitchell	LARAINE STEPHENS
Lyman Spencer	BERT CONVY
Betty Denton	PAMELA SUSAN SHOOP
Joanne Vail	ELLEN BRY
Kim Everly	JENIFER SHAW
Ginny O'Neil	KATHERINE BAUMANN
Jessie Mathews	LAURA TEWES
Kyle Jessop	BUCKY DENT
J. R. Denton	TERRY COOK
Herself	TEXI WATERMAN
Himself	RON CHAPMAN
Herself	JERRI MOTE
Dora	IRMA HALL
Frank Rand	GAVIN TROSTER
Tyler	HARLAN JORDAN
Tom	RANDY MOORE
Mary Lou	JAKI MORRISON

and the Dallas Cowboys Cheerleaders

To salvage his job and the circulation of his magazine, an editor decides to publish an exposé revealing the inside story of the famed cheerleading squad and plants his reporter/girlfriend among the girls. This was the highest rated TV movie for the 1978–79 season.

0938
CHARLESTON
1/15/79 Robert Stigwood Productions/RSO, Inc. (2 hours)

Producer: Beryl Vertue
Director: Karen Arthur
Teleplay: Nancy Lynn Schwartz
Photography: Ric Waite
Music: Elmer Bernstein
Art Director: Tom J. John
Editor: Bud Friedkin

Stella Farrell	DELTA BURKE
Gregg Morgan	JORDAN CLARKE
James Harris	RICHARD LAWSON

Minerva	LYNNE MOODY
Valerie Criss	PATRICIA PEARCY
Mrs. Farrell (Aunt Louisa)	MARTHA SCOTT
Beaudine Croft	MANDY PATINKIN
Cluskey	RICHARD BRADFORD
Miss Fay	LUCILLE BENSON
Gabriel	BEN HALLEY, JR.
Tom Doder	DENNIS BURKLEY
Rev Dr. Palmer	ANCEL COOK
Lt. Beeson	ALAN McRAE
Rev. Duchamp	ROCKNE TARKINGTON

Narrated by DOUG HALE

and: William Norren, Sam Cotten, Charles "Honi" Coles

A tacky road-company version of *Gone with the Wind* involving a southern belle who is determined to hang onto her aristocratic family's mansion following the Civil War. Its dubious distinction comes from its feminist viewpoint and the fact that its producer, director and writer were women (the last died before completing it) and that its stars were virtual unknowns.

0939
MURDER IN MUSIC CITY
1/16/79 Frankel Films Inc. (2 hours)

Executive Producer: Ernie Frankel
Producer: Jimmy Sangster
Director: Leo Penn
Teleplay: Jimmy Sangster and Ernie Frankel
Photography: Alan Stensvold
Music: Earle Hagen
Art Director: Allen Jones
Editor: Sidney M. Katz

Sonny Hunt	SONNY BONO
Samantha Hunt	LEE PURCELL
Mrs. Bloom	LUCILLE BENSON
Billy West	CLAUDE AKINS
Peggy Ann West	BELINDA MONTGOMERY
Dana Morgan	MORGAN FAIRCHILD
Chigger Wade	MICHAEL MacRAE
Jim Feegan	HARRY BELLAVER
Sam Prine	KIM OWEN
Lt. Culver	T. TOMMY CUTRER
and as Themselves	CHARLIE DANIELS LARRY GATLIN BARBARA MANDRELL RONNIE MILSAP BOOTS RANDOLPH RAY STEVENS MEL TILLIS

A brash songwriter who buys a detective business as a tax shelter finds himself and his photographer's model bride involved in a puzzling murder—when a dead body turns up in their honeymoon suite—and a trail that leads them to Nashville.

0940
CAPTAIN AMERICA
1/19/79 Universal (2 hours)

Executive Producer: Allan Balter
Producer: Martin Goldstein
Director: Rod Holcomb
Teleplay: Don Ingalls
From a story by Don Ingalls and Chester Krumholz
Photography: Ronald W. Browne
Music: Mike Post and Pete Carpenter
Art Director: Lou Montejano
Editor: Mike Murphy

Steve Rogers	REB BROWN
Dr. Simon Mills	LEN BIRMAN
Dr. Wendy Day	HEATHER MENZIES
Lou Brackett	STEVE FORREST
Tina Hayden	ROBIN MATTSON
Rudy Sandrini	JOSEPH RUSKIN
Harley	LANCE LeGAULT
Charles Barber	FRANK MARTH
Jerry	CHIP JOHNSON
Jeff Hayden	DAN BARTON
Throckmorton	NOCONA ARANDA
Ortho	MICHAEL McMANUS
Lester Wiant	JAMES INGERSOLL

and: Jim Smith, Ken Chandler, Jason Wingreen, Buster Jones, June Dayton, Diane Webster

The legendary comic-strip crimefighter's ex-Marine son takes up where his dad left off, righting wrongs, defending the American ideal and pursuing an arch-criminal who plans to decimate Phoenix with a neutron bomb in this pilot for a proposed series.

0941
A LAST CRY FOR HELP
1/19/79 Myrt-Hal Production/Viacom (2 hours)

Executive Producer: Hal Sitowitz
Producer: Douglas Benton
Director/Writer: Hal Sitowitz
Photography: Dennis Dalzell
Music: Miles Goodman
Art Director: Adrian Gorton
Editor: Leon Carrere

Sharon Muir	LINDA PURL
Joan Muir	SHIRLEY JONES
Dr. Ben Abbot	TONY LoBIANCO
Ralph Muir	MURRAY HAMILTON
Jeff Burgess	GRANT GOODEVE
Connie	KAREN LAMM
Mr. Burgess	MORGAN WOODWARD
Budd	ROBIN STRAND
Sandy	CINDY EILBACHER
Carol	DELTA BURKE
Willie	RENEE BROWN
Peter	CHIP LUCIA
Kathy	CANDY MOBLEY
Mandy	STACEY KUHNE
Jessie	MELISSA SHERMAN
Ms. Harrison	MOLLY DODD

A pretty high school coed, fearing that she is not living up to her parents' expectations and that she is a disappointment to her friends, withdraws into a world of her own and attempts suicide.

0942
SALVAGE
1/20/79 Bennett-Katleman Productions/Columbia Pictures (2 hours)

Executive Producers: Harve Bennett and Harris Katleman
Producers: Mike Lloyd Ross and Norman S. Powell
Director: Lee Philips
Teleplay: Mike Lloyd Ross
Photography: Fred Koenekamp
Music: Walter Scharf
Art Directors: Ross Bellah and John Beckman
Editor: Ronald LeVine

Harry Broderick	ANDY GRIFFITH
Skip Carmichael	JOEL HIGGINS
Melanie Slozer	TRISH STEWART
Klinger	RICHARD JAECKEL
Mack	J. JAY SAUNDERS
Fred	RALEIGH BOND

Lorene	JACQUELINE SCOTT
Bill Kelly	PETER BROWN
Hank Beddoes	LEE DeBROUX
Commentator	RICHARD EASTHAM

A hotshot junkman decides to go to the moon with his two young companions in a homemade rocket to recover millions of dollars worth of discarded space equipment in this lighthearted pilot to the series which began the following week as "Salvage 1," with Griffith and his associates using the rocket for other weekly adventures.

0943
INSTITUTE FOR REVENGE
1/22/79 Gold-Driskill Productions/Columbia Pictures (90 min)

Executive Producers: Bill Driskill and Otto Salamon
Producer: Bert Gold
Director: Ken Annakin
Teleplay: Bill Driskill
From a story by Bill Driskill and Otto Salamon
Photography: Roland (Ozzie) Smith
Music: Lalo Schifrin
Art Directors: Ross Bellah and Robert Lawrence
Editors: J. Terry Williams and Robert M. Ross

John Schroeder	SAM GROOM
Lilah	LAUREN HUTTON
JoAnn	LANE BINKLEY
Bradley	T. J. McCAVITT
Wellington	ROBERT COOTE
Bodyguard	MURRAY SALEM
Counselor Barnes	LESLIE NIELSEN
Frank Anders	RAY WALSTON
Alan Roberto	GEORGE HAMILTON
Pilot	DENNIS O'FLAHERTY
Senator	ROBERT EMHARDT
Power Broker	JAMES KAREN
Voice of IFR	JOHN HILLERMAN

and: Harlee McBride, Ron Roy, Lisle Wilson, Ernie Fuentes, John Yates, Gavin Mooney, Rawn Hutchinson, Paul Lawrence, Jim Hess, John Davey, Anne Bellamy, Patience Cleveland, Natalie Core

A sophisticated computer named IFR (the film's title is its nickname) supervises an organization dedicated to correcting wrongs against the defenseless and assigns human operatives to track down the evildoers and bring them to justice nonviolently. This fanciful pilot was for a series that never materialized.

0944
MANDRAKE
1/24/79 Universal (2 hours)

Producer: Rick Husky
Director: Harry Falk
Teleplay: Rick Husky
Photography: Vincent A. Martinelli
Music: Morton Stevens
Art Director: John T. Bruce
Editors: Fredric Knudsten and Edward A. Williams

Mandrake	ANTHONY HERRERA
Stacy	SIMONE GRIFFETH
Lothar	JI-TU CUMBUKA
Alec Gordon	HANK BRANDT
Jennifer Lindsay	GRETCHEN CORBETT

William Romero	PETER HASKELL
Arkadian	ROBERT REED
Dr. Malcolm Lindsay	DAVID HOOKS
Dr. Nolan	HARRY BLACKSTONE, JR.

and: James Hong, Sab Shimono, Donna Benz, David Hollander

Suave Mandrake the Magician, the long-time comic-strip favorite, came to television in this pilot movie, to fight not only TV crime but also a madman trying to blackmail a business tycoon for ten million dollars after arranging for a series of rollercoaster murders.

0945
AND YOUR NAME IS JONAH
1/28/79 Charles Fries Productions (2 hours)

Executive Producer: Charles Fries
Producers: Norman Felton and Stanley Rubin
Associate Producer: Michael Bortman
Director: Richard Michaels
Teleplay: Michael Bortman
Photography: David Myers
Music: Fred Karlin
Art Director: Herman Zimmerman
Editor: David Newhouse

Jenny Corelli	SALLY STRUTHERS
Danny Corelli	JAMES WOODS
Connie	RANDEE HELLER
Grandpa	TITOS VANDIS
Grandma	PENNY STANTON
Mrs. Marquardt	RUTH MANNING
Jonah	JEFF BRAVIN
Dickie	ROBERT DAVI
Jenny's Mother	ERICA YOHN
Audiologist	LEE KESSLER
Larry	ANTHONY PONZINI
Kathe	ROBIN PEARSON ROSE
Paul	BERNARD BRAGG

and: Rose Barbato, Paula Shaw, Tracee Lyles, Jeremy Licht, Dick Rossner, Michael Fuller, Hilary Martin, Kathleen Hughes, Michael Griswold, Billy Seago

Drama about a New York couple whose seven-year-old son is discovered to be profoundly deaf after having been incorrectly diagnosed as mentally retarded and institutionalized for three years.

0946
THE CORN IS GREEN
1/29/79 Warner Bros. (2 hours)

Producer: Neil Hartley
Associate Producer: Eric Rattray
Director: George Cukor
Teleplay: Ivan Davis*
Based on the play by Emlyn Williams

Photography: Ted Scaife
Music: John Barry
Art Director: Carmen Dillon
Editors: Richard Marden and John Wright

Lilly Moffat	KATHARINE HEPBURN
Morgan Evans	IAN SAYNOR
The Squire	BILL FRASER
Mrs. Watty	PATRICIA HAYES
Miss Ronberry	ANNA MASSEY
John Goronwy Jones	ARTRO MORRIS
Sara Pugh	DOROTHEA PHILLIPS
Bessie Watty	TOYAH WILCOX

Idwal	HUW RICHARDS	
Robbart	BRYN FON	
Gwyn	DYFAN ROBERTS	
Ivor	ROBIN JOHN	

In this remake of the 1944 Bette Davis movie, reuniting Katharine Hepburn and director George Cukor for the tenth time in thirty-seven years (he directed her in her first movie, *Bill of Divorcement*), Lilly Moffat, the strong-willed spinster teacher, goes again on her mission to educate the illiterate youth of a turn-of-the-century North Wales mining community and finds one with a spark of genius. Katharine Hepburn won an Emmy Award nomination for her performance, as did costume designer David Walker.

*The script originally was credited to James Costigan.

0947

THE TRIANGLE FACTORY FIRE SCANDAL
1/30/79 Alan Landsburg Productions/Don Kirshner Productions (2 hours)

Executive Producer: Alan Landsburg and Don Kirshner
Producer: Paul Freeman
Associate Producer: Merrill Grant
Director: Mel Stuart
Teleplay: Mel and Ethel Brez
Photography: Matthew F. Leonetti
Music: Walter Scharf
Production Designer: Alan Manser
Editor: Corky Ehlers

Feldman	TOM BOSLEY
Lou Ribin	DAVID DUKES
Florence	TOVAH FELDSHUH
Sonya Levin	LAUREN FROST
Rose	JANET MARGOLIN
Gina	STACEY NELKIN
Vinnie	TED WASS
Connie	STEPHANIE ZIMBALIST
Bessie	CHARLOTTE RAE
Mrs. Levin	ERICA YOHN
Mr. Levin	MILTON SELZER
Max Levin	MICHAEL MULLINS
Roselli	JEROME GUARDINO
Loretta	VALERIE LANDSBURG
Mo Pincus	LARRY GELMAN

Ian Saynor and Katharine Hepburn in **THE CORN IS GREEN (1979)**

Frieda LIN SHAYE
Edith JUDITH MARIE
BERGAN

and: Bart Burns, Sean Roche, Olivia Barash, Rhoda Gemignani, Eric Mason, Milt Oberman, Dave Shelley, Wil Albert, Mario Gallo, Lilah McCarthy, Scott Mulhern, John O'Connell, Constance Pfeifer, Bill Sorrells, Naomi Stevens, Pamela Toll, Ron Vernan, Patrick Wright

A dramatic retelling of the 1911 holocaust in which 146 workers died in New York's garment district and ultimately laid the groundwork for the establishment of the ILGWU. The real-life catastrophe took a mere eleven minutes; the movie, with its soap opera plots and assorted inaccuracies (like several key references by some of the ladies to the popularity of Charlie Chaplin who at the time was totally unknown and did not make his first American movie until three years later), took two agonizing hours to unreel. Three technical Emmy Award nominations went to *The Triangle Factory Fire Scandal,* which won in the category of Outstanding Achievement in Hairstyling.

0948
THE GIRLS IN THE OFFICE
2/2/79 ABC Circle Films (2 hours)

Producer: Barry Oringer
Director: Ted Post
Teleplay: Richard Danus
From the book by Jack Olsen
Photography: Andrew Costikyan
Music: John Parker
Production Design: Steven P. Sardanis
Editor: Tom Stevens

Rita Massaro SUSAN SAINT
JAMES
Lee Rawlins BARBARA EDEN
Mike Holden TONY ROBERTS
Karen Heineman ROBYN DOUGLASS
Tracy Beaumont PENNY PEYSER
Beau Galloway JOE PENNY
Bill Pearson JONATHAN
GOLDSMITH
Ben Nayfak DAVID WAYNE

and: Merrill L. Conway, Jacki Morrison, Hugh Gorian, Nik Hagler, John Conlee, Don Dalesandro, Gaetana Campbell, Yvonne McCord, David Wurst

A romantic comedy about four women employees of an ultra-modern Houston department store who discover that they must choose between love and success.

0949
MR. HORN
2/3, 2/5/79 Lorimar Productions (4 hours)

Executive Producer: Lee Rich
Producer: Robert L. Jacks
Director: Jack Starrett
Teleplay: William Goldman
Photography: Jorge Stahl, Jr.
Music: Jerry Fielding
Art Director: Agustine Ytuarte
Editor: Michael McCroskey

Tom Horn DAVID
CARRADINE
Al Sieber RICHARD
WIDMARK
Ernestina Crawford KAREN BLACK
Sheriff Ed Smalley RICHARD MASUR
Lt. Henry Lawton CLAY TANNER
John Noble PAT McCORMICK
Gen. George Crook JACK STARRETT
Marshal Joe LeFlors JOHN DURREN
Capt. Emmet Crawford JEREMY SLATE
Geronimo ENRIQUE LUCERO

David Carradine and Enrique Lucero in MR. HORN (1979)

Gen. Nelson Miles STAFFORD
MORGAN
Mr. Nickell DON COLLIER
Mickey Free LEWIS JAMES
OLIVER

and: George Reynolds, William Smith, Jr., Ian McLean, Regino Herrera, Noye Murayama, Romero Rameriz, Alexis Jacks, Marilyn Starr, Dan Vadis, Sunshine Parker, Michael Tanner, Seamon Glass, Lou Cutell, Blackie Dammett, Billy Murphy, Tiger Williams, John Dayton, John Malloy, John Alderman, Leon Fredericks, James Steward, Jon Ian Jacobs

A sprawling Western saga based on the legend of frontier folk hero Tom Horn, his role in the trackdown of Geronimo in the 1880s with his mentor and pal Al Sieber, the fabled Indian scout, his later days as a Pinkerton detective and the way he was used by both sides in turn-of-the-century cattle wars, leading to his tragic death.

Richard Widmark in MR. HORN (1979)

0950
FLATBED ANNIE & SWEETIEPIE: LADY TRUCKERS
2/10/79 Moonlight Productions Inc./Filmways (2 hours)

Producer: Frank von Zerneck
Director: Robert Greenwald
Teleplay: Robie Robinson
Photography: William K. Jurgensen
Music: Don Peake
Art Director: Jack Bissell
Editor: Jack Tucker

Flatbed Annie	ANNIE POTTS
C. W. Douglas	HARRY DEAN STANTON
Ginny LaRosa ("Sweetiepie")	KIM DARBY
Uncle Wally	ARTHUR GODFREY
Jack LaRosa	FRED WILLARD
Deputy Miller	BILLY CARTER
Farner	RORY CALHOUN
Munroe	AVERY SCHREIBER
Mr. Murray	RANCE HOWARD
Georgina	JULIE MANNIX
Al	DON PIKE
Nick	ROBERT HERRON
Hospital Attendant	LORNA THAYER

Two young women join forces to save an expensive trucking rig from the repossessor and keep it out of the clutches of hijackers.

0951
ELVIS
2/11/79 Dick Clark Productions (3 hours)

Executive Producer: Dick Clark
Producer: Anthony Lawrence
Associate Producer: James Ritz
Director: John Carpenter
Teleplay: Anthony Lawrence
Photography: Donald M. Morgan
Music: Joe Renzetti
Elvis' Vocals Sung by Ronnie McDowell
Art Directors: Tracy Bousman and James Newport
Editor: Tom Walls

Elvis Presley	KURT RUSSELL
Gladys Presley	SHELLEY WINTERS
Vernon Presley	BING RUSSELL
Red West	ROBERT GRAY
Col. Tom Parker	PAT HINGLE
Priscilla Presley	SEASON HUBLEY
Bonnie	MELODY ANDERSON
D. C. Fontana	ED BEGLEY, JR.
Scotty	JAMES CANNING
Sam Phillips	CHARLES CYPHERS
Jim Denny	PETER HOBBS
Sonny West	LES LANNOM
Bill Black	ELLIOTT STREET
Ed Sullivan	WILL JORDAN
Joe Esposito	JOE MANTEGNA
Hank Snow	GALEN THOMPSON
Marion	ELLEN TRAVOLTA
Natalie Wood	ABI YOUNG
Lisa Marie Presley	FELICIA FENSKE
Elvis as a boy	RANDY GRAY
Grandma	MEG WYLIE
Himself	CHARLIE HODGE

and: Nora Boland, Robert Christopher, Mark Dennis, William Angus Erwin, Mario Gallo, Larry Geller, Del Hinkley, Jim Greenleaf, Ted Lehman, Jack McCulloch, Larry Pennell, Ed Ruffalo, Ken Smolka, David Hunt Stafford, Dennis Stewart, Dick Young

An affectionate biography of Presley from his boyhood through his spectacular rise to fame and ending with the Las Vegas nightclub appearance in 1969 that began Elvis' resurgence and his final epoch. Kurt Russell, cinematographer Donald M. Morgan, and makeup specialist Marvin G. Westmore each won an Emmy Award nomination.

0952
CRISIS IN MID-AIR
2/13/79 CBS Entertainment (2 hours)

Producer: Roger Lewis
Director: Walter Grauman
Teleplay: Sean Baine
Photography: John M. Nicholaus
Music: Robert Drasnin
Art Director: Albert Heschong
Editor: Anthony DiMarco

Nick Culver	GEORGE PEPPARD
Betsy Culver	KAREN GRASSLE
Tim Donovan	DESI ARNAZ, JR.
Frank Piovano	MICHAEL CONSTANTINE
Brian Haley	GREG MORRIS
Billy Coleman	FABIAN FORTE
Brad Mullins	DANA ELCAR
Bret Loebner	ALAN FUDGE
Jenny Sterling	DENISE DuBARRY
Dr. Denvers	MARTIN MILNER
Adam Travis	DON MURRAY
Attorney	JAMES RAY
Maggie Johnson	MARGARET IMPERT
Pope	CHIP LUCIA
Dowdell	BRIAN FARRELL

and: James Blendick, Hank Rolike, Cynthia Pepper, Sandra Giles, Grett Dunham, William Dozier, Steve Eastin

A drama involving an aging air traffic controller who is haunted by a recent mid-air collision for which an investigator is trying to hold him responsible.

0953
MURDER BY NATURAL CAUSES
2/17/79 Richard Levinson/William Link Productions (2 hours)

Executive Producers: Richard Levinson and William Link

Producer: Robert A. Papazian
Director: Robert Day
Teleplay: Richard Levinson and William Link
Photography: Jack Swain
Music: Dick DeBenedictis
Art Director: Richard Y. Haman
Editor: Frank Morriss

Arthur Sinclair	HAL HOLBROOK
Allison Sinclair	KATHERINE ROSS
George Brubaker	RICHARD ANDERSON
Gil Weston	BARRY BOSTWICK
Marty Chambers	BILL FIORE
Eddie	PHIL LEEDS
Helen Carrington	EVE McVEAGH
Maid	JEFF DONNELL
Garden Party Hostess	MAIDA SEVERN
Director	LLOYD McLINN
Television Actress	VICTORIA CARROLL
Technician	JESSICA RAINS

and: Judith Marie Bergan, Vivian Brown, Rosanna Huffman, Dany Marrou, Margery Nelson

An elaborate mystery involving a famous mentalist, his unfaithful wife who is trying literally to scare him to death, the best friend of the family, and the wife's ham-actor lover—not only an intriguing who (or whether) dunnit but also a literate, adult dramatic puzzle with an endless series of twists.

0954
SILENT VICTORY: THE KITTY O'NEIL STORY
2/24/79 The Channing-Debin-Locke Company
(2 hours)

Executive Producers: David Debin and Duffy Hambleton
Producer: R. J. Louis
Associate Producer: Judith Gill
Director: Lou Antonio
Teleplay: Steven Gethers
Photography: Michel Hugo
Music: Jimmie Haskell
Art Director: W. Stewart Campbell
Stunt Coordinator and Technical Advisor: Duffy Hambleton
Editor: Jerrold Ludwig

Kitty O'Neil	STOCKARD CHANNING
Duffy Hambleton	JAMES FARENTINO
Mrs. O'Neil	COLLEEN DEWHURST
Tom Buchanan	EDWARD ALBERT
Mr. O'Neil	BRIAN DENNEHY
Charlie	JIM ANTONIO
Himself	DR. SAMMY LEE
Accountant	RICHARD BALIN
Interviewer	HILDY BROOKS
Warren Porter	GEORGE PETRIE
Doctor	NOBEL WILLINGHAM
Orchestra Leader	LISA BLAKE RICHARDS
Kitty (age 2–4)	ANGELIQUE ANTONIO
Kitty (age 8–10)	ELKIN ANTONIO

and: Robby Weaver, Norman Field, Ken Kane, Dick Sondergard, Sybil Scotford, George Boyd, Janice Karman, Mel Gallagher, Jim Normandin, Gene Tyburn, George Wilbern, Terry Kingsley, Janet Winter, Franco Spolar, Jack Lucarelli

The real-life account of a deaf girl who overcomes her handicap to become one of Hollywood's top stuntwomen and holder of the women's world land-speed record in a rocket-powered racing car. Colleen Dew-

hurst was Emmy Award-nominated as Outstanding Supporting Actress, and Lou Antonio was nominated as Outstanding Director.

0955
WOMEN AT WEST POINT
2/27/79 Green/Epstein Production-Alan Sacks
Production (2 hours)

Executive Producers: Jim Green and Allen Epstein
Producer: Alan Sacks
Director: Vincent Sherman
Teleplay: Ann Marcus and Ellis Marcus
From a story by Juleen Compton
Photography: Sol Negrin
Music: Charles Bernstein
Art Director: Gene Rudolph
Editor: Grant Hoag

Jennifer Scott	LINDA PURL
Molly Dahl	LESLIE ACKERMAN
J. J. Palfrey	JAMESON PARKER
Doug Davidson	ANDREW STEVENS
Pete Greenway	EDWARD EDWARDS
Commandant	BERNARD BARROW
Bea Scott	JOAN KAYE
Maj. James Kirk	PAUL GLEASON
Vincent Cavelli	VICTOR BEVINE
Tom Fenton	JACK BLESSING
Harvey Hagan	LEE TOOMBS
Liz Grote	CHERYL FRANCIS
Susan Zachary	MICHELLE RAUM
Russell Baker	ROBERT TOWNSEND
Ebberly	PETER ARMSTRONG
Mrs. Dahl	SHEILA WALSH
Colonel Dahl	JIM MITCHELL
Ms. Atwood	ANNE BYRNE HOFFMAN

A fictionalized drama about the first women to enter the U.S. Military Academy in 1976 and the reactions they faced. Filmed entirely at West Point.

Kurt Russell in ELVIS (1979)

0956
THE ORDEAL OF PATTY HEARST
3/4/79 Finnegan Associates/David Paradine
Television, Inc. (3 hrs.)

Executive Producer: Marvin Minoff
Producer: William Finnegan
Associate Producer: Pat Finnegan
Director: Paul Wendkos
Teleplay: Adrian Spies
Photography: Hector Figuera
Music: John Rubinstein
Art Director: Joe Aubel
Technical Advisor: Charles Bates
Editor: Ken Zemke

Charles Bates	DENNIS WEAVER
Patty Hearst	LISA EILBACHER
Steven Weed	DAVID HASKELL
Randolph Hearst	STEPHEN ELLIOTT
Catherine Hearst	DOLORES SUTTON
Cinque	FELTON PERRY
Gabi	TISA FARROW
Pato	JONATHAN BANKS
Gelina	ANNE DeSALVO
Carmella	KATHRYN BUTTERFIELD
Fahizah	KAREN LANDRY
Lucy Brawley	NANCY WOLFE
Cujo	BRENDAN BURNS

and: Walker Edmiston, Roy Poole, Redmond Gleeson, Ric Mancini

The Patricia Hearst story—through the eyes of FBI Special Agent Charles Bates—from her abduction on February 4, 1974, until her capture nineteen months later.

0957
JENNIFER: A WOMAN'S STORY
3/5/79 Marble Arch Productions (2 hours)

Executive Producer: Martin Starger
Producer: Doris Quinlan
Director: Guy Green
Teleplay: Richard Gregson
Photography: Michel Hugo
Music: William Goldstein
Art Director: Ray Beal
Editor: Samuel E. Beetley

Jennifer Prince	ELIZABETH MONTGOMERY
Don Prince	BRADFORD DILLMAN
Lee Devlin	SCOTT HYLANDS
George Black	JAMES BOOTH
Dr. Robin Symon	ROBIN GAMMELL
Jack Dent	MICHAEL GOODWIN
Prof. Eric Wohlstrom	JOHN BEAL
Kay	DORIS ROBERTS
Joan Russell	KATE MULGREW
Dick Leonard	ARTHUR FRANZ
Neil Turner	BASIL HOFFMAN

and: Dennis Dimster, Tracey Gold, Ted Gehring, Hope Clarke, Momo Yashima, James Reynolds, Loel Lawrence, Fil Formicola, Whitney Hall, Ken Hill, Woody Skaggs

The widow of a wealthy shipbuilder tries to hold onto his business and becomes involved with boardroom intrigue in her bitter struggle to maintain control of the company. The British TV series "The Foundation" was the basis of this movie.

0958
GOLD OF THE AMAZON WOMEN
3/6/79 MI-KA Productions, Inc. (2 hours)

Executive Producer: Stanley Ralph Ross
Producer: Alfred Leone
Director: Mark L. Lester
Teleplay: Sue Donen
Photography: David Quaid
Music: Gil Melle
Art Director: Karl Hueglin
Editor: Michael A. Luciano

Tom Jensen	BO SVENSON
Queen Na-Eela	ANITA EKBERG
Clarence Blasko	DONALD PLEASENCE
Luis Rodriguez	RICHARD ROMANUS
Noboro	ROBERT MINOR
Reina	MAGGIE JEAN SMITH
Taimi	BOND GIDEON
Oriana	SUSAN E. MILLER
Lee-Leeo	YASMINE
Polani	MARY PETERS
Heintz Ginther	IAN EDWARD
Barari	SARITA BUTTERFIELD
Jorn Abramson	CHARLES REYNOLDS

and: John Anthony Sarno, Carl Low, Fred Berkoff, Joseph Gilbert, Robert Ross

Two fortune hunters searching for treasure in the South American jungles stumble upon a primitive society of statuesque women, descendants of a legendar_

Blythe Danner and Michael Moriarty in TOO FAR TO GO (1979)

warrior tribe, who follow the pair back to present-day Manhattan. Anita Ekberg, screen sex queen of the 1950s, returned to moviemaking in this one after many years out of the limelight.

0959
THE CHILD STEALER
3/9/79 The Production Company/Columbia Pictures (2 hours)

Executive Producers: Mike Wise and Franklin R. Levy
Producer: Hugh Benson
Director: Mel Damski
Teleplay: Sue Milburn
Photography: Robert Moreno
Music: Jimmie Haskell
Art Director: Ross Bellah
Editor: John Farrell

David Rodman	BEAU BRIDGES
Jan Rodman	BLAIR BROWN
Karen	CRISTINA RAINES
Jack Farnham	DAVID GROH
Lew Beck	EUGENE ROCHE
Mrs. Benson	MARJ DUSAY
Andrea Rodman	LAURI HENDLER
Pam Rodman	TRACEY GOLD
Hoskins	LEE WALLACE
Gersh	PHILLIP R. ALLEN
Frank Demas	ALAN FUDGE
Dan Miller	WILLIAM BRYANT
Houghton	ROBERT DoQUI
Jordan	ARTHUR A. ROSENBERG

A young mother battles to get her children back after her ex-husband kidnaps them and the law won't help her in her efforts.

0960
TOO FAR TO GO
3/12/79 Sea Cliff Productions (2 hours)

Executive Producer: Robert Geller
Producer: Chiz Schultz
Associate Producer: David Kappes
Director: Fielder Cook
Teleplay: William Hanley
Based on the short stories by John Updike
Photography: Walter Lassally
Music: Elizabeth Swados
Art Director: Leon Munier
Editor: Eric Albertson

Richard Maple	MICHAEL MORIARTY
Joan Barlow Maple	BLYTHE DANNER
Rebecca Kuehn	GLENN CLOSE
Jack Dennis	KEN KERCHEVAL
Henry Mills	JOSEF SOMMER
Marion Sales	KATHRYN WALKER
Judith Maple (age 19)	DORAN CLARK
Judith Maple (age 14)	LORI LAUGHLIN
Richie Maple (age 17)	TIM HOLCOMB
Richie Maple (age 12)	MARK MORING
John Maple (age 15)	ADAM STORKE
John Maple (age 10)	JASON SCOTT
Margaret (Bean) Maple (age 13)	MARGARET SCHULTZ
Margaret (Bean) Maple (age 8)	PATTI DAWSON
Man at Pool	ROBERT GELLER

and: Thomas Hill, Alice Beardsley, Mitch McGuire, Paul Milikin, John C. Becher, Reed Birney, John Buckwalter, Anne Martin

An incisive study of the dissolution of a twenty-year marriage, from seventeen John Updike stories that were published in *The New Yorker* beginning in 1956

and later in *Harper's*, *The Atlantic Monthly*, *Playboy* and others.

0961
THE CRACKER FACTORY
3/16/79 Roger Gimbel Productions/EMI Television (2 hours)

Executive Producers: Roger Gimbel and Tony Converse
Producer: Richard Shapiro
Associate Producer: John A. Martinelli
Director: Burt Brinckerhoff
Teleplay: Richard Shapiro
Based on the novel by Joyce Rebeta-Burditt
Photography: Michel Hugo
Music: Billy Goldenberg
Art Director: Alexander A. Mayer
Editor: John A. Martinelli

Cassie Barrett	NATALIE WOOD
Dr. Edwin Alexander	PERRY KING
Charlie Barrett	PETER HASKELL
Clara	SHELLEY LONG
Helen	VIVIAN BLAINE
Eleanor	MARIAN MERCER
Tinkerbell	JULIET MILLS
Father Dunhill	JOHN HARKINS
Alice	BARBARA TARBUCK
Greg	SHANE BUTTERWORTH
Steven	DAVID COMFORT
Jenny	TONYA CROWE
Bobby	ROBERT PERAULT
Gloria	BEBE DRAKE-HOOKS
Dalton	ELSA RAVEN
Pomeroy	PEGGY REA

and: Art Evans, Donald Hotton, Sidney Lassick, Delia Salvi

This film depicts the problems of a suburban housewife, suffering from fits of depression and alcoholism, and her stay in a psychiatric center after a feeble suicide attempt.

0962
WILLA
3/17/79 GJL Productions Inc./Dove Inc. (2 hours)

Executive Producer: Jerry Leider
Producers: Michael Viner and Burt Nodella
Directors: Joan Darling and Claudio Guzman
Teleplay: Carmen Culver
Photography: Matthew F. Leonetti
Music: John Barry
Special songs written and sung by Susie Allanson, Keith Carradine, The Incredible Bongo Band, Merle Kilgore, Jerry Naylor, The Bellamy Brothers, Jimmy Witherspoon and Hank Williams, Jr.
Production Designer: C. E. Guzman
Editor: Patrick Kennedy

Willa Barnes	DEBORAH RAFFIN
Joe Welch	CLU GULAGER
Darla Jean	CLORIS LEACHMAN
Mae	DIANE LADD
Mrs. Stanch	NANCY MARCHAND
Eunice	MARY WICKES
Phil	BOB SEAGREN
Virgil	JOHN AMOS
Hank	HANK WILLIAMS, JR.
Buck	GARY BISIG
Junior	GARY GRUBBS
Mrs. Beaudry	FREDDYE CHAPMAN

and: Corey Feldman, Megan Jeffers, Tommy Aguilar, Trudy Marshall, Piccola Martin, Four Scott

A truck-stop waitress, determined to make a better life for her young children after being abandoned by her husband, leaves hash-slinging behind her to embark on a new career as a trucker in the rig her late father used to drive.

0963
THE JERICHO MILE
3/18/79 ABC Circle Film (2 hours)

Producer: Tim Zimmerman
Director: Michael Mann
Teleplay: Patrick J. Nolan and Michael Mann
From a story by Patrick J. Nolan
Photography: Rexford Metz
Music: Jimmie Haskell
Additional music: James Di Pasquale
Art Director: Stephen Berger
Editor: Arthur Schmidt

Rain Murphy	PETER STRAUSS
R. C. Stiles	RICHARD LAWSON
Cotton Crown	ROGER E. MOSLEY
Dr. D	BRIAN DENNEHY
Warden Earl Gulliver	BILLY GREEN BUSH
Jerry Beloit	ED LAUTER
Dr. Bill Janowski	GEOFFREY LEWIS
Wylene	BEVERLY TODD
OAU Chairman	WILLIAM PRINCE
Rubio	MIGUEL PINERO
Joker Gibb	RICHARD MOLL
OAU Official	EDMUND PENNEY
Jimmy-Jack	BURTON GILLIAM
Brother Lateef	JI-TU CUMBUKA
Moo-Moo	WILMORE THOMAS

and: LeRoy Haskins, Gaddis Franklin, Jr., John E. Jackson, Robert L. Jones, Gilbert Tewsbury, Benny L. Rapisura, Eluterio Rodarte, Steven White, Jimmy Coppola, Terry Lee Dawson, Joe Campoy

A runner, serving a life sentence at Folsom Prison, works at becoming the world's fastest miler and wins a chance to compete for a spot on the Olympic team. Peter Strauss won the Emmy Award for his work in this film which also was nominated as the year's Outstanding Drama. Patrick Nolan and Michael Mann received Emmy Awards for their teleplay as did editor Arthur Schmidt.

0964
FAST FRIENDS
3/19/79 Columbia Pictures TV (2 hours)

Executive Producers: Jed Green and Allen Epstein
Producer: Sandra Harmon
Director: Steven Hilliard Stern
Teleplay: Sandra Harmon
Photography: Howard R. Schwartz
Music: Donald Pearce
Art Directors: Ross Bellah and Zoltan Muller
Editor: Kurt Hirschler

Diana Hayward	CARRIE SNODGRESS
Deke Edwards	DICK SHAWN
Connie Burton	EDIE ADAMS
Bernie	JED ALLAN
Sylvia	VIVIAN BLAINE
Marcy	DENISE DuBARRY
Pat McKenna	TOM HALLICK
Amy	ELAYNE HEILVEIL
Matt Morgan	DAVID LETTERMAN
David York	MICHAEL PARKS
Jenny Roman	SUSAN HELDFOND
Susan	MACKENZIE PHILLIPS
Josh	MEENO PELUCE

Alan Berkowitz   BRUCE STIDHAM
Bill Owens   PAT PROFT

and: Joseph Hardin, Mitch Hara, Russ Marin, Michael Payne, Roscoe Born, Joel Lawrence

A young divorcée struggles to provide for her young son and make a new life for herself in the backstage jungle of a TV talk show, becoming fast friends with its head writer whose job is to see that its host, a woman-chasing egomaniac, stays at the top of the ratings.

0965
NO OTHER LOVE
3/24/79 Tisch/Avnet Productions, Inc. (2 hours)

Producers: Steve Tisch and Jon Avnet
Director: Richard Pearce
Teleplay: Edwin Francis Kaplan
Photography: David Myers
Music: Charles Gross
Art Director: Jack DeGovia
Editors: Gary Griffin and Bill Yahrus

Andrew Madison   RICHARD THOMAS
Janet Michaels   JULIE KAVNER
Pat Hollister   FRANCES LEE McCAIN
Les Hollister   NORMAN ALDEN
Jean Michaels   ELIZABETH ALLEN
DeFranco   M. EMMET WALSH
David Michaels   ROBERT LOGGIA
Bruce Michaels   SCOTT JACOBY
Mrs. Walker   MARILYN COLEMAN
Neil   NEIL COOPER
Brian   BILLY DRAGO
Richard   BRAD GORMAN
Justice of the Peace   JOHN D. GOWAN
Mrs. Oberman   CYNTHIA ANNE HOPPENFELD

and: Corkie Harris, Doris Hess, Julie Krauss, Sylvia Sage, John O'Leary, Glenn Robards, Woody Skaggs, Mark Taylor

A drama about a young, marginally retarded girl and boy who meet, plan to marry, and convince the world that they are entitled to a life of their own—despite the attempts by the girl's parents to separate them.

0966
SOONER OR LATER
3/25/79 Laughing Willow Co. Inc./NBC-TV (2 hours)

Producer: Carole Hart
Director: Bruce Hart
Teleplay: Carole and Bruce Hart
Photography: Edward R. Brown
Music: Stephen Lawrence
Songs by Stephen Lawrence and Bruce Hart
Art Director: Stephen Hendrickson
Editors: Eric Albertson and Patrick McMahon

Jessie Walters   DENISE MILLER
Michael Skye   REX SMITH
Lois Walters   BARBARA FELDON
Bob Walters   JUDD HIRSCH
Grandma   LILIA SKALA
Eddie Nova   MOREY AMSTERDAM
Cosmetic Saleslady   VIVIAN BLAINE
Teacher   LYNN REDGRAVE
Caroline   MARY BETH MANNING

and: Mari Danziger, Edward Green, Paul Mones, Grace Davies, Tara King, Cheryl D. Francis, Emily Bindiger, Mark Cunningham, Lenny Mancuso, Egleton Leroy Woodside, Jr.

An anxious thirteen-year-old girl dreams of being a grown-up and tries to make herself look older in order to attract the rock idol she's fallen for.

0967
THE DARKER SIDE OF TERROR
4/3/79 Shaner/Ramrus Production-Bob Banner Associates (2 hours)

Executive Producer: Bob Banner
Producers: Al Ramrus and John Herman Shaner
Associate Producer: Clyde Phillips
Director: Gus Trikonis
Teleplay: Al Ramrus and John Herman Shaner
Photography: Donald M. Morgan
Music: Paul Chihara
Art Director: William Sandell
Editor: Ann Mills

Prof. Paul Corwin/The Clone   ROBERT FORSTER
Margaret Corwin   ADRIENNE BARBEAU
Professor Meredith   RAY MILLAND
Prof. Sidney Hillstrom   DAVID SHEINER
Lieut. Merholz   JOHN LEHNE
Ann Sweeney   DENISE DuBARRY
Roger   JACK DeMAVE
Ed Linnick   THOMAS BELLIN
Jenny   HEATHER HOBBS
Watchman   EDDIE QUILLAN

A psychological thriller about a research biologist who, angered when an associate is given a position over him based on stolen research findings, agrees to assist his former professor in a cloning experiment in which a duplicate of himself is created—and which then, with a mind and will of its own, falls in love with the biologist's wife.

0968
THE SEEDING OF SARAH BURNS
4/7/79 Michael Klein Productions (2 hours)

Executive Producer: Michael Klein
Producer: Robert A. Papazian
Director: Sandor Stern
Teleplay: Sandor Stern
From a story by Marc Ray and Sandor Stern
Photography: William Cronjager
Music: Jimmie Haskell
Song: "Open A Window (Unlock the Door)" by Will Jennings and Richard Kerr
Sung by Richard Kerr
Art Director: Elizabeth Bousman
Editor: Ina Massari

Sarah Burns   KAY LENZ
Dr. Samuel Melman   MARTIN BALSAM
Karen Lovell   CASSIE YATES
Alex Lovell   CHARLES SIEBERT
Tim   CLIFF DeYOUNG
Mrs. Angstrom   VIRGINIA KISER
Roger Deems   BRYAN GORDON
Linda   CAITLIN O'HEANEY
Terri   JORDAN MICHALS
Bonnie   MARGARET LADD
Jill   RUTH COX
Penny   PEGGY LEE BRENNAN
Flora   MAXINE STUART

and: John Dennis, Catherine Hickland, Judy Reich, Jessica Davis, Lin Shaye, Donna Raye, Judy Kerr

A young woman decides to volunteer for a proposed embryo transplant to help a couple who are unable to have a child, and then has second thoughts about giving up the baby.

0969
THE LEGEND OF THE GOLDEN GUN
4/10/79 A Bennett-Katleman Production/Columbia Pictures (2 hours)

Executive Producers: Harve Bennett and Harris Katleman
Producer: B. W. Sandefeur
Director: Alan J. Levi
Teleplay: James D. Parriott
Photography: Gerald Perry Finnerman
Music: Jerrold Immel
Art Directors: Ross Bellah and Robert Peterson
Editor: Robert F. Shugrue

John Colton   JEFFREY OSTERHAGE
Book (Joshua Brown)   CARL FRANKLIN
Jim Hammer   HAL HOLBROOK
General Custer   KEIR DULLEA
William Quantrill   ROBERT DAVI
Maggie Oakley   MICHELLE CAREY
Jake Powell   JOHN McLIAM
Sara Powell   ELISSA LEEDS
Judge Harrison Harding   R. G. ARMSTRONG
Buffalo Bill   R. L. TOLBERT
William Ford   WILLIAM BRYANT
Captain Marks   J. BRIAN PIZER
Sturges   REX HOLMAN
Photographer   MICHAEL YAMAHA

and: Budge Taylor, Walt Davis, Michael Yama, David Holbrook

This engaging Western, a pilot for a prospective series and an homage to the cowboy movies of yore, has a handsome, dazzlingly blond young farmer team up with a Bible-quoting runaway slave to track down the infamous Quantrill. He learns how to shoot from a legendary gunslinger who convinces him to be a fighter for law and justice and save the seventh bullet in his special gun for evil. "Imagine 'Star Wars' as a Western" was the publicity ploy for this one, which envoked the names of the greats of the Old West and had General Custer himself turning up with a twinkle in his eye, a corn-cob pipe in his mouth, and, like a later military figure, promising Sitting Bull: "I shall return."

0970
LIKE NORMAL PEOPLE
4/13/79 Christiana Productions/20th Century-Fox (2 hours)

Producer: Joanna Lee
Associate Producer: Donie Nelson
Director: Harvey Hart
Teleplay: Joanna Lee
Based on the book by Robert Meyers
Photography: Charles F. Wheeler
Music: John Addison
Art Director: Stan Jolley
Editor: Harry Keller

Roger Meyers   SHAUN CASSIDY
Virginia Rae Hensler   LINDA PURL
Bill Stein   ZALMAN KING
Robert Meyers, Jr.   JAMES KEACH
Robert Meyers   MICHAEL McGUIRE
Roz Meyers   HOPE LANGE
Aunt Kate   MAUREEN ARTHUR
Lloyd Davis   JACK MURDOCK
Roger (age 11)   JIMMY GATHERUM
Grandma Teresa   DOREEN LANG
Dorothy   McKEE ANDERSON
Billie   MIRIAM BYRD NETHERY

and: Carmen Zapata, Fritzi Burr, Rhea Pearlman, Walter Brooke, Frankie Kabott, Dick Billingsley, Dago Dimster, Danny Williams, Ken Medlock, Michael Hughes, Fred D. Scott, Christopher Ciampa, Julie Anne Haddock

Carol Burnett and Ned Beatty in FRIENDLY FIRE (1979)

This fact-based drama about a pair of mentally retarded young adults who face angry resistance when they decide to marry is virtually identical to the TV movie *No Other Love* which premiered three weeks earlier. Rock singer and teen idol Shaun Cassidy made his dramatic acting debut in this film.

0971
THE BILLION DOLLAR THREAT
4/15/79 David Gerber Productions/Columbia Pictures (2 hours)

Executive Producer: David Gerber
Producer: Jay Daniel
Director: Barry Shear
Teleplay: Jimmy Sangster
Photography: Jack Woolf
Music: Richard Shores
Art Directors: Ross Bellah and Dale Hennessy
Special Effects: Joe Unsinn
Editors: Mel Shapiro and Robbie L. Shapiro

Robert Sands	DALE ROBINETTE
Miles Larson	RALPH BELLAMY
Ely	KEENAN WYNN
Horatio Black	PATRICK MACNEE
Benjamin	ROBERT W. TESSIER
Holly	BETH SPECHT
Ivy	KAREN SPECHT
Marcia Buttercup	RONNIE CAROL
Harold Darling	STEPHEN KEEP
Harry	WILLIAM BRYANT
Ming	MARIANNE MARKS
Charlie	READ MORGAN

and: Harold Sakata, Walt Davis, Jason Corbett, Ned Wilson, Robert Lone, Fil Formicola, Bob Hastings, Than Wyenn, Davis Roberts, Read Morgan, Elven Havard, Cliff Carnell, George Spicer, Seth Foster

A James Bondish superspy is assigned to thwart the devious plans of a master agent who is threatening to destroy the planet unless he is paid one billion dollars within forty-eight hours. This lighthearted thriller was the pilot for a proposed series.

0972
TRANSPLANT
4/17/79 Time-Life Television (2 hours)

Executive Producer: David Susskind
Producer: Douglas Benton
Director: William A. Graham
Teleplay: John Gay
Based on the book by Philip Dossick
Photography: Jorden Cronenweth
Music: Fred Karlin
Art Director: Julian Sacks
Editor: Greyfox

John Hurley	KEVIN DOBSON
Dr. Kroner	GRANVILLE VAN DUSEN
Jim Clark	RONNY COX
Noreen	BIBI BESCH
Ann Hurley	MELINDA DILLON
Miss Mills	JOAN LANCASTER
Janice Hurley	HELEN HUNT
Mrs. Wiggins	DEE CROXTON
Gladys	BARI SILVERN
Dr. Scofield	WOODY ENEY
Jean Clark	LINDA ALPER
Joanie Hurley	MELISSA HOWARD
Sylvia	MELINDA CORDELL
Dr. Samuels	DAVID BYRD
Barbara	KATHLEEN DOYLE
Boris	ORVILLE SHERMAN
Mildred	PATIENCE CLEVELAND
Dr. Sofier	DAVID DARRELL

and: Robina Suwol, Carole H. Field, Frank Downing, Michael O'Dwyer, Stephen Liss, Lindy Davis

A fact-based story of a hard-driving young executive who rebels against his failing heart and undergoes a risky transplant.

0973
FRIENDLY FIRE
4/22/79 Marble Arch Productions (3 hours)

Executive Producer: Martin Starger
Producers: Philip Barry and Fay Kanin
Director: David Greene
Teleplay: Fay Kanin
Based on the book and *New Yorker* article by C. D. B. Bryan
Photography: Harry May
Music: Leonard Rosenman
Art Directors: Lawrence G. Paull and Kirk Axtel
Editor: Michael Economou

Peg Mullen	CAROL BURNETT
Gene Mullen	NED BEATTY
C. D. B. Bryan	SAM WATERSTON
Michael Mullen	DENNIS ERDMAN
John Mullen	TIMOTHY HUTTON
Pat Mullen	FANNY SPIES
Mary Mullen	SHERRY HURSEY
Father Shimon	MICHAEL FLANAGAN
Huddleston	HILLY HICKS
Col. Schindler	WILLIAM JORDAN
Col. Georgi	VERNON WEDDLE
Sgt. Fitzgerald	JACK RADER
Alan Hulting	ROBERT WAHLER
Young Hamilton	DAVID KEITH
Dietrich	BERNARD BEHRENS
Hamilton	FORD RAINEY
Ralph Jenner	PHILLIP R. ALLEN

and: Virginia Kiser, Macon McCalman, Joe Lowry, Mark Taylor, Jenny Sullivan, Dan Shore, Bob Boyles, Jerry Hardin, Craig Shreeve, Joe Medalis, Norman Bartold, Paul Baxley, Kevin Hooks, Jorge Cervera, Jr., Charles Cyphers, William Bogert, Woody Eney, Mary Gregory, Nicholas Coster, Henry Brown, Marcia Shepard, Michael Bond, Steve Benedict, Charles Bracy, Mark Montgomery, Warren Munson, Steve Bonino, John Hilner, Cosie Costa, Hank Ross, Wyatt Knight, Kevin Geer, Frank Bruno, Demetre Phillips

A drama about a rural American couple who become increasingly embittered as they cope with governmental indifference in their search for the truth behind the death of their son in Vietnam—killed by friendly fire from American artillery. Based on the true story of war activist Peg Mullen. Emmy Awards: Outstanding Drama, Best Director (David Greene), Best Music Score (Leonard Rosenman), Outstanding Film Sound Editing (William H. Wistrom). Carol Burnett and Ned Beatty also were nominated, as was writer Fay Kanin.

0974
SANCTUARY OF FEAR
4/23/79 Marble Arch Productions (2 hours)
(subsequently titled *The Girl in the Park*)

Executive Producer: Martin Starger
Producer: Philip Barry
Director: John Llewellyn Moxey
Teleplay: Don Mankiewicz and Gordon Cotler
Based on the novel *Father Brown, Detective* by G. K. Chesterton
Photography: Ronald Lautore
Music: Jack Elliott and Allyn Ferguson
Art Director: Robert Gundlach
Editor: John Wright

Father Brown	BARNARD HUGHES
Carol Bain	KAY LENZ
Lt. Bellamy	MICHAEL McGUIRE
Monsignor Kerrigan	GEORGE HEARN
Father Wembley	ROBERT SCHENKKAN
Jack Coburn	DAVID RASCHE
Judge Potter	FRED GWYNNE
Mrs. Glidden	ELIZABETH WILSON
Russell Heyman	DONALD SYMINGTON
Jerry Stone	SAUL RUBINEK
Eli Clay	PETER MALONEY
Whitney Fowler	JEFFREY DeMUNN
Beth	MAUREEN SILLIMAN
Grace	ALICE DRUMMOND

and: Thomas Hill, Sydney Hibbert, David Ramsey, Robin Mary Paris, Gary Boyer, Sudie Bond, Richard Hughes, Mary Boylan

An amiable Manhattan parish priest with a bent for crime-solving comes to the aid of a damsel in distress, a young actress who is innocently embroiled in a series of bizarre incidents and cannot find a sympathetic ear among the police. This pilot for a proposed "Father Brown" series updated the G. K Chesterton creation, introduced in 1911 in a collection of short stories, who played detective fictionally through 1935 in pastoral England. The character was transplanted to New York City of the 1970s for this movie, originally to have been shown as *Father Brown, Detective* (the title used when Alec Guinness played the part in the 1954 film), and then was switched to *Sanctuary of Death* before its final name was settled on.

0975
YOU CAN'T GO HOME AGAIN
4/25/79 CBS Entertainment (2 hours)

Executive Producer: Bob Markell
Director: Ralph Nelson
Teleplay: Ian McLellan Hunter
Based on the novel by Thomas Wolfe
Photography: Jack Priestley
Music: Charles Gross
Art Director: David Chapman
Editor: Murray Solomon

Esther Jack	LEE GRANT
George Webber	CHRIS SARANDON
Foxhall Edwards	HURD HATFIELD
Amy Carlton	TAMMY GRIMES
Milliken	CHRISTOPHER MURNEY
Judge Bland	ROLAND WINTERS
Fritz Jack	PAUL SPARER
Tim Wagner	MALACHY McCOURT
Piggy Logan	ROBERT ABERDEEN
Sam Pennock	SETH ALLEN
Sol	SCOTT BAKER
Minister	JOHN C. BECHER
Higgins	JOHN BENTLEY
Sidney	RONALD BISHOP
First Officer	ELIF DAGFIN
Else von Kohler	FRANCESCA DeSAPIO
Mayor Kennedy	ALFRED HINCKLEY

and: Michael Egan, Rex Everhart, John Favorite, Arthur French, Desiree Gould, John Hallow, Edward C. Henry, Ray Hill, Tom Hill, Beej Johnson, Juergen Kuehn, Eileen Letchworth, Abby Lewis, Paul Milikin, Mack R. Miller, Gordon Oas-Helm, Ralph Redpath, William Robertson, John Seymour, Martin Shakar, Myrna Stennett, Jeremiah Sullivan, Vincent Van Lynn, Kai Wulff, Frank Young

Wolfe's literary classic, telling of the struggles of a young writer determined to be a success in New York's literary world of the 1920s, his married lover and the brilliant editor who sees him as a blossoming genius. The story parallels the life of Wolfe himself and his affair with stage designer Aline Bernstein (here called Esther Jack). Editor Maxwell Perkins was the fictional Foxhall Edwards' real-life counterpart.

0976
I KNOW WHY THE CAGED BIRD SINGS
4/28/79 Tomorrow Entertainment (2 hours)

Executive Producer: Thomas W. Moore
Producer: Jean Moore Edwards
Director: Fielder Cook
Teleplay: Leonora Thuna and Maya Angelou
Based on the autobiography by Maya Angelou
Photography: Ralph B. Woolsey
Music: Peter Matz
Art Director: Carl Anderson
Editor: Frank J. Urioste

Freeman	PAUL BENJAMIN
Vivian	DIAHANN CARROLL
Grandmother Baxter	RUBY DEE
Bailey, Sr.	ROGER E. MOSLEY
Momma	ESTHER ROLLE
Miss Flowers	MADGE SINCLAIR
Maya	CONSTANCE GOOD
Bailey, Jr.	JOHN M. DRIVER II
Uncle Willie	SONNY JIM GAINES
Principal	ART EVANS

and: J. Don Ferguson, Georgia Allen, Darleen Taylor, Darryl Williams, Tommie Stewart, Jack Stevens, Monica Kyles, Frankie Mitchell

Maya Angelou's eloquent reminiscences of her days as a gifted youngster growing up in the South during the Depression years where she and her older brother were raised by their grandmother after the divorce of their parents.

0977
BEACH PATROL
4/30/79 Spelling-Goldberg Productions (90 min)

Executive Producers: Aaron Spelling and Leonard Goldberg
Producer: Philip Fehrle
Director: Bob Kelljan
Teleplay: Ronald Austin and James D. Buchanan
Photography: Arch R. Dalzell
Music: Barry DeVorzon
Art Directors: Seymour Klate and Paul Sylos
Editor: Jack Harnish

Russ Patrick	ROBIN STRAND
Marty Green	JONATHON FRAKES
Jan Plummer	CHRISTINE DeLISLE
Earl (Hack) Hackman	RICHARD HILL
Sgt. Lou Markowski	MICHAEL GREGORY
Wes Dobbs	PAUL BURKE
The Banker	MICHAEL V. GAZZO
Wild Boy	PANCHITO GOMEZ
Wanda	MIMI MAYNARD
Tall Girl	PRINCESS O'MAHONEY

and: Lillian Adams, Bella Bruck, X Brands, Georgie Paul, Chuck Tamburro, Terry Leonard

A "Rookies"-in-dune-buggies series pilot in which a comely lady cop is transferred from the narcotics division and assigned to a special police team patrolling California's beaches, only to spot a fugitive drug king pin and find herself targeted for murder.

0978
SAMURAI
4/30/79 Danny Thomas Productions/Universal (90 min)

Executive Producers: Danny Thomas, Ron Jacobs and Fernando Lamas
Producer: Allan Balter
Director: Lee H. Katzin

Teleplay: Jerry Ludwig
Photography: Vincent A. Martinelli
Music: Fred Karlin
Art Director: Paul Peters
Editor: Albert J. Zuniga

Lee Cantrell	JOE PENNY
Frank Boyd	DANA ELCAR
Hana Mitsubishi Cantrell	BEULAH QUO
Takeo Chisato	JAMES SHIGETA
Amory Bryson	CHARLES CIOFFI
Harold Tigner	GEOFFREY LEWIS
Lt. Al DeNisco	NORMAN ALDEN
Cathy Berman	MORGAN BRITTANY
Irving Berman	RALPH MANZA
Tommy	SHANE SINUTKO
Peter Lacey	MICHAEL PATAKI
Richardson	JAMES McEACHIN
Professor Owens	PHILIP BAKER HALL

and: Bob Minor, Randolph Roberts, Diana Webster, Don Keefer

A young San Francisco lawyer, an assistant district attorney by day, straps on his samurai sword at night to do battle with a power-mad tycoon who is plotting to destroy San Francisco with an earthquake machine, in this pilot for a prospective martial arts series.

0979
TORN BETWEEN TWO LOVERS
5/2/79 Alan Landsburg Productions (2 hours)

Executive Producer: Tom Kuhn
Producers: Linda Otto and Joan Barnett
Director: Delbert Mann
Teleplay: Doris Silverton
Based on a story by Doris Silverton and Rita Lakin
Photography: Ronald Lautore
Music: Ian Fraser
Art Director: David Jaquest
Editor: Gene Milford

Diane Conti	LEE REMICK
Ted Conti	JOSEPH BOLOGNA
Paul Rassmussen	GEORGE PEPPARD
Andy Conti	DERRICK JONES
Nina Dworski	MURPHY CROSS
Sherry Saunders	MOLLY CHEEK
Joseph Conti	GIORGIO TOZZI
Mrs. Conti	KAY HAWTREY
Frank Conti	MARTIN SHAKAR
Steffie Conti	ANDREA MARTIN
Penny	MARY LONG
Norma Conti	LOIS MARKLE
Leonard Shaeffer	TOM HARVEY
Alex Conti	JESS OSUNA
Doctor	SEAN McCANN

A women's picture, dealing with a happily married suburbanite who becomes romantically attached to a handsome architect she meets at Chicago's airport. Its distinction comes from Lee Remick's presence and her reteaming with director Delbert Mann with whom she worked a similar magic on *Breaking Up* (1978) as well as *A Girl Named Sooner* (1975). The title was inspired by Peter Yarrow's hit song.

0980
ANATOMY OF A SEDUCTION
5/8/79 Moonlight Productions Inc./Filmways (2 hours)

Producer: Frank Von Zerneck
Director: Steven Hilliard Stern
Teleplay: Alison Cross
Photography: Howard R. Schwartz
Music: Hagood Hardy
Art Director: James Bissell
Editor: Melvin Shapiro

Maggie Kane	SUSAN FLANNERY
Ed	JAMESON PARKER
Nina	RITA MORENO
Mark Kane	ED NELSON
Ricky Kane	MICHAEL LeCLAIR
Dan Sawyer	ALLAN MILLER
Harry Jackson	ROGER C. CARMEL
Maitre d'	SANDY BARON
Howard	BRYAN O'BRYNE
Michael	RON PRINCE
Businessman	ROD COLBIN
Desk Clerk	BARRY MICHLIN
Allan	ERNEST HARODA

and: Peter Turgeon, Eldon Quick, Joseph Sheen, Pilar Del Ray, Frank Wagner

A romantic drama about the love affair between a divorced woman and the college-age son of her best friend, alienating her teenage son who is just a few years younger than her lover.

0981
HANGING BY A THREAD
5/8–9/79 Irwin Allen Productions/Warner Bros. (4 hours)

Producer: Irwin Allen
Director: Georg Fenady
Teleplay: Adrian Spies
Photography: John M. Nicholaus
Music: Richard LaSalle
Art Director: Duane Alt
Editor: Jamie Caylor

Paul Craig	SAM GROOM
Sue Grainger	PATTY DUKE ASTIN
Anita Minton	JOYCE BULIFANT
Eddie Minton	OLIVER CLARK
Alan Durant	BERT CONVY
Jim Grainger	BURR DeBENNING
Mr. Durant	PETER DONAT
Ellen Craig	DONNA MILLS
Lawton	CAMERON MITCHELL
Mitchell	ROGER PERRY
Tommy Craig	MICHAEL SHARRETT
Jim Croft	TED GEHRING
Charles Minton	LONNY CHAPMAN
Mrs. Durant	JAQUELINE HYDE
Marty	BRENDON BOONE
Turk	STEVEN MARLOW
Maggie Porter	ELIZABETH ROGERS

and: Paul Fix, Deanna Lund, Randy Grant, James Gavin, Doug Llewelyn

Irwin Allen, filmdom's "disaster master," strands a party of friends in a disabled sightseeing tram dangling above a mountain gorge to sweat out a rescue while reliving (through flashbacks) past jealousies, simmering conflicts and forgotten secrets as the cable begins snapping wire by wire.

0982
THE WILD WILD WEST REVISITED
5/9/79 CBS Entertainment (2 hours)

Executive Producer: Jay Bernstein
Producer: Robert L. Jacks
Director: Burt Kennedy
Teleplay: William Bowers
Photography: Robert B. Hauser
Music: Jeff Alexander
Title theme by Richard Markowitz
Art Director: Albert Heschong
Editor: Michael McCroskey

James T. West	ROBERT CONRAD
Artemus Gordon	ROSS MARTIN
Michelito Loveless, Jr.	PAUL WILLIAMS
Robert T. Malone	HARRY MORGAN
Capt. Sir David Edney	RENE AUBERJONOIS
Carmelita	JO ANN HARRIS
Penelope	TRISHA NOBLE
Alan	ROBERT SHIELDS
Sonya	LORENE YARNELL
Hugo Kaufman	JEFF McKAY
Gabrielle	SUSAN BLU
Nadia	PAULA USTINOV
Pres. Grover Cleveland	WILFORD A. BRIMLEY
Russian Tsar	TED HARTLEY
Queen Victoria	JAQUELINE HYDE
Spanish King	ALBERTO MORIN
Joseph	SKIP HOMEIER
Lola	JOYCE JAMESON

and: John Wheeler, Mike Wagner, Jeff Redford

The intrepid team of Old West government intelligence agents are brought out of retirement after ten years to hunt down a cunning new adversary, the son of their former arch-enemy who is suspected of cloning imposters to be substituted for the crowned heads of Europe and perhaps even the President of the United States. This lighthearted romp revived the popular Western series that ran from 1965 to 1969 and reunited the show's original stars, Robert Conrad and Ross Martin.

0983
THE POWER WITHIN
5/11/79 Aaron Spelling Productions (90 min)

Executive Producers: Aaron Spelling and Douglas S. Cramer
Producer: Alan S. Godfrey
Supervising Producer: E. Duke Vincent
Associate Producer: Michael S. McClean
Director: John Llewellyn Moxey
Teleplay: William Clark
Photography: Emil Oster
Music: John Addison
Art Directors: Tom Trimble and Paul Sylos
Editor: Dennis C. Duckwall

Chris Darrow	ART HINDLE
Gen. Tom Darrow	EDWARD BINNS
Bill Camelli	JOE RASSULO
Stephens	ERIC BRAEDEN
Danton	DAVID HEDISON
Dr. Joanna Mills	SUSAN HOWARD
Capt. Ed Holman	RICHARD SARGENT
Marvalee	KAREN LAMM
Grandma	ISABELL McCLOSKEY
Small Boy	K. C. MARTEL
Guard No. 1	CHRIS WALLACE
Guard No. 2	BILL SORRELIS

A prospective pilot about a daredevil flyer, barnstorming for county fairs, who becomes a human dynamo after being struck by lightning and is menaced by enemy agents determined to find out the secret of his incredible strength. This was called *Power Man* not only in production but in all publicity and in *TV Guide* ads virtually until moments before its initial airing.

0984
THE NIGHT RIDER
5/11/79 Stephen J. Cannell Productions/Universal (90 min)

Executive Producers: Stephen J. Cannell and Alex Beaton
Producer: J. Rickley Dumm
Supervising Producer: Bill Phillips
Director: Hy Averback
Teleplay: Stephen J. Cannell

Gena Rowlands and Bette Davis in STRANGERS: THE STORY OF A MOTHER AND DAUGHTER (1979)

Photography: Steve Poster
Music: Mike Post and Pete Carpenter
Art Director: John J. Jeffries
Editor: Christopher Nelson

Lord Thomas Earl	DAVID SELBY
Robert	PERCY RODRIGUES
Regina Kenton	KIM CATTRALL
Dan Kenton	GEORGE GRIZZARD
Tru Sheridan	ANTHONY HERRERA
Lady Earl	ANNA LEE
Alex Sheridan	PERNELL ROBERTS
Chock Hollister (Young Thomas)	MICHAEL SHARRETT
Billy "Bowlegs" Baines	HARRIS YULIN
Marie Hollister	HILDY BROOKS
Hans Klaus	CURT LOWENS
Jim Hollister	VAN WILLIAMS
Doc Ellis	STUART NISBET
Donald White (Hotel Clerk)	GARY ALLEN

and: Sydney Penny, Whit Bissell, Edward Knight, Maria Diane, Susan Davis

The Mark of Zorro was updated for this pilot for a prospective series that tells of a New Orleans gentleman who turns masked rider to fight for law and order and avenge his family's killing by four men who wanted their silver mine.

0985
THE ULTIMATE IMPOSTER
5/12/79 Universal (2 hours)

Producer: Lionel E. Siegel
Director: Paul Stanley
Teleplay: Lionel E. Siegel
Based on the novel *The Capricorn Man* by William Zacha, Sr.
Photography: Vincent A. Martinelli
Music: Dana Kaproff
Art Director: Lou Montejano
Editors: Clay Bartels and Fred Baratta

Frank Monihan	JOSEPH HACKER
Eugene Danziger	KEITH ANDES
Dr. Jake McKeever	MACON McCALMAN
Beatrice Tate	ERIN GRAY
Danielle Parets	TRACY BROOKS SWOPE
Ruben Parets	JOHN VAN DREELEN
Lai-Ping	ROSALIND CHAO
Tennis Pro	BOBBY RIGGS
Papich	NORMAN BURTON
"Red" Cottle	ROBERT PHILLIPS
Sergeant Williger	GREG BARNETT

Joe Maslan	THOMAS BELLIN
Dominic	LOREN BERMAN
Tony	BILL CAPIZZI
Esteban	CANDY CASTILLO
Felipe	MARK GARCIA
Carl Lathrop	GRAYDON GOULD
Martin	CHIP JOHNSON

and: Joseph Hardin, Mike Kulcsar, Betty Kwan, Harry Pugh, Roberto Ramirez, Tommy Reamon, Bob Thomas, Chuck Tamburro, W. T. Zacha

A series pilot about a secret agent who is armed with skills learned by a computer-brain link-up—lasting only seventy-two hours at a time—and is sent to rescue a Russian submarine commander, a defector who has been kidnapped by an agent for another nation.

0986
STRANGERS: THE STORY OF A MOTHER AND DAUGHTER
5/13/79 Chris-Rose Productions (2 hours)

Producers: Robert W. Christiansen and Rick Rosenberg
Associate Producer: Ric Rondell
Director: Milton Katselas
Teleplay: Michael de Guzman
Photography: James Crabe
Music: Fred Karlin
Production Designers: Harry Horner and Albert Brenner
Art Director: Spencer Deverill
Editor: Millie Moore

Lucy Mason	BETTE DAVIS
Abigail Mason	GENA ROWLANDS
Mr. Meecham	FORD RAINEY
Wally Ball	DONALD MOFFAT
Dr. Henry Blodgett	WHIT BISSELL
Mr. Willis	ROYAL DANO
Mrs. Brighton	KATE RIEHL
Louis Spencer	KRISHAN TIMBERLAKE
Joan Spencer	RENEE McDONNELL
Mildred Sloate	SALLY KEMP
Bartender	DON FOSSE
Third Kid	SON SALO
Clerk	JOHN ZUMINO

A drama about a dying woman who returns to the home of her widowed mother after an absence of twenty years and how their bitter estrangement slowly turns to love. This double tour-de-force for Bette Davis and Gena Rowlands was a heralded first effort for writer Michael de Guzman, and premiered rightly on Mother's Day, 1979. Bette Davis won the Emmy Award for her performance.

0987
SON RISE: A MIRACLE OF LOVE
5/14/79 A Rothman-Wohl Production/Filmways (2 hours)

Executive Producers: Bernard Rothman and Jack Wohl
Producer: Richard M. Rosenbloom
Director: Glenn Jordan
Teleplay: Stephen Kandel
Based on the book by Barry Neil Kaufman
Photography: Matthew F. Leonetti
Music: Gerald Fried
Song "Is There Room in Your World for Me?" by Gene and Paul Nelson
Sung by Debby Boone
Art Director: James H. Spencer
Editor: Sidney M. Katz

Barry Kaufman	JAMES FARENTINO
Suzie Kaufman	KATHRYN HARROLD

Abe Kaufman	STEPHEN ELLIOTT
Dr. Bob Clark	HENRY OLEK
Nancy	KERRY SHERMAN
Raun Kaufman	MICHAEL AND CASEY ADAMS
Thea Kaufman	MISSY FRANCIS
Bryn Kaufman	SHELLEY BALIK
Dr. Fields	ERICA YOHN

and: Don Chastain, Richard Doyle, Rachel Bard, Barbara Carney, Amentha Dymally, Sue Ann Gilfillan, Sean Griffin, Enid Kent, Mark Ross, Nancy Steen, Fred Stuthman, Reba Waters, Jack Wohl, June Whitley Taylor, William Wintersole

A poignant true story of a couple who discover that their son is an autistic child but refuse to believe gloomy medical prognoses and devise their own ways of treating him. Remarkable performances were gotten from the two youngsters who played the boy, 3½-year-old twin great-grandsons of veteran director King Vidor.

0988
THE SACKETTS
5/15–16/79 Douglas Netter/M.B. Scott Productions in association with Shalako Enterprises, Inc. (4 hours)

Producers: Douglas Better and Jim Byrnes
Director: Robert Totten
Teleplay: Jim Byrnes
Based on the novels *The Daybreakers* and *Sackett* by Louis L'Amour
Photography: Jack A. Whitman, Jr.
Music: Jerrold Immel
Production Designer: Johannes Larson
Art Director: Tambi Larsen
Editor: Howard A. Smith

Tell Sackett	SAM ELLIOTT
Orrin Sackett	TOM SELLACK
Tye Sackett	JEFF OSTERHAGE
Tom Sunday	GLENN FORD
Cap Roundtree	BEN JOHNSON
Don Luis Alvarado	GILBERT ROLAND
Jonathan Pritts	JOHN VERNON
Rosie	RUTH ROMAN
Ira Bigelow	JACK ELAM
Benson Bigelow	GENE EVANS
Beldon	L. Q. JONES
Kid Newton	PAUL KOSLO
Ma Sackett	MERCEDES McCAMBRIDGE
Jack Bigelow	SLIM PICKENS
Tuthill	PAT BUTTRAM
Wes Bigelow	JAMES GAMMON
Reed Carney	BUCK TAYLOR
Simpson	LEE DeBROUX
Laura Pritts	MARCY HANSON
Druscilla	ANA ALICIA
Ange Kerry	WENDY RASTATTER

and: Shug Fisher, Frank Ramirez, Ramon Chavez, Henry Capps, Tim Waters, Brian Libby, Kimo Owens, Malcolm Watt, Pam Earnhardt, Buddy Totten, James O'Connell, Don Collier, R. L. Tolbert, Bruce Fischer, Anakorita, Billy Cardi, Mark Wales, Patrick Mahoney, John Copeland, Rusty Lee, Dick Kyker, Earl W. Smith, Melvin Todd, Dave Herrera, Mai Gray, Bill Hart, C. B. Clark, Monique St. Pierre, Richard Jamison, Ken Plankey, Russell Cox, Jr., James Almanzar

A traditional sagebrush saga based on two novels by Louis L'Amour, the foremost Western author on the contemporary scene, and the first dramatized for television of the seventy-four he has written (eleven are about the Sackett family). This four-hour movie focuses on the three Sackett brothers in New Mexico territory after the Civil War, seeking their fortunes, avenging a family killing, driving cattle, and fighting for law and order.

0989
WALKING THROUGH THE FIRE
5/15/79 A Time-Life Television Production (2 hours)

Executive Producer: David Susskind
Producer: Stan Hough
Director: Robert Day
Teleplay: Sue Grafton
Based on the book by Laurel Lee
Photography: Richard C. Glouner
Music: Fred Karlin
Art Director: Paul Barnes
Editor: Gerald Ludwig

Laurel Lee	BESS ARMSTRONG
Richard Lee	TOM MASON
Dr. Maitland	RICHARD MASUR
Carla	SWOOSIE KURTZ
Dr. Freeman	KEN KERCHEVAL
Ruth Moore	JUNE LOCKHART
Dr. Goodwin	J. D. CANNON
Dr. Rand	BONNIE BEDELIA
Dr. Levinson	DANIEL BENTON
William Francis	HAL FREDERICK
Matthew Lee	BOBBY JACOBY
Anna Lee	LAURA JACOBY
Jeannie	LOUISE HOVEN
Delia	BARBARA ALLEN
Dr. Fowler	NOEL CONLON
Dr. Baker	MICHAEL PRINCE

and: Tanya Boyd, Betty Jinnette, Karen Werner, Isabel Cooley

A young mother battles Hodgkin's disease, endangering both her own life and that of her unborn baby, based on Laurel Lee's chronicle of her own seemingly hopeless struggle.

0990
THE RETURN OF MOD SQUAD
5/18/79 A Thomas/Spelling Production (2 hours)

Executive Producers: Danny Thomas and Aaron Spelling
Producer: Lyn Loring
Associate Producer: Shelley Hull
Director: George McGowan
Teleplay: Robert James
Photography: Arch R. Dalzell
Music: Shorty Rogers and Mark Snow
Art Directors: Jan van Tamelen and Paul Sylos
Editors: Stan Wohlbert and Dennis C. Duckwall

Pete Cochrane	MICHAEL COLE
Linc Hayes	CLARENCE WILLIAMS III
Julie Barnes	PEGGY LIPTON
Adam Greer	TIGE ANDREWS
Frank Webber	TOM BOSLEY
Jason Hayes	TODD BRIDGES
Keith Starr	VICTOR BUONO
Cook	TOM EWELL
Marty	JOHN KARLEN
Buck Prescott	ROSS MARTIN
Himself	SUGAR RAY ROBINSON
Richie Webber	MARK SLADE
Dan	ROY THINNES
Barney Metcalf	SIMON SCOTT
Kate Kelsey	JESS WALTON
Jake (Bartender)	TAYLOR LARCHER
Johnny Sorella	RAFAEL CAMPOS
Bingo	BRYON STEWART
Willie	HOPE HOLLIDAY
Phil	THOMAS DILLION

With an eye toward reviving the hit series that ran from 1968 to 1973, "Mod Squad" producers Danny Thomas and Aaron Spelling joined forces once again after going their separate ways for many years to call ex-undercover cops Pete, Linc and Julie back to the force when a series of sniper attacks are made on their old boss, but the three soon find that they themselves are the intended victims of a gunman who lives in their old "flower child" world of the 1960s. This ploy to pump new life into old successes followed the pattern set previously (and unsuccessfully) by those behind "Maverick," "Gilligan's Island," "Wild Wild West," "Lassie," "The Millionaire"—and, theatrically, "Star Trek" and "Get Smart."

0991
LOVE'S SAVAGE FURY
5/20/79 Aaron Spelling Productions (2 hours)

Executive Producers: Aaron Spelling and Douglas S. Cramer
Producer: Ronald Lyon
Director: Joseph Hardy
Teleplay: Calvin Clements, Jr.
Photography: Richard L. Rawlings
Music: Johnn Addison
Art Directors: Alfeo Bocchicchio and Paul Sylos
Editor: John M. Woodcock

Laurel Taggart	JENNIFER O'NEILL
Col. Zachary Willis	PERRY KING
Lyle Taggart, Sr.	RAYMOND BURR
Col. Marston	ROBERT REED
Dolby	CONNIE STEVENS
Sergeant Weed	ED LAUTER
Ferris	HOWARD McGILLIN
Jewel	VERNEE WATSON
Opal	DEBORAH MORGAN
Lyle Taggart, Jr.	JEFFREY BYRON
Dr. Tighe	ROBERT CORNTHWAITE
Capt. Brody	ED POWERS

and: Slim Gaillard, Erica Welles, Mark Hicher

This outrageous carbon copy of *Gone with the Wind* had a petulant, self-centered Southern belle fighting not only to keep herself the center of attraction among her countless beaux but also to hold on to the family homestead when the Union Army comes marching through, and then it veers off into a search for a cache of gold and a look at prison camp life under the bluecoats. "Not since *Gone with the Wind* has there been a romantic drama with the epic sweep of *Love's Savage Fury*" a voice intoned solemnly before the letters of the title, ripping a page from the classic to which its producers dared compare it, swept majestically across the TV screen.

0992
A VACATION IN HELL
5/21/79 A David Greene/Finnegan Associates Production (2 hours)

Executive Producer: David Greene
Producers: Pat and Bill Finnegan
Director: David Greene
Teleplay: Shelley Katz and D. B. Ledrov
Photography: Harry May
Music: Gil Melle
Art Director: Joe Aubel
Editors: Ken Zemke and Parkie Zingh

Denise	PRISCILLA BARNES
Evelyn	BARBARA FELDON
Barbara	ANDREA MARCOVICCI
Margaret	MAUREEN McCORMICK

| Alan | MICHAEL BRANDON |
| Native | ED KA'AHEA |

A dream vacation at a posh tropical resort turns into a nightmare for four women and a man who wander off into the jungle on a remote part of the island and wage a desperate fight for survival.

0993
HOT ROD
5/25/79 ABC Circle Films (2 hours)

Producer: Sam Manners
Writer/Director: George Armitage
Photography: Andrew Davis
Music: Michael Simpson
Art Director: Michael Baugh
Editors: William Neel and Carroll Sax

Brian Edison	GREGG HENRY
Sheriff Marsden	PERNELL ROBERTS
Jenny	ROBIN MATTSON
Sonny Munn	GRANT GOODEVE
T. L. Munn	ROBERT CULP
Johnny Hurricane	ROYCE APPLEGATE
Sprout	TOPO SWOPE
Clay	ED BEGLEY, JR.
Cannonball	BRUCE M. FISCHER
Barry Hogue	ERIK HOLLAND
Violet	JULIE GIBSON

A free-wheeling drag racer enters a local championship meet and finds himself head-to-head with the tyrannical town boss who has already arranged for his own son to win.

0994
DUMMY
5/27/79 The Konigsberg Company/Warner Bros. (2 hours)

Executive Producer: Frank Konigsberg
Producers: Sam Manners and Ernest Tidyman
Director: Frank Perry
Teleplay: Ernest Tidyman
Photography: Gayne Rescher
Music: Gil Askey
Art Director: Bill Cassidy
Editors: Donald R. Rode and Benjamin A. Weissman

Lowell Myers	PAUL SORVINO
Donald Lang	LeVAR BURTON
Ragoti	BRIAN DENNEHY
Jean Markin	ROSE GREGORIO
Asst. D.A. Smith	GREGG HENRY
Julius Lang	STEVEN WILLIAMS
Mrs. Harrod	HELEN MARTIN
Detective Romain	JONATHAN PILURS
Sgt. Alonzo Hobbs	PAUL BUTLER
Ernestine Williams	FRANKIE HILL
Dr. Romney	ALLEN HAMILTON
Dr. Morris	PATRICK BILLINGSLEY
Judge	JAMES O'REILLY

The real-life account of an illiterate deaf-and-dumb black youth who was accused of murdering a prostitute and the relationship that developed between him and his court-appointed attorney who is also deaf, and the events leading up to his precedent-setting trial where he was determined incompetent by the law because his severe handicaps prevented him from defending himself or testifying to his innocence. *Dummy* was nominated for an Emmy Award in the category of Outstanding Drama or Comedy Special.

0995
THE BEST PLACE TO BE
5/27–28/79 A Ross Hunter Production (4 hours)

Producers: Ross Hunter and Jacque Mapes
Associate Producer: Marvin Miller
Director: David Miller
Teleplay: Stanford Whitmore
Based on the novel by Helen Van Slyke
Photography: Terry K. Meade
Music: Henry Mancini
Song "Free Now" written and sung by Chris Mancini
Production Designer: Jack DeShields
Editor: Richard Bracken

Sheila Callahan	DONNA REED
Bill Reardon	EFREM ZIMBALIST, JR.
Rose Price	MILDRED DUNNOCK
Sally Cantrell	BETTY WHITE
Dr. Mancini	JOHN PHILLIP LAW
Maryanne Callahan	STEPHANIE ZIMBALIST
Patrick Callahan	MICHAEL SHANNON
Rick Jawlosky	GREGORY HARRISON
Tommy Callahan	TIMOTHY HUTTON
Bob Stockwood	LLOYD BOCHNER
Emily Stockwood	MADLYN RHUE
Paul Bellinger	RICK JASON
Kitty Rawlings	ALICE BACKES
Jean Callahan	PEGGY CONVERSE
William Callahan	LEON AMES
Dottie Parker	COLEEN GRAY
Betty Callahan	SUSAN WALDEN
Sean Callahan	LIAM SULLIVAN

and: Redmond Gleeson, Booth Colman, Jay Claussen, Pat Corley, Richard Rorke, Jon Montoya, Marguerite DeLain, Eduardo Noriega, Angelina Estrada, Marcus K. Mukai, Johnny Haymer, Jack Grapes, Raymond O'Keefe, Frank Arno, Gloria Stuart, June Whitley Taylor, Taldo Kenyon, Harriet E. MacGibbon, Julie Dolan, Steve Eastin, Charles Walker, Jimmy Weldon, Michael Sloane, Christopher Carson, Mike Hammett, Thomas Logan, Chris Mancini

A lavish romantic drama in true Ross Hunter style about a young widow whose life is complicated by a hippie daughter, a rebellious teenage son and an ill-starred love affair with a younger man—and then a former suitor comes back into the picture. The film not only marked Donna Reed's TV movie debut but also brought her back to television after a twelve-year absence.

0996
THE HOUSE ON GARIBALDI STREET
5/28/79 Charles Fries Productions (2 hours)

Executive Producers: Charles Bloch and Steve Shagan
Production Supervised by Charles Fries and Malcolm Stuart
Producer: Mort Abrahams
Director: Peter Collinson
Teleplay: Steve Shagan
Based on the book by Isser Harel
Photography: Allejandro Ulloa
Music: Charles Bernstein
Production Designers: Fernando Gonzalez and Disley Jones
Art Director: Giorgio Desideri
Editor: Gene Fowler, Jr.

Michael	TOPOL
Ari	NICK MANCUSO
Hedda	JANET SUZMAN
Isser Harel	MARTIN BALSAM
David Ben-Gurion	LEO McKERN
Gen. Lischke	CHARLES GRAY
Arthur Lubinsky	DERREN NESBITT
Adolph Eichmann	ALFRED BURKE
Aaron Lazar	JOHN BENNETT
Doctor	JOHN CATER
Inspector Contreras	FERNANDO HILBECK
Meged	EDWARD JUDD
Rodriques	ALBERTO BERCO
Primo	ALBERTO DeMENDOZA
Dani	RICARDO PALACIOS
Dieter Eichmann	RICHARD WREN
Vera Eichmann	MARIA ISBERT
Nicholaus Eichmann	SIMON SHEPHERD
Vincente	JORGE BOSSO

and: Wolf Kohler, Ian Serra, Carl Rapp, Paco Belloch, Gareth Hunt, Antonio Canal, Dennis Vaughn

A dramatization, filmed in Spain, about the events leading up to the capture of Nazi war criminal Adolph Eichmann by Israeli agents in Argentina in 1960. Two of them, Topol and Janet Suzman, are best known to American moviegoers as Academy Award nominees for their roles in *Fiddler on the Roof* and *Nicholas and Alexandra* respectively, while Martin Balsam portrays the author of the book on which this film was based, who at the time was the head of Israeli Intelligence.

0997
SURVIVAL OF DANA
5/29/79 EMI Television Programs, Inc. (2 hours)

Executive Producers: Roger Gimbel and Tony Converse
Producer: Mark Trabulus
Director: Jack Starrett
Teleplay: Frank E. Norwood
From a story by Tom Lazarus and Frank E. Norwood
Photography: Bruce Logan
Music: Craig Safan
Art Director: Peter M. Wooley
Editor: Joy Wilson

Dana Lee	MELISSA SUE ANDERSON
Donny Davis	ROBERT CARRADINE
Madeline Lee	MARION ROSS
Rona Sims	TALIA BALSAM
Arnold Denker	MICHAEL PATAKI
Roy "Skates" Snider	KEVIN BRESLIN
Francis "Bear" Honfi	JUDGE REINHOLD
Anthony Cavachi	DAN SPECTOR
Lorna Sims	BARBARA BABCOCK
Mrs. Blake	SHELBY LEVERINGTON
Joanie	DAWN JEFFORY
Coach Tanner	TRENT DOLAN
Paul	SCOTT McGINNIS
Big	GARY CERVANTES
Bill Snider	PAUL HAMPTON
Mrs. Honfi	ELLEN BLAKE
Mr. Honfi	HOWARD VANN
Little Big	JOSHUA GALLEGOS
Mrs. Davis	EDITH FIELDS
Principal	JUNE WHITLEY TAYLOR
Clerk	LAURA FANNING
Lynn	JENNIFER STARRETT

A pretty high school girl moves to a new town and falls in with the wrong crowd in this contemporary drama of teenage values in an affluent society.

0998
STUNT SEVEN
5/30/79 A Martin Poll Production (2 hours)

Producers: Martin Poll and William Craver
Associate Producer: Ralph S. Singleton

Director: John Peyser
Teleplay: David Shaw
Photography: Frank Holgate
Music: Bill Conti
Additional Music: Jack Eskew
Art Director: David Chapman
Editor: Murray Solomon

Hill Singleton	CHRISTOPHER CONNELLY
Skip Hartman	CHRISTOPHER LLOYD
Wally Ditweiler	BOB SEAGREN
Kenny Uto	SOON-TECK OH
Horatio Jennings	BRIAN BRODSKY
Dinah Lattimore	JUANIN CLAY
Elena Sweet	MORGAN BRITTANY
Frank Wallach	BILL MACY
Phil Samson	PETER HASKELL
Boudreau	PATRICK MACNEE
Rebecca Wayne	ELKE SOMMER
John Heinlein	MORGAN PAULL
Monica	LYNDA BEATTIE
Ilya	SANTY JOSOL
Harrison	ROBERT RITCHIE

An intrepid team of stunt experts stage a daring air, sea and land rescue of a kidnapped movie star from the clutches of a suave, modern-day pirate who rules a sovereign fortress state in the middle of the Gulf of Mexico. This was a pilot for a prospective adventure series.

0999
THIS MAN STANDS ALONE
5/30/79 A Roger Gimbel Production for EMI Television/Abby Mann Productions (90 min)*

Executive Producer: Abby Mann
Producer: Harry R. Sherman
Writer/Director: Jerrold Freedman
Photography: Tak Fujimoto
Music: Fred Karlin
Art Director: Herman Zimmerman
Editor: John F. Link II

Tom Haywood	LOUIS GOSSETT, JR.
Marvin Tayman	CLU GULAGER
Minnie Haywood	MARY ALICE
Fred Tayman	BARRY BROWN
George Tayman	BARTON HEYMAN
Harris McIntyre	JAMES McEACHIN
Sheriff Harvey Johnson	LONNY CHAPMAN
Rufus	PHILLIP MICHAEL THOMAS
Mrs. Cartwright	HELEN MARTIN
Sergeant Hunt	JOHN CRAWFORD
Deputy Poole	BURTON GILLIAM
Reverend Farrell	CLEBERT FORD
Albert Jackson	NICK SMITH
Loretta Tayman	MARY KAY PASS
Factory Worker	ROYCE CLARK

This dramatization of the true story of a black civil rights activist who, following Martin Luther King's assassination, goes home to a small southern town and runs for sheriff against a popular segregationist was "inspired" by events in the life of Sheriff Thomas E. Gilmore but was emasculated by severe last-minute editing by the network.

*Originally filmed as a two-hour telefeature under the title *Lawman Without a Gun*.

1000
THE LAST GIRAFFE
6/7/79 A Westfall Production (2 hours)

Executive Producer: Charles G. Mortimer, Jr.
Producers: Jonathan Bernstein and Warren Littlefield
Associate Producer: Clive Reed
Director: Jack Couffer
Teleplay: Sherman Yellen
Based on the book *Raising Daisy Rothschild* by Jock and Betty Leslie-Melville
Photography: Ted Scaife
Music: Fred Karlin
Song "Now I Know Where I Belong" by Fred Karlin and Norman Gimbel
Sung by Mary Macgregor
Art Director: Tony Reading
Editor: David Garfield

Betty Leslie-Melville	SUSAN ANSPACH
Jock Leslie-Melville	SIMON WARD
Fielding	GORDON JACKSON
Mwenga	DON WARRINGTON
Taj	SAEED JAFFREY
Atherton	JOHN HALLAM
Kamua	RUDOLPH WALKER

An engaging tale of the efforts of an American wildlife photographer and her safari guide husband to save the endangered Rothschild giraffe of Kenya by adopting an orphaned animal whose mother had been slain by a notorious poacher.

1001
HOLLOW IMAGE
6/24/79 A Titus Production (2 hours)

Executive Producer: Herbert Brodkin
Supervising Producer: Robert Berger
Producers: Thomas DeWolfe and Stephen A. Rotter
Director: Marvin J. Chomsky
Teleplay: Lee Hunkins
Photography: Alan Metzger
Music: Don Sebesky
Songs "Too Many Springs" by Don Sebesky and Alan and Marilyn Bergman and "Makin' It to the Top" by Don Sebesky and Thomas DeWolfe
Art Director: Charles Bennett
Editor: Robert M. Reitano

Paul Hendrix	ROBERT HOOKS
Harriet Gittens	SAUNDRA SHARP
Danny York	DICK ANTHONY WILLIAMS
Ivy	HATTIE WINSTON
Sweet Talk (Ralph Simmons)	MORGAN FREEMAN
Monica	ANNA MARIA HORSFORD
Scotty	SAMUEL E. WRIGHT
Mamma	MINNIE GENTRY
Sandy	LAURIE CHOCK

A black career girl who has made it in the fashion world is torn between her new life "downtown" and her roots in Harlem with an old flame. This was the first TV play by Miss Hunkins and the winner of the 1979 ABC Theatre Award.

THE MINI-SERIES

MS01
THE BLUE KNIGHT
November 13–16, 1973 Lorimar Productions (4 hours)*

Executive Producer: Lee Rich
Producer: Walter Coblenz
Associate Producer: Neil T. Maffeo
Director: Robert Butler
Teleplay: E. Jack Neuman
Based on the novel by Joseph Wambaugh
Photography: Michael Margulies
Music: Nelson Riddle
Art Director: Hilyard Brown
Editors: Marjorie Fowler, Samuel E. Beetley and Gene Fowler, Jr.

Bumper Morgan	WILLIAM HOLDEN
Cassie Walters	LEE REMICK
Sgt. Cruz Segovia	JOE SANTOS
Glenda	EILEEN BRENNAN
Harry Debbs	EMILE MEYER
Det. Charlie Bronski	SAM ELLIOTT
Rudy Garcia	ERNEST ESPARZA III
Laila	ANNE ARCHER
Neil Grogan	VIC TAYBACK
Zoot Lafferty	GEORGE DiCENZO
Harold Wagner	MARIO ROCCUZZO
Celia Louise	JA'NET DuBOIS
Yasser Hafiz	JAMIE FARR
Lt. Hilliard	RAYMOND GUTH
Knobby Booker	JOHN QUADE
Judge Redford	KATHERINE BARD
Elmira Gooch	LUCILLE BENSON
Freddie Opp	JOHN SYLVESTER WHITE

and: Harry Arnie, Janit Baldwin, Jim Beach, Nanci Beck, Norland Benson, Danny "Big Black," Arell Blanton, Helen Boll, Roxanne Bonilla, Simmy Bow, Claire Brennan, Donald Calfa, Thomas Paul Carey, Ric Carrot, Stanley Clay, Richard Collier, Lou Cutell, Larry Duran, Joseph X. Flaherty, Alan Fudge, John Furlong, Eddra Gale, Janie Greenspun, Margie Haber, Stan Haze, Monika Henreid, Janear Hines, Jan-Minika Hughes, J. S. Johnson, Richard Kalk, Wayne King, Rand Kirby, Dudley Knight, Jon Korkes, Maryann Krakow, Bob Lauher, Paul Lawrence, Norma Lee, Patrick Dennis-Leigh, Gloria LeRoy, David Lipp, Jay W. MacIntosh, Arthur Malet, David Moody, Karmine Murcelo, Douglas O'-Dell, Tim O'Denning, Rudy Ramos, Paul Reid Roman, Nick St. Nicholas, Richard Saradet, Christopher Seitz, Kenneth Smedberg, Michael Stearns, Jack Tesler, Russell Thorson, Tom Tolbert, Dino Washington, Lee Weaver, Jason Wingreen, Kenneth Wolger, Richard Wright, Clint Young, E. Jack Neuman

Veteran actor William Holden made his dramatic debut on TV in the role of Bumper Morgan, a twenty-year veteran of the Los Angeles Police Department on his last few days on the force before his retirement, and won an Emmy Award for his performance. The mini-series form as subsequently established began with this four-hour film that was shown initially in one-hour segments on four consecutive nights. This is a movie version of the best-selling novel by Joseph Wambaugh, the ex-cop who turned writer to successfully tell of his experiences here and on the series "Police Story" and its two spin-offs, "Police Woman" and "Joe Forrester," as well as "The Blue Knight" series with George Kennedy taking over the lead role from William Holden. In addition to Holden's Emmy, statuettes were given to director Robert Butler (for Part III) and to editors Marjorie and Gene Fowler and Samuel E. Beetley. Lee Remick also received a nomination for her performance as Bumper Morgan's ever-patient girlfriend Cassie Walters.

*Subsequently edited down to 2 hours for syndication.

MS02
MOSES—THE LAWGIVER
June 21, 28, July 5, 12, 26, Aug. 2, 1975 ATV, Ltd. for ITC and RAI Television (6 hours)

Producer: Vincenzo Labella
Director: Gianfranco DeBosio
Teleplay: Anthony Burgess, Vittorio Bonicelli, Bernardino Zapponi, Gianfranco DeBosio
Photography: Marcello Gatti
Music: Ennio Morricone
Conducted by Bruno Nicolai
Songs and Dances: Dov Seltzer
Choreography: Oshra El Kayam
Special Effects: Mario Bava
Art Director: Pier Luigi Basile
Costumes: Enrico Sabbatini
Editor: Alberto Galletti

Moses	BURT LANCASTER
Aaron	ANTHONY QUAYLE
Miriam	INGRID THULIN
Zipporah	IRENE PAPAS
Young Moses	WILLIAM LANCASTER
Egyptian Princess	MARIANGELA MELATO
Mernephta (Pharaoh)	LAURENT TERZIEFF
Cotbi	SIMONETTA STEFANELLI
Joshua	AHARON IPALE
Mernephta's Wife	MELBA ENGLANDER
Ramses II	MARIO FERRARI
Koreb	ANTONIO PIOVANELLI
Eliseba	MARINA BERTI
Dathan	YOUSEG SHILOAH
Jethro	SHMUEL RODENSKY

and: Paul Muller, Jose Quaglio, Umberto Raho, John Francis Lane, Paul Verani, Jaques Herlin, Giancarlo Badese, Cosimo Cinieri, Renato Chiantoni, Didi Lukof, Enzo Fieramonte, Andrea Aureli, Percy Hogan, Fausto DiBella, Galia Kohn, Umberto Raho, Dina Doronne, Marco Steiner, Yossi Warjansky, Almos Tapshir, Haim Bashi, Haim Banai.

This biblical spectacular, which ran in hour-long segments over a six-week period and then turned up theatrically in a severely edited version not long after its initial TV showing, marked Burt Lancaster's TV acting debut, as well as that of his son, William (as Young Moses), best known as the writer of the hit movie *The Bad News Bears*. A multi-national cast, working in Israel and the Negev, found itself trapped during the 1973 Arab-Israeli War while filming this leisurely paced but very expensive production.

MS03
RICH MAN, POOR MAN
February 1–2, 9, 16, 23, March 1, 8, 15, 1976 Universal (12 hours)

Executive Producer: Harve Bennett
Producer: Jon Epstein
Directors: David Greene (Parts 1, 2, 7, 8) and Boris Sagal (Parts 3, 4, 5, 6)
Teleplay: Dean Reisner
Based on the novel by Irwin Shaw
Photography: Howard R. Schwartz
Music: Alex North
Art Director: John E. Childberg II
Editors: Douglas Stewart and Richard Bracken

Rudy Jordache	PETER STRAUSS
Tom Jordache	NICK NOLTE
Julie Prescott	SUSAN BLAKELY
Axel Jordache	EDWARD ASNER
Al Fanducci	DICK BUTKUS
Arnold Simms	MICHAEL EVANS
Sue Prescott	GLORIA GRAHAME
Mary Jordache	DOROTHY McGUIRE
Teddy Boylan	ROBERT REED

Claude Tinker	DENNIS DUGAN	Asher Berg	CRAIG STEVENS	Phil McGee	GAVAN O'HERLIHY
Mr. Tinker	FRANK ALETTER	Smitty	NORMAN FELL	Billy	LEIGH McCLOSKEY
Miss Lenaut	JOSETTE BANZET	Gloria Bartley	JO ANN HARRIS	Wesley	MICHAEL MORGAN
Dr. Tinker	JOHN FURLONG	Linda Quales	LYNDA DAY		
Buddy	MIKE BAIRD		GEORGE		
Martin	MARTIN ASH	Joey Quales	GEORGE MAHARIS		
Theatre Manager	WILLIAM	Lou Martin	ANTHONY		
	BRONDER		CARBONE		
Bayard Nichols	STEVE ALLEN	Pete Tierney	ROY JENSON		
Willie Abbott	BILL BIXBY	Papadakis	ED BARTH		
Virginia Calderwood	KIM DARBY	Falconetti	WILLIAM SMITH		
Clothilde	FIONNUALA	Sid Gossett	MURRAY		
	FLANAGAN		HAMILTON		
Brad Knight	TIM McINTIRE	Marsh Goodwin	VAN JOHNSON		
Duncan Calderwood	RAY MILLAND	Irene Goodwin	DOROTHY MALONE		
Bill Denton	LAWRENCE	Roy Dwyer	HERBERT		
	PRESSMAN		JEFFERSON, JR.		
Teresa Santoro	TALIA SHIRE	Col. Deiner	ANDREW DUGGAN		
Harold Jordache	BO BRUNDIN	Kate	KAY LENZ		
Augie	JULIUS HARRIS	Pinky	HARVEY JASON		
Jay Ledbetter	BEN ARCHIBEK	Martha	HELEN CRAIG		

The overwhelming success of this star-laden TV adaptation of Irwin Shaw's 1970 best-seller that was shown as six two-hour motion pictures over a seven-week period assured the future of the "Novel for Television" mini-series genre. Stars of varying magnitudes were made of the production's three leading players—Peter Strauss, Susan Blakely and Nick Nolte (each Emmy Award-nominated)—as the two Jordache brothers and the girl involved at one time or another with each during the twenty years from the end of World War II until the late 1960s in this odyssey examining the shifting social and moral values in America. It also spawned a weekly series, "Rich Man, Poor Man— Book II" (which had nothing to do with Shaw's original book), running during the 1976–77 television season with Strauss continuing his original role.

Burt Lancaster and Anthony Quayle in MOSES—THE LAWGIVER (1975)

Susan Blakely and Peter Strauss in RICH MAN, POOR MAN (1976)

Emmy Awards were won by Edward Asner and Fionnuala Flanagan for acting, David Greene for directing (Part 8), and Alex North for his music score. Among the other nominations (twenty in all) were one for Best Limited Series as well as to Dorothy McGuire, Ray Milland, Bill Bixby, Robert Reed, Van Johnson and Norman Fell (in various specialized acting categories), director Boris Sagal (for Part 5), writer Dean Reisner, cinematographer Howard R. Schwartz, costumer Charles Waldo, and editors Douglas Stewart and Richard Bracken.

MS04
CAPTAINS AND THE KINGS
September 30, October 7, 14, 28, November 4, 11, 1976 Universal (9 hours)

Executive Producer: Roy Huggins
Producer: Jo Swerling, Jr.
Directors: Douglas Heyes (first three and last three hours) and Allen Reisner
Teleplay: Douglas Heyes
Adapted by Stephen and Elinor Karpf
From the novel by Taylor Caldwell
Photography: Isidore Mankofsky, Ric Waite and Vilis Lapenieks
Music: Elmer Bernstein
NBC Best Sellers Theme: Elmer Bernstein
Art Directors: John W. Curso and Joseph J. Jennings
Editors: Larry Lester, Edwin F. England, Christopher Nelson and Lawrence J. Vallario

Joseph Armagh	RICHARD JORDAN
Rory Armagh	PERRY KING
Bernadette Hennessey	
Armagh	PATTY DUKE ASTIN
R. J. Squibbs	RAY BOLGER
Elizabeth Healey	BLAIR BROWN
Father Hale	JOHN CARRADINE
Moira Armagh	KATHERINE CRAWFORD
Ed Healey	CHARLES DURNING
Sen. Enfield Bassett	HENRY FONDA
Sister Angela	CELESTE HOLM
Judge Newell Chisholm	JOHN HOUSEMAN
Sean Armagh	DAVID HUFFMAN
"Old Syrup"	BURL IVES
Haroun (Harry) Zieff	HARVEY JASON
Tom Hennessey	VIC MORROW
Martinique	BARBARA PARKINS
Katherine Hennessey	JOANNA PETTET
Marjorie Chisholm Armagh	JANE SEYMOUR
Mrs. Finch	ANN SOTHERN
Charles Desmond	ROBERT VAUGHN
O'Herlihy	NEVILLE BRAND
Braithwaite	PERNELL ROBERTS
Strickland	JOE KAPP
Peg	LINDA KELSEY
Young Bernadette	ELIZABETH CHESHIRE
Young Joseph	JOHNNY DORAN
Sean (as a child)	KRISTOPHER MARQUIS

Mary Armagh (as a child)	MISSY GOLD
Miss Emmy	BEVERLY D'ANGELO
Clair Montrose	PETER DONAT
Kevin Armagh	DOUGLAS HEYES, JR.
Gannon	STEFAN GIERASCH
Courtney Wickersham	TERRY KISER
Governor Skerritt	CLIFTON JAMES
Brian Armagh	CLIFF DeYOUNG
Governor Hackett	ALAN HEWITT
Honora Houlihan	JENNY SULLIVAN
Boland	SEAN McCLORY
President Garfield	RICHARD MATHESON
Orestes Bradley	GEORGE GAYNES
Abraham Lincoln	FORD RAINEY
Jay Regan	WILLIAM PRINCE
Ann-Marie	ANN DUSENBERRY
Father Scanlon	PHILIP BOURNEUF
Claudia Desmond Armagh	CYNTHIA SIKES
James Spaulding	KERMIT MURDOCK
Young Courtney	JOHN HERBSLEB
Young Rory	PATRICK LABORTEAUX
Preston	MILLS WATSON
Cpl. Lincoln Douglas	ROGER ROBINSON
Teddy Roosevelt	LEE JONES-DeBROUX
Wounded Texan	ROBERT DONNER
Captain Muldoon	KEN SWOFFORD
President McKinley	STEPHEN COIT
Foreign Gentleman	GIORGIO TOZZI
Plover	SEVERN DARDEN
William Jennings Bryan	BYRON WEBSTER
Rosemary Armagh	TRACEY GOLD
Cara Leslie	SIAN-BARBARA ALLEN
Aggie	SALLY KIRKLAND
Dr. Harris Herbert	BILL QUINN
Pearl Gray	CONNIE KRESKI

and: Ted Gehring, John DeLancie, William Bryant, Todd Martin, Martin Kove, Alex Sharp, Jack Stryker, Duane Grey, Norman Bartold, Boyd Morgan, Woody Skaggs, June Whitley Taylor, Roberta Storm, Alex Wipf, Walt Davis, James O'Connell, George Berkeley, Barbara Morrison, William Gordon, Charles H. Gray, Bernard Behrens, Charles O. Lynch, Richard Herd, Macon McCalman, George Skaff, Rod Haase, Ned Wilson, John Dennis Johnston, Eldon Quick, Sandy Ward, Terrence Locke, Walter O. Miles

The nine-hour serialization of Taylor Caldwell's novel about an Irish immigrant and the establishment of his family name through the accumulation of wealth and power during the years from 1857 to 1912, along with his goal of having his son elected the first Catholic President of the United States, gained a huge television following because of its thinly disguised similarities to the Kennedy family saga. Richard Jordan and Perry King, as father and son (although they are basically the same age), became stars of sorts because of their performances. Patty Duke Astin won another of her assorted Emmy Awards for her work as Jordan's breakdown-prone wife, and cinematographer Ric Waite received one for photographing Part 1 (of six). The production also was nominated as Outstanding Series of 1976–77, as were actors Richard Jordan and Charles Durning, composer Elmer Bernstein, art director Joseph R. Jennings and set designer Jerry Adams (the last two for their work on Part 2).

MS05
ONCE AN EAGLE
December 2, 9, 16, 23, 30, 1976 January 6, 13, 1977 Universal (9 hours)*

Executive Producer: William Sackheim
Producer: Peter S. Fischer
Directors: E. W. Swackhamer and Richard Michaels

Teleplay: Peter S. Fischer
Based on the novel by Anton Myrer
Photography: J. J. Jones
Music: Dana Kaproff
NBC Best Sellers Theme: Elmer Bernstein
Art Director: William Campbell
Editors: Chuck McClelland, John Elias and
Howard S. Deane

Sam Damon	SAM ELLIOTT
Courtney Massengale	CLIFF POTTS
Tommy Caldwell	DARLEEN CARR
Emily Pawlfrey Massengale	AMY IRVING
George Caldwell	GLENN FORD
Ed Caldwell	RALPH BELLAMY
Harry Sheppard	DANE CLARK
General McKelvey	ANDREW DUGGAN
Marge Krisler	LYNDA DAY GEORGE
Jack Delvin	GARY GRIMES
Alvin Merrick	CLU GULAGER
Ben Krisler	ROBERT HOGAN
Kitty Damon	KIM HUNTER
Earl Preis	DAVID HUDDLESTON
Joyce	JULIET MILLS
Columbine Crawford	HARRIET NELSON
Sen. Bert McConnadin	ALBERT SALMI
Captain Townsend	JOHN SAXON
Lin Tso-Han	JAMES SHIGETA
General Bannerman	BARRY SULLIVAN
Alma Caldwell	PHYLLIS THAXTER
Colonel Avery	FORREST TUCKER
Colonel Terwilliger	DAVID WAYNE
Gen. Duke Pulleyne	WILLIAM WINDOM
Dave Shifkin	ANTHONY ZERBE
George Varney	JOHN ANDERSON
Reb Rayburne	ANDREW ROBINSON
Sam (as a boy)	JEFF COTLER
Peggy Damon	TRACIE SAVAGE
Celia Harrodson	LYNNE MARTA
Krazewski	DENNIS BURKLEY
Brewster	WILL SELTZER
Cheryl Logan	JANE ELLIOT
Nurse Pomeroy	PATRICIA STICH
Michele	PATTI D'ARBANVILLE
Paul Sinclair	HAYDEN ROARKE
Maynard Lambert	RON MASAK
J. L. Cleghorne	JAMES CROMWELL
Dr. McCabe	GEORGE WYNER
Mae Lee Cleghorne	CATHEY PAINE
Ryetower	KIP NIVEN
Joe Brand	KARIO SALEM
Adam Brand	CARMEN ARGENZIANO
Sergeant Stoner	TOM REESE
Bill Nickerson	LEE JONES-DeBROUX
Donny Damon	ANDREW STEVENS
Capt. Lasovitch	JIM ANTONIO
Jinny Massengale	MELANIE GRIFFITH
Captain Jerome	BEN PIAZZA
General Jacklyn	KENT SMITH
Sergeant Ives	JORDAN RHODES
Sergeant Chepenek	GEORGE MURDOCK
Captain Nagasay	FRANK MICHAEL LIU
Lee McConnadin	RANDALL CARVER
Helene McConnadin	ANNE BELLAMY

and: Bert Kramer, Simon Scott, Jennifer Shaw, Rick
Podell, George Loros, Chick Vennera, Lew Brown,
Gary Springer, Rod Porter, Rori Gwynne, Geoffrey
Binney, Rod McCary, Shelley Morrison, Richard
Forbes, John Waldron, Sari Price, John Fujioka,
Frank Farmer, Jan Burrell, John Waldron, William
Bryant, William H. Bassett, Suzanne Horton, Clint
Ritchie, Smith Evans, Sean McClory, Stacy Keach, Sr.

The saga of two soldiers—one compassionate, one
ruthless—from 1918 through World War II was
adapted from Anton Myrer's sweeping 1968 best-seller
for a nine-(later six-) hour serialization that juggled
wartime action with assorted romantic interludes. Veteran Glenn Ford was the stabilizing influence for his
four younger co-stars, with all the others in the huge
cast "guest starring" in alphabetical order. Cinematographer J. J. Jones received the film's lone Emmy
Award nomination for his photography of Part 1 (of
seven).

*Edited to 6 hours over three nights in initial rerun.

MS06
ARTHUR HAILEY'S THE MONEYCHANGERS
December 4–5, 12, 19, 1976 Ross Hunter
Productions/Paramount (6½ hours)*

Producers: Ross Hunter and Jacque Mapes
Associate Producer: Marvin Miller
Director: Boris Sagal
Teleplay: Dean Riesner and Stanford Whitmore
Based on the novel by Arthur Hailey
Photography: Joseph Biroc
Music: Henry Mancini
Art Director: Jack DeShields
Editor: Richard Bracken

Anne Baxter and Kirk Douglas in THE MONEYCHANGERS (1976)

Alex Vandervoort	KIRK DOUGLAS
Roscoe Heyward	CHRISTOPHER PLUMMER
Edwina Dorsey	ANNE BAXTER
Jerome Devereaux	RALPH BELLAMY
Miles Eastin	TIMOTHY BOTTOMS
Avril Devereaux	JOAN COLLINS
Margot Bracken	SUSAN FLANNERY
Tony Bear	ROBERT LOGGIA
Celia Vandervoort	MARISA PAVAN
Beatrice Heyward	JEAN PETERS
Nolan Wainwright	PERCY RODRIGUES
Lewis Dorsey	HAYDEN ROARKE
Wizard Wong	JAMES SHIGETA
Juanita Nunez	AMY TIVELL
Harold Austin	PATRICK O'NEAL
George Quartermain	LORNE GREENE

and Special Guest Star Appearance by

Dr. McCartney	HELEN HAYES
Fergus Gatwick	ROGER BOWEN
Danny Kerrigan	DOUGLAS V. FOWLEY
Stanley Inchbeck	BASIL HUFFMAN
Deacon Euphrates	LINCOLN KILPATRICK

and: Leonard Carmino (Ben Rosselli), Woodrow Parfrey (Mr. Tottenhoe), Stan Shaw (John Dinkerwell), Joseph R. Sicari (Jules LaRocca), Nancy Hseuh (Moonbeam), Bing Russell (Timberwell), Lynette Metty (Teller), Virginia Grey (Miss Callahan), Jon Lormer (Depositor), Burt Mustin (Jack Henderson), Marla Gibbs (Mrs. Euphrates), Redmond Gleeson (Vernon Jax), Miiko Taka (Mom), Barry Coe (TV Newsman)

This four-part adaptation of Arthur Hailey's tale of power and greed in the banking business as two ambitious vice presidents become rivals when an imminent board room vacancy arises won an Emmy Award nomination as Outstanding Series of the 1976–77 season as well as an Emmy for Christopher Plummer as one of the antagonists. Other nominations went to Susan Flannery (as Kirk Douglas' lawyer girlfriend), to Joseph Biroc for his photography, and to Phil Normann for his graphics and opening titles. Of interest: Jean Peters returned to films here after spending nearly twenty years in retirement—most of them as Mrs. Howard Hughes.

*Edited down to 6 hours over three nights in initial rerun.

MS07
ROOTS
January 23–30, 1977 A David L. Wolper Production (12 hours)

Executive Producer: David L. Wolper
Producer: Stan Margulies
Directors: David Greene, John Erman, Marvin J. Chomsky, Gilbert Moses
Teleplay: William Blinn, Ernest Kinoy, James Lee, M. Charles Cohen
Adapted by William Blinn
Based on the novel by Alex Haley
Photography: Stevan Larner, Joseph M. Wilcots

Music: Quincy Jones and Gerald Fried
Art Directors: Jan Scott, Joseph R. Jennings
Editors: Neil Travis, James T. Heckert, Peter Kirby

Nyo Boto	MAYA ANGELOU
The Wrestler	JI-TU CUMBUKA
The Kintango	MOSES GUNN
Omoro	THALMUS RASULALA
Brima Cesay	HARRY RHODES
Gardner	WILLIAM WATSON
Fanta	REN WOODS
Kunta Kinte	LeVAR BURTON
Binta	CICELY TYSON
Capt. Thomas Davies	EDWARD ASNER
Kadi Touray	O. J. SIMPSON
Slater	RALPH WAITE
Fiddler	LOUIS GOSSETT, JR.
William Reynolds	ROBERT REED
John Reynolds	LORNE GREENE
Mrs. Reynolds	LYNDA DAY GEORGE
Ames	VIC MORROW
John Carrington	PAUL SHENAR
Kunta Kinte as Adult (Toby)	JOHN AMOS
Bell	MADGE SINCLAIR
Grill	GARY COLLINS
Trumbull	LEE JONES DeBROUX
Jennova	TANYA L. BOYD
Fanta as Adult	BEVERLY TODD
Harlan	THAYER DAVID
The Drummer	RAYMOND ST. JACQUES

Lloyd Bridges in ROOTS (1977)

Ben Vereen in ROOTS (1977)

Tom Moore	CHUCK CONNORS
Missy Anne Reynolds	SANDY DUNCAN
Noah	LAWRENCE HILTON-JACOBS
Ordell	JOHN SCHUCK
Kizzy	LESLIE UGGAMS
Melissa	ROXIE ROKER
Ada	ELMA JACKSON
Mrs. Moore	CAROLYN JONES
Squire James	MACDONALD CAREY
Mingo	SCATMAN CROTHERS
Mathilda	OLIVIA COLE
Stephen Bennett	GEORGE HAMILTON
Sir Eric Russell	IAN McSHANE
Sister Sara	LILLIAN RANDOLPH
Sam Bennett	RICHARD ROUNDTREE
Chicken George	BEN VEREEN
Reverend	WALLY TAYLOR
Leonard	DAVID ROBERTS
Evan Brent	LLOYD BRIDGES
Tom	GEORG STANFORD BROWN
Ol' George Johnson	BRAD DAVIS
Lewis	HILLY HICKS
Jemmy Brent	DOUG McCLURE
Irene	LYNNE MOODY
Martha Johnson	LANE BINKLEY
Sam Harvey	RICHARD McKENZIE
Virgil	AUSTIN STOKER
Lila Harvey	SALLY KEMP
Sen. Arthur Johnson	BURL IVES
Sheriff Biggs	JOHN QUADE
Drake	CHARLES CYPHERS
Bud	TODD BRIDGES

The dramatization of Alex Haley's chronicle of his family history from his ancestors' life in tribal Africa of the eighteenth century to their emancipation in the post-Civil War South became an overnight phenomenon—the subject of educational programs as well as newspaper editorials—that attracted, as it progressed, the largest viewing audience ever for a dramatic TV program. It won an unprecedented thirty-seven Emmy Award nominations and was chosen the Outstanding Dramatic Series of the 1976–77 season, and won Emmys for Louis Gossett, Jr. as Best Actor, Edward Asner as Best Supporting Actor and Olivia Cole as Best Supporting Actress, as well as for director David Greene (Part 1), writers Ernest Kinoy and William Blinn (Part 2), editor Neil Travis (Part 1), and Quincy Jones and Gerald Fried for their music score (Part 1). Other acting nominations include: John Amos, LeVar Burton (UCLA drama student in his dramatic acting debut), Ben Vereen, Leslie Uggams, Madge Sinclair, Moses Gunn, Robert Reed, Ralph Waite, Sandy Duncan and Cicely Tyson plus Marvin J. Chomsky (director, Part 3), John Erman (director, Part 2), Gilbert Moses (director, Part 6), Stevan Larner (cinematographer, Part 2), Joseph M. Wilcots (cinematographer, Part 7), James Lee (teleplay, Part 5), M. Charles Cohen (teleplay, Part 8), James Lee (teleplay, Part 5), Neil Travis (editor, Part 2) (also winner for Part 1), Peter Kirby (editor, Part 3), James T. Heckert (editor, Part 8).

MS08
SEVENTH AVENUE
February 10, 17, 24, 1977 Universal (6 hours)

Executive Producer: Franklin Barton
Producer: Richard Irving
Directors: Richard Irving and Russ Mayberry (Part 3)
Teleplay: Laurence Heath
Based on the novel by Norman Bogner

Photography: Jack Priestley
Music: Nelson Riddle
NBC Best Sellers Theme: Elmer Bernstein
Production Designer: Philip Rosenberg
Art Director: Loyd S. Papez
Editor: Robert F. Shugrue

Jay Blackman	STEVEN KEATS
Rhoda Gold Blackman	DORI BRENNER
Eva Meyers	JANE SEYMOUR
Myrna Gold	ANNE ARCHER
Al Blackman	KRISTOFFER TABORI
Joe Vitelli	HERSCHEL BERNARDI
Frank Topo	RICHARD DIMITRI
Finklestein	JACK GILFORD
Morris Blackman	MICHAEL KELLIN
Harry Lee	ALAN KING
Douglas Fredericks	RAY MILLAND
Dave Shaw	PAUL SORVINO
Gus Farber	ELI WALLACH
John Meyers	WILLIAM WINDOM
Mrs. Gold	LEORA DANA
Marty Cass	JOHN PLESHETTE
Credan	LOU CRISTOLO
Howart Horton	RICHARD KLINE
Edward Gold	ROBERT SYMONDS
Celia Blackman	ANNA BERGER
Paula	ELLEN GREENE
Barney Green	JOSH MOSTEL
Moll	GLORIA GRAHAME
Sergeant Rollins	BROCK PETERS
Ray Boone	RON MAX
Neal Blackman	JOSHUA FREUND
Detective Clever	GRAHAM BECKEL

The third in NBC's Best Seller series, this three-part serialization of Norman Bogner's novel about a poor young man from New York's lower East Side who becomes a power in the garment industry in the post-Depression era won Emmy Award nominations for Steven Keats and Dori Brenner.

MS09
THE RHINEMANN EXCHANGE
March 10, 17, 24, 1977 Universal (5 hours)*

Executive Producer: George Eckstein
Producer: Richard Collins
Director: Burt Kennedy
Teleplay: Richard Collins
Based on the novel by Robert Ludlum
Photography: Alex Phillips, Jr.
Music: Michel Colombier
NBC Best Sellers Theme: Elmer Bernstein
Art Director: William H. Tuntke
Editors: Anthony Redman and Rod Stevens

David Spaulding	STEPHEN COLLINS
Leslie Jenner Hawkewood	LAUREN HUTTON
Walter Kendall	CLAUDE AKINS
General Swanson	VINCE EDWARDS
Erich Rhinemann	JOSE FERRER
Col. Edmund Pace	LARRY HAGMAN
Amb. Henderson Granville	JOHN HUSTON
Bobby Ballard	RODDY McDOWALL
Asher Feld	LEN BIRMAN
Colonel Barton	GENE EVANS
Geoffrey Moore	JEREMY KEMP
Franz Altmuller	WERNER KLEMPERER

LeVar Burton in ROOTS (1977)

Irene	TRICIA NOBLE
Alex Spaulding	WILLIAM PRINCE
Dietrich	JOHN VAN DREELEN
Anna	ISELA VEGA
The Creole	VICTORIA RACIMO
Mrs. Cameron	KATE WOODVILLE
Heinrich Stolz	BO BRUNDIN
Daniel Meehan	RAMON BIERI
Lieutenant Fuentes	PEDRO ARMENDARIZ, JR.
Dr. Eugene Lyons	RENE AUBERJONOIS

and: Ben Wright, Anthony Charnota, John Hoyt, Charles Siebert, Thayer David, Zitto Kazann, John Chappell, Mark deVries, John Ashton

Double-dealing and espionage in World War II as an intelligence officer is dispatched by the U.S. government to arrange an exchange in Argentina of industrial diamonds needed by the Germans for a secret gyroscope needed by our side.

*Edited to 4 hours over two nights in initial rerun.

MS10
JESUS OF NAZARETH
April 3, 1977 (Palm Sunday) (3 hours, 10 min)
April 10, 1977 (Easter Sunday) (3 hours, 20 min)*
A Sir Lew Grade Production for ITV

Executive Producer: Bernard J. Kingham
Producer: Vincenzo Labella
Associate Producer: Dyson Lovell
Director: Franco Zeffirelli
Teleplay: Anthony Burgess, Suso Cecchi D'Amico and Franco Zeffirelli
With additional dialogue by David Butler
Photography: Armando Nannuzzi and David Watkin
Music: Maurice Jarre
Played by The National Philharmonic Orchestra
Art Director: Gianni Quaranta
Editor: Reginald Mills

Jesus Christ	ROBERT POWELL
Mary Magdalene	ANNE BANCROFT
The Centurion	ERNEST BORGNINE
The Adultress	CLAUDIA CARDINALE
Herodias	VALENTINA CORTESE
Simon Peter	JAMES FARENTINO
Balthasar	JAMES EARL JONES
Barabbas	STACY KEACH
Quintilius	TONY LoBIANCO
Joseph of Arimathea	JAMES MASON
Judas	IAN McSHANE
Nicodemus	LAURENCE OLIVIER
Melchior	DONALD PLEASENCE
Herod Antipas	CHRISTOPHER PLUMMER
Caiaphas	ANTHONY QUINN
Gaspar	FERNANDO REY
Simeon	RALPH RICHARDSON
Pontius Pilate	ROD STEIGER
Herod the Great	PETER USTINOV
John the Baptist	MICHAEL YORK
The Virgin Mary	OLIVIA HUSSEY

and: Cyril Cusack, Ian Holm, Yorgo Voyagis, Ian Bannen, Regina Bianchi, Marina Berti, Oliver Tobias, Maria Carta, Lee Montague, Renato Rascel, Norman Bowler, Robert Beatty, John Phillips, Ken Jones, Nancy Nevinson, Renato Terra, Roy Holder, Jonathan Adams, Christopher Reich, Lorenzo Monet, Robert Davey, Oliver Smith, George Camiller, Murray Salem, Tony Vogal, Isabel Mestres, Michael Cronin, Forbes Collins, Martin Benson

A reverent retelling of the biblical tale with an all-star cast, winning Emmy Award nominations for Outstanding Drama (1977–78) and for James Farentino as Best Supporting Actor in a Drama.

*Expanded to 8 hours over four nights in 1979 rerun.

MS11
TESTIMONY OF TWO MEN
May 1977 Universal (Operation Prime Time)
(6 hours)

Producer: Jack Laird
Directors: Larry Yust (Parts 1 and 3) and Leo Penn (Part 2)
Teleplays: James M. Miller (Part 1), William Hanley (Part 2) and William Hanley, James M. Miller and Jennifer Miller (Part 3)
Based on the novel by Taylor Caldwell
Photography: Isidore Mankofsky (Parts 1 and 3) and Jim Dickson (Part 2)
Music: Michel Colombier (Parts 1 and 3) and Gerald Fried (Part 2)
Art Directors: William H. Tuntke (Part 1) and John E. Chilberg II
Editors: Robert F. Shugrue (Part 1), John Elias (Part 2) and Jim Benson (Part 3)

Jonathan Ferrier	DAVID BIRNEY
Marjorie Ferrier/Hilda Eaton	BARBARA PARKINS
Martin Eaton	STEVE FORREST
Dr. Jim Spaulding	RALPH BELLAMY
Peter Heger	THEODORE BIKEL
Dr. Louis Hedler (and narrator)	TOM BOSLEY
Howard Best	BARRY BROWN
Kenton Campion	J. D. CANNON
Father McGuire	DAN DAILEY
David Paxton	LEONARD FREY
Harald Ferrier	DAVID HUFFMAN
Father Frank McNulty	RANDOLPH MANTOOTH
Jonas Witherby	RAY MILLAND
Jeremiah Hadley	CAMERON MITCHELL
Edna Beamish	TRISHA NOBLE
Myrtle Heger	KATHLEEN NOLAN
Flora Bumpstead Eaton	MARGARET O'BRIEN
Jenny Heger	LAURIE PRANGE
Adrian Ferrier	WILLIAM SHATNER
Amelia Foster	INGA SWENSON
Jane Robson	JOAN VAN ARK
Mavis Eaton	LINDA PURL
Priscilla "Prissy" Madden Witherby	DEVON ERICSON
Francis Campion	KARIO SALEM
Elizabeth Best	LYNN TUFELD
Jerome Eaton	JOHN DeLANCIE

and: Robert Foulke, Herb Vigran, Joel Parks, Regis J. Cordic, Logan Ramsey, Jeff Corey

The initial production in an off-network project started by a group of independent stations pooling their resources for high quality drama to compete with the networks themselves. This ambitious post-Civil War costume saga intertwines several stories of lust, power, greed and murder as it tells of "two surgeons' passion for their work and their women" over a thirty-six-year period. An Emmy Award nomination went to costumer Bill Jobe for his stunning ante-bellum creations.

MS12
WASHINGTON: BEHIND CLOSED DOORS
September 6–11, 1977 Paramount (12½ hours)

Executive Producer: Stanley Kallis
Supervising Producers: Eric Bercovici and David W. Rintels

Producer: Norman Powell
Director: Gary Nelson
Teleplay: David W. Rintels and Eric Bercovici
Based on the book *The Company* by John Ehrlichman
Photography: Joseph Biroc and Jack Swain
Music: Dominic Frontiere and Richard Markowitz (Part 4)
Art Directors: Jack DeShields and James Claytor
Editors: Gerald J. Wilson, Harry Kaye and Arthur Hilton

William Martin	CLIFF ROBERTSON
Richard Monckton	JASON ROBARDS
Sally Whalen	STEFANIE POWERS
Frank Flaherty	ROBERT VAUGHN
Linda Martin	LOIS NETTLETON
Bob Bailey	BARRY NELSON
Carl Tessler	HAROLD GOULD
Adam Gardiner	TONY BILL
Esker Scott Anderson	ANDY GRIFFITH
Myron Dunn	JOHN HOUSEMAN
Roger Castle	DAVID SELBY
Jennie Jamison	MEG FOSTER
Eli McGinn	PETER COFFIELD
Joe Wisnovsky	BARRY PRIMUS
Kathy Ferris	DIANA EWING
Wanda Elliott	LARA PARKER
Tucker Tallford	JOHN LEHNE
Simon Cappell	ALAN OPPENHEIMER
Hank Ferris	NICHOLAS PRYOR
Lawrence Allison	FRANK MARTH
Bennett Lowman	JOHN RANDOLPH
Jack Atherton	LINDEN CHILES
Brewster Perry	GEORGE GAYNES
Elmer Morse	THAYER DAVID
Walter Tulloch	PHILLIP R. ALLEN
Lars Haglund	SKIP HOMEIER
Alex Coffee	MICHAEL ANDERSON, JR.
Ozymandias	JOE SIROLA
Paula Stoner Gardiner	FRANCES LEE McCAIN
Mrs. Monckton	JUNE DAYTON
Dorothy Kemp	JEAN HOWELL

and: Danna Hansen, Rick Gates, Madison Arnold, Borah Silver, Karen Smith-Bercovici, Joseph Hacker, Regis J. Cordic, John Kerr, Mary LaRoche, Fred Sadoff, Charles MacCauley, J. Jay Saunders

A lavish fictionalized retelling of the Watergate story mixing political intrigue and personal drama and centering on the rise of a power-hungry U.S. President and the men with whom he surrounded himself in order to keep his grip on his office. Robert Vaughn received an Emmy Award for his performance as the President's Chief of Staff, with other nominations going to the show itself as Outstanding Series, to Jason Robards for his portrayal of President Richard Monckton with its overt Nixonian images, director Gary Nelson, cinematographers Joseph Biroc and Jack Swain, art directors Jack DeShields and James Claytor and set decorator Barbara Kreiger.

MS13
HAROLD ROBBINS' 79 PARK AVENUE
October 16–18, 1977 Universal (6 hours)

Executive Producer: George Eckstein
Producer/Director: Paul Wendkos
Teleplay: Richard DeRoy (Part 1), Jack Guss (Part 2), Lionel Siegel (Part 3)
Developed for television by Richard DeRoy
Based on the novel by Harold Robbins
Photography: Enzo A. Martinelli
Music: Nelson Riddle
Art Director: Loyd S. Papez
Editors: Robert F. Shugrue (Parts 1 and 3) and Rod Stephens (Part 2)

Marja Fludjicki/Marianne	LESLEY ANN WARREN
Ross Savitch	MARC SINGER
Mike Koshko	DAVID DUKES
Kaati Fludjicki	BARBARA BARRIE
Vera Keppler	POLLY BERGEN
Armand Perfido	RAYMOND BURR
Ben Savitch	MICHAEL CONSTANTINE
John Stevens	LLOYD HAYNES
Paulie Fludjicki	SCOTT JACOBY
Brian Whitfield	PETER MARSHALL
Frank Millerson	ALEX ROCCO
Peter Markevich	ALBERT SALMI
Harry Vito	JOHN SAXON
John Hackson DeWitt	ROBERT WEBBER
Joker Martin	JACK WESTON
Joey Rannis	SANDY HELBERG
Myrna Savitch	MARGARET FAIRCHILD
Frannie	JANE MARIA ROBBINS
Hal Roper	ANDY ROMANO
Candy Berkowski	DENISE GALIK
Laura Koshko	VERONICA HAMMEL
Angie Harding	PAMELA SHOOP

and: Ross Marin, Al Checcio, Richard Self, Gypsi D. Young, Francey Nealy

A poor New York teenager of the mid-1930s is forced into prostitution despite sincere efforts to make a living otherwise, and ultimately she becomes the city's most famous madam. An Emmy Award nomination went to Yvonne Wood for her period costumes.

MS14
ASPEN
November 5–7, 1977 Universal (6 hours) (subsequently retitled *The Innocent and the Damned*)

Executive Producer: Michael Klein
Producer: Jo Swerling, Jr.
Director: Douglas H. Heyes
Teleplay: Douglas H. Heyes
Based on material from the novels *Aspen* by Bert Hirschfeld and *The Adversary* by Bart Spicer
Photography: Isidore Mankofsky
Music: Tom Scott and Mike Melvoin
Art Director: John W. Corso
Editors: Larry Lester, Edwin F. England and Lawrence J. Vallario

Tom Keating	SAM ELLIOTT
Lee Bishop	PERRY KING
Carl Osborne	GENE BARRY
Joan Carolinian	MARTINE BESWICK
Horton Paine	JOSEPH COTTEN
Max Kendrick	ROGER DAVIS
Sam Dinehart	LEE DeBROUX
Abe Singer	GEORGE DiCENZO
Alex Budde	ANTHONY FRANCIOSA
Kit Pepe	JESSICA HARPER
Jon Osborne	DOUG HEYES, JR.
Budd Townsend	BO HOPKINS
Joseph Merrill Drummond	JOHN HOUSEMAN
Owen Keating	JOHN McINTIRE
Gloria Osborne	MICHELLE PHILLIPS
Judge Miles Kendrick	WILLIAM PRINCE
Angela Morelli	DEBI RICHTER
Vanessa Faye	STEPHANIE BLACKMORE
Coker	DON COLLIER
Ralston	PEPPER MARTIN
Jackie Camerovsky	CONNIE KRESKI
Mrs. Morelli	CORINNE MICHAELS
TV Interviewer	MARALEE BECK

and: Wings Hauser, Susan Lawson, Michael Carr, Leslie Simms, Raul Martinez, Stephen Coit, Marion Wright, Todd Martin, Michael Mancini, Mark Heyes, Lynn Topping, Terry Donahue, Dana Baker, Roberta McElroy, Angus Duncan, John R. Walsh, Jeff Harlan, Gary Pagett, John R. McKee, Sheila Cann, Penny Ciarlo, Martha Gerwetz, Cassandra Lampert, Emma Trekman, Sandy Ward

A chic Colorado ski resort in the 1960s is the setting for illicit love, corruption and a sensational murder trial in this melodrama woven together from two novels (actually the title of one, the plot of the other) and subsequently spiced up with a new, more intriguing title the second time around. Involved are an ambitious young attorney, a drifter accused of murdering a teenage sexpot, a land developer whose bored daughter has become a jet setter, and an unctuous ex-gangster trying to make a land killing.

*Subsequently retitled *The Innocent and the Damned*.

MS15
BLACK BEAUTY
January 31–February 4, 1978 Universal (5 hours)

Executive Producer: Peter S. Fischer
Producer: Ben Bishop
Associate Producer: Norman Fox
Director: Daniel Haller
Teleplay: Peter S. Fischer
Based on the novel by Anna Sewell
Photography: John J. Jones and Terry K. Meade
Music: John Addison
Art Director: Loyd S. Papez
Editors: Skip Lusk and Michael S. Murphy

Lewis Barry	EDWARD ALBERT
Annie Gray	EILEEN BRENNAN
Samuel Livingston	LONNY CHAPMAN
Howard Jakes	KEN CURTIS
Martin Tremaine	DON DeFORE
John Manly	WILLIAM DEVANE
Jonas McBride	JACK ELAM
Nicholas Skinner	MEL FERRER
Enos Sutton	FARLEY GRANGER
Reuben Smith	CLU GULAGER
Horace Tompkins	VAN JOHNSON
Amelia Gordon	DIANE LADD
Polly Barker	ZOHRA LAMPERT
Tom Gray	MARTIN MILNER
Henry Gordon	CAMERON MITCHELL
Elizabeth Sutton	DIANA MULDAUR
Jerry Barker	WARREN OATES
Phyllis Carpenter	GLYNNIS O'CONNOR
Ruth Manly	JENNY O'HARA
Mr. Carmichael	BROCK PETERS
Peter Blantyre	CHRISTOPHER STONE
Luke Gray (as an adult)	KRISTOFFER TABORI
Mr. York	FORREST TUCKER
Mr. Dowling (and narrator)	DAVID WAYNE

and: Jane Actman, Harry Carey, Jr., John DeLancie, Dennis Dimster, Chris Gardner, Ike Eisenmann, Simone Griffith, Benny Medina, Stuart Silbar, Daniel Tamm, Garrison True, Michael Odom, Peter Breck, Luke Sickle, Sandra Walker, Kelly Morgan, Lee Ann Fahey, Miles Shearer, John Sullivan, Bill Nave

A sentimental, all-star retelling (the ninth and most lavish filming since 1906) of Anna Sewell's beloved animal classic, stretched out in its premiere showing over five nights in hourly episodes.

MS16
KING
February 12–14, 1978 Abby Mann Productions/Filmways (6 hours)

Executive Producer: Edward S. Feldman
Producer: Paul Maslansky
Director: Abby Mann
Teleplay: Abby Mann
Photography: Michael Chapman
Additional Photography: Gerald Hirschfield
Music: Billy Goldenberg
Production Designer: James H. Spencer
Editors: Byron "Buzz" Brandt, Richard Meyer and David Berlatsky

Martin Luther King, Jr.	PAUL WINFIELD
Coretta King	CICELY TYSON
Himself	TONY BENNETT
Philip Harrison	ROSCOE LEE BROWNE
Chief Frank Holloman	LONNY CHAPMAN
Martin Luther King, Sr.	OSSIE DAVIS
Robert F. Kennedy	CLIFF DeYOUNG
Damon Lockwood	AL FREEMAN, JR.
William Sullivan	CLU GULAGER
Stanley Levison	STEVEN HILL
John F. Kennedy	WILLIAM JORDAN
Lyndon Johnson	WARREN KEMMERLING
Jerry Waring	LINCOLN KILPATRICK
Bull Conner	KENNETH McMILLAN
Andrew Young	HOWARD ROLLINS
David Beamer	DAVID SPIELBERG
J. Edgar Hoover	DOLPH SWEET
Malcolm X	DICK ANTHONY WILLIAMS*
Himself	JULIAN BOND
Himself	RAMSEY CLARK
Rev. Fred Shuttlesworth	ROGER ROBINSON
Mrs. Alberta King	FRANCES FOSTER
Ralph Abernathy	ERNIE BANKS
A. D. King	ART EVANS
Rosa Parks	YOLANDA KING
Mayor Richard Daley	PATRICK HINES
Det. Ed Redditt	CHARLES KNOX ROBINSON
Sheriff Corruthers	ROY JENSON

and: Sheila Frazier, Terry Alexander, Ernie Hudson, Donzaleigh Abernathy, Maynard Jackson, Linda Hopkins, Matt Bennett, Alveda King Beale, Christine King, Bernice King, Dexter King, Martin Luther King III, Harriet Karr, Leon Hall, Tony Holmes, LaDonna Carter, Hope Clarke

A drama about the career of Martin Luther King, Jr. from his days as a Baptist minister in the South of the 1950s until his assassination in 1968. Aside from Billy Goldenberg's Emmy Award-winning score, there were nominations for Paul Winfield and Cicely Tyson as Best Actor and Actress for their performances as Martin and Coretta King, Ossie Davis as Best Supporting Actor for his portrayal of Martin Luther King, Sr., and Abby Mann for his directing and for his writing (two nominations), as well as for the editors of the film and for the production itself as Outstanding Series (1977–78).

*Replaced Harry Belafonte.

MS17
THE AWAKENING LAND
February 19–21, 1978 Warner Bros. (7 hours)

Executive Producers: Harry Bernsen and Tom Kuhn
Producer: Robert E. Relyea
Director: Boris Segal

Teleplay: James Lee Barrett ("The Trees" and "The Fields") and Liam O'Brien ("The Town")
Based on the trilogy of novels by Conrad Richter
Photography: Michel Hugo
Music: Fred Karlin
Production Designer: Jack DeShields
Dance Movement and Dialogue Supervision: Marge Champion
Editor: Bernard J. Small

Sayward Luckett Wheeler	ELIZABETH MONTGOMERY
Portius Wheeler (The Solitary)	HAL HOLBROOK
Genny Luckett	JANE SEYMOUR
Jake Tench	STEVEN KEATS
Jary Luckett	LOUISE LATHAM
Worth Luckett	TONY MOCKUS
Achsa Luckett	DERIN ALTAY
Sulie Luckett	MICHELLE STACY
Louie Scurrah	BARNEY McFADDEN
Will Beagle	W. H. MACY
Granny McWhirter	JEANNETTE NOLAN
Angus Witherspoon	JAMES O'REILLY
Reverend Hutchins	CHARLES TYNER
Mistress Bartram	DORRIE KAVANAUGH
Isaac Barker	BERT REMSEN
Cora Barker	SANDRA WHEELER
George Roebuck	ART KASSUL
Zephron Brown	LOUIS BLANTE
Danny Goldring	GEORGE HOLCOMB
Allen Hamilton	CHARLES GOWAN
Resolve Wheeler	SEAN FRYE
Kinzie Wheeler	JOHNNY TIMKO
Huldah Wheeler	PIA ROMANS
Sulie Wheeler	THERESA LANDRETH
Chancey Wheeler	DENNIS DIMSTER
Dezia Wheeler	TRACY KLERONOMOS
Rosa Tench	KATY KURTZMAN
Dr. Pearsall	BYRNE PIVEN
Huldah (Adult)	DEVON ERICSON
Resolve (Adult)	MARTIN SCANLAN
Kinzie (Adult)	PAUL SWANSON
Aunt Cornelia	JOAN TOMPKINS

A lusty frontier saga about a pioneer woman and her love for her family, the man she marries and the land on which she lives, dramatized from Conrad Richter's Pulitzer Prize-winning triology. Emmy Award nominations went to Elizabeth Montgomery (her tenth), Hal Holbrook and Jeanette Nolan for their acting, Michel Hugo for his cinematography, Fred Karlin for his music score and Bernard J. Small for his film editing. The drama's authenticity came in part from the unusual speech patterns and dialects adapted for the actors by former dancer Marge Champion who drew upon an apparent family heritage for dialogue realism.

MS18
LOOSE CHANGE*
February 26–28, 1978 Universal (6 hours)
(Subsequently retitled *Those Restless Years* and edited to 4 hours)

Executive Producer: Jules Irving
Producer: Michael Rhodes
Director: Jules Irving
Teleplay: Corinne Jacker and Charles E. Israel (Part 1), Jennifer Miller (Part 2), Corinne Jacker and Jennifer Miller (Part 3)
Based on the novel by Sara Davidson
Photography: John Elsenbach (Part 1) and Harry L. Wolf (Parts 2 and 3)
Music: Don Costa
Art Director: William Campbell
Editors: John Elias, John F. Schreyer and Gene Foster

Late Evans	CRISTINA RAINES
Tanya Berensen	SEASON HUBLEY
Jenny Reston	LAURIE HEINEMAN
Tom Feiffer	THEODORE BIKEL
Rob Kagan	GUY BOYD
John Campbell	JOHN GETZ
Hank Okrun	GREGG HENRY
Irene Evans	JUNE LOCKHART
Peter Lane	STEPHEN MACHT
Joe Norman	BEN MASTERS
Sol Berenson	JOSHUA SHELLEY
Judy Berenson	JUDY STRANGIS
Mark Stewart	MICHAEL TOLAN
Dr. Moe Sinden	DAVID WAYNE
Hilda	KATE REID
Roxanne	PAULA WAGNER
Mrs. Berenson	PEGGY McKAY
Timmy Reston	RICHARD STANLEY
Marita Kagan	MARIA ELENA CORDERO
Dave Goodwin	ROBERT SYMONDS

and: James Blendick, Allan Migicovsky, Alice Hirson, Carl Franklin, Gary Swanson, Jon Lormer, Victor Mohica, Milt Kogan, Hunter Von Leer

A novel for television focusing on a ten-year period in the lives and loves of three best girlfriends—an author, an artist and a political activist—maturing during the turbulent 1960s.

*Subsequently cut to 4 hours and retitled *Those Restless Years*.

MS19
HOLOCAUST
April 16–19, 1978 Titus Productions, Inc. (9½ hours)

Executive Producer: Herbert Brodkin
Producer: Robert Berger
Associate Producer: Pia I. Arnold
Director: Marvin J. Chomsky
Teleplay: Gerald Green
Photography: Brian West
Music: Morton Gould
Production Designer: Wilfrid J. Shingleton
Art Directors: Theo Harisch and Jurgen Kiebach
Supervising Editor: Stephen A. Rotter

Adolph Eichmann	TOM BELL
Rudi Weiss	JOSEPH BOTTOMS
Helena Slomova	TOVAH FELDSHUH
Herr Palitz	MARIUS GORING
Berta Weiss	ROSEMARY HARRIS
Heinz Muller	ANTHONY HAYGARTH
Heinrich Himmler	IAN HOLM
Uncle Sasha	LEE MONTAGUE
Erik Dorf	MICHAEL MORIARTY
Marta Dorf	DEBORAH NORTON
Lowy	GEORGE ROSE
Uncle Kurt Dorf	ROBERT STEPHENS
Inga Helms Weiss	MERYL STREEP
Moses Weiss	SAM WANAMAKER
Reinhard Heydrich	DAVID WARNER
Josef Weiss	FRITZ WEAVER
Karl Weiss	JAMES WOODS
Hoefle	SEAN ARNOLD
Hans Frank	JOHN BAILEY
Anna Weiss	BLANCHE BAKER
Frau Lowy	KATE JAENICKE
Dr. Kohn	CHARLES KORVIN

and: Michael Beck, John Collin, David Daker, Vernon Dobtscheff, Edward Hardwicke, Nigel Hawthorne, Werner Kreindl, Stanley Lebor, Jeremy Levy, T. P. McKenna, Hans Meyer, Nora Minor, Irene Prador, George Pravda, Oscar Quitak, Osman Ragheb, John Rees, Llewellyn Rees, Toby Salaman, Murray Salem,

Nina Sandt, Cyril Shaps, Robert Sherman, Gabor Vernon, Peter Vogel.

Chosen as the Outstanding Limited Series (1977–78) at Emmy Award time, this original drama about two German families that are affected by events between 1935 and 1945 rivaled *Roots* in its impact on viewers in this country and sparked controversy throughout Europe as it premiered on television in one country after another. Gerald Green also won an Emmy Award for his teleplay about a Jewish family's desperate fight for survival and the parallel story of a young German lawyer, a family friend, who rises to power as an influential Nazi official. Michael Moriarty (the lawyer), Meryl Streep (the Catholic girl who marries into the Jewish family), and one-time sex symbol Carroll Baker's daughter Blanche (making her acting debut as the family's youngest daughter who becomes a Nazi victim after going mad following an assault) won Emmy statuettes for their performances, as did Marvin J. Chomsky for his direction, Morton Gould for his music score and Peggy Farrell and Edith Almoslino for their costumes. Emmy nominations (sixteen in all) also were given to Fritz Weaver, Rosemary Harris, Sam Wanamaker, David Warner and Tovah Feldshuh as well as production designer Wilfrid J. Shingleton and supervising editor Stephen A. Rotter.

MS20
ARTHUR HAILEY'S WHEELS
May 7-9, 14-15, 1978 Universal (10 hours)

Executive Producer: Roy Huggins
Producer: Robert F. O'Neill
Associate Producer: Gary B. Witney
Director: Jerry London
Teleplay: Millard Lampell, Hank Searls, Robert Hamilton and Nancy Lynn Schwartz
Based on the novel by Arthur Hailey
Photography: Jacques R. Marquette
Music: Morton Stevens
Art Director: William H. Tuntke
Editors: James T. Heckart, Jamie Caylor, Ed England, Gene Ranney and Larry Lester

Adam Trenton	ROCK HUDSON
Erica Trenton	LEE REMICK
Barbara Lipton	BLAIR BROWN
Peter Flodenhale	JOHN BECK
Lowell Baxter	RALPH BELLAMY
Matt Zaleski	SCOTT BRADY
Merv Rucks	JOHN DURREN
Caroline Horton	MARJ DUSAY
Jody Horton	LISA EILBACHER
Smokey Stevenson	ANTHONY FRANCIOSA
Kirk Trenton	JAMES CARROLL JORDAN
Teresa Chapman	ADELE MARA
Greg Trenton	HOWARD McGILLIN
Hub Hewitson	TIM O'CONNOR
Rusty Horton	GERALD S. O'LOUGHLIN
Waggoner	ALLAN RICH
Dr. Patterson	DAVID SPIELBERG
Rollie Knight	HAROLD SYLVESTER
Ursula	JESSICA WALTER
Leonard Wingate	FRED WILLIAMSON
Emerson Vale	ANTHONY COSTELLO
Ernie Johnson	RAMON BIERI
Sir Phillip Sturdevant	JAMES BOOTH
Parkland	JOHN CRAWFORD
Brett DeLossanto	STEWART MOSS
Damiano	CLIFF EMERICH

and: Debi Richter, Bob Hastings, Al C. White, Carole Mallory, James Ray, Richard Venture, Ray Singer, Marilyn Devlin, Dave Shelley, Ellen Travolta, Sheila DeWindt, Danna Hansen, Randy Kirby

Olivia Hussey, Mark Neely, Eleanor Parker, Andrew Stevens and Patricia Neal in THE BASTARD (1978)

The slick Hailey novel about passion and intrigue at the corporate level of the automotive industry emerged an elegantly produced soap opera in this project, the biggest ever handled by a single director and highlighted by the Emmy-nominated performance of Lee Remick as the bored wife who finds that playing second-fiddle to her executive husband's development of a new car leaves her plenty of time for some extramarital sex, alcohol and drugs. This ten-hour movie was filmed in an unprecedented sixty-one different locations around southern California with a star-laden cast heading a roster of over 150 speaking roles. It subsequently gained the dubious distinction of being truncated in its repeat showing by four hours with absolutely no publicity—and with no viewer complaints as Parts 3 and 4 simply were dropped without notice.

MS21
THE DAIN CURSE
May 22–24, 1978 A Martin Poll Production
(6 hours)

Executive Producer: Bob Markell
Producer: Martin Poll
Co-Producer: William C. Gerrity
Director: E. W. Swackhamer
Teleplay: Robert Lenski
Based on the novel by Dashiell Hammett
Photography: Andrew Laszlo
Music: Charles Gross
Art Directors: John Robert Lloyd and Gene Rudolf
Editor: Murray Solomon

Hamilton Nash	JAMES COBURN
Ben Feeney	HECTOR ELIZONDO
Owen Fitzstephan	JASON MILLER
Aaronia Haldorn	JEAN SIMMONS
The Old Man	PAUL STEWART
Alice Dain Leggett	BEATRICE STRAIGHT
Gabrielle Leggett	NANCY ADDISON
Sergeant O'Gar	TOM BOWER
Jack Santos	DAVID CANARY
Marshall Cotton	BEESON CARROLL
Eric Collinson	MARTIN CASSIDY
Tom Vernon	BRIAN DAVIES
Daisy Cotton	RONI DENGEL
Mr. Leggett	PAUL HARDING
Maria Grosso	KAREN LUDWIG
Mickey	MALACHY McCOURT
Tom Fink	BRENT SPINER
Judge Cochran	RON WEYAND
Minnie Hershey	HATTIE WINSTON
Hubert Collinson	ROLAND WINTERS
Joseph Haldorn	ELLIS RABB

Actor James Coburn returned to TV acting after fourteen years to star as Dashiell Hammett's fictional detective Hamilton Nash in this complex tale of the 1920s that has the private eye looking into a diamond robbery and finding himself involved with a young woman's obsession with a deadly family curse. The Mystery Writers of America gave the film their annual Edgar Award (for Edgar Allan Poe) as the Best Television Program of 1978, and director E. W. Swackhamer and recent Oscar winner Beatrice Straight both received Emmy Award nominations for the movie.

MS22
THE BASTARD*
May 1978 Universal (Operation Prime Time)
(4 hours)

Executive Producer: John Wilder
Producer: Joe Byrne
Director: Lee H. Katzin
Teleplay: Guerdon Trueblood
Based on the novel by John Jakes
Photography: Michel Hugo
Music: John Addison
Art Director: Loyd S. Papez
Editors: Robert F. Shugrue and Michael Murphy

Phillipe Charboneau/Philip Kent	ANDREW STEVENS
Benjamin Franklin	TOM BOSLEY
Anne Ware	KIM CATTRALL
Benjamin Edes	BUDDY EBSEN
Bishop Francis	LORNE GREENE
Alicia	OLIVIA HUSSEY
Captain Plummer	CAMERON MITCHELL
Captain Caleb	HARRY MORGAN
Marie Charboneau	PATRICIA NEAL
Lady Amberly	ELEANOR PARKER
Solomon Sholto	DONALD PLEASENCE
Paul Revere	WILLIAM SHATNER
Abraham Ware	BARRY SULLIVAN
Dan O'Brien	NOAH BEERY
Girard	PETER BONERZ
Lord North	JOHN COLICOS
Samuel Adams	WILLIAM DANIELS

Will Campbell	JAMES GREGORY	
Lucas	HERBERT JEFFERSON, JR.	
Roger Amberly	MARK NEELY	
Johnny Malcolm	KEENAN WYNN	

Narrated by RAYMOND BURR

and: Jim Antonio, William Bassett, Roger Bowen, Robert Burke, George Chandler, Sam Chew, Jr., John DeLancie, Johnny Doran, Ike Eisenmann, Peter Elbling, Charles Haid, Alex Henteloff, Russell Johnson, Claude Earl Jones, Monte Landis, Alan Napier, John Mark Robinson, Elizabeth Shepherd, Carol Tru Foster, James Whitmore, Jr., Michael Alldredge, Beege Barkette, Albert Carrier, Damon Douglas, Stephen Furst, James Garrett, Phil Hall, Keith McConnell, Richard Peel, Peggy Rea, Clint Ritchie, Benjamin Stewart, Pamela White

The first of prolific writer John Jakes' seven-part American Bicentennial series was adapted into a film swashbuckler in which the illegitimate son of a French nobleman fights to regain his rightful inheritance amid the dangers and intrigues when American Colonists were overthrowing British rule. This fictionalized account of the Revolutionary War period follows him from Europe to the New World where he encounters Benjamin Franklin, Paul Revere, Samuel Adams and other legendary colonial figures. The leading role was given to newcomer Andrew Stevens (actress Stella Stevens' son), with support from a dozen or so seasoned veterans. Emmy Award nominations went to Loyd S. Papez for his art direction and to Richard Feldman for his set decoration.

*Shown in some locations as *The Kent Chronicles.*

MS23
EVENING IN BYZANTIUM
August 1978 Universal (Operation Prime Time)
(4 hours)

Executive Producer: Glen A. Larson
Supervising Producer: Michael Sloan
Producer: Robert F. O'Neill
Director: Jerry London
Teleplay: Glen A. Larson and Michael Sloan
Based on the novel by Irwin Shaw
Photography: Michael Margulies
Music: Stu Phillips
Art Director: Loyd S. Papez
Editor: Buford Hayes

Jess Craig	GLENN FORD
Brian Murphy	EDDIE ALBERT
Bret Easton	VINCE EDWARDS
Ian Wadleigh	PATRICK MACNEE
Fabricio	GREGORY SIERRA
Jerry Olson	HARRY GUARDINO
Danny	MICHAEL COLE
Walter Klein	SIMON OAKLAND
Sonia Murphy	GLORIA DeHAVEN
Inspector LeDioux	MARCEL HILLAIRE
Inspector DuBois	CHRISTIAN MARQUAND
Monsieur Carroll	LEE BERGERE
Leonardo	LEN BIRMAN
Jack Conrad	JAMES BOOTH
Roger Tory	GEORGE LAZENBY
Constance Dobson	SHIRLEY JONES
Gail McKinnon	ERIN GRAY
Penny Craig	CYNTHIA FORD

John Macklin	ANTHONY COSTELLO
William Bast	WILLIAM DOZIER

and: Nick Dyrenforth, George Skaff, Sid Haig, Ben Frommer, Chris Winfield, Carol Baxter, Edward Olmos, Byron Morrow

Operation Prime Time's third production and first contemporary project deals with power plays at the Cannes Film Festival, where a once famed producer is trying to finance a new movie, and international terrorism which comes straight from his secret script. Action, violence and sexual intrigue are among the ingredients liberally laced into the tale which stars Glenn Ford as the idealistic producer with the politically provocative script and cover girl and TV commercial model Erin Gray as an aggressive writer who chases him for an interview.

MS24
CENTENNIAL
October 1978–February 1979 Universal
(26½ hours)*

Executive Producer: John Wilder
Adapted by John Wilder from the novel by James A. Michener

Basic Cast:

Lame Beaver	MICHAEL ANSARA
Jim Lloyd	WILLIAM ATHERTON
Herman Bockweiss	RAYMOND BURR
Clay Basket	BARBARA CARRERA

Eddie Albert and Glenn Ford in EVENING IN BYZANTIUM (1978)

Robert Conrad in CENTENNIAL (1978)

Richard Chamberlain in CENTENNIAL (1978)

Alexander McKeag	RICHARD CHAMBERLAIN	Old Sioux	CHIEF DAN GEORGE	Clemma Zendt	ADRIANNA LaRUSSO
Pasquinel	ROBERT CONRAD	Alvarez	HENRY DARROW	Messmore Garrett	CLINT RITCHIE
Col. Frank Skimmerhorn	RICHARD CRENNA	Jim Bridger	REB BROWN	Martin Zendt	MARK NEELY
Oliver Seccombe	TIMOTHY DALTON	Blue Leaf	MARIA POTTS	Muerice	ART METRANO
John Skimmerhorn	CLIFF DeYOUNG	Rude Water	ROBERT TESSIER	Finlay Perkin	CLIVE REVILL
Capt. Maxwell Mercy	CHAD EVERETT	General Asher	PERNELL ROBERTS	Philip Wendell	DOUG McKEON
Sidney Andermann	SHARON GLESS	Young Lame Beaver	RAY TRACEY	Tranquilino Marquez	A MARTINEZ
Prof. Lewis Venor	ANDY GRIFFITH	Broken Thumb	JORGE RIVERO	Serafina Marquez	SILVANA GALLENDO
Cisco Calendar	MERLE HAGGARD	Elly Zendt	STEPHANIE ZIMBALIST		
Levi Zendt	GREGORY HARRISON			Reverend Holly	ROBERT PHALEN
		Mother Zendt	IRENE TEDROW	Mr. Norris	LOU FRIZZELL
Paul Garrett (and narrator)	DAVID JANSSEN	Rebecca Stolfitz	DEBI RICHTER	Matt	CLAUDE EARL JONES
Hans Brumbaugh	ALEX KARRAS	Laura Lou Booker	LAURA WINSTON		
Sheriff Axel Dumire	BRIAN KEITH	Lisette Mercy	KAREN CARLSON	Beeley Garrett	TIGER THOMPSON
Lise Bockweiss	SALLY KELLERMAN	Spade Larkin	JAMES SLOYAN	Soren Sorenson	SANDY McPEAK
		John McIntosh	MARK HARMON	Earl Grebe	CLAUDE JARMAN
Jacques Pasquinel	STEPHEN McHATTIE	General Wade	MORGAN WOODWARD	Alice Grebe	JULIE SOMMARS
				Magnes Volkema	BO BRUNDIN
Maude Wendell	LOIS NETTLETON	Lost Eagle	NICK RAMUS	Vesta Volkema	LYNN BORDEN
Samuel Purchase	DONALD PLEASENCE	Abel Tanner	BARNEY McFADDEN	Sheriff Bogardus	GEOFFREY LEWIS
				Judge Hart	DANA ELCAR
Lucinda McKeag Zendt	CRISTINA RAINES	Nacho Gomez	RAFAEL CAMPOS	William Bellamy	WILLIAM BOGERT
Charlotte Buckland	LYNN REDGRAVE	Nate Person	GLYNN TURMAN	Truinfador Marquez	ALEX COLON
Morgan Wendell	ROBERT VAUGHN	Gompert	ROBBY WEAVER	Beeley Garrett (adult)	ALAN VINT
Joe Bean	CLINT WALKER	Amos Calendar	JESSE VINT	Philip Wendell (adult)	MORGAN PAULL
R. J. Poteet	DENNIS WEAVER	Bufe Coker	LES LANNOM	Colonel Salcedo	JOAQUIN MARTINEZ
Mervin Wendell	ANTHONY ZERBE	Laseter	SCOTT HYLANDS		
		Mule Canby	GREG MULLAVEY	Aunt Agusta	GALE SONDERGAARD
Also:		Young Jim Lloyd	MICHAEL LeCLAIR		
Dr. Richard Butler	ROBERT WALDEN	Emma Lloyd	JAY W. MacINTOSH	Flor Marquez	KARMIN MURCELO
Marcel Pasquinel	KARIO SALEM	Claude Richards	ROBERT DOUGLAS	Nate Person III	ROBERT DoQUI

Defense Attorney	JAMES HAMPTON
Prosecutor	JAMES McMULLEN
Dennis	MARSHALL THOMPSON
Manolo Marquez	RENE ENRIQUEZ
Holmes	ROYCE D. APPLEGATE
Judge	RICHARD O'BRIEN
Hank Garvey	JAMES BEST

Chapter 1: "Only the Banks Live Forever" (3 hours) (10/1/78)

Chapter 2: "The Yellow Apron" (2 hours) (10/7/78)
Producer: Howard Alston
Director: Virgil W. Vogel**
Teleplay: John Wilder
Photography: Duke Callaghan
Music: John Addison
Art Director: Jack Senter
Editor: Robert Watts

Chapter 3: "The Wagon and the Elephant" (2 hours) (10/28/78)
Producer: Malcolm R. Harding
Director: Paul Krasny
Teleplay: Jerry Ziegman
Photography: Duke Callaghan
Music: John Addison
Production Design: Jack Senter
Art Directors: Mark Mansbridge, Sherman Loudermilk, Lou Montejano and Seymour Klate
Editor: Robert F. Shugrue

Chapter 4: "For As Long As the Water Flows" (2 hours) (11/4/78)

Chapter 5: "The Massacre" (2 hours) (11/11/78)
Producer: Malcolm R. Harding
Director: Paul Krasny
Teleplay: Jerry Ziegman (Chapter 4) and Charles Larson (Chapter 5)
Photography: Duke Callaghan
Music: John Addison
Art Directors: Sherman Loudermilk, Mark Mansbridge and Lou Montejano
Editor: Ralph Schoenfeld

Chapter 6: "The Longhorns" (2 hours) (12/3/78)
Producer: John Wilder
Director: Virgil W. Vogel
Teleplay: John Wilder
Photography: Ronald Browne
Music: John Addison
Art Director: John P. Bruce
Editor: Bill Parker

Chapter 7: "The Shepherds" (2 hours) (12/10/78)
Producer: Malcolm R. Harding
Director: Virgil W. Vogel
Teleplay: Charles Larson
Photography: Jacques R. Marquette
Music: John Addison
Production Design: Jack Senter
Art Director: John Corso
Editor: Robert Watts

Chapter 8: "The Storm" (2 hours) (1/14/79)

Chapter 9: "The Crime" (2 hours) (1/21/79)
Producer: Malcolm R. Harding
Director: Harry Falk
Teleplay: Charles Larson
Photography: Charles W. Short
Music: John Addison
Art Director: Jack Senter
Editors: Howard Deane and Bill Parker

Chapter 10: "The Winds of Fortune" (2 hours) (1/28/79)
Producer: Malcolm R. Harding
Director: Harry Falk

Teleplay: Charles Larson
Photography: Charles W. Short
Music: John Addison
Production Design: Jack Senter
Art Director: Loyd S. Papez
Editor: John Elias

Chapter 11: "The Winds of Death" (2 hours) (2/3/79)
Producer: Malcolm R. Harding
Director: Bernard McEveety
Teleplay: Jerry Ziegman
Photography: Duke Callaghan
Music: John Addison
Production Design: Jack Senter
Art Director: Loyd S. Papez
Editor: Ralph Schoenfeld

Chapter 12: "The Scream of Eagles" (3 hours) (2/4/79)
Producer: George E. Crosby
Supervising Producer: Richard Caffey
Director: Virgil W. Vogel
Teleplay: John Wilder
Photography: Duke Callaghan
Music: John Addison
Production Design: Jack Senter
Art Directors: John Corso and Loyd S. Papez
Editor: Robert Watts

An epic mini-series about the making of America—the most ambitious project ever filmed for television—this filming of James Michener's 1,100-page saga that spanned the decades from the late eighteenth century to the present ended up as a 26½ hour movie irregularly scheduled over four months and molded into nine self-contained TV movies, each of which could be shown later independently of the others. Heralded in network publicity as "a story of reckless daring and reckless loving, of struggle and pain, of laughter and triumph; it's the story of the land, and the people who turned it into a nation," *Centennial* not only was (and is) the most expensive film ever made for television—its $25-million budget was four times that of *Roots*—but had the biggest "name" cast ever assembled for a dramatic presentation, with David Janssen tying the whole project together as the overall narrator and star of the final "chapter" as the current-day descendant of those who founded the fictional town of Centennial, Colorado. *Centennial* received Emmy Award nominations for Film Editing (Chapter 1) and Art Direction (Chapter 7).

*Shown in two- and three-hour segments irregularly over four months.

**Replaced Sam O'Steen.

MS25
THE IMMIGRANTS
November 1978 Universal (Operation Prime Time) (4 hours)

Executive Producer: Robert A. Cinader
Producers: Gino Grimaldi and Hannah Shearer
Director: Alan J. Levi
Teleplay: Richard Collins
Based on the novel by Howard Fast
Photography: Frank Thackery
Music: Gerald Fried
Art Director: George Renne
Editors: Albert Zuniga and Ed Williams

Dan Lavetta	STEPHEN MACHT
Jean Seldon Lavetta	SHARON GLESS
May Ling	AIMEE ECCLES
Thomas Seldon	RICHARD ANDERSON
Maria Cassala	INA BALIN
Chris Noel	LLOYD BOCHNER
Pete Lomas	KEVIN DOBSON
Mark Levy	MICHAEL DURRELL
Calvin Braderman	RODDY McDOWALL
Mary Seldon	KATHLEEN NOLAN
Anthony Cassala	PERNELL ROBERTS
Alan Brocker	JOHN SAXON
Feng Wo (and narrator)	YUKI SHIMODA
Sarah Levy	SUSAN STRASBERG
Grant Whittier	BARRY SULLIVAN
Joseph Lavetta	AHARON IPALE
Anna Lavetta	MICHELE MARSH
Tony	PAUL SYLVAN
Gregory Pastore	JOE BENNETT
Mrs. Whittier	MONICA LEWIS
So-Toy	BEULAH QUO
Joseph (as a boy)	SHANE SINUTKO
Dan Lavetta (as a boy)	ARI MACHT
Barbara	CYNTHIA EILBACHER
Doctor	DON KEEFER
Somers	REGIS J. CORDIC
Clancy	HARRY TOWNES

and: Walt Davis, Byron Morrow, C. Russ McGinn, June Barret, Jordan Suffin

Howard Fast's number one best-seller—the rags-to-riches-to-rags saga of a young Italian immigrant who battles his way out of the San Francisco earthquake to become a shipping magnate, rise to the top of Nob Hill's society through a loveless marriage to the daughter of the city's wealthiest family, and find happiness with an Oriental mistress despite the collapse of his fortune during the Wall Street crash. It made spectacular way to television on the strength of sincere performances by a solid cast of actors who knew they would be upstaged by the legendary earthquake, re-created on the Universal backlot with new special effects intercut with footage from the studio's earlier *Earthquake,* from MGM's *San Francisco* (with individually colored frames for matching shots), and from existing newsreel footage of the actual event in 1906.

MS26
THE WORD
November 12–15, 1978 Charles Fries Productions/Stonehenge (8 hours)

Executive Producers: Charles Fries and Dick Berg
Producer: David Manson
Director: Richard Lang
Teleplay: Dick Berg, Robert L. Joseph, S. S. Schweitzer and Richard Fielder
Based on the novel by Irving Wallace
Photography: Michel Hugo
Music: Alex North
Art Director: Herman Zimmerman
Editor: David Newhouse

Steve Randall	DAVID JANSSEN
George Wheeler	JAMES WHITMORE
Angela Monti	FLORINDA BOLKAN
Ogden Towery	EDDIE ALBERT
Naomi Dunn	GERALDINE CHAPLIN
Cedric Plummer	HURD HATFIELD
Nathan Randall	JOHN HUSTON
Florian Knight	JOHN McENERY
LeBrun	RON MOODY
Claire Randall	DIANA MULDAUR
Tony Nicholson	KATE MULGREW
Barbara Randall	JANICE RULE
Sarah Randall	MARTHA SCOTT
Maertin de Vroome	NICOL WILLIAMSON
Tom Carey	DAVID ACKROYD
Maria	LAURA BETTI
Heldering	BO BRUNDIN
Henri Aubert	DONALD MOFFAT
Abbot Petropolous	NEHEMIAH PERSOFF
Lori Cook	CATHERINE BURNS

Diana Muldaur, David Janssen and Martha Scott in THE WORD (1978)

Peter Ajemian   NICHOLAS COSTER
Dr. Jeffries   ROLAND CULVER
Herself   TESSIE O'SHEA

and: Walter Gottell, Alexa Kenin, John Korkes, Alan Miller, Lynn Farleigh, Chris Lloyd, Mario Scaccia, John Van Dreelan

Intrigue surrounding the discovery and publication of a controversial document that appears to be a long-lost ancient eye-witness account of the life of Christ, with David Janssen playing a public relations executive hired to promote this new version of the Bible. International film beauty Florinda Balkan made her American acting debut in this movie, and composer Alex North received an Emmy Award nomination for his score.

MS27
PEARL
November 16–17, 19, 1978 A Silliphant-Konigsberg Production/Warner Bros. (6 hours)

Executive Producers: Stirling Silliphant and Franklin Konigsberg
Producer: Sam Manners
Director: Hy Averback
Second Unit Director: Alex Singer
Teleplay: Stirling Silliphant
Photography: Gayne Rescher
Music: John Addison
Art Director: W. Stewart Campbell
Editor: Donald R. Rode

Midge Forrest   ANGIE DICKINSON
Col. Jason Forrest   DENNIS WEAVER
Capt. Cal Lanford   ROBERT WAGNER
Dr. Karel Lang   LESLEY ANN WARREN

Holly Nagata   TIANA
    ALEXANDRA
Lt. Doug North   GREGG HENRY
Sally Colton   KATHERINE
    HELMOND
Pvt. Zylowski   ADAM ARKIN
Sgt. Otto Chain   BRIAN DENNEHY
Sgt. Walder   MAX GAIL
Shirley   CHAR FONTANE
Lily (General's Wife)   AUDRA LINDLEY
Comm. John North   RICHARD
    ANDERSON
Mary North   MARION ROSS
Harrison   ALLAN MILLER
Pvt. John Finger   CHRISTIAN VANCE
Patricia North   MARY FRANCES
    CROSBY
Lt. Christopher   CHIP LUCIA
Cerruti   DAVID ELLIOTT
Looper   LES LANNOM

Narrated by JOSEPH CAMPANELLA

A romantic drama looking suspiciously like *From Here to Eternity* (a mini-series version of which turned up some weeks after this one premiered) and interweaving the lives and passions of three military couples living in Honolulu in December 1941.

MS28
BACKSTAIRS AT THE WHITE HOUSE
January 29, February 5, 12, 19, 1979 Ed Friendly Productions (9 hours)

Executive Producer: Ed Friendly
Producer/Director: Michael O'Herlihy
Associate Producer/Assistant Director: Robert Enrietto

Teleplay: Gwen Bagni and Paul Dubov
Based on the book *My Thirty Years Backstairs at the White House* by Lillian Rogers Parks with Francis Spatz Leighton
Photography: Robert L. Morrison
Music: Morton Stevens
Art Director: Richard Y. Haman
Set Decorator: Anne D. McCulley
Costumes: Bill Thomas
Editors: Paul LaMastra and Roy E. Peterson

Maggie Rogers   OLIVIA COLE
Lillian Rogers Parks   LESLIE UGGAMS
Levi Mercer   LOUIS GOSSETT, JR.
John Mays   ROBERT HOOKS
Ike Hoover   LESLIE NIELSEN
Mrs. Jaffray   CLORIS
    LEACHMAN
Emmett Rogers, Sr.   PAUL WINFIELD
Helen (Nellie) Taft   JULIE HARRIS
William Howard Taft   VICTOR BUONO
Woodrow Wilson   ROBERT VAUGHN
Ellen Wilson   KIM HUNTER
Edith Galt Wilson   CLAIRE BLOOM
Florence Harding   CELESTE HOLM
Warren G. Harding   GEORGE KENNEDY
Calvin Coolidge   ED FLANDERS
Grace Coolidge   LEE GRANT
Herbert Hoover   LARRY GATES
Lou Hoover   JAN STERLING
Eleanor Roosevelt   EILEEN HECKART
Franklin Delano Roosevelt   JOHN ANDERSON
Harry S. Truman   HARRY MORGAN
Bess Truman   ESTELLE PARSONS
Mamie Eisenhower   BARBARA BARRIE
Dwight Eisenhower   ANDREW DUGGAN
Young Emmett   KEVIN HOOKS
Young Lillian   TANIA JOHNSON

Coates	HARI RHODES
Jackson	BILL OVERTON
Annie Gilhooley	HELEN CARROLL
Dixon	DAVID DOWNING
Frazer	JAMES A. WATSON, JR.
Mrs. Colgate	DANA WYNTER
Mr. Johnson	JOHN RANDOLPH
Harry Daugherty	BARRY SULLIVAN
Navy Secretary	FORD RAINEY
Mrs. Long	DIANE SHALET
Bridgit	KATHLEEN DOYLE
Wheatley Parks	HARRISON PAGE
Alexander Woollcott	TOM CLANCY
Louis Howe	WOODROW PARFREY
Krim	RICHARD ROAT
Miss Mesbitt	LOUISE LATHAM
Roy Clayton	JAMES CRITTENDEN
Miss Lahan	BIBI BESCH
Mrs. Walker	MARGED WAKELY
Margaret Truman	NANCY MORGAN
Miss Clare	ANN DORAN
Mrs. Wallace	HEATHER ANGEL

and: Dan Mason, Emmaline Henry, Anna Mathias, Brendan Dillon, Joe Lowry, Harry Townes, Tom Scott, Noble Willingham, Frank McCarthy, Lee Kessler, Carson Sipes, Bill Barrett, Ron Recasner, Bill Quinn, Stymie Beard, Gerry Black, Bebe Drake-Hooks, Guy Christopher, Betty Bridges, Ron Kelly, Harry Gayle Sanders, Marilyn Chris

A lovingly filmed version of the book by Lillian Rogers Parks, the crippled seamstress-maid who, along with her mother, served for fifty-two years as a White House domestic during eight presidential administrations. A mixture of pop history of the twentieth century and the private lives of the various First Families (as portrayed by an all-star cast) as seen through the eyes of the various maids and butlers, played by many of the same black actors who had appeared in and "died" in the initial *Roots* and thus were not available for the sequel to that mini-series that, in calculated programming, was scheduled in part against *Backstairs at the White House*. There were eleven Emmy Award nominations for the film: Outstanding Limited Series, Best Actress (Olivia Cole), Best Actor (Louis Gossett, Jr.), Best Supporting Actress (both Eileen Heckart and Celeste Holm), Best Supporting Actor (both Ed Flanders and Robert Vaughn), Outstanding Teleplay (Part 1), Outstanding Art Direction/Set Decoration (Part 1), and two other technical awards. These made *Backstairs at the White House* the single most honored program of the 1978–79 TV season.

MS29
FROM HERE TO ETERNITY
February 14, 21, 28, 1979 Bennett-Katleman Productions/Columbia Pictures (6 hours)

Executive Producers: Harve Bennett and Harris Katleman
Producer/Director: Buzz Kulik
Teleplay: Don McGuire and Harold Gast
Based on the novel by James Jones and the screenplay by Daniel Taradash
Photography: Gerald Perry Finnerman
Music: Walter Scharf
Big Band Music arranged by Shorty Rodgers
Sung by Helen O'Connell and The Modernaires
Production Supervisor: Carl Pingitore
Art Directors: Ross Bellah and Robert Peterson
Costumes: Grady Hunt
Editors: Les Green, Robert L. Swanson and Michael B. Hoggan

Karen Holmes	NATALIE WOOD
Sgt. Milt Warden	WILLIAM DEVANE
Pvt. Robert E. Lee Prewitt	STEVE RAILSBACH

Capt. Dana Holmes	ROY THINNES
Angelo Maggio	JOE PANTOLINO
Lorene Rogers	KIM BASINGER
Fatso Judson	PETER BOYLE
Cpl. Cheney	WILL SAMPSON
PFC Hanson	RICK HURST
Gert Kipfer	SALOME JENS
Sgt. Maylon Stark	ANDREW ROBINSON
Lt. Ross	DAVID SPIELBERG
Col. Jake Delbart	RICHARD VENTURE
Gen. Barney Slater	ANDY GRIFFITH
Sgt. Doehm	RICHARD BRIGHT
Cpl. Lewis	CHRISTOPHER MURNEY
Cpl. Kowalski	GENE SCHERER
Major Thompson	JOHN CRAWFORD
Cpl. Levy	WYNN IRWIN
Violet	MORGAN KESLER
Sgt. McKay	RON MAX
Sgt. Preem	KENNETH WHITE
Cpl. Herbert	GARY SWANSON
Della	DEA ST. LAMONT
Chip Holmes	JONATHAN B. WOODWARD

and: Tech Murdock, Jonathan LaPage, Mariko Tse, Donegan Smith, Russ Marin, Carmen Argenziano, Robert Davi, Jerry Day, Sally Kim, Bebe Louie, Clem Low, Karin Mani, Victoria Perry, Julia Sabre, Allen G. Wood.

An expanded new version of the 1953 movie classic taken from James Jones' memorable first novel dealing with military life in Hawaii on the eve of the attack on Pearl Harbor. The Burt Lancaster-Deborah Kerr-Montgomery Clift-Frank Sinatra-Donna Reed roles were here played by (respectively) William Devane, Natalie Wood, Steve Railsbach, Joe Pantolino and Kim Basinger. A series which spun off from this mini-series was planned for the fall of 1979 with William Devane and Roy Thinnes continuing their roles and Barbara Hershey taking over for Natalie Wood.

MS30
ROOTS: THE NEXT GENERATIONS
February 18-23, 25, 1979 A David L. Wolper Production (14 hours)

Executive Producer: David L. Wolper
Producer: Stan Margulies
Directors: John Erman, Charles S. Dubin, Georg Stanford Brown and Lloyd Richards
Teleplay: Ernest Kinoy, Sidney A. Glass, Thad Mumford, Daniel Wilcox, and John McGreevey
Developed by Ernest Kinoy
Based on the books *Roots* and *Search* by Alex Haley
Photography: Joseph M. Wilcots
Music: Gerald Fried
Art Director: Robert MacKichan
Editors: John W. Wheeler, Robbe Roberts, Neil Travis and David Saxon

Tom Harvey	GEORG STANFORD BROWN
Mrs. Warner	OLIVIA De HAVILLAND
Col. Frederick Warner	HENRY FONDA
Earl Crowther	PAUL KOSLO
Chicken George	AVON LONG
Irene Harvey	LYNNE MOODY
Beeman Jones	GREG MORRIS
Andy Warner	MARC SINGER
Jim Warner	RICHARD THOMAS
Carrie Barden	FAY HAUSER
John Dolan	BRIAN MITCHELL
Elizabeth Harvey	DEBBI MORGAN
Lucy Damson	KATHLEEN DOYLE
Sally Harvey	JA'NET DUBOIS

Sam Wesley	SLIM GAILLARD
Bob Campbell	HARRY MORGAN
Lee Garnet	ROGER E. MOSLEY
Will Palmer	STAN SHAW
Bertha Palmer	IRENE CARA
R. S. M. Boyce	JAMES DALY
Dad Jones	OSSIE DAVIS
Queen Haley	RUBY DEE
Simon Haley	DORIAN HAREWOOD
Detroit	KENE HOLLIDAY
Mr. Goldstein	GEORGE VOSKOVEC
Aleck Haley	HAL WILLIAMS
Cynthia Palmer	BEVER-LEIGH BANFIELD
Frank Warner (age 20)	E. LAMONT JOHNSON
Bubba Haywood	BERNIE CASEY
Francey	PAM GRIER
Big Slew Johnson	ROSEY GRIER
Capt. Bowker	GERALD S. O'LOUGHLIN
Boyd Moffatt	PERCY RODRIGUES
Lt. Hamilton Ten Eyck	JOHN RUBINSTEIN
Mrs. Andy Warner	DIANA DOUGLAS
Judge Quartermain	JASON WINGREEN
Sister Scrap Scott	MAIDIE NORMAN
Calloway	BRUCE FRENCH
Lyle Pettijohn	ROBERT CULP
Mrs. Hickinger	DINA MERRILL
Ab Decker	BROCK PETERS
Cynthia Palmer	BEAH RICHARDS
Dr. Horace Huguley	PAUL WINFIELD
Cousin Georgia	LYNN HAMILTON
Alex Haley (age 8)	CHRISTOFF ST. JOHN
D. L. Lewis	LOGAN RAMSEY
Sheriff Duffy	DENNIS FIMPLE
Nan Branch Haley	DEBBIE ALLEN
Alex Haley (17–25)	DAMON EVANS
Cmdr. Robert Munroe	ANDY GRIFFITH
Zeona (Mrs. Simon Haley)	DIAHANN CARROLL
Nelson	RAFER JOHNSON
Lila	CARMEN McRAE
Scotty	JOHN HANCOCK
Mrs. Lydia Branch	DELLA REESE
Daisy	THELMA HOPKINS
Mel Klein	MILT KOGAN
Dodie Brattle	BARBARA BARRIE
George Lincoln Rockwell	MARLON BRANDO
Dr. Lewis	JAMES BRODERICK
Odile Richards	LEE CHAMBERLAIN
Dr. Vansina	MICHAEL CONSTANTINE
Bernie Raymond	NORMAN FELL
Malcolm X	AL FREEMAN, JR.
Alex Haley	JAMES EARL JONES
Sister Will Ada	CLAUDIA McNEIL
Singer	LINDA HOPKINS
Pianist	BOBBY SHORT
Mrs. Bulfinch	JANE ROSE
George Haley	HOWARD ROLLINS
Ebou Manga	JOHNNY SEKKA

The unparalleled success of *Roots* in 1977 prompted this continuation of Alex Haley's saga, beginning with the events where its predecessor ended in 1882 and bringing the story to the present with James Earl Jones playing Haley and Marlon Brando as American Nazi leader George Lincoln Rockwell, who agreed to an interview in the 1960s with Haley for *Playboy*. Brando won an Emmy (as Outstanding Supporting Actor) for his ten-minute cameo part, his television acting debut. *Roots: The Next Generations* covered fourteen television hours, two more than its predecessor, with only Georg Stanford Brown and Lynne Moody (as Tom Harvey and his wife Irene, Alex Haley's great-great-grandparents) continuing the roles they began in

Marlon Brando and James Earl Jones in ROOTS: THE NEXT GENERATIONS (1979)

Moxey	JAMES CALLAHAN
Fran Lonigan	DEVON ERICSON
Loretta Lonigan	JESSICA HARPER
Davey Cohen	SAM WEISMAN
Weary Riley	DAVID WILSON
Phil Rolfe	JED COOPER
Young Studs	DAN SHOR
Young Danny	KEVIN O'BRIEN
Young Davey	COREY PEPPER
Young Weary	FREDERIC LEHNE
Young Paulie	KEITH GORDON
Young Red Kelly	GLENN WITHROW
Paulie Haggerty	MICHAEL K. HAGGERTY
Father Gilhooley	DOLPH SWEET
Eileen Haggerty	LAURIE HEINEMAN
Helen Borax	LESLIE ACKERMAN
Davey's Father	RICHARD B. SCHULL
Sally (Prostitute)	NORA HEFLIN
Nurse	ANNE SEYMOUR

and: Jay W. McIntosh, Bob Neill, John Chilton, Shelly Juttner, Steffan Zacharias, Meridict Baer, Annie O'Neill, June Whitley Taylor, Darrell Larsen, Bob Hastings, Camille Ashland, Angelo Rossito, Betty Cole, Jade McCall, John Furlong, Pamela Hayden

The television adaptation drawn from James T. Farrell's once-banned-for-being-oh-so-racy '30s trilogy *(Young Lonigan, The Young Manhood of Studs Lonigan* and *Judgment Day)* about the struggles and growing pangs of a self-destructive Depression-era Chicago youth introduced to TV viewers the rough-hewn Harry Hamlin, who not long before had made an auspicious debut in films in *Movie, Movie.* Superior in every way to the previous B-movie filming of the Farrell classic in 1960, with another virtual unknown, Christopher Knight, in the lead (Knight remained an unknown), this six-hour version nonetheless failed to catch fire despite Reginald Rose's literate teleplay and the strong performances of veterans like Charles Durning and Colleen Dewhurst as Studs' parents. Emmy Award nominations went to *Studs Lonigan* for Outstanding Art/Set Direction for both Part 1 and Part 3 (it won for the latter).

MS32
THE CHISHOLMS
March 29, April 5, 12, 19, 1979 Alan Landsburg Productions (6 hours)

Executive Producers: Alan Landsburg and David Dortort
Producer: Paul Freeman
Director: Mel Stuart
Created by David Dortort
Teleplay: Evan Hunter
Based on his novel
Photography: Jacques R. Marquette
Music: Elmer Bernstein
Based on themes from "Appalachin Spring," "Billy the Kid" and "Rodeo" by Aaron Copland
Art Director: Fred Price
Editors: Corky Ehlers and Arthur Stafford

Hadley Chisholm	ROBERT PRESTON
Minerva Chisholm	ROSEMARY HARRIS
Will Chisholm	BEN MURPHY
Gideon Chisholm	BRIAN KERWIN
Beau Chisholm	JIMMY VAN PATTEN
Bonnie Sue Chisholm	STACEY NELKIN
Annabel Chisholm	SUSAN SWIFT
Lester Hackett	CHARLES FRANK
Elizabeth Chisholm	GLYNNIS O'CONNOR
Kewedinok	SANDRA GRIEGO

Roots. Brown also directed several hours of the sequel. Like its predecessor, *Roots: The Next Generations* was an Emmy Award winner as Outstanding Limited Series, with other nominations going to Ruby Dee as Outstanding Supporting Actress, to Al Freeman, Jr. and Paul Winfield as Outstanding Supporting Actor (in competition with Brando), to writer Ernest Kinoy (for Part 1) and to the makeup experts (for Part 3).

MS31
STUDS LONIGAN
March 7, 14, 21, 1979 Lorimar Productions (6 hours)

Executive Producers: Lee Rich and Philip Capice
Producer: Harry R. Sherman
Director: James Goldstone
Teleplay: Reginald Rose
Based on the trilogy by James T. Farrell
Photography: Terry K. Meade
Music: Ken Lauber
Art Director: Jan Scott
Costumes: Bill Jobe
Editors: Edward A. Biery, Jeff Godison and Ken Zemke

Bill Lonigan (Studs)	HARRY HAMLIN
Mary Lonigan	COLLEEN DEWHURST
Danny O'Neill	BRAD DOURIF
Paddy Lonigan	CHARLES DURNING
Lucy Scanlon	LISA PELIKAN
Catherine Banahan	DIANA SCARWID
Martin Lonigan	JOHN FRIEDRICH

Robert Preston and Rosemary Harris (top); Ben Murphy (center); Jimmy Van Patten, Susan Swift, Stacey Nelkin and Brian Kerwin in THE CHISHOLMS (1979)

Timothy Oates	DAVID HAYWARD	Judge Wilson	CHARLES L. CAMPBELL
Jimmy Jackson	ANTHONY ZERBE		
Andrew Blake	BRIAN KEITH	Howahkan	JOE (RUNNING FOX) GARCIA
Fiddler Ephraim	DOUG KERSHAW		
Harlow Cooper	TOM TAYLOR	Franz Schwarzenbacher	CHRISTOPHER ALLPORT
Brian Cassidy	GAVIN TROSTER		
Luke Cassidy	JAMES D. O'REILLY	Mrs. Hackett	PEG SMALL
Jeremy Stokes	DEAN HILL		
Squire Bailey	DAVID ALLEN		
Benjamin Lowery	DENNIS KENNEDY		
Doc Simpson	JAMES HARRELL		
Millie Bain	MAUREEN STEINDLER		
Jonah Comyns	JERRY HARDIN		
Sarah Comyns	KATIE HANDLEY		

and: Mike Genovese, Tenaya Torres, Geno Silva, Ron Godines, Billy Drago, Don Shanks, Jack Wallace, Roger Frazier, Richard L. Jamison

The sprawling saga of a close-knit pioneer family's hazardous trek from their home in Virginia to Fort Laramie, Wyoming, and ultimately California.

MS33
IKE

May 3–4, 6, 1979 ABC Circle Films (6 hours)

Executive Producer: Melville Shavelson
Producer: Bill McCutchen
Directors: Melville Shavelson (U.S. and North African sequences) and Boris Sagal (European scenes)
Teleplay: Melville Shavelson
Based on official files of the United States Army, historical sources in The National Archives, and the autobiography *Past Forgetting* by Kay Summersby Morgan
Photography: Arch R. Dalzell and Freddie Young
Music: Fred Karlin
Choreography: Marge Champion (Europe) and Miriam Nelson (U.S.)
Art Directors: Ward Preston and Peter Murton
Editors: John M. Woodcock, Paul Dixon and Bill Lenny

Gen. Dwight D. Eisenhower	ROBERT DUVALL
Kay Summersby	LEE REMICK
Gen. George C. Marshall	DANA ANDREWS
Gen. Walter Bedell Smith	J. D. CANNON
Capt. Ernest (Tex) Lee	PAUL GLEASON
Maj. Richard Arnold	LAURENCE LUCKINBILL
Gen. George S. Patton	DARREN McGAVIN
Winston Churchill	WENSLEY PITHEY
Field Marshal Sir Bernard Montgomery	IAN RICHARDSON
Franklin Delano Roosevelt	STEVE ROBERTS
Gen. Mark Clark	WILLIAM SCHALLERT
Field Marshal Alfred Jodl	WOLFGANG PREISS
Mamie Eisenhower	BONNIE BARTLETT
Gen. Lucian Truscott	CHARLES H. GRAY
Himself	LOWELL THOMAS
Gen. Charles DeGaulle	VERNON DOBTCHEFF
Gen. Omar Bradley	RICHARD T. HERD
Mrs. Westerfield	K CALLAN
Gen. Arthur Tedder	TERRENCE ALEXANDER
Gen. "Freddie" DeGuingand	CHARLES GRAY
Sergeant Hunt	CLIFTON JONES
Admiral	WHIT BISSELL
General String	MICHAEL MALNICK
Mickey McKeogh	VINCENT MARZELLO
Noel Coward	FRANCIS MATTHEWS
Gertrude Lawrence	PATRICIA MICHAEL
Sergeant Mooney	MAJOR WILEY

Eisenhower the military man is the focus of this TV mini-series, his relationship with the other wartime leaders, and, very discreetly, his personal relationship with his driver, Kay Summersby. *Ike* came up with five Emmy Award nominations: Outstanding Cinematography (Part 2), Outstanding Film Editing (Part 3), and three others in the technical category.

MS34
THE REBELS

May 1979 Universal (Operation Prime Time) (4 hours)

Executive Producer: Robert A. Cinader
Producers: Gino Grimaldi and Hannah Shearer
Associate Producer: Bernadette Joyce
Director: Russ Mayberry
Teleplay: Sean Bain and Robert A. Cinader
Based on the novel by John Jakes
Photography: Frank Thackery

Music: Gerald Fried
Art Director: William Campbell
Editors: John Kaufman and Skip Lusk

Philip Kent	ANDREW STEVENS
Judson Fletcher	DON JOHNSON
Eph Tait	DOUG McCLURE
John Hancock	JIM BACKUS
Duke of Kentland	RICHARD BASEHART
Mrs. Brumple	JOAN BLONDELL
Benjamin Franklin	TOM BOSLEY
Breen	RORY CALHOUN
Dr. Church	MACDONALD CAREY
Anne Kent	KIM CATTRALL
Henry Knox	JOHN CHAPPELL
John Adams	WILLIAM DANIELS
Mrs. Harris	ANNE FRANCIS
George Washington	PETER GRAVES
Charlotte Waverly	PAMELA HENSLEY
Peggy McLean	GWEN HUMBLE
General Howe	WILFRID HYDE-WHITE
Baron von Steuben	NEHEMIAH PERSOFF
John Waverly	WILLIAM SMITH
Ambrose Waverly	WARREN STEVENS
Thomas Jefferson	KEVIN TIGHE
Sam Gill	BOBBY TROUP
Angus Fletcher	FORREST TUCKER
Rachel	TANYA TUCKER
Lafayette	MARC VAHANIAN
Seth McLean	ROBERT VAUGHN

Narrated by WILLIAM CONRAD

and: David Matthau, Ben Davidson, Paul Fix, Debi Richter, Chip Johnson, Duncan Gamble, Ted Gehring, Sammy Jackson, Gordon Steel, Timothy O'Hagen, John Rayner, Tom Williams

A second helping of elegantly mounted fiction about the America Revolution as written by the prolific John Jakes. This sequel to *The Bastard* (1978) continues the saga of Philip Kent, the illegitimate son of an English nobleman, who has renounced his patrician birthright to become a Colonial soldier fighting for America's independence, befriending a southern aristocrat and his earthy buddy to help thwart a plot to assassinate George Washington. Andrew Stevens as Kent, Kim Cattrall as his wife, and Tom Bosley and Ben Franklin are the only performers back from the original four-hour film. William Daniels, who played Samuel Adams in *The Bastard,* is back as John Adams in *The Rebels,* being destined, it seems, to play the entire Adams family (he also was John Adams in *1776* on stage and screen and was John Quincy Adams in the television special *The Adams Chronicles*).

MS35
BLIND AMBITION
May 20–23, 1979 Time-Life Television Productions
(8 hours)

Executive Producer: David Susskind
Producers: George Schaefer and Renee Valente
Director: George Schaefer
Teleplay: Stanley R. Greenberg
Based on the books *Blind Ambition* by John Dean and *Mo* by Maureen Dean
Photography: Edward R. Brown
Music: Walter Scharf (Parts 1 and 2) and Fred Karlin (Parts 3 and 4)
Art Director: Michael Baugh
Editors: Arthur David Hilton, Peter Parasheles and John Wright

John Dean	MARTIN SHEEN
Maureen Dean	THERESA RUSSELL
Charles Colson	MICHAEL CALLAN
L. Patrick Gray	LONNY CHAPMAN

Lee Remick and Robert Duvall in IKE (1979)

G. Gordon Liddy	WILLIAM DANIELS
Fred Fielding	CLIFFORD DAVID
Charles Shaffer	ED FLANDERS
Donald Segretti	FRED GRANDY
Jeb Stuart Magruder	CHRISTOPHER GUEST
John Ehrlichman	GRAHAM JARVIS
Henry Peterson	EDWARD MALLORY
John J. Caufield	GERALD S. O'LOUGHLIN
George Simonson	ALAN OPPENHEIMER
H. R. Haldeman	LAWRENCE PRESSMAN
John Mitchell	JOHN RANDOLPH
Robert Mardian	PETER MARK RICHMAN
Herbert Kalmbach	WILLIAM SCHALLERT
Ronald Ziegler	JAMES SLOYAN
Richard M. Nixon	RIP TORN
Richard Kleindienst	WILLIAM WINDOM
Hugh Sloan	RALPH BYERS
Gordon Strachman	PATRICK COLLINS
Egil Krogh	KIP NIVEN
Carol Thompson	GARN STEPHENS
J. Edgar Hoover	LOGAN RAMSEY
E. Howard Hunt	JAMES GREENE
Press Briefing Secretary	MITZI HOAG

Jane Thomas	LEE KESSLER
Dwight Chapin	DAWSON MAYS
Frederick LaRye	DARRELL ZWERLING
Mrs. Pat Nixon	CATHLEEN CORDELL
Jack Garfield	TERRY McGOVERN
Liz Garfield	JENNY O'HARA
Judge John Sirica	AL CHECCO
Maureen Dean's Mother	ROSEMARY DeCAMP
Sam Dash	DAVID SHEINER

and: Josette Banzet, Ross Bickell, Stuart Gillard, Harry Basch, Brian Farrell, James Karen, Jo DeWinter, Alan Haufrect, Anne Ramsey, Patricia Stitch, Jack Collins, Don Herbert, Mario Machado, Janice Kent, Hal Fishman, Janet Langhart, John Barbour, Ray Briehm, Larry Carroll, Larry McCormick, Hettie Lynn Hurtes

The Watergate crisis as viewed by John Dean and his wife Maureen, based on their personal accounts—his best-seller, her book on how it affected their marriage —and distilled into an eight-hour drama with all of the political figures of the day parading by as Dean relates his story to his attorney when his world based on blind ambition begins crashing down on him. Sheen, whose gamut of portrayals ran from Robert Kennedy (in *The Missiles of October*) to Pretty Boy Floyd, is Dean during his years as counsel to President Nixon. Theresa Russell, who had starred in only two theatrical movies,

made her TV acting debut as Maureen Dean. Rip Torn's offbeat interpretation of Richard Nixon seems to have been based on personal feeling rather than on actual conversations and speeches and occasionally threatened to derail the entire concept of the drama. *Blind Ambition* was nominated for an Emmy as the Outstanding Limited Series of the 1978–79 season. A second nomination went to the film for Art Direction/Set Decoration (Part 3).

MS36
A MAN CALLED INTREPID
May 20–22, 1979 Lorimar Productions/Astral Bellevue Pathe Ltd. (6 hours)

Executive Producers: Lee Rich, Philip Capice and Harold Greenberg
Producer: Peter Katz
Director: Peter Carter
Teleplay: William Blinn
Based on the novel by William Stevenson
Photography: Brian West
Music: Robert Farnon
Production Design: Keith Wilson
Art Director: Claude Bonniere
Editors: Tony Lower and Martin Pepler

Sir William Stephenson	DAVID NIVEN
Evan Michaelian	MICHAEL YORK
Madelaine	BARBARA HERSHEY
Col. Juergen	PAUL HARDING
Sister Luke	FLORA ROBSON
Gubbins	PETER GILMORE
Mrs. Wainwright	RENEE ASHERSON
Winston Churchill	NIGEL STOCK
Alexander Korda	FERDY MAYNE
Cynthia	GAYLE HUNNICUTT
Anna	SHIRLEY STEEDMAN
Deidra	BELINDA MAYNE
Nils Bohr	LARRY REYNOLDS
Albert Einstein	JOSEPH GOLLAND
Heisenberg	CHRIS WIGGINS
Bill Donovan	DICK O'NEIL
J. Edgar Hoover	KEN JAMES
Willoughby	SHANE RIMMER

and: Reg Lye, Bruce Boa, Leon Green, Collin Fox, Brian Strimer, Paul Shelley, Edward Dentith, David King, Jo Dunlop, John Quentin, Spencer Banks, Sue Vanner, Ian Sharp, Jack McKenzie, Judy Wiles, William Greaves, Adrian Gibbs, Roger Owen, Tony Stephens, Christopher Jenkinson, Marianne Stone, Lincoln Wright

A fanciful suspense drama inspired by William Stevenson's best-selling account about the formation of an Allied espionage network during World War II by a wealthy Canadian using his own funds. David Niven made his TV movie debut as the man behind the operation.

Alphabetized listing of titles followed in each case by release year in parentheses and catalogue index number referring to its chronological position in the previous section. A second date where indicated is that of production year if a wide discrepancy between the film's making and its release exists. Italicized titles indicate a subsequent name change under which the film now shows in syndication. "MS" numbers refer to mini-series.

ABDUCTION OF SAINT ANNE, THE (1975) 0507 *(They've Kidnapped Anne Benedict)*
ADVENTURES OF DON QUIXOTE, THE (1973) 0324
ADVENTURES OF NICK CARTER, THE (1972) 0213
ADVENTURES OF THE QUEEN (1975) 0518
AFFAIR, THE (1973) 0356
ALEXANDER: THE OTHER SIDE OF DAWN (1977) 0720
ALIAS SMITH AND JONES (1971) 0105
ALL CREATURES GREAT AND SMALL (1975) 0511
ALL MY DARLING DAUGHTERS (1972) 0257
ALL THE KIND STRANGERS (1974) 0476
ALL TOGETHER NOW (1975) 0512
ALOHA MEANS GOODBYE (1974) 0463
ALONG CAME A SPIDER (1970) 0068
ALPHA CAPER, THE (1973) 0340
AMATEUR NIGHT AT THE DIXIE BAR AND GRILL (1979) 0935
AMAZING HOWARD HUGHES, THE (1977) 0712
AMELIA EARHART (1976) 0662
ANATOMY OF A SEDUCTION (1979) 0980
AND I ALONE SURVIVED (1978) 0910
AND NO ONE COULD SAVE HER (1973) 0293
AND YOUR NAME IS JONAH (1979) 0945
ANY SECOND NOW (1969) 0033
AQUARIANS, THE (1970) 0091
ARE YOU IN THE HOUSE ALONE? (1978) 0875
ART OF THE CRIME, THE (1975) 0596
ARTHUR HAILEY'S THE MONEYCHANGERS (1976) MS06
ARTHUR HAILEY'S WHEELS (1978) MS20
ASPEN (1977) MS14 *(The Innocent and the Damned)*
ASSAULT ON THE WAYNE (1971) 0107
ASSIGNMENT: MUNICH (1972) 0225
ATTACK ON TERROR: THE FBI VERSUS THE KU KLUX KLAN (1975) 0522
AUTOBIOGRAPHY OF MISS JANE PITTMAN, THE (1974) 0389
AWAKENING LAND, THE (1978) MS17

BABE (1975) 0584
BACKSTAIRS AT THE WHITE HOUSE (1979) MS28
BAD RONALD (1974) 0467
BAFFLED! (1973) 0283
BAIT, THE (1973) 0307
BALLAD OF ANDY CROCKER, THE (1969) 0052
BANACEK: DETOUR TO NOWHERE (1972) 0223
BANJO HACKETT: ROAMIN' FREE (1976) 0628
BANYON (1971) 0126
BARBARY COAST, THE (1975) 0558
BASTARD, THE (1978) MS22 (also known as *The Kent Chronicles*)
BATTERED (1978) 0877
BEACH PATROL (1979) 0977
BEASTS ARE ON THE STREETS, THE (1978) 0852
BEAUTY AND THE BEAST (1976) 0676
BEG, BORROW . . . OR STEAL (1973) 0315
BEHIND THE BADGE (see KILLING AFFAIR, A)
BENNY AND BARNEY: LAS VEGAS UNDERCOVER (1977) 0684
BERLIN AFFAIR (1970) 0093
BERMUDA DEPTHS, THE (1978) 0807
BEST PLACE TO BE, THE (1979) 0995
BETRAYAL (1974) 0488
BETRAYAL (1978) 0903
BEYOND THE BERMUDA TRIANGLE (1975) 0587
BIG BOB JOHNSON AND HIS FANTASTIC SPEED CIRCUS (1978) 0862
BIG RIPOFF, THE (1975) 0536
BIG ROSE (1974) 0421
BILLION DOLLAR THREAT, THE (1979) 0971
BILLY: PORTRAIT OF A STREET KID (1977) 0750
BIRDMEN, THE (1971) 0140 *(Escape of the Birdmen)*
BIRDS OF PREY (1973) 0281
BJ AND THE BEAR (1978) 0882
BLACK BEAUTY (1978) MS15
BLACK MARKET BABY (1977) 0765
BLACK NOON (1971) 0164
BLACK WATER GOLD (1970) 0061
BLIND AMBITION (1979) MS35
BLOOD SPORT (1973) 0364
BLUE KNIGHT, THE (1973) MS01
BLUE KNIGHT, THE (1975) 0564
BORGIA STICK, THE (1967) 0012
BORN INNOCENT (1974) 0448
BORROWERS, THE (1973) 0369
BOUNTY MAN, THE (1972) 0250
BOY IN THE PLASTIC BUBBLE, THE (1976) 0669
BRAND NEW LIFE, A (1973) 0292
BRAVOS, THE (1972) 0192
BREAKING UP (1978) 0797

BREAKOUT (1970) 0102
BRENDA STARR (1976) 0630
BRIAN'S SONG (1971) 0177
BRIDGER (1976) 0648
BRIEF ENCOUNTER (1974) 0475
BRINK'S: THE GREAT ROBBERY (1976) 0616
BROCK'S LAST CASE (1973) 0301
BROTHERHOOD OF THE BELL, THE (1970) 0083
BUD AND LOU (1978) 0905
BUT I DON'T WANT TO GET MARRIED! (1970) 0087

CABLE CAR MURDER, THE (1971) 0172 *(Cross Current)*
CAGE WITHOUT A KEY (1975) 0537
CALIFORNIA KID, THE (1974) 0456
CALL HER MOM (1972) 0210
CALL OF THE WILD, THE (1976) 0640
CALL TO DANGER (1973) 0297
CAN HELEN BE SAVED? (1974) 0393
CANNON (1971) 0129
CAPTAIN AMERICA (1979) 0940
CAPTAINS AND THE KINGS (1976) MS04
CAPTAINS COURAGEOUS (1977) 0783
CARTER'S ARMY (1970) 0066
CASE OF RAPE, A (1974) 0401
CAT CREATURE, THE (1973) 0367
CAT ON A HOT TIN ROOF (1976) 0678
CATCHER, THE (1972) 0226
CATHOLICS (1973) 0361
CENTENNIAL (1978) MS24
CENTURY TURNS, THE (see HEC RAMSEY)
CHADWICK FAMILY, THE (1974) 0437
CHALLENGE, THE (1970) 0070
CHALLENGERS, THE (1970) 0072
CHAMPIONS: A LOVE STORY (1979) 0936
CHARLESTON (1979) 0938
CHARLIE COBB: NICE NIGHT FOR A HANGING (1977) 0735
CHARLIE'S ANGELS (1976) 0614
CHASE (1973) 0319
CHILD STEALER, THE (1979) 0959
CHILDREN OF THE LOTUS EATERS (see PSYCHIATRIST: GOD BLESS THE CHILDREN, THE)
CHISHOLMS, THE (1979) MS32
CHRISTMAS MIRACLE IN CAUFIELD, U.S.A. (1977) 0793
CHRISTMAS TO REMEMBER, A (1978) 0929
CINDY (1978) 0832
CIRCLE OF CHILDREN, A (1977) 0705
CITY, THE (1971) 0134
CITY, THE (1977) 0687
CITY BENEATH THE SEA (1971) 0111
CLASS OF '63 (1973) 0308

GIRL ON THE LATE, LATE SHOW, THE (1974) 0426
GIRL WHO CAME GIFT-WRAPPED, THE (1974) 0388
GIRLS IN THE OFFICE, THE (1979) 0948
GIRLS OF HUNTINGTON HOUSE, THE (1973) 0291
GLASS HOUSE, THE (see TRUMAN CAPOTE'S THE GLASS HOUSE)
GLASS MENAGERIE, THE (1973) 0371
GO ASK ALICE (1973) 0280
GO WEST, YOUNG GIRL (1978) 0842
GODCHILD, THE (1974) 0483
GOLD OF THE AMAZON WOMEN (1979) 0958
GOLDENROD (1977) 0731
GOOD AGAINST EVIL (1977) 0729
GOODBYE RAGGEDY ANN (1971) 0157
GOODNIGHT MY LOVE (1972) 0246
GRASS IS ALWAYS GREENER OVER THE SEP-TIC TANK, THE (1978) 0891
GREAT AMERICAN BEAUTY CONTEST, THE (1973) 0287
GREAT AMERICAN TRAGEDY, A (1972) 0247
GREAT EXPECTATIONS (1974) 0481
GREAT HOUDINIS, THE (1976) 0658
GREAT ICE RIP-OFF, THE (1974) 0473
GREAT MAN'S WHISKERS, THE (1973) (1969) 0289
GREAT NIAGARA, THE (1974) 0454
GREAT WALLENDAS, THE (1978) 0810
GREATEST GIFT, THE (1974) 0471
GREATEST THING THAT ALMOST HAP-PENED, THE (1977) 0769
GREEN EYES (1977) 0683
GRIFFIN AND PHOENIX (1976) 0606
GUESS WHO'S SLEEPING IN MY BED? (1973) 0349
GUIDE FOR THE MARRIED WOMAN, A (1978) 0884
GUILTY OR INNOCENT: THE SAM SHEPPARD MURDER CASE (1975) 0593
GUN, THE (1974) 0477
GUN AND THE PULPIT, THE (1974) 0427

HANGED MAN, THE (1964) 0002
HANGED MAN, THE (1974) 0413
HANGING BY A THREAD (1979) 0981
HAPPILY EVER AFTER (1978) 0870
HAPPINESS IS A WARM CLUE (1973) 0327 (The Return of Charlie Chan)
HARDCASE (1972) 0204
HARNESS, THE (1971) 0167
HAROLD ROBBINS' 79 PARK AVENUE (1977) MS13
HAROLD ROBBINS' THE PIRATE (1978) 0906
HARPY (1971) 0125
HATFIELDS AND THE McCOYS, THE (1975) 0505
HAUNTS OF THE VERY RICH (1972) 0233
HAUSER'S MEMORY (1970) 0098
HAVING BABIES (1976) 0659
HAVING BABIES II (1977) 0770
HAVING BABIES III (1978) 0826
HAWAII FIVE-O (1968) 0019
HAWKINS ON MURDER (1973) 0306 (Death and the Maiden)
HEALERS, THE (1974) 0447
HEAT OF ANGER (1972) 0218
HEATWAVE! (1974) 0387
HEC RAMSEY (1972) 0240 (The Century Turns)
HEIDI (1968) 0023
HEIST, THE (1972) 0259
HELTER SKELTER (1976) 0617
HEY, I'M ALIVE (1975) 0589
HIGH RISK (1976) 0635
HIJACK! (1973) 0336
HIT LADY (1974) 0461
HITCHED (1973) 0321
HITCHHIKE! (1974) 0403
HOLLOW IMAGE (1979) 1001
HOLOCAUST (1978) MS19

HOME FOR THE HOLIDAYS (1972) 0258
HOME OF OUR OWN, A (1975) 0582
HOME TO STAY (1978) 0844
HOMECOMING, THE (1971) 0188
HONEYMOON WITH A STRANGER (1969) 0059
HONKY TONK (1974) 0425
HONOR THY FATHER (1973) 0300
HORROR AT 37,000 FEET, THE (1973) 0288
HOSTAGE HEART, THE (1977) 0749
HOT ROD (1979) 0993
HOUND OF THE BASKERVILLES, THE (1972) 0208
HOUSE ON GARIBALDI STREET, THE (1979) 0996
HOUSE ON GREENAPPLE ROAD, THE (1970) 0063
HOUSE THAT WOULD NOT DIE, THE (1970) 0092
HOUSTON, WE'VE GOT A PROBLEM (1974) 0407
HOW AWFUL ABOUT ALLAN (1970) 0084
HOW I SPENT MY SUMMER VACATION (1967) 0007
HOW TO BREAK UP A HAPPY DIVORCE (1976) 0657
HOW TO PICK UP GIRLS! (1978) 0899
HOW TO STEAL AN AIRPLANE (1971) (1968) 0181 (Only One Day Left Before Tomorrow)
HOWLING IN THE WOODS, A (1971) 0163
HUCKLEBERRY FINN (1975) 0542
HUMAN FEELINGS (1978) 0885
HUNCHBACK OF NOTRE DAME, THE (1978) 0863
HUNTED LADY, THE (1977) 0780
HUNTER (1973) (1971) 0273
HUNTERS ARE FOR KILLING (1970) 0079
HUNTERS OF THE REEF (1978) 0853
HURRICANE (1974) 0449
HUSTLING (1975) 0523

I HEARD THE OWL CALL MY NAME (1973) 0372
I KNOW WHY THE CAGED BIRD SINGS (1979) 0976
I LOVE A MYSTERY (1973) (1967) 0296
I LOVE YOU, GOODBYE (1974) 0398
I WANT TO KEEP MY BABY (1976) 0673
I WILL FIGHT NO MORE FOREVER (1975) 0549
IF TOMORROW COMES (1971) 0180
IKE (1979) MS33
IMMIGRANTS, THE (1978) MS25
IMMORTAL, THE (1969) 0041
IMPATIENT HEART, THE (1971) 0150
IMPOSTER, THE (1975) 0538
IN BROAD DAYLIGHT (1971) 0155
IN NAME ONLY (1969) 0053
IN SEARCH OF AMERICA (1971) 0127
IN TANDEM (1974) 0446 (Movin' On)
IN THE GLITTER PALACE (1977) 0702
IN THE MATTER OF KAREN ANN QUINLAN (1977) 0759
IN THIS HOUSE OF BREDE (1975) 0527
INCIDENT IN SAN FRANCISCO (1971) 0119
INCIDENT ON A DARK STREET (1973) 0275
INCREDIBLE HULK, THE (1977) 0772
INCREDIBLE JOURNEY OF DOCTOR MEG LAUREL, THE (1979) 0932
INCREDIBLE ROCKY MOUNTAIN RACE, THE (1977) 0788
INDICT AND CONVICT (1974) 0376
INITIATION OF SARAH, THE (1978) 0814
INNOCENT AND THE DAMNED, THE (see ASPEN)
INSTITUTE FOR REVENGE (1979) 0943
INTIMATE STRANGERS (1977) 0775
INTRUDERS, THE (1970) 0095
INVASION OF JOHNSON COUNTY, THE (1976) 0646
INVISIBLE MAN, THE (1975) 0560
IRONSIDE (1967) 0014

ISHI: THE LAST OF HIS TRIBE (1978) 0928
ISLANDER, THE (1978) 0874
ISN'T IT SHOCKING? (1973) 0338
ISTANBUL EXPRESS (1968) 0021
IT COULDN'T HAPPEN TO A NICER GUY (1974) 0478
IT HAPPENED AT LAKE WOOD MANOR (1977) 0781 (Panic at Lakewood Manor)
IT HAPPENED ONE CHRISTMAS (1977) 0786
IT'S GOOD TO BE ALIVE (1974) 0402

JAMES A. MICHENER'S DYNASTY (1976) 0612
JAMES AT 15 (1977) 0748
JAMES DEAN (1976) 0604
JANE EYRE (1971) 0128
JARRETT (1973) 0310
JENNIFER: A WOMAN'S STORY (1979) 0957
JERICHO MILE, THE (1979) 0963
JESUS OF NAZARETH (1977) MS10
JIGSAW (1972) 0224
JOHNNY, WE HARDLY KNEW YE (1977) 0693
JORDAN CHANCE, THE (1978) 0919
JOURNEY FROM DARKNESS (1975) 0524
JUDGE AND JAKE WYLER, THE (1972) 0260
JUDGE DEE AND THE MONASTERY MUR-DERS (1974) 0493
JUDGE HORTON AND THE SCOTTSBORO BOYS (1976) 0622
JUST A LITTLE INCONVENIENCE (1977) 0761
JUST AN OLD SWEET SONG (1976) 0650
JUST ME AND YOU (1978) 0855

KANSAS CITY MASSACRE, THE (1975) 0576
KATE BLISS AND THE TICKER TAPE KID (1978) 0856
KATE McSHANE (1975) 0546
KATHERINE (1975) 0579
KATIE: PORTRAIT OF A CENTERFOLD (1978) 0888
KEEFER (1978) 0830
KEEGANS, THE (1976) 0627
KENT CHRONICLES, THE (see BASTARD, THE)
KEY WEST (1973) 0366
KILL ME IF YOU CAN (1977) 0758
KILLDOZER (1974) 0390
KILLER BEES (1974) 0405
KILLER BY NIGHT (1972) 0190
KILLER ON BOARD (1977) 0766
KILLER WHO WOULDN'T DIE, THE (1976) 0619
KILLING AFFAIR, A (1977) 0757 (Behind the Badge)
KILLING STONE (1978) 0843
KING (1978) MS16
KINGSTON: THE POWER PLAY (1976) 0651
KISS ME, KILL ME (1976) 0631
KISS MEETS THE PHANTOM OF THE PARK (1978) 0893
KOJAK AND THE MARCUS-NELSON MUR-DERS (see MARCUS-NELSON MURDERS, THE)
KUNG FU (1972) 0214

LACY AND THE MISSISSIPPI QUEEN (1978) 0850
LADY OF THE HOUSE (1978) 0903
LANIGAN'S RABBI (1976) 0643
LARRY (1974) 0440
LAST ANGRY MAN, THE (1974) 0435
LAST CHILD, THE (1971) 0149
LAST CRY FOR HELP, A (1979) 0941
LAST DAY, THE (1975) 0519
LAST DINOSAUR, THE (1977) 0697
LAST GIRAFFE, THE (1979) 1000
LAST HOURS BEFORE MORNING (1975) 0552
LAST HURRAH, THE (1977) 0776
LAST OF THE GOOD GUYS (1978) 0827
LAST OF THE MOHICANS (1977) 0779
LAST SURVIVORS, THE (1975) 0530
LAST TENANT, THE (1978) 0865
LAW, THE (1974) 0465
LAW AND ORDER (1976) 0629
LAW OF THE LAND (1976) 0624

PLAYMATES (1972) 0237
PLEASURE COVE (1979) 0934
POLICE STORY, THE (1973) 0313
POOR DEVIL (1973) 0290
PORTRAIT OF A DEAD GIRL (see McCLOUD: WHO KILLED MISS U.S.A.?)
POSSESSED, THE (1977) 0714
POWDERKEG (1971) 0133
POWER WITHIN, THE (1979) 0983
PRAY FOR THE WILDCATS (1974) 0386
PRESCRIPTION: MURDER (1968) 0017
PRESIDENT'S MISTRESS, THE (1978) 0816
PRESIDENT'S PLANE IS MISSING, THE (1973) 0346
PRIEST KILLER, THE (1971) 0136
PRINCE OF CENTRAL PARK, THE (1977) 0739
PROBE (1972) 0209 (Search)
PROFANE COMEDY, THE (see SET THIS TOWN ON FIRE)
PROMISE HIM ANYTHING . . . (1975) 0566
PSYCHIATRIST: GOD BLESS THE CHILDREN, THE (1970) 0103 (Children of the Lotus Eater)
PUNCH AND JODY (1974) 0484
PURSUIT (1972) 0263

QB VII (1974) 0442
QUARANTINED (1970) 0074
QUEEN OF THE STARDUST BALLROOM (1975) 0517
QUEST, THE (1976) 0633
QUESTION OF GUILT, A (1978) 0820
QUESTION OF LOVE, A (1978) 0908
QUESTOR TAPES, THE (1974) 0385
QUINNS, THE (1977) 0745

RAID ON ENTEBBE (1977) 0685
RAINBOW (1978) 0901
RANGERS, THE (1974) 0492
RANSOM FOR A DEAD MAN (1971) 0120
RANSOM FOR ALICE! (1977) 0732
REAL AMERICAN HERO, A (1978) 0917
REBELS, THE (1979) MS34
RED ALERT (1977) 0723
RED BADGE OF COURAGE, THE (1974) 0487
RED PONY, THE (1973) 0312
REFLECTIONS OF MURDER (1974) 0482
RELENTLESS (1977) 0752
RELUCTANT HEROES, THE (1971) 0173
REMEMBER WHEN (1974) 0419
RETURN OF CHARLIE CHAN, THE (see HAPPINESS IS A WARM CLUE)
RETURN OF JOE FORRESTER, THE (1975) 0561
RETURN OF MOD SQUAD, THE (1979) 0990
RETURN OF THE GUNFIGHTER (1967) 0009
RETURN OF THE WORLD'S GREATEST DETECTIVE, THE (1976) 0642
RETURN TO EARTH (1976) 0634
RETURN TO FANTASY ISLAND (1978) 0803
RETURNING HOME (1975) 0555
REVENGE (1971) 0165
REVENGE FOR A RAPE (1976) 0672
RHINEMANN EXCHANGE, THE (1977) MS09
RICHIE BROCKELMAN: MISSING 24 HOURS (1976) 0663
RICH MAN, POOR MAN (1976) MS03
RING OF PASSION (1978) 0813
RITUAL OF EVIL (1970) 0073
RIVER OF GOLD (1971) 0123
RIVER OF MYSTERY (1971) (1969) 0146
ROBINSON CRUSOE (1974) 0485
ROCKFORD FILES, THE (1974) 0422
ROGER & HARRY: THE MITERA TARGET (1977) 0715 (Love for Ransom)
ROLL, FREDDY, ROLL! (1974) 0490
ROLLING MAN (1972) 0239
ROOKIES, THE (1972) 0222
ROOTS (1977) MS07
ROOTS: THE NEXT GENERATIONS (1979) MS30

ROSEMARY'S BABY II (see LOOK WHAT'S HAPPENED TO ROSEMARY'S BABY)
ROSETTI AND RYAN: MEN WHO LOVE WOMEN (1977) 0725
RUBY AND OSWALD (1978) 0815 (Four Days in Dallas)
RUN A CROOKED MILE (1969) 0051
RUN, SIMON, RUN (1970) 0100
RUNAWAY! (1973) 0337
RUNAWAY BARGE, THE (1975) 0541
RUNAWAYS, THE (1975) 0543

SACKETTS, THE (1979) 0988
SALVAGE (1979) 0942
SAM HILL: WHO KILLED THE MYSTERIOUS MR. FOSTER? (1971) 0112
SAMURAI (1979) 0978
SAN FRANCISCO INTERNATIONAL (1970) 0085
SAN PEDRO BUMS, THE (1977) 0719
SANCTUARY OF FEAR (1979) 0974 (The Girl in the Park)
SANDCASTLES (1972) 0245
SARAH T.—PORTRAIT OF A TEENAGE ALCOHOLIC (1975) 0514
SARGE: THE BADGE OR THE CROSS (1971) 0116
SATAN'S SCHOOL FOR GIRLS (1973) 0334
SATAN'S TRIANGLE (1975) 0504
SAVAGE (1973) 0322
SAVAGE BEES, THE (1976) 0674
SAVAGES (1974) 0450
SAY GOODBYE, MAGGIE COLE (1972) 0236
SCALPLOCK (1966) 0003
SCORPIO LETTERS, THE (1967) 0011
SCOTT FREE (1976) 0660
SCREAM OF THE WOLF (1974) 0382
SCREAM, PRETTY PEGGY (1973) 0357
SCREAMING WOMAN, THE (1972) 0201
SEARCH (see PROBE)
SEARCH FOR THE GODS (1975) 0534
SECOND CHANCE (1972) 0206
SECRET LIFE OF JOHN CHAPMAN, THE (1976) 0682
SECRET NIGHT CALLER, THE (1975) 0520
SECRETS (1977) 0699
SECRETS OF THREE HUNGRY WIVES (1978) 0883
SEE HOW SHE RUNS (1978) 0809
SEE HOW THEY RUN (1964) 0001
SEE THE MAN RUN (1971) 0183
SEEDING OF SARAH BURNS, THE (1979) 0968
SENIOR YEAR (1974) 0418
SENSITIVE, PASSIONATE MAN, A (1977) 0734
SERGEANT MATLOVICH VS. THE U.S. AIR FORCE (1978) 0866
SERPICO: THE DEADLY GAME (1976) 0623
SET THIS TOWN ON FIRE (1973) (1969) 0271 (The Profane Comedy)
SEVEN IN DARKNESS (1969) 0040
SEVENTH AVENUE (1977) MS08
79 PARK AVENUE (see HAROLD ROBBINS' 79 PARK AVENUE)
SEX AND THE MARRIED WOMAN (1977) 0751
SEX SYMBOL, THE (1974) 0451
SHADOW IN THE STREETS, A (1975) 0508
SHADOW ON THE LAND (1968) 0026
SHADOW OVER ELVERON (1968) 0018
SHARK KILL (1976) 0638
SHARON: PORTRAIT OF A MISTRESS (1977) 0771
SHE CRIED "MURDER!" (1973) 0335
SHE LIVES (1973) 0331
SHE WAITS (1972) 0200
SHELL GAME (1963) 0563
SHERIFF, THE (1971) 0130
SHERLOCK HOLMES IN NEW YORK (1976) 0661
SHIRTS/SKINS (1973) 0341
SHOOTOUT IN A ONE-DOG TOWN (1974) 0380
SHORT WALK TO DAYLIGHT (1972) 0248
SIDEKICKS (1974) 0417

SIEGE (1978) 0841
SILENCE, THE (1975) 0588
SILENT GUN, THE (1969) 0058
SILENT NIGHT, LONELY NIGHT (1969) 0057
SILENT VICTORY: THE KITTY O'NEIL STORY (1979) 0954
SIX-MILLION DOLLAR MAN, THE (1973) 0304
SKI LIFT TO DEATH (1978) 0825
SKY HEI$T (1975) 0569
SKYWAY TO DEATH (1974) 0383
SMASH-UP ON INTERSTATE 5 (1976) 0677
SMILE, JENNY, YOU'RE DEAD (1974) 0391
SMUGGLERS, THE (1968) 0030
SNATCHED (1973) 0284
SNOOP SISTERS, THE (1972) 0265 (Female Instinct)
SNOWBEAST (1977) 0713
SOLE SURVIVOR (1970) 0062
SOME KIND OF MIRACLE (1979) 0933
SOMEONE I TOUCHED (1975) 0526
SOMEONE IS WATCHING ME! (1978) 0911
SOMETHING EVIL (1972) 0197
SOMETHING FOR A LONELY MAN (1968) 0025
SOMETHING FOR JOEY (1977) 0711
SON RISE: A MIRACLE OF LOVE (1979) 0987
SOONER OR LATER (1979) 0966
SOUND OF ANGER, THE (1968) 0028
SPECIAL KIND OF LOVE, A (see SPECIAL OLYMPICS)
SPECIAL OLYMPICS (1978) 0821 (A Special Kind of Love)
SPECIALISTS, THE (1975) 0495
SPECTRE (1977) 0727
SPELL, THE (1977) 0698
SPIDER-MAN (1977) 0753
SPLIT SECOND TO AN EPITAPH (1968) 0020
SPY KILLER, THE (1969) 0050
SST—DEATH FLIGHT (1977) 0700 (SST: Disaster in the Sky)
STALK THE WILD CHILD (1976) 0665
STANDING TALL (1978) 0804
STARSKY AND HUTCH (1975) 0556
STEEL COWBOY (1978) 0915
STEP OUT OF LINE, A (1971) 0118
STICKING TOGETHER (1978) 0839
STONESTREET: WHO KILLED THE CENTERFOLD MODEL? (1977) 0690
STORY OF JACOB AND JOSEPH, THE (1974) 0430
STORY OF PRETTY BOY FLOYD, THE (1974) 0444
STORYTELLER, THE (1977) 0785
STOWAWAY TO THE MOON (1975) 0502
STRANGE AND DEADLY OCCURRENCE, THE (1974) 0455
STRANGE HOMECOMING (1974) 0468
STRANGE NEW WORLD (1975) 0573
STRANGE POSSESSION OF MRS. OLIVER, THE (1977) 0701
STRANGER, THE (1973) 0295
STRANGER IN OUR HOUSE (1978) 0897
STRANGER ON THE RUN (1967) 0015
STRANGER WHO LOOKS LIKE ME, THE (1974) 0408
STRANGER WITHIN, THE (1974) 0457
STRANGERS IN 7A, THE (1972) 0255
STRANGERS: THE STORY OF A MOTHER AND DAUGHTER (1979) 0986
STREET KILLING (1976) 0649
STREETS OF SAN FRANCISCO, THE (1972) 0230
STRIKE FORCE (1975) 0548
STUDS LONIGAN (1979) MS31
STUNT SEVEN (1979) 0998
SUDDENLY, LOVE (1978) 0913
SUDDENLY SINGLE (1971) 0156
SUMMER OF MY GERMAN SOLDIER (1978) 0895
SUMMER WITHOUT BOYS, A (1973) 0363
SUNSHINE (1973) 0353
SUNSHINE CHRISTMAS (1977) 0787
SUNSHINE PATRIOT, THE (1968) 0029
SUPERDOME (1978) 0799

SURVIVAL OF DANA (1979) 0997
SWEET HOSTAGE (1975) 0580
SWEET, SWEET RACHEL (1971) 0148
SWISS FAMILY ROBINSON, THE (1975) 0550
SWITCH (1975) 0535
SYBIL (1976) 0670

TAIL GUNNER JOE (1977) 0695
TARANTULAS: THE DEADLY CARGO (1977) 0794
TARGET RISK (1975) 0496
TASTE OF EVIL, A (1971) 0153
TATTERED WEB, A (1971) 0143
TELETHON (1977) 0774
TELL ME MY NAME (1977) 0791
TELL ME WHERE IT HURTS (1974) 0411
TENAFLY (1973) 0286
TERRACES (1977) 0744
TERROR IN THE SKY (1971) 0138
TERROR ON THE BEACH (1973) 0332
TERROR ON THE 40th FLOOR (1974) 0452
TERROR OUT OF THE SKY (1978) 0930
TESTIMONY OF TWO MEN (1977) MS11
THADDEUS ROSE AND EDDIE (1978) 0823
THAT CERTAIN SUMMER (1972) 0251
THEN CAME BRONSON (1969) 0037
THEY CALL IT MURDER (1971) 0185
THEY ONLY COME OUT AT NIGHT (1975) 0554
THEY'VE KIDNAPPED ANNE BENEDICT (see ABDUCTION OF SAINT ANNE, THE)
THIEF (1971) 0152
THIEF OF BAGHDAD, THE (1978) 0907
THINGS IN THEIR SEASON (1974) 0486
THIRD GIRL FROM THE LEFT, THE (1973) 0344
THIS MAN STANDS ALONE (1979) 0999
THIS WAS THE WEST THAT WAS (1974) 0491
THOSE RESTLESS YEARS (see LOOSE CHANGE)
THOU SHALT NOT COMMIT ADULTERY (1978) 0898
THREE ON A DATE (1978) 0817
THREE'S A CROWD (1969) 0054
3,000 MILE CHASE, THE (1977) 0738
THURSDAY'S GAME (1974) (1971) 0432
TIME MACHINE, THE (1978) 0900
TIME TRAVELERS (1976) 0613
TO ALL MY FRIENDS ON SHORE (1972) 0215
TO KILL A COP (1978) 0837
TOM SAWYER (1973) 0317
TOMA (1973) 0316
TOO FAR TO GO (1979) 0960
TOO MANY SUSPECTS (see ELLERY QUEEN)
TOP SECRET (1978) 0859
TORN BETWEEN TWO LOVERS (1979) 0979
TRACKERS, THE (1971) 0184
TRANSPLANT (1979) 0972

TRAPPED (1973) 0355
TRAPPED BENEATH THE SEA (1974) 0466
TRAVIS LOGAN, D.A. (1971) 0124
TREE GROWS IN BROOKLYN, A (1974) 0423
TRIAL OF CHAPLAIN JENSEN, THE (1975) 0515
TRIAL OF LEE HARVEY OSWALD, THE (1977) 0760
TRIAL RUN (1969) 0032
TRIANGLE FACTORY FIRE SCANDAL, THE (1979) 0947
TRIBE, THE (1974) 0489
TRIBES (1970) 0094
TRILOGY OF TERROR (1975) 0531
TROUBLE COMES TO TOWN (1973) 0274
TRUE GRIT (1978) 0852
TRUMAN CAPOTE'S THE GLASS HOUSE (1972) 0203
TURN OF THE SCREW (1974) 0433
TURNING POINT OF JIM MALLOY, THE (1975) 0547
21 HOURS AT MUNICH (1976) 0667
TWICE IN A LIFETIME (1974) 0415
TWIN DETECTIVES (1976) 0625
TWO-FIVE, THE (1978) 0838
TWO FOR THE MONEY (1972) 0216
TWO ON A BENCH (1971) 0162

UFO INCIDENT, THE (1975) 0583
ULTIMATE IMPOSTER, THE (1979) 0985
U.M.C. (1969) 0039 *(Operation Heartbeat)*
UNDERGROUND MAN, THE (1974) 0443
UNWED FATHER (1974) 0406
USERS, THE (1978) 0870

VACATION IN HELL (1979) 0992
VANISHED (1971) 0122
VEGA$ (1978) 0840
VERY MISSING PERSON, A (1972) 0219
VICTIM, THE (1972) 0254
VICTORY AT ENTEBBE (1976) 0679
VIRGINIA HILL STORY, THE (1974) 0479
VISIONS . . . (1972) 0242 *(Visions of Death)*
VOYAGE OF THE YES, THE (1973) 0278

WAKE ME WHEN THE WAR IS OVER (1969) 0043
WALKING THROUGH THE FIRE (1979) 0989
WANTED: THE SUNDANCE WOMAN (1976) 0656 *(Mrs. Sundance Rides Again)*
WAR BETWEEN THE TATES, THE (1977) 0737
WAR OF CHILDREN, A (1972) 0262
WASHINGTON: BEHIND CLOSED DOORS (1977) MS12
WEEKEND NUN, THE (1972) 0267
WEEKEND OF TERROR (1970) 0101

WELCOME HOME, JOHNNY BRISTOL (1972) 0202
WHAT ARE BEST FRIENDS FOR? (1973) 0373
WHAT'S A NICE GIRL LIKE YOU . . . ? (1971) 0187
WHEELS (see ARTHUR HAILEY'S WHEELS)
WHEN EVERY DAY WAS THE FOURTH OF JULY (1978) 0828
WHEN MICHAEL CALLS (1972) 0205
WHERE HAVE ALL THE PEOPLE GONE? (1974) 0460
WHO IS THE BLACK DAHLIA? (1975) 0528
WHOLE WORLD IS WATCHING, THE (1969) 0036
WHO'LL SAVE OUR CHILDREN? (1978) 0923
WIDOW (1976) 0601
WILD AND WOOLY (1978) 0819
WILD WILD WEST REVISITED, THE (1979) 0982
WILD WOMEN (1970) 0090
WILLA (1979) 0962
WILMA (1977) 0790
WINCHESTER '73 (1967) 0013
WINDS OF KITTY HAWK, THE (1978) 0925
WINGS OF FIRE (1967) 0010
WINNER TAKE ALL (1975) 0529
WINTER KILL (1974) 0434
WITH THIS RING (1978) 0846
WOMAN CALLED MOSES, A (1978) 0917
WOMAN HUNTER, THE (1972) 0231
WOMAN OF THE YEAR (1976) 0644
WOMAN WHO CRIED MURDER, THE (see DEATH SCREAM)
WOMEN AT WEST POINT (1979) 0955
WOMEN IN CHAINS (1972) 0199
WONDER WOMAN (1974) 0410
WORD, THE (1978) MS26

YESTERDAY'S CHILD (1977) 0694
YOU CAN'T GO HOME AGAIN (1979) 0975
YOU LIE SO DEEP, MY LOVE (1975) 0525
YOU'LL NEVER SEE ME AGAIN (1973) 0299
YOUNG COUNTRY, THE (1970) 0081
YOUNG JOE, THE FORGOTTEN KENNEDY (1977) 0755
YOUNG PIONEERS (1976) 0607
YOUNG PIONEERS' CHRISTMAS (1976) 0680
YOUNG LAWYERS, THE (1969) 0047
YOUR MONEY OR YOUR WIFE (1972) 0266
YUMA (1971) 0121

ZIEGFELD: THE MAN AND HIS WOMEN (1978) 0854
ZUMA BEACH (1978) 0879

THE ACTORS

(Premiere date follows film title. A second title in
parentheses indicates that by which the film is now
shown. A second date in parentheses refers to year
made if there is a great difference between the film's
production and its initial showing.)

PHILIP ABBOTT
Tail Gunner Joe (1977) 0695
Escape from Brogan County (1977) 0764
Cops and Robin (1978) 0833

WALTER ABEL
The Man Without a Country (1973) 0325

SHARON ACKER
A Clear and Present Danger (1970) 0082
Hec Ramsey (The Century Turns) (1972) 0240
The Stranger (1973) 0295
The Hanged Man (1974) 0413
The Hostage Heart (1977) 0749

BETTYE ACKERMAN
Companions in Nightmare (1968) 0024
Heat of Anger (1972) 0218
Murder or Mercy (1974) 0438
Doctors' Private Lives (1978) 0831

DAVID ACKROYD
Exo-Man (1977) 0740
The Dark Secret of Harvest Home (1978) 0805
The Word (1978) MS26
And I Alone Survived (1978) 0910

BROOKE ADAMS
The Daughters of Joshua Cabe (1975) 0509
Who Is the Black Dahlia? (1975) 0528
Murder on Flight 502 (1975) 0594

DON ADAMS
The Love Boat (1976) 0652

EDIE ADAMS
Evil Roy Slade (1972) 0211
The Return of Joe Forrester (1975) 0561
Superdome (1978) 0799
Fast Friends (1979) 0964

JULIE ADAMS
The Trackers (1971) 0184
Go Ask Alice (1973) 0280

NANCY ADDISON
The Dain Curse (1978) MS21

LUTHER ADLER
The Sunshine Patriot (1968) 0029
The Psychiatrist: God Bless the Children
(Children of the Lotus Eater) (1970) 0103

JENNY AGUTTER
A War of Children (1972) 0262
The Man in the Iron Mask (1977) 0691

PHILIP AHN
Hawaii Five-O (1968) 0019
Kung Fu (1972) 0214

CLAUDE AKINS
Lock, Stock and Barrel (1971) 0142
River of Mystery (1971) 0146
The Night Stalker (1972) 0193
The Norliss Tapes (1973) 0294
The Death Squad (1974) 0379
In Tandem (Movin' On) (1974) 0446
Medical Story (1975) 0575
Eric (1975) 0591
Kiss Me, Kill Me (1976) 0631
Yesterday's Child (1977) 0694
The Rhinemann Exchange (1977) MS09
Killer on Board (1977) 0766
Tarantulas: The Deadly Cargo (1977) 0794
Little Mo (1978) 0869
BJ and the Bear (1978) 0882
Murder in Music City (1979) 0939

JOSH ALBEE
Tom Sawyer (1973) 0317
The Runaways (1975) 0543
Helter Skelter (1976) 0617
A Question of Love (1978) 0908

EDDIE ALBERT
See the Man Run (1971) 0183
Fireball Forward (1972) 0220
The Borrowers (1973) 0369

Switch (1975) 0535
Promise Him Anything . . . (1975) 0566
Evening in Byzantium (1978) MS23
The Word (1978) MS26

EDWARD ALBERT
Killer Bees (1974) 0405
Death Cruise (1974) 0470
Black Beauty (1978) MS15
The Millionaire (1978) 0927
Silent Victory: The Kitty O'Neil Story (1979)
0954

JACK ALBERTSON
The Monk (1969) 0045
A Clear and Present Danger (1970) 0082
Once Upon a Dead Man (1971) 0139
Congratulations, It's a Boy! (1971) 0141
Lock, Stock and Barrel (1971) 0142
The Comedy Company (1978) 0834

LOLA ALBRIGHT
Delta County, U.S.A. (1977) 0726
Terraces (1977) 0744

ALAN ALDA
Truman Capote's The Glass House (1972) 0203
Playmates (1972) 0237
Isn't It Shocking? (1973) 0338
Kill Me If You Can (1977) 0758

ROBERT ALDA
Last Hours Before Morning (1975) 0552
Perfect Gentlemen (1978) 0829

JANE ALEXANDER
Welcome Home, Johnny Bristol (1972) 0202
Miracle on 34th Street (1973) 0370
This Was the West That Was (1974) 0491
Death Be Not Proud (1975) 0510
Eleanor and Franklin (1976) 0598
A Circle of Children (1977) 0705
Eleanor and Franklin: The White House Years
(1977) 0706
A Question of Love (1978) 0908
Lovey: A Circle of Children, Part II (1978)
0920

341

DEBORAH ALLEN
The Greatest Thing That Almost Happened (1977) 0769
Roots: The Next Generations (1979) MS30

ELIZABETH ALLEN
No Other Love (1979) 0965

MARTY ALLEN
Mister Jerico (1970) 0075
Benny and Barney: Las Vegas Undercover (1977) 0684

SIAN-BARBARA ALLEN
The Family Rico (1972) 0228
Scream, Pretty Peggy (1973) 0357
Eric (1975) 0591
The Lindbergh Kidnapping Case (1976) 0605
Captains and the Kings (1976) MS04
Smash-Up on Interstate 5 (1976) 0677

STEVE ALLEN
Now You See It, Now You Don't (1968) 0022
Rich Man, Poor Man (1976) MS03

VALERIE ALLEN
The Borgia Stick (1967) 0012

JUNE ALLYSON
See the Man Run (1971) 0183
Letters from Three Lovers (1973) 0339
Curse of the Black Widow (Love Trap) (1977) 0754
Three on a Date (1978) 0817
Vega$ (1978) 0840

DON AMECHE
Shadow Over Elveron (1968) 0018
Gidget Gets Married (1972) 0189

LEON AMES
Sherlock Holmes in New York (1976) 0661
The Best Place to Be (1979) 0995

JOHN AMOS
Future Cop (1976) 0626
Roots (1977) MS07
Cops and Robin (1978) 0833
Willa (1979) 0962

MOREY AMSTERDAM
Sooner or Later (1979) 0966

BARBARA ANDERSON
Ironside (1967) 0014
Split Second To an Epitaph (1968) 0020
Visions . . . (Visions of Death) (1972) 0242
The Six-Million Dollar Man (1973) 0304
Don't Be Afraid of the Dark (1973) 0342
Strange Homecoming (1974) 0468
You Lie So Deep, My Love (1975) 0525
SST—Death Flight (SST: Disaster in the Sky) (1977) 0700
Doctors' Private Lives (1978) 0831

JOHN ANDERSON
Scalplock (1966) 0003
Set This Town on Fire (The Profane Comedy) (1973) (1969) 0271
Call to Danger (1973) 0297

Brock's Last Case (1973) 0301
Heatwave! (1974) 0387
Smile, Jenny, You're Dead (1974) 0391
Manhunter (1974) 0404
Dead Man on the Run (1975) 0544
Death Among Friends (Mrs. R—Death Among Friends) (1975) 0568
The Dark Side of Innocence (1976) 0639
Bridger (1976) 0648
Once an Eagle (1976) MS05
Tail Gunner Joe (1977) 0695
Peter Lundy and the Medicine Hat Stallion (1977) 0773
The Last Hurrah (1977) 0676
Donner Pass: The Road to Survival (1978) 0899
The Deerslayer (1978) 0926
Backstairs at the White House (1979) MS28

DAME JUDITH ANDERSON
The Borrowers (1973) 0369
The Underground Man (1974) 0443

LONI ANDERSON
The Magnificent Magnet of Santa Mesa (1977) 0741
Three on a Date (1978) 0817

MICHAEL ANDERSON, JR.
The House That Would Not Die (1970) 0052
In Search of America (1971) 0127
The Family Rico (1972) 0228
The Daughters of Joshua Cabe (1972) 0229
Coffee, Tea or Me? (1973) 0329
Shootout in a One-Dog Town (1974) 0380
Kiss Me, Kill Me (1976) 0631
Washington: Behind Closed Doors (1977) MS12

MELISSA SUE ANDERSON
Little House on the Prairie (1974) 0424
The Loneliest Runner (1976) 0681
James at 15 (1977) 0748
The Survival of Dana (1979) 0997

RICHARD ANDERSON
Along Came a Spider (1970) 0068
Dead Men Tell No Tales (1971) 0186
The Astronaut (1972) 0191
The Longest Night (1972) 0227
Say Goodbye Maggie Cole (1972) 0236
The Night Strangler (1973) 0277
Jarrett (1973) 0310
Partners in Crime (1973) 0320
The Immigrants (1978) MS25
Pearl (1978) MS27
Murder by Natural Causes (1979) 0953

WARNER ANDERSON
Gidget Grows Up (1969) 0060

KEITH ANDES
The Ultimate Imposter (1979) 0985

DANA ANDREWS
The Failing of Raymond (1971) 0175
A Shadow in the Streets (1975) 0508
The First 36 Hours of Dr. Durant (1975) 0565
The Last Hurrah (1977) 0776
Ike (1979) MS33

EDWARD ANDREWS
The Over-the-Hill Gang (1969) 0042
The Intruders (1970) 0095
Travis Logan, D.A. (1971) 0124
The Streets of San Francisco (1972) 0230
How to Break Up a Happy Divorce (1976) 0657
Don't Push, I'll Charge When I'm Ready (1977) (1969) 0789
Lacy and the Mississippi Queen (1978) 0850

HARRY ANDREWS
Destiny of a Spy (1969) 0046
The Story of Jacob and Joseph (1974) 0430
The Four Feathers (1978) 0796

TIGE ANDREWS
Skyway to Death (1974) 0383
Raid on Entebbe (1977) 0685
The Return of Mod Squad (1979) 0990

MAYA ANGELOU
Roots (1977) MS07

MICHAEL ANSARA
How I Spent My Summer Vacation (1967) 0007
Powderkeg (1971) 0133
Call to Danger (1973) 0297
Ordeal (1973) 0348
Shootout in a One-Dog Town (1974) 0380
The Barbary Coast (1975) 0558
Centennial (1978) MS24

SUSAN ANSPACH
I Want to Keep My Baby (1976) 0673
The Secret Life of John Chapman (1976) 0682
Rosetti and Ryan: Men Who Love Women (1977) 0725
Mad Bull (1977) 0792
The Last Giraffe (1979) 1000

LOU ANTONIO
Sole Survivor (1970) 0062
Partners in Crime (1973) 0320
Dog and Cat (1977) 0746

ANNE ARCHER
The Blue Knight (1973) MS01
The Mark of Zorro (1974) 0469
The Log of the Black Pearl (1974) 0494
A Matter of Wife . . . or Death (1976) 0620
The Dark Side of Innocence (1976) 0639
Seventh Avenue (1977) MS08
Harold Robbins' The Pirate (1978) 0906

EVE ARDEN
In Name Only (1969) 0053
A Very Missing Person (1972) 0219
All My Darling Daughters (1972) 0257
A Guide for the Married Woman (1978) 0884

ADAM ARKIN
It Couldn't Happen to a Nicer Guy (1974) 0478
All Together Now (1975) 0512
Pearl (1978) MS27

ALAN ARKIN
The Other Side of Hell (1978) 0802
The Defection of Simas Kudirka (1978) 0806

BESS ARMSTRONG
Getting Married (1978) 0849
How to Pick Up Girls! (1978) 0899
Walking Through the Fire (1979) 0989

DESI ARNAZ, JR.
Mr. and Mrs. Bo Jo Jones (1971) 0170
The Voyage of the Yes (1973) 0278
She Lives (1973) 0331
Having Babies (1976) 0659
Flight to Holocaust (1977) 0710
Black Market Baby (1977) 0765
To Kill a Cop (1978) 0837
The Courage and the Passion (1978) 0857
How to Pick Up Girls! (1978) 0899
Crisis in Mid-Air (1979) 0952

LUCIE ARNAZ
Who Is the Black Dahlia? (1975) 0528
Death Scream (The Woman Who Cried
Murder) (1975) 0577

JAMES ARNESS
The Macahans (1976) 0599

ELIZABETH ASHLEY
Harpy (1971) 0125
The Face of Fear (1971) 0151
When Michael Calls (1972) 0205
Second Chance (1972) 0206
The Heist (1972) 0259
Your Money or Your Wife (1972) 0266
The Magician (1973) 0311
One of My Wives Is Missing (1976) 0609
The War Between the Tates (1977) 0737
A Fire in the Sky (1978) 0909

LUKE ASKEW
Manhunter (1974) 0404
Night Games (1974) 0414
This Was the West That Was (1974) 0491
Attack on Terror: The FBI Versus the Ku
Klux Klan (1975) 0522
A Matter of Wife . . . or Death (1976) 0620
The Quest (1976) 0633
The Invasion of Johnson County (1976) 0646

EDWARD ASNER
The Doomsday Flight (1966) 0005
Daughter of the Mind (1969) 0056
The House on Greenapple Road (1970) 0063
The Old Man Who Cried Wolf (1970) 0088
The Last Child (1971) 0149
They Call It Murder (1971) 0185
Haunts of the Very Rich (1972) 0233
The Police Story (1973) 0313
The Girl Most Likely To . . . (1973) 0351
The Imposter (1975) 0538
Death Scream (The Woman Who Cried
Murder) (1975) 0577
Hey, I'm Alive! (1975) 0589
Rich Man, Poor Man (1976) MS03
Roots (1977) MS07
The Life and Assassination of the Kingfish
(1977) 0709
The Gathering (1977) 0784

ARMAND ASSANTE
Human Feelings (1978) 0885
Lady of the House (1978) 0904
Harold Robbins' The Pirate (1978) 0906

FRED ASTAIRE
The Over-the-Hill Gang Rides Again (1970)
0096
A Family Upside Down (1978) 0836

JOHN ASTIN
Two on a Bench (1971) 0162
Evil Roy Slade (1972) 0211
Skyway to Death (1974) 0383
Only with Married Men (1974) 0472
The Dream Makers (1975) 0497
Operation Petticoat (1977) 0747

PATTY DUKE ASTIN (see Patty Duke)

WILLIAM ATHERTON
Centennial (1978) MS24

RICHARD ATTENBOROUGH
David Copperfield (1970) 0080

RENE AUBERJONOIS
Once Upon a Dead Man (1971) 0139
The Birdmen (Escape of the Birdmen) (1971)
0140
Shirts/Skins (1973) 0341
Panache (1976) 0636
The Rhinemann Exchange (1977) MS09
The Dark Secret of Harvest Home (1978) 0804
The Wild Wild West Revisited (1979) 0982

SKYE AUBREY
Vanished (1971) 0122
The City (1971) 0134
Ellery Queen: Don't Look Behind You (1971)
0171
A Very Missing Person (1972) 0219
The Longest Night (1972) 0227
The Phantom of Hollywood (1974) 0397

PAM AUSTIN
Evil Roy Slade (1972) 0211

LEW AYRES
Hawaii Five-O (1968) 0019
Marcus Welby, M.D. (A Matter of
Humanities) (1969) 0038
Earth II (1971) 0176
She Waits (1972) 0200
The Stranger (1973) 0295
The Questor Tapes (1974) 0385
Heatwave! (1974) 0387
Francis Gary Powers: The True Story of the
U-2 Spy Incident (1976) 0655
Suddenly, Love (1978) 0913

LAUREN BACALL
Perfect Gentlemen (1976) 0829

JIM BACKUS
Wake Me When the War Is Over (1969) 0043
Getting Away From It All (1972) 0196
Magic Carpet (1972) 0252
The Girl Most Likely To . . . (1973) 0351
Miracle on 34th Street (1973) 0370
The Return of Joe Forrester (1975) 0561
The Rebels (1979) MS34

MAX BAER, JR.
The Birdmen (Escape of the Birdmen) (1971)
0140

BARBARA BAIN
Murder Once Removed (1971) 0160
Goodnight My Love (1972) 0246
Savage (1973) 0322
A Summer Without Boys (1973) 0363

BLANCHE BAKER
Holocaust (1978) MS19

DIANE BAKER
The Dangerous Days of Kiowa Jones (1966)
0006
Trial Run (1969) 0032
The D.A.: Murder One (1969) 0055
The Old Man Who Cried Wolf (1970) 0088
Do You Take This Stranger? (1971) 0108
Sarge: The Badge or the Cross (1971) 0116
Congratulations, It's a Boy! (1971) 0141
A Little Game (1971) 0161
Killer by Night (1972) 0190
The Police Story (1973) 0313
A Tree Grows in Brooklyn (1974) 0423
The Dream Makers (1975) 0497
The Last Survivors (1975) 0530

JOE DON BAKER
Mongo's Back in Town (1971) 0182
That Certain Summer (1972) 0251
To Kill a Cop (1978) 0837

STANLEY BAKER
Robinson Crusoe (1974) 0485

INA BALIN
The Lonely Profession (1969) 0044
Desperate Mission (1971) 0178
Call to Danger (1973) 0297
The Police Story (1973) 0313
Panic on the 5:22 (1974) 0480
Danger in Paradise (1977) 0718
The Immigrants (1978) MS25

CARL BALLANTINE
The Girl Most Likely To . . . (1973) 0351

MARTIN BALSAM
Hunters Are for Killing (1970) 0079
The Old Man Who Cried Wolf (1970) 0088
Night of Terror (1972) 0241
A Brand New Life (1973) 0292
The Six-Million Dollar Man (1973) 0304
Trapped Beneath the Sea (1974) 0466
Miles to Go Before I Sleep (1975) 0498
Death Among Friends (Mrs. R—Death
Among Friends) (1975) 0568
The Lindbergh Kidnapping Case (1976) 0605
Raid on Entebbe (1977) 0685
Contract on Cherry Street (1977) 0777
The Storyteller (1977) 0785
Siege (1978) 0841
Rainbow (1978) 0901
The Millionaire (1978) 0927
The Seeding of Sarah Burns (1979) 0968
The House on Garibaldi Street (1979) 0996

ANNE BANCROFT
Jesus of Nazareth (1977) MS10

JOY BANG
The Psychiatrist: God Bless the Children
(Children of the Lotus Eater) (1970) 0103

IAN BANNEN
Jane Eyre (1971) 0128
Jesus of Nazareth (1977) MS10

ADRIENNE BARBEAU
The Great Houdinis (1976) 0658
Having Babies (1976) 0659
Red Alert (1977) 0723
Return to Fantasy Island (1978) 0803
Crash (1978) 0894
Someone Is Watching Me! (1978) 0911
The Darker Side of Terror (1979) 0967

PRISCILLA BARNES
The Time Machine (1978) 0899
A Vacation in Hell (1979) 0992

BARBARA BARRIE
Harold Robbins' 79 Park Avenue (1977) MS13
Tell Me My Name (1977) 0791
Summer of My German Soldier (1978) 0895
Backstairs at the White House (1979) MS28
Roots: The Next Generations (1979) MS30

GENE BARRY
Prescription: Murder (1968) 0017
Istanbul Express (1968) 0021
Do You Take This Stranger? (1971) 0108
The Devil and Miss Sarah (1971) 0179
Ransom for Alice! (1977) 0732
Aspen (The Innocent and the Damned) (1977)
MS14

JOHN DREW BARRYMORE
Winchester '73 (1967) 0013

RICHARD BASEHART
Sole Survivor (1970) 0062
City Beneath the Sea (1971) 0111
The Birdmen (Escape of the Birdmen) (1971)
0140
The Death of Me Yet (1971) 0159
Assignment: Munich (1972) 0225
The Bounty Man (1972) 0250
Maneater (1973) 0365
Time Travelers (1976) 0613
21 Hours at Munich (1976) 0667
Flood (1976) 0675
Stonestreet: Who Killed the Centerfold Model?
(1977) 0690
The Critical List (1978) 0872
The Rebels (1979) MS34

KIM BASINGER
Dog and Cat (1977) 0746
The Ghost of Flight 401 (1978) 0818
Katie: Portrait of a Centerfold (1978) 0889
From Here to Eternity (1979) MS29

ALAN BATES
The Story of Jacob and Joseph (narrator)
(1974) 0430

KATHY BAUMANN
The Great American Beauty Contest (1973)
0287
Letters from Three Lovers (1973) 0339
Death Among Friends (Mrs. R—Death
Among Friends) (1975) 0568
Flight to Holocaust (1977) 0710
Dallas Cowboys Cheerleaders (1979) 0937

BARBARA BAXLEY
The Law (1974) 0465
The Imposter (1975) 0538

ANNE BAXTER
Stranger on the Run (1967) 0015
Companions in Nightmare (1968) 0024
Marcus Welby, M.D. (A Matter of
Humanities) (1969) 0038
The Challengers (1970) 0072
Ritual of Evil (1970) 0073
If Tomorrow Comes (1971) 0180
The Catcher (1972) 0226
Lisa, Bright and Dark (1973) 0360
Arthur Hailey's The Moneychangers (1976)
MS06
Little Mo (1978) 0869

MEREDITH BAXTER (BIRNEY)
The Cat Creature (1973) 0367
The Stranger Who Looks Like Me (1974) 0408
Target Risk (1975) 0496
The Imposter (1975) 0538
The Night That Panicked America (1975) 0586
Little Women (1978) 0881

JOHN BEAL
The Legend of Lizzie Borden (1975) 0513
Eleanor and Franklin: The White House Years
(1977) 0706
Jennifer: A Woman's Story (1979) 0957

NED BEATTY
Footsteps (Footsteps: Nice Guys Finish Last)
(1972) 0238
The Marcus-Nelson Murders (1973) 0305
Dying Room Only (1973) 0333
The Execution of Private Slovik (1974) 0412
Attack on Terror: The FBI Versus the Ku
Klux Klan (1975) 0522
The Deadly Tower (1975) 0581
Tail Gunner Joe (1977) 0695
Lucan (1977) 0728
A Question of Love (1978) 0908
Friendly Fire (1979) 0973

JOHN BECK
The Silent Gun (1969) 0058
Lock, Stock and Barrel (1971) 0142
Sidekicks (1974) 0417
The Law (1974) 0465
Attack on Terror: The FBI Versus the Ku
Klux Klan (1975) 0522
The Call of the Wild (1976) 0640
Arthur Hailey's Wheels (1978) MS20
The Time Machine (1978) 0900

BONNIE BEDELIA
Then Came Bronson (1969) 0037
Sandcastles (1972) 0245
Hawkins on Murder (Death and the Maiden)
(1973) 0306
Message to My Daughter (1973) 0368
Heatwave! (1974) 0387
A Question of Love (1978) 0908
Walking Through the Fire (1979) 0989

NOAH BEERY
The Alpha Caper (1973) 0340
Sidekicks (1974) 0417
Savages (1974) 0450
Francis Gary Powers: The True Story of the
U-2 Spy Incident (1976) 0655
The Bastard (1978) MS22

ED BEGLEY
The Silent Gun (1969) 0058

CHRISTINE BELFORD
Vanished (1971) 0122
Banacek: Detour to Nowhere (1972) 0223
Cool Million (Mask of Marcella) (1972) 0244
Kate McShane (1975) 0546
The Million Dollar Rip-Off (1976) 0653
To Kill a Cop (1978) 0837

TOM BELL
Holocaust (1978) MS19

RALPH BELLAMY
Wings of Fire (1967) 0010
The Immortal (1969) 0041
Something Evil (1972) 0197
The Log of the Black Pearl (1975) 0494
Adventures of the Queen (1975) 0518
Search for the Gods (1975) 0534
Murder on Flight 502 (1975) 0594
McNaughton's Daughter (1976) 0608
Return to Earth (1976) 0634
Nightmare in Badham County (1976) 0666
The Boy in the Plastic Bubble (1976) 0669
Once an Eagle (1976) MS05
Arthur Hailey's The Moneychangers (1976)
MS06
Testimony of Two Men (1977) MS11
Charlie Cobb: Nice Night for a Hanging (1977)
0735
Arthur Hailey's Wheels (1978) MS20
The Clone Master (1978) 0873
The Millionaire (1978) 0927
The Billion Dollar Threat (1979) 0971

KATHLEEN BELLER
Something for Joey (1977) 0711
Having Babies III (1978) 0826
Are You in the House Alone? (1978) 0875

DIRK BENEDICT
Journey from Darkness (1975) 0524
Cruise into Terror (1978) 0811

PAUL BENJAMIN
Friendly Persuasion (1975) 0567
Judge Horton and the Scotsboro Boys (1976)
0672
One in a Million: The Ron LeFlore Story
(1978) 0878
I Know Why the Caged Bird Sings (1979)
0976

JOAN BENNETT
Gidget Gets Married (1972) 0189
The Eyes of Charles Sand (1972) 0217
Suddenly, Love (1978) 0913

ROBBY BENSON
Remember When (1974) 0419
All the Kind Strangers (1974) 0476
The Virginia Hill Story (1974) 0479
Death Be Not Proud (1975) 0510
The Death of Richie (1977) 0686

BARBI BENTON
The Great American Beauty Contest (1973)
0287
The Third Girl from the Left (1973) 0344
Murder at the Mardi Gras (1978) 0847

JOHN BERADINO
Do Not Fold, Spindle or Mutilate (1971) 0166
Moon of the Wolf (1972) 0235
A Guide for the Married Woman (1978) 0884

TOM BERENGER
Johnny, We Hardly Knew Ye (1977) 0693

EDGAR BERGEN
The Hanged Man (1964) 0002
The Homecoming (1971) 0188

POLLY BERGEN
Death Cruise (1974) 0470
Murder on Flight 502 (1975) 0594
Harold Robbins' 79 Park Avenue (1977) MS13
Telethon (1977) 0774
How to Pick Up Girls! (1978) 0899

HELMUT BERGER
Victory at Entebbe (1976) 0679

SENTA BERGER
See How They Run (1964) 0001
Istanbul Express (1968) 0021

MILTON BERLE
Seven in Darkness (1969) 0040
Evil Roy Slade (1972) 0211
The Legend of Valentino (1975) 0595

HERSCHEL BERNARDI
But I Don't Want to Get Married! (1970) 0087
No Place to Run (1972) 0232
Sandcastles (1972) 0245
The Story of Jacob and Joseph (1974) 0430
Seventh Avenue (1977) MS08

KEN BERRY
Wake Me When the War Is Over (1969) 0043
The Reluctant Heroes (1971) 0173
Every Man Needs One (1972) 0264
Letters from Three Lovers (1973) 0339
The Love Boat II (1977) 0692

BIBI BESCH
Victory at Entebbe (1976) 0679
Peter Lundy and the Medicine Hat Stallion (1977) 0773
Betrayal (1978) 0903
Backstairs at the White House (1979) MS28
Transplant (1979) 0972

TED BESSELL
Two on a Bench (1971) 0162
Your Money or Your Wife (1972) 0266
Scream, Pretty Peggy (1973) 0357
What Are Best Friends For? (1973) 0373

JAMES BEST
Run, Simon, Run (1970) 0100
Savages (1974) 0450
The Runaway Barge (1975) 0541
The Savage Bees (1976) 0674
Centennial (1978) MS24

MARTINE BESWICK
Longstreet (1971) 0117
Crime Club (1975) 0545
Strange New World (1975) 0573

Aspen (The Innocent and the Damned) (1977) MS14
Devil Dog: The Hound of Hell (1978) 0896
My Husband Is Missing (1978) 0914

LYLE BETTGER
Return of the Gunfighter (1967) 0009

CARL BETZ
The Monk (1969) 0045
In Search of America (1971) 0127
The Deadly Dream (1971) 0144
Set This Town on Fire (The Profane Comedy) (1973) (1969) 0271
Killdozer (1974) 0390
The Daughters of Joshua Cabe Return (1975) 0509
Brink's: The Great Robbery (1976) 0616

RAMON BIERI
Sarge: The Badge or the Cross (1971) 0116
Owen Marshall, Counselor-at-Law (A Pattern of Morality) (1971) 0135
Hunter (1973) 0373
Outrage! (1973) 0359
It's Good to Be Alive (1974) 0402
Lucas Tanner (1974) 0445
The Gun (1974) 0477
Crossfire (1975) 0540
McNaughton's Daughter (1976) 0608
The Rhinemann Exchange (1977) MS09
The San Pedro Bums (1977) 0719
Panic in Echo Park (1977) 0743
A Love Affair: The Eleanor and Lou Gehrig Story (1978) 0800
Arthur Hailey's Wheels (1978) MS20
True Grit (1978) 0852

THEODORE BIKEL
Killer by Night (1972) 0190
Murder on Flight 502 (1975) 0594
Victory at Entebbe (1976) 0679
Testimony of Two Men (1977) MS11
Loose Change (Those Restless Years) (1978) MS18

TONY BILL
Haunts of the Very Rich (1972) 0233
Having Babies II (1977) 0770
Washington: Behind Closed Doors (1977) MS12
The Initiation of Sarah (1978) 0814
With This Ring (1978) 0846
Are You in the House Alone? (1978) 0875

EDWARD BINNS
The Sheriff (1971) 0130
Hunter (1973) 0273
The Power Within (1979) 0983

DAVID BIRNEY
Murder or Mercy (1974) 0438
Only with Married Men (1974) 0472
Serpico: The Deadly Game (1976) 0623
Testimony of Two Men (1977) MS11
Someone Is Watching Me! (1978) 0911

BILL BIXBY
Congratulations, It's a Boy! (1971) 0141
The Couple Takes a Wife (1972) 0261
The Magician (1973) 0311
Shirts/Skins (1973) 0341
The Barbary Coast (1975) 0558
Rich Man, Poor Man (1976) MS03

The Invasion of Johnson County (1976) 0646
The Great Houdinis (1976) 0658
Fantasy Island (1977) 0688
Black Market Baby (1977) 0765
The Incredible Hulk (1977) 0772

KAREN BLACK
Trilogy of Terror (1975) 0531
The Strange Possession of Mrs. Oliver (1977) 0701
Mr. Horn (1979) 0949

SIDNEY BLACKMER
Do You Take This Stranger? (1971) 0108

VIVIAN BLAINE
Katie: Portrait of a Centerfold (1978) 0888
The Cracker Factory (1979) 0961
Sooner or Later (1979) 0966

LINDA BLAIR
Born Innocent (1974) 0448
Sarah T.—Portrait of a Teenage Alcoholic (1975) 0514
Sweet Hostage (1975) 0500
Victory at Entebbe (1976) 0679
Stranger in Our House (1978) 0897

AMANDA BLAKE
Betrayal (1974) 0488

WHITNEY BLAKE
The Stranger Who Looks Like Me (1974) 0408
Strange Homecoming (1974) 0468
Returning Home (1975) 0555
Law and Order (1976) 0629

RONEE BLAKELY
Desperate Women (1978) 0890

SUSAN BLAKELY
Rich Man, Poor Man (1976) MS03
Secrets (1977) 0699

SUSAN BLANCHARD
The Magnificent Magnet of Santa Mesa (1977) 0741
The New Maverick (1978) 0879

DAN BLOCKER
Something for a Lonely Man (1968) 0025

JOAN BLONDELL
Winchester '73 (1967) 0013
The Dead Don't Die (1975) 0503
Winner Take All (1975) 0529
Death at Love House (1976) 0647
Battered (1978) 0877
The Rebels (1979) MS34

CLAIRE BLOOM
Backstairs at the White House (1979) MS28

VERNA BLOOM
Where Have All the People Gone? (1974) 0460
Sarah T.—Portrait of a Teenage Alcoholic (1975) 0514
The Blue Knight (1975) 0564
Contract on Cherry Street (1977) 0777

MARGARET BLYE
Melvin Purvis, G-Man (1974) 0431
Mayday at 40,000 Feet (1976) 0668

LLOYD BOCHNER
Scalplock (1966) 0003
Stranger on the Run (1967) 0015
Crowhaven Farm (1970) 0099
They Call It Murder (1971) 0185
Satan's School for Girls (1973) 0334
Richie Brockelman: Missing 24 Hours (1976) 0663
Terraces (1977) 0744
The Immigrants (1978) MS25
A Fire in the Sky (1978) 0909
The Best Place to Be (1979) 0995

RAY BOLGER
Captains and the Kings (1976) MS04
The Entertainer (1976) 0610
Three on a Date (1978) 0817

FLORINDA BOLKAN
The Word (1978) MS26

TIFFANY BOLLING
Key West (1973) 0366

JOSEPH BOLOGNA
Honor Thy Father (1973) 0300
Woman of the Year (1976) 0644
Torn Between Two Lovers (1979) 0979

BEULAH BONDI
She Waits (1972) 0200

PETER BONERZ
How to Break Up a Happy Divorce (1976) 0657
The Bastard (1978) MS22

SONNY BONO
Murder on Flight 502 (1975) 0594
Murder in Music City (1979) 0939

SORRELL BOOKE
The Borgia Stick (1967) 0012
Owen Marshall, Counselor-at-Law (A Pattern of Morality) (1971) 0135
The Adventures of Nick Carter (1972) 0213
Dr. Max (1974) 0428
The Last Angry Man (1974) 0435
Adventures of the Queen (1975) 0518
The Manhunter (1976) (1968) 0618
Brenda Starr (1976) 0630
The Amazing Howard Hughes (1977) 0712
The Greatest Thing That Almost Happened (1977) 0769

PAT BOONE
The Pigeon (1969) 0048

RICHARD BOONE
In Broad Daylight (1971) 0155
Deadly Harvest (1972) 0234
Hec Ramsey (The Century Turns) (1972) 0240
Goodnight My Love (1972) 0246
The Great Niagara (1974) 0454
The Last Dinosaur (1977) 0697

JAMES BOOTH
Arthur Hailey's Wheels (1978) MS20
Evening in Byzantium (1978) MS23

SHIRLEY BOOTH
The Smugglers (1968) 0030

ERNEST BORGNINE
Sam Hill: Who Killed the Mysterious Mr. Foster? (1971) 0112
The Trackers (1971) 0184
Twice in a Lifetime (1974) 0415
Future Cop (1976) 0626
Jesus of Nazareth (1977) MS10
Fire! (1977) 0717
The Ghost of Flight 401 (1978) 0818
Cops and Robin (1978) 0833

TOM BOSLEY
Marcus Welby, M.D. (A Matter of Humanities) (1969) 0038
Night Gallery (1969) 0049
A Step Out of Line (1971) 0118
Vanished (1971) 0122
Congratulations, It's a Boy! (1971) 0141
Mr. and Mrs. Bo Jo Jones (1971) 0170
The Streets of San Francisco (1972) 0230
No Place to Run (1972) 0232
Miracle on 34th Street (1973) 0370
The Girl Who Came Gift-Wrapped (1974) 0388
Death Cruise (1974) 0470
Who Is the Black Dahlia? (1975) 0528
The Last Survivors (1975) 0530
The Night That Panicked America (1975) 0586
The Love Boat (1976) 0652
Testimony of Two Men (1977) MS11
Black Market Baby (1977) 0765
The Bastard (1978) MS22
With This Ring (1978) 0846
The Triangle Factory Fire Scandal (1979) 0947
The Rebels (1979) MS34
The Return of Mod Squad (1979) 0990

BARRY BOSTWICK
The Chadwick Family (1974) 0437
The Quinns (1977) 0745
Murder by Natural Causes (1979) 0953

BENJAMIN BOTTOMS
Stalk the Wild Child (1976) 0665

JOSEPH BOTTOMS
Trouble Comes to Town (1973) 0274
Unwed Father (1974) 0406
Stalk the Wild Child (1976) 0665
Holocaust (1978) MS19

SAM BOTTOMS
Savages (1974) 0450
Cage Without a Key (1977) 0537

TIMOTHY BOTTOMS
Arthur Hailey's The Moneychangers (1976) MS06
The Gift of Love (1978) 0916

BARBARA BOUCHET
Cool Million (Mask of Marcella) (1972) 0244

LEE BOWMAN
Fame Is the Name of the Game (1966) 0004

BRUCE BOXLEITNER
The Chadwick Family (1974) 0437
A Cry for Help (1975) 0516
The Macahans (1976) 0599
Kiss Me, Kill Me (1976) 0631
Murder at the World Series (1977) 0708
Happily Ever After (1978) 0870

STEPHEN BOYD
Carter's Army (1970) 0066
Key West (1973) 0366
The Lives of Jenny Dolan (1975) 0585

PETER BOYLE
The Man Who Could Talk to Kids (1973) 0345
Tail Gunner Joe (1977) 0695
From Here to Eternity (1979) MS29

LANE BRADBURY
Dial Hot Line (1970) 0076
Maybe I'll Come Home in the Spring (1971) 0115
Serpico: The Deadly Game (1976) 0623
Just a Little Inconvenience (1977) 0761
A Real American Hero (1978) 0917

RICHARD BRADFORD
U.M.C. (Operation Heartbeat) (1969) 0039

SCOTT BRADY
The D.A.: Murder One (1969) 0055
The Night Strangler (1973) 0277
Roll, Freddy, Roll! (1974) 0490
The Kansas City Massacre (1975) 0576
Law and Order (1976) 0629
Arthur Hailey's Wheels (1978) MS20
When Every Day Was the Fourth of July (1978) 0828
To Kill a Cop (1978) 0837

ERIC BRAEDEN
Honeymoon with a Stranger (1969) 0059
The Mask of Sheba (1970) 0077
The Judge and Jake Wyler (1972) 0260
Death Race (1973) 0354
Death Scream (The Woman Who Cried Murder) (1975) 0577
The New, Original Wonder Woman (1975) 0590
Code Name: Diamond Head (1977) 0716
Happily Ever After (1978) 0870
The Power Within (1979) 0983

NEVILLE BRAND
Lock, Stock and Barrel (1971) 0142
Marriage: Year One (1971) 0154
The Adventures of Nick Carter (1972) 0213
Two for the Money (1972) 0216
No Place to Run (1972) 0232
Hitched (1973) 0321
Killdozer (1974) 0390
Death Stalk (1975) 0506
The Barbary Coast (1975) 0558
The Quest (1976) 0633
Captains and the Kings (1976) MS04
Fire! (1977) 0717
Captains Courageous (1977) 0783

JOCELYN BRANDO
A Question of Love (1978) 0907

MARLON BRANDO
    Roots: The Next Generations (1979) MS30

MICHAEL BRANDON
    The Impatient Heart (1971) 0150
    The Strangers in 7A (1972) 0255
    The Third Girl from the Left (1973) 0344
    Hitchhike! (1974) 0403
    The Red Badge of Courage (1974) 0487
    Queen of the Stardust Ballroom (1975) 0517
    Cage Without a Key (1975) 0537
    James Dean (1976) 0604
    Scott Free (1976) 0660
    Red Alert (1977) 0723
    The Comedy Company (1978) 0864
    A Vacation in Hell (1979) 0992

ROSANNO BRAZZI
    Honeymoon with a Stranger (1969) 0059

EILEEN BRENNAN
    Playmates (1972) 0237
    The Blue Knight (1973) MS01
    My Father's House (1975) 0570
    The Night That Panicked America (1975) 0586
    The Death of Richie (1977) 0686
    Black Beauty (1978) MS15

WALTER BRENNAN
    The Over-the-Hill Gang (1969) 0042
    The Young Country (1970) 0081
    The Over-the-Hill Gang Rides Again (1970)
        0096
    Two for the Money (1972) 0216
    Home for the Holidays (1972) 0258

DORI BRENNER
    All Together Now (1975) 0512
    I Want To Keep My Baby (1976) 0673
    Seventh Avenue (1977) MS08

DAVID BRIAN
    The Manhunter (1976) (1968) 0618

BETH BRICKELL
    San Francisco International (1970) 0085
    The Great Man's Whiskers (1973) (1969) 0289
    Brock's Last Case (1973) 0301

BEAU BRIDGES
    The Man Without a Country (1973) 0325
    The Stranger Who Looks Like Me (1974) 0408
    Medical Story (1975) 0575
    The Four Feathers (1978) 0796
    The President's Mistress (1978) 0816
    The Child Stealer (1979) 0959

JEFF BRIDGES
    Silent Night, Lonely Night (1969) 0057
    In Search of America (1971) 0127

LLOYD BRIDGES
    Silent Night, Lonely Night (1969) 0057
    The Silent Gun (1969) 0058
    The Love War (1970) 0078
    Do You Take This Stranger? (1971) 0108
    A Tattered Web (1971) 0143
    The Deadly Dream (1971) 0144
    Haunts of the Very Rich (1972) 0233
    Trouble Comes to Town (1973) 0274
    Crime Club (1973) 0302
    Death Race (1973) 0354

Stowaway to the Moon (1975) 0502
The Return of Joe Forrester (1975) 0561
Roots (1977) MS07
Telethon (1977) 0774
The Great Wallendas (1978) 0810
The Critical List (1978) 0872

MORGAN BRITTANY
    The Amazing Howard Hughes (1977) 0712
    Delta County, U.S.A. (1977) 0726
    The Initiation of Sarah (1978) 0814
    Samurai (1979) 0978
    Stunt Seven (1979) 0998

JAMES BROLIN
    Marcus Welby, M.D. (A Matter of
        Humanities) (1969) 0038
    Short Walk to Daylight (1972) 0248
    Class of '63 (1973) 0308
    Trapped (1973) 0355
    Steel Cowboy (1978) 0915

CHARLES BRONSON
    Raid on Entebbe (1977) 0685

GERALDINE BROOKS
    Ironside (1967) 0014

STEPHEN BROOKS
    Two for the Money (1972) 0216

KEVIN BROPHY
    Lucan (1977) 0728

BARRY BROWN
    The Psychiatrist: God Bless the Children
        (Children of the Lotus Eater) (1970) 0103
    The Birdmen (Escape of the Birdmen) (1971)
        0140
    The Bravos (1972) 0192
    The Disappearance of Aimee (1976) 0671
    Testimony of Two Men (1977) MS11
    This Man Stands Alone (1979) 0999

CHELSEA BROWN
    Dial Hot Line (1970) 0076

BLAIR BROWN
    Captains and the Kings (1976) MS04
    Eleanor and Franklin: The White House Years
        (1977) 0706
    Charlie Cobb: Nice Night for a Hanging (1977)
        0735
    The 3,000 Mile Chase (1977) 0738
    The Quinns (1977) 0745
    Arthur Hailey's Wheels (1978) MS20
    And I Alone Survived (1978) 0910
    The Child Stealer (1979) 0959

GEORG STANFORD BROWN
    The Young Lawyers (1969) 0047
    Ritual of Evil (1970) 0073
    The Rookies (1972) 0222
    Dawn: Portrait of a Teenage Runaway (1976)
        0654
    Roots (1977) MS07
    Roots: The Next Generations (1979) MS30

PAMELA BROWN
    Dracula (1974) 0395
    In This House of Brede (1975) 0527

PETER BROWN
    Hunters Are for Killing (1970) 0079
    Salvage (1979) 0942

REB BROWN
    The Girl Most Likely To . . . (1973) 0351
    The Law (1974) 0465
    Let's Switch (1975) 0499
    Strange New World (1975) 0573
    Centennial (1978) MS24
    Captain America (1979) 0940

KATHIE BROWNE
    Berlin Affair (1970) 0093

ROSCOE LEE BROWNE
    The Big Ripoff (1975) 0536
    King (1978) MS16
    Dr. Scorpion (1978) 0822

EDGAR BUCHANAN
    Something for a Lonely Man (1968) 0025
    The Over-the-Hill Gang (1969) 0042
    The Over-the-Hill Gang Rides Again (1970)
        0096
    Yuma (1971) 0121

HORST BUCHHOLZ
    The Savage Bees (1976) 0674
    Raid on Entebbe (1977) 0685
    Return to Fantasy Island (1978) 0803

BROOKE BUNDY
    Along Came a Spider (1970) 0068
    Travis Logan, D.A. (1971) 0124
    The Adventures of Nick Carter (1972) 0213
    Short Walk to Daylight (1972) 0248
    Man on the Outside (1975) 0572
    Francis Gary Powers: The True Story of the
        U-2 Spy Incident (1976) 0655
    Crash (1978) 0894

VICTOR BUONO
    Goodnight My Love (1972) 0246
    Crime Club (1973) 0302
    Brenda Starr (1976) 0630
    High Risk (1976) 0635
    Man from Atlantis (1977) 0704
    Backstairs at the White House (1979) MS28
    The Return of Mod Squad (1979) 0990

PAUL BURKE
    Crowhaven Farm (1970) 0099
    The Rookies (1972) 0222
    Lieutenant Schuster's Wife (1972) 0243
    Crime Club (1973) 0302
    Little Ladies of the Night (1977) 0689
    Wild and Wooly (1978) 0819
    Beach Patrol (1979) 0977

CAROL BURNETT
    The Grass Is Always Greener over the Septic
        Tank (1978) 0891
    Friendly Fire (1979) 0973

CATHERINE BURNS
    Two for the Money (1972) 0216
    The Catcher (1972) 0226
    Night of Terror (1972) 0241
    Amelia Earhart (1976) 0662
    The Word (1978) MS26

GEORGE BURNS
The Comedy Company (1978) 0864

MICHAEL BURNS
Stranger on the Run (1967) 0015
Gidget Gets Married (1972) 0189
Brock's Last Case (1973) 0301
The Magnificent Magnet of Santa Mesa (1977) 0741

RAYMOND BURR
Ironside (1967) 0014
Split Second to an Epitaph (1968) 0020
The Priest Killer (1971) 0136
Mallory: Circumstantial Evidence (1976) 0603
Kingston: The Power Play (1976) 0651
Harold Robbins' 79 Park Avenue (1977) MS13
The Jordan Chance (1978) 0919
The Bastard (narrator) (1978) MS22
Centennial (1978) MS24
Love's Savage Fury (1979) 0991

ELLEN BURSTYN
Thursday's Game (1974) (1971) 0432

LeVAR BURTON
Roots (1977) MS07
Billy: Portrait of a Street Kid (1977) 0750
Battered (1978) 0877
One in a Million: The Ron LeFlore Story (1978) 0878
Dummy (1979) 0994

RICHARD BURTON
Divorce His/Divorce Hers (1973) 0285
Brief Encounter (1974) 0475

WENDELL BURTON
Murder Once Removed (1971) 0160
Go Ask Alice (1973) 0280
The Red Badge of Courage (1974) 0487
Journey from Darkness (1975) 0524
Medical Story (1975) 0575

GARY BUSEY
Blood Sport (1973) 0364
The Execution of Private Slovik (1974) 0412
The Law (1974) 0465

RED BUTTONS
Breakout (1970) 0102
The New, Original Wonder Woman (1975) 0590
Louis Armstrong—Chicago Style (1976) 0600
Telethon (1977) 0774
Vega$ (1978) 0840
The Users (1978) 0880

PAT BUTTRAM
The Hanged Man (1964) 0002
The Sacketts (1979) 0988

RUTH BUZZI
In Name Only (1969) 0053

EDD BYRNES
The Silent Gun (1969) 0058
Mobile Two (1975) 0574
Telethon (1977) 0774
Vega$ (1978) 0840

JOHN BYNER
Three on a Date (1978) 0817
A Guide for the Married Woman (1978) 0884

JAMES CAAN
Brian's Song (1971) 0177

SEBASTIAN CABOT
The Spy Killer (1969) 0050
Foreign Exchange (1970) 0064
Miracle on 34th Street (1973) 0370

SID CAESAR
Flight to Holocaust (1977) 0710
Curse of the Black Widow (Love Trap) (1977) 0754

RORY CALHOUN
Flight to Holocaust (1977) 0710
Flatbed Annie & Sweetiepie: Lady Truckers (1979) 0950
The Rebels (1979) MS34

MICHAEL CALLAN
In Name Only (1969) 0053
Donner Pass: The Road to Survival (1978) 0889
Blind Ambition (1979) MS35

CHARLIE CALLAS
The Snoop Sisters (Female Instinct) (1972) 0265
Switch (1975) 0535

CORINNE CALVET
The Phantom of Hollywood (1974) 0397

JOANNA CAMERON
The Great American Beauty Contest (1973) 0287
Night Games (1974) 0414
It Couldn't Happen to a Nicer Guy (1974) 0478
High Risk (1976) 0635

JOSEPH CAMPANELLA
Any Second Now (1969) 0033
The Whole World Is Watching (1969) 0036
A Clear and Present Danger (1970) 0082
Owen Marshall, Counselor-at-Law (A Pattern of Morality) (1971) 0135
Murder Once Removed (1971) 0160
You'll Never See Me Again (1973) 0299
Honor Thy Father (narrator) (1973) 0300
Drive Hard, Drive Fast (1973) (1969) 0328
The President's Plane Is Missing (1973) 0346
Skyway to Death (1974) 0383
Unwed Father (1974) 0406
Terror on the 40th Floor (1974) 0452
Hit Lady (1974) 0461
Journey from Darkness (1975) 0524
Sky Hei$t (1975) 0569
Return to Fantasy Island (1978) 0803
Ring of Passion (1978) 0813
Pearl (narrator) (1978) MS27

GLEN CAMPBELL
Strange Homecoming (1974) 0468

DAVID CANARY
Incident on a Dark Street (1973) 0275
Melvin Purvis, G-Man (1974) 0431
The Dain Curse (1978) MS21

DYAN CANNON
The Virginia Hill Story (1974) 0479
Lady of the House (1978) 0904

J. D. CANNON
U.M.C. (Operation Heartbeat) (1969) 0039
The D.A.: Murder One (1969) 0055
Sam Hill: Who Killed the Mysterious Mr. Foster? (1971) 0112
Cannon (1971) 0129
Testimony of Two Men (1977) MS11
Killing Stone (1978) 0843
Ike (1979) MS33
Walking Through the Fire (1979) 0989

DIANA CANOVA
The Love Boat II (1977) 0692
With This Ring (1978) 0846

CLAUDIA CARDINALE
Jesus of Nazareth (1977) MS10

HARRY CAREY, JR.
Black Beauty (1978) MS15
Kate Bliss and the Ticker Tape Kid (1978) 0856

MACDONALD CAREY
Gidget Gets Married (1972) 0189
Ordeal (1973) 0348
Who Is the Black Dahlia? (1975) 0528
Roots (1977) MS07
Stranger in Our House (1978) 0897
The Rebels (1979) MS34

MICHELE CAREY
The Norliss Tapes (1973) 0294
Savage (1973) 0322
Delta County U.S.A. (1977) 0726
The Legend of the Golden Gun (1979) 0969

PHILIP CAREY
Scream of the Wolf (1974) 0382

LEN CARIOU
Who'll Save Our Children? (1978) 0923

LYNN CARLIN
Silent Night, Lonely Night (1969) 0057
A Step Out of Line (1971) 0118
Mr. and Mrs. Bo Jo Jones (1971) 0170
The Morning After (1974) 0399
The Last Angry Man (1974) 0435
Terror on the 40th Floor (1974) 0452
The Lives of Jennie Dolan (1975) 0585
Dawn: Portrait of a Teenage Runaway (1976) 0654
James at 15 (1977) 0748

KAREN CARLSON
Night Chase (1970) 0097
Cage Without a Key (1975) 0537
The First 36 Hours of Dr. Durant (1975) 0565
Tail Gunner Joe (1977) 0695
It Happened One Christmas (1977) 0786
Centennial (1978) MS24

RICHARD CARLSON
The Doomsday Flight (1966) 0005

JUDY CARNE
Dead Men Tell No Tales (1971) 0186
QB VII (1974) 0442
Only with Married Men (1974) 0472

ART CARNEY
The Snoop Sisters (Female Instinct) (1972) 0265
Death Scream (The Woman Who Cried Murder) (1975) 0577
Katherine (1975) 0579
Lanigan's Rabbi (1976) 0643

LESLIE CARON
QB VII (1974) 0442

DARLEEN CARR
All My Darling Daughters (1972) 0257
The Horror at 37,000 Feet (1973) 0288
My Darling Daughters' Anniversary (1973) 0352
The Chadwick Family (1974) 0437
Law of the Land (1976) 0624
Once an Eagle (1976) MS05
Young Joe, the Forgotten Kennedy (1977) 0755

DAVID CARRADINE
Maybe I'll Come Home in the Spring (1971) 0115
Kung Fu (1972) 0214
Mr. Horn (1979) 0948

KEITH CARRADINE
Man on a String (1972) 0212
Kung Fu (1972) 0214
The Godchild (1974) 0483

JOHN CARRADINE
Daughter of the Mind (1969) 0056
Crowhaven Farm (1970) 0099
The Night Strangler (1973) 0277
The Cat Creature (1973) 0367
Stowaway to the Moon (1975) 0502
Death at Love House (1976) 0647
Captains and the Kings (1976) MS04
Tail Gunner Joe (1977) 0695
Christmas Miracle in Caufield U.S.A. (1977) 0793

ROBERT CARRADINE
Footsteps (Footsteps: Nice Guys Finish Last) (1972) 0238
Go Ask Alice (1973) 0280
The Hatfields and the McCoys (1975) 0505
The Survival of Dana (1979) 0997

BARBARA CARRERA
Centennial (1978) MS24

DIAHANN CARROLL
Death Scream (The Woman Who Cried Murder) (1975) 0577
Roots: The Next Generations (1979) MS30
I Know Why the Caged Bird Sings (1979) 0976

BILLY CARTER
Flatbed Annie & Sweetiepie: Lady Truckers (1979) 0950

JACK CARTER
The Lonely Profession (1969) 0044
The Family Rico (1972) 0228
The Sex Symbol (1974) 0451
The Great Houdinis (1976) 0658
The Last Hurrah (1977) 0776
Human Feelings (1978) 0885
Rainbow (1978) 0901

LYNDA CARTER
The New, Original Wonder Woman (1975) 0590
A Matter of Wife . . . or Death (1976) 0620

TERRY CARTER
McCloud: Who Killed Miss U.S.A.? (Portrait of a Dead Girl) (1970) 0071
Two on a Bench (1971) 0162

ALLEN CASE
The Magician (1973) 0311
Man from Atlantis (1977) 0704

BERNIE CASEY
Brian's Song (1971) 0177
Gargoyles (1972) 0256
Panic on the 5:22 (1974) 0480
Mary Jane Harper Cried Last Night (1977) 0763
It Happened at Lake Wood Manor (1977) 0781
Ring of Passion (1978) 0813
Love Is Not Enough (1978) 0860
Roots: The Next Generations (1979) MS30

JOHNNY CASH
Thaddeus Rose and Eddie (1978) 0823

JUNE CARTER CASH
Thaddeus Rose and Eddie (1978) 0823

ROSALIND CASH
A Killing Affair (Behind the Badge) (1977) 0757

SEYMOUR CASSEL
The Hanged Man (1964) 0002

JACK CASSIDY
Your Money or Your Wife (1972) 0266
The Phantom of Hollywood (1974) 0397
Death Among Friends (Mrs. R—Death Among Friends) (1975) 0568
Benny and Barney: Las Vegas Undercover (1977) 0684

SHAUN CASSIDY
Like Normal People (1979) 0970

TED CASSIDY
Genesis II (1973) 0318
Planet Earth (1974) 0441
Benny and Barney: Las Vegas Undercover (1977) 0684

RICHARD CASTELLANO
Incident on a Dark Street (1973) 0275
Honor Thy Father (1973) 0300

KIM CATTRALL
Good Against Evil (1977) 0729
The Bastard (1978) MS22
The Night Rider (1979) 0984
The Rebels (1979) MS34

JOAN CAULFIELD
The Magician (1973) 0311
The Hatfields and the McCoys (1975) 0505

ENZO CERUSICO
Magic Carpet (1972) 0252
Don't Push, I'll Charge When I'm Ready (1977) (1969) 0789

SUZY CHAFFEE
Ski Lift to Death (1978) 0825

GEORGE CHAKIRIS
Return to Fantasy Island (1978) 0803

RICHARD CHAMBERLAIN
F. Scott Fitzgerald and "The Last of the Belles" (1974) 0377
The Count of Monte Cristo (1975) 0501
The Man in the Iron Mask (1977) 0691
Centennial (1978) MS24

LEE CHAMBERLIN
Long Journey Back (1978) 0922
Roots: The Next Generations (1979) MS30

GOWER CHAMPION
Sharon: Portrait of a Mistress (1977) 0771

STOCKARD CHANNING
The Girl Most Likely To . . . (1973) 0351
Lucan (1977) 0728
Silent Victory: The Kitty O'Neil Story (1979) 0954

GERALDINE CHAPLIN
The Word (1978) MS26

SYDNEY CHAPLIN
The Woman Hunter (1972) 0231
Medical Story (1975) 0575

LONNY CHAPMAN
The Dangerous Days of Kiowa Jones (1966) 0006
Marriage: Year One (1971) 0154
The Screaming Woman (1972) 0201
Visions (Visions of Death) (1973) 0242
Hunter (1973) 0273
Big Rose (1974) 0421
Hurricane (1974) 0449
The Last Survivors (1975) 0530
Alexander: The Other Side of Dawn (1977) 0720
Black Beauty (1978) MS15
King (1978) MS16
Terror Out of the Sky (1978) 0930
Hanging by a Thread (1979) 0982
Blind Ambition (1979) MS35

LINDEN CHILES
Hitchhike! (1974) 0403
Panic on the 5:22 (1974) 0480
Death Be Not Proud (1975) 0510
Adventures of the Queen (1975) 0518
Who Is the Black Dahlia? (1975) 0528
Helter Skelter (1976) 0617
James at 15 (1977) 0748
Washington: Behind Closed Doors (1977) MS12

CHARLES CIOFFI
Mongo's Back in Town (1971) 0182
See the Man Run (1971) 0183
Nicky's World (1974) 0439
Kate McShane (1975) 0546
Return to Earth (1976) 0634
Tail Gunner Joe (1977) 0695
Dog and Cat (1977) 0746
Just a Little Inconvenience (1977) 0761
Samurai (1979) 0978

CANDY CLARK
James Dean (1976) 0604
Amateur Night at the Dixie Bar and Grill (1979) 0935

DANE CLARK
The Face of Fear (1971) 0151
The Family Rico (1972) 0228
Say Goodbye Maggie Cole (1972) 0236
The Return of Joe Forrester (1975) 0561
Murder on Flight 502 (1975) 0594
James Dean (1976) 0604
Once an Eagle (1976) MS05

DICK CLARK
Telethon (1977) 0774
Deadman's Curve (1978) 0812

MATT CLARK
The Execution of Private Slovik (1974) 0412
Melvin Purvis, G-Man (1974) 0431
The Great Ice Rip-Off (1977) 0473
This Was the West That Was (1974) 0491
The Kansas City Massacre (1975) 0576
Dog and Cat (1977) 0746
Lacy and the Mississippi Queen (1978) 0850

SUSAN CLARK
Something For a Lonely Man (1968) 0025
The Challengers (1970) 0072
The Astronaut (1972) 0191
Trapped (1973) 0355
Babe (1975) 0584
McNaughton's Daughter (1976) 0608
Amelia Earhart (1976) 0662

JILL CLAYBURGH
The Snoop Sisters (Female Instinct) (1972) 0265
Hustling (1975) 0523
The Art of Crime (1975) 0596
Griffin and Phoenix (1976) 0606

PAUL CLEMENS
A Death in Canaan (1978) 0824

LEE J. COBB
Heat of Anger (1972) 0218
Double Indemnity (1973) 0343
Dr. Max (1974) 0428

Trapped Beneath the Sea (1974) 0466
The Great Ice Rip-Off (1974) 0473

JAMES COBURN
The Dain Curse (1978) MS21

ROBERT COLBERT
City Beneath the Sea (1971) 0111
The Killer Who Wouldn't Die (1976) 0619

DENNIS COLE
Powderkeg (1971) 0133
Connection (1973) 0298
The Barbary Coast (1975) 0558

MICHAEL COLE
The Last Child (1971) 0149
Beg, Borrow . . . or Steal (1973) 0315
Evening in Byzantium (1978) MS23
The Return of Mod Squad (1979) 0990

OLIVIA COLE
Roots (1977) MS07
Backstairs at the White House (1979) MS28

DABNEY COLEMAN
Brotherhood of the Bell (1970) 0083
Savage (1973) 0322
Dying Room Only (1973) 0333
The President's Plane Is Missing (1973) 0346
Bad Ronald (1974) 0467
Attack on Terror: The FBI Versus the Ku Klux Klan (1975) 0522
Returning Home (1975) 0555
Kiss Me, Kill Me (1976) 0631
Maneaters Are Loose! (1978) 0845
More Than Friends (1978) 0886

JOHN COLICOS
Goodbye Raggedy Ann (1971) 0157
A Matter of Wife . . . or Death (1976) 0620
The Bastard (1978) MS22

GARY COLLINS
Quarantined (1970) 0074
Getting Away from It All (1972) 0196
Houston, We've Got a Problem (1974) 0407
Roots (1977) MS07
The Night They Took Miss Beautiful (1977) 0768

JOAN COLLINS
Drive Hard, Drive Fast (1973) (1968) 0328
Arthur Hailey's The Moneychangers (1976) MS06

STEPHEN COLLINS
Brink's: The Great Robbery (1976) 0616
The Rhinemann Exchange (1977) MS09

CORINNE COMACHO
The Mask of Sheba (1970) 0077
Gidget Gets Married (1972) 0189
What Are Best Friends For? (1973) 0373
Planet Earth (1974) 0441
The Specialists (1975) 0495

ANJANETTE COMER
The Young Lawyers (1969) 0047
Banyon (1971) 0126

Five Desperate Women (1971) 0145
The Deadly Hunt (1971) 0147
Night Games (1974) 0414
Terror on the 40th Floor (1974) 0452
Death Stalk (1975) 0506

DIDI CONN
Genesis II (1973) 0318
Three on a Date (1978) 0817
Murder at the Mardi Gras (1978) 0847

CHRISTOPHER CONNELLY
In Name Only (1969) 0053
Incident in San Francisco (1971) 0119
The Last Day (1975) 0519
Charlie Cobb: Nice Night for a Hanging (1977) 0735
Murder in Peyton Place (1977) 0762
The Incredible Rocky Mountain Race (1977) 0788
Crash (1978) 0894
Stunt Seven (1979) 0998

CHUCK CONNORS
The Birdmen (Escape of the Birdmen) (1971) 0140
Night of Terror (1972) 0241
Set This Town on Fire (The Profane Comedy) (1973) (1969) 0271
The Horror at 37,000 Feet (1973) 0288
The Police Story (1973) 0313
Banjo Hackett: Roamin' Free (1976) 0628
Nightmare in Badham County (1976) 0666
Roots (1977) MS07
The Night They Took Miss Beautiful (1977) 0768
Standing Tall (1978) 0804

MIKE CONNORS
Beg, Borrow . . . or Steal (1973) 0315
The Killer Who Wouldn't Die (1976) 0619
Revenge for a Rape (1976) 0672
Long Journey Back (1978) 0922

ROBERT CONRAD
The D.A.: Murder One (1969) 0055
Weekend of Terror (1970) 0101
The D.A.: Conspiracy to Kill (1971) 0106
Five Desperate Women (1971) 0145
The Adventures of Nick Carter (1972) 0213
The Last Day (1975) 0519
Smash-Up on Interstate 5 (1976) 0677
Centennial (1978) MS24
The Wild Wild West Revisited (1979) 0982

WILLIAM CONRAD
The Brotherhood of the Bell (1970) 0083
The D.A.: Conspiracy to Kill (1971) 0106
Cannon (1971) 0129
O'Hara, U.S. Treasury: Operation Cobra (1971) 0131
Attack on Terror: The FBI Versus the Ku Klux Klan (narrator) (1975) 0522
The Macahans (narrator) (1976) 0599
The City (narrator) (1977) 0687
Night Cries (1978) 0808
Keefer (1978) 0830
The Rebels (narrator) (1979) MS34

HANS CONRIED
Wake Me When the War Is Over (1969) 0043

MICHAEL CONSTANTINE
The Impatient Heart (1971) 0150
Suddenly Single (1971) 0156
Deadly Harvest (1972) 0234
Say Goodbye, Maggie Cole (1972) 0236
The Bait (1973) 0307
Big Rose (1974) 0421
Death Cruise (1974) 0470
The Secret Night Caller (1975) 0520
The Night That Panicked America (1975) 0586
Conspiracy of Terror (1976) 0621
Twin Detectives (1976) 0625
Wanted: The Sundance Woman (Mrs.
    Sundance Rides Again) (1976) 0656
Billy: Portrait of a Street Kid (1977) 0750
Harold Robbins' 79 Park Avenue (1977) MS13
Summer of My German Soldier (1978) 0895
Harold Robbins' The Pirate (1978) 0906
Crisis in Mid-Air (1979) 0952
Roots: The Next Generations (1979) MS30

EDDIE CONSTANTINE
Raid on Entebbe (1977) 0685

RICHARD CONTE
The Challengers (1970) 0072

FRANK CONVERSE
Dr. Cook's Garden (1971) 0109
A Tattered Web (1971) 0143
In Tandem (Movin' On) (1974) 0446
Killer on Board (1977) 0768
Cruise into Terror (1978) 0811
Sergeant Matlovich Vs. the U.S. Air Force
    (1978) 0866

BERT CONVY
Death Takes a Holiday (1971) 0158
The Girl On the Late, Late Show (1974) 0426
The Love Boat II (1977) 0692
SST—Death Flight (SST: Disaster in the Sky)
    (1977) 0700
Thou Shalt Not Commit Adultery (1978) 0898
Dallas Cowboys Cheerleaders (1979) 0937
Hanging by a Thread (1979) 0981

GARY CONWAY
The Judge and Jake Wyler (1972) 0260

KEVIN CONWAY
Johnny, We Hardly Knew Ye (1977) 0693
The Deadliest Season (1977) 0707

TIM CONWAY
Roll, Freddy, Roll! (1974) 0490

JACKIE COOGAN
Cool Million (Mask of Marcella) (1972) 0244
The Phantom of Hollywood (1974) 0397
The Specialists (1975) 0495
Sherlock Holmes in New York (1976) 0661

ELISHA COOK
The Movie Murderer (1970) 0067
Night Chase (1970) 0097
The Night Stalker (1972) 0193
Mad Bull (1977) 0792

JACKIE COOPER
Shadow on the Land (1968) 0026
Maybe I'll Come Home in the Spring (1971)
    0115

The Astronaut (1972) 0191
The Day the Earth Moved (1974) 0453
The Invisible Man (1975) 0560
Mobile Two (1975) 0574
Operation Petticoat (1977) 0747

ROBERT COOTE
Institute for Revenge (1979) 0943

GLENN CORBETT
The Stranger (1973) 0295
The Log of the Black Pearl (1975) 0494
Law of the Land (1976) 0624

GRETCHEN CORBETT
Farewell to Manzanar (1976) 0611
The Savage Bees (1976) 0674
Secrets of Three Hungry Wives (1978) 0883
Mandrake (1979) 0944

ELLEN CORBY
A Tattered Web (1971) 0143
The Homecoming (1971) 0188
The Story of Pretty Boy Floyd (1974) 0444

ALEX CORD
The Scorpio Letters (1967) 0011
Genesis II (1973) 0318
Fire! (1977) 0717

JEFF COREY
The Movie Murderer (1970) 0067
A Clear and Present Danger (1970) 0082
Something Evil (1972) 0197
Set This Town on Fire (The Profane Comedy)
    (1973) (1969) 0271
The Gun and the Pulpit (1974) 0427
Banjo Hackett: Roamin' Free (1976) 0628
Testimony of Two Men (1977) MS11
Curse of the Black Widow (Love Trap) (1977)
    0754
Captains Courageous (1977) 0783
Harold Robbins' The Pirate (1978) 0906

VALENTINA CORTESE
Jesus of Nazareth (1977) MS10

BILL COSBY
To All My Friends on Shore (1972) 0215
Top Secret (1978) 0859

HOWARD COSELL
The 500-Pound Jerk (1973) 0270
Connection (1973) 0298

MARICLARE COSTELLO
The Execution of Private Slovik (1974) 0412
The Gun (1974) 0477
Conspiracy of Terror (1976) 0621
Raid on Entebbe (1977) 0685
A Sensitive, Passionate Man (1977) 0734

JOSEPH COTTEN
Split Second to an Epitaph (1968) 0020
The Lonely Profession (1969) 0044
Cutter's Trail (1970) 0069
Assault on the Wayne (1971) 0107
Do You Take This Stranger? (1971) 0108
City Beneath the Sea (1971) 0111
The Screaming Woman (1972) 0201

The Devil's Daughter (1973) 0272
The Lindbergh Kidnapping Case (1976) 0605
Aspen (The Innocent and the Damned) (1977)
    MS14
Return to Fantasy Island (1978) 0803

TOM COURTENAY
I Heard an Owl Call My Name (1973) 0372

RONNY COX
Connection (1973) 0298
A Case of Rape (1974) 0401
Who Is the Black Dahlia? (1975) 0528
Having Babies (1976) 0659
Corey: For the People (1977) 0736
The Girl Called Hatter Fox (1977) 0767
Lovey: A Circle of Children, Part II (1978)
    0920
Transplant (1979) 0972

WALLY COX
Ironside (1967) 0014
Quarantined (1970) 0074
The Young Country (1970) 0081
Magic Carpet (1972) 0252
The Night Strangler (1973) 0277

YVONNE CRAIG
Jarrett (1973) 0310

BOB CRANE
The Delphi Bureau (1972) 0221

NORMA CRANE
Night Gallery (1969) 0049
The Movie Murderer (1970) 0067

BRODERICK CRAWFORD
The Challenge (1970) 0070
A Tattered Web (1971) 0143
The Adventures of Nick Carter (1972) 0213
The Phantom of Hollywood (1974) 0397
Look What's Happened to Rosemary's Baby
    (1976) 0664
Mayday at 40,000 Feet (1976) 0668

JOAN CRAWFORD
Night Gallery (1969) 0049

JOHN CRAWFORD
Return of the Gunfighter (1967) 0009
Killer by Night (1972) 0190
Strange Homecoming (1974) 0468
The Swiss Family Robinson (1975) 0550
Guilty or Innocent: The Sam Sheppard Murder
    Case (1975) 0593
The Macahans (1976) 0599
The Two-Five (1978) 0838
Arthur Hailey's Wheels (1978) MS20
Desperate Women (1978) 0890
From Here to Eternity (1979) MS29

KATHERINE CRAWFORD
The Doomsday Flight (1966) 0005
How to Steal an Airplane (1971) (1968) 0181
Gemini Man (Code Name: Minus One) (1976)
    0632
Captains and the Kings (1976) MS04

RICHARD CRENNA
Thief (1971) 0152
Footsteps (Footsteps: Nice Guys Finish Last)
(1972) 0238
Double Indemnity (1973) 0343
Nightmare (1974) 0378
Shootout in a One-Dog Town (1974) 0380
Honky Tonk (1974) 0425
A Girl Named Sooner (1975) 0571
The War Between the Tates (1977) 0737
Centennial (1978) MS24
Devil Dog: The Hound of Hell (1978) 0896
First You Cry (1978) 0902
A Fire in the Sky (1978) 0909

LINDA CRISTAL
The Dead Don't Die (1975) 0503

BING CROSBY
Dr. Cook's Garden (1971) 0109

CATHY LEE CROSBY
Wonder Woman (1974) 0410
Keefer (1978) 0830

GARY CROSBY
Wings of Fire (1967) 0010
O'Hara, U.S. Treasury: Operation Cobra
(1971) 0131
Sandcastles (1972) 0245
Partners in Crime (1973) 0320
Three on a Date (1978) 0817

KATHRYN CROSBY
The Initiation of Sarah (1978) 0814

MARY FRANCIS CROSBY
With This Ring (1978) 0846
A Guide for the Married Woman (1978) 0884
Pearl (1978) MS27

SCATMAN CROTHERS
Man on the Outside (1975) 0572
Roots (1977) MS07
Vega$ (1978) 0840

PAT CROWLEY
The Return of Joe Forrester (1975) 0561
Return to Fantasy Island (1978) 0803
A Family Upside Down (1978) 0836
The Millionaire (1978) 0927

BRANDON CRUZ
But I Don't Want to Get Married! (1970) 0087

BILLY CRYSTAL
SST—Death Flight (SST: Disaster in the Sky)
0700
Human Feelings (1978) 0885

JOHN CULLUM
The Man Without a Country (1973) 0325

ROBERT CULP
The Hanged Man (1964) 0002
See the Man Run (1971) 0183
A Cold Night's Death (1973) 0282
Outrage! (1973) 0359
Houston, We've Got a Problem (1974) 0407
Strange Homecoming (1974) 0468

A Cry for Help (1975) 0516
Flood (1976) 0675
Spectre (1977) 0727
Last of the Good Guys (1978) 0827
Roots: The Next Generations (1979) MS30
Hot Rod (1979) 0993

BOB CUMMINGS
Gidget Grows Up (1969) 0060
The Great American Beauty Contest (1973)
0287
Partners in Crime (1973) 0320

QUINN CUMMINGS
Night Terror (1977) 0696
Intimate Strangers (1977) 0775

KEENE CURTIS
The Magician (1973) 0311
Strange New World (1975) 0573
The Magnificent Magnet of Santa Mesa (1977)
0741

TONY CURTIS
The Third Girl from the Left (1973) 0355
The Count of Monte Cristo (1975) 0501
The Big Ripoff (1975) 0536
Vega$ (1978) 0840
The Users (1978) 0880

PETER CUSHING
The Great Houdinis (1976) 0658

CYRIL CUSACK
Catholics (1973) 0361
Jesus of Nazareth (1977) MS10
Les Miserables (1978) 0931

DAN DAILEY
Mr. and Mrs. Bo Jo Jones (1971) 0170
The Daughters of Joshua Cabe Return (1975)
0509
Testimony of Two Men (1977) MS11

BILL DAILY
In Name Only (1969) 0053
Murder at the Mardi Gras (1978) 0847

ABBY DALTON
Magic Carpet (1972) 0252

TIMOTHY DALTON
Centennial (1978) MS24

JAMES DALY
U.M.C. (Operation Heartbeat) (1969) 0039
The Storyteller (1977) 0785
Roots: The Next Generations (1979) MS30

TYNE DALY
In Search of America (1971) 0127
A Howling in the Woods (1971) 0163
Heat of Anger (1972) 0218
The Man Who Could Talk to Kids (1973)
0345
Larry (1974) 0440
The Entertainer (1976) 0610
Intimate Strangers (1977) 0775

BARBARA DANA
Daughter of the Mind (1969) 0056
The Other Side of Hell (1978) 0802

BILL DANA
Rosetti and Ryan: Men Who Love Women
(1977) 0725
A Guide for the Married Woman (1978) 0884

LEORA DANA
Seventh Avenue (1977) MS08

RODNEY DANGERFIELD
Benny and Barney: Las Vegas Undercover
(1977) 0684

WILLIAM DANIELS
Murdock's Gang (1973) 0314
A Case of Rape (1974) 0401
Sarah T.—Portrait of a Teenage Alcoholic
(1975) 0514
One of Our Own (1975) 0559
Francis Gary Powers: The True Story of the
U-2 Spy Incident (1976) 0655
Killer on Board (1977) 0766
The Bastard (1978) MS22
Big Bob Johnson and His Fantastic Speed
Circus (1978) 0861
Sergeant Matlovich Vs. the U.S. Air Force
(1978) 0866
The Rebels (1979) MS34
Blind Ambition (1979) MS35

BLYTHE DANNER
Dr. Cook's Garden (1971) 0109
F. Scott Fitzgerald and "The Last of the
Belles" (1973) 0377
Sidekicks (1974) 0417
A Love Affair: The Eleanor and Lou Gehrig
Story (1978) 0800
Are You in the House Alone? (1978) 0875
Too Far to Go (1979) 0960

ROYAL DANO
The Dangerous Days of Kiowa Jones (1966)
0006
Run, Simon, Run (1970) 0100
Moon of the Wolf (1972) 0235
Huckleberry Finn (1975) 0542
The Manhunter (1976) 0618
Murder in Peyton Place (1977) 0762
Donner Pass: The Road to Survival (1978)
0889
Strangers: The Story of a Mother and
Daughter (1979) 0986

CESARE DANOVA
Honeymoon with a Stranger (1969) 0059
Death Cruise (1974) 0470
A Matter of Wife . . . or Death (1976) 0620

RAY DANTON
Banyon (1971) 0126
A Very Missing Person (1972) 0219
Runaway! (1973) 0337

KIM DARBY
Ironside (1967) 0014
The People (1972) 0198
The Streets of San Francisco (1972) 0230
Don't Be Afraid of the Dark (1973) 0342
The Story of Pretty Boy Floyd (1974) 0444

This Was the West That Was (1974) 0491
Rich Man, Poor Man (1976) MS03
Flatbed Annie & Sweetiepie: Lady Truckers
   (1979) 0950

SEVERN DARDEN
The Movie Murderer (1970) 0067
Playmates (1972) 0237
The Man Who Died Twice (1973) 0323
Skyway to Death (1974) 0383
The New, Original Wonder Woman (1975)
   0590
The Disappearance of Aimee (1976) 0671
Captains and the Kings (1976) MS04
Victory at Entebbe (1976) 0679
Outside Chance (1978) 0912

JOAN DARLING
Owen Marshall, Counselor-at-Law (A Pattern
   of Morality) (1971) 0135

JAMES DARREN
City Beneath the Sea (1971) 0111
The Lives of Jenny Dolan (1975) 0585

HENRY DARROW
Brock's Last Case (1973) 0301
Hitchhike! (1974) 0403
Night Games (1974) 0414
Aloha Means Goodbye (1974) 0463
The Invisible Man (1975) 0560
Centennial (1978) MS24

HOWARD da SILVA
Smile, Jenny, You're Dead (1974) 0391

CLAUDE DAUPHIN
Berlin Affair (1970) 0093
Les Miserables (1978) 0931

NIGEL DAVENPORT
The Picture of Dorian Gray (1973) 0326
Dracula (1974) 0395

JOHN DAVIDSON
Coffee, Tea or Me? (1973) 0329
Shell Game (1975) 0563
Roger & Harry: The Mitera Target (Love for
   Ransom) (1977) 0715

BETTE DAVIS
Madame Sin (1972) 0195
The Judge and Jake Wyler (1972) 0260
Scream, Pretty Peggy (1973) 0357
The Disappearance of Aimee (1976) 0671
The Dark Secret of Harvest Home (1978) 0805
Strangers: The Story of a Mother and
   Daughter (1979) 0986

BRAD DAVIS
Sybil (1976) 0670
The Secret Life of John Chapman (1976) 0682
Roots (1977) MS07

CLIFTON DAVIS
Little Ladies of the Night (1977) 0689
Superdome (1978) 0799
Cindy (1978) 0832

JIM DAVIS
Vanished (1971) 0122
The Trackers (1971) 0184
Deliver Us from Evil (1973) 0330
Satan's Triangle (1975) 0504
Law of the Land (1976) 0624
Just a Little Inconvenience (1977) 0761
Killing Stone (1978) 0843

OSSIE DAVIS
The Outsider (1967) 0016
Night Gallery (1969) 0049
The Sheriff (1971) 0130
Billy: Portrait of a Street Kid (1977) 0750
King (1978) MS16
Roots: The Next Generations (1979) MS30

ROGER DAVIS
The Young Country (1970) 0081
River of Gold (1971) 0123
Killer Bees (1974) 0405
This Was the West That Was (narrator) (1974)
   0491
Aspen (The Innocent and the Damned) (1977)
   MS14

SAMMY DAVIS, JR.
The Pigeon (1969) 0048
The Trackers (1971) 0184
Poor Devil (1973) 0290

BRUCE DAVISON
Owen Marshall, Counselor-at-Law (A Pattern
   of Morality) (1971) 0135
The Affair (1973) 0356
The Last Survivors (1975) 0530
The Gathering (1977) 0784
Deadman's Curve (1978) 0812
Summer of My German Soldier (1978) 0895

RICHARD DAWSON
How to Pick Up Girls! (1978) 0899

LARAINE DAY
Murder on Flight 502 (1975) 0594
Return to Fantasy Island (1978) 0803

LYNDA DAY (see Lynda Day George)

JIMMY DEAN
The Ballad of Andy Crocker (1969) 0052
Rolling Man (1972) 0239
The City (1977) 0687

BURR DeBENNING
The House of Greenapple Road (1970) 0063
City Beneath the Sea (1971) 0111
The Face of Fear (1971) 0151
Adventures of the Queen (1975) 0518
Brink's: The Great Robbery (1976) 0616
Hanging by a Thread (1979) 0981

ROSEMARY DeCAMP
The Time Machine (1978) 0900
Blind Ambition (1979) MS35

YVONNE DeCARLO
The Girl on the Late, Late Show (1974) 0476
The Mark of Zorro (1974) 0469

DON DeFORE
Black Beauty (1978) MS15

GLORIA DeHAVEN
Call Her Mom (1972) 0210
Who Is the Black Dahlia? (1975) 0528
Banjo Hackett: Roamin' Free (1976) 0628
Sharon: Portrait of a Mistress (1977) 0771
Evening in Byzantium (1978) MS23

OLIVIA de HAVILLAND
The Screaming Woman (1972) 0201
Roots: The Next Generations (1979) MS30

DOM DeLUISE
Evil Roy Slade (1972) 0211
Only with Married Men (1974) 0472

DANIELLE DeMETZ
Wake Me When the War Is Over (1969) 0043

JOYCE DeWITT
With This Ring (1978) 0846

CLIFF DeYOUNG
Sunshine (1973) 0353
The Night That Panicked America (1975) 0586
The Lindbergh Kidnapping Case (1976) 0605
Captains and the Kings (1976) MS04
The 3,000 Mile Chase (1977) 0738
Sunshine Christmas (1977) 0787
King (1978) MS15
Centennial (1978) MS24
The Seeding of Sarah Burns (1979) 0968

RUBY DEE
Deadlock (1969) 0034
The Sheriff (1971) 0130
It's Good to Be Alive (1974) 0402
Roots: The Next Generations (1979) MS30
I Know Why the Caged Bird Sings (1979)
   0976

SANDRA DEE
The Daughters of Joshua Cabe (1972) 0229
Houston, We've Got a Problem (1974) 0407
The Manhunter (1976) (1968) 0618
Fantasy Island (1977) 0688

JOHN DEHNER
Winchester '73 (1967) 0013
Something for a Lonely Man (1968) 0025
Quarantine (1970) 0074
Honky Tonk (1974) 0425
The Big Ripoff (1975) 0536
Danger in Paradise (1977) 0718

WILLIAM DEMAREST
Don't Be Afraid of the Dark (1973) 0342
The Millionaire (1978) 0926

BRIAN DENNEHY
Johnny, We Hardly Knew Ye (1977) 0693
It Happened at Lake Wood Manor (1977) 0781
Ruby and Oswald (1978) 0815
A Death in Canaan (1978) 0824
A Real American Hero (1978) 0917
Pearl (1978) MS27

Silent Victory: The Kitty O'Neil Story (1979) 0954
The Jericho Mile (1979) 0963
Dummy (1979) 0994

SANDY DENNIS
The Man Who Wanted to Live Forever (1970) 0104
Something Evil (1972) 0197
Perfect Gentlemen (1978) 0829

BRUCE DERN
Sam Hill: Who Killed the Mysterious Mr. Foster? (1971) 0112

PETER DEUEL (Peter Duel)
Marcus Welby, M.D. (A Matter of Humanities) (1969) 0038
The Young Country (1970) 0081
The Psychiatrist: God Bless the Children (Children of the Lotus Eater) (1970) 0103
Alias Smith and Jones (1971) 0105
How to Steal an Airplane (Only One Day Left Before Tomorrow) (1971) (1968) 0181

WILLIAM DEVANE
Crime Club (1973) 0302
The Bait (1973) 0307
Fear on Trial (1975) 0578
Red Alert (1977) 0723
Black Beauty (1978) MS15
From Here to Eternity (1979) MS29

ANDY DEVINE
The Over-the-Hill Gang (1969) 0042
The Over-the-Hill Gang Rides Again (1970) 0096

COLLEEN DEWHURST
The Story of Jacob and Joseph (1974) 0430
Silent Victory: The Kitty O'Neil Story (1979) 0954
Studs Lonigan (1979) MS31

SUSAN DEY
Terror on the Beach (1973) 0332
Cage Without a Key (1975) 0537
Mary Jane Harper Cried Last Night (1977) 0763
Little Women (1978) 0881

KHIGH DHEIGH
Hawaii Five-O (1968) 0019
Judge Dee and the Monastery Murders (1974) 0493

GEORGE DiCENZO
The Norliss Tapes (1973) 0294
The Blue Knight (1973) MS01
The Swiss Family Robinson (1975) 0550
Last Hours Before Morning (1975) 0552
Helter Skelter (1976) 0617
The Hostage Heart (1977) 0749
Aspen (The Innocent and the Damned) (1977) MS14
To Kill a Cop (1978) 0837
The Jordan Chance (1978) 0919

ANGIE DICKINSON
The Love War (1970) 0078
Thief (1971) 0152

See the Man Run (1971) 0183
The Norliss Tapes (1973) 0294
Pray for the Wildcats (1974) 0386
A Sensitive, Passionate Man (1977) 0734
Overboard (1978) 0876
Pearl (1978) MS27

BRADFORD DILLMAN
Fear No Evil (1969) 0035
Black Water Gold (1970) 0061
Longstreet (1971) 0117
Five Desperate Women (1971) 0145
Revenge (1971) 0165
The Eyes of Charles Sand (1972) 0217
The Delphi Bureau (1972) 0221
Moon of the Wolf (1972) 0234
Deliver Us from Evil (1973) 0330
Murder or Mercy (1974) 0438
The Disappearance of Flight 412 (1974) 0458
Adventures of the Queen (1975) 0518
Force Five (1975) 0553
Widow (1976) 0601
Street Killing (1976) 0649
Kingston: The Power Play (1976) 0651
The Hostage Heart (1977) 0749
Jennifer: A Woman's Story (1979) 0957

MELINDA DILLON
The Critical List (1978) 0872
Transplant (1979) 0972

BOB DISHY
It Couldn't Happen to a Nicer Guy (1974) 0478

IVAN DIXON
Fer-De-Lance (1974) 0464

KEVIN DOBSON
The Immigrants (1978) MS25
Transplant (1979) 0972

TAMARA DOBSON
Murder at the World Series (1977) 0708

ELINOR DONAHUE
In Name Only (1969) 0053
Gidget Gets Married (1972) 0189
Mulligan's Stew (1977) 0742
Doctors' Private Lives (1978) 0831

TROY DONAHUE
Split Second to an Epitaph (1968) 0020
The Lonely Profession (1969) 0044

JAMES DONALD
Destiny of a Spy (1969) 0046
David Copperfield (1970) 0080

JAMES DOUGLAS
A Clear and Present Danger (1970) 0082

KIRK DOUGLAS
Mousey (1974) 0409
Arthur Hailey's The Moneychangers (1976) MS06
Victory at Entebbe (1976) 0679

MELVYN DOUGLAS
Companions in Nightmare (1968) 0024
Hunters Are for Killing (1970) 0079
Death Takes a Holiday (1971) 0158
The Death Squad (1974) 0379
Murder or Mercy (1974) 0438
Intimate Strangers (1977) 0775

MICHAEL DOUGLAS
When Michael Calls (1972) 0205
The Streets of San Francisco (1972) 0230

ROBERT DOUGLAS
The Questor Tapes (1974) 0385
Centennial (1978) MS24

BRAD DOURIF
Sergeant Matlovich Vs. the U.S. Air Force (1978) 0866

DAVID DOYLE
Incident on a Dark Street (1973) 0275
The Police Story (1973) 0313
Money to Burn (1973) 0347
Blood Sport (1973) 0364
Miracle on 34th Street (1973) 0370
The Stranger Within (1974) 0457
The First 36 Hours of Dr. Durant (1975) 0565
Charlie's Angels (1976) 0614
Black Market Baby (1977) 0765
Wild and Wooly (1978) 0819

ALFRED DRAKE
Your Money or Your Wife (1972) 0266

CHARLES DRAKE
The Smugglers (1968) 0030
The Screaming Woman (1972) 0201
Partners in Crime (1973) 0320
Scream, Pretty Peggy (1973) 0357
The Return of Joe Forrester (1975) 0561
The Lives of Jenny Dolan (1975) 0585

TOM DRAKE
City Beneath the Sea (1971) 0111
The Return of Joe Forrester (1975) 0561
A Matter of Wife . . . or Death (1976) 0620
Mayday at 40,000 Feet (1976) 0668

ALEX DREIER
Sweet, Sweet Rachel (1971) 0148
Murdock's Gang (1973) 0314

RICHARD DREYFUSS
Two for the Money (1972) 0216
Victory at Entebbe (1976) 0679

JAMES DRURY
Breakout (1970) 0102
Alias Smith and Jones (1971) 0105
The Devil and Miss Sarah (1971) 0179

DON DUBBINS
Run, Simon, Run (1970) 0100
Banacek: Detour to Nowhere (1972) 0223
Outrage! (1973) 0359

HOWARD DUFF
The D.A.: Murder One (1969) 0055
In Search of America (1971) 0127
A Little Game (1971) 0161
The Heist (1972) 0259
Snatched (1973) 0284
In the Glitter Palace (1977) 0702
Ski Lift to Death (1978) 0825
Battered (1978) 0877

PATRICK DUFFY
The Stranger Who Looks Like Me (1974) 0408
Man from Atlantis (1977) 0704

DENNIS DUGAN
The Girl Most Likely To . . . (1973) 0351
Death Race (1973) 0354
Rich Man, Poor Man (1976) MS03
Richie Brockelman: Missing 24 Hours (1976) 0663

ANDREW DUGGAN
Hawaii Five-O (1968) 0019
The Forgotten Man (1971) 0137
Two on a Bench (1971) 0162
The Homecoming (1971) 0188
Jigsaw (1972) 0224
The Streets of San Francisco (1972) 0230
Firehouse (1973) 0269
The Last Angry Man (1974) 0435
Panic on the 5:22 (1974) 0480
Attack on Terror: The FBI Versus the Ku
   Klux Klan (1975) 0522
Rich Man, Poor Man (1976) MS03
Once an Eagle (1976) MS05
Tail Gunner Joe (1977) 0695
The Deadliest Season (1977) 0707
Pine Canyon Is Burning (1977) 0722
The Hunted Lady (1977) 0780
Overboard (1978) 0875
The Time Machine (1978) 0900
A Fire in the Sky (1978) 0909
The Incredible Journey of Dr. Meg Laurel
   (1979) 0932
Backstairs at the White House (1979) MS28

PATTY DUKE (Patty Duke Astin)
My Sweet Charlie (1970) 0065
Two on a Bench (1971) 0162
If Tomorrow Comes (1971) 0180
She Waits (1972) 0200
Deadly Harvest (1972) 0234
Nightmare (1974) 0378
Rich Man, Poor Man (1976) MS04
Look What's Happened to Rosemary's Baby
   (Rosemary's Baby II) (1976) 0664
Fire! (1977) 0717
Rosetti and Ryan: Men Who Love Women
   (1977) 0725
Curse of the Black Widow (Love Trap) (1977)
   0754
Killer on Board (1977) 0766
The Storyteller (1977) 0785
Having Babies III (1978) 0826
A Family Upside Down (1978) 0836
Hanging by a Thread (1979) 0981

DAVID DUKES
Harold Robbins' 79 Park Avenue (1977) MS13
Go West, Young Girl (1978) 0842
A Fire in the Sky (1978) 0909
Some Kind of Miracle (1979) 0933
The Triangle Factory Fire Scandal (1979) 0947

KEIR DULLEA
Black Water Gold (1970) 0061
Law and Order (1976) 0629
The Legend of the Golden Gun (1979) 0969

FAYE DUNAWAY
The Disappearance of Aimee (1976) 0671

SANDY DUNCAN
Roots (1977) MS07

JAMES DUNN
Shadow over Elveron (1968) 0018

MILDRED DUNNOCK
A Brand New Life (1973) 0292
A Summer Without Boys (1973) 0363
Murder or Mercy (1974) 0438
The Best Place to Be (1979) 0995

CHARLES DURNING
Connection (1973) 0298
The Trial of Chaplain Jensen (1975) 0515
Queen of the Stardust Ballroom (1975) 0517
Switch (1975) 0535
Captains and the Kings (1976) MS04
Special Olympics (1978) 0821
Studs Lonigan (1979) MS31

DAN DURYEA
Winchester '73 (1967) 0013
Stranger on the Run (1967) 0015

MARJ DUSAY
Climb an Angry Mountain (1972) 0268
Most Wanted (1976) 0615
Murder in Peyton Place (1977) 0762
Arthur Hailey's Wheels (1978) MS20
The Child Stealer (1979) 0959

ANN DUSENBERRY
Captains and the Kings (1976) MS04
Stonestreet: Who Killed the Centerfold Model?
   (1977) 0690
Little Women (1978) 0881

ROBERT DUVALL
Fame Is the Name of the Game (1966) 0004
Ike (1979) MS33

SHIRLEY EATON
The Scorpio Letters (1967) 0011

BUDDY EBSEN
The Daughters of Joshua Cabe (1972) 0229
The Horror at 37,000 Feet (1973) 0288
Tom Sawyer (1973) 0317
The President's Plane Is Missing (1973) 0346
Smash-Up on Interstate 5 (1976) 0677
Leave Yesterday Behind (1978) 0848
The Bastard (1978) MS22
The Critical List (1978) 0872

HERB EDELMAN
In Name Only (1969) 0053
The Feminist and the Fuzz (1971) 0110
The Neon Ceiling (1971) 0113
Banyon (1971) 0126
Once Upon a Dead Man (1971) 0139

The Strange and Deadly Occurrence (1974)
   0455
Crossfire (1975) 0540
Smash-Up on Interstate 5 (1976) 0677
Special Olympics (1978) 0821
The Comedy Company (1978) 0864

BARBARA EDEN
The Feminist and the Fuzz (1971) 0110
A Howling in the Woods (1971) 0163
The Woman Hunter (1972) 0231
Guess Who's Sleeping in My Bed? (1973) 0349
The Stranger Within (1974) 0457
Let's Switch (1975) 0499
How to Break Up a Happy Divorce (1976)
   0657
Stonestreet: Who Killed the Centerfold Model?
   (1977) 0690
The Girls in the Office (1979) 0948

JENNIFER EDWARDS
Heidi (1968) 0023
Go Ask Alice (1973) 0280

VINCE EDWARDS
Sole Survivor (1970) 0062
Dial Hot Line (1970) 0076
Do Not Fold, Spindle or Mutilate (1971) 0166
Firehouse (1973) 0269
Death Stalk (1975) 0506
The Rhinemann Exchange (1977) MS09
Cover Girls (1977) 0721
Evening in Byzantium (1978) MS23
The Courage and the Passion (1978) 0857

RICHARD EGAN
The House That Would Not Die (1970) 0092
Shootout in a One-Dog Town (1974) 0380

SAMANTHA EGGAR
Double Indemnity (1973) 0343
All the Kind Strangers (1974) 0476
The Killer Who Wouldn't Die (1976) 0619
Ziegfeld: The Man and His Women (1978)
   0854

CINDY EILBACHER
A Clear and Present Danger (1970) 0082
Crowhaven Farm (1970) 0099
The Great Man's Whiskers (1973) (1969) 0289
Bad Ronald (1974) 0467
The Death of Richie (1977) 0686
Donner Pass: The Road to Survival (1978)
   0889
A Fire in the Sky (1978) 0909
The Immigrants (1978) MS25
A Last Cry for Help (1979) 0941

LISA EILBACHER
Bad Ronald (1974) 0467
Panache (1976) 0636
Spider-Man (1977) 0753
Arthur Hailey's Wheels (1978) MS20
The Ordeal of Patty Hearst (1979) 0956

IKE EISENMANN
Banjo Hackett: Roamin' Free
Black Beauty (1978) MS15
The Bastard (1978) MS22
Devil Dog: The Hound of Hell (1978) 0896
Terror Out of the Sky (1978) 0930

ANITA EKBERG
Gold of the Amazon Women (1979) 0958

BRITT EKLAND
The Great Wallendas (1978) 0810
Ring of Passion (1978) 0813

JACK ELAM
The Over-the-Hill Gang (1969) 0042
The Daughters of Joshua Cabe (1972) 0229
The Red Pony (1973) 0312
Shootout in a One-Dog Town (1974) 0312
Sidekicks (1974) 0417
Huckleberry Finn (1975) 0542
The New Daughters of Joshua Cabe (1976) 0641
Black Beauty (1978) MS15
Lacy and the Mississippi Queen (1978) 0850
The Sacketts (1979) 0988

DANA ELCAR
The Borgia Stick (1967) 0012
The Sound of Anger (1968) 0028
Deadlock (1969) 0034
The Whole World Is Watching (1969) 0036
The D.A.: Murder One (1969) 0055
San Francisco International (1970) 0085
Sarge: The Badge or the Cross (1971) 0116
The Death of Me Yet (1971) 0159
The Bravos (1972) 0192
Fireball Forward (1972) 0220
Hawkins on Murder (Death and the Maiden) (1973) 0306
Dying Room Only (1973) 0333
Heatwave! (1974) 0387
Senior Year (1974) 0418
Panic on the 5:22 (1974) 0480
Law of the Land (1976) 0624
Gemini Man (Code Name: Minus One) (1976) 0632
Centennial (1978) MS24
Crisis in Mid-Air (1979) 0952
Samurai (1979) 0978

FLORENCE ELDRIDGE
First You Cry (1978) 0902

TAINA ELG
The Great Wallendas (1978) 0810

HECTOR ELIZONDO
The Impatient Heart (1971) 0150
Wanted: The Sundance Woman (Mrs. Sundance Rides Again) (1976) 0656
The Dain Curse (1978) MS21

DENHOLM ELLIOTT
Madame Sin (1972) 0195

SAM ELLIOTT
The Challenge (1970) 0070
Assault on the Wayne (1971) 0107
The Blue Knight (1973) MS01
I Will Fight No More Forever (1975) 0549
Once an Eagle (1976) MS05
Aspen (The Innocent and the Damned) (1977) MS14
The Sacketts (1979) 0988

STEPHEN ELLIOTT
The Gun (1974) 0477
The Invasion of Johnson County (1976) 0646

Young Joe, the Forgotten Kennedy (1977) 0755
Sergeant Matlovich Vs. the U.S. Air Force (1978) 0866
Overboard (1978) 0876
Betrayal (1978) 0903
Some Kind of Miracle (1979) 0933
The Ordeal of Patty Hearst (1979) 0956
Son-Rise: A Miracle of Love (1979) 0987

MONIE ELLIS
Gidget Gets Married (1972) 0189

GEORGIA ENGEL
A Love Affair: The Eleanor and Lou Gehrig Story (1978) 0800

LEIF ERICKSON
Terror in the Sky (1971) 0138
The Deadly Dream (1971) 0144
The Family Rico (1972) 0228
The Daughters of Joshua Cabe (1972) 0229

DEVON ERICSON
The Dream Makers (1975) 0497
The Runaway Barge (1975) 0541
Eleanor and Franklin (1976) 0598
Testimony of Two Men (1977) MS11
The Awakening Land (1978) MS17
Ishi: The Last of His Tribe (1978) 0928
Studs Lonigan (1979) MS31

JOHN ERICSON
The Bounty Man (1972) 0250
Tenafly (1973) 0296

STUART ERWIN
Shadow over Elveron (1968) 0018

ERIK ESTRADA
Fire! (1977) 0717

DAMON EVANS
Roots: The Next Generations (1979) MS30

EDITH EVANS
David Copperfield (1970) 0080
QB VII (1974) 0442

GENE EVANS
Dragnet (1969) (1966) 0031
The Intruders (1970) 0095
The Bounty Man (1972) 0250
Shootout in a One-Dog Town (1974) 0380
Sidekicks (1974) 0417
The Last Day (1975) 0519
Matt Helm (1975) 0562
The Macahans (1976) 0599
The Rhinemann Exchange (1977) MS09
Fire! (1977) 0717
Kate Bliss and the Ticker Tape Kid (1978) 0856
The Sacketts (1979) 0988

LINDA EVANS
Female Artillery (1973) 0279
Nakia (1974) 0436
Nowhere to Run (1978) 0801
Standing Tall (1978) 0804

MAURICE EVANS
U.M.C. (Operation Heartbeat) (1969) 0039
The Brotherhood of the Bell (1970) 0083

MIKE EVANS
Killer by Night (1972) 0190
Call Her Mom (1972) 0210
The Voyage of the Yes (1973) 0278
Rich Man, Poor Man (1976) MS03

CHAD EVERETT
Return of the Gunfighter (1967) 0009
In the Glitter Palace (1977) 0702
Centennial (1978) MS24

JASON EVERS
The Young Lawyers (1969) 0047
Fer-De-Lance (1974) 0464

GREG EVIGAN
BJ and the Bear (1978) 0882

TOM EWELL
Promise Him Anything . . . (1975) 0566
The Return of Mod Squad (1979) 0990

FABIAN (FORTE)
Getting Married (1978) 0849
Katie: Portrait of a Centerfold (1978) 0888
Crisis in Mid-Air (1979) 0952

SHELLEY FABARES
U.M.C. (Operation Heartbeat) (1969) 0039
Brian's Song (1971) 0177
Two for the Money (1972) 0216
Sky Hei$t (1975) 0569
Pleasure Cove (1979) 0934

NANETTE FABRAY
Fame Is the Name of the Game (1966) 0004
But I Don't Want to Get Married! (1970) 0087
Magic Carpet (1972) 0252
The Couple Takes a Wife (1972) 0261

DOUGLAS FAIRBANKS, JR.
The Crooked Hearts (1972) 0253

MORGAN FAIRCHILD
The Initiation of Sarah (1978) 0814
Murder in Music City (1979) 0939

PETER FALK
Prescription: Murder (1968) 0017
A Step Out of Line (1971) 0118
Ransom for a Dead Man (1971) 0120
Griffin and Phoenix (1976) 0606

JAMES FARENTINO
Wings of Fire (1967) 0010
The Sound of Anger (1968) 0028
The Whole World Is Watching (1969) 0036
Vanished (1971) 0122
The Longest Night (1972) 0227
The Family Rico (1972) 0228
Cool Million (Mask of Marcella) (1972) 0244
The Elevator (1974) 0396
Crossfire (1975) 0540
Jesus of Nazareth (1977) MS10

The Possessed (1977) 0714
Silent Victory: The Kitty O'Neil Story (1979) 0954
Son-Rise: A Miracle of Love (1979) 0987

MIKE FARRELL
The Longest Night (1972) 0227
She Cried "Murder!" (1973) 0335
The Questor Tapes (1974) 0385
Live Again, Die Again (1974) 0400
McNaughton's Daughter (1976) 0608
Battered (1978) 0877

SHARON FARRELL
Quarantined (1970) 0074
The Eyes of Charles Sand (1972) 0217
The Underground Man (1974) 0443

MIA FARROW
Goodbye Raggedy Ann (1971) 0157

FARRAH FAWCETT (Farrah Fawcett Majors)
The Feminist and the Fuzz (1971) 0110
The Great American Beauty Contest (1973) 0287
The Girl Who Came Gift Wrapped (1974) 0388
Murder on Flight 502 (1975) 0594
Charlie's Angels (1976) 0614

ALAN FEINSTEIN
Alexander: The Other Side of Dawn (1977) 0720
The Hunted Lady (1977) 0780
The Users (1978) 0880

BARBARA FELDON
Getting Away From It All (1972) 0196
Playmates (1972) 0237
What Are Best Friends For? (1973) 0373
Let's Switch (1975) 0499
A Guide for the Married Woman (1978) 0884
Sooner or Later (1979) 0966
A Vacation in Hell (1979) 0992

TOVAH FELDSHUH
Scream, Pretty Peggy (1973) 0357
The Amazing Howard Hughes (1977) 0712
Holocaust (1978) MS19
Terror Out of the Sky (1978) 0930
The Triangle Factory Fire Scandal (1979) 0947

NORMAN FELL
The Hanged Man (1964) 0002
Three's a Crowd (1969) 0054
The Heist (1972) 0259
Thursday's Game (1974) (1971) 0432
Death Stalk (1975) 0506
Rich Man, Poor Man (1976) MS03
Richie Brockelman: Missing 24 Hours (1976) 0663
Roots: The Next Generations (1979) MS30

PAMELYN FERDIN
Daughter of the Mind (1969) 0056
The Forgotten Man (1971) 0137
A Tree Grows in Brooklyn (1974) 0423
Miles to Go Before I Sleep (1975) 0498

JOSE FERRER
The Aquarians (1970) 0091
Banyon (1971) 0126

The Cable Car Murder (Cross Current) (1971) 0172
The Marcus-Nelson Murders (1973) 0305
The Missing Are Deadly (1975) 0500
Medical Story (1975) 0575
The Art of Crime (1975) 0596
The Rhinemann Exchange (1977) MS09
Exo-Man (1977) 0740

MEL FERRER
Tenafly (1973) 0286
Sharon: Portrait of a Mistress (1977) 0771
Black Beauty (1978) MS15

LOU FERRIGNO
The Incredible Hulk (1977) 0772

SALLY FIELD
Maybe I'll Come Home in the Spring (1971) 0115
Marriage: Year One (1971) 0154
Mongo's Back in Town (1971) 0182
Home for the Holidays (1972) 0258
Hitched (1973) 0321
Bridger (1976) 0648
Sybil (1976) 0670

PETER FINCH
Raid on Entebbe (1977) 0685

JOHN FINK
Ransom for a Dead Man (1971) 0120
Home for the Holidays (1972) 0258
Linda (1973) 0350
Who Is the Black Dahlia? (1975) 0528
The Lindbergh Kidnapping Case (1976) 0605
High Risk (1976) 0635

FRANK FINLAY
The Adventures of Don Quixote (1973) 0324
The Thief of Baghdad (1978) 0907

CARRIE FISHER
Come Back, Little Sheba (1977) 0795
Leave Yesterday Behind (1978) 0848

GAIL FISHER
Every Man Needs One (1972) 0264

GERALDINE FITZGERALD
Yesterday's Child (1977) 0694
The Quinns (1977) 0745

PAUL FIX
Winchester '73 (1967) 0013
Set This Town on Fire (The Profane Comedy) (1973) (1969) 0271
Guilty or Innocent: The Sam Sheppard Murder Case (1975) 0593
The City (1977) 0687
Just Me and You (1978) 0855
Hanging by a Thread (1979) 0981

FANNY FLAGG
The New, Original Wonder Woman (1975) 0590
Sex and the Married Woman (1977) 0751

FIONNUALA FLANAGAN
The Picture of Dorian Gray (1973) 0326
The Godchild (1974) 0483
The Legend of Lizzie Borden (1975) 0513
Rich Man, Poor Man (1976) MS03
Nightmare in Badham County (1976) 0666
Mary White (1977) 0778

ED FLANDERS
Goodbye Raggedy Ann (1971) 0157
The Snoop Sisters (Female Instinct) (1972) 0265
Hunter (1973) 0273
Indict and Convict (1974) 0376
Things in Their Season (1974) 0486
The Legend of Lizzie Borden (1975) 0513
Attack on Terror: The FBI Versus the Ku Klux Klan (1975) 0522
Eleanor and Franklin (1976) 0598
The Amazing Howard Hughes (1977) 0712
Mary White (1977) 0778
Backstairs at the White House (1979) MS28
Blind Ambition (1979) MS35

SUSAN FLANNERY
Arthur Hailey's The Moneychangers (1976) MS06
Anatomy of a Seduction (1979) 0980

RHONDA FLEMING
Last Hours Before Morning (1975) 0552

LOUISE FLETCHER
Can Ellen Be Saved? (1974) 0393
Thou Shalt Not Commit Adultery (1978) 0898

JAY C. FLIPPEN
Fame Is the Name of the Game (1966) 0004
The Sound of Anger (1968) 0028
The Old Man Who Cried Wolf (1970) 0088
Sam Hill: Who Killed the Mysterious Mr. Foster? (1971) 0112

JOE FLYNN
The Girl Most Likely To . . . (1973) 0351

NINA FOCH
Prescription: Murder (1968) 0017
Gidget Grows Up (1969) 0060
Female Artillery (1973) 0279
The Great Houdinis (1976) 0658

HENRY FONDA
Stranger on the Run (1967) 0015
The Red Pony (1973) 0312
The Alpha Caper (1973) 0340
Captains and the Kings (1976) MS04
Home to Stay (1978) 0844
Roots: The Next Generations (1979) MS30

JOAN FONTAINE
The Users (1978) 0880

GLENN FORD
The Brotherhood of the Bell (1970) 0083
Jarrett (1973) 0310
The Disappearance of Flight 412 (1974) 0458
The Greatest Gift (1974) 0471
Punch and Jody (1974) 0484
Once an Eagle (1976) MS05
The 3,000 Mile Chase (1977) 0738
Evening in Byzantium (1978) MS23
The Sacketts (1979) 0988

HARRISON FORD
The Intruders (1970) 0095
James A. Michener's Dynasty (1976) 0612
The Possessed (1977) 0714

PAUL FORD
In Name Only (1969) 0053

FREDERIC FORREST
Larry (1974) 0440
Promise Him Anything . . . (1975) 0566
Ruby and Oswald (1978) 0815

STEVE FORREST
The Hanged Man (1974) 0413
The Hatfields and the McCoys (1975) 0505
Wanted: The Sundance Woman (Mrs.
Sundance Rides Again) (1976) 0656
Last of the Mohicans (1977) 0779
Testimony of Two Men (1977) MS11
Maneaters Are Loose (1978) 0845
The Deerslayer (1978) 0926
Captain America (1979) 0940

CONSTANCE FORSLUND
The Legend of Valentino (1975) 0595
Big Bob Johnson and His Fantastic Speed
Circus (1978) 0861
Pleasure Cove (1979) 0934

ROBERT FORSTER
Banyon (1971) 0126
The Death Squad (1974) 0379
Nakia (1974) 0436
The City (1977) 0687
Standing Tall (1978) 0804
The Darker Side of Terror (1979) 0967

ROSEMARY FORSYTH
The Brotherhood of the Bell (1970) 0083
City Beneath the Sea (1971) 0111
The Death of Me Yet (1971) 0159
My Father's House (1975) 0570

JOHN FORSYTHE
See How They Run (1964) 0001
Shadow on the Land (1968) 0026
Murder Once Removed (1971) 0160
The Letters (1973) 0303
Lisa, Bright and Dark (1973) 0360
Cry Panic (1974) 0394
The Healers (1974) 0447
Terror on the 40th Floor (1974) 0452
The Deadly Tower (1975) 0581
Charlie's Angels (voice) (1976) 0614
Amelia Earhart (1976) 0662
Tail Gunner Joe (1977) 0695
Cruise into Terror (1978) 0811
With This Ring (1978) 0846
The Users (1978) 0880

BRIGITTE FOSSEY
The Man Who Died Twice (1973) 0323

GLORIA FOSTER
To All My Friends on Shore (1972) 0215
Top Secret (1978) 0859

JODIE FOSTER
Smile, Jenny, You're Dead (1974) 0391

MEG FOSTER
The Death of Me Yet (1971) 0159
Sunshine (1973) 0353
Things In Their Season (1974) 0486
Promise Him Anything . . . (1975) 0566
James Dean (1976) 0604
Washington: Behind Closed Doors (1977)
MS12
Sunshine Christmas (1977) 0787

BERNARD FOX
The Hound of the Baskervilles (1972) 0208

ROBERT FOXWORTH
The Devil's Daughter (1973) 0272
Frankenstein (1973) 0276
Mrs. Sundance (1974) 0381
The Questor Tapes (1974) 0385
The FBI Story: The FBI Versus Alvin Karpis,
Public Enemy Number One (1974) 0474
James Dean (1976) 0604
It Happened at Lake Wood Manor (1977) 0781
Death Moon (1978) 0858

ANTHONY FRANCIOSA
Fame Is the Name of the Game (1966) 0004
The Deadly Hunt (1971) 0147
Earth II (1971) 0176
The Catcher (1972) 0226
This Was the West That Was (1974) 0491
Matt Helm (1975) 0562
Curse of the Black Widow (Love Trap) (1977)
0754
Aspen (The Innocent and the Damned) (1977)
MS14
Arthur Hailey's Wheels (1978) MS20

ANNE FRANCIS
Wild Women (1970) 0090
The Intruders (1970) 0095
The Forgotten Man (1971) 0137
Mongo's Back In Town (1971) 0182
Fireball Forward (1972) 0220
Haunts of the Very Rich (1972) 0233
Cry Panic (1974) 0394
The FBI Story: The FBI Versus Alvin Karpis,
Public Enemy Number One (1974) 0474
The Last Survivors (1975) 0530
A Girl Named Sooner (1975) 0571
Banjo Hackett: Roamin' Free (1976) 0628
Little Mo (1978) 0869
The Rebels (1979) MS34

JAMES FRANCISCUS
Shadow Over Elveron (1968) 0018
Trial Run (1969) 0032
Night Slaves (1970) 0086
Longstreet (1971) 0117
The 500-Pound Jerk (1973) 0270
Aloha Means Goodbye (1974) 0463
The Dream Makers (1975) 0497
The Trial of Chaplain Jensen (1975) 0515
One of My Wives Is Missing (1976) 0609
Secrets of Three Hungry Wives (1978) 0883
Harold Robbins' The Pirate (1978) 0906

CHARLES FRANK
The Silence (1975) 0588
Panache (1976) 0636
Tarantulas: The Deadly Cargo (1977) 0794
Ski Lift to Death (1978) 0825
Go West, Young Girl (1978) 0842
The New Maverick (1978) 0868
A Guide for the Married Woman (1978) 0884
The Chisholms (1979) MS32

GARY FRANK
Senior Year (1974) 0418

BONNIE FRANKLIN
The Law (1974) 0465
A Guide for the Married Woman (1978) 0884

PAMELA FRANKLIN
See How They Run (1964) 0001
David Copperfield (1970) 0080
The Letters (1973) 0303
Satan's School for Girls (1973) 0334
Crossfire (1975) 0540
Eleanor and Franklin (1975) 0598

EDUARD FRANZ
Brotherhood of the Bell (1970) 0083
Panic on the 5:22 (1974) 0480

AL FREEMAN, JR.
My Sweet Charlie (1970) 0065
King (1978) MS16
Roots: The Next Generations (1979) MS30

MONA FREEMAN
Welcome Home, Johnny Bristol (1972) 0202

VICTOR FRENCH
Cutter's Trail (1970) 0069
Little House on the Prairie (1974) 0424
The Tribe (1974) 0489
Amateur Night at the Dixie Bar & Grill (1979)
0935

LEONARD FREY
Shirts/Skins (1973) 0341

JONATHAN FRID
The Devil's Daughter (1973) 0272

SQUIRE FRIDELL
The Strangers in 7A (1972) 0255
Rosetti and Ryan: Men Who Love Women
(1977) 0725
Human Feelings (1978) 0885

LOU FRIZZELL
Banacek: Detour to Nowhere (1972) 0223
Streets of San Francisco (1972) 0230
Footsteps (Footsteps: Nice Guys Finish Last)
(1972) 0238
Runaway (1973) 0337
Letters from Three Lovers (1973) 0339
Money to Burn (1973) 0347
Manhunter (1974) 0404
Crossfire (1975) 0540
Returning Home (1975) 0555
Farewell to Manzanar (1976) 0611
Lucan (1977) 0728
Ruby and Oswald (1978) 0815
Centennial (1978) MS24
Devil Dog: The Hound of Hell (1978) 0896
Steel Cowboy (1978) 0915

PENNY FULLER
Women in Chains (1972) 0199

ROBERT FULLER
    Emergency (1972) 0194
    Donner Pass: The Road to Survival (1978)
        0889

MARTIN GABEL
    Smile, Jenny, You're Dead (1974) 0391
    Contract on Cherry Street (1977) 0777

EVA GABOR
    Wake Me When the War Is Over (1969) 0043

MAX GAIL
    The Priest Killer (1971) 0136
    Curse of the Black Widow (Love Trap) (1977)
        0754
    Like Mom, Like Me (1978) 0887
    Desperate Women (1978) 0889
    Pearl (1978) MS27

DON GALLOWAY
    Ironside (1967) 0014
    Split Second to an Epitaph (1968) 0020
    The Priest Killer (1971) 0136
    Lieutenant Schuster's Wife (1972) 0243
    You Lie So Deep, My Love (1975) 0525
    Cover Girls (1977) 0721
    Ski Lift to Death (1978) 0825

KAZ GARAS
    The Sheriff (1971) 0130
    The City (1971) 0134
    Wonder Woman (1974) 0410
    Last Hours Before Morning (1975) 0552
    Murder in Peyton Place (1977) 0762

ALLEN GARFIELD
    Footsteps (Footsteps: Nice Guys Finish Last)
        (1972) 0238
    The Marcus-Nelson Murders (1973) 0305
    The Virginia Hill Story (1974) 0479
    Serpico: The Deadly Game (1976) 0623
    The Million Dollar Rip-Off (1976) 0653
    Nowhere to Run (1978) 0801
    Ring of Passion (1978) 0813

BEVERLY GARLAND
    Cutter's Trail (1970) 0069
    Say Goodbye, Maggie Cole (1972) 0236
    The Weekend Nun (1972) 0267
    The Voyage of the Yes (1973) 0278
    Unwed Father (1974) 0406
    The Healers (1974) 0447
    The Day the Earth Moved (1974) 0453

JAMES GARNER
    The Rockford Files (1974) 0422
    The New Maverick (1978) 0868

PEGGY ANN GARNER
    Betrayal (1978) 0903

TERI GARR
    Law and Order (1976) 0629

LEIF GARRETT
    Strange Homecoming (1974) 0468
    The Last Survivors (1975) 0530
    Flood (1976) 0675
    Peter Lundy and the Medicine Hat Stallion
        (1977) 0773

SEAN GARRISON
    The Outsider (1967) 0016
    Seven in Darkness (1969) 0040
    The Challengers (1970) 0072
    Breakout (1970) 0102
    The Adventures of Nick Carter (1972) 0213
    Cover Girls (1977) 0721

GREER GARSON
    Little Women (1978) 0880

LORRAINE GARY
    The City (1971) 0134
    The Marcus-Nelson Murders (1973) 0305
    Partners in Crime (1973) 0320
    Pray for the Wildcats (1974) 0386
    Man on the Outside (1975) 0572
    Lanigan's Rabbi (1976) 0643
    Crash (1978) 0894

LARRY GATES
    Sarge: The Badge or the Cross (1971) 0116
    Aloha Means Goodbye (1974) 0463
    Kate McShane (1975) 0546
    Backstairs at the White House (1979) MS28

JOHN GAVIN
    Cutter's Trail (1970) 0069
    Doctors' Private Lives (1978) 0831
    The New Adventures of Heidi (1978) 0921

MARVIN GAYE
    The Ballad of Andy Crocker (1969) 0052

BEN GAZZARA
    When Michael Calls (1972) 0205
    Fireball Forward (1972) 0220
    The Family Rico (1972) 0228
    Pursuit (1972) 0263
    Maneater (1973) 0365
    QB VII (1974) 0442
    The Death of Richie (1977) 0686
    The Trial of Lee Harvey Oswald (1977) 0760

MICHAEL GAZZO
    Brink's: The Great Robbery (1976) 0616
    Beach Patrol (1979) 0977

WILL GEER
    The Brotherhood of the Bell (1970) 0083
    Sam Hill: Who Killed the Mysterious Mr.
        Foster? (1971) 0112
    Brock's Last Case (1973) 0301
    Savage (1973) 0322
    Isn't It Shocking? (1973) 0338
    The Hanged Man (1974) 0413
    Honky Tonk (1974) 0425
    Hurricane (1974) 0445
    The Night That Panicked America (1975) 0586
    Law and Order (1976) 0629
    A Woman Called Moses (1978) 0918

CHRISTOPHER GEORGE
    The Immortal (1969) 0041
    The House on Greenapple Road (1970) 0063
    Escape (1971) 0132
    Dead Men Tell No Tales (1971) 0186
    Man on a String (1972) 0212
    The Heist (1972) 0259
    The Last Survivors (1975) 0530
    Mayday at 40,000 Feet (1976) 0668
    Cruise into Terror (1978) 0811

LYNDA DAY GEORGE (Lynda Day)
    The Sound of Anger (1968) 0028
    Fear No Evil (1969) 0035
    The House on Greenapple Road (1970) 0063
    Cannon (1971) 0129
    The Sheriff (1971) 0130
    Set This Town on Fire (The Profane Comedy)
        (1973) (1969) 0271
    She Cried "Murder!" (1973) 0335
    Panic on the 5:22 (1974) 0480
    The Trial of Chaplain Jensen (1975) 0515
    The Barbary Coast (1975) 0558
    Death Among Friends (Mrs. R—Death
        Among Friends) (1975) 0568
    Rich Man, Poor Man (1976) MS03
    Twin Detectives (1976) 0625
    Mayday at 40,000 Feet (1976) 0668
    Once an Eagle (1976) MS05
    Roots (1977) MS07
    Murder at the World Series (1977) 0708
    It Happened at Lake Wood Manor (1977) 0781
    Cruise into Terror (1978) 0811

GIL GERARD
    Ransom for Alice! (1977) 0732
    Killing Stone (1978) 0843

RICHARD GERE
    Strike Force (1975) 0548

LISA GERRITSEN
    A Howling in the Woods (1971) 0163
    Locusts (1974) 0462

ALICE GHOSTLEY
    Two on a Bench (1971) 0162

HENRY GIBSON
    Evil Roy Slade (1972) 0211
    Every Man Needs One (1972) 0264
    The New, Original Wonder Woman (1975)
        0590
    Escape from Brogan County (1977) 0764
    The Night They Took Miss Beautiful (1977)
        0768
    Amateur Night at the Dixie Bar & Grill (1979)
        0935

JOHN GIELGUD
    Probe (Search) (1972) 0209
    Frankenstein: The True Story (1973) 0362
    QB VII (1974) 0442
    Les Miserables (1978) 0931

MELISSA GILBERT
    Little House on the Prairie (1974) 0424
    Christmas Miracle in Caufield U.S.A. (1977)
        0793

JACK GILFORD
    Seventh Avenue (1977) MS08

ANITA GILLETTE
    A Matter of Wife . . . or Death (1976) 0620
    It Happened at Lake Wood Manor (1977) 0781

RICHARD GILLILAND
    Unwed Father (1974) 0406
    The Family Kovack (1974) 0429
    Operation Petticoat (1977) 0747
    Little Women (1978) 0881

VIRGINIA GILMORE
The Brotherhood of the Bell (1970) 0083

HERMIONE GINGOLD
Banyon (1971) 0126
A Death of Innocence (1971) 0174

LILLIAN GISH
Twin Detectives (1976) 0625

PAUL MICHAEL GLASER
Trapped Beneath the Sea (1974) 0466
Starsky and Hutch (1975) 0556
The Great Houdinis (1976) 0658

SHARON GLESS
All My Darling Daughters (1972) 0257
My Darling Daughters' Anniversary (1973) 0352
Switch (1975) 0535
Richie Brockelman: Missing 24 Hours (1976) 0663
The Islander (1978) 0874
Centennial (1978) MS24
Crash (1978) 0894
The Immigrants (1978) MS25

GEORGE GOBEL
Benny and Barney: Las Vegas Undercover (1977) 0684
A Guide for the Married Woman (1978) 0884

PAULETTE GODDARD
The Snoop Sisters (Female Instinct) (1972) 0265

ARTHUR GODFREY
Flatbed Annie & Sweetiepie: Lady Truckers (1979) 0950

THOMAS GOMEZ
Shadow over Elveron (1968) 0018

RUTH GORDON
Isn't It Shocking? (1973) 0338
The Great Houdinis (1976) 0658
Look What's Happened to Rosemary's Baby (1976) 0664
The Prince of Central Park (1977) 0739
Perfect Gentlemen (1978) 0829

MARIUS GORING
Holocaust (1978) MS19

CLIFF GORMAN
Class of '63 (1973) 0308
Strike Force (1975) 0548
The Silence (1975) 0588
Brink's: The Great Robbery (1976) 0616
Having Babies II (1977) 0770

FRANK GORSHIN
Sky Hei$t (1975) 0569

MARJOE GORTNER
The Marcus-Nelson Murders (1973) 0305
Pray for the Wildcats (1974) 0386
The Gun and the Pulpit (1974) 0427
Mayday at 40,000 Feet (1976) 0668

LOUIS GOSSETT, JR. (Lou Gossett)
Companions in Nightmare (1968) 0024
It's Good to Be Alive (1974) 0402
Sidekicks (1974) 0417
Delancey Street: The Crisis Within (1975) 0551
Roots (1977) MS07
Little Ladies of the Night (1977) 0689
To Kill a Cop (1978) 0837
The Critical List (1978) 0872
Backstairs at the White House (1979) MS28
This Man Stands Alone (1979) 0999

HAROLD GOULD
Ransom for a Dead Man (1971) 0120
Medical Story (1975) 0575
How to Break Up a Happy Divorce (1976) 0657
Washington: Behind Closed Doors (1977) MS12

ROBERT GOULET
The Couple Takes a Wife (1972) 0261

GLORIA GRAHAME
Escape (1971) 0132
Black Noon (1971) 0164
The Girl on the Late, Late Show (1974) 0426
Rich Man, Poor Man (1976) MS03
Seventh Avenue (1977) MS08

FARLEY GRANGER
The Challengers (1970) 0072
The Lives of Jenny Dolan (1975) 0585
Widow (1976) 0601
Black Beauty (1978) MS15

STEWART GRANGER
Any Second Now (1969) 0033
The Hound of the Baskervilles (1972) 0208

LEE GRANT
Night Slaves (1970) 0086
The Neon Ceiling (1971) 0113
Ransom for a Dead Man (1971) 0120
Lieutenant Schuster's Wife (1972) 0243
Partners in Crime (1973) 0320
What Are Best Friends For? (1973) 0373
Perilous Voyage (1976) (1968) 0645
The Spell (1977) 0698
Backstairs at the White House (1979) MS28
You Can't Go Home Again (1979) 0975

KAREN GRASSLE
Little House on the Prairie (1974) 0424
The President's Mistress (1978) 0816
Battered (1978) 0877
Crisis in Mid-Air (1979) 0952

PETER GRAVES
Call to Danger (1973) 0297
The President's Plane Is Missing (1973) 0346
Scream of the Wolf (1974) 0382
The Underground Man (1974) 0443
Where Have All the People Gone? (1974) 0460
Dead Man on the Run (1975) 0544
SST—Death Flight (SST: Disaster in the Sky) (1977) 0700
The Rebels (1979) MS34

TERESA GRAVES
Get Christie Love! (1974) 0384

COLEEN GRAY
Ellery Queen: Don't Look Behind You (1971) 0171
The Best Place to Be (1979) 0995

ERIN GRAY
Evening in Byzantium (1978) MS23
The Ultimate Imposter (1979) 0985

LINDA GRAY
Murder in Peyton Place (1977) 0762
The Grass Is Always Greener over the Septic Tank (1978) 0891

LORNE GREENE
Destiny of a Spy (1969) 0046
The Harness (1971) 0167
Nevada Smith (1975) 0557
Man on the Outside (1975) 0572
Arthur Hailey's The Moneychangers (1976) MS06
SST—Death Flight (SST: Disaster in the Sky) (1977) 0700
The Trial of Lee Harvey Oswald (1977) 0760
Roots (1977) MS07
The Bastard (1978) MS22

JULIE GREGG
Mobile Two (1975) 0574

JAMES GREGORY
Hawaii Five-O (1968) 0019
A Very Missing Person (1972) 0219
The Weekend Nun (1972) 0267
Miracle on 34th Street (1973) 0370
The Abduction of Saint Anne (They've Kidnapped Anne Benedict) (1975) 0507
Francis Gary Powers: The True Story of the U-2 Spy Incident (1976) 0655
The Bastard (1978) MS22

JOEL GREY
Man on a String (1972) 0212

VIRGINIA GREY
The Lives of Jenny Dolan (1975) 0585
Arthur Hailey's The Moneychangers (1976) MS06

PAM GRIER
Roots: The Next Generations (1979) MS30

ROOSEVELT GRIER
Carter's Army (1970) 0066
Desperate Mission (1971) 0178
Second Chance (1972) 0206
To Kill a Cop (1978) 0837
Roots: The Next Generations (1979) MS30

ANDY GRIFFITH
The Strangers in 7A (1972) 0255
Go Ask Alice (1973) 0280
Pray for the Wildcats (1974) 0386
Winter Kill (1974) 0434
Savages (1974) 0450
Street Killing (1976) 0649
The Girl in the Empty Grave (1977) 0756
Washington: Behind Closed Doors (1977) MS12
Deadly Game (1977) 0782
Centennial (1978) MS24

Salvage (1979) 0942
From Here to Eternity (1979) MS29
Roots: The Next Generations (1979) MS30

GARY GRIMES
Once an Eagle (1976) MS05

TAMMY GRIMES
The Other Man (1970) 0089
The Horror at 37,000 Feet (1973) 0288
The Borrowers (1973) 0369
You Can't Go Home Again (1979) 0975

GEORGE GRIZZARD
Travis Logan, D.A. (1971) 0124
Indict and Convict (1974) 0376
The Stranger Within (1974) 0457
Attack on Terror: The FBI Versus the Ku
    Klux Klan (1975) 0522
The Lives of Jenny Dolan (1975) 0585
The Night Rider (1979) 0984

CHARLES GRODIN
Just Me and You (1978) 0855
The Grass Is Always Greener over the Septic
    Tank (1978) 0891

DAVID GROH
Smash-Up on Interstate 5 (1976) 0677
Victory at Entebbe (1976) 0679
Murder at the Mardi Gras (1978) 0847
The Child Stealer (1979) 0959

SAM GROOM
Betrayal (1974) 0488
Winner Take All (1975) 0529
Beyond the Bermuda Triangle (1975) 0587
Time Travelers (1976) 0613
Sharon: Portrait of a Mistress (1977) 0771
Institute for Revenge (1979) 0943
Hanging by a Thread (1979) 0981

HARRY GUARDINO
The Lonely Profession (1969) 0044
The Last Child (1971) 0149
The Police Story (1973) 0313
Partners in Crime (1973) 0320
Indict and Convict (1974) 0376
Get Christie Love! (1974) 0384
Street Killing (1976) 0649
Having Babies (1976) 0659
Contract on Cherry Street (1977) 0777
Evening in Byzantium (1978) MS23
Pleasure Cove (1979) 0934

CLU GULAGER
San Francisco International (1970) 0085
Truman Capote's The Glass House (1972) 0203
Footsteps (Footsteps: Nice Guys Finish Last)
    (1972) 0238
Call to Danger (1973) 0297
Smile, Jenny, You're Dead (1973) 0391
Houston, We've Got a Problem (1974) 0407
Hit Lady (1974) 0461
The Killer Who Wouldn't Die (1976) 0619
Once an Eagle (1976) MS05
Charlie Cobb: Nice Night for a Hanging (1977)
    0735
Black Beauty (1978) MS15
King (1978) MS16
Ski Lift to Death (1978) 0825
Sticking Together (1978) 0839

A Question of Love (1978) 0907
Willa (1979) 0962
This Man Stands Alone (1979) 0999

MOSES GUNN
Carter's Army (1970) 0066
The Sheriff (1971) 0130
Haunts of the Very Rich (1972) 0233
Law of the Land (1976) 0624
Roots (1977) MS07

FRED GWYNNE
Captains Courageous (1977) 0783

BUDDY HACKETT
Bud and Lou (1978) 0905

JOAN HACKETT
The Young Country (1970) 0081
How Awful About Allan (1970) 0084
The Other Man (1970) 0089
Five Desperate Women (1971) 0145
Class of '63 (1973) 0308
Reflections of Murder (1974) 0482
Stonestreet: Who Killed the Centerfold Model?
    (1977) 0690
The Possessed (1977) 0714
Pleasure Cove (1979) 0934

GENE HACKMAN
Shadow on the Land (1968) 0026

JEAN HAGEN
Alexander: The Other Side of Dawn (1977)
    0720

MERLE HAGGARD
Huckleberry Finn (1975) 0542
Centennial (1978) MS24

DAN HAGGERTY
Desperate Women (1978) 0890
Terror Out of the Sky (1978) 0930

LARRY HAGMAN
Three's a Crowd (1969) 0054
Vanished (1971) 0122
A Howling in the Woods (1971) 0163
Getting Away From It All (1972) 0196
No Place to Run (1972) 0232
The Alpha Caper (1973) 0340
Blood Sport (1973) 0364
What Are Best Friends For? (1973) 0373
Sidekicks (1974) 0417
Hurricane (1974) 0449
Sarah T.—Portrait of a Teenage Alcoholic
    (1975) 0514
The Big Ripoff (1975) 0536
The Return of the World's Greatest Detective
    (1976) 0642
The Rhinemann Exchange (1977) MS09
Intimate Strangers (1977) 0775
The President's Mistress (1978) 0816
Last of the Good Guys (1978) 0827

GRAYSON HALL
Gargoyles (1972) 0256
The Great Ice Rip-Off (1974) 0473

HUNTZ HALL
Escape (1971) 0132

MONTY HALL
The Courage and the Passion (1978) 0857

BRETT HALSEY
Crash (1978) 0894

MARK HAMILL
Sarah T.—Portrait of a Teenage Alcoholic
    (1975) 0514
Delancey Street: The Crisis Within (1975) 0551
Eric (1975) 0591
Mallory: Circumstantial Evidence (1976) 0603
The City (1977) 0687

BERNIE HAMILTON
Stranger on the Run (1967) 0015
A Clear and Present Danger (1970) 0082

GEORGE HAMILTON
The Dead Don't Die (1975) 0503
Roots (1977) MS07
The Strange Possession of Mrs. Oliver (1977)
    0701
Killer on Board (1977) 0766
The Users (1978) 0880
Institute for Revenge (1979) 0943

MARGARET HAMILTON
The Night Strangler (1973) 0277

MURRAY HAMILTON
Vanished (1971) 0122
Cannon (1971) 0129
A Tattered Web (1971) 0143
The Harness (1971) 0167
The Failing of Raymond (1971) 0175
Deadly Harvest (1972) 0234
Incident on a Dark Street (1973) 0275
Murdock's Gang (1973) 0314
Rich Man, Poor Man (1976) MS03
Murder at the World Series (1977) 0708
Killer on Board (1977) 0766
A Last Cry for Help (1979) 0941

HARRY HAMLIN
Studs Lonigan (1979) MS31

NICHOLAS HAMMOND
Law of the Land (1976) 0624
Spider-Man (1977) 0753

SUSAN HAMPSHIRE
David Copperfield (1970) 0080
Baffled! (1973) 0283

TY HARDIN
Fire! (1977) 0717

JUNE HARDING
Dial Hot Line (1970) 0076

DORIAN HAREWOOD
Foster and Laurie (1975) 0592
Panic in Echo Park (1977) 0743
Siege (1978) 0841
Roots: The Next Generations (1979) MS30

VALERIE HARPER
Thursday's Game (1974) (1971) 0432
Night Terror (1977) 0696

PAT HARRINGTON
Savage (1973) 0322
The Affair (1973) 0356
The Healers (1974) 0447
Let's Switch (1975) 0499
Benny and Barney: Las Vegas Undercover
(1977) 0684
The Critical List (1978) 0872

JONATHAN HARRIS
Once Upon a Dead Man (1971) 0139
Last of the Good Guys (1978) 0827

JULIE HARRIS
The House on Greenapple Road (1970) 0063
How Awful About Allan (1970) 0084
Home for the Holidays (1972) 0258
The Greatest Gift (1974) 0471
Backstairs at the White House (1979) MS28

JULIUS HARRIS
Incident in San Francisco (1971) 0119
A Cry for Help (1975) 0516
Rich Man, Poor Man (1976) MS03
Victory at Entebbe (1976) 0679
Ring of Passion (1978) 0813
To Kill a Cop (1978) 0837
BJ and the Bear (1978) 0882

ROSEMARY HARRIS
Holocaust (1978) MS19
The Chisholms (1979) MS32

GREGORY HARRISON
Trilogy of Terror (1973) 0531
Centennial (1978) MS24
The Best Place to Be (1979) 0995

REX HARRISON
The Adventures of Don Quixote (1973) 0324

MARIETTE HARTLEY
Earth II (1971) 0176
Sandcastles (1972) 0245
Genesis II (1973) 0318
The Killer Who Wouldn't Die (1976) 0619
The Last Hurrah (1977) 0776

DAVID HARTMAN
San Francisco International (1970) 0085
The Feminist and the Fuzz (1971) 0110
I Love a Mystery (1973) (1967) 0296
You'll Never See Me Again (1973) 0299
Miracle on 34th Street (1973) 0370
Lucas Tanner (1974) 0445

PETER HASKELL
Love, Hate, Love (1971) 0114
The Eyes of Charles Sand (1972) 0217
The Phantom of Hollywood (1974) 0397
The Night They Took Miss Beautiful (1977)
0768
Superdome (1978) 0799
The Jordan Chance (1978) 0919
Mandrake (1979) 0944
The Cracker Factory (1979) 0961
Stunt Seven (1979) 0998

MARILYN HASSETT
Quarantined (1970) 0074

SIGNE HASSO
The Magician (1973) 0311
QB VII (1974) 0442
Shell Game (1975) 0563
Sherlock Holmes in New York (1976) 0661

RICHARD HATCH
Crime Club (1973) 0302
F. Scott Fitzgerald and "The Last of the
Belles" (1974) 0377
The Hatfields and the McCoys (1975) 0505
Deadman's Curve (1978) 0812

HURD HATFIELD
Thief (1971) 0132
The Norliss Tapes (1973) 0294
The Word (1978) MS26
You Can't Go Home Again (1979) 0975

JACK HAWKINS
Jane Eyre (1971) 0128
QB VII (1974) 0442

JILL HAWORTH
The Ballad of Andy Crocker (1969) 0052
Home for the Holidays (1972) 0258

HELEN HAYES
Do Not Fold, Spindle or Mutilate (1971) 0166
The Snoop Sisters (Female Instinct) (1972)
0265
Arthur Hailey's The Moneychangers (1976)
MS06
Victory at Entebbe (1976) 0679
A Family Upside Down (1978) 0836

DICK HAYMES
Betrayal (1974) 0488

LLOYD HAYNES
Assault on the Wayne (1971) 0107
Look What's Happened to Rosemary's Baby
(Rosemary's Baby II) (1976) 0664
Harold Robbins' 79 Park Avenue (1977) MS13

KATHRYN HAYS
Breakout (1970) 0102
Yuma (1971) 0121

ROBERT HAYS
Young Pioneers (1976) 0607
Young Pioneers' Christmas (1976) 0680
Delta County, U.S.A. (1977) 0726
The Initiation of Sarah (1978) 0814

SUSAN HAYWARD
Heat of Anger (1972) 0218
Say Goodbye, Maggie Cole (1972) 0236

JOEY HEATHERTON
The Ballad of Andy Crocker (1969) 0052

PAUL HECHT
The Imposter (1975) 0538
Fear on Trial (1975) 0578
Street Killing (1976) 0649
The Savage Bees (1976) 0674

EILEEN HECKART
The Victim (1972) 0254
The FBI Story: The FBI Versus Alvin Karpis
Public Enemy Number One (1974) 0474
Sunshine Christmas (1977) 0787
Suddenly, Love (1978) 0913
Backstairs at the White House (1979) MS28

DAVID HEDISON
Crime Club (1973) 0302
The Cat Creature (1973) 0367
Adventures of the Queen (1975) 0518
The Lives of Jenny Dolan (1975) 0585
The Art of Crime (1975) 0596
Murder in Peyton Place (1977) 0762
The Power Within (1979) 0983

VAN HEFLIN
The Last Child (1971) 0149

ELAYNE HEILWIEL
Birds of Prey (1973) 0281
Winter Kill (1974) 0434
A Cry for Help (1975) 0516
The Secret Life of John Chapman (1976) 0682
Fast Friends (1979) 0964

ANN HELM
A Tattered Web (1971) 0143

KATHERINE HELMOND
Dr. Max (1974) 0428
Larry (1974) 0440
Locusts (1974) 0462
The Legend of Lizzie Borden (1975) 0513
The Family Nobody Wanted (1975) 0521
Cage Without a Key (1975) 0537
The First 36 Hours of Dr. Durant (1975) 0565
James Dean (1976) 0604
Wanted: The Sundance Woman (Mrs.
Sundance Rides Again) (1976) 0656
Little Ladies of the Night (1977) 0689
Getting Married (1978) 0849
Pearl (1978) MS27

MARIEL HEMINGWAY
I Want to Keep My Baby (1976) 0673

FLORENCE HENDERSON
The Love Boat (1976) 0652

PAUL HENREID
The Failing of Raymond (1971) 0175
Death Among Friends (Mrs. R—Death
Among Friends) (1975) 0568

GREGG HENRY
Loose Change (Those Restless Years) (1978)
MS18
Murder at the Mardi Gras (1978) 0847
Pearl (1978) MS27
Hot Rod (1979) 0993
Dummy (1979) 0994

PAMELA HENSLEY
The Law (1974) 0465
Death Among Friends (Mrs. R—Death
Among Friends) (1975) 0568
Kingston: The Power Play (1976) 0651
The Rebels (1979) MS34

KATHARINE HEPBURN
The Glass Menagerie (1973) 0371
Love Among the Ruins (1975) 0533
The Corn Is Green (1979) 0946

ANTHONY HERRERA
Helter Skelter (1976) 0617
Mandrake (1979) 0944
The Night Rider (1979) 0984

EDWARD HERRMANN
Eleanor and Franklin (1976) 0598
Eleanor and Franklin: The White House Years
(1977) 0706
A Love Affair: The Eleanor and Lou Gehrig
Story (1978) 0800

BARBARA HERSHEY
Flood (1976) 0675
In the Glitter Palace (1977) 0702
Just a Little Inconvenience (1977) 0761
Sunshine Christmas (1977) 0787
A Man Called Intrepid (1979) 0S36

DWAYNE HICKMAN
Don't Push, I'll Charge When I'm Ready
(1972) (1969) 0789

ARTHUR HILL
The Other Man (1970) 0089
Vanished (1971) 0122
Owen Marshall, Counselor-at-Law (A Pattern
of Morality) (1971) 0135
Ordeal (1973) 0348
Death Be Not Proud (1975) 0530
Judge Horton and the Scottsboro Boys (1976)
0622
Tell Me My Name (1977) 0792

MARIANNA HILL
Death at Love House (1976) 0647
Relentless (1977) 0752

WENDY HILLER
David Copperfield (1970) 0080

JOHN HILLERMAN
Sweet, Sweet Rachel (1971) 0921
The Great Man's Whiskers (1973) (1969) 0289
The Law (1974) 0465
Ellery Queen (1975) 0539
The Invasion of Johnson County (1976) 0646
Relentless (1977) 0752
Kill Me If You Can (1977) 0758
A Guide for the Married Woman (1978) 0884
Betrayal (1978) 0903
Institute for Revenge (voice) (1979) 0943

ART HINDLE
Law and Order (1976) 0629
The Clone Master (1978) 0873
Some Kind of Miracle (1979) 0933
The Power Within (1979) 0983

PAT HINDLE
The Ballad of Andy Crocker (1969) 0052
A Clear and Present Danger (1970) 0082
The City (1971) 0134
Sweet, Sweet Rachel (1971) 0148
If Tomorrow Comes (1971) 0180
Trouble Comes to Town (1973) 0274
The Last Angry Man (1974) 0435
The Secret Life of John Chapman (1976) 0682
Escape from Brogan County (1977) 0764
Sunshine Christmas (1977) 0787
Tarantulas: The Deadly Cargo (1977) 0794
Elvis (1979) 0951

JUDD HIRSCH
The Law (1974) 0465
Fear on Trial (1975) 0578
The Legend of Valentino (1975) 0595
The Keegans (1976) 0627
Sooner or Later (1979) 0966

HAL HOLBROOK
The Whole World Is Watching (1969) 0036
A Clear and Present Danger (1970) 0082
Travis Logan, D.A. (1971) 0124
Suddenly Single (1971) 0156
Goodbye Raggedy Ann (1971) 0157
That Certain Summer (1972) 0251
The Awakening Land (1978) MS17
Murder by Natural Causes (1979) 0953
The Legend of the Golden Gun (1979) 0969

WILLIAM HOLDEN
The Blue Knight (1973) MS01
21 Hours in Munich (1976) 0667

GEOFFREY HOLDER
The Man Without a Country (1973) 0325

KENE HOLLIDAY
Roots: The Next Generations (1979) MS30

EARL HOLLIMAN
Tribes (1970) 0094
Alias Smith and Jones (1971) 0105
Cannon (1971) 0129
Desperate Mission (1971) 0178
Trapped (1973) 0355
Cry Panic (1974) 0394
I Love You, Goodbye (1974) 0398
Alexander: The Other Side of Dawn (1977)
0720

STANLEY HOLLOWAY
Run a Crooked Mile (1969) 0051

CELESTE HOLM
The Delphi Bureau (1972) 0221
The Underground Man (1974) 0443
Death Cruise (1974) 0470
Captains and the Kings (1976) MS04
The Love Boat II (1977) 0692
Backstairs at the White House (1979) MS28

SKIP HOMEIER
The Challenge (1970) 0070
Two for the Money (1972) 0216
The Voyage of the Yes (1973) 0278
Helter Skelter (1976) 0617
Washington: Behind Closed Doors (1977)
MS12
Overboard (1978) 0876
The Wild Wild West Revisited (1979) 0982

OSCAR HOMOLKA
One of Our Own (1975) 0559

ROBERT HOOKS
Carter's Army (1970) 0066
Vanished (1971) 0122
The Cable Car Murder (Cross Current) (1971)
0172
Two for the Money (1972) 0216
Trapped (1973) 0355
The Killer Who Wouldn't Die (1976) 0619
Just an Old Sweet Song (1976) 0650
To Kill a Cop (1978) 0837
The Courage and the Passion (1978) 0857
A Woman Called Moses (1978) 0918
Backstairs at the White House (1979) MS28
Hollow Image (1979) 1001

PETER HOOTEN
Night of Terror (1972) 0241
One of Our Own (1975) 0559
Dr. Strange (1978) 0871

ANTHONY HOPKINS
QB VII (1974) 0442
All Creatures Great and Small (1975) 0511
Dark Victory (1976) 0602
The Lindbergh Kidnapping Case (1976) 0605
Victory at Entebbe (1976) 0679

BO HOPKINS
The Runaway Barge (1975) 0541
The Kansas City Massacre (1975) 0576
Charlie's Angels (1976) 0614
The Invasion of Johnson County (1976) 0646
Dawn: Portrait of a Teenage Runaway (1976)
0654
Aspen (The Innocent and the Damned) (1977)
MS14
Thaddeus Rose and Eddie (1978) 0823
Crisis in Sun Valley (1978) 0834

ROBERT HORTON
The Dangerous Days of Kiowa Jones (1966)
0006
The Spy Killer (1969) 0050
Foreign Exchange (1970) 0064

JOHN HOUSEMAN
Fear on Trial (1975) 0578
Captains and the Kings (1976) MS04
Washington: Behind Closed Doors (1977)
MS12
Aspen (The Innocent and the Damned) (1977)
MS14

CLINT HOWARD
The Red Pony (1973) 0312
Huckleberry Finn (1975) 0542
The Death of Richie (1977) 0686
Cotton Candy (1978) 0892

KEN HOWARD
Manhunter (1974) 0404
Superdome (1978) 0799
The Critical List (1978) 0872
A Real American Hero (1978) 0917

RON HOWARD
The Migrants (1974) 0392
Locusts (1974) 0462
Huckleberry Finn (1975) 0542

SUSAN HOWARD
The Silent Gun (1969) 0058
Quarantined (1970) 0074
Savage (1973) 0322
Indict and Convict (1974) 0376
Night Games (1974) 0414
Killer on Board (1977) 0766
Superdome (1978) 0799
The Power Within (1979) 0983

TREVOR HOWARD
Catholics (1973) 0361
The Count of Monte Cristo (1975) 0501

SALLY ANN HOWES
The Hound of the Baskervilles (1972) 0208
Female Artillery (1973) 0279

SEASON HUBLEY
She Lives (1973) 0331
The Healers (1974) 0447
SST—Death Flight (SST: Disaster in the Sky) (1977) 0700
Loose Change (Those Restless Years) (1978) MS18
Elvis (1979) 0951

DAVID HUDDLESTON
Sarge: The Badge or the Cross (1971) 0116
The Priest Killer (1971) 0136
Suddenly Single (1971) 0156
The Homecoming (1971) 0188
Tenafly (1973) 0286
Brock's Last Case (1973) 0286
Hawkins on Murder (Death and the Maiden) (1973) 0306
Heatwave! (1974) 0387
The Gun and the Pulpit (1974) 0427
The Oregon Trail (1976) 0597
Shark Kill (1976) 0638
Sherlock Holmes in New York (1976) 0661
Once an Eagle (1976) MS05
Kate Bliss and the Ticker Tape Kid (1978) 0856

ROCK HUDSON
Once Upon a Dead Man (1971) 0139
Arthur Hailey's Wheels (1978) MS20

DAVID HUFFMAN
F. Scott Fitzgerald and "The Last of the Belles" (1974) 0377
The Gun (1974) 0477
Eleanor and Franklin (1975) 0598
Amelia Earhart (1976) 0662
Captains and the Kings (1976) MS04
Look What's Happened to Rosemary's Baby (Rosemary's Baby II) (1976) 0664
Testimony of Two Men (1977) MS11
In the Matter of Karen Ann Quinlan (1977) 0759
The Winds of Kitty Hawk (1978) 0924

BARNARD HUGHES
The Borgia Stick (1967) 0012
Dr. Cook's Garden (1971) 0109
The Borrowers (1973) 0369
The UFO Incident (1975) 0583
Guilty or Innocent: The Sam Sheppard Murder Case (1975) 0593
Ransom for Alice! (1977) 0732
Kill Me If You Can (1977) 0758
Tell Me My Name (1977) 0791
See How She Runs (1978) 0809
Sanctuary of Fear (1979) 0974

ARTHUR HUNNICUTT
The Trackers (1971) 0184
The Bounty Man (1972) 0250
Climb an Angry Mountain (1972) 0268
Mrs. Sundance (1974) 0381
The Daughters of Joshua Cabe Return (1975) 0509

GAYLE HUNNICUTT
The Smugglers (1968) 0030
A Man Called Intrepid (1979) MS36

MARSHA HUNT
Fear No Evil (1969) 0035
Jigsaw (1972) 0224

KIM HUNTER
Dial Hot Line (1970) 0076
In Search of America (1971) 0127
The Magician (1973) 0311
Unwed Father (1974) 0406
Born Innocent (1974) 0448
Bad Ronald (1974) 0467
Ellery Queen (1975) 0539
The Dark Side of Innocence (1976) 0639
Once an Eagle (1976) MS05
Backstairs at the White House (1979) MS28

TAB HUNTER
San Francisco International (1971) 0085
Katie: Portrait of a Centerfold (1978) 0888

CHET HUNTLEY
Vanished (1971) 0122

JOHN HURT
Spectre (1977) 0727

OLIVIA HUSSEY
Jesus of Nazareth (1977) MS10
The Bastard (1978) MS22
Harold Robbins' The Pirate (1978) 0906

RUTH HUSSEY
My Darling Daughters' Anniversary (1973) 0352

JOHN HUSTON
Sherlock Holmes in New York (1976) 0661
The Rhinemann Exchange (1977) MS09
The Word (1978) MS26

WILL HUTCHINS
The Horror at 37,000 Feet (1973) 0288
The Quest (1976) 0633

JIM HUTTON
The Deadly Hunt (1971) 0147
The Reluctant Heroes (1971) 0173
They Call It Murder (1971) 0185
Call Her Mom (1972) 0210
Don't Be Afraid of the Dark (1973) 0342
The Underground Man (1974) 0443
Ellery Queen (1975) 0539
Flying High (1978) 0867

LAUREN HUTTON
The Rhinemann Exchange (1977) MS09
Someone Is Watching Me! (1978) 0911
Institute for Revenge (1979) 0943

WILFRID HYDE-WHITE
The Sunshine Patriot (1968) 0029
Fear No Evil (1969) 0035
Run a Crooked Mile (1969) 0051
Ritual of Evil (1970) 0073
A Brand New Life (1973) 0292
The Great Houdinis (1976) 0658
The Rebels (1979) MS34

DIANA HYLAND
Scalplock (1966) 0003
Ritual of Evil (1970) 0073
The Boy in the Plastic Bubble (1976) 0669

SCOTT HYLANDS
Earth II (1971) 0176
Truman Capote's The Glass House (1972) 0203
Terror on the Beach (1973) 0332
The First 36 Hours of Dr. Durant (1975) 0565
With This Ring (1978) 0846
Centennial (1978) MS24
The Winds of Kitty Hawk (1978) 0925
Jennifer: A Woman's Story (1979) 0957

STEVE IHNAT
The Whole World Is Watching (1969) 0036
The D.A.: Conspiracy to Kill (1971) 0106
Sweet, Sweet Rachel (1971) 0148
Hunter (1973) 0273

JOHN IRELAND
The Phantom of Hollywood (1974) 0397
The Girl on the Late, Late Show (1974) 0426
The Millionaire (1978) 0927

AMY IRVING
James Dean (1976) 0604
James A. Michener's Dynasty (1976) 0612
Panache (1976) 0636
Once an Eagle (1976) MS05

BURL IVES
The Sound of Anger (1968) 0028
The Whole World Is Watching (1969) 0036
The Man Who Wanted to Live Forever (1970) 0104
Captains and the Kings (1976) MS04
Roots (1977) MS07
The Bermuda Depths (1978) 0807
The New Adventures of Heidi (1978) 0921

GORDON JACKSON
Spectre (1977) 0727
The Last Giraffe (1979) 1000

KATE JACKSON
Satan's School for Girls (1973) 0334
Killer Bees (1974) 0405
Death Cruise (1974) 0470
Death Scream (The Woman Who Cried Murder) (1975) 0577
Charlie's Angels (1976) 0614
Death at Love House (1976) 0647
James at 15 (1977) 0748

SHERRY JACKSON
Wild Women (1970) 0090
Hitchhike! (1974) 0403
The Girl on the Late, Late Show (1974) 0426
Returning Home (1975) 0555

LOU JACOBI
The Judge and Jake Wyler (1972) 0260
Coffee, Tea or Me? (1973) 0329

SCOTT JACOBY
No Place to Run (1972) 0232
That Certain Summer (1972) 0251
The Man Who Could Talk to Kids (1973) 0345
Bad Ronald (1974) 0467
Smash-Up on Interstate 5 (1976) 0677
Harold Robbins' 79 Park Avenue (1977) MS13
No Other Love (1979) 0965

LAWRENCE HILTON-JACOBS
Roots (1977) MS07
The Comedy Company (1978) 0864

RICHARD JAECKEL
The Deadly Dream (1971) 0144
Firehouse (1973) 0269
The Red Pony (1973) 0312
Partners in Crime (1973) 0320
Born Innocent (1974) 0448
The Last Day (1975) 0519
Go West, Young Girl (1978) 0842
Champions: A Love Story (1979) 0936
Salvage (1979) 0942

SAM JAFFE
Night Gallery (1969) 0049
Quarantined (1970) 0074
The Old Man Who Cried Wolf (1979) 0088
Sam Hill: Who Killed the Mysterious Mr. Foster? (1971) 0112
QB VII (1974) 0442

DEAN JAGGER
The Lonely Profession (1969) 0044
Brotherhood of the Bell (1970) 0083
Incident in San Francisco (1971) 0119
Truman Capote's The Glass House (1972) 0203
The Delphi Bureau (1972) 0221
The Stranger (1973) 0295
I Heard the Owl Call My Name (1973) 0372
The Hanged Man (1974) 0413
The Lindbergh Kidnapping Case (1976) 0605

DAVID JANSSEN
Night Chase (1970) 0097
O'Hara, U.S. Treasury: Operation Cobra (1971) 0131
The Longest Night (1972) 0227
Moon of the Wolf (1972) 0235
Birds of Prey (1973) 0281
Hijack! (1973) 0336
Pioneer Woman (1973) 0374
Smile, Jenny, You're Dead (1974) 0391
Fer-De-Lance (1974) 0464
Stalk the Wild Child (1976) 0665
Mayday at 40,000 Feet (1976) 0668
A Sensitive, Passionate Man (1977) 0734
Superdome (1978) 0799
Nowhere to Run (1978) 0801
Centennial (1978) MS24
The Word (1978) MS26

CLAUDE JARMAN
Centennial (1978) MS24

HARVEY JASON
Rich Man, Poor Man (1976) MS03
Captains and the Kings (1976) MS04

RICK JASON
The Monk (1969) 0045
Who Is the Black Dahlia? (1975) 0528
The Best Place to Be (1979) 0995

HERB JEFFERSON, JR.
The Law (1974) 0465
Rich Man, Poor Man (1976) MS03
The Bastard (1978) MS22

SALOME JENS
In the Glitter Palace (1977) 0702
Sharon: Portrait of a Mistress (1977) 0771
From Here to Eternity (1979) MS29

KAREN JENSEN
Congratulations, It's a Boy! (1971) 0141
I Love a Mystery (1973) (1967) 0296
Louis Armstrong—Chicago Style (1976) 0600

ARTE JOHNSON
Twice in a Lifetime (1974) 0415
Bud and Lou (1978) 0905

BEN JOHNSON
The Red Pony (1973) 0312
Runaway! (1973) 0337
Blood Sport (1973) 0364
Locusts (1974) 0462
The Savage Bees (1976) 0674
The Sacketts (1979) 0988

CELIA JOHNSON
Les Miserables (1978) 0931

DON JOHNSON
The City (1977) 0687
Cover Girls (1977) 0721
Ski Lift to Death (1978) 0825
The Two-Five (1978) 0838
Katie: Portrait of a Centerfold (1978) 0888
First You Cry (1978) 0902
Amateur Night at the Dixie Bar & Grill (1979) 0935
The Rebels (1979) MS34

MELODIE JOHNSON (Melody Johnson)
Fame Is the Name of the Game (1966) 0004
Powderkeg (1971) 0133
I Love a Mystery (1973) (1967) 0296

RAFER JOHNSON
The Loneliest Runner (1976) 0681
Roots: The Next Generations (1979) MS30

RUSSELL JOHNSON
The Movie Murderer (1970) 0067
Vanished (1971) 0122
The Horror at 37,000 Feet (1973) 0288
Beg, Borrow . . . or Steal (1973) 0315
Aloha Means Goodbye (1974) 0463
Adventures of the Queen (1975) 0518
You Lie So Deep, My Love (1975) 0525
Nowhere To Hide (1977) 0733
The Ghost of Flight 401 (1978) 0818
The Bastard (1978) MS22

VAN JOHNSON
The Doomsday Flight (1966) 0005
San Francisco International (1970) 0085
Call Her Mom (1972) 0210

The Girl on the Late, Late Show (1974) 0426
Rich Man, Poor Man (1976) MS03
Black Beauty (1978) MS15
Superdome (1978) 0799
Getting Married (1978) 0849

CAROLYN JONES
Roots (1977) MS07
Little Ladies of the Night (1977) 0689

DEAN JONES
The Great Man's Whiskers (1973) (1969) 0289
Guess Who's Sleeping in My Bed? (1973) 0349
When Every Day Was the Fourth of July (1978) 0828

HENRY JONES
Something for a Lonely Man (1968) 0025
The Movie Murderer (1970) 0067
Love, Hate, Love (1971) 0114
The Daughters of Joshua Cabe (1972) 0229
The Letters (1973) 0303
Letters from Three Lovers (1973) 0339
Roll, Freddy, Roll (1974) 0490
Who Is the Black Dahlia? (1975) 0528
Tail Gunner Joe (1977) 0695

JAMES EARL JONES
The UFO Incident (1975) 0583
Jesus of Nazareth (1977) MS10
The Greatest Thing That Almost Happened (1977) 0769
Roots: The Next Generations (1979) MS30

L. Q. JONES
Fireball Forward (1972) 0220
Mrs. Sundance (1974) 0381
Manhunter (1974) 0404
Attack on Terror: The FBI Versus the Ku Klux Klan (1975) 0522
Banjo Hackett: Roamin' Free (1976) 0628
Standing Tall (1978) 0804
The Sacketts (1979) 0988

SHIRLEY JONES
Silent Night, Lonely Night (1969) 0057
But I Don't Want to Get Married! (1970) 0087
The Girls of Huntington House (1973) 0291
The Family Nobody Wanted (1975) 0521
Winner Take All (1975) 0529
The Lives of Jenny Dolan (1975) 0585
Yesterday's Child (1977) 0694
Evening in Byzantium (1978) MS23
Who'll Save Our Children? (1978) 0923
A Last Cry for Help (1979) 0941

TOM JONES
Pleasure Cove (1979) 0933

TOMMY LEE JONES
Charlie's Angels (1976) 0614
Smash-Up on Interstate 5 (1976) 0677
The Amazing Howard Hughes (1977) 0712

RICHARD JORDAN
Captains and the Kings (1976) MS04
The Defection of Simas Kudirka (1978) 0806
Les Miserables (1978) 0931

VICTOR JORY
Perilous Voyage (1976) (1968) 0645
Devil Dog: The Hound of Hell (1978) 0896

LOUIS JOURDAN
Fear No Evil (1969) 0035
Run a Crooked Mile (1969) 0051
Ritual of Evil (1970) 0073
The Great American Beauty Contest (1973) 0287
The Count of Monte Cristo (1975) 0501
The Man in the Iron Mask (1977) 0691

RAUL JULIA
McCloud: Who Killed Miss U.S.A.? (Portrait of a Dead Girl) (1970) 0071
Death Scream (The Woman Who Cried Murder) (1975) 0577

KATY JURADO
Any Second Now (1969) 0033
A Little Game (1971) 0161

KATHERINE JUSTICE
Prescription: Murder (1968) 0017
The Psychiatrist: God Bless the Children (Children of the Lotus Eater) (1970) 0103
Dead Man on the Run (1975) 0544

GABE KAPLAN
The Love Boat (1976) 0652

JOE KAPP
Climb an Angry Mountain (1972) 0268
Captains and the Kings (1976) MS04
Nakia (1974) 0436
Smash-Up on Interstate 5 (1976) 0677

ALEX KARRAS
Hardcase (1972) 0204
The 500-Pound Jerk (1973) 0270
Babe (1975) 0584
Mulligan's Stew (1977) 0742
Mad Bull (1977) 0792
Centennial (1978) MS24

KURT KASZNAR
The Smugglers (1968) 0030
Once Upon a Dead Man (1971) 0139
The Snoop Sisters (Female Instinct) (1972) 0265
Suddenly, Love (1978) 0913

BILL KATT
Night Chase (1970) 0097
The Daughters of Joshua Cabe (1972) 0229
Can Ellen Be Saved? (1974) 0393

JULIE KAVNER
Katherine (1975) 0579
No Other Love (1979) 0965

LAINIE KAZAN
A Love Affair: The Eleanor and Lou Gehrig Story (1978) 0800

STACY KEACH
All the Kind Strangers (1974) 0476
James A. Michener's Dynasty (1976) 0612
Jesus of Nazareth (1977) MS10

STEVEN KEATS
The Story of Pretty Boy Floyd (1974) 0444
The Dream Makers (1975) 0497

Promise Him Anything . . . (1975) 0566
Seventh Avenue (1977) MS08
The Last Dinosaur (1977) 0697
The Awakening Land (1978) MS17
Zuma Beach (1978) 0879

LILA KEDROVA
Cool Million (Mask of Marcella) (1972) 0244

HARVEY KEITEL
The Virginia Hill Story (1974) 0479

BRIAN KEITH
Second Chance (1972) 0206
The Quest (1976) 0633
The Loneliest Runner (1976) 0681
In the Matter of Karen Ann Quinlan (1977) 0759
Centennial (1978) MS24
The Chisholms (1979) MS32

SALLY KELLERMAN
Centennial (1978) MS24

MIKE KELLIN
A Clear and Present Danger (1970) 0082
Assignment: Munich (1972) 0225
The Catcher (1972) 0226
Connection (1973) 0298
The Art of Crime (1975) 0596
Seventh Avenue (1977) MS08

BRIAN KELLY
Berlin Affair (1970) 0093
Drive Hard, Drive Fast (1973) (1969) 0328

JACK KELLY
Vega$ (1978) 0840
The New Maverick (1978) 0868

NANCY KELLY
The Imposter (1975) 0538
Murder at the World Series (1977) 0708

PATSY KELLY
The Pigeon (1969) 0048

LINDA KELSEY
The Picture of Dorian Gray (1973) 0326
Eleanor and Franklin (1976) 0598
Captains and the Kings (1976) MS04
Eleanor and Franklin: The White House Years (1977) 0706
Something for Joey (1977) 0711

JEREMY KEMP
The Rhinemann Exchange (1977) MS09

ARTHUR KENNEDY
The Movie Murderer (1970) 0067
A Death of Innocence (1971) 0174
Crawlspace (1972) 0207
The President's Plane Is Missing (1973) 0346
Nakia (1974) 0436

GEORGE KENNEDY
See How They Run (1964) 0001
Sarge: The Badge or the Cross (1971) 0116
The Priest Killer (1971) 0136

A Great American Tragedy (1972) 0247
Deliver Us from Evil (1973) 0330
A Cry in the Wilderness (1974) 0420
The Blue Knight (1975) 0564
Backstairs at the White House (1979) MS28

ROGER KERN
Trapped Beneath the Sea (1974) 0466
Young Pioneers (1976) 0607
Young Pioneers' Christmas (1976) 0680

JOHN KERR
Yuma (1971) 0121
The Longest Night (1972) 0227
Incident on a Dark Street (1973) 0275
Washington: Behind Closed Doors (1977) MS12

LANCE KERWIN
The Healers (1974) 0447
The Greatest Gift (1974) 0471
Reflections of Murder (1974) 0482
Amelia Earhart (1976) 0662
The Loneliest Runner (1976) 0681
The Death of Richie (1977) 0686
James at 15 (1977) 0748
Young Joe, the Forgotten Kennedy (1977) 0755

MARGOT KIDDER
Suddenly Single (1971) 0156
The Bounty Man (1972) 0250
Honky Tonk (1974) 0425

RICHARD KIEL
The Barbary Coast (1975) 0558

RICHARD KILEY
Night Gallery (1969) 0049
Incident in San Francisco (1971) 0119
Murder Once Removed (1971) 0160
Jigsaw (1972) 0224
Friendly Persuasion (1975) 0567
The Macahans (1976) 0599

ARON KINCAID
Black Water Gold (1970) 0061
Planet Earth (1974) 0441

ANDREA KING
Prescription: Murder (1968) 0017

ALAN KING
Seventh Avenue (1977) MS08
How to Pick Up Girls! (1978) 0899

PERRY KING
Foster and Laurie (1975) 0592
Rich Man, Poor Man (1976) MS04
Aspen (The Innocent and the Damned) (1977) MS14
The Cracker Factory (1979) 0961
Love's Savage Fury (1979) 0991

ZALMAN KING
The Dangerous Days of Kiowa Jones (1966) 0006
Stranger on the Run (1967) 0015
The Young Lawyers (1969) 0047
The Intruders (1970) 0095
Smile, Jenny, You're Dead (1974) 0391
Like Normal People (1979) 0969

EARTHA KITT
Lieutenant Schuster's Wife (1972) 0243
To Kill a Cop (1978) 0837

ALF KJELLIN
Francis Gary Powers: The True Story of the
U-2 Spy Incident (1976) 0655

WERNER KLEMPERER
Wake Me When the War Is Over (1969) 0043
Assignment: Munich (1972) 0225
The Rhinemann Exchange (1977) MS09

JACK KLUGMAN
Fame Is the Name of the Game (1966) 0004
Poor Devil (1973) 0290
The Underground Man (1974) 0443
One of My Wives Is Missing (1976) 0609

SHIRLEY KNIGHT
The Outsider (1967) 0016
Shadow Over Elveron (1968) 0018
Friendly Persuasion (1975) 0567
Medical Story (1975) 0575
Return to Earth (1976) 0634
21 Hours in Munich (1976) 0667
The Defection of Simas Kudirka (1978) 0806
Champions: A Love Story (1979) 0936

DON KNOTTS
I Love a Mystery (1973) (1967) 0296

PATRIC KNOWLES
The D.A.: Murder One (1969) 0055

ALEXANDER KNOX
Run a Crooked Mile (1969) 0051

HARVEY KORMAN
Three's a Crowd (1969) 0054
Suddenly Single (1971) 0156
The Love Boat (1976) 0652
Bud and Lou (1978) 0905

YAPHET KOTTO
Night Chase (1970) 0097
Raid on Entebbe (1977) 0685

JACK KRUSCHEN
Istanbul Express (1968) 0021
Emergency (1972) 0194
Deadly Harvest (1972) 0234
The Log of the Black Pearl (1975) 0494
The Incredible Rocky Mountain Race (1977)
0788
The Time Machine (1978) 0899

KATY KURTZMAN
Mulligan's Stew (1977) 0742
When Every Day Was the Fourth of July
(1978) 0828
Hunters of the Reef (1978) 0853
The New Adventures of Heidi (1978) 0921
Long Journey Back (1978) 0922

NANCY KWAN
Hawaii Five-O (1968) 0019

CHERYL LADD (Cheryl Jean Stopplemoor)
Satan's School for Girls (1973) 0334

DIANE LADD
The Devil's Daughter (1973) 0272
Black Beauty (1978) MS15
Thaddeus Rose and Eddie (1978) 0822
Willa (1979) 0962

FERNANDO LAMAS
The Lonely Profession (1969) 0044
Powderkeg (1971) 0133
Murder on Flight 502 (1975) 0594

KAREN LAMM
The Hatfields and the McCoys (1975) 0505
The Night They Took Miss Beautiful (1977)
0768
It Happened at Lake Wood Manor (1977) 0781
Christmas Miracle in Caufield, U.S.A. (1977)
0793
A Last Cry for Help (1979) 0941
The Power Within (1979) 0983

DOROTHY LAMOUR
Death at Love House (1976) 0647

ZOHRA LAMPERT
Connection (1973) 0298
One of Our Own (1975) 0559
Black Beauty (1978) MS15
Lady of the House (1978) 0904

BURT LANCASTER
Moses—The Lawgiver (1975) MS02
Victory at Entebbe (1976) 0679

ELSA LANCHESTER
In Name Only (1969) 0053

MARTIN LANDAU
Welcome Home, Johnny Bristol (1972) 0202
Savage (1973) 0322

JESSIE ROYCE LANDIS
Mr. and Mrs. Bo Jo Jones (1971) 0170

MICHAEL LANDON
Little House on the Prairie (1974) 0424
The Loneliest Runner (1976) 0681

SUE ANE LANGDON
The Victim (1972) 0254

HOPE LANGE
Crowhaven Farm (1970) 0099
That Certain Summer (1972) 0251
The 500-Pound Jerk (1973) 0270
I Love You, Goodbye (1974) 0398
Fer-De-Lance (1974) 0464
The Secret Night Caller (1975) 0520
The Love Boat II (1977) 0692
Like Normal People (1979) 0970

FRANK LANGELLA
The Mark of Zorro (1974) 0469

ROBERT LANSING
Killer by Night (1972) 0190
The Astronaut (1972) 0191
Crime Club (1975) 0545
Widow (1976) 0601
The Deadly Triangle (1977) 0724

JOHN LARCH
The City (1971) 0134
Winter Kill (1974) 0434
The Chadwick Family (1974) 0437
Bad Ronald (1974) 0467
The Desperate Miles (1975) 0532
Ellery Queen (1975) 0539
Future Cop (1976) 0626
The Critical List (1978) 0872

MICHAEL LARRAIN
Dial Hot Line (1970) 0076
The Last Child (1971) 0149

LOUISE LASSER
Coffee, Tea or Me? (1973) 0329
Isn't It Shocking? (1973) 0338
Just Me and You (1978) 0855

PIPER LAURIE
In the Matter of Karen Ann Quinlan (1977)
0759
Rainbow (1978) 0901

ED LAUTER
Class of '63 (1973) 0308
The Migrants (1974) 0392
The Godchild (1974) 0483
Satan's Triangle (1975) 0504
A Shadow in the Streets (1975) 0508
Last Hours Before Morning (1975) 0552
The Clone Master (1978) 0873
The Jericho Mile (1979) 0963

LINDA LAVIN
The Morning After (1974) 0399
Like Mom, Like Me (1978) 0887

JOHN PHILLIP LAW
The Best Place to Be (1979) 0995

PETER LAWFORD
How I Spent My Summer Vacation (1967)
0007
A Step Out of Line (1971) 0118
The Deadly Hunt (1971) 0147
Ellery Queen: Don't Look Behind You (1971)
0171
The Phantom of Hollywood (1974) 0397
Fantasy Island (1977) 0688

CAROL LAWRENCE
Three on a Date (1978) 0817
Stranger in Our House (1978) 0897

VICKI LAWRENCE
Having Babies (1976) 0659

GEORGE LAZENBY
Cover Girls (1977) 0721
Evening in Byzantium (1978) MS23

CLORIS LEACHMAN

Silent Night, Lonely Night (1969) 0057
Suddenly Single (1971) 0156
Haunts of the Very Rich (1972) 0233
A Brand New Life (1973) 0292
Crime Club (1973) 0302
Dying Room Only (1973) 0333
The Migrants (1974) 0392
Hitchhike! (1974) 0403
Thursday's Game (1974) (1971) 0432
Death Sentence (1974) 0459
Someone I Touched (1975) 0526
A Girl Named Sooner (1975) 0571
Death Scream (The Woman Who Cried
Murder) (1975) 0577
The New, Original Wonder Woman (1975)
0590
The Love Boat (1976) 0652
It Happened One Christmas (1977) 0786
Long Journey Back (1978) 0922
Backstairs at the White House (1979) MS28
Willa (1979) 0962

MICHAEL LEARNED

Hurricane (1974) 0449
It Couldn't Happen to a Nicer Guy (1974)
0478
Widow (1976) 0601
Little Mo (1978) 0869

ANNA LEE

Eleanor and Franklin (1976) 0598
The Night Rider (1979) 0984

CHRISTOPHER LEE

Poor Devil (1973) 0290
Harold Robbins' The Pirate (1978) 0906

GYPSY ROSE LEE

The Over-the-Hill Gang (1969) 0042

MICHELE LEE

Only with Married Men (1974) 0472
Dark Victory (1976) 0602
Bud and Lou (1978) 0905

RON LEIBMAN

The Art of Crime (1975) 0596
A Question of Guilt (1978) 0820

JANET LEIGH

The Monk (1969) 0045
Honeymoon with a Stranger (1969) 0059
The House on Greenapple Road (1970) 0063
The Deadly Dream (1971) 0144
Murdock's Gang (1973) 0314
Murder at the World Series (1977) 0708
Telethon (1977) 0774

MARGARET LEIGHTON

Frankenstein: The True Story (1973) 0362
Great Expectations (1974) 0481

PAUL LeMAT

Firehouse (1973) 0269

HARVEY LEMBECK

Raid on Entebbe (1977) 0685

JACK LEMMON

The Entertainer (1976) 0610

KAY LENZ

The Weekend Nun (1972) 0267
Lisa, Bright and Dark (1973) 0360
A Summer Without Boys (1973) 0363
Unwed Father (1974) 0406
The Underground Man (1974) 0443
The FBI Story: The FBI Versus Alvin Karpis,
Public Enemy Number One (1974) 0474
Journey from Darkness (1975) 0524
Rich Man, Poor Man (1976) MS03
The Initiation of Sarah (1978) 0814
The Seeding of Sarah Burns (1979) 0968
Sanctuary of Fear (1979) 0974

RICK LENZ

Owen Marshall, Counselor-at-Law (A Pattern
of Morality) (1971) 0135
Hec Ramsey (The Century Turns) (1972) 0240

SHELDON LEONARD

Top Secret (1978) 0850
The Islander (1978) 0874

MICHAEL LERNER

Magic Carpet (1972) 0252
Firehouse (1973) 0269
Reflections of Murder (1974) 0482
The Dream Makers (1975) 0497
Sarah T.—Portrait of a Teenage Alcoholic
(1975) 0514
A Cry for Help (1975) 0516
Starsky and Hutch (1975) 0556
Dark Victory (1976) 0602
F. Scott Fitzgerald in Hollywood (1976) 0637
Scott Free (1976) 0660
Killer on Board (1977) 0766
A Love Affair: The Eleanor and Lou Gehrig
Story (1978) 0800
Ruby and Oswald (1978) 0815
Vega$ (1978) 0840

BETHEL LESLIE

Dr. Cook's Garden (1971) 0109
The Last Survivors (1975) 0530
The Gift of Love (1978) 0916

JOAN LESLIE

The Keegans (1976) 0627

AL LETTIERI

The Hanged Man (1964) 0002
Footsteps (Footsteps: Nice Guys Finish Last)
(1972) 0238

GEOFFREY LEWIS

Moon of the Wolf (1972) 0235
Honky Tonk (1974) 0425
The Gun and the Pulpit (1974) 0427
The Great Ice Rip-Off (1974) 0473
Attack on Terror: The FBI Versus the Ku
Klux Klan (1975) 0522
The New Daughters of Joshua Cabe (1976)
0641
The Great Houdinis (1976) 0658
The Deadly Triangle (1977) 0724
The Hunted Lady (1977) 0780
When Every Day Was the Fourth of July
(1978) 0828
Centennial (1978) MS24
The Jericho Mile (1979) 0962
Samurai (1979) 0977

ABBEY LINCOLN

Short Walk to Daylight (1972) 0248

HAL LINDEN

Mr. Inside/Mr. Outside (1973) 0309
The Love Boat (1976) 0652
How to Break Up a Happy Divorce (1976)
0657

VIVECA LINDFORS

A Question of Guilt (1978) 0820

JOANNE LINVILLE

The House on Greenapple Road (1970) 0063
Secrets (1977) 0699
The Critical List (1978) 0872
The Users (1978) 0877

PEGGY LIPTON

The Return of Mod Squad (1979) 0990

CLEAVON LITTLE

The Homecoming (1971) 0188
Money to Burn (1973) 0347
The Day the Earth Moved (1974) 0453

FRANK MICHAEL LIU

If Tomorrow Comes (1971) 0180
All My Darling Daughters (1972) 0257
Once an Eagle (1976) MS05
Code Name: Diamond Head (1977) 0716

KATHY LLOYD

Owen Marshall, Counselor-at-Law (A Pattern
of Morality) (1971) 0135
Incident on a Dark Street (1973) 0275
Lacy and the Mississippi Queen (1978) 0850

NORMAN LLOYD

The Dark Secret of Harvest Home (1978) 0805

TONY LoBIANCO

Mr. Inside/Mr. Outside (1973) 0309
The Story of Jacob and Joseph (1974) 0430
A Shadow in the Streets (1975) 0508
Jesus of Nazareth (1977) MS10
Goldenrod (1977) 0731
The Last Tenant (1978) 0865
A Last Cry for Help (1979) 0941

JUNE LOCKHART

But I Don't Want to Get Married! (1970) 0087
The Bait (1973) 0307
Who Is the Black Dahlia? (1975) 0528
Curse of the Black Widow (Love Trap) (1977)
0754
Loose Change (Those Restless Years) (1978)
MS18
The Gift of Love (1978) 0916
Walking Through the Fire (1979) 0989

GARY LOCKWOOD

Earth II (1971) 0176
Manhunter (1974) 0404
The FBI Story: The FBI Versus Alvin Karpis,
Public Enemy Number One (1974) 0474
The Ghost of Flight 401 (1978) 0818
The Incredible Journey of Dr. Meg Laurel
(1979) 0932

ROBERT LOGGIA

Mallory: Circumstantial Evidence (1976) 0603
Street Killing (1976) 0649
Scott Free (1976) 0660

Arthur Hailey's The Moneychangers (1976)
MS06
Raid on Entebbe (1977) 0685
No Other Love (1979) 0965

ERBERT LOM
Mister Jerico (1970) 0075

JLIE LONDON
Emergency (1972) 0194

VON LONG
Roots: The Next Generations (1979) MS30

ICHARD LONG
The Girl Who Came Gift-Wrapped (1974)
0388
Death Cruise (1974) 0470

LAUDINE LONGET
How to Steal an Airplane (Only One Day Left
Before Tomorrow) (1971) (1968) 0181

ICHARD LOO
Marcus Welby, M.D. (A Matter of
Humanities) (1969) 0038
Kung Fu (1972) 0214

RINI LOPEZ
The Reluctant Heroes (1971) 0173

ACK LORD
The Doomsday Flight (1966) 0005
Hawaii Five-O (1968) 0019

ARJORIE LORD
The Missing Are Deadly (1975) 0500
Harold Robbins' The Pirate (1978) 0906

OPHIA LOREN
Brief Encounter (1974) 0475

YN LORING
Black Noon (1971) 0164
The Horror at 37,000 Feet (1973) 0288
The Desperate Miles (1975) 0532
The Kansas City Massacre (1975) 0576

INA LOUISE
But I Don't Want to Get Married! (1970) 0087
Call to Danger (1973) 0297
Death Scream (The Woman Who Cried
Murder) (1975) 0577
Look What's Happened to Rosemary's Baby
(Rosemary's Baby II) (1976) 0664
Nightmare in Badham County (1976) 0666
SST—Death Flight (SST: Disaster in the Sky)
(1977) 0700

YRNA LOY
Death Takes a Holiday (1971) 0158
Do Not Fold, Spindle or Mutilate (1971) 0166
The Couple Takes a Wife (1972) 0261
Indict and Convict (1974) 0376
The Elevator (1974) 0396

LAURENCE LUCKINBILL
The Delphi Bureau (1972) 0221
Death Sentence (1974) 0459
Panic on the 5:22 (1974) 0480
Winner Take All (1975) 0529
The Lindbergh Kidnapping Case (1976) 0605
Ike (1979) MS33

PAUL LUKAS
The Challenge (1970) 0070

KEYE LUKE
Kung Fu (1972) 0214
The Cat Creature (1973) 0367
Judge Dee and the Monastery Murders (1974)
0493

BARBARA LUNA
Winchester '73 (1967) 0013
Women in Chains (1972) 0199
The Hanged Man (1974) 0413 ·
They Only Come Out at Night (1975) 0554
Brenda Starr (1976) 0630
Pleasure Cove (1979) 0934

IDA LUPINO
Women in Chains (1972) 0199
The Strangers in 7A (1972) 0255
Female Artillery (1973) 0279
I Love a Mystery (1973) (1967) 0296
The Letters (1973) 0304

PAUL LYNDE
Gidget Grows Up (1969) 0060
Gidget Gets Married (1972) 0189

CAROL LYNLEY
Shadow on the Land (1968) 0026
The Smugglers (1968) 0030
The Immortal (1969) 0041
Weekend of Terror (1970) 0101
The Cable Car Murder (Cross Current) (1971)
0172
The Night Stalker (1972) 0193
The Elevator (1974) 0396
Death Stalk (1975) 0506
Flood (1976) 0675
Fantasy Island (1977) 0688
Having Babies II (1977) 0770
Cops and Robin (1978) 0833
The Beasts Are on the Streets (1978) 0851

SUE LYON
But I Don't Want to Get Married! (1970) 0087
Smash-Up on Interstate 5 (1976) 0677
Don't Push, I'll Charge When I'm Ready
(1977) (1969) 0789

JANET MacLACHLEN
Trouble Comes to Town (1973) 0274
Louis Armstrong—Chicago Style (1976) 0600
Dark Victory (1976) 0602

GAVIN MacLEOD
The Intruders (1970) 0095
Only with Married Men (1974) 0472
Ransom for Alice! (1977) 0732

FRED MacMURRAY
The Chadwick Family (1974) 0437
Beyond the Bermuda Triangle (1975) 0587

HEATHER MacRAE
Connection (1973) 0298
Secrets of Three Hungry Wives (1978) 0883

MEREDITH MacRAE
Three on a Date (1978) 0817

ANDREA McARDLE
Rainbow (1978) 0900

DIANE McBAIN
Donner Pass: The Road to Survival (1978)
0889

FRANCES LEE McCAIN
Secrets (1977) 0699
Washington: Behind Closed Doors (1977)
MS12
The Trial of Lee Harvey Oswald (1977) 0760
Ziegfeld: The Man and His Women (1978)
0854
No Other Love (1979) 0965

DAVID McCALLUM
Hauser's Memory (1970) 0098
She Waits (1972) 0200
Frankenstein: The True Story (1973) 0362
The Invisible Man (1975) 0560

MERCEDES McCAMBRIDGE
Killer By Night (1972) 0190
Two for the Money (1972) 0216
The Girls of Huntington House (1973) 0291
The President's Plane Is Missing (1973) 0346
Who Is the Black Dahlia? (1975) 0528
The Sacketts (1979) 0988

CHUCK McCANN
The Girl Most Likely To . . . (1973) 0351
A Cry for Help (1975) 0516
How to Break Up a Happy Divorce (1976)
0657
Sex and the Married Woman (1977) 0751

KEVIN McCARTHY
U.M.C. (Operation Heartbeat) (1969) 0039
A Great American Tragedy (1972) 0247
Exo-Man (1977) 0740
Mary Jane Harper Cried Last Night (1977)
0763

LEIGH J. McCLOSKEY
Rich Man, Poor Man (1976) MS03
Dawn: Portrait of a Teenage Runaway (1976)
0654
Alexander: The Other Side of Dawn (1977)
0720
The Bermuda Depths (1978) 0807
Doctors' Private Lives (1978) 0831

DOUG McCLURE
The Longest Hundred Miles (1967) 0008
Terror in the Sky (1971) 0138
The Birdmen (Escape of the Birdmen) (1971)
0140
The Death of Me Yet (1971) 0159
Playmates (1972) 0237
The Judge and Jake Wyler (1972) 0260
Shirts/Skins (1973) 0341
Death Race (1973) 0354
Satan's Triangle (1975) 0504
Roots (1977) MS07

SST—Death Flight (SST: Disaster in the Sky)
(1977) 0700
Wild and Wooly (1978) 0819
The Rebels (1979) MS34

KENT McCORD
The Outsider (1967) 0016
Shadow Over Elveron (1968) 0018
Dragnet (1969) (1966) 0031
Emergency (1972) 0194
Beg, Borrow . . . or Steal (1973) 0315
Pine Canyon Is Burning (1977) 0722
Telethon (1977) 0774

RUTH McDEVITT
In Search of America (1971) 0127
The Girl Most Likely To . . . (1973) 0351
Skyway to Death (1974) 0383
Winter Kill (1974) 0434
The Abduction of Saint Anne (They've
Kidnapped Anne Benedict) (1975) 0507
My Father's House (1975) 0570
Man on the Outside (1975) 0572

RODDY McDOWALL
Night Gallery (1969) 0049
Terror in the Sky (1971) 0138
A Taste of Evil (1971) 0153
What's a Nice Girl Like You . . . ? (1971)
0187
The Elevator (1974) 0396
Flood (1976) 0675
The Rhinemann Exchange (1977) MS09
The Immigrants (1978) MS25
The Thief of Baghdad (1978) 0907

JAMES McEACHIN
Deadlock (1969) 0034
The D.A.: Conspiracy to Kill (1971) 0106
The Neon Ceiling (1971) 0113
Welcome Home, Johnny Bristol (1972) 0202
Short Walk to Daylight (1972) 0248
That Certain Summer (1972) 0251
The Judge and Jake Wyler (1972) 0260
Tenafly (1973) 0286
The Alpha Caper (1973) 0340
The Dead Don't Die (1975) 0503
Samurai (1979) 0978
This Man Stands Alone (1979) 0999

DARREN McGAVIN
The Outsider (1967) 0016
The Challenge (1970) 0070
The Challengers (1970) 0072
Berlin Affair (1970) 0093
Tribes (1970) 0094
Banyon (1971) 0126
The Death of Me Yet (1971) 0159
The Night Stalker (1972) 0193
Something Evil (1972) 0197
The Rookies (1972) 0222
Say Goodbye, Maggie Cole (1972) 0236
The Night Strangler (1973) 0277
The Six-Million Dollar Man (1973) 0304
Brink's: The Great Robbery (1976) 0616
Law and Order (1976) 0629
The Users (1978) 0880
Ike (1979) MS33

JOHN McGIVER
The Feminist and the Fuzz (1971) 0110
Sam Hill: Who Killed the Mysterious Mr.
Foster? (1971) 0112
The Great Man's Whiskers (1973) (1969) 0289
Tom Sawyer (1973) 0317

PATRICK McGOOHAN
The Man in the Iron Mask (1977) 0691

CHARLES McGRAW
O'Hara, U.S. Treasury: Operation Cobra
(1971) 0131
The Devil and Miss Sarah (1971) 0179
The Night Stalker (1972) 0193
The Longest Night (1972) 0224
Hawkins on Murder (Death and the Maiden)
(1973) 0306
Money to Burn (1973) 0347
Perilous Voyage (1976) (1968) 0645

VONETTA McGEE
The Norliss Tapes (1973) 0294
Superdome (1978) 0799

WALTER McGINN
Delancey Street: The Crisis Within (1975) 0551
The Night That Panicked America (1975) 0586
Guilty or Innocent: The Sam Sheppard Murder
Case (1975) 0593
Serpico: The Deadly Game (1976) 0623
Eleanor and Franklin: The White House Years
(1977) 0706
The Deadliest Season (1977) 0707
Kill Me If You Can (1977) 0758

BIFF McGUIRE
The Underground Man (1974) 0443
The Turning Point of Jim Malloy (1975) 0547
Law and Order (1976) 0629
Kingston: The Power Play (1976) 0651
Francis Gary Powers: The True Story of the
U-2 Spy Incident (1976) 0655
Roger & Harry: The Mitera Target (Love for
Ransom) (1977) 0715
In the Matter of Karen Ann Quinlan (1977)
0759

DOROTHY McGUIRE
She Waits (1972) 0200
The Runaways (1975) 0543
Rich Man, Poor Man (1976) MS03
Little Women (1978) 0881
The Incredible Journey of Dr. Meg Laurel
(1979) 0932

STEPHEN McHATTIE
Search for the Gods (1975) 0534
James Dean (1976) 0604
Look What's Happened to Rosemary's Baby
(Rosemary's Baby II) (1976) 0664
Centennial (1978) MS24

JOHN McINTIRE
Longstreet (1971) 0117
Powderkeg (1971) 0133
Linda (1973) 0350
The Healers (1974) 0447
The New Daughters of Joshua Cabe (1976)
0641
Aspen (The Innocent and the Damned) (1977)
MS14
Crisis in Sun Valley (1978) 0834
The Jordan Chance (1978) 0919

VIRGINIA McKENNA
Beauty and the Beast (1976) 0676

CATHERINE McLEOD
Vanished (1971) 0122

ALLYN ANN McLERIE
A Tree Grows in Brooklyn (1974) 0423
Born Innocent (1974) 0448
Someone I Touched (1975) 0526
Death Scream (The Woman Who Cried
Murder) (1975) 0577
The Entertainer (1976) 0610

JOHN McMARTIN
Ritual of Evil (1970) 0073
Fear on Trial (1975) 0578
The Defection of Simas Kudirka (1978) 0806

BARBARA McNAIR
The Lonely Profession (1969) 0044

STEPHEN McNALLY
The Whole World Is Watching (1969) 0036
The Lonely Profession (1969) 0044
Vanished (1971) 0122
Call to Danger (1973) 0297
Nakia (1974) 0436
Most Wanted (1976) 0615

CLAUDIA McNEIL
Incident in San Francisco (1971) 0119
Moon of the Wolf (1972) 0235
The Migrants (1974) 0392
Cry Panic (1974) 0394
Roots: The Next Generations (1979) MS30

JAMES VINCENT McNICHOL
Champions: A Love Story (1979) 0936

KRISTY McNICHOL
The Love Boat II (1977) 0692
Like Mom, Like Me (1978) 0887
Summer of My German Soldier (1978) 0895

CARMEN McRAE
Roots: The Next Generations (1979) MS30

IAN McSHANE
The Lives of Jenny Dolan (1975) 0585
Roots (1977) MS07
Jesus of Nazareth (1977) MS10
Code Name: Diamond Head (1977) 0716
Harold Robbins' The Pirate (1978) 0906

STEPHEN MACHT
Amelia Earhart (1976) 0662
Raid on Entebbe (1977) 0685
Loose Change (Those Restless Years) (1978)
MS18
Ring of Passion (1978) 0813
Hunters of the Deep (1978) 0853
The Immigrants (1978) MS25

PATRICK MACNEE
Mister Jerico (1970) 0075
Matt Helm (1975) 0562
Sherlock Holmes in New York (1976) 0661
Evening in Byzantium (1978) MS23
The Billion Dollar Threat (1979) 0971
Stunt Seven (1979) 0998

GEORGE MACREADY
Fame Is the Name of the Game (1966) 0004
The Young Lawyers (1969) 0047
Night Gallery (1969) 0049
Daughter of the Mind (1969) 0056

BILL MACY
All Together Now (1975) 0512
Death at Love House (1976) 0647
Stunt Seven (1979) 0998

KATHLEEN MAGUIRE
The Borgia Stick (1967) 0012
The Chadwick Family (1974) 0437

GEORGE MAHARIS
Escape to Mindanao (1968) 0027
The Monk (1969) 0045
The Victim (1972) 0254
Murder on Flight 502 (1975) 0594
Rich Man, Poor Man (1976) MS03
Look What's Happened to Rosemary's Baby
(Rosemary's Baby II) (1976) 0664
SST—Death Flight (SST: Disaster in the Sky)
(1977) 0700
Return to Fantasy Island (1978) 0803
Crash (1978) 0894

LEE MAJORS
The Ballad of Andy Crocker (1969) 0052
Weekend of Terror (1970) 0101
The Six-Million Dollar Man (1973) 0304
Francis Gary Powers: The True Story of the
U-2 Spy Incident (1976) 0655
Just a Little Inconvenience (1977) 0761

MAKO
The Challenge (1970) 0070
If Tomorrow Comes (1971) 0180
The Streets of San Francisco (1972) 0230
Judge Dee and the Monastery Murders (1974)
0493
Farewell to Manzanar (1976) 0611

KARL MALDEN
The Streets of San Francisco (1972) 0230
Captains Courageous (1977) 0783

DOROTHY MALONE
The Pigeon (1969) 0048
Rich Man, Poor Man (1976) MS03
Little Ladies of the Night (1977) 0689
Murder in Peyton Place (1977) 0762
Katie: Portrait of a Centerfold (1978) 0888

MO MALONE
The Trial of Lee Harvey Oswald (1977) 0760
The Winds of Kitty Hawk (1978) 0925

NANCY MALONE
The Outsider (1967) 0016
San Francisco International (1970) 0085
Set This Town on Fire (The Profane Comedy)
(1973) (1969) 0291
The Girls of Huntington House (1973) 0291
Skyway to Death (1974) 0383
A Tree Grows in Brooklyn (1974) 0423
Lucas Tanner (1974) 0445
Like Mom, Like Me (1978) 0887

NICK MANCUSO
Dr. Scorpion (1978) 0822
The House on Garibaldi Street (1979) 0996

RANDOLPH MANTOOTH
Vanished (1971) 0012
Marriage: Year One (1971) 0154

The Bravos (1972) 0192
Emergency (1972) 0194
Testimony of Two Men (1977) MS11

ADELE MARA
Arthur Hailey's Wheels (1978) MS20

NANCY MARCHAND
Some Kind of Miracle (1979) 0933
Willa (1979) 0962

ANDREA MARCOVICCI
Cry Rape! (1973) 0358
Smile, Jenny, You're Dead (1974) 0391
Some Kind of Miracle (1979) 0933
A Vacation in Hell (1979) 0992

JANET MARGOLIN
The Last Child (1971) 0149
Family Flight (1972) 0249
Pray for the Wildcats (1974) 0386
Planet Earth (1974) 0441
Lanigan's Rabbi (1976) 0643
Murder in Peyton Place (1977) 0762
Sharon: Portrait of a Mistress (1977) 0771
The Triangle Factory Fire Scandal (1979) 0947

STUART MARGOLIN
The Intruders (1970) 0095
The Rockford Files (1974) 0422
The California Kid (1974) 0456
This Was the West That Was (1974) 0491
Lanigan's Rabbi (1976) 0643
Perilous Voyage (1976) (1968) 0645

MONTE MARKHAM
Death Takes a Holiday (1971) 0158
The Astronaut (1972) 0191
Visions (Visions of Death) (1972) 0242
Hustling (1975) 0523
Ellery Queen (1975) 0539
Relentless (1977) 0752

JOHN MARLEY
Istanbul Express (1968) 0021
Incident in San Francisco (1971) 0119
The Sheriff (1971) 0130
In Broad Daylight (1971) 0155
The Family Rico (1972) 0228
The Alpha Caper (1973) 0340
Telethon (1977) 0774

SCOTT MARLOWE
Night Slaves (1970) 0086
Travis Logan, D.A. (1971) 0124
The Critical List (1978) 0872

CHRISTIAN MARQUAND
Victory at Entebbe (1976) 0679
Evening in Byzantium (1978) MS23

KENNETH MARS
Second Chance (1972) 0206
Guess Who's Sleeping in My Bed (1973) 0349
Someone I Touched (1975) 0526
The New, Original Wonder Woman (1975)
0590

JEAN MARSH
Jane Eyre (1971) 0128

E. G. MARSHALL
A Clear and Present Danger (1970) 0082
Vanished (1971) 0122
The City (1971) 0134
Ellery Queen: Don't Look Behind You (1971)
0171
Pursuit (1972) 0263
Money to Burn (1973) 0347
The Abduction of Saint Anne (They've
Kidnapped Anne Benedict) (1975) 0507

PENNY MARSHALL
The Feminist and the Fuzz (1971) 0110
The Crooked Hearts (1972) 0253
The Couple Takes a Wife (1972) 0261
Let's Switch (1975) 0499
More Than Friends (1978) 0886

PETER MARSHALL
Harold Robbins' 79 Park Avenue (1977) MS13
A Guide for the Married Woman (1978) 0884

WILLIAM MARSHALL
U.M.C. (Operation Heartbeat) (1969) 0039
The Mask of Sheba (1970) 0077
Rosetti and Ryan: Men Who Love Women
(1977) 0725

ANA MARTIN
Return of the Gunfighter (1967) 0009

DEWEY MARTIN
Assault on the Wayne (1971) 0107

PAMELA SUE MARTIN
The Girls of Huntington House (1973) 0291
The Gun and the Pulpit (1974) 0427
Human Feelings (1978) 0885

ROSS MARTIN
The Sheriff (1971) 0130
The Crooked Hearts (1972) 0253
Happiness Is a Warm Clue (The Return of
Charlie Chan) (1973) (1970) 0327
Dying Room Only (1973) 0333
Skyway to Death (1974) 0383
Yesterday's Child (1977) 0694
Wild and Wooly (1978) 0819
The Wild Wild West Revisited (1979) 0982
The Return of Mod Squad (1979) 0988

STROTHER MARTIN
Hawkins on Murder (Death and the Maiden)
(1973) 0306
Steel Cowboy (1978) 0915

A MARTINEZ
Hunters Are for Killing (1970) 0079
Probe (Search) (1972) 0209
The Abduction of Saint Anne (They've
Kidnapped Anne Benedict) (1975) 0507
Death Among Friends (Mrs. R—Death
Among Friends) (1975) 0568
Mallory: Circumstantial Evidence (1976) 0603
Exo-Man (1977) 0740
Centennial (1978) MS24

JAMES MASON
Frankenstein: The True Story (1973) 0362
Great Expectations (1974) 0481
Jesus of Nazareth (1977) MS10

MARTIN MILNER
Emergency (1972) 0194
Runaway! (1973) 0337
Hurricane (1974) 0449
The Swiss Family Robinson (1975) 0550
Flood (1976) 0675
SST—Death Flight (SST: Disaster in the Sky)
(1977) 0700
Black Beauty (1978) MS15
Little Mo (1978) 0869
Crisis in Mid-Air (1979) 0962

YVETTE MIMIEUX
Death Takes a Holiday (1971) 0158
Black Noon (1971) 0164
Hit Lady (1974) 0461
The Legend of Valentino (1975) 0595
Snowbeast (1977) 0713
Ransom for Alice! (1977) 0732
Devil Dog: The Hound of Hell (1978) 0896
Outside Chance (1978) 0912

NICO MINARDOS
The Challengers (1970) 0072
Sarge: The Badge or the Cross (1971) 0116
River of Mystery (1971) 0146

SAL MINEO
The Dangerous Days of Kiowa Jones (1966)
0006
Stranger on the Run (1967) 0015
The Challengers (1970) 0072
In Search of America (1971) 0127
How to Steal an Airplane (Only One Day Left
Before Tomorrow) (1971) (1968) 0181
The Family Rico (1972) 0228

CAMERON MITCHELL
Thief (1971) 0152
The Delphi Bureau (1972) 0221
The Rookies (1972) 0222
Hitchhike (1974) 0403
The Hanged Man (1974) 0413
The Girl on the Late, Late Show (1974) 0426
The Swiss Family Robinson (1975) 0550
The Quest (1976) 0633
Flood (1976) 0675
Testimony of Two Men (1977) MS11
The Hostage Heart (1977) 0749
Black Beauty (1978) MS15
The Bastard (1978) MS22
Return to Fantasy Island (1978) 0803
Hanging By a Thread (1979) 0981

DONALD MITCHELL
Ironside (1967) 0014
Split Second to an Epitaph (1968) 0020
The Priest Killer (1971) 0136
Short Walk to Daylight (1972) 0248

SCOEY MITCHLLL
The Voyage of the Yes (1973) 0278
Cindy (1978) 0832

CHRISTOPHER MITCHUM
Flight to Holocaust (1977) 0710

MARY ANN MOBLEY
Istanbul Express (1968) 0021
The Girl on the Late, Late Show (1974) 0426

RICARDO MONTALBAN
The Longest Hundred Miles (1967) 0008
The Pigeon (1969) 0048
Black Water Gold (1970) 0061
The Aquarians (1970) 0091
Sarge: The Badge or the Cross (1971) 0116
The Face of Fear (1971) 0151
Desperate Mission (1971) 0178
Fireball Forward (1972) 0220
Wonder Woman (1974) 0410
The Mark of Zorro (1974) 0469
McNaughton's Daughter (1976) 0608
Fantasy Island (1977) 0688
Captains Courageous (1977) 0783
Return to Fantasy Island (1978) 0803

BELINDA MONTGOMERY
Ritual of Evil (1970) 0073
The D.A.: Conspiracy to Kill (1971) 0106
Lock, Stock and Barrel (1971) 0142
The Bravos (1972) 0192
Women in Chains (1972) 0199
The Devil's Daughter (1973) 0272
Crime Club (1973) 0302
Letters from Three Lovers (1973) 0339
Man from Atlantis (1977) 0704
The Hostage Heart (1977) 0749
Murder in Music City (1979) 0939

ELIZABETH MONTGOMERY
The Victim (1972) 0254
Mrs. Sundance (1974) 0381
A Case of Rape (1974) 0401
The Legend of Lizzie Borden (1975) 0513
Dark Victory (1976) 0602
A Killing Affair (Behind the Badge) (1977)
0757
The Awakening Land (1978) MS17
Jennifer: A Woman's Story (1979) 0957

LEE H. MONTGOMERY
The Harness (1971) 0167
Female Artillery (1973) 0279
Runaway! (1973) 0337
A Cry in the Wilderness (1974) 0420
Man on the Outside (1975) 0572
True Grit (1978) 0852

LYNNE MOODY
Nightmare in Badham County (1976) 0666
Roots (1977) MS07
Charleston (1979) 0938
Roots: The Next Generations (1979) MS30

RON MOODY
David Copperfield (1970) 0080
The Word (1978) MS26

ARCHIE MOORE
The Hanged Man (1964) 0002
My Sweet Charlie (1970) 0065

MARY TYLER MOORE
Run a Crooked Mile (1969) 0051
First You Cry (1978) 0902

ROGER MOORE
Sherlock Holmes in New York (1976) 0661

TERRY MOORE
Quarantined (1970) 0074
Smash-Up on Interstate 5 (1976) 0677

AGNES MOOREHEAD
The Ballad of Andy Crocker (1969) 0052
Marriage: Year One (1971) 0154
Suddenly Single (1971) 0156
Rolling Man (1972) 0239
Night of Terror (1972) 0241
Frankenstein: The True Story (1973) 0362

RITA MORENO
Anatomy of a Seduction (1979) 0978

HARRY MORGAN
Dragnet (1969) (1966) 0031
But I Don't Want to Get Married! (1970) 0087
The Feminist and the Fuzz (1971) 0110
Ellery Queen: Don't Look Behind You (1971)
0171
Hec Ramsey (The Century Turns) (1972) 0240
Sidekicks (1974) 0417
The Last Day (narrator) (1975) 0519
Exo-Man (1977) 0740
The Magnificent Magnet of Santa Mesa (1977)
0741
Maneaters Are Loose! (1978) 0845
The Bastard (1978) MS22
Murder at the Mardi Gras (1978) 0847
Kate Bliss and the Ticker Tape Kid (1978)
0856
Backstairs at the White House (1978) MS28
Roots: The Next Generations (1979) MS30
The Wild Wild West Revisited (1979) 0982

JAYE P. MORGAN
The Adventures of Nick Carter (1972) 0213

MICHAEL MORIARTY
A Summer Without Boys (1973) 0363
The Glass Menagerie (1973) 0371
The Deadliest Season (1977) 0707
Holocaust (1978) MS19
The Winds of Kitty Hawk (1978) 0925
Too Far to Go (1979) 0960

ROBERT MORLEY
Great Expectations (1974) 0481

GREG MORRIS
Doomsday Flight (1966) 0005
Killer By Night (1972) 0190
Flight to Holocaust (1977) 0710
Vega$ (1978) 0840
Crisis in Mid-Air (1979) 0952
Roots: The Next Generations (1979) MS30

KAREN MORROW
The Boy in the Plastic Bubble (1976) 0669

VIC MORROW
A Step Out of Line (1971) 0118
Travis Logan, D.A. (1971) 0124
River of Mystery (1971) 0146
Truman Capote's The Glass House (1972) 0203
The Weekend Nun (1972) 0267
The Police Story (1973) 0313
Tom Sawyer (1973) 0317
Nightmare (1974) 0378
The California Kid (1974) 0456
Death Stalk (1975) 0506
The Night That Panicked America (1975) 0586
Captains and the Kings (1976) MS04
Roots (1977) MS07
The Man with the Power (1977) 0730
The Hostage Heart (1977) 0749

Curse of the Black Widow (Love Trap) (1977)
0754
Wild and Wooly (1978) 0880

ROGER E. MOSLEY
The Other Side of Hell (1978) 0802
Cruise into Terror (1978) 0811
The Jericho Mile (1979) 0963
Roots: The Next Generations (1979) MS30
I Know Why the Caged Bird Sings (1978)
0976

DONNY MOST
Huckleberry Finn (1975) 0542
With This Ring (1978) 0846

DIANA MULDAUR
McCloud: Who Killed Miss U.S.A.? (Portrait
of a Dead Girl) (1970) 0071
Call to Danger (1973) 0297
Ordeal (1973) 0348
Planet Earth (1974) 0441
Charlie's Angels (1976) 0614
Pine Canyon Is Burning (1977) 0722
The Deadly Triangle (1977) 0724
Black Beauty (1978) MS15
To Kill a Cop (1978) 0837
Maneaters Are Loose! (1978) 0845
The Word (1978) MS26

EDWARD MULHARE
Gidget Grows Up (1969) 0060

BEN MURPHY
Alias Smith and Jones (1971) 0105
The Letters (1973) 0303
Runaway! (1973) 0337
Heatwave! (1974) 0387
This Was the West That Was (1974) 0491
Gemini Man (Code Name: Minus One) (1976)
0632
Bridger (1976) 0648
The Chisholms (1979) MS32

MARY MURPHY
Footsteps (Footsteps: Nice Guys Finish Last)
(1972) 0238
I Love You, Goodbye (1974) 0398
The Stranger Who Looks Like Me (1974) 0408
Born Innocent (1974) 0448
Katherine (1975) 0579

MICHAEL MURPHY
The Crooked Hearts (1972) 0253
The Autobiography of Miss Jane Pittman
(1974) 0389
I Love You, Goodbye (1974) 0398

ROSEMARY MURPHY
A Case of Rape (1974) 0401
Lucas Tanner (1974) 0445
Eleanor and Franklin (1976) 0598
Eleanor and Franklin: The White House Years
(1977) 0706

DON MURRAY
The Borgia Stick (1967) 0012
Daughter of the Mind (1969) 0056
The Intruders (1970) 0095
The Girl on the Late, Late Show (1974) 0426

The Sex Symbol (1974) 0451
A Girl Named Sooner (1975) 0571
Rainbow (1978) 0901
Crisis in Mid-Air (1979) 0952

JAN MURRAY
Roll, Freddy, Roll! (1974) 0490
Banjo Hackett: Roamin' Free (1976) 0628

TONY MUSANTE
Toma (1973) 0316
The Desperate Miles (1975) 0532
Nowhere To Hide (1977) 0733
My Husband Is Missing (1978) 0915

GEORGE NADER
Nakia (1974) 0436

J. CARROLL NAISH
The Hanged Man (1964) 0002
Cutter's Trail (1970) 0069

LAURENCE NAISMITH
The Scorpio Letters (1967) 0011
Run a Crooked Mile (1969) 0051

TOM NARDINI
Incident in San Francisco (1971) 0119
Harpy (1971) 0125

MILDRED NATWICK
Do Not Fold, Spindle or Mutilate (1971) 0166
The Snoop Sisters (Female Instinct) (1972)
0265
Money to Burn (1973) 0347

PATRICIA NEAL
The Homecoming (1971) 0188
Things in Their Season (1974) 0486
Eric (1975) 0591
Tail Gunner Joe (1977) 0695
A Love Affair: The Eleanor and Lou Gehrig
Story (1978) 0800
The Bastard (1978) MS22

BARRY NELSON
The Borgia Stick (1967) 0012
Seven in Darkness (1969) 0040
Climb an Angry Mountain (1972) 0268
Washington: Behind Closed Doors (1977)
MS12

DAVID NELSON
Smash-Up on Interstate 5 (1976) 0677

ED NELSON
A Little Game (1971) 0161
The Screaming Woman (1972) 0201
Banacek: Detour to Nowhere (1972) 0223
Tenafly (1973) 0286
Runaway! (1973) 0337
Linda (1973) 0350
Houston, We've Got a Problem (1974) 0407
The Deadly Are Missing (1975) 0500
Murder in Peyton Place (1977) 0762
Superdome (1978) 0799
Doctors' Private Lives (1978) 0831
Leave Yesterday Behind (1978) 0848
Crash (1978) 0894
Anatomy of a Seduction (1979) 0980

GENE NELSON
Family Flight (1972) 0249
A Brand New Life (1973) 0292

HARRIET NELSON
Smash-Up on Interstate 5 (1976) 0677
Once an Eagle (1976) MS05

RICK NELSON
The Over-the-Hill Gang (1969) 0042
Three on a Date (1978) 0817

FRANCO NERO
The Legend of Valentino (1975) 0595
21 Hours in Munich (1976) 0667
Harold Robbins' The Pirate (1978) 0906

LOIS NETTLETON
Any Second Now (1969) 0033
Weekend of Terror (1970) 0101
The Forgotten Man (1971) 0137
Terror in the Sky (1971) 0138
Women in Chains (1972) 0199
Fear on Trial (1975) 0578
Washington: Behind Closed Doors (1977)
MS12
Centennial (1978) MS24

BOB NEWHART
Thursday's Game (1974) (1971) 0432

BARRY NEWMAN
Night Games (1974) 0414
Sex and the Married Woman (1977) 0751

JULIE NEWMAR
McCloud: Who Killed Miss U.S.A.? (Portrait
of a Dead Girl) (1970) 0071
The Feminist and the Fuzz (1971) 0110
A Very Missing Person (1972) 0219
Terraces (1977) 0744

DENISE NICHOLAS
Five Desperate Women (1971) 0145
Ring of Passion (1978) 0813

LESLIE NIELSEN
See How They Run (1964) 0001
Shadow Over Elveron (1968) 0018
Hawaii Five-O (1968) 0019
Companions in Nightmare (1968) 0024
Trial Run (1969) 0032
Deadlock (1969) 0034
Night Slaves (1970) 0086
The Aquarians (1970) 0091
Hauser's Memory (1970) 0098
Incident in San Francisco (1971) 0119
They Call It Murder (1971) 0185
Snatched (1973) 0284
The Letters (1973) 0303
Happiness Is a Warm Clue (The Return of
Charlie Chan) (1973) (1970) 0327
Can Ellen Be Saved? (1974) 0393
Brink's: The Great Robbery (1976) 0616
Little Mo (1978) 0869
Backstairs at the White House (1979) MS28
Institute for Revenge (1979) 0943

LEONARD NIMOY
Assault on the Wayne (1971) 0107
Baffled! (1973) 0283
The Alpha Caper (1973) 0340
The Missing Are Deadly (1975) 0500

DAVID NIVEN
A Man Called Intrepid (1979) MS36

JEANETTE NOLAN
Alias Smith and Jones (1971) 0105
Longstreet (1971) 0117
Say Goodbye, Maggie Cole (1972) 0236
Hijack! (1973) 0336
The Desperate Miles (1975) 0532
Babe (1975) 0584
Law and Order (1976) 0629
The New Daughters of Joshua Cabe (1976) 0641
The Awakening Land (1978) MS17

LLOYD NOLAN
Wings of Fire (1967) 0010
Isn't It Shocking? (1973) 0338
The Abduction of Saint Anne (They've Kidnapped Anne Benedict) (1975) 0507
Flight to Holocaust (1977) 0710
Fire! (1977) 0717

NICK NOLTE
Winter Kill (1974) 0434
The California Kid (1974) 0456
Death Sentence (1974) 0459
The Runaway Barge (1975) 0541
Rich Man, Poor Man (1976) MS03

CHRISTOPHER NORRIS
Mr. and Mrs. Bo Jo Jones (1971) 0170
The Great American Beauty Contest (1973) 0287
Senior Year (1974) 0418
Mayday at 40,000 Feet (1976) 0668
Lady of the House (1978) 0904
Suddenly, Love (1978) 0913

SHEREE NORTH
Then Came Bronson (1969) 0037
Vanished (1971) 0122
Rolling Man (1972) 0239
Trouble Comes to Town (1973) 0274
Snatched (1973) 0284
Maneater (1973) 0365
Key West (1973) 0366
Winter Kill (1974) 0434
Shadow on the Street (1975) 0508
Most Wanted (1976) 0615
They Night They Took Miss Beautiful (1977) 0768
A Real American Hero (1978) 0917

KIM NOVAK
The Third Girl from the Left (1973) 0344
Satan's Triangle (1975) 0504

FRANCE NUYEN
Black Water Gold (1970) 0061
The Horror at 37,000 Feet (1973) 0288
Code Name: Diamond Head (1977) 0716
Return to Fantasy Island (1978) 0803
Death Moon (1978) 0858

CARRIE NYE
Divorce His/Divorce Hers (1973) 0285
The Users (1978) 0880

HUGH O'BRIAN
Wild Women (1970) 0090
Harpy (1971) 0125
Probe (Search) (1972) 0209
Murder on Flight 502 (1975) 0594
Benny and Barney: Las Vegas Undercover (1977) 0684
Fantasy Island (1977) 0688
Murder at the World Series (1977) 0708
Cruise into Terror (1978) 0811

EDMOND O'BRIEN
The Hanged Man (1964) 0002
The Doomsday Flight (1966) 0005
The Outsider (1967) 0016
The Intruders (1970) 0095
River of Mystery (1971) 0146
What's a Nice Girl Like You . . . ? (1971) 0187
Jigsaw (1972) 0224
Isn't It Shocking? (1973) 0338

MARGARET O'BRIEN
Split Second to an Epitaph (1968) 0020
Testimony of Two Men (1977) MS11

PAT O'BRIEN
The Over-the-Hill Gang (1969) 0042
Welcome Home, Johnny Bristol (1972) 0202
The Adventures of Nick Carter (1972) 0213
Kiss Me, Kill Me (1976) 0631

ARTHUR O'CONNELL
Seven in Darkness (1969) 0040
A Taste of Evil (1971) 0153
Shootout in a One-Dog Town (1974) 0380

CARROLL O'CONNOR
Fear No Evil (1969) 0035
The Last Hurrah (1977) 0776

GLYNNIS O'CONNOR
Senior Year (1974) 0418
All Together Now (1975) 0512
Someone I Touched (1975) 0526
The Boy in the Plastic Bubble (1976) 0669
Black Beauty (1978) MS15
Little Mo (1978) 0868
The Chisholms (1979) MS32

TIM O'CONNOR
The House on Greenapple Road (1970) 0063
Incident in San Francisco (1971) 0119
The Failing of Raymond (1971) 0175
Visions (Visions of Death) (1972) 0242
The Stranger (1973) 0295
Manhunter (1974) 0404
Winter Kill (1974) 0434
Ellery Queen (1975) 0539
They Only Come Out at Night (1975) 0554
Tail Gunner Joe (1977) 0695
The Man with the Power (1977) 0730
Arthur Hailey's Wheels (1978) MS20

GEORGE O'HANLON, JR.
Where Have All the People Gone? (1974) 0406
The Missing Are Deadly (1975) 0500
Smash-Up on Interstate 5 (1976) 0677

MAUREEN O'HARA
The Red Pony (1973) 0312

DAN O'HERLIHY
The People (1972) 0198
QB VII (1974) 0442
Banjo Hackett: Roamin' Free (1976) 0628
Good Against Evil (1977) 0729
Deadly Game (1977) 0782

GERALD S. O'LOUGHLIN
The D.A.: Murder One (1969) 0055
Murder at the World Series (1977) 0708
Something for Joey (1977) 0711
A Love Affair: The Eleanor and Lou Gehrig Story (1978) 0799
Arthur Hailey's Wheels (1978) MS20
Crash (1978) 0893
Roots: The Next Generations (1979) MS30
The Return of Mod Squad (1979) 0990
Blind Ambition (1979) MS35

PATRICK O'NEAL
Companions in Nightmare (1968) 0024
Cool Million (Mask of Marcella) (1972) 0244
Crossfire (1975) 0540
The Killer Who Wouldn't Die (1976) 0619
Twin Detectives (1976) 0625
Arthur Hailey's The Moneychangers (1976) MS06
The Deadliest Season (1977) 0707
Sharon: Portrait of a Mistress (1977) 0771
The Last Hurrah (1977) 0776
To Kill a Cop (1978) 0837
Like Mom, Like Me (1978) 0887

RYAN O'NEAL
Love, Hate, Love (1971) 0114

JENNIFER O'NEILL
Love's Savage Fury (1979) 0991

MILO O'SHEA
And No One Could Save Her (1973) 0293
QB VII (1974) 0442
Peter Lundy and the Medicine Hat Stallion (1977) 0773

JENNIFER O'NEILL
Love's Savage Fury (1979) 0991

MILO O'SHEA
And No One Could Save Her (1973) 0293
QB VII (1974) 0442
Peter Lundy and the Medicine Hat Stallion (1977) 0773

MAUREEN O'SULLIVAN
The Crooked Hearts (1972) 0253
The Great Houdinis (1976) 0658

ANNETTE O'TOOLE
The Girl Most Likely To . . . (1973) 0351
The Entertainer (1976) 0610
The War Between the Tates (1977) 0737

SIMON OAKLAND
The Cable Car Murder (Cross Current) (1971) 0172
The Night Stalker (1972) 0193
The Night Strangler (1973) 0277
Toma (1973) 0316
Key West (1973) 0366
Young Joe, the Forgotten Kennedy (1977) 0755
Evening in Byzantium (1978) MS23

WARREN OATES
Something for a Lonely Man (1968) 0025
The Movie Murderer (1970) 0067
The Reluctant Heroes (1971) 0173
Black Beauty (1978) MS15
True Grit (1978) 0852

ODETTA
The Autobiography of Miss Jane Pittman (1974) 0389

SUSAN OLIVER
Carter's Army (1970) 0066
Do You Take This Stranger? (1971) 0108
Amelia Earhart (1976) 0662

LAURENCE OLIVIER
David Copperfield (1970) 0080
Love Among the Ruins (1975) 0533
Cat on a Hot Tin Roof (1976) 0678
Jesus of Nazareth (1977) MS10
Come Back, Little Sheba (1977) 0795

JAMES OLSON
Paper Man (1971) 0168
Incident on a Dark Street (1971) 0275
Manhunter (1974) 0404
A Tree Grows in Brooklyn (1974) 0423
The Sex Symbol (1974) 0451
The Family Nobody Wanted (1975) 0521
Someone I Touched (1975) 0526
Man on the Outside (1975) 0572
Strange New World (1975) 0573
Law and Order (1976) 0629
The Spell (1977) 0698

DAVID OPATOSHU
The Smugglers (1968) 0030
The D.A.: Murder One (1969) 0055
Incident in San Francisco (1971) 0119
Conspiracy of Terror (1976) 0621
Francis Gary Powers: The True Story of the

LARA PARKER
My Darling Daughters' Anniversary (1973) 0352
The Chadwick Family (1974) 0437
Adventures of the Queen (1975) 0518
The Incredible Hulk (1977) 0772
Washington: Behind Closed Doors (1977) MS12

BARBARA PARKINS
A Taste of Evil (1971) 0153
Snatched (1973) 0284
Law of the Land (1976) 0624
Captains and the Kings (1976) MS04
Young Joe, the Forgotten Kennedy (1977) 0755
Testimony of Two Men (1977) MS11
Ziegfeld: The Man and His Women (1978) 0853
The Critical List (1978) 0872

MICHAEL PARKS
Stranger on the Run (1967) 0015
Then Came Bronson (1969) 0037
The Young Lawyers (1969) 0047
Can Ellen Be Saved? (1974) 0393
The Story of Pretty Boy Floyd (1974) 0444
Perilous Voyage (1976) (1968) 0645
The Savage Bees (1976) 0674
Murder at the World Series (1977) 0708
Escape from Brogan County (1977) 0764

Night Cries (1978) 0808
Hunters of the Reef (1978) 0853
Rainbow (1978) 0901
Fast Friends (1979) 0963

JERRY PARIS
But I Don't Want to Get Married! (1970) 0087
Every Man Needs One (1972) 0264

ESTELLE PARSONS
Terror on the Beach (1973) 0332
The Gun and the Pulpit (1974) 0427
The UFO Incident (1975) 0583
Backstairs at the White House (1979) MS28

NEVA PATTERSON
Message to My Daughter (1973) 0368
The Stranger Who Looks Like Me (1974) 0408
The Runaways (1975) 0543
Nowhere to Run (1978) 0801

MARISA PAVAN
Cutter's Trail (1970) 0069
Arthur Hailey's The Moneychangers (1976) MS06
The Trial of Lee Harvey Oswald (1977) 0760

E. J. PEAKER
Three's a Crowd (1969) 0054
Getting Away From It All (1972) 0196

LISA PELIKAN
I Want to Keep My Baby (1976) 0673
Perfect Gentlemen (1978) 0829
True Grit (1978) 0852
Studs Lonigan (1979) MS31

GEORGE PEPPARD
The Bravos (1972) 0192
Banacek: Detour to Nowhere (1972) 0223
One of Our Own (1975) 0559
Guilty or Innocent: The Sam Sheppard Murder Case (1975) 0593
Crisis in Mid-Air (1979) 0952
Torn Between Two Lovers (1979) 0979

ANTHONY PERKINS
How Awful About Allan (1970) 0084
First You Cry (1978) 0902
Les Miserables (1978) 0931

VIC PERRIN
Dragnet (1969) (1966) 0031
The UFO Incident (narrator) (1975) 0583

VALERIE PERRINE
The Couple Takes a Wife (1972) 0261
Ziegfeld: The Man and His Women (1978) 0854

NEHEMIAH PERSOFF
The Dangerous Days of Kiowa Jones (1966) 0006
Escape to Mindanao (1968) 0027
Cutter's Trail (1970) 0069
Lieutenant Schuster's Wife (1972) 0243
The Sex Symbol (1974) 0451
The Stranger Within (1974) 0457
Eric (1975) 0591
Killing Stone (1978) 0843

Ziegfeld: The Man and His Women (1978) 0854
The Word (1978) MS26
The Rebels (1979) MS34

DONNA PESCOW
Human Feelings (1978) 0885
Rainbow (1978) 0901

BERNADETTE PETERS
The Islander (1978) 0874

BROCK PETERS
Welcome Home, Johnny Bristol (1972) 0202
Seventh Avenue (1977) MS08
SST—Death Flight (SST: Disaster in the Sky) (1977) 0700
Black Beauty (1978) MS15
The Incredible Journey of Dr. Meg Laurel (1979) 0932
Roots: The Next Generations (1979) MS30

JEAN PETERS
Arthur Hailey's The Moneychangers (1976) MS06

PAUL PETERSON
Something for a Lonely Man (1968) 0025
Gidget Grows Up (1969) 0060

PASCALE PETIT
Berlin Affair (1970) 0093

JOANNA PETTET
The Delphi Bureau (1972) 0221
Footsteps (Footsteps: Nice Guys Finish Last) (1972) 0238
The Weekend Nun (1972) 0267
Pioneer Woman (1973) 0374
A Cry in the Wilderness (1974) 0420
The Desperate Miles (1975) 0532
The Dark Side of Innocence (1976) 0639
Captains and the Kings (1976) MS04
Sex and the Married Woman (1977) 0757

JO ANN PFLUG
A Step Out of Line (1971) 0118
They Call It Murder (1971) 0185
The Night Strangler (1973) 0277
Scream of the Wolf (1974) 0382
The Underground Man (1974) 0443

MACKENZIE PHILLIPS
Miles to Go Before I Sleep (1975) 0498
Eleanor and Franklin (1976) 0598
Fast Friends (1979) 0964

MICHELLE PHILLIPS
The Death Squad (1974) 0379
The California Kid (1974) 0456
Aspen (The Innocent and the Damned (1977) MS14
The Users (1978) 0880

ROBIN PHILLIPS
David Copperfield (1970) 0080

BEN PIAZZA
Fer-De-Lance (1974) 0464
Fear on Trial (1975) 0578

Once an Eagle (1976) MS05
When Every Day Was the Fourth of July
    (1978) 0828
The Critical List (1978) 0872

SLIM PICKENS
    Sam Hill: Who Killed the Mysterious Mr.
        Foster? (1971) 0112
    Desperate Mission (1971) 0178
    The Devil and Miss Sarah (1971) 0179
    Rolling Man (1972) 0239
    Hitched (1973) 0321
    Twice in a Lifetime (1974) 0415
    The Gun and the Pulpit (1974) 0427
    Babe (1975) 0584
    Banjo Hackett: Roamin' Free (1976) 0628
    The Sacketts (1979) 0988

MOLLY PICON
    Murder on Flight 502 (1975) 0594

WALTER PIDGEON
    How I Spent My Summer Vacation (1967)
        0007
    The House on Greenapple Road (1970) 0063
    The Mask of Sheba (1970) 0077
    The Screaming Woman (1972) 0201
    Live Again, Die Again (1974) 0400
    The Girl on the Late, Late Show (1974) 0426
    You Lie So Deep, My Love (1975) 0525
    Murder on Flight 502 (1975) 0594
    The Lindbergh Kidnapping Case (1976) 0605

DONALD PLEASENCE
    The Count of Monte Cristo (1975) 0501
    Jesus of Nazareth (1977) MS10
    Goldenrod (1977) 0731
    The Dark Secret of Harvest Home (narrator)
        (1978) 0805
    The Defection of Simas Kudirka (1978) 0806
    The Bastard (1978) MS22
    Centennial (1978) MS24
    Gold of the Amazon Women (1979) 0958

JOHN PLESHETTE
    Seventh Avenue (1977) MS08
    The Trial of Lee Harvey Oswald (1977) 0760
    The Users (1978) 0879

SUZANNE PLESHETTE
    Wings of Fire (1967) 0010
    Along Came a Spider (1970) 0068
    Hunters Are for Killing (1970) 0079
    River of Gold (1971) 0123
    In Broad Daylight (1971) 0155
    The Legend of Valentino (1975) 0595
    Law and Order (1976) 0629
    Richie Brockelman: Missing 24 Hours (1976)
        0663
    Kate Bliss and the Ticker Tape Kid (1978)
        0856

EVE PLUMB
    The House on Greenapple Road (1970) 0063
    Dawn: Portrait of a Teenage Runaway (1976)
        0654
    Alexander: The Other Side of Dawn (1977)
        0720
    Telethon (1977) 0774
    Little Women (1978) 0881
    Secrets of Hungry Wives (1978) 0883

CHRISTOPHER PLUMMER
    Arthur Hailey's The Moneychangers (1976)
        MS06
    Jesus of Nazareth (1977) MS10

MICHAEL J. POLLARD
    The Smugglers (1968) 0030

DON PORTER
    The Norliss Tapes (1973) 0294
    The Morning After (1974) 0399
    Murder or Mercy (1974) 0438
    The Legend of Lizzie Borden (1975) 0513
    Last Hours Before Morning (1975) 0532
    Christmas Miracle in Caufield, U.S.A. (1977)
        0793
    The President's Mistress (1978) 0816

NYREE DAWN PORTER
    Jane Eyre (1971) 0128

TOM POSTON
    The Magnificent Magnet of Santa Mesa (1977)
        0741
    A Guide for the Married Woman (1978) 0884

ANNIE POTTS
    Black Market Baby (1977) 0765
    Flatbed Annie & Sweetiepie: Lady Truckers
        (1979) 0950

CLIFF POTTS
    San Francisco International (1970) 0085
    Magic Carpet (1972) 0252
    Live Again, Die Again (1974) 0400
    A Case of Rape (1974) 0401
    Trapped Beneath the Sea (1974) 0466
    Nevada Smith (1975) 0557
    Once an Eagle (1976) MS05
    Danger in Paradise (1977) 0718
    Love's Dark Ride (1978) 0835
    Little Women (1978) 0881

JANE POWELL
    The Letters (1973) 0303
    Mayday at 40,000 Feet (1976) 0668

ROBERT POWELL
    Jesus of Nazareth (1977) MS10
    The Four Feathers (1978) 0796

TARYN POWER
    The Count of Monte Cristo (1975) 0501

STEFANIE POWERS
    Five Desperate Women (1971) 0145
    Sweet, Sweet Rachel (1971) 0148
    Paper Man (1971) 0168
    Ellery Queen: Don't Look Behind You (1971)
        0171
    Hardcase (1972) 0204
    No Place to Run (1972) 0232
    Shoutout in a One-Dog Town (1974) 0380
    Skyway to Death (1974) 0383
    Manhunter (1974) 0404
    Night Games (1974) 0414
    Sky Hei$t (1975) 0569
    Return to Earth (1976) 0634
    Washington: Behind Closed Doors (1977)
        MS12
    Nowhere to Run (1978) 0801
    A Death in Canaan (1978) 0824

ROBERT PRATT
    Dial Hot Line (1970) 0076
    The Neon Ceiling (1971) 0113
    Marriage: Year One (1971) 0154
    Hec Ramsey (The Century Turns) (1972) 0240
    Magic Carpet (1972) 0252

ANNE PRENTISS
    In Name Only (1969) 0053

PAULA PRENTISS
    The Couple Takes a Wife (1972) 0261
    Having Babies II (1977) 0770

LAWRENCE PRESSMAN
    Cannon (1971) 0129
    The Snoop Sisters (Female Instinct) (1972)
        0265
    The Marcus-Nelson Murders (1973) 0305
    Winter Kill (1974) 0434
    The First 36 Hours of Dr. Durant (1975) 0565
    Rich Man, Poor Man (1976) MS03
    Man from Atlantis (1977) 0704
    Mulligan's Stew (1977) 0742
    The Trial of Lee Harvey Oswald (1977) 0760
    The Gathering (1977) 0784
    Like Mom, Like Me (1978) 0887
    Blind Ambition (1979) MS35

HARVE PRESNELL
    The Great Man's Whiskers (1973) (1969) 0289

ROBERT PRESTON
    My Father's House (1975) 0570
    The Chisholms (1979) MS32

VINCENT PRICE
    What's a Nice Girl Like You . . . ? (1971)
        0187

BARRY PRIMUS
    Big Rose (1974) 0421
    Roger & Harry: The Mitera Target (Love for
        Ransom) (1977) 0715
    Washington: Behind Closed Doors (1977)
        MS12

WILLIAM PRINCE
    Key West (1973) 0366
    Night Games (1974) 0414
    Sybil (1976) 0670
    Captains and the Kings (1976) MS04
    The Rhinemann Exchange (1977) MS09
    Johnny, We Hardly Knew Ye (1977) 0693
    Aspen (The Innocent or the Damned) (1977)
        MS14
    The Jericho Mile (1979) 0963

VICTORIA PRINCIPAL
    Last Hours Before Morning (1975) 0552
    Fantasy Island (1977) 0688
    The Night They Took Miss Beautiful (1977)
        0768

ANDREW PRINE
    Split Second to an Epitaph (1968) 0020
    Along Came a Spider (1970) 0068
    Night Slaves (1970) 0086
    Wonder Woman (1974) 0410
    Law of the Land (1976) 0624
    Tail Gunner Joe (1977) 0695

Last of the Mohicans (1977) 0779
Christmas Miracle in Caufield, U.S.A. (1977) 0793
Donner Pass: The Road to Survival (1978) 0889

FREDDIE PRINZE
The Million Dollar Ripoff (1976) 0653

DOROTHY PROVINE
The Sound of Anger (1968) 0028

JULIET PROWSE
Second Chance (1972) 0206

NICHOLAS PRYOR
Force Five (1975) 0553
Fear on Trial (1975) 0578
Washington: Behind Closed Doors (1977) MS12
Night Terror (1977) 0696
The Life and Assassination of the Kingfish (1977) 0709
Having Babies II (1977) 0770
Rainbow (1978) 0901

RICHARD PRYOR
The Young Lawyers (1969) 0047
Carter's Army (1970) 0066

LEE PURCELL
Hijack! (1973) 0336
The Amazing Howard Hughes (1977) 0712
Stranger in Our House (1978) 0897
Murder in Music City (1979) 0937

LINDA PURL
Bad Ronald (1974) 0467
The Oregon Trail (1976) 0597
Eleanor and Franklin (1976) 0598
Young Pioneers (1976) 0607
Having Babies (1976) 0659
Young Pioneers' Christmas (1976) 0680
Testimony of Two Men (1977) MS11
Little Ladies of the Night (1977) 0689
Black Market Baby (1977) 0765
A Last Cry for Help (1979) 0941
Women at West Point (1979) 0955
Like Normal People (1979) 0970

DENVER PYLE
Hitched (1973) 0321
Sidekicks (1974) 0417
Murder or Mercy (1974) 0438
Death Among Friends (Mrs. R—Death Among Friends) (1975) 0568

RANDY QUAID
Getting Away From It All (1972) 0196
The Great Niagara (1974) 0454

ROBERT QUARRY
The Millionaire (1978) 0927

ANTHONY QUAYLE
Destiny of a Spy (1969) 0046
Jarrett (1973) 0310
QB VII (1974) 0442
Great Expectations (1974) 0481
Moses—The Lawgiver (1975) MS02
21 Hours at Munich (1976) 0667

KATHLEEN QUINLAN
Can Ellen Be Saved? (1974) 0393
Lucas Tanner (1974) 0445
Where Have All the People Gone? (1974) 0460
The Missing Are Deadly (1975) 0500
The Abduction of Saint Anne (They've Kidnapped Anne Benedict) (1975) 0507
The Turning Point of Jim Malloy (1975) 0547
Little Ladies of the Night (1977) 0689

ANTHONY QUINN
The City (1971) 0134
Jesus of Nazareth (1977) MS10

ELLIS RABB
The Dain Curse (1978) MS21

DEBORAH RAFFIN
Nightmare in Badham County (1976) 0666
Ski Lift to Death (1978) 0825
How to Pick Up Girls! (1978) 0899
Willa (1979) 0962

STEVE RAILSBACK
Helter Skelter (1976) 0617
From Here to Eternity (1979) MS29

CRISTINA RAINES
Sunshine (1973) 0353
Loose Change (Those Restless Years) (1978) MS18
Centennial (1978) MS24
The Child Stealer (1979) 0959

DACK RAMBO
River of Gold (1971) 0123
Hit Lady (1974) 0461
Good Against Evil (1977) 0729

CHARLOTTE RAMPLING
Sherlock Holmes in New York (1976) 0661

TONY RANDALL
Kate Bliss and the Ticker Tape Kid (1978) 0856

JOHN RANDOLPH
The Borgia Stick (1967) 0012
A Step Out of Line (1971) 0118
The Cable Car Murder (Cross Current) (1971) 0172
A Death of Innocence (1971) 0174
The Family Rico (1972) 0228
The Judge and Jake Wyler (1972) 0260
Partners in Crime (1973) 0320
Tell Me Where It Hurts (1974) 0411
Adventures of the Queen (1975) 0518
The Runaways (1975) 0543
The New, Original Wonder Woman (1975) 0590
F. Scott Fitzgerald in Hollywood (1976) 0637
Tail Gunner Joe (1977) 0695
Secrets (1977) 0699
Lucan (1977) 0728
Nowhere to Hide (narrator) (1977) 0733
Washington: Behind Closed Doors (1977) MS12
Kill Me If You Can (1977) 0758
The Gathering (1977) 0784
Nowhere to Run (1978) 0801

Doctors' Private Lives (1978) 0831
The Winds of Kitty Hawk (1978) 0925
Backstairs at the White House (1979) MS28
Blind Ambition (1979) MS35

ROBERT RANDOM
Scalplock (1966) 0003
Cutter's Trail (1970) 0069

THALMUS RASULALA
The Bait (1973) 0307
The Autobiography of Miss Jane Pittman (1974) 0389
Last Hours Before Morning (1975) 0552
Roots (1977) MS07
Killer on Board (1977) 0766
The President's Mistress (1978) 0816

ALDO RAY
Deadlock (1969) 0034
Promise Him Anything . . . (1975) 0566

WILLIAM REDFIELD
Companions in Nightmare (1968) 0024
Fear on Trial (1975) 0578

CORIN REDGRAVE
David Copperfield (1970) 0080

LYNN REDGRAVE
Turn of the Screw (1974) 0433
Centennial (1978) MS24
Sooner or Later (1979) 0966

MICHAEL REDGRAVE
Heidi (1968) 0023
David Copperfield (1970) 0080

JOYCE REDMAN
Les Miserables (1978) 0931

DONNA REED
The Best Place to Be (1979) 0994

ROBERT REED
The City (1971) 0134
Assignment: Munich (1972) 0225
Haunts of the Very Rich (1972) 0233
Snatched (1973) 0284
The Man Who Could Talk to Kids (1973) 0345
Pray for the Wildcats (1974) 0386
The Scret Night Caller (1975) 0520
Rich Man, Poor Man (1976) MS03
Law and Order (1976) 0629
Lanigan's Rabbi (1976) 0643
Nightmare in Badham County (1976) 0666
The Boy in the Plastic Bubble (1976) 0669
Revenge for a Rape (1976) 0672
Roots (1977) MS07
The Love Boat II (1977) 0692
SST—Death Flight (SST: Disaster in the Sky) (1977) 0700
The Hunted Lady (1977) 0780
Thou Shalt Not Commit Adultery (1978) 0898
Bud and Lou (1978) 0905
Mandrake (1979) 0944

TRACY REED
Incident in San Francisco (1971) 0119
The Great American Beauty Contest (1973) 0287
Aloha Means Goodbye (1974) 0463
Top Secret (1978) 0859

DELLA REESE
The Voyage of the Yes (1973) 0278
Twice in a Lifetime (1974) 0415
The Return of Joe Forrester (1975) 0561
Roots: The Next Generations (1979) MS30

KATE REID
Hawkins on Murder (Death and the Maiden) (1973) 0306
She Cried "Murder!" (1973) 0335
Death Among Friends (Mrs. R—Death Among Friends) (1975) 0568
Loose Change (Those Restless Years) (1978) MS18

CHARLES NELSON REILLY
Call Her Mom (1972) 0210

CARL REINER
Medical Story (1975) 0575

ROB REINER
Thursday's Game (1974) (1971) 0432
More Than Friends (1978) 0886

LEE REMICK
And No One Could Save Her (1973) 0293
The Blue Knight (1973) MS01
QB VII (1974) 0442
Hustling (1975) 0523
A Girl Named Sooner (1975) 0571
Breaking Up (1978) 0797
Arthur Hailey's Wheels (1978) MS20
Torn Between Two Lovers (1978) 0979
Ike (1979) MS33

ANNE REVERE
Two for the Money (1972) 0216

CLIVE REVILL
The Great Houdinis (1976) 0658
Centennial (1978) MS24

ALEJANDRO REY
Seven in Darkness (1969) 0040
Money to Burn (1973) 0347
Satan's Triangle (1975) 0504

FERNANDO REY
Jesus of Nazareth (1977) MS10

BURT REYNOLDS
Hunters Are for Killing (1970) 0079
Run, Simon, Run (1970) 0100

BARBARA RHOADES
The Silent Gun (1969) 0058
The Judge and Jake Wyler (1972) 0260
Hunter (1973) 0273
The Police Story (1973) 0313

What Are Best Friends For? (1973) 0373
Crime Club (1975) 0545
Conspiracy of Terror (1976) 0621
Twin Detectives (1976) 0625
The Great Houdinis (1976) 0658

HARI RHODES (Harry Rhodes)
Deadlock (1969) 0034
Earth II (1971) 0176
Trouble Comes to Town (1973) 0274
A Dream for Christmas (1973) 0375
The Return of Joe Forrester (1975) 0561
Matt Helm (1975) 0562
Mayday at 40,000 Feet (1976) 0668
Roots (1977) MS07
The Hostage Heart (1977) 0749
A Woman Called Moses (1978) 0918
Backstairs at the White House (1979) MS28

MADLYN RHUE
Stranger on the Run (1967) 0015
Poor Devil (1973) 0290
The Sex Symbol (1974) 0451
Medical Center (1975) 0575
The Manhunter (1976) (1968) 0618
The Best Place to Be (1979) 0995

BEAH RICHARDS
Footsteps (Footsteps: Nice Guys Finish Last) (1972) 0238
Outrage (1973) 0359
A Dream for Christmas (1973) 0375
Just an Old Sweet Song (1976) 0650
Ring of Passion (1978) 0812

KIM RICHARDS
James at 15 (1977) 0748
Devil Dog: The Hound of Hell (1978) 0896

PAUL RICHARDS
Savage (1973) 0322

RALPH RICHARDSON
David Copperfield (1970) 0080
Frankenstein: The True Story (1973) 0362
The Man in the Iron Mask (1977) 0691
Jesus of Nazareth (1977) MS10

MARK RICHMAN (Peter Mark Richman)
The House on Greenapple Road (1970) 0063
McCloud: Who Killed Miss U.S.A.? (Portrait of a Dead Girl) (1970) 0071
Yuma (1971) 0121
Mallory: Circumstantial Evidence (1976) 0603
The Islander (1978) 0874
Blind Ambition (1979) MS35

DIANA RIGG
In This House of Brede (1975) 0527

JOHN RITTER
The Night That Panicked America (1975) 0586
Leave Yesterday Behind (1978) 0847

CHITA RIVERA
The Marcus-Nelson Murders (1973) 0305

ADAM ROARKE
The Keegans (1976) 0627

JASON ROBARDS
Washington: Behind Closed Doors (1977) MS12
A Christmas to Remember (1978) 0929

PERNELL ROBERTS
The Silent Gun (1969) 0058
San Francisco International (1970) 0085
The Bravos (1972) 0192
The Adventures of Nick Carter (1972) 0213
Dead Man on the Run (1975) 0544
The Deadly Tower (1975) 0581
The Lives of Jenny Dolan (1975) 0585
Charlie Cobb: Nice Night for a Hanging (1977) 0735
Centennial (1978) MS24
The Immigrants (1978) MS25
The Night Rider (1979) 0984
Hot Rod (1979) 0993

RACHEL ROBERTS
Destiny of a Spy (1969) 0046
Baffled! (1973) 0283
Great Expectations (1974) 0481
A Circle of Children (1977) 0705

TONY ROBERTS
The Lindbergh Kidnapping Case (1976) 0605
Rosetti and Ryan: Men Who Love Women (1977) 0725
The Girls in the Office (1979) 0948

CLIFF ROBERTSON
The Sunshine Patriot (1968) 0029
The Man Without a Country (1973) 0325
A Tree Grows in Brooklyn (1974) 0423
My Father's House (1975) 0570
Return to Earth (1976) 0634
Washington: Behind Closed Doors (1977) MS12
Overboard (1978) 0876

DALE ROBERTSON
Scalplock (1966) 0003
Melvin Purvis: G-Man (1974) 0431
The Kansas City Massacre (1975) 0576

DALE ROBINETTE
The Deadly Triangle (1977) 0724
Dog and Cat (1977) 0746
Crisis in Sun Valley (1978) 0834
The Beasts Are on the Streets (1978) 0851
The Billion Dollar Threat (1979) 0971

CHARLES KNOX ROBINSON
The Screaming Woman (1972) 0201
Banacek: Detour to Nowhere (1972) 0223
Set This Town on Fire (The Profane Comedy) (1973) (1968) 0271
The Six-Million Dollar Man (1973) 0304
Fer-De-Lance (1974) 0464
Man on the Outside (1975) 0572
Francis Gary Powers: The True Story of the U-2 Spy Incident (1976) 0655
Nowhere to Hide (1977) 0733
A Killing Affair (1977) 0757
The Trial of Lee Harvey Oswald (1977) 0760

CHRIS ROBINSON
The Aquarians (1970) 0091
Travis Logan, D.A. (1971) 0124
Sweet, Sweet Rachel (1971) 0148
The FBI Story: The FBI Versus Alvin Karpis, Public Enemy Number One (1974) 0474

EDWARD G. ROBINSON
U.M.C. (Operation Heartbeat) (1969) 0039
The Old Man Who Cried Wolf (1970) 0088

SUGAR RAY ROBINSON
City Beneath the Sea (1971) 0111
Telethon (1977) 0774
The Return of Mod Squad (1979) 0990

FLORA ROBSON
Les Miserables (1978) 0931
A Man Called Intrepid (1979) MS36

ALEX ROCCO
Hustling (1975) 0523
The Blue Knight (1975) 0564
Harold Robbins' 79 Park Avenue (1977) MS13
A Question of Guilt (1978) 0820
The Grass Is Always Greener over the Septic
Tank (1978) 0892

EUGENE ROCHE
Crawlspace (1972) 0207
Winter Kill (1974) 0434
The Last Survivors (1975) 0530
Crime Club (1975) 0545
The Art of Crime (1975) 0596
Mallory: Circumstantial Evidence (1976) 0603
The Possessed (1977) 0714
Corey: For the People (1977) 0736
The Ghost of Flight 401 (1978) 0818
The New Maverick (1978) 0868
The Winds of Kitty Hawk (1978) 0925
The Child Stealer (1979) 0959

MARCIA RODD
How to Break Up a Happy Divorce (1976)
0657

PERCY RODRIGUES
The Old Man Who Cried Wolf (1970) 0088
The Forgotten Man (1971) 0137
Genesis II (1973) 0318
The Last Survivors (1975) 0530
The Lives of Jenny Dolan (1975) 0585
Most Wanted (1976) 0615
Arthur Hailey's The Moneychangers (1976)
MS06
Ring of Passion (1978) 0813
Roots: The Next Generations (1979) MS30
The Night Rider (1979) 0984

WAYNE ROGERS
Attack on Terror: The FBI Versus the Ku
Klux Klan (1975) 0522
Having Babies II (1977) 0770
It Happened One Christmas (1977) 0786
Thou Shalt Not Commit Adultery (1978) 0898

GILBERT ROLAND
The Mark of Zorro (1974) 0469
The Deadly Tower (narrator) (1975) 0581
The Sacketts (1979) 0987

ESTHER ROLLE
Summer of My German Soldier (1978) 0895
I Know Why the Caged Bird Sings (1979)
0976

RUTH ROMAN
The Old Man Who Cried Wolf (1970) 0088
Incident in San Francisco (1971) 0119
Go Ask Alice (1973) 0280
Punch and Jody (1974) 0484
The Sacketts (1979) 0987

RICHARD ROMANUS
Night Chase (1970) 0097
Night Terror (1977) 0696
Gold of the Amazon Women (1979) 0957

CESAR ROMERO
Don't Push, I'll Charge When I'm Ready!
(1977) (1969) 0789

NED ROMERO
Winchester '73 (1967) 0013
The Priest Killer (1971) 0136
I Will Fight No More Forever (1975) 0549
Peter Lundy and the Medicine Hat Stallion
(1977) 0773
Last of the Mohicans (1977) 0779
The Deerslayer (1978) 0926

MICKEY ROONEY
Evil Roy Slade (1972) 0211

GEORGE ROSE
Holocaust (1978) MS19

KATHARINE ROSS
The Longest Hundred Miles (1967) 0008
Wanted: The Sundance Woman (Mrs.
Sundance Rides Again) (1976) 0656
Murder by Natural Causes (1979) 0953

RICHARD ROUNDTREE
Firehouse (1973) 0269
Roots (1977) MS07

GENA ROWLANDS
A Question of Love (1978) 0907
Strangers: The Story of a Mother and
Daughter (1979) 0986

JOHN RUBINSTEIN
The Psychiatrist: God Bless the Children
(Children of the Lotus Eaters) (1970) 0103
A Howling in the Woods (1971) 0163
Something Evil (1972) 0197
The Streets of San Francisco (1972) 0230
All Together Now (1975) 0512
Corey: For the People (1977) 0736
Happily Ever After (1978) 0870
Roots: The Next Generations (1979) MS30

PAUL RUDD
Johnny, We Hardly Knew Ye (1977) 0693

JANICE RULE
Shadow on the Land (1968) 0026
Trial Run (1969) 0032
The Devil and Miss Sarah (1971) 0179
The Word (1978) MS26

BARBARA RUSH
Suddenly Single (1971) 0156
The Eyes of Charles Sand (1972) 0217
Moon of the Wolf (1972) 0235
Crime Club (1973) 0302
The Last Day (1975) 0519

JOHN RUSSELL
Alias Smith and Jones (1971) 0105

KURT RUSSELL
Search for the Gods (1975) 0534
The Deadly Tower (1975) 0581
The Quest (1976) 0633
Christmas Miracle in Caufield, U.S.A. (1977)
0793
Elvis (1979) 0951

ROSALIND RUSSELL
The Crooked Hearts (1972) 0252

THERESA RUSSELL
Blind Ambition (1979) MS35

MITCHELL RYAN
Chase (1973) 0319
The Entertainer (1976) 0610
Escape from Brogan County (1977) 0764
Peter Lundy and the Medicine Hat Stallion
(1977) 0773
Christmas Miracle in Caufield, U.S.A. (1977)
0793
Having Babies III (1978) 0826
Sergeant Matlovich Vs. the U.S. Air Force
(1978) 0866

ROBERT RYAN
The Man Without a Country (1973) 0325

ALFRED RYDER
U.M.C. (Operation Heartbeat) (1969) 0039
The D.A.: Murder One (1969) 0055
Probe (Search) (1972) 0209
The Abduction of Saint Anne (They've
Kidnapped Anne Benedict) (1975) 0507
Sergeant Matlovich Vs. the U.S. Air Force
(1978) 0866

EVA MARIE SAINT
The Macahans (1976) 0599
A Christmas to Remember (1978) 0929

RAYMOND ST. JACQUES
The Monk (1969) 0045
Search for the Gods (1975) 0534
Roots (1977) MS07
Secrets of Three Hungry Wives (1978) 0883

SUSAN SAINT JAMES
Fame Is the Name of the Game (1966) 0004
Alias Smith and Jones (1971) 0105
Once Upon a Dead Man (1971) 0139
Magic Carpet (1972) 0252
Scott Free (1976) 0660
Night Cries (1978) 0808
Desperate Women (1978) 0890
The Girls in the Office (1979) 0948

JILL ST. JOHN
Fame Is the Name of the Game (1966) 0004
How I Spent My Summer Vacation (1967) 0007
The Spy Killer (1969) 0050
Foreign Exchange (1970) 0064
Brenda Starr (1976) 0630
Telethon (1977) 0774

SOUPY SALES
Don't Push, I'll Charge When I'm Ready! (1977) (1969) 0789

ALBERT SALMI
Kung Fu (1972) 0214
Female Artillery (1973) 0279
Night Games (1974) 0414
The Manhunter (1976) (1968) 0618
Once an Eagle (1976) MS05
Harold Robbins' 79 Park Avenue (1977) MS13

JENNIFER SALT
Gargoyles (1972) 0256
The Great Niagara (1974) 0454

WILL SAMPSON
Relentless (1977) 0752
The Hunted Lady (1977) 0780
Standing Tall (1978) 0804
Vega$ (1978) 0840
From Here to Eternity (1979) MS29

ISABEL SANFORD
The Great Man's Whiskers (1973) (1969) 0289

RENI SANTONI
Powderkeg (1971) 0133
Indict and Convict (1974) 0376
Panic on the 5:22 (1974) 0480

JOE SANTOS
The Blue Knight (1973) MS01
The Rockford Files (1974) 0422
The Girl on the Late, Late Show (1974) 0426
A Matter of Wife . . . or Death (1976) 0620

CHRIS SARANDON
Thursday's Game (1974) (1971) 0432
You Can't Go Home Again (1979) 0975

SUSAN SARANDON
F. Scott Fitzgerald and "The Last of the Belles" (1974) 0377

DICK SARGENT
Melvin Purvis: G-Man (1974) 0431
Fantasy Island (1977) 0688
The Power Within (1979) 0983

MICHAEL SARRAZIN
The Doomsday Flight (1966) 0005
Frankenstein: The True Story (1973) 0362

JOHN SAVAGE
All the Kind Strangers (1974) 0476
The Turning Point of Jim Malloy (1975) 0547
Eric (1975) 0591

TELLY SAVALAS
Mongo's Back in Town (1971) 0182
Visions (Visions of Death) (1972) 0242
The Marcus-Nelson Murders (1973) 0305
She Cried "Murder!" (1973) 0335

JOHN SAXON
The Doomsday Flight (1966) 0005
Winchester '73 (1967) 0013
Istanbul Express (1968) 0021
The Intruders (1970) 0095
Snatched (1973) 0284
Linda (1973) 0350
Can Ellen Be Saved? (1974) 0393
Planet Earth (1974) 0441
U-2 Spy Incident (1976) 0655
Raid on Entebbe (1977) 0685
Ziegfeld: The Man and His Women (1978) 0854

MARIE OSMOND
The Gift of Love (1978) 0916

JEFFREY OSTERHAGE
True Grit (1978) 0852
The Legend of the Golden Gun (1979) 0969
The Sacketts (1979) 0988

JUDY PACE
The Young Lawyers (1969) 0047
Brian's Song (1971) 0177

GERALDINE PAGE
Live Again, Die Again (1974) 0400
Something for Joey (1977) 0711

JANIS PAIGE
The Turning Point of Jim Malloy (1975) 0547
The Return of Joe Forrester (1975) 0561
Lanigan's Rabbi (1976) 0643

JACK PALANCE
Dracula (1974) 0395
The Godchild (1974) 0483
The Hatfields and the McCoys (1975) 0505

LILLI PALMER
Hauser's Memory (1970) 0098

LUCIANA PALUZZI
Now You See It, Now You Don't (1968) 0022
Powderkeg (1971) 0133

IRENE PAPAS
Moses—The Lawgiver (1975) MS02

ELEANOR PARKER
Maybe I'll Come Home in the Spring (1971) 0115
Vanished (1971) 0122
Home for the Holidays (1972) 0258
The Great American Beauty Contest (1973) 0287
Fantasy Island (1977) 0688
The Bastard (1978) MS22

FESS PARKER
Climb an Angry Mountain (1972) 0268

JAMESON PARKER
Women at West Point (1979) 0953
Anatomy of a Seduction (1979) 0980
Crossfire (1975) 0540
Strange New World (1975) 0573
Once an Eagle (1976) MS05
Raid on Entebbe (1977) 0685
Harold Robbins' 79 Park Avenue (1977) MS13
The Immigrants (1978) MS25

WILLIAM SCHALLERT
Escape (1971) 0132
Man on a String (1972) 0212
Partners in Crime (1973) 0320
Hijack! (1973) 0336
Remember When (1974) 0419
Death Sentence (1974) 0459
Promise Him Anything . . . (1975) 0566
Dawn: Portrait of a Teenage Runaway (1976) 0654
Tail Gunner Joe (1977) 0695
Little Women (1978) 0881
Ike (1979) MS33
Blind Ambition (1979) MS35

ROY SCHEIDER
Assignment: Munich (1972) 0225

MAXIMILLIAN SCHELL
Heidi (1968) 0023

JOHN SCHUCK
Once Upon a Dead Man (1971) 0139
Hunter (1973) 0273
Roots (1977) MS07

BRENDA SCOTT
The Hanged Man (1964) 0002
Sweet, Sweet Rachel (1971) 0148
Chase (1973) 0319

DEBRALEE SCOTT
Lisa, Bright and Dark (1973) 0360
A Summer Without Boys (1973) 0363
Senior Year (1974) 0418
Death Moon (1978) 0858

GEORGE C. SCOTT
Jane Eyre (1971) 0128
Fear on Trial (1975) 0578
Beauty and the Beast (1976) 0676

MARTHA SCOTT
The Devil's Daughter (1973) 0272
Thursday's Game (1974) (1971) 0432
The Abduction of Saint Anne (They've Kidnapped Anne Benedict) (1975) 0507
Medical Story (1975) 0575
The Word (1978) MS26
Charleston (1979) 0938

JEAN SEBERG
Mousey (1974) 0409

DAVID SELBY
Washington: Behind Closed Doors (1977) MS12
Telethon (1977) 0774
The Night Rider (1979) 0984

TOM SELLECK
The Movie Murderer (1970) 0067
Returning Home (1975) 0555
Most Wanted (1976) 0615
Superdome (1978) 0798
The Sacketts (1979) 0988

JANE SEYMOUR
Frankenstein: The True Story (1973) 0362
Captains and the Kings (1976) MS04
Benny and Barney: Las Vegas Undercover (1977) 0684
Seventh Avenue (1977) MS07
Killer on Board (1977) 0766
The Four Feathers (1978) 0796
The Awakening Land (1978) MS17
Love's Dark Ride (1978) 0835
Dallas Cowboys Cheerleaders (1979) 0937

MICHAEL SHANNON
Future Cop (1976) 0626
Cops and Robin (1978) 0833
The Best Place to Be (1979) 0995

SAUNDRA SHARP
Minstrel Man (1977) 0703
The Greatest Thing That Almost Happened (1977) 0769
Night Cries (1978) 0808
Are You in the House Alone? (1978) 0875
Hollow Image (1979) 1001

CORNELIA SHARPE
Cover Girls (1977) 0721

WILLIAM SHATNER
Sole Survivor (1970) 0062
Vanished (1971) 0122
Owen Marshall, Counselor-at-Law (A Pattern of Morality) (1971) 0135
The People (1972) 0198
The Hound of the Baskervilles (1972) 0208
Incident on a Dark Street (1973) 0275
Go Ask Alice (1973) 0280
The Horror at 37,000 Feet (1973) 0288
Pioneer Woman (1973) 0374
Indict and Convict (1974) 0376
Pray for the Wildcats (1974) 0386
The Barbary Coast (1975) 0558
Perilous Voyage (1976) (1968) 0645
Testimony of Two Men (1977) MS11
The Bastard (1978) MS22
Little Women (1978) 0881
Crash (1978) 0894

ARTIE SHAW
Crash (1978) 0894

STAN SHAW
Street Killing (1976) 0649
Arthur Hailey's The Moneychangers (1976) MS06
Roots: The Next Generations (1979) MS30

DICK SHAWN
Evil Roy Slade (1972) 0211
Fast Friends (1979) 0964

MARTIN SHEEN
Then Came Bronson (1969) 0037
Goodbye Raggedy Ann (1971) 0157
Mongo's Back in Town (1971) 0182
Welcome Home, Johnny Bristol (1972) 0202

That Certain Summer (1972) 0251
Pursuit (1972) 0263
Crime Club (1973) 0302
Letters from Three Lovers (1973) 0339
Catholics (1973) 0361
Message to My Daughter (1973) 0368
The Execution of Private Slovik (1974) 0412
The Story of Pretty Boy Floyd (1974) 0494
The California Kid (1974) 0456
The Last Survivors (1975) 0530
Sweet Hostage (1975) 0580
Blind Ambition (1979) MS35

PAUL SHENAR
The Execution of Private Slovik (1974) 0412
The Night That Panicked America (1975) 0586
The Keegans (1976) 0627
Gemini Man (Code Name: Minus One) (1976) 0632
Roots (1977) MS07
The Hostage Heart (1977) 0749
Ziegfeld: The Man and His Women (1978) 0854
The Courage and the Passion (1978) 0857
Suddenly, Love (1978) 0913

CYBILL SHEPHERD
A Guide for the Married Woman (1978) 0884

BOBBY SHERMAN
Skyway to Death (1974) 0383

BROOKE SHIELDS
The Prince of Central Park (1977) 0739

JAMES SHIGETA
Escape to Mindanao (1968) 0027
U.M.C. (Operation Heartbeat) (1969) 0039
The Young Lawyers (1969) 0047
The Questor Tapes (1974) 0385
Matt Helm (1975) 0562
The Killer Who Wouldn't Die (1976) 0619
Once an Eagle (1976) MS05
Arthur Hailey's The Moneychangers (1976) MS06
Samurai (1979) 0978

TALIA SHIRE
Foster and Laurie (1975) 0592
Rich Man, Poor Man (1976) MS03
Kill Me If You Can (1977) 0758
Daddy, I Don't Like It Like This (1978) 0862

SALLIE SHOCKLEY
A Tattered Web (1971) 0143
The Longest Night (1972) 0227
A Great American Tragedy (1972) 0247

SYLVIA SIDNEY
Do Not Fold, Spindle or Mutilate (1971) 0166
The Secret Night Caller (1975) 0520
Winner Take All (1975) 0529
Death at Love House (1976) 0647
Raid on Entebbe (1977) 0685
Snowbeast (1977) 0713
Siege (1978) 0841

HENRY SILVA
Black Noon (1971) 0164
Drive Hard, Drive Fast (1973) (1969) 0328
Contract on Cherry Street (1977) 0777

PHIL SILVERS
The Night They Took Miss Beautiful (1977) 0768

JEAN SIMMONS
Heidi (1968) 0023
The Dain Curse (1978) MS21

O. J. SIMPSON
Roots (1977) MS07
A Killing Affair (Behind the Badge) (1977) 0757

CHRISTINA SINATRA
Fantasy Island (1977) 0688

FRANK SINATRA
Contract on Cherry Street (1977) 0777

MADGE SINCLAIR
Roots (1977) MS07
One in a Million: The Ron LeFlore Story (1978) 0878
I Know Why the Caged Bird Sings (1979) 0976

MARC SINGER
Things in Their Season (1974) 0486
Journey from Darkness (1975) 0524
Something for Joey (1977) 0711
Harold Robbins' 79 Park Avenue (1977) MS13
Sergeant Matlovich Vs. the U.S. Air Force (1978) 0866
Roots: The Next Generations (1979) MS30

JOSEPH SIROLA
Visions (Visions of Death) (1972) 0242
Cry Rape! (1973) 0358
High Risk (1976) 0635
Washington: Behind Closed Doors (1977) MS12

LILIA SKALA
Ironside (1967) 0014
Split Second to an Epitaph (1968) 0020
The Sunshine Patriot (1968) 0029
Probe (Search) (1972) 0209
Eleanor and Franklin (1976) 0598
Sooner or Later (1979) 0966

TOM SKERRITT
The Birdmen (Escape of the Birdmen) (1971) 0140
The Last Day (1975) 0519
Maneaters Are Loose! (1978) 0845

JEREMY SLATE
Wings of Fire (1967) 0010
The Cable Car Murder (Cross Current) (1971) 0172
The Man Who Died Twice (1973) (1970) 0323
Stowaway to the Moon (1975) 0502
Stranger in Our House (1978) 0897
Mr. Horn (1979) 0949

WALTER SLEZAK
Heidi (1968) 0023

CHARLES MARTIN SMITH
    Law of the Land (1976) 0624
    Cotton Candy (1978) 0892

JACLYN SMITH
    Probe (Search) (1972) 0209
    Switch (1975) 0535
    Charlie's Angels (1976) 0614
    Escape from Brogan County (1977) 0764
    The Users (1978) 0880

KENT SMITH
    How Awful About Allan (1970) 0084
    The Last Child (1971) 0149
    The Night Stalker (1972) 0193
    Probe (Search) (1972) 0209
    The Crooked Hearts (1972) 0253
    The Judge and Jake Wyler (1972) 0260
    The Snoop Sisters (Female Instinct) (1972) 0265
    The Affair (1973) 0356
    The Cat Creature (1973) 0367
    Murder or Mercy (1974) 0438
    The Disappearance of Flight 412 (1964) 0458
    Once an Eagle (1976) MS05

WILLIAM SMITH
    The Over-the-Hill Gang (1969) 0042
    Crowhaven Farm (1970) 0099
    The Rockford Files (1974) 0422
    The Sex Symbol (1974) 0451
    Death Among Friends (Mrs. R—Death Among Friends) (1975) 0568
    Rich Man, Poor Man (1976) MS03
    The Manhunter (1976) (1968) 0618
    The Rebels (1979) MS34

JAMIE SMITH-JACKSON
    Go Ask Alice (1973) 0280
    Satan's School for Girls (1973) 0334
    The Affair (1973) 0356
    Lisa, Bright and Dark (1973) 0360
    Remember When (1974) 0419
    The Wild Child (1976) 0665
    Night Cries (1978) 0808
    Having Babies II (1978) 0826

WILLIAM SMITHERS
    The Monk (1969) 0045
    The Brotherhood of the Bell (1970) 0083
    The Neon Ceiling (1971) 0113

CARRIE SNODGRESS
    The Whole World Is Watching (1969) 0036
    Silent Night, Lonely Night (1969) 0057
    The Impatient Heart (1971) 0150
    Love's Dark Ride (1978) 0835
    Fast Friends (1979) 0964

SUZANNE SOMERS
    Sky Hei$t (1975) 0569
    It Happened at Lake Wood Manor (1977) 0781
    Happily Ever After (1978) 0870
    Zuma Beach (1978) 0879

JULIE SOMMARS
    Five Desperate Women (1971) 0145
    The Harness (1971) 0167
    How to Steal an Airplane (1971) (1968) 0181
    Centennial (1978) MS24

ELKE SOMMER
    Probe (Search) (1972) 0209

GALE SONDERGAARD
    The Cat Creature (1973) 0367
    Centennial (1978) MS24

JACK SOO
    The Monk (1969) 0045
    She Lives (1973) 0331

LOUISE SOREL
    River of Mystery (1971) 0146
    Every Man Needs One (1972) 0264
    Happiness Is a Warm Clue (The Return of Charlie Chan) (1973) (1970) 0327
    The President's Plane Is Missing (1973) 0346
    Get Christie Love! (1974) 0384
    The Girl Who Came Gift-Wrapped (1974) 0388
    The Healers (1974) 0447
    The Mark of Zorro (1974) 0469
    One of Our Own (1975) 0559
    Widow (1976) 0601
    Perilous Voyage (1976) (1968) 0645
    When Every Day Was the Fourth of July (1978) 0828

PAUL SORVINO
    Tell Me Where It Hurts (1974) 0411
    It Couldn't Happen to a Nicer Guy (1974) 0478
    Seventh Avenue (1977) MS08
    Dummy (1979) 0994

ANN SOTHERN
    The Outsider (1967) 0016
    Congratulations, It's a Boy! (1971) 0141
    A Death of Innocence (1971) 0174
    The Weekend Nun (1972) 0267
    The Great Man's Whiskers (1973) (1969) 0289
    Captains and the Kings (1976) MS04

DAVID SOUL
    The Disappearance of Flight 412 (1974) 0458
    Starsky and Hutch (1975) 0556
    Little Ladies of the Night (1977) 0689

SISSY SPACEK
    The Girls of Huntington House (1973) 0291
    The Migrants (1974) 0392
    Katherine (1975) 0579

DAVID SPIELBERG
    Night of Terror (1972) 0241
    Toma (1973) 0316
    Force Five (1975) 0553
    The Lindbergh Kidnapping Case (1976) 0605
    The 3,000 Mile Chase (1977) 0738
    In the Matter of Karen Ann Quinlan (1977) 0759
    The Storyteller (1977) 0785
    King (1978) MS16
    Arthur Hailey's Wheels (1978) MS20
    Sergeant Matlovich Vs. the U.S. Air Force (1978) 0866
    From Here to Eternity (1979) MS29

ROBERT STACK
    The Strange and Deadly Occurrence (1974) 0455
    Adventures of the Queen (1975) 0518
    Murder on Flight 502 (1975) 0594
    Most Wanted (1976) 0615

JAMES STACY
    Paper Man (1971) 0168
    Heat of Anger (1972) 0218
    Ordeal (1973) 0348
    Just a Little Inconvenience (1977) 0761

TERENCE STAMP
    The Thief of Baghdad (1978) 0907

BARBARA STANWYCK
    The House That Would Not Die (1970) 0092
    A Taste of Evil (1971) 0153
    The Letters (1973) 0303

KIM STANLEY
    U.M.C. (Operation Heartbeat) (1969) 0039

MAUREEN STAPLETON
    Tell Me Where It Hurts (1974) 0411
    Queen of the Stardust Ballroom (1975) 0517
    Cat on a Hot Tin Roof (1976) 0678
    The Gathering (1977) 0784

ROD STEIGER
    Jesus of Nazareth (1977) MS10

JAMES STEPHENS
    True Grit (1978) 0852

ROBERT STEPHENS
    QB VII (1974) 0442
    Holocaust (1978) MS19

LARAINE STEPHENS
    The Screaming Woman (1972) 0201
    The Adventures of Nick Carter (1972) 0213
    Jarrett (1973) 0310
    The Girl on the Late, Late Show (1974) 0426
    The Rangers (1974) 0492
    Matt Helm (1975) 0562
    The Courage and the Passion (1978) 0857
    Crash (1978) 0894
    Dallas Cowboys Cheerleaders (1979) 0937

JAN STERLING
    Having Babies (1976) 0659
    Backstairs at the White House (1979) MS28

TISHA STERLING
    Night Slaves (1970) 0086
    Powderkeg (1971) 0133
    A Death of Innocence (1971) 0174
    Snatched (1973) 0284
    Betrayal (1974) 0488
    Kiss Me, Kill Me (1976) 0631
    In the Glitter Palace (1977) 0702

FRANCES STERNHAGEN
    Who'll Save Our Children? (1978) 0923

ANDREW STEVENS
    The Last Survivors (1975) 0530
    The Oregon Trail (1976) 0597
    Once an Eagle (1976) MS05
    Secrets (1977) 0699
    The Bastard (1978) MS22
    Women at West Point (1979) 0955
    The Rebels (1979) MS34

CONNIE STEVENS
Mister Jerico (1970) 0075
Call Her Mom (1972) 0210
Playmates (1972) 0237
Every Man Needs One (1972) 0264
The Sex Symbol (1974) 0451
Love's Savage Fury (1979) 0991

CRAIG STEVENS
McCloud: Who Killed Miss U.S.A.? (Portrait of a Dead Girl) (1970) 0071
The Snoop Sisters (Female Instinct) (1972) 0265
The Elevator (1974) 0396
Killer Bees (1974) 0405
Rich Man, Poor Man (1976) MS03
The Love Boat II (1977) 0692
Secrets of Three Hungry Wives (1978) 0883

INGER STEVENS
The Borgia Stick (1967) 0012
The Mask of Sheba (1970) 0077
Run, Simon Run (1970) 0100

STELLA STEVENS
In Broad Daylight (1971) 0155
Climb an Angry Mountain (1972) 0268
Linda (1973) 0350
Honky Tonk (1974) 0425
The Day the Earth Moved (1974) 0453
The New, Original Wonder Woman (1975) 0590
Kiss Me, Kill Me (1976) 0631
Wanted: The Sundance Woman (Mrs. Sundance Rides Again) (1976) 0656
Charlie Cobb: Nice Night for a Hanging (1977) 0735
Murder in Peyton Place (1977) 0762
The Night They Took Miss Beautiful (1977) 0768
Cruise into Terror (1978) 0811
The Jordan Chance (1978) 0919

McLEAN STEVENSON
Shirts/Skins (1973) 0341

JAMES STEWART
Hawkins on Murder (Death and the Maiden) (1973) 0306

PAUL STEWART
Carter's Army (1970) 0066
City Beneath the Sea (1971) 0111
The Dain Curse (1978) MS21
The Nativity (1978) 0924

DOROTHY STICKNEY
The Homecoming (1971) 0188

DEAN STOCKWELL
Paper Man (1971) 0168
The Failing of Raymond (1971) 0175
The Adventures of Nick Carter (1972) 0213
The Return of Joe Forrester (1975) 0561
A Killing Affair (Behind the Badge) (1977) 0757

GUY STOCKWELL
The Sound of Anger (1969) 0028
The Disappearance of Flight 412 (1974) 0458

LARRY STORCH
Hunters Are for Killing (1970) 0079
The Woman Hunter (1972) 0231
The Couple Takes a Wife (1972) 0261
The Incredible Rocky Mountain Race (1977) 0788

BEATRICE STRAIGHT
The Borrowers (1973) 0369
Killer on Board (1977) 0766
The Dain Curse (1978) MS21

MARC STRANGE
Shadow on the Land (1968) 0026

LEE STRASBERG
The Last Tenant (1978) 0865

SUSAN STRASBERG
Marcus Welby, M.D. (A Matter of Humanities) (1969) 0038
Hauser's Memory (1970) 0098
Mr. and Mrs. Bo Jo Jones (1971) 0170
Frankenstein (1973) 0276
Toma (1973) 0316
SST—Death Flight (SST: Disaster in the Sky) (1977) 0700
The Immigrants (1978) MS25

PETER STRAUSS
The Man Without a Country (1973) 0325
Attack on Terror: The FBI Versus the Ku Klux Klan (1975) 0522
Rich Man, Poor Man (1976) MS03
Young Joe, the Forgotten Kennedy (1977) 0755
The Jericho Mile (1979) 0963

MERYL STREEP
The Deadliest Season (1977) 0707
Holocaust (1978) MS19

GAIL STRICKLAND
Ellery Queen (1975) 0539
My Father's House (1975) 0570
The Dark Side of Innocence (1976) 0639
The Gathering (1977) 0784
A Love Affair: The Eleanor and Lou Gehrig Story (1978) 0799
The President's Mistress (1978) 0816
Ski Lift to Death (1978) 0825

WOODY STRODE
Breakout (1970) 0102
Key West (1973) 0366

MICHAEL STRONG
Vanished (1971) 0122
Travis Logan, D.A. (1971) 0124
Queen of the Stardust Ballroom (1975) 0517
Overboard (1978) 0876

DON STROUD
Split Second to an Epitaph (1968) 0020
Something for a Lonely Man (1968) 0025
The D.A.: Conspiracy to Kill (1971) 0106
The Deadly Dream (1971) 0144
The Daughters of Joshua Cabe (1972) 0229
Rolling Man (1972) 0239
The Elevator (1974) 0396

The Return of Joe Forrester (1975) 0561
High Risk (1976) 0635
Katie: Portrait of a Centerfold (1978) 0888

SHEPPARD STRUDWICK
The Man Without a Country (1973) 0325

SALLY STRUTHERS
Aloha Means Goodbye (1974) 0463
Hey, I'm Alive! (1975) 0589
The Great Houdinis (1976) 0658
Intimate Strangers (1977) 0775
My Husband Is Missing (1978) 0915
And Your Name Is Jonah (1979) 0945

BARRY SULLIVAN
The Immortal (1969) 0041
Night Gallery (1969) 0049
The House on Greenapple Road (1970) 0063
Yuma (1971) 0121
Cannon (1971) 0129
Kung Fu (1972) 0214
The Magician (1973) 0311
Savage (1973) 0322
Letter from Three Lovers (1973) 0339
Hurricane (1974) 0449
Once an Eagle (1976) MS05
The Bastard (1978) MS22
The Immigrants (1978) MS25
Backstairs at the White House (1979) MS28

SUSAN SULLIVAN
No Place to Run (1972) 0232
The City (1977) 0687
Roger & Harry: The Mitera Target (Love for Ransom) (1977) 0715
The Magnificent Magnet of Santa Mesa (1977) 0741
Having Babies II (1977) 0770
The Incredible Hulk (1977) 0772
Deadman's Curve (1978) 0812
Having Babies III (1978) 0826
The Comedy Company (1978) 0864
The New Maverick (1978) 0868

DONALD SUTHERLAND
The Sunshine Patriot (1968) 0029

JAMES SUTORIUS
A Death in Canaan (1978) 0824
Siege (1978) 0841
A Question of Love (1978) 0908

BO SVENSON
The Bravos (1972) 0192
Frankenstein (1973) 0276
You'll Never See Me Again (1973) 0299
Hitched (1973) 0321
Target Risk (1975) 0496
Snowbeast (1977) 0713
Gold of the Amazon Women (1979) 0958

GLORIA SWANSON
Killer Bees (1974) 0405

INGA SWENSON
Earth II (1971) 0176
Testimony of Two Men (1977) MS11
Ziegfeld: The Man and His Women (1978) 0854

LORETTA SWIT
Shirts/Skins (1973) 0341
The Last Day (1975) 0519
The Hostage Heart (1977) 0749

BRENDA SYKES
The Sheriff (1971) 0130

KRISTOFFER TABORI
Truman Capote's The Glass House (1972) 0203
Family Flight (1972) 0249
Terror on the Beach (1973) 0332
QB VII (1974) 0442
Seventh Avenue (1977) MS08
Black Beauty (1978) MS15

NITA TALBOT
The Movie Murderer (1970) 0067
They Call It Murder (1971) 0185
What Are Best Friends For? (1973) 0373
The Rockford Files (1974) 0422

AKIM TAMIROFF
Then Came Bronson (1969) 0037

VIC TAYBACK
Partners in Crime (1973) 0320
The Alpha Caper (1973) 0340
The Blue Knight (1973) MS01
Dark Victory (1976) 0602
Little Ladies of the Night (1977) 0689
Getting Married (1978) 0849

ELIZABETH TAYLOR
Divorce His/Divorce Hers (1973) 0285
Victory at Entebbe (1976) 0679

KENT TAYLOR
The Phantom of Hollywood (1974) 0397

RENEE TAYLOR
Woman of the Year (1976) 0644

ROBERT TAYLOR
Return of the Gunfighter (1967) 0009

ROD TAYLOR
Powderkeg (1971) 0133
Family Flight (1972) 0249
The Oregon Trail (1976) 0597
A Matter of Wife . . . or Death (1976) 0620

LAURA TEWES
Dallas Cowboys Cheerleaders (1979) 0937

PHYLLIS THAXTER
Incident in San Francisco (1971) 0119
The Longest Night (1972) 0227
Once an Eagle (1976) MS05

ROY THINNES
The Other Man (1970) 0089
The Psychiatrist: God Bless the Children
(Children of the Lotus Eaters) (1970) 0103
Black Noon (1971) 0164
The Horror at 37,000 Feet (1973) 0288
The Norliss Tapes (1973) 0294
Satan's School for Girls (1973) 0334
Death Race (1973) 0354

The Manhunter (1976) (1968) 0618
Secrets (1977) 0699
Code Name: Diamond Head (1977) 0716
From Here to Eternity (1979) MS29
The Return of Mod Squad (1979) 0990

LOWELL THOMAS
Amelia Earhart (1976) 0662
Ike (1979) MS33

MARLO THOMAS
It Happened One Christmas (1977) 0786

RICHARD THOMAS
The Homecoming (1971) 0188
The Red Badge of Courage (1974) 0487
The Silence (1975) 0588
Getting Married (1978) 0849
Roots: The Next Generations (1979) MS30
No Other Love (1979) 0965

TERRY-THOMAS
I Love a Mystery (1973) (1967) 0296

MARSHALL THOMPSON
Centennial (1978) MS24

SADA THOMPSON
The Entertainer (1976) 0610

INGRID THULIN
Moses—The Lawgiver (1975) MS02

GENE TIERNEY
Daughter of the Mind (1969) 0056

KEVIN TIGHE
Emergency (1972) 0194
The Rebels (1979) MS34

BEVERLY TODD
Deadlock (1969) 0034
Roots (1977) MS07
The Ghost of Flight 401 (1978) 0818
Having Babies III (1978) 0826
The Jericho Mile (1979) 0963

ANGEL TOMPKINS
Probe (Search) (1972) 0209
You Lie So Deep, My Love (1975) 0525

FRANCHOT TONE
See How They Run (1964) 0001
Shadow over Elveron (1968) 0018

RIP TORN
The President's Plane Is Missing (1973) 0346
Attack on Terror: The FBI Versus the Ku
Klux Klan (1975) 0522
Betrayal (1978) 0903
Steel Cowboy (1978) 0915
Blind Ambition (1979) MS35

AUDREY TOTTER
The Outsider (1967) 0016
U.M.C. (Operation Heartbeat) (1969) 0039
The Nativity (1978) 0924

GIORGIO TOZZI
One of Our Own (1975) 0559
Captains and the Kings (1976) MS04
Torn Between Two Lovers (1979) 0979

JOHN TRAVOLTA
The Boy in the Plastic Bubble (1976) 0669

DOROTHY TRISTAN
Isn't It Shocking? (1973) 0338
The Trial of Chaplain Jensen (1975) 0515
Journey from Darkness (1975) 0524
Fear on Trial (1975) 0578
Griffin and Phoenix (1976) 0606

BOBBY TROUP
Dragnet (1969) (1966) 0031
Emergency (1972) 0194
Benny and Barney: Las Vegas Undercover
(1977) 0684
The Rebels (1979) MS34

TOM TRYON
Winchester '73 (1967) 0013

FORREST TUCKER
Alias Smith and Jones (1971) 0105
Welcome Home, Johnny Bristol (1972) 0202
Footsteps (Footsteps: Nice Guys Finish Last)
(1972) 0238
Jarrett (1973) 0310
Once an Eagle (1976) MS05
The Incredible Rocky Mountain Race (1977)
0788
Black Beauty (1978) MS15
A Real American Hero (1978) 0917
The Rebels (1979) MS34

TANYA TUCKER
Amateur Night at the Dixie Bar & Grill (1979)
0935
The Rebels (1979) MS34

TOM TULLY
Any Second Now (1969) 0033
Hijack! (1973) 0336

ANN TURKEL
Matt Helm (1975) 0562

GLYNN TURMAN
Carter's Army (1970) 0066
In Search of America (1971) 0127
The Blue Knight (1975) 0564
Minstrel Man (1977) 0703
Katie: Portrait of a Centerfold (1978) 0888
Centennial (1978) MS24

RITA TUSHINGHAM
Green Eyes (1977) 0683

JEFF TYLER
Tom Sawyer (1973) 0317

SUSAN TYRELL
Lady of the House (1978) 0904

CICELY TYSON
Marriage: Year One (1971) 0154
The Autobiography of Miss Jane Pittman
(1974) 0389
Just an Old Sweet Song (1976) 0650
Roots (1977) MS07
Wilma (1977) 0790
King (1978) MS16
A Woman Called Moses (1978) 0918

LESLIE UGGAMS
Roots (1977) MS07
Backstairs at the White House (1979) MS28

ROBERT URICH
Killdozer (1974) 0390
The Specialists (1975) 0495
Vega$ (1978) 0840
Leave Yesterday Behind (1978) 0848

PETER USTINOV
Jesus of Nazareth (1977) MS10
The Thief of Baghdad (1978) 0907

JOAN VAN ARK
The Judge and Jake Wyler (1972) 0260
Big Rose (1974) 0421
Shell Game (1975) 0563
The Last Dinosaur (1977) 0697
Testimony of Two Men (1977) MS11

LEE VAN CLEEF
Nowhere To Hide (1977) 0733

TRISH VAN DEVERE
Stalk the Wild Child (1976) 0665
Beauty and the Beast (1976) 0676
Sharon: Portrait of a Mistress (1977) 0771

GRANVILLE VAN DUSEN
Dr. Max (1974) 0428
A Cry for Help (1975) 0516
Someone I Touched (1975) 0526
The Night That Panicked America (1975) 0586
James A. Michener's Dynasty (1976) 0612
The War Between the Tates (1977) 0737
Breaking Up (1978) 0797
Dr. Scorpion (1978) 0822
Love's Dark Ride (1978) 0835

DICK VAN DYKE
The Morning After (1974) 0399

PETER VAN EYCK
Heidi (1968) 0023

JO VAN FLEET
The Family Rico (1972) 0228
Satan's School for Girls (1973) 0334

DICK VAN PATTEN
Hec Ramsey (The Century Turns) (1972) 0240
The Crooked Hearts (1972) 0253
The Love Boat (1976) 0652
With This Ring (1978) 0846

JIMMY VAN PATTEN
The Chisholms (1979) MS32

JOYCE VAN PATTEN
But I Don't Want to Get Married! (1970) 0087
Winter Kill (1974) 0434
The Stranger Within (1974) 0457
Let's Switch (1975) 0499
Winner Take All (1975) 0529
To Kill a Cop (1978) 0837
Murder at the Mardi Gras (1978) 0847
The Comedy Company (1978) 0864

BRENDA VACCARO
Travis Logan, D.A. (1971) 0124
What's a Nice Girl Like You . . . ? (1971)
0187
Honor Thy Father (1973) 0300
Sunshine (1973) 0353
The Big Ripoff (1975) 0536

KAREN VALENTINE
Gidget Grows Up (1969) 0060
The Daughters of Joshua Cabe (1972) 0229
Coffee, Tea or Me? (1973) 0329
The Girl Who Came Gift-Wrapped (1974)
0388
The Love Boat (1976) 0652
Having Babies (1976) 0659
Murder at the World Series (1977) 0708
Return to Fantasy Island (1978) 0803
Go West, Young Girl (1978) 0842

RAF VALLONE
Honor Thy Father (1973) 0300
Catholics (1973) 0361

VIVIAN VANCE
Getting Away From It All (1972) 0196
The Great Houdinis (1976) 0658

TITOS VANDIS
Genesis II (1973) 0318
Get Christie Love! (1974) 0384
The Last Angry Man (1974) 0435
In Tandem (Movin' On) (1974) 0446
Satan's Triangle (1975) 0504
Roger & Harry: The Mitera Target (Love for
Ransom) (1977) 0715
The San Pedro Bums (1977) 0719
The 3,000 Mile Chase (1977) 0738
Mad Bull (1977) 0792
And Your Name Is Jonah (1979) 0945

DIANE VARSI
The People (1972) 0198

ROBERT VAUGHN
The Woman Hunter (1972) 0231
Kiss Me, Kill Me (1976) 0631
Captains and the Kings (1976) MS04
Washington: Behind Closed Doors (1977)
MS12
The Islander (1978) 0874
Centennial (1978) MS24
Backstairs at the White House (1979) MS28
The Rebels (1979) MS34

ELENA VERDUGO
The Alpha Caper (1973) 0340

BEN VEREEN
Louis Armstrong—Chicago Style (1976) 0600
Roots (1977) MS07

JOHN VERNON
Trial Run (1969) 0032
Escape (1971) 0132
Cool Million (Mask of Marcella) (1972) 0244
Hunter (1973) 0273
The Questor Tapes (1974) 0385
Mousey (1974) 0409
The Virginia Hill Story (1974) 0479
The Imposter (1975) 0538
The Swiss Family Robinson (1975) 0550
The Barbary Coast (1975) 0558
Matt Helm (1975) 0562
Mary Jane Harper Cried Last Night (1977)
0763
The Sacketts (1979) 0988

VICTORIA VETRI
The Pigeon (1969) 0048
Night Chase (1970) 0097
Incident in San Francisco (1971) 0119

ABE VIGODA
The Devil's Daughter (1973) 0272
Toma (1973) 0316
The Story of Pretty Boy Floyd (1974) 0444
Having Babies (1976) 0659
The Comedy Company (1978) 0864
How to Pick Up Girls! (1978) 8999

HERVE VILLECHAIZE
Fantasy Island (1977) 0688
Return to Fantasy Island (1978) 0803

JAN-MICHAEL VINCENT
Tribes (1970) 0094
The Catcher (1972) 0226
Sandcastles (1972) 0245
Deliver Us from Evil (1973) 0330

LYLE WAGGONER
Letters from Three Lovers (1973) 0339
The New, Original Wonder Woman (1975)
0590
The Love Boat II (1978) 0692

LINDSAY WAGNER
The Rockford Files (1974) 0422
The Incredible Journey of Dr. Meg Laurel
(1979) 0932

ROBERT WAGNER
How I Spent My Summer Vacation (1967)
0007
City Beneath the Sea (1971) 0111
The Cable Car Murder (Cross Current) (1971)
0172
Killer by Night (1972) 0190
Madame Sin (1972) 0195
The Streets of San Francisco (1972) 0230
The Affair (1973) 0356
The Abduction of Saint Anne (They've
Kidnapped Anne Benedict) (1975) 0507
Switch (1975) 0535
Death at Love House (1976) 0647
Cat on a Hot Tin Roof (1976) 0678
The Critical List (1978) 0872
Pearl (1978) MS27

JAMES WAINWRIGHT
Once Upon a Dead Man (1971) 0139
Jigsaw (1972) 0225
The President's Plane Is Missing (1973) 0346
Killdozer (1974) 0390
Bridger (1976) 0648
A Woman Called Moses (1978) 0920

RALPH WAITE
The Borgia Stick (1967) 0012
The Secret Life of John Chapman (1976) 0682
Roots (1977) MS07
Red Alert (1977) 0723

ROBERT WALDEN
The Marcus-Nelson Murders (1973) 0305
Shirts/Skins (1973) 0341
Larry (1974) 0440
The Great Ice Rif-Off (1974) 0473
Panic on the 5:22 (1974) 0480
The Kansas City Massacre (1975) 0576
The Hostage Heart (1977) 0749
Centennial (1979) MS24

CLINT WALKER
Yuma (1971) 0121
Hardcase (1972) 0204
The Bounty Man (1972) 0250
Scream of the Wolf (1974) 0382
Killdozer (1974) 0390
Snowbeast (1977) 0713
Centennial (1978) MS24

JIMMIE WALKER
The Greatest Thing That Almost Happened
(1977) 0769
Telethon (1977) 0774

KATHRYN WALKER
The Winds of Kitty Hawk (1978) 0925
Too Far to Go (1979) 0960

NANCY WALKER
Every Man Needs One (1972) 0264
Thursday's Game (1974) (1971) 0432
Death Scream (The Woman Who Cried
Murder) (1975) 0577
Human Feelings (1978) 0885

ELI WALLACH
A Cold Night's Death (1973) 0282
Indict and Convict (1974) 0376
Seventh Avenue (1977) MS08
Harold Robbins' The Pirate (1978) 0906

RAY WALSTON
Institute for Revenge (1979) 0943

JESSICA WALTER
The Immortal (1969) 0041
Three's a Crowd (1969) 0054
They Call It Murder (1971) 0185
Women in Chains (1972) 0199
Home for the Holidays (1972) 0258
Hurricane (1974) 0449
Having Babies (1976) 0659
Victory at Entebbe (1976) 0679
Black Market Baby (1977) 0765
Wild and Wooly (1978) 0819
Arthur Hailey's Wheels (1978) MS20
Dr. Strange (1978) 0871
Secrets of Three Hungry Wives (1978) 0883

SAM WANAMAKER
Mousey (1974) 0409
The Law (1974) 0465
Holocaust (1978) MS19

SIMON WARD
Dracula (1974) 0395
All Creatures Great and Small (1975) 0511
The Four Feathers (1978) 0796
The Last Giraffe (1979) 1000

JACK WARDEN
The Face of Fear (1971) 0151
Brian's Song (1971) 0177
What's a Nice Girl Like You . . . ? (1971)
0187
Man on a String (1972) 0212
Lieutenant Schuster's Wife (1972) 0243
Remember When (1974) 0419
The Godchild (1974) 0483
Journey from Darkness (1975) 0524
They Only Come Out at Night (1975) 0554
Raid on Entebbe (1977) 0685

MARLENE WARFIELD
Goodbye Raggedy Ann (1971) 0157

DAVID WARNER
Holocaust (1978) MS19

JENNIFER WARREN
Banjo Hackett: Roamin' Free (1976) 0628
Shark Kill (1976) 0638
First You Cry (1978) 0902
Steel Cowboy (1978) 0915
Champions: A Love Story (1979) 0936

LESLEY ANN WARREN
Seven in Darkness (1969) 0040
Love, Hate, Love (1971) 0114
Assignment: Munich (1972) 0225
The Daughters of Joshua Cabe (1972) 0229
The Letters (1973) 0303
The Legend of Valentino (1975) 0595
Betrayal (1978) 0903
Harold Robbins' 79 Park Avenue (1977) MS13
Pearl (1978) MS27

SAM WATERSTON
The Glass Menagerie (1973) 0371
Reflections of Murder (1974) 0482
Friendly Fire (1979) 0973

DAVID WAYNE
The Catcher (1972) 0226
The FBI Story: The FBI Versus Alvin Karpis,
Public Enemy Number One (1974) 0474
Ellery Queen (1975) 0539
Once an Eagle (1976) MS05
In the Glitter Palace (1977) 0702
Black Beauty (1978) MS15
Murder at the Mardi Gras (1978) 0847
Loose Change (Those Restless Years) (1978)
MS18
The Gift of Love (1978) 0916
The Girls in the Office (1979) 0948

PATRICK WAYNE
Sole Survivor (1970) 0062
Yesterday's Child (1977) 0694
Flight to Holocaust (1977) 0710
The Last Hurrah (1977) 0776
Three on a Date (1978) 0817

DENNIS WEAVER
McCloud: Who Killed Miss U.S.A.? (Portrait
of a Dead Girl) (1970) 0071
The Forgotten Man (1971) 0137
Duel (1971) 0169

Rolling Man (1972) 0239
Female Artillery (1973) 0279
The Great Man's Whiskers (1973) (1969) 0289
Terror on the Beach (1973) 0332
Intimate Strangers (1977) 0775
The Islander (1978) 0874
Centennial (1978) MS24
Pearl (1978) MS27
Ishi: The Last of His Tribe (1978) 0928
The Ordeal of Patty Hearst (1979) 0956

FRITZ WEAVER
The Borgia Stick (1967) 0012
Berlin Affair (1970) 0093
Heat of Anger (1972) 0218
The Snoop Sisters (Female Instinct) (1972)
0265
Hunter (1973) 0273
The Legend of Lizzie Borden (1975) 0513
Captains Courageous (1977) 0783
Holocaust (1978) MS19

JACK WEBB
Dragnet (1969) (1966) 0031
O'Hara, U.S. Treasury: Operation Cobra
(narrator) (1971) 0131

ROBERT WEBBER
The Movie Murderer (1970) 0067
Hauser's Memory (1970) 0098
Thief (1971) 0152
Hawkins on Murder (Death and the Maiden)
(1973) 0306
Double Indemnity (1973) 0343
Murder or Mercy (1974) 0438
Death Stalk (1975) 0506
Harold Robbins' 79 Park Avenue (1977) MS13

TUESDAY WELD
Reflections of Murder (1974) 0482
F. Scott Fitzgerald in Hollywood (1976) 0637
A Question of Guilt (1978) 0820

ORSON WELLES
It Happened One Christmas (1977) 0786
A Woman Called Moses (narrator) (1978) 0918

ADAM WEST
The Eyes of Charles Sands (1972) 0217
Poor Devil (1973) 0290
Nevada Smith (1975) 0557

JACK WESTON
Fame Is the Name of the Game (1966) 0004
Now You See It, Now You Don't (1968) 0022
I Love a Mystery (1973) (1967) 0296
Deliver Us from Evil (1973) 0330
Harold Robbins' 79 Park Avenue (1977) MS13

BETTY WHITE
Vanished (1971) 0122
With This Ring (1978) 0846
The Best Place to Be (1979) 0995

LEONARD WHITING
Frankenstein: The True Story (1973) 0362

STUART WHITMAN
The Man Who Wanted to Live Forever (1970)
0104
City Beneath the Sea (1971) 0111
Revenge (1971) 0165

The Woman Hunter (1972) 0231
The Man Who Died Twice (1973) (1970) 0323
The Cat Creature (1973) 0367
Go West, Young Girl (1978) 0842
Harold Robbins' The Pirate (1978) 0906

JAMES WHITMORE
The Challenge (1970) 0070
If Tomorrow Comes (1971) 0180
I Will Fight No More Forever (1975) 0549
The Word (1978) MS26

JOHNNY WHITTAKER
Something Evil (1972) 0197
Mulligan's Stew (1977) 0742

RICHARD WIDMARK
Vanished (1971) 0122
Brock's Last Case (1973) 0301
The Last Day (1975) 0519
Mr. Horn (1979) 0949

LARRY WILCOX
Mr. and Mrs. BoJo Jones (1971) 0170
The Great American Beauty Contest (1973) 0287
The Girl Most Likely To . . . (1973) 0351
Death Stalk (1975) 0506
Sky Hei$t (1975) 0569
Relentless (1977) 0752

COLLIN WILCOX-JONES
The Man Who Could Talk to Kids (1973) 0345
The Autobiography of Miss Jane Pittman (1974) 0389
A Cry in the Wilderness (1974) 0420
The Lives of Jenny Dolan (1975) 0585

HENRY WILCOXON
Sarge: The Badge or the Cross (1970) 0116
The Tribe (1974) 0489
The Log of the Black Pearl (1975) 0494
When Every Day Was the Fourth of July (1978) 0828

CORNEL WILDE
Gargoyles (1972) 0256

GENE WILDER
Thursday's Game (1974) (1971) 0432

MICHAEL WILDING
Frankenstein: The True Story (1973) 0362

ANSON WILLIAMS
Lisa, Bright and Dark (1973) 0360

BILL WILLIAMS
The Phantom of Hollywood (1974) 0397

BILLY DEE WILLIAMS
Carter's Army (1970) 0066
Brian's Song (1971) 0177

CINDY WILLIAMS
The Migrants (1974) 0392
Suddenly, Love (1978) 0913

CLARENCE WILLIAMS III
The Return of Mod Squad (1979) 0990

DICK ANTHONY WILLIAMS
The Storyteller (1977) 0785
King (1978) MS16
A Woman Called Moses (1978) 0918
Some Kind of Miracle (1979) 0933
Hollow Image (1979) 1001

EMLYN WILLIAMS
David Copperfield (1970) 0080

HANK WILLIAMS, JR.
Willa (1979) 0962

JOHN WILLIAMS
The Hound of the Baskervilles (1972) 0208

PAUL WILLIAMS
Flight to Holocaust (1977) 0710
The Wild Wild West Revisited (1979) 0982

VAN WILLIAMS
The Runaways (1975) 0543
The Night Rider (1979) 0984

FRED WILLIAMSON
Deadlock (1969) 0034
Arthur Hailey's Wheels (1978) MS20

NICOL WILLIAMSON
The Word (1978) MS26

CHILL WILLS
The Over-the-Hill Gang (1969) 0042
The Over-the-Hill Gang Rides Again (1970) 0096

WILLIAM WINDOM
Prescription: Murder (1968) 0017
U.M.C. (Operation Heartbeat) (1969) 0039
The House on Greenapple Road (1970) 0063
Assault on the Wayne (1971) 0107
Escape (1971) 0132
A Taste of Evil (1971) 0153
Marriage: Year One (1971) 0154
The Homecoming (1971) 0188
Second Chance (1972) 0206
A Great American Tragedy (1972) 0247
Pursuit (1972) 0263
The Girls of Huntington House (1973) 0291
The Day the Earth Moved (1974) 0453
The Abduction of Saint Anne (They've Kidnapped Anne Benedict) (1975) 0507
Journey from Darkness (1975) 0524
Guilty or Innocent: The Sam Sheppard Murder Case (1975) 0593
Bridger (1976) 0648
Richie Brockelman: Missing 24 Hours (1976) 0663
Once an Eagle (1976) MS05
Seventh Avenue (1977) MS08
Hunters of the Deep (1978) 0853
Blind Ambition (1979) MS35

MARIE WINDSOR
Wild Women (1970) 0090
Manhunter (1974) 0404

PAUL WINFIELD
The Horror at 37,000 Feet (1973) 0288
It's Good to Be Alive (1974) 0402
Green Eyes (1977) 0683
King (1978) MS16
Backstairs at the White House (1979) MS28
Roots: The Next Generations (1979) MS30

HENRY WINKLER
Katherine (1975) 0579

KATHERINE (KITTY) WINN
The House That Would Not Die (1970) 0092
Man on a String (1972) 0212
Message to My Daughter (1973) 0368
Miles to Go Before I Sleep (1975) 0498
Most Wanted (1976) 0615
The Last Hurrah (1977) 0776

MARE WINNINGHAM
Special Olympics (1978) 0821

JONATHAN WINTERS
Now You See It, Now You Don't (1968) 0022

ROLAND WINTERS
Miracle on 34th Street (1973) 0370
The Dain Curse (1978) MS21
You Can't Go Home Again (1979) 0975

SHELLEY WINTERS
Revenge (1971) 0165
A Death of Innocence (1971) 0174
The Adventures of Nick Carter (1972) 0213
The Devil's Daughter (1973) 0272
Big Rose (1974) 0421
The Sex Symbol (1974) 0451
The Initiation of Sarah (1978) 0814
Elvis (1979) 0951

JOSEPH WISEMAN
The Outsider (1967) 0016
The Mask of Sheba (1970) 0077
Pursuit (1972) 0263
Men of the Dragon (1974) 0416
QB VII (1974) 0442
Murder at the World Series (1977) 0708

JANE WITHERS
All Together Now (1975) 0512

MICHAEL WITNEY
The Catcher (1972) 0226

LANA WOOD
Black Water Gold (1970) 0061
The Over-the-Hill Gang Rides Again (1970) 0096
O'Hara, U.S. Treasury: Operation Cobra (1971) 0131
QB VII (1974) 0442
Who Is the Black Dahlia? (1975) 0528
Nightmare in Badham County (1976) 0666
Little Ladies of the Night (1977) 0689
Corey: For the People (1977) 0736
A Question of Guilt (1978) 0820

NATALIE WOOD
The Affair (1973) 0356
Cat on a Hot Tin Roof (1976) 0678
From Here to Eternity (1979) MS29
The Cracker Factory (1979) 0961

DONALD WOODS
Istanbul Express (1968) 0021

JAMES WOODS
Footsteps (Footsteps: Nice Guys Finish Last)
(1972) 0238
A Great American Tragedy (1972) 0247
Foster and Laurie (1975) 0592
F. Scott Fitzgerald in Hollywood (1976) 0637
The Disappearance of Aimee (1976) 0671
Raid on Entebbe (1976) 0685
Holocaust (1978) MS19
The Gift of Love (1978) 0916
The Incredible Journey of Dr. Meg Laurel
(1979) 0932
And Your Name Is Jonah (1979) 0944

KATHARINE (KATE) WOODVILLE
Fear No Evil (1969) 0035
The Aquarians (1970) 0091
The Healers (1974) 0447
Widow (1976) 0601
The Lindbergh Kidnapping Case (1976) 0605
The Rhinemann Exchange (1977) MS09
Keefer (1978) 0830

JOANNE WOODWARD
Sybil (1976) 0670
Come Back, Little Sheba (1977) 0795
See How She Runs (1978) 0809
A Christmas to Remember (1978) 0929

JO ANN WORLEY
The Feminist and the Fuzz (1971) 0110
What's a Nice Girl Like You . . . ? (1971)
0187

TERESA WRIGHT
Crawlspace (1972) 0207
The Elevator (1974) 0396
Flood (1976) 0675

JANE WYATT
See How They Run (1964) 0001
Weekend of Terror (1970) 0101
You'll Never See Me Again (1973) 0299
Tom Sawyer (1973) 0317
Katherine (1975) 0579
Amelia Earhart (1976) 0662
Superdome (1978) 0798
A Love Affair: The Eleanor and Lou Gehrig
Story (1978) 0799
The Nativity (1978) 0924
The Millionaire (1978) 0927

JANE WYMAN
The Failing of Raymond (1971) 0175
The Incredible Journey of Dr. Meg Laurel
(1979) 0932

KEENAN WYNN
The Young Lawyers (1969) 0047
The House on Greenapple Road (1970) 0063
Assault on the Wayne (1971) 0107
Cannon (1971) 0129
Terror in the Sky (1971) 0138
Assignment: Munich (1972) 0225
Hijack! (1973) 0336
Hit Lady (1974) 0461
Target Risk (1975) 0496
The Lindbergh Kidnapping Case (1976) 0605
The Quest (1976) 0633
Sex and the Married Woman (1977) 0751
The Bastard (1978) MS22
The Billion Dollar Threat (1979) 0971

DANA WYNTER
Companions in Nightmare (1968) 0024
Any Second Now (1969) 0033
Owen Marshall, Counselor-at-Law (A Pattern
of Morality) (1971) 0135
Connection (1973) 0298
The Questor Tapes (1974) 0385
The Lives of Jenny Dolan (1975) 0585
Backstairs at the White House (1979) MS28

RICHARD YNIQUEZ
Tribes (1970) 0094
Man on a String (1972) 0212
Fireball Forward (1972) 0220
The Deadly Tower (1975) 0581
Shark Kill (1976) 0638
The Hunted Lady (1977) 0780
Crash (1978) 0894

MICHAEL YORK
Great Expectations (1974) 0461
Jesus of Nazareth (1977) MS10
A Man Called Intrepid (1979) MS36

SUSANNAH YORK
Jane Eyre (1971) 0128

BURT YOUNG
The Great Niagara (1974) 0454
Hustling (1975) 0523
Serpico: The Deadly Game (1976) 0623
Woman of the Year (1976) 0644
Daddy, I Don't Like It Like This (1978) 0862

GIG YOUNG
Companions in Nightmare (1968) 0024
The Neon Ceiling (1971) 0113
The Great Ice Rip-Off (1974) 0473

The Turning Point of Jim Malloy (1975) 0547
Sherlock Holmes in New York (1976) 0661
Spectre (1977) 0727

ROBERT YOUNG
Marcus Welby, M.D. (A Matter of
Humanities) (1969) 0038
Vanished (1971) 0122
All My Darling Daughters (1972) 0257
My Darling Daughters' Anniversary (1973)
0352
Little Women (1978) 0881

STEPHEN YOUNG
The Mask of Sheba (1970) 0077
The Death Squad (1974) 0379

HARRIS YULIN
Melvin Purvis: G-Man (1974) 0431
The Greatest Gift (1974) 0471
The FBI Story: The FBI Versus Alvin Karpis,
Public Enemy Number One (1974) 0474
The Trial of Chaplain Jensen (1975) 0515
The Kansas City Massacre (1975) 0576
James A. Michener's Dynasty (1976) 0612
Victory at Entebbe (1976) 0679
Roger & Harry: The Mitera Target (Love for
Ransom) (1977) 0715
Ransom for Alice! (1977) 0732
When Every Day Was the Fourth of July
(1978) 0829
The Night Rider (1979) 0984

ANTHONY ZERBE
The Priest Killer (1971) 0136
The Hound of the Baskervilles (1972) 0208
Snatched (1973) 0284
She Lives (1973) 0331
The Healers (1974) 0447
Once an Eagle (1976) MS05
In the Glitter Palace (1977) 0702
KISS Meets the Phantom of the Park (1978)
0893
Centennial (1978) MS24
The Chisholms (1979) MS32

EFREM ZIMBALIST, JR.
Who Is the Black Dahlia? (1975) 0528
A Family Upside Down (1978) 0836
Terror Out of the Sky (1978) 0930
The Best Place to Be (1979) 0995

STEPHANIE ZIMBALIST
Yesterday's Child (1977) 0694
In the Matter of Karen Ann Quinlan (1977)
0759
The Gathering (1977) 0784
Forever (1978) 0798
Centennial (1978) MS24
Long Journey Back (1978) 0922
The Triangle Factory Fire Scandal (1979) 0947
The Best Place to Be (1979) 0995

THE DIRECTORS

EDWARD A. ABROMS
The Imposter (1975) 0538

ADELL ALDRICH
Daddy, I Don't Like It Like This (1978) 0862

COREY ALLEN
See the Man Run (1971) 0183
Cry Rape! (1973) 0358
Yesterday's Child (1973) 0694

IRWIN ALLEN
City Beneath the Sea (1971) 0111

JOHN A. ALONZO
Champions: A Love Story (1979) 0936

KEN ANNAKIN
Murder at the Mardi Gras (1978) 0846
Harold Robbins' The Pirate (1978) 0906
Institute for Revenge (1979) 0943

LOU ANTONIO
Someone I Touched (1975) 0526
Lanigan's Rabbi (1976) 0643
Something for Joey (1977) 0711
The Girl in the Empty Grave (1977) 0756
The Critical List (1978) 0872
A Real American Hero (1978) 0917
Silent Victory: The Kitty O'Neil Story (1979) 0954

GEORGE ARMITAGE
Hot Rod (1979) 0993

JACK ARNOLD
Sex and the Married Woman (1977) 0751

KAREN ARTHUR
Charleston (1979) 0938

JOHN ASTIN
Rosetti and Ryan: Men Who Love Women (1977) 0725
Operation Petticoat (1977) 0747

HY AVERBACK
Richie Brockelman: Missing 24 Hours (1976) 0663
The Love Boat II (1977) 0692
The Magnificent Magnet of Santa Mesa (1977) 0741
The New Maverick (1978) 0867
A Guide for the Married Woman (1978) 0882
Pearl (1978) MS27
The Night Rider (1979) 0984

JOHN BADHAM
The Impatient Heart (1971) 0150
Isn't It Shocking? (1973) 0338
The Law (1974) 0465
The Gun (1974) 0477
Reflections of Murder (1974) 0482
The Godchild (1974) 0483
The Keegans (1976) 0627

REZA BADIYI
The Eyes of Charles Sand (1972) 0217

ROY BAKER
The Spy Killer (1969) 0050
Foreign Exchange (1970) 0064

EARL BELLAMY
The Pigeon (1969) 0048
Desperate Mission (1971) 0178
The Trackers (1974) 0148
Flood (1976) 0635
Fire! (1977) 0717
Desperate Women (1978) 0889

KEVIN BILLINGTON
And No One Could Save Her (1973) 0293

BRUCE BILSON
The Girl Who Came Gift-Wrapped (1974) 0388
Dead Man on the Run (1975) 0544
The New Daughters of Joshua Cabe (1976) 0641
BJ and the Bear (1978) 0882
Pleasure Cove (1979) 0934
Dallas Cowboys Cheerleaders (1979) 0937

BILL BIXBY
The Barbary Coast (1975) 0558
Three on a Date (1978) 0817

NOEL BLACK
Mulligan's Stew (1977) 0742

PAUL BOGART
In Search of America (1971) 0127
Tell Me Where It Hurts (1974) 0411
Winner Take All (1975) 0529

ALAN BRIDGES
Brief Encounter (1974) 0475

BURT BRINCKERHOFF
The Cracker Factory (1979) 0961

GEORG STANFORD BROWN
Roots: The Next Generations (1979) MS30

JIM BURROWS
More Than Friends (1978) 0886

ROBERT BUTLER
Death Takes a Holiday (1971) 0158
The Blue Knight (1973) MS01
Strange New World (1975) 0573
Dark Victory (1976) 0602
James Dean (1976) 0604
Mayday at 40,000 Feet (1976) 0668
In the Glitter Palace (1977) 0702
A Question of Guilt (1978) 0820
Lacy and the Mississippi Queen (1978) 0850

MICHAEL CACOYANNIS
The Story of Jacob and Joseph (1974) 0430

MICHAEL CAFFEY
Seven in Darkness (1969) 0040
The Silent Gun (1969) 0058
The Devil and Miss Sarah (1971) 0179
The Hanged Man (1974) 0413

JOHN CARPENTER
Someone Is Watching Me! (1978) 0910
Elvis (1979) 0951

PETER CARTER
A Man Called Intrepid (1979) MS36

GILBERT CATES
To All My Friends on Shore (1972) 0215
The Affair (1973) 0356
Johnny, We Hardly Knew Ye (1977) 0693

DON CHAFFEY
The Gift of Love (1978) 0916

MARVIN CHOMSKY
Assault on the Wayne (1971) 0107
Mongo's Back in Town (1971) 0182
Fireball Forward (1972) 0220
Family Flight (1972) 0249
Female Artillery (1973) 0279
The Magician (1973) 0311
Mrs. Sundance (1974) 0381
The FBI Story: The FBI Versus Alvin Karpis, Public Enemy Number One (1974) 0474
Attack on Terror: The FBI Versus the Ku Klux Klan (1975) 0522
Kate McShane (1975) 0546
Brink's: The Great Robbery (1976) 0616
A Matter of Wife . . . and Death (1976) 0620
Law and Order (1976) 0629
Victory at Entebbe (1976) 0679
Roots (1977) MS07
Little Ladies of the Night (1977) 0689
Danger in Paradise (1977) 0718
Holocaust (1978) MS19
Hollow Image (1979) 1001

RICHARD A. COLLA
The Whole World Is Watching (1969) 0036
McCloud: Who Killed Miss U.S.A.? (1970) 0071
The Other Man (1970) 0089
Sarge: The Badge or the Cross (1971) 0116
The Priest Killer (1971) 0136
Tenafly (1973) 0286
The Questor Tapes (1974) 0385
Live Again, Die Again (1974) 0400
The Tribe (1974) 0489
The UFO Incident (1975) 0583

ROBERT COLLINS
The Life and Assassination of the Kingfish (1976) 0709
Serpico: The Deadly Game (1976) 0623

PETER COLLINSON
The House on Garibaldi Street (1979) 0996

RICHARD COMPTON
Deadman's Curve (1978) 0812

JAMES L. CONWAY
Last of the Mohicans (1977) 0779
The Incredible Rocky Mountain Race (1977) 0788
Donner Pass: The Road to Survival (1978) 0889

FIELDER COOK
Sam Hill: Who Killed the Mysterious Mr. Foster? (1971) 0112
Goodbye Raggedy Ann (1971) 0157
The Homecoming (1971) 0188
Miracle on 34th Street (1973) 0370
This Was the West That Was (1974) 0491
Miles to Go Before I Sleep (1975) 0498
Judge Horton and the Scottsboro Boys (1976) 0622
Beauty and the Beast (1976) 0676
A Love Affair: The Eleanor and Lou Gehrig Story (1977) 0800
Too Far to Go (1979) 0960
I Know Why the Caged Bird Sings (1979) 0976

ALAN COOKE
The Hunchback of Notre Dame (1978) 0863

JACKIE COOPER
Having Babies III (1978) 0826
Perfect Gentlemen (1978) 0829
Rainbow (1978) 0901

JACK COUFFER
The Last Giraffe (1979) 1000

BARRY CRANE
The Hound of the Baskervilles (1972) 0208

WES CRAVEN
Stranger in Our House (1978) 0897

MICHAEL CRICHTON
Pursuit (1972) 0263

GEORGE CUKOR
Love Among the Ruins (1975) 0533
The Corn Is Green (1979) 0946

DAN CURTIS
The Night Strangler (1973) 0277
The Norliss Tapes (1973) 0294
Scream of the Wolf (1974) 0382
Dracula (1974) 0395
Melvin Purvis: G-Man (1974) 0431
Turn of the Screw (1974) 0433
The Great Ice Rip-Off (1974) 0473
Trilogy of Terror (1975) 0531
The Kansas City Massacre (1975) 0576
Curse of the Black Widow (1977) 0754
When Every Day Was the Fourth of July (1978) 0828

MEL DAMSKI
Long Journey Back (1978) 0922
The Child Stealer (1979) 0959

MARC DANIELS
Planet Earth (1974) 0441

JOAN DARLING
Willa (1979) 0962

HERSCHEL DAUGHERTY
Winchester '73 (1967) 0013
The Victim (1972) 0254
She Cried "Murder!" (1973) 0335
Twice in a Lifetime (1974) 0415

ROBERT DAY
The House on Greenapple Road (1970) 0063
Ritual of Evil (1970) 0073
Banyon (1971) 0126
In Broad Daylight (1971) 0155
Mr. and Mrs. Bo Jo Jones (1971) 0170
The Reluctant Heroes (1971) 0173
The Great American Beauty Contest (1973) 0287
Death Stalk (1975) 0506
The Trial of Chaplain Jensen (1975) 0515
Switch (1975) 0535
A Home of Our Own (1975) 0582
Twin Detectives (1976) 0625
Kingston: The Power Play (1976) 0651
Having Babies (1976) 0765
The Initiation of Sarah (1978) 0814
The Grass Is Always Greener Over the Septic Tank (1978) 0891
Murder by Natural Causes (1979) 0953
Walking Through the Fire (1979) 0989

GIANFRANCO DeBOSIO
Moses—The Lawgiver (1975) MS02

FRANK DeFELITTA
Trapped (1973) 0355

PHILIP DeGUERE
Dr. Strange (1978) 0871

IVAN DIXON
Love Is Not Enough (1978) 0860

LAWRENCE DOHENY
Houston, We've Got a Problem (1974) 0407

WALTER DONIGER
Mad Bull (1977) 0792

CLIVE DONNER
Spectre (1977) 0727
The Thief of Baghdad (1978) 0907

RICHARD DONNER
Senior Year (1974) 0418
Lucas Tanner (1974) 0445
A Shadow in the Streets (1975) 0508
Sarah T.—Portrait of a Teenage Alcoholic (1975) 0514

GORDON DOUGLAS
Nevada Smith (1975) 0557

CHARLES S. DUBIN
Murder Once Removed (1971) 0160
Murdock's Gang (1973) 0314
The Deadly Triangle (1977) 0724
Roots: The Next Generations (1979) MS30

DARYL DUKE
The Psychiatrist: God Bless the Children (1970) 0103
Happiness Is a Warm Clue (1973) (1970) 0327
The President's Plane Is Missing (1973) 0346
I Heard the Owl Call My Name (1973) 0372
A Cry for Help (1975) 0516
They Only Come Out at Night (1975) 0554
Griffin and Phoenix (1976) 0606

INCE EDWARDS
Maneater (1973) 0365

ARRY ELIKANN
The Great Wallendas (1978) 0810

EORGE ENGLUND
A Christmas to Remember (1978) 0929

JHN ERMAN
Letters from Three Lovers (1973) 0339
Green Eyes (1977) 0683
Roots (1977) MS07
Alexander: The Other Side of Dawn (1977)
0720
Just Me and You (1978) 0855
Roots: The Next Generations (1979) MS30

ARRY FALK
Three's a Crowd (1969) 0054
The Death Squad (1974) 0379
Men of the Dragon (1974) 0416
The Abduction of Saint Anne (1975) 0507
Mandrake (1979) 0944
Centennial (1979) MS24

EORG FENADY
Hanging by a Thread (1979) 0981

HEODORE J. FLICKER
Playmates (1972) 0237
Guess Who's Sleeping in My Bed? (1973) 0349
Just a Little Inconvenience (1977) 0761
Last of the Good Guys (1978) 0827

AMES FRAWLEY
Delancey Street: The Crisis Within (1975) 0551

ERROLD FREEDMAN
A Cold Night's Death (1973) 0282
Blood Sport (1973) 0364
The Last Angry Man (1974) 0435
Some Kind of Miracle (1979) 0933
This Man Stands Alone (1979) 0999

ICK FRIEDENBERG
The Deerslayer (1978) 0925

AVID FRIEDKIN
River of Gold (1971) 0123

IMOTHY GALFAS
Revenge for a Rape (1976) 0165
Maneaters Are Loose! (1978) 0845

ILA GARRETT
Terraces (1977) 0744

RUCE GELLER
The Savage Bees (1976) 0624

TEVE GETHERS
Billy: Portrait of a Street Kid (1977) 0750

RANK D. GILROY
The Turning Point of Jim Malloy (1975) 0547

BERNARD GIRARD
Hunters Are for Killing (1970) 0079

JACK GOLD
Catholics (1973) 0361

JAMES GOLDSTONE
Scalplock (1966) 0003
Ironside (1967) 0014
Shadow over Elveron (1968) 0018
A Clear and Present Danger (1970) 0082
Cry Panic (1974) 0394
Dr. Max (1974) 0428
Things in Their Season (1974) 0486
Journey from Darkness (1975) 0524
Eric (1975) 0591
Studs Lonigan (1979) MS31

WILLIAM A. GRAHAM
The Doomsday Flight (1966) 0005
Trial Run (1969) 0032
Then Came Bronson (1969) 0037
The Intruders (1970) 0095
Congratulations, It's a Boy! (1971) 0141
Thief (1971) 0152
Marriage: Year One (1971) 0154
Jigsaw (1972) 0224
Magic Carpet (1972) 0252
Birds of Prey (1973) 0281
Mr. Inside/Mr. Outside (1973) 0309
The Police Story (1973) 0323
Shirts/Skins (1973) 0341
Get Christie Love! (1974) 0384
Larry (1974) 0440
Trapped Beneath the Sea (1974) 0466
Beyond the Bermuda Triangle (1975) 0587
Shark Kill (1976) 0638
21 Hours at Munich (1976) 0667
Minstrel Man (1977) 0703
The Amazing Howard Hughes (1977) 0712
Contract on Cherry Street (1977) 0777
Cindy (1978) 0832
One in a Million: The Ron LeFlore Story
(1978) 0878
And I Alone Survived (1978) 0910
Transplant (1979) 0972

ALEX GRASSHOFF
The Last Dinosaur (1977) 0697

WALTER GRAUMAN
Daughter of the Mind (1969) 0056
The Old Man Who Cried Wolf (1970) 0088
Crowhaven Farm (1970) 0099
The Forgotten Man (1971) 0137
Paper Man (1971) 0168
They Call It Murder (1971) 0185
Dead Men Tell No Tales (1971) 0186
The Streets of San Francisco (1972) 0230
Manhunter (1974) 0404
Force Five (1975) 0553
Most Wanted (1976) 0615
Are You in the House Alone? (1978) 0875
Crisis in Mid-Air (1979) 0952

GUY GREEN
The Incredible Journey of Doctor Meg Laurel
(1979) 0932
Jennifer: A Woman's Story (1979) 0957

DAVID GREENE
Madame Sin (1972) 0195
The Count of Monte Cristo (1975) 0501
Ellery Queen (1975) 0539
Rich Man, Poor Man (1976) MS03

Roots (1977) MS07
Lucan (1977) 0728
The Trial of Lee Harvey Oswald (1977) 0760
Friendly Fire (1979) 0973
A Vacation in Hell (1979) 0992

BUD GREENSPAN
Wilma (1977) 0790

ROBERT GREENWALD
Sharon: Portrait of a Mistress (1977) 0771
Katie: Portrait of a Centerfold (1978) 0888
Flatbed Annie & Sweetiepie: Lady Truckers
(1979) 0950

TOM GRIES
Earth II (1971) 0176
Truman Capote's The Glass House (1972) 0203
Call to Danger (1973) 0297
Connection (1973) 0298
QB VII (1974) 0442
The Healers (1974) 0447
Helter Skelter (1976) 0617

CLAUDIO GUZMAN
Willa (1979) 0962

STUART HAGMANN
She Lives (1973) 0331
Tarantulas: The Deadly Cargo (1977) 0794

WILLIAM HALE
How I Spent My Summer Vacation (1967)
0007
Nightmare (1974) 0378
The Great Niagara (1974) 0454
Crossfire (1975) 0540
The Killer Who Wouldn't Die (1976) 0619
Stalk the Wild Child (1976) 0665
Red Alert (1977) 0723

DANIEL HALLER
The Desperate Miles (1975) 0532
Black Beauty (1978) MS15
Little Mo (1978) 0869

JOSEPH HARDY
A Tree Grows in Brooklyn (1974) 0423
Great Expectations (1974) 0481
Last Hours Before Morning (1975) 0552
The Silence (1975) 0588
James at 15 (1977) 0748
The Users (1978) 0880
Love's Savage Fury (1979) 0991

DEAN HARGROVE
The Big Ripoff (1975) 0536
The Return of the World's Greatest Detective
(1976) 0642

CURTIS HARRINGTON
How Awful About Allan (1970) 0074
The Cat Creature (1973) 0367
Killer Bees (1974) 0405
The Dead Don't Die (1975) 0503
Devil Dog: The Hound of Hell (1978) 0896

HARRY HARRIS
The Runaways (1975) 0543
Swiss Family Robinson (1975) 0550

BRUCE HART
Sooner or Later (1979) 0966

HARVEY HART
The Young Lawyers (1969) 0047
Can Ellen Be Saved? (1974) 0393
Murder or Mercy (1974) 0438
Panic on the 5:22 (1974) 0480
Street Killing (1976) 0649
The City (1977) 0687
Goldenrod (1977) 0731
The Prince of Central Park (1977) 0739
Captains Courageous (1977) 0783
Standing Tall (1978) 0804
Like Normal People (1979) 0970

ANTHONY HARVEY
The Glass Menagerie (1973) 0371
The Disappearance of Aimee (1976) 0671

SIDNEY HAYERS
Mister Jerico (1970) 0075

RICHARD T. HEFFRON
Do You Take This Stranger? (1971) 0108
Toma (1973) 0316
Outrage! (1973) 0359
The Morning After (1974) 0399
The Rockford Files (1974) 0422
The California Kid (1974) 0456
Locusts (1974) 0462
I Will Fight No More Forever (1975) 0549
Death Scream (1975) 0577
Young Joe, The Forgotten Kennedy (1977) 0755
See How She Runs (1978) 0809
True Grit (1978) 0852

GORDON HESSLER
Scream, Pretty Peggy (1973) 0357
Skyway to Death (1974) 0383
Hitchhike (1974) 0403
A Cry in the Wilderness (1974) 0420
Betrayal (1974) 0488
The Strange Possession of Mrs. Oliver (1977) 0701
Secrets of Three Hungry Wives (1978) 0883
KISS Meets the Phantom of the Park (1978) 0893

DOUGLAS HEYES
The Lonely Profession (1969) 0044
Powderkeg (1971) 0133
Drive Hard, Drive Fast (1973) (1969) 0328
Captains and the Kings (1976) MS04
Aspen (1977) MS14

RON HOLCOMB
Captain America (1979) 0938

LEONARD J. HORN
Split Second to an Epitaph (1968) 0020
Climb an Angry Mountain (1972) 0268
Hunter (1973) 0273
The Bait (1973) 0307
Hijack! (1973) 0336
Nakia (1974) 0436
The New, Original Wonder Woman (1975) 0590

CY HOWARD
It Couldn't Happen to a Nicer Guy (1974) 0478

RON HOWARD
Cotton Candy (1978) 0892

ROY HUGGINS
The Young Country (1970) 0081

PETER HUNT
The Beasts Are on the Streets (1978) 0851
Flying High (1978) 0867

WARIS HUSSEIN
Divorce His/Divorce Hers (1973) 0285

PETER HYAMS
Rolling Man (1972) 0239
Goodnight My Love (1972) 0246

JULES IRVING
Loose Change (1978) MS18
The Jordan Chance (1978) 0919

RICHARD IRVING
Prescription: Murder (1968) 0017
Istanbul Express (1968) 0021
Breakout (1970) 0102
Ransom for a Dead Man (1971) 0120
The Six-Million Dollar Man (1973) 0304
The Art of Crime (1975) 0596
Seventh Avenue (1977) MS08
Exo-Man (1977) 0740

JERRY JAMESON
Heatwave! (1974) 0387
The Elevator (1974) 0396
Hurricane (1974) 0449
Terror on the 40th Floor (1974) 0452
The Secret Night Caller (1975) 0520
The Deadly Tower (1975) 0581
The Lives of Jenny Dolan (1975) 0585
The Call of the Wild (1976) 0640
The Invasion of Johnson County (1976) 0646
Superdome (1978) 0799
A Fire in the Sky (1978) 0909

KENNETH JOHNSON
The Incredible Hulk (1977) 0772

LAMONT JOHNSON
Deadlock (1969) 0034
My Sweet Charlie (1970) 0065
That Certain Summer (1972) 0251
The Execution of Private Slovik (1974) 0412
Fear on Trial (1975) 0578

GLENN JORDAN
Frankenstein (1973) 0276
The Picture of Dorian Gray (1973) 0326
Shell Game (1975) 0563
One of My Wives Is Missing (1976) 0609
Delta County, U.S.A. (1977) 0726
Sunshine Christmas (1977) 0787
Les Miserables (1978) 0931
Son Rise: A Miracle of Love (1979) 0987

HAL JORDAN
In the Matter of Karen Ann Quinlan (1977) 0759

JAN KADAR
The Other Side of Hell (1978) 0802

JEREMY KAGAN
Unwed Father (1974) 0406
Judge Dee and the Monastery Murders (1974) 0493
Katherine (1975) 0579

MILTON KATSELAS
Strangers: The Story of a Mother and Daughter (1979) 0986

LEE H. KATZIN
Along Came a Spider (1970) 0068
Visions (1972) 0242
The Voyage of the Yes (1973) 0278
The Stranger (1973) 0295
Ordeal (1973) 0348
Savages (1974) 0450
Strange Homecoming (1974) 0468
The Last Survivors (1975) 0530
Sky Hei$t (1975) 0569
The Quest (1976) 0633
Man from Atlantis (1977) 0704
Relentless (1977) 0752
The Bastard (1978) MS22
Zuma Beach (1978) 0879
Terror Out of the Sky (1978) 0930
Samurai (1979) 0978

BOB KELLJAN
Dog and Cat (1977) 0746
Beach Patrol (1979) 0977

BURT KENNEDY
Shootout in a One-Dog Town (1974) 0380
Sidekicks (1974) 0417
All the Kind Strangers (1974) 0476
The Rhinemann Exchange (1977) MS09
Kate Bliss and the Ticker Tape Kid (1978) 0856
The Wild Wild West Revisited (1979) 0982

IRVIN KERSHNER
Raid on Entebbe (1977) 0685

BRUCE KESSLER
Murder in Peyton Place (1977) 0762
Cruise into Terror (1978) 0831
The Two-Five (1978) 0838
Death Moon (1978) 0858

RICHARD KINON
The Love Boat (1976) 0652

ALF KJELLIN
The Deadly Dream (1971) 0144
The Girls of Huntington House (1973) 0291

RANDAL KLEISER
All Together Now (1975) 0512
Dawn: Portrait of a Teenage Runaway (1976) 0654
The Boy in the Plastic Bubble (1976) 0669
The Gathering (1977) 0784

JOHN KORTY
The People (1972) 0198
Go Ask Alice (1973) 0280
Class of '63 (1973) 0308
The Autobiography of Miss Jane Pittman (1974) 0389
Farewell to Manzanar (1976) 0611
Forever (1978) 0798

TOM KOTANI
The Last Dinosaur (1977) 0697
The Bermuda Depths (1978) 0807

BERNARD KOWALSKI
Terror in the Sky (1971) 0138
Black Noon (1971) 0164
Women in Chains (1972) 0199
Two for the Money (1972) 0216
The Woman Hunter (1972) 0231
In Tandem (1974) 0446
Flight to Holocaust (1977) 0710
The Nativity (1978) 0924

PAUL KRASNY
The D.A.: Conspiracy to Kill (1971) 0106
The Adventures of Nick Carter (1972) 0213
The Letters (1973) 0303
Big Rose (1974) 0421
The Islander (1978) 0874
Centennial (1978) MS24

WILLIAM KRONICK
The 500-Pound Jerk (1973) 0270

BUZZ KULIK
Vanished (1971) 0122
Owen Marshall, Counselor At Law (1971) 0135
Brian's Song (1971) 0177
Incident on a Dark Street (1973) 0275
Pioneer Woman (1973) 0374
Remember When (1974) 0419
Bad Ronald (1974) 0467
Cage Without a Key (1975) 0537
Matt Helm (1975) 0562
Babe (1975) 0584
The Lindbergh Kidnapping Case (1976) 0605
Corey: For the People (1977) 0736
Kill Me If You Can (1977) 0758
Ziegfeld: The Man and His Women (1978) 0854
From Here to Eternity (1979) MS29

HARVEY LAIDMAN
Steel Cowboy (1978) 0915

MICHAEL LANDON
It's Good to Be Alive (1974) 0402
Little House on the Prairie (1974) 0424
The Loneliest Runner (1976) 0681
Killing Stone (1978) 0843

ALAN LANDSBURG
Black Water Gold (1970) 0061

RICHARD LANG
Fantasy Island (1977) 0688
The Hunted Lady (1977) 0780
Nowhere to Run (1978) 0801
Night Cries (1978) 0808
Dr. Scorpion (1978) 0822
Vega$ (1978) 0840
The Word (1978) MS26

PHILIP LEACOCK
The Birdmen (1971) 0140
When Michael Calls (1972) 0205
The Daughters of Joshua Cabe (1972) 0229
Baffled! (1973) 0283
The Great Man's Whiskers (1973) (1969) 0289
Dying Room Only (1973) 0333

Key West (1973) 0366
Killer on Board (1977) 0766
Wild and Wooly (1978) 0819

PAUL LEAF
Top Secret (1978) 0859
Sergeant Matlovich Vs. the U.S. Air Force (1978) 0866

MARK L. LESTER
Gold of the Amazon Women (1979) 0958

ALAN J. LEVI
Gemini Man (1976) 0632
Go West, Young Girl (1978) 0842
The Immigrants (1978) MS25
The Legend of the Golden Gun (1979) 0969

GENE LEVITT
Any Second Now (1969) 0033
Run a Crooked Mile (1969) 0051
Alias Smith and Jones (1971) 0105
Cool Million (1972) 0244
The Phantom of Hollywood (1974) 0397

ROBERT MICHAEL LEWIS
The Astronaut (1972) 0191
The Alpha Caper (1973) 0340
Money to Burn (1973) 0347
Message to My Daughter (1973) 0368
Pray for the Wildcats (1974) 0386
The Day the Earth Moved (1974) 0453
The Invisible Man (1975) 0560
Guilty or Innocent: The Sam Sheppard Murder Case (1975) 0593
The Night They Took Miss Beautiful (1977) 0768
Ring of Passion (1978) 0813

NORMAN LLOYD
Companions in Nightmare (1968) 0024
The Smugglers (1968) 0030

JERRY LONDON
Killdozer (1974) 0390
McNaughton's Daughter (1976) 0608
Cover Girls (1977) 0721
Arthur Hailey's Wheels (1978) MS20
Evening in Byzantium (1978) MS23

JAMES MacTAGGART
Robinson Crusoe (1974) 0485

DON McDOUGALL
Escape to Mindanao (1968) 0027
The Aquarians (1970) 0091
The Heist (1972) 0259
The Mark of Zorro (1974) 0469
The Missing Are Deadly (1975) 0500

BERNARD McEVEETY
A Step Out of Line (1971) 0118
Killer by Night (1972) 0190
The Macahans (1976) 0599
The Hostage Heart (1977) 0749
Centennial (1979) MS24

VINCENT McEVEETY
Cutter's Trail (1970) 0069
Wonder Woman (1974) 0410
The Last Day (1975) 0519

GEORGE McGOWAN
The Monk (1969) 0045
The Ballad of Andy Crocker (1969) 0052
Carter's Army (1970) 0066
The Love War (1970) 0078
The Over-the-Hill Gang Rides Again (1970) 0096
Run, Simon, Run (1970) 0100
Love, Hate, Love (1971) 0114
Cannon (1971) 0129
The Face of Fear (1971) 0151
If Tomorrow Comes (1971) 0180
Welcome Home, Johnny Bristol (1972) 0202
Murder on Flight 502 (1975) 0594
Return to Fantasy Island (1978) 0803
The Return of Mod Squad (1979) 0990

ANDREW McLAGLEN
The Log of the Black Pearl (1975) 0494
Stowaway to the Moon (1975) 0502
Banjo Hackett: Roamin' Free (1976) 0628
Murder at the World Series (1977) 0708

ABBY MANN
King (1978) MS16

DELBERT MANN
Heidi (1968) 0023
David Copperfield (1970) 0080
Jane Eyre (1971) 0128
She Waits (1972) 0200
No Place to Run (1972) 0232
The Man Without a Country (1973) 0325
A Girl Named Sooner (1975) 0591
Francis Gary Powers: The True Story of the U-2 Spy Incident (1976) 0655
Tell Me My Name (1977) 0791
Breaking Up (1978) 0797
Love's Dark Ride (1978) 0835
Home to Stay (1978) 0844
Thou Shalt Not Commit Adultery (1978) 0898
Torn Between Two Lovers (1979) 0979

MICHAEL MANN
The Jericho Mile (1979) 0963

ALEX MARCH
The Dangerous Days of Kiowa Jones (1966) 0006
Firehouse (1973) 0269

STUART MARGOLIN
Suddenly Single (1978) 0156

ROBERT MARKOWITZ
The Deadliest Season (1977) 0707
The Storyteller (1977) 0785

LESLIE H. MARTINSON
The Challengers (1970) 0072
How to Steal an Airplane (1971) (1968) 0181

RUSS MAYBERRY
Probe (1972) 0209
A Very Missing Person (1972) 0219
Fer-De-Lance (1974) 0464
Seventh Avenue (1977) MS08
Stonestreet: Who Killed the Centerfold Model? (1977) 0690
The 3,000 Mile Chase (1977) 0738
The Rebels (1979) MS34

PETER MEDAK
The Third Girl from the Left (1973) 0344

DON MEDFORD
Incident in San Francisco (1971) 0119
The Clone Master (1978) 0873

RICHARD MICHAELS
Once an Eagle (1976) MS05
Charlie Cobb: Nice Night for a Hanging (1977) 0735
Having Babies II (1977) 0770
Leave Yesterday Behind (1978) 0848
My Husband Is Missing (1978) 0914
And Your Name Is Jonah (1979) 0945

DAVID MILLER
The Best Place to Be (1979) 0995

MICHAEL MILLER
Outside Chance (1978) 0912

ROBERT ELLIS MILLER
Just an Old Sweet Song (1976) 0650
Ishi—The Last of His Tribe (1978) 0928

WALTER C. MILLER
The Borrowers (1973) 0369

ALLEN H. MINER
The Catcher (1972) (1970) 0226

DAVID MOESSINGER
Mobile Two (1975) 0574

ROBERT MOORE
Thursday's Game (1974) (1971) 0432

GILBERT MOSES
Roots (1977) MS07
The Greatest Thing That Almost Happened (1977) 0769

JOHN LLEWELLYN MOXEY
San Francisco International (1970) 0085
The House That Would Not Die (1970) 0092
Escape (1971) 0132
The Last Child (1971) 0149
A Taste of Evil (1971) 0153
The Death of Me Yet (1971) 0159
The Night Stalker (1972) 0193
Hardcase (1972) 0204
The Bounty Man (1972) 0250
Home for the Holidays (1972) 0258
Genesis II (1973) 0318
The Strange and Deadly Occurrence (1974) 0455
Where Have All the Strangers Gone? (1974) 0460
Foster and Laurie (1975) 0592
Charlie's Angels (1976) 0614
Conspiracy of Terror (1976) 0621
Nightmare in Badham County (1976) 0666
Smash-Up on Interstate 5 (1976) 0677
Panic in Echo Park (1977) 0743
Intimate Strangers (1977) 0775
The President's Mistress (1978) 0816
The Courage and the Passion (1978) 0857
Sanctuary of Fear (1979) 0974
The Power Within (1979) 0983

ALAN MYERSON
The Love Boat (1976) 0652

JAMES NEILSON
Return of the Gunfighter (1967) 0009
Tom Sawyer (1973) 0317

GARY NELSON
The Girl on the Late, Late Show (1974) 0426
Medical Story (1975) 0575
Panache (1976) 0636
Washington: Behind Closed Doors (1977) MS12
To Kill a Cop (1978) 0837

GENE NELSON
Wake Me When the War Is Over (1969) 0043
The Letters (1973) 0303

RALPH NELSON
Lady of the House (1978) 0904
You Can't Go Home Again (1979) 0975

MIKE NEWELL
The Man in the Iron Mask (1977) 0691

JOHN NEWLAND
The Deadly Hunt (1971) 0147
Crawlspace (1972) 0207
Don't Be Afraid of the Dark (1973) 0342
A Sensitive, Passionate Man (1977) 0734
Overboard (1978) 0876

B. W. L. NORTON
Gargoyles (1972) 0256

CHRIS NYBY III
The Rangers (1974) 0492
Pine Canyon Is Burning (1977) 0722

MICHAEL O'HERLIHY
Deadly Harvest (1972) 0234
Young Pioneers (1976) 0607
Kiss Me, Kill Me (1976) 0631
Young Pioneers' Christmas (1976) 0680
Peter Lundy and the Medicine Hat Stallion (1977) 0773
Backstairs at the White House (1979) MS28

SAM O'STEEN
A Brand New Life (1973) 0292
I Love You, Goodbye (1974) 0398
Queen of the Stardust Ballroom (1975) 0577
High Risk (1976) 0635
Look What's Happened to Rosemary's Baby (1976) 0664

ANTHONY PAGE
F. Scott Fitzgerald in Hollywood (1976) 0637

NORMAN PANAMA
Coffee, Tea or Me? (1973) 0329

JERRY PARIS
But I Don't Want to Get Married! (1970) 0087
The Feminist and the Fuzz (1971) 0110
Two on a Bench (1971) 0162
What's a Nice Girl Like You . . . ? (1971) 0187

Call Her Mom (1972) 0210
Evil Roy Slade (1972) 0211
The Couple Takes a Wife (1972) 0261
Every Man Needs One (1972) 0264
Only with Married Men (1974) 0472
How to Break Up a Happy Divorce (1976) 0657

EDWARD PARONE
Promise Him Anything . . . (1975) 0566

RICHARD PEARCE
Siege (1978) 0841
No Other Love (1979) 0965

LARRY PEERCE
The Stranger Who Looks Like Me (1974) 0408

LEO PENN
Quarantined (1970) 0074
Testimony of Two Men (1977) MS11
The Dark Secret of Harvest Home (1978) 0805
Murder in Music City (1979) 0939

FRANK PERRY
Dummy (1979) 0993

BILL PERSKY
Roll, Freddy, Roll! (1974) 0490
How to Pick Up Girls! (1978) 0899

DANIEL PETRIE
Silent Night, Lonely Night (1969) 0057
The City (1971) 0134
A Howling in the Woods (1971) 0163
Moon of the Wolf (1972) 0235
Hec Ramsey (1972) 0240
Trouble Comes to Town (1973) 0274
Mousey (1974) 0409
The Gun and the Pulpit (1974) 0427
Returning Home (1975) 0555
Eleanor and Franklin (1976) 0598
Sybil (1976) 0670
Eleanor and Franklin: The White House Years (1977) 0706
The Quinns (1977) 0745

JOSEPH PEVNEY
My Darling Daughters' Anniversary (1973) 0352
Who Is the Black Dahlia? (1975) 0528

JOHN PEYSER
Honeymoon with a Stranger (1969) 0059
Stunt Seven (1979) 0998

LEE PHILIPS
Getting Away From It All (1972) 0196
The Girl Most Likely To . . . (1973) 0351
The Stranger Within (1974) 0457
The Red Badge of Courage (1974) 0487
Sweet Hostage (1975) 0580
Louis Armstrong—Chicago Style (1976) 0600
James A. Michener's Dynasty (1976) 0612
Wanted: The Sundance Woman (1976) 0656
The Spell (1977) 0698
The War Between the Tates (1977) 0737
Special Olympics (1978) 0821
The Comedy Company (1978) 0862
Salvage (1979) 0942

FRANK A. PIERSON
The Neon Ceiling (1971) 0113

ERNEST PINTOFF
Human Feelings (1978) 0885

TED POST
Night Slaves (1970) 0086
Dr. Cook's Garden (1971) 0109
Yuma (1971) 0121
Five Desperate Women (1971) 0145
Do Not Fold, Spindle or Mutilate (1971) 0166
The Bravos (1972) 0192
Sandcastles (1972) 0245

MICHAEL PRESSMAN
Like Mom, Like Me (1978) 0887

RICHARD QUINE
The Specialists (1975) 0495

ALAN RAFKIN
Let's Switch (1975) 0499

ALVIN RAKOFF
The Adventures of Don Quixote (1973) 0324

ALLEN REISNER
Your Money or Your Wife (1972) 0266
Captains and the Kings (1976) MS04
Mary Jane Harper Cried Last Night (1977) 0763
Cops and Robin (1978) 0833

DAVID LOWELL RICH
See How They Run (1964) 0001
Wings of Fire (1967) 0010
The Borgia Stick (1967) 0012
Marcus Welby, M.D. (1969) 0038
The Mask of Sheba (1970) 0077
Berlin Affair (1970) 0093
The Sheriff (1971) 0130
Assignment: Munich (1972) 0225
Lieutenant Schuster's Wife (1972) 0243
All My Darling Daughters (1972) 0257
The Judge and Jake Wyler (1972) 0260
Set This Town on Fire (1973) (1969) 0271
The Horror at 37,000 Feet (1973) 0288
Brock's Last Case (1973) 0301
Crime Club (1973) 0302
Beg, Borrow . . . or Steal (1973) 0315
Satan's School For Girls (1973) 0334
Runaway! (1973) 0337
Death Race (1973) 0354
The Chadwick Family (1974) 0437
The Sex Symbol (1974) 0451
Aloha Means Goodbye (1974) 0463
The Daughters of Joshua Cabe Return (1975) 0509
Adventures of the Queen (1975) 0518
You Lie So Deep, My Love (1975) 0525
Bridger (1976) 0648
The Secret Life of John Chapman (1976) 0682
SST—Death Flight (1977) 0700
Ransom For Alice! (1977) 0732
Telethon (1977) 0774
The Defection of Simas Kudirka (1978) 0806
A Family Upside Down (1978) 0836
Little Women (1978) 0881

LLOYD RICHARDS
Roots: The Next Generations (1979) MS30

TONY RICHARDSON
A Death in Canaan (1978) 0824

MICHAEL RITCHIE
The Outsider (1967) 0016
The Sound of Anger (1968) 0028

SUTTON ROLEY
Sweet, Sweet Rachel (1971) 0148
Snatched (1973) 0284
Satan's Triangle (1975) 0504

BOB ROSENBAUM
Yesterday's Child (1977) 0694

STUART ROSENBERG
Fame Is the Name of the Game (1966) 0004

BORIS SAGAL
U.M.C. (1969) 0039
Destiny of a Spy (1969) 0046
Night Gallery (1969) 0049
The D.A.: Murder One (1969) 0055
The Movie Murderer (1970) 0067
Hauser's Memory (1970) 0098
The Harness (1971) 0167
The Failing of Raymond (1971) 0175
Hitched (1973) 0321
Deliver Us from Evil (1973) 0330
Indict and Convict (1974) 0376
A Case of Rape (1974) 0401
The Greatest Gift (1974) 0471
The Dream Makers (1974) 0497
The Runaway Barge (1975) 0541
Man on the Outside (1975) 0572
The Oregon Trail (1976) 0597
Rich Man, Poor Man (1976) MS03
Mallory: Circumstantial Evidence (1976) 0603
Sherlock Holmes in New York (1976) 0661
Arthur Hailey's The Moneychangers (1976) MS06
The Awakening Land (1978) MS17

JAY SANDRICH
The Crooked Hearts (1972) 0253
What Are Best Friends For? (1973) 0373

RICHARD C. SARAFIAN
Shadow on the Land (1968) 0026
One of Our Own (1975) 0559
A Killing Affair (1977) 0757

JOSEPH SARGENT
The Sunshine Patriot (1968) 0029
The Immortal (1969) 0041
Tribes (1970) 0094
Maybe I'll Come Home in the Spring (1971) 0115
Longstreet (1971) 0117
Man on a String (1972) 0212
The Marcus-Nelson Murders (1973) 0305
The Man Who Died Twice (1973) 0323
Sunshine (1973) 0353
Hustling (1975) 0523
Friendly Persuasion (1975) 0567
The Night That Panicked America (1975) 0586

RON SATLOF
Benny and Barney: Las Vegas Undercover (1977) 0684

GEORGE SCHAEFER
A War of Children (1972) 0262
F. Scott Fitzgerald and "The Last of the Belles" (1974) 0377
In This House of Brede (1975) 0527
Amelia Earhart (1976) 0662
The Girl Called Hatter Fox (1977) 0767
First You Cry (1978) 0902
Who'll Save Out Children? (1978) 0923
Blind Ambition (1979) MS35

ROBERT SCHEERER
Poor Devil (1973) 0290
Target Risk (1975) 0496
It Happened at Lake Wood Manor (1977) 0781
Happily Ever After (1978) 0870

HENNING SCHELLERUP
The Time Machine (1978) 0900

LAWRENCE SCHILLER
Hey, I'm Alive! (1975) 0589

JOEL SCHUMACHER
The Virginia Hill Story (1974) 0479
Amateur Night at the Dixie Bar and Grill (1979) 0935

ALEX SEGAL
My Father's House (1975) 0570

RALPH SENESKY
A Dream for Christmas (1973) 0375
The Family Kovack (1974) 0429
Death Cruise (1974) 0470
The Family Nobody Wanted (1975) 0521
The New Adventures of Heidi (1978) 0921

NICHOLAS SGARRO
The Man with the Power (1977) 0730

DON SHARP
The Four Feathers (1978) 0796

MELVILLE SHAVELSON
The Legend of Valentino (1975) 0595
The Great Houdinis (1976) 0658
Ike (1979) MS33

BARRY SHEAR
Night Gallery (1969) 0049
Ellery Queen: Don't Look Behind You (1971) 0171
Short Walk to Daylight (1972) 0248
Jarrett (1973) 0310
Punch and Jody (1974) 0484
Strike Force (1975) 0548
Starsky and Hutch (1975) 0556
The San Pedro Bums (1977) 0719
Keefer (1978) 0830
Crash (1978) 0894

JAMES SHELDON
Gidget Grows Up (1969) 0060
With This Ring (1978) 0846

VINCENT SHERMAN
The Last Hurrah (1977) 0076
Lady of the House (1978) 0904
Women at West Point (1979) 0955

DON SIEGEL
The Hanged Man (1964) 0002
Stranger on the Run (1967) 0015

GERALD SETH SINDELL
Harpy (1971) 0125

ALEXANDER SINGER
The First 36 Hours of Dr. Durant (1975) 0565
Time Travelers (1976) 0613
The Million Dollar Rip-Off (1976) 0653
Hunters of the Reef (1978) 0853

HAL SITOWITZ
A Last Cry for Help (1979) 0941

JACK SMIGHT
The Screaming Woman (1972) 0201
Banacek: Detour To Nowhere (1972) 0223
The Longest Night (1972) 0227
Partners in Crime (1973) 0320
Double Indemnity (1973) 0343
Linda (1973) 0350
Frankenstein: The True Story (1973) 0362

ALLEN SMITHEE
The Challenge (1970) 0070

STEVEN SPIELBERG
Night Gallery (1969) 0049
Duel (1971) 0169
Something Evil (1972) 0197
Savage (1973) 0322

PAUL STANLEY
Sole Survivor (1970) 0062
River of Mystery (1971) 0146
Nicky's World (1974) 0439
Crisis in Sun Valley (1978) 0834
The Ultimate Imposter (1979) 0985

JACK STARRETT
Night Chase (1970) 0097
Roger & Harry: The Mitera Target (1977) 0715
Nowhere to Hide (1977) 0733
Thaddeus Rose and Eddie (1978) 0823
Big Bob Johnson and His Fantastic Speed Circus (1978) 0861
Mr. Horn (1979) 0949
Survival of Dana (1979) 0997

LEN STECKLER
Mad Bull (1977) 0792

SANDOR STERN
The Seeding of Sarah Burns (1979) 0968

LEONARD STERN
Once Upon a Dead Man (1971) 0139
The Snoop Sisters (1972) 0265

STEVEN HILLIARD STERN
Escape from Brogen County (1977) 0764
The Ghost of Flight 401 (1978) 0818
Doctors' Private Lives (1978) 0831
Getting Married (1978) 0849
Fast Friends (1979) 0964
Anatomy of a Seduction (1979) 0980

LESLIE STEVENS
I Love a Mystery (1973) (1967) 0296

MEL STUART
Brenda Starr (1976) 0630
Ruby and Oswald (1978) 0815
The Triangle Factory Fire (1979) 0947
The Chisholms (1979) MS32

E. W. SWACKHAMER
In Name Only (1969) 0053
Gidget Gets Married (1972) 0189
Death Sentence (1974) 0459
Death at Love House (1976) 0647
Once an Eagle (1976) MS05
Night Terror (1977) 0696
Spider-Man (1977) 0753
The Dain Curse (1978) MS21
The Winds of Kitty Hawk (1978) 0925

JEANNOT SZWARC
Night of Terror (1972) 0241
The Weekend Nun (1972) 0267
The Devil's Daughter (1973) 0272
You'll Never See Me Again (1973) 0299
Lisa, Bright and Dark (1973) 0360
A Summer Without Boys (1973) 0363
Crime Club (1975) 0545
Code Name: Diamond Head (1977) 0716

DON TAYLOR
Something for a Lonely Man (1968) 0025
Wild Women (1970) 0090
Heat of Anger (1972) 0218
Night Games (1974) 0414
Honky Tonk (1974) 0425
A Circle of Children (1977) 0705

JUD TAYLOR
Weekend of Terror (1970) 0101
Suddenly Single (1971) 0156
Revenge (1971) 0165
The Rookies (1972) 0222
Say Goodbye, Maggie Cole (1972) 0236
Hawkins on Murder (1973) 0306
Winter Kill (1974) 0434
The Disappearance of Flight 412 (1974) 0458
Search for the Gods (1975) 0534
Future Cop (1976) 0626
Return to Earth (1976) 0634
Woman of the Year (1976) 0644
Tail Gunner Joe (1977) 0695
Mary White (1977) 0778
Christmas Miracle in Caufield, U.S.A. (1977) 0793
The Last Tenant (1978) 0865
Lovey: A Circle of Children, Part II (1978) 0920

PETER TEWKSBURY
Second Chance (1972) 0206

J. LEE THOMPSON
A Great American Tragedy (1972) 0247
The Blue Knight (1975) 0564
Widow (1976) 0601

ROBERT C. THOMPSON
Bud and Lou (1978) 0905

JERRY THORPE
Dial Hot Line (1970) 0076
Lock, Stock and Barrel (1971) 0142

The Cable Car Murder (1971) 0172
Kung Fu (1972) 0214
Smile Jenny, You're Dead (1974) 0391
The Dark Side of Innocence (1976) 0639
I Want to Keep My Baby (1976) 0673
The Possessed (1977) 0714
Sticking Together (1978) 0839
A Question of Love (1978) 0908

RICHARD THORPE
The Scorpio Letters (1967) 0011

ROBERT TOTTEN
The Red Pony (1973) 0312
Huckleberry Finn (1975) 0542
The Sacketts (1979) 0988

JOHN TRENT
The Man Who Wanted to Live Forever (1970) 0104

GUS TRIKONIS
The Darker Side of Terror (1979) 0967

MICHAEL TUCHNER
Summer of My German Soldier (1978) 0895

VIRGIL W. VOGEL
The Return of Joe Forrester (1975) 0561
Law of the Land (1976) 0624
Centennial (1978) MS24

HERB WALLERSTEIN
Snowbeast (1977) 0713

CLYDE WARE
The Story of Pretty Boy Floyd (1974) 0444
The Hatfields and the McCoys (1975) 0505

JACK WEBB
Dragnet (1969) (1966) 0031
O'Hara, U.S. Treasury: Operation Cobra (1971) 0131
Emergency! (1972) 0194
Chase (1973) 0319

DON WEIS
The Longest Hundred Miles (1967) 0008
Now You See It, Now You Don't (1968) 0022
The Millionaire (1978) 0927

PAUL WENDKOS
Hawaii Five-O (1968) 0019
Fear No Evil (1969) 0035
The Brotherhood of the Bell (1970) 0083
Travis Logan, D.A. (1971) 0127
A Tattered Web (1971) 0143
A Little Game (1971) 0161
A Death of Innocence (1971) 0174
The Delphi Bureau (1972) 0221
The Family Rico (1972) 0228
Haunts of the Very Rich (1972) 0233
Footsteps (1972) 0238
The Strangers in 7A (1972) 0255
Honor Thy Father (1973) 0306
Terror on the Beach (1973) 0332
The Underground Man (1974) 0443
The Legend of Lizzie Borden (1975) 0513
Death Among Friends (1975) 0568
The Death of Richie (1977) 0686
Secrets (1977) 0699

Good Against Evil (1977) 0729
Harold Robbins' 79 Park Avenue (1977) MS13
Betrayal (1978) 0903
A Woman Called Moses (1978) 0918
The Ordeal of Patty Hearst (1979) 0956

PETER WERNER
Battered (1978) 0877

WILLIAM WIARD
Scott Free (1976) 0660
Ski Lift to Death (1978) 0825

DONALD WRYE
The Man Who Could Talk to Kids (1973) 0345
Born Innocent (1974) 0448
Death Be Not Proud (1975) 0510
The Entertainer (1976) 0610
It Happened One Christmas (1977) 0786

CLAUDE WHATHAM
All Creatures Great and Small (1975) 0511

TRACY KEENAN WYNN
Hit Lady (1974) 0461

JEAN YARBROUGH
The Over-the-Hill Gang (1969) 0042

LARRY YUST
Testimony of Two Men (1977) MS11

FRANCO ZEFFIRELLI
Jesus of Nazareth (1977) MS10